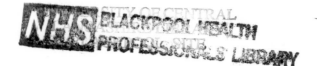
The Blackpool, Fylde & Wyre

Health Library

This book is due for return on or before the last date shown below
to avoid overdue charges.
Books may be renewed (twice only) unless required by other readers.
Renewals may be made in person or by telephone, quoting reader number
and the number on the barcode below.

WE WANT TO HEAR FROM YOU!!

By sharing your opinions about this book, you will help us ensure that you are getting the most value for your textbook dollars. After you've used the book for awhile, please fill out this form fold, tape and drop it in the mail.

Course Title:_____ Text Title & Author:_____

1. Are you a major in this subject? ❏ yes ❏ no ❏ undecided
   Were you required to purchase this text? ❏ yes ❏ no

2. Did you purchase this book: ❏ for yourself? ❏ for yourself and at least one other student?
   Was a copy available when you needed one? ❏ yes ❏ no

3. Was a study guide available for purchase? ❏ yes ❏ no ❏ don't know
   If yes, did you purchase it? ❏ yes ❏ no
   Might you purchase it in the future? ❏ yes ❏ no

4. Were any other supplements to the text available (for example, software, a workbook, etc.)?
   ❏ yes ❏ no   If yes, what? _____
   Did you purchase any other supplement? ❏ yes ❏ no

5. How far along in the course are you? ❏ only starting ❏ less than midway
   ❏ more than midway ❏ completed

6. How much have you used this text? ❏ only skimmed it   ❏ read/studied a few chapters
   ❏ read/studied most chapters ❏ read/studied entire text

7. Have you read the introductory material (such as the preface)? ❏ yes ❏ no
   Do you feel you know how to effectively use this book? ❏ yes ❏ no

8. Even if you've only skimmed the text, please rate your perception of it in terms of the following:

a) Value as a reference	❏ highly valuable	❏ somewhat valuable	❏ not valuable
b) Readability	❏ consistently clear	❏ sometimes clear	❏ generally unclear
c) Illustrations/photos	❏ very effective	❏ somewhat effective	❏ ineffective
d) Design/use of color	❏ very effective	❏ somewhat effective	❏ ineffective
e) Study help in the text	❏ very effective	❏ somewhat effective	❏ ineffective
f) Level	❏ too difficult	❏ appropriate	❏ too easy/not challenging
g) Problems	❏ too difficult	❏ appropriate	❏ too easy/not challenging
h) OVERALL PERCEPTION:	❏ better than average	❏ average	❏ less than average

9. Do you find the examples in the text relevant to you? ❏ yes ❏ no
   Note any that you find particularly relevant _____

10. By looking at the text, do you think it treats the subject as interestingly as possible?
    ❏ yes ❏ no ❏ hard to tell

11. What do you like most about this book?_____
    What *don't* you like about this book? _____

12. At the end of the semester, what do you intend to do with this text?
    ❏ keep for future reference ❏ sell back to bookstore or other students ❏ unsure

THANK YOU FOR YOUR HELP!

WILEY

Look What Students Are Saying About Westen

"I like the delineation of psychology between biology and culture. This adds an understanding of how questions in the field evolve." -Amy Polage, University of New Mexico

"I found the author's writing style to be extremely refreshing, especially in the context of many of the other textbooks I have read.... I was engaged by the real-life examples and the author's personal statements at the close of the chapter. If other students take the time to read their texts, they should have no problem finding this text interesting, especially in comparison to other books." -Mike Guildoo, Ohio State University

"It was easy to read and understand. It didn't drag on that often. It seemed like the author tried to explain things so that it could be understood instead of babbling in a language I don't know." -Joel Johnson, University of Tennessee

"As textbooks go, it was intelligent and insightful. I thought the author's use of examples was very helpful." -John T. Farrar, University of Oklahoma

"I feel the author did an excellent job in terms of writing style; to be better he'd have to be speaking to me in person." -Mark C. Waits, Southern Illinois University, Carbondale

"Writing style was great—good examples and stories, clear language. Sounds a bit less formal than other texts. Almost conventional, easy to follow...I like the unbiased view—it is good to not shield students from disagreements—it gives a better picture of what the field of psychology is like." -Kelly Mutchler, University of Minnesota

"In my opinion, Westen's attempt to try to help the reader understand sets this book above the rest. Most text books are dry, and quickly become boring. That was not the case here. I found myself very interested in what he had to say." -Matthew S. Jordan, Ohio State University

"This text flows logically and clearly in a comprehensible progression. He presents it in a non-threatening fashion. My current text is choppy, disorganized and overwhelming in the first chapter...I prefer Westen. At the risk of being redundant, it is clear, concise, logical, interesting, objective, and non-intimidating." -Laurel Dunseth, Johnson County CC

On cross-cultural coverage: "Score: 10. This aspect is also important because it shows you the diversity among cultures around the world. It does help you learn the material because it lets you see how different cultures create different people." -Adrienne Walton, Canisius College

"The Westen text is good because it is not as dry as some texts can be. I really enjoyed the author's writing style because he came across as real and personable. I really liked how the author gave his own opinion at the end of the chapter; in many texts I often wonder what the author thinks." -Joanna Myers, University of Oklahoma

"Westen's style is great! He brings in personal examples and uses easy-to-understand analogies, while still getting important ideas across without the use of textese." -Londa Jill Smith, Ohio State University

PSYCHOLOGY
MIND, BRAIN, & CULTURE

DREW WESTEN
HARVARD UNIVERSITY

John Wiley & Sons, Inc.

New York   Chichester   Brisbane   Toronto   Singapore

EXECUTIVE EDITOR Christopher Rogers
SENIOR DEVELOPMENTAL EDITOR Nancy Perry
MARKETING MANAGER Rebecca Herschler
PRODUCTION SERVICE HRS/Electronic Text Management
DESIGN SUPERVISOR Ann Renzi
TEXT AND COVER DESIGN HRS/Electronic Text Management
MANUFACTURING MANAGER Mark Cirillo
PHOTO EDITOR Mary Ann Price
FINE ART CONSULTANT Steven Diamond
ILLUSTRATION COORDINATOR Anna Melhorn
ANATOMICAL ART DEVELOPMENT Arthur Ciccone
ART STUDIO Precision Graphics
COVER ART "It's How You Play the Game" 1992 by Rosamond W. Purcell

This book was set in Sabon by HRS/Electronic Text Management and printed and bound by Von Hoffman, Inc. The cover was printed by NEBC.

The text, figure, and photo credits appear on page C-1, which constitutes a continuation of the copyright page.

Recognizing the importance of preserving what has been written, it is a policy of John Wiley & Sons, Inc. to have books of enduring value published in the United States printed on acid-free paper, and we exert our best efforts to that end.

The paper on this book was manufactured by a mill whose forest management programs include sustained yield harvesting of its timberlands. Sustained yield harvesting principles ensure that the number of trees cut each year does not exceed the amount of new growth.

Library of Congress Cataloging in Publication Data:
Westen, Drew, 1959–
Psychology: mind brain and culture/ Drew I. Westen.
p.   cm.
Includes bibliographical references.
ISBN 0-471-05411-9 (alk. paper)
1. Psychology.   I. Title.
BF121.W44   1995
150–dc20

Printed in the United States of America

10 9 8 7 6 5 4 3 2 1

PREFACE

Psychology: Mind, Brain, & Culture emerged from my several years of teaching introductory psychology at the University of Michigan. Nothing is more exciting to a teacher than watching students become absorbed in a discipline, intermingling its concepts with their own. What I wanted to do was to translate a style of teaching into the written word, a style that is at once personal and informal, engaging students by presenting material relevant to their own concerns and interests, yet highly conceptual and scientifically rigorous. In some ways this is where I live, as a clinician and researcher, confronted in a hospital and a private office with patients for whom the personal relevance of psychological knowledge is what really matters, and in a university, where the task is to try to know something and study it systematically. Translating a lecture style into a book is no easy task because so much of effective teaching happens through interaction, eye contact, and humor, which elude capture on the written page. So this has been quite a challenge.

AIMS AND CORRESPONDING FEATURES

What I wanted to do was to write a textbook with four objectives: to focus on both the biological basis of psychology and the role of culture in shaping basic psychological processes; to provide a conceptual orientation that would capture the excitement and tensions in the field; to use an integrative approach that would avoid the dangers of "faculty psychology"; and to employ a language that would be sophisticated but engaging. The features of the book follow from these four aims.

Biology and Culture: A Micro to Macro Approach

A consistent theme of the book, introduced in the first chapter, is that biology and culture form the boundaries of psychology, and that understanding people means attending simultaneously to biological processes, psychological experience, and the cultural and historical context. The focus on biological and neural underpinnings echoes one of the major trends in contemporary psychological research, as technological developments allow progressively more sophisticated understanding of the neural substrates of psychological experience. The focus on culture has been a central feature of this book since I began work on it in 1987, long before the current interest in diversity. *Cross-cultural material is not tacked onto this book; it is integral to it.* My first book, published in 1985, was on culture and personality, and a background in anthropology and sociology informs my understanding of the way people think, feel, learn, behave, and develop.

Each chapter of this book contains two extended discussions that show the way psychological experience is situated between the nervous system and cultural experience.

- "From Mind to Brain" integrates concepts and findings from biopsychology and neuroscience into every chapter, discussing such issues as the way people can react to a stimulus with two different emotional responses because two distinct neural systems underlie emotion, or the way damage to the brain can alter personality.

- "A Global Vista" uses ethnographic examples and cross-cultural studies to explore psychological phenomena in other cultures, with implications for their universality or culture-specificity. For example, menopause has a very different meaning, and hence different symptoms, in a Mayan village than it does in North America, and parenting styles fostering autonomy that are adaptive in Western, technologically developed societies are not necessarily optimal everywhere. In addition, cross-cultural research is integrated into the structure of each chapter, so that students do not balkanize cross-cultural issues as distinct from the "psychology of white people" but instead ask cross-cultural questions from the start.

These special features flow integrally from the text and are not presented as isolated "boxes." In this way, students will not get the message that the material is somehow superfluous or added on.

Conceptual Orientation

The book is conceptually oriented. It attempts, within the limits of my biases and expertise, to give a fair and compelling account of the different perspectives psychologists take in understanding psychological phenomena. I have a healthy respect for each approach and assume that if thousands of my colleagues find an approach compelling, it probably contains something that students should know about without my own predilections getting in the way.

• From the start, therefore, students are challenged to think about psychological phenomena from multiple perspectives. Chapter 1 is not perfunctory; it introduces four perspectives—*psychodynamic, behavioral, cognitive,* and *evolutionary*—in enough depth to allow students to begin conceptualizing psychological data rather than simply memorizing a list of facts, names, or studies. Furthermore, Chapter 1 includes a section on the "psychology of psychology," which turns the four perspectives on the field itself and challenges students to use psychological principles to explain why psychologists think as they do.

• At the same time, I have avoided slavishly introducing paragraphs on each perspective in every chapter, since some perspectives obviously apply better to certain phenomena than to others. For example, Chapter 6 on memory is organized primarily around a cognitive information-processing model. It does, however, conclude with an evolutionary perspective that challenges the view of an all-purpose, general processing brain, suggesting that the brain may have modules that process very specific information relevant to survival and reproduction.

• The book is also realistic about psychology as a discipline and does not shield students from tensions in the field, such as the division between clinicians and researchers or the antagonisms that sometimes exist between adherents of different viewpoints.

Integrative Approach

Solo-authoring an introductory text is probably presumptive evidence of mental instability, but I could not have produced this book any other way because my aim was to engage students in the enterprise of thinking about the whole person, not just the parts. As one psychologist put it (Holt, 1976), the human psyche is not the handiwork of an obsessive-compulsive god who created cognition on one day, affect on another, motivation on another, and so forth, and made sure they all stayed neatly in their own territories. Too often our efforts to classify and label lead us to try to separate the inseparable. The integrative bent of the book stems primarily from my own work as a researcher, which has focused on integrating clinical and experimental perspectives as well as concepts and methods from different psychological traditions.

Wherever possible, this book tries to delineate some of the links that our best intellectual efforts often obscure. For example, Chapter 11 on emotion, stress, and coping concludes by asking how we might begin to pull together the "cold" cognitive models presented in the chapters on learning, memory, thought, and intelligence with the "hot" models of emotion, stress, and motivation presented in the chapters that immediately follow them. The result is a modified information-processing model that describes the operation of implicit and explicit memory, thought, emotion, and motivation. Chapter 14 on social development also provides an integrative approach as it reviews the major theories that emphasize either cognition or emotion in moral development. It then offers a preliminary conceptualization of the relative roles of thought and emotion in the evolving experience of morality.

Language

Above all, I wanted to avoid writing in "textese," a language that presents dry summaries of data for students to memorize instead of engaging them in *thinking* about psychology. *Psychology: Mind, Brain, & Culture* offers a solid and comprehensive account of the principles of psychology in what I hope is an accessible, lively, and thought-provoking style.

- Throughout the book, I aim at clarity and introduce terminology only when it enlightens, not obscures. I am not shy about using metaphor or weaving a narrative, but not a single term in this book is defined by context alone. If students need to understand a concept, they will see the definition in the same sentence in which the word is boldfaced. I have also tried to keep the language at a level appropriate to college students, but if they have to look up an occasional word, I will not lose sleep over it. (I had to look up a few in writing it!)

- As a teacher and writer, I try to make use of one of the most robust findings in psychology: that memory and understanding are enhanced when target information is associated with vivid and personally relevant material. Each chapter begins, then, with an experiment, a case, or an event that lets students know why the topic is important and why anyone might be excited about it. None of the cases is invented; this is real material, and the questions raised in the opening study or vignette reemerge throughout each chapter. Chapter 1, for example, begins with the case of a teenage girl who lost 50 IQ points as her brain degenerated with a seizure disorder, but who began a steady recovery when her mother, who had abandoned her, returned. The issues raised by this case, such as the relation between meaning and mechanism and between nature and nurture, are at the heart of psychology.

Other Features

Three other features deserve some mention here: research focus, commentaries, and pedagogy.

- **Research focus.** This book takes psychological science seriously. A student should come out of an introductory psychology class not only with a sense of the basic questions and frameworks for answering them but also with an appreciation for how to obtain psychological knowledge. Thus, Chapter 2 is devoted to research methods; the style reflects an effort to engage, not intimidate, so students may see how methods actually make a difference. The statistical supplement that immediately follows it, which even the most seriously math-phobic can understand, is included in the body of the text rather than cast off at the end as an impenetrable appendix. In addition, throughout each chapter, students read about specific studies so that they can learn about the logic of scientific investigation. The research presented in this book is also up to date; like Sisyphus, I have been pushing the boulder of citations up the hill every year for eight years, updating and rethinking as it acquires new weight. At the same time, I have included many classic citations and have tried to convey the way theories and hypotheses have evolved, not just their latest renditions for the sake of appearing current.

• **Commentaries.** I have made every effort to present controversies in a balanced and dispassionate way. The danger in doing so, however, is that one loses one's voice, and the last thing I wanted to write was a book with intellectual laryngitis. Thus, I periodically comment on issues of method that bear on the conclusions being reached (such as the use of questionnaires in coping research to assess coping strategies that are frequently unavailable to conscious introspection). Or, after presenting both sides of a debate, I let the reader know where I stand on controversial issues (such as the existence of repressed memories of sexual abuse). I have presented versions of some of these commentaries on National Public Radio's "All Things Considered."

• **Pedagogy.** I have tried to avoid pedagogy that is condescending or unnecessary. For example, in my experience students never follow up on annotated recommendations for future reading, so I have not cluttered the ends of chapters with them. (If they want to follow up, they should read the studies cited in the chapter.) Similarly, because all terms are defined in the text, there is no need to list key terms at the end of the chapter; students can use the index and the glossary if they have trouble locating them. I worked very hard, however, to make sure that the chapter summaries include the key concepts presented in the chapter and will be helpful to students in studying for exams.

ORGANIZATION

I tried to organize *Psychology: Mind, Brain, & Culture* in a way that would be convenient for most instructors and yet faithful to an internal design. Of course, different instructors organize things differently, but I do not think many will find the organization idiosyncratic.

• After introducing the main issues in the field (Chapter 1) and the research methods used to study psychological phenomena (Chapter 2), the text describes the biological underpinnings of psychological experience (Chapter 3).

• The next several chapters are devoted, broadly speaking, to knowing: sensation and perception (Chapter 4), learning (Chapter 5), memory (Chapter 6), thought and language (Chapter 7), and intelligence (Chapter 8).

• Chapter 9 explores the nature of consciousness, including attention, conscious and unconscious processes, and states of consciousness.

• The next two chapters move from the "cold" to the "hot": motivation (Chapter 10) and emotion, stress, and coping (Chapter 11).

• Chapter 12 on personality pulls together various strands presented thus far to examine theories of the whole person and describes research on individual differences.

• Chapters 13 and 14 then explore development, the first focusing on physical and cognitive development, and the second on social and personality development.

- Then we turn to psychological disorders, to their nature (Chapter 15) and treatment (Chapter 16).

- The last two chapters are on social psychology, examining attitudes and social cognition (Chapter 17) and interpersonal processes (Chapter 18).

Teaching the material in the order presented is probably optimal, for chapters do build on each other. For example, the consciousness chapter presupposes knowledge of the distinction posed in Chapter 6 between implicit and explicit memory. However, if instructors want to rearrange the order of chapters, they can certainly do so, as material mentioned from a previous chapter is cross-referenced so that students can easily find any information they need.

ILLUSTRATION AND DESIGN

When I began this enterprise, I had no idea what it meant to put together a whole textbook. As a person with minimal use of his right hemisphere, I assumed that some editorial type would come up with figures and tables. This assumption was obviously an example of a well-known psychological phenomenon, wishful thinking. After eight years of working on this project, I think I finally figured out how to educate the right hemisphere, even if mine does not work so well. I took tremendous care to select and design only figures and tables that actually add something and that do not just make the pages look less ominous. The same is true of photo selection, which involved collaboration of the author, editors, and a very talented photo research department committed to finding images that would provoke thought and not simply provide momentary respite from the prose. We also worked with the best designers in the business to create a design that is sophisticated and readable. Focus groups of college students helped us hone all these elements.

SUPPLEMENTARY MATERIALS

Accompanying the text is an integrated supplements package that includes the following components.

Study Guide

By Alastair Younger, University of Ottawa. The Study Guide offers students an easy way to review the material and test their knowledge of it. Each chapter in the text has a corresponding chapter in the Study Guide. Six tools help students master the material: chapter outlines, learning objectives, key terms, fill-in exercises, critical thinking exercises, and sample test questions with answers.

Instructor's Manual

By Herbert Friedman, The College of William and Mary. For each text chapter, this comprehensive resource includes an outline, learning objectives, a chapter overview, suggested lecture organizers, lecture lead-ins, lecture extenders, a lecture organizer, discussion questions, and an activities section.

Test Bank

By Matthew Mendel, (Ph.D., University of Michigan). All the test items have been meticulously proofread and reviewed for coordination with the text. The nearly 2000 test items include approximately 5 essay questions and approximately 100 multiple-choice questions for each chapter. Multiple-choice questions are linked to the text's learning objectives and range from relatively factual items to those that truly challenge students to think and apply what they have learned. Each question is page-referenced to its source in the text. Answers to multiple-choice questions are provided.

Diploma IV Computerized Test Bank

This easy-to-use test-generation program fully supports graphics and prints tests and student answer sheets quickly and easily. All the test item files can be transferred easily to another program. In addition to the test-generating program, *Exam,* this system includes *gradebook* and *calendar* functions, and *Proctor.* The *Proctor* function allows PC users to give tests online (students use the computer to take the test) and provides the results to the instructor.

Transparencies

This set of 165 full-color illustrations is provided in a form suitable for projection in any size classroom or lecture hall.

Wiley *Psychology* Videodisk

By Henry Cross, Colorado State University, at the university's Office of Instructional Services and an advisory board. This videodisk contains 58 minutes of video and computer animation (averaging two minutes per segment), and approximately 1200 still images of lecture aids, photographs, and line art. Active learning activities take full advantage of the power of videodisk technology for use in large lecture halls. An Instructor's Manual contains teaching hints and barcodes to access the disk's images.

The Brain: Teaching Modules (Annenberg/CPB)

Qualified adopters can enhance their lectures with flexible, targeted excerpts from *The Brain.* This Peabody Award-winning series artfully blends interviews with world-famous brain scientists and dramatic reenactments of landmark cases in medical history. Edited into 30 teaching modules of 2 to 11 minutes each, they are provided on two videocassettes. A Teacher's Manual has been prepared by Sheldon Solomon, Skidmore College, to coordinate with *Psychology: Mind, Brain, & Culture.*

ACKNOWLEDGMENTS

This project began many years ago—in 1987—and several people have played important roles in getting if off the ground. The initial plan for the book was to co-write it with a very talented writer, Jean Stein, who helped draft the first half of the book. Her involvement ended a year after the project began, and the writing and content are now very different because of the many rounds of revisions the book has undergone since then. Nevertheless, many flashes of sparkle, felicitous turns of phrase, and clear passages remain from her efforts, for which I am extremely grateful. Several other people also contributed in the early stages, notably Judy Block, Barbara Misle, Carol Holden, and Karen Schenkenfeldter. Like Jean, they helped lay the foundations, and their efforts, too, are greatly appreciated. In this past year, I gained substantially from the help of two very able research assistants, Lauren Korfine and Patricia Harney. Others who helped research the first draft include Caroline Burns, Marcia Hissong, Alfred Kellam, Doug Leber, and Stuart Segal. Several others more recently helped with the daunting task of finding missing citations for the bibliography (yes, there were a few), most notably Colleen Coffey, who did a considerable amount of eleventh-hour detective work.

Reviewers

Over the past eight years, this book has been shaped by the insightful comments of dozens of colleagues and would look nothing like it does now without their tireless efforts. In particular, I would like to thank Walt Lonner of Western Washington University, who advised me on cross-cultural coverage for many chapters and gave feedback on several. I would also like to offer special thanks to Paul Watson of the University of Tennessee for his uncanny ability throughout the years to notice where my prose was getting sloppy, my thoughts confused, or my coverage idiosyncratic. Special thanks also go to the following:

Gordon Allen	Miami University
Harvard L. Armus	University of Toledo
Robert Batsell	Southern Methodist University
Carol M. Batt	Sacred Heart University
Col. Johnston Beach	United States Military Academy-West Point
John B. Best	Eastern Illinois University
John Bonvillian	University of Virginia
Robert Brown	Georgia State University
Mark Byrd	University of Canterbury (New Zealand)
Barbara K. Canaday	Southwestern College
George A. Cicala	University of Delaware
John M. Clark	Macomb Community College
Margaret Cleek	University of Wisconsin-Madison
Peter Ditto	Kent State University
Allen Dobbs	University of Alberta
Eugene B. Doughtie	University of Houston
J. Gregor Fetterman	Arizona State University
Nelson Freedman	Queens University
Herbert Friedman	The College of William and Mary
Mauricio Gaborit, S.J.	St. Louis University
Adrienne Ganz	New York University
Mark Garrison	Kentucky State University
Marian Gibney	Phoenix College

William E. Gibson	Northern Arizona University
Marvin Goldfried	State University of New York-Stony Brook
Mary Alice Gordon	Southern Methodist University
Charles R. Grah	Austin Peay State University
Mary Banks Gregerson	George Washington University
Timothy Jay	North Adams State College
James Johnson	Illinois State University
Lance K. Johnson	Pasadena City College
Lynne Kiorpes	New York University
Stephen B. Klein	Mississippi State University
Keith Kluender	University of Wisconsin-Madison
James M. Knight	Humboldt State University
James Kopp	University of Texas-Arlington
Emma Kraidman	Franciscan Children's Hospital, Boston
Philip Langer	University of Colorado-Boulder
Peter Leppmann	University of Guelph
Alice Locicero	Tufts University
Richard M. Martin	Gustavus Adolphus College
Donald McBurney	University of Pittsburgh
Eleanor Midkiff	Eastern Illinois University
David Mitchell	Southern Methodist University
David I. Mostofsky	Boston University
John Mullennix	Wayne State University
John Nezlek	The College of William and Mary
J. Faye Pritchard	La Salle University
Freda Rebelsky	Boston University
Bradley C. Redburn	Johnson County Community College
Daniel Roenkert	Western Kentucky University
Lawrence Rosenblum	University of California-Riverside
Kenneth W. Rusiniak	Eastern Michigan University
Ina Samuels	University of Massachusetts-Boston
Karl E. Scheibe	Wesleyan University
Richard Schiffman	Rutgers University
Robert Sekuler	Brandeis University
Norman Simonson	University of Massachusetts-Amherst
Steven Sloman	Brown University
J. Diedrick Snoek	Smith College
Sheldon Solomon	Skidmore College
Perry Timmermans	San Diego City College
D. Rene Verry	Millikin University
Paul Watson	University of Tennessee-Chatanooga
Russell H. Weigel	Amherst College
Joel Weinberger	Adelphi University
Cheryl Weinstein	Harvard Medical School
Paul Wellman	Texas A & M University
Macon Williams	Illinois State University
Jeremy M. Wolfe	Massachusetts Institute of Technology
Todd Zakrajsek	Albion College
Thomas Zentall	University of Kentucky

Student Focus Groups

Toward the end of the writing process, we were very fortunate in our effort to enlist the help of a wide range of students across the country to see what they thought of the writing, the pedagogy, and the overall conceptual approach of this text. A great deal of work on the part of those students and their faculty went into this final review stage, and the unique perspective of our ultimate customer, the student, helped me fine-tune the last draft. I am very grateful to all the students who read the words and thought about the ideas with great care, and I especially appreciate the time and effort of the faculty coordinators for administering these student focus groups and summarizing their results. My heartfelt gratitude to the following:

Canisius College
Coordinator: Harvey Pines
Student Participants: Kristen A. Breen, Tanii Anitra Chin, Robyn A. Filipink, Adrienne Walton, Heather Zajac

Johnson County Community College
Coordinator: Toby Klinger
Student Participants: Danita L. Coovert, Laurel Dunseth, Casey Hutchins, Thomas F. J. McGuire, Anne F. Rhoads, Peter Widhalm

Ohio State University
Faculty Coordinator: Alexis Collier
Graduate Teaching Assistant Coordinators: Mary Beth DeWitt, Londa Jill Smith
Student Participants: L. Estep, Eric Gamble, Marilyn A. Greenwood, Michael Guildoo, Matthew S. Jordan, Marissa Moy, Kerry A. Nixon, Prasenjit Ray, Tom Price, Jodi E. Scott, Rita P. Thompson, Joseph W. Vasquez

Southern Illinois University-Carbondale
Coordinator: Gordon Pitz
Student Participants: Jonathan Crosby, Amy M. Forst, Margaret Gors, Christina P. Iles, Thomas L. Reinsager, Mark C. Waits

University of Minnesota-Minneapolis
Coordinator: Gail Peterson
Student Participants: Nathan Chan, Kelly Mutchler, A. Sheldon

University of New Mexico-Albuquerque
Coordinator: Robert J. Sutherland
Student Participants: Georgia Gersh, Byron LaShawn Laurie, John Leak, Amy L. Polage, Kimberly Ravenscraft

University of Oklahoma-Norman
Coordinator: Richard Reardon
Student Participants: John Farrar, Jennifer Katzung, Joanna Myers, Jenny Wilson, Michelle Wray

University of Tennessee-Knoxville
Coordinator: William H. Calhoun
Co-coordinator: Paul Busby
Student Participants: Tracy L. Brown, Jeff Crumpley, Julie Ellis, Eugene Johnson, Jodi Johnson, Elizabeth Anne McSwiney, Daniel C. Oliver, Carrie Price, D. M. Rice, Amy Rigsby, Janna Sanders, Shelley R. Smith, Deanna Taylor, Ginger Walker

Finally, I'd like to offer my deep appreciation to the extraordinary team at Wiley. Foremost, Chris Rogers has shepherded this project for several years and helped elaborate its vision. He has been a wonderful friend and editor, a rare combination of scholar, businessman, and empathic soul who understands the torment of textbook authorship. This book would not have happened without him and his extraordinary confluence of editorial and interpersonal skills. Karen Dubno was also helpful in making sure the book came out on time and in the best possible shape, especially through her management of the review process and help with design decisions. Nancy Perry's contributions have been invaluable in monitoring the book's development and attending to every level of detail. I have never met an editor whose judgment is always so consistently thoughtful and trustworthy in matters ranging from content and writing to color and design. Anna Melhorn and Mary Ann Price have done a superb job developing the art work and photography programs, respectively. They performed an impressive balancing act in giving me autonomy while sharing their expertise whenever my defective right hemisphere led me astray. My thanks also go to Art Ciccone, who helped render accurate technical illustrations; the artists at Precision Graphics, who did an extraordinary job of turning my sketches into illustrations that are both aesthetically appealing and edifying; Ann Renzi, who supervised the design; Charlotte Hyland and Pamela Kennedy-Oborski, who carefully oversaw production; and David Kear, Francine Banner, Anne Dempsey, Matthew van Hattem, and Pui Szeto, who helped pull the final project together. Finally, I would like to thank Edward A. Burke of HRS for creating the book's clear, engaging design; and Lorraine Burke, Erica Smythe, and the staff at HRS for the work they did in producing this book.

One last person deserves my deepest thanks, for she has probably done more to improve my writing than anyone since my twelfth-grade English teacher: Harriett Prentiss. I thought I was just about done with this book a year ago, until, as development editor, she carefully examined the syntax of every sentence, the coherence of every paragraph, and the flow of every section. Her contributions were manifold. The reader has as much to thank Harriett for as I do.

ABOUT THE AUTHOR

Drew Westen is Associate Professor of Psychology at the Harvard Medical School and Chief Psychologist at the Cambridge Hospital, in Cambridge, Massachusetts. He received his undergraduate degree from Harvard, an M.A. in Social and Political Thought from the University of Sussex (England), and a Ph.D. in Clinical Psychology from the University of Michigan, where he taught introductory psychology for several years. While at the University of Michigan, he was honored two years in a row as the best teaching professor at the university, and was the recipient of the first Golden Apple Award for outstanding undergraduate teaching. His primary research is on the cognitive, emotional, and motivational processes that allow people to maintain intimate relationships, with a focus on people with personality disorders, who have interpersonal problems. Much of his theoretical work has attempted to bridge perspectives, particularly cognitive, psychodynamic, and evolutionary. His series of videotaped lectures on abnormal psychology, called *Is Anyone Really Normal?*, was published by the Teaching Company, in collaboration with the Smithsonian Institution. He also provides psychological commentaries on political issues for "All Things Considered" on National Public Radio. His main love outside of psychology is music. He writes comedy music and has performed as a stand-up comic in Boston.

DEDICATION

To my mother, and in memory of my father, who graced the dinner table with talk of people and ideas.

Contents
in Brief

Contents

Chapter 5

**Learning
174**

Chapter 6

**Memory
212**

Chapter 7

Thought and Language 254

Chapter 8

Intelligence
294

Chapter 9

Consciousness
330

Chapter 10

Motivation
364

Chapter 11

Emotion, Stress, and Coping
404

Chapter 12

Personality
446

Chapter 13

Physical and Cognitive Development 488

Chapter 14

**Social
Development
530**

Chapter 15

Psychological Disorders
574

Chapter 16

Treatment of Psychological Disorders 620

Chapter 17

**Attitudes
and Social
Cognition
660**

Chapter 18

**Interpersonal
Processes
698**

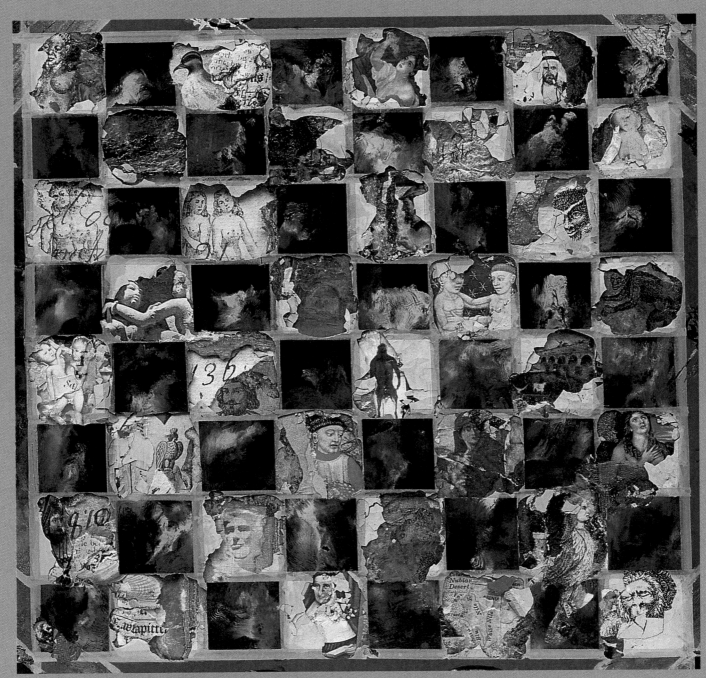

Rosamond Purcell, "It's How You Play the Game," *1992*

Chapter 1

PSYCHOLOGY: THE STUDY OF MENTAL PROCESSES AND BEHAVIOR

A 15-year-old girl we shall call Susan was hospitalized in a psychiatric unit because of severe adjustment problems. The most notable characteristic of her case was a dramatic change in her IQ score: In less than five years it had dropped 50 points, from 120 to 70. IQ is a measure of intelligence, and 120 is quite high, whereas 70 is on the border of mental retardation. As IQ scores in adolescence and adulthood typically remain fairly stable, a change of even 10 or 15 points in such a short time span is remarkable.

Susan had a poorly controlled case of epilepsy, a disorder characterized by abnormal patterns of electrical activity in the brain. Essentially, what happens in epilepsy is that nerve cells in the brain discharge or "fire" without appropriate stimulation. This leads to alterations in consciousness and behavior called seizures, such as psychological absence from reality for seconds or moments or violent muscle movements. Except in a small number of cases, epilepsy can be controlled with medication (Scheuer & Pedley, 1990), but Susan's was one of those cases.

Susan was peculiar in a number of ways. She was extremely egocentric, focusing only on her own perspective and interrupting conversations with her own concerns. She had difficulty sticking to the subject, and would often blurt out inappropriate thoughts. Her response to questions was often characterized by long delays before answering. Finally, she was overly preoccupied with religion, a phenomenon observed in a small percentage of people with epilepsy (Daiguji, 1990; Tucker et al., 1987).

According to Susan, her only problem was that her mother no longer lived with her; Susan's mother had abandoned the family five years earlier, and Susan had never recovered emotionally. As soon as her mother returned, she insisted, she would be fine again. However, the medical team treating Susan—I was one of them—had a different prognosis. We suspected Susan had a degenerative neurological condition—a deteriorating brain illness—that was responsible for both the epilepsy and her plummeting IQ score.

Several months after her release from the hospital, something strange happened: Susan's IQ rose almost 30 points, her social and academic difficulties diminished somewhat, and her seizures decreased in frequency. She would never return to normal, but the change was extraordinary. When I heard of this dramatic improvement, I presumed that her doctors had probably hit upon a new medication, but like many psychological hypotheses, this one turned out to be wrong. In fact, what prompted Susan's dramatic improvement was just what she had predicted: Her mother had returned.

Susan's case is unusual because rarely does an environmental change lead to such a remarkable improvement in brain functioning. Yet it illustrates one of the central issues that has vexed philosophers for over two millennia and psychologists for over a century—namely, the relation between mental events and physical events, between meaning and mechanism.

Humans are complex creatures whose psychological experience lies at the intersection of biology and culture. To paraphrase a leading figure in twentieth-century psychology, Erik Erikson (1963), psychologists must practice "triple bookkeeping" to understand an individual at any given time, simultaneously tracking biological events, psychological experience, and the cultural and historical context. Susan had **lesions,** or damaged areas, throughout various regions of her brain, but she also had emotional "lesions"—a broken heart as well as a broken brain. The confluence of these misfortunes created a syndrome that probably neither alone would have produced. Yet even this interaction of mind and brain does not fully account for Susan's syndrome, for in most cultures in human history, people have lived in small communities with their extended families, and mothers do not have the option of moving far away from their children. Had she lived in another place or another time, then, Susan may not have experienced either a rapid decline or a remarkable recovery.

At the intersection of biology and culture, then, lies **psychology,** the systematic study of mental processes and behavior. To understand psychology requires a constant movement between the micro-level of biology and the macro-level of culture. This chapter begins by exploring these boundaries and borders within which humans (and psychologists) operate. We then examine the theoretical perspectives that lie at the heart of psychology, which have focused, and often divided, the attention of the scientific community for a century. We conclude by placing these psychological perspectives in a broader context and examining the range of phenomena psychologists investigate, from the first smiles of infancy to the roots of violence.

THE BOUNDARIES AND BORDERS OF PSYCHOLOGY

Biology and culture establish both the possibilities and the constraints within which people think, feel, and act. On the one hand, all psychological processes have their basis in the activity of cells in the brain, so the structure of the brain sets the parameters or limits of human potential. Most ten-year-olds cannot solve algebra problems, as the neural circuitry essential for abstract thought has not yet matured. Similarly, the human capacity for love has its roots in the innate propensity of infants to develop an emotional attachment with their caretakers. These are biological givens.

On the other hand, most adults throughout human history would find algebra problems as mystifying as would a preschooler because their culture never provided the groundwork for this kind of reasoning, and though love may be a basic potential, the way people love depends on the values, beliefs, and practices of their society. In some cultures, people seek and expect romance in their marriages, whereas in others, they do not select a spouse based on affection or attraction at all.

FROM MIND TO BRAIN

THE BOUNDARY WITH NATURE

The biological boundary of psychology is the province of **biopsychology**, which investigates the physical basis of psychological phenomena such as motivation, emotion, and stress. Within this field, neuropsychologists and other neuroscientists (some of whom are physicians or biologists rather than psychologists) focus on the relation between the workings of the brain and mental processes and behavior. Instead of studying thoughts, feelings, fears, or wishes, neuroscientists investigate the electrical and chemical processes in the nervous system that underlie these mental events.

The connection between mind and brain became increasingly clear during the nineteenth century when doctors began observing patients with severe head injuries. Language and memory were often greatly curtailed in these patients, who might also show dramatic alterations in their personalities. A genteel businessman and devoted father, for example, could suddenly become affectionless, lewd, and cantankerous following a severe blow to the head. These observations led researchers to experiment by producing lesions surgically in animals in different neural regions to observe the effects on behavior.

One of the major issues in neuroscience since its origins in the nineteenth century is **localization of function,** the extent to which different parts of the brain control different aspects of functioning. In 1836, a physician named Marc Dax presented a paper in which he noted that lesions on the left side of the brain were associated with aphasia, or language disorders. The notion that language was localized to the left side of the brain (the left hemisphere) developed momentum as discoveries accumulated, linking specific language functions to specific regions of the left hemisphere. Paul Broca (1824–1880) discovered that brain-injured people with lesions in the front section of the left hemisphere were often unable to speak fluently but could comprehend language. Next, Carl Wernicke (1848–1904) showed that damage to an area a few centimeters behind the section Broca had discovered could lead to another kind of aphasia. In this form of aphasia, the person can neither understand language nor speak comprehensibly (Figure 1.1). Individuals with this form of aphasia may speak fluently, apparently following rules of grammar, but the words they utter make little sense ("I saw the bats and cuticles as the dog lifted the hoof, the pauser").

One of the metaphors that underlies neuropsychological thinking is that the brain is like an electronic machine with a complex series of circuits. Particular experiences or behaviors reflect patterns or sequences in the activation of cells, and these patterns depend, in turn, on the way cells are "wired" together. To offer an analogy, no single point on a television screen means anything on its own because each pixel or dot can be used in millions of different configurations. The *pattern* in which that dot is activated gives it meaning, just as the pattern of firing of cells determines the meaning of a neural event.

Contemporary neuropsychologists no longer believe that complex psychological functions "happen" exclusively in a single localized part of the brain. Rather, they believe that the circuits for complex psychological events, such as emotions or thoughts, are distributed throughout the brain, with each part contributing to the total experience. A man who sustains lesions to one area may be unable consciously to distinguish his wife's face from the face of any other woman—a disabling condition indeed—but may react physiologically to her face with a higher heart rate or pulse (Bruyer, 1991). Technological advances over the last two decades have allowed researchers to pinpoint lesions precisely, and even to watch computerized portraits of the brain light up with activity (or fail to light up, in cases of neural damage) as people perform psychological tasks (Gur, Erwin, & Gur, 1992).

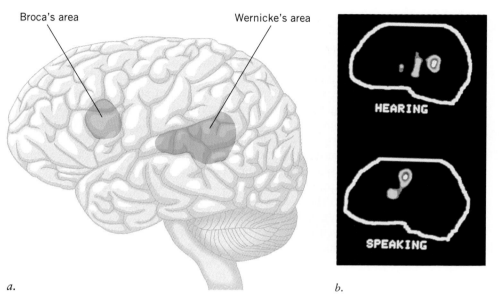

FIGURE 1.1
Broca's and Wernicke's areas. (a) Discovery of different effects of lesions to Broca's and Wernicke's areas led to increased sophistication about localization of function. Both produce aphasia, but Broca's aphasia involves difficulty producing speech, whereas Wernicke's aphasia typically involves difficulty comprehending language. (b) A PET scan is a computerized imaging technique that allows researchers and doctors to study the functioning of the brain as the person responds to stimuli. The PET scans here show activity in Wernicke's and Broca's areas.

A GLOBAL VISTA

THE BOUNDARY WITH CULTURE

Humans are not only collections of cells; they are also members of collectivities, which similarly impose their stamp on psychological functioning. The emergence of agriculture and cities, generally known as civilization, occurred less than ten thousand years ago. Before that time, and in much of this planet's southern hemisphere until well into the twentieth century, humans lived in small bands composed largely of their kin. Several bands often joined into larger tribes in order to trade mates, protect territory, wage war on other groups, or participate in communal rituals.

The anthropologists who first studied these "exotic" cultures in Africa, Australia, North America, and elsewhere were struck by their differentness from our own, and they raised a central issue that psychology has been slow to address: To what extent do cultural differences create psychological differences? What can we make of someone who becomes terrified because he believes that a quarrel with kin has offended the forest and may bring disaster upon his family? Does he share our psychological nature, or does each society produce its own psychology?

The first theorists to address this issue were psychologically sophisticated anthropologists like Margaret Mead and Ruth Benedict, who were interested in the relation between culture and personality (LeVine, 1982). Impressed with the wide variation of cultural beliefs and practices across the globe, they argued that individual psychology is fundamentally shaped by cultural values, ideals, and ways of thinking. As Benedict put it, "The life history of the individual is first and foremost an accommodation to the patterns and standards traditionally handed down in the community" (1934, p. 2). As children develop, they learn to behave in ways that conform to cultural standards. The openly competitive, confident, self-interested style generally rewarded in North American society would be unthinkable in Japan, where communal sentiments are much stronger. Japanese manufacturing companies do not lay off workers during economic downturns as do their North American and European counterparts, because they believe corporations are like families and should treat their employers accordingly. Even ways of thinking—using witchcraft to explain disease, or manipulating things that do not exist in reality, such as negative numbers—are shaped through interactions with others and become woven into the individual's own psychological fabric (Vygotsky, 1978; Wertsch & Kanner, 1992).

At midcentury, **psychological anthropologists,** who study psychological phenomena in other cultures by observing people as they behave in their daily lives (see Bock, 1988; Suarez-Orozco and Spindler, 1994), turned their interest to the way economic realities shape childrearing practices, which in turn mold personality (Kardiner, 1945; Whiting & Child, 1953). Then as now, people in much of the Third World were leaving their ancestral homelands seeking work in large cities. Working as a laborer in a factory requires different attitudes toward time, mobility, and individuality than farming or foraging. A laborer must be able and willing to punch a time clock, move where the work is, work for wages, and spend all day without the company of kin (see Inkeles & Smith, 1974). Notions that we take for granted—such as arriv-

Margaret Mead was a leading figure among anthropologists and psychologists trying to understand the relation between personality and culture. Here she is pictured among the Manus in the late 1920s.

ing at the job within a prescribed span of minutes—are not "natural" to human beings. Punctuality is necessary for shiftwork in a factory or for changing from class to class in a modern school, and we consider it an aspect of character or personality. Yet punctuality was probably not even recognized as a dimension of personality in most cultures before the contemporary era and was certainly not a prime concern of parents in rearing their children.

Working in a factory requires attitudes, behaviors, and personality traits such as punctuality that require years, if not generations, to form.

After the 1950s, interest in the relation between culture and psychological attributes waned for decades. Within psychology, however, a small group of researchers developed the field of **cross-cultural psychology,** which attempts to test psychological hypotheses in different cultures (Berry et al., 1992; Lonner & Malpass, 1994; Triandis, 1980, 1994). Interest in cross-cultural psychology has blossomed recently as issues of diversity have come to the fore in the political arena. Psychologists have been more self-consciously asking whether decades of experimental research on topics such as memory, motivation, psychological disorders, or obedience have yielded results about *people* or about a particular *group* of people. Do individuals in all cultures experience depression? Do toddlers learn to walk and talk at the same time cross-culturally? Do people dream in all cultures, and if so, what is the function of dreaming? Only cross-cultural comparisons can distinguish between psychological processes that are universal and those that are culturally specific.

Generalizing about human nature requires studying its many varieties.

The Philosophical Roots of Psychological Questions

Questions about human nature, such as whether psychological attributes are the same everywhere, were once the province of philosophy. Early in this century, however, just as philosophers were wrestling with the limitations of what they could know about topics like morality, justice, and the nature of knowledge, psychologists began to apply the methods and technologies of natural science to psychological questions. They reasoned that if physics can discover the atom and if industry can mass-produce automobiles, then psychological science can uncover basic laws of human and animal behavior that transcend time and culture.

The fact that psychology was born from the womb of philosophy is of no small consequence. Many of the issues that remain at the heart of contemporary psychological research and controversy are classic philosophical questions. One of these is whether human action is the product of free will or determinism. Those who champion free will follow in the footsteps of the seventeenth-century French philosopher Rene Descartes (1596–1650), who contended that human action follows from human intention—that is, that people choose a course of action and act on it. In contrast, proponents of determinism, from the Greek philosopher Democritus onward, assert that behavior follows lawful patterns like everything else in the universe, from falling rocks to planets revolving around the sun. Psychological determinists believe that the actions of humans and other animals are determined by physical forces, internally by genetic processes and externally by environmental events.

If this issue had an easy solution, philosophers would have found it, but it does not. Subjectively, we have the experience of free will. I could choose to stop writing—or you to stop reading—at this very moment. Yet here we are, continuing into the next sentence. Why? What determined our choice to forge ahead? And how can mental processes exercise control over physical processes such as moving a pen or turning a page? Humans are material beings, part of nature like birds, plants, and water. When we choose to move, our limbs exert a force that counters gravity and disturbs molecules of air. How can a nonmaterial force—will—displace material forces? Although no one has ever proposed a satisfactory solution to the **mind-body problem** (the question of how mental and physical events interact), psychological phenomena such as the decline and subsequent rise of Susan's IQ put the mind-body problem in a new light. They draw scientific attention to the processes through which psychological meaning (despair at her mother's absence) becomes transformed into mechanism (physiological events, such as seizure activity).

Indeed, the classic philosophical question of free will versus determinism reverberates through many contemporary psychological discussions. Research into the genetics of personality and personality disturbances provides an intriguing, if disquieting, example. People with antisocial personality disorder have minimal conscience and a proclivity toward aggressive or criminal behavior, as was the case with a man who boasted in an initial psychiatric evaluation about the way he had terrorized his former girlfriend for an hour by brandishing a knife and telling her in exquisite detail the ways he intended to slice her flesh. This man could undoubtedly have exercised his free will to continue or discontinue his behavior at any moment, and hence was morally (and legally) responsible for his acts. He knew what he was doing, he was not hearing voices commanding him to behave aggressively, and he thoroughly enjoyed his victim's terror. A determinist, however, could offer an equally compelling case. Like many violent men, he was the son of violent alcoholic parents, who had beaten him severely as a child. Both physical abuse in childhood and parental alcoholism (which may have both genetic and environmental influence) render an individual more likely to develop antisocial personality disorder (see Cadoret et al., 1986; Zanarini et al., 1990). In the immediate moment, perhaps, he had free will, but over the long run, he may have had no choice but to be the person he was.

The prisons are filled with people whose genetic and environmental background predisposed them to criminality. Whether they are responsible for their actions is as much a question for philosophers as for psychologists.

THE ROLE OF PERSPECTIVES IN PSYCHOLOGY

We have thus far examined the boundaries of psychology with biology and culture, which provide the inner and outer context for mental processes and behavior, and have explored the way psychological questions border on the philosophical. We now move inward from the borders to examine the theoretical perspectives that guide the way psychologists formulate questions and attempt to answer them.

A tale is told of several blind men in India who came upon an elephant. They had no knowledge of what an elephant was, and eager to understand the beast, they reached out to explore it. One man grabbed its trunk and concluded, "An elephant is like a snake." Another touched its ear and proclaimed, "An elephant is like a leaf." A third, examining its leg, disagreed: "An elephant," he asserted, "is like the trunk of a tree." Psychologists are in some ways like those blind men, struggling with imperfect instruments to try to understand the beast we call human nature and typically touching only part of the animal while trying to grasp the whole. In this chapter and throughout the book, we examine four perspectives that guide psychological thinking, offering sometimes competing and sometimes complementary frameworks or points of view on phenomena ranging from antisocial personality disorder to the way people make decisions when choosing a mate.

These perspectives are similar in many respects to the intuitive perspectives people take in daily life. The importance of perspective can be illustrated by a simple perceptual phenomenon. Consider Figure 1.2. Does it depict a vase? The profiles of two faces? The answer depends on one's perspective on the whole picture. This picture was used by a German school of psychologists known as **Gestalt** psychologists, who believed that perception is not a passive experience through which people take photographic snapshots of details of the world around them. Rather, they argued, perception is an active experience of imposing order on an overwhelming panorama of details by seeing them as parts of larger wholes.

On simple perceptual tasks, then, the way people understand specific facts or details depends upon their interpretation of the object as a whole, be it a vase or two

FIGURE 1.2
An ambiguous figure. The indentation in the middle could be either an indentation in a vase or a nose. In science as in everyday perception, knowledge involves understanding "facts" in the context of a broader interpretive framework.

profiles. This is equally true of complex scientific observations, which always occur within the context of a broader view, a theoretical perspective. To take a clinical example (that is, an example from the therapeutic practice of psychology), a patient with an irrational fear, or phobia, of elevators may be told by one psychologist that her problem stems from the way thoughts and feelings were connected in her mind as a child. A second psychologist informs her that her problem results from an unfortunate connection between something in her environment, an elevator, and her learned response, avoidance of elevators. A third—examining the same data, no less—concludes that she has faulty wiring in her brain that leads to irrational anxiety.

What can we make of this state of affairs, in which experts seriously disagree on the meaning and implications of a simple symptom? And what confidence could anyone have in seeking psychological help? The alternative is even less attractive: A psychologist with no perspective at all would be totally baffled and could only recommend to this patient that she take the stairs. Perspectives in psychology are like imperfect lenses through which one can view some aspect of reality. They are frequently too convex or concave, and they often leave their wearers blind to data on the periphery of their understanding, but without them, we are all totally blind.

The relationship between "facts" and scientific interpretations has been described at length by Thomas Kuhn, a philosopher of science. Kuhn (1970) observed that science does not progress through the accumulation of facts, as many had believed. Rather, scientific progress depends on the development of better and better paradigms. A **paradigm** is a broad system of theoretical assumptions that a scientific community uses to make sense of a domain of experience. For example, the scientific community of physicists develops paradigms to make sense of the domain of the physical world; economists develop paradigms to explain market forces.

A paradigm has several key components. First, it includes a set of theoretical assertions that provide a **model** or abstract picture of the object of study. In economics, this model includes laws of supply and demand, which can be graphically depicted, much as vectors in physics. Second, a paradigm includes a set of shared metaphors that compare the object under investigation to another that is readily apprehended (such as "the mind is like a computer"). Third, a paradigm includes a set of methods that members of the scientific community agree will, if properly executed, produce valid and useful data. In astronomy, the community of scientists agrees that telescopic investigation provides a window to studying events in space.

According to Kuhn, the social sciences, among them psychology, differ from the natural sciences in that they lack an accepted paradigm upon which most members of the scientific community agree. Instead, he proposes, the social sciences are still splintered into several schools of thought, or what we have simply called **perspectives**. The four psychological perspectives we shall examine offer the same kind of broad orienting approach as a scientific paradigm, and they share its three essential features. Focusing on these particular perspectives is not to say that other, less comprehensive approaches have not contributed to psychological knowledge, or that nothing can be studied without them. A researcher interested in a specific question, such as whether preschool programs for economically disadvantaged children will improve their functioning later in life (Chafel, 1992), does not need to endorse a broader outlook. But perspectives generally guide psychological investigations.

In the following sections we examine the **psychodynamic, behaviorist, cognitive, and evolutionary perspectives**. These perspectives have evolved in many respects independently, and each addresses phenomena ignored by the others, yet all four will undoubtedly contribute someday to an integrated paradigm. Table 1.1 presents an overview of the four perspectives.

TABLE 1.1 PRINCIPLES, METAPHORS, AND METHODS OF THE FOUR PERSPECTIVES ON PSYCHOLOGY

PERSPECTIVE	BASIC PRINCIPLES	METAPHORS	METHODS
Psychodynamic	Behavior is largely the result of unconscious processes, motivation, and early experiences.	Consciousness is like the tip of an iceberg; the mind is like a battleground for warring factions.	Interpretation of verbal discourse, slips of the tongue, dreams, fantasies, actions, and postures; case studies; limited experimentation.
Behaviorist	Behavior is learned and selected by its environmental consequences.	Humans and other animals are like machines; the mind is like a black box.	Experimentation with humans and other animals.
Cognitive	Behavior is the product of information processing: storage, transformation, and retrieval of data.	The mind is like a computer; enduring patterns of thought are like software.	Experimentation with humans; computer modeling.
Evolutionary	Psychological processes reflect evolutionary process of natural selection.	Life is like a race for survival and reproduction.	Deduction of explanations for traits and behaviors; cross-species and cross-cultural comparisons; limited experimentation.

The Psychodynamic Perspective

A friend has been dating a man for five months and has even jokingly tossed around the idea of marriage. Suddenly, her boyfriend tells her he has found someone else. She is shocked, feels flooded with sadness and anger, and cries uncontrollably, but a day later asserts that she does not care: "He didn't mean that much to

Sigmund Freud poring over a manuscript in his home office in Vienna around 1930.

me anyway." When you try to console her about the rejection she must be feeling, she says, "Rejection? Hey, I don't know why I put up with him as long as I did," and jokes that "bad character is a genetic abnormality carried on the Y-chromosome" (more on that later). You know she really cared about him, and you conclude that she is being defensive, that she really feels rejected. You draw these conclusions because you have grown up in a culture heavily influenced by the psychoanalytic theory of Sigmund Freud.

In the late nineteenth century, Sigmund Freud (1856–1939), a Viennese physician, developed a theory of mental life and behavior and an approach to treating psychological disorders known as **psychoanalysis.** Since then, many psychologists have maintained Freud's emphasis on **psychodynamics,** or the dynamic interplay of mental forces. Psychodynamic psychologists make several basic assumptions. First, people's actions are determined by the way thoughts, feelings, and wishes are connected in their minds. Second, many of these mental events occur outside of conscious awareness. And third, these mental processes may conflict with one another, leading to compromises among competing motives. Thus, people are unlikely to know precisely the chain of psychological events that leads to their conscious thoughts, intentions, feelings, or behaviors.

Origins of the Psychodynamic Approach

Freud originated his theory in response to patients whose symptoms, although real, were not based on physiological malfunctioning. Scientific thinking at the time had no way to explain patients who were preoccupied with irrational guilt after the death of a parent or were so paralyzed with fear that they could not leave their homes. Freud made a deceptively simple deduction, one that changed the face of intellectual history: If the symptoms were not consciously created and maintained, and if they had no physical basis, only one possibility remained—their basis must be unconscious.

Just as people have conscious motives or wishes, Freud argued, they also have powerful unconscious motives that underlie their conscious intentions. The reader has undoubtedly had the infuriating experience of waiting for half an hour as traffic crawls on the highway, only to find that nothing was blocking the road at all—just an accident in the opposite lane. Why do people slow down and gawk at accidents on the highway? Is it because they are concerned? Perhaps. But Freud would suggest that people derive an unconscious titillation or excitement—or at least satisfy a morbid curiosity—from viewing a gruesome scene, even though they may work hard to deny to themselves that they have such socially unacceptable feelings.

Metaphors of the Psychodynamic Approach

Freud considered the relation between conscious awareness and unconscious mental forces analogous to the visible tip of an iceberg and the vast, submerged hulk that lies out of sight beneath the water. Before Freud's time, most people believed their own and others' actions were directed by their conscious wishes and beliefs. In contrast, Freud emphasized that these conscious desires themselves may reflect *unconscious* conflicts and compromises.

One patient, for example, came to a psychotherapist because she was always choosing men who were unobtainable. She explained that she was only attracted to men who were exciting, charismatic, and ultrasuccessful. As she explored her dating history in therapy, however, a pattern emerged: If she could actually win these "special" men, she became uninterested. Exploring her childhood history revealed that her father was a flashy, charismatic, and highly successful businessman whose love and respect she felt she never could obtain. As an adult, she was attracted to men much like her father, but she was also afraid that they would reject her as her father had. Her way of resolving this unconscious conflict was to look for men like her father but reject them as soon as they showed interest. Recent research, in fact, supports the view that the relationship between children and their caretakers is crucial in shaping later social relationships and that these patterns of relating may be transmitted from generation to generation through parent-child interactions beginning in infancy (Bretherton, 1985, 1990; Main, 1990; Main, Kaplan, & Cassidy, 1985; von Izjendoorn, in press).

Another psychodynamic metaphor is that the mind is a battleground in which warring factions struggle for expression. Imagine a young man growing up in a culture such as our own, which views homosexuality with considerable hostility. The young man nevertheless has sexual feelings only toward other males, which conflict with societal norms or rules and with his conscience, which has been shaped by social and parental attitudes. What does he do in the face of this conflict? The conflict can be so painful that it apparently contributes to a high suicide rate among homosexual teenagers (Coleman & Remafedi, 1989).

One option for this man is to acknowledge his homosexual feelings and ultimately accept them, a path that increasing numbers of gays and lesbians are now choosing. Alternatively, he may resolve the conflict unconsciously. For instance, he might **repress** his wishes, that is, keep himself unaware of them to avoid emotional discomfort. Freud maintained, however, that things are rarely that simple. Unconscious motives may be out of sight, but they are not out of mind. They will continue to press for satisfaction, and the stronger their force, the more intense will be the efforts to disavow them. For example, the man might convince himself that he is not really homosexual and might join a crusade against homosexuality. He thus exerts considerable effort trying to eradicate the homosexuality outside of him, when his real aim is to stifle the homosexual feelings and impulses within.

Methods and Data of the Psychodynamic Perspective

The methods used by psychodynamic psychologists flow from their aims. Psychodynamic understanding seeks to interpret meanings, that is, to infer underlying wishes, fears, and patterns of thought from an individual's conscious, verbalized thought and behavior. Based on this goal, a psychodynamic psychologist observes a patient's dreams, fantasies, posture, and subtle behavior toward the therapist. The psychodynamic perspective thus lends itself to the case study method, which entails in-depth observation of a small number of people.

The data of psychoanalysis can be thoughts, feelings, and actions that occur anywhere, from jockeying for power in corporate boardrooms to a young child biting his brother for refusing to vacate a hobbyhorse. The use of any and all forms of information about a person reflects the psychodynamic assumption that people reveal themselves in everything they do (which is why psychoanalysts may not always be the most welcome guests at dinner parties). Many psychodynamic psychologists rely exclusively on clinical data to test or support their theories, but a growing number believe in applying scientific methods as well (Fisher & Greenberg, 1985; Shedler, Mayman, & Manis, 1993; Westen, 1990).

The Behaviorist Perspective

You are enjoying an intimate dinner at a little Italian place on Main Street when your partner springs on you an unexpected piece of news: He (or she) is leaving. Your stomach turns and you leave in tears. One evening a year or two later, your new flame suggests dining at that same restaurant. Your reaction? Just as before, your stomach turns and your appetite suddenly disappears.

The second broad perspective that developed in psychology early in this century, **behaviorism,** argues that the aversion to that quaint Italian trattoria, like many reactions and dispositions to act in various ways, is the result of learning—in this case, instant, one-trial learning. Whereas the psychodynamic perspective emphasizes internal mental events, behaviorism focuses on the relation between objects or events in the environment (**stimuli**) and an organism's response to those events. Indeed, John Watson (1878–1958), a pioneer of American behaviorism, considered mental events outside the province of a scientific psychology altogether, and B. F. Skinner (1904–1990) who developed behaviorism into a full-fledged perspective years later, stated, "There is no place in a scientific analysis of behavior for a mind or self" (1990, p. 1209).

Origins of the Behaviorist Approach

At the same time Freud was developing psychoanalytic theory, Ivan Pavlov (1849–1936), a Russian physiologist, was conducting experiments on the digestive processes of dogs. During the course of his experiments, Pavlov made an important and quite accidental discovery: Once his dogs became accustomed to hearing a particular sound at mealtime, they began to salivate automatically whenever they heard it, just as they would salivate if food were presented. The process that had shaped this new response was learning. In fact, behaviorists argue that human and animal behaviors—from salivation in Pavlov's laboratory to losing your appetite upon hearing the name of a restaurant associated with rejection—are largely acquired by learning. Psychologists today have even begun to identify the biochemical changes in brain cells and the neural circuits involved in learning (Lavond, Kim, & Fitzgerald, 1993; Matthies, 1989).

The behaviorist perspective, particularly as it developed in the United States, sought to do away with two ideas propounded by the philosopher Descartes. Descartes stressed the role of reason in human affairs; he believed that thought can be independent of experience and can generate knowledge that is not derived from experience. To be human is to reflect upon one's experience, and to reflect is to create new insights about oneself and the world. As noted earlier, Descartes also proposed a dualism of mind and body, in which mental events and physical events can have different causes. The mind, or soul, is free to think and choose, while the body is constrained by the laws of nature.

Behaviorists countered Descartes's focus on mental processes by asserting that human behavior, no less than animal behavior, can be understood entirely without reference to internal states such as thoughts and feelings. Further, they aimed to circumvent **Cartesian dualism** (the doctrine of dual spheres of mind and body) by demonstrating that human conduct follows laws of behavior, just as the law of gravity can explain why things fall down instead of up.

The task for behaviorists was to discern the ways in which environmental events, or stimuli, control behavior. John Locke (1632–1704), a seventeenth-century British philosopher, contended that at birth the mind is a *tabula rasa*, a blank slate upon which experience writes itself. In a similar vein, John Watson was later to claim that if he were given 12 healthy infants at birth, he could turn them into whatever he wanted, doctors or thieves, regardless of any innate dispositions or talents, simply by controlling their environments (Watson, 1925).

The Environment and Behavior

The belief that behavior is under the control of environmental stimuli rather than under the control of conscious or unconscious processes dovetailed with the philosophy of science that informed behaviorism. The dramatic progress of the natural sciences in the nineteenth century had led many psychologists to believe that the time had come to wrest the study of human nature away from philosophers and put it into the hands of scientists. For behaviorists, psychology is the *science of behavior,* and the proper method for conducting psychological research should be the same as that for other sciences—rigorous application of scientific method, particularly experimentation.

Scientists can directly observe a rat running a maze, a baby sucking on a plastic nipple to make a mobile turn, or even the rise of a dog's heart rate when it hears a bell that has previously preceded a painful electric shock. However, no one can directly observe unconscious motives. To have a science, behaviorists argued, one must be able to make observations on a reliable and calibrated instrument that others can use to make precisely the same observations. If two observers can view the same data very differently, as often occurs with psychodynamic inferences, then prediction and hypothesis testing are impossible.

According to behaviorists, psychologists cannot even study *conscious* thoughts in a scientific way because no one has access to them except the subject. In the early part of this century, a school of thought known as **structuralism** arose in Germany. The structuralists attempted to understand the way conscious sensations, feelings, and images fit together, much as atoms combine into molecules in chemistry. The originator of structuralism, Wilhelm Wundt (1832–1920), is sometimes viewed as the father of psychology because he founded the first psychological laboratory in 1879. Wundt's ideas spread to the United States, where the primary research tool used by his followers was a method called **introspection,** in which trained subjects verbally reported everything that went through their minds when presented with a stimulus or task. Behaviorists questioned the scientific value of such observations, which could not be independently verified. They proposed an alternative to psychodynamic and introspectionist methods: Study observable behaviors and environmental events, and build a science around the way people and animals *behave.* Hence the term behaviorism.

Perhaps the most systematic behaviorist theory was developed by B. F. Skinner. Building on the work of earlier behaviorists, Skinner observed that the behavior of organisms can be controlled by environmental conditions that either increase (reinforce) or decrease (**punish**) their likelihood of occurring, and that subtle alterations in these conditions (such as the timing of an aversive consequence) can have dramatic effects on behavior. Most dog owners can attest that swatting a dog with a rolled-up newspaper after it grabs a piece of steak from the dinner table can be very useful in suppressing the dog's unwanted behavior, but not if the punishment comes an hour later. Skinner believed that all human and animal behavior can ultimately be understood as learned responses to environmental events, and that behaviors are selected on the basis of their consequences. Researchers from a behaviorist perspective have discovered that this kind of learning-by-consequences can be used to control some very unlikely "behaviors" in humans, such as headaches and heart rate (Holroyd & Penzien, 1990; Lisspers & Ost, 1990; Larkin, Manuck, & Kasprowicz, 1990).

Metaphors, Methods, and Data of Behaviorism

A primary metaphor of behaviorism is that humans and other animals are like machines. In the same way that pushing a button starts the coffee maker brewing, presenting food triggered an automatic or reflexive response in Pavlov's dogs. Similarly, opening this book probably triggered the learned behavior of underlining and note taking. Many behaviorists also view the mind as a black box whose mechanisms can never be observed. A stimulus enters the box, and a response comes out; what happens inside is not the behaviorist's business. Other behaviorists are interested in what might occur in that box but are not convinced that current technologies render it accessible to scientific investigation; hence, they prefer to study what *can* be observed, the relation between what goes into it and what comes out.

The primary method of behaviorism is the experimental method. The experimental method entails framing a hypothesis or prediction about the way certain environmental events will affect behavior, then creating a laboratory situation to test that hypothesis. For instance, a behaviorist experiment may place two rats in sim-

Wilhelm Wundt is often called the "father of psychology" for his pioneering laboratory research. This portrait was painted in Leipzig, where he founded the first psychological laboratory.

B. F. Skinner offered a comprehensive behaviorist analysis of topics ranging from animal behavior to language development in children. In Walden Two, he even proposed a utopian vision of a society based on behaviorist principles.

FIGURE 1.3
A standard T-maze from a behaviorist experiment. The experimenter controls the rat's behavior by giving or eliminating rewards, in one arm or the other of the "T."

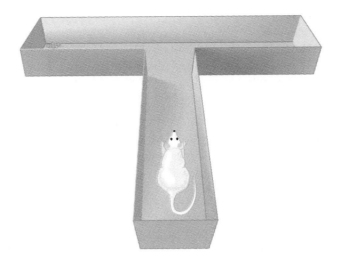

ple T-mazes, shaped like the letter "T," as shown in Figure 1.3. The two mazes are identical in all respects but one: Pellets of food lie at the end of the left arm of the first rat's maze, but not the second. After a few trials (efforts at running through the maze), the rat that obtains the reward will be more likely to turn to the left and run the maze faster. The experimenter can now systematically modify the situation, again observing the results over several trials. What happens if the rat is rewarded only every third time? Every fourth time? Will it run faster or slower, or will it complete the maze at the same rate? By creating and testing such contingencies, behaviorists aim to uncover general laws of learning. Similarly, researchers can compare the number of trials necessary to teach a child to solve a problem when candy is given to the child immediately after, or 30 seconds after a correct response. Because these data can be measured quantitatively, experimenters can test the accuracy of their predictions with great precision.

Behaviorism was the dominant perspective in psychology, particularly in North America, from the 1920s to the 1960s. In its purest forms, however, it has lost some favor in the last two decades as psychology has once again become concerned with the study of mental processes. Many psychologists have come to believe that thoughts *about* the environment are just as important in predicting behavior as the environment itself (Rotter, 1966, 1990; Mischel, 1990; Bandura, 1977, 1991). Other theorists define behavior quite broadly, to include thoughts as covert or hidden behaviors. Nevertheless, traditional behaviorist theory continues to have widespread applications, from helping people quit smoking or drinking to enhancing children's learning in school.

The Cognitive Perspective

When from a long distant past nothing subsists, after the people are dead, after the things are broken and scattered, still, alone, more fragile, but with more vitality, more unsubstantial, more persistent, more faithful, the smell and taste of things remain poised a long time, like souls, ready to remind us, waiting and hoping for their moment, amid the ruins of all the rest; and bear unfaltering, in the tiny and almost impalpable drop of their essence, the vast structure of recollection.

Marcel Proust, *Remembrance of Things Past*

The past 20 years have witnessed a cognitive revolution in psychology (Dember, 1974). Today the study of **cognition,** or thought, dominates psychology in the same way that the study of behavior did at midcentury. Indeed, when the chairpersons of psychology departments across the country were asked to rank the ten most important contemporary psychologists, eight were cognitive (Korn, Davis, & Davis, 1991). Poets and literary figures such as Proust, of course, foreshadowed psychologists' interest in thought and memory, and the cognitive approach has its own psychological ancestors as well. Wundt's introspection experiments were cognitive, in that people were trained to report their thought processes while, for example, solving problems. This "think aloud" procedure is still used in research by contemporary cognitive psychologists. Gestalt psychology, too, was arguably a cognitive psychology, in its focus on the way people organize sensory information into meaningful units. Nevertheless, in large measure the **cognitive perspective** owes its contemporary form to a technological development—the computer.

Many cognitive psychologists use the metaphor of the computer to understand and model the way the mind works. From this perspective, thinking is a form of **information processing:** The environment provides inputs, which are transformed, stored, and retrieved using various mental "programs," leading to specific response outputs. Just as the computer database of a book store may code its inventory according to genre, title, author, and so forth, human memory systems also encode information in order to store it. The coding system we use affects how easily we can later access information. Thus, most people would find it hard to name the fortieth president of the United States but easy to tell which recent president was in his seventies when he left office. The reason is that most people have given Ronald Reagan's age more priority in coding information about him in memory than the numerical order of his presidency.

The cognitive perspective can also be useful in understanding decision-making processes. For example, when people enter a car showroom, they have a set of attributes in their minds: smooth ride, sleek look, good gas mileage, affordable price, and so forth. At the same time, they must process a great deal of external auditory information (the salesman's description of one car as a "real steal," for instance) and match it with stored linguistic knowledge. This allows them to comprehend the meaning of his speech, such as the connotation of real steal (from both his viewpoint and theirs). In making a decision, they must process the information they are receiving, taking into account both the importance of particular attributes and the quality of each car on those dimensions.

Origins of the Cognitive Approach

The philosophical roots of the cognitive perspective lie in a series of questions raised by the ancient Greek philosophers and pondered again by British and European philosophers over the last three centuries (see Gardner, 1985). These questions center on the origins of knowledge. Descartes, like Plato, reflected on the remarkable truths of arithmetic and geometry and noted that the purest and most useful abstractions—such as a circle, a hypotenuse, pi, or a square root—could never be observed by the senses. Rather, this kind of knowledge appeared to be generated by the mind itself. Other philosophers, notably Locke, argued, on the contrary, that all knowledge is derived from experience. Complex ideas, Locke proposed, ultimately emerge from the mental manipulation of simple ideas; these simple ideas are products of the senses, of observation.

The behaviorists roundly rejected Descartes's view of an active, reasoning mind with knowledge independent of experience. Cognitive psychologists, however, have shown more interest in some of the questions raised by Descartes and other **rationalist** philosophers, that is, philosophers who emphasize the role of reason in creating knowledge. For example, cognitive psychologists have studied the way people form abstract concepts or categories. These concepts are in part derived from experience, but they often differ from any particular instance the person has ever perceived, which means that they must be mentally constructed (Medin, 1989). For

People categorize an object that resembles a dog by comparing it to examples of dogs, generalized views of dogs, or characteristic features of dogs stored in memory.

example, children can recognize that a bulldog is a dog even if they have never seen one before, because they have an abstract concept of "dog" stored in memory that goes beyond the details of any specific dogs they have seen.

Metaphors, Methods, and Data of Cognitive Psychology

Both the cognitive and behaviorist perspectives view organisms as machines that respond to environmental input with predictable output. Some cognitive theories even propose that a stimulus evokes a series of mini-responses inside the head, much like the responses the behaviorist studies outside the head (Anderson, 1983). But the metaphors used by cognitive psychologists differ from those of behaviorists. As noted earlier, many behaviorists view the mind as a black box whose contents are unobservable and therefore problematic for a scientific psychology. Most behaviorists actually object entirely to the concept of mind. The cognitive perspective, in contrast, has filled the box with software—with mental programs that produce output. In fact, the cognitive perspective is often more interested in how mental programs operate than in either the particular stimulus or the end result.

Like behaviorism, the primary method of the cognitive perspective is experimental, but with an important difference. Cognitive psychologists use experimental procedures to infer mental processes at work. For example, when people try to retrieve information from a list (such as the names of states), do they scan all the relevant information in memory until they hit the right item? One way cognitive psychologists have explored this question is by presenting subjects with a series of word lists to memorize that vary in length, such as those in Figure 1.4. Then they ask the subjects if particular words were on the lists. If subjects take longer to recognize that a word was *not* on a longer list–which they do–it implies that they are scanning the lists sequentially, and that additional words on the list take additional time (Sternberg, 1975).

Cognitive psychologists originally tended to study processes such as memory and decision making that had little to do with emotion or motivation. In more recent years, however, the cognitive perspective has emerged as a full-fledged per-

LIST A	LIST B
Nevada	Texas
Arkansas	Colorado
Tennessee	Missouri
Texas	South Carolina
North Dakota	Alabama
Nebraska	California
Michigan	Washington
Rhode Island	Idaho
Massachusetts	
Idaho	
New York	
Pennsylvania	

FIGURE 1.4
Two lists of words used in a study of memory scanning. Presenting subjects with two lists of state names provides a test of the memory scanning hypothesis. Iowa is not on either list. If an experimenter asks subjects whether Iowa is on the list, they take longer to respond to List A than List B because they have to scan more items in memory. The cognitive perspective focuses on the way information is stored and retrieved from memory in tasks like this.

spective that offers explanations for a wide range of phenomena. Cognitive research on emotion, for example, documents that the way people think about events, and the concepts they hold about feared or desired states, play a substantial role in generating emotions (Cantor, 1990; Lazarus, 1993).

The Evolutionary Perspective

- The impulse to eat in humans has a biological basis.
- The sexual impulse in humans has a biological basis.
- Caring for one's offspring has a biological basis.
- The fact that most males are interested in sex with females, and vice versa, has a biological basis.
- The higher incidence of aggressive behavior in males than in females has a biological basis.
- The tendency to care more for one's own offspring than for the offspring of other people has a biological basis.

Many people fully agree with the first of these statements but have growing doubts as the list proceeds. The degree to which inborn processes determine human behavior is a classic issue in psychology, called the **nature-nurture controversy.** Advocates of the "nurture" position maintain that behavior is primarily learned and not biologically ordained. Other psychologists, however, point to the similarities in behavior between humans and other animals, from chimpanzees to birds, arguing that some behavioral similarities are so striking that they must reflect, to some degree, the biological nature of humans and other animals. Indeed, anyone who thinks that the sight of two male teenagers "duking it out" behind the local high school for the attention of a popular girl is distinctively human should observe the behavior of rams and baboons. As we shall see, many if not most psychological processes reflect an *interaction* of nature and nurture, as in the case of Susan's epileptic seizures, which waxed and waned with her mother's presence. Human life is like a gray fabric, with strands of genetics (white) and environmental influence

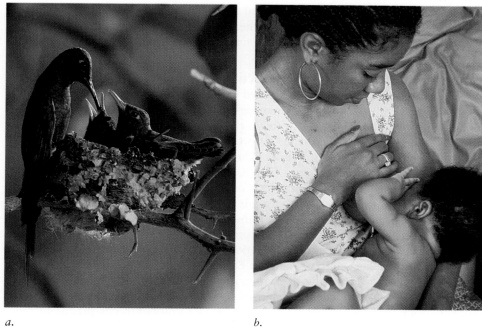

a.   b.

The notion that birds instinctively care for their children (a) is widely accepted, but the corresponding claim that humans have innate mechanisms that elicit caretaking behavior (b) is more controversial.

Similar behavior in humans and other animals suggests common evolutionary roots.

(black) so tightly interwoven that one can rarely discern the separate threads (Kagan & Snidman).

The **evolutionary perspective** argues that many human behavioral proclivities, from the need to eat to concern for one's children, became prevalent in human populations because they helped our ancestors survive and produce offspring that would be more likely to survive. Why, for example, was Susan, whose case opened this chapter, so devastated by her mother's absence? From an evolutionary perspective, a deep emotional bond between parents and children prevents them from straying too far away from each other while children are immature and vulnerable. Breaking this bond leads to tremendous distress. Evolutionary psychologists believe most enduring human attributes—from physical traits such as the presence of two eyes rather than one, which allows perception of depth, to cognitive and emotional tendencies, such as a child's distress at the absence of her caregivers—at some time served a function for humans as biological organisms (Buss, 1991). The implication of this point of view for psychological theory is that to understand human mental processes and behaviors requires insight into their evolution.

Origins of the Evolutionary Perspective

The evolutionary perspective is rooted in the writings of Charles Darwin, whose *On the Origin of Species* (1859) theorized that current species are the product of millions of years of evolution. Although the concept of evolution was not entirely new, Darwin took it a step further by proposing that evolution occurs through a mechanism he called **natural selection**. The theory of natural selection suggests that natural forces select traits in organisms that are **adaptive**—that is, that help organisms adjust to their environment. This occurs naturally because organisms with fewer adaptive features for their particular environmental circumstance, or **niche**, are less likely to survive and reproduce; they thus have fewer offspring who survive in the next generation and themselves reproduce.

A classic example of natural selection occurred in Birmingham, Liverpool, Manchester, and other industrial cities in England (Bishop & Cook, 1975). A light-colored variety of peppered moth common in rural areas of Britain also populated most cities, but as England industrialized in the nineteenth century, light-colored moths became scarce in industrial regions and dark-colored moths predominated.

Charles Darwin revolutionized human self-understanding in 1859 by rewriting the family tree.

a.   *b.*

FIGURE 1.5

The natural selection of moth color. As environmental conditions changed in industrial England, so, too, did the moth population. In (a), where two pepper moths rest on the dark bark of an oak tree in Manchester, the darker moth is better camouflaged. With industrialization, the darker moths became better adapted to their environments. In contrast, (b) shows a light-colored oak bark typical of rural Wales, where the light moth is extremely difficult to see and hence better able to evade its predators.

How did this happen? With industrialization, the air became sooty, darkening the bark of the trees on which these moths spent much of their time. Light-colored moths were thus easily noticed and eaten by their predators. Prior to industrialization, moths that had darker coloration were selected *against* by nature because they were conspicuous against light-colored bark. Now, however, they were better able to blend into the background of the dark tree trunks (Figure 1.5), and as a result, they survived to pass on their coloration to the next generation. Over decades, the moth population changed to reflect the differential selection of light and dark varieties. Moreover, since England has been cleaning up its air through more stringent pollution controls in the past 20 years, the trend has begun to reverse.

The peppered moth story highlights a crucial point about evolution: Because adaptation is always relative to a specific niche, evolution is not synonymous with progress. A trait or behavior that is highly adaptive can suddenly become maladaptive with even a seemingly small change in the environment. A new insect that enters a geographical region can eliminate a flourishing crop, just as the arrival of a bellicose tribe (or nation) into a previously peaceful region can render prior attitudes toward war and peace maladaptive. People have used Darwinian ideas to justify racial and class prejudices ("people on welfare must be naturally unfit"), but sophisticated evolutionary arguments contradict the view that adaptation or fitness can ever be absolute. Adaptation is always relative to a niche.

Ethology, Sociobiology, and Evolutionary Psychology

If Darwin's theory of natural selection can be applied to characteristics such as the color of a moth, can it also apply to behaviors? It stands to reason that certain behaviors, such as the tendency of moths to rest on trees in the first place, evolved because they helped members of the species to survive. The field of **ethology,** which studies animal behavior from a biological and evolutionary perspective (Hinde, 1982), began in the middle of this century to apply this sort of evolutionary approach to understanding animal behavior. For example, several species of birds emit warning cries to alert their flock of approaching predators, and some even band together to attack. Konrad Lorenz, an ethologist who befriended a flock of black jackdaws, was once attacked by the flock when he was carrying a wet black bathing suit. Convinced that they were not simply offended by the style, Lorenz hypothesized that jackdaws have an inborn or **innate** tendency to become distressed

It is seldom that I laugh at an animal, and when I do, I usually find out afterwards that it was at myself, at the human being whom the animal has portrayed in a more or less pitiless caricature, that I have laughed. We stand before the monkey house and laugh, but we do not laugh at the sight of a caterpillar or a snail, and when the courtship antics of a lusty greylag gander are so incredibly funny, it is only [because] our human youth behaves in a very similar fashion.

(Lorenz, 1979, p. 39)

whenever they see a creature dangling a black object resembling a jackdaw, and they respond by attacking (Lorenz, 1979).

If animal behaviors can be explained by their adaptive advantage, can the same logic be applied to human behavior? About two decades ago, Harvard biologist E. O. Wilson (1975) christened a new, and controversial, field called **sociobiology,** which explores possible evolutionary and biological bases of human social behavior. Sociobiologists and **evolutionary psychologists,** who apply evolutionary thinking to a wide range psychological phenomena, note that genetic transmission is not limited to physical traits, such as height, body type, or vulnerability to heart disease. Parents also pass onto their children behavioral and mental tendencies. Some of these are universal, such as the capacity to perceive certain wavelengths of light to which the eye is attuned, or the need to eat and sleep. Others differ across individuals. As we shall see in later chapters, recent research in **behavioral genetics,** a field that examines the genetic and environmental bases of differences between individuals on psychological traits, suggests that heredity is a surprisingly strong determinant of many personality traits and intellectual skills, such as the tendency to be outgoing, aggressive, or musically talented (Loehlin, 1992; Loehlin et al., 1988; Pedersen, McClearn, Plomin, & Nesselroade, 1991).

The basic notion of sociobiological theory, common to all contemporary evolutionary theories, is that evolution selects creatures that maximize their **reproductive success.** Reproductive success refers to the capacity to survive and produce offspring. Over many generations, organisms with greater reproductive success will have many more descendants because they will survive and reproduce more than other organisms, including other members of their own species. Central to evolutionary views is that the human brain, like the eye or the heart, has been "designed" by nature to solve certain problems involved in survival and reproduction, such as selecting mates, using language, competing for scarce resources, and cooperating with kin, neighbors, and coalition partners (Tooby & Cosmides, 1992).

Metaphors, Methods, and Data of the Evolutionary Perspective

The metaphors and methods of evolutionary psychologists differ from those of the other three perspectives. The major metaphor is borrowed from the sixteenth-century philosopher Thomas Hobbes (1538–1679): Wittingly or unwittingly, we are all runners in a race, competing for survival, sexual access to partners, and resources for ourselves and our kin. Evolutionary methods are frequently deductive, beginning. with an observation of something that already exists in nature and trying to explain it with logical arguments. For instance, evolutionary psychologists might take as their starting point the fact that people care for their kin and try to deduce an explanation. This method is in contrast to experimentation, in which investigators create circumstances in the laboratory and test the impact of changing these conditions on behavior.

Many psychologists have challenged the deductive methods of evolutionary psychologists, just as they have criticized psychodynamic explanations of individual cases. They argue that predicting behavior in the laboratory is much more difficult and convincing than explaining what has already happened. Others worry that evolutionary claims could be used, as they were in the late nineteenth century, to support reactionary political agendas, justifying the oppression of women, various ethnic groups, and the poor as outcomes of natural selection. These are legitimate concerns, but they do not invalidate carefully constructed evolutionary arguments. No other theory has ever, in fact, offered a compelling explanation for why people take care of their kin and offspring, even though this is one of the most universal dispositions of human beings across the globe. Evolutionary psychologists are, however, increasingly making use of experimental procedures used by other psychologists (Buss et al., 1992).

PUTTING PSYCHOLOGICAL PERSPECTIVES IN PERSPECTIVE

Throughout this chapter we have seen that what psychologists study, how they study it, and what they observe is determined not only by the reality "out there" but also by the conceptual lenses they wear. In many cases adherents of one perspective know very little—and may even have stereotypic views or gross misconceptions—about other perspectives. At different points in the history of psychology, however, some attempts at integration have occurred. As early as 1950, psychologists John Dollard and Neal Miller tried to wed psychoanalysis and behaviorism by applying principles of learning to mental processes. More recently, Paul Wachtel (1977, 1987) has argued that people learn to repress painful thoughts or memories much as they learn other behaviors, and has suggested ways to integrate behaviorist and psychodynamic principles in treating patients.

The clinical practice of psychology has seen a thoroughgoing integration of behaviorist and cognitive principles in an approach called **cognitive behaviorism** (Bandura, 1977, 1986; McKeachie, 1976; Mischel, 1973). Cognitive-behavioral clinicians accept the behaviorist principle that learning is the basis of behavior but also emphasize the role of mental processes in determining the way individuals respond to their environment. For example, people often develop the skill to perform an action (such as skiing) by observing other people doing it, but they will not perform it unless they believe they can do it and that they will enjoy it (Bandura, 1986; Mischel, 1973; Rotter, 1954). Some cognitive psychologists have also taken up the task of trying to integrate behaviorist theories of learning with more cognitive conceptualizations, by considering the cognitive and neural events that occur as organisms learn (Anderson, 1995).

Behaviorism and cognitive psychology might seem at first like strange bedfellows, because behaviorists reject mentalistic explanations. Even behaviorists who are comfortable acknowledging the existence of mental events often deny that such events could play a *causal* role in human affairs; they tend to see mental processes as products or byproducts of environmental stimulation or behavior, not as independent causes of behavior. What these two approaches share, however, is an **empiricist** view of psychology, that is, a belief that the road to scientific knowledge is systematic observation, and ideally, experimental observation.

The Psychology of Psychology

Why do different psychologists hold such varying points of view? Why do some look for the causes of behavior in unconscious processes while others deny the importance of mental processes altogether? To some extent, these questions are probably unanswerable. No one knows, for example, why some people look at an ambiguous figure and see a vase while others see faces. Nevertheless, if we turn psychology on itself, each perspective offers insights into why psychologists believe what they believe, and why some readers may already find themselves gravitating toward certain ways of understanding psychological events.

Psychodynamic psychologists would point to some basic differences in personality between people who prefer to work with patients to understand the meanings of their symptoms and those who prefer to study behavior experimentally. Experimental psychologists tend to enjoy solving intellectual puzzles and to focus on details, such as the specifics of designing a study. They tend to be less interested in subjective personal experience and to be more at home with thought than emotion. Psychodynamic clinicians, on the other hand, tend to align at the other end of the spectrum on these dimensions. A psychoanalyst would find it no accident that experimental psychologists have historically focused on sensation, perception, behavior, and cognition, and have spent comparatively less time examining emotion. A psychodynamic psychologist would also point out the extent to which psychologists' views are shaped by their desires to be liked and respected by their mentors, who are powerful authority figures. As a result, psychologists trained at one university or by one mentor may almost uniformly hold one perspective, whereas those trained elsewhere may tend to find a different perspective compelling. One would, no doubt, similarly find introductory psychology professors' theoretical biases frequently mirrored in their students.

For the behaviorist, behavior goes where its consequences lead it. If students believe what their mentors teach, they do so because of the overt and subtle reinforcement of grades, nods of agreement, praise, and letters of recommendation. Much as those of us who teach psychology endeavor to lead students to draw their own conclusions, students are remarkably adept at ferreting out our biases and discovering their virtues. The behaviorist would add that the topics psychologists study and the approaches they use to understand them are systematically controlled by the agencies that fund research: If a perspective or topic is no longer "in," psychologists who study it will not be reinforced for their behavior.

From a cognitive perspective, the tenacity with which psychologists cling to their preferred perspective, often in the face of discrepant findings, is an example of a conservative bias in all cognition. Individuals tend to change their beliefs, particularly those that they rely upon frequently, only if the evidence is extremely compelling. People are much more likely to view counterexamples as exceptions to the rule and hence dismiss them and overemphasize cases that support their beliefs.

Evolutionary psychologists would point out that the human cognitive system is itself a product of evolution (Tooby & Cosmides, 1992). They would agree that a conservative cognitive bias leads people to hold onto views that are important to them until faced with overwhelming evidence to the contrary. But they would argue that this bias reflects the adaptive advantage of entering into situations with expectations and expertise, rather than trying to assess every new situation without the benefit of past experience.

Biopsychology and cross-cultural psychology, as the inner and outer bounds of psychology, also provide insight into why psychologists think as they do. From a biopsychological standpoint, individuals show striking differences in their cognitive strengths, weaknesses, and proclivities (Gardner, 1983; Hartlage & Telzrow, 1985). Some people think more visually, whereas others tend to think in words. Some think intuitively and globally, whereas others are more likely to analyze details. Such differences, based on both the innate wiring of the brain and on social and learning experiences, are likely to influence profoundly the way individual psychologists think about psychological issues and the perspectives they find compelling.

From a cultural standpoint, psychologists' beliefs are inseparable from broader movements and ideologies. At times, psychology shapes popular culture, as with Freud's ideas about repression and Skinner's concept of reinforcement. At other times, psychologists borrow concepts and technologies from the broader culture or from other disciplines, as in cognitive psychology's appropriation of the computer metaphor. From this point of view, areas of research or theoretical perspectives that are prominent are likely to be those which, whether true or not in some ultimate sense, are congruent with ways of thinking that are current at a particular historical time. Computer metaphors and an emphasis on cognition, for example, would not likely have held much favor during the Romantic era in the late eighteenth century, when philosophers exalted emotion over reason.

Historian of science Frank Sulloway (1994) recently carried out a complex and historically rich empirical study of the reasons individual scientists believe as they do, and happened upon a striking finding. Among hundreds of scientists who wrote during periods of scientific revolution in several disciplines, he found one variable remarkably predictive of whether they allied themselves with the old perspective or the new revolutionary one: birth order. First-born children tended to be conservative, rejecting radical new views and advocating caution in rejecting the old order. Later-born children as scientists were more rebellious, jumping on the bandwagon of new approaches. Neither stand is uniformly better than the other: Later-borns embraced farfetched views that were ultimately rejected as well as perspectives that supplanted the older anachronistic views of their first-born peers. Sulloway's data suggest that the experience of being a first-born leads a person to identify with the views of authorities, whereas being a later-born renders a researcher more prone to challenge scientific elders (Figure 1.6).

(a) Acceptance and rejection of Darwinian theory by birth order (1859–1870)

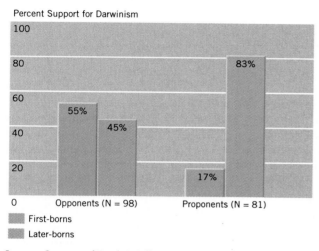

First-borns

Later-borns

SOURCE: Courtesy of Frank J. Sulloway.

(b) Percent of first-borns and later-borns supporting various scientific revolutions

EVENT	YEARS	PERCENT FIRST-BORNS SUPPORTING	PERCENT LATER-BORNS SUPPORTING
Copernican revolution	1543–1609	33	67
Relativity theory (Einstein)	1905–1914	46	71
Phrenology	1799–1875	44	88
Darwinian theory	1859–1870	35	71
Evolution prior to Darwin	1714–1859	9	47
Harvey's theory of blood circulation	1628–1653	64	91

SOURCE: Adapted from Sulloway, 1994.

FIGURE 1.6
The link between birth order and acceptance of revolutionary views in science. As (a) shows, the proponents of the Darwinian revolution were overwhelmingly later-borns. Part (b) shows that the same holds across a remarkably diverse array of scientific revolutions, including one that was erroneous (phrenology, which proposed a link between character and the shape of the skull).

The Many Faces of Psychology

The reader will no doubt be tempted at times to conclude that a particular perspective is the right one and that the others must be mistaken. This condition unfortunately afflicts most of us who make our careers putting on a set of theoretical lenses to understand a psychological phenomenon and then forget that we are bespectacled. Before succumbing to this fate, be forewarned that the different perspectives often contribute in unique ways, often determined by the object under investigation. Deciding that one perspective is valid in all situations is like choosing to use a telescope instead of a microscope without knowing whether the objects of study are amoebas or asteroids.

Psychology has many subfields, and the perspectives psychologists adopt differ from one area to another. For example, **developmental psychology** studies the way thought, feeling, and behavior develop through the lifespan, from infancy to death. Developmental psychologists use all four major perspectives, often in combination. Developmental psychologists researching the influence of television on children's aggressive behavior tend to take a cognitive or cognitive-behavioral approach, guided by the hypothesis that what children observe influences the way they behave (Singer, 1986). Research on the close ties that form between infants and their mothers, on the other hand, has drawn heavily on the work of John Bowlby (1969, 1988), who was both a psychoanalyst and an ethologist. **Social psychology** examines interactions of individual psychology and social phenomena. Social psychologists study phenomena such as prejudice, mob violence, peer pressure, and the way people process information about themselves and others. Social psychology has been increasingly influenced in recent years by the cognitive perspective (Markus & Zajonc, 1985).

Psychologists in applied subdisciplines (fields that apply psychological knowledge to practical issues) often have a dominant perspective but draw on other perspectives as the problem at hand requires. **Clinical psychology** focuses on the nature and treatment of psychological processes that lead to emotional distress. A clinician treating an anxious patient may both explore the patient's thoughts and fears shaped in childhood (a psychodynamic intervention) and teach the patient relaxation techniques (a behaviorist strategy). **Industrial/organizational psychology (I/O psychology)** examines the behavior of people in organizations and attempts to help solve organizational problems such as low productivity or interpersonal friction. An I/O psychologist might address a leader's psychodynamics or teach cognitive and behavioral skills, such as communication skills. **Educational psychology** examines psychological processes in learning and in learning disabilities, and applies psychological knowledge in educational settings. Psychologists who assess a child for learning disabilities need to understand cognitive processes and their neural basis, but they also must be cognizant of the way emotional distress at home can create roadblocks to learning.

As theory, technology, and the needs of society change, new subdisciplines emerge or grow in importance. A rapidly expanding area of research and practice today is **health psychology** (Taylor, 1991). At the intersection of psychology and medicine, health psychology examines psychological factors involved in health and disease. Some health psychologists study the way stress or personality traits contribute to disease. Others treat stress-related problems or develop programs to help people minimize psychological contributions to illness (such as smoking, drinking, or overeating).

Psychology's composition as a discipline and its role in society have changed dramatically in recent decades. In 1940, 70 percent of new PhDs in psychology were **experimental psychologists** primarily interested in studying processes such as human and animal learning. By the 1980s, the majority of psychology PhDs were working in settings such as clinics, schools, and industry (Howard et al., 1986), and

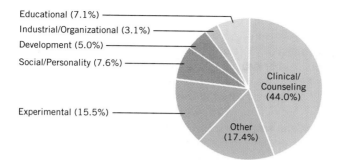

FIGURE 1.7

Proportions of doctoral psychologists in different fields (1991). Psychologists come in a number of stripes. Unlike 50 years ago, the majority are now clinicians, who apply the practice of psychology to helping people change dysfunctional patterns of thinking, feeling, and behaving. Data on which pie chart is based are from American Psychological Association, Office of Research (November 1994). [Table 1: Major fields of all doctoral psychologists and new psychology doctorate recipients: 1981–1991]. Unpublished analyses. (Original source: National Science Foundation, Division of Science Resources Studies, unpublished analyses).

a new contingent of psychologists were receiving an advanced degree called a Doctor of Psychology (PsyD) developed exclusively to train practitioners. Figure 1.7 describes the percentage of psychologists in different subdisciplines today.

The shift in the composition of the field has had important implications both within psychology and without. Within, tensions have traditionally existed between research psychologists, who work primarily in universities and consider themselves scientists, and clinicians, who work in health settings or private practice and consider themselves practitioners. The two groups have widely different conceptions of people: Two-thirds of clinicians have either a psychodynamic or an eclectic theoretical orientation that relies to some extent on psychodynamic theory, which most academic researchers reject as unscientific or erroneous (see Pope et al., 1987).

Clinicians and researchers also tend to have different philosophies of science. Most academic psychologists believe experimentation must be the basis of a scientific psychology and that clinical observation is too unsystematic and inferential to be scientifically useful. In contrast, many clinicians believe that an experimentally derived psychology focuses too heavily on phenomena that can be reproduced in limited experiments and ignores complex, real-life phenomena. The tensions between researchers and clinicians became so severe in recent years that a large group of researchers left psychology's professional organization, the American Psychological Association, and founded their own organization, the American Psychological Society, which publishes a journal called—tellingly—*Psychological Science.*

Commentary: How to Grasp an Elephant from Trunk to Tail Without Getting Skewered on the Tusks

The perspectives clinicians and researchers find compelling in part reflect their database and their aims. A cognitive psychologist collecting experimental data on subjects' ability to remember word pairs is likely to have little use for psychodynamic concepts. Similarly, a clinician trying to make sense of a troubled teenage diabetic's life-threatening refusal to eat appropriately, even though he is well aware of the likely consequences, is unlikely to find a complete answer in experimentally derived cognitive models. Both the researcher and the clinician would benefit from a paradigm that fostered rigorous experimentation as well as helped psychologists interpret the meanings of what people think, feel, say, and do.

Many readers may have wondered, in reading the renditions of the four perspectives described in this chapter, where the author stands on them. Does he see vases, profiles, or simply random collections of white and black dots? Forewarned is forearmed: The best way for readers to inoculate themselves against the subtle intrusions of an author's biases in any field is to know what they are. My own point of view reflects, and is shaped by, the fact that I am both a researcher and a clinician. Much of my work has been at the intersection of cognition and psychodynamics, looking at the way thoughts, feelings, and motives are connected in the mind, and the way these connections influence individuals' capacity to maintain intimate relationships. My understanding of motivation and emotion, however, is heavily influenced by evolutionary and behaviorist principles, particularly the idea that human emotions have evolved to regulate our behavior in adaptive ways, and that they do so by rewarding or punishing various courses of action. As a freshman in college I took a year-long course on the evolutionary bases of human social behavior taught by one of the leaders of that emerging approach, which forever sensitized me to questions about the adaptive functions and evolution of psychological processes. Thus, I am a hybrid—in the vernacular, a mutt—and the words psychodynamic, behavioral, cognitive, and evolutionary have all appeared in the titles of articles I have written for professional journals.

An advantage of being a mutt is recognizing some of the limitations of the pure-bred positions and the impact that inbreeding can have on the health of a perspective. I sometimes find my fingers tapping impatiently when psychoanalysts and evolutionary psychologists spin elaborate theoretical yarns without subjecting their hypotheses to rigorous scientific scrutiny (such as the evolutionary hypothesis that rape is a reproductive strategy used by lower-class males with little access to females, which ignores the fact that rapists are not all indigent, childless men sitting alone in their rooms at night). I am equally struck by the limitations of cognitive theories that minimize the role of emotion and motivation. When people think about issues that matter to them—which is most of the time—their thinking is frequently biased toward the conclusions they want to reach, as when fans on opposite sides of a college football stadium see a pass interference call entirely differently, or lovers fail to see each others' foibles and failings (until they are ready to break up, at which point they may see nothing but foibles and failings).

I am probably least sympathetic to the underlying assumptions of the behaviorist perspective, or at least of its most radical proponents, because experimental studies on thought and memory and my patients' life stories have impressed me with the richness and importance of the thoughts, feelings, and personal meanings that guide human action. As a clinician, however, I consider the therapeutic contributions of the behaviorist perspective extremely important and frequently attend the annual convention of the Association for the Advancement of Behavior Therapy as well as that of the American Psychoanalytic Association. Being a mutt requires a high tolerance for ambiguity and conflict, but I am motivated by the contradictions among these approaches to search for ways to integrate them, as I believe a whole elephant is more valuable than part of one.

WHAT IS TO COME

Psychology is a field with broad vision, which nonetheless teems with blind men and elephants. Moving about this jungle is our task in the remainder of the book, as we move from the micro-level of the nerve cell in Chapter 3 to the macro-level of social forces in the final chapter. First, however, we will examine the increasingly sophisticated methods psychologists use in their efforts to understand mental life and behavior.

Summary

The Boundaries and Borders of Psychology

1. **Psychology** is the systematic study of mental processes and behavior. Understanding a person means practicing "triple bookkeeping": simultaneously examining the person's biological makeup, psychological experience and functioning, and the cultural and historical moment.

2. **Biopsychology** examines the physical basis of psychological phenomena such as motivation, emotion, and stress. **Cross-cultural psychology** attempts to test psychological hypotheses in different cultures. Biology and culture form the boundaries, or constraints, within which psychological processes operate.

3. A classic question inherited from philosophy is whether human action is characterized by **free will** or **determinism**, that is, whether people freely choose their actions or whether behavior follows lawful patterns. A related issue is the **mind-body problem**, the question of how mental and physical events interact, a contemporary version of which addresses the genetics of personality.

The Role of Perspectives in Psychology

4. A **paradigm** is a broad system of theoretical assumptions employed by a scientific community to try to make sense of a domain of experience. Psychology lacks a unified paradigm but has a number of schools of thought or **perspectives**, broad ways of understanding psychological phenomena. A psychological perspective, like a paradigm, includes theoretical propositions, shared metaphors, and accepted methods of observation.

5. The **psychodynamic perspective** originated with Sigmund Freud. Its primary aim is to interpret meanings, many of which may be unconscious. The primary method is the case study, and the primary metaphors are the mind as a battleground for warring factions, and an iceberg with consciousness the tip.

6. The **behaviorist perspective** focuses on the relation between environmental events (or **stimuli**) and the responses of the organism. The behaviorist B.F. Skinner proposed that all behavior can ultimately be understood as learned responses and that behaviors are selected on the basis of their consequences. The metaphor underlying behaviorism is the machine, with the mind a black box; the source of data is laboratory experimentation.

7. The **cognitive perspective** focuses on the way people process, store, and retrieve information. **Information processing** refers to taking input from the environment and transforming it into meaningful output. The metaphor underlying the cognitive perspective is the mind as computer, complete with software. The primary method of the cognitive perspective is experimental.

8. The **nature-nurture** question refers to the extent to which inborn biological processes and environmental events shape mental processes and behavior. Many if not most psychological processes reflect an *interaction* of nature and nurture.

9. The **evolutionary perspective** argues that many human behavioral proclivities exist because they helped our ancestors survive and produce offspring that

would likely survive. It proposes the mechanism of **natural selection,** through which natural forces select traits in organisms that help them adjust to their environment. The basic notion of evolutionary theory is that evolution selects creatures that maximize their **reproductive success,** defined as the capacity to survive and reproduce. The primary methods are deductive and comparative.

Putting Psychological Perspectives in Perspective

10. Although the four major perspectives largely developed independently, some areas of integration have occurred, particularly in clinical psychology, where ideology is sometimes tempered by practical considerations in treating patients as effectively as possible. **Cognitive behaviorism** accepts many behaviorist principles but emphasizes as well the role of thought processes, such as expectations, in learning.

11. Psychology has many subfields, such as developmental, social, clinical, industrial–organizational, educational, and health psychology. Perhaps someday the four perspectives will contribute to an integrated paradigm that can guide research and practice across these domains.

George Segal, "Machine of the Year," 1983

Chapter 2

RESEARCH METHODS IN PSYCHOLOGY

*I*n a study conducted in 1977, pairs of male and female college students talked to each other from separate rooms through an intercom system (Snyder et al., 1977). They had never met, but the male students thought they knew what their partner looked like from a photograph the researchers had given them. Actually, the photo was not of the partner: Half the **subjects** (participants in a study whose responses are being assessed) received a picture of a college-age woman whom other students had rated as physically very attractive, whereas the other half received an unattractive mug-shot. Not surprisingly, those males who believed their partners were attractive were more sociable and sexually warm toward them.

The more interesting finding came from studying the responses of the females. Judges who listened to the taped conversations with the males' comments edited out found that the women who were believed to be attractive behaved in a friendly, sociable, witty, and appealing manner. Conversely, women who were treated as if they were unattractive behaved unattractively.

This experiment provides a classic example of a **self-fulfilling prophecy,** a false definition of a situation that evokes behavior that, in turn, makes the false conception become true (Merton, 1957). Self-fulfilling prophecies occur in many situations. In classrooms, simply leading teachers to believe that certain students have tremendous untapped potential can cause those students to make impressive gains in learning (Rosenthal & Jacobson, 1968). Teachers who think particular children are talented may interpret small steps as giant leaps and hence give them opportunities to flourish by paying them extra attention, grading papers more meticulously, and so forth. In the process, such students develop positive beliefs and expectations about themselves and their abilities that color the way they respond, potentially confirming the teacher's expectations (see Jussim, 1986).

The intercom experiment illustrates the power of psychological research to take important questions into the laboratory, study them, and provide insight into the nature and causes of psychological phenomena. The methods psychologists use to learn about thought, feeling, and behavior are the topic of this chapter. We begin by describing the features of good psychological research. How do researchers take a topic such as self-fulfilling prophecies and turn it into a researchable question? How do they know when the results of their study apply to the real world? Then we describe the two major types of research, experimental and descriptive. Next, we discuss how to distinguish a good research study from a bad one. In the process, we examine a wide range of research techniques, from the procedures researchers use to study the brain in action to those that allow them to test the universality of psychological generalizations across cultures. We conclude by examining the relation between methods and perspectives in psychology, considering how the observations of experimenters, clinicians, and researchers who study psychological processes as they occur in nature can be integrated.

CHARACTERISTICS OF GOOD PSYCHOLOGICAL RESEARCH

The tasks of a psychological researcher trying to understand human nature are similar to the tasks we all face in our daily lives as we try to predict other people's behavior. A student named Elizabeth, for example, is running behind on a term paper that is due the following week. She wants to ask her professor for an extension, but she does not want to risk his forming a negative impression of her. Her task, then, is one of prediction: How will he behave?

To make her decision, she can rely on her observations of the way her professor normally behaves, or she can experiment by saying something and seeing how he responds. Elizabeth has observed her professor on many occasions and has a clear impression—a theory about him—that he tends to be rigid. She has noticed that when students arrive late to class, he looks angry, and that when they ask to meet with him outside of class, he often seems inflexible in scheduling appointments. She thus expects—hypothesizes—that he will not give her an extension. Not sure, however, that her observations are entirely accurate, she tests her hypothesis by speaking with him casually after class one day. She mentions a friend who is feeling very stressed because she is having trouble finishing the term paper on time, and she watches for his reaction (his facial expressions, his words, and the length of time he takes to respond). The professor surprises her by suggesting that the friend ask him for an extension because wading through the other papers will take him two weeks anyway. Elizabeth laughs and reveals the identity of her "friend."

In this scenario, Elizabeth is doing exactly what psychologists do: observing a psychological phenomenon (her professor's behavior), constructing a theory, using the theory to develop a hypothesis, measuring psychological processes (the professor's flexibility and his attitude toward extensions), and testing the hypothesis. Although psychologists are likely to be more systematic in applying the scientific method and to have more sophisticated tools, the logic of investigation is basically the same.

Like an architect or carpenter, researchers have a number of tools at their disposal. Just as a carpenter would not use a hammer to drive a nail, turn a screw, and loosen a bolt, a researcher would not rely exclusively on any single method to lay a solid empirical foundation for a theory. Nevertheless, most of the methods psychologists use—the tools of their trade—share certain features, notably a theoretical framework, standardized procedures, generalizability, and objective measurement (Figure 2.1). We examine each of these in turn.

The methods of psychological researchers are not altogether different from the observational and experimental methods of people in their daily lives as they try to predict and understand behavior.

FIGURE 2.1
Characteristics of good psychological research. Studies vary tremendously in design, but most good research shares certain attributes.

A THEORETICAL FRAMEWORK	A STANDARDIZED PROCEDURE	GENERALIZABILITY	OBJECTIVE MEASUREMENT
Systematic way of organizing and explaining observations	Procedure that is the same for all subjects except where variation is introduced to test a hypothesis	Sample that is representative of the population	Measures that are reliable (that produce consistent results)
Hypothesis that flows from the theory		Procedure that is sensible and relevant to circumstances outside the laboratory	Measures that are valid (that assess the dimensions they purport to assess)

Theoretical Framework

Psychologists study some phenomena because of their practical importance. They may, for example, conduct studies on the impact of divorce on children (Kalter, 1987, 1990; Mulholland et al., 1991; Wallerstein, 1988) or the effect of the human immunodeficiency virus (HIV), which causes AIDS, on the nervous system (Greenwood, 1991). In most cases, however, research is grounded firmly in theory. A **theory** is a systematic way of organizing and explaining observations that includes a set of propositions or statements about the relations among various phenomena. For example, a theory might propose that having a pessimistic attitude promotes poor physical health because pessimists do not take good care of themselves and tax their bodies' defenses against disease by keeping themselves in a state of constant physiological stress. People frequently assume that a theory is simply a fact that has not yet been proven. As suggested in Chapter 1, however, a theory is always a mental construction, an imperfect rendering of reality by a scientist or community of scientists, which can have more or less evidence to support it. The scientist's thinking is the mortar that holds the bricks of reality in place.

In most research, theory provides the framework for the researcher's specific hypothesis. A **hypothesis** is a tentative belief or educated guess about the relationship between two or more variables. A **variable** is any phenomenon that can change or vary from one situation to another or differ from person to person. Researchers measure variables they believe have important connections with each other. For example, a research team interested in the links between optimism, pessimism, and health decided to test the hypothesis that optimism (variable 1) is related to speed of recovery from heart surgery (variable 2). The researchers found that patients undergoing coronary artery bypass operations who are optimistic are quicker to recover than people who are pessimistic (Scheier & Carver, 1993).

Optimism and health are variables because people are more or less optimistic and they recover more or less quickly. A variable that can be placed on a continuum—such as degree of optimism, intelligence, shyness, or rate of recovery—is called a **continuous variable**. In contrast, some variables are comprised of groupings, classifications, or categories, such as gender, species, or whether or not a person has had a heart attack. A **categorical variable** of this sort cannot easily be placed on a continuum; a subject is either male or female and is not easily located on a continuum between the two.

Standardized Procedures

In addition to being grounded in theory, good psychological research uses **standardized procedures**; that is, it applies the same procedures to research subjects in the same way. In the study of self-fulfilling prophecies described earlier, the experimenters used an intercom system for all subjects. Had they allowed some subjects to talk by phone and others by intercom, the clearer sound of the phone connection might have made some subjects respond more warmly to their partner.

Generalizability from a Sample

Psychological research typically studies the behavior of a particular group or subset of people in order to learn something about a larger **population**. The population might be as broad as all humans or as narrow as preschool children with working mothers. A **sample** is a subgroup of the population that is likely to be **representative** of the population as a whole (i.e., similar enough to other members of the population that conclusions drawn from the sample are likely to be true of the rest of the population).

A representative sample contributes to the generalizability of a study's conclusions. **Generalizability** refers to the applicability of the findings to the entire population of interest to the researcher. The study of self-fulfilling prophecies used college students as subjects. Would middle-aged subjects have been as heavily swayed by their partner's appearance? What about married subjects? And although male subjects behaved very differently depending on the perceived attractiveness of their partner, would female subjects be so shallow—especially since, cross-culturally, females focus less on physical attractiveness than males in evaluating potential mates (Buss et al., 1988)? Answering these questions would require collecting data with samples drawn from these other populations.

For a study to be generalizable, its procedures must also be sound, or **valid**, and to be valid, a study must meet two criteria. First, it must convincingly test the hypothesis it is supposed to test. In other words, it must employ methods—including measures and standardized procedures—that effectively test the hypothesis. This is often called **internal validity**, that is, validity of the design itself. Second, the study must establish **external validity**, which means that the findings can be generalized to situations outside, or external to, the laboratory. The study of self-fulfilling prophecies would have received little interest from psychologists had it not appeared to be a good analog of similar processes in everyday life.

Objective Measurement

As in all scientific endeavors, objectivity is important in psychological research. The reader of a study wants to be confident that the results are not simply the experimenter's subjective impression but could be verified by others. Variables must therefore be defined in a way that enables researchers to quantify or categorize them. For example, one group of researchers wanted to study conflicts between adolescents and their parents in divorced and nondivorced families (Smetana et al., 1991). Prior studies had found that divorced mothers who had not remarried tended to be more permissive and less controlling with their children than mothers in intact marriages (Hetherington, 1989). Based on the theory that conflict often emerges in adolescence as teenagers struggle for autonomy, the researchers hypothesized that adolescents would experience less conflict with divorced mothers, who would not encroach as much on their desires for autonomy.

To test this hypothesis, the researchers had to overcome a major hurdle: how to measure objectively the degree of parent-child conflict. They decided to interview the mother and adolescent separately, to ask each to list and describe all the conflicts between the two of them they could think of, and to rate the severity and frequency of each conflict on a scale from 1 (*not at all bad*) to 5 (*very, very bad*). To put this research problem in the language of variables, the researchers were interested in the relation between a categorical variable (whether the mother was divorced) and a continuous variable (degree of mother-adolescent conflict). The results shown in Table 2.1 reveal that both mothers and adolescents reported higher rates of conflict in the married than in the divorced families.

To study a variable, then, we must first devise a technique to measure it. A **measure** is a concrete way of assessing a variable; it is a way of bringing an often abstract concept down to earth. In the research linking optimism to health, the investigators used a questionnaire to measure optimism. The questionnaire included items such as, "I hardly ever expect things to go my way" and "In uncertain times, I usually expect the best." The investigation measured recovery from heart attack by assessing behavior (for example, how quickly the subject began to sit up in bed, to walk around the hospital room after surgery, or to return to work). In the study of self-fulfilling prophecies, the investigators asked judges to rate subjects' behaviors on several dimensions, such as friendliness and wit.

Psychologists often use measures that resemble the measures people intuitively use in assessing psychological processes. Recall the example of Elizabeth, who wanted to predict whether her professor would respond favorably to her request for an extension. When she asked him about a friend who needed an extension, she observed his facial expressions and the speed with which he responded, listening carefully for delays in response time that could indicate conflict or conscious efforts to control his feelings. Psychologists similarly measure facial expressions, often by attaching electrodes to the muscles of the face, and they use reaction time to measure the amount of mental activity needed to solve a problem.

For some variables, measurement is not a problem. Researchers typically have little difficulty distinguishing males from females. For most characteristics, however, such as optimism and health, measurement is much more complex. In these cases, researchers need to know two characteristics of a measure: whether it is reliable and whether it is valid.

Reliability

Reliability refers to a measure's ability to produce consistent results. A highly reliable measure yields an assessment of a variable that does not fluctuate substantially despite the presence of random factors that may influence results, such as the day the subject took the test, whether the subject had a good night's sleep, or who is coding the data (Anastasi, 1988). If a single subject received different scores on the same measure depending on these random factors, the accuracy of that person's score on any particular occasion would be doubtful.

TABLE 2.1 CONFLICTS BETWEEN EARLY ADOLESCENTS AND THEIR MOTHERS				
VARIABLE	ADOLESCENTS' RATINGS		MOTHERS' RATINGS	
	Married Families	Divorced Families	Married Families	Divorced Families
Number of conflicts generated	4.06	3.60	3.94	2.87
Conflict frequency	3.50	3.42	3.93	3.52
Conflict severity	2.55	2.03	2.78	2.76

Source: Adapted from Smetana et al., 1991.

Note. The table shows the average number, frequency, and severity of conflicts reported by early adolescents (average age 12-13) and their mothers in married and divorced families. Findings were largely similar for mid-adolescents (average age 15-16).

Reliability in this technical sense is not altogether different from reliability in its everyday meaning. A test is unreliable if we cannot count on it to behave consistently, just as a plumber is unreliable if we cannot count on him consistently to show up when he says he will. An unreliable measure may sometimes work, just as an unreliable plumber may sometimes work, but we can never predict when either will perform adequately.

Three kinds of reliability are especially important. **Test-retest reliability** assesses the temporal stability of a test—that is, its tendency to yield relatively similar scores for the same individual over time. If a measure is reliable, subjects who are retested should not receive scores that are highly discrepant from their initial scores. Another kind of reliability is **internal consistency.** A measure is internally consistent if several ways of asking the same question yield similar results. For example, suppose a researcher asks two questions designed to assess self-esteem: "Do you like yourself?" and "Do you think you are a good person?" If subjects who answer "yes" to the first question are not especially likely to answer the second in the affirmative, then the test would not be internally consistent; that is, the two items are not really asking the same question. A third kind of reliability is **inter-rater reliability.** If two different interviewers rate a subject on some dimension, both should give the subject similar scores. To make sure that a test has inter-rater reliability, raters must be trained to use precise definitions of the phenomena they are measuring. This often requires developing detailed coding procedures to guarantee that different raters are similarly "calibrated," like two thermometers recording temperature in the same room.

The distinctions among these kinds of reliability may be clarified by returning to the plumbing analogy. A plumber establishes his test-retest reliability by showing up when he says he will on different occasions and by performing competently on each occasion. He establishes internal consistency by fixing an overflowing commode with as much dispatch as he would a stopped-up sink. He can boast inter-rater reliability if his customers agree in their assessment of his work. If he fails any of these reliability tests, he is unlikely to be called again, just as an unreliable measure will not be used in another study.

Validity

When the term **validity** is applied to a psychological measure, it refers to that measure's ability to assess the variable it is supposed to measure. For example, readers are all familiar with IQ tests, which are supposed to measure intelligence. One way psychologists have tried to demonstrate the validity of IQ test scores is to show that they consistently predict other phenomena, such as school performance, that require intellectual ability. As we will see in Chapter 8, IQ tests and similar tests such as the Scholastic Aptitude Test (the SAT) are, in general, highly predictive of school success (Anastasi, 1988), although they are not without their critics (Elliott, 1988). Some of the measures people intuitively use in their daily lives have much less certain validity, as when Elizabeth initially presumed that her professor's inflexibility in arranging meetings with students was a good index of his general flexibility (rather than, for example, simply a tight schedule).

To ensure the validity of a psychological measure, researchers subject it to considerable validation research. **Validation** means demonstrating that a measure consistently relates to some objective criterion or to other measures that have themselves already demonstrated their validity. For example, the Affect Intensity Measure (AIM) is a self-report measure of emotional intensity on which subjects report how strongly they typically experience their emotions (Larsen & Diener, 1987). To assess the validity of the instrument, the psychologists who developed the AIM measured the extent to which subjects responded physiologically to emotion-arousing events in the laboratory (assessed by measuring variables such as heart rate) and the extent to which their moods actually fluctuated in daily life. Subjects who described themselves as emotionally intense on the AIM tended to be the most physiologically reactive in the laboratory and reported more intense emotions when their emotional experiences were monitored at various times throughout a normal day. These findings supported the validity of the AIM.

Multiple Measures

One of the best ways to obtain an accurate assessment of a variable is to employ multiple measures of it. **Multiple measures** are important because no psychological measure is perfect. A measure that assesses a variable accurately 80 percent of the time is excellent—but it is also inaccurate 20 percent of the time. In fact, built into every measure is a certain amount of **error**, or discrepancy between the phenomenon as measured and the phenomenon as it really is. Multiple measures therefore provide a safety net for catching errors. In the adolescent-mother conflict study described earlier, the researchers assessed not only the number of conflicts subjects reported but also their frequency and intensity. This turned out to be important because some of these measures picked up differences that the others did not. The investigators also assessed conflict directly by videotaping family members as they discussed family conflicts. They coded the videotaped interactions on dimensions such as degree of conflict, extent to which subjects listened to each other, and amount of anger expressed.

Virtually all good psychological studies share the ingredients of psychological research outlined here—a theoretical framework, standardized procedure, generalizability, and objective measurement. Nevertheless, studies vary considerably in design and goals. The following sections examine two broad types of research: experimental research that tries to demonstrate cause-and-effect relationships, and research that attempts to describe psychological phenomena and the relations among them. As we will see, the line between these two types is not hard and fast. Many studies categorized as descriptive have implications for cause and effect, and some experimental studies simply attempt to document the existence of certain phenomena, such as different types of memory.

EXPERIMENTAL RESEARCH

In **experimental research**, investigators manipulate some aspect of a situation and examine the impact of this manipulation on the way subjects respond. The virtue of experimental methods is that they can assess cause and effect directly. To demonstrate causation, the researcher must show that two variables tend to occur together and that the presence of one of them precedes and leads to the other. An experiment can demonstrate causation by proving that manipulating one variable leads to predicted changes in another. Telling male subjects that the woman with whom they are interacting is the attractive woman in a photograph consistently leads to differences not only in their behavior but in the woman's behavior as well. This establishes a cause-and-effect relationship between a belief and a subsequent chain of events, demonstrating the power of false beliefs in creating self-fulfilling prophecies.

The logic of experimentation is actually quite straightforward and was used implicitly by Elizabeth when she tested her professor's flexibility. An experimenter manipulates variables that are outside the subjects' control or independent of their actions; these are known as **independent variables.** The aim is to assess the impact of these manipulations on the way subjects respond. Because subjects' responses depend on both the subject and the independent variable, they are known as **dependent variables.** Thus, the independent variable is the variable the experimenter manipulates, and the dependent variable is the one the experimenter measures to see if the manipulation had an effect. To assess cause and effect, experimenters present subjects with different possible values, or **conditions,** of the independent variable and study the resulting variations in the way subjects respond. In the study of self-fulfilling prophecies, the experimenters used an independent variable (perceived attractiveness) with two conditions (attractive or unattractive) and tested the impact on the behavior of both the men and women (dependent variables).

Consider a series of classic studies conducted in the 1950s by Harry Harlow and his colleagues (Harlow & Zimmerman, 1959). They were interested in determining which of two theories better explained why infant monkeys become emotionally attached to their mothers. One theory hypothesized that the basis for this attachment was the mother's role as the source of food. An alternative theory suggested that infant monkeys are drawn by the security and comfort mothers provide their young. To test these two hypotheses, the researchers conducted an experiment in which infant monkeys were separated from their mothers and raised in social isolation. Each monkey shared its cage with two surrogate or replacement "mothers," one made of wire and the other also made of wire but covered with terry cloth (and hence softer).

The independent variable—the variable manipulated by the researchers—was the placement of the milk bottle. In one experimental condition, a bottle was attached to the wire mother, whereas in the other condition it was attached to the cloth mother (Figure 2.2). The dependent variable was the infant monkeys' response, notably the amount of time they spent on each of the two mothers and which mother they turned to when frightened. The researchers found that no matter whether the wire or the cloth surrogate was the source of milk, the infants showed a clear preference for the cloth surrogate. Harlow and his colleagues concluded that in the development of attachment to the mother, security and comfort were more important than simple nourishment.

Experiments vary widely in both their designs and their goals, but the steps in conceiving and executing them are roughly the same, from the starting point of framing a hypothesis to the ultimate evaluation of findings (Figure 2.3). Although these steps relate specifically to the experimental method, many of them are applicable to descriptive methods as well.

FIGURE 2.2
Surrogate mother in Harlow's monkey studies. Monkeys were separated from birth from their mothers and given the choice of spending time with a wire mother or a terrycloth mother. Regardless of which "mother" fed the baby monkey, it preferred the soft terrycloth mother, suggesting that security, not nourishment, is the basis of attachment in monkeys.

Framing a Hypothesis

The first step in constructing an experiment is to develop a hypothesis that predicts the relationship between two or more variables. For example, Gordon Bower and his associates have investigated the impact of mood on memory (Bower, 1981, 1989; Gilligan & Bower, 1984). Based on a cognitive theory of the way people store and retrieve memories, they hypothesized that people who are in a positive mood while learning information will be more likely to remember pleasant aspects of that information. Conversely, people in a negative mood while learning will be more likely to remember negative information. This hypothesis states a relationship between two variables: induced *mood state* when learning material (the independent variable) and later ability to *recall* that material (the dependent variable).

Operationalizing Variables

The second step in experimental research is to operationalize the variables. **Operationalizing** means turning an abstract concept into a concrete variable as defined by some set of actions or operations. Bower operationalized the independent variable, mood state, by hypnotizing subjects to feel either happy or sad (the two conditions of the independent variable). He then had the subjects read about a psychiatric patient recounting various happy and sad memories. Bower operationalized the dependent variable, the ability to recall either positive or negative information, as the number of positive and negative memories the subject could recall 20 minutes later.

FIGURE 2.3
Steps in conducting an experiment. Conducting an experiment requires systematically going through a series of steps, from the initial framing of a hypothesis to drawing conclusions about the data obtained. The process is circular, as the conclusion of one study is generally the origin of another.

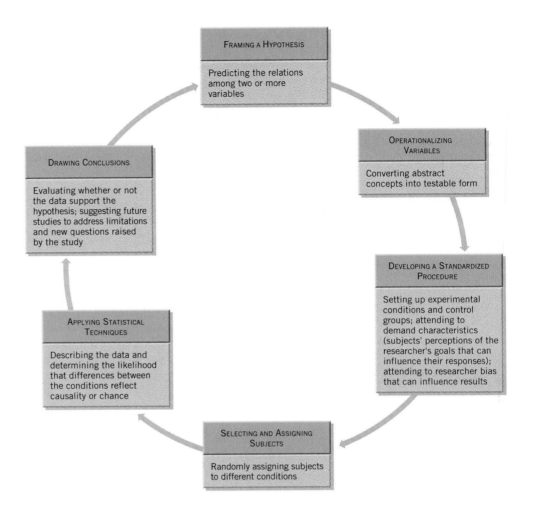

Developing a Standardized Procedure

The next step in constructing an experiment is to develop a standardized procedure for all subjects, so that the only things that vary from subject to subject are the independent variables and the performance of subjects on the dependent variables. Standardized procedures maximize the likelihood that any differences observed in subjects' behavior can be attributed to the experimental manipulation, so the investigator can draw inferences about cause and effect. In Bower's study, the experiment would have been contaminated, or ruined, if different subjects had heard different stories with varying numbers of positive and negative memories. These differences might have influenced the number of positive and negative memories subjects could recall. Bower's method of inducing happy or sad mood states also had to be standardized. If the experimenter induced a negative mood in one subject by hypnotizing him and in another by asking him to try to imagine his mother dying, differences in recall could stem from the different ways mood was induced rather than from its positive or negative nature.

Control Groups

Experimental research typically involves dividing subjects into groups who experience different conditions of the independent variable and then comparing the responses of the different groups. In Bower's experiment, the two groups consisted of subjects who were hypnotized to be in a happy mood and those who were hypnotized to be in a sad mood. Experiments often include another kind of group or condition, called a control group. Instead of being exposed to the experimental manipulation, subjects in the **control group** experience a neutral condition. Although Bower's experiment did not have a control group, a control condition for this experiment could have been a group of subjects who were brought under hypnosis but were not given any mood induction. By comparing subjects who were induced to feel sad while reading the story with those who were not induced to feel anything, Bower could have seen whether sad subjects recall more sad memories (or fewer happy ones) than relatively neutral subjects. Examining the performance of subjects who have not been exposed to the experimental condition gives researchers a clearer view of the direct impact of the experimental manipulation.

Protecting against Bias

Researchers try to anticipate and control the many sources of bias that can affect the results of a study. Investigators must sometimes ensure that subjects do not know too much about the study because this knowledge could influence their performance. Some subjects try to respond in the way they think the experimenter wants them to respond. (They are nice people, but lousy subjects.) The degree to which subjects' perceptions of the researcher's goals influence their responses is known as the **demand characteristics** of a study. To prevent demand characteristics from biasing the results, psychologists sometimes conduct **blind studies**, in which subjects are kept unaware of, or blind to, important aspects of the research. In the study of self-fulfilling prophecies, subjects were kept blind to the hypothesis because if they had known it, the men would surely have ignored the photograph when interacting with the women.

Blind studies are especially valuable in researching the effect of medications on psychological symptoms such as anxiety or depression. Researchers in these studies have to contend with **placebo effects**, in which an intervention such as giving a subject a pill produces an effect because subjects *believe* it will produce an effect. Subjects who think they are taking a medication often find that their symptoms disappear after they have taken only an inert or inactive substance such as a sugar pill (a placebo). Simply believing that a treatment is effective can sometimes prove as effective as the drug itself. In a **single-blind study**, subjects are kept blind to crucial information, such as the condition to which they are being exposed (in this case, placebo versus medication). It is called single-blind because the subject is blind, but the experimenter is not.

The design of an experiment should also guard against researcher bias. Experimenters are usually committed to the hypotheses they set out to test, and being human, they can be predisposed to interpret their results in a positive light. An experimenter who expects an antianxiety medication to be more effective than a placebo may inadvertently overrate improvement in subjects who receive the medication. The best way to avoid the biases of both subjects and investigators is to perform a **double-blind study** in which subjects and researchers alike are blind to the experimental condition to which each subject has been exposed until the research is completed.

Selecting and Assigning Subjects

Having developed standardized procedures, the researcher is now ready to find subjects representative of the population of interest. Experimenters typically place subjects randomly in each of the experimental conditions (such as sad mood, happy mood, or neutral mood). Random assignment of subjects is essential for internal validity; it minimizes differences between subjects in different groups that cannot be attributed to the independent variable. If all subjects in the sad condition were male and all those in the happy condition were female, Bower could not tell whether his subjects' responses were determined by mood or by sex. In this case the sex of the subjects would be a **confounding variable**, a variable that could produce effects that are confused, or confounded, with the effects of the independent variable. The presence of confounding variables compromises the internal validity of a study by making inferences about causality impossible.

Ideally, samples psychologists use to test general hypotheses about mental and behavioral processes should be representative of the human population as a whole. From a practical point of view, however, collecting data on subjects from multiple cultures, or even from a true cross-section of a single society, is very difficult. Because so many researchers are based on college campuses, the most frequently studied population is largely white, middle-class, 18- to 20-year-old Americans—a fact that led one somewhat cynical observer to call psychology the "science of the behavior of the college sophomore" (Rubenstein, 1982). Although this constraint is too seldom acknowledged in research studies, it undoubtedly limits the generalizability of many research findings.

Should one therefore discount all North American or European psychological research because it depends on student subjects? To do so, a critic would need a good reason to believe that people in other cultures or other age groups would respond differently on the particular task at hand. In the case of Bower's research, for example, there is little reason to suspect that the relation between mood state and recall would differ from a Canadian college student to an Australian aborigine, although the only way to know is to test the hypothesis cross-culturally. In contrast, findings of a study assessing the way people take turns speaking in face-to-face group discussions (Stasser & Taylor, 1991) are likely to depend on cultural norms about turn-taking or status; hence, they are more likely to vary cross-culturally.

Applying Statistical Techniques to the Data

Once an investigator has selected subjects and conducted an experiment, the next step is to analyze the data. When psychologists present and analyze data, they are typically confronted with two tasks. First, they must describe the findings in a way that summarizes their essential features (called **descriptive statistics**); second, they must draw inferences from the sample to the population as a whole (**inferential statistics**). Descriptive statistics are a way of taking what may be a staggeringly large set of observations, sometimes made over months or years, and turning them into a summary form that the researcher and others reading the research can comprehend in a table or graph.

Inferential statistics are used to help sort out whether the findings of a study reflect a true phenomenon or simply random fluctuations in it. In experimental research, the goal is to test for differences between groups or conditions to see if the independent variable really had an impact on the way subjects responded. Figure 2.4 shows the results of Bower's study in which subjects heard about the psychiatric patient while they were either happy or sad. As this figure reveals, the average number of positive and negative memories recalled by subjects varied according to mood. Happy subjects recalled almost 8 happy story incidents but fewer than 6.5 sad ones, whereas sad subjects recalled over eight sad but fewer than six happy incidents. The supplement that immediately follows this chapter addresses descriptive and inferential statistics in enough detail to allow the reader to make sense of most articles in psychological journals. (Fight the urge to skip it—it is comprehensible even to the seriously math phobic and is even occasionally interesting.)

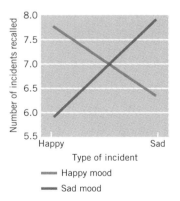

FIGURE 2.4
The influence of mood on memory. Happy subjects stored and later retrieved more happy incidents, while sad subjects differentially remembered sad incidents. SOURCE: *Bower, 1981.*

Drawing Conclusions

The final step in experimental research, drawing conclusions, involves evaluating whether or not the hypothesis was supported—that is, whether the independent and dependent variables were related as predicted. It also entails interpreting the findings in light of the broader theoretical framework of the study and assessing their generalizability. Most studies conclude by acknowledging their limitations and pointing toward future research that might address unanswered questions.

Limitations of Experimental Research

Because experimenters can manipulate variables one at a time and observe the effects of each manipulation, experiments provide the cleanest findings of any method in psychology. No other method in psychological research can determine cause and effect so unambiguously. Furthermore, because experiments can be **replicated,** or repeated, to see if the same findings emerge with a different sample, results can be corroborated or refined.

Experimental methods do, however, have their limitations. First, for both practical and ethical reasons, many complex phenomena cannot be tested in the laboratory. A psychologist who wants to know whether divorce has a negative impact on children's intellectual development cannot manipulate people into divorcing in order to test the hypothesis. Researchers frequently have to examine phenomena as they exist in nature rather than bring them into the laboratory.

When experiments are impractical, psychologists sometimes employ **quasi-experimental designs,** which share the logic and many features of the experimental method but do not afford the experimenter as much control over all relevant variables (Campbell & Stanley, 1963). An experimenter interested in the impact of divorce on memory, for example, might compare the ability of children from divorced and nondivorced families to retrieve positive and negative memories. The researcher would also test to be sure the two groups did not differ on variables that could potentially influence the results, such as age, gender, and socioeconomic status (social class). Although quasi-experimental designs cannot provide the degree of certainty about cause-and-effect relationships that experiments offer, they are probably the most common designs used in psychology. Reality, unfortunately, is both the object of scientific inquiry and its major impediment.

A second limitation of the experimental method centers on the problem of external validity. Researchers can never be certain how closely the phenomena observed in a laboratory parallel their real-life counterparts. In some instances, such as the study with which this chapter opened, the implications seem clear: If brief exposure to a photograph can induce a self-fulfilling prophecy, imagine what years of prejudice or discrimination can do. In other cases, however, external validity is more problematic. Do the principles that operate in a laboratory study of memory apply when a person reflects on past events to decide whether or not to stay in a relationship (Ceci & Bronfenbrenner, 1991; Neisser, 1976; Rogoff & Lave, 1984)?

A third limitation is emphasized by psychologists who take a **hermeneutic,** or interpretive, stance on methodology (Messer et al., 1988). They argue that the aim of a science of human mental life and behavior is not *predicting* behavior but *understanding* the highly idiosyncratic personal meanings that lead to an individual's actions. One person may commit suicide because he feels he is a failure; another may kill himself to get back at a relative or spouse; another may do so to escape intense or chronic psychic pain; still another individual might take his life because cultural norms demand it in the face of a wrongdoing or humiliation. From a hermeneutic point of view, explaining a behavior such as suicide means understanding the subjective meanings behind it, not predicting it from some combination of variables. Many psychodynamic psychologists take a hermeneutic approach, arguing that complex meanings of this sort are not amenable to experimental study and are more likely to be uncovered through long-term exploration. Patients typically discuss much more intimate experiences, and in much more depth, than they ever would with an experimenter, who they meet only briefly and in a highly structured situation that does not encourage the elaboration of personal meanings.

Despite its limitations, the experimental method is the bread and butter of psychology. No method in psychology is more definitive than a well-executed experiment. Nevertheless, few would desire a steady diet of bread and butter, and scientific investigation is nourished by multiple methods with multiple sources of data.

DESCRIPTIVE RESEARCH

The second major type of research, **descriptive research,** attempts to describe phenomena as they exist rather than to manipulate variables to test cause and effect. Descriptive studies answer questions such as the following: Do people in different cultures focus on the same traits in describing personality (Paunonen et al., 1992)? Do children who are inhibited in the second year of life, who seem fearful and unsociable, remain inhibited two to three years later (Broberg et al., 1990)? Do young women with anorexia nervosa (a disorder characterized by a life-threatening aversion to eating) have personality characteristics that distinguish them from their peers (Bruch, 1973)? Do adolescents who make suicide attempts differ in their life experiences from other teenagers (Kienhorst et al., 1992)? To answer such questions, psychologists use a variety of research methods, including case studies, naturalistic observation, survey research, and correlational methods. Table 2.2 summarizes the major uses and limitations of these descriptive methods as well as the experimental method.

Case Study Methods

A **case study** is an in-depth observation of one subject or a small group of subjects. Case study methods are useful when trying to learn about phenomena that are not yet well understood and thus require exploration or complex psychological phenomena that are difficult to produce experimentally. The most famous case studies in psychology were Sigmund Freud's studies of his early patients. Freud sought to discover the origin of his patients' symptoms (such as a little boy's fear of horses or a physically healthy woman's inability to breastfeed her baby) in their past experiences. Researchers tend to describe cases they believe are representative of a population, much as Freud used the case of a little boy who was afraid of horses to set forth some hypotheses about the origins of phobias. Single-case designs can also be used in combination with quantitative or experimental procedures. For example, some researchers assess change in patients over time by coding videotaped psychotherapy sessions for qualities such as emotion, self-esteem, or defensiveness (Hilliard, 1993).

Case studies are often useful when large numbers of subjects are not available, either because they do not exist or because obtaining them would be extremely difficult. For example, extensive case studies of patients who have undergone surgery to sever the tissue connecting the right and left hemispheres of the brain (in order to control severe epileptic seizures) have yielded important information about the specific functions of the two hemispheres.

TABLE 2.2 COMPARISON OF RESEARCH METHODS		
METHOD	**USES**	**LIMITATIONS**
Experimental	Demonstrates causal relationship.	Generalizability: Results may not apply to other cases. Many complex phenomena cannot be tested. Does not offer insight into personal meanings.
Descriptive		
Case study	Reveals individual psychological dynamics. Allows study of complex phenomena not easily reproduced experimentally. Provides data to build hypotheses.	Generalizability. Replicability: The study may not be repeatable. Researcher bias. Cannot establish causation.
Naturalistic observation	Reveals phenomena as they occur outside of the laboratory. Provides data to build hypotheses.	Generalizability. Replicability. Observer effects: The presence of an observer may alter the behavior of the subjects. Researcher bias. Cannot establish causation.
Survey research	Reveals attitudes or self-reported behaviors of a large sample of people.	Self-report bias. Cannot establish causation.
Correlational methods	Reveals relationships between variables as they exist in nature.	Cannot establish causation.

Case study methods are limited by their small sample size and the possibility of researcher bias. Because case study research gains its insights from examining only a small group of subjects, generalization to a larger population is always uncertain. An investigator who conducts intensive research on one young woman with anorexia nervosa and finds that her self-starvation behavior is strongly tied to her wishes for control might be tempted to conclude that control issues are central in cases of this disorder. They may well be, but they may also be idiosyncratic to this particular person. One way to minimize this limitation is to use a multiple case study method (Rosenwald, 1988), extensively examining a small sample of subjects individually and drawing generalizations across subjects.

A second limitation is that case studies are susceptible to researcher bias; that is, investigators tend to see what they expect to see. A psychotherapist who believes anorexic patients have conflicts with sexuality will undoubtedly see such conflicts in her anorexic patients because they are operative in everyone. In writing up the case, she may select examples that demonstrate these conflicts and miss other issues that might be just as salient to another observer. Because no one else is privy to the data of a case, no other investigator can examine the data directly and draw any different conclusions unless the therapy sessions are videotaped. In the case study, the data are always filtered through the psychologist's theoretical lens.

Case studies are probably most useful either at the beginning or at the end of a series of studies that employ quantitative methods with larger samples. Exploring individual cases can be crucial in deciding what questions to ask or what hypotheses to test because they allow the researcher to immerse herself in the phenomenon as it appears in real life. A case study can also flesh out the meaning of quantitative findings by providing a detailed analysis of representative examples.

Naturalistic Observation

A second descriptive method, **naturalistic observation**, is the in-depth observation of a phenomenon in its natural setting. Psychologists who take an evolutionary perspective frequently use naturalistic observation. A researcher interested in the social and mating behavior of baboons might spend a year in the field observing and videotaping baboon interactions (Smuts, 1990). Observing the way male baboons compete for females may suggest hypotheses about the evolution of these behaviors, or it may suggest parallels with the way male humans form hierarchies or compete for females.

Psychologists also observe humans by using naturalistic methods, as in the classic studies of Genevan school children by the Swiss psychologist Jean Piaget (1926). Piaget and his colleagues conducted their research in playgrounds and classrooms, taking detailed notes on who spoke to whom, for how long, and on what topics. Piaget found that young children often speak in "collective monologues," talking all at once; they may neither notice whether they are being listened to nor address their comments to a particular listener. Naturalistic observation has an advantage over experimental methods in that its findings are clearly applicable outside the laboratory.

Most people behave somewhat differently when they are aware that someone is watching, and one limitation of observational methods is that the very fact of being watched may influence behavior, if only subtly. Researchers sometimes try to minimize this bias by employing covert observation (inserting themselves into the environment in ways that make them less noticeable) or by becoming participant-observers (interacting naturally with subjects in their environment and thus tending to elicit more typical behavior). Naturalistic observation shares other limitations

Naturalistic observation allows researchers to observe behavior as it occurs naturally. Left, Jean Piaget observes children on a playground; right, Jane Goodall watches chimpanzees interacting.

with the case study method, such as the problem of generalizability. When can a psychologist conclude that after she has seen one baboon troop, she has seen them all? Researcher bias can also pose limitations since observers' theoretical biases can influence what they look for and therefore what they see. As with case studies, this limitation can be minimized by observing several groups of subjects or by videotaping interactions, so that more than one coder can independently rate the data.

Finally, like other descriptive studies, naturalistic observation primarily describes behaviors; it cannot demonstrate *why* observed behaviors take place. Based on extensive observation, the best an investigator can do is make a convincing argument about the way one variable influences another because researchers using this method do not have the luxury of doing something to subjects and seeing what they do in response, as in experimental designs.

Survey Research

A third type of descriptive research, **survey research,** involves asking a large sample of subjects questions, usually about their attitudes or behaviors. For instance, in 1976, a team of researchers embarked on a massive study of over 2200 Americans to see whether conceptions of mental health and attitudes about treatment for emotional problems had changed since administration of similar survey twenty years earlier (Veroff et al., 1981). Survey research can yield rigorous quantitative findings by attaching numbers to subjects' responses, such as the number of times they saw a mental health professional or their attitudes toward people with mental illness rated on a seven-point scale. The two most frequently used tools of survey researchers are **questionnaires,** which subjects fill out by themselves, and **interviews,** in which researchers ask questions using a standard format.

Selection of the sample is extremely important in survey research, as when pollsters want to be sure that their predictions of election results accurately reflect a large and heterogeneous population. Researchers typically want a **random sample,** a sample of subjects selected from the general population in a relatively arbitrary way that does not introduce any systematic bias. A researcher seeking a random sample of residents of Montreal, for instance, might choose names out of the phone book.

Random selection, however, does not always guarantee that a sample will accurately reflect the **demographic characteristics** (such as gender, race, and socioeconomic status) of the population in which the researcher is interested. A telephone survey based on a random sample of Montreal residents listed in the phone book may overrepresent people who happen to be home answering the phone during the day (such as older people). Where proportional representation of different subpopulations is important, researchers select a stratified random sample. A **stratified random sample** specifies the percentage of subjects to be drawn from each population category (age, race, etc.) and then randomly selects subjects from *within* each category. Researchers often use census data to provide demographic information on the population of interest, and they match this information as closely as possible in their sample. The 1976 mental health study was stratified along a number of lines, including age, sex, race, marital status, region of the country, and education.

The major problem with survey methods is that they rely on subjects to report on themselves truthfully and accurately. Unfortunately, people tend to describe their behaviors and attitudes in more flattering terms than others would use to describe them (Greenwald, 1984; John & Robins, 1994). How many people are likely to admit their addiction to *General Hospital* or *Leave It to Beaver* reruns? In part, their answers may be biased by their conscious efforts to present themselves in the best possible light. They may also unconsciously shade the truth because they want to seem intelligent or industrious. In addition, subjects may honestly misjudge themselves. How many women, in their interactions with men, would expect their behavior to be heavily influenced by the man's perception of their attractiveness? The results of a questionnaire and a laboratory experiment on self-fulfilling prophecies could thus be widely discrepant. Similarly, measuring people's attitudes toward the handicapped by means of a questionnaire leads to a much more benign view of these attitudes than measuring how far subjects *sit* from a handicapped person when entering a room.

Correlational Research

The aim of the fourth type of descriptive research, **correlational research,** is to determine the degree to which two or more variables are related, so that knowing the value of one allows a prediction of the other. For example, one study provided data on the extent to which people who frequently experience one emotion, such as guilt, experience others, such as shame (Izard et al., 1993). On a scale from 1 (*never*) to 5 (*very often*), subjects completed questionnaires asking them to rate how frequently in their lives they experience various emotions.

Do people who frequently feel guilty also often feel ashamed, fearful, or angry? To answer this question, the researchers correlated guilt with other emotions. To **correlate** two variables means to assess the extent to which being high or low on one measure predicts being high or low on another. The statistic that allows a researcher to make this assessment is called a correlation coefficient. A **correlation coefficient** measures the extent to which two variables are related, and it can be either positive or negative. A **positive correlation** means that the higher individuals measure on one variable, the higher they are likely to measure on the other. This also means, of course, that the lower they score on one variable, the lower they will score on the other. A **negative correlation** means that the higher subjects measure on one variable, the *lower* they will measure on the other. Correlations can be depicted on **scatterplot graphs,** which show the scores of every subject along two dimensions (Figure 2.5).

Correlation coefficients vary between +1.0 and -1.0. A strong correlation—one with a value close to either positive or negative 1.0—means that a psychologist who knows a person's score on one variable can predict that person's score on the other

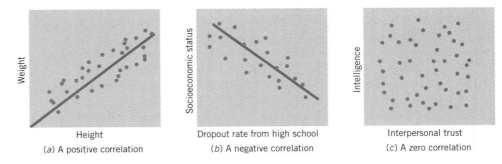

Weight / Height	Socioeconomic status / Dropout rate from high school	Intelligence / Interpersonal trust
(a) A positive correlation	(b) A negative correlation	(c) A zero correlation

FIGURE 2.5

Positive, negative, and zero correlations. A correlation expresses the relation between two variables. The panels above depict three kinds of correlations on hypothetical scatterplot graphs, which show the way data points fall (that is, are scattered) along the axes on two dimensions. Panel (a) shows a positive correlation between height and weight. Comparing the dots (which represent individual subjects) on the right with those on the left shows that those on the left are lower on both variables. The dots scatter around the line that summarizes them, which is the correlation coefficient. Panel (b) shows a negative correlation between socioeconomic status and dropout rate from high school. The higher the socioeconomic status, the lower the dropout rate. Panel (c) shows a zero correlation, between intelligence and the extent to which the individual believes people can be trusted. The dots are randomly distributed across the diagram: Being high on one dimension predicts nothing about whether the subject is high or low on the other.

TABLE 2.3 CORRELATIONS AMONG VARIOUS EMOTIONS

	Guilt	Shame	Fear	Anger	Joy
Guilt	—	.61	.54	.51	-.23
Shame	—	—	.51	.26	-.30
Fear	—	—	—	.41	-.14
Anger	—	—	—	—	-.31
Joy	—	—	—	—	—

Source: Adapted from Izard et al., 1993.

Note. The dashes represent correlations between a variable and itself (e.g., fear with fear), which by definition are 1.0 (a perfect correlation). Note that only half a table is needed to present a correlation matrix, for any correlations below the dashes would be redundant, having already been presented elsewhere in the table.

variable with confidence. For instance, one would expect a strong negative correlation between level of alcohol in a person's blood and that person's ability to recite the alphabet backwards; the higher the alcohol level, the fewer letters accurately recited backwards. A weak correlation hovers close to zero, either on the positive or the negative side. Variables with a very weak correlation cannot be used to predict one another. A correlation of zero means that the two variables are totally unrelated, such as adult weight and IQ score.

To return to the study of emotions, we would expect people who tend to feel one unpleasant emotion frequently to experience other unpleasant feelings as well. That is, we would hypothesize a positive correlation between guilt and fear, or between guilt and shame. Table 2.3 displays the correlations among various emotions, presented as a **correlation matrix**—that is, a table presenting the correlations among a number of variables. The strongest positive correlation (.61) is between shame and guilt: People who tend to feel guilty do tend to feel ashamed as well. The strongest negative correlation (-.31) is between anger and joy. This is a weak correlation, which means, somewhat counterintuitively, that knowing that a person frequently has unpleasant feelings does *not* guarantee that the individual lacks positive feelings.

The virtue of correlational research is that it allows investigators to study a whole range of phenomena that vary in nature—from personality characteristics to attitudes—that cannot be produced in the laboratory. Like the other descriptive methods, however, correlational research can only describe relationships among variables. When two variables correlate with each other, the researcher must infer the relation between them: Does one cause the other, or does some third variable explain the correlation?

Media reports on research often disregard or misunderstand the fact that *correlation does not imply causation*. If a study shows a correlation between drug use and poor grades, the media often report that "scientists have found that drug use leads to bad grades." An equally valid hypothesis might be that some underlying aspect of personality (such as alienation) or home environment (such as poor parenting, abuse, neglect, or chaos) produces both drug use *and* bad grades (Shedler & Block, 1990). Similarly, in 1986 the Meese Commission, established by President Ronald Reagan, reviewed the evidence linking pornography to violence, particularly crimes against women, and concluded that pornography leads to rape and other crimes. Just because rapists read pornography, however, does not prove that pornography leads to rape. Many people who do not commit rapes also read pornography. In rapists, both pornographic viewing and violent sexual behavior may reflect a third variable, disturbed sexuality (see Mould, 1990).

FROM MIND TO BRAIN

RESEARCHING THE BRAIN

Thus far, we have explored the major types of research designs used by psychologists. We now examine how these designs help address two issues raised in Chapter 1 that recur throughout this book: the relation between mind and brain, and the cross-cultural generalizability of psychological findings.

As we saw in Chapter 1 various regions of the brain are specialized for particular functions. Discovering these functions is no easy task, however, because under normal conditions the various structures work together as an integrated whole. Case studies of patients who have suffered disease or damage to particular neural regions (lesion studies) provide one window to the normal workings of the nervous system; psychologists can infer what a structure does by seeing what happens when it is *not* working. Physicians discovered the promise of lesion studies in the mid nineteenth century when they observed patients with left-hemisphere damage who had speech or language impairments. In the middle of the present century, neurosurgeons began to learn about the functions of different parts of the brain by stimulating them during surgery using a mild electrical current. This procedure was necessary to "map" the brain of a given patient to avoid damaging essential regions, such as those involved in language. Researchers using experimental methods with animals learn about the functions of different structures by lesioning them or the neural tissue that leads to and from them and assessing the effects.

Currently, researchers use a number of other technologically sophisticated methods to pinpoint the location of lesions and to study the brain as it is functioning (Raichle, 1994). The **electroencephalogram** (**EEG**), the first such instrument developed, has been in use since the early 1930s. Electrodes placed on the scalp record ongoing electrical activity in the brain. The EEG is frequently employed in diagnosing disorders such as epilepsy as well as in studying neural activity during sleep. A second method, **computerized axial tomography** (commonly known as a **CT scan**), produces a series of X-ray pictures.

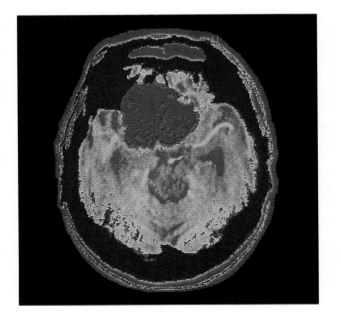

FIGURE 2.6
A CT scan of a patient with a brain tumor (shown in purple).

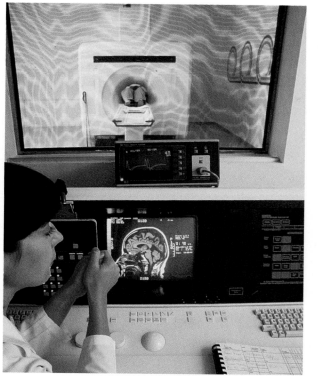

An MRI scan.

A CT scanner rotates an X-ray tube around a person's head along various planes parallel to the top of the skull, producing a series of pictures that a computer combines into a composite visual image. The CT scan shown in Figure 2.6 reveals a brain tumor. CT scans can pinpoint the location of abnormalities such as neuronal atrophy (degeneration) and abnormal tissue growths (tumors). A related technology, **magnetic resonance imaging (MRI)**, can accomplish similar tasks without using X rays and can sometimes yield clearer pictures than CT scans.

Still another diagnostic technique, **positron emission tomography (PET)**, enables observation of the brain in action. To produce a PET scan, radioactive glucose is injected into the bloodstream. (The amount injected is not dangerous.) Nerve cells use glucose for energy, and they replenish their supply of glucose from the bloodstream. As these cells make use of glucose that has been radioactively "tagged," a computer produces a color portrait of the active parts of the brain. Researchers and clinicians can thus examine ongoing activity in various regions in patients suffering from disorders such as schizophrenia (a severe mental disorder) or Parkinson's disease (a severe disorder of movement, which often begins with a mild tremor in the hands or head). Using a PET scan, researchers can isolate structures that are more or less active in these patients than in normals (Bench et al., 1990; Kuperman et al., 1990; Raichle, 1995). Researchers can also see exactly what parts of the brain are utilized during tasks such as remembering, listening to music, or solving a problem, thereby allowing the experimental investigation of neural processes.

Some investigators have begun using this technology to study the neuropsychology of intelligence, comparing brain activity on various cognitive tasks in subjects with differing levels of IQ. The results of one such study were paradoxical (Haier et al., 1988). As Figure 2.7 shows, the brain of a subject

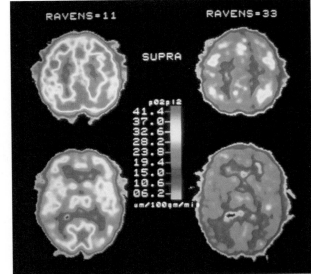

FIGURE 2.7
IQ and brain activity as measured by PET. A computerized image lights up in color as areas of the brain become active. Subjects with higher IQ (right) show less activation, suggesting that they have to work less hard while solving problems.

with a higher IQ shows *less* overall activity during an abstract reasoning task than does the brain of a lower IQ subject. As the researchers suggest, more intelligent subjects may be able to solve the problem more efficiently and with less effort.

A GLOBAL VISTA

CROSS-CULTURAL RESEARCH

As we saw in Chapter 1, human nature is constrained on one side by biology and on the other by culture, as humans are both physiological organisms and members of larger groups. To some degree, human nature is the same everywhere because the genetic blueprints are so similar, but the expression of those blueprints can look as varied as an adobe hut and a high-rise apartment. Ascertaining the extent to which psychological findings in one culture apply to people around the globe presents more difficult challenges than might first appear.

Like anthropological fieldwork, in which an investigator lives in another culture and observes daily events, many cross-cultural investigations involve naturalistic observation. This approach can be supplemented with quantitative methods, as when researchers wanted to explore the origins of social behavior in infants reared in a culture very different from their own (Tronick et al., 1992). They studied Efe pygmies in the tropical rain forests of Zaire, who survive by hunting, gathering food, and trading with neighboring agricultural peoples. The Efe establish camps composed of huts arranged in a semicircle, usually consisting of about 20 people. Researchers armed with laptop computers recorded minute-by-minute observations of the social life of Efe infants and toddlers in the camps. They found that unlike Western children, who are groomed for independence, Efe children are surrounded by other people virtually every hour of their lives, which prepares them well for a communal lifestyle as adults.

Other researchers rely on correlational and experimental methods to investigate psychological phenomena across cultures. In the 1940s an anthropologist at Yale University created the Human Relations Area Files, a database on hundreds of cultures taken from detailed observations by anthropologists. Information in the files is indexed under categories such as supernatural beliefs, treatment of outsiders, rituals, infant care, and child-rearing practices. The files allow researchers to test hypotheses by correlating variables with each other across cultures. Studies since the 1950s have examined the correlations between various child-rearing variables and cultural practices (Whiting & Child, 1953). For example, harsh childhood discipline correlates with beliefs in malevolent deities (Rohner, 1986). Apparently, cultural views of the gods are not independent of children's views of the godlike figures in their lives—their parents. Cross-cultural psychologists have also applied experimental procedures in other countries, to test whether the findings of studies on phenomena like self-fulfilling prophecies replicate cross-culturally (see Berry et al., 1992; Triandis, 1994).

Psychologists interested in the cross-cultural validity of their theories face many difficulties, however, in transporting research from one culture to another. The same stimulus may mean very different things to people in different cultures. What might a shepherd from the Middle East make of the intercom system used in the study of self-fulfilling prophecies or of the photos rated attractive or unattractive by American undergraduates? To create an equivalent experimental design often requires using a *different* design, but then is it really the same experiment?

Similarly, when employing a questionnaire cross-culturally, researchers must be very careful about the translation because even minor changes or ambiguities could make cross-cultural comparisons invalid. To minimize distortions in translation, researchers use a procedure called back-translation. In this procedure, a bilingual speaker translates the items into the target language, and another bilingual translates it back into the original language (usually English). Then they repeat the process until the translation back into English matches the original. Even this procedure is not always adequate because sometimes concepts simply differ too much across cultures to make the items equivalent. Asking a subject to rate the item "I have a good relationship with my brother" would be inappropriate in Japan, where speakers distinguish between older and younger brothers and lack a general term to denote both (Brislin, 1986). Once again reality poses obstacles to research, but we have to try to hurdle them if we want to learn about the psychology of *people* rather than of particular *peoples*.

Among the Efe, as in many cultures, children are rarely alone.

HOW TO EVALUATE A STUDY CRITICALLY

Having explored the major research designs, we now turn to the question of how to be an informed consumer of research. In deciding whether to "buy" the results of a study, the same maxim applies as in buying a car: *caveat emptor*, let the buyer beware. The popular media often report that "Researchers at Harvard have found . . . ," followed by conclusions that are tempting to take at face value. In reality, most studies have their limitations. To evaluate a study critically, the reader must examine the research carefully (Figure 2.8) and attempt to answer seven questions.

Does the Theoretical Framework Make Sense?

The first step in evaluating a study is to consider whether the theory and the specific hypothesis to be tested make sense. Do the authors specify precisely what they mean by the concepts they use? Do all definitions of the same concept refer to the same thing? For example, if the study explores the relation between social class and intelligence, does the article explain why social class and intelligence should have some relationship to one another? Do the authors clearly and consistently define both social class and intelligence?

FIGURE 2.8

How to evaluate a study critically. Examining a study critically means considering every aspect of the investigation, from the theory underlying it to its ethics.

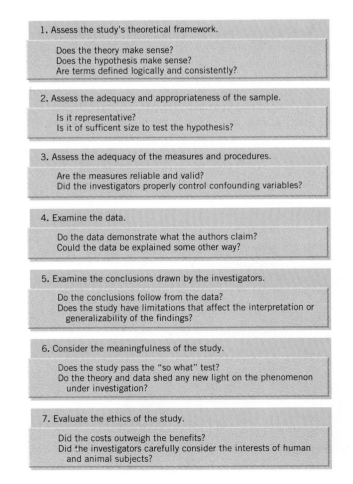

1. Assess the study's theoretical framework.

Does the theory make sense?
Does the hypothesis make sense?
Are terms defined logically and consistently?

2. Assess the adequacy and appropriateness of the sample.

Is it representative?
Is it of sufficent size to test the hypothesis?

3. Assess the adequacy of the measures and procedures.

Are the measures reliable and valid?
Did the investigators properly control confounding variables?

4. Examine the data.

Do the data demonstrate what the authors claim?
Could the data be explained some other way?

5. Examine the conclusions drawn by the investigators.

Do the conclusions follow from the data?
Does the study have limitations that affect the interpretation or
generalizability of the findings?

6. Consider the meaningfulness of the study.

Does the study pass the "so what" test?
Do the theory and data shed any new light on the phenomenon
under investigation?

7. Evaluate the ethics of the study.

Did the costs outweigh the benefits?
Did the investigators carefully consider the interests of human
and animal subjects?

Is the Sample Adequate and Appropriate?

The next step is to examine the sample and determine whether it adequately represents the population from which it is drawn. If researchers want to know about self-fulfilling prophecies among undergraduates, then a sample of undergraduates is perfectly appropriate. If they want to generalize to other populations, however, they need to use multiple samples to determine whether the same effects hold. Another important question is whether the sample is large enough to allow for adequate statistical tests of the findings' significance (Chapter 2 Supplement).

Were the Measures and Procedures Adequate?

The third question is whether the procedures and measures were well suited to the hypothesis being tested. Do the measures assess what they were designed to assess? Were proper control groups chosen to rule out alternative explanations and to assure the validity of the study? Did the investigators fail to notice any confounding variables that might have influenced the results? For example, if the study involved interviewing subjects, were some of the interviewers male and some female? If so, did the sex of the interviewer have an effect on the way subjects responded?

Are the Data Conclusive?

Another step in evaluating a study is to examine the data presented. Do they demonstrate what the author claims? Typically, data in research articles are presented in a section entitled "Results," usually in the form of graphs, charts, or tables. In evaluating a study critically, the reader should carefully examine the data presented in these figures and ask whether any alternative interpretations could explain the results as well as or better than the researcher's explanation. Often, data permit many interpretations, and the findings may fit a pattern that the researcher has not considered.

Are the Broader Conclusions Warranted?

Still another question is whether the researcher's broad conclusions fit both the theory presented and the data of the study. Does the study have limitations that render the conclusions invalid or seriously circumscribed? An experiment may nicely test a phenomenon in a very specific domain, but then the investigator may try to generalize the findings to other areas with different properties. One should be wary of a research article that describes the effects of overcrowding on rats and then tries to draw broad conclusions about the need for human population control.

Does the Study Say Anything Meaningful?

The sixth question in evaluating a study is the "so what?" test: Are the results meaningful? Does the fact that college freshmen rated their mothers more feminine than their fathers really matter? Does the study tell us anything we did not already know? Does it lead to questions for future research? The meaningfulness of a study typically depends on the importance, usefulness, and adequacy of the theoretical perspective from which it derives.

Is the Study Ethical?

A final question concerns ethics. If the study uses human or animal subjects, does it treat them humanely, and do the ends of the study—the incremental knowledge it produces—justify the means? Psychologists were once free to make those determinations on their own, and the vast majority have always considered the welfare of their subjects carefully in designing studies. Today, however, the American Psychological Association (APA) publishes guidelines that govern psychological research practices (APA, 1973, 1982, 1990), and universities and other institutions have boards that review proposals for psychological studies, with the power to reject them on ethical grounds.

The ethical issues involved in research are not always black and white. For example, in 1991, Jacob, Krahn, and Leonard published a study of problem solving in alcoholic fathers and their adolescent children. Subjects were offered a sizable honorarium ($400) to participate in the study. During one procedure, alcoholic beverages were made available to subjects in order to explore the impact of alcohol consumption on the parent-child interaction. Not surprisingly, the alcoholics availed themselves of this opportunity, with a mean consumption of 3.4 ounces.

The study was very strong methodologically and overcame numerous problems of previous research. For instance, many studies have used college students as subjects. Yet even college students who display symptoms of alcohol abuse may not be a representative sample. Some students abuse alcohol during college because of its novelty, peer pressure, and cultural norms of college behavior, but they later have normal drinking patterns. Studies that *have* used actual alcoholics as subjects have often relied on self-reports. Unfortunately, self-reports of alcohol consumption are notoriously unreliable among alcoholics, who may be unwilling or unable (because of denial or memory lapses) to provide accurate information. Thus, Jacob and colleagues could argue that their study was of particular value in offering new insights into an important topic.

Other psychologists, however, expressed concerns about the ethics of the research. The study essentially paid alcoholics to drink, thereby colluding in a disorder that has substantial negative consequences for families (Koocher, 1991; Stricker, 1991). As one commentator noted, $400 is a substantial payment for participation in a study, especially since roughly one-quarter of the subjects were unemployed (Koocher, 1991). Jacob and colleagues responded that they had safeguarded the welfare of the subjects in a number of ways, such as sending them home in taxis to prevent them from driving under the influence (Jacob & Leonard, 1991). Furthermore, most subjects drank less than two drinks during the procedure, hardly an amount likely to influence the lives of men who had been drinking heavily for 10 to 20 years. Nevertheless, this example demonstrates the ambiguity that sometimes arises when researchers are confronted with ethical decisions.

Deception in Psychological Research

Many studies, like the one with which this chapter opened, keep subjects blind to the aims of the investigation until the end, and some even deceive subjects, giving them a cover story so that demand characteristics will not bias their responses. Had the experimenters told subjects they were interested in self-fulfilling prophecies, for example, they could never have obtained valid results.

From an ethical standpoint, these practices, and particularly the use of deception, raise questions about **informed consent**—the subject's ability to agree (or refuse) to participate in an informed manner. Can subjects really give informed consent to a study whose aims they do not know? Some psychologists argue that "the use of intentional deception in the research setting is unethical, imprudent, and unwarranted scientifically" (Baumrind, 1985). Others, however, point to evidence demonstrating that subjects in deception experiments actually tend to enjoy the experience more, to learn more from their participation, and to consider the deception unobjectionable when they are "debriefed" at the end (Christensen, 1988).

Only a small proportion of experiments involve deception, and APA guidelines permit deception only if a study meets four conditions: (1) The research is of great importance and cannot be conducted without the use of deception; (2) participants can be expected to find the procedures reasonable upon being informed of them after the experiment is completed; (3) subjects can withdraw from the experiment at any time; and (4) experimenters debrief the subjects afterward, explaining the purposes of the study and removing any stressful after-effects. Many universities address the issue of consent in deception experiments by giving subjects the option of participating only in experiments that do not involve deception. That way, any subject who is deceived by an experimenter has given prior consent to be deceived.

Ethics and Animal Research

A larger ethical controversy concerns the use of nonhuman animal subjects for psychological research (Bowd, 1990; Ulrich, 1991). By lesioning a region of the cat's brain, for example, researchers can sometimes learn a tremendous amount about the function of similar regions in the human brain. Conducting such an experiment, however, has an obvious cost to the animal. This raises questions about the moral status of animals—that is, whether they have rights (Plous, 1991; Rollin, 1985). Again the question is one of balancing costs and benefits: To what extent do the costs to animals justify the benefits to humans? The most vexing aspect of this philosophical dilemma is that, unlike human subjects, animals cannot give informed consent.

To what extent can humans use, and even breed, other sentient creatures (that is, animals who feel) to satisfy intellectual or other human interests? Groups such as Mobilization for Animals (1984) argue that animal research in psychology has produced little of value to humans, especially considering the enormous suffering that animals have undergone. Most psychologists dispute this claim (Miller, 1985). They note that animal research has led to important advances in behavioral treatment, biofeedback, potential treatment for serious disorders such as Alzheimer's disease, a degenerative brain illness that ultimately leads to death, and the understanding of such phenomena as stress, weight gain, and the effects of aging on learning and memory. The difficulty lies in balancing the interests of humans and other animals and advancing science while staying within sensible ethical boundaries (Bowd, 1990). As in research with human subjects, institutional review boards examine proposals for experiments with nonhuman subjects and may similarly veto proposals they deem unethical.

Observers disagree on the ethics of animal research, and passions run high.

SOME CONCLUDING THOUGHTS

The four major perspectives in psychology make use of different combinations of methods. Psychologists with a behaviorist or cognitive perspective are almost uniformly committed to experimental investigation. This emphasis on experimentation as a way of understanding the nature of things derives from Sir Francis Bacon, a British philosopher who was writing as England took its first steps into the modern age in the sixteenth century. According to Bacon, the best way to test whether one genuinely understands nature is to bend it to do something it normally does not do (Smith, 1992). Scientists who understand the laws of physics—or behavior—ought to be able to "bend nature" in a laboratory to do something scientifically interesting or practically useful. The philosopher of science Karl Popper (1963), among others, has argued that the criterion that distinguishes science is the formulation and evaluation of testable hypotheses. Preferably, these hypotheses should not be intuitively obvious, so they can put a theory to the test and potentially prove it wrong. From this standpoint, the behavioral and cognitive perspectives have the greatest scientific support, since psychodynamic and evolutionary psychologists have relied on case studies and naturalistic observation more than on experimental methods.

On the other hand, the phenomena that most readily lend themselves to experimental investigation may not necessarily be the most important. For instance, psychodynamic theory suggests that people who are chronically angry may deal with their anger in one of at least three ways. They may express anger directly and appear hostile; they may deny the feeling entirely and report that they rarely feel angry; or they may control their aggressive impulses by behaving in precisely the opposite manner, with exaggerated sweetness or politeness. This hypothesis is extremely difficult to test. Even if we could reliably diagnose angry people, we could interpret the entire spectrum of behavior, from aggressive to neutral to sweet, as confirmation of the theory. Should the hypothesis therefore be discarded simply because it is difficult to assess? To do so would confuse the truth-value of a hypothesis with its testability. A sophisticated theory of human nature may include many accurate propositions that are difficult to test empirically precisely because humans are complex creatures.

Philosophers of science sometimes distinguish between the **context of discovery** (in which phenomena are observed, hypotheses are framed, and theories are built) and the **context of justification** (in which hypotheses are tested empirically). Descriptive methods such as case studies, naturalistic observation, and correlational studies are often more useful in the context of discovery precisely because the investigator is *not* structuring the situation. The more experimenters exert control, the less they see behavior that is unconstrained—behavior as it occurs in nature. Freud's observations of the intimate thoughts and feelings of hundreds of patients led him to postulate the existence of unconscious processes. Because experimental methods did not point to the importance of these processes, a century passed before experimental psychologists recognized that such processes exist, are central to human cognition, and can be studied experimentally (see Bowers & Meichenbaum, 1984; Kihlstrom, 1987; Schacter, 1992; Weinberger, in press).

In the context of justification, in which hypotheses are tested, the best designs are experimental, quasi-experimental, and correlational. By using inferential statistics, researchers can begin to separate their beliefs from reality. It could be argued, however, that psychology, as a human science, has a second context of justification: an interpretive, or hermeneutic, one. A theory that cannot help psychologists interpret the meanings behind people's actions better than another theory—or better than a layperson's understanding—is probably as inadequate as a theory that cannot generate testable hypotheses.

The road to psychological knowledge is paved in many directions. Just as an optimal study uses multiple measures, so an optimal science of mental life and behavior uses multiple methods of observation. Different methods serve different purposes, just as do various perspectives. The remainder of this text examines the discoveries to which the various methodologies have led, beginning with the biological bases of mental processes and behavior.

Summary

Characteristics of Good Psychological Research

1. Good psychological research typically has a number of features: a theoretical framework, standardized procedures, generalizability, and objective measurement.

2. A **theory** is a systematic way of organizing and explaining observations, which includes a set of propositions about the relations among various phenomena. A **hypothesis** is a tentative belief or educated guess that purports to predict or explain the relationship between two or more **variables**; variables are phenomena that differ or change across circumstances or individuals. A variable that can be placed on a continuum is called a **continuous** variable. A variable comprised of groupings or categories is called **categorical**.

3. A **sample** is a subgroup of a **population** that is likely to be **representative** of the population as a whole. **Generalizability** refers to the applicability of findings based on a sample to the entire population of interest to the researcher. For a study's findings to be generalizable, its methods must be sound, or **valid**.

4. A **measure** is a concrete way of assessing a variable. A good measure is both reliable and valid. **Reliability** refers to a measure's ability to produce consistent results. The **validity** of a measure refers to its ability to assess the construct it is intended to measure.

Experimental Research

5. In **experimental research**, investigators manipulate some aspect of a situation and examine the impact of this manipulation on the way subjects respond in order to assess cause and effect. **Independent variables** are the variables the experimenter manipulates, and **dependent variables** are the subjects' responses which the experimenter measures to see if the manipulation had an effect.

6. Conducting a study entails a series of steps: framing the hypothesis, operationalizing variables, developing a standardized procedure, selecting subjects, testing the results for statistical significance, and drawing conclusions. **Operationalizing** means turning an abstract concept into a concrete variable defined by some set of actions, or operations.

7. A **control group** is not exposed to experimental manipulations but experiences a neutral condition instead. Researchers frequently perform **blind studies** in which subjects are kept unaware of or "blind" to important aspects of the research. In a **single-blind study,** only subjects are kept blind; in **double-blind studies,** subjects and researchers alike are blind.

8. A **confounding variable** is a variable that could produce effects that are confused with the effects of the independent variable.

9. Limitations of experimental studies include the difficulty of bringing complex phenomena into the laboratory, the question of external validity (applicability of the results to phenomena in the real world), and an inattention to personal meanings. A **hermeneutic,** or interpretive, stance on methodology argues that the aim of a science of human action is not the *prediction* of behavior but the *understanding* of the highly idiosyncratic personal meanings that lead to an individual's actions.

Descriptive Research

10. Unlike experimental studies, **descriptive** methods cannot unambiguously demonstrate cause and effect. They describe phenomena as they already exist rather than manipulate variables to test the effects. Descriptive methods include case studies, naturalistic observation, survey research, and correlational methods.

11. A **case study** is an in-depth observation of one subject or a small group of subjects. **Naturalistic observation** is the in-depth observation of a phenomenon in its natural setting. Both case studies and naturalistic observation are vulnerable to researcher bias, the tendency of investigators to see what they are expecting to see. **Survey research** involves asking a large sample of subjects questions, often about attitudes or behaviors, using **questionnaires** or **interviews**.

12. **Correlational research** assesses the degree to which two variables are related, in an effort to see whether knowing the value of one can lead to prediction of the other. A **correlation coefficient** measures the extent to which two variables are related; it may be positive or negative. A **positive correlation** between two variables means that the higher individuals measure on one variable, the higher they are likely to measure on the other. A **negative correlation** means that the higher subjects measure on one variable, the lower they will measure on the other, and vice versa. Correlation does not demonstrate causation.

13. Researchers studying the relation between mental and neural processes use a number of methods, including case studies of patients with brain damage, experimental lesion studies with animals, **eletroencephalograms (EEGs)**, and computerized scanning techniques.

14. Researchers studying psychological phenomena cross-culturally use a variety of methods, including naturalistic observation, correlational studies linking one cultural trait to another, and experiments.

How to Evaluate a Study Critically

15. To evaluate a study, a critical reader should answer several questions: (1) What is the study's theoretical framework? Does it make sense, and do the hypotheses flow sensibly from it? (2) Is the sample adequate and appropriate? (3) What measures and procedures were used? Are they valid and reliable? (4) Are the data conclusive? (5) Are the broader conclusions warranted? (6) Does the study say anything meaningful? (7) Is the study ethical?

Some Concluding Thoughts

16. Psychologists with a behaviorist or cognitive perspective are almost uniformly committed to experimental investigation, whereas psychodynamic and evolutionary psychologists have tended to rely on case studies and naturalistic observation more than on experimental methods. The optimal path to psychological knowledge is through the use of multiple methods.

STATISTICAL PRINCIPLES IN PSYCHOLOGICAL RESEARCH

Statistics are far more intuitive than most people believe and are quite comprehensible, even to people who do not consider mathematics their strong suit. As described in Chapter 2, psychologists use descriptive statistics to summarize quantitative data in a form that is relatively understandable, and they employ inferential statistics to tell whether the results reflect anything other than chance. We discuss each in turn.

SUMMARIZING THE DATA: DESCRIPTIVE STATISTICS

The first step in describing subjects' responses on a variable is usually to chart a frequency distribution. A **frequency distribution** is exactly what it sounds like—a method of organizing the data to show how frequently subjects received each of the many possible scores. In other words, a frequency distribution represents the way scores were distributed across the sample. The kind of frequency distribution that a professor might observe on a midterm examination (in a very small class, for illustration) is shown in Table 2S.1 and again graphically in Figure 2S.1. The graph, called a **histogram**, plots ranges of scores along the x axis and the frequency of scores in each range on the y axis. The rounded-out version of the histogram drawn with a line is the familiar "curve."

TABLE 2S.1 DISTRIBUTION OF TEST SCORES ON A MIDTERM EXAMINATION

98
92
87
87
84
78
74
70
<u>60</u>
730

$$\text{Mean} = \frac{730}{9} \frac{\text{(total of scores)}}{\text{(\# of students)}} = 81.1$$

Note. The mean is the average of all scores (in this case, 81.1). The mode is the most common score (87). The median is the score in the middle of the distribution, with half of all scores above it and half below it (84).

Measures of Central Tendency

Perhaps the most important descriptive statistics are **measures of central tendency**, which provide an index of the way a typical subject responded on a measure. The three most common measures of central tendency are the mean, the mode, and the median. The **mean** is simply the statistical average of the scores of all subjects, computed by adding up all the subjects' scores and dividing by the number of subjects. The mean is the most commonly reported measure of central tendency and is the most intuitively descriptive of the average subject.

Sometimes, however, the mean may be misleading. For example, suppose as part of a larger study, a researcher wanted to know how much money the typical rural family in Peru earns per year, and found, in a sample of 10 families, that 8 earned $2000 per year, 1 earned $100,000 per year, and 1 earned $300,000 (Table 2S.2). Relying strictly on mean income as the measure of central tendency, the researcher would conclude that rural Peruvians are, on the average, a wealthy group, with a mean annual income of $41,600. However, this would misrepresent the majority whose meager incomes were averaged in with their wealthy landowning neighbors.

FIGURE 2S.1

Histogram showing a frequency distribution of test scores. A frequency distribution shows graphically the frequency of each score (how many times it occurs) distributed across the sample.

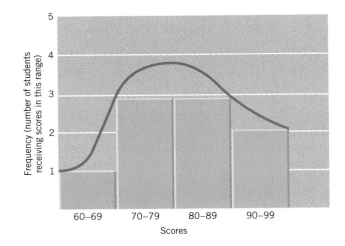

In this case, both the mode and the median would be more useful measures of central tendency. The **mode** (or modal score) refers to the most common score observed in the sample. In this case, $2000 would be the modal income because 8 of 10 families had an income of $2000. In Table 2S.1, the modal test score is 87, whereas the mean is 81.1. One or two students with particularly low scores for this sample pulled down the class mean.

The **median** refers to the score that falls in the middle of the distribution of scores, with half of subjects scoring below it and half above it. Reporting the median essentially allows one to ignore extreme scores on each end of the distribution that would bias a portrait of the typical subject. In the Peruvian example, median income, like modal income, would be $2000 because $2000 falls in the middle of

---

TABLE 2S.2 WHEN A MEAN IS MISLEADING

FAMILY #	INCOME PER FAMILY PER YEAR (IN DOLLARS)
1	2000
2	2000
3	2000
4	100,000
5	2000
6	2000
7	2000
8	300,000
9	2000
10	2000

$$\text{Mean} = \frac{\text{sum of all incomes} = \$416,000}{\text{number of families} = 10} = \$41,600$$

Mode = $2000

the distribution. Half of the families sampled earn $2000 or less, and half earn $2000 or more, even though those who earn more earn substantially more. Median test score on the hypothetical midterm examination in Table 2S.1 is 84; half the scores fall above and half below.

Variability

As the test score and Peruvian income examples demonstrate, another important descriptive statistic is a measure of the **variability** of scores—that is, how much subjects' scores differ from each other. Variability influences the choice of measure of central tendency. The simplest measure of variabilty is the **range** of scores, which refers to the difference between the highest and the lowest value observed on the variable. In the Peruvian case, values of the income variable run from $2000 to $300,000, for a range of $298,000.

The range can be a biased estimate of variability, however, in much the same way as the mean can be a biased estimate of central tendency. Income does range considerably in this sample, but for the majority of Peruvians studied, variability is minimal (ranging from $2000 to $2000—no variability at all). Hence, a more useful measure is the **standard deviation (SD)**, which again is just what it sounds like: the amount that the average subject deviates from the mean of the sample. Table 2S.3 shows how to compute a standard deviation.

The Normal Distribution

When researchers collect data on continuous variables (such as weight or IQ) and plot them on a histogram as described in Chapter 2, the data generally approximate a normal distribution, like the distribution of IQ scores shown in Figure 2S.2. In a **normal distribution**, the scores of most subjects fall in the middle of the bell-shaped distribution, and progressively fewer subjects have scores at either extreme. In other words, most people are about average on most dimensions, and very few are extremely above or below average. Thus, most people have an average IQ

TABLE 2S.3 THE STANDARD DEVIATION

SCORE	DEVIATION FROM THE MEAN	D^2
98	98-91 = 7	49
94	94-91 = 3	9
91	91-91 = 0	0
87	87-91 = -4	16
85	85-91 = -6	36
455	0	110

Mean = 455/5 = 91

Standard deviation = $\sqrt{\dfrac{\Sigma D^2}{N}} = \sqrt{\dfrac{110}{5}} = \sqrt{22} = 4.7$

Note. The table presents the scores of five students on an examination (Column 1). Computing a standard deviation is actually quite intuitive. The first step is to calculate the mean score, which in this case is 91. The next step is to calculate the difference, or deviation, between each subject's score and the mean score, as shown in Column 2. The standard deviation is the average deviation of subjects from the mean. The only complication is that taking the average of the deviations would always produce a mean deviation of zero because the sum of deviations is by definition zero (see the total in Column 2). Thus, the next step is to square the deviations (Column 3). The standard deviation is then actually computed by taking the square root of the sum of deviations squared (ΣD^2) divided by the number of subjects (N).

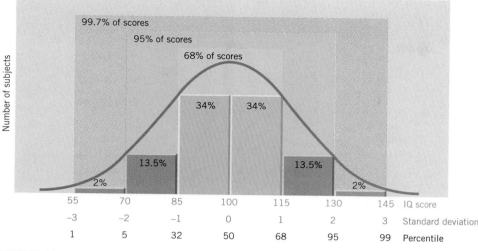

FIGURE 2S.2

A normal distribution. IQ scores approximate a normal distribution, which looks like a bell-shaped curve, with 68 percent of scores within one standard deviation of the mean (represented by the area under the curve in blue). The curve is a smoothed-out version of a histogram. An individual's score can be represented alternatively by the number of standard deviations it diverges from the mean in either direction or by a percentile score, which shows the percentage of scores that fall below it (to the left on the graph).

(100), whereas very few have an IQ of 70 or 130. In a distribution of scores that is completely normal, the mean, mode, and median are all the same.

Subjects' scores on a variable that is normally distributed can be described in terms of how far they are from average—that is, their deviation from the mean. Thus, a subject's IQ could be described as either 85 or as one standard deviation below the mean, for the standard deviation in IQ is about 15. A subject two standard deviations below the mean would have an IQ of 70, which is bordering on mental retardation. In a perfectly normal distribution, which IQ approximates, the standard deviation is 16. For normal data, 68 percent of subjects fall within one standard deviation of the mean (34 percent on either side of it), 95 percent fall within two standard deviations, and over 99.7 percent fall within three standard deviations. Thus, an IQ above 145 is a very rare occurrence.

Knowing the relation between standard deviations and percentages of subjects whose scores lie on different parts of a distribution allows researchers to report **percentile scores**, which indicate the percentage of scores that fall below a score. Thus, a subject whose score is three standard deviations above the mean is in the 99th percentile, whereas an average subject (whose score does not deviate from the mean) is in the 50th percentile.

TESTING THE HYPOTHESIS: INFERENTIAL STATISTICS

When researchers find a difference between the responses of subjects in one condition and another, they must determine whether these differences likely occurred by chance or whether they reflect a true causal relationship. Similarly, if they discover a correlation between two variables, they need to know the likelihood that the two variables simply correlated by chance. As the philosopher David Hume (1711–1776) demonstrated two centuries ago, we can never be entirely sure about the answer to questions like these. If someone believes that all swans are white and observes 99 swans that are white and none that are not, can the person conclude with certainty that the hundredth swan will also be white? The issue is one of prob-

How many swans must one observe before concluding that all swans are white?

ability: If the person has observed a representative sample of swans, what is the likelihood that, given 99 white swans, a black one will emerge next?

Statistical Significance

Psychologists deal with this issue in their research by using tests of **statistical significance.** These procedures determine whether the results of a study are likely to have occurred simply by chance and cannot be meaningfully generalized to a population, or whether they reflect true properties of the population. Statistical significance has nothing to do with practical or theoretical significance. A researcher may demonstrate with a high degree of certainty that, on the average, females spend more time shopping in malls than males, but who cares? Statistical significance means only that a finding is unlikely to be an accident of chance.

Beyond description of the data, then, the researcher's second task in presenting and analyzing data is to draw inferences from the sample to the population as a whole using inferential statistics. Inferential statistics help sort out whether or not the findings of a study really show anything. Researchers report the likelihood that their results mean something in terms of a **probability value** (or **p-value**). A p-value represents the probability that the results obtained with the sample were just a matter of chance. In other words, a p-value is an index of the probability that the findings obtained would not apply to the population and instead reflect only the peculiar characteristics of the particular sample.

To illustrate, one study tested the hypothesis that children increasingly show signs of morality and empathy during their second year of life (Zahn-Waxler et al., 1992). The investigators trained 27 mothers to dictate reports into a tape recorder of any episode in which their one year olds either witnessed or caused distress. Typical incidents involving witnessing distress were the mother burning herself on the stove or another child crying; examples of the child causing distress included pulling the cat's tail, teasing a sibling, or biting the mother's breast while nursing. The mothers dictated descriptions of these events over the course of the next year, including in each report an account of the way their child responded to the other person's distress. Coders then rated the child's behavior using categories such as prosocial behavior, defined as efforts to help the person in distress.

Table 2S.4 shows the percentage of times the child behaved prosocially during these episodes at each of three periods: Time 1 (13–15 months of age), Time 2 (18–20 months), and Time 3 (23–25 months). As the table shows, the percentage of times the child behaved prosocially increased dramatically over the course of the second year of life, whether the child witnessed or caused the distress. When the investigators analyzed the changes in percentages over time for both types of distress (witnessed and caused), they found the differences statistically significant. A jump from 9 to 49 prosocial behaviors in 12 months was not likely to be accidental.

By convention, psychologists accept the results of a study whenever the probability of findings attributable to chance is less than 5 percent. This is typically expressed as $p < .05$. Thus, the smaller the p-value, the more certain one can feel about the results. A researcher would rather be able to say that the chances of her findings being spurious are 1 in 1000 ($p<.001$) than 1 in 100 ($p<.01$). Nevertheless, researchers can never be *certain*, as Hume's warning about the hundredth swan makes clear, that their results are true of the population as a whole. Nor can they be sure if they performed the study with 100 different subjects they would not obtain different findings. This is why replication—repeating a study to see if the same results occur again—is extremely important in science. For example, in his studies of mood and memory described in Chapter 2, Bower hit an unexpected black swan. His initial series of studies yielded compelling results, but some of these findings failed to replicate in later experiments. He ultimately had to alter parts of his theory that the initial data had supported (Bower, 1989).

The best way to ensure that a study's results are not accidental is to use a large sample. The larger the sample, the more likely the sample is to reflect the actual properties of the population. Suppose 30 people in the world are over 115 years old and researchers want to know about hearing ability in this population. If the researchers test 25 of them, they can be much more certain that their findings are generalizable to this population than if they study a sample of only two of them. These two could have been born with hearing deficits that have no connection to their age or could be atypical in their hearing ability.

The importance of large numbers in sampling is intuitively obvious to most people, and certainly to people who schedule sporting events. In tennis matches, for example, decisions as to who moves on to the next round are not made on the basis of a single game because a variety of factors could influence the outcome of any single game other than the ability of the players. These include such irrelevant or chance variables as fluctuations in concentration, momentary physical condition (such as a dull pain in the foot), lighting, wind, or which player served first. Like good statisticians, the Wimbledon elite know that a single game, or even a single set,

---

TABLE 2S.4 CHILDREN'S PROSOCIAL RESPONSE TO ANOTHER PERSON'S DISTRESS DURING THE SECOND YEAR OF LIFE

	PERCENTAGE OF EPISODES THE CHILD BEHAVED PROSOCIALLY		
TYPE OF INCIDENT	TIME 1	TIME 2	TIME 3
Witnessed distress	9	21	49
Caused distress	7	10	52

Source: Adapted from Zahn-Waxler et al., 1992.

is not a large enough set of observations to make a reliable assessment of who the better player is. Hence, as in other sports where this approach is practical, they rely on a best-of-three or best-of-five series.

Common Tests of Statistical Significance

The choice of which inferential statistics to use depends on the design of the study and particularly on whether the variables assessed are continuous or categorical. If both sets of variables are continuous, the researcher simply correlates them to see whether they are related and tests the probability that a correlation of that magnitude could occur by chance. For many kinds of research, however, the investigator wants to compare two or more groups of subjects, such as males and females, or subjects exposed to several different experimental conditions. In this case, the independent variables are categorical (male/female, condition 1/condition 2). If the dependent variables are also categorical, the appropriate statistic is a **chi-square** test (or X^2). A chi-square compares the observed data with the results that would be expected by chance and tests the likelihood that the differences between observed and expected are accidental. For example, suppose a researcher wants to know whether patients with antisocial personality disorders are more likely than the general population to have had academic difficulties in elementary school. In other words, she wants to know whether one categorical variable (diagnosis: antisocial versus normal) predicts another (presence or absence of academic difficulties, defined as having failed a grade in elementary school). The researcher collects a sample of 50 male patients with the disorders (since the incidence is much higher in males, and gender could be a confounding variable) and compares them with 50 males of similar socioeconomic status (since difficulties in school are correlated with social class). She finds that of her antisocial sample, 20 failed a grade in elementary school, whereas only 2 of the comparison subjects did (Table 2S.5). The likelihood is extremely small that this difference could have emerged by chance, and the chi-square test would therefore show that the differences are statistically significant.

In many cases, the independent variables are categorical, but the dependent variables are continuous. This was the case in Bower's study, described in Chapter 2, which placed subjects in one of two conditions (positive versus negative mood) and compared the number of positive or negative pieces of information they could remember from a vignette (continuous variables). The question to be answered statistically is the following: Across subjects, what is the likelihood that the mean number of positive or negative items recalled in the two conditions differed by

FIGURE 2S.5 TYPICAL DATA APPROPRIATE FOR A CHI-SQUARE ANALYSIS

| | | SCHOOL FAILURE | |
		Present	Absent
DIAGNOSTIC GROUP	Antisocial	20	30
	Normal	2	48

FIGURE 2S.5

Typical data appropriate for a chi-square analysis. A chi-square is the appropriate statistic when testing the relation between two categorical variables. In this case, the variables are diagnosis (presence or absence of antisocial personality disorder) and school failure (presence or absence of a failed grade). The chi-square tests the likelihood that the relative abundance of school failure in the antisocial group occurred by chance.

chance? If subjects in a positive mood remembered 10 positive facts on the average, whereas those in a negative mood remembered only 3 positive items, is this likely to be accidental, or does it truly depend on the condition to which they were exposed?

When comparing the mean scores of two groups, researchers use a t-test. A **t-test** is actually a special case of a statistical procedure called **analysis of variance**, (**ANOVA**), which can be used to compare the means of two or more groups. ANOVA assesses the likelihood that mean differences between groups occurred by chance. To put it another way, ANOVA assesses the extent to which variation in scores is attributable to the independent variable. Once again, a larger sample is helpful in determining whether mean differences between groups are real or random. If Bower tested only two subjects in each condition and found mean differences, he could not be confident of the findings because the results could simply reflect the idiosyncrasies of these four subjects. If he tested 30, however, and the differences between the two conditions were large and consistent across subjects, the ANOVA would be statistically significant.

SOME CONCLUDING THOUGHTS

We have now surveyed the ways researchers study psychological phenomena and the statistical procedures they use to describe and analyze their data. The remaining chapters explore the findings uncovered by these methods.

SUMMARY

Descriptive Statistics

1. The most important descriptive statistics are **measures of central tendency**, which provide an index of the way a typical subject responded on a measure. The **mean** is the statistical average of the scores of all subjects. The **mode** is the most common or frequent score or value of the variable observed in the sample. The **median** is the score that falls right in the middle of the distribution of scores, with half of subjects scoring below it and half above it.

2. **Variability** refers to the extent to which subjects tend to vary from each other in their scores. The **standard deviation** refers to the amount that the average subject deviates from the mean of the sample.

Inferential Statistics

3. To assess the results of a study, psychologists use tests of **statistical significance** to determine whether the results are likely to have occurred simply by chance. A **probability value**, or **p-value**, represents the probability that the findings obtained were accidental or just a matter of chance. By convention, psychologists accept p-values that fall below .05, that is, that have a probability of being accidental of less than 5 percent. The best way to ensure that a study's results are not accidental is to use a large enough sample that random fluctuations will cancel each other out.

4. The choice of which inferential statistics to use depends on the design of the study and particularly on whether the variables assessed are continuous or categorical. Common statistical tests are **chi-square** and **analysis of variance (ANOVA)**.

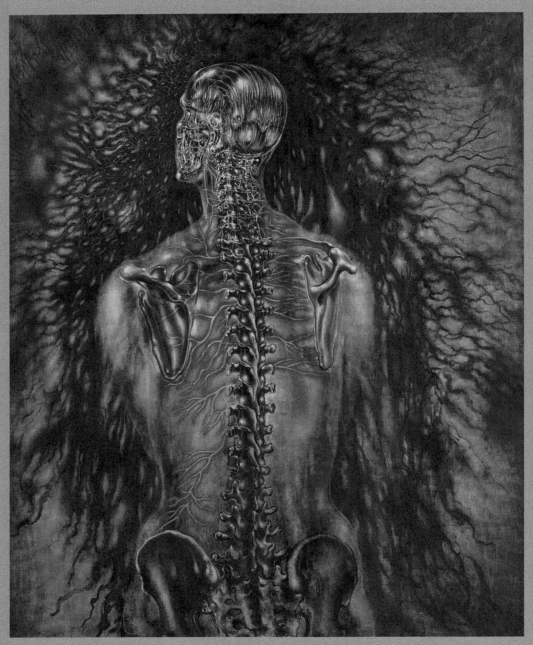

Pavel Tchelitchew, "Anatomical Painting," 1946, Whitney Museum of American Art

Chapter 3

BIOLOGICAL BASES OF MENTAL LIFE AND BEHAVIOR

*I*n 1917, an epidemic broke out in Vienna that quickly spread throughout the world. The disease was a mysterious sleeping-sickness called encephalitis lethargica. *Encephalitis* refers to any inflammation of the central nervous system that results from infection. In the case of encephalitis lethargica, the infection was thought to be viral, although the viral agent was never discovered. The infection sent its victims into extreme states of arousal: Some were so underaroused that they seemed to sleep for weeks, while others became so hyperaroused they could not sleep. The epidemic lasted 10 years and affected approximately 5 million people (Sacks, 1973). Roughly one-third of those who contracted encephalitis lethargica died in the acute phase of the illness.

Most of the survivors of the epidemic developed some form of postencephalitic brain disorder, leaving many in a virtual state of sleep for almost

40 years. These survivors were aware of their surroundings, but they did not seem to be fully awake. They were motionless and speechless, without energy, motivation, emotion, or appetite. They evidenced repetitive stereotyped movements, such as tics and compulsions, as well as involuntary spasms, vocalizations, and occasional explosive outbursts. Most of the time, they just stared. And they remained in that stuporous state until the development of a new drug in the 1960s, L-dopa, which suddenly awakened many from their slumbers by restoring a chemical in the brain that the virus had destroyed.

Ms. B contracted a severe form of encephalitis lethargica when she was 18 (Sacks, 1973). Although she recovered in a few months, she began to show signs of the postencephalitic disorder four years later. For almost half a century she was unable to perform any voluntary movements, to speak, or even to blink, for long periods of time. Ms. B was not in a coma—she was aware of the events around her—but she could not react to them physically or emotionally.

Ms. B began to come alive within days of receiving L-dopa. After one week, she started to speak. Within two weeks she was able to write, stand up, and walk between parallel bars. Eventually her emotions returned, and she reestablished contact with her family—or what was left of it. She had fallen asleep a vibrant young woman of 22 and awakened a woman of 67. Unlike some of her fellow victims, she seemed remarkably free of bitterness and anger at having lost most of her life. Not all patients responded to L-dopa treatment. Some deteriorated severely after short periods of health, experiencing debilitating side effects of the drug. The drug thus had to be stopped, leading to a return to their stuporous state.

To comprehend Ms. B's experience requires an understanding of the **nervous system**, the interacting network of nerve cells that underlies all psychological activity. We begin by examining the neuron, or nerve cell, and the way nerve cells communicate with each other to produce thought, feeling, and behavior. After exploring the way hormones work with neurons to create psychological experience, we then look at how billions of nerve cells are organized in the central nervous system (the brain and spinal cord) and the peripheral nervous system (neurons in the rest of the body). We conclude with a brief discussion of the role of biology and genetics in understanding human mental life and behavior. Throughout, we wrestle with some thorny questions about the translation of physical mechanisms into psychological meanings, considering whether our subjective experience is little more than a shadow cast by our neurons, hormones, and genes.

NEURONS: BASIC UNITS OF THE NERVOUS SYSTEM

Nerve cells, or **neurons**, are the basic units of the nervous system. Appreciating a sunset, swaying to music, pining for a lover five hundred miles away, or praying for forgiveness—all of these acts reflect the coordinated action of thousands or millions of neurons. We do not, of course, experience ourselves as systems of interacting nerve cells, any more than we experience hunger as the depletion of sugar in the bloodstream. We think, we feel, we hurt, we want. But we do all these things through the silent, behind-the-scenes activity of our neurons, whose function is to carry information from cell to cell within the nervous system as well as to and from muscles and organs.

No one knows precisely how many neurons are in the nervous system; the best estimates range from 10 to 100 billion in the brain alone (Stevens, 1979). Each of these neurons may connect with thousands of other cells. In some parts of the nervous system, neurons have so many connections that information sent by one cell can affect 15 to 30,000 other neurons, although the average neuron transmits information to about 1000 others (Damasio, 1994).

The nervous system is composed of three kinds of neurons: sensory neurons, motor neurons, and interneurons. **Sensory neurons** (also called afferent neurons) transmit information from receptors that detect events in the environment (a cool breeze) or inside the body (a sore throat) to the brain, either directly or by way of the spinal cord. **Motor neurons** (or efferent neurons) transmit commands from the brain to the glands and musculature of the body, most often through the spinal cord. Motor neurons carry out both voluntary actions and vital bodily functions such as digestion and heartbeat. **Interneurons** connect other neurons with each other; they are found mainly in the brain and spinal cord.

Anatomy of a Neuron

No two neurons are exactly alike in their form, size, and shape, but their cellular structure is basically the same. The main part of the neuron is the **cell body**, or soma (Figure 3.1). The cell body includes a nucleus that contains the genetic material of the cell (the chromosomes) as well as other microstructures vital to cell functioning. The neuron is surrounded by a membrane made of lipids (fats) and proteins, which are involved in transporting chemicals across the membrane and receiving signals from other cells.

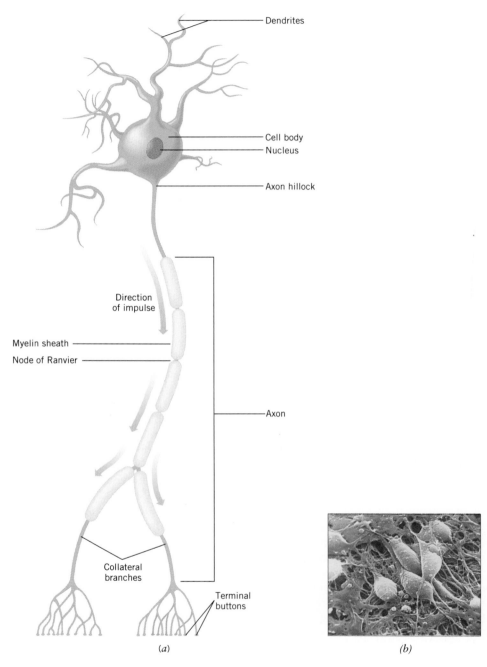

FIGURE 3.1
*The anatomy of a neuron. (a) The branched fibers called dendrites receive
neural information from other neurons and pass it down the axon. The
terminal buttons then release neurotransmitters, chemicals that transmit
information to other cells. (b) An actual neuron, magnified by electron
microscope.*

Branchlike extensions of the cell body, called **dendrites**, receive information
from other cells. Their form is well suited to this function. By extending their
branches to numerous other cells, they increase the surface area of the neuron that
is available to receive information. If a neuron receives enough stimulation through
its dendrites and cell body, it passes information to other neurons through its **axon**,
a long extension (occasionally as long as several feet), which frequently has two or
more offshoots, or collateral branches.

The axons of many neurons are covered with a **myelin sheath**, a coat of cells composed primarily of lipids. Myelinated axons give some portions of the brain a white appearance (hence the term *white matter*). The "gray matter" of the brain gets its color from cell bodies, dendrites, and unmyelinated axons. The myelin sheath insulates the axon from chemical or physical stimuli that might interfere with the transmission of nerve impulses and speeds the transmission of messages. Between the cells that form the myelin sheath are small spaces called **nodes of Ranvier**. When a neuron **fires** (is activated enough to send information on to other neurons), the electrical impulse appears to jump from node to node, like an express train that does not have to stop at every station.

Not all axons are myelinated at birth. The transmission of impulses along these axons is slow and arduous, which helps explain why babies have such poor motor control. As myelination occurs in areas of the nervous system involved in motor action, an infant becomes capable of reaching and pointing. Similar lack of motor control characterizes demyelinating diseases such as multiple sclerosis. Degeneration of the myelin sheath on large clusters of axons causes jerky, uncoordinated movement, although at times the symptoms disappear when the disease goes into remission. Multiple sclerosis and other diseases that progressively strip axons of their myelin may be fatal, particularly if they strike the neurons that control basic life-support processes such as the beating of the heart.

At the end of an axon are **terminal buttons**, which send signals from a neuron to adjacent cells. These messages are typically received by the dendrites or cell bodies of other neurons, although they may also be received by muscle or gland cells. Connections between neurons occur at what are called **synapses**. Two neurons do not actually touch at a synapse; instead, a space exists between the two, called the **synaptic cleft**. Neurons communicate at the synapse through a complex process that involves both electrical and chemical changes.

Having outlined the anatomy of the neuron, we now more carefully examine the way neurons fire. We then explore the manner in which neurons communicate with each other to produce the psychological experience of a sunset, a song, love, or repentance.

Firing of a Neuron

The nerve impulse that travels down the length of an axon is electrochemical, and it is the product of a change in the differential electrical charge between the inside and outside of the neuron's cell membrane. A combination of chemicals normally exists on both the inside and outside of a neuron's cell membrane. Important among these chemicals are sodium (Na+), potassium (K+), and chloride (Cl-) ions. (An ion is an atom or small molecule that carries an electrical charge.) The cell membrane of a neuron is typically not permeable to positively charged sodium ions; in other words, they cannot get through the membrane, and thus they tend to accumulate outside the neuron. The result is that the electrical charge is normally more positive on the outside of the cell than on the inside.

This "resting" condition, in which the neuron is not firing, is called the **resting potential**; it is called a "potential" because the cell has a stored-up source of energy (Carlson, 1991). At its resting potential, the electrical charge inside the neuron is about −70 millivolts (mv). (A volt is a standard unit of electricity, and a millivolt is one-thousandth of a volt.) Normally, then, the potential across the cell membrane is polarized, just as a battery has two poles: The negative charge is on the inside, and the positive charge is on the outside.

When a neuron's dendrites or cell body are stimulated by an impulse from other neurons, one of two things can happen. The stimulation can reduce the polarization across the membrane, decreasing the voltage discrepancy between the inside and the outside. For instance, the resting potential might move from −70 to −60 mv. Alternatively, stimulation from another neuron can increase polarization. Typically, a decrease in polarization (**depolarization**) stems from an influx of positive sodium ions. This causes the charge inside the cell membrane to become less negative. The opposite state of affairs, increasing the electrical difference between the inside and outside of the cell, is called **hyperpolarization**. This condition usually results from an outflow of potassium ions, which are also positively charged; the result is that the charge on the inside of the membrane becomes even more negative.

These brief voltage changes occur along dendrites and the cell body and then spread down the cell membrane, much as sound waves are set in motion with the strike of a kettledrum. These spreading voltage changes, which occur when the neural membrane receives a signal from another cell, are called **graded potentials**, and they have two notable characteristics. First, their strength diminishes as they travel along the cell membrane away from the source of the stimulation, just as the sound of a drum grows weaker with distance. Second, graded potentials are cumulative or additive. If a neuron is simultaneously depolarized by +2 mv at one point on a dendrite and hyperpolarized -2 mv at an adjacent point, the two graded potentials add to 0 and essentially cancel each other out. In contrast, if a dendrite or several dendrites of a neuron are depolarized at multiple points, a progressively greater influx of positive ions occurs.

If the cumulative effect of these depolarizations is strong enough, something important happens, beginning at a point on the neuron known as the **axon hillock,** at the juncture of the axon and the cell body (Figure 3.1, p. 76). The axon hillock acts somewhat like a computer, adding up the total voltage change from all the graded potentials sent along the dendrites and cell body. If the charge across the membrane at the axon hillock crosses a certain threshold—to about −50 mv from its resting state of −70 mv—a sudden change in the cell membrane occurs. For a flicker of an instant, the membrane is totally permeable to positive sodium ions, which have accumulated outside the membrane. Sodium ions pour in, changing the charge on the inside of the cell from −70 mv to about +50 mv (Figure 3.2). Thus, the charge on the inside of the cell becomes momentarily positive. An outpouring of positive potassium ions then rapidly restores the neuron to its resting potential, rendering the charge inside the cell negative once again.

This temporary shift in the polarity of the membrane, and subsequent restoration of the resting potential, is called an **action potential**, which occurs as a nerve fires. The action potential, or nerve impulse, spreads from the axon hillock, where it originated, down the length of the axon to the terminal buttons. The action potential differs from graded potentials in two ways: It does not diminish with distance, and it is not cumulative. Rather, an action potential has an **all-or-none** quality; that is, an action potential either occurs, or it does not. In this sense, the firing

FIGURE 3.2

An action potential. This figure depicts the firing of a neuron as recorded by two electrodes, one inside the membrane of the axon and the other just outside the membrane. When a neuron is depolarized to about -50 millivolts, an influx of positively charged ions briefly creates an action potential. An outpouring of positive ions then restores the neuron to its resting potential.

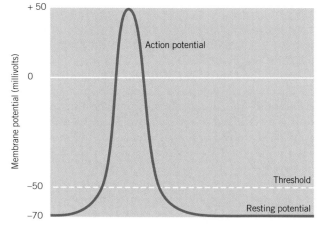

of a neuron is like the firing of a gun. Unless the trigger is pulled hard enough, the amount of pressure placed on the trigger below that threshold does not matter. Once the threshold is crossed, however, the trigger gives way, the gun fires, and the trigger springs back, ready to be pulled once more. Stronger stimulation does not make a neuron fire harder, any more than keeping a trigger depressed once it has fired will make the bullet go farther.

If neurons do not fire harder in response to stronger stimuli than to weaker ones, how can a person distinguish between a dim light and a bright one? The answer, in part, has to do with the frequency of firing and the number of neurons that fire. A bright light causes a sudden rash of firings of visual neurons. Thousands of neurons near each other fire simultaneously at a high rate until the light fades. In contrast, a dim light causes fewer neurons to fire at a lower rate.

Transmission of Impulses between Cells

Neurons generally communicate with other neurons chemically, which can in turn create an electrical event. This intercellular communication typically takes place at the synapse. Figure 3.3 presents a simplified diagram of a synaptic connection between two neurons. The neuron that is sending an impulse is called the **presynaptic neuron** (that is, *before* the synapse); the cell receiving the impulse is the **postsynaptic neuron**.

Within the terminal buttons of a neuron are small sacs called **synaptic vesicles**, which contain **neurotransmitters**, chemical substances that transmit information from one cell to another. When the presynaptic neuron fires, the synaptic vesicles in its terminal buttons move toward the presynaptic membrane. Some of them adhere to the membrane and break open, releasing neurotransmitters into the synaptic cleft. Some of these chemical molecules then bind with special protein molecules in the postsynaptic membrane, called **receptors**.

Receptors act like locks that can be opened only by particular keys. In this case, the keys are neurotransmitters that flow through the synaptic cleft. When a receptor binds with the neurotransmitter that fits it—in both molecular structure and electrical charge—the chemical and electrical balance of the postsynaptic cell membrane changes, producing a graded potential.

The effect of a neurotransmitter depends on the type of receptor it fits. Each neurotransmitter has several receptors it can activate, and different receptors produce different effects from the same neurotransmitter. Neurotransmitters tend to have one of two effects: They either increase or decrease neural firing. **Excitatory neurotransmitters** depolarize the postsynaptic cell membrane, making an action potential more likely. (That is, they "excite" the neuron.) In contrast, **inhibitory neurotransmitters** hyperpolarize the membrane (increase its polarization); this reduces (inhibits) the likelihood that the postsynaptic neuron will fire. Excitatory neurotransmitters, as suggested above, are the keys that open the floodgates, whereas inhibitory neurotransmitters are the keys that turn in the other direction, fortifying the barricade. Neurotransmitters share the task of neural communication across the synapse with other chemical substances that influence the response of the postsynaptic cell. Table 3.1 (p. 81) lists several neurotransmitters and their effects; the list is not exhaustive, and our knowledge of exact effects remains incomplete. We now briefly examine four neurotransmitters: dopamine, acetylcholine, serotonin, and endorphins.

Dopamine

The neurotransmitter **dopamine** has wide-ranging effects, including control of movement, attention, thought, and emotion. The presence of dopamine in certain parts of the brain is essential to the experience of pleasure that makes people perform behaviors for which they have been rewarded. A depletion or excess of

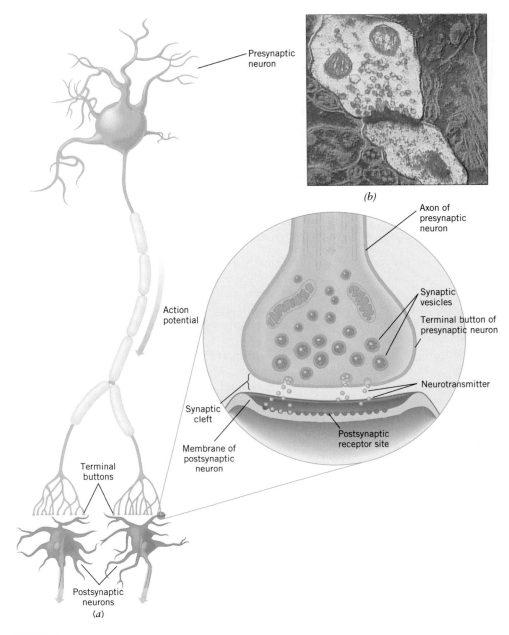

FIGURE 3.3
(a) Transmission of a nerve impulse. When an action potential occurs, the nerve impulse travels along the axon until it reaches the synaptic vesicles. The synaptic vesicles release neurotransmitters into the synaptic cleft. The neurotransmitters then bind with postsynaptic receptors and produce a graded potential on the membrane of the postsynaptic neuron. (b) An electron micrograph of a synapse.

dopamine in the brain produces symptoms ranging from jerky muscle movements to psychosis (loss of contact with reality, such as hallucinations) and depression.

Degeneration of the dopamine-releasing neurons in a part of the brain called the substantia nigra (literally, "dark substance") causes **Parkinson's disease,** a disorder characterized by uncontrollable tremors, repetitive movements, and difficulty initiating movements. Physicians discovered that the substantia nigra was the culprit in this disorder when they noticed the lack of this region's typical coloration in an autopsied Parkinson's patient; the dark color is normally a byproduct of chemical reactions involving dopamine (Carlson, 1991). Disordered movement is the most

TABLE 3.1 PARTIAL LIST OF NEUROTRANSMITTERS

CHEMICAL	PSYCHOLOGICAL FUNCTION
Dopamine	Emotional arousal, voluntary movements, learning and memory
Serotonin	Sleep and emotional arousal; implicated in aggression
Endorphins	Pain relief and elevation of mood
Epinephrine	Emotional arousal, anxiety, and fear; involved in activation of the sympathetic nervous system
Norepinephrine	Emotional arousal, anxiety, and fear; involved in activation of the sympathetic nervous system
Acetylcholine (ACh)	Muscle contractions, learning, and memory
Gamma aminobutyric acid (GABA)	Inhibition of brain excitability and anxiety
Enkephalins	Pain relief

Note. Knowledge of neurotransmitters is relatively recent, and several may actually serve primarily as neuromodulators rather than neurotransmitters per se. Neuromodulators moderate the postsynaptic cell's response to the neurotransmitter it has just received; that is, they can increase or decrease its impact.

visible sign of Parkinson's disease; other psychological symptoms of the disorder include depression and a general slowing of thought (Cummings, 1992; Guze & Barrio, 1991; Rao et al., 1992).

Because the victims of encephalitis lethargica described at the beginning of this chapter showed Parkinsonian symptoms, researchers believed the dopamine-rich neurons in the substantia nigra and areas of the brain connected to it had been destroyed. They therefore administered L-dopa, a chemical that readily converts to dopamine and had recently proven effective in treating Parkinson's disease. Dopamine itself cannot be administered because it cannot cross the blood-brain barrier, which normally protects the brain from foreign substances in the blood.

Unfortunately, only a small percentage of even L-dopa gets past the blood-brain barrier. The rest enters the peripheral nervous system and causes side effects such as nausea, vomiting, and shortness of breath. The L-dopa that does make its way into the brain can have unwanted consequences because the brain uses dopamine for neural transmission in many regions and for different purposes. L-dopa can thus reduce Parkinsonian symptoms, but it can also produce psychotic thinking or movement disorders other than Parkinson's. For example, Ms. B, the victim of the 1917 encephalitis epidemic, developed a "touching tic," in which she had to touch everything she passed.

Researchers have been experimenting with **brain grafting**, or neural tissue transplants, as a treatment for Parkinson's disease and other neurological conditions (Lindvall, 1991; Madrazo et al., 1987; Ridley & Baker, 1991). Early work using rats as experimental subjects found that producing lesions in the substantia nigra induced Parkinson-like symptoms. When researchers transplanted dopamine-rich tissue from the substantia nigra of rat embryos or from other parts of the rat's own body to the lesioned area, results were very encouraging, with considerable relief of Parkinsonian symptoms (Wyatt et al., 1985; Ziegler, 1985). Such success in animal subjects holds the promise of treating Parkinson's disease and other degenerative brain diseases in humans (Dunnett, 1991; Nilsson et al., 1990).

Acetylcholine

Another neurotransmitter that has been the focus of tissue transplant studies is **acetylcholine (ACh)**, which is involved in learning and memory. Transplanting tissue rich in ACh has led to markedly improved cognitive functioning in impaired rats. The results of one such study are reproduced in Figure 3.4 (Gage & Björklund, 1985). Old rats with neuronal transplants performed substantially better on a learning task than similarly-aged rats without infusion of new ACh-rich tissue (Björklund & Gage, 1985). Other studies using rats and monkeys as subjects have similarly demonstrated that transplanted tissue rich in dopamine or other neurotransmitters can generate new connections among neurons, producing marked behavioral changes (Iwashita et al., 1994; Mickley et al., 1991; Nilsson et al.,1990; Schnell et al., 1994; Tuszynski et al., 1991).

Serotonin

Like other neurotransmitters, **serotonin** serves a variety of functions. It is involved in the regulation of mood, sleep, eating, and arousal, and it appears to

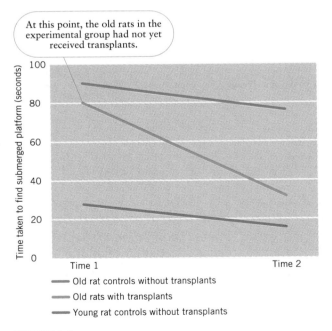

FIGURE 3.4

Neural transplants and learning in aged rats. The investigators compared three groups: old rats without transplants, old rats with transplants, and unimpaired young rat controls. The investigators tested the rats' learning ability by seeing how long they would take to learn to swim to a platform submerged under water. Old rats who were given transplants showed remarkable improvements in their ability to learn this task compared to untreated old rats, as measured by their response time. SOURCE: Adapted from Björklund & Gage, 1985.

play a role in the regulation of pain as well. Decreased availability of serotonin is common in severe depression, which often responds favorably to medications that increase serotonin activity. Several studies have shown low serotonin levels to be a risk factor for suicide (Roy, 1993). People who are depressed often have trouble with sleeping and eating, in part because the disruption of serotonin levels that often occurs in depression can also affect these other functions. Oversleeping, difficulty falling asleep, overeating, and undereating are common symptoms of depression.

Serotonin plays an inhibitory role in most sites in the nervous system. For example, it is apparently involved in inhibiting both aggression and depression. In rhesus monkeys, low serotonin levels are associated with increased aggression (Higley et al., 1992). Similar findings have emerged in studies of antisocial adult humans and delinquent children (Kruesi et al., 1992).

People who are severely depressed often show decreased serotonin activity.

Endorphins

For centuries the Chinese have practiced acupuncture, relieving pain by inserting and rotating needles in specific body locations. Although Western medical science has had difficulty explaining why acupuncture works, the reason for its effectiveness may lie in a class of chemicals in the brain known as **endorphins** (Grossman, 1985; Watkin & Mayer, 1982). The word "endorphin" comes from *endogenous* (meaning "produced within the body") and *morphine*, a chemical substance derived from opium that elevates mood and reduces pain (Lipman et al., 1990; Smith et al., 1992; Steinberg & Sykes, 1985). Endorphins are neurotransmitters that are chemically similar to morphine.

The body produces endorphins in response to many forms of physical stress or injury. Often a person reports feeling minimal pain shortly after tearing a muscle or ligament or breaking a bone but then experiences excruciating pain when this natural painkiller wears off. In fact, opium and similar narcotic drugs kill pain and elevate mood because they activate receptors in the brain specialized for endorphins. Essentially, narcotics "pick the locks" normally opened by endorphins. Endorphins appear to be involved in runner's high, the state of euphoria some runners report after a prolonged period of exercise (Thoren et al., 1990; Vives & Oltras, 1992). People's pain thresholds tend to increase directly following exercise such as a long-distance run (Janal et al., 1984), and their moods are often elevated.

THE ENDOCRINE SYSTEM

Understanding the biological bases of psychologically meaningful events requires more than an examination of the way neurotransmitter substances bind with receptors in individual neurons. We now turn to some of the broader biological structures involved in psychological functioning, beginning with the **endocrine system,** a collection of ductless glands (glands that secrete chemicals directly into the bloodstream) that control various body functions (Figure 3.5).

Neurotransmitters released by synaptic vesicles are not the only chemicals that transmit psychologically important information throughout the body. **Hormones** are chemicals secreted directly into the bloodstream by the endocrine glands. Like neurotransmitters, they bind with receptors in cell membranes in various parts of the body. The chemical structure of some hormones, in fact, is similar or identical to that of neurotransmitters. The hormone **adrenalin,** for example, is the same compound as the neurotransmitter **epinephrine;** similarly, the hormone noradrenalin is the same compound as norepinephrine.

Whereas the nervous system relies on electrochemical transmission of impulses to transmit messages between cells, the endocrine system provides another method

Acupuncture has been used for centuries in the East and has since been transplanted to the West.

FIGURE 3.5
The major endocrine glands. The endocrine system is a series of ductless glands that rely on hormonal communication to activate cells throughout the body.

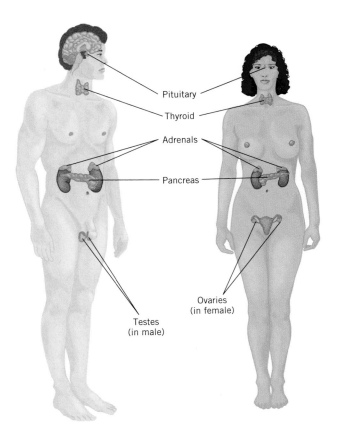

Pituitary
Thyroid
Adrenals
Pancreas
Ovaries (in female)
Testes (in male)

of intercellular communication that is far more global, that is, not limited to connections among a relatively small number of individual cells. The difference between the communication that takes place through the two systems is analogous to the difference between word of mouth and mass media (which can communicate information to hundreds of millions of people at once). The endocrine system "broadcasts" its signals by releasing hormones into the bloodstream.

In many instances, the endocrine and nervous systems function simultaneously. When a person faces an emergency, the adrenal glands release adrenalin into the bloodstream. At the same time, neurons are sending "word-of-mouth" impulses by releasing epinephrine and its close cousin, norepinephrine, into synapses at strategic locations in the nervous system. These parallel actions ready the body for emergency by, among other things, quickening heart rate and diverting blood to the muscles and away from internal organs. People typically remain in a slightly aroused state and continue to feel "jittery" even after a crisis is over because the bloodstream contains higher than normal hormone levels of adrenalin for up to a few hours even though the neurons stopped firing hours earlier.

The endocrine system performs many functions other than readying the body for response to emergency. Endocrine glands located throughout the body help regulate continuous life processes such as creating and calling up energy reserves. They are also involved in other psychological processes such as emotion. Table 3.2 summarizes the functions of some of these glands, which we briefly examine here.

The **pituitary gland** is a reddish-gray, oval structure, about the size of a pea, located in the brain. It is often referred to as the "master gland" because some of the hormones it releases stimulate and regulate the hormonal action of other endocrine glands. Because of its location in the brain, the pituitary gland is connected more directly to the central nervous system than other endocrine glands. Its connection to neural circuits involved in emotion means that the pituitary gland can

TABLE 3.2 THE ENDOCRINE GLANDS AND SOME OF THEIR FUNCTIONS

GLAND	FUNCTION
Pituitary	
Anterior (front) region	Growth; metabolism (transformation of food into energy); regulation of adrenal, thyroid, and gonadal hormone secretion; milk production in females
Posterior (back) region	Blood pressure; urine production; uterine contraction during delivery in females
Thyroid	Growth; energy level; mood
Adrenal	Adaptation to prolonged stress (increases metabolism of proteins and fats)
Pancreas	Control of blood-sugar level
Gonads	Reproduction; primary and secondary sex characteristics; sex drive

influence, and be influenced by, emotional states. Chronic fear or stress, for example, can produce hormonal changes, and hormonal changes can make an individual more vulnerable to anxiety or depression.

The **thyroid gland**, located next to the trachea and larynx in the neck, releases a hormone that controls metabolism (transformation of food into energy). The thyroid gland also affects energy levels and mood (Haggerty et al., 1993). People who have **hypothyroidism**, an underactive thyroid gland (*hypo* means "under"), sometimes require artificial replacement of thyroid hormones to relieve lethargy and depression. One study found a 10 percent incidence of undiagnosed hypothyroidism in patients complaining of these psychological symptoms (Gold & Pearsall, 1983).

The **adrenal glands** are located above the kidneys (the Latin *ad renal* means "toward the kidney"). They secrete adrenalin and other hormones during emergency situations. Another endocrine gland, the **pancreas**, is located near the stomach; it produces various hormones that control blood-sugar level.

The **gonads** control sexual development and behavior. The male gonads, or **testes**, are located in the testicles; the most important hormone they produce is **testosterone**. The female gonads, the **ovaries**, produce **estrogens**. In both sexes, these hormones control not only sex drive but also the development of secondary sex characteristics such as growth of breasts in females, deepened voice in males, and pubic hair in both sexes.

THE PERIPHERAL NERVOUS SYSTEM

We now turn to the nervous system, which underlies all psychological functioning. The nervous system has two major divisions, the central nervous system and the peripheral nervous system. These divisions and their functions are shown in Figures 3.6 and 3.7. The **central nervous system (CNS)** consists of the brain and spinal cord; the **peripheral nervous system (PNS)** consists of neurons that convey messages to and from the central nervous system. The peripheral nervous system has two subdivisions, the somatic and the autonomic nervous system.

The Somatic Nervous System

The **somatic nervous system** brings information to the central nervous system and carries out its commands. Sensory neurons receive information through receptors in the eyes, ears, skin, muscles, and other parts of the body such as the tongue. Motor neurons direct the action of skeletal muscles. Because the somatic nervous system is involved in intentional actions such as standing up or shaking someone's hand, it is often called the voluntary nervous system. However, the somatic nervous system also directs some involuntary or automatic actions, such as adjustments in posture or balance.

The Autonomic Nervous System

The **autonomic nervous system (ANS)** serves visceral (internal bodily) structures that carry out basic life processes, such as digestion and respiration. It consists of two parts, the sympathetic and the parasympathetic nervous system. Although these systems are integrated and work in tandem, in many ways they create directly opposite reactions in the body and perform largely complementary functions. In broadest strokes, one can think of the sympathetic nervous system as an emergency system and the parasympathetic nervous system as a "business as usual" system (Figure 3.8, page 88).

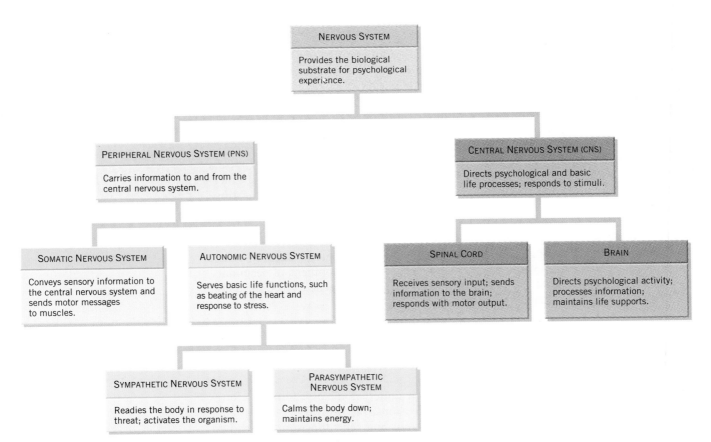

FIGURE 3.6 *Divisions of the nervous system.*

The Sympathetic Nervous System

The **sympathetic nervous system** is typically activated in response to threats to the organism. Its job is to ready the body for fight or flight, which it does in several ways. It stops digestion, since diverting blood away from the stomach allows more blood to be directed to the muscles, which may need extra oxygen for an emergency response. It increases heart rate, dilates the pupils, and causes hairs on the body and head to stand erect. It is also involved in other states of intense activation, such as ejaculation in males.

By preparing the organism to respond to emergencies, the sympathetic nervous system serves an important adaptive function, but the sympathetic cavalry sometimes comes to the rescue when least wanted. A surge of anxiety, tremors, profuse sweating, dry mouth, and palpitating heart may have helped prepare our ancestors to flee from a hungry lion, but they are less welcome when a person is trying to deliver a speech. Similar physiological reactions occur in panic attacks, a type of anxiety disorder characterized by extreme anxiety, tremors, sweating, and palpitating heart (Chapter 15).

Anxiety reactions such as panic attacks exemplify some of the complex interactions of mind and brain, of psychological experience and its neurological substrate (that is, its basis in the nervous system). As we will see in later chapters, people vary tremendously in their genetic proclivity to experience unpleasant emotions such as anxiety, and a biological vulnerability clearly underlies some anxiety disorders. Some people tend toward an overactivation of epinephrine and related neurotransmitters, which leaves them vulnerable to anxiety symptoms. Panic attacks and other anxiety disorders frequently respond to biochemical treatments—to medications that block the action of neurotransmitters involved in sympathetic arousal—sometimes even allowing a person with severe stage fright to perform calmly before an audience of hundreds. These drugs can work in different ways. They may bind with receptors in postsynaptic membranes, "locking up" the postsynaptic membrane and preventing depolarization. Others stop the neurotransmitter from being released in the first place or increase the activity of inhibitory neurotransmitters that inhibit the firing of neurons involved in anxiety reactions (Bunney, 1981; Nibuya & Kanba, 1990; Olivier et al., 1992; Schreiber & de Vry, 1993).

Matters are not always so simple, however. Neural processes undoubtedly underlie every psychological event; no thought or feeling can occur without them. Thus, even an experience that has clear environmental causes, such as a toddler becoming profoundly distressed when her parents leave for an evening at the movies, is in some sense biological. Just because a medication can block anxiety does not, therefore, mean that the anxiety stems from a genetically overactive neurotransmitter system. Many anxiety symptoms are less the result of a bad job of

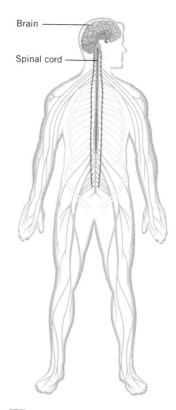

Brain

Spinal cord

Central nervous system
Peripheral nervous system
Autonomic
Somatic

FIGURE 3.7
The nervous system. The nervous system consists of the brain, the spinal cord, and the neurons of the peripheral nervous system that carry information to and from these central nervous system structures.

The sympathetic nervous system is involved in fight-or-flight responses in the face of threat.

FIGURE 3.8
The sympathetic and parasympathetic divisions of the autonomic nervous system. The sympathetic division tends to be activated in times of threat or arousal. The parasympathetic division tends to be activated in times of relaxation or eating, and it functions to conserve and maintain energy.

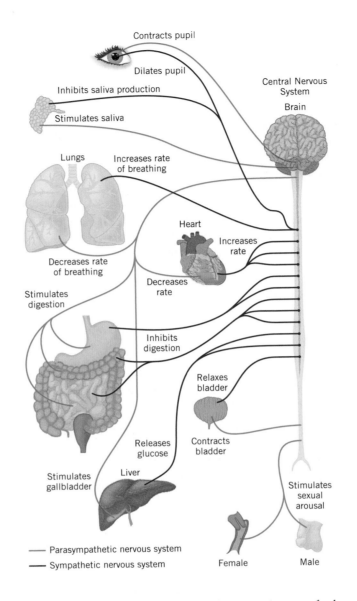

wiring in the brain than of learned associations or faulty cognitive patterns, which can be addressed with psychotherapy (see Beck & Emery, 1985; Chambless & Gillis, 1993; Clum et al., 1993; Rapee, 1987; Zinbarg et al., 1992). And experiencing some traumatic events, such as a rape or a massive earthquake, can alter the brain itself, leading to permanent symptoms such as being easily startled.

The Parasympathetic Nervous System

The **parasympathetic nervous system** supports activities that maintain the body's store of energy, such as regulating blood-sugar levels, secreting saliva, and eliminating wastes; it also participates in activities such as regulating heart rate and pupil size. Though not always antagonistic, the relationship between the sympathetic and parasympathetic nervous systems is in many ways a balancing act. When an emergency has passed, the parasympathetic nervous system resumes control, calming the body's systems and reversing sympathetic responses. This means returning to the normal business of storing and maintaining resources.

A good illustration of the way these two systems interact, and how their interaction can be derailed, is sexual activity. In males, the parasympathetic nervous system controls the flow of blood to the penis and is thus responsible for engorging blood vessels that produce an erection; in females, it controls vaginal lubrication.

However, ejaculation in males is controlled by the sympathetic nervous system. The sympathetic system may also be important in the female experience of orgasm. The capacity to become excited and experience orgasm thus depends on the synchronized activation of the parasympathetic and sympathetic nervous systems. If a man experiences sympathetic activation too early, he loses his capacity to sustain an erection and may ejaculate prematurely. Conversely, if sympathetic activation does not occur, ejaculation will not take place (Kimble, 1988). In women, poor coordination of sympathetic and parasympathetic activity may inhibit vaginal lubrication and thus hinder sexual pleasure.

In a society that places a premium on sexual performance, a few disappointing sexual experiences can disrupt the delicate balance between sympathetic and parasympathetic activation. For example, a man who experiences a brief period of difficulty maintaining sexual excitement may begin to see himself as a failure sexually and may become more anxious with each encounter. The anxiety, in turn, can inhibit the parasympathetic activation that normally leads to erection, setting in motion a cycle in which sympathetic activation and feelings of anxiety fuel one another and create a full-fledged problem in sexual functioning. This example also illustrates the interaction of psychological experience, physiological processes, and culture. A transitory psychobiological dysfunction (failure to sustain an erection) can lead a person to feel inadequate based on cultural standards, producing anxiety, which then contributes to biological dysfunction.

THE CENTRAL NERVOUS SYSTEM

The peripheral nervous system carries information to and from the central nervous system and carries out its directives. Understanding the central nervous system requires some knowledge of its evolution, from a single fluid-filled tube (the spinal cord) to a multistructured organ (Kolb & Whishaw, 1990; MacLean, 1982).

Evolution of the Central Nervous System

The earliest vertebrates (animals with spinal cords) were little more than stimulus-response machines. Sensory information from the environment entered the upper side of the spinal cord, and neurons exiting the underside directed a reflexive or automatic behavioral response. Through evolution, the front end of the spinal cord became specialized to respond to special features of the sensory environment, allowing more sophisticated processing of information and more flexible motor responses (Figure 3.9). Presumably one end of this cord developed because these organisms moved forward, head first.

This first primitive brain, or brainstem, had three parts. The foremost section, called the forebrain, was specialized for sensation at a very immediate level—smell and perhaps taste. The middle region, or midbrain, controlled sensation for distant stimuli—vision and audition (hearing). The back of the brainstem, or hindbrain, was specialized for equilibrium and balance (Sarnat & Netsky, 1974). The hindbrain was also the connecting point between the brain and spinal cord and allowed messages to travel between the two. This rough division of labor in the primitive central nervous system still applies in fish and amphibians as well as in the spinal cord and brainstem of humans. Many human reflexes, for example, occur precisely as they did (and do) in simple vertebrates, with sensory information entering one side of the spinal cord (toward the back of the body in humans, who stand erect) and motor impulses exiting the other.

As mammals evolved, the most dramatic changes occurred in the hindbrain and forebrain. The hindbrain sprouted an expanded cerebellum, which increased the animal's capacity to integrate complex motor movements. Climbing trees and for-

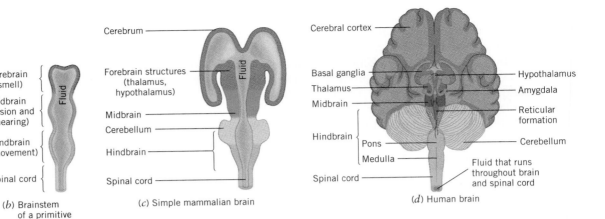

FIGURE 3.9
Evolution of the brain. The brain evolved from a simple spinal cord (a), through a primitive brain or brainstem, to the mammalian brain (c), the most sophisticated form of which is the human brain (d).
SOURCE: *Adapted from Kolb & Whishaw, 1990.*

aging for food on land required far more capacity for fine motor coordination than swishing back and forth in water for locomotion, leading to evolutionary changes in the size of the cerebellum. The forebrain of mammals is also very different from its ancestral prototype. It evolved many new structures, most notably those that comprise the **cerebrum**, the part of the brain most involved in complex thought, which greatly expanded the capacity for processing information and initiating movement (see Finlay & Darlington, 1995). Thus, even simple mammals such as hedgehogs and opossums are able to discriminate and respond to more subtle features of the environment than fish, whose less developed cerebrum renders them less "cerebral" (Diamond & Hall, 1969).

In higher mammals, and especially in humans, considerable evolution has occurred in the many-layered surface of the cerebrum known as the **cortex** (from the Latin word for "bark"). Eighty percent of the human brain's volume is cortex (Kolb & Whishaw, 1990). The human cortex has come to assume control over many of the functions carried out in other animals by lower neural structures, which suggests the need for care in generalizing research findings from animals to humans. For example, although the midbrain remains the visual and auditory brain of birds, in mammals the cortex assumes a much more central role in visual and auditory processing.

The human brain and the brains of other animals differ dramatically, but most of the differences result from additions to, rather than replacement of, the original brain structures. Thus, the brainstem in humans (which includes most of the structures below the cerebrum) is almost identical to the brainstem of sheep (Kolb & Whishaw, 1990), but the two species differ tremendously in the size and structure of their cortex. Much of the sheep's cortex is devoted to direct processing of sensory information, while a greater part of the human cortex is devoted to the formation of complex thoughts, perceptions, and plans for action. Nevertheless, human behavior, like the behavior of all other mammals, bears the distinct imprint of the same relatively primitive structures that guide motivation in other animals.

The central nervous system, then, is hierarchically organized, with an overall structure that follows its evolution. The most primitive centers are regulated by, and integrated into, the functions of higher regions, which are similarly regulated by still more advanced areas of the brain. From the lower to the higher parts, behavioral and cognitive precision progressively increase (Luria, 1973). The spinal cord can respond on its own with a reflex when the skin is pricked without even communicating with the brain, but more complex cognitive activity also occurs as the person makes sense of what has happened. We reflexively withdraw from a pinprick, but if the reason is a vaccine injection, we inhibit our response. Responding appropri-

How the brain works.

The nervous system is a collection of circuits.

ately requires the integrated functioning of structures from the spinal cord up through the cortex.

We now examine the major structures of the central nervous system, beginning with the spinal cord. We then describe the structures of the hindbrain, midbrain, and forebrain, focusing special attention on the cerebral cortex, whose evolution has permitted the complexity of human thought—such as the ability to understand the brain itself.

Before proceeding, however, a caveat is in order. One of the major debates since the origins of modern neuroscience in the nineteenth century has centered on the extent to which functions are localized to specific parts of the brain. Different regions are indeed specialized for different functions. For example, a severe blow to the head that damages the left side of the brain can affect language, whereas damage to the back of the cortex can affect vision. Knowing that a lesion at the back of the cortex can produce blindness suggests that this region is involved in vision and that its integrity is necessary for normal visual functioning—but not that it is the brain's "center" for vision. Every thought, feeling, or psychological attribute is always the result of a network of neurons acting in combination.

The Spinal Cord

Although neurons in the spinal cord can produce reflex actions, the **spinal cord** acts primarily as a relay station: It sends information from sensory neurons in various parts of the body to the brain, and it takes motor commands back to the muscles. The spinal cord is segmented, with each segment controlling a different part of the body. By and large, the upper segments control the upper parts of the body, and the lower segments, the lower body (Figure 3.10).

In humans, as in the earliest vertebrates, sensory information enters one side of the spinal cord (toward the back of the body), and motor impulses exit the other (toward the front). Bundles of axons from these sensory and motor neurons join together to form 31 **spinal nerves** that carry information to and from segments of the spinal cord to the periphery. Within the spinal cord, bundles of axons send impulses to and from the brain, relaying sensory messages and motor commands.

When the spinal cord is severed, the result is thus both loss of feeling and paralysis at all levels below the injury, which can no longer communicate with the brain. Even with less severe lesions, physicians can often pinpoint the location of spinal damage simply by patients' descriptions of their symptoms. If a patient complains of a lack of feeling in the upper part of the foot, and nerve damage to the foot or brain has been ruled out, the sacral segment (lowest segment) of the spinal cord has probably been damaged (Figure 3.10).

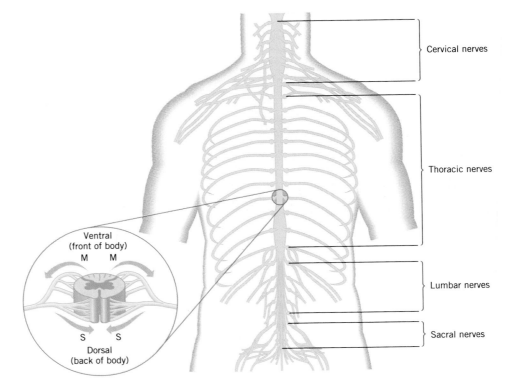

Cervical nerves

Thoracic nerves

Lumbar nerves

Sacral nerves

Ventral
(front of body)
M   M

Dorsal
(back of body)

FIGURE 3.10
The spinal cord. Segments of the spinal cord relay information to and from different parts of the body. Sensory fibers relay information to the dorsal (back) of the spine, and motor neurons transmit information from the ventral (front) of the spinal cord to the periphery.

The Hindbrain

Directly above the spinal cord in humans are several structures that comprise the **hindbrain**: the medulla oblongata, cerebellum, and parts of the reticular formation. Another small hindbrain structure, the pons, is not yet well understood (Figure 3.11). As in other animals, hindbrain structures serve several crucial functions, such as linking the brain to the spinal cord, controlling the supply of air and blood to cells in the body, and regulating arousal level.

Medulla Oblongata

Anatomically, the lowest of the brainstem structures, the **medulla oblongata** (or simply **medulla**), is actually an extension of the spinal cord. Although quite small—about an inch and a half long and three-fourths of an inch wide at its broadest part—the medulla is essential to life, controlling such vital physiological functions as heartbeat, circulation, and respiration. Neither humans nor other animals can survive destruction of the medulla.

The medulla is the link between the spinal cord and the rest of the brain. Here, bundles of axons (usually called **tracts** in the brain, and **nerves** elsewhere) cross over from each side of the body to the opposite side of the brain. As a result, most of the sensations experienced on the right side of the body, as well as the capacity to move the right side, are controlled by the left side of the brain, and vice versa.

Cerebellum

The **cerebellum** (Latin for "little cerebrum") is a large structure at the back of the brain. The cerebellum coordinates smooth, well-sequenced movements. It is

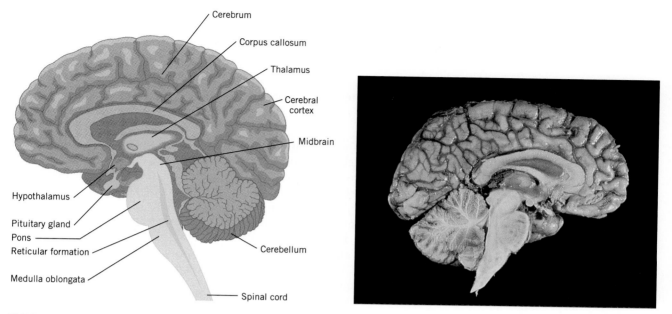

Cerebrum
Corpus callosum
Thalamus
Cerebral cortex
Midbrain
Hypothalamus
Pituitary gland
Pons
Reticular formation
Medulla oblongata
Cerebellum
Spinal cord

FIGURE 3.11
Cross-section of the human brain. The drawing and accompanying photo show a view of the cerebral cortex and the more primitive structures below the cerebrum. Not shown here are the limbic system and basal ganglia, which are subcortical structures within the cerebrum.

also involved in maintaining equilibrium and regulating postural reflexes, which are especially important to upright creatures. Staggering and slurred speech in an inebriated person stem in large measure from the effects of alcohol on cerebellar functioning. The cerebellum also takes a pounding when the head is repeatedly snapped back in boxing. The cumulative effect over the span of a career may be permanent damage, leading to a movement disorder or slurred speech, particularly if a boxer refuses to retire as his reflexes slow and he absorbs more punches on the chin.

Reticular Formation

The **reticular formation** (sometimes called the reticular activating system), is a diffuse network of neural nuclei and fibers (axons) that extends from the lowest parts of the medulla in the hindbrain to the upper end of the midbrain. The reticular formation sends fibers to many parts of the brain and to the spinal cord. The major function of the reticular formation is to maintain consciousness and regulate activity states throughout the central nervous system. Reticular damage can affect both sleep patterns and the ability to be alert or attentive. Parts of the reticular formation are also involved in movement and muscle control.

The Midbrain

The **midbrain** consists of the tectum and tegmentum. The **tectum** includes structures involved in vision and hearing. In humans and other mammals, these structures are largely involved in orienting to visual and auditory stimuli with eye and body movements. In birds, reptiles, and other animals, the tectum is the part of the brain responsible for both vision and hearing. The **tegmentum**, which includes parts of the reticular formation and other neural structures, serves a variety of functions, mostly related to movement.

Repeated battering of the brain in boxing can lead to damage to the cerebellum.

The Forebrain

The **forebrain**, which allows complex emotional reactions, thought processes, and movement patterns, consists of the hypothalamus, thalamus, and cerebrum. Within the cerebrum are the basal ganglia and limbic system, which are called **subcortical** structures (*sub*, or *below*, the cortex). The cortex is complex enough that we will devote a separate section to it.

Hypothalamus

Situated directly above the midbrain and adjacent to the pituitary gland is the **hypothalamus**. Although the hypothalamus accounts for only 0.3 percent of the brain's total weight, this tiny structure helps regulate a wide range of behaviors, including eating, sleeping, sexual activity, and emotional experience. In nonhuman animals, it is involved in species-specific behaviors, such as responses to predators. Electrical stimulation of the hypothalamus has been shown to produce rage attacks (hissing, growling, and biting) in cats (Bandler, 1982; Crescimanno et al., 1986; Gralewicz, 1983; Lu et al., 1992). The hypothalamus works closely with the pituitary gland and thus plays an important role in endocrine functioning, largely by activating pituitary hormones.

One of the most important functions of the hypothalamus is **homeostasis**— keeping vital processes such as body temperature, blood-sugar (glucose) level, and metabolism within a fairly narrow range. For example, as people ingest food, the hypothalamus detects a rise in glucose level and responds by shutting off hunger sensations. Just as researchers in a good experiment often rely on multiple measures, the hypothalamus makes use of several different sources of feedback, or information about the vital processes it is regulating. This redundancy is advantageous from an evolutionary standpoint, for if the system relied only on one measure and that measure failed, the result could be catastrophic. In regulating eating, for instance, the hypothalamus not only receives information from receptors elsewhere in the body about blood glucose levels, but it has glucose receptors itself. Artificially altering the action of these receptors in cats (by injecting a chemical that blocks glucose receptors in the hypothalamus, for example) can produce ravenous eating as the hypothalamus attempts to maintain homeostasis in the face of misleading information (Batuev & Gafurov, 1993; Berridge & Zajonc, 1991; Katafuchi et al., 1985).

Thalamus

The **thalamus** is located above the hypothalamus. It performs a number of functions, the most important of which is to relay sensory information to higher brain centers. In this capacity, the thalamus acts like a switchboard that routes information from neurons connected to visual, auditory, taste, and touch receptors throughout the body to appropriate regions of the brain.

The Limbic System

The **limbic system** is a set of structures with diverse functions. Various limbic regions appear to be involved in emotional reactions, motivation, learning, and memory. The limbic system includes the **septal area**, the **amygdala**, and the **hippocampus** (Figure 3.12). The role of the **septal area** is unclear, though early research linked it to the experience of pleasure (Milner, 1991; Olds & Milner, 1954). Stimulating a section of the septal area proved to be a powerful reinforcer for rats, who would walk across an electrified grid to receive the stimulation.

The **amygdala** is an almond-shaped structure (amygdala is Latin for "almond") involved in many emotional processes, especially learning and remembering emotionally significant events (LeDoux, 1990, 1995; Sarter & Markowitsch, 1985). Lesioning the amygdala in rats, for example, inhibits learned fear responses; without an intact amygdala, they no longer fear a stimulus they had previously connected with pain (Davis, 1992).

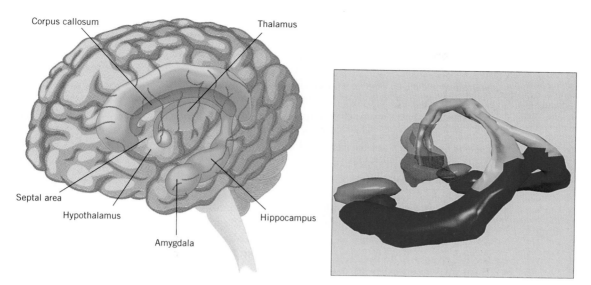

FIGURE 3.12
The limbic system. The limbic system, located within the cerebrum, consists of the septal area, amygdala, and hippocampus. The drawing shows the parts of the limbic system, and the photo shows the way it looks using computer imaging.

The **hippocampus** is particularly important in memory. In a famous case study by Brenda Milner and her colleagues (Milner et al., 1968; Scoville & Milner, 1957), a man identified as H. M. underwent surgery at the age of 27 to control intractable, life-threatening epileptic seizures. The surgeon removed sections of H. M.'s cortex and some underlying neural structures, including the hippocampus. The surgery was successful in reducing his seizures, but H. M. became unable to remember new information—or perhaps more accurately, he was unable to *know* that he had learned anything, even though he was capable of certain kinds of learning and memory (Chapter 6). Every time he met Dr. Milner, who studied him over 20 years, he had to be reintroduced; invariably, he would smile politely and tell her that it was a pleasure to make her acquaintance. At one time, however, H. M.'s father took him to visit his mother in the hospital. Afterward, H. M. did not remember anything of the visit, but he "expressed a vague idea that something might have happened to his mother" (Milner et al., 1968, p. 216). By the next day, though, he had no recollection even of his sense of uneasiness.

The Basal Ganglia

The **basal ganglia** are a set of structures located near the thalamus and hypothalamus that are involved in movement. Damage to the basal ganglia can cause changes in posture and muscle tone or various kinds of abnormal movements. The basal ganglia have been implicated in Parkinson's disease and in the encephalitis lethargica that struck millions earlier in this century. The dopamine-rich neurons of the substantia nigra (in the midbrain) normally project to the basal ganglia. When these neurons die, as in Parkinson's, they stop sending signals to the basal ganglia, which in turn cease functioning properly to regulate movement. Some neural circuits involving the basal ganglia appear to inhibit movement, whereas others initiate it, since lesions in different sections of the basal ganglia can either release movements or block them. Damage to the basal ganglia can also lead to disorders of mood and memory, as higher regions of the brain involved in these functions fail to receive necessary activation from the basal ganglia (see Decker et al., 1991; Federoff et al., 1992; Krishnan, 1993; Sano, 1991).

The Cerebral Cortex

Although many components of normal behaviors are produced below the cortex—in the spinal cord and medulla up through the limbic system and basal ganglia—the cerebral cortex coordinates and integrates these components (Kolb & Whishaw, 1990). The cortex consists of a 3-millimeter-thick layer of densely packed interneurons; it is grayish in color and highly convoluted (that is, filled with twists and turns). The convolutions appear to serve a purpose. Just as crumpling a piece of paper into a tight wad reduces its size, the folds and wrinkles of the cortex allow a relatively large area of cortical cells to fit into the compact region between the skull and lower brain structures. The hills and valleys of these convolutions are known as **gyri** (plural of **gyrus**) and **sulci** (plural of **sulcus**), respectively.

In humans, the cortex performs three functions. First, it allows the flexible construction of sequences of voluntary movements involved in activities such as changing a tire or playing a piano concerto. Second, it permits subtle discriminations among complex sensory patterns; without a cerebral cortex, the words "gene" and "gem" would be indistinguishable. Third, the cortex makes possible symbolic thinking—the ability to use symbols, such as words or pictorial signs, to represent an object or concept with a complex meaning. The capacity to think symbolically enables people to have conversations about things that do not exist or are not presently in view; it is the foundation of human thought and language.

Primary and Association Areas

The cortex consists of several regions that are specialized for different functions, such as vision, hearing, and body sensation. Each of these areas can be divided into two zones, called primary and association cortex. The **primary areas** receive direct sensory information or initiate motor movements, whereas the **association areas** are involved in constructing perceptions, ideas, and plans.

The primary areas do the initial cortical processing of sensory information. Neurons in these zones receive sensory information, usually via the thalamus, which comes from sensory receptors in the ears, eyes, skin, and muscles. As we will see in Chapter 4, a sensation is not an organized pattern or image. When a person sees a safety pin lying on her dresser, the primary or sensory areas receive the simple visual sensations that make up the contours of the safety pin. Activation of circuits in the visual association cortex leads to recognition of the object as a safety pin rather than a needle or a formless shiny object.

Neurons in the primary sensory areas tend to have the greatest specificity of function; that is, they may be wired to fulfill very particular tasks. Often from birth, these neurons are specialized to register very basic attributes of a stimulus, such as the angle at which it is presented. For example, particular neurons in the primary visual cortex are specialized to respond to horizontal lines but will not fire in response to vertical lines; other neurons respond only to vertical lines (Hubel & Wiesel, 1963). Although some neurons in the association cortex are equally specific in their functions, in much of the association cortex this is not the case, as in the association areas involved in organizing simple visual sensations into meaningful patterns. The brain may be wired from birth to detect the contours of objects like safety pins, but a person must learn what a safety pin is and does.

Lobes of the Cerebral Cortex

The cerebrum is divided into two roughly symmetrical halves or **hemispheres**, which are separated by the **longitudinal fissure**. (A fissure is a deep sulcus or valley.) A band of fibers called the **corpus callosum** connects the **right** and **left hemispheres**. Each hemisphere consists of four sections or **lobes**: the occipital, parietal, frontal, and temporal lobes. Thus, a person has a right and left occipital lobe, a right and left parietal lobe, and so forth (Figure 3.13).

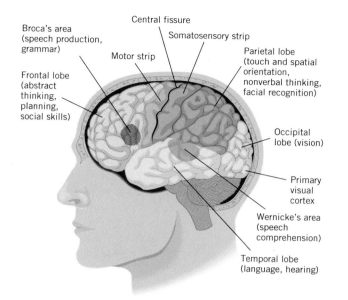

FIGURE 3.13
The lobes of the cerebral cortex. The cortex has four lobes, each specialized for different functions, and each containing primary and association areas

The Occipital Lobes   The **occipital lobes**, located in the rear portion of the cortex, are specialized for vision. Primary areas of the occipital lobes receive visual information from the thalamus. The thalamus, in turn, receives input from the receptors in the retina via the optic nerve. The primary areas respond to relatively simple features of a visual stimulus, such as its color or orientation. In contrast, visual association areas organize these simple characteristics into more complex patterns.

The visual association cortex projects (that is, sends neural fibers carrying messages) to several areas throughout the cortex that receive other types of sensory information, such as auditory or tactile. Areas that receive information from more than one sensory system are called **polysensory association areas**. The existence of a polysensory area that processes both visual and auditory information helps us associate the sight of a car stopping suddenly with the sound of squealing tires, although the simultaneous activation of the two systems contributes as well (see Damasio, 1994).

The Parietal Lobes   The **parietal lobes** are located in front of the occipital lobes. They are involved in a number of functions, including the sense of touch and the experience of one's own body in space and in movement. Damage to the primary area of the parietal lobes could make a person unable to feel a thimble on her finger, whereas damage to the association area could render her unable to recognize the object she was feeling as a thimble or to understand what the object does. The primary area of the parietal lobe, called the **somatosensory cortex**, lies directly behind the **central fissure**, which divides the parietal lobe from the frontal lobe. Different sections of the somatosensory cortex receive information from different parts of the body (Figure 3.14). Thus, one section registers sensations from the hand, whereas another processes sensations from the foot.

The Frontal Lobes   The **frontal lobes** are involved in a number of functions, including coordination of movement, attention, planning, social skills, abstract thinking, memory, and some aspects of personality (see Goldman-Rakic, 1995; Russell & Roxanas, 1990; Stuss & Benson, 1984). Figure 3.14 shows the **motor cortex**, the primary zone of the frontal lobe. Through its projections to the basal ganglia, cerebellum, and spinal cord, the motor cortex is the cortical region that initiates voluntary movement. The motor cortex and the adjacent somatosensory cortex send and receive information from the same parts of the body. The motor cortex sends sig-

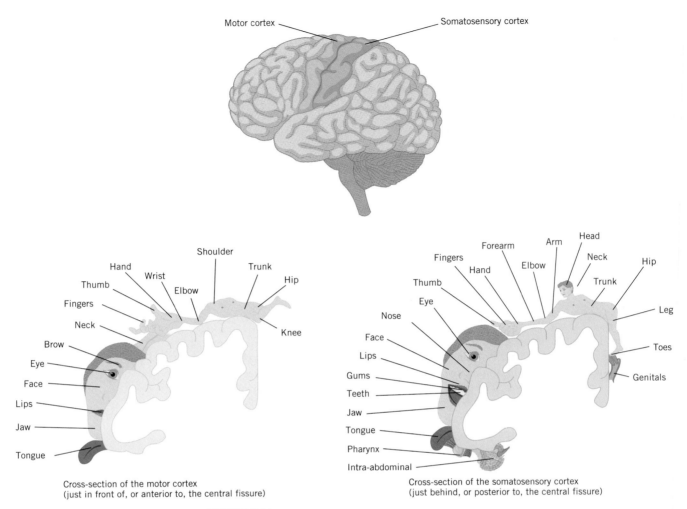

FIGURE 3.14

The motor and somatosensory cortex. The motor cortex directly initiates movement through its projections to the spinal cord. The somatosensory cortex receives sensory information from the spinal cord, largely via the thalamus. Both the motor and somatosensory cortex devote space according to the importance, neural density (number of neurons), and complexity of the anatomical regions to which they are connected. SOURCE: *Penfield & Rasmussen, 1978.*

nals to particular muscles that initiate movement, and the somatosensory cortex receives sensory information from the muscles, skin, and joints of those parts of the body.

As the figure indicates, the amount of space devoted to different parts of the body in the motor and somatosensory cortexes is not directly proportional to their size. Parts of the body that produce fine motor movements or have particularly dense and sensitive receptors are more highly represented in the motor and somatosensory cortexes. These body parts tend to serve important or complex functions and thus require more processing capacity. In humans, the hands, which are crucial to exploring objects and using tools, occupy considerable territory, whereas a section of the back of similar size occupies a relatively small space.

In the frontal lobes, the primary zones are motor rather than sensory areas. The association cortex is involved in planning and putting together sequences of behavior; neurons in the primary areas then issue specific "commands" to motor neurons throughout the body. Thus, the pattern in the frontal lobes is reversed from the other lobes: The primary areas of the occipital, temporal, and parietal lobes analyze the basic characteristics of sensory inputs before the association cortex is activated. In the frontal lobes, in contrast, the primary areas tend to be activated last, after the association areas have put together some kind of behavioral plan.

Damage to the frontal lobes can lead to a wide array of problems, from paralysis to difficulty thinking abstractly, coordinating complex sequences of behavior, and adjusting socially. Lesions in other parts of the brain that project to the frontal lobes can produce similar symptoms if the frontal lobes fail to receive normal activation. For example, the victims of encephalitis lethargica could not initiate movements even though their frontal lobes were probably intact because projections from the basal ganglia that normally activate the frontal lobes were impaired from dopamine depletion. Similarly, the slowing of thought in some Parkinson's patients may reflect a "break" in the neural circuits that generally regulate thinking, particularly abstract thinking.

In most individuals, the left frontal lobe is also involved in language. **Broca's area**, located in the left frontal lobe at the base of the motor cortex, is involved in speaking, for it is specialized for movements of the mouth and tongue necessary for speech production. It also plays a pivotal role in the use and understanding of grammar. Damage to Broca's area causes **Broca's aphasia**, in which a person may have difficulty speaking, putting together grammatical sentences, and articulating words but may nevertheless be able to comprehend language. The individual may have difficulty comprehending complex sentences, however, if subjects and objects cannot be discerned from context because lesions to this area disrupt grammar. A person with Broca's aphasia might thus have tremendous difficulty decoding the sentence, "The cat, which was under the hammock, chased the bird, which was flying over the dog."

The Temporal Lobes The **temporal lobes**, located in the lower side portion of the cortex, are important in audition (hearing) and language. For most people the left hemisphere of the temporal lobe is specialized for language, although some linguistic functions are shared by the right hemisphere. **Wernicke's area**, located in the left temporal lobe, is involved in language comprehension. Damage to Wernicke's area may produce **Wernicke's aphasia**, in which the individual has difficulty understanding what words and sentences mean. When these individuals speak, the result is often "word salad": They may speak fluently and expressively, as if their speech were meaningful, but the words are tossed together so that they make little sense.

FROM MIND TO BRAIN

THE IMPACT OF FRONTAL AND TEMPORAL LOBE DAMAGE ON PERSONALITY

If damage to the brain can affect such specific functions as language, what can it do to the complex patterns of emotion, thought, and behavior that constitute an individual's personality? Psychologists define personality much as laypeople do, as both a person's reputation (the way people tend to perceive him) and the enduring psychological attributes (mental processes) that create this reputation. Personality thus includes an individual's characteristic ways of feeling, of thinking about himself and the world, and of behaving. We hold people responsible for their personalities and tend to associate personality more with the "mind" or the "soul" than with the brain. We condemn people for aspects of their personality or character in a way that we do not for mental retardation or physical handicaps.

But is personality really so independent of the brain that serves as its material embodiment? Can a damaged brain create a damaged soul for which a person bears no more responsibility than for paralysis caused by an automobile accident? In fact, damage to parts of the brain can alter personality so

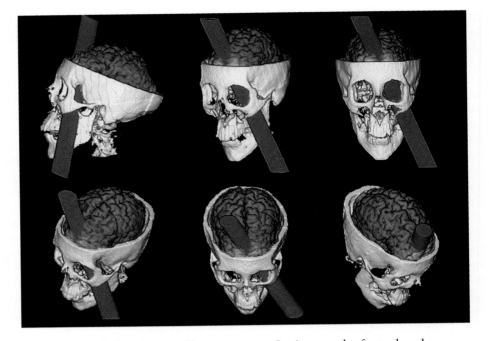

Computerized images from six angles reconstruct the likely path of the rod through Phineas Gage's frontal lobes.

that someone is literally a different person. Lesions to the frontal and temporal lobes provide striking examples.

Patients with frontal damage often make tactless comments and are described as callous, grandiose, boastful, and unable to understand other people's perspectives. They are also prone to lewd, bawdy, or childish joking (Ron, 1989; Russell & Roxanas, 1990; Stuss et al., 1992). A famous early report of symptoms of this sort was the case of a construction worker named Phineas Gage. In 1848 an explosion sent a metal bar of more than an inch in diameter through his skull, damaging association areas of his frontal lobes. Previously known to be a decent, conscientious man, Gage was described following the accident as childish, irreverent, unable to control his impulses, and constantly devising plans that he would abandon within moments (Blumer & Benson, 1984; Damasio, 1994). According to his doctor, the balance between his intellect and "animal propensities" had been disrupted.

Another broad class of personality alterations associated with frontal lobe lesions includes indifference, listlessness, and slowness. A 46-year-old man suffered a skull fracture in a car accident and consequently had a portion of his left frontal lobe removed. Although his physical and cognitive abilities returned to normal, his personality changed dramatically. Prior to the accident, his friends described him as friendly, active in the community, talkative, animated, and happy. He was a warm, loving father and husband and a successful salesperson. After his injury, he became quiet, spent most of his time alone smoking, and spoke only in response to questions. His changed behavior makes neuropsychological sense, since the frontal lobes are involved in initiating activity. The patient spoke in an intelligent but very "matter of fact" manner, and he was completely without concern for his wife and children, who eventually stopped seeing him because of his utter indifference (Blumer & Benson, 1984).

Another form of brain pathology associated with specific types of personality change is temporal lobe epilepsy, a seizure disorder characterized by abnormal electrical activity in the brain that begins in the temporal lobe. Some forms of epilepsy bring about personality changes, such as mood shifts, a tendency to ruminate on repetitive thoughts, and excessive religiosity (Lezak, 1983). A 43-year-old businessman began to experience seizures and personality changes after he suffered a head injury in a car accident. Just prior to each seizure, he would become suspicious of people and fight with his friends for no apparent reason. Although he was described as talkative before his injury, afterward he became excessively verbose, preoccupied with irrelevant details, and could literally spend hours discussing small, tangential details before returning to the point he was trying to make. His inability to maintain a fluent conversation, as well as his quickness to become angry, eventually led to a breakdown in communication with his wife and periods of marital separation (Blumer & Benson, 1984).

These cases challenge the way most of us intuitively understand ourselves and other people, particularly in the West, where cultural beliefs emphasize the separation of mind and body and the responsibility of the individual. How does a person respond to a once loving spouse or father who no longer seems to care? Is he the same husband or father, or does the same body now house a different person? Is he accountable for the way he behaves? As we shall see, the moral and philosophical issues become even more complex in the face of evidence that personality is partly innate and that some people are born with a proclivity to behave antisocially or indifferently to other people.

Cerebral Lateralization

We have seen that the left frontal and temporal lobes tend to play a more important role in speech and language than their right hemisphere counterparts. This raises the question of whether other cortical functions are **lateralized** (that is, localized on one or the other side of the brain), and if so, how extensive this lateralization is.

Caution is in order in making global generalizations, for most functions that are popularly considered to be lateralized are actually represented on both sides of the brain in most people. However, some division of labor between the hemispheres does exist, with each side **dominant** for (that is, in more control of) certain functions. Figure 3.15 highlights some of these differences. In general (at least for right-handed people), the left hemisphere is dominant for language, logic, complex motor behavior, and probably some aspects of consciousness (particularly verbal aspects).

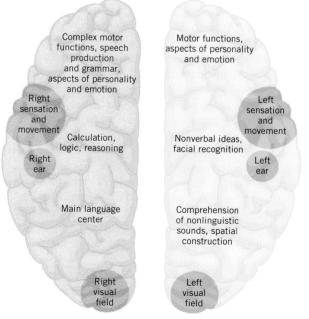

Left hemisphere   Right hemisphere

FIGURE 3.15

Cerebral lateralization. Although the two hemispheres share many functions, various functions tend to be lateralized to one of the two hemispheres. In general, the left hemisphere is more analytical, whereas the right hemisphere is more global and intuitive.

Drawing by Sidney Harris

Left hemisphere functions are considered more analytical—breaking down thoughts and perceptions into component parts and attempting to analyze the relations among them. Lateralization for language is wired into the organism and is already present to some extent at birth (Hahn, 1987; Previc, 1991).

The right hemisphere is specialized for visual-spatial and other nonlinguistic functions. Studies indicate that it is involved in visual mapping, tactile perception, facial identification, and the recognition of nonlinguistic sounds such as music. The right hemisphere's specialization for nonlinguistic sounds also seems to hold in non-human animals that communicate orally with other members of their species. Japanese macaque monkeys, for example, have a right ear advantage for understanding species-specific calls but not for other environmental sounds (Petersen et al., 1984). The right ear is connected primarily to the left hemisphere, which means that "language" between Japanese macaques is lateralized to the left hemisphere. Processing other sounds such as bird calls, however, is primarily localized to the right hemisphere in macaques. This kind of lateralization for the sounds of their own species occurs in birds as well (Sherman et al., 1982).

Damage to the right hemisphere can lead to some unusual problems. For example, lesions in a temporal-parietal region, particularly on the right, can result in an inability to recognize faces, a disorder known as **prosopagnosia** (Bruyer, 1991; Sergent & Signoret, 1992). One woman with prosopagnosia was unable to recognize her husband by sight. As soon as he spoke, she knew who he was because her left temporal lobe was intact, but without his speaking, he was a total stranger.

Split-Brain Studies

Much of what psychologists know about cerebral lateralization comes from case studies of **split-brain** subjects—patients whose corpus callosum has been surgically cut, blocking communication between the two hemispheres. Severing this connective tissue is a radical treatment for severe epileptic seizures that spread from one hemisphere to another and cannot be controlled by any other means.

In their everyday behavior, split-brain patients generally appear normal (Sperry, 1984). However, their two hemispheres actually operate independently, and each may be oblivious to what the other is doing. Under certain experimental circumstances, the disconnection between the two minds housed in one brain becomes apparent. To understand the results of these experiments, bear in mind that the left hemisphere, which is the center for most speech functions, receives information from the right visual field and that the right hemisphere receives information from the left visual field. Normally, whether the right or left hemisphere receives the information makes little difference because once the message reaches the brain, the left and right hemispheres freely pass the information between them. Severing the corpus callosum, however, blocks this sharing of information (Gazzaniga, 1967).

Figure 3.16a depicts a typical split-brain experiment. A split-brain subject is seated at a table, and the surface of the table is blocked from view by a screen so the subject cannot see objects on it. The experimenter asks the subject to focus on a point in the center of the screen. A word (here, "key") is quickly flashed on the left side of the screen. When information is flashed for only about 150 milliseconds, the eyes do not have time to move, ensuring that the information is sent to only one hemisphere. The subject is unable to identify the word verbally because the information never reached his left hemisphere, which is dominant for speech. He can, however, select a key with his left hand from an array of objects hidden behind the screen because the left hand receives information from the right hemisphere, which "saw" the key. Thus, the right hand literally does not know what the left hand is doing—and neither does the left hemisphere. Figure 3.16b illustrates the way visual information from the left and right visual fields is transmitted to the brain in normal and split-brain patients.

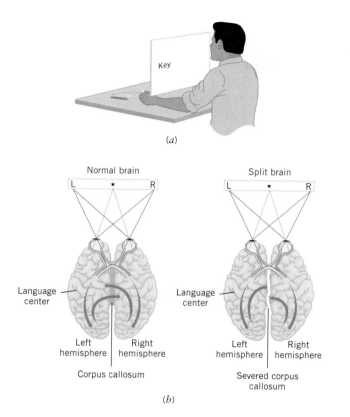

FIGURE 3.16

A split-brain study. In a typical split-brain study (a), a subject with a severed corpus callosum sees the word "key" flashed on the left portion of the screen. Although he cannot name what he has seen, as speech is lateralized to the left hemisphere, he is able to use his left hand to select the key from a number of objects because the right hemisphere, which has "seen" the key, controls the left hand. Part (b) illustrates the way information from the left and right visual fields is transmitted to the brain in normal and split-brain subjects. When subjects focus vision on a point in the middle of the visual field (such as the star in the diagram), anything on the left of this fixation point (for instance, point L) will be sensed by receptors on the right half of each eye. These receptors are located in the retina, at the back of the eye. This information is subsequently processed by the right hemisphere. Conversely, receptors in the left part of each eye's retina register information from the right visual field and pass this information along to the left hemisphere for processing. In the normal brain, information is readily transmitted via the corpus callosum between the two hemispheres. In the split-brain patient, the severed neural route means the right and left hemispheres "see" different things.
SOURCE: *Part (a) adapted from Gazzaniga, 1967.*

This research raises an intriguing question: Can a person with two independent hemispheres be literally of two minds, with two centers of conscious awareness, like Siamese twins joined at the cortex? Consider the case of a 10-year-old boy with a split brain (LeDoux et al., 1977). In one set of tests, the boy was asked about his sense of himself, his future, and his likes and dislikes. The examiner asked the boy questions in which a word or words were replaced by the word "blank." The missing words were then projected to one hemisphere or the other. For example, when the boy was asked, "Who *blank*?" the missing words "are you" were projected to the left or the right hemisphere. Not surprisingly, the boy could only answer verbally when inquiries were made to the left hemisphere, although the right hemisphere could answer by spelling out words with letter tiles with the left hand (because the right hemisphere is usually not entirely devoid of language) when the question was flashed to the right hemisphere. Thus, the boy could describe his moods, his preferences, and his aspirations with both hemispheres.

Many times the views expressed by the right and left hemispheres overlapped, but not always. On one day when the boy was in a pleasant mood, his hemispheres tended to agree (both, for example, reporting high self-esteem). On another day when the boy seemed anxious and behaved aggressively, the hemispheres were in disagreement. In general, his right hemisphere responses were consistently more negative than those of the left, as if the right hemisphere tended to be in a worse mood. Researchers using other methods have also reported that the two hemispheres differ in their processing of positive and negative emotions (Davidson, 1992; Fox, 1991).

Sex Differences in Lateralization

Psychologists have long known that females score higher on tests of verbal fluency, perceptual speed, and manual dexterity than males, whereas males score higher on tests of mathematical ability and spatial processing (Bradbury, 1989; Maccoby & Jacklin, 1974; Nicholson, 1984). In one study of students under age 13 with exceptional mathematical ability (measured by scores of 700 or above on the SAT), boys outnumbered girls 13 to 1 (Benbow & Stanley, 1983). On the other hand, males are much more likely than females to develop learning disabilities with reading and language comprehension. Although these sex differences may not be particularly large (Hyde, 1990; Tallal, 1991), they have been documented in several countries and have not consistently decreased over the last two decades despite social changes pushing toward equality of the sexes (see Bradbury, 1989; Randhawa, 1991). Psychologists have thus debated whether such discrepancies in performance could be based in part on innate differences between the brains of men and women.

Some neuropsychological evidence suggests that women's and men's brains do differ in ways that may affect cognitive functioning. At a hormonal level, research with human and nonhuman primates indicates that the presence of testosterone and estrogen in the bloodstream early in development influences aspects of brain development (Clark & Goldman-Rakic, 1989; Gorski & Barraclough, 1963). Indeed, the amounts of androgens (male hormones) present in early life have been shown to be associated with spatial abilities in men (Hines, 1982). Adult levels of testosterone also appear to be related, although in complex ways, to spatial and mathematical functioning in men and women (Gouchie & Kimura, 1991). Some evidence even suggests that women's spatial abilities, as measured on at least some tasks, are lower during high-estrogen periods of the menstrual cycle, whereas motor skills, on which females typically have an advantage, are superior during high-estrogen periods (Kimura, 1987). Recent MRI studies have shown subtle differences between men's and women's brains while performing linguistic tasks (Shaywitz et al., 1995).

Although neuropsychological evidence suggests innate differences, culture plays an important role in shaping the skills and interests of males and females as well. Parents tend to talk to little girls more, and they encourage boys to play with mechanical objects and discourage them from many verbal activities such as writing poetry. By the elementary school years, girls have already learned to think they cannot succeed in mathematics and to attribute any success they have in mathematical pursuits to luck (Stipek & Gralinski, 1991). Furthermore, despite efforts to remove gender biases from textbooks, a study comparing high school chemistry textbooks from the early 1970s with their current editions found that males are still shown three times more often in illustrations and examples than females, subtly perpetuating the view of chemistry as a male discipline (although the ratio had dropped from 5:1) (Bazler & Simonis, 1991). Some of the most interesting evidence of the impact of culture comes from a study that followed girls from ages 11 to 18 (Newcombe & Dubas, 1992). The best predictors of spatial ability at age 16 were two psychological attributes at age 11: wishing to be a boy and having a view of what one would like to be that fit more masculine than feminine stereotypes. To what extent these psychological attributes themselves could be influenced by biology is, however, unknown.

A GLOBAL VISTA

ENVIRONMENT, CULTURE, AND THE BRAIN

As we have seen, changes in the brain can influence psychological functioning, as when occipital lobe damage renders a person unable to see visual images, or when frontal lobe damage gave Phineas Gage the personality and charm of a drunken sailor. But can causality run the other way? Can psychological, environmental, or cultural experiences influence the brain or even change its structure?

Over the last three chapters, we have already seen some hints that they can. Chapter 1 opened with the case of a young girl whose epileptic seizures diminished in response to her mother's return. A similar finding emerged in Harry Harlow's experiments raising monkeys with surrogate mothers (Chapter 2): Monkeys separated from their mothers for long periods of time developed abnormal EEGs (see Gabbard, 1992). In both cases, social deprivation altered the physiology of the brain—which in turn altered mental processes and behavior.

A fascinating line of research indicates that early sensory enrichment or deprivation can affect the brain in fundamental ways, including its growth (Rosenzweig et al., 1972). In one series of studies, young male rats were raised in one of two conditions (Cummins et al., 1977). The experimenters exposed one group to an enriched environment, with 6 to 12 rats sharing an open-mesh cage filled with a variety of toys. Another group was raised in isolation in small, individual cages with no toys. After periods ranging from 18 to 120 days, depending on the experimental design, the experimenters sacrificed the rats and weighed their forebrains. The brains of enriched rats tended to be heavier than those of the deprived rats, indicating that the presence of environmental stimuli can alter the course of neural development. Another study linked early postnatal stimulation to accelerated growth of dendrites (Shapiro & Vukovich, 1970). Newborn rats that were frequently handled, stroked, and subjected to experiences such as noise and flashing lights showed much greater dendritic development than rats that were not exposed to such stimulation. The actual structure of the brain thus depends in part on environmental input.

Sex differences in cognitive abilities may partially reflect differences in the brain.

Subsequent research has documented the impact of enriched versus socially isolated environments on the later availability of neurotransmitters in different parts of the brain (Heritch et al., 1990). Environmental enrichment appears to affect only certain classes of neurotransmitters and certain neural pathways, namely, those that link one part of the cortex to another (rather than, for example, connections between subcortical structures and the cortex, which seem to be relatively impervious to environmental conditions) (Myhrer et al., 1992). More primitive parts of the brain essential for survival tend to have more genetically hard-wired circuits than the cortical regions that permit complex thought and learning (Damasio, 1994).

Does the environment shape the structure of the brain in humans as well? Recent evidence suggests that it does. The brain undergoes considerable development, particularly in childhood, both in the myelinization of axons and in the sprouting of multiple connections among its billions of neurons. In fact, the brain triples in weight in the first two years and quadruples to its adult weight by age 14 (Winson, 1985). Increasing evidence suggests that social, cultural, and environmental experience shapes the development of the brain. Subtle environmental and cultural influences on the brain can be seen with language. For instance, many native Asian-language speakers have difficulty distinguishing "la" from "ra" because Asian languages do not distinguish these units of sound. One study found that Japanese people who heard sound frequencies between "la" and "ra" did not hear them as *either* "la" or "ra," as do Americans (Goto, 1971). If children do not learn certain linguistic patterns in the first few years of life (such as the "la/ra" distinction, the French "r," or the Hebrew "ch"), these patterns may be laid down with different and much less efficient neural machinery later on (Lenneburg, 1967).

One study tested this hypothesis by assessing lateralization of speech production in deaf subjects who lost their hearing at different points in early childhood (Marcotte & Morere, 1990). Subjects who lost their hearing after the third year of life—who had thus been exposed to verbal language during those early years—showed the same left hemisphere dominance for speech as subjects with normal hearing. In contrast, subjects who were deaf from birth or who lost their hearing before the third year showed varying and atypical patterns of lateralization. This suggests that hearing speech in the first three years of life may be critical to the organization of linguistic centers in the brain.

An even more startling possibility is that cultural factors may alter the division of labor between the two cerebral hemispheres. The available data are inconclusive, but the kind of language a person speaks and reads may

Chinese pictographic writing may be responsible for decreased lateralization of language in Chinese readers.

influence the actual organization of information in the brain (Keung & Hoosain, 1989; Shimada & Otsuka, 1981; Zhang & Peng, 1983).   For instance, unlike most languages, Chinese writing is pictographic; instead of spelling words out phonetically with letters, Chinese written language represents objects or concepts with pictorial images.   One would expect such pictorial information to be more heavily processed in the right hemisphere than in the left, where Western languages are processed.   Indeed, some experimental and clinical evidence suggests that language may be less lateralized among users of the pictographic Chinese language than among Westerners (Hatta, 1977; Tzen et al., 1979).

The Chinese language also differs from most other languages in that it is a tone language, which means that intonation—the rising and falling of the voice—is used to distinguish otherwise identical words.   In Mandarin Chinese, for example, saying the word "mao" with a rising tone means "cat," and with a falling tone, "hat."   The processing of tone, like music, is typically more lateralized to the right hemisphere in the West.   A study of Chinese subjects suffering from Broca's aphasia, however, suggests that being a native Chinese speaker may shift this function to the left hemisphere.   These patients, with documented left hemisphere damage, had considerable difficulty producing tone (Packard, 1986).   Although the data are not entirely conclusive, they suggest that cultural factors, and without doubt environmental experiences, can literally alter the structure of the brain.

MIND, BRAIN, AND GENE

This chapter has focused on the neural basis of thought, feeling, and behavior and has explored the complex relations between mind and brain in normal and abnormal functioning.   In normal functioning, sensory neurons bring information from the environment to the central nervous system, which in turn may respond with autonomic or motor responses.   These responses result from the activity of neural circuits linking evolutionarily primitive regions of the brain with more recently evolved subcortical and cortical regions, such as the basal ganglia and motor cortex of the frontal lobes.   The nearly instantaneous firing of millions of neurons provides the physiological basis for all our psychological processes, from the aesthetic appreciation of a Monet to the capacity to operate a computer.

In abnormal functioning, damage to the nervous system may alter or disrupt psychological experience.   **Tumors**, or abnormal tissue growths, may put pressure on brain structures and thus damage or destroy existing cells.   The psychological impact may be as varied as blurred vision, searing headaches, or explosive emotional outbursts that seem to come from nowhere.   Vascular disease (disease of blood vessels) can lead to **strokes**, in which blood flow to regions of the brain is interrupted.   If blood flow to a part of the brain is cut off for more than about 10 minutes, the cells in that area will die.   As a result, the person may become paralyzed, lose the capacity for speech, or die if the stroke destroys neural regions vital for life support such as the medulla or hypothalamus.

Similar psychological changes can result from trauma to the nervous system caused by automobile accidents, blows to the head, or falls that break the neck. Infection caused by viruses, bacteria, or parasites can also destroy parts of the brain, as in malaria, where delirium or death may result as malarial protozoa cause the capillaries in the brain to hemorrhage or burst.   For survivors of the mysterious Viennese sleeping sickness, a viral assault on the brain and subsequent discovery of L-dopa not only altered the course of their lives but also dramatically influenced their sense of meaning in life and their self-concepts.   How does a person who has lost 40 or 50 years find meaning in her existence and her tragedy, and what happens when the reawakened self-concept of a teenager confronts the reality of an aged body?

Having thus described the structure and function of the nervous system, we conclude our examination of the biological bases of mental life and behavior with a brief discussion of the influence of genetics on psychological functioning. Few people would argue with the view that hair and eye color are heavily influenced by genetics or that genetic vulnerabilities contribute to heart disease, cancer, and diabetes. Yet as we saw in Chapter 1, as soon as one suggests genetic roots to human behaviors and dispositions or to differences between individuals, clouds of controversy begin to collect. In part, the controversy reflects realistic concerns about branding certain people or races as genetically defective. In part, too, resistance to notions about biological contributions to psychological dispositions, and particularly to individual differences between people, is based in a strongly held cultural belief that "all men are created equal" and that anyone can do almost anything with hard work and perseverance.

Genetics

Psychologists interested in genetics study the way observable psychological attributes or qualities (**phenotypes**) reflect underlying genetic blueprints (**genotypes**). The **gene** is the unit of hereditary transmission. A single gene may control eye color or heart rate; however, genetic contributions to most complex phenomena, such as intelligence or personality, reflect the action of many genes.

Genes are encoded in the DNA (deoxyribonucleic acid) contained within the nucleus of every cell in the body. Genes are arranged along **chromosomes**—strands of paired DNA that spiral around each other (Figure 3.17). Human cells have 46 chromosomes, except sperm cells in males and egg cells in females, each of which has 23 unpaired chromosomes. The union of a sperm and an egg creates a cell with 46 chromosomes, half from the mother and half from the father. This single cell contains the blueprint for an organism that will emerge several months later, replete with billions of specialized cells and an array of behavioral proclivities.

Children receive a somewhat random selection of half the genetic material of each parent, which means that the probability of sharing any particular gene with a parent is 1 out of 2, or .50. This number represents the **degree of relatedness**

DNA research: reading nature's code.

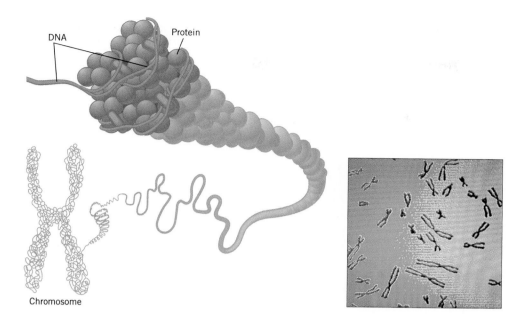

DNA
Protein

Chromosome

FIGURE 3.17
Human chromosomes. A drawing and magnified photograph of human chromosomes.

between parent and offspring. Because children and their parents are related by .50, and parents and *their* parents are related by .50, the degree of relatedness between grandchildren and grandparents is .25, or .5 x .5. In other words, a grandmother passes on half of her genes to her daughter, who passes on half of those genes to her child; the likelihood that the grandchild got any particular gene from her maternal grandmother through her mother is thus .25. Siblings are also related by .50 because they have a .25 chance of sharing a gene from their mother and a .25 chance from their father; added together, they are related by .50 on the average. Table 3.3 shows the degree of relatedness for various relatives.

The fact that relatives differ in degree of relatedness enables researchers to tease apart the relative contributions of heredity and environment to phenotypic differences between individuals. If the similarity between relatives on attributes such as intelligence or conscientiousness correlates highly with their degree of relatedness, this suggests genetic influence, especially if the relatives did not share a common upbringing (such as siblings adopted into different families). Particularly important for research on the genetic basis of behavioral differences are identical and fraternal twins. **Monozygotic (MZ)**, or **identical, twins** develop from the union of the same sperm and egg. They share the same genetic makeup, so their degree of genetic relatedness is 1.0. In contrast, **dizygotic (DZ)**, or **fraternal, twins** develop from the union of two sperm with two separate eggs. Like other siblings, their degree of relatedness is .50, for they have a 50 percent chance of sharing the same gene for any characteristic.

Behavioral Genetics

A relatively new field called behavioral genetics has produced rapid advances in our understanding of the relative roles of genetics and environment in shaping mental processes and behavior. Recent evidence suggests that genetic influences are far greater than were once believed in a number of domains, including personality, intelligence, and mental illness (Fuller & Thompson, 1978; Gottesman, 1991; Kendler & Diehl, 1993; McGue et al., 1993; Plomin & Rende, 1991). Twin studies provide psychologists a golden opportunity to examine the role of genetics because MZ and DZ twins typically share similar environments but differ in their degree of genetic relat-

TABLE 3.3 DEGREE OF RELATEDNESS AMONG SELECTED RELATIVES

RELATION	DEGREE OF RELATEDNESS
Identical (MZ) twin	1.0 (1/1)
Fraternal (DZ) twin	.50 (1/2)
Parent/child	.50 (1/2)
Sibling	.50 (1/2)
Grandparent/grandchild	.25 (1/4)
Half-sibling	.25 (1/4)
First cousin	.125 (1/8)
Nonbiological parent/adopted child	0

edness. If a psychological attribute is genetically transmitted, MZ twins should be much more likely than DZ twins and other siblings to share it. This method is not free of bias, however, because identical twins may receive more similar treatment than fraternal twins, since they look the same. Thus, as a way of assessing the relative roles of heredity and environment, behavioral geneticists also compare twins reared together in the same family with twins who were adopted away and hence reared apart (Bouchard et al., 1991; Loehlin, 1989, 1992; Lykken et al., 1992; Tellegen et al., 1988).

The findings from these studies have allowed psychologists to estimate the extent to which differences among individuals on psychological dimensions such as intelligence and personality are **heritable**, that is, determined by genetic factors. A **heritability coefficient** quantifies the degree to which a trait is heritable. A coefficient of 0 indicates no heritability at all, whereas a coefficient of 1.0 indicates that a trait is completely heritable.

Heritability connotes the degree to which genetic *variability* among individuals in a population (variability in genotype) contributes to variability of an observed trait (variability in phenotype). This is easily confused with the degree to which a trait is genetically *determined*. The fact that humans have two eyes is genetically determined. For all practical purposes, however, humans show no variability in the expression of the trait of two-eyedness because virtually all humans are born with two eyes. Thus, the heritability of two-eyedness is 0; genetic variability is not correlated with phenotypic or observed variability because virtually no variability exists. In contrast, the trait of eye *color* has a very high degree of heritability (approaching 1.0) in a heterogeneous population.

Several studies of the personality characteristics of twins have produced heritability estimates from .15 to .50 (that is, up to 50 percent heritability) on a broad spectrum of traits, including conservatism, neuroticism, nurturance, assertiveness, and aggressiveness (Plomin & Rende, 1991). Some findings have been remarkable and highly counterintuitive. For example, identical twins reared apart, who may never have even met each other, tend to have very similar vocational interests and levels of job satisfaction (Arvey et al., 1989; Moloney et al., 1991). Researchers have even found a genetic influence on religious attitudes, beliefs, and values (Waller et al., 1990). Heritability estimates for IQ are over 50 percent.

In interpreting the findings of behavioral genetics, some caveats are in order. As emphasized by a leading behavioral geneticist, but too readily forgotten, heritability in the range of 50 percent means that environmental factors are equally impor-

Jerry Levey and Mark Newman, separated at birth, met when a colleague did a double-take at a firefighters' convention.

tant—they account for the other 50 percent (Plomin & Rende, 1991). Furthermore, heritability estimates frequently include a hidden environmental component. Some people are, from the start, more emotional, active, or shy than others. These basic dispositions influence not only the way they act but also the way others respond to them. If an infant is genetically predisposed to be passive and unassertive, caretakers may react by becoming more active. They may treat the child as more helpless and intervene more frequently than they would with a more assertive and independent child, and the child in turn may respond by becoming even *more* passive. This complex interaction of genetic proclivities and environmental responses is all included under genetic effects in estimating heritability. The relative roles of heredity and environment, and estimates of heritability, also vary from population to population. Children who are severely malnourished may show less heritability of IQ than others because malnutrition or extreme deprivation can place constraints on intellectual potential as assessed by IQ tests and thus reduce the potential impact of hereditary differences.

SOME CONCLUDING THOUGHTS

If one message emerges from this chapter, it is probably that nothing is simple. Psychological experiences do not merely reflect neuropsychological processes. The grief of losing a parent or lover is not adequately explained as the activation of neural circuits in the hypothalamus, limbic system, and cortex. On the other hand, neuropsychological processes are crucial to understanding psychological functioning. Without understanding the structure and function of the brain, we cannot understand the human capacity for memory or the reason a stroke victim has mysteriously lost both the ability to talk and the ability to move his right arm.

Similarly, psychological qualities such as intelligence and personality cannot be explained as mere reflections of genetic programs. Genes and environment interact in staggeringly complex ways, which psychologists are just beginning to unravel. At the same time, however, the genetic basis of human nature and human variability is clearly substantial. Believing that anyone can become a violin virtuoso or that the eradication of aggression is simply a matter of education or reshaping social institutions is a myth—a comforting and perhaps useful one, but a myth nonetheless. As Sir Francis Bacon asserted, knowledge is power. By understanding the biological bases of human mental life and behavior, we may be better able to control aspects of ourselves that we wish to temper or develop and to ameliorate some of the misfortunes that come with being human.

Summary

Neurons: Basic Units of the Nervous System

1. The firing of billions of nerve cells provides the physiological basis for all our psychological processes—thinking, feeling, and behaving.

2. **Neurons**, or nerve cells, are the basic units of the nervous system. **Sensory neurons** carry sensory information from sensory receptors to the central nervous system. **Motor neurons** transmit commands from the brain to the glands and muscles of the body. **Interneurons** connect neurons with each other.

3. Neurons all have a **cell body, dendrites** (branchlike extensions of the cell body), and **axons** that carry information to other neurons. Axons are often covered with **myelin** for more efficient electrical transmission. Located on the axons are **terminal buttons,** which contain **neurotransmitters**, chemicals that transmit information across the **synapse** (the space between neurons through which they communicate).

4. The "resting" condition in which a neuron is not firing is called the **resting potential**. When a neuron is stimulated by another neuron, it either becomes **depolarized** (the inside of the cell becomes less negative) or **hyperpolarized** (the inside of the cell becomes more negative). The spreading voltage changes that occur when the neural membrane receives signals from other cells are called **graded potentials**. If enough depolarizing graded potentials accumulate to cross a threshold, the neuron will **fire**. This **action potential** leads to the release of neurotransmitters and similar substances (such as dopamine, serotonin, endorphins, norepinephrine, and acetylcholine). These chemical messages are in turn received by **receptors** in the cell membrane of other neurons, which in turn can excite or inhibit those neurons.

The Endocrine System

5. The **endocrine system** is a collection of ductless glands that control various bodily functions through the secretion of **hormones**. The endocrine system complements the cell-to-cell communication of the nervous system by sending global messages through the bloodstream.

The Peripheral Nervous System

6. The **peripheral nervous system (PNS)** consists of neurons that carry messages to and from the central nervous system. The peripheral nervous system has two subdivisions, the somatic nervous system and the autonomic nervous system. The **somatic nervous system** consists of the sensory neurons that receive information through sensory receptors in the skin, muscles, and other parts of the body such as the eyes, and the motor neurons that direct the action of skeletal muscles. The **autonomic nervous system** controls basic life processes such as the beating of the heart, the working of the digestive system, and breathing. It consists of two parts, the **sympathetic nervous system** (which is activated in response to threats) and the **parasympathetic nervous system** (which returns the body to normal and works to maintain the body's energy resources).

The Central Nervous System

7. The **central nervous system (CNS)** is hierarchically organized, with an overall structure that follows its evolution. Evolutionarily more recent centers control and rechannel many of the processes that occur at lower levels. The CNS consists of the brain and spinal cord.

8. Aside from carrying out reflexes, the **spinal cord** acts primarily as a relay station, taking information from the sensory neurons in various parts of the body, relaying it to higher centers in the central nervous system, and in turn sending commands back to the muscles and organs.

9. Several structures comprise the **hindbrain**. The **medulla oblongata** controls vital physiological functions such as heartbeat, circulation, and respiration, and forms a link between the spinal cord and the rest of the brain. The **cerebellum** helps coordinate smooth, well-sequenced movements. The **reticular formation** maintains consciousness and helps regulate activity states throughout the central nervous system, including sleep cycles.

10. The **midbrain** consists of the tectum and tegmentum. The **tectum** includes structures involved in orienting to visual and auditory stimuli. The **tegmentum** includes parts of the reticular formation and other nuclei with a variety of functions, mostly related to movement.

11. The **forebrain** consists of the hypothalamus, thalamus, and cerebrum. The **hypothalamus** is involved in regulating a wide range of behaviors, including eating, sleeping, sexual activity, and emotional experience. The **thalamus** serves as a relay station for sensory information.

12. The **cerebrum** includes a number of **subcortical** structures as well as an outer layer, or **cortex**. The subcortical structures are the limbic system and the basal ganglia. Structures of the **limbic system** are involved in emotion, motivation, learning, and memory. **Basal ganglia** structures are involved in the control of movement. Damage to the basal ganglia can affect posture, muscle tone, and movement, leading to such disorders as Parkinson's disease.

13. In humans, the **cerebral cortex** allows the flexible construction of sequences of voluntary movements, enables people to discriminate complex sensory patterns, and provides the capacity to think symbolically. The **primary areas** of the cortex receive direct information and initiate motor movements. The **association areas** are involved in putting together perceptions, ideas, and plans.

14. The **right** and **left hemispheres** of the cerebral cortex are connected by a fibrous structure called the **corpus callosum**. Each hemisphere consists of four sections or lobes. The **occipital lobes** are specialized for vision. The **parietal lobes** are involved in a number of functions, including the sense of touch and the experience of one's own body in space and in movement. The functions of the **frontal lobes** include coordination of movement, attention, planning, social skills, conscience, abstract thinking, memory, and aspects of personality. The **temporal lobes** are important in audition and language. Some psychological functions are **lateralized**, or primarily processed by one hemisphere.

15. Cultural and environmental factors can modify not only behavior but also the structure of the brain.

Mind, Brain, and Gene

16. Environment and genes interact in staggeringly complex ways that psychologists are just beginning to understand. Psychologists interested in genetics study the way observable psychological attributes or qualities (**phenotypes**) reflect underlying genetic blueprints (**genotypes**). Studies in **behavioral genetics** suggest that a substantial portion of the variation among individuals on many psychological attributes such as intelligence and personality are **heritable**, that is, determined by genetic factors.

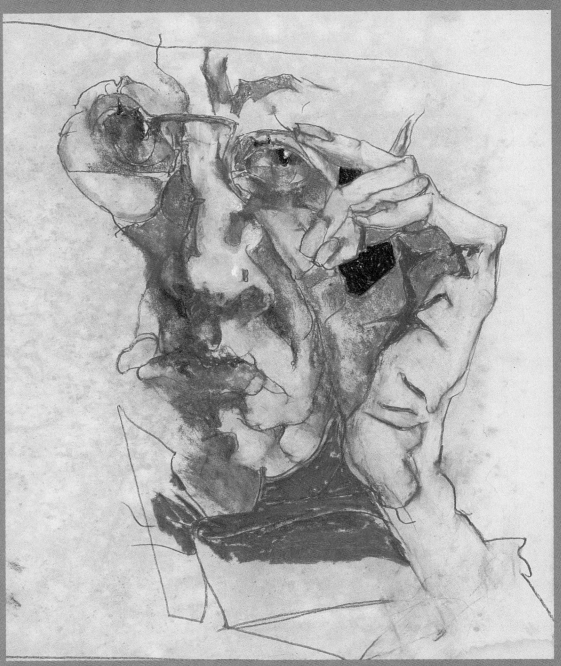

Horst Janssen, "Self-Portrait," Claude Bernard Gallery, Ltd.

Chapter 4

SENSATION AND PERCEPTION

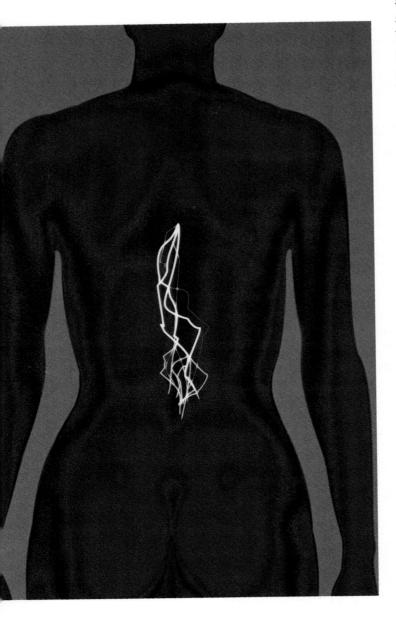

A woman in her early twenties damaged her knee in a fall. Following surgery, she experienced sharp, burning pain so excruciating that she could not eat or sleep, causing her to lose 20 pounds in four weeks. The pain ran from her ankle to the middle of her thigh, and the slightest touch—even a light brush with a piece of cotton—provoked a feeling of intense burning. Surgical attempts to relieve her pain led to no relief or to temporary relief followed by even more severe pain (Gracely et al., 1992). Tragically, her pain persisted indefinitely.

Another case had a happier ending. A 50-year-old man suffered from chronic lower back pain, and after unsuccessful attempts to treat it with exercise and medication, he underwent surgery. Like roughly 1 percent of patients who undergo this procedure (Sachs et al., 1990), he, too, developed severe burning pain and extraordinary sensitivity to any kind of stimulation of the skin. Fortunately, however, extensive physical therapy and other treatments led to elimination of the pain within three months.

These patients suffered from a disorder called **painful neuropathy** (which literally means a painful disorder, or pathology, of the neurons). Painful neuropathy can result from an accident or from surgery, but the effects are the same: The brain interprets signals from receptors in the skin or joints that normally indicate light touch, pressure, or movement as excruciating pain. Researchers are unclear whether the problem lies in the peripheral or the central nervous system. Physical trauma might cause a rewiring of peripheral nerves, so that they connect with the wrong sensory receptors and hence transmit an erroneous message to the brain. Alternatively, the brain may make a paradoxical adaptation to nerve damage by becoming hypersensitive to any stimulation of the affected region (Gracely et al., 1992).

Whether the damage is peripheral or central, this syndrome raises some intriguing questions about the way the nervous system translates information about the world into psychological experience. Does the intensity of sensory experience normally mirror the intensity of physical stimulation? In other words, when pain increases, or the light in a theater seems extremely bright following a movie, how much does this reflect changes in reality versus changes in our perception of reality? And if neurons can become accidentally rewired so that touch is misinterpreted as burning pain, could attaching neurons from the ear to the primary region of the occipital lobes produce visual images of sound?

These are some of the central questions underlying the study of sensation and perception. **Sensation** refers to the process by which the sense organs gather information about the environment. **Perception** is the closely related process by which the brain organizes and interprets these sensations. Sensations are immediate experiences of qualities (such as red or hot), whereas perceptions are always experiences of objects or events (Schiffman, 1990). To clarify the distinction, consider Figure 4.1. The photograph makes little sense until you recognize a Dalmatian, nose to the ground, walking toward a tree in the upper left corner. When people first look at this photo, their eyes transmit information to the brain about which parts of the picture are white and which are black; this is sensation. Sorting out the pockets of white and black into a meaningful picture is perception. The distinction is useful, although in reality it is somewhat artificial, since sensory and perceptual processes form an integrated whole (Zeki, 1992), translating physical reality into psychological reality.

We begin the chapter with sensation, exploring basic processes that apply to all **sensory modalities** (that is, the different senses that provide ways of knowing about stimuli). We then discuss each sense individually, focusing on the two senses that allow sensation at a distance (vision and audition, or hearing) and more briefly exploring olfaction (smell), gustation (taste), touch, and proprioception (the sense of the body's position and motion). Next we turn to perception. We start with the way the brain organizes sensations so that we see shapes rather than random patterns of light, depth rather than two dimensions, and constant forms rather than objects that seemingly change in size and shape as we approach them or view them from a different angle. We conclude by considering the role of interpretation in perception and the influence of experience, expectations,

FIGURE 4.1
From sensation to perception. Most people take several moments to make sense of this picture. While sensation occurs immediately, perception takes longer, requiring interpretation of patterns of white and black into the form of a Dalmatian.

and needs on the way people interpret sensory signals. Does a hamburger taste the same to someone who is starving as to someone who is sated? Does an X ray of a finger look different to a radiologist than to a layperson? And do people learn to organize sensations into meaningful three-dimensional shapes, or are fundamental perceptual processes innate?

BASIC PRINCIPLES

Throughout this discussion, three general principles repeatedly emerge. First, there is no one-to-one correspondence between physical and psychological reality. What is "out there" is not directly reproduced "in here." The relation between physical stimuli and the psychological experience of them is not, of course, random; it is quite orderly. Yet the inner world is not simply a photograph of the outer. The experience of patients with painful neuropathy is unusual, since brushing a ball of cotton against the skin should not produce the sensation of burning. However, even in normal people, the degree of pressure or pain experienced when a pin presses against the skin does not precisely match the actual pressure exerted. Up to a certain point, light pressure is not experienced at all, and pressure only feels like pain when it crosses a certain threshold. The inexact correspondence between physical and psychological reality is one of the fundamental findings of **psychophysics**, the branch of psychology that studies the relation between attributes of the physical world and our psychological experience of them.

Second, sensation and perception are active. Sensation may seem passive—images are cast on the retina at the back of the eye, pressure is imposed on the skin. Yet sensation is first and foremost an act of translation, converting external energy into an internal representation of it. Not only is the process of sensation itself inherently active, but the perceiver is active in another sense as well: People orient themselves to stimuli to capture sights, sounds, and smells that are relevant to them. We turn our ears toward potentially threatening sounds to magnify their impact on our senses, just as we turn our noses toward the smell of baking bread. We also selectively focus our consciousness on parts of the environment that are particularly relevant to our needs and goals (Chapter 9).

Like sensation, perception is an active process, which organizes and interprets sensations. The world as subjectively experienced by an individual—the **phenomenological world**—is a joint product of external reality and the person's creative efforts to understand and depict it mentally. People often assume that perception is analogous to photographing a scene or tape-recording a sound and that they need only open their eyes and ears to capture what is "really" there. In fact, perception is probably more like stitching a quilt than taking a photograph. The phenomenological world must be constructed, or synthesized from sensory experience. The quiltmaker creates something whole from pieces and patches.

If perception is a creative, constructive process, to what extent do people perceive the world in the same way? Does red appear to one person as it does to another? If one person loves garlic and another hates it, are the two loving and hating the same taste, or does garlic have a different taste to each? The constructive nature of perception raises the equally intriguing question of whether, or to what extent, people see the world as it really is. Plato argued that what we perceive is little more than shadows on the wall of a cave, cast by the movement of an unseen reality in the dim light. What does it mean to say that a cup of coffee is hot? And is grass *really* green? A person who is color-blind for green, whose visual system lacks the capacity to discriminate certain wavelengths of light, will not see the grass as green. Is greenness, then, an attribute of the object (grass), the perceiver, or some interaction between the observer and the observed? These are philosophical questions at the heart of sensation and perception.

The third general principle is that sensation and perception are adaptive. For humans as for other animals, sensation is the organism's point of contact with its surroundings. From an evolutionary perspective, the ability to see, hear, or touch is the product of millions of adaptations that left our senses exquisitely crafted to serve functions that facilitate survival and reproduction (Tooby & Cosmides, 1992). Frogs have "bug detectors" in their visual systems; rabbits have "hawk detectors." Similarly, human infants have an innate tendency to attend to forms that resemble the human face, and over the course of their first year they become remarkably expert at reading emotions from other people's faces (Chapter 13). Attending to parental facial cues (such as concern or fear) can mean the difference between approaching or escaping a predator, and it is crucial for adjusting to the social milieu.

The specific ways sensory systems are constructed reflects evolutionary pressures. Consider the placement of the eyes (Figure 4.2). Among vertebrates, the eyes can be placed frontally, as in humans, or laterally (on the sides), as in rabbits. Frontal placement is common in predators, who rely on sensory input from two eyes to pinpoint distance. Lateral placement is more common among animals who are frequently prey, for it provides them with an expanded field of vision. If they do not have eyes in the back of their head, at least they have something approximating it (Sekuler & Blake, 1994).

SENSING THE ENVIRONMENT

Although each sensory system is attuned to particular forms of energy, all sensory modalities share certain common features. First, they must translate physical stimulation into sensory signals. Second, they all have thresholds below which a person does not sense anything despite external stimulation. Children know this intuitively when they tiptoe through a room to "sneak up" on someone, who suddenly hears them and turns around. The tiptoeing sounds are continuous as the child approaches, but the person senses nothing until the sound crosses a threshold. Third, sensation, though seemingly effortless, requires constant decision making, as the individual tries to distinguish meaningful from irrelevant stimulation. Alone at night, people often wonder, "Did I hear something?" Their answers depend not only on the intensity of the sound but also on their propensity to impute meaning to small variations in sound. Fourth, sensing the world requires the ability to detect changes in stimulation, to notice when a bag of groceries has gotten heavier or a light has dimmed. Finally, efficient sensory processing means "turning down the volume" on information that is redundant; the nervous system tunes out messages that continue without change. We examine each of these processes in turn.

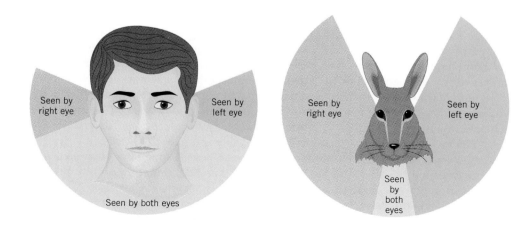

FIGURE 4.2
Eye placement and field of vision. Frontal placement of the eyes allows depth perception but reduces the field of vision. Lateral eye placement has the opposite result. Regardless of eye placement, animals expand their range of vision by moving their eyes and heads. SOURCE: Adapted from Sekuler & Blake, 1994, pp. 28-29.

FIGURE 4.3
Echolocation in the bat. Bats use echolocation to detect stimuli in the dark, such as insects. They send out pulses of sound waves and home in by sensing the echoes that bounce off their prey. As they prepare to intercept, they send out pulses at a more rapid rate to get the precise coordinates. SOURCE: *Griffin, 1959, p. 86.*

Transduction

Sensation requires converting energy in the world into internal signals that are psychologically meaningful. The more the brain processes these signals, from sensation to perception to cognition, the more meaningful they become. All sensation begins with an environmental stimulus, a form of energy capable of exciting the nervous system. We actually register only a tiny fraction of the energy surrounding us, and different species have developed the capacity to process different types of information. Honeybees can sense the Earth's magnetic field and essentially relocate important landmarks, such as places they have found food, by their compass coordinates (Collett & Baron, 1994). Bats are nocturnal creatures, but instead of relying on vision in darkness like cats, they "see with their ears," using a process called echolocation. Creatures using **echolocation** (such as bats, whales, and porpoises) obtain information about the size, location, and movement of objects by emitting waves of sound (mechanical energy that causes particles of air or water to vibrate) and sensing the echoes as these waves bounce off objects (Griffin, 1959; Schiffman, 1996). The ears and brains of bats evolved to detect very tiny air movements caused by echoes from small flying insects, upon which bats feed. As the bat approaches its prey, it emits faster pulses of sound to help it locate the insect in space (Figure 4.3). SONAR (sound navigation and ranging) uses similar principles to navigate the ocean. Instruments such as SONAR, or Geiger counters for detecting X-ray radiation, expand the range of the senses to detect energy for which they lack the sensitivity.

Specialized cells in the nervous system respond to different forms of energy and generate action potentials in adjacent sensory neurons. In the eye, for example, these cells respond to particles of light; in the ear, to the movement of molecules of air. The function of these specialized cells, called **receptors**, is to transform energy in the environment into neural impulses that can be interpreted by the brain (Loewenstein, 1960; Miller et al., 1961). The process of converting physical energy or stimulus information into neural impulses is called **transduction**.

The brain then interprets the impulses generated by sensory receptors as light, sound, smell, taste, touch, or motion. It essentially reads a neural code—a pattern of neural firing—and translates the code into a psychologically meaningful "language." In 1826, Johannes Müller proposed that whether a neural message is experienced as light, sound, or some other sensation results less from differences in stimuli than from the particular neurons excited by them. Müller's hypothesis, known as the **doctrine of specific nerve energies**, appears to be bolstered by reports of syndromes such as painful neuropathy, in which, as described earlier, a cotton ball can produce a sensation of burning instead of light touch because receptors presumably become rewired to different neural fibers. For each sense, discrete neural pathways normally carry sensory information to specific regions in the brain. Extending and revising Müller's doctrine, psychologists now recognize that the nature of a sensation depends on the parts of the brain it activates. Electrical stimulation of the primary visual cortex produces visual sensations as surely as shining a light in the eye, whereas stimulation of the auditory cortex produces sensations experienced as sound. The stimulus is the same—electrical current—but the pathways are different.

Within each sensory modality, the brain codes sensory stimulation for intensity and quality. The neural code for **intensity**, or strength, of a sensation varies by sensory modality but usually involves the number of sensory neurons that fire, the frequency with which each neuron fires, or some combination of the two (Chapter 3). The neural code for **quality**, or nature, of the sensation (such as color, pitch, taste, or temperature) is often more complicated, relying on both the specific type of receptors involved and the pattern of neural impulses generated. For example, some receptors respond to warmth and others to cold, but a combination of both leads to the sensation of extreme heat. Remarkably, the brain synthesizes millions of simple on/off decisions (made by sensory neurons that receive information from receptors and either fire or do not fire) to perceive the lines and shapes of a Cezanne landscape or words on a printed page. It does this so quickly and automatically that we are unaware of anything but the end product.

Absolute Thresholds

Even if a sensory system has the capacity to respond to a stimulus, the individual may not experience the stimulus if it is too weak. The minimum amount of physical energy needed for an observer to notice a stimulus is called an **absolute threshold**. One way psychologists measure absolute thresholds is by presenting a particular stimulus (light, sound, taste, odor, pressure) at varying intensities and determining the level of stimulation necessary for the person to detect it about 50 percent of the time. A psychologist trying to identify the absolute threshold for sound of a particular pitch would present subjects with sounds at that pitch, some so soft they would never hear them and others so loud they would never miss them. In between would be sounds they would hear some or most of the time. The volume at which most subjects heard the sound half the time but missed half the time would be defined as the absolute threshold; above this point, people sense stimulation most of the time. The absolute thresholds for many senses are remarkably low, such as a small flame burning 30 miles away on a clear night (Table 4.1).

Despite the "absolute" label, absolute thresholds are not constant values; they vary from person to person and situation to situation. One reason for this variation is the presence of **noise**, which, in its technical sense, refers to irrelevant, distracting information (not just to loud sounds). Some noise is external; to pick out the ticking of a watch at a concert is far more difficult than in a quiet room. Other noise is internal, created by the occasional random firing of neurons. Other factors affecting absolute thresholds include psychological states, such as experience, expectations, motivation, and level of fatigue (Harder et al., 1989; Singh, 1989). A person whose home has been burglarized, for example, is likely to be highly attuned to night-time sounds and to "hear" suspicious noises more readily, whether or not they actually occur.

Signal Detection

The ability to detect a stimulus in a background of noise is known as signal detection (Greene & Swets, 1966; Swets, 1992). According to **signal detection theory**, sensation is not a passive process that occurs when the amount of stimulation crosses a

TABLE 4.1 EXAMPLES OF ABSOLUTE THRESHOLDS	
SENSE	**THRESHOLD**
Vision	A flame 30 miles away on a dark, clear night
Hearing	A watch ticking 20 feet away in a quiet place
Smell	A drop of perfume in a six-room house
Taste	A teaspoon of sugar in two gallons of water
Touch	A wing of a fly falling on the cheek from a height of 1 centimeter

Source: Adapted from Brown et al., 1962.

critical threshold; rather, experiencing a sensation means making a *judgment* about whether a stimulus is present or absent. Does a noise downstairs, a blip on a radar screen, or a small irregularity on a brain scan signal something dangerous? According to signal detection theory, two distinct processes are at work in detection tasks. The first is an initial sensory process, reflecting the observer's **sensitivity** to the stimulus—how well the person sees, hears, or feels the stimulus. The second is a decision process, reflecting the observer's **response bias** (or **decision criterion**), which refers to the subject's readiness to report detecting a stimulus when uncertain.

To assess response bias, signal detection researchers present subjects with stimuli at low intensities, as in the traditional procedure for measuring absolute thresholds, but they add trials in which *no* stimulus is presented. What subjects experience on each trial is some mixture of stimulus energy (the signal), which may or may not be present, and noise, which randomly waxes and wanes. Sometimes the noise alone is enough to lead the subject to say she heard or saw something because its effect crosses the decision criterion. At other times, the signal is present but too weak to be detected, and the noise level is too low to augment it.

Subjects in signal detection experiments make two kinds of errors. They may respond with a false alarm, reporting a stimulus when none was presented, or they may miss, not reporting an actual stimulus. Similarly, subjects may give two kinds of correct response. They may hit, reporting an actual stimulus, or they may provide a correct negative, reporting no stimulus when none was presented. Accuracy in sensing a signal involves a tradeoff between sensitivity to stimuli that are presented and vulnerability to reporting stimuli that have not been presented. Thus, an observer who tends to overreport sensations will have a high number of hits but also a high number of false alarms, and an observer who tends to underreport will have a lower number of hits but also a lower number of false alarms.

Whether a person has a low or high response bias for reporting "yes" depends on many factors. One is expectations: If a patient complains of shooting pain in the extremities, heart pain, and shortness of breath, her doctor is more likely to hear an irregular heartbeat. Another factor that influences response bias is motivation. Two neurologists who review the MRI scan of a woman who is experiencing blinding headaches may come to different conclusions about a possible irregularity. The neurologist who recently lost a patient by mistaking a tumor for noise will have a low threshold for reporting "yes" because the psychological cost of setting it higher is too great. The other, who recently performed exploratory surgery when in fact no tumor was present and left the patient with partial paralysis, will have a much higher criterion for reporting "yes." To distinquish the relative contributions of sensivity and response bias, psychologists experimentally manipulate the costs and benefits of over- or underreporting stimulation (Figure 4.4).

Difference Thresholds

Thus far, we have focused on absolute thresholds, the lowest level of stimulation required to sense a stimulus. Above this threshold, another kind of threshold is the **difference threshold**—the lowest level of stimulation required to sense that a *change* in stimulation has occurred. To put it another way, the difference threshold is the difference in intensity between two stimuli necessary to produce a **just noticeable difference** (or **jnd**), such as the difference between two lightbulbs of slightly different wattage. The absolute threshold is actually a special case of the difference threshold, in which the difference is between no intensity and a very weak stimulus. As we have seen, absolute thresholds are generally extremely low, such as a drop of perfume in a six-room house.

Beyond the absolute threshold, however, the jnd depends not only on the intensity of the new stimulus but also on the level of stimulation already present. The more intense the existing stimulus, the larger the change must be to be noticeable.

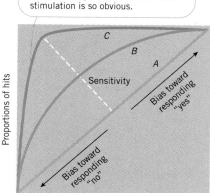

Note that at high stimulus intensities, a "no" response bias does not appreciably diminish the number of hits because presence or absence of stimulation is so obvious.

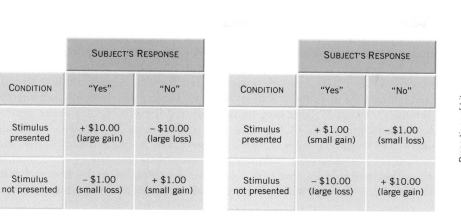

CONDITION	SUBJECT'S RESPONSE	
	"Yes"	"No"
Stimulus presented	+ $10.00 (large gain)	− $10.00 (large loss)
Stimulus not presented	− $1.00 (small loss)	+ $1.00 (small gain)

(*a*) Matrix that will produce a "yes" bias

CONDITION	SUBJECT'S RESPONSE	
	"Yes"	"No"
Stimulus presented	+ $1.00 (small gain)	− $1.00 (small loss)
Stimulus not presented	− $10.00 (large loss)	+ $10.00 (large gain)

(*b*) Matrix that will produce a "no" bias

(*c*) ROC curve

FIGURE 4.4

Signal detection. Psychologists alter response biases experimentally by changing the relative conse-
quences of making one type of error or the other. These differential consequences can be described in
a payoff matrix, which shows the costs and benefits of hitting and missing. Parts (a) and (b) contrast
two payoff matrices, one that leads to a "yes" bias and the other to a "no" bias, by paying subjects
different amounts for different types of correct or incorrect responses. To assess sensitivity to a stimu-
lus (c), researchers plot the proportion of hits against the proportion of misses on a receiver operating
characteristic curve (ROC curve), which literally shows the way the receiver operates under different
conditions. If the signal is so low that it is imperceptible, subjects will be as likely to hit as to miss
because their responses are essentially random. This situation is represented along the diagonal (line
A), where the proportion of hits equals the proportion of misses. At a somewhat higher stimulus
intensity (line B), subjects have a better hit-to-miss ratio because their responses are influenced by the
detectable presence or absence of the signal; they are no longer just guessing. At very high signal inten-
sities (line C), people rarely give wrong answers. The sensitivity of the observer to different signal
intensities is thus represented by the dotted line, which shows how far the subject's ROC curve
diverges from the diagonal, which represents chance responding.

A person carrying a 2-pound backpack will easily notice the addition of a half-pound book, but adding the same book to a 60-pound backpack will not make the pack feel any heavier—that is, it will not produce a just noticeable difference.

In 1834, the German physiologist Ernst Weber recognized not only this lack of a one-to-one relationship between the physical and psychological worlds but also the existence of a consistent relationship between them. Regardless of the magnitude of two stimuli, the second must differ by a constant proportion from the first for it to be perceived as different. In other words, as the magnitude of a stimulus increases, additional stimulation must be correspondingly larger for the person to recognize a change. This relationship is called **Weber's law**, which can be expressed mathematically as

$$\Delta I \,/\, I \,=\, k,$$

where I = the intensity of the stimulus, ΔI = the increment of intensity necessary to produce a jnd at that intensity, and k = a constant.

To put it still another way, the ratio of change in intensity to initial intensity required to produce a jnd—expressed as a fraction, such as one unit/ten units—is a constant for a given sensory modality. This constant, known as a **Weber fraction**, varies depending on the individual, context, stimulus, and sensory modality. For example, the Weber fraction for perceiving changes in brightness is 1/60. This means that the average person can perceive an increment of one candle added to 60 but requires two candles if 120 are already present, 3 if 180 are present, and so forth, to produce a jnd. The Weber fraction for a sound of middle pitch is 1/10, so a person can hear an extra voice in a chorus of 10 but would require two voices to notice an increase in loudness in a chorus of 20. Over 150 years ago, Weber was thus hot on the trail of the relation between reality and psychological experience.

Weber's brother-in-law, Gustav Fechner, was an intellectual jack of many trades and founder of psychophysics. Fechner (1860) broadened the application of Weber's law by linking the subjective experience of intensity of stimulation with the actual magnitude of a stimulus. He assumed that for any given stimulus, all jnds are created equal; that is, each additional jnd feels subjectively like one incremental unit in intensity. Using Weber's law, he then plotted these subjective units against the actual incremental units of stimulus intensity necessary to produce each jnd (Figure 4.5). The result was a logarithmic function, which simply means that as one variable (in this case, subjective intensity) increases arithmetically (1, 2, 3, and so forth), the other variable (in this case, objective intensity) increases geometrically (60, 120, 180, etc.). **Fechner's law** thus held that the subjective magnitude of a sensation (S) grows as a proportion (k) of the logarithm of the objective intensity of the stimulus (I), or

$$S = k \log I.$$

This means that people experience only a small percentage of actual increases in stimulus intensity, but this percentage is predictable. Thus, knowing the Weber constant and the intensity of the stimulus, a psychologist can predict the perceived intensity of a subject's sensation, which is truly remarkable.

Fechner's law held up for a century but was modified by S. S. Stevens (1961, 1975) because it did not apply to all stimuli and sensory modalities. For example, the relation between perceived pain and stimulus intensity is the opposite of most other psychophysical relations: The greater the pain, the *less* incremental intensity is required for a jnd. This makes adaptive sense, since increasing pain means increasing danger and should thus demand increasing attention. In part on a dare from a colleague (Stevens, 1956), Stevens set out to prove that people can accurately rate subjective intensity on a numerical scale. He instructed subjects to listen to a series of tones of differing intensity and asked them simply to assign numbers to the tones to indicate their relative loudness. What he discovered was a lawful relation between the self-reports and stimulus intensity across a much wider range of sensory modes and intensities than Fechner's law could accommodate.

Stevens's power law states that subjective intensity (S) grows as a proportion (k) of the actual intensity (I) raised to some power (b). Expressed mathematically,

$$S = k I^b.$$

FIGURE 4.5
Fechner's law. According to Fechner's law, as subjective units of sensation increase by increments of one, objective units increase geometrically (that is, by a factor of more than one), leading to a logarithmic curve.
Source: *Adapted from Guilford, 1954, p. 38.*

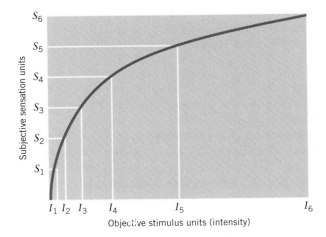

In other words, as perceived intensity grows arithmetically, the actual magnitude of a stimulus grows exponentially—that is, by some power (squared, cubed, etc.). The exponent varies, however, for different senses, just as the Weber fraction varies. Where the exponent is less than one (for example, for brightness it is .33), the results are usually similar to Fechner's law. Where the exponent is larger than one, however, as is the case for sensations produced by electric shock (where the exponent is 3.5), the magnitude of sensations grows quite rapidly as stimulation increases (Figure 4.6). Thus, Stevens's power law can predict subjective experiences of pain intensity as readily as brightness.

Although the formulas have become more precise, the take-home message from Weber, Fechner, and Stevens is basically the same: Sensation bears a relation to physical stimulation, and the relation is orderly and predictable, but psychological experience is not a photograph, tape recording, or wax impression of external reality.

Sensory Adaptation

A final process shared by all sensory systems is called adaptation. You walk into a crowded restaurant, and the noise level is overwhelming, yet within a few minutes, you do not even notice it. Driving into an industrial city, you notice an unpleasant odor that smells like sulfur and wonder how anyone tolerates it, but a short time later, you are no longer aware of it. These are examples of **sensory adaptation**, the tendency of sensory systems to respond less to stimuli that continue without change. From an evolutionary perspective, sensory adaptation makes sense. When constant sensory inputs provide no new information about the environment, the nervous system ignores them. Given all the stimuli with which an organism is bombarded at any particular moment, a creature that paid as much notice to constant stimulation as to changes that might be adaptively significant would be at a disadvantage.

Although sensory adaptation generally applies across senses, the nervous system is wired to circumvent it in some important instances. The visual system has ways to keep its receptors from adapting; otherwise, stationary objects in a person's field of vision would disappear from sight. The eyes are constantly moving, making tiny quivering motions, which guarantees that different receptors are always being stimulated. Similarly, although we may adapt to mild pain, we generally do not adapt to severe pain (Miller & Kraus, 1990), which again makes evolutionary sense.

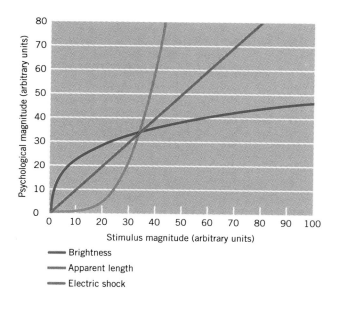

FIGURE 4.6
Stevens's power law. Stevens's power law plots subjective magnitude of stimulation as an exponential function of stimulus magnitude. Here, these functions are shown for brightness (where the exponent is .33), apparent length (where the exponent is 1.0, so the function is linear), and electric shock (where the exponent is 3.5). SOURCE: *Stevens, 1961, p. 11.*

VISION

We will use vision as our major example of sensory processes because it is the best understood of the senses. We begin by discussing the form of energy (light) transduced by the visual system. We then examine the organ responsible for transduction (the eye) and trace the neural pathways that take raw information from receptors and convert it into sensory knowledge. We also consider the mechanisms by which the sensory organ (eye) and the brain code stimulus energy into qualities (in this case, color) that allow objects to be distinguished from other objects in the environment and identified.

The Nature of Light

Light is just one form of electromagnetic radiation, the form to which the eye is sensitive. Other forms of electromagnetic radiation to which we are blind include infrared, ultraviolet, radio, and X-ray radiation. Electromagnetic energy travels in waves, created by the oscillation of electrically charged particles. Different forms of radiation have waves of different lengths, or **wavelengths**, which means simply that their particles oscillate with more or less frequency. Some of these wavelengths, such as gamma rays, are as short as the diameter of an atom; others are quite long, such as radio waves, which may oscillate once in a mile. Wavelengths are measured in **nanometers (nm)**, that is, billionths of a meter (Figure 4.7). The physical dimension of wavelength translates into the psychological dimension of color, just as the physical intensity of light is related to the subjective sensation of brightness.

The reason we are sensitive only to some forms of electromagnetic radiation is that the receptors in the eye are tuned to detect only a very restricted portion of the electromagnetic spectrum, ranging from roughly 380 to 750 nm. Other organisms are sensitive to different regions of the spectrum. Bees and iguanas see ultraviolet light, and rattlesnakes use infrared radiation to track prey (Alberts, 1989; Backhaus, 1992; Newman & Hartline, 1982).

Light is a useful form of energy to sense for a number of reasons (Sekuler & Blake, 1994). Like other forms of electromagnetic radiation, light travels very quickly (186,000 miles, or roughly 300,000 kilometers, per second), so sighted organisms can see things almost immediately after they happen. Light also travels in straight lines, which means that it preserves the geometric organization of the objects it illuminates; the image an object casts on the retina resembles its actual structure. Perhaps most importantly, light interacts with the molecules on the sur-

FIGURE 4.7

The electromagnetic spectrum. Humans sense only a small portion of the electromagnetic spectrum (enlarged in the figure), light. Light at different wavelengths is experienced as different colors.

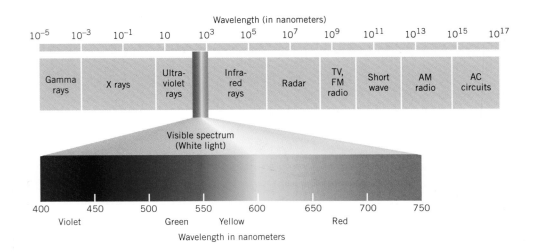

face of many objects and is either absorbed or reflected. The light that is reflected reaches the eyes and creates a visual pattern. Objects that reflect a lot of light appear light, whereas those that absorb much of the light that hits them appear dark.

The Eye

Two basic processes occur in the eyes (Figure 4.8). First, the cornea, pupil, and lens focus light on the retina. Then the retina transduces this visual image into neural impulses that are relayed to and interpreted by the brain.

Focusing Light

Light enters the eye through the **cornea**, a tough, transparent tissue covering the front of the eyeball. Under water, people cannot see clearly because the cornea is constructed to bend, or refract, light rays traveling through air, not water. That is why a diving mask allows clearer vision: It puts a layer of air between the water and the cornea (Sekuler & Blake, 1994).

From the cornea, light passes through a chamber of fluid known as the **aqueous humor**, which supplies oxygen and other nutrients to the cornea and lens, much as blood does to other structures of the body. Unlike blood, however, the fluid in the aqueous humor is clear, so light can pass through it. Next, light travels through an opening in the center of the **iris** (the pigmented tissue that gives the eye its blue, green, or brown color); this opening is the **pupil**. Muscle fibers in the iris cause the pupil to constrict or dilate to regulate the amount of light entering the eye, much as the f-stop aperture regulates the amount of light entering a camera. The size of the pupil also changes with different autonomic states, such as fear, excitement, and sexual arousal. Experienced gamblers (and perhaps Don Juans) can use pupil size to read other people's emotional states (Hess, 1965).

The next step in focusing light occurs in the **lens**, an elastic, disc-shaped structure about the size of a lima bean. Muscles attached to the lens stretch and relax the lens to focus on objects at various distances. The lens flattens for distant objects and becomes more spherical for closer objects, a process known as **accommodation**. The light is then projected through the **vitreous humor** (a clear, gelatinous liquid) onto the **retina**, a light-sensitive layer of tissue at the back of the eye. The retina receives a constant flow of images as people turn their heads and eyes or move through space.

Abnormalities in the eye sometimes make accommodation difficult, affecting **visual acuity**, or sharpness of the image. Since lightwaves normally diverge, or spread out over a distance, the eye has to focus them on a single point in the retina to produce a clear image. **Nearsightedness**, or **myopia**, occurs when the cornea and lens focus this image in front of the retina; by the time rays of light reach the retina, they have begun to cross, leading to a blurred image (Figure 4.9). The opposite occurs in **farsightedness**, or **hyperopia**. The eye focuses light on a point beyond the

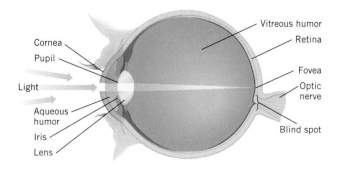

FIGURE 4.8
Anatomy of the human eye. The cornea, pupil, and lens focus a pattern of light onto the retina, which then transduces the retinal image into neural signals carried to the brain by the optic nerve.

FIGURE 4.9
Normal vision, nearsightedness, and farsightedness. In (a), the cornea and lens focus the image on the retina, producing normal vision. In (b), the image is focused in front of the retina (myopia), whereas in (c), it is focused behind the retina (hyperopia).

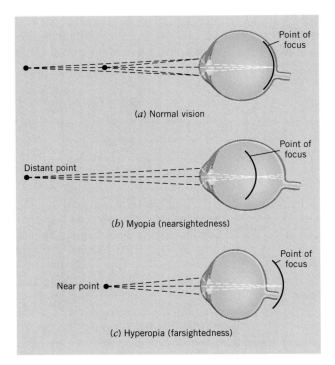

retina, leading to decreased acuity at close range. Both abnormalities are common at all ages and usually are readily corrected with lenses that alter the optics of the eye. With advancing age, however, losses in visual acuity become more pronounced. The lens becomes more opaque and loses some of its ability to accommodate (Fukada et al., 1990), and the diameter of the pupil shrinks so that less light reaches the retina. Cataracts, which are common in older people, occur when the lens becomes so opaque that the person becomes almost blind. As a result of age-related changes, the retina of a normal 65 year old receives only about one-third as much light as that of a 20 year old (Kline & Schieber, 1985).

The Retina

The eye is like a camera insofar as it has an opening to adjust the amount of incoming light, a lens to focus light, and the equivalent of a photosensitive film—the retina. (The analogy is incomplete, however, because the eye, unlike a camera, works best when it is moving; it takes motion pictures rather than stills.) The retina transduces light energy into neural impulses, transforming a pattern of light reflected off objects into psychologically meaningful information.

Structure of the Retina   The retina is a multi-layered structure about as thick as a sheet of paper (Figure 4.10). The innermost layer (at the back of the retina) contains two types of light receptors, or **photoreceptors** ("photo" is from the Greek word for light), called **rods** and **cones**, which are so named for their appearance. Each retina contains approximately 120 million rods and 8 million cones. When a rod or cone absorbs light energy, it generates an electrical signal, stimulating the neighboring **bipolar cells**. These cells in turn combine the information from many receptors and excite **ganglion cells**, which integrate information from multiple bipolar cells. The long axons of these ganglion cells bundle together to form the **optic nerve**, which carries visual information to the brain.

The lens focuses light most directly on the central region of the retina, the **fovea**, which is most sensitive to small detail and thus provides maximal visual acuity for

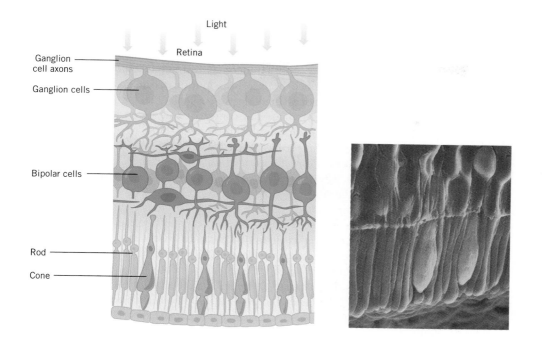

Light

Retina

Ganglion cell axons

Ganglion cells

Bipolar cells

Rod

Cone

FIGURE 4.10
The retina. Light passes through layers of neurons to reach photoreceptors, called rods and cones, which respond to different wavelengths of light. These receptors in turn connect to bipolar cells, which pass information to the ganglion cells, whose axons form the optic nerve. The photo shows rods and cones magnified thousands of times. Above them are bipolar cells.

stimuli directly in sight. In contrast, the point on the retina where the optic nerve leaves the eye, the **optic disk** (or **blind spot**), has no receptor cells (Figure 4.11). Generally, people are unaware of their blind spots. Different images usually fall on the blind spots of the two eyes, so one eye sees what the other does not. In addition, the eyes are always moving, providing information about the missing area. The visual system is also wired to ignore the blind spot; the brain automatically uses visual information from the rest of the retina to fill in the gap.

Rods and Cones Rods and cones have distinct functions. Rods are more sensitive to light than cones, allowing vision in dim light. The images produced by rods are in black, white, and gray. Cones are specialized for color vision, but they require more light to be activated, which is why we see little or no color in dim light. Nocturnal animals, such as owls, tend to have mostly rods, whereas daytime animals, and most other birds, have mostly cones (Schiffman, 1996). Humans see both in black-and-white and in color, depending on the amount of light.

FIGURE 4.11
The blind spot. Close your right eye, fix your gaze on the circle, and slowly move the book toward and away from you. The plus sign will disappear when it falls in the blind spot of the left retina.

Rods and cones also differ in their distribution on the retina and their connections to bipolar cells. Cones are concentrated in the center of the retina, in the fovea. Thus, in bright light an object is seen best if looked at directly, focusing the image on the fovea. A single cone may connect with a single bipolar cell. This allows perception of fine detail, since precise information from each cone is preserved and passed on for higher processing.

In contrast, rods are concentrated off the center of the retina. Thus, in dim light, objects are seen most clearly by looking slightly away from them, focusing the image away from the center of the retina. (You can test this yourself tonight by looking at the stars. Fix your eyes directly on a bright star and then focus your gaze slightly off to the side of it. The star will appear brighter when the image is cast away from the fovea.) Furthermore, a single bipolar cell may receive information from many rods. Thus, a bipolar cell can be activated by many different rods or combinations of rods, so that the resulting image is not very precise. On the other hand, the sum of the energy collected by many rods can easily cause an action potential in sensory neurons excited by them, so these cells will fire in very dim light.

How do photoreceptors transform light into sight? Both rods and cones contain photosensitive pigments that change chemical structure, or bleach, in response to light (Rushton, 1962; Wald, 1968). The process is called **bleaching** because photoreceptors are normally pigmented, but this pigment breaks down when exposed to light, leading to loss of their characteristic color. This chemical change in the photoreceptors then triggers action potentials in the bipolar cells connected to them.

Bleaching must, however, be reversed before a photoreceptor is restored to full sensitivity. Pigment regeneration takes time, which is why people often have to feel their way around the seats when entering a dark theater on a bright day. Adjusting to a dimly illuminated setting is called **dark adaptation**. The cones adapt relatively quickly, usually within about five minutes, depending on the duration and intensity of light to which the eye was previously exposed. Rods, in contrast, take about fifteen minutes to adapt, and since they are especially useful in dim light, vision may remain less than optimal in the theater for several minutes. **Light adaptation**, the process of adjusting to bright light after exposure to darkness, is much faster; readapting to bright sunlight upon leaving a theater takes only about a minute (Matlin, 1983).

Receptive Fields   Once the rods and cones have responded to patterns of light, the nervous system must somehow convert these patterns into a neural code to allow the brain to reconstruct the image. This is done by the ganglion cells. Each ganglion cell has a **receptive field**, a region within which a neuron responds to appropriate stimulation, such as a particular section of the retina (Hartline, 1938). Unless a stimulus falls within its receptive field, a neuron will not fire. Neurons at higher levels of the visual system (that is, in the brain) also have receptive fields, as do neurons in other sensory systems.

Psychologists have learned about the receptive fields of ganglion cells and the neurons in the brain to which they pass information through a technique called single cell recording. In **single cell recording**, researchers insert a tiny electrode into the brain of a cat, monkey, or other animal close enough to a neuron to detect when it fires. Then, holding the animal's head still, they flash light to different parts of the visual field to see what kind of stimulation is required for the ganglion cell to fire. By placing electrodes in many places, psychologists can map the receptive fields of ganglion cells.

Using this method, researchers discovered that these receptive fields have a center and a surrounding area, like a target (Figure 4.12). For some ganglion cells, presenting light to the center of the receptive field turns the cell "on" (that is, produces repeated firing), whereas presenting light within the receptive field but outside the center turns the cell "off." For other ganglion cells the pattern is just the opposite: Light in the center inhibits neural firing, whereas light in the periphery excites the

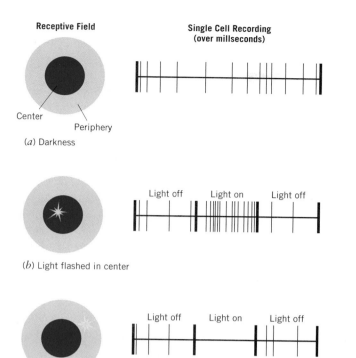

(a) Darkness

(b) Light flashed in center

(c) Light flashed in periphery

FIGURE 4.12
Single cell recording. In (a), the neuron spontaneously fires occasionally in darkness. In (b), it fires repeatedly when light is flashed to the center of its receptive field. In (c), firing stops when light is flashed in the periphery of its receptive field; that is, light outside the center inhibits firing.
SOURCE: *Adapted from Sekuler & Blake, 1994, p. 68.*

neuron.   This antagonistic relationship between stimulation of the center and periphery of the receptive field is called **lateral inhibition.** Lateral inhibition is responsible in part for the phenomenon seen in **Hermann grids** (Figure 4.13), in which the intersections of white lines in a dark grid appear gray, and the intersections of black lines in a white grid appear gray (Spillman, 1994). Essentially, white surrounded by black on four corners appears whiter than white surrounded by black on only two sides, and vice versa. Similar contrast effects can be seen in Figure 4.14.

Why do receptive fields have this concentric circular organization, with on and off regions that inhibit each other? As described at the beginning of the chapter, our sensory systems are attuned to changes and differences. The concentric organization of ganglion cells allows humans and other animals to perceive edges and changes in brightness and texture that signal where one surface ends and another begins. A neuron that senses light in its center but not in its periphery will fire

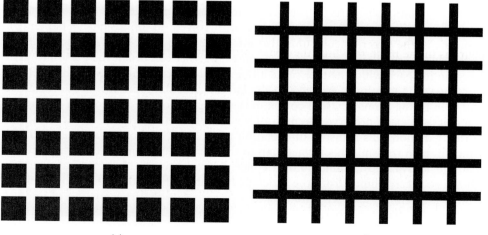

(a)   (b)

Hermann grids. White lines against a black grid appear to have gray patches at their intersections (a), whereas black lines against a white grid appear to have slightly whiter patches at their intersections (b).

FIGURE 4.13

FIGURE 4.14
Contrast effects. Gray against a light background appears darker than the same shade against a dark background because of lateral inhibition.

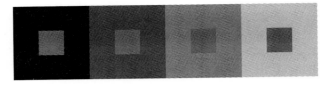

rapidly if the light is bright and covers much of the center. If light is also present in the periphery of the receptive field, however, this will inhibit neural firing, essentially transmitting the information that the image is continuous in this region of space, with no edges.

The receptive fields of neurons in the fovea tend to be very small, allowing perception of very small objects, whereas receptive fields increase in size with distance from the center of the retina (Wiesel & Hubel, 1960). This is why looking straight at the illusory patches of darkness or lightness in Hermann grids makes them disappear: Receptive fields of neurons in the fovea can be so small that the middle of each line is surrounded by the same shade for the vast majority of neurons regardless of whether it is at an intersection.

Neural Pathways

Transduction in the eye, then, starts with the focusing of images onto the retina. When photoreceptors bleach in response, they excite bipolar cells, which in turn trigger action potentials in ganglion cells with particular receptive fields. The axons from these ganglion cells comprise the optic nerve, which transmits information from the retina to the brain.

From the Eye to the Brain

Impulses from the optic nerve first pass through the **optic chiasm** ("chiasm" comes from the Greek word for "cross"), where the optic nerve splits (Figure 4.15). Information from the left half of each retina (which comes from the right visual field) goes to the left hemisphere and vice versa. Once past the optic chiasm, combined information from the two eyes travels to the brain via the **optic tracts**, which are simply a continuation of the axons from ganglion cells that constitute the optic nerve. From there, visual information flows along two separate pathways within each hemisphere. One small pathway projects to a clump of neurons in the midbrain known as the **superior colliculus**. In less complex animals, this is the primary vision center; in more complex creatures, such as humans, the cerebral cortex eclipsed that role through evolution. The superior colliculus in humans is involved in controlling eye movements. Its neurons respond to the presence or absence of visual stimulation in parts of the visual field but cannot identify specific objects; thus, this second pathway appears to be involved in blindsight (Chapter 3). Neurons in the superior colliculus also integrate input from the eyes and the ears, so that weak stimulation from the two senses together can orient the person toward a region in space which neither sense alone could detect (Stein & Meredith, 1990).

The second pathway projects to the **lateral geniculate nucleus** of the thalamus and then to the primary visual cortex in the occipital lobes. Neurons in the lateral geniculate nucleus preserve the map of visual space in the retina. That is, neighboring ganglion cells transmit information to thalamic neurons next to each other, which in turn transmit this retinal map to the cortex. Neurons in the lateral geniculate nucleus have the same kind of concentric receptive fields as retinal neurons. They also receive input from the reticular formation; thus, the extent to which an animal is attentive, aroused, and awake may modulate the transmission of impulses from the thalamus to the visual cortex (Burke & Cole, 1978; Harth, 1985; Humphrey & Saul, 1992).

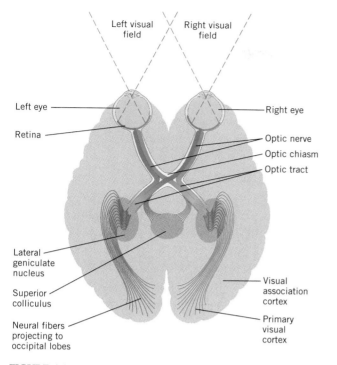

Left visual field

Right visual field

Left eye

Right eye

Retina

Optic nerve

Optic chiasm

Optic tract

Lateral geniculate nucleus

Superior colliculus

Visual association cortex

Neural fibers projecting to occipital lobes

Primary visual cortex

FIGURE 4.15

Visual pathways. The optic nerve carries visual information from the retina to the optic chiasm, where the optic nerve splits. The brain processes information from the right visual field in the left hemisphere and vice versa because of the way some visual information crosses and some does not cross over to the opposite hemisphere at the optic chiasm. The optic tract then carries information to the lateral geniculate nucleus of the thalamus, where neurons project to the primary occipital cortex. A small pathway from the optic tract carries information simultaneously to the superior colliculus.

Visual Cortex

From the lateral geniculate nucleus, visual information travels to the primary visual cortex in the occipital lobes. The cortex does not give "equal time" to all regions of the visual field. In fact, much of the primary visual cortex is devoted to information from the fovea (Drasdo, 1977), just as the somatosensory cortex in the parietal lobes overrepresents regions such as the hands which have many receptors and transmit especially important information (Chapter 3). Whereas neurons in the retina and lateral geniculate nucleus respond to edges and differences in texture or light intensity, neurons in the primary cortex analyze more complex information. The mechanisms through which they do this were discovered by David Hubel and Thorsten Wiesel (1959, 1979), who won a Nobel Prize for their efforts.

Hubel and Wiesel discovered **feature detectors** in the cortex, neurons that fire only when stimulation in their receptive field matches a particular pattern or orientation. **Simple cells** are feature detectors that respond most vigorously to lines of a specific orientation, such as horizontal or vertical, in an exact location in the visual field (Figure 4.16). **Complex cells** are feature detectors that generally cover a larger receptive field and respond when a stimulus of the proper orientation falls anywhere within their receptive field, not just at a particular location. They may also fire only when the stimulus moves in a particular direction. Still other cells, called **hypercomplex cells**, require that a stimulus be of a specific size or length to fire. Other neurons in the visual cortex respond selectively to color, contrast, and texture (Livingstone & Hubel, 1988).

FIGURE 4.16
Feature detectors. A simple cell that responds to vertical lines will show more rapid firing the closer a visual image in its receptive field matches its preferred orientation. SOURCE: *Sekuler & Blake, 1994, p. 119.*

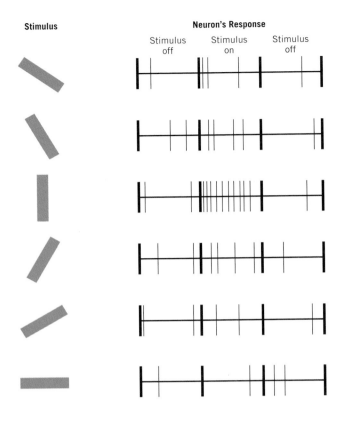

Neurons from the primary visual cortex project to association cortex in the occipital lobes, where specialized neural modules simultaneously attend to features such as form, color, and motion (Zeki, 1992). These modules then connect with each other and with information from other senses to allow identification of objects and their functions.

Perceiving in Color

"Roses are red, violets are blue...." Well, not exactly. Color is a psychological property, not a quality of the stimulus. Grass is not green to a cow or a dog because these animals lack color receptors; in contrast, most insects, reptiles, fish, and birds have excellent color vision (Nathans, 1987). As Sir Isaac Newton demonstrated in research with prisms in the sixteenth century, white light (such as sunlight and light from incandescent lamps) is composed of all the wavelengths that constitute the colors in the visual spectrum. A rose appears red because it absorbs certain wavelengths and reflects others, and humans have receptors that detect electromagnetic radiation in that range of the spectrum.

Actually, color has three psychological dimensions: hue, brightness, and saturation. **Hue** is what people commonly mean by color, that is, whether an object appears blue, red, violet, and so on. **Brightness** refers to a color's intensity, whereas **saturation** is its purity (the extent to which it is diluted with white or black or "saturated" with its own wavelength, like a sponge in water). People of all cultures perceive the same colors or hues, although cultures vary widely in the number and specificity of their color labels (Chapter 7).

Retinal Transduction of Color

How does the visual system translate wavelength into the subjective experience of color? The first step in transduction of color occurs in the retina, where cones with different photosensitive pigments respond to wavelengths of varying frequencies. In 1802, a British physician named Thomas Young proposed that human color vision is trichromatic—that is, that the colors we see reflect blends of three colors to which our retinas are sensitive. Modified 50 years later by Hermann von Helmholtz, the **Young-Helmholtz** (or **trichromatic**) **theory of color** holds that the eye contains three types of receptors, each maximally sensitive to wavelengths of light that produce sensations of blue, green, or red.

Another century later, Nobel Prize winner George Wald and others confirmed experimentally the existence of three different types of cones in the retina (Brown & Wald, 1964; Dartnall et al., 1983; Schnapf et al., 1989). Each cone responds to a range of wavelengths but fires most persistently at a particular point on the spectrum (Figure 4.17). Short-wavelength cones (S-cones) are maximally sensitive to wavelengths of about 450 nm, which are perceived as blue. Middle-wavelength cones (M-cones), which produce the sensation of green, are most sensitive to wavelengths of about 525 nm. Long-wavelength cones (L-cones), which produce red sensations, are most sensitive to wavelengths of about 555 nm (Brown & Wald, 1964). Mixing these three primary colors of light—red, green, and blue—produces the roughly one thousand color shades humans can discriminate.

This list of primary colors differs from the list of primary colors children learn in elementary school from mixing paints (blue, red, and yellow) because mixing paint and mixing light alter the wavelengths perceived in different ways, one subtracting and the other adding parts of the spectrum. Mixing paints is called **subtractive color mixture** because each new paint added actually blocks out, or subtracts, wavelengths reflected onto the retina. For example, yellow paint appears yellow because its pigment absorbs most wavelengths and reflects only those perceived as yellow; the same is true of blue paint. When blue and yellow paints are mixed, only the wavelengths that fall between blue and yellow are reflected, which people perceive as green.

Subtractive color mixture mixes colors before they reach the eye. In contrast, **additive color mixture** takes place in the eye itself, as light of differing wavelengths simultaneously strikes the retina and thus expands (adds to) rather than contracts the perceived section of the spectrum. Newton discovered additive color mixture by using two prisms to funnel two colors simultaneously into the eye. Color television works on an additive principle. A television picture is composed of minute blue, green, and red dots, which the eye blends from a distance. When struck by an elec-

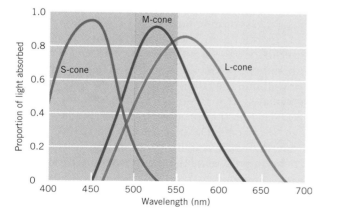

FIGURE 4.17

Cone response curves. All three kinds of cones respond to a range of frequencies—that is, they absorb light waves of many lengths, which contributes to bleaching—but they are maximally sensitive at particular frequencies and thus produce different color sensations.

The Impressionists made heavy use of additive color mixture, as in this painting of Venice by the French painter Paul Signac.

tron beam inside the set, the spots light up. From a distance, the spots combine to produce multicolored images (although the dots can be seen at very close range).

Processing of Color in the Brain

The trichromatic theory accurately predicted the nature of retinal receptors, but it had its limits. For example, the physiologist Ewald Hering noted that trichromatic theory offered no explanation for a peculiar phenomenon that occurs with **afterimages**, visual images that persist after a stimulus has been removed. Hering wondered why the colors of the afterimage were different in predictable ways from those of the original image (Figure 4.18).

Why does this occur? Hering (1878, 1920) proposed a theory, subsequently modified substantially by other researchers, known as opponent-process theory (DeValois, 1975; Hurvich & Jameson, 1957). **Opponent-process theory** argues that all colors are derived from three antagonistic color systems: black-white, blue-yellow, and red-green. The black-white system contributes to brightness and saturation, whereas the other two systems are responsible for hue.

Hering proposed his theory in opposition to trichromatic theory, but subsequent research suggests that the two theories are complementary. Trichromatic theory applies to the retina, whereas opponent-process theory applies at higher visual centers in the brain. Researchers have found that some neurons in the lateral geniculate nucleus of monkeys (whose visual system is similar to that of humans) are **color-opponent cells**, excited by wavelengths that produce one color but inhibited by wavelengths of the other member of the pair (DeValois & DeValois, 1975). For example, some red-green neurons increase their activity when wavelengths experienced as red are in their receptive fields and decrease their activity when exposed to green; others are excited by green and inhibited by red. Psychologists now recognize that the pattern of activation of several color-opponent neurons together determines the color experienced (Abramov & Gordon, 1994).

Opponent-process theory neatly explains afterimages, which result from a rebound effect in color-opponent cells. Recall that across sensory modalities, the sensory system adapts, or responds less, to constant stimulation. In the visual system, adaptation begins with bleaching in the retina. Photoreceptors take time to resynthesize their photoreceptive pigments once they have bleached and cannot fire

FIGURE 4.18
*Afterimage. Stare at the yellow and red globe for three minutes, centering
your eyes on the white dot in the middle, and then look at the white space
on the page to the right of it. The afterimage is the traditional blue and
green globe, reflecting the operation of antagonistic color-opponent cells in
the lateral geniculate nucleus.*

continuously in response to constant stimulation. Thus, staring at a stimulus of one
color leads to adaptation to it, facilitating sensation of its opponent color. The
afterimage of yellow therefore appears blue (and vice versa), red appears green, and
black appears white.

Opponent-process theory also explains another phenomenon that interested
Hering: color-blindness (or, more accurately, color deficiency). Few people are
entirely blind to color; those who are (because of genetic abnormalities that leave
them with only one kind of cone) can only detect brightness, not color. Most color-
deficient people confuse red and green (Figure 4.19). Red-green color-blindness is

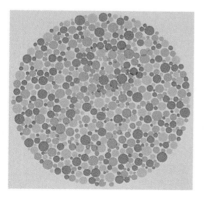

FIGURE 4.19
*Color-blindness. In this common test for color-blindness, a green 3 is pre-
sented against a background of orange and yellow dots. The pattern of
stimulation normally sent to the lateral geniculate nucleus by S-, M-, and L-
cones allows discrimination of these colors. People who are red-green
color-blind see only a random array of dots.*

sex-linked, about 10 times more prevalent in males than females, and generally reflects a deficiency of either M-cones or L-cones, which makes red-green distinctions impossible at higher levels of the nervous system (Weale, 1982; Wertenbaker, 1981).

HEARING

If a tree falls in a forest, does it make a sound if no one hears it? To answer this question requires an understanding of hearing, or **audition**, and the physical qualities it reflects. Like vision, hearing allows sensation from a distance and is thus of tremendous adaptive value. Hearing also allows the richest form of communication, spoken language. As with our discussion of vision, we begin by considering the stimulus energy underlying hearing, sound. Next we examine the organ that transduces it, the ear, and the neural pathways for auditory processing.

The Nature of Sound

When a tree falls in the forest, the crash produces vibrations in adjacent air molecules, which in turn collide with each other. A guitar string being plucked, a piece of paper rustling, or a tree falling to the ground all produce sound because they create vibrations in the air. Like ripples on a pond, these rhythmic pulsations of acoustic energy (sound) spread outward from the vibrating object as **sound waves**. Sound waves grow weaker as their distance increases from the original disturbance, but they travel at a constant speed, roughly 1130 feet (or 340 meters) per second. Because sound travels more slowly than light, fans in center field sometimes hear the crack of a bat after seeing the batter hit the ball, whereas the difference between the speed of light and the speed of sound is imperceptible at close range. Unlike light, sound travels through most objects; thus, unwanted sound is more difficult to shut out. When sound is reflected off an object, it produces an echo. When it is absorbed by an object, such as carpet, it is muffled. Everyone sounds like Pavarotti in the shower because tile absorbs so little sound, creating echoes and resonance that give fullness to even a mediocre voice.

Frequency

Acoustic energy has three important properties, frequency, complexity, and amplitude. When a person hits a tuning fork, the prongs of the fork move rapidly inward and outward, putting pressure on the air molecules around them, which collide with the molecules next to them. Each round of expansion and contraction of the distance between molecules of air is known as a **cycle**. The number of cycles per second determines the sound wave's frequency. **Frequency** is just what it sounds like—a measure of how often (that is, how *frequently*), a wave cycles. Frequency is expressed in **Hertz**, or **Hz** (named after the German physicist, Heinrich Hertz). One Hz equals one cycle per second, so a 1500-Hz tone has 1500 cycles per second. The frequency of a simple sound wave corresponds to the psychological property of **pitch** (the quality of a tone, from low to high). Generally, the higher the frequency, the higher the pitch. When frequency is doubled—that is, when the number of cycles per second is twice as frequent—the pitch perceived is an octave higher.

The human auditory system is sensitive to a wide range of frequencies. Young adults can hear frequencies from about 15 to 20,000 Hz, but as with most senses, capacity diminishes with aging. Frequencies used in music range from the lowest note on an organ (16 Hz) to the highest note on a grand piano (over 4000 Hz). Human voices range from about 100 Hz to about 3500 Hz, and our ears are most sensitive to sounds in that frequency range. Other species are sensitive to different ranges. Dogs hear frequencies ranging from 15 to 50,000 Hz, which is why they

People see fireworks from a distance before they hear them because light travels faster than sound.

are responsive to "silent" whistles with frequencies that fall above the range humans can sense. Elephants can hear ultralow frequencies over considerable distances. So, does a tree falling in the forest produce a sound? It produces sound waves, but the waves only become sound if creatures in the forest have receptors tuned to them.

Complexity

Sounds rarely consist of waves of uniform frequency. Rather, most sounds are a combination of sound waves, each with a different frequency. The **complexity** of a sound wave—the extent to which it is composed of multiple frequencies—corresponds to the psychological property of **timbre**, or texture of the sound. People recognize each other's voices, as well as the sounds of different musical instruments, from their characteristic timbre. Timbre allows people to distinguish the middle C of a piano from the same pitch played by a flute. The dominant part of each wave produces the predominant pitch (in this case, middle C), but overtones (additional frequencies) give the instrument its distinctive sound. Synthesizers imitate conventional instruments by electronically adding the right overtones to pure frequencies (Hilts, 1980). Much of the music on popular radio stations today is synthesized, with many of the nonpercussive sounds actually played on a keyboard and mixed with special computer software. Adding instrumentation is as easy as saying, "Let's try putting some strings in the background."

The sounds instruments produce, whether in a rock band or a symphony, are music to our ears because we learn to interpret particular temporal patterns and combinations of sound waves as music. What people hear as music and as random auditory noise depends on their culture. The scales and harmonic structures that are standard in contemporary jazz would have been musically incomprehensible to Mozart, just as rock 'n' roll was denounced by incredulous parents of teenagers in the 1960s as senseless noise.

Amplitude

In addition to frequency and complexity, sound waves have amplitude. **Amplitude** refers to the height and depth of a wave—that is, the difference between its maximum and minimum pressure level (Figure 4.20). The amplitude of a sound wave corresponds to the psychological property of **loudness**; the greater the amplitude, the louder the sound. Amplitude is measured in **decibels** (**dB**). Zero decibels is the absolute threshold above which people can hear a 1000 Hz tone.

Like the visual system, the human auditory system has an astonishing range, handling energy levels that can differ by a factor of 10 billion or more (Bekesy & Rosenblith, 1951). The decibel scale is logarithmic, condensing a huge range of intensities into a manageable metric, just as the sensory system does. A loud scream is 100,000 times more intense than a sound at the absolute threshold, whereas it is only 100 dB different. Conversation is usually held at 50 to 60 dB. Sounds over 130 dB are likely to be experienced as painful, and prolonged exposure to sounds over about 90 dB, such as subway cars rolling into the station or amplifiers at a rock concert, can produce permanent hearing loss (Figure 4.21).

Frequency, complexity, and amplitude then, are the stimulus qualities that shape auditory experience. Just as vision has the characteristics of hue, brightness, saturation, and audition has the qualities of pitch, timbre, and loudness.

The Ear

Transduction of sound occurs in the ear, which consists of an outer, middle, and inner ear (Figure 4.22). The outer ear collects and magnifies sound in the air, the middle ear converts waves of air pressure into infinitesimal movements of tiny bones, and the inner ear transforms these movements into waves in fluid that generate neural signals.

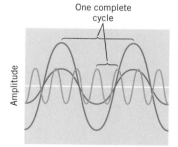

One complete cycle

Amplitude

Frequency

— High frequency, low amplitude (soft tenor or soprano)

— Low frequency, low amplitude (soft bass)

— Low frequency, high amplitude (loud bass)

FIGURE 4.20
Frequency and amplitude. Sound waves can differ in both frequency (pitch) and amplitude (loudness). A cycle can be represented as the length of time or distance between peaks of the curve.

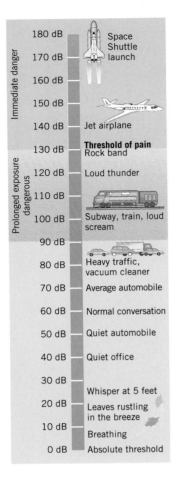

FIGURE 4.21
Loudness. This figure shows the loudness of various common sounds in decibels.

Transduction

The hearing process begins in the outer ear, where sound waves are funneled into the ear by the **pinna**, the skin-covered cartilage that protrudes from the sides of the head. The pinna is not essential for hearing, but its irregular shape is useful for locating sounds in space, which bounce off its folds differently when they come from various locations (Batteau, 1967). Just inside the skull is the other part of the outer ear, the **auditory canal**, a passageway about an inch long. As sound waves resonate in the auditory canal, they are amplified by up to a factor of two.

At the end of the auditory canal is a thin, flexible membrane, known as the **eardrum**, or **tympanic membrane**. The eardrum marks the outer boundary of the middle ear. When sound waves reach the eardrum, they set it in motion. The movements of the eardrum are extremely small—.00000001 centimeter, or about the width of a hydrogen molecule, in response to a whisper (Sekuler & Blake, 1994). The eardrum essentially reproduces in microcosm the cyclical vibration of the object that created the noise. Its fidelity in doing so, however, requires that the air pressure on both sides of it (in the outer and middle ear) be roughly the same. For example, if the pressure is greater on the inside, as can occur when an airplane begins its descent and a person's head is blocked from a head cold, internal pressure damps the vibrations of the eardrum. The normal mechanism for equalizing air pressure is the **Eustachian tube**, which connects the middle ear to the throat.

When the eardrum vibrates, it sets in motion three tiny bones in the middle ear, called **ossicles**. These bones, named for their distinctive shapes, are called the malleus, incus, and stapes, which translate from the Latin into hammer, anvil, and stirrup, respectively. The ossicles further amplify the sound two or three times before transmitting vibrations to the inner ear. The stirrup pounds against a membrane called the **oval window**, which forms the beginning of the inner ear.

The inner ear consists of two sets of fluid-filled cavities hollowed out of the temporal bone of the skull: the semicircular canals (involved in balance) and the cochlea (involved in hearing). The temporal bone is the hardest bone in the body and serves as natural soundproofing for its vibration-sensitive cavities. Chewing during a meeting sounds louder to the person eating than to those nearby because it rattles the temporal bone and thus augments the sounds from the ears.

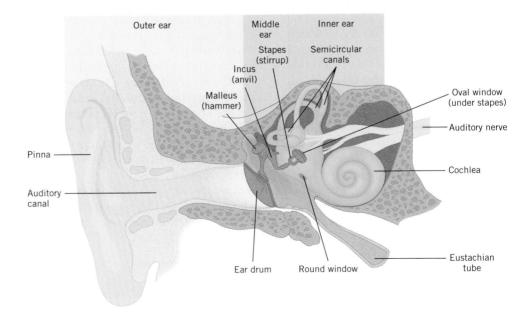

FIGURE 4.22
The ear. The ear consists of outer, middle, and inner sections, which perform the functions of directing the sound, amplifying it (and protecting against damage from loud noise), and turning mechanical energy into neural signals, respectively.

The **cochlea** (Figure 4.23) is a three-chambered tube shaped like a snail. When the stirrup pounds against the oval window, the oval window vibrates, causing pressure waves in the cochlear fluid. These waves flex the **basilar membrane**, which separates two of the cochlea's chambers. Attached to the basilar membrane are the ear's 15,000 receptors for sound, called **hair cells** (because they terminate in tiny bristles, or cilia). Above the hair cells is another membrane, the **tectorial membrane**, which also moves as waves of pressure travel through the cochlear fluid. The cilia bend as the basilar and tectorial membranes move in different directions. This triggers action potentials in sensory neurons forming the **auditory nerve**, which transmits auditory information to the brain. Thus, mechanical energy—the movement of cilia and membranes—is transduced into neural energy.

With hearing as with other senses, sensory deficits can arise either from problems with parts of the sense organ that channel stimulus energy or with the receptors and neural circuits that convert this energy into psychological experience. Failure of

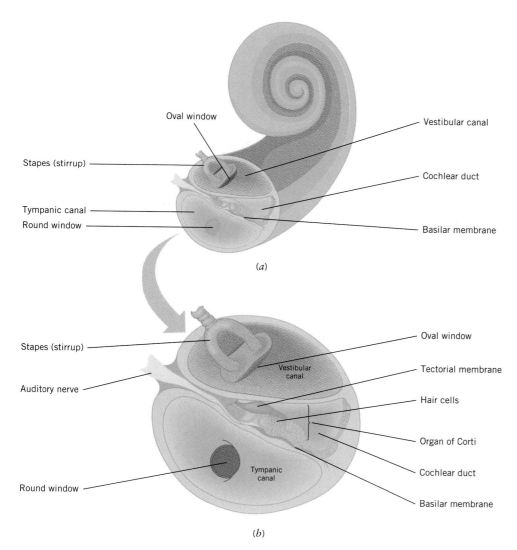

FIGURE 4.23

The cochlea. The cochlea's chambers (the vestibular canal, the cochlear duct, and the tympanic canal) are filled with fluid. When the stirrup pounds against the oval window, it vibrates, causing pressure waves in the fluid of the vestibular canal. These pressure waves spiral up the vestibular canal and down the tympanic canal, flexing the basilar membrane and to a lesser extent the tectorial membrane. Transduction occurs in the Organ of Corti, which includes these two membranes and the hair cells sandwiched between them. At the end of the tympanic canal is the round window, which pushes outward to disperse pressure when the sound waves have passed through the cochlea.

the outer or middle ear to conduct sound to the receptors in the hair cells is called **conduction loss**; failure of receptors in the inner ear or of neurons in any auditory pathway in the brain is referred to as **sensorineural loss**. The most common problems with hearing result from exposure to noise or reflect changes in the receptors with aging, which occur in most sensory systems (Chapter 13). A single exposure to an extremely loud noise, such as a firecracker, an explosion, or a gun firing at close range, can do permanent damage to the hair cell receptors in the inner ear.

Sensing Pitch and Loudness

Precisely how does auditory transduction transform the physical properties of sound frequency and amplitude into the psychological experiences of pitch and loudness? Two theories, both proposed in the nineteenth century and once considered opposing explanations, together appear to explain the available data. The first, called **place theory**, holds that different areas of the basilar membrane are maximally sensitive to different frequencies (Bekesy, 1959, 1960; Helmholtz, 1863). Place theory was initially proposed by Herman von Helmholtz (of trichromatic color fame), who had the mechanism wrong but the idea right. A Hungarian scientist named Georg von Bekesy discovered the mechanism a century after Helmholtz by recognizing that when the stapes hits the oval window, a wave travels down the basilar membrane like a carpet being shaken at one end (Figure 4.24). Shaking a carpet rapidly (at high frequency) produces a peak in the wave early, whereas shaking it slowly produces a peak in the wave toward the other end of the carpet. Similarly, high-frequency tones, which produce rapid strokes of the stapes, maximally displace the basilar membrane close to the oval window, whereas low-frequency tones cause a peak in basilar movement toward the far end of the basilar membrane. Peak vibration leads to peak firing of hair cells at a particular location. Hair cells at different points on the basilar membrane thus transmit information about different frequencies to the brain, just as rods and cones transduce electromagnetic energy at different frequencies. As with light, the more intense a sound, the more neurons will fire.

Bekesy's work earned him a Nobel Prize, but place theory has one problem: At very low frequencies the entire basilar membrane vibrates fairly uniformly, so that

FIGURE 4.24

Place theory. The frequency with which the stapes strikes the oval window affects the location of peak vibration on the basilar membrane. The lower the tone, the farther the maximum displacement on the membrane is from the oval window. SOURCE: *Sekuler & Blake, 1994, p. 315.*

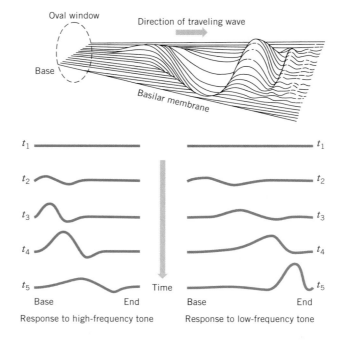

for very low tones, location of peak vibration cannot account for pitch. The second theory of pitch, **frequency theory**, overcomes this problem, asserting that the more frequently a sound wave cycles, the more frequently the basilar membrane vibrates and its hair cells fire. According to its original version, the entire basilar membrane and attached hair cells vibrate at the same rate as the original sound wave. Thus, a 250 Hz tone causes the membrane to vibrate at 250 cycles per second, which causes a similar rate of neural firing. However, as we have seen, the basilar membrane does not vibrate at a uniform rate. Moreover, neurons cannot fire fast enough to match the pace of sound waves. The solution to this latter problem is the volley principle—named after a military practice in the days before automatic weapons, in which infantrymen staggered their shots to give each other time to reload (Figure 4.25). The **volley principle** means that neurons stagger their responses, so that the combined pattern produces a signal of a particular frequency (Wever, 1949). In other words, several neurons together produce a rate of neural firing that none alone could match. As in place theory, the mechanism for converting sound intensity into loudness in frequency theory is the number of neurons firing; more neurons firing at each point in a volley produce a louder sensation without changing the pitch.

Today many researchers believe that pitch perception is mediated by two neural mechanisms, a place code at high frequencies and a frequency code at low frequencies. Both mechanisms probably operate at intermediate frequencies (Goldstein, 1989).

Neural Pathways

Neurons in the auditory system are similar in many respects to those in the visual system. Firing depends on input from several hair cells, just as firing in ganglion cells reflects the summed activity of many photoreceptors. Neurons comprising the auditory nerve also carry information specifying stimulus quality (pitch), as do fibers in the optic nerve (color). Thus, a neuron will respond to a range of frequencies if the sound is intense enough, but it will most readily respond to a characteristic frequency to which it is tuned. Neurons activated by hair cells near the oval window respond to high frequencies, whereas those activated by hair cells on the other end of the basilar membrane fire more readily for low tones. At each pitch, some neurons respond to relatively low intensities of sound, whereas others fire more at high sound levels, which allows the auditory system to be responsive to an enormous range of sound energy.

Information transmitted by the ears along the two auditory nerves ultimately finds its way to the auditory cortex in the temporal lobes, but it makes several stops along the way (Figure 4.26). The auditory nerve from each ear projects to the medulla, where the majority of its fibers cross over to the other hemisphere. (Recall that the medulla is the section of the hindbrain that connects the spinal cord with the brain, where sensory and motor neurons cross from one side of the body to the other). Some information from each ear, however, does not cross over; thus, information from both ears is represented on both sides of the brain. Auditory tracts project to the midbrain and on to the thalamus. There, like visual neurons, auditory neurons synapse with neurons from the reticular formation, which presumably modulate their input to the cortex depending on level of arousal.

The thalamus relays information to the auditory cortex in the temporal lobes, which has sections devoted to different frequencies, much as sites in the primary visual cortex process different parts of the retinal image. Some cortical neurons also respond to the "movement" of sounds—whether frequency changes, moving up or down—similar to the way some complex cells in the visual cortex respond to movement in space. Just as the cortical region corresponding to the fovea is disproportionately large, so, too, is the region of the primary auditory cortex tuned to sound frequencies in the middle of the spectrum—the same frequencies involved in speech

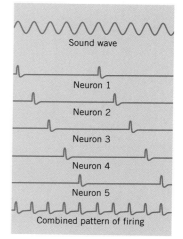

FIGURE 4.25
The volley principle. When a sound of high frequency reaches the cochlea, each of several neurons may fire, collectively producing a response of higher frequency than any neuron alone. SOURCE: *Adapted from Wever, 1949, p. 167.*

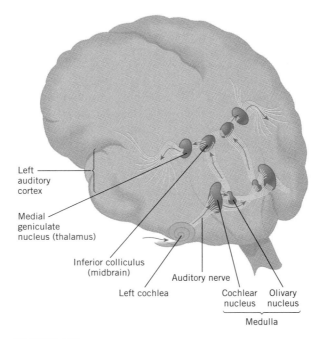

FIGURE 4.26

Auditory pathways. Axons from neurons in the inner ear project to the cochlear nucleus in the medulla. From there, most cross over to a structure called the olivary nucleus on the opposite side, although some remain uncrossed. At the olivary nucleus, information from the two ears begins to be integrated. Information from the olivary nucleus then passes to a midbrain structure (the inferior colliculus) and on to the medial geniculate nucleus, a part of the thalamus, before reaching the auditory cortex.

(Sekuler & Blake, 1994). Indeed, in humans and other animals, some cortical neurons in the left temporal lobe respond exclusively to particular sounds characteristic of the language of the species, whether monkey calls or human speech.

Neurons in the thalamus and primary cortex are also involved in **sound localization**, that is, identification of the spatial location of a sound. Sound localization requires the integration of information from both ears because the brain uses two main cues for localizing sound: differences between the two ears in loudness of the sound and differences in timing of the sound (Middlebrooks & Green, 1991; Stevens & Newman, 1934). Particularly for high-frequency sounds, relative loudness in the ear closer to the source provides information about its location because the head blocks some of the sound from hitting the other ear (Figure 4.27). Loudness is less useful for localizing lower-frequency sounds because their waves are so long that the head does not effectively block them. For example, a 900-Hz sound (a relatively low tone) cycles about every 40 centimeters, which is twice the diameter of the average head, so it curves right around the head (Sekuler & Blake, 1994). Localization of sounds at low frequencies relies more on the difference in the arrival time of the sound at the two ears. A sound coming from the left reaches the left ear a split second before reaching the right, particularly if it is moving slowly—that is, at a low frequency. Timing differences are less useful for localizing sounds at high frequencies because they travel so quickly between the two ears. The ability to move the head toward sounds is also crucial for localizing sounds. Neurologically, the basis for sound localization lies in neurons that respond to relative differences in the signals from the two ears.

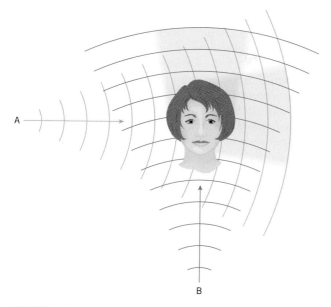

FIGURE 4.27
Sound localization. At high frequencies, sounds on one side of the head can be localized by relative intensity in the two ears because the head casts a "sound shadow" on one side but not the other, as in sound (A). With sound (B), the shadow is behind the head, so it does not lead to any relative differences between the ears. At low frequencies, the slight difference between the time a sound reaches one ear, as in (A), provides a cue for sound localization.

OTHER SENSES

Vision and audition are the most highly specialized senses in humans, occupying the greatest amount of brain space and showing the most cortical evolution. Our other senses, however, serve important adaptive functions. These include smell, taste, the skin senses (pressure, temperature, and pain), and the proprioceptive senses (body position and motion).

Smell

Smell (**olfaction**) serves a number of functions in humans, such as detection of danger (e.g., the smell of something burning), discrimination of palatable and unpalatable or spoiled foods, and the recognition of familiar others. Smell plays a less important role in humans than in most other animals, who rely heavily on olfaction to mark territory and track other animals. Many species communicate through scent messages called **pheromones** (Chapter 10). Pheromones regulate the sexual behavior of many animals and direct a variety of behaviors in insects (Edwards et al., 1991; Mason et al., 1989; Shorey, 1976; Stoddard, 1980). We humans, in contrast, often try to "cover our tracks" in the olfactory domain, using perfumes and deodorants to mask odors that our mammalian ancestors might have found informative or appealing.

Nevertheless, vestiges of this ancient reproductive mechanism remain, and humans appear both to secrete and sense olfactory cues related to reproduction. In experiments using sweaty hands or articles of clothing, subjects can identify the gender of another person by smell alone with remarkable accuracy (Doty et al., 1982;

Russell, 1976; Wallace, 1977). The tendency of menstrual cycles of women living in close proximity to synchronize is also mediated by smell (McClintock, 1971). In one study, researchers collected underarm secretions of female volunteers at several points in their menstrual cycles (Preti et al., 1986). A mixture of alcohol and secretions from "donor" subjects was then dabbed on the upper lips of subjects in the experimental condition. The experimenters applied this mixture three times a week for 10 weeks. Secretions from the start of the donors' cycles were applied the first week, secretions from midcycle were applied the second week, and so on. The menstrual cycles of the women in the experimental condition began to synchronize with their donors after a few weeks, while the cycles of women in a control condition (whose lips were dabbed with alcohol only) showed no such changes.

The environmental stimuli for olfaction are invisible molecules of gas emitted by substances and suspended in the air. Although the nose is the sense organ for smell, the vapors that give rise to olfactory sensations can enter the **nasal cavities** (the region hollowed out of the bone in the skull that contains smell receptors) through either the nose or the mouth (Figure 4.28). When food is chewed, vapors travel up the back of the mouth into the nasal cavity; this process actually accounts for much of the taste.

Transduction of smell occurs in the **olfactory epithelium**, a thin pair of structures (one on each side) less than a square inch in diameter at the top of the nasal cavities. Chemical molecules in the air become trapped in the mucus of the epithelium, where they make contact with olfactory receptor cells, which transduce the stimulus into olfactory sensations. Humans have approximately 10 million olfactory receptors

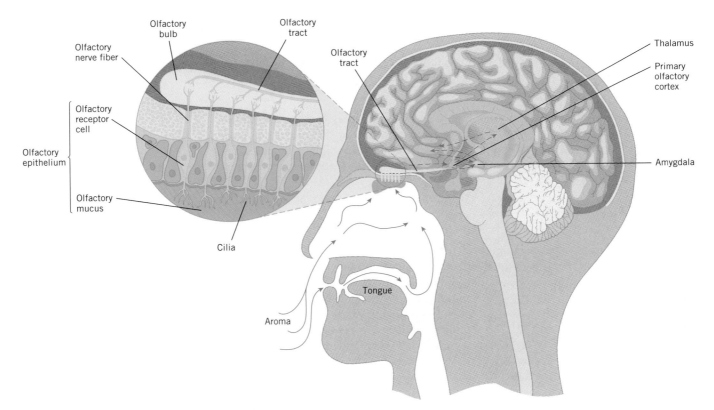

FIGURE 4.28

Olfaction. Molecules of air enter the nasal cavities through the nose and throat, where smell is transduced by receptors in the olfactory epithelium. Axons of receptor cells form the olfactory nerve, a relatively short nerve that projects to the olfactory bulb. From there, information passes through the olfactory tract to the primary olfactory cortex. This region connects with the thalamus and amygdala, which in turn connect with higher olfactory centers in a more evolutionarily recent region of the frontal lobe.

(Engen, 1982), in comparison with dogs, whose 200 million receptors enable them to track humans and other animals with their noses (Marshall & Moulton, 1981). Olfactory receptors differ from all other sensory receptors in the body in that they are actually neurons, which directly connect the external world with the brain. Psychologists have long debated whether a small number of receptors coding different qualities combine to produce complex smells, or whether the olfactory epithelium contains hundreds or thousands of receptors that bind only with very specific molecules. Recent research on the genes that produce proteins involved in smell transduction supports the latter hypothesis, that many receptors are responsive to chemicals with very specific molecular structures (Bartoshuk & Beauchamp, 1994; Buck & Axel, 1991).

The axons of olfactory receptor cells form the **olfactory nerve**, which transmits information to the **olfactory bulbs**, multilayered structures that combine information from receptor cells. Olfactory information then travels to the primary olfactory cortex, a primitive region of the cortex deep in the frontal lobes. Unlike other senses, smell is not relayed through the thalamus on its way to the cortex, although the olfactory cortex has projections to both the thalamus and the limbic system, so that smell is connected to both taste and emotion. Animals that respond to pheromonal cues have a second or accessory olfactory system, with its own olfactory bulbs and tracts, that projects directly to the amygdala and on to the hypothalamus, thus contributing to regulation of reproductive behavior (Carlson, 1991). Recent evidence suggests that humans may have a similar secondary olfactory system, which, if operative, has no links to consciousness and thus influences reproductive behavior unconsciously (Bartoshuk & Beauchamp, 1994).

Taste

The sense of smell is sensitive to molecules in the air, whereas taste (**gustation**) is sensitive to molecules soluble in saliva. At the dinner table, the contributions of the nose and mouth to taste are indistinguishable except when the nasal passages are blocked and food loses much of its taste. From an evolutionary perspective, the function of taste is to protect the organism from ingesting toxic substances and to regulate intake of nutrients such as sugars and salt. The gustatory system is exquisitely tuned for performing these functions. For example, toxic substances often taste bitter, and foods high in sugar, which is necessary for energy for the muscles and nervous system, are usually sweet. The tendency to reject bitter substances and to ingest sweet substances is present even in newborns, despite their lack of experience with taste (Bartoshuk & Beauchamp, 1994).

Transduction of taste occurs in the **taste buds** (Figure 4.29). Roughly 10,000 taste buds are distributed throughout the mouth and throat (Miller, 1995), although

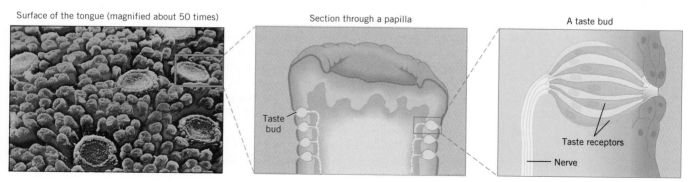

FIGURE 4.29
Taste buds. Taste buds, the majority of which are located on the papillae of the tongue, contain receptor cells that bind with chemicals in the saliva and stimulate gustatory neurons.

most by far are located in the bumps on the surface of the tongue called **papillae** (Latin for pimple). Soluble chemicals that enter the mouth penetrate tiny pores in the papillae and stimulate the taste receptors. Each taste bud contains between 50 and 150 receptor cells (Margolskee, 1995). Like olfactory receptors, taste receptors are unusual among sensory receptors in that they wear out by repeated contact and are frequently replaced (every 10 or 11 days for taste receptors; Graziadei, 1969). Regeneration is essential, or a burn to the tongue would result in permanent loss of taste.

Taste receptors stimulate neurons whose axons carry information, via the cranial nerves (nerves in the head), to the medulla and pons in the hindbrain. From there, gustatory information travels to one of two destinations in the brain, each with its own function (Sekuler & Blake, 1994). One pathway leads to the thalamus and on to the primary gustatory cortex deep within a region between the temporal and parietal lobes. This pathway allows the identification of tastes. The second pathway, which has no access to consciousness, is to the limbic system. This pathway allows immediate affective and behavioral responses to tastes (such as spitting out bitter substances). It also appears to be involved in learned aversions to tastes that become associated through experience with nausea. As in blindsight (Chapter 3), people with damage to the cortical pathway cannot identify substances by taste but react with appropriate facial expressions to bitter and sour substances if this second, more primitive, pathway is intact.

Most researchers agree that the gustatory system responds to four basic tastes—sweet, sour, salty, and bitter—and that different receptors are maximally sensitive to each of these, at least at low levels of stimulation. Cross-cultural evidence supports this conclusion: People of different cultures diverge in their taste preferences and beliefs about basic flavors, but they vary only minimally in identifying substances as sweet, sour, salty, or bitter (Laing et al., 1993). Matters are not, however, quite so simple. For example, researchers have discovered at least four types of receptors that produce the same sensation—bitter—but in response to very different substances. Apparently, as plants and insects evolved toxic chemicals to protect against predation, animals that ate them evolved specific mechanisms for detecting these substances but relied on the same sensation, bitterness, to discourage their ingestion (Bartoshuk & Beauchamp, 1994). Furthermore, the mechanisms by which four basic tastes produce hundreds of different taste sensations are not well understood. Presumably, complex tastes reflect the pattern of activity across thousands of nerve fibers leading from the tongue as well as sensory signals from the nasal cavities (Erickson, 1968; Erickson et al., 1990).

Skin Senses

The approximately 18 square feet of skin covering the human body constitutes a complex, multilayered organ. The skin senses help protect the body from injury, aid in identifying objects, help maintain body temperature, and facilitate social interaction through hugs, kisses, holding, and handshakes. What we colloquially call the sense of touch is actually a mix of at least three qualities: pressure, temperature, and pain. Receptors in the skin respond to different aspects of these qualities, such as light or deep pressure on the skin, or warm or cold stimulation. Microscopic studies reveal that the human body contains approximately 5 million touch receptors of various types (Figure 4.30). Although receptors are specialized for different qualities, as with other senses, most skin sensations are complex, reflecting stimulation across many receptors (Goldstein, 1989).

In most cases, several receptors in the skin feed into a single sensory neuron, which in turn synapses with other neurons in the spinal cord (Chapter 3). Having multiple inputs makes sensory neurons highly sensitive, since receptor input is additive; that is, more stimulation adds up to more neural firing. The qualities sensory

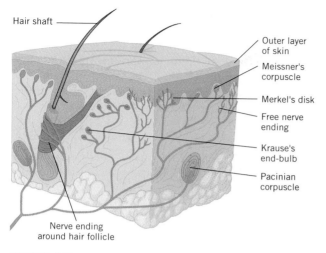

Hair shaft

Outer layer
of skin

Meissner's
corpuscle

Merkel's disk

Free nerve
ending

Krause's
end-bulb

Pacinian
corpuscle

Nerve ending
around hair follicle

FIGURE 4.30

*The skin and its receptors. Several different types of receptors transduce
tactile stimulation, such as Meissner's corpuscles, which respond to brief
stimulation (as when a ball of cotton moves across the skin), and Merkel's
disks, which detect steady pressure.*

neurons convey to the nervous system (soft pressure, warmth, cold, and so forth)
depend on the receptors to which they are connected. Thus, when receptors reat-
tach to the wrong nerve fibers, as presumably occurs in some cases of painful neuropathy, the result can be a misinterpretation of sensory information. Like neurons
in other sensory modalities, the neurons mediating the sense of touch also have
receptive fields. These receptive fields distinguish both spatial location of a stimulus (where the stimulation occurred on the skin) and temporal properties (how long
it occurred).

Sensory neurons synapse with spinal interneurons that directly stimulate motor
neurons, allowing reflexive action; they also synapse with neurons that carry information up the spinal cord to the medulla, where neural tracts cross over. From there
sensory information travels to the thalamus and is subsequently routed to the primary touch center in the brain, the somatosensory cortex. The somatosensory cortex contains a map of the body (Chapter 3); cortical touch neurons have receptive
fields corresponding to different body regions. Similar to the complex cells in the
visual system, some of these neurons respond to edges of objects of particular orientations, whereas others respond to movement in particular directions.

The different skin senses transduce different forms of stimulation. Pressure
receptors, called **mechanoreceptors**, transduce mechanical energy, like the receptors
in the ear. Temperature receptors respond to thermal energy. Pain receptors do not
directly transform external stimulation into psychological experience; rather, they
respond to a range of internal and external bodily states, from valves in the circula-
tory system that do not open appropriately to damaged flesh. We briefly examine
each of these skin senses.

Pressure

People experience pressure when the skin is mechanically displaced. Sensitivity
to pressure varies considerably over the surface of the body. The most sensitive
regions are the face and fingers, and the least sensitive, the back and legs. These disparities in sensitivity are directly reflected in the relative space accorded neurons
representing these areas in the somatosensory cortex. The hands are the skin's
foveas, providing tremendous acuity; they have small receptive fields that allow fine
discriminations, and substantial space is devoted to them in the primary cortex (see
Johnson & Lamb, 1981). The hands turn what could be a passive sensory process—

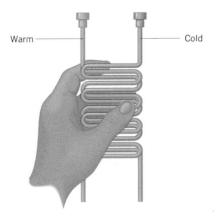

Warm ——— Cold

FIGURE 4.31
Experiencing intense heat. Warm and cold receptors activated simultaneously produce a sensation of intense heat.

responding to indentations produced in the skin by external stimulation—into an active process. As the hands move over objects, pressure receptors register the indentations created in the skin and hence allow perception of texture. Just as eye movements allow people to read written words, so do finger movements allow blind people to read the raised dots that constitute Braille. In other animals, the somatosensory cortex emphasizes other body zones that provide important information for adaptation, such as the whiskers in cats (Kaas, 1987).

Temperature

When people sense the temperature of an object, they are actually sensing the difference between the temperature of the skin and the object—which is why a pool of 80-degree water feels warm to someone who has been standing in the cold rain but chilly to someone lying on a hot beach. Temperature sensation actually relies on two sets of receptors, one for cold and one for warmth (see Levine & Shefner, 1991; Spray, 1986). Cold receptors, however, not only detect coolness but are also involved in the experience of extreme temperatures, both hot and cold. Subjects who grasp two pipes twisted together, one containing warm water and the other cold, experience intense heat (Figure 4.31). As with pressure, the pattern of stimulation, rather than the activation of specific receptors alone, codes for the quality of the sensation.

Pain

People spend billions of dollars a year fighting pain, but pain serves an important function: It prevents tissue damage. Indeed, people who are insensitive to pain because of nerve damage, congenital abnormality (genetic defect), or psychological efforts to numb themselves are at serious risk of injury and infection. Young children with congenital pain insensitivity have reportedly chewed off their tongues and the tips of their fingers and been severely burned leaning against hot stoves or climbing into scalding bathwater (Jewesbury, 1951). Adults with this disorder learn to compensate by attending carefully to cues from other sensory systems, but injury is unavoidable. One woman developed numbness and a limp because her joints and spine were so damaged from not adjusting to normal pain sensations when standing or sleeping (Baxter & Olszewski, 1960; Melzack, 1973). On the other hand, persistent pain can be debilitating. Some estimates suggest that as many as one-third of North Americans suffer from persistent or recurrent pain, and the cost in suffering, productivity, and dollars is immense (Miller & Kraus, 1990).

In contrast to other sensory modalities, pain has no specific physical stimulus; the skin does not transduce "pain waves." Sounds that are too loud, lights that are too bright, pressure that is too intense, temperatures that are too extreme, and other stimuli can all elicit pain. Although pain transduction is not well understood, the most important receptors for pain appear to be the **free nerve endings** toward the surface of the skin (Schiffman, 1996). According to one prominent theory, when cells are damaged, they release chemicals that stimulate the free nerve endings in the skin, which in turn transmit pain messages to the brain (Price, 1988). Recent research supports the role of one such chemical, called **substance P** (for pain), in pain sensation. In one study, researchers found that pinching the hindpaws of rats led to the release of substance P in the spinal cord (Beyer et al., 1991). The concentration of substance P increased with the amount of painful stimulation and returned to baseline when the stimulation stopped. Other researchers found that rats injected with substance P responded with biting, scratching, and distress vocalizations, all of which are generally associated with painful stimulation (DeLander & Wahl, 1991).

Experiencing Pain Of all the senses, pain is probably the most affected by beliefs, expectations, and emotional state, and the least reducible to level of stimulation

(Sternbach, 1968). Anxiety can increase pain (Oberle et al., 1990), whereas intense fear, stress, or concentration on other things can inhibit it (al Absi & Rokke, 1991; Melzack & Wall, 1983). Cultural norms and expectations also influence the subjective experience and behavioral expression of pain (Bates, 1987; Morse & Morse, 1988; Zatzick & Dimsdale, 1990). For example, on the island of Fiji, women of two subcultures experience labor pain quite differently (Morse & Park, 1988). The native Fijiian culture is sympathetic to women in labor and provides both psychological support and herbal remedies for labor pain. In contrast, an Indian subculture on the island considers childbirth a defiling event and offers little sympathy or support. Interestingly, women from the Indian group rate the pain of childbirth significantly lower than native Fijiians. Cultural recognition of pain apparently influences the extent to which people can acknowledge it. Similarly, anecdotal evidence in the West suggests that people in subcultures that provide no support for pain and encourage a "stiff upper lip" show fewer signs of pain and attend less to daily aches and pains than subcultures that dwell on pain.

The phenomenological experience of pain is not always initiated by peripheral sensory stimulation. A striking example is phantom limb pain, experienced by a substantial number of amputees. **Phantom limb pain** is pain felt in a limb that no longer exists. The pain does not originate from severed nerves in the stump. Even if the stump is completely anesthetized, the pain persists, and medications that should ease the pain often fail to do so (Melzack, 1970).

A Japanese boy walks on fire at Mt. Takao. Pain is as much a state of mind as a state of receptors.

Gate Control Theory A theory that tries to account for both phantom limb pain and the influence of cognition and emotion on pain is gate-control theory (Melzack, 1973, 1980; Melzack & Wall, 1965). Although its initial formulation was not entirely correct, subsequent modifications have proven useful in understanding and treating pain (Schiffman, 1996). According to **gate-control theory,** two different kinds of neural fibers (sensory neurons) open and close spinal "gateways" for pain. Large-diameter fibers (called L-fibers), which transmit neural information very quickly, carry information about many forms of tactile stimulation as well as sharp pain. Once they transmit a message, they close the pain gate by inhibiting the firing of the neurons with which they synapse. Small-diameter fibers (S-fibers) synapse with the same neurons, carrying information about dull pain and burning to the brain. Because their small axons conduct electricity more slowly, however, their messages may arrive at a closed gate if competing sensory input from L-fibers has inhibited pain transmission.

Gate-control theory thus explains why rubbing the area around a burn or cut, or even pinching a nearby region of skin, can alleviate pain. These actions stimulate L-fibers, which close the gates to incoming signals from S-fibers. This mechanism may also explain the efficacy of acupuncture in alleviating pain. Evidence supporting gate-control theory comes from studies in which electrical stimulation of L-fibers has relieved pain in some chronic pain patients (Long, 1991). According to gate-control theory, messages from the brain to the spinal cord can also close the gates, which means that mental states such as calm (or conversely, anxiety) can modulate pain sensations arising from the peripheral nervous system. Finally, gate-control theory offers an explanation of phantom limb pain. If L-fibers are destroyed by amputation, the gates remain open, allowing random firing of neurons at the amputation site to trigger action potentials, thus leading to the experience of pain in the missing limb (Melzack, 1973).

Pain Control Because mental as well as physiological processes contribute to pain, treatment may require attention to both mind and matter—both the psychology and neurophysiology of pain. The Lamaze method of childbirth, for example, teaches women to relax through deep breathing and muscle relaxation and to distract themselves by focusing their attention elsewhere. The Lamaze method also teaches the woman's "coach" (partner) to stimulate L-fibers through gentle massage. These procedures are effective: Lamaze-trained women experience less pain during labor (Leventhal et al., 1989), and they show a general increase in pain tolerance (as measured by the length of time they can keep their hands submerged in ice water), especially if their coach provides encouragement (Whipple et al., 1990; Worthington et al., 1983).

Many other techniques target the mental components of pain (although, of course, the distinction between mental and physical is in some sense arbitrary, since cognitive and emotional changes translate into physiological changes through gate-control or other mechanisms). Though not a panacea, distraction is generally a useful strategy for increasing pain tolerance (Anderson et al., 1991; McCaul & Malott, 1984). Health care professionals often keep up a stream of chatter while giving patients injections in order to distract and relax them. Something as simple as a pleasant view can affect pain tolerance in hospitalized patients. In one study, surgery patients whose rooms overlooked lush plant life had shorter stays and required less medication than patients whose otherwise identical rooms looked out on a brick wall (Ulrich, 1984). Environmental psychologists, who apply psychological knowledge to building and landscape design, use such information to help architects design hospitals (Saegert & Winkel, 1990). Hypnosis (Chapter 9) can also be useful in controlling pain (Evans, 1990; Hilgard & Hilgard, 1975). Research suggests that hypnotic procedures can help burn victims tolerate debriding (removing dead tissue and changing dressings on wounds), which can be so painful that patients writhe in agony even on the maximum dosage of opioid medications such as morphine (Patterson et al., 1992). Whether hypnosis might similarly be useful for treating painful neuropathy is unknown.

FROM MIND TO BRAIN

PERSONALITY AND PAIN

If mental states can affect pain sensation, are some people vulnerable to chronic pain by virtue of their personalities? Despite long-standing controversy in this area, researchers have identified a personality style that appears to be shared by many chronic pain patients (Keller & Butcher, 1992). Chronic pain patients tend to blame their physical condition for all life's difficulties while denying emotional and interpersonal problems. They tend to have difficulty expressing anger, to be anxious and depressed, and to be needy and dependent. A methodological difficulty in studying such patients, however, is distinguishing the causes from the effects of chronic pain, since unending pain could produce many of these personality traits (Gamsa, 1990).

A team of researchers addressed this methodological problem by studying patients at risk for developing chronic pain prospectively, that is, before they developed chronic pain (Dworkin et al., 1992). Subjects suffered from herpes zoster (shingles), a viral disease infection that results from reactivation of latent chicken pox virus. The nature and duration of the pain associated with herpes zoster varies widely, but some patients experience disabling chronic pain. To see if they could predict which patients would develop chronic pain, the investigators gave a sample of 19 recently diagnosed herpes zoster patients a series of questionnaires and tests, including measures of depression, anxiety, life stress, attitudes toward their illness, and pain severity. Physicians provided data on the severity of subjects' initial herpes zoster outbreaks.

The researchers contacted the patients several times over the next year to ask about their pain experiences. Six patients reported ongoing pain three months after the acute outbreak, while twelve did not (the researchers could not locate one patient). Although these two groups (pain, no pain) did not differ in the initial severity of their symptoms, they did differ significantly on a number of psychological dimensions assessed *at the time of their initial diagnosis.* In confirmation of the portrait painted by previous studies, chronic pain patients were more depressed and anxious and less satisfied with their lives than patients without pain, and they were more likely to dwell on their illness and resist physicians' reassurances.

Chronic pain is by no means "all in the head." It most likely reflects an interaction of psychological factors, physiological vulnerabilities, and disease or injury. But this research suggests that the way people experience themselves and the world does, in fact, affect their vulnerability to their own sensory processes.

Proprioceptive Senses

Aside from the five traditional senses—vision, hearing, smell, taste, and touch—two additional senses, called **proprioceptive senses**, register body position and movement. **Kinesthesia** provides information about the movement and position of the limbs and other parts of the body relative to each other. Kinesthesia is essential in guiding every complex movement, from walking, which requires instantaneous adjustments of the two legs, to drinking a cup of coffee. Some of the receptors for kinesthesia are in the joints; these cells transduce information about the position of the bones. Other receptors, in the tendons and muscles, transmit messages about muscle tension that signal body position (Gandevia et al., 1992; Neutra & LeBlond, 1969).

The other proprioceptive sense, the **vestibular sense**, provides information on the position of the body in space by sensing gravity and movement. The ability to sense gravity is a very early evolutionary development, found in nearly all animals. The existence of this sense again exemplifies the way psychological characteristics have evolved to match characteristics of the environment that impact on adaptation. Gravity affects movement, so humans and other animals have receptors to transduce it, just as they have receptors for light.

Without the capacity to sense position of the body in space and position of the limbs relative to each other, this skier would be on his way to the hospital rather than the lodge.

The vestibular sense organs are in the inner ear, above the cochlea (see Figure 4.22, p. 140). Two organs transduce vestibular information: the semicircular canals and the vestibular sacs. The **semicircular canals** sense acceleration or deceleration in any direction as the head moves. The **vestibular sacs** sense gravity and the position of the head in space. Vestibular receptors are hair cells that register movement, much as hair cells in the ear transduce air movements. The neural pathways for the vestibular sense are not well understood, although impulses from the vestibular system travel to several regions of the hindbrain, notably the cerebellum, which is involved in smooth movement, and to a region deep in the temporal cortex (Carlson, 1991).

The vestibular and kinesthetic senses work in tandem, sensing different aspects of movement and position. Proprioceptive sensations are also integrated with messages from other sensory systems, especially touch and vision. For example, even when the proprioceptive senses are intact, walking can be difficult if tactile stimulation from the feet is shut off (as when the legs fall asleep). The integration of visual and vestibular information is perhaps most apparent when it is not working correctly, as with motion sickness, which appears to result in part from the discrepancy between random movements registered by the vestibular organs and reports of a more stabilized image from the visual system.

PERCEPTION

The line between sensation and perception is thin—sometimes barely perceptible—and we probably have already crossed it in discussing the psychology of pain perception. Indeed, for some senses, such as taste and smell, a distinction between sensation and perception can hardly be maintained because sensations automatically give rise to impressions about the object being sensed (the taste of butter, the smell of bacon). For these senses, the association areas of the cortex that give meaning to stimuli occupy smaller regions than for vision and hearing. In general, however, perception involves activation of association areas of the cortex, thus integrating prior knowledge with current sensation.

The hallmarks of perception are organization and interpretation. (Many psychologists consider attention a third aspect of perception, but since attention is also involved in memory, thought, consciousness, motivation, and emotion, we address it later, in Chapter 9.) Perception organizes a continuous array of sensations into meaningful units. When we speak, we produce a dozen meaningful linguistic sounds (called phonemes) per second (such as "walk" and "-ing") and are capable of understanding 10 to 40 phonemes per second (Pinker, 1994). When we listen to a symphony or popular song, we can easily follow the melody despite the presence of other instruments or voices. This requires organization of sensations. Beyond organization, perception requires interpretation of the information organized. A scrawl on a piece of paper is not just a set of lines of particular orientation but a series of letters and words. A melodic pattern in the middle of a song or symphony is not just a novel set of notes but a variation on an earlier theme.

In this final section, we again emphasize the visual system, since the bulk of work in perception has used visual stimuli, but most of the same principles hold across sensory modalities. We begin by discussing three types of perceptual organization: form perception, depth perception, and perceptual constancy. Next we address two influences on interpretation: experience and motivation.

Organization

If you put this book on the floor, it does not blur into the floor or appear two-dimensional. If you walk slowly away from it, it does not seem to diminish in size, even though it casts a progressively smaller image on the retina. These are examples of perceptual organization. **Perceptual organization** integrates sensations into **percepts** (meaningful perceptual units, such as images of particular objects), puts these percepts in perspective and locates them in space, and prevents stimuli from changing their appearance as the perceiver examines them from another vantage point. **Form perception** refers to the organization of sensations into meaningful shapes and patterns; you perceive the book not as part of the floor but as a distinct object. **Depth perception** is the organization of perception in three dimensions; you perceive the book as having height, width, and breadth, and being at a particular distance, even though the retinal image is two-dimensional. **Perceptual constancy** refers to the organization of changing sensations into percepts that are relatively stable in size, shape, and color; you do not perceive the book as changing in size as you walk away or view it from a different angle, even though its retinal image changes. We examine each aspect of perceptual organization in turn.

Form Perception

Form perception—the way sensations are organized into meaningful shapes and patterns—was first studied systematically in Germany in the early twentieth century by the **Gestalt psychologists**. As noted in Chapter 1, *Gestalt* is a German word that translates loosely to "whole" or "form"; Gestalt psychologists were concerned with meaningful patterns or wholes. Proponents of the Gestalt approach argued that perceptions are more than the sum of their sensory parts. Based on the results of numerous experiments conducted in the 1920s and 1930s, the Gestalt psychologists proposed six major perceptual rules the brain follows automatically and unconsciously as it organizes sensory input into meaningful wholes: figure-ground, similarity, proximity, good continuation, simplicity, and closure.

A fundamental rule of form perception is **figure-ground perception**, namely that people inherently differentiate between figure (the object they are viewing) and ground (or background), such as words in black ink against a white page. The relationship between figure and ground, however, can be ambiguous, as in Figure 4.32. Such ambiguity highlights the distinction between sensation and perception, since the retinal image is the same whether one sees an old woman or a young woman; what changes is the interpretation of this image. To focus simultaneously on figure and ground is impossible. While you may see an old woman and a young woman in rapid sequence, you cannot see them at the same time. In fact, one sign of psychosis (a gross disturbance in the capacity to perceive reality) is blurring figure and ground on perceptual tests. For example, a psychotic patient looking at Figure 4.32 might respond that it looks like "an old young woman." Apparently, the psychotic person cannot control the ideas that automatically come to mind and organize them. The figure–ground principle applies to other senses as well. When people attend to the voice of a waiter in a noisy restaurant, his voice becomes figure and all other sounds, ground.

A second fundamental rule of form perception is **similarity**: The brain tends to group similar elements within a perceptual field, such as the circles that form the letter R in Figure 4.33a. Another principle, **proximity** (nearness), means that, other things being equal, the brain groups objects together that are close to each other. In Figure 4.33b, the first six lines have no particular organization, whereas the same six lines arranged somewhat differently in the second part of the panel are perceived as three pairs. The Gestalt rule of **good continuation** states that, if possible, the brain organizes stimuli into continuous lines or patterns rather than discontinuous elements. For example, in Figure 4.33c, the figure appears to show an *X* on top of a circle, rather than pieces of a pie with lines extending beyond the pie's perimeter. Similarity, proximity, and good continuation are all rules of perceptual grouping that distinguish objects from each other. Like the figure-ground principle, perceptual grouping principles apply to sense modalities other than vision. For example,

FIGURE 4.32
Whether this drawing appears to depict a young woman or an old woman depends on what the perceiver considers figure or ground. SOURCE: *Boring, 1930, p. 42.*

FIGURE 4.33
Gestalt principles of form perception. The Gestalt psychologists discovered a set of laws of perceptual organization, including (a) similarity, (b) proximity, (c) good continuation, (d) simplicity, and (e) closure. SOURCE: *Part (e) adapted from Kanizsa, 1976.*

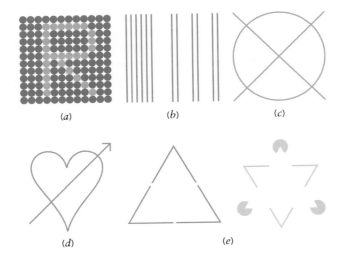

good continuation allows people to hear a series of notes as a melody, similarity allows them to recognize a melody played on a violin while other instruments are playing, and proximity groups notes played together as a chord.

According to the Gestalt rule of **simplicity**, people tend to perceive the simplest pattern possible. Most people perceive Figure 4.33*d* as a heart with an arrow through it because that is the simplest interpretation. Alternatively, the figure could be a line sticking out of a curved line perpendicular to it attached to other curved lines, and so forth. Finally, the rule of **closure** states that people tend to perceive incomplete figures as complete. If part of a familiar pattern or shape is missing, perceptual processes complete the pattern, as in the triangle shown in Figure 4.33*e*. The second part of Figure 4.33*e* demonstrates another type of closure, sometimes called subjective or cognitive contour (Albert, 1993; Kanizsa, 1976). People see two overlapping triangles, but in fact, neither one exists; the brain simply fills in the gaps to perceive familiar patterns. Covering the incomplete black circles at each angle of the triangle reveals that the solid white triangle is entirely an illusion.

The Gestalt principles exemplify the way psychological regularities reflect the regularities of nature (Sekuler & Blake, 1994). In nature, the parts of objects tend to be near each other and attached. Thus, the principles of proximity and good continuation are useful perceptual rules of thumb. Similarly, objects often partially block or occlude other objects, as when a squirrel crawls up the bark of a tree. The principle of closure leads humans and other animals to assume the existence of the part of the tree that is covered by the squirrel's body.

Sometimes the brain's efforts to organize sensations into coherent and accurate percepts fail. This is the case with **perceptual illusions**, in which normal perceptual processes produce perceptual misinterpretations. Impossible figures are one such type of illusion, which produce conflicting cues for three-dimensional organization, as illustrated in Figure 4.34. The second part of the figure shows a painting called *Concave and Convex* by M. C. Escher, an artist who made explicit use of psychological research on perception in his work (Ernst, 1976). Recognizing the impossibility of these figures takes time because the brain attempts to impose order by using principles such as simplicity on data that allow no simple solution. Each portion of an impossible figure is credible, but as soon as the brain organizes sensations in one way, another part of the figure invalidates it.

Depth Perception

A second aspect of perceptual organization is depth perception. We focus again on the visual system, although auditory cues also localize objects in space, as do kinesthetic sensations about the extension of the body while touching an object. Two kinds of visual information provide information about depth and distance:

(a) *(b)*

FIGURE 4.34
Impossible figures. The brain cannot form a stable percept because each time it does, another segment of the figure renders the percept impossible. Escher, who painted the impossible figure in (b), made use of perceptual research.

binocular cues (visual input integrated from the two eyes) and **monocular cues** (visual input from a single eye alone).

Binocular Cues   Because the eyes are in slightly different locations, all but the most distant objects produce a different image on each retina, or a **retinal disparity**. To demonstrate this to yourself, hold your finger about 6 inches from your nose and alternately close your left and right eye. You will note that each eye sees your finger in a slightly different position. Now, do the same for a distant object; you will note only minimal differences between the views. Retinal disparity is greatest for close objects and diminishes as objects move away.

How does the brain translate retinal disparity into depth perception? Most cells in the primary visual cortex are **binocular cells,** which receive information from both eyes. Some of these cells respond most vigorously when the same input arrives from each eye, whether the input is a vertical line, a horizontal line, or a line moving in one direction. Other binocular cells respond to different sorts of disparities between the eyes. Like many cells receptive to particular orientations, binocular cells require environmental input early in life to assume their normal functions. Researchers have learned about binocular cells by allowing kittens to see with only one eye at a time, covering one eye or the other on alternate days. As adults, these cats are unable to use binocular cues for depth (Blake & Hirsch, 1975; Packwood & Gordon, 1975).

Two other binocular cues, convergence and accommodation, are actually more kinesthetic than visual, since they rely on sensation of muscle movement in the eyes. When looking at a close object (such as your finger 6 inches in front of your face), the eyes converge, whereas distant objects require ocular divergence; this provides a depth cue called **convergence**. Objects at different distances also cause the lens to assume different shapes to maximize visual acuity (**accommodation**). Thus, the brain uses information about eye-muscle movements that control ocular convergence and lens accommodation to gauge distance.

Monocular Cues   Although binocular cues are extremely important for depth perception, people do not crash their cars whenever an eyelash momentarily gets into one eye because they can still rely on monocular cues. The photographs in Figure 4.35 illustrate the main monocular depth cues that arise even when looking at a nonmoving scene. **Interposition** occurs when one object blocks part of another, leading to perception of the occluded object as more distant. **Elevation** refers to the fact that objects farther away are higher on a person's plane of view and thus appear higher up toward the horizon. Another monocular cue is **texture gradient**: When looking at textured surfaces, such as cobblestones or grained wood, the pattern or texture appears coarser at close range and finer and more densely packed at greater distances. A similar mechanism for monocular depth perception is **linear perspective**: Parallel lines appear to converge in the distance. **Shading** also provides monocular depth cues, since two-dimensional objects do not cast shadows. The brain assumes that light comes from above and hence interprets shading differently toward the top or the bottom of an object. Another cue is **aerial perspective**: Since

FIGURE 4.35

Monocular depth cues. The photo of the Taj Mahal in India (a) illustrates all of the monocular cues to depth perception: interposition (the trees blocking the sidewalks and the front of the building), elevation (the most distant object being the highest), texture gradient (the relative clarity of the breaks in the walkway closer to the camera), linear perspective (the convergence of the lines of the walkway surrounding the water), shading (the indentations of the arches toward the top of the building), aerial perspective (the lack of detail of the birds in the distance), familiar size (the person standing on the walkway who seems tiny), and relative size (the diminishing size of the trees as they get further away). Several other photos show just how much we rely on monocular cues automatically including (b) texture, linear perspective, and aerial perspective; (c) interposition and shading; (d) linear perspective; (e) familiar size; and (f) relative size and interposition.

(a)   *(b)*

FIGURE 4.36
Artistic use of monocular cues for depth perception has developed tremendously since Giotto's "Flight into Egypt" painted in the fifteenth century (a). In the Cyclorama exhibit in Atlanta (b), which depicts the Battle of Atlanta during the U.S. Civil War, the artists had such mastery of monocular cues for depth perception that visitors cannot easily tell where actual three dimensional objects (soldiers, trees, etc.) end and a painted background begins.

light scatters as it passes through space, and especially through moist or polluted air, objects at greater distances appear fuzzier than those nearby. Two other cues rely on the individual's knowledge of the size of familiar objects. **Familiar size** refers to the tendency to assume an object is its usual size; thus, people perceive familiar objects that appear small as distant. Closely related is **relative size:** When looking at two objects known to be of similar size, people perceive the smaller object as farther away.

Artists working in two-dimensional media rely on monocular depth cues to represent a three-dimensional world. Humans have used interposition and elevation to convey depth for thousands of years. Other cues, however, such as linear perspective, were not discovered until as late as the fifteenth century, so that art before that time appears flat to the modern eye (Figure 4.36). Although some monocular cues appear to be innate, cross-cultural research suggests that perceiving three dimensions in two-dimensional drawings is partially learned, influenced by artistic conventions and experience with different kinds of two-dimensional media (Berry et al., 1992). Some people in technologically less developed cultures who have never seen photography initially have difficulty recognizing even their own images in two-dimensional form.

A final monocular depth cue arises from movement. When people move, images of nearby objects sweep across their field of vision faster than objects farther away. This disparity in apparent velocity produces a depth cue called **motion parallax**. The relative motion of nearby versus distant objects is particularly striking when looking out the window of a moving car or train. Nearby trees appear to speed by, whereas distant objects barely seem to move.

Depth cues generally lead to accurate inferences about depth and distance, but they can also give rise to perceptual illusions. A classic example is the moon illusion, in which the moon seems larger on the horizon than at its zenith (Figure 4.37). The moon illusion appears to result from depth cues such as relative size; the moon seems larger against a backdrop of large buildings than against a backdrop of stars that provide no depth cues.

Perceptual Constancy

Thus far, we have explored two ways that perception organizes sensations: It organizes them into patterns, and it organizes them in space. A third form of perceptual organization, **perceptual constancy**, refers to the perception of objects as relatively stable despite changes in the stimulation of sensory receptors. We recognize that a radio is blaring in the car behind us by the pounding bass, even though we can barely hear the song, just as we know the sofa does not change its shape as we view it from different angles (shape constancy). Here we examine two kinds of visual constancy, color and size constancy.

FIGURE 4.37
The moon illusion. The moon appears larger against a city skyline than high in the sky, where, among other things, no depth cues exist.

Color Constancy   **Color constancy** refers to the tendency to perceive the color of objects as stable despite changing illumination.   An apple appears the same color in the kitchen as it does in the sunlight, even thought the light illuminating it is very different.   A similar phenomenon occurs with achromatic color (black and white). Snow against a dark shadow appears whiter than coal appears in sunlight, even though the amount of light reflected off the coal may be greater (Schiffman, 1996). In perceiving the brightness of an object, the brain essentially computes the amount of light reflectance *relative* to the amount of illumination.   In other words, perceptual mechanisms adjust for the amount of light when determining brightness.   For chromatic colors, the mechanism is more complicated, but color constancy does not work if the light contains only a narrow band of wavelengths.   Being in a room with only red lightbulbs causes even familiar objects to appear red.

Size Constancy   A second type of perceptual constancy is **size constancy**: Familiar objects do not appear to change in size when viewed from different distances.   The closer an object is, the larger an image it casts on the retina; a car 10 feet away will cast a retinal image five times as large as that cast by the same car 50 feet away.   Yet people do not wonder how the car 50 feet away can possibly carry full-sized passengers.   Just as the size of familiar objects provides a monocular cue for distance, perceived distance influences judgments about size (Figure 4.38).   Helmholtz (1909)

FIGURE 4.38
In (a), the man and the pyramids appear to be of normal size because the pyramids are off in the distance. The photo in (b) is perceptually confusing because the distance cues have been distorted by doctoring the photo.

was the first to recognize that the brain adjusts for distance when assessing the size of familiar objects, just as it adjusts for color and brightness. He called this process "unconscious inference" because people have no consciousness of the computations involved.

A GLOBAL VISTA

CULTURE AND PERCEPTUAL ILLUSIONS

Size constancy, like other processes of perceptual organization, can sometimes produce perceptual illusions. This appears to be the case with the **Müller-Lyer illusion,** in which two lines of equal length appear different in size (Figure 4.39a). According to one prominent theory, the angled lines provide linear perspective cues that make the vertical line appear closer or farther away (Gregory, 1978). The brain then adjusts for distance, interpreting the fact that the retinal images of the two vertical lines are the same size as evidence that the line on the right is longer. Similar principles explain the three-dimensional version of the illusion (Figure 4.39b), which adds shading cues for depth perception.

If the Müller-Lyer illusion relies on depth cues such as linear perspective that are not recognized in all cultures, will people in some cultures be more susceptible to the illusion than others? That is, does vulnerability to an illusion depend on culture and experience, or is it rooted in the structure of the brain? A team of psychologists and anthropologists set out to answer these questions three decades ago in what turned out to be a classic study (Segall et al., 1966).

Two hypotheses that guided the investigators are especially relevant. The first is that the nature of architecture in a culture influences the tendency to experience particular illusions. According to this hypothesis, people reared in cultures lacking roads that join at angles, rectangular buildings, and houses with angled roofs lack experience with the kinds of cues that give rise to the Müller-Lyer illusion and hence will be less susceptible to it. Second, individuals from cultures that do not use sophisticated two-dimensional cues (such as linear perspective) to represent three dimensions in pictures should also be less vulnerable to perceptual illusions of this sort.

The researchers presented subjects from 14 non-Western and three Western societies with several stimuli designed to elicit perceptual illusions. They found that Western subjects were consistently more likely to experience

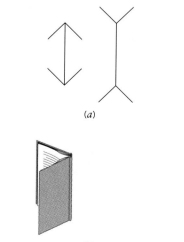

(a)

(b)

FIGURE 4.39
The Müller-Lyer illusion. In its original version (a), the line on the right appears longer than the line on the left. In a three-dimensional variant (b), the first two books appear closer together than the second two, even though the spines of each are equidistant. SOURCE: *Part (b) Adapted from De Lucia & Hochberg, 1991.*

(a)

People from this African village (a) are less susceptible to illusions involving straight lines than people who live in "carpentered worlds," such as Paris (b), who are familiar with angled buildings and streets.

(b)

the Müller-Lyer illusion than non-Western subjects, but they were no more likely to experience other illusions unrelated to angles and sophisticated depth cues. Subsequent studies have replicated their findings with the Müller-Lyer illusion (Pedersen & Wheeler, 1983; Segall et al., 1990). Teasing apart the relative impact of architecture and exposure to pictures is difficult, but the available data support both hypotheses (Berry et al., 1992).

Size constancy is involved in another famous illusion, the **Ponzo illusion**, which also appears to be influenced by culture and experience (Figure 4.40). Linear perspective cues indicate that the upper bar is larger because it seems farther away. Cross-culturally, people who live in environments in which lines converge in the distance (such as railroad tracks and long straight highways)

FIGURE 4.40
The Ponzo illusion. Converging lines that signal depth lead to the perception of the upper red bar as larger since it appears to be farther away. The bars are actually identical in length.

appear to be more susceptible to this illusion than people from environments with relatively few converging lines (Brislin & Keating, 1976). Thus, although sensory processes are rooted in biology, cultural and environmental influences affect perception.

Interpretation

The processes of perceptual organization we have examined—form perception, depth perception, and perceptual constancy—organize sensations into stable, recognizable forms, but they do not endow them with meaning. In other words, perceptual organization does not classify objects or determine their emotional or adaptive significance. Generating meaning from sensory experience is the task of **perceptual interpretation**.

Perceptual interpretation lies at the intersection of sensation and memory, as the brain interprets current sensations in light of past experience. This can occur at a very primitive level—reacting to a bitter taste, recoiling from an object coming toward the face, or responding emotionally to a familiar voice—without either consciousness or cortical involvement. Much of the time, however, interpretation involves classification of stimuli—a moving object is a dog, a pattern of tactile stimulation is a soft caress—that requires interaction between primary and association cortex. In this final section, we examine two influences on interpretation: experience and motivation.

The Influence of Experience

To what degree does perception rely on past experience? This question leads us back to the nature-nurture debate that runs through nearly every domain of psychology. The German philosopher Immanuel Kant argued that humans innately experience the world using certain categories, such as time, space, and causality. For example, when a person slams a door and the door frame shakes, we naturally make a causal inference, that slamming the door led to rattling of the frame. In this view, people automatically infer causality, prior to any learning.

In psychology, the theory of **direct perception**, championed by James Gibson (1966, 1979), similarly holds that perception requires little prior knowledge and that sensory information intrinsically carries meaning. For example, with respect to perceptual organization, Gibson argued that the image on the retina provides constancy cues that do not require prior knowledge. Objects do not appear to change size, among other reasons, because their size relative to other objects reflected on the retina does not change. With respect to perceptual interpretation, Gibson argued that the senses were designed to respond to aspects of the environment relevant to adaptation, so that the meaning of stimuli is inherent in sensory experience. In other words, stimuli present themselves to the senses, and their meaning for adaptation is often obvious: An object coming rapidly toward the face is dangerous; food with a sweet taste affords energy; a stimulus that is intensely hot is dangerous.

Laboratory evidence of direct perception comes from studies using the **visual cliff**. The visual cliff is a clear table with a "shallow" checkerboard on one side and a "deep" checkerboard that appears to drop off like a cliff on the other (Figure 4.41). Infants are reluctant to crawl to the side of the table that looks deep even when they have just begun crawling and have no experience with precipices (E. Gibson & Walk, 1960). According to the theory of direct perception, both the understanding of depth cues and the meaning of falling off a cliff are native endowments of the human species.

FIGURE 4.41
The visual cliff. Infants are afraid to crawl over the "cliff" even when they have just begun to crawl and therefore have no experience leading them to fear it.

Another possible example of innate perceptual meaning may be the way people across the globe evaluate colors. Two decades ago researchers found that preschool children in the United States from various racial groups tended to prefer light- to dark-skinned people and to favor the color white over black (Williams & Morland, 1976). An obvious explanation was that the children had simply learned the racist biases of their culture. Yet previous research had established, across several continents and languages, that people all over the world associate the color white with more positive feelings than black and that this bias emerged by the preschool years in Japan, France, Italy, Germany, and Great Britain. Subsequent research shows that native African children share the same bias (Williams & Best, 1990). The investigators speculate that, beyond culturally imposed meanings, the pan-cultural preference for light over dark may reflect a generalization from light and dark cycles of the day. For young children as well as for adults, light is associated with safety, whereas darkness generates universal meanings of danger. Whether this association is innate or learned in infancy is unclear. Or perhaps the answer is more complex. Nature may have endowed humans with a tendency to dislike the dark, just as it has endowed them with a susceptibility to fear of snakes and spiders (Chapter 5). The degree to which children generalize this tendency to skin color, however, likely depends on cultural messages.

Nature and Nurture   Answers to the nature-nurture question have become more sophisticated as psychologists have come to recognize that the nervous system has certain innate potentialities—such as seeing in depth or localizing sound auditorially—but that these potentialities require environmental input to develop. In one set of studies, researchers reared kittens in darkness for their first five months of life except for five hours each day, during which they placed the kittens in a cylinder with either horizontal or vertical stripes (Blakemore & Cooper, 1970). The kittens saw only the stripes, since they wore a big collar that kept them from seeing even their own bodies. As adults, the kittens reared in horizontal environments were unable to perceive vertical lines, and they lacked cortical feature detectors responsive to vertical lines; the opposite was true of kittens reared in a vertical environment. Although these cats were genetically programmed to have both vertical and horizontal feature detectors, their brains adapted to a world without certain features to detect.

Other studies have outfitted infant kittens and monkeys with translucent goggles that allow light to pass through, but only in diffuse, unpatterned form. When the animals are adults and the goggles are removed, they are able to perform simple perceptual tasks without difficulty, such as distinguishing colors, brightness, and size. However, they have difficulty with more complex tasks; for example, they are unable to distinguish forms or to track moving objects (Riesen, 1960, 1965; Wiesel, 1982). Similar findings have emerged in studies of humans who were born blind but subsequently obtained sight in adulthood as a result of surgery (Gregory, 1978; Sacks, 1993; von Senden, 1960). Most of these individuals can discern figure from ground, sense colors, and follow moving objects, but a considerable number cannot recognize objects they previously knew by touch and hence remain functionally blind.

Early experiences are not the only experiences that shape the neural systems underlying sensation and perception. In one study, monkeys who were taught to make fine pitch discriminations showed increases in the size of the cortical regions responsive to pitch (Recanzone et al., 1993). Intriguing research with humans finds that practice at discriminating letters manually in Braille produces changes in the brain. A larger region of the cortex of Braille readers is devoted to the fingertips with which they read (Pascual-Leone & Torres, 1993). Thus, experience can alter the structure of the brain, making it more or less responsive to subsequent sensory input.

Bottom-Up and Top-Down Processing   Beyond neuronal changes, to what extent does experience influence perception? Psychologists have traditionally taken two

Kittens reared in a horizontal world lost their innate capacity to see vertical lines.

opposing stands, which now appear to be complementary. (This seems to be the case with a number of classic debates about sensation and perception.) One view emphasizes the role of sensory data, whereas the other emphasizes the influence of prior experience. **Bottom-up processing** refers to processing that begins "at the bottom" with raw sensory data that feed "up" to the brain. A bottom-up explanation of visual perception argues that the brain forms perceptions by combining the responses of multiple feature detectors in the primary cortex, which themselves integrate input from neurons lower in the visual system. **Top-down processing** starts "at the top," from the observer's expectations and knowledge. Theorists who focus on top-down processing maintain that the brain organizes and interprets incoming sensations based on prior knowledge and expectations rather than waiting for percepts to form based on their isolated features.

Both approaches have considerable empirical support. Research on motion perception provides an example of the accuracy of bottom-up processing. Psychologists trained monkeys to report the direction in which a display of dots moved while the researchers observed the response of individual neurons previously identified as feature detectors for movement of a particular speed and direction (Newsome et al., 1989). They discovered that the "decisions" made by individual neurons about the direction the dots moved were as accurate—and sometimes more so—than the decisions of the monkeys! Perceptual decisions on simple tasks of this sort may require little involvement of higher mental processes. On the other hand, reading these words provides a good example of top-down processing, since reading would be incredibly cumbersome if people had to detect every letter of every word from the bottom up rather than expecting and recognizing patterns.

A fascinating study demonstrates precisely how expectations can have a top-down influence on the cortical neurons that register sensory stimulation (Mistlin & Perrett, 1990). The researchers were studying a cortical region in macaque monkeys that responds to both visual and tactile stimulation when they noticed that neurons in this region responded differently to expected and unexpected stimuli. To study the phenomenon, they compared the activation level of neurons when the monkey touched a very familiar metal stimulus (part of its chair) or an unfamiliar metal stimulus. In both conditions, the monkey's vision was blocked, but its chair was in an expected location. As can be seen in Figure 4.42, touching the expected stimulus produced little neural activity, whereas touching the unexpected object led to firing of the cortical cell, demonstrating the impact of expectations on perception.

Trying to explain perception by either bottom-up or top-down processes alone presents a paradox. You would not be able to identify the shapes in Figure 4.43*a*

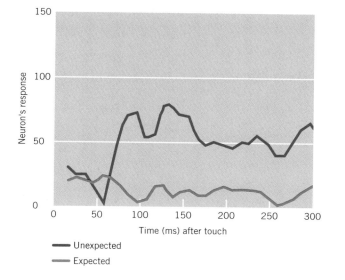

FIGURE 4.42
Expectations and neural firing. Expectations modulate the firing of a neuron in the macaque cortex. SOURCE: Adapted from Mistlin & Perrett, 1990.

FIGURE 4.43
Top-down and bottom-up-processing. In isolation (perceiving from the bottom up), the designs in (a) would have no meaning, but the broader design in (b), the dog, cannot be recognized without recognizing these component parts.

unless you knew they were part of a dog. Yet you would not recognize Figure 4.43*b* as a dog unless you could process information about the specific parts shown in the first panel of the figure. Without bottom-up processing, external stimuli would have no effect on perception; we would hallucinate rather than perceive. Without top-down processing, experience would have no effect on perception. How, then, do people ever recognize and classify objects?

According to current thinking, perception proceeds in both directions simultaneously. For example, features of the environment create patterns of stimulation in the primary cortex. These patterns in turn stimulate neural circuits in the association cortex that represent various objects, such as a friend's face. If the perceiver expects to see that face, or if a large enough component of the neural network representing the face gets activated, the brain essentially forms a "hypothesis" about an incoming pattern of sensory stimulation, even though all the data are not yet in from the feature detectors. Contemporary models of human cognition suggest that all information processing, from sensation and perception through complex thinking, involves processes that occur in parallel and mutually activate each other (Chapter 7).

Expectations and Perception Experience with the environment shapes perception by creating perceptual expectations. These expectations, called **perceptual set**, make particular interpretations more likely. Two aspects of perceptual set are the current context and enduring knowledge structures. Context plays a substantial role in perceptual interpretation in nearly every sensory modality. Consider, for example, how readily you understood the meaning of *substantial role* in the last sentence. Had someone uttered that phrase in a bakery, you would have assumed they meant *substantial roll* unless the rest of the sentence provided a context suggesting otherwise. In the tactile realm, the same pattern of stimulation can have very different meanings—for example, if a hug comes from a relative or a relative stranger. Figure 4.44 illustrates the importance of context in the visual mode. Context is especially

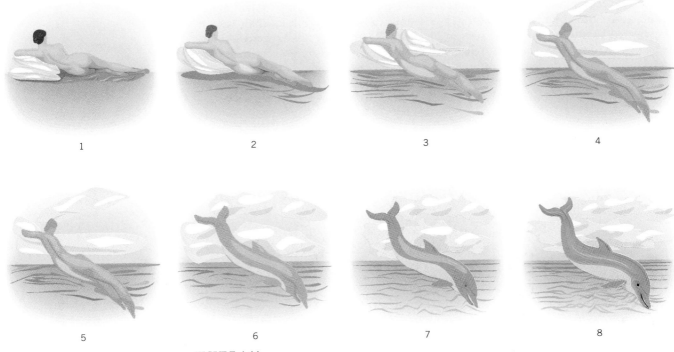

FIGURE 4.44
The impact of context on perception. Look at drawings 1, 2, 3, and 4, in that order (top row, left to right). Now look at drawings 5, 6, 7, and 8, in reverse order (bottom row, right to left). Drawing 4 most likely seems to be a woman's body and drawing 5, a porpoise, yet drawing 4 and 5 are identical. The same pattern of stimulation can be interpreted in many ways depending on context.

Schemas produce expectations that can sometimes lead perception astray. Turn the book over and the abnormality in one photo of Bill Clinton is readily apparent.

important in perceiving spoken language (Chapter 7), since even the most careful speaker drops syllables, slurs sounds, or misses words altogether, and many words (such as role and roll) have the same sound but different meanings.

Another way prior experience shapes perception is through enduring structures of knowledge. Knowledge is not stored in memory in isolated bits. Rather, it is organized by patterns of thought that render the environment relatively predictable, called **schemas** (Neisser, 1976). Schemas are organized into categories, such as things (chairs, dogs), people (introverts, ministers), or situations (funerals, dining out). Because schemas allow people to anticipate what they will encounter, they increase both the speed and efficiency of perception. For example, people process information extremely quickly when shown photographs of real-world scenes, such as a kitchen, a city street, or a desk top (Figure 4.45). In one study, subjects could recall almost half the objects in familiar scenes after viewing them for only one-tenth of a second (Biederman et al., 1973). In contrast, subjects in a second condition who viewed the scenes cut into six equal pieces and randomly reassembled had difficulty both identifying and remembering the objects in the picture. Schemas can also, however, produce perceptual errors. For example, before reading further, look briefly at part (c) of Figure 4.45. People rarely notice the unexpected object in the

| (a) | (b) | (c) |

FIGURE 4.45

Schemas. Subjects have no trouble remembering objects in (a) a photo of a normal Chinatown street because the scene activates a "city street schema" that guides perception and memory. Without a schema, they would have much more difficulty with (b). Schemas can also lead to perceptual failures, as in (c), in which people frequently fail to notice a misplaced object.

upper right-hand corner (the fire hydrant) because it is incongruent with their activated "restaurant" schema (Biederman et al., 1981, 1982).

A Different Perspective: The New Look, Motivation, and Perception

We have seen that expectations influence perception. People tend to see what they expect to see, hear the words they expect to hear, and so forth. But people often hear the words they *want* to hear, too. In other words, motivation, like cognition, exerts a top-down influence on perception. This was the argument of a school of perceptual thought in the late 1940s called the New Look in perception (in contrast to the "old look," which paid more attention to pinnas than to personality). The **New Look** integrated perceptual research with personality theory, especially psychodynamic theory, and focused on the influence of motives on perception. Many of the questions raised by the New Look school are once again at the forefront of psychological inquiry (see, for example, Bruner, 1992; Greenwald, 1992; Uleman & Bargh, 1989).

One way the New Look researchers investigated the effects of need states on perception was to see what happened to perceptual processes when people were deprived—of food, water, money, or other necessities. One experiment examined the effects of food and water deprivation on word identification (Wispe & Drambarean, 1953). The experimenters placed subjects in one of three groups. Some went without food for 24 hours prior to the experiment, some ate nothing for 10 hours, and others ate just beforehand. The researchers then rapidly flashed two kinds of words on a screen: neutral words (e.g., *serenade* and *hunch*) and words related to food (e.g., *lemonade* and *munch*). The three groups did not differ in their responses to the neutral words. However, both of the deprived groups perceived the need-related words at shorter exposure times than the nondeprived subjects. Thus, to a hungry person, the world is a hamburger. Outside the laboratory, people are often intensely aware of the aroma of food outside a restaurant when they are hungry but oblivious to it when their stomachs are full.

In another classic study, researchers compared the perceptual experiences of children from poor and wealthy families (Bruner & Goodman, 1946). They asked children to adjust the size of a circle of light to match the sizes of various coins—a penny, a nickel, a dime, and a quarter. Children from wealthier families tended to see the coins as smaller than they actually are, whereas children from poor families overestimated the size of the coins. The investigators argued that the need for money among children from poor homes influenced their perception of its size. This finding has been replicated in other cultures, such as Hong Kong (Dawson, 1975).

New Look researchers tested the impact of motivation on perception in another, more controversial way. Psychodynamic theory proposes that many motives are outside conscious awareness but influence conscious thought, feeling, and behavior nevertheless. To test this theory, researchers studied a phenomenon called **perceptual defense**, an unconscious tendency to resist perceiving anxiety-provoking stimuli. Few other topics in the recent history of experimental psychology have produced as sustained and bitter a controversy, which pitted those who believed in the existence of unconscious processes against those who did not (Erdelyi, 1985).

Early research testing the perceptual defense hypothesis typically compared the time subjects took to identify emotionally neutral words, such as *house* or *tree*, with comparable time for presumably anxiety-provoking words, such as *bitch* and *raped*. For example, in one study the experimenter flashed words very briefly from two lists, one neutral and one emotionally loaded (McGinnis, 1949). Exposure time started at .01 second and increased gradually until the subject correctly identified the words. As predicted, the emotionally threatening words required longer exposure than the neutral words, suggesting that the perceptual system defends against consciously perceiving anxiety-evoking stimuli.

Some critics offered alternative hypotheses to explain these and similar findings, arguing that the anxiety-provoking words were less familiar and thus more difficult to identify, or that the findings might merely reflect a response bias against saying objectionable words. Additional research did not, however, support these alternative explanations (Erdelyi, 1974). Other critics of the concept (e.g., Spence, 1967) focused on purely logical difficulties: How could a subject defend against perceiving a threatening stimulus without first perceiving it as threatening? New Look researchers responded that perception is a complex process with many stages prior to conscious experience, a proposition that is now widely accepted. Thus, a process inhibiting a word from consciousness could occur subsequent to an early, unconscious identification of the word and its emotional implications (Chapter 9).

SOME CONCLUDING THOUGHTS

Although the New Look was highly controversial, perhaps its main point is no longer in doubt: The way we come to know reality is rarely divorced from our reasons for knowing, and these reasons are rooted in motivation—that is, in the goals we bring to the perceptual process. Evolution has equipped humans with a nervous system remarkably attuned to stimuli of importance. If people did not need to eat or to worry about what they put in their mouths, they would not have a sense of taste. If they did not need to find food, escape danger, and communicate, they would not need to see and hear. And if their skin were not vulnerable to damage, they would not need to feel pain. What is meaningful and significant, however, is not only a product of biology. It also reflects cultural forces and idiosyncratic personal experiences.

Thus, although sensation and perception lie on a continuum of information processing that extends to memory and thought, they are also inextricably linked to the motivational processes that drive human thought and behavior. In the next few chapters, we examine a number of psychological processes that dovetail with sensation and perception. First, we describe the ways humans and other animals learn from their experience. Next, we explore the cognitive processes that guide perception and integrate perceptual experience into enduring knowledge structures. We then examine the motivational and emotional processes that ultimately provide the impetus for applying the knowledge delivered by our senses.

Summary

1. **Sensation** refers to the process by which sense organs gather information about the environment. **Perception** refers to the process by which the brain selects, organizes, and interprets sensations.

Basic Principles

2. Three basic principles apply across all sensory modalities. First, there is no one-to-one correspondence between physical and psychological reality. Second, sensation and perception are active, not passive. Third, sensation and perception are adaptive.

Sensing the Environment

3. Sensation begins with an environmental stimulus; all sensory systems have specialized cells called **receptors** that respond to environmental stimuli and typical-

ly generate action potentials in adjacent sensory neurons. This process is called **transduction**. Within each sensory modality, the brain codes sensory stimulation for intensity and quality.

4. The minimum amount of physical energy needed for an observer to perceive a stimulus is called an **absolute threshold**. **Signal detection theory** argues that the ability to detect a stimulus depends not only on characteristics of the stimulus, such as its intensity, but also on characteristics of the observer. Whether or not a person detects a signal depends first on the observer's sensitivity to it, and second on a **decision process** reflecting the observer's **response bias**—how readily the person reports detecting a stimulus when uncertain.

5. The **difference threshold** refers to the lowest level of stimulation required to sense that a *change* in stimulation has occurred (a **just noticeable difference**, or **jnd**). **Weber's law** states that regardless of the magnitude of two stimuli, the second must differ by a constant proportion from the first for it to be perceived as different. **Fechner's law** holds that the subjective magnitude of a stimulus grows as a proportion of the logarithm of the objective magnitude. **Stevens's power law** states that subjective intensity grows as a proportion of the actual intensity raised to some power—that is, that sensation increases in a linear fashion as actual intensity grows exponentially.

6. **Sensory adaptation** is the tendency of sensory systems to respond less to stimuli that continue without change.

Vision

7. The eyes are sensitive to a small portion of the electromagnetic spectrum called light. In vision, light is focused on the retina by the **cornea, pupil,** and **lens**. **Rods** are very sensitive to light, allowing vision in dim light; **cones** are especially sensitive to particular wavelengths, producing the psychological experience of color. Cones are concentrated at the **fovea**, the region of the retina where light is most directly focused by the lens. The **ganglion cells** of the retina transmit visual information via the **optic nerve** to the brain. Ganglion cells, like other neurons involved in sensation, have **receptive fields**, a region of stimulation to which the neuron responds. **Feature detectors** are specialized cells of the primary cortex in the occipital lobes that respond only when stimulation in their receptive field matches a particular pattern or orientation, such as horizontal or vertical lines.

8. The property of light that is transduced into color is **wavelength**. The **Young-Helmholtz** or **trichromatic theory** proposes that the eye contains three types of receptors, sensitive to red, green, or blue. **Opponent-process theory** argues for the existence of pairs of opposite primary colors linked in three systems: a blue-yellow system, a red-green system, and a black-white system. Both theories appear to be involved in color perception, with trichromatic theory operative at the level of the retina and opponent-process theory operative at higher neural levels.

Hearing

9. Hearing, or **audition**, occurs as a vibrating object sets air particles in motion. Each round of expansion and contraction of the air is known as a **cycle**. The number of cycles per second determines a sound wave's **frequency**, which corresponds to the psychological property of **pitch**. **Amplitude** refers to the height and depth of the wave and corresponds to the psychological property of **loudness**. Sound waves travel through the auditory canal to the **eardrum**, where they are amplified; transduction occurs by way of **hair cells** attached to the **basilar**

membrane that respond to vibrations in the fluid-filled **cochlea**. This mechanical process triggers action potentials in the **auditory nerve**, which are then transmitted to the brain.

10. Two theories, once considered opposing, explain the psychological qualities of sound. **Place theory**, which holds that different areas of the basilar membrane respond to different frequencies, appears to be most accurate for high frequencies. **Frequency theory**, which asserts that the basilar membrane's rate of vibration reflects the frequency with which a sound wave cycles, explains sensation of low-frequency sounds. In both theories, the neural code for loudness is the number of neurons firing.

Other Senses

11. The environmental stimuli for smell, or **olfaction**, are invisible molecules of gas emitted by substances and suspended in the air. As air enters the nose, it flows into the **olfactory epithelium**, where hundreds of different types of receptors respond to various kinds of molecules, producing complex smells. The axons of olfactory receptor cells constitute the **olfactory nerve**, which transmits information to the **olfactory bulbs** under the frontal lobes and on to the primary olfactory cortex, a primitive region of the cortex deep in the frontal lobes.

12. Taste, or **gustation**, is sensitive to molecules soluble in saliva. Much of the experience of taste, however, is really contributed by smell. Taste occurs as receptors in the **taste buds** on the tongue and throughout the mouth transduces chemical information into neural information, which is integrated with olfactory information in the brain.

13. Touch actually includes three senses: pressure, temperature, and pain. The human body contains approximately 5 million touch receptors of at least seven different types. Sensory neurons synapse with spinal interneurons that directly stimulate motor neurons, allowing reflexive action, as well as with neurons that carry information up the spinal cord to the medulla, where nerve tracts cross over. From there, sensory information travels to the thalamus and is subsequently routed to the primary touch center in the brain, the somatosensory cortex, which contains a map of the body. Pain is greatly affected by beliefs, expectations, and emotional state. **Gate-contol theory** holds that the experience of pain is affected by neural fibers that can "close the gate" on pain, preventing messages from other fibers getting through.

14. The **proprioceptive senses** provide information about the body's position and movement. **Kinesthesia** provides information about the movement and position of the limbs and other parts of the body relative to each other. The **vestibular sense** provides information on the position of the body in space by sensing gravity and movement.

Perception

15. The hallmarks of perception are organization and interpretation. **Perceptual organization** involves form and depth perception and perceptual constancy. **Form perception** refers to the organization of sensations into meaningful shapes and patterns (**percepts**). **Depth perception** is the organization of perception in three dimensions. **Perceptual constancy** refers to the organization of changing sensations into percepts that are relatively stable in size, shape, and color.

16. Principles of form perception include the Gestalt principles of figure–ground perception, similarity, proximity, good continuation, simplicity, and closure. Depth perception organizes two-dimensional retinal images into a three-dimensional world primarily through **binocular** and **monocular visual cues**. Two types

of perceptual constancy are size and color constancy, which refer to the perception of unchanging size and color despite momentary changes in the retinal image. The processes that organize perception leave perceivers vulnerable to **perceptual illusions**, some of which appear to be innate, whereas others depend on culture and experience.

17. **Perceptual interpretation** involves generating meaning from sensory experience. Perceptual interpretation lies at the intersection of sensation and memory, as the brain interprets current sensations in light of past experience. Perception is neither entirely innate nor entirely learned. The nervous system has certain innate potentialities, but these potentialities require environmental input to develop. Experience can alter the structure of the brain, making it more or less responsive to subsequent sensory input.

18. **Bottom-up processing** refers to processing that begins "at the bottom," with raw sensory data that feeds "up" to the brain. **Top-down processing** starts "at the top," from the observer's expectations and knowledge. According to current thinking, perception proceeds in both directions simultaneously. Experience with the environment shapes perceptual interpretation by creating perceptual expectations called **perceptual set**. Two aspects of perceptual set are current context and enduring knowledge structures called **schemas**. The **New Look** school of perception demonstrated that motives, like expectations, can influence perception, and particularly perceptual interpretation.

Paul Buckley, "Unlocking the Door," *1992*

Chapter 5

LEARNING

*A*n experiment by John Garcia and his colleagues adds a new twist to all the stories ever told about wolves and sheep. The researchers fed a wolf a muttonburger containing odorless, tasteless capsules of lithium chloride, a chemical that induces nausea. Displaying a natural preference for mutton, the animal wolfed it down but half an hour later became sick and vomited (Garcia & Garcia y Robertson, 1985; Gustavson, et al., 1976).

Several days later, the researchers introduced a sheep into the wolf's compound. At the sight of one of its favorite dishes, the wolf went straight for the sheep's throat. But on contact, the wolf abruptly drew back. It slowly circled the sheep. Soon it attacked from another angle, going for the

hamstring. This attack, however, was as short-lived as the last. After an hour in the compound together, the wolf still had not attacked the sheep—and in fact, the sheep had made a few short charges at the wolf. Lithium chloride seems to have been the real wolf in sheep's clothing.

Although the effects of a single dose of a toxic chemical do not last forever, Garcia's research illustrates the powerful impact of **learning**, which refers to any enduring change in the way an organism responds based on its experience. Why is learning important? The main reason is that the environment does not stand still; it varies from place to place and from moment to moment. Knowing how to distinguish edible from inedible foods, or to recognize enemies and predators, is essential for survival. The range of possible foods or threats is simply too great to be prewired into the brain, although many animal species have natural preferences and aversions that guide their learning, such as young children's attraction to sweets or fear of strangers. Not only is the natural environment complex and variable but so, too, is the social environment. In some Islamic cultures, a woman who shows her legs may be beaten; in other cultures, revealing skin may be a way to attract a mate. Even within a culture, the standards of appropriate behavior change across situations and over time. A skirt length that is acceptable in one context or during one era, for example, may be considered inappropriate or scandalous in another.

Theories of learning tend to share three assumptions. The first is that experience shapes behavior. Particularly in complex organisms such as humans, the vast majority of responses are learned rather than innate. The migration patterns of Pacific salmon may be instinctive, but the migration of college students to Daytona Beach during spring break is not. Second, learning is adaptive. Just as nature eliminates organisms that are not well suited to their environments, the environment naturally selects those behaviors in an individual that are adaptive and weeds out those that are not (Skinner, 1977). Behaviors useful to the organism (such as avoiding fights with larger members of its species) will be reproduced because of their consequences (safety from bodily harm). A third assumption is that careful experimentation can uncover laws of learning, many of which apply to human and nonhuman animals alike. Learning theorists believe that the way to test a theory is to see whether predictions logically derived from it hold true in the laboratory.

Since the turn of the century, the nature of learning has captured the imagination of generations of researchers. Psychologists have applied learning theories in the classroom to try to increase the pace and efficiency of learning and in the clinic to alter unwanted behaviors and emotional responses such as phobias. Learning theory is the foundation of the behaviorist perspective, and the bulk of this chapter explores the behaviorist concepts of classical and operant conditioning. The remainder examines cognitive approaches that emphasize the role of thought and social experience in learning.

CLASSICAL CONDITIONING

Classical conditioning (sometimes called Pavlovian or respondent conditioning) was the first kind of learning to be studied systematically. In the late nineteenth century, the Russian physiologist Ivan Pavlov (1849–1936) was studying the digestive systems of dogs (research for which he won a Nobel prize). During the course of his work, he noticed a peculiar phenomenon. Like humans and other animals, dogs normally salivate when presented with food, which is a simple reflex. A **reflex** is a behavior that is elicited automatically by an environmental stimulus, as when a doctor tests a knee-jerk reflex with a rubber hammer. A **stimulus** is something in the environment that elicits a response. Pavlov noticed that if an environmental stimulus, such as a bell ringing, repeatedly occurred just as a dog was about to be fed, the dog would start to salivate, even if food were not actually presented. As Pavlov understood it, the dog had learned to associate the bell with food, and because food produced the reflex of salivation, the bell also came to produce the reflex.

Pavlov's Model

An innate reflex such as salivation to food is an unconditioned reflex. **Conditioning** is a form of learning; hence, an **unconditioned reflex** is a reflex that occurs naturally, without any learning having taken place. The stimulus that produces the response in an unconditioned reflex is called an **unconditioned stimulus, (UCS).** An unconditioned stimulus activates a reflexive response without any learning having taken place; that is, it is unlearned, or unconditioned. An **unconditioned response (UCR)** is a response that does not have to be learned. In Pavlov's experiment, the UCS was food, and the UCR was salivation.

Pavlov's basic experimental set-up is illustrated in Figure 5.1. Shortly before the UCS (the food) was presented, Pavlov presented a neutral stimulus—that is, a stim-

FIGURE 5.1

Pavlov's dogs. Pavlov's research with dogs documented the phenomenon of classical conditioning. Actually, his dogs became conditioned to salivate in response to many aspects of the experimental situation and not just to bells; the sight of the experimenter and the harness, too, could elicit the conditioned response.

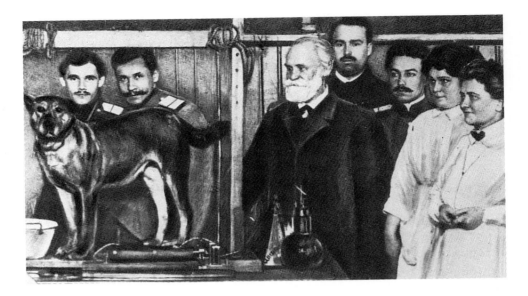

ulus that normally does not elicit a response related to the UCS (in this case, ringing a bell). After several pairings of the bell with the unconditioned stimulus (the food), the sound of the bell alone came to evoke a conditioned response, salivation (Figure 5.2). A **conditioned response (CR)** is a response that has been learned. By pairing the UCS (the food) with the sounding of a bell, the bell became a **conditioned stimulus (CS)**, or a stimulus that the organism learns to associate with the unconditioned stimulus. Figure 5.3 summarizes the classical conditioning process.

Why did such a seemingly simple discovery earn Pavlov a central place in the history of psychology? The reason is that classical conditioning is not restricted to laboratories and explains a wide array of learned responses. For example, a house cat that was repeatedly sprayed with flea repellent squinted reflexively as the repellent got in her eyes. She associated the repellent in her eyes (the UCS) with the sound of the spray can (the CS) and came to squint and meow piteously whenever her owner used an aerosol spray. If you are beginning to feel somewhat superior to the poor cat wasting all those meows and squints on a spray can, consider whether you have ever been at your desk, engrossed in work, when you glanced at the clock and discovered that it was dinner time. If so, you probably noticed some physiological responses—stomach growling, perhaps mouth watering—that had not been present before you looked at the clock. Through repeated pairings of stimuli associated with a particular time of day and the event of dinner, you have been classically conditioned to associate a time of day indicated on a clock (the CS) with food (the UCS).

FIGURE 5.2

Acquisition of a classically conditioned response. Initially, the dog did not salivate in response to the sound of the bell. By the third conditioning trial, however, the conditioned stimulus (the bell) had begun to elicit a conditioned response (salivation), which was firmly established by the fifth or sixth trial. SOURCE: Pavlov, 1927.

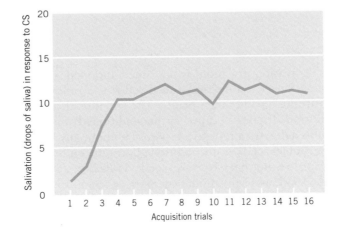

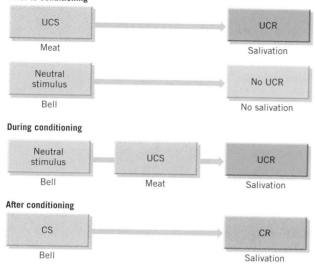

FIGURE 5.3
Classical conditioning. In classical conditioning, an initially neutral stimulus comes to elicit a conditioned response.

Classical conditioning can have a profound impact on human behavior. For example, chemotherapy for cancer often produces nausea as a side effect. As a result, chemotherapy patients frequently develop aversions to foods that become inadvertently associated with the nausea, which can contribute to serious weight loss. **Acquisition**, or initial learning, of this conditioned response can occur rapidly with only one or two exposures to the food paired with nausea (Bernstein, 1991), much as Garcia's wolf took little time to acquire an aversion to the taste of sheep. Some patients even begin to feel nauseous at the sound of a nurse's voice, the sight of the clinic, or the thought of treatment, although acquisition of these conditioned responses generally requires repeated exposure (Bovbjerg et al., 1990).

Other important physiological processes can be conditioned as well. Several researchers have studied the impact of classical conditioning on the **immune system**, a system of cells throughout the body that fight disease (e.g., Ader & Cohen, 1985, 1993; Grochowicz et al., 1991). Just as certain drugs can influence the functioning of these cells, so, too, can neutral stimuli (such as saccharin-flavored water) that have become associated with administration of these drugs. In other words, enhanced or diminished immune reactions can become conditioned responses. For example, aside from producing nausea, chemotherapy for cancer tends to suppress immune functioning. A study of female cancer patients found that changes in immune functioning also occur in response to cues associated with chemotherapy (Bovbjerg et al., 1990). The experimenters compared the immune response of blood taken from subjects at two different times: a few days before chemotherapy and the morning before chemotherapy after the patient was hospitalized (and hence exposed to the stimuli associated with prior chemotherapy experiences). The results were striking. Blood taken the morning of hospitalization showed weakened immune functioning when exposed to germs. Thus, immune suppression appeared to be a conditioned response to hospital cues (the CS) that had been paired with an aversive UCS (chemotherapy).

Conditioned Emotional Responses

Emotional responses can also be classically conditioned. Consider the automatic smile that comes to a person's face when hearing a special song, or the fear of elevators that a person develops after being trapped in one. **Conditioned emotional responses** occur by pairing a formerly neutral stimulus with an unconditioned or previously conditioned stimulus. Conditioned emotional responses are commonplace in everyday life, as when sweaty palms, a pounding heart, and a feeling of anx-

Drawing by John Chase

iety arise after an instructor walks into a classroom and begins handing out a few printed pages of questions.

One of the most famous examples of classical conditioning was the case of little Albert. The study was performed by John Watson, considered the founder of American behaviorism, and his colleague, Rosalie Rayner (1920). The study was neither methodologically nor ethically beyond reproach, but its findings were provocative and served as a catalyst for decades of research. When Albert was 9 months old, Watson and Rayner presented him with a variety of objects, including a dog, a rabbit, a white rat, masks (including a Santa Claus mask), and a fur coat. Albert showed no fear in response to any of these objects; in fact, he played regularly with the rat— a budding behaviorist, no doubt. A few days later, Watson and Rayner tested little Albert's response to a loud noise (the UCS) by banging on a steel bar directly behind his head. Albert reacted by jumping, falling forward, and whimpering.

About two months later, Watson and Rayner selected the white rat to be the CS in their experiment and proceeded to condition a fear response in Albert. Each time Albert reached out to touch the rat, they struck the steel bar, creating the same loud noise that had initially startled him. After only a few pairings of the noise and the rat, Albert learned to fear the rat.

Studies since Watson and Rayner's time have suggested classical conditioning as an explanation for some human **phobias**, that is, irrational fears of specific objects or situations (Merckelbach et al., 1991; Ost, 1991; Wolpe, 1958). Many people develop severe emotional reactions (including fainting) to hypodermic needles through exposure to injections in childhood. Even adult knowledge that injections are necessary may have little impact on the fear, which is elicited automatically.

Stimulus Generalization and Discrimination

Once an organism has learned to associate a CS with a UCS, it may also respond to similar stimuli in the same way. This phenomenon, called **stimulus generalization**, occurs when an organism produces a conditioned response to other stimuli that have not been paired with the original unconditioned stimulus. For instance, in Watson and Rayner's experiment, the pairing of the rat and the loud noise produced a fear in little Albert not only of the rat but also of other furry or hairy objects, including the rabbit, the dog, the fur coat, and even Santa's face. In other words, Albert's fear of the rat had *generalized* to other furry objects. As one might guess, the more a stimulus resembles the original conditioned stimulus, the more likely stimulus generalization will take place. Thus, Albert generalized his fear response to furry objects but not to wooden blocks.

Through classical conditioning, little Albert developed a fear of rats and other furry objects—even Santa's face (a disabling phobia for a child, indeed).

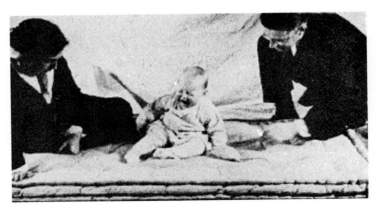

Courtesy of Prof. Benjamin Harris

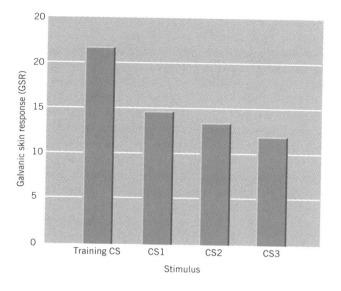

FIGURE 5.4
Stimulus generalization. Galvanic skin response (a measure of physiological arousal) varies according to the similarity of the conditioned stimuli to the training stimulus. In this case, the training stimulus was a tone of a particular frequency. CS1 is most similar to the training stimulus, whereas CS3 is least similar to it. (Here, GSR is measured in millimeters on an electronically generated recording sheet.) SOURCE: Hovland, 1937.

Many years ago researchers demonstrated the importance of similarity in stimulus generalization in an experiment with human subjects (Hovland, 1937). They paired a tone (the CS) with a mild electrical shock (the UCS). With repeated pairings, subjects produced a measurable conditioned response to the tone known as a **galvanic skin response** or **GSR** (an electrical measure of the amount of sweat on the skin, associated with arousal or anxiety). The experimenter then presented tones of varying frequencies that had not been paired with shock and measured the resulting GSR. Tones with a frequency similar to the CS evoked the most marked GSR, whereas dissimilar tones evoked progressively smaller responses (Figure 5.4). Current research efforts are attempting to build mathematical models that can predict the extent of generalization from properties of the CS and the test stimuli (Thomas, 1993).

The capacity for stimulus generalization is highly adaptive. A child who associates feelings of comfort and relief with the neighborhood police officer will seek out other officers when she needs help because they, too, evoke feelings of relief. Generalization is not always adaptive, however. A major component of adaptive learning is knowing when to generalize and when to be more specific or discriminating. Maladaptive patterns in humans often involve inappropriate generalization from one set of circumstances to others, as when a person who has been frequently criticized by a parent responds negatively to all authority figures.

Most of the time, however, people do not generalize quite so broadly. Instead, like other animals, they discriminate between stimuli. **Stimulus discrimination** is the learned tendency to respond to a restricted range of stimuli or only to the stimulus used during training. In many ways, stimulus discrimination is the opposite of stimulus generalization. Pavlov's dogs did not salivate in response to just *any* sound, and people do not get hungry when the clock reads four o'clock even though it is not far from six o'clock.

Extinction

In the acquisition or initial learning of a conditioned response, each pairing of the CS and UCS is known as a **conditioning trial**. Although one-trial learning sometimes occurs, as with the wolf who ate tainted mutton, classically conditioned responses most frequently emerge over several conditioning trials. But what happens if the CS repeatedly occurs without the UCS? What would have happened if

Watson and Rayner had, on the second, third, and all subsequent trials exposed little Albert to the white rat without the loud noise?

Albert's learned fear response would eventually have been *extinguished*, or eliminated, from his behavioral repertoire. **Extinction** in classical conditioning refers to the process by which a CR is weakened by presentation of the CS without the UCS. If a dog has come to associate the sounding of a bell with presentation of food, it will eventually stop salivating at the bell tone if the bell rings enough times without the presentation of food. However, the association is only weakened, not obliterated. If days later the dog once more hears the bell, it is likely to salivate again. This is known as **spontaneous recovery**—the reemergence of a previously extinguished conditioned response. The spontaneous recovery of a CR is short-lived, however, and will rapidly extinguish again without renewed pairings of the CS and UCS.

Factors That Affect Classical Conditioning

Classical conditioning does not occur every time a bell rings or a wolf gets sick on lamb chops. Several factors influence the extent to which classical conditioning will occur. These include the interstimulus interval, the individual's learning history, and the organism's preparedness to learn (Chance, 1988).

Interstimulus Interval

The **interstimulus interval** is the duration of time between presentation of the CS and the UCS. If too much time intervenes between presentation of these two stimuli, the animal is unlikely to associate them, and conditioning is thus less likely to occur. For most motor and skeletal responses, the optimal interval between the CS and UCS is very brief; about half a second, for instance, is most effective in conditioning humans to blink their eyes in response to a puff of air (Ross & Ross, 1971). Longer intervals of up to several seconds are more effective in conditioning other responses, such as fear.

The temporal relationship between the CS and the UCS—that is, which stimulus comes first—is also crucial (Figure 5.5). Maximal conditioning occurs when the onset of the CS precedes the UCS, known as **forward conditioning**. Less effective than forward conditioning is **simultaneous conditioning**, in which the CS and UCS are presented at the same time. A third pattern, **backward conditioning**, is the least effective of all. Here, the CS is presented after the UCS has occurred.

The Individual's Learning History

Another factor that influences classical conditioning is the individual's learning history. An extinguished response tends to be easier to learn the second time around because the stimulus was once associated with the response. Suppose a person developed an aversion to bacon upon coincidentally coming down with the flu shortly after eating a bacon, lettuce, and tomato sandwich. If the aversion is eventually extinguished, it is likely to be easily reinstated—and difficult to extinguish—if bacon and nausea ever occur together again.

Sometimes previous conditioning can also hinder learning. Consider a dog that has been conditioned to salivate at the sound of a bell. The researcher now wants to condition the dog to associate the food with an additional stimulus, a flash of light. The dog will probably have difficulty learning this new association, even if the light flashes before each feeding and the bell sounds only with every third or fourth feeding. This phenomenon is known as blocking. **Blocking** refers to the failure of a stimulus (such as a flash of light), to elicit a conditioned response when it is combined with another stimulus that is already effective in eliciting the response (Kamin, 1969;

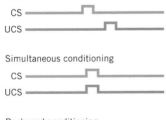

Forward conditioning

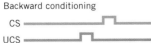

Simultaneous conditioning

Backward conditioning

FIGURE 5.5
Forward, simultaneous, and backward conditioning. In forward conditioning, the CS is presented before the UCS. In simultaneous conditioning, the CS is presented at the same time as the UCS. In backward conditioning, the CS is presented immediately after the UCS.

Pearce, 1987). If a bell is already associated with food, a flashing light is of little consequence unless it provides additional, nonredundant information.

Preparedness to Learn: An Evolutionary Perspective

A third influence on classical conditioning bears the imprint of evolution. The early behaviorists, such as Watson, believed that the laws of classical conditioning could link virtually any stimulus to any response. Yet subsequent research suggested that some responses can be conditioned much more readily to certain stimuli than to others and that this contributes to adaptation. A single experience of nausea after eating a particular food is sufficient to cause a permanent distaste for it, even if the cause of the nausea is completely unrelated to what has been eaten.

A classic study by Garcia and Koelling (1966) documented the relative ease with which certain stimuli are associated. The experimenters used three conditioned stimuli: light, sound, and taste (flavored water). For one group of rats, these stimuli were paired with the UCS of radiation, which produces nausea. For the other group, the stimuli were paired with a different UCS, electric shock. The experimenters then exposed the rats to each of the three conditioned stimuli by themselves to test the strength of the conditioned response. The results can be seen in Figure 5.6. Rats that experienced nausea after exposure to radiation developed an aversion to the flavored water but not to either the light or sound cues. In contrast, rats exposed to electric shock developed avoidance reactions to the audiovisual conditioned stimuli but not to the taste cues. In other words, the rats learned to associate sickness in their stomachs with a taste stimulus, and an aversive tactile stimulus (electrical shock) with audiovisual stimuli.

Why should animals be prepared, or biologically programmed, to learn some associations more easily than others (a phenomenon called **prepared learning**)? Why do people readily connect a taste with nausea when they have gotten sick? And why are phobias of spiders, snakes, and similar animals more common than phobias of flowers or telephones (Marks, 1969; Ohman et al., 1976; Seligman, 1971)?

From an evolutionary perspective, animals appear to have become prone to connect certain stimuli and responses through natural selection. The proclivity to develop a taste aversion to a food that induces illness provides a clear survival advantage. A bird lucky enough to survive after eating a poisonous caterpillar is less prone to partake of another and hence is more likely to survive and reproduce. Humans may have been predisposed to learn fear responses to creatures such as snakes and spiders because some of these posed a real threat when people lived clos-

UNCONDITIONED STIMULUS	CONDITIONED STIMULUS		
	Light	Sound	Taste
Shock	Avoidance	Avoidance	No avoidance
X-Rays	No avoidance	No avoidance	Avoidance

FIGURE 5.6

Preparedness to learn. Garcia and Koelling's experiment examined the impact of biological constraints on learning in rats exposed to shock or X-rays. Rats associated nausea with a taste stimulus rather than with audiovisual cues and associated an aversive tactile event with sights and sounds rather than with taste stimuli. The results demonstrated that animals are prepared to learn certain associations in classical conditioning. SOURCE: Adapted from Garcia & Koelling, 1966.

er to nature than they do today. Other associations appear to be more readily learned as well. Experimental data suggest that humans may be biologically predisposed to associate aversive experiences more readily with angry than with smiling faces (Dimberg, 1990).

Biological preparedness, of course, has its limits, especially in humans. One study, for example, found people equally likely to develop a fear of handguns as of snakes (Honeybourne et al., 1993). The fear of snakes may be innate, but the fear of handguns is not. Where biological predispositions leave off, learning begins as a way of naturally selecting adaptive responses.

Snakes strike terror in the human psyche, even though most people have never had unpleasant encounters with them.

FROM MIND TO BRAIN

WHAT DO ORGANISMS LEARN IN CLASSICAL CONDITIONING?

In some ways, to contrast innate with learned responses is to set up a false dichotomy because the capacity to learn—to form associations—is itself a product of natural selection. Precisely what organisms learn when they are classically conditioned, however, has been a topic of considerable debate. Like other behaviorists, Pavlov was influenced by associationism, the philosophical school that focused on the way thoughts and ideas become associated with each other. Pavlov (1927) hypothesized that in classical conditioning the CS essentially becomes a *signal* to an organism that the UCS is about to occur, and he offered a neurological explanation of how this may happen. With innate reflexes, he argued, the sensations associated with a UCS (such as meat) are processed in one brain structure, which is connected with another that controls the UCR (salivation). In classical conditioning, physiological connections are formed between nervous system centers responsive to the CS (a bell) and the UCS, so that the organism ultimately responds to the CS as if it were the UCS. This explanation is called **stimulus substitution** because the CS acts as a substitute for the UCS.

Subsequent research has challenged Pavlov's view that classical conditioning is nothing more than stimulus substitution. Although the CR and the UCR are usually similar, they are rarely identical. Dogs typically do not salivate as much in response to a bell as to the actual presentation of food. In other cases, a CR is not just different in degree from the UCR but different in kind. It can even be directly opposite, as in a phenomenon known as paradoxical conditioning. In **paradoxical conditioning**, the CR is actually the body's attempt to counteract the effects of a stimulus that is about to occur. For example, the sight of drug paraphernalia in a heroin addict can activate physiological reactions that reduce the effect of the heroin he is about to inject (Caggiula et al., 1991; Siegel, 1984). This conditioning process produces a conditioned tolerance, or decreased sensitivity, to the drug with repeated use, as the body counteracts dosages that were previously effective.

A study of opiate addicts compared the effects of self-injection (which included exposure to drug paraphernalia, the CS) with an intravenous injection provided by the researchers (Ehrman et al., 1992). Only those subjects who self-injected with their personal paraphernalia demonstrated evidence of drug tolerance; that is, their bodies showed signs of counteracting the impact of the drugs. This paradoxical reaction may be involved in the increased tolerance that leads addicts to take progressively higher doses of a drug to achieve the same effect.

On the other hand, research has confirmed Pavlov's speculation that classical conditioning alters the action of neurons that link stimuli with responses (Matthies, 1989). Studies on the molecular or cellular basis of learning often use the marine snail, Aplysia, an organism so simple that its neurons can actually be

The marine snail, Aplysia, has afforded researchers the opportunity to study the molecular basis of learning.

observed under a microscope. Studies with Aplysia suggest that learning occurs through increases and decreases in the amount of neurotransmitter that a neuron releases at its terminal buttons (Kandel, 1989; Kandel & Schwartz, 1982). For example, when an organism has learned to associate a flash of light with an electric shock, certain neurons release their neurotransmitters more readily than before. In Aplysia, repeated classical conditioning trials increase serotonin release in affected neurons (Kandel, 1989). Related research implicates changes in the postsynaptic membranes that are often set in motion by the greater availability of neurotransmitters such as serotonin in the synapse (Woody, 1986). Thus, learning actually alters cellular structure, transforming an environmental event into a physical change in the nervous system.

OPERANT CONDITIONING

In 1898, Edward Thorndike placed a hungry cat in a box that had a mechanical latch and then placed food in full view just outside the box. The cat meowed, paced back and forth, and rubbed against the walls of the box. In the course of its distressed behavior, the cat happened to trip the latch. Immediately, the door to the box opened, and the cat gained access to the food. Thorndike repeated the experiment, and with continued repetitions the cat became more adept at tripping the latch. Eventually, it was able to leave its cage almost as soon as food appeared.

Thorndike proposed a law of learning, which he called the law of effect, to account for this phenomenon. The **law of effect** makes intuitive sense: An animal's tendency to reproduce a behavior depends on that behavior's effect on the environment and the impact of that effect on the animal. If tripping the latch had not had the effect of helping the cat reach the food, the cat would not have learned to keep brushing up against the latch. More simply, the law of effect states that behavior is controlled by its consequences.

The behavior of Thorndike's cats exemplifies a second form of conditioning known as instrumental or operant conditioning. Thorndike used the term **instrumental conditioning** because the behavior is instrumental to achieving a more satisfying state of affairs. B. F. Skinner, who spent years experimenting with and systematizing the ways in which behavior is controlled by the environment, introduced the term **operant conditioning**, which means learning to operate on the environment to produce a consequence. **Operants** are behaviors that are *emitted* rather than *elicited* by the environment. In Pavlov's dogs, food elicited salivation. In contrast,

Thorndike's cat spontaneously emitted the behavior of brushing up against the latch, which resulted in an effect that conditioned future behavior. The behavior in operant conditioning *precedes* the environmental event that produces conditioning. This differs from classical conditioning, in which a stimulus precedes a response. Pavlov's dogs could salivate only after a bell sounded, and no matter how much they salivated, they could not get to a piece of meat unless the experimenter put it within reach. In contrast, Thorndike's cat could feed itself through its own actions.

The basic idea behind operant conditioning, then, is that behavior is selected by its environmental consequences. In this section, we explore two types of environmental consequences that produce operant conditioning: **reinforcement**, which increases the probability that a response will occur, and **punishment**, which diminishes its likelihood.

Reinforcement

Reinforcement means just what the name implies: Something in the environment fortifies, or reinforces, a behavior. A **reinforcer** is an environmental consequence that occurs after an organism has produced a response, which makes the response more likely to recur. Psychologists distinguish two kinds of reinforcement, positive and negative.

Positive Reinforcement

Positive reinforcement is the process whereby presentation of a stimulus (a reward or payoff) makes a behavior more likely to occur again. For example, in B.F. Skinner's classic studies (1938), a pigeon was placed in a cage with a target mounted on one side (Figure 5.7). The pigeon spontaneously pecked around in the cage. This behavior was not a response to any particular stimulus; pecking is simply innate avian behavior. If by chance the pigeon pecked at the target, however, a pellet of grain dropped into a bin. If the pigeon happened to peck at the target again, it was once more rewarded with a pellet. The pellet is a **positive reinforcer**—an environmental consequence that, when presented, strengthens the probability that a response will recur. The pigeon would thus gradually peck at the target more frequently since this operant became associated with the positive reinforcer.

Positive reinforcement is not limited to pigeons. In fact, it controls much of human behavior, as when students learn to exert effort studying by being reinforced

FIGURE 5.7

Apparatus for operant conditioning. In (a), a pigeon is placed in a cage with a target on one side, which can be used for operant conditioning. In (b), B. F. Skinner experiments with a rat placed in a so-called Skinner Box, with a similar design, in which pressing a bar may result in reinforcement.

(a)   *(b)*

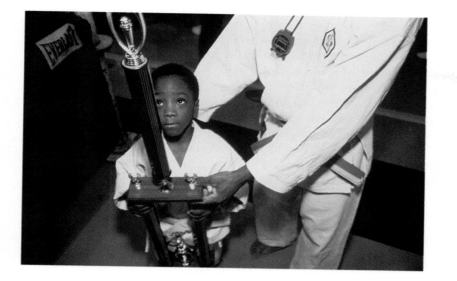

A young boy receives positive reinforcement for his karate skills. He might receive less praise for hitting and kicking in other contexts.

with praise and good grades, or salespeople learn to appease obnoxious customers and laugh at their jokes because doing so yields them commissions.

Negative Reinforcement

Negative reinforcement is the process whereby termination of an aversive stimulus makes a behavior more likely to occur. The basic principle of negative reinforcement is that eliminating something aversive can itself be a reinforcer or reward. Just as the presentation of a positive reinforcer rewards a response, the *removal* of an aversive stimulus (a negative reinforcer) rewards a response. **Negative reinforcers,** then, are aversive or unpleasant stimuli that strengthen a behavior by their removal. Hitting the snooze button on an alarm clock is negatively reinforced by the termination of the alarm; cleaning the kitchen is negatively reinforced by the elimination of sights and smells that are less than pleasing.

Negative reinforcement occurs in both escape learning and avoidance learning. In **escape learning,** the organism is reinforced by the cessation of an aversive event that already exists; that is, the organism escapes an aversive situation. For example, a rat presses a lever and terminates an electric shock, or a person applies lotion to her skin to relieve sunburn pain. **Avoidance learning** occurs as an organism prevents an *expected* aversive event from happening; in other words, avoidance of a potentially aversive situation reinforces the operant. For example, a rat presses a lever when it hears a tone that signals that a shock is about to occur, or a person puts on sunscreen before going out in the sun to avoid a sunburn.

Shaping

Outside the laboratory, positive and negative reinforcement provide the basis for some very complex behaviors—as well as for some creative training procedures. One procedure, called **shaping,** teaches a new behavior by reinforcing closer and closer approximations to the desired response. Skinner (1951) described a shaping procedure that can be used to teach a dog to touch its nose to a cupboard door handle. The first step is to bring a hungry dog into the kitchen and immediately reward with food any spontaneous movement he makes to face toward the cupboard; the dog will soon face the cupboard most of the time. (In Skinnerian terms, a "hungry" dog is one that has not been fed for some time. Hunger is a subjective, and hence unmeasurable, state. Skinner and other behaviorists were determined to avoid describing stimuli as pleasant or unpleasant, or attributing mental states such as hunger to animals, because they wished to base psychological science on strictly

Shaping procedures can lead animals—and humans—to strike some unusual poses.

observable behaviors.) The next step is to reward the dog whenever it moves toward the cupboard, then to reward it when it moves its head in such a way that its nose comes closer to the cupboard, and finally to reward the dog only for touching its nose to the cupboard handle. This shaping procedure should take no more than five minutes, even for a beginner.

The same shaping techniques can be used to teach more complex behaviors. The key, as a trainer, is to begin by conditioning the animal to do something it can readily do. Gradually, the trainer reinforces only certain ways of performing the desired behavior, so that the animal eventually produces a very specific operant. With humans, shaping is common in all kinds of teaching. A tennis instructor may at first praise a student any time he holds the racquet in a way that resembles a good grip and gets the ball over the net. Gradually, however, the instructor compliments only proper form and well-placed shots, progressively shaping the student's behavior.

Chaining

Another procedure for eliciting complex behavior is **chaining**. In chaining, a sequence of already-established behaviors is reinforced step by step. Whereas shaping involves progressively modifying a specific behavior to produce a new response, chaining requires putting together a sequence of existing responses in a particular order. When I was a child, my brother Marc displayed a natural gift for applying this operant technique. Marc would awaken at four o'clock in the morning (who knows why), and while everyone else slept soundly, he devised a way to train the family cat to wake me by licking my face. This trick does not come naturally to most felines, and so it required several steps to accomplish. The cat already knew how to climb, jump, and lick. Marc's goal was to get the cat to perform these behaviors in a particular sequence. First, Marc placed pieces of cat food on the stairs leading up to my bedroom. After several trials, the cat learned to climb the stairs on its own. The next step was to reinforce the operant of jumping onto my bed; again, a few judiciously placed bits of cat food did the trick. This same reward, placed gently in the proper location, was also sufficient for training the cat to lick me on the face. Once this occurred enough times, the cat seemed to be reinforced simply by licking my cheek. (Marc seemed quite amused and was apparently reinforced for his little foray into behaviorism as well.)

Shaping and chaining can lead to maladaptive as well as adaptive behavior. In one experiment, rats were trained to jump onto a platform and extend their noses over the edge so far that they fell (Rasey & Iversen, 1993). In humans, gang members may reinforce progressively more dangerous behavior in each other through shaping and chaining, as they increasingly "up the ante" from petty crimes and fistfights to felonies and drive-by shootings.

Punishment

Reinforcement is one type of environmental consequence that controls behavior through operant conditioning; the other is punishment (Figure 5.8). Whereas reinforcement always *increases* the likelihood of a response—either by the presentation of a reward or the removal of an aversive stimulus—punishment *decreases* the probability that a response will recur. Thus, if Skinner's pigeon received an electric shock each time it pecked at the target, the operant of pecking would be less likely to be emitted again because it resulted in an aversive outcome. Parents intuitively apply this behavioral technique when they "ground" a teenager for staying out past curfew. The criminal justice system also operates on a system of punishment, attempting to discourage illicit behaviors by imposing penalties.

Like reinforcement, punishment takes two forms: positive and negative. In positive punishment, such as spanking, exposure to an aversive event as a consequence of a behavior renders the operant less likely to recur. Negative punishment involves

Punishment is not always effective, as evidenced by the recidivism rates for violent crime.

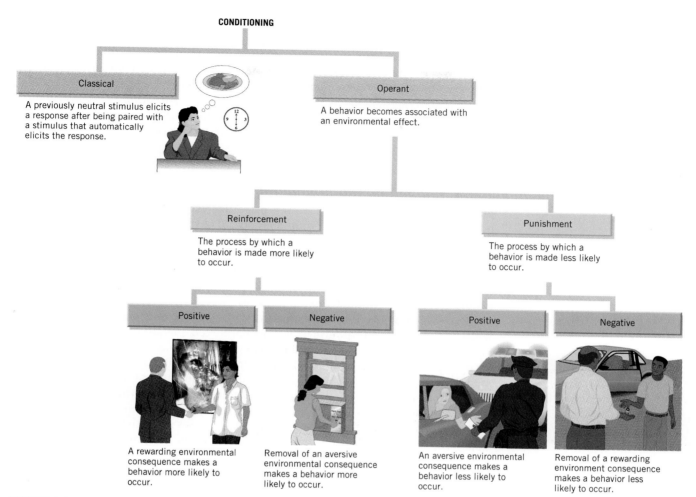

FIGURE 5.8

Conditioning processes. Behaviorists distinguish two kinds of conditioning, classical and operant. In operant conditioning, the environment influences behavior through reinforcement and punishment.

losing, or not obtaining, a reinforcer as a consequence of behavior, as when an employee fails to receive a pay increase because of frequent lateness or absenteeism.

Punishment is commonplace in human affairs, but it is frequently applied ineffectively (Chance, 1988; Newsom et al., 1983; Skinner, 1953). One common problem in using punishment with animals and young children is that the learner may have difficulty distinguishing which operant is being punished. People who yell at their dog for coming after it has been called several times are actually punishing good behavior—coming when called. The dog associates the punishment with its action, not its inaction, and is likely to adjust its behavior accordingly. A second and related problem associated with punishment is that the learner may come to fear the person meting out the punishment (via classical conditioning) rather than the action (via operant conditioning). A child who is harshly punished by his father may become afraid of his father instead of changing his behavior.

A third drawback is that punishment does not eliminate existing rewards for a behavior. In nature, unlike the laboratory, a single action may have multiple consequences, and behavior can be controlled by any number of them. A teacher who punishes the class clown may not suppress inappropriate behavior reinforced by the attention of classmates. Sometimes, too, punishing one behavior (such as stealing) may inadvertently reinforce another (such as lying).

Fourth, people typically use punishment when they are angry, which can lead both to poorly designed punishment (from a learning point of view) and to the potential for abuse. An angry parent may punish a child for misdeeds just discovered but that occurred a considerable time earlier. The time interval between the child's action and the consequence may render the punishment ineffective because the child does not adequately connect the two events. Parents also frequently punish inconsistently, depending on their mood, which may prevent the child from learning what behavior is being punished, under what circumstances, and how to avoid it.

Finally, aggression that is used to punish behavior often leads to further aggression. The child who is punished corporally, as by hitting or beating, typically learns a much deeper lesson—that problems can be solved with violence. In fact, the more physical punishment parents use, the more aggressively their children behave at home (Larzelere, 1986). Correlation does not, of course, prove causation; aggressive children may provoke punitive parenting. Nevertheless, the weight of evidence suggests that violent parents tend to create violent children. Parents who augment their physical strength with a paddle or belt may be finding a convenient outlet for their sadistic or poorly controlled aggressive impulses, but they are not benefiting their children, regardless of their rationalizations.

Punishment tends to be most effective when it is accompanied by reasoning and when the person being punished is also reinforced for an alternative, acceptable behavior. Explaining helps a child correctly connect an action with a punishment. Having other positively reinforced behaviors to draw on allows the child to generate alternative responses. Similarly, juvenile delinquents and adult criminals who are punished for their crimes are more likely to alter their behavior if they have skills (such as literacy and job skills) and experiences (such as success at something other than criminal activity) that make alternative responses attractive.

We have spoken thus far as if reinforcement and punishment were unilateral techniques, in which one person (a trainer) conditions another person or animal (a learner). In fact, in human social interactions, each partner continuously uses operant conditioning techniques to mold the behavior of the other. Indeed, one person's punishment is often another's negative reinforcement. When a child behaves in a way its parents find upsetting, the parents are likely to punish the child. But the parents' behavior is itself being conditioned because the operant of punishing the child will be negatively reinforced if it causes the child's bad behavior to cease. Thus, the child is negatively reinforcing the parents' use of punishment just as the parents are punishing the child's behavior.

A GLOBAL VISTA

REWARD AND PUNISHMENT IN TWO CULTURES

Rewards and punishments are used in different ways by different communities to maintain social order and preserve cultural values. In all cultures, parents must teach their children to avoid danger and to observe the community's moral precepts. Adults also condition each other's observance of social norms, using methods ranging from mild forms of censure, such as looking away when someone makes an inappropriate remark, to imprisoning or executing individuals for behavior considered deviant or dangerous. The caning of American teenager Michael Fay in Singapore for vandalism in 1994 brought wide media attention to cultural differences in the application of punishment. Faced with increasing violence at home, many Americans endorsed Singapore's use of corporal punishment to maintain social order. Was Fay's punishment effective? Whether he subsequently avoids vandalism is

Among the Gusii of Kenya, parents rely heavily on punishment to control children's behavior

unknown, but the punishment did apparently lead to his avoidance of Singapore—which he left promptly.

The operant techniques societies use to maintain social control vary in part with the dangers and threats that confront them. The Gusii of Kenya, with a history of tribal warfare, face threats not only from outsiders but also from natural forces, including wild animals. Gusii parents tend to rely more on punishment and fear than on rewards in conditioning appropriate social behavior in their children. Caning, food deprivation, and withdrawing shelter and protection are common forms of punishment. One Gusii mother warned her child, "If you don't stop crying, I shall open the door and call a hyena to come and eat you!" (LeVine & LeVine, 1963, p. 166). Death from wild animals is a real fear, and therefore making this threat gains compliance from Gusii children.

In contrast, the Mixtecans of Juxtlahuaca, Mexico, are a highly cohesive community, with little internal conflict, and social norms that encourage cooperation. Their social patterns appear adaptive, for the Mixtecans are dominated by the nearby Spanish Mexicans, who control the official government and many economic resources in their region. The Mixtecans do not generally impose fines or jail sentences or use physical punishment to deter aggression in either adults or children. Rather, they tend to rely on soothing persuasion. An anthropologist reported an incident of aggression that occurred among a group of Mixtecan males, in which one man assaulted several others while he was under the influence of alcohol (Romney, 1963). Instead of retaliating, the victims simply worked together to calm him down. Social ostracism is the most feared punishment, and social ties within the community are very strong, so responses that reinforce these ties are effective in maintaining social order.

In the United States, fear of ostracism or stigma was once a more powerful force in maintaining control over antisocial behavior, especially in small communities. Today, even incarceration does not appear to be an adequate deterrent to many forms of crime, especially violent crime. Although one reason is the inconsistent application of punishment, another may be the fact that incarceration no longer carries the intense stigma it once had, so that prison is no longer as effective a punishment.

Extinction in Operant Conditioning

Although cultures apply operant learning principles in a multitude of ways, many of the basic processes appear to be cross-culturally universal. One such process is extinction. Just as in classical conditioning, operant responses can be extinguished. If an animal has learned to associate an operant with a pattern of reinforcement or punishment and this pattern is broken after enough conditioning trials, the animal will ultimately stop responding in the way it has learned. For example, a rat that once received a pellet of food every time it pressed a bar may stop bar-pressing if it does not receive food after 25 presses. Similarly, a salesperson accustomed to large and regular commissions will find a new job if sales revenues drop precipitously, because of a lack of reinforcement.

Knowing how to extinguish behavior is important in everyday life, particularly for parents. Consider the case of a 21-month-old boy who had a serious illness requiring around-the-clock attention (Williams, 1959). After recovering, the child continued to demand this level of attention even though it was no longer necessary. His demands were especially troublesome at bedtime, when he screamed and cried unless a parent sat with him until he fell asleep, which could take up to two hours.

Relying on the learning principle that behavior that is not reinforced will be extinguished, the parents began following a new bedtime regimen. In the first trial of the extinction series, they spent a relaxed and warm good-night session with their son, closed the door when they left the room, and refused to respond to the wails and screams that followed. After 45 minutes, the boy fell asleep (Figure 5.9). On the second trial, he fell asleep immediately. The next several bedtimes were accompanied by tantrums that steadily grew shorter, so that by the tenth trial, the parents fully enjoyed the sounds of silence.

As in classical conditioning, however, spontaneous recovery, in which a previously learned behavior recurs without reinforcement, sometimes occurs. In fact, the boy cried and screamed again one day when his aunt attempted to put him to bed. She reinforced this behavior by returning to his room; as a result, his parents had to repeat their extinction procedure.

Schedules of Reinforcement

In the examples of operant conditioning we have discussed, an animal (or person) is rewarded or punished every time it performs a behavior. This type of operant procedure is called a **continuous reinforcement schedule**, in which the environmental consequence is the same each time an animal emits a behavior. In other

FIGURE 5.9

Extinction of tantrum behavior in a 21-month-old child. As shown in curve A, the child initially cried for long periods of time, but very few trials of nonreinforced crying were required to extinguish the behavior. In curve B, the behavior was again quickly extinguished following its spontaneous recovery. SOURCE: Williams, 1959, p. 269.

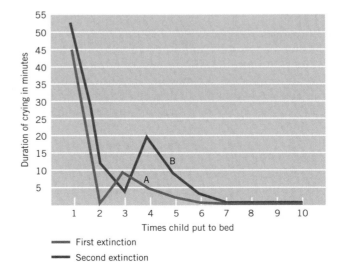

words, the behavior is continuously reinforced. A child reinforced for altruistic behavior on a continuous schedule of reinforcement might be praised every time she shares, just as a pigeon might receive a piece of grain each time it pecks a target. However, such consistent reinforcement rarely occurs in nature or in human life. The more usual case is that an action sometimes leads to reinforcement but other times does not. Such reinforcement schedules are known as **partial** or **intermittent schedules of reinforcement** because the organism is not reinforced each time it produces a particular response. It is reinforced only part of the time, or intermittently. (These are called schedules of reinforcement, but the same types of principles apply with punishment.)

Which is more effective, continuous or intermittent reinforcement? Intuitively, one would think that continuous schedules would be more effective. This is generally true during response acquisition, that is, initial learning of a response, because the connection between behavior and consequence is more predictable and clear. In maintaining behavior, however, partial reinforcement is usually superior. To illustrate, suppose you have a relatively new car, and every time you turn the key the engine starts. If one day, however, you try to start the car 10 times in a row and the engine will not turn over, you will probably give up and call a towing company. In contrast, if you are the proud owner of a rusted-out 1972 Chevy and are accustomed to 10 turns of the ignition before the car finally cranks up, you may try 20 or 30 times before calling the tow truck. Thus, behaviors maintained under partial schedules are usually more resistant to extinction.

Behaviorist researchers, notably Skinner and his colleagues, have categorized intermittent reinforcement schedules according to whether payoffs are tied to the number of operant responses emitted or whether rewards are delivered according to intervals of time (Ferster & Skinner, 1957; Skinner, 1938). The former are known as **ratio schedules** because the animal is reinforced for some proportion of responses (with a ratio of reinforced to total responses), while the latter are called **interval schedules**. Reinforcement schedules are often studied with a **cumulative response recorder**, an instrument that tallies the number of times a subject produces a response such as pressing a bar or pecking a target. Figure 5.10 illustrates typical cumulative response recordings for the four reinforcement schedules to be discussed here: fixed ratio, variable ratio, fixed interval, and variable interval.

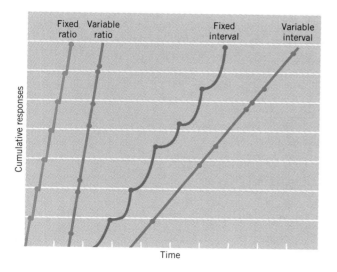

FIGURE 5.10
Schedules of reinforcement. The figure shows cumulative response records for fixed ratio, variable ratio, fixed interval, and variable interval reinforcement schedules. A cumulative response record graphs the total number of responses that have been emitted at any point in time. Different schedules of reinforcement produce different patterns of responding.

Fixed Ratio Schedules

In a **fixed ratio (FR) schedule** of reinforcement, an organism receives reinforcement for a fixed proportion of the responses it emits. Piecework employment uses a fixed ratio schedule of reinforcement: A person receives payment for every bushel of apples picked (an FR-1 schedule) or for every 10 scarves woven (an FR-10 schedule). Workers weave the first nine scarves without reinforcement because the payoff will occur when the tenth scarf is completed. As shown in Figure 5.10, FR schedules tend to result in rapid responding, with a brief pause after each reinforcement.

Variable Ratio Schedules

In **variable ratio (VR) schedules**, as in fixed ratio schedules, an animal receives a reward for some percentage of responses, but the number of responses required before each reinforcement is unpredictable (that is, variable). Variable ratio schedules specify an average number of responses that will be rewarded. Thus, a pigeon on a VR-5 schedule may be rewarded on its fourth, seventh, thirteenth, and twentieth responses, averaging one reward for every five responses. Variable ratio schedules generally produce rapid, constant responding and are probably the most common in daily life. People cannot predict that they will be rewarded or praised for every fifth good deed, but they do receive occasional, irregular social reinforcement, which is enough to reinforce altruistic behavior in most people. Similarly, students may not receive a good grade each time they study hard for an examination, but many study nonetheless because they learn that the *average* rate of reinforcement is higher than if they do not study.

Fixed Interval Schedules

In a **fixed interval (FI) schedule**, an animal receives reinforcement for its responses only after a fixed amount of time. For example, a rat that presses a bar is reinforced by delivery of a pellet of food every 10 minutes. The rat may press the bar 100 times or one time during that 10 minutes. Doing so does not make a difference in the delivery of the pellet, just as long as it presses the bar after the 10-minute interval has ended.

An animal on an FI schedule of reinforcement will ultimately learn to stop responding except toward the end of each interval, producing the scalloped cumulative response pattern shown in Figure 5.10. Fixed interval schedules affect human performance in the same way. For example, workers whose boss comes by only at two o'clock are likely to relax the rest of the day. Schools rely heavily on FI schedules, leading some students to procrastinate between exams and to pull "all-nighters" when the reinforcement (or punishment) is imminent. Politicians, too, seem to resemble rats in their response patterns (Figure 5.11). Periodic adjournment of Congress on a fixed interval appears to reinforce bill-passing (the congressional equivalent of bar-pressing), producing precisely the same scalloped response record (Waldrop, 1972).

Variable Interval Schedules

The **variable interval (VI) schedule**, like the fixed interval schedule, ties reinforcement to an interval of time after which a response by the organism leads to reinforcement; however, in a VI schedule, the animal cannot predict how long that time interval will be. Thus, a rat might receive reinforcement for bar-processing, but only at 5, 6, 20, and 40 minutes.

Variable interval schedules are more effective than fixed interval schedules in maintaining consistent performance. Random, unannounced governmental inspections of working conditions in a plant are much more effective in getting management to maintain safety standards than inspections at fixed intervals. In the classroom, pop quizzes make similar use of VI schedules.

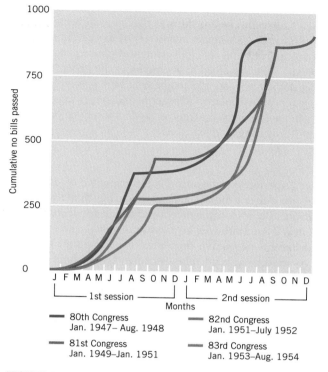

FIGURE 5.11

The effects of a fixed interval schedule on the U.S. Congress. Adjournment serves as a powerful reinforcer for members of the U.S. House of Representatives, who seem to respond to this fixed interval schedule of reinforcement with a flurry of last-minute activity before being reinforced. As the graph shows, the pattern looked the same over several years investigated. The scalloped curve is remarkably similar to the fixed interval cumulative response recording derived from studying rats and pigeons in Figure 5.10. SOURCE: *Weisberg & Waldrop, 1972, p. 23.*

Factors Affecting Operant Conditioning

Schedules of reinforcement thus affect the way humans and other animals behave. They do this by controlling the degree of contingency between the reward or punishment and the operant. An animal must learn that reinforcement is more likely to follow a response than a nonresponse. Animals may, however, mistakenly connect an operant and an environmental event. Skinner (1948) described this as **superstitious behavior**. In one study, he placed pigeons on a schedule in which grain was delivered at regular time intervals, no matter what behavior the pigeons performed. Each pigeon developed its own operant response. One bird turned counterclockwise about the cage, another repeatedly thrust its head in an upper corner of the cage, and a third tossed its head as if lifting an invisible bar (1948, p. 168). Skinner compared these behaviors to human actions such as wearing a lucky outfit to a basketball game or performing a sequence of actions when up to bat in baseball. According to Skinner, such behaviors develop because the delivery of a reinforcer strengthens whatever behavior an organism happens to be engaged in at the time.

Aside from the degree of contingency between an operant and its consequences, several other variables influence the acquisition, maintenance, and extinction of operant behaviors. These include the interval between the operant and its consequences, the presence of discriminative stimuli, and preparedness to learn certain behaviors.

The Interval between the Operant and Its Consequence

A second factor that influences operant conditioning is the interval between the operant and the outcome. Parents often recognize intuitively that the shorter the time between the production of an operant and its environmental consequences, the more likely conditioning is to occur. When a child misbehaves at the grocery store, parents rarely wait until the next day to address the problem. This principle holds true for reinforcement as well as for punishment: A pigeon that gains access to a container of grain two minutes after pecking at a target is far less likely to continue to peck than if the behavior were immediately reinforced.

Discriminative Stimuli

Another factor that influences operant conditioning is the presence of discriminative stimuli. Neither humans nor other animals are so inflexible that they emit the same operant in every situation. Professors receive a paycheck for lecturing to their classes, but if they lecture new acquaintances at a cocktail party, the environmental consequences are quite different. Similarly, domestic cats learn that the dining room table is a great place to stretch out and relax—except when their owners are home.

A stimulus signaling the occurrence of particular contingencies of reinforcement is called a **discriminative stimulus**. For the professor, the classroom situation signals that lecturing behavior will be reinforced; for the cat, the presence of humans is a discriminative stimulus signaling punishment. In both cases, the behavior emitted depends on the stimulus, a phenomenon known as **stimulus control**. One study demonstrated stimulus control with rats who were rewarded for turning clockwise when they were placed in one chamber and turning counterclockwise when placed in another (Richards et al., 1990). The two chambers controlled the rats' behavior, much as red and green lights control the flow of traffic.

Species-Specific Behavior and Preparedness

Just as some stimulus-response connections are easier than others to acquire in classical conditioning, certain behaviors are more readily learned by some species than others in operant conditioning. This point was vividly illustrated by Keller and Marian Breland, who learned operant conditioning techniques while working with Skinner. The Brelands went on to apply these procedures in their own animal training business but initially with mixed success. In one case, they trained pigs to deposit wooden coins in a large "piggy bank" in order to obtain food:

> Pigs condition very rapidly.... [T]hey have ravenous appetites (naturally), and in many ways are among the most tractable animals we have worked with. However, this particular problem behavior developed in pig after pig, usually after a period of weeks or months, getting worse every day. At first the pig would eagerly pick up one dollar, carry it to the bank, run back, get another, carry it rapidly and neatly, and so on.... Thereafter, over a period of weeks the behavior would become slower and slower. He might run over eagerly for each dollar, but on the way back, instead of carrying the dollar and depositing it simply and cleanly, he would repeatedly drop it, root it, drop it again, root it along the way, pick it up, toss it up in the air, drop it, root it some more, and so on. (p. 683)

The Brelands observed that the pigs' "rooting" behavior—nuzzling the coin with their snouts—eventually replaced the conditioned behavior of depositing coins in the bank to such an extent that the hungry pigs were not getting enough food. The Brelands had similar experiences with porpoises that swallowed the balls they were supposed to manipulate, cats that would stalk their food slots, and raccoons that tried to wash the tokens they were supposed to deposit in banks. All these operants were more closely related to instinctive, species-specific behaviors than the operants the Brelands were attempting to condition.

Pigs, like other animals, return to species-specific behavior despite the best efforts of trainers.

Species-specific behavior also influences the way animals respond to negative reinforcement. Conditioning a rat to press a lever in order to avoid an electric shock may be difficult because a rat's natural response to shock is either to crouch and freeze or run away—both of which interfere with bar-pressing. According to some theorists, an animal can be trained to perform certain operants in response to an aversive stimulus but only as long as those operants are already within its inborn, species-specific repertoire of behaviors (Bolles, 1970).

Species-specific behavioral proclivities suggest an evolutionary explanation: Pigs' rooting behavior normally allows them to obtain food, and a "frozen" animal is less likely to be noticed by a predator than a frenetic one searching for levers to press. Through natural selection, humans and other animals are prepared, or innately predisposed, to learn particular behaviors and responses to stimuli (Seligman, 1970, 1971). As in classical conditioning, prepared operant conditioning is not easily extinguished.

Characteristics of the Learner

Another set of variables affecting operant conditioning are the characteristics of the learner. In humans as in other species, individuals differ in their response to conditioning (Ferre & Garcia-Sevilla, 1987). Individual rats vary, for example, in their tendency to behave aggressively or to respond with fear or avoidance to environmental events (Carbonell et al., 1987). Rats can also be selectively bred for their ability to learn mazes (Innis, 1992).

The importance of the learner's characteristics was illustrated in an experiment that attempted to train three octopi named Albert, Bertram, and Charles to pull a lever in their saltwater tanks in order to obtain food (Dews, 1959). The usual shaping procedures worked successfully on Albert and Bertram, who were first rewarded for approaching the lever, then for touching it with a tentacle, and finally for tugging at it. With Charles, however, things were different. Instead of simply pulling the lever to obtain food, Charles tugged at it with such force that he broke it. In addition, Charles spent a great deal of time "with eyes above the surface of the water, directing a jet of water at any individual who approached the tank" (1959, p. 62).

The situation is not altogether different in humans, who may vary even more widely than Albert, Bertram, and Charles. Differences in the ease with which conditioning occurs may account in part for many personality differences (Ax, 1990–1991; Eysenck, 1967). Some evidence suggests that individuals with antisocial personality disorder, who show a striking disregard for society's standards, respond differently to reward and punishment than other people (Newman et al., 1990; Scerbo et al., 1990). They appear less likely to experience anxiety when faced with potential punishment, which may lead to poor impulse control and a weak conscience.

The Relation between Classical and Operant Conditioning

As we have seen, the difference between operant and classical conditioning is that in classical conditioning the response follows an environmental event (the stimulus), whereas in operant conditioning the environmental event (reinforcement or punishment) follows the response (operant). Operant conditioning typically involves voluntary behavior, whereas classical conditioning involves involuntary behavior usually controlled by the autonomic nervous system.

The distinction is not, however, always quite so clear. In **biofeedback**, psychologists feed information back to patients about their biological processes, allowing them to gain operant control over autonomic responses such as heart rate, body temperature, and blood pressure (Larkin et al., 1992; Musso et al., 1991; Stroebel, 1985). Physiological responses that patients continuously monitor using special elec-

Biofeedback allows patients to gain operant control of autonomic processes.

tronic devices can be reinforced, such as changes in muscle tension or blood pressure. Biofeedback can help patients overcome such chronic problems as asthma, hypertension, migraine headaches, and rheumatoid arthritis (Blanchard et al., 1986; Nicholson & Blanchard, 1993; Lehrer et al., 1992; Young, 1992). In one study, patients treated for chronic back pain with biofeedback showed substantial improvement in comparison to control subjects (Flor et al., 1986). They also maintained these benefits at followup over two years later, reporting less need for treatment, less disruption of their life from pain, and fewer pain-related thoughts (Table 5.1).

In daily life, the distinction between operant and classical conditioning is also frequently far from clear, especially when complex behaviors are involved, for almost any learned behavior involves both classical and operant conditioning (Mowrer, 1947). A person who has a car accident, for instance, may develop a conditioned fear response to riding in cars, an example of classical conditioning. The

TABLE 5.1 THE EFFECTS OF BIOFEEDBACK ON CHRONIC BACK PAIN

DOMAINS DISRUPTED BY PAIN	BIOFEEDBACK GROUP	CONTROL GROUP
Life in general	14.3	38.9
Work	19.9	48.6
Sex	2.0	45.0

CHANGES AT FOLLOWUP IN TREATED GROUP	PRETREATMENT	POST-TREATMENT
Hours in pain per day	15.5	8.7
Interference with life	35.0	15.0
Negative pain-related thoughts	40.7	29.0

Source: Adapted from Flor et al., 1986, pp. 198–199.

Note. Back pain treated with biofeedback interfered substantially less in the lives of experimental subjects than in untreated controls. At followup, patients in the biofeedback condition continued to show substantial gains as compared with their initial pain reports prior to treatment.

individual may also develop the operant response of avoiding cars (avoidance learning), since the behavior is reinforced by the avoidance of an aversive experience.

Why Are Reinforcers Reinforcing?

Skinner and earlier behaviorists hoped to demonstrate empirical relationships between environmental events and an organism's responses without making reference to mental events. Indeed, they considered the mind a black box—unknowable, unobservable, and scientifically irrelevant. All one can observe is what goes into it and what comes out of it. Their aim was to uncover a set of laws about the way environmental variables are related to behavioral variables but not to offer a theory of the mental mechanisms that account for these lawful relationships. Other psychologists, however, have asked the question: What makes a reinforcer reinforcing or a punisher punishing? No single answer has achieved widespread acceptance, but three are worth considering.

Reinforcers as Drive Reducers

One theory relies on the concept of **drive**, a state that impels or "drives" the organism to act. Clark Hull (1943, 1951, 1952) used the term to refer to unpleasant tension states caused by deprivation of basic needs such as food and water. He proposed that stimuli that reduce drives are reinforcing. According to **drive-reduction theory**, reinforcers are stimuli associated with the reduction of drives. This theory makes intuitive sense and explains why an animal that is not hungry will typically not press a bar for pellets of food. However, it requires additional principles to explain why behaviors related to basic needs may be learned even when drives are not currently activated; lions can learn to hunt in packs and humans can learn to manipulate numbers on a computer even when their stomachs are full (Smith, 1984). Indeed, optimal learning does not typically occur under intense arousal.

Primary and Secondary Reinforcers

Drives help explain why some stimuli such as food, sex, and water, are reinforcing. Such stimuli are known as **primary reinforcers** because they innately reinforce behavior. Another kind of reinforcer, known as a **secondary reinforcer**, gains its power to reinforce through its associative connection with a primary reinforcer. If a neutral stimulus is paired enough times with a primary reinforcer, it may come to have the same or similar reinforcement value as the primary reinforcer. For instance, various words become connected with reinforcement through social interaction. Children often experience pleasant consequences while being told they are good, so that the word "good" itself becomes a secondary reinforcer. Smiles are reinforcing in all cultures.

Many secondary reinforcers are culturally defined. Blue ribbons for the biggest melon or best science project, gold medals for athletic performance, thank-you notes, and parades for heroes are all examples of secondary reinforcers in our own culture. In cultures that use money, children gradually learn to associate it with many things that are reinforcing. In noncash economies, alternative forms of currency acquire secondary reinforcement value. In the Gusii community in Kenya, for example, cattle and other livestock are the primary form of economic exchange. Cattle, rather than cash, are thus associated with marriage, happiness, and social status (LeVine & LeVine, 1963), and the smell of the barnyard carries very different connotations among the Gusii than among North Americans.

The Role of Feelings

A third explanation of why reinforcers are reinforcing stresses the role of feelings. For example, a student cheats on a test and receives a very high grade for which he is praised several times by his teacher. The more she praises him, the guiltier he feels. Paradoxically, despite previous conditioning to respond to praise as a reinforcer, the student may actually be less likely to cheat again than if he were not praised so profusely. Why?

The explanation harkens back to Thorndike's law of effect. It holds that feelings, including such emotions as sadness or joy as well as sensory experiences of pleasure or pain, provide the basis for conditioning (see Dollard & Miller, 1950; Mowrer, 1960; Wachtel, 1977; Westen, 1985, 1994). An operant that is followed by a pleasurable feeling will be reinforced, whereas one that is followed by unpleasant feelings will be less likely to recur. Whether a stimulus is reinforcing or punishing may depend on the *meaning* of the stimulus to the person, which determines whether the stimulus arouses pleasant or unpleasant feelings. The teacher's praise—normally a positive reinforcer—was punishing because it evoked guilt, which in turn decreased the probability that the response would recur. Although this view violates the intention of behaviorists to avoid discussing mental processes, it fits with an intuitive understanding of operant conditioning: Positive reinforcement occurs because a consequence *feels good*, negative reinforcement occurs because termination of an unpleasant stimulus *feels better*, and punishment reflects a consequence that *feels bad*.

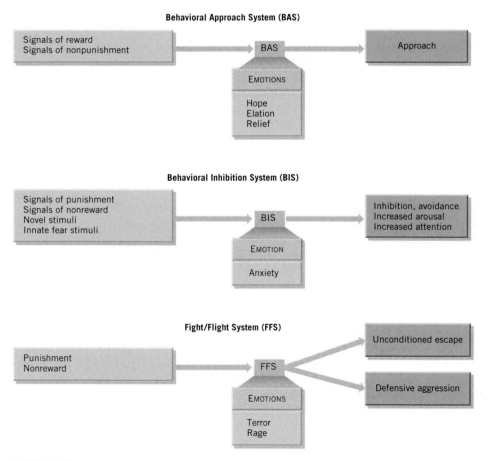

FIGURE 5.12

Gray's three behavioral systems. The behavioral approach system (BAS) orients the person (or animal) to stimuli associated with reward; approach is motivated by the positive emotions of hope, elation, and relief. The behavioral inhibition system (BIS) orients the person to avoidance and vigilance against threat. The BIS addresses potential dangers and involves anxiety. The fight/flight system (FFS) is a more evolutionarily primitive system that orients the person to escape currently punishing stimuli. It is associated with terror and rage. SOURCE: Adapted from Gray, 1988, pp. 278–279.

Neuropsychological evidence supports the proposition that feelings play a central role in operant conditioning. Gray (1987, 1990) argues that anatomically distinct pathways in the nervous system control different forms of conditioning and are associated with different emotional states (Figure 5.12). The **behavioral approach system** is associated with pleasurable emotional states and is responsible for approach-oriented operant behavior. The **behavioral inhibition system** is associated with anxiety and is involved in avoidance learning. The behavioral approach system involves neural circuits in which dopamine is the primary neurotransmitter, whereas the behavioral inhibition system relies on norepinephrine pathways. Administering chemicals that block the activity of norepinephrine (and hence reduce anxiety) inhibits the functioning of the behavioral inhibition system; giving antianxiety medications to dogs diminishes the power of conditioning using electric shock (Scott, 1980). These medications block the dogs' fear of being shocked, making them less likely to avoid a stimulus they previously associated with fear. Gray also describes a third, more evolutionarily primitive system, the **fight/flight system**, which is related to rage and terror.

Although psychodynamic conceptions have largely been aversive stimuli to learning theorists, someday we may have an integrated account of learning that includes many of the concepts studied by psychodynamic psychologists. For example, when a person raised in a violent home has difficulty recalling memories of abuse, a number of learning mechanisms may be operating. The memories are linked to emotions such as fear, anxiety, and rage, so that recalling them elicits a conditioned emotional response. This emotional response may be so unpleasant that it elicits avoidance or escape responses, one of which is to block off conscious access to these memories. If this "operant" of repression, or cognitive avoidance, successfully reduces the unpleasant emotion, it will be negatively reinforced, that is, strengthened by the removal of an aversive emotional state, and hence likely to be maintained or used again. Related thoughts may similarly evoke these memories, and these thoughts may become discriminative stimuli that alert the person to activate repressive mechanisms. If autonomic processes that are inaccessible to consciousness can come under operant control through biofeedback, it seems likely that the attentional mechanisms that bring thoughts, memories, or associations to consciousness can similarly come under the control of conditioning processes.

COGNITIVE-SOCIAL THEORY

The idea that feelings provide a basis for operant conditioning takes us far from the radical behaviorism that dominated experimental psychology for several decades. The radical behaviorist goal was to avoid entirely any mention of mental processes. However, by the 1960s, many researchers and theorists began to doubt that a psychological science could be built strictly on observable behaviors without reference to thought. Consider, for example, the role of cognitive processes in classical conditioning. Why does an organism respond to a previously neutral stimulus with a conditioned response?

A cognitive explanation suggests that a conditioned stimulus has predictive value to the organism—that is, the presence of the CS alerts the animal to prepare for the UCS. In other words, the CS predicts the presence of the UCS. When a UCS (electrical shock) frequently occurs in the absence of a CS (a tone), rats are unlikely to develop a conditioned fear response to the CS, regardless of the number of times the CS has been paired with the UCS (Rescorla, 1988; Rescorla & Holland, 1982; Rescorla & Wagner, 1972). Rats will not become afraid of a stimulus unless it is highly predictive of an aversive event. Blocking—the failure of a stimulus to lead to a CR when another stimulus already elicits the response—lends itself to a similar cognitive explanation. If an organism can already predict that the UCS is about to occur based on one stimulus (such as a bell), it does not require any other predictor (such as a flash of light).

The cognitive perspective can explain other conditioning phenomena as well. Stimulus discrimination and generalization reflect an animal's formation of a concept of what "counts" as a particular type of stimulus, which may be relatively general (any furry object) or relatively specific (a white rat). Cognitive explanations also help make sense of operant conditioning phenomena. Pieceworkers on a fixed ratio schedule (such as payment for every fifth bushel of apples) continue to work between reinforcements because they *know* they will be paid at the end. A cognitive psychologist can readily explain the paradoxical superiority of intermittent over continuous reinforcement schedules in maintaining behavior. With intermittent schedules, the animal develops the expectation that reinforcement will only come intermittently, so that lack of reinforcement on several trials does not signal a change in environmental contingencies. In contrast, when the owner of a new car suddenly finds the engine will not turn over, he has reason to stop trying after three or four attempts because he knows the engine should start on a new car and that he has been continuously reinforced by this car in the past.

The recognition that thought is integral to learning led to the development of cognitive-social theory (sometimes called cognitive-social learning or cognitive-behavioral theory). This theory grew out of behaviorism and incorporated many of its principles while at the same time suggesting learning mechanisms other than classical and operant conditioning. **Cognitive-social theory** stresses the roles of cognition and social learning.

The Role of Cognition

The first basic tenet of cognitive-social theory is that cognition mediates between stimulus and response or between the environment and behavior. Cognitive-social theorists do not deny that the environment has a crucial impact on the way organisms respond. However, in animals that have the capacity for complex sensory discrimination and thinking, it is not the environment per se but the way the organism *construes* the environment that is crucial to learning.

One of the first research programs to question the radical behaviorist dismissal of mental events was conducted by Edward Tolman. In a paper entitled "Cognitive Maps in Rats and Men" (1948), Tolman described learning that occurred when rats were placed in a maze without any reinforcement, similar in certain respects to the kind of learning that occurs when viewers watch the evening news. In one experiment, Tolman simply let rats wander through a maze in 10 trials on 10 consecutive days without any reinforcement (Tolman & Honzik, 1930). A control group spent the same amount of time in the maze, but these rats received a food reinforcement in each of their 10 trials. The rats that were reinforced learned quite rapidly to travel to the end of the maze with few errors, whereas the behavior of the unreinforced rats was, not surprisingly, less predictable. On the eleventh day, Tolman made food available for the first time to the previously unreinforced rats and recorded the number of errors they made. As Figure 5.13 shows, his findings were striking: These rats immediately took advantage of their familiarity with the maze and were able to obtain food just as efficiently as the rats who had undergone earlier reinforcement trials. A third group of rats who still received no reinforcement continued to wander aimlessly through the maze.

To explain what had happened, Tolman suggested that the rats who were familiar with the maze even without reinforcement had formed **cognitive maps**, mental representations or images, of the maze. They formed these maps prior to conditioning, which suggested that they had been learning about their environment even in the absence of reinforcement. Once the rats were reinforced, their learning mere-

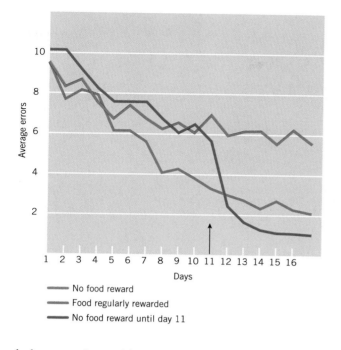

— No food reward
— Food regularly rewarded
— No food reward until day 11

FIGURE 5.13
Latent learning. Rats that were not rewarded until the eleventh trial immediately showed equal performance with rats that had been rewarded from the start. This suggests that they were learning the maze prior to reinforcement and were forming a cognitive map that allowed them to navigate it as soon as they received reinforcement. *SOURCE: Tolman & Honzik, 1930, p. 267.*

ly became observable. Tolman called learning that has occurred but is not currently manifest in behavior **latent learning**.

To Tolman and later cognitive-social theorists, latent learning was evidence that thinking mediates between the environment and behavior. He argued that the black box of behaviorism—the mysterious and scientifically unknowable mental machinery that occurs between stimulus and response—was the locus of significant happenings that were a legitimate object of psychological study. Thus emerged the view that humans and other animals are constantly processing information about the world around them and forming mental representations of classes of stimuli.

Expectancies

Cognitive-social theory proposes that expectations, or **expectancies,** of the consequences of behavior are what render it more or less likely to occur. If a behavior has a positive **outcome expectancy**, that is, if the person expects it to produce a reinforcing consequence, the individual is likely to perform it, as long as she has the competence to do so (Mischel, 1973). Julian Rotter (1954) first defined expectancies as "the probability [as assessed] by the individual that a particular reinforcement will occur as a function of a specific behavior on his part" (p. 107). Rotter argued that people act in a goal-directed way because they expect future reinforcement for certain behaviors.

Although many expectancies are specific to concrete situations ("If I ask this professor for an extension, he will refuse"), others are generalized ("You can't ask people for anything in life—they'll always turn you down"). Rotter was particularly interested in **generalized expectancies** that influence a broad spectrum of behavior. He used the term **locus of control of reinforcement** (or simply **locus of control**) to refer to the generalized expectancies people hold about whether or not their own behavior will bring about the outcomes they seek (Rotter, 1954, 1990). Individuals with an **internal locus of control** believe they are the masters of their own fate, whereas individuals with an **external locus of control** believe their lives are determined by forces outside (that is, external to) themselves. Figure 5.14 shows some of the items included in Rotter's questionnaire for assessing locus of control.

Why are cognitive factors such as expectancies important to understanding learning? Why should locus of control matter to a learning theorist? The answer, according to cognitive-social theorists, is that learning how to behave in various sit-

FIGURE 5.14
Items from Rotter's locus of control questionnaire, called the Internal-External Scale. The scale presents subjects with a series of choices between two responses, one of which is internal and the other, external. SOURCE: *Rotter, 1971.*

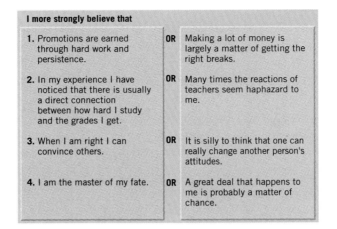

I more strongly believe that		
1. Promotions are earned through hard work and persistence.	**OR**	Making a lot of money is largely a matter of getting the right breaks.
2. In my experience I have noticed that there is usually a direct connection between how hard I study and the grades I get.	**OR**	Many times the reactions of teachers seem haphazard to me.
3. When I am right I can convince others.	**OR**	It is silly to think that one can really change another person's attitudes.
4. I am the master of my fate.	**OR**	A great deal that happens to me is probably a matter of chance.

uations means learning to *anticipate* the links between actions and their consequences. People who believe they control their own destiny are much more likely to learn to do so.

Locus of control expectancies differ across cultures and depend on social and ecological circumstances. Research comparing locus of control in Chinese and American adolescents finds that Chinese subjects have a more internal locus of control for failure but a more external locus of control for success. In other words, they take more responsibility for their failures and less for their successes than their American counterparts (Chiu, 1988). This expectancy likely reflects hundreds of years of Chinese history of living in densely populated agricultural areas. In such environments, excessive pride and self-centeredness are highly disruptive, and fulfilling responsibilities to others is valued, since these behaviors are essential to survival and harmonious group living.

Learned Helplessness and Explanatory Style

The powerful impact of expectancies even on the behavior of nonhuman animals was demonstrated graphically in a series of studies by Martin Seligman (1975), who harnessed dogs so that they could not escape electric shocks. Not surprisingly, the dogs whimpered and howled for some time and tried to escape the shocks, until finally they gave up. They lay on the floor without struggle, manifesting physiological stress responses and behaviors that reminded Seligman of human depression. A day later he placed the dogs in a shuttlebox from which they could easily escape the shocks. They made no effort to escape, however, and failed to learn even when they did occasionally escape. The dogs had developed the expectancy that they could not get away; they had learned to be helpless. **Learned helplessness** consists of the expectancy that one cannot escape aversive events and the motivational and learning deficits that accrue from this belief. Seligman argued by analogy that learned helplessness plays a role in human depression, in which people similarly tend to feel that they are helpless to improve their lives.

In humans, learned helplessness is not an automatic outcome of uncontrollable aversive events. Seligman and his colleagues subsequently developed the concept of explanatory styles to account for the fact that some people have a positive, active coping attitude in the face of failure or disappointment, whereas others become depressed and helpless (Peterson & Seligman, 1984). **Explanatory style** refers to the way people make sense of bad events. Individuals with a depressive or **pessimistic explanatory style** blame themselves; that is, they make the inference or attribution that the causes of their misfortune are internal rather than external, which leads to lowered self-esteem. They also tend to see these causes as stable (unlikely to change) and global (broad, general, and widespread in their impact). When a person with a pessimistic style does poorly on a biology exam, he may blame it on his own stupidity—an explanation that is internal, stable, and global. Most people, in contrast, would offer explanations to themselves that permit hope and encourage further effort, such as "I didn't study hard enough," "The exam was ridiculous," or "I just had a bad day."

Numerous studies document that pessimists have a higher incidence of depression and lower achievement in school than optimists (Peterson & Seligman, 1984). Pessimistic students tend to have vague academic goals and to take fewer active steps than optimists (such as seeking help from fellow students or from the professor) after doing poorly on an assignment (Peterson, 1989). In trying to understand the origins of these patterns, one research team measured the explanatory style of parents of 52 disabled and 40 nondisabled elementary school children (Vanden Belt & Peterson, 1991). They asked parents to attribute causes to negative scenarios regarding their children. The data, displayed in Table 5.2, show that a composite measure of parental explanatory style (a general measure of pessimism) negatively correlated with children's academic achievement. It also negatively correlated with teachers' assessments of their behavior, happiness, and ability to cope with failure, live up to their potential, and meet challenges. In other words, the more pessimistic the parents, the less successful and happy the child. The same pattern held for both disabled and nondisabled children. These data suggest that children may learn an optimistic or pessimistic style at home and that these learned beliefs affect their academic performance.

As we have seen, cognitive variables such as expectancies are heavily influenced by cultural factors, and this is true of explanatory style as well. Within our own culture, people from fundamentalist religious backgrounds (both Christian and Jewish) tend to have more optimistic explanatory styles than nonfundamentalists (Sethi & Seligman, 1993). They seem to believe that their fate is in the hands of God and that God is basically good. Across cultures, variations in explanatory style can be quite dramatic. Of relevance is a classic study in the early 1960s that examined value orientations in five North American groups: Texans, Mormons, Hispanics, Zuni Indians, and Navaho Indians (Kluckhohn & Strodtbeck, 1961). The researchers presented subjects with short stories that posed a problem or dilemma and asked them to indicate which of several solutions was most appropriate.

TABLE 5.2 PARENTAL EXPLANATORY STYLE AND CLASSROOM PERFORMANCE

	Correlation with Parental Explanatory Style	
	DISABLED	NONDISABLED
Academic achievement	−.27	−.42
Behavior in classroom	−.28	−.32
Ability to meet challenges	−.21	−.43
Ability to cope with failure	−.15	−.32
Performance in relation to potential	−.27	−.39
Happiness	−.25	−.42

Source: Vanden Belt & Peterson, 1991, p. 337.

Note. The table shows the correlations between parental explanatory style and classroom performance of disabled and nondisabled students. The data show that the higher the parents' score on pessimism, the lower the functioning of the child, whether or not disabled, although the link is stronger for the nondisabled group.

Although broad generalizations should be advanced with caution (since all of these cultures have changed dramatically over the last 30 years and variation among individuals exists within all cultures), the results have important implications for understanding the impact of culture on explanatory style. Hispanic subjects, like members of most cultures in human history, tended to believe that humans should not tamper with nature. Texans preferred mastery over nature, whereas the Navajo stressed a peaceful coexistence between humans and their natural environment. People who have different attitudes about the extent to which they can and should master events are likely to respond very differently to situations in which they are helpless. The Hispanic subjects in this study would likely respond more philosophically to negative situations outside their control, whereas for the Texans, helplessness would probably engender not only frustration or depression but also lowered self-esteem. On the other hand, people who believe they *can* control nature are more likely to develop technologies to do so.

The Role of Social Learning

Alongside the emphasis on cognition, a second basic tenet of cognitive-social theory is that much of learning occurs socially, through mechanisms other than classical and operant conditioning. Individuals learn many things from the people around them—that is, they undergo **social learning**—without being conditioned. They may develop ideas about what a beautiful woman or handsome man looks like from the pages of magazines, or they may remember something they heard on television that is of no immediate relevance to their well-being.

A major form of social learning is **observational learning**—learning by observing the behavior of others. The impact of observational learning in humans is enormous, from learning how to give a speech, to learning how to feel and act when someone tells an inappropriate joke, to learning what kind of clothes, haircuts, or foods are fashionable. Albert Bandura (1967) provides a tongue-in-cheek example of observational learning in the story of a lonesome farmer who bought a parrot to keep him company. The farmer spent many long hours trying to teach the parrot to repeat the phrase, "Say uncle," but to no avail. Even hitting the parrot with a stick whenever it failed to respond correctly had no effect. Finally, the farmer gave up; in disgust, he relegated the parrot to the chicken coop. Not long afterward, the farmer was walking by the chicken coop when he heard a terrible commotion. Looking in, he saw his parrot brandishing a stick at the chickens and yelling, "Say uncle! Say uncle!"

Observational learning in which a human or other animal learns to reproduce behavior exhibited by a model is called **modeling** (Bandura, 1967). The most well-known modeling studies were done by Bandura and his colleagues on children's aggressive behavior (1961, 1963). In these studies, children observed an adult model interacting with a large inflatable doll called Bobo. One group of children watched the model behave in a subdued manner, while other groups observed the model verbally and physically attack the doll in real life, on film, or in a cartoon. A control group observed no model at all. Children who observed the model acting aggressively displayed nearly twice as much aggressive behavior as those who watched the nonaggressive model (Figure 5.15). The children had learned to reproduce the adult's behavior through modeling.

Whether people will imitate a model is influenced by a number of factors, such as the model's prestige, likeability, and attractiveness. The extent to which people actually perform modeled behavior also depends on the behavior's likely outcome. This outcome expectancy is itself often learned through an observational learning mechanism known as **vicarious conditioning**, in which a person learns the consequences of an action by observing its consequences for someone else. For example,

In Bandura's classic Bobo studies, children learned by observation.

children learn what not to do at home by observing what happens when their siblings talk back to their parents or break curfews.

In a classic study of vicarious conditioning, Bandura and his colleagues (1963) had nursery school children observe an aggressive adult model named Rocky. Rocky took food and toys that belonged to someone named Johnny. In one condition, Johnny punished Rocky; in the other, Rocky packed all of Johnny's toys in a sack, singing "Hi ho, hi ho, it's off to play I go" as the scene ended. Later, when placed in an analogous situation, the children who saw Rocky punished displayed relatively little aggressive behavior. In contrast, those who saw Rocky rewarded behaved much more aggressively. Because Rocky's aggressive behavior exemplified what the children had previously learned was bad behavior, even those who followed his lead displayed some ambivalence when they saw his behavior rewarded. One girl voiced strong disapproval of Rocky's behavior but then ended the experimental session by asking the researcher, "Do you have a sack?" More recent research shows that people who are empathic and helpful to others tended to have parents who modeled similar behavior when they were children (Penner & Rioux, 1995).

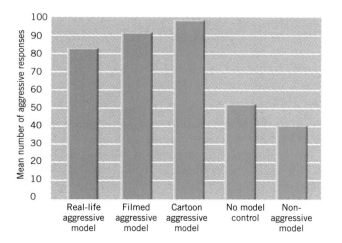

FIGURE 5.15
Social learning of aggressive behavior through modeling. This figure shows the average number of aggressive responses made by children after observing an adult model playing with an inflatable doll in each of five experimental conditions: real-life aggressive model, filmed aggressive model, cartoon aggressive model, no model control, and nonaggressive model. As can be seen, children tend to perform the behaviors of adult models. SOURCE: Bandura, 1967, p. 45.

Another form of social learning is direct **tutelage**—teaching concepts or procedures primarily through verbal explanation or instruction. This process is responsible for most formal education and is occurring at this very moment. Social learning processes, such as learning from a textbook, work in tandem with conditioning, since most readers have been reinforced for learning in this manner and may be reinforced by noticing that the chapter is just about over.

SOME CONCLUDING THOUGHTS

We have come a long way from the early behaviorists' view that the environment automatically stamps behaviors into the organism. Nevertheless, behaviorism has had, and continues to have, a tremendous impact on theories of learning and has been applied to many everyday problems. Conditioning research has led to treatments for a variety of psychological problems, from snake phobias to inappropriate classroom or dinner-table behavior (Chapter 16). Behaviorist learning principles have also been put to use in an educational technique known as programmed learning. In **programmed learning**, which is now typically computerized, students proceed at their own rate, receiving reinforcement (such as "Good job!") when successfully mastering an assignment. Many software programs, such as those used for word processing, include self-teaching disks derived from this behaviorist innovation (Lippert, 1989). Beyond all else, perhaps the main legacy of behaviorism is a hard-nosed attitude toward psychological observation and explanation, and a skeptical attitude toward theoretical speculation without empirical support.

As important as behaviorist research has been, however, explanations of learning have shifted dramatically in a cognitive direction. Many contemporary learning theorists view learning not primarily as a set of behavioral tendencies evoked by different situations but as the accumulation and mental organization of knowledge (see Canfield & Ceci, 1992). Psychologists now speak more freely of thoughts, emotions, motives, goals, and stresses that interact to produce behavioral outcomes. In the following chapters we examine these phenomena, beginning with the memory processes that allow humans and other animals to store information about past experiences in order to direct their future behavior.

Summary

1. **Learning** refers to any enduring change in the way an organism responds based on its experience. Learning theories assume that experience shapes behavior, that learning is adaptive, and that uncovering laws of learning requires systematic experimentation. Learning theory is the foundation of the behaviorist perspective.

Classical Conditioning

2. **Conditioning** is a type of learning studied by behaviorists. **Classical conditioning** refers to learning in which an environmental stimulus produces a response in an organism. An innate reflex is an **unconditioned reflex**. The stimulus that produces the response in an unconditioned reflex is called an **unconditioned stimulus**, or **UCS**. An **unconditioned response (UR)** is a response that does not have to be learned. A **conditioned response (CR)** is a response that has been learned. A **conditioned stimulus (CS)** is a stimulus that the organism learns to associate with the unconditioned stimulus.

3. **Stimulus generalization** occurs when an organism produces a conditioned response to stimuli that have not been paired with the original unconditioned stimulus but are similar to the conditioned stimulus. **Stimulus discrimination** is the learned tendency to respond to a very restricted range of stimuli or to only the one used during training. **Extinction** results if the CS repeatedly occurs without the UCS.

4. Factors that influence classical conditioning include the **interstimulus interval** (the time between presentation of the CS and the UCS), the individual's learning history, and the organism's biological **preparedness** to learn.

5. Research suggests that classical conditioning increases the action of neurotransmitters at the synapse: Learning actually produces changes in cells.

Operant Conditioning

6. Thorndike's **law of effect** states that an animal's tendency to produce a behavior depends on that behavior's effect on the environment. Skinner elaborated this idea into the concept of **operant conditioning**. **Operants** are behaviors that are emitted rather than elicited by the environment. A consequence is said to lead to **reinforcement** if it increases the probability that a response will recur. A **reinforcer** is an environmental consequence that occurs after an organism has produced a response, which makes the response more likely to recur.

7. **Positive reinforcement** is the process whereby presentation of a stimulus (a reward or payoff) makes a behavior more likely to recur. A **positive reinforcer** is an environmental consequence that, when presented, increases the probability that a response will recur. Whereas the *presentation* of a positive reinforcer rewards a response, the *removal* of a negative reinforcer rewards a response. **Negative reinforcement** is the process whereby termination of an aversive stimulus (a negative reinforcer) makes a behavior more likely to recur. **Negative reinforcers** are aversive or unpleasant stimuli that strengthen a behavioral tendency by their removal. Whereas reinforcement always increases the probability that a response will recur, **punishment** decreases the probability.

8. The mechanisms of learning appear similar across cultures, although cultures apply these principles in various ways, using different strategies for punishing and reinforcing behavior.

9. In a **continuous schedule of reinforcement**, the environmental consequence is the same each time an animal emits a behavior. In an **intermittent schedule of reinforcement**, reinforcement does not occur every time the organism emits a particular response. In a **fixed ratio (FR) schedule of reinforcement**, an organism receives reinforcement at a fixed rate, according to the number of operant responses emitted. As in the fixed ratio schedule, an animal on a **variable ratio (VR) schedule** receives a reward for some percentage of responses, but the number of responses required before each reinforcement is unpredictable. In a **fixed interval (FI) schedule**, an animal receives reinforcement for its responses only after a fixed amount of time. In a **variable interval (VI) schedule**, the animal cannot predict how long that time interval will be.

10. Several factors influence operant conditioning, including the degree of contingency between operant and consequence (that is, how consistently they are paired); the interval between the behavior and the environmental consequence; the presence of **discriminative stimuli** (stimuli that signal to an organism that particular contingencies of reinforcement are in effect); prepared learning (the tendency of animals to produce certain species-specific behaviors or to connect particular behaviors and responses); and characteristics of the learner.

11. Why reinforcers have their effects is a matter of debate. Some theorists view reinforcers as drive-reducers, associated with elimination of need deprivation. Others argue that most reinforcers derive their power from their association with stimuli that are innately reinforcing. A third theory suggests that pleasurable and painful feelings are responsible for reinforcement and punishment.

Cognitive-Social Theory

12. **Cognitive-social theory** proposes that cognition mediates between the environment and behavior and that much of learning is social. Tolman demonstrated that rats formed **cognitive maps** or mental images of their environment and that these were responsible for **latent learning**—learning that has occurred but is not currently manifest in behavior.

13. Cognitive-social theory proposes that expectations or **expectancies** of the consequences of behaviors are what render behaviors more or less likely to occur. **Locus of control** refers to the generalized expectancies people hold about whether or not their own behavior will bring about the outcomes they prefer. **Learned helplessness** includes the expectancy that one cannot escape aversive events and the motivational and learning deficits that accrue from it. **Explanatory style** refers to the way people make sense of bad events. Individuals with a depressive or **pessimistic explanatory style** see the causes of bad events as internal, stable, and global.

14. Psychologists have studied several kinds of **social learning** (learning that takes place as a direct result of social interaction), including **observational learning** (learning by observing the behavior of others) and **tutelage** (direct instruction). A kind of observational learning in which a human or other animal learns to reproduce behavior exhibited by a model is known as **modeling**. In **vicarious conditioning**, a person learns the consequences of an action by observing its consequences for someone else.

15. Behaviorists have left a substantial legacy through their work on conditioning and its applications, including a skeptical attitude toward theoretical speculation without empirical support. Nevertheless, many psychologists now believe that learning entails the accumulation and organization of thoughts and feelings as well as behavioral tendencies.

Jan Sawka, "The Memories II," 1987

Chapter 6

MEMORY

Jimmie was a fine-looking man, with a curly bush of gray hair, a healthy and handsome forty-nine-year-old. He was cheerful, friendly, and warm.

"Hi, Doc!" he said. "Nice morning! Do I take this chair here?" He was a genial soul, very ready to talk and to answer any question I asked him. He told me his name and birth date, and the name of the little town in Connecticut where he was born. . . . He recalled, and almost relived, his war days and service, the end of the war, and his thoughts for the future. . . .

With recalling, Jimmie was full of animation; he did not seem to be speaking of the past but of the present. . . . A sudden, improbable suspicion seized me.

"What year is this, Mr. G.?" I asked, concealing my perplexity in a casual manner.

"Forty-five, man. What do you mean?" He went on, "We've won the war, FDR's dead, Truman's at the helm. There are great times ahead."

"And you, Jimmie, how old would you be?"

Oddly, uncertainly, he hesitated a moment as if engaged in calculation.

"Why, I guess I'm nineteen, Doc. I'll be twenty next birthday."

(Sachs, 1970, pp. 21–23)

*J*immie was, in fact, 20 years behind the times; he was nearly 50 years old. His **amnesia**, or memory loss, resulted from Korsakoff's syndrome, a disorder related to chronic alcoholism that arises from the deterioration of subcortical structures involved in memory. Jimmie suffered from **anterograde amnesia**, a loss of memory for events since the damage to the brain. (**Retrograde amnesia**, in contrast, is the loss of memory of events prior to the damage.) Jimmie had no difficulty recalling incidents from World War II, but he could not remember anything since 1945, when he succumbed to Korsakoff's.

Curiously, though, amnesics like Jimmie are still able to form certain kinds of new memories (Squire & Zola-Morgan, 1991; Squire, 1986). If asked to recall a seven-digit phone number long enough to walk to another room and dial it, they have no difficulty doing so—although a minute after completing the call, they will not remember having picked up the phone. Or suppose Jimmie, who grew up before the days of computers, were to play a computer game every day for a week. Like most people, he would steadily improve at it, demonstrating that he was learning and remembering new skills. Astonishingly, however, he would still greet the computer each day with the same, "Gee, what's this thing?"

Case studies of neurologically impaired patients support experimental studies of normal subjects to suggest that memory is not a single entity or process that one can have or lose. Rather, memory is composed of several systems. How many systems, and how independent they are from one another, are questions at the heart of contemporary research on memory.

This chapter begins by briefly laying out the basic cognitive model that has guided research on memory for three decades. We then explore the various memory systems outlined by this information-processing model, from initial brief stores that hold sensations for a flicker of an instant, through long-term systems that can retain information for a lifetime. In doing so, we consider the implications of memory research for questions such as the accuracy of eyewitness testimony in court and the existence of repressed memories in victims of childhood sexual abuse. We conclude with a discussion of the limits of the information-processing model and some thoughts on the evolution of memory.

MEMORY AND INFORMATION PROCESSING

The cognitive perspective has dominated psychologists' view of memory for the past three decades, although in recent years it has become integrated with an understanding of the neuropsychology of memory (Polster et al., 1991; Raajmakers & Shriffrin, 1992). As discussed in Chapter 1, the cognitive perspective focuses on information processing and is predicated on an analogy between the mind and the input, processing, storage, and output functions of computers.

Figure 6.1 presents an information-processing model of memory. The first stage is the presentation of a stimulus, such as an unfamiliar road sign. When people see a stimulus like a sign on the road, its image is held momentarily in their visual sensory register. **Sensory registers** hold information about a perceived stimulus for a split second after the stimulus disappears, allowing a mental model or representa-

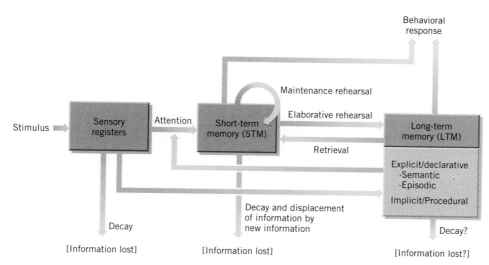

FIGURE 6.1

An information-processing model of memory. Stimulus information enters the sensory registers and may receive attention or exit the system. Some information enters STM or activates information in LTM. Other information is lost from STM and presumably never encoded in LTM.

tion of it to remain in memory briefly for further processing. A sensory register probably exists for each sensory modality.

Many of the stimuli people perceive in the course of a day register so briefly that they drop out of the memory system without further processing or storage. Others, however, make a greater impression. The road sign may depict what look like falling rocks on a mountain road. Information about these objects is passed along to **short-term memory (STM)**, which stores information for roughly 20–30 seconds. Short-term memory is also called **working memory** because it functions like a mental "sketch pad" on which people make mental notes, solve problems, and hold relevant information in consciousness for a brief period (Baddeley, 1986; Goldman-Rakic, 1995).

As can be seen in Figure 6.1, some information from short-term memory is lost from the system and is never processed further. If you hold a phone number in your mind momentarily, you may forget it within seconds, and it will never be retrievable. Some of the information that enters STM, however, goes on to be processed in **long-term memory (LTM)**, where memories for facts, images, thoughts, feelings, skills, and experiences may reside for as long as a lifetime. Recovering information from long-term memory, known as **retrieval**, involves bringing it back into short-term memory (which is often used in information-processing models as a synonym for consciousness).

In the past decade, cognitive psychologists have made three changes in this basic information-processing model. First, they have come to view memory not as a single process or function but as a set of **memory systems**—discrete but interdependent processing units responsible for different kinds of remembering. This view fits with contemporary neuropsychological theories, which suggest that the central nervous system consists of **modules**, coordinated but independently functioning systems of neurons. These modules function in parallel rather than one at a time (Fodor, 1983; Gazzaniga, 1989; Grigsby & Schneiders, 1991; Rumelhart et al., 1986). For instance, when people simultaneously hear thunder and see lightning, they process the sound using auditory modules and the image with visual modules. When they then remember the episode, however, they experience the activation of both modules at the same time, so that they have no awareness that the brain has been operating in parallel.

Second, psychologists now recognize other forms of remembering that do not involve retrieval into consciousness. An amnesic who learns to play a computer game with increasing precision, or a child who learns to tie a shoe, is storing new information in long-term memory. When this information is remembered, however, it is expressed directly in skilled behavior, rather than retrieved into conscious short-term memory.

Third, not all information in the model follows the path just described, as shown in Figure 6.1. Some information from the sensory registers may be transferred directly to long-term memory, bypassing short-term memory or consciousness altogether. This phenomenon accounts for the familiar experience of finding oneself humming a tune that was playing in the background at a grocery store without even noticing that it was playing. Further, the model is not unidirectional. Cognitive psychologists initially believed that information passes from STM to LTM and is then retrieved. What has become clear, however, is that the process of selecting the sensory information that will be processed in short-term memory in the first place is actually influenced by long-term memory. Long-term memory often determines which of the current incoming data are relevant to the task at hand and hence will receive conscious attention (Chapter 9).

This information-processing model provides a useful roadmap of memory and will be used as the framework for organizing this chapter. In the next several pages, we consider each stage in the model, from sensory registration to short-term memory and long-term memory. In the process, we examine the way information is represented in memory.

SENSORY REGISTRATION

Suppose you grab a handful of quarters (say, six or seven) from your pocket at the laundromat and, while looking away, stretch out your hand so that all of the coins are visible. If you then glance for a second at your hand but look away before stopping to count the change, you are still likely to be able to report accurately the number of coins in your hand because the image is held momentarily in your sensory register. To date, most research has focused on visual (or iconic) and auditory (echoic) sensory registration.

The term **iconic storage** is used to describe visual sensory registration: For a brief period after an image disappears from vision, people retain a mental image (or "icon") of what they have seen (Foley & Mulhern, 1991; Neisser, 1967, 1976). This visual trace is remarkably accurate and contains considerably more information than people can report, for it fades from memory long before they can verbalize what they have seen (Baddeley & Patterson, 1971).

George Sperling of Harvard University demonstrated iconic storage in a classic series of experiments published in 1960. Sperling used an instrument called a tachistoscope to flash a grid of 12 letters on a screen for 15–500 milliseconds—that is, up to half a second (Figure 6.2). Then, at the sound of a tone, subjects were to report what they had seen. The delay between disappearance of the image and the sounding of the tone varied from virtually no time to one second.

In one experiment (the "whole report" design), Sperling simply asked subjects to report as many of the letters as they could remember at the sound of the tone. In a second, "partial report" experiment, Sperling told subjects that they would hear one of three different tones after the image disappeared. If they heard the high-pitched tone, they were to report the letters in the top row; if the tone had a medium pitch, they were to report the middle row; and if the tone was low, they were to report the bottom row. Until the tone sounded, subjects did not know which row they would be asked to report. Thus, they had to "read" the row from iconic storage to provide an accurate report.

The difference in results between the two experiments was striking. In the whole report design, subjects typically remembered no more than four of the 12 letters they had seen, or 33 percent. In the partial report design, subjects accurately reported roughly three out of the four items they were asked to recall (or 75 percent), if the tone sounded a fraction of a second after the image disappeared. If the tone was delayed longer, however, accuracy declined rapidly. The partial report

DISPLAY	TONE	RESPONSE
M Q T Z	High	
R F G A	Medium	If low tone was sounded
N S L C	Low	"N, S, L, C"

FIGURE 6.2

Iconic memory. Subjects briefly viewed a grid of 12 letters and then heard a tone after a short delay. Depending on whether a high, medium, or low tone sounded, they were instructed to report the top, middle, or bottom row. If the tone sounded within half a second, they were 75% accurate, by reading the icon in their mind. If the tone sounded beyond that time, their accuracy dropped substantially because the icon was no longer available. SOURCE: Sperling, 1960.

Glance briefly at Renoir's Luncheon of the Boating Party *and try counting the number of people from the momentary iconic memory.*

design allowed subjects to focus their attention on one part of the image while it was still in iconic storage and thus to retain it in short-term memory even after the icon had faded. In contrast, subjects in the whole report design could only report what they could "see" for the fraction of a second that the icon was present (about three or four letters). Subjects for whom the bell tolled too late could not read anything off the icon.

The duration of icons varies from approximately half a second to two seconds, depending on the individual, the content of the image, and the circumstances (Neisser, 1976). Presenting another image or even a flash of light directly after the first image disappears erases the original icon (Schiller, 1965), much as a new movie recorded on an old videotape erases previous material.

The auditory counterpart of iconic storage is called **echoic storage** (Battacchi et al., 1981; Darwin et al., 1972; Neisser, 1967). Most readers have probably had the experience of hearing a voice or a sound "echo" in their minds after the actual sound has stopped. Some researchers have suggested that humans may have two types of echoic memory systems, one for nonspeech and the other for speech sounds, lateralized to the right and left hemispheres of the brain, respectively (Ardila et al., 1986; Deutsch, 1970; Kimura & Folb, 1970). As with iconic storage, echoic storage is apparently relatively brief (Cowan, 1984) and is quickly erased if another auditory stimulus is presented.

REPRESENTATION

When information passes through the sensory registers to be processed and stored, it does so in the form of a **mental representation**, a mental model of a stimulus or category of stimuli. In neuropsychological terms, a representation is a patterned firing of a circuit of neurons that forms the neural code for a stimulus or concept, such as dog, sister, or a road sign indicating falling rocks. Information can be represented in various ways, though most representations are sensory or verbal.

Sensory Representations

Sensory representations store information in a sensory mode, such as the sound of a dog barking or the image of a city's skyline. The cognitive maps discovered in rats running mazes (Chapter 5) are a form of visual representation. People rely on visual representations to recall where they put their keys last night or what information was on a page of notes relevant to answering an examination question. Some psychologists have argued that visual representations are like pictures that can be mentally scrutinized or manipulated (Kosslyn, 1983; Tye, 1991). If asked, "How many light fixtures are in your home?" most people could answer, despite never having counted, by forming a mental image of the rooms in the house and simply counting the fixtures as they travel mentally from room to room.

Several studies support this theory. In one, the experimenters showed subjects pictures of a well-known stimulus, such as a capital R, rotated between 0 and 360 degrees (Figure 6.3). The task was to tell whether the letter was shown normally or in mirror image. The time subjects took to answer—the dependent variable—varied directly with the degree of rotation from upright. In other words, the more the rotation, the longer the reaction time. This indicated that subjects were mentally rotating an image of the letter to come to a conclusion (Cooper & Shepard, 1973; Cooper, 1975, 1976). In a more recent study, subjects underwent a PET scan (Chapter 2) while either perceiving or imagining a visual pattern (Kosslyn et al., in press). The results showed that imagining a visual pattern (such as a letter) activates the same parts of the primary visual cortex as actually perceiving it, thus clearly documenting the existence of visual representations.

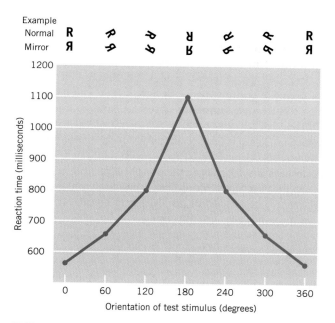

FIGURE 6.3

The manipulation of visual representations. The investigators asked subjects to determine whether the "R" they saw at different degrees of rotation was forward or backward. The dependent variable was the amount of time required to accomplish the task. The figure graphs reaction time as a function of degrees of rotation. As can be seen, the more subjects had to rotate the letter mentally, the longer they took to complete the task. Peak reaction time was at 180 degrees, which requires the furthest rotation.
SOURCE: *Adapted from Cooper & Shepard, 1973.*

A person with eidetic memory could retrieve the image from memory and report the number of people in this scene from nineteenth century Osaka, Japan.

An extreme example of visual representation is **eidetic imagery**, or photographic memory. An individual with eidetic imagery might look at a painting and hold it so clearly in memory as to later describe each person in it. Only a small fraction of the population possesses eidetic memory, and for reasons psychologists do not yet understand, this ability is far less common among adults than among preadolescent children (Giray, 1985; Gray & Gummerman, 1975; Haber, 1979).

Visual representations are not the only sensory representations. The auditory mode is also important for encoding information, particularly language. Some forms of auditory information would be difficult to represent in other modes. For instance, most readers would be able to retrieve pieces of Beethoven's Fifth Symphony or Michael Jackson's "Beat It" quite easily. In both cases, the representation that is retrieved is a series of patterned segments of sound, such as the *di-di-di-dah* that opens Beethoven's Fifth.

Other types of sensory representations have rarely been studied, although people undoubtedly rely on them as well (Hill & Bliss, 1967; Schab, 1991). When a chef spices a stew to taste, he compares his current gustatory perception to a representation of the way the food is supposed to taste. Emotions must also be stored and represented in memory, as is apparent when recalling the loss of a significant other or the feeling of being surrounded by family at Thanksgiving.

Verbal Representations

Although many representations are stored in sensory modes, much of the time people think with words using verbal **representations**, either in lieu of or along with other modes. Try to imagine what "liberty" or "mental representation" means without thinking in words. Other experiences, in contrast, are virtually impossible to describe or remember verbally, such as the smell of bacon.

Representational modes are like languages that permit discourse within our own minds. The content of our thoughts and memories—a bird, an angry friend, a beautiful sunset—can be described or translated into many languages, but some languages simply cannot capture certain experiences the way others can. Fortunately, we are all "multilingual" and frequently process information simultaneously using multiple sensory and verbal representations. This is another example of parallel processing of information by interdependent modules in the brain (Chapter 3).

SHORT-TERM MEMORY

A century ago, William James (1890) described short-term memory (which he called "primary memory") as "the trailing edge of the conscious present." Short-term memory refers to a set of brief memory stores that holds information in consciousness for roughly 20–30 seconds (unless the person makes a conscious effort to maintain it longer). After that time, the information is either stored for longer-term use, or it disappears from consciousness. STM is spared in amnesics like Jimmie, who can momentarily hold information in consciousness until distracted.

Characteristics of Short-Term Memory

Short-term memory is distinguished by four characteristics (Bower, 1975): It is active, rapidly accessed, preserved in the sequence presented, and limited in capacity. Short-term memory is active: Information remains in STM only so long as the person is consciously processing, examining, or manipulating it. People use short-term memory as a "workspace" to process new information and to call up relevant information from long-term memory. The workspace conception of STM is supported by research showing that STM is disrupted by the active processing of other tasks (Peterson & Peterson, 1959). The experimenters in one study presented college-aged subjects with lists of four, six, or eight words and asked them to recall the lists eight seconds later (Morris, et al., 1990). During the eight seconds, subjects in one condition were given an additional task, to decide quickly whether simple sentences were true or false (such as, "A sparrow can build a nest" or "A cat does not hunt mice"). Subjects given the sentence task recalled significantly fewer words than subjects who were not distracted (Figure 6.4). Taking away a person's conscious workspace apparently makes the job of remembering much more difficult.

The second characteristic of short-term memory, rapid access, is easily demonstrated. You can probably repeat the last sentence you just read without looking back but would likely take longer to recall the first characteristic of short-term memory, which is no longer immediately available to consciousness and has to be accessed from long-term memory. In this respect, the difference between STM and LTM is the difference between pulling a file from the top of the desk versus searching for it in a file drawer, or between searching for information in an open computer file versus a file stored on the hard drive.

Third, STM preserves the temporal sequence of information. Subjects provided with a list such as "fly, ten, chair, foot, seven" will generally remember it (and repeat it if asked) in just that order (Morris, 1986). Finally, short-term memory has limited capacity. On the average, people can hold about seven pieces of information in STM at a time, with a normal range from five to nine items (Miller, 1956). Hermann Ebbinghaus (1885) was the first to note the seven-item limit to short-term memory in research conducted in the late nineteenth century. Ebbinghaus pioneered the study of memory using the most convenient and reliable subject he could find—himself—with a method that involved inventing some 2,300 nonsense syllables (such as pir and vup). The purpose of using nonsense syllables was to try to control the possible influence of prior knowledge on memory. He randomly placed groups of syllables in lists of varying lengths and then attempted to memorize the lists. Ebbinghaus found that he could memorize up to seven syllables, but no more, in a

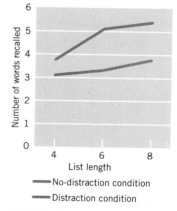

- No-distraction condition
- Distraction condition

FIGURE 6.4

Disruption of short-term memory. This figure shows the number of items subjects could maintain in short-term memory. Subjects in the distraction condition, who had to make a decision about the accuracy of a sentence while holding information in STM, recalled fewer items than those who were not distracted by a competing task. SOURCE: Adapted from Morris et al., 1990.

Like the counter at a diner, short-term memory is rapidly accessed but limited in capacity.

single trial. The limits of STM seem to be neurologically based, as they are similar in other cultures, including those with very different languages (Yu et al., 1985).

Because of STM's limited capacity, psychologists have often likened it to a lunch counter (Bower, 1975). If only seven seats are available at the counter, some customers will have to get up before new customers can be seated. Similarly, new information "bumps" previous short-term memories from consciousness. Figure 6.5 illustrates this bumping effect: A person presented with seven digits stores them in STM. After 20 seconds, the memory of these digits begins to fade or decay, but it can probably still be retrieved. However, if new numbers are presented, they will replace the numbers that first entered short-term memory. With limited space at the counter, the waitress does not encourage customers to sip their coffee at their leisure when others are waiting to sit.

Controlling Information in Short-Term Memory

Because STM's capacity is limited, use of this conscious workspace requires controlling the information in it. This is apparent to anyone who has tried to solve an arithmetic problem mentally ("Wait a minute—she went *how* many miles at 36 miles per hour?"). The STM waitress tends to choose the customers who can linger at the STM counter and to fit as many on a stool as possible. In fact, two conscious processes allow more efficient use of STM: rehearsal and chunking (Atkinson & Schiffrin, 1968).

Rehearsal

When people look up a phone number and try to hold it in their minds long enough to get to the phone to dial it, they employ a method of controlling the information in STM known as **rehearsal**. Rehearsal for STM involves repeating the information again and again to prevent it from fading. This kind of rehearsal is called **maintenance rehearsal**, since its purpose is to maintain information in STM. Rehearsal is also important in transferring information to LTM—which will not surprise anyone who has ever memorized a poem, lines from a play, or a math formula by repeating it over and over. As we shall see, however, maintenance rehearsal is less useful for storing information in LTM than is thinking about, or elaborating, the information's meaning while rehearsing, a procedure known as **elaborative rehearsal**.

Chunking

Because STM's capacity is limited to seven pieces of information, most people would find a number like *1062363392* difficult to hold in mind. One way to increase the workspace, however, is to store information in larger units rather than as isolated letters or digits, a process known as **chunking**. (Yes, the term arose just as it sounds, reflecting the process of sticking memory units into "chunks.") Chunking is essential in everyday life, particularly in cultures that rely upon literacy, requiring momentary memory for telephone numbers, social security numbers, or written words and phrases. Consider the following sequence of letters:

DJIBMNYSEWSJSEC

This string would be impossible for most people to hold in STM—unless they are interested in business and recognize some meaningful chunks: *DJ* for Dow-Jones, *IBM* for International Business Machines, *NYSE* for New York Stock Exchange, *WSJ* for *Wall Street Journal*, and *SEC* for Securities and Exchange Commission. In this example, chunking effectively reduces the number of pieces of information to store in STM from fifteen to six, by putting two or three customers on each stool.

(a) **7 6 3 8 8 2 6**

(b) **7** 6 3 8 8 2 **6** (20 seconds later)

(c) **9 1 8** 8 8 2 **6** (25 seconds later)

FIGURE 6.5
Short-term memory. In an experimental task, the subject is asked to recall a string of seven digits but is instructed not to rehearse (a). Without rehearsal, 20 seconds later, the representations of the digits have begun to fade but are likely still to be retrievable (b). At 25 seconds, however, the experimenter introduces three more digits, which "bump" three of the still-fading digits from the short-term memory store (c).

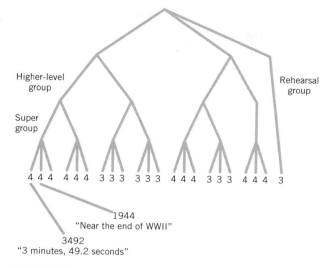

FIGURE 6.6

Chunking. An ordinary subject (SF) demonstrates extraordinary control of information in STM. SF grouped sequences of digits into hierarchically organized groups. Except for the group of five digits at the end that he rehearsed mentally, SF coded sequences of digits into groups of three or four digits, which, in turn, he combined into "super groups." These super groups were then combined into higher-level groups. SOURCE: Adapted from Ericcson & Chase, 1982.

The value of chunking as a memory aid was demonstrated in a remarkable study done with an undergraduate student of average intelligence called SF (Ericsson and Chase, 1982; see also Ericsson, 1985). The goal was to increase SF's capacity to memorize strings of digits. Early in the study, SF noticed that he could group some of the digits to resemble running times for races. (SF was a long-distance runner.) He now had a method for chunking groups of three or four numbers into larger, meaningful numbers. For instance, SF remembered the number 3492 as "3 minutes and 49.2 seconds," close to the world record for running a mile. Not all of the numbers he was asked to memorize lent themselves to running times, however, so he also incorporated ages and dates into his system. Thus, the number 893 became "89.3 years old, a very old person," and 1944 became "near the end of World War II." The next step was to group the running times, ages, and dates into larger units called "super groups," consisting of three groups of three- or four-digit numbers (Figure 6.6). Any number SF could not organize meaningfully he remembered by simple rehearsal. SF began the study with unexceptional memory abilities, but after about 20 months of practice (one hour a day, three to five days a week), he had increased the number of digits he could remember in one presentation from seven to 80.

LONG-TERM MEMORY

To remember a string of 80 digits, SF relied upon short-term memory and a set of conscious strategies. Those strategies actually drew upon long-term memory for information such as track records and historically significant dates. We now explore the nature of long-term memory, starting with a phenomenon called the serial position effect, in which STM and LTM operate in tandem.

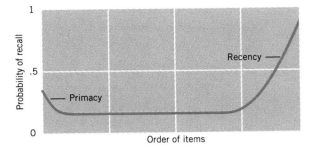

FIGURE 6.7
Primacy and recency effects. Items earlier in a list and those at the end show a heightened probability of recall in comparison to those in the middle. A likely explanation is that the primacy effect results from rehearsal, which transfers early information into LTM, whereas the recency effect reflects the storage of the most recent information in STM. Source: *Atkinson & Schiffrin, 1968.*

The Serial Position Effect

One way to test long-term memory is through free recall tasks, in which the experimenter presents subjects with a list of several words, one at a time, and later asks them to recall as many as possible. Researchers who first employed this technique noticed a curious pattern to the responses: Subjects were more likely to remember the earlier and later items on the list than the words in the middle (Atkinson & Schiffrin, 1968). This phenomenon, known as the **serial position effect**, can be graphed in a curve showing probability of recall (Figure 6.7). Psychologists have posed various explanations for the serial position effect, but most agree that both LTM and STM are implicated. When subjects learn a list of words (or other items) presented one at a time, they use rehearsal strategies to remember them (Rundus, 1971). The first words on the list receive considerable rehearsal, but as the number of words steadily increases, the subject has less opportunity to rehearse each one (Figure 6.8). This phenomenon, in which words at the beginning of the list are more likely to be committed to long-term memory than words that appear later, is known as the **primacy effect**.

Item Presented	Rehearsal
1. Reaction	Reaction, Reaction, Reaction, Reaction
2. Hoof	Hoof, Reaction, Hoof, Reaction
3. Blessing	Blessing, Hoof, Reaction
4. Research	Research, Reaction, Hoof, Research
5. Candy	Candy, Hoof, Research, Reaction
6. Hardship	Hardship, Hoof, Hardship, Hoof
7. Kindness	Kindness, Candy, Hardship, Hoof
8. Nonsense	Nonsense, Kindness, Candy, Hardships
.	.
.	.
20. Cellar	Cellar, Alcohol, Misery, Cellar

FIGURE 6.8
Rehearsal and the primacy effect. A subject rehearses aloud, demonstrating the way patterns of rehearsal produce a primacy effect. This partial listing of the items rehearsed by one subject shows that early items receive more rehearsal than later items and hence are more likely to be stored in long-term memory. Source: *Rundus, 1971.*

Items at the end of a list are also remembered better than those in the middle, a phenomenon known as the **recency effect**, originally studied by Mary Calkins (1905), the first female president of the American Psychological Association and a pioneer in memory research (see Madigan & O'Hara, 1992). Since STM has a limited capacity, each successive word in the list bumps a previously presented word from STM. Because the last words on the list are not displaced by new words, however, they are likely to be remembered.

Long-Term Memory Systems

Long-term memory appears to be composed of multiple systems. Many psychologists now distinguish between two types of long-term memory (Figure 6.9), explicit and implicit (Graf & Schacter, 1987; Polster et al., 1991; Schacter, 1992).

Explicit Memory

Explicit memory, also called **declarative memory** (see Squire, 1986), refers to knowledge that can be consciously brought to mind and "declared." Explicit memory is conscious memory for facts and events. Jimmie, who suffered from Korsakoff's disease, could still retrieve explicit memories from the 1940s and before, but he could no longer **consolidate**, or solidify, new explicit memories.

Explicit memories may be semantic or episodic (Tulving, 1972, 1987). **Semantic memory** refers to general world knowledge or facts, such as the knowledge that summers are hot in Katmandu or NaCl is the chemical formula for table salt (Tulving, 1972). **Episodic memory** consists of memories of particular episodes or events from personal experience. Episodic memories are connected with a time or date and typically include much more personal or autobiographical elements than semantic memories. When people remember what they did on their 18th birthday or what they ate yesterday, they are retrieving episodic memories.

One type of episodic memory studied extensively from both psychodynamic and cognitive perspectives is **early memories**, memories of events that took place many

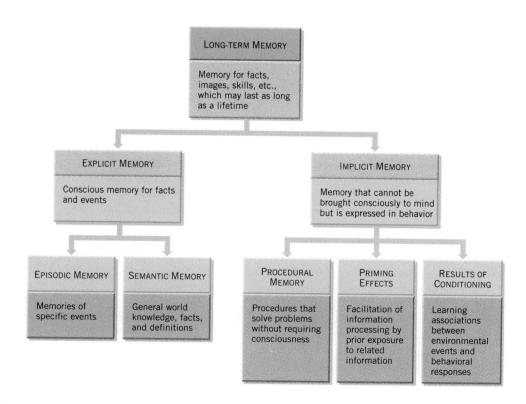

FIGURE 6.9
A tentative classification of long-term memory. Explicit memory can be retrieved verbally as a proposition (e.g., "a day lasts 24 hours") or as the experience of an event in many representational modes. Implicit memory includes procedural memory and priming effects. It also includes the results of conditioning, which are expressed in behavior.

Most people remember little or nothing from their first few years of life.

years ago (see Bruhn, 1992). According to psychodynamic psychologists, the way people represent themselves, other people, and relationships in their early memories can provide information about their personality (Mayman, 1967). Psychodynamic research has documented, for example, that people who expect relationships to be frightening or abusive, and whose relationships frequently match their expectations, tend to have early memories filled with themes of people being hurt or victimized (Ryan, 1982; Urist, 1980; Nigg et al., 1992). From an information-processing perspective, this makes sense as well, for as we shall see, the way people recall events depends on the way they organize these events in their minds. A person who is sensitive to potential abuse in relationships—whether or not she was ever actually abused—is likely to recall unhappy childhood experiences and to expect to be treated unfairly or malevolently as an adult (see Higgins, 1990).

Implicit Memory

Implicit memory cannot be brought to mind consciously but is expressed in behavior (Roediger, 1990; Schacter, 1992). One of the most important kinds of implicit memory is **procedural memory**, that is, "how to" knowledge of procedures or skills. People are often astonished to find that even though they have not skated for 20 years, the skills are reactivated easily, almost as if their use had never been interrupted.

Although procedural memories require no consciousness, they are frequently acquired consciously. A beginning guitar player must often "think out" a piece and consciously use a particular fingering, but gradually these conscious efforts become unconscious and effortless. A more advanced guitarist may not even be able to describe the chord structure of a complicated piece he can play by memory, and his performance may actually be inhibited by thinking consciously about what he is doing. Through repeated use, many motor skills become automatic and thus procedural. Writing while listening to a lecture is a common example of procedural knowledge.

Another kind of implicit memory emerges in experiments on **priming effects**, in which prior exposure to the same or similar information facilitates the processing of new information. Subjects show priming effects even when they do not consciously remember being exposed to the prime word. For instance, subjects in one experiment were told that they were participating in a study of picture and word perception (Bowers & Schacter, 1990). In the so-called word perception task, which was really a priming procedure, subjects rated each word in a list of 24 for its pleasantness or counted the number of t's in it. The 24 words were carefully chosen: Each began with a different three-letter stem, which could form the basis of many other words. For example, REASON, CHECK, and PENNY might be on the list; the stems REA-, CHE-, and PEN- could also be completed to make READY, CHEESE, and PENGUIN. After the subjects studied the list for ten minutes, they completed distracter tasks designed to eliminate the words from short-term memory.

The experimenters then gave them a stem-completion task consisting of 75 stems to complete. Twelve of the stems were from words in the initial list presented ten minutes earlier, while the other 63 were new. The priming hypothesis would predict that subjects would complete more of the stems with words from the prior list than control subjects who had never seen the words. The prediction was confirmed: Control subjects completed about 12 percent of the stems with words from the initial list, while experimental subjects completed about 30 percent with the priming words.

The experiment had an additional twist: The investigators told half of the subjects at the beginning that they would be tested later on the study words; the other half were not informed. The experimenters also told half of each group that some of the stems could be completed with the words they had just studied. Neither

An expert guitarist like Carlos Santana can improvise much faster than he can consciously think.

telling subjects that they would be tested nor informing them that some stems could be completed with study words affected priming. Thus, priming appears to have its effects with or without conscious effort.

FROM MIND TO BRAIN
THE NEUROPSYCHOLOGY OF MEMORY

Some of the most definitive evidence for the existence of separate memory systems comes from neurological data demonstrating that different neural pathways underlie distinct kinds of memory (Squire & Zola-Morgan, 1991; Squire, 1992). Recall from Chapter 3 the case of H. M., who suffered severe anterograde amnesia after surgical removal of his temporal lobes and hippocampus. Despite his inability to store new memories, H. M. was nevertheless able to learn new procedural skills, such as writing words upside-down. Each new time H. M. was asked to perform this task, he had no recollection that he had ever performed it before, yet his speed improved with each test. Psychologists have now reported similar cases many times, documenting that the neural structures involved in the consolidation of episodic memories (memories of events) are not the same ones involved in solidifying or consolidating procedural memories (memories of how to perform a task).

H. M.'s case also demonstrates that STM and LTM are neurologically distinct. Like Jimmy, H. M. had minimal capacity to consolidate new long-term, conscious, declarative memories, yet his short-term memory was largely intact. He could recall seven pieces of information for several seconds like anyone else and could maintain this information for a considerable period of time through rehearsal. However, if distracted and thus blocked from continuously rehearsing the information in STM, he would lose it forever and have no recognition that he had just been rehearsing it moments earlier.

Recent research suggests that an area of association cortex in the frontal lobes, the **prefrontal cortex**, plays a pivotal role in short-term, or working, memory (Friedman & Goldman-Rakic, 1994; Fuster, 1989; Goldman-Rakic, 1995). Much of this research has studied monkeys on tasks such as choosing between two food wells, one of which is filled in front of them, the other left empty. Before they can make a choice, the food wells are hidden from view for several seconds. Brain-imaging studies show that areas of the prefrontal cortex become activated at different points during this task, with some regions particularly active during the period when the food wells are hidden and the monkeys must keep them in mind. When the monkeys are watching the food well being filled, areas of the parietal lobes that process spatial position of the two wells light up on brain scans along with the prefrontal cortex, but only the prefrontal neurons remain active between the time the experimenter hides the food wells and the time the monkeys choose between the wells. These studies suggest that short-term memory is distributed across neural circuits in different cortical regions but that the prefrontal cortex is particularly important in holding information briefly in mind. Bolstering this conclusion are experiments in which monkeys with prefrontal lesions perform poorly on such tasks and studies of humans with prefrontal damage, who show difficulty keeping relevant information in mind. Other studies of patients with brain damage suggest that the two kinds of explicit memory, semantic and episodic, may rely upon different neural mechanisms as well. Patients with retrograde amnesia, who lose their capacity to remember events from the past, may nevertheless maintain intact vocabularies. Researchers have begun to track down the precise neural structures involved in long-term memory by using a combination of methods, including case studies, brain imaging, examination of autopsied brains, and experimental studies with animals. The H. M. case demonstrated that consolidation of explicit memories depends on areas deep within the temporal lobe—the hippocampus, the amygdala, or the tissue surrounding them—because removal of this neural region produced amnesia. More recent research has provided evidence that the hippocampus and adjacent anatomically related regions of the cortex, and not the amygdala, mediate the consolidation of explicit memories (Squire, 1992).

In one series of experiments, researchers lesioned very specific cortical and subcortical regions of monkeys' temporal lobes (Squire & Zola-Morgan, 1991). They gave one group of monkeys large bilateral lesions (that is, lesions in both hemispheres), similar to those sustained by H. M. The damaged area included the hippocampus, the amygdala, and the regions of the cortex surrounding each. The researchers labeled this lesion H⁺A⁺, with H referring to the hippocampus, A to the amygdala, and + to the adjacent cortical regions (Figure 6.10). Other monkeys had only some of those structures removed (e.g., just the amygdala, or just the amygdala and the area adjacent to it). The researchers then tested the monkeys on memory tasks that were identical or analogous to those used to evaluate memory in human patients.

As a test of recognition memory, the investigators first showed the monkey a single object, and then, after a delay of several minutes, presented the original object along with a new one. If the monkey chose the new object, he received a food reward (Figure 6.11). Monkeys with H⁺A⁺ lesions showed severe impairment. On average, they chose the correct object only 50 percent of the time, ten minutes after seeing the initial object, which is no better than chance. Monkeys with lesions to the hippocampus and adjacent cortex (H⁺) also performed poorly, but they were not as impaired as H⁺A⁺ monkeys. Monkeys whose amygdalas were left intact but who had lesions to the hippocampus, the cortex adjacent to it, and the cortex surrounding the amygdala (H⁺⁺) were just as impaired as H⁺A⁺ monkeys. Lesioning the amygdala with-

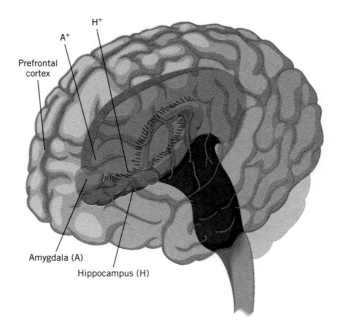

FIGURE 6.10
Tracking down the anatomy of memory. Researchers lesioned different combinations of the amygdala, hippocampus, and adjacent tissue in monkeys to determine which regions play a role in memory. The figure shows the analogous structures in the human brain.

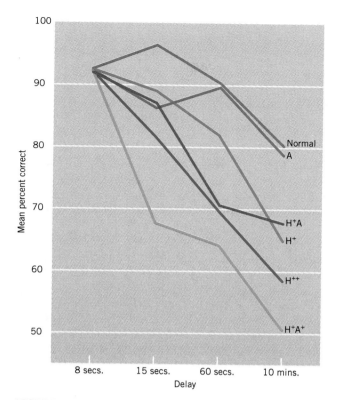

FIGURE 6.11

The hippocampus and memory consolidation. This graph shows the performance of monkeys on a test of recognition memory. Lesions to the amygdala alone produced no deficits in memory. Lesions to the hippocampus, amygdala, and adjacent cortex to each produced the most severe deficits. However, differences between the H^{++} and H$^+$A$^+$ groups were not significant.
A = Lesion to amygdala only.
H$^+$ A = Lesion to hippocampus, cortex adjacent to hippocampus, and amygdala.
H$^+$ = Lesion to hippocampus and adjacent cortex.
H^{++} = Lesion to hippocampus, adjacent cortex, and cortex surrounding amygdala.
H$^+$ A$^+$ = Lesion to hippocampus, amygdala, and cortex adjacent to each.
SOURCE: Reprinted with permission from Squire, L.R. & Zola-Morgan, S. (1991). The medial temporal lobe memory system, Science, 253. Copyright 1991 American Association for the Advancement of Science.

out lesioning the surrounding cortex, in contrast, had no effect on memory. The researchers concluded that the hippocampus is crucial to the consolidation of explicit memory, as is surrounding cortical tissue containing pathways to the hippocampus, but the amygdala is not involved.

Encoding and Long-Term Memory

Most people have had the embarrassing experience of meeting someone at a party, repeating the individual's name in greeting, conversing for several minutes, and then having no recollection of the person's name. Why do we retain some information for years and lose other information within a matter of seconds? If information is to be stored for long-term use, it must be **encoded,** or cast into a representational form or "code" that can be readily accessed from memory. As with

STM, the way people rehearse and mentally represent information play important roles in its retention.

Rehearsal and Levels of Processing

One factor that influences the storage and retrieval of long-term memories is the extent and manner of rehearsal—that is, how, how much, and at what intervals the person rehearses. Any student who has ever crammed for a test knows that rehearsal is important for storing information in LTM. As noted earlier, however, the simple, repetitive rehearsal that maintains information momentarily in STM is not optimal for storage in LTM. Effective LTM rehearsal requires forming associative links to previously stored information. The degree to which information is elaborated, reflected upon, or processed in a meaningful way during memory storage is referred to as the level or **depth of processing** (Craik & Tulving, 1975; Jelicic & Bonke, 1991).

According to some psychologists, the durability of new information in memory is a function of the depth to which it is processed. Information may be processed at a shallow, structural level (focusing on physical characteristics of the stimulus), at a somewhat deeper, phonemic level (focusing on simple characteristics of the language used to describe it), or at the deepest, semantic level (focusing on the meaning of the stimulus). At a shallow structural level, for instance, people may walk by a restaurant and notice the typeface and colors of its sign. At a phonemic level, they may read the sign to themselves and notice that it sounds Spanish. Processing material deeply, in contrast, means paying attention to its meaning or significance—noticing, for instance, that this is the restaurant a friend has been recommending for months. The undergraduate, SF, who learned to memorize strings of numbers did so by processing them deeply, dividing them into meaningful units. He thus used his LTM as an auxiliary to his STM.

Advocates of depth of processing theory originally argued that deeper processing is necessary for storage and retrieval from LTM; that is, the more a person thinks about something while committing it to memory, the more likely he will be to recall it. While this is generally true, subsequent research has demonstrated that the best encoding strategy depends on what the person later needs to retrieve (see Anderson, 1995). If a subject is asked to recall shallow information (such as whether a word was originally presented in capital letters), shallow encoding tends to be more useful.

The way a person rehearses information, then, influences retention and retrieval. Another variable related to rehearsal is of practical significance from an educational point of view: the **spacing of rehearsal** (the interval between rehearsal sessions). Students intuitively know that if they cram the night before a test, the information is likely to be available to them when they need it the next day. But is this optimal for long-term retention of the information? In fact, it is not, and the study strategy that maximizes grades in the short run is inefficient for maximizing long-term knowledge (Anderson, 1995; Glenberg, 1976). If a student has eight hours to allocate to study material on a topic like memory, she is wiser to study two hours a week for four weeks than to study eight hours one night if she wants to remember the information a year later. For a student who has to take a licensing examination at the end of a program of study, such as law or medicine, this is probably the better strategy. (The best, of course, would be to cram the night before and continue to study the material once the test is over.)

Multiple Representations and Representational Modes

The ability to retain information in LTM also depends on the modes used to encode it. People frequently store information using several modes. For instance, many people remember phone numbers not only by memorizing the digits but also by forming a mental map of the pattern of buttons they need to push. They may even be alerted that they have dialed the wrong number by hearing a sound pattern when pushing the buttons that does not match the expected pattern, suggesting auditory as well as visual storage. In general, the more ways information is represented in memory, the easier it is to bring back to mind because if one route to memory fails, others are available (see Paivio, 1991).

Mnemonic Devices

The fact that multiple representations provide multiple paths for accessing a piece of information is of practical use in trying to improve memory. This principle underlies many **mnemonic devices** (memory aids), named after the Greek word, *mneme* (which means "memory"). One mnemonic device is the **method of loci**, which uses visual imagery as a memory aid. Psychologists attribute this technique to the ancient Greek poet Simonides, who was attending a banquet when he was reportedly summoned from the banquet hall to receive a message. In his absence, the roof collapsed, killing everyone. The bodies were mangled beyond recognition, but Simonides was able to identify the guests by their physical placement around the banquet table. He thus realized that images could be remembered by fitting them into an orderly arrangement of locations (Bower, 1970).

To use the method of loci, you must first decide on a series of "snapshot" mental images of locations with which you are very familiar. For instance, locations in your bedroom might be your pillow, your closet, the top of your dresser, and under the bed. Now, suppose that you need to do the following errands: pick up vitamin C pills, buy milk, return a book to the library, and speak to your course advisor about changing a class. You can remember these items by visualizing each in one of your loci. Thus, you might picture the vitamin C pills spilled all over your pillow, a bottle of milk poured over the best outfit in your closet, the book lying on top of your dresser, and your course advisor hiding under your bed. Often, the more ridiculous the image, the easier it is to remember. While you are out doing your errands, you can mentally flip through your imagined loci to bring back the mental images.

A second mnemonic technique, called the **peg method**, also uses imagery. Here, people "hang" information to be remembered on mental pegs such as numbers. For example, you create a number rhyme that you cannot possibly forget, such as "One is a bun, two is a shoe, three is a tree, four is door," and so forth. Note that each number in this rhyme is associated with an object that can easily be visualized. Like the various locations in the method of loci approach, these images then act as mental pegs with which you can associate the items that you need to remember. To return to the list of errands, you might hang the first item, vitamin C, on the "one is a bun" image by visualizing a hamburger bun full of vitamin C pills. You might likewise visualize a shoe full of milk, your library book caught in the branches of a tree, and so forth.

A strategy developed to help students remember information learned in textbooks is called the **SQ3R method**, for the five steps involved in the method: survey, question, read, recite, and review (Robinson, 1961; Martin, 1985). SQ3R fosters active, rather than passive learning while reading. The first step is to survey or glance through the organization of the chapter, looking at headings and the summary, so that you know the gist of it and therefore organize the material more efficiently as you encode. Questioning refers to turning the headings into questions; this orients you to the content of each section and makes reading more interesting. For example, for the subheading, "Long-term Memory Systems," you might ask yourself, "What evidence could demonstrate the existence of separate memory systems? Could patients with different brain lesions have one kind of LTM intact and another disrupted?" The third step is to read, trying to find answers to the questions that you posed. Fourth, recite the answers to these questions as well as other relevant information in each section before going on to the next section. Finally, when you have finished the chapter, review the material by recalling your questions and answers and actively thinking about the material, relating the new material learned to things that you know about and that interest you. (The only catch is that you may need a mnemonic to help you remember the acronym SQ3R.)

The mnemonics we have described—the method of loci, the peg method, and the SQ3R method—share certain key principles. One is that visual imagery is helpful in remembering verbal material, probably because it codes information into a second, and vivid, representational mode. Second, organizing material in a way that

(a)

FIGURE 6.12

Networks of association. Long-term memory is organized into networks of association, ideas that are mentally connected with each other by repeatedly occurring together. Part (a) shows a network for kitchen appliances. Part (b) shows how one network connects with another.

is meaningful and readily associated with past memories is crucial to remembering. Whether this involves mentally locating objects in a familiar room or turning headings into questions, new information becomes associated with well-known material and is hence more easily accessed. As William James suggested a century ago (1890),

> [T]he more other facts a fact is associated with in the mind, the better possession of it our memory retains. Each of its associates becomes a hook to which it hangs, a means to fish it up by when sunk beneath the surface. Together, they form a network of attachments by which it is woven into the entire tissue of our thought. The 'secret of a good memory' is thus the secret of forming diverse and multiple associations with every fact we care to retain. (p. 662, italics deleted)

How Information Is Stored in Long-Term Memory

As in the previous chapter on learning, once again we return to the time-worn concept of associations. Associations are crucial to remembering because the pieces of information stored in memory form **networks of association**, that is, clusters of interconnected information. For example, the phrase "kitchen appliances" evokes images of refrigerators, stoves, microwaves, coffee makers, and so on. Each of these items is stored in memory under the general rubric *kitchen appliance* and is associated with the others because it is similar in function and location (Figure 6.12*a*). Each piece of information along a network is called a **node**. Nodes may be thoughts, images, concepts, propositions, smells, tastes, memories, emotions, or any

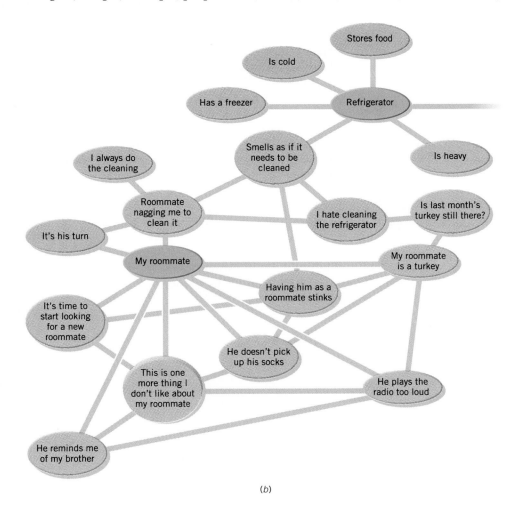

(*b*)

other piece of information. One node may have connections to many other nodes, just as each appliance has its own set of associations. Thus, networks of associations can become extremely complex (Figure 6.12*b*).

Spreading Activation

One theory that attempts to explain the workings of networks of association, and particularly their role in retrieval, is **spreading activation** (Collins & Loftus, 1975). According to spreading activation theory, activating one node in a network (that is, presenting some stimulus that leads to firing in the neural circuits that represent that stimulus) triggers activation in closely related nodes. If the activation is intense enough, these nodes become conscious.

This theory can explain many priming effects. For example, presenting the word "dog" to a subject leads to shorter reaction times when subjects are later asked to identify "terrier" and "collie" as words. According to the theory, activating one node in a network (such as "dog") spreads activation to related nodes, with the greatest activation in nodes most closely associated with the one that has been directly activated (the prime). Terrier and collie are likely to receive more activation than Siamese, because they are directly associated with dog, whereas the route to Siamese is less direct (dog leads to cat, and cat leads to Siamese).

Spreading activation does not always start with a perception such as hearing a spoken word. Activation may also begin with a thought, fantasy, or wish, which in turn activates other nodes. For example, a psychotherapy patient trying to decide whether to divorce his wife found the song, "Reunited and It Feels So Good" coming to mind on days when he leaned toward reconciliation. On days when he was contemplating divorce, however, he found himself inadvertently singing a different tune: "Fifty Ways to Leave Your Lover."

Considerable research supports the theory of spreading activation. The investigators in one study presented subjects with word pairs to learn, including the pair "ocean-moon" (see Nisbett & Wilson, 1977). Later, when asked to name a laundry detergent, a higher percentage of subjects named the brand "Tide," compared to control subjects who had not been exposed to the same pairs of words. The researchers offered an intriguing explanation (Figure 6.13). The network of associations linked to ocean and moon included the word "tide." Priming with the words ocean-moon thus activated the network, spreading activation to tide, which was associated with another network of associations (laundry detergents).

Freud actually proposed a theory very similar to spreading activation many years ago (see Erdelyi, 1985; Pribram & Gill, 1976; Freud, 1895). He distinguished two kinds of thought, which he called primary and secondary process. **Primary process thought** involves associations that become connected through experience and are activated automatically when a person thinks about a related idea. **Secondary process thought**, in contrast, is rational and characterizes conscious thought (as when people solve algebra problems or decide which apartment to choose). Contemporary cognitive psychologists draw a similar distinction between

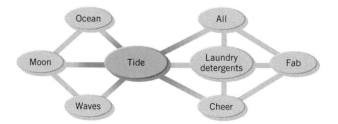

FIGURE 6.13
Spreading activation. Tide stands at the intersection of two activated networks of association and is thus doubly activated. In contrast, All, Fab, and Cheer only receive activation from one network.

information that is effortless and associative and that which is conscious, effortful, and goal directed (Schneider & Schiffrin, 1977; Schiffrin & Schneider, 1977; Strayer & Kramer, 1990). Freud argued that an inability to rein in associations and use secondary process thought underlies psychotic thinking. People with schizophrenia often seem unintelligible because they mix ideas and categories of thought. Their thought is dominated by associations, as they jump from one to another.

Hierarchical Organization of Long-Term Memory

Although activating a "kitchen appliance" node on a network of associations can trigger some idiosyncratic thoughts, networks of association are far from haphazard jumbles of information. To access information in memory, the mind must store that information in an organized fashion. In this sense, LTM can be compared to a filing cabinet. In any filing system, certain files are used frequently, whereas others are consulted only occasionally if at all. People typically keep earnings statements and business expenses for tax purposes, but once April 15 rolls by, they file this information at the back of the bottom drawer, where it will not take up valuable space. Similarly, important information (such as a good friend's phone number) is frequently brought into STM, where each use provides a form of rehearsal for LTM, rendering it highly accessible (Alba & Hasher, 1983; Kintsch & van Dijk, 1978). In contrast, information used less often gets buried deep in our mental archives, so that after many years, it may be virtually irretrievable.

Information that is seldom used can be difficult to access.

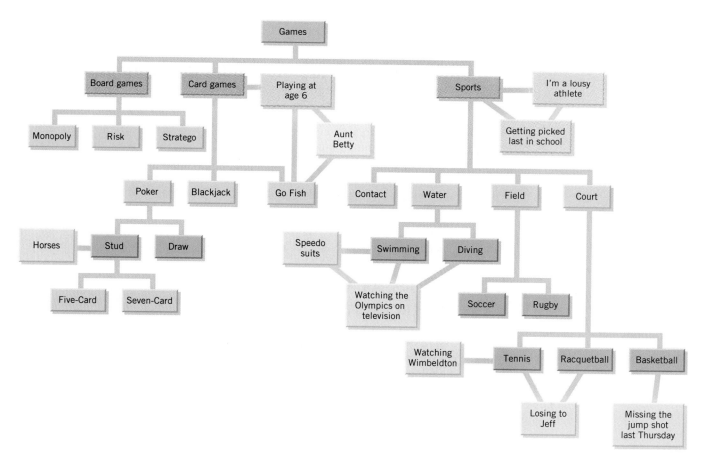

FIGURE 6.14
Hierarchical organization of information in long-term memory. Information about games may be hierarchically organized (although also linked with associated information). Blue lines indicate hierarchical connections. Orange fading lines indicate nonhierarchical, associative connections (such as specific episodic memories).

As the filing cabinet metaphor suggests, information in LTM also tends to be filed **hierarchically**: Broad categories are composed of narrower subcategories, which in turn consist of even more specific categories, until ultimately, the bottom level is filled with discrete facts. Memories appear to be organized similarly, although probably not quite so neatly. Stored in a person's general file for games, for instance, may be information stored at several levels (Figure 6.14). At the broadest level is knowledge about games in general. At a lower level are different categories of games, such as board games, card games, and athletic sports. At still a lower level are more specific board games and card games, as well as types of sports, such as contact sports, water sports, and so forth. This hierarchical structure is very complex, for each level also contains pieces of information, or nodes, that are related to multiple networks of association. The category "card games" might trigger a wealth of associations ranging from playing poker in a smoke-filled room to playing Go Fish as a child.

The idea that memory is hierarchically organized has received support from studies using a simple measure, reaction time, as a dependent variable (Meyer & Schvaneveldt, 1976). If attributes are encoded at one level of generalization, retrieving information at that level is easier and faster. Thus, subjects asked whether birds have feathers are likely to respond more quickly than if asked whether penguins have feathers. The latter decision requires that they first think about what penguins look like, then categorize them as birds, and then use their general information about birds to decide whether all birds have feathers or whether the rule has exceptions. Each step up and down a hierarchy or across networks of association requires extra time, although this is generally imperceptible in everyday life. From a neuropsychological standpoint, reaction time is probably a good measure of travel up and down hierarchies because the more steps, the more synapses must be crossed, and the more synapses, the longer the reaction time (in milliseconds).

Although hierarchical storage is generally quite efficient, it can occasionally lead to errors. For instance, when asked:

Which is farther north, Seattle or Montreal?

most people say Montreal (Stevens & Coupe, 1978). In fact, Seattle is farther north. People mistakenly assume that Montreal is north of Seattle because they go to their general level of knowledge about Canada and the United States and remember that Canada is north of the United States. In reality, some parts of the United States are farther north than many parts of Canada. A better strategy in this case would be to visualize a map of North America and scan it for Seattle and Montreal.

MEMORY AS A CONSTRUCTIVE AND RECONSTRUCTIVE PROCESS

We have spoken in detail about the way memories are organized in LTM but not of the end-product of remembering, the memory itself. Most people think of memories as analogous to mental photographs that can be examined like pictures in an album. A class of episodic memories that seemingly exemplifies this intuitive view of memory is **flashbulb memories**, vivid memories of exciting or highly consequential events (Brown & Kulik, 1977; Winograd & Neisser, 1993; Pillemer, 1990; Weaver, 1993). Most Americans who have been around long enough to remember the assassination of John F. Kennedy in 1963, for instance, can recall precisely where they were and what they were doing when they heard the news, almost as if a camera had recorded that moment in time Many people report similar vivid memories of the assassination of Martin Luther King in 1968, the explosion of the space shuttle Challenger in 1986, as well as personal events such as the death of a loved one or a romantic encounter (Rubin & Kozin, 1984; Pillemer, 1984).

Flashbulb memories are so clear and vivid that we tend to think of them as totally accurate; however, considerable evidence suggests that most memories, including flashbulb memories, are not of snapshot clarity or accuracy and in fact can be entirely incorrect (Neisser, 1991). Memory is not a matter of opening a mental scrapbook; rather, it is a constructive or reconstructive process in which we build or rebuild a mental representation of an event by combining our general store of information with specific recollections of an event.

People who survive an event like a powerful earthquake often report that the scene is indelibly etched in memory.

Schemas and the Construction of Memory

When students walk into a classroom on the first day of class and a person resembling a professor begins to lecture, they generally find this rather unremarkable. Instead, they listen and take notes in a routine fashion. The reason they are not surprised that one person has assumed control of the situation and begun talking is that they have a schema for events that normally transpire in a classroom. As discussed in Chapter 4, schemas are patterns of thought that render the environment relatively predictable. In other words, schemas constitute general knowledge about particular situations or domains (Alba & Hasher, 1983; Wilcox & Williams, 1990).

People use schemas to process new information and enter it into their memory systems. To see this process at work, consider the following passage:

> Business had been slow since the oil crisis. Nobody seemed to want anything really elegant anymore. Suddenly the door opened and a well-dressed man entered the showroom floor. John put on his friendliest and most sincere expression and walked toward the man. (Rumelhart, 1980, p. 43)

Most readers gradually realize that this paragraph is about selling cars through a process of generating and rejecting or confirming hypotheses. The first sentence suggests that the passage is somehow related to the economy and that it probably has something to do with the auto or gas industry. The second sentence narrows the choices: The word "elegant" relates to cars but not generally to gas stations. The phrase "showroom floor" in the third sentence supports the hypothesis that the passage relates to the auto industry. Finally, John's reaction in the fourth sentence confirms this interpretation because our general knowledge structures—that is, schemas—about car salesmen often include "insincere."

Just as schemas provide frameworks for understanding new information, they are also involved in the formation and retrieval of memories. Schemas affect the way people remember in two ways: by influencing the information they encode and by shaping the way they reconstruct data that they have already stored (Rumelhart, 1980; Rumelhart & Ortony, 1977).

Schemas and Encoding

Schemas influence the way people initially construe an event and thus the manner in which they encode it in LTM. Harry Triandis (1994) relates an account of two Englishmen engaged in a friendly game of tennis in nineteenth-century China. The two were sweating and panting under the hot August sun. As they finished their final set, a Chinese friend sympathetically asked, "Could you not get two servants to do this for you?" Operating from a different set of schemas, their Chinese friend encoded this event rather differently than would an audience at Wimbledon.

A brief experiment illustrates the influence of schemas on the encoding of memories in our own culture:

The procedure is actually quite simple. First you arrange things into different groups. Of course, one pile may be sufficient depending on how much there is to do. If you have to go somewhere else due to lack of facilities, that is the next step, otherwise you are pretty well set. It is important not to overdo things. That is, it is better to do too few things at once than too many.... After the procedure is completed, one arranges the materials into different groups again. Then they can be put into their appropriate places. Eventually they will be used once more and the whole cycle will then have to be repeated. (Bransford & Johnson, 1977, p. 400)

Most readers would have difficulty comprehending this paragraph, let alone remembering its component parts five minutes later. But try rereading the passage with the title, "Washing Clothes." The title activates a schema that organizes the information and allows it to be stored efficiently.

Schemas and Retrieval

Titling a paragraph also aids memory because of the influence of schemas on retrieval. Schemas not only provide hooks on which to hang information during encoding, but they also provide hooks for fishing information out of LTM. Many schemas have "slots" for particular kinds of information (Minsky, 1975). A person shopping for stereo equipment who is trying to recall the various compact disk players she saw that day is likely to remember the names Sony and Pioneer but not Frank Sylvester (the salesman at one of the stores). Unlike Sony, Frank Sylvester does not fit into the slot "brand names of compact disk players." Readers who use word-processing programs will readily recognize the computer analogy: At various points, the program instructs the user to select an item from a list (such as a file from a list of filenames) and rejects items that do not conform to its specifications. The program usually provides procedures for adding new options to the list as well (such as creating new files), which then become standard options to fill the slot.

Like word-processing programs, too, the slots in schemas often have **default values**, or standard answers, that fill in missing information the person did not notice or bother to store at the time. When asked if the cover of this book gives the author's name, you are likely to report that it does (default value = yes), even if you never really noticed, because the author's name normally appears on a book cover. In fact, people are generally unable to tell which pieces of information in a memory are truly remembered and which reflect the operation of default values. Thus, memory is less like opening the pages of a photo album than reconstructing the skeleton of a dinosaur from bone fragments and general knowledge about its bone structure.

Many years ago, memory researcher Frederic Bartlett (1932) conducted an experiment demonstrating the impact of schemas on retrieval. British subjects read a North American Indian folk tale, waited 15 minutes, and then attempted to reproduce it verbatim. Their errors were systematic: Subjects distorted the story so that it fit their cultural conceptions of what was logical and conventional. In other words, they drew upon their schemas to reconstruct the story, which were quite different from the schemas of members of the culture that generated the story. Figure 6.15 presents the text of one of these folk tales and a subject's reconstruction, illustrating the way cultural schemas about ghosts, for example, influence memory reconstruction.

A half century later, researchers demonstrated the reconstructive role of schemas using a visual task (Brewer & Treyens, 1981). The experimenter instructed college student subjects to wait (one at a time) in a "graduate student's office" similar to the one depicted in Figure 6.16, while the experimenter excused himself to check on something. The experimenter returned in 35 seconds and led the student to a different room where he asked the subject either to write down a description of the graduate student's office or to draw a picture of it, including as many objects as could be recalled. The room contained a number of objects (e.g., bookshelves, coffee pot, desk) that would fit most subjects' schema of a graduate student's office. Several objects, however, were conspicuous—or rather, inconspicuous—in their absence, such as a filing cabinet, a coffee cup, books on the shelves, a window, pens and pencils, and curtains. Many subjects assumed the presence of these default items, however, and "remembered" seeing them even though they had not actually been present.

Without schemas, life would seem like one random event after another, and efficient memory would be impossible. Yet as the research just described shows, schemas can lead people to misclassify information, to believe they have seen what they really have not seen, and to fail to notice things that might be important. For example, read the following sentence:

> Now is the time for all good men to
> to come to the aid of their countrymen.

The extra "to" at the beginning of the second line is easily overlooked because of the schema-based expectation that it is not there. Students often fail to notice typographical errors in their papers for the same reason. As we have seen in earlier discussions of the active structuring of perception (Chapter 4) and the development of paradigms and perspectives in science (Chapter 1), people process information in the context of general knowledge structures, and these structures both make cogni-

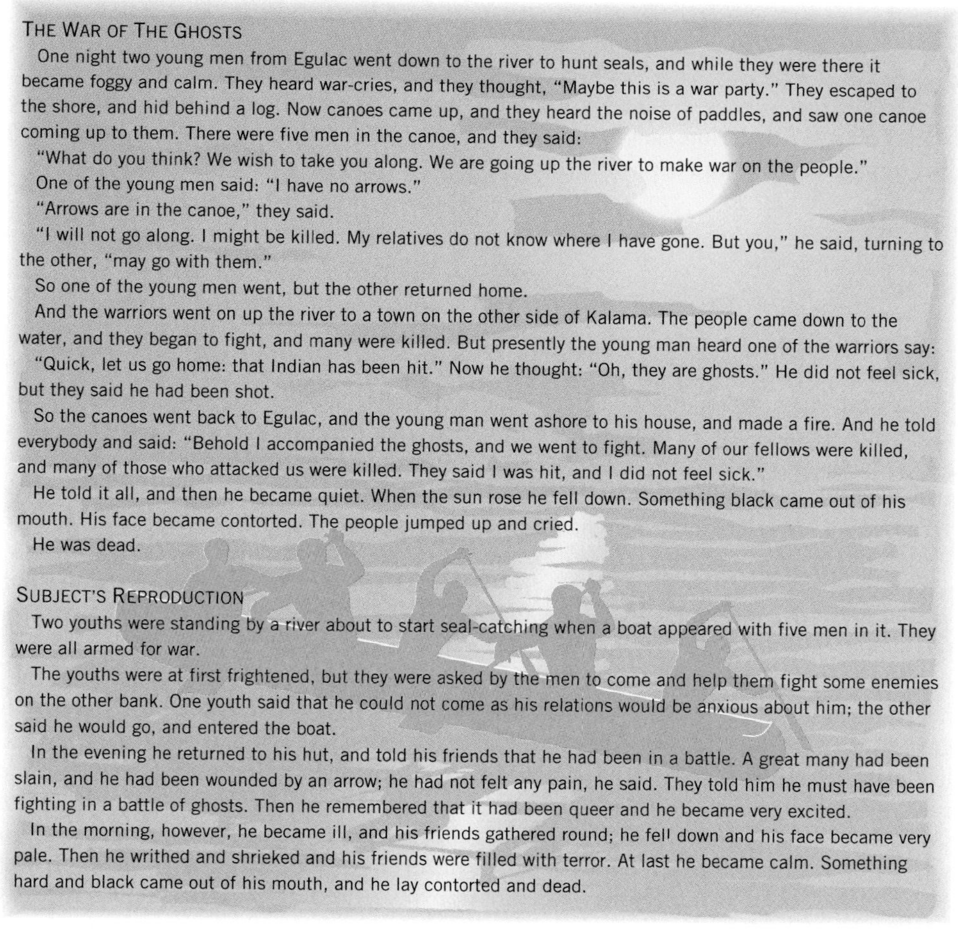

THE WAR OF THE GHOSTS

One night two young men from Egulac went down to the river to hunt seals, and while they were there it became foggy and calm. They heard war-cries, and they thought, "Maybe this is a war party." They escaped to the shore, and hid behind a log. Now canoes came up, and they heard the noise of paddles, and saw one canoe coming up to them. There were five men in the canoe, and they said:

"What do you think? We wish to take you along. We are going up the river to make war on the people."

One of the young men said: "I have no arrows."

"Arrows are in the canoe," they said.

"I will not go along. I might be killed. My relatives do not know where I have gone. But you," he said, turning to the other, "may go with them."

So one of the young men went, but the other returned home.

And the warriors went on up the river to a town on the other side of Kalama. The people came down to the water, and they began to fight, and many were killed. But presently the young man heard one of the warriors say:

"Quick, let us go home: that Indian has been hit." Now he thought: "Oh, they are ghosts." He did not feel sick, but they said he had been shot.

So the canoes went back to Egulac, and the young man went ashore to his house, and made a fire. And he told everybody and said: "Behold I accompanied the ghosts, and we went to fight. Many of our fellows were killed, and many of those who attacked us were killed. They said I was hit, and I did not feel sick."

He told it all, and then he became quiet. When the sun rose he fell down. Something black came out of his mouth. His face became contorted. The people jumped up and cried.

He was dead.

SUBJECT'S REPRODUCTION

Two youths were standing by a river about to start seal-catching when a boat appeared with five men in it. They were all armed for war.

The youths were at first frightened, but they were asked by the men to come and help them fight some enemies on the other bank. One youth said that he could not come as his relations would be anxious about him; the other said he would go, and entered the boat.

In the evening he returned to his hut, and told his friends that he had been in a battle. A great many had been slain, and he had been wounded by an arrow; he had not felt any pain, he said. They told him he must have been fighting in a battle of ghosts. Then he remembered that it had been queer and he became very excited.

In the morning, however, he became ill, and his friends gathered round; he fell down and his face became very pale. Then he writhed and shrieked and his friends were filled with terror. At last he became calm. Something hard and black came out of his mouth, and he lay contorted and dead.

FIGURE 6.15

The effect of schemas on comprehension and memory. The way a subject from one culture comprehends and remembers a story from another reflects the schemas he uses, which may be quite different from those of the original culture. SOURCE: *Bartlett, 1932.*

FIGURE 6.16
The influence of schemas on memory. Subjects asked to recall this graduate student's office frequently remembered many items that actually were not in it but were in their office schemas.
SOURCE: *Brewer & Treyens, 1981.*

tion possible and distort it. Whether perceiving a sunset, remembering an elementary school experience, or studying human nature or astrophysics, we are constantly and actively ordering our experience. In this ordering lies both our knowledge and our ignorance, and separating the two is not an easy task.

Schemas in Eyewitness Testimony

Understanding the role of schemas in the reconstruction of memories has an important legal application: How accurate is eyewitness testimony? Numerous studies have explored this question experimentally, usually by showing subjects a short film or slides of an event such as a car accident (Loftus, 1979; Wells & Loftus, 1984; Wells & Turtle, 1987). The experimenter then asks subjects specific questions about the scene, sometimes introducing information that was not present in the actual scene or contradicting what the subjects saw.

Even seemingly minor variations in the wording of a question can determine what subjects "remember" from a scene. One study simply substituted the definite article "the" for the indefinite article "a" in the question, "Did you see the/a broken headlight?" Using the definite article increased both the likelihood that subjects would recall seeing a broken headlight and their certainty that they had, even if they never actually observed one (Loftus & Zanni, 1975). In another study, subjects gave higher estimates of the speed automobiles were travelling at the time of a collision if they were asked, "About how fast were the cars going when they smashed each other?" than if the word *hit* was substituted for *smashed*. Using the word *smashed* also increased the likelihood that they would remember seeing broken glass when questioned a week later, even when no broken glass was at the scene (Loftus & Palmer, 1974). Clearly, new information presented after an event has already occurred can influence memory of the event.

Such findings have important implications for courtroom examinations as well as for police interrogations of eyewitnesses. Some psychologists argue—and testify in court—that these findings demonstrate the unreliability of eyewitness testimony.

An accident can become more severe if a lawyer asks the right questions.

Others, however, have failed to replicate these results or have qualified them on a number of grounds (e.g., Elliot, 1985; Gruneberg & Sykes, 1993; Kohnken & Maass, 1988; McCloskey & Egeth, 1983; Smith & Ellsworth, 1987; Yuille, 1980). For instance, individuals vary in their susceptibility to misleading information. People with poor memories are especially susceptible to misinformation (Loftus et al., 1992). Susceptibility also varies with cognitive development, although the relationship is not as simple as it might seem (Ceci & Bruck, 1993). Older children may at times actually be more vulnerable to suggestions than younger children because they possess knowledge about some topics that can lead them to draw erroneous inferences (Lindberg, 1991). Further, some aspects of a memory may be more reliable than others. The emotional stress of witnessing a traumatic event can lead to heightened processing (and hence better memory) of core details of the event but less extensive processing of peripheral details (Christianson, 1992). A sharp attorney could thus attack the credibility of a witness's entire testimony by establishing that her memory of peripheral details is faulty even though she clearly remembers the central aspects of the event.

A GLOBAL VISTA

CROSS-CULTURAL VARIATION IN MEMORY—BETTER, WORSE, OR JUST DIFFERENT?

The account of information processing presented thus far is based almost exclusively on studies of subjects in Western, technologically advanced societies. Do the general principles of memory from these samples apply cross-culturally, or do memory and thought differ depending on the cultural, historical, and ecological context?

When Western anthropologists first began observing preliterate tribes in the nineteenth century, they were struck most by the differences between so-called "primitive thought" and our own. Sir James Frazer (1922) argued that "primitives" think just as rationally as Westerners but that the premises from which they reason are less accurate. For example, "if one starts from the premise that a person's discarded clothing, hair, or nail-clippings retain some spiritual connection with him, it is quite rational to conclude that one can affect the person by doing something to these objects," as in voodoo (Bock, 1988, p. 19). Other anthropologists argued that the thought processes of people at different levels of technological development actually differ. Lucien Levy-Bruhl (1923) contrasted the mystical thought of the "primitive mind" with the rational thought of the modern intellect.

Levy-Bruhl was thoroughly vilified by later anthropologists for his ethnocentrism, as he exaggerated the differences on both sides; "we" are not so rational, and "they" are not so mystical as he presumed. Nevertheless, Levy-Bruhl and other ethnographers uncovered some striking cognitive phenomena in tribal cultures on every continent that require explanation. Perhaps the most remarkable was the tendency to treat inanimate objects as if they were animate and to believe that moral transgressions could affect events in nature. Observers of the Iroquois in the eighteenth century noted their tendency to address pleas to inanimate objects. In 1745, one European observed an Iroquois man having trouble trying to drive stakes into the ground. The man then implored the ground not to give him trouble, explaining to the European that although his tribe lacked the iron tools of Europeans, "we have other means which we have learned from our Grandfathers, and we have it much easier if we talk to spirits and call them friends, and mingle threats therein, then we succeed" (cited in Druke, 1980). Similarly, people in tribal societies often believe that moral transgressions can influence natural forces. The Salteaux Indians of North America, for example, would search for a culprit if food became scarce and frequently attributed illness to human causes such as witchcraft (Hallowell, 1955).

Subsequent experimental studies comparing the memory processes of people from literate and preliterate societies have produced inconsistent findings, largely because people tend to do better on tasks that resemble the demands of their everyday lives (see Cole et al., 1968; Doob, 1964). Members of hunter-gatherer societies who must remember the location of edible berries tend to be adept at doing so. Thus, psychologists and anthropologists have tended to move away from global comparisons of thought and memory in literate and preliterate societies and instead have turned their attention to the influence of culture and ecology on the way people process information and the kinds of information they remember. From this viewpoint, culture imposes certain ways of organizing information, which tend to be useful or adaptive in responding to ecological demands. Cross-cultural variations in performance on memory tasks appear to arise less from differences in memory capacities than from variations in the way people organize information schematically (that is, in the way they use schemas). For example, echoing Bartlett's "War of the Ghosts"(Figure 6.15), one research team found that Kpelle tribespeople have excellent recall for narrative material *if* it parallels the way stories are structured in their culture (Cole & Scribner, 1974).

Another study examined differences between subjects *within* a culture. The study compared rural Zambian women with urban Zambian schoolboys in their ability to recall time-relevant information in a story (Deregowski, 1970). The daily life of rural Zambian women is free of references to time, while the day of a Zambian schoolboy is highly time structured. Results revealed no differences in recall for non-time-related information. However, schoolboys were significantly more likely to recall information about time. Thus, people tend to remember information that matters to them, and they organize information in memory to match the demands of their environment and the beliefs of their culture.

People in most cultures in human history have believed in the magical power of ritual, such as animal sacrifice. Here, Haitians participate in a voodoo ritual.

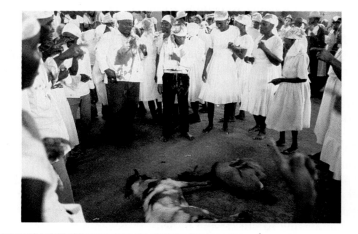

RETRIEVAL

Using memory adaptively requires not only encoding and manipulating information but also retrieving it. Retrieval of explicit memories involves bringing information back from LTM into consciousness, or STM. Korsakoff's patients like Jimmie have difficulty storing and consolidating new memories, but they have little trouble retrieving old ones.

Researchers distinguish between two kinds of retrieval, recall and recognition. **Recall** is the spontaneous retrieval of material from LTM, as when a person brings to mind memories of her wedding day or the name of the capital of Egypt. **Recognition** refers to the explicit knowledge of whether something has been previously encountered or learned. The difference between recall and recognition is exemplified by the difference between fill-in-the-blank and multiple-choice tests. Fill-in-the-blank questions require recall, whereas multiple-choice items usually require only recognition. The greater difficulty of recall over recognition is illustrated by the **tip-of-the-tongue phenomenon**, the experience of trying to remember a piece of information such as a name, knowing that "it's in there," but not being quite able to call it to mind (Brennan, et al., 1990; Brown & McNeill, 1966).

Encoding Specificity and Retrieval

One factor that influences the ease of retrieval is the match between the way information is encoded and the manner in which it is later retrieved; this is known as the **encoding specificity principle** (Tulving & Thompson, 1973). For example, if you study expecting a multiple-choice test, you may memorize specific definitions and details without trying to understand the underlying concepts. If you are then unexpectedly faced with essay questions, you may do poorly because you encoded the information at a more shallow level than you need.

According to the encoding specificity principle, the contexts in which people encode and retrieve information can also affect the ease of retrieval. One study presented scuba divers with different lists of words, some while the divers were under water and others while they were above (Godden & Baddeley, 1975). Divers had better recall for lists they had encoded under water when they were under water at retrieval; conversely, lists encoded above water were better recalled above water. Encoding specificity may similarly influence memory when students take exams: Recalling material from lectures is easier if students are sitting in the same lecture room on examination day. Having the same context during encoding and retrieval facilitates recall because the context provides **retrieval cues**, stimuli or thoughts that can be used to facilitate recall. To return to the filing cabinet analogy, something has to cue the mind to open a particular drawer and look under a particular heading.

Encoding specificity also applies to the internal "context." In other words, a person's physical or emotional state can also provide retrieval cues, a phenomenon termed **state-dependent memory**. Results of experiments on state-dependent memory have been equivocal, but a number have found that information encoded while subjects are in a particular emotional or physical state (e.g., euphoric, sad, terrified, or highly aroused) is best recalled when they are in the same state at retrieval (see Bower, 1981; Eich, 1980). This appears to be true of drug-induced states as well, which create specific patterns of internal stimulation that can serve as retrieval cues.

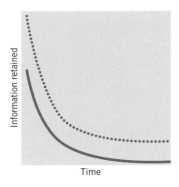

FIGURE 6.17
Forgetting. Forgetting follows a standard (logarithmic) pattern, with rapid initial loss of information followed by gradual decline. Increasing the amount of time initially studying the information (the dotted line) increases retention, but forgetting occurs at the same rate. In other words, increased study shifts the curve upward, but it does not eliminate forgetting.

Forgetting

The flipside of memory is **forgetting**, the inability to retrieve information from memory. Some memories are particularly resistant to forgetting; you may never forget who wrote *Romeo and Juliet* or how to drive a car. Many long-term memories, however, seemingly become irretrievable. Ebbinghaus (1885) documented over a century ago that forgetting follows a typical pattern, with rapid initial loss of information after initial learning and gradual decline thereafter (Figure 6.17). Researchers have recently discovered that the decline of memory is logarithmically related to the length of time between learning and retrieval, which essentially means that the rate of forgetting is high right after initial learning but eventually becomes very slow (Wixted & Ebbesen, 1991). Spending more time studying information initially can increase the amount of information retained at first testing and thereafter, but the information will be forgotten at the same pace. Interestingly, this forgetting curve seems to apply whether the period of time is hours or years. The same curve emerged when researchers studied people's ability to remember the names of old television shows: They rapidly forgot the names of shows canceled within the last seven years, but the rate of forgetting trailed off after that (Squire, 1989).

Why do people forget? Psychologists have offered several explanations. The **decay theory** of forgetting explains the loss of memories as a result of a fading of the memory trace. The process by which memories are formed produces physiochemical changes in the central nervous system (a memory trace), presumably resulting in the formation of a neural circuit that constitutes the memory. According to decay theory, these neurophysiological changes fade with disuse, much as muscles atrophy if immobilized in a cast for several months (Anderson, 1995) or a wilderness path grows over unless continually trodden. The decay theory is difficult to corroborate or disprove empirically, but some studies show a similar pattern of rapid and then more gradual deactivation of neural pathways in the hippocampus, which is involved in memory consolidation, suggesting a possible physiological basis for decay (see Anderson, 1995).

A second cause of forgetting that is better supported empirically is interference. According to **interference theory**, memories stored under similar categories tend to interfere with each other. To return again to the filing cabinet metaphor, storing too many documents under the same heading makes finding the right one difficult.

Cognitive psychologists distinguish two kinds of interference. **Proactive interference** refers to the interference of previously stored memories with the retrieval of new information, as when a person calls a new romantic partner by the name of an old one (a common but dangerous memory lapse). In **retroactive interference**, new information interferes with retrieval of old information, as when people have difficulty recalling their home phone numbers from past residences. One reason children take years to memorize multiplication tables, even though they can learn the names of cartoon characters or classmates with astonishing speed, is the tremendous interference involved, because every number is paired with so many others (Anderson, 1995). Interference tends to be highest when two sets of information are similar in form and function, such as multiples of 7, or two phone numbers. A person's address and phone number rarely interfere with each other because they are different categories of knowledge; in the language of schemas, addresses and phone numbers fill different slots. Similarly, social security numbers rarely interfere with phone numbers, even though both use digits.

Another cause of forgetting, central to psychodynamic theory, is motivated forgetting, or repression. Forgetting things one does not want to remember happens frequently, as when one "overlooks" a dentist appointment. If dentists were handing out $100 bills instead of filling teeth, few people would forget their appointments. Freud was among the first to note that people rarely remember events from early childhood (roughly before age three), a phenomenon known as **childhood amnesia**. He attributed childhood amnesia to repression: Many thoughts, feelings,

... AND, AS YOU GO OUT INTO THE WORLD, I PREDICT THAT YOU WILL, GRADUALLY AND IMPERCEPTIBLY, FORGET ALL YOU EVER LEARNED AT THIS UNIVERSITY."

Drawing by Sidney Harris

and wishes that occur before the development of a conscience would be considered immoral and lead to guilt afterwards, so repression systematically blocks these early memories from consciousness.

Repression does not, however, provide the only explanation for childhood amnesia. From a cognitive perspective, young children do not use the same kinds of hierarchical categories as adults when classifying information; they are prone to tossing papers more haphazardly and inefficiently into their mental filing cabinets (Chapter 13). Adults also tend to encode information verbally—using language—so that information from childhood filed under different representational modes cannot be accessed using the adult filing system. In this sense, retrieving childhood memories is like trying to find a book in the library using the Library of Congress number when it is catalogued by the Dewey decimal system. Furthermore, as adults, most people are not exposed to many of the stimuli that they experienced as little children (such as their bedrooms, mobiles, and toys), so they have few cues to retrieve information encoded in childhood.

Commentary: Repressed Memories of Sexual Abuse

The concept of repression has long been a lightning rod for disagreement between psychodynamic and other psychologists and more generally between clinicians and experimental researchers. Nearly all clinicians who work with survivors of extreme trauma, regardless of their theoretical orientation, take as axiomatic that repression is a common outcome of overwhelmingly traumatic events (see, e.g., McCann and Pearlman, 1990). Experimental psychologists, in contrast, have long been skeptical of repression, pointing to the lack of experimental evidence documenting its existence (Holmes, 1990).

The concept of repression is now the centerpiece of renewed controversy for social and political reasons: It is at the heart of claims of childhood sexual abuse and counterclaims of false memories. The controversy stems from the outrage of alleged perpetrators who maintain that charges of sexual abuse against them have been fabricated in psychotherapy by unscrupulous, poorly trained clinicians. A group of these individuals has formed and financed a False Memory Syndrome Foundation and has enlisted the support of many prominent experimental psychologists dubious about the concept of repression and concerned about the limitations of memories reconstructed in psychotherapy (e.g., Loftus, 1993). Actually, most victims of repeated or severe sexual abuse in childhood have at least some memories of the abuse prior to psychotherapy, although their memories are often fragmented (Herman, 1992). Their recollection of childhood events tends to have gaps of months or years, and the memories they do recall of traumatic experiences frequently come to them in flashbacks, in physical forms (such as the sensation of gagging that initially attended the experience of being forced to perform oral sex), or in nightmares. One patient interviewed for research purposes had such severe amnesia for childhood events that she could not recognize herself in pictures from childhood.

The question of false memories is exceedingly difficult to address scientifically for a number of reasons. First, distinguishing true from false allegations is difficult under any circumstances. Second, passions on the subject of childhood sexual abuse run high, and understandably so. Millions of women and men have had their lives destroyed by sexually predatory adults. Their stories, particularly those that involve incest, produce anxiety, horror, and disgust in scientists and laypeople alike, which can foster either empathy or denial that such a thing could really happen.

Third, a cardinal feature of sexual abuse is the perpetrator's insistence on secrecy and the attempt to discredit victims who tell their story. Discrediting the victim is as characteristic of childhood sexual abuse as it is of political torture, persecution, and genocide (Herman, 1992). The attempt to discredit the victim is a tactic of neo-

A U.S. soldier forces German civilians to confront mass murder in a concentration camp. He apparently understood that shame, guilt, and disgust can prevent people from recognizing truths that are too painful to acknowledge. If the mind can play tricks on people who believe they have been the victims of sexual abuse, perhaps it can play similar tricks on the rest of us as we decide whether or not to believe them.

Nazi revisionists who deny that the Holocaust occurred and has been seen more recently in the ardent denials of Serbian rapists and mass-murderers in Bosnia. Complicating matters, however, is that for every hundred genuine perpetrators of sexual abuse who are exposed for their crimes, some number of innocent people are unfairly accused. Unfortunately, we do not know what that number is. Some divorcing parents make accusations against their former spouses as a tactic in custody disputes. And some poorly trained therapists, many of whom have unresolved feelings about their own childhood experiences, look for abuse whenever an adult female patient steps into their office complaining of anxiety or depression and may convince nontraumatized patients that their symptoms reflect a history of childhood abuse (Loftus, 1993).

Fourth, the controversy over repressed versus fabricated memories of abuse cannot be divorced from the larger context of gender. Most abuse victims are female, and most perpetrators are male. The power differential between men and women has undoubtedly contributed to the extent to which abuse victims have historically been silenced, and no doubt contributes to the sympathetic hearing that alleged abusers are currently receiving from the public and many psychological researchers.

In fact, empirical evidence for the existence of repressed traumatic memories is now beginning to accumulate. Among a large sample of adults reporting histories of childhood sexual abuse, roughly 60 percent identified some period during childhood in which they were amnesic for the abuse (Briere & Conte, 1993). The earlier and more severe the trauma, the more likely were subjects to have repressed it at some point. Another study found that 19 percent of women treated for substance abuse who acknowledged a history of childhood abuse similarly reported a period of amnesia for the events (Loftus et al., 1994).

Perhaps the clearest empirical evidence for repressed memories comes from a study that tracked down women who had been treated at a hospital for sexual molestation when they were children (Williams, 1992, 1994). Seventeen years after their documented abuse, 38 percent were amnesic for the incident, even though many reported other traumas, including later incidents of sexual abuse. When asked if any family members had ever gotten into trouble for their sexual behavior, one subject, who denied sexual abuse, reported that before she was born an uncle had apparently molested a little girl and was stabbed to death by the girl's mother. Examination of newspaper reports 17 years earlier found that the subject herself had been one of the uncle's two victims, and that the mother of the other victim had indeed stabbed the perpetrator.

Clinical experience suggests the need for caution on both sides of this issue. Several years ago, like many clinicians, I began to see cases in which patients gradually retrieved memories of abusive childhood experiences through flashbacks, dreams, and careful examination of gaps in their memories. This occurred before television coverage of the controversy and before I knew to assess abuse histories more systematically. It is therefore highly unlikely that the return of these repressed memories reflected anything other than my patients' painful and courageous efforts to come to terms with their past. A few years later, however, when I had become sensitized to issues of abuse and had conducted research on its effects, I treated a woman who had many signs of abuse, such as long gaps in her memory and violent images that occasionally came to mind like pictures on a screen. During one session, I repeatedly probed some very suspicious memories and their possible links to her violent imagery. With some exasperation, she finally chided, "You know, I wasn't sexually abused, if that's what you're looking for."

Perhaps the moral of the story is that psychologists should always attend both to the phenomenon they are studying—in this case, repressed memories—and to their own needs, fears, and cognitive biases. Clinicians need to be aware of the research on the limits of reconstructive memory, not to mention the influence of their own emotional processes on the way they understand their patients. On the other hand, cognitive researchers who may have had little or no exposure to real sexual abuse victims, should be very circumspect before overstepping the limits of their own vantage point. In matters of public policy, experimental psychologists, like clinicians, need to examine carefully their own psychologies before trying to write—or write off—the life histories of others.

CHALLENGES TO THE INFORMATION-PROCESSING MODEL

Although this chapter has drawn from many perspectives, the information-processing model has provided the general framework for understanding memory processes. In this final section, we first consider the limitations of this model and then explore some recent challenges to it from an evolutionary perspective.

Limitations of the Model

As useful as the information-processing model is, particularly as it continues to evolve to accommodate neuropsychological findings, it is only as powerful as the metaphor on which it rests—the idea that the mind is like a computer. In all the ways humans differ from computers, this model may lead to misunderstandings of human cognition (Dreyfus, 1979, 1986; Searle, 1984; see Nadeau, 1991).

First, computers do not feel, wish, or desire. Consequently, the biases that emotion and motivation impose on our memory systems cannot be easily represented in computer models of information processing. Unlike computers, people not only can be motivated to forget painful memories, but they often remember things as they wish they had happened rather than as they really were. Thus, people on two sides of an argument may remember themselves as winning it. Indeed, most people have a basic bias that leads them to overestimate their own contributions to positive events and underestimate their role in negative ones (Epstein, 1992; Greenwald & Pratkanis, 1984).

A second limitation relates to the role of consciousness. Because consciousness is not a characteristic of computers, cognitive psychologists have only recently taken it into account, and somewhat as an afterthought. A number of ambiguities and confusions have resulted. Cognitive psychologists often equate activation with consciousness or the propensity to obtain consciousness; yet many active processes—such as schemas, procedural knowledge, and repressed memories—can clearly be activated without conscious awareness. Similarly, theorists (e.g., Squire, 1986) frequently equate declarative knowledge (knowledge of facts and episodes) with explicit knowledge (knowledge that can be consciously retrieved). Many types of declarative knowledge, however, cannot become conscious. Repressed memories certainly constitute declarative knowledge—they refer to events, episodes, and general knowledge—but they are not conscious. Many schemas have declarative content (they provide information about what things mean or what they are like), yet people do not have access to their own schematic processes. Further, priming studies typically rely on activation of declarative information (such as word lists), but priming is viewed as an example of implicit, not explicit knowledge. In reality, implicit and explicit memory probably each have declarative and procedural components. Skills that are exercised consciously, such as telling oneself to calm down in an upsetting situation or figuring out how to solve a problem, may represent conscious procedural knowledge.

A third limitation pertains to the external validity of experimental studies of memory, that is, the extent to which findings from the laboratory adequately reflect memory processes in real life. Ebbinghaus had good reason to use nonsense syllables to study memory: He was trying to study memories in the laboratory that were as unaffected as possible by previous knowledge. Creating artificial tasks using nonsense syllables, word lists, and so forth has been useful for many purposes, but researchers now disagree on whether models based on such tasks adequately reflect the complexity of memory as people use it in their everyday lives (Banaji & Crowder, 1989; Conway, 1991; Ceci & Bronfenbrenner, 1991; Klatzky, 1991; Neisser, 1978; Rogoff & Lave, 1985; Tulving, 1991).

Finally, in attempting to model the memory systems of individual information processors, the information-processing approach tends to ignore the cultural context of memory (see Cole, 1975; Middleton & Edwards, 1990). As noted earlier, shared cultural concepts organize knowledge and hence shape the schemas and thought processes people use in their daily lives. The way individuals classify information—such as types of kin, colors, and plants—reflects cultural systems of categorization. Culture also shapes such abstract conceptions as beliefs about the nature of personality, the nature of supernatural entities, and the meaning of life (Baumeister, 1991; Tyler, 1969; Price-Williams, 1975; Shweder, 1991). If members of preliterate societies use moral transgressions to explain droughts or typhoons, they do so less because of peculiarities in their individual thought processes than because of the collective representations, or collective schemas, they have internalized from their culture. Computers, unlike people, are engineered, not reared.

Cultures not only shape the way individuals store and retrieve memories, but they also collectively store memories and provide memory aids that supplement the brains of individuals. In preliterate societies, collective memories are preserved through oral history and tradition. Literate societies possess a number of ways of storing information that usually extend memory beyond the limits of any individual's memory. Textbooks are collective memory systems, as are libraries. Even such simple devices as lists increase memory capacity to an extraordinary degree (Goody, 1977). Thus, culture influences both the way people organize memory internally and the way they harness it externally.

In preliterate societies, oral tradition shapes the way people think and serves as an archive for collective memories.

A Different Perspective: The Evolution of Information Processing

Another challenge to the information-processing approach comes from the evolutionary perspective. As we have seen, culture sensitizes people to information that is important to their survival and to the demands of their society. But could humans be *innately* sensitized to certain kinds of information? And could the way they think about potential mates, family members, and other people reflect millions of years of evolution?

The capacity for sophisticated information processing has substantial adaptive value and likely evolved through natural selection. An expanding cortex served our ancestors well, fostering the use of progressively more sophisticated tools, communication skills, and implements of warfare. This much is uncontroversial. For years, however, cognitive psychologists have viewed the capacity for memory and thought as essentially content-independent. That is, the mind is a general information-processing machine that can take almost any input, manipulate it, and remember it with appropriate encoding and rehearsal. Although researchers have amended the information-processing model to account for independent memory systems or neural modules that process different kinds of information, the model has remained content-independent.

Today, a new and quite radical view of cognition has begun to emerge in evolutionary circles—the view that the mind has evolved content-specific mechanisms that facilitate the remembering and processing of very particular kinds of information (Tooby & Cosmides, 1992). Few would doubt that the eye's capacity to detect certain wavelengths of light reflects the natural selection of adaptations in its structure that proved useful for survival and reproduction. Similarly, the fact that taste buds detect qualities such as bitter and salty undoubtedly reflects the adaptive value of being able to recognize and remember foods that cause illness or prevent it by providing essential nutrients.

But what about the proposition that people have innate information-processing modules, constructed over the course of evolution, which encode and process spe-

The symbols differ, but everywhere people attend to status cues.

cific kinds of information such as one's own or others' position in status hierarchies, or indicators that one's mate is being unfaithful? As we have seen in previous chapters, the human mind is indeed attuned to certain kinds of information and is more likely to form some types of associations than others. Neuropsychological data indicate that people have specialized mechanisms for recognizing emotions (Etcoff, 1984). The right parietal lobe is also specialized for facial recognition, so that individuals who suffer damage to this region often cannot recognize people's faces (Chapter 3). In human evolution, the ability to recognize faces would certainly have conferred an adaptive advantage, facilitating investment of resources in one's own offspring or genetically related individuals and permitting our ancestors to make very quick judgments about who they needed to fear and who they could trust. This specialized capacity for discriminating and remembering facial features may work in tandem with an innate tendency in humans to feel more comfortable with stimuli that are familiar (on familiarity and comfort, see Zajonc, 1960).

Similarly, we saw in Chapter 5 that humans, like other animals, more readily associate episodes of nausea with tastes than with sounds. Could the human mind be similarly designed to process and remember subtle social cues that indicate a person's position in a status hierarchy or his willingness to respond altruistically in the face of threats to the community? Humans, like other primates, are universally attuned to status. Although the indices of status differ across cultures (clothing, physical appearance, and so forth), adolescents everywhere spontaneously rank themselves and their peers by their position in social hierarchies and tend to agree on their relative ranks. People everywhere also attend to two salient dimensions of personality, agreeableness and conscientiousness, that reflect on their peers' ability to be good social partners (Buss, 1991). Research is just beginning in these areas, but the evidence that does exist may challenge the view that evolution created an all-purpose brain, rather than a brain designed by natural selection to solve specific problems of adaptation.

SOME CONCLUDING THOUGHTS

The information-processing model and the computer metaphor, like all models and metaphors, provide an imperfect lens through which to view human mental life and behavior, yet they have led to considerable advances in the understanding of memory and an enormous body of research. In the next chapter we extend our investigation of information processing to the mechanisms by which people transform and manipulate information in the process of thinking, making decisions, and trying to meet their goals. These cognitive operations provide what many argue is the property that separates humans from all other animals: the capacity for complex thinking. In the process, we discuss the pivotal role of language in human thought, itself a remarkable product of millions of years of evolution.

Summary

Memory and Information Processing

1. Contemporary cognitive models view memory as a series of **memory systems**, sets of discrete but interdependent processing units responsible for different kinds of remembering. This fits well with a modular conception of the nervous system.

Sensory Registration

2. In the information-processing model, the **sensory register** refers to the split-second mental representation (an image, sound, etc.) of a perceived stimulus that remains very briefly after that stimulus disappears. **Iconic storage** describes visual sensory registration, and **echoic storage** describes auditory sensory registration.

Representation

3. Information that passes through the sensory registers to be processed and stored is put into the form of a **mental representation**—an internal model of a stimulus or category of stimuli. Most representations are verbal or sensory.

Short-Term Memory

4. **Short-term memory (STM)** stores information for roughly 20 to 30 seconds, unless the information is maintained through **rehearsal** (repeating the information again and again). This form of rehearsal, which merely maintains information in STM, is called **maintenance rehearsal**. It differs from the **elaborative rehearsal** optimal for storing information in long-term memory, which involves elaboration of the information's meaning. Another way of controlling the information that remains in STM is **chunking**, grouping pieces of information into larger units or chunks.

5. Short-term memory is active, rapidly accessed, preserved in the sequence in which it was presented, and limited in capacity.

Long-Term Memory

6. If information is to be stored for long-term use, it needs to be **encoded**, put into a code or representational form that can be stored and readily accessed from memory. Memories in **long-term memory (LTM)** may last a lifetime. **Explicit memory** is conscious memory for facts and events, and includes two types of knowledge: **Semantic memory** refers to general world knowledge or facts, while **episodic memory** consists of memories of particular episodes or events from personal experience. Research with human amnesics and experiments with monkeys indicates that the hippocampus and adjacent cortical tissue are crucial to the consolidation of explicit memory.

7. **Implicit memory** is memory that cannot be brought to mind consciously but is expressed in behavior. One of the most important kinds of implicit memory is **procedural memory**, "how to" knowledge of procedures or skills. Another example of implicit memory emerges in experiments on **priming effects**, in which processing of specific information is facilitated by prior exposure to the same or similar information.

8. One way information is stored in LTM is along **networks of association**, clusters of information connected to each other. A piece of information along a network is called a **node**. The theory of **spreading activation** holds that activating one node in a network triggers activation in closely related nodes and renders them more likely to become conscious. Information in long-term memory also tends to be filed **hierarchically** into categories and subcategories.

Memory as a Constructive and Reconstructive Process

9. Memory is also organized in **schemas**, patterns of thought that render the environment relatively predictable. Schemas influence both encoding and retrieval. Remembering is a constructive or reconstructive process that uses existing schemas to help rebuild a mental representation of an event.

10. Culture influences the way people store, retrieve, and manipulate information mentally. Cultural knowledge systems organize schemas, and hence influence the way people process information. Cultural differences in memory generally reflect the adaptive demands of different environments.

Retrieval

11. Recovering information from long-term memory is called **retrieval**. **Recall** is the spontaneous retrieval of material from LTM. **Recognition** refers to the explicit knowledge of whether something has been previously encountered or learned.

12. **Forgetting**, the inability to retrieve information from memory, appears to have a number of causes, including decay (the memory trace fades), interference, and repression. **Proactive interference** refers to the interference of old memories that have already been stored with the retrieval of new information. In **retroactive interference**, new information interferes with the retrieval of old information.

Challenges to the Information-Processing Model

13. The information-processing model has provided the basis for decades of fruitful research, but it is not without its limitations, notably those that stem from the metaphor of the mind as a computer. Computers lack motivation, consciousness, and culture. Many psychologists have also questioned the external validity or generalizability of research using procedures such as word lists and nonsense syllables.

14. An evolutionary perspective may advance the information-processing model by suggesting the presence of modules for detecting specific types of information particularly relevant for survival and reproduction.

Sol Aquino, "They're Only Words," 1981

Chapter 7

THOUGHT AND LANGUAGE

Men are all alike.
IN WHAT WAY
They're always bugging us about something or other.
CAN YOU THINK OF A SPECIFIC EXAMPLE
Well, my boyfriend made me come here.
YOUR BOYFRIEND MADE YOU COME HERE
He says I'm depressed much of the time.
I AM SORRY TO HEAR YOU ARE DEPRESSED
It's true. I'm unhappy.
DO YOU THINK COMING HERE WILL HELP YOU NOT TO BE
    UNHAPPY
I need some help; that much seems certain.
WHAT WOULD IT MEAN TO YOU IF YOU GOT SOME HELP
Perhaps I could learn to get along with my mother.
TELL ME MORE ABOUT YOUR FAMILY
My mother takes care of me.
WHO ELSE IN YOUR FAMILY TAKES CARE OF YOU
My father.
YOUR FATHER
You are like my father in some ways.
WHAT RESEMBLANCE DO YOU SEE
*You are not very aggressive, but I think you don't want me to notice
that.*
WHAT MAKES YOU THINK I AM NOT VERY AGGRESSIVE
You don't argue with me.
DOES IT PLEASE YOU TO BELIEVE I AM AFRAID OF YOU
My father is afraid of everybody.
WHAT ELSE COMES TO MIND WHEN YOU THINK OF
YOUR FATHER
Bullies.
DOES THAT HAVE ANYTHING TO DO WITH THE FACT
THAT YOUR BOYFRIEND MADE YOU COME HERE

(Weizenbaum, 1966, p. 37)

This dialogue is not between a therapist and a client, nor even between two people. It is between a person and a computer running a program called ELIZA, which was developed at the Massachusetts Institute of Technology in the 1960s. The ELIZA program follows a procedure that resembles elements of human thought: It (she?) takes in data, recognizes patterns, selects key elements of those patterns, and uses stored information to determine the appropriate response, much as humans do. ELIZA is also a decent conversationalist, whose use of language demonstrates that it "recognizes" words and knows what rules to use to maintain a dialogue.

So precisely what distinguishes ELIZA's conversations from ours? We address this question as we examine the nature of thought, language, and the relation between the two. Thinking makes possible human activities ranging from the mundane (tying a shoe or planning a dinner) to the profound (programming a computer or understanding Einstein's law of relativity). We begin by exploring the basic units of thought, such as mental images and propositions, and the way people manipulate these units to reason, solve problems, and make decisions. Then we turn to language, the system of symbols that mediates much of human thought. What might thought look like without language? Has evolution created a brain specifically attuned to linguistic information? We conclude by considering whether some of our close cousins in the animal kingdom, especially chimpanzees, can also use language.

UNITS OF THOUGHT: IMAGES, CONCEPTS, AND PROPOSITIONS

Virtually everything people do involves thinking, whether they are sitting on a park bench daydreaming or trying to solve a mathematical problem. **Thinking** means representing things mentally and operating on these representations. The units of thought, or mental representations, that people manipulate when they think can be mental images, mental models, concepts, or propositions.

Mental Images and Mental Models

Although much of human thought is verbal, as we have seen, many cognitive processes rely on **mental images**, visual representations such as the image of a street or a geometric form (Chapters 5 and 6). By operating on mental images, people can find a house they once visited or figure out how to carry a large desk through a narrow doorway without getting its legs (or theirs) caught. People also make frequent use of **mental models**, representations of systems that enable them to describe, explain, and predict the way things work. Mental models may be quite simple, like most people's understanding of automobiles ("If the car doesn't start, there's a problem somewhere under the hood") or quite complex, such as the mental models used by mechanics to troubleshoot a car that is making a peculiar sound. Although mental models often rely heavily on mental images, they do not always do so. For example, the mental models of relationships people use in their interactions with significant others do not rely primarily on visual images (Bowlby, 1962; Bretherton, 1990; Main, 1991).

Thinking makes use of representations in sensory modes other than visual. When people find themselves spontaneously harmonizing with the radio, they are doing an impressive bit of musical thinking, unconsciously manipulating auditory representations using procedural knowledge such as rules of harmonic structure. Remarkably, most people cannot articulate these rules verbally, even though they can use them effortlessly. As we shall see, the same is true of language, which most people can speak grammatically long before they learn the formal rules of grammar.

Concepts and Categories

Much of human thought takes place using concepts. A **concept** is a mental representation of a class of objects, ideas, or events that share common properties (Anderson, 1991; Medin, 1989; Murphy & Medin, 1985). Some concepts can be visualized, but the concept is broader than its visual image. For example, the concept *car* stands for a class of vehicles that have four wheels, seating space for at least two individuals, and a roughly similar shape. Other concepts, like *honest*, defy visualization or representation in any other sensory mode, although they may have visual associations (such as an image of an honest face). The process of grouping objects considered equivalent and excluding those that are not is called **categorization**. Categorization is an ongoing process that occurs every moment, as people simplify and sort the multitude of objects and experiences they encounter.

Some concepts, like car, salt, or triangle, are relatively **well-defined concepts**, which means they have properties that clearly set them apart from other concepts. A triangle can be defined as "a plane geometry figure with three sides and three angles," and anything that does not fit this definition is not a triangle. Most of the concepts used in daily life, however, are not well defined (Fehr & Russell, 1991; Holland et al., 1986; Rosch, 1978). Rather, they are **fuzzy concepts**, which are not easily defined by a precise set of features. Consider the concept *good*. This concept takes on different meanings when applied to a meal or a person: Few of us look for tastiness in a person or honesty and sensitivity in a meal. Similarly, the concept *adult* is fuzzy around the edges, at least in North America and Europe: At what point does a person stop being an adolescent and become an adult? Is a person an adult at voting age? at drinking age? at marriage?

For years, philosophers and psychologists have wrestled with the question of whether people categorize objects or situations by comparing them to a list of features or to prominent examples of the concept (Huttenlocher & Hedges, 1994; Medin & Smith, 1985; Smith & Medin, 1981). For example, when a person stands in a zoo wondering whether an unfamiliar animal is a dog or a horse, does she consult mental lists of the attributes of dogs and horses, or does she compare the mystery beast with her images of typical canines and equines? Even with well-defined concepts, people may, in practice, find categorization easier and more efficient by comparing an object with an example.

Many concepts do have defining features, and the more an instance matches those features, the more likely a person is to categorize it accordingly. Some features are absolutely central, or **core features**, whereas others are more peripheral (Figure 7.1). Rather than consulting a list of defining features, however, people often categorize using **prototypes**, that is, particularly good or typical examples of a category (Huttenlocher & Hedges, 1994; Rosch, 1978). If asked whether Windsor, Ontario, is a city, most people do not consult a list of features such as minimum population size. Instead, if they have seen or heard of Windsor, they compare it with their image of a crowded, bustling, prototypical example, such as New York City, or with a generalized portrait extracted from experience with several cities,

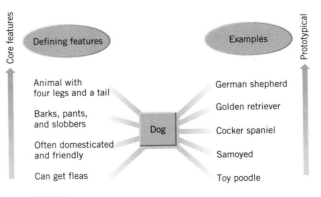

FIGURE 7.1

Categorization. Psychologists disagree on the extent to which people represent concepts in terms of defining features or prototypical examples. Defining features probably range from core features that are central to the definition to those that are merely characteristic, just as examples range from the prototypical to the less typical.

At what point does a creature become categorized as "human?"

such as Los Angeles, Toronto, New York, and London. To what degree people rely on idealized prototypes versus real examples (such as New York City) when they categorize is not clear.

What *is* clear is that specific instances of a concept like "city" (Toronto, Los Angeles, Windsor) differ in the degree to which they resemble the prototype and that people more easily categorize typical members of a category. When subjects are asked whether "robin," "wren," and "penguin" are birds, they answer more quickly if the object is prototypical (such as robin) rather than less typical of the concept (like penguin) because atypical examples require more thought.

Are these two views of categorization—one advocating defining features and the other, example-based categorization—irreconcilable? In reality, people probably represent concepts in both ways much of the time and use different procedures, or some combination of them, to categorize objects at different times. If a person has difficulty classifying a novel object by matching it with a prototype, she may switch to feature-based categorization, as when deciding whether a pomegranate is a fruit. Conversely, a judge may decide a case by analogizing to prominent cases from the past (prototype matching) if the situation lacks features that place it definitively within the rubric of a particular legal principle (defining features).

People readily recognize robins as birds. Categorizing penguins takes a little more thought—and hence measurably more time.

Hierarchies of Concepts

Just as concepts vary in the extent to which they can be readily defined, they also differ in their degree of specificity. In other words, concepts are hierarchically ordered. We categorize all pets that pant, slobber, and bark as dogs, but we can further subdivide the concept *dog* into more specific categories such as *collie*, *chihuahua*, and *St. Bernard*. Similarly, *dog* can be situated within larger, more general categories such as *mammal* and *vertebrate* (Figure 7.2).

Thinking with concepts requires choosing the right level of abstraction. A woman walking down the street in a bright purple raincoat belongs to the categories *mammal*, *vertebrate*, and *human* just as clearly as she belongs to the category *woman*. Yet are we more likely to say, "Look at that woman in the purple raincoat" than "Look at that vertebrate in the purple raincoat." The level people naturally tend to use in categorizing objects is known as the **basic level**, which is the most inclusive level at which objects share distinctive common attributes (Corter & Gluck, 1992; Rosch, 1978). In other words, it is the broadest level of a hierarchy that has attributes that "stand out." Thus, *woman* is a basic-level object; so are *dinner*, *car*, and *bird*. At times, however, people categorize at a more specific or **subordinate level** (for instance, *robin* instead of *bird*). Alternatively, robins, wrens, and penguins can be classified at the larger or **superordinate level**, *animal*. The superordinate level is one level more abstract than the basic level, and members of this class share fewer common features (Table 7.1).

Those of us who have trouble telling a robin from a wren are most comfortable using the more generic *bird* as the basic-level category. Thus, basic levels tend to vary according to an individual's (or a culture's) familiarity with a conceptual domain. The more a person knows about a particular domain, the more specific the basic level tends to be (Dougherty, 1978; Geoghehan, 1976; Mervis & Rosch, 1981; Russell, 1991; Tanaka & Taylor, 1991). Clinical psychologists, whose job requires them to focus on subtle nuances of behavior, are unlikely to describe a person as "nice," "friendly," or "conscientious," even though these terms may be basic in everyday speech. The basic level of categorization also fluctuates according to the situational context. During the workday, a furniture maker may refer to chairs according to specific types or constructions (for instance, an oak ladder-back reproduction); however, when the day ends and he is ready to rest his feet, "chair" will suffice (Holland et al., 1986). Basic-level categories also vary to some extent across cultures. While *love* is a basic-level concept for most Westerners, the Native American Utku distinguish love-for-those-who-need-protection and love-for-those-who-are-charming-or-admired at the basic level (Russell, 1991).

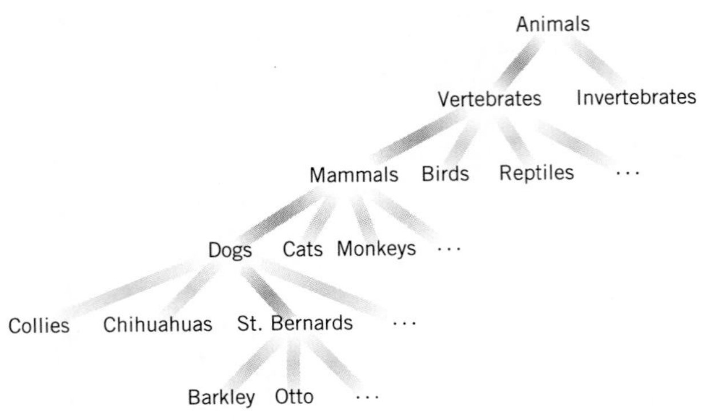

FIGURE 7.2

A hierarchy of concepts. Many concepts are organized hierarchically, from superordinate categories like animals, down to very specific examples.

TABLE 7.1 SUPERORDINATE, BASIC-LEVEL, AND SUBORDINATE CATEGORIES

SUPERORDINATE	BASIC-LEVEL	SUBORDINATE
Furniture	Chair	Kitchen chair Living room chair
	Table	Kitchen table End table Dining room table
	Lamp	Floor lamp Desk lamp
Mammal	Dog	Collie Bull terrier Golden retriever
	Cat	Tiger Tabby Burmese
	Elephant	African elephant Indian elephant

Source: Adapted from Rosch, 1978, p. 33.

Failure to use the appropriate level of categorization can sound jarring, as when a dinner guest asked for a piece of quiche by requesting that someone "pass the pie." Problems reaching the appropriate level of abstraction are common in schizophrenia. Individuals with this disorder often interpret words too abstractly or too concretely (Rapaport, et al., 1945). One patient glanced at the ceiling, terrified, when a psychologist told him that he needed to go to court because criminal charges were "hanging over his head" (Holden, personal communication, 1992).

A GLOBAL VISTA

CULTURE AND CATEGORIZATION

The concepts we use seem natural to us: Blue jays, cardinals, and robins "obviously" go together (as do the Blue Jays, Cardinals, and Dodgers). To a large extent, culture shapes not only the categories people consider basic but also the way they group things together. One tribe of Australian aborigines has a category that includes women, fire, and dangerous things (Lakoff, 1985). This category would make little sense to members of other societies, but to the aborigines it seems perfectly natural. In their mythology, the sun—a woman—is the wife of the moon. Because the sun gives off heat, it is associated with fire, and since fire is dangerous, both the sun and women are linked to dangerous things.

Many preliterate societies include animals as members of their tribe, ignoring the distinction that seems natural to contemporary Westerners between human and nonhuman. For example, a Papuan from New Guinea included the crested dove, the black cockatoo, and a particular iguana as members of his tribe (Kitagawa, 1962, pp. 42–43). The Nuer of the Sudan

In her tribe in Australia, this little girl, by virtue of her gender, will one day find herself in a category that includes "dangerous things."

categorize twins as birds (Evans-Pritchard, 1956). Once again the differences between these ways of ordering the world and our own reflect less some peculiarity of the "primitive mind" than the differing collective representations or categories that members of different cultures internalize and use in their thinking. Many contemporary Christians would have a difficult time explaining to a Papuan or Nuer just how Jesus could simultaneously be a man, a god, a spirit, and the Son of God.

One study examined the influence of culture on categorization, comparing the thought processes of 100 college students from New Mexico with 80 illiterate Manu farmers from a small village in Liberia, Africa (Irwin et al., 1974). One way of assessing subjects' ability to categorize and think abstractly, used in the West, is card sorting. The psychologist presents subjects with a deck of cards with different geometric forms printed on them (squares, triangles, etc.). The geometric forms vary in color and number. The task for the subject is to figure out the three dimensions on which the cards vary and sort them by category—that is, by form, color, and number. After the subject has sorted the cards one way, the psychologist informs him whether his sort is correct or incorrect and asks him now to re-sort them another way. The subject has a certain amount of time (in this study, five minutes) within which to sort the cards in all three correct ways.

Previous research had found that many preliterate people did poorly on this task, which was often attributed to inferior cognitive skills caused by a lack of formal education. The experimenters in this study wondered, however, whether the apparent superiority of Western-educated subjects would disappear if the task involved materials more familiar to the Manu. One extremely familiar object in their culture is rice, which comes in different forms that the Manu can readily discriminate. Thus, the experimenters adapted the sorting task to fit Manu experience by presenting subjects with bowls of rice. The bowls varied on three dimensions: amount, type (long-grain and short-grain), and roughness (polished versus unpolished). The task, then, was to sort the rice using each of these three categories. The researchers hypothesized that the Manus would do better on the rice task, whereas North American subjects would do better on the card sort task. To test this hypothesis, half the subjects in each sample received the rice task, and half, the card sort.

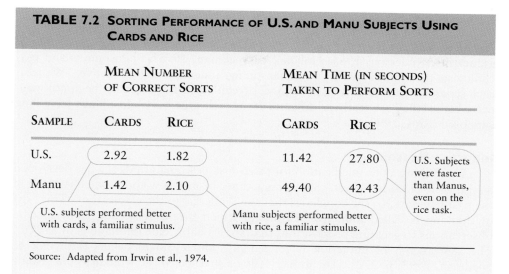

TABLE 7.2 SORTING PERFORMANCE OF U.S. AND MANU SUBJECTS USING CARDS AND RICE

| SAMPLE | MEAN NUMBER OF CORRECT SORTS | | MEAN TIME (IN SECONDS) TAKEN TO PERFORM SORTS | | |
	CARDS	RICE	CARDS	RICE	
U.S.	2.92	1.82	11.42	27.80	U.S. Subjects were faster than Manus, even on the rice task.
Manu	1.42	2.10	49.40	42.43	

U.S. subjects performed better with cards, a familiar stimulus.

Manu subjects performed better with rice, a familiar stimulus.

Source: Adapted from Irwin et al., 1974.

The results generally supported the hypothesis: North American subjects performed much better and faster on card sorting, which is more familiar to them, than rice sorting (Table 7.2). The opposite was true for the Manu farmers. Interestingly, however, the Western subjects were faster on both tasks than the Manus, and their performance was generally superior. Whether this reflects the difference between educated and uneducated, Western and non-Western, or select (college) and nonselect (cross-section of a farm population) cannot be determined from this study. What is clear, however, is that people in different cultures categorize objects in different ways depending on their use of, and familiarity with objects in their environment.

Propositions

Most thinking entails relating concepts to one another in a meaningful fashion. One way of doing this is by forming propositions. **Propositions** are the smallest units of meaning that can stand alone as an assertion and be judged true or false. The concept *dog* is neither true nor false; nor is *mammal*. The proposition *dogs are mammals*, however, relates the two concepts in a meaningful way and can be judged for its accuracy.

REASONING, PROBLEM SOLVING, AND DECISION MAKING

Mental images, mental models, concepts, and propositions are thus the building blocks of thought. In the next several pages, we explore how people use these building blocks to reason, solve problems, and make decisions.

Reasoning

Reasoning refers to the process by which people generate and evaluate logical arguments (Anderson, 1985; Holyoak & Spellman, 1993). Philosophers and psychologists distinguish two kinds of reasoning: inductive and deductive. We treat each separately, although as we shall see, psychologists have recently begun to wonder whether they are really as different from each other as philosophers have long supposed (Rips, 1990).

Inductive Reasoning

After taking a new medication for three days, a woman finds she has developed a strange rash on her chest. She cannot think of any new foods she has eaten in the past few days, so she concludes that she is allergic to the medication. This type of thinking is called **inductive reasoning**, which means reasoning from specific observations to generate propositions that are probably true (Holland et al., 1986). The central aim of induction is to generate and evaluate beliefs (Holyoak & Spellman, 1993, p. 273). The inductive logic that led to the woman's conclusions might be summarized as follows:

In the past three days I have developed a rash.

In the past three days I have been taking a new medication.

In the past three days I have not been exposed to any foods that might cause an allergy.

Therefore, I must be allergic to the new medication.

Inductive reasoning relies on probabilities. An inductive conclusion does not *necessarily* follow from the propositions that support it because the premises are only probable, not certain. For example, the woman with the rash may have been exposed to chicken pox, so that the symptoms appeared coincidentally with her new medication schedule. Because inductive reasoning is based on probabilities, psychologists have investigated the extent to which people intuitively apply laws of probability and principles of statistical reasoning derived from these laws when they reason inductively (Nisbett & Ross, 1980). Most of us are not very astute intuitive statisticians, but instruction in statistical rules and probability theory can improve our ability to reason inductively in everyday life (Fong & Nisbett, 1991; Lehman et al., 1988; Nisbett, 1993). One study investigated the extent to which undergraduate training improves everyday reasoning (Lehman & Nisbett, 1990). The researchers tested undergraduates in the first semester of their freshman year and again in the second semester of their senior year. Among other tasks, they asked subjects questions that relied on statistical reasoning and understanding of scientific method, such as the importance of large samples and control groups (Figure 7.3). After four years of college, the statistical-methodological reasoning abilities of students majoring in the natural sciences and the humanities improved only slightly, while the abilities of psychology and other social science majors improved dramatically (Figure 7.4). (This may be something to write home about.)

Deductive Reasoning

Deductive reasoning is logical reasoning that draws conclusions from assumptions or premises. In contrast to inductive reasoning, it starts with an idea rather than an observation. For instance, if you understand the general premise that all dogs have fur (which is part of the definition of "dog") and you know that Barkley is a dog, then you can deduce that Barkley has fur, even though you have never made Barkley's acquaintance. Unlike inductive reasoning, deductive reasoning can lead to *certain* rather than simply *probable* conclusions, as long as the premises are correct and the reasoning is logical.

Choose the BEST answer.

FIGURE 7.3
Statistical and methodological reasoning questions. With training, students improve in their reasoning abilities in college.
SOURCE: *Lehman et al., 1988.*

1. After the first two weeks of the major league baseball season, newspapers begin to print the top ten batting averages. Typically, after two weeks, the leading batter has an average of about .450. Yet no batter in major league history has ever averaged .450 at the end of a season. Why do you think this is?

a. A player's high average at the beginning of the season may be just a lucky fluke.

b. A batter who has such a hot streak at the beginning of the season is under a lot of stress to maintain his performance record. Such stress adversely affects his playing.

c. Pitchers tend to get better over the course of the season, as they get more in shape. As pitchers improve, they are more likely to strike out batters, so batters' averages go down.

d. When a batter is known to be hitting for a high average, pitchers bear down more when they pitch to him.

e. When a batter is known to be hitting for a high average, he stops getting good pitches to hit. Instead, pitchers "play the corners" of the plate because they don't mind walking him.

2. The city of Minneapolis has had an unpopular police chief for a year and a half. He is a political appointee who is a crony of the mayor, and he had little previous experience in police administration when he was appointed. The mayor has recently defended the chief in public, announcing that in the time since he took office, the crime rate has decreased by 12 percent. Which of the following pieces of evidence would most deflate the mayor's claim that his chief is competent?

a. An independent survey of the citizens of Minneapolis shows that 40 percent more crime is reported by respondents in the survey than is reported in police records.

b. Common sense indicates that there is little a police chief can do to lower crime rates. These are for the most part due to social and economic conditions beyond the control of officials.

c. The crime rates of the two cities closest to Minneapolis in location and size have decreased by 18 percent in the same period.

d. The police chief has been discovered to have business contacts with people who are known to be involved in organized crime.

answers: 1, a, 2, c

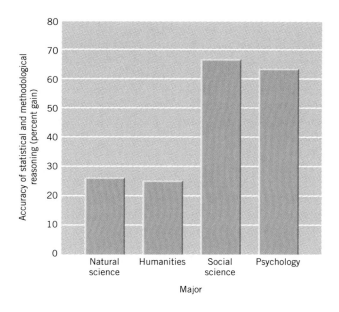

FIGURE 7.4
Gains in statistical and methodological reasoning for different majors. Undergraduates who majored in subjects placing a premium on statistical and methodological reasoning showed substantially higher gains in reasoning than subjects in other majors. SOURCE: *Lehman & Nisbett, 1990.*

FIGURE 7.5
Card selection task. If each card has a number on one side and a letter on the other, which cards must be turned over to verify or disprove the rule, "If a card has an A on one side, then it has a 3 on the other"? SOURCE: Wason, 1968.

The formal statement of deductive reasoning used by philosophers is called a syllogism. A **syllogism** consists of two premises that lead to a logical conclusion. A classic example of a syllogism is the following:

Premise: All men are mortal.

Premise: Socrates is a man.

Therefore: Socrates is mortal.

Restated in generic form, the syllogism appears as

Premise: All *A*s are *B*.

Premise: *C* is an *A*.

Therefore: *C* is a *B*.

Just as people trained in statistical principles are better able to reason inductively, so can experts trained in rules of logic perform deductive tasks more rapidly and effectively than novices (Galotti et al., 1986). To reason deductively, one must focus on the pertinent information and manipulate the relevant units of thought—propositions—systematically. Thinking logically requires preserving the meaning of each proposition while mentally moving it around or testing its implications. Failing to do so with the Socrates syllogism would produce the following:

Premise: All men are mortal

Premise: Socrates is a man.

Therefore: All men are Socrates.

Few people would accept this conclusion, regardless of the logic, because they know it is absurd; however, if the syllogism is expressed in terms of *A*s and *B*s, the error is easy to make:

Premise: All *A*s are *B*.

Premise: *C* is an *A*.

Therefore: All *A*s are *C*.

Both the form (abstract or concrete) and content (familiar or unfamiliar) of deductive reasoning problems influence the ease with which people solve them (Cosmides, 1989; Wilkins, 1982), as illustrated in the card problem presented in Figure 7.5. Subjects in this study are shown four cards and told that each card has a letter on one side and a number on the other. They are also told that the cards conform to the following rule: *If a card has an A on one side, then it has a 3 on the other side.* The task: Turn over only those cards necessary to discover whether the rule is true or false (Johnson-Laird et al., 1972; Wason, 1968).

While most people correctly conclude that they must turn over the card with the *A* on it (a number other than *3* would falsify the rule), few also realize that they must turn over the *2* card: Finding an *A* on the opposite side of this card would disprove the rule just as surely as would turning over the *A* card and finding something other than a *3*. (If your self-esteem has just plummeted, take heart—I did not get this right on the first try either.) If the same type of problem is posed with more familiar contents, reasoning deductively becomes easier (Cosmides, 1989; Cox & Griggs, 1982; Johnson-Laird et al., 1972). Consider the situation faced by a bouncer in a bar who must decide whose identification to check (Figure 7.6). When the card problem is put in terms of the bouncer's dilemma, most people find it relatively easy to solve (Griggs & Cox, 1982).

The fact that the content of a syllogism can influence the ability to solve it has led some psychologists to question whether induction and deduction are really different forms of reasoning (Rips, 1990). If people can reason more accurately about the properties of men and Socrates than about *A*s and *B*s, perhaps this means that they are really intermingling deduction and induction—or at least using their inductive knowledge about empirical realities as a check on their logical deductions (Oakhill et al., 1989). And where do the premises of deductive logic come from, such as the proposition that all dogs have fur? Usually from induction—from seeing several dogs

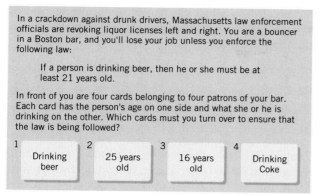

In a crackdown against drunk drivers, Massachusetts law enforcement officials are revoking liquor licenses left and right. You are a bouncer in a Boston bar, and you'll lose your job unless you enforce the following law:

If a person is drinking beer, then he or she must be at least 21 years old.

In front of you are four cards belonging to four patrons of your bar. Each card has the person's age on one side and what she or he is drinking on the other. Which cards must you turn over to ensure that the law is being followed?

1 | 2 | 3 | 4
Drinking beer | 25 years old | 16 years old | Drinking Coke

Answer: 1 and 3

FIGURE 7.6
Card selection task with familiar content. SOURCE: Adapted from Griggs & Cox, 1982.

and realizing they all have fur. So perhaps deduction is just an extension of inductive reasoning, carrying it one step further. If that is the case, the distinction between induction as involving probabilities and deduction as allowing certainty also breaks down; if a premise is only probably true, the conclusion can only be probably true.

Problem Solving

People are constantly confronted with problems to solve in daily life. Your next-door neighbor plays his stereo too loud, your psychology grades are lower than you would like, or you are having difficulty with a relationship. Although syllogisms might momentarily seem insightful ("All men are trouble, Bob is a man, therefore Bob is trouble"), inductive and deductive reasoning are unlikely to provide solutions. Instead of inferring the correct conclusion based on propositions, the task in problem solving is to move from a current, unsatisfactory state to a state in which the problem is eliminated. Thus, **problem solving** can be defined as the process of transforming one situation into another that meets a goal (Gilhooly, 1989; Greeno, 1978).

Problem solving has three components (Figure 7.7). In the **initial state**, a problem exists; this state differs in some unsatisfactory way from a **goal state** in which the problem is solved. To get from the initial state to the goal state, the individual uses **operators**, mental and behavioral processes aimed at transforming the initial state until it eventually approximates the goal state (Anderson, 1993; Miller et al., 1960; Newell & Simon, 1972; Simon, 1978).

Some problems are termed **well-defined problems** because the initial state, goal state, and operators are easily determined. Probably the best examples of well-defined problems are the math problems students confront countless times in their school careers (Kintsch & Greeno, 1985). In real life, however, few problems are so clearly set forth. Sometimes, in fact, simply determining what the problem *is* can be a problem. Consider, for example, the problem of finding a suitable boyfriend or girlfriend. Defining the goal (someone to spend Friday nights with? a companion? a sexual partner? a potential spouse?) and determining the operators (join clubs? go to a bar? answer the personal ads?) are themselves problems. Not surprisingly, this kind of problem is called an **ill-defined problem** because both the information needed to solve the problem and the criteria that determine whether the

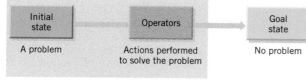

Initial state → Operators → Goal state
A problem | Actions performed to solve the problem | No problem

The problem space

FIGURE 7.7
The problem-solving process. Problem solving means transforming an initial problem state, using operators, to attain a goal state.

goals are attained are vague (Simon, 1978). Business executives and government officials often confront ill-defined problems, such as how to raise morale, how to reduce expenditures while maintaining essential services, or how to stay in power.

Steps in Problem Solving

Once a problem is defined, how does one get from the initial state to the goal state? In general, problem solving is a four-step process (Holland et al., 1986; Newell, 1969; Reiman & Chi, 1989). The first step is to compare the initial state with the goal state in order to identify precise differences between the two states. Thus, if the initial state is that your neighbor's stereo is on too loud and you find this annoying (the problem), the goal state may be to get your neighbor to turn down his stereo. The second step is to identify possible operators and select the one that seems most likely to reduce the differences. You may decide, for instance, that your best strategy is to knock on your neighbor's door and politely ask him to lower the volume (Figure 7.8).

The third step is to apply the operator or operators, responding to ensuing challenges or roadblocks by establishing subgoals. **Subgoals** are mini-goals on the way to achieving an overall goal. In dealing with the noisy neighbor, a subgoal might be to establish an initial positive rapport with him so he will be more willing to change his behavior for you. The final step is to continue using operators until all differences between the initial state and the goal state are eliminated.

Actually, the solution to a problem, or even the goal itself (when the problem is ill defined), often develops during the course of problem solving (Duncker, 1946). For instance, although your original goal may have been to get your neighbor to play his stereo softly, you may realize as you are choosing operators that you can live with noise up until 10 P.M. Similarly, when you approach your neighbor, you may find that the operator you have initially chosen is ineffective. Your neighbor may not be at home, or he may respond by getting angry rather than cooperating. Problem solving often requires rapid and creative thinking.

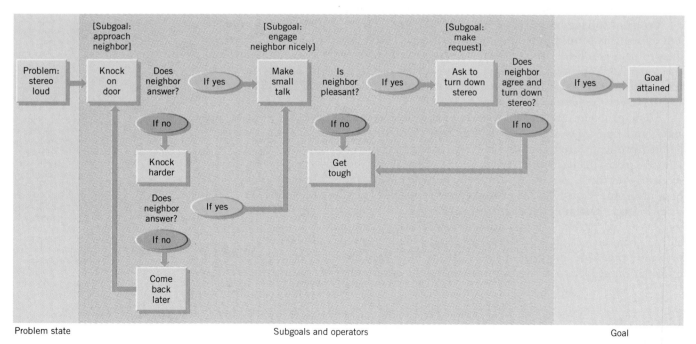

Problem state   Subgoals and operators   Goal

FIGURE 7.8

Solving a problem. The problem is that your neighbor is blasting his stereo. Like most problems, this one consists of several subproblems, which involve subgoals. You consider or attempt a number of operators to solve the subproblems and reach your goal state. At each step, you compare reality with the subgoal and continue to try operators until you solve the problem.

Problem-Solving Strategies

Problem solving would be an impossible task if people had to try every potential operator in every situation until they found one that worked. Instead, they experiment with various operators mentally by employing **problem-solving strategies**, techniques that serve as guides for solving a problem (Demorest, 1986; Mayer, 1983; Reimann & Chi, 1989). Problem-solving strategies are a type of procedural knowledge. Among the most important of these strategies are algorithms and heuristics.

Algorithms are systematic problem-solving procedures that inevitably produce a solution (Anderson, 1995). Computers use algorithms in memory searches, as when a spelling-check command checks every word in a file against an internal dictionary. Humans also use algorithms to solve problems, such as counting the number of guests coming to a barbeque and multiplying by two to determine how many hot dogs to buy. While algorithms are guaranteed to find a solution (as long as one exists), they are generally impractical to use except in solving relatively simple problems. Imagine solving for the square root of 16,129 by methodically squaring 1, then 2, then 3, and so forth, each time checking to see if the answer is 16,129. You would eventually arrive at the right answer, but only on your 127th try.

Because algorithms are so unwieldy, people more often rely on **heuristics**, cognitive shortcuts or "rules of thumb." Although they do not carry the same guarantee of success, heuristic strategies are often easier and more economical in terms of effort expended. For example, **hypothesis testing** is a common heuristic, which involves formulating a hypothesis and then testing it to see if it solves the problem (Klayman & Ha, 1989). In the noisy neighbor example, your hypothesis might be that most people try to be good neighbors, so your neighbor will probably be cooperative. If so, you will select "asking politely" as your operator.

Hypotheses reflect people's perceptions, expectations, and biases. If their intuitions are right, then hypothesis testing can be a useful shortcut; if they are wrong, this heuristic can lead them astray. One study examined the relationship between medical students' hypothesis-testing skills and their cost-effectiveness in ordering diagnostic tests (Durand et al., 1991). Researchers presented third-year medical students with case studies and asked them to generate hypotheses about possible diagnoses and to list the tests they would order. Students whose hypotheses were logically organized suggested fewer and less expensive tests than their less organized peers.

Decision Making

People are constantly called upon to make decisions, from the mundane ("Should I buy the cheaper brand or the one that tastes better?") to the consequential ("What career should I choose?"). **Decision making** is the process by which an individual weighs the pros and cons of different alternatives in order to make a choice.

According to information-processing models, when people make decisions, they consider the utility (the value) of the outcomes of different options, as well as the probability (the estimated likelihood) of each outcome. If you have located three apartments near campus and must choose one, the attributes you are likely to value might include rent, proximity to campus, attractiveness, availability of parking, and whether the landlord allows pets. To make a thoroughly rational decision, you would begin by assigning a numerical weight to each attribute according to its importance (Edwards, 1977). Thus, if budget is the most important factor, rent would be assigned the highest numerical weight. Then, for each apartment, you would assign a **utility value** to each attribute, that is, a number representing the extent to which the potential choice (the apartment) fulfills the criterion (such as proximity to campus), say, from −10 to +10 (Table 7.3).

Next, you multiply the numerical weight of the attribute (how important it is) by its utility value (how well the option fulfills the criterion) for each option (apartment) to arrive at a weighted utility value. A **weighted utility value** is a combined measure of the importance of an attribute and the extent to which a given option sat-

TABLE 7.3 CALCULATING WEIGHTED UTILITY VALUE

Attributes (in order of importance)	Importance (numerical weight)	216 GREEN ST.		16 CEDAR ST.		1010 CALIFORNIA ST.	
		Utility Value	Weighted Utility Value	Utility Value	Weighted Utility Value	Utility Value	Weighted Utility Value
Rent	5	+10	×5=50	+8	×5 = 40	+5	×5=25
Location	4	0	×4= 0	+3	×4 = 12	+10	×4=40
Livability	3	+8	×3=24	+3	×3 = 9	+1	×3= 3
Parking	2	+10	×2=20	+10	×2 = 20	−2	×2=−4
Pets	1	+10	×1=10	−10	×1 =−10	+10	×1=10
			104		71		74

Source: Adapted from Edwards, 1977. Copyright © 1977 IEEE.

Note. Multiplying the utility value of each of several attributes by their importance yields weighted utility values for three apartments on five dimensions. Adding together the weighted utilities leads to a preference for the apartment at 216 Green Street.

isfies it. Suppose, for example, the attribute of parking has a weight of 2, and parking at 1010 California Street is inconvenient enough to have a utility value of −2; then its weighted utility value will be 2 × −2, or −4. Once you have rated and weighted all of the attributes, determining which alternative has the highest overall weighted utility value is simply a matter of adding up the totals.

In the real world, of course, people do not always get their first choice, and trying for something that is probably unattainable may have heavy costs. For example, the Green Street apartment may have so many applicants that no matter how high a rating it earns, it may be a poor selection if you have only a slight chance of getting it and must have a place to live by a certain date. Making a rational decision, then, involves a combined assessment of the value and probability of the different options, known as **expected utility**. The expected utility of an alternative is obtained by multiplying the weighted utility by the expected probability of that outcome (see Table 7.4). If you have a 10 percent chance of getting the Green Street apartment, the expected utility of that choice is .10 x 104, or 10.4. By comparison, if you have a 50 percent chance of getting the Cedar Street apartment and a 90 percent chance of getting the California Street apartment, the expected utilities of those alternatives are, respectively, 35.5 and 66.6. If you need to make a decision within a very short time, then the one to choose is 1010 California.

Decision making can, of course, have much weightier consequences than selecting the right apartment. Anthropologists use decision-making models to explain the way groups of people choose to earn their livelihood. One model contrasts two strategies for deciding how to allocate time and effort on different modes of subsistence such as hunting, fishing, or farming (Coombs, 1980). The first strategy is to maximize the minimum possible payoffs. That is, people allocate their time, effort, and other resources to provide the highest nutritional rewards in the worst circumstances, even if another strategy generally gives a greater yield, because the higher yield strategy does not protect against famine. Populations with minimal capacities for food storage, such as nomadic groups, are likely to choose this strategy because they cannot count on carrying food reserves from one season to the next. In contrast, groups with greater capacity to store food may choose a strategy that maxi-

TABLE 7.4 CALCULATING EXPECTED UTILITY

	ALTERNATIVE APARTMENTS		
	216 GREEN ST.	16 CEDAR ST.	1010 CALIFORNIA ST.
Weighted utility value	104	71	74
Probability of getting apartment	×.10	×.50	×.90
Expected utility =	10.4	35.5	66.6

Source: Adapted from Edwards, 1977. Copyright © 1977 IEEE.

Note. Although the apartment on California Street has the highest weighted utility value, its improbability makes it the worst choice among the three options.

mizes *average* yield, even if this means they sometimes have a rough year. They may choose, for example, to plant a crop that occasionally fails if its usual payoff is large.

This anthropological model of decision making dovetails with behaviorist and evolutionary explanations of decision-making strategies. Suppose a tribe without storage capacity chooses a subsistence strategy that does not yield enough to support the population during one season. The tribe will either starve or migrate. The only populations left in the area will be those that have chosen strategies that maximize minimum payoffs. Thus, operant conditioning (reinforcement of effective strategies)—or from another perspective, natural selection (adaptation to a niche)—chooses populations who choose wisely.

Factors That Interfere with Rational Thinking

Knowing how to solve problems and make rational decisions is one thing, but carrying them out is another. Everyday decision making is filled with irrationality. For example, people tend to take more risks when their prospects are bad than when

Nomadic tribes often make decisions that protect against the worst case scenario.

they are good, even though prudence might dictate just the opposite (Tversky & Kahneman, 1981). In a simulated tax collection experiment, subjects who expected to receive a tax refund were significantly less likely to write off questionable expenses than those who believed their deductions would not cover their taxes. These findings suggest that if the government maximized withholding during the year so that taxpayers would expect a refund, fewer would write off questionable expenses. The practical import of this study could be tremendous: Eliminating income tax noncompliance could reduce the U.S. annual budget deficit by half (Robben et al., 1990).

Psychologists have discovered a number of other cognitive biases and constraints on rational problem solving and decision making (Gilovich, 1991). Particularly common are heuristics gone awry, confirmation bias, and functional fixedness.

Representativeness and Availability Heuristics

Heuristics can be efficient methods for reasoning, solving problems, and making decisions, but they can also lead to errors. One such heuristic is the **representativeness heuristic**, a strategy used to decide whether an object or incident belongs in a particular class. The representativeness heuristic relies on the object's resemblance to a prototype (that is, how much the object is "representative" of a category) and ignores information about its probability of occurring. To see the representativeness heuristic at work, consider the following personality description:

> Steve is very shy and withdrawn, invariably helpful, but with little interest in people, or in the world of reality. A meek and tidy soul, he has a need for order and structure, and a passion for detail. (Tversky & Kahneman, 1974, p. 1124)

Is Steve most likely a farmer, a salesman, an airline pilot, a librarian, or a physician? Most people believe he is probably a librarian, even if they are informed that librarians are much less common in the population from which Steve has been drawn than are the other occupations. Although Steve's attributes seem typical or representative of a librarian, if the population has 50 salesmen for every librarian, the chances are high that Steve is a salesman, even though he fits the prototype of a librarian.

Another heuristic that can lead to judgment errors is the availability heuristic (MacLeod & Campbell, 1992; Tversky & Kahneman, 1973). The **availability heuristic** judges the frequency of a class of events or the likelihood of something happening on the basis of its availability in memory (that is, its ease of retrieval). People essentially assume that events or occurrences that they can recall easily are common and typical. This can introduce a serious bias in judgment, however, because familiar or vivid occurrences come to mind more readily than less familiar or less striking events. For instance, most North Americans believe that driving to a family holiday gathering a few hours away is safer than flying to the Middle East, with its history of terrorist activity. Statistically, however, the chances of fatality are much greater driving in the United States and Canada during the holidays. In large part, the error in judgment occurs because exposure to mass media, especially television, makes isolated examples of violence in the Middle East extremely vivid and therefore more available in memory (Wober, 1987).

Confirmation Bias

Another limitation on rational thinking is the **confirmation bias**, the tendency for people to believe, and search for confirmation of, what they already believe (see Klayman & Ha, 1989; Oakhill & Garnham, 1993). In one study, the experimenters presented subjects with three numbers (2, 4, and 6) and asked them to discover the rule used to construct this sequence of numbers by generating their own sets of numbers (Wason, 1960). After each response, the experimenters told subjects whether or not their number sets illustrated the rule, so they received immediate and ongoing feedback. The rule was actually very simple: any three numbers, in sequence

FIGURE 7.9a
The candle problem. Use the objects on the table to mount a candle on the wall so that when it is lit, no wax drips on the floor. (Solution is on next page)

from smallest to largest. To discover this rule, subjects would have had to test a variety of sequences until only this rule remained. Instead, most subjects did just the opposite. Early on, they formed a hypothesis such as "Add 2 to each number to form the next number" and then generated other sequences that confirmed this rule until they were sure they were right.

Functional Fixedness

An experiment published in 1946 asked subjects to mount a candle on a wall so that when it was lit no wax would drip on the floor (Duncker, 1946). On a table lay a few small candles, some tacks, and a box of matches (Figure 7.9*a*). The experiment was designed to test **functional fixedness**, the tendency for people to ignore other possible functions of an object when they have a fixed function in mind. The tendency here, of course, was to see a matchbox as only a matchbox. In fact, if the matches were *out* of the matchbox, subjects solved the problem more easily because they then recognized that the box could be used as something other than a container for matches. The tendency to see or use objects only in accustomed ways is thus another limitation on rational thinking (see Figure 7.10).

Parallel Distributed Processing

Although human thought is prone to errors, it is generally remarkably fast and efficient. How do people think as quickly as they do? How, for example, do they continuously monitor and adjust the position of their car on a winding road, while

FIGURE 7.10
The two-string problem. You are standing between two dangling ropes, with nothing else in the room but a chair and a pair of pliers. Your goal is to hold onto both ropes at the same time, one in each hand. The ropes are far enough apart that grabbing one and reaching the other is impossible, even with your feet. What do you do? SOURCE: Maier, 1931.
Solution: Use the pliers as a weight to set one string in motion.

FIGURE 7.9*b*
Solution to the candle problem.
SOURCE: *Duncker, 1946.*

processing the complex meanings of a conversation with a passsenger? A major development in the field of cognitive science, **parallel distributed processing (PDP)** models of cognition, offer an explanation (Rumelhart et al., 1986). PDP models rest on two propositions. The first is that many cognitive processes occur simultaneously, that is, in *parallel*, rather than one at a time. The second is that the meaning of a representation to a person is not contained in some specific locus in the brain. Rather, it is spread out, or *distributed*, throughout an entire network of interacting processing units, with each unit attending to some small aspect of the representation.

PDP models differ from traditional information-processing models in two respects. First, the underlying metaphor is no longer really the mind as computer but the mind as brain. PDP models assume that when the brain represents knowledge, it does so through the interaction of hundreds, thousands, or millions of neurons. When neurons interact, they may either excite or inhibit other neurons, through the action of excitatory and inhibitory neurotransmitters (Chapter 3). PDP models postulate similar cognitive mechanisms, as when a person differentiates between the words "got" and "sot." Both words share "ot," but if the context is a sentence like, "He _ot paid today," then the context will spread activation to "g" and away from "s" because only "got" fits. That is, activation provided by context increases the likelihood of one interpretation of the initial consonant and inhibits the other.

PDP models also differ from traditional models by deemphasizing serial processing, the kind of processing that begins with sensory registration and goes through stages of short-term memory, long-term memory, and retrieval to short-term memory. According to PDP models, any information that becomes conscious has already had numerous elements of it processed simultaneously and unconsciously without passing through all the stages in the standard model. Advocates of parallel processing models contend that human information processing is simply too fast, and the requirements of the environment too instantaneous, to make serial processing viable. For example, in typing the word "vacuum," the right hand does nothing until the first "u," yet high-speed videotapes of skilled typists find that the right hand has moved into position to hit the "u" by the time the left hand is typing the "v." This happens so quickly that the typist cannot possibly be aware of it. Thus, even while the typist is focusing on the action of the left hand, recognition of the word "vacuum" has activated parallel systems that prepare the right hand for action (Rumelhart et al., 1986).

A relatively simple perceptual phenomenon illustrates the power of a PDP model. Figure 7.11 shows words with letters that are ambiguous because they are slanted or pieces are blotted out. Most readers can easily discern the correct letters and read the words. In fact, such ambiguity is the rule in reading handwriting, where many letters are not perfectly drawn. According to PDP models, people can read the words in Figure 7.11 because they simultaneously process information about the letters and the words. In the top line, the second letter of each word could either be an "a" or an "h." Both letters are thus activated by information-processing units whose job is letter recognition. At the same time, however, a word-recognition processing unit recognizes that an "a" would render the first word a nonword, and an "h" would do the same for the second word. The two processing modules interact, so that extra activation spreads to the "h" option in "the," and the impossibility of "tae" as a word leads to inhibition of "a" as an option in that word. At an even broader level, the phrase "the cat" is also being processed, and because no other phrase is possible using that configuration of letters, the mind is even more likely to perceive the first word as "the" (because what else would precede "cat" and has three letters?), further spreading activation to the "h" in "the." This all happens so quickly that we are only aware of reading "the cat" and have no idea of the underlying cognitive processes. Similar processes account for the fact that we can readily decode the second word in the figure as "RED," even though substantial pieces of the letters are covered.

FIGURE 7.11
Parallel distributed processing. People are able to decipher ambiguous, degraded, or distorted messages by simultaneously processing parts (such as letters) and wholes (words and phrases).
SOURCE: *Rumelhart, 1984, p. 8.*

PDP models can also be used to explain more complex phenomena, such as inductive reasoning (Golden & Rumelhart, 1993; Read & Marcus-Newhall, 1993). Consider the woman who was trying to infer the cause of her rash. She reasoned that (1) she developed a rash after taking a new medication, (2) she had not been exposed to any foods that could cause an allergic reaction, and therefore, (3) she must be allergic to the medication. From a PDP perspective, each of these propositions is associated with a degree of confidence, which can be represented with a number from 0 to 1 (Rips, 1990). Her confidence that she has taken the medication is, say, 1.0, whereas her confidence that she has not eaten any foods to which she is allergic is .60. This leaves her quite convinced of her induction (at, say, .75); that is, she feels subjectively that it is probably true. If she subsequently realizes that she may have inadvertently eaten shellfish (to which she is allergic) in an hors d'oeuvre, her confidence in the second proposition ("I have not eaten any food to which I am allergic") plummets to .20, leading to a substantial downward revision in her confidence that the medication has caused the rash (say, to .35), and perhaps to a decision to restart the medication. The continuously changing subjective estimates of probability that underlie inductive reasoning are unconscious, as is the way they combine to produce a conscious conclusion. From a PDP perspective, induction and deduction may represent a continuum of subjective certainty rather than an absolute dichotomy, where people's confidence in their reasoning ranges from none (0) to complete (1).

Using Computers to Simulate Thought

PDP models grew out of efforts to simulate human thought using computers. In the 1960s, cognitive scientists designed a computer program called the General Problem Solver (GPS) to model human problem solving (Ernst & Newell, 1969; Newell & Simon, 1972). GPS's heir, SOAR (State, Operator, And Result) learns from trial and error, so it can solve problems with increasing efficiency without additional input from its programmers (Lindsay, 1991; Waldrop, 1988).

Advances in **artificial intelligence**—that is, in the use of computers to perform tasks that require intelligence when performed by humans (Alty, 1989; Wagman, 1991)—have produced programs ranging from ELIZA, which we met at the beginning of this chapter, to SOAR, to expert systems that perform highly specialized tasks requiring in-depth, expert knowledge of a field (Denning, 1986; Hernandez, 1990). Some of these expert programs can diagnose certain diseases with a reliability approaching that of many doctors. Computer programs can also model language acquisition as it occurs in young children (Anderson, 1983; Van Someren, 1984) and recognize and simulate speech (Michaelis & Wiggins, 1982; Tucker & Jones, 1991).

As promising as these advances are, some critics argue that computers are still far from being able to simulate human thought or intelligence adequately and may never be able to do so. Hubert and Stewart Dreyfus (1986) note that one limitation of computer "thinking" is the shallow nature of the understanding that underlies it. For instance, ELIZA was programmed to carry out conversations according to routine formulas. When Hubert Dreyfus typed, "I'm feeling happy" and then corrected himself by typing, "No, elated," ELIZA responded, "Don't be so negative" because it was programmed to respond with that rebuke whenever the word "no" was in the input.

An additional limitation is that computers are not conscious of their thoughts, and hence any comparison between the brain and a computer misses a fundamental aspect of human cognition (Chapter 6). When people know something and are conscious of it, they know that they know it. Conscious experiences are endowed with subjective meaning (Searle, 1987). Computers may produce a pattern of electrical activity that provides an *analog* of processes in the brain, but the subjective experience of knowledge differentiates human and artificial intelligence.

When choosing a mate, people often have criteria in mind, but their choices are guided as much by their heart and gut as by their head.

A Different Perspective: Psychodynamic and Behavioral Views of Decision Making

Although information-processing models offer the most systematic and well-researched approach to thinking, they are not without challenge. From a psychodynamic perspective, the rational decision maker of information-processing theory exists only in the mind of the cognitive psychologist. Most problems and decisions involve motivation and emotion, and many judgments are influenced by needs and wishes, all of which are absent from the information-processing account. For example, a child with a learning disability who suffers repeated setbacks in school might "solve" this problem by convincing himself that he does not care about success or failure and hence stop making any effort. Similarly, when assessing the probability of victory in an upcoming game, students from competing universities tend to make dramatically different predictions, which are distorted by their wishes.

Because rational models of problem solving and decision making were formulated before cognitive psychologists became concerned with consciousness, these models tend to assume that people are aware of their goals and consciously weigh the utility value of different options. From a psychodynamic perspective, however, many goals or motives can impinge on any single decision, problem, or judgment. Some of these motives may be quite irrational and may not be represented in conscious awareness at all. Is anyone so rational in choosing a mate as information-processing theory proposes? When you picked your last boyfriend or girlfriend, did you consciously assign weighted utility values— +10 for sense of humor, +5 for intelligence, +8 for thoughtfulness—and perform a rational cost-benefit analysis? Many adults whose parents were alcoholics gravitate toward alcoholic mates, despite the misery that their parents' alcoholism caused them as children. Cues associated with alcoholism seem to be important *implicit* criteria in their mate selection, but these are neither rational nor conscious.

Research suggests, in fact, that people often make decisions based less on their thoughts than on their feelings and that thinking can sometimes *interfere* with sound judgment. In one study, subjects rated five brands of strawberry jam previously rated by *Consumer Reports* as the 1st, 11th, 24th, 32nd, and 44th best. (Subjects used a nine-point scale, from 1 = disliked to 9 = liked.) The investigators asked subjects in the experimental group to list their reasons for liking or disliking each jam prior to making their ratings; subjects in the control group made their ratings without any instructions. When subjects' ratings were compared to those of the *Consumer Reports* experts, an interesting pattern emerged: The rankings of subjects who made their ratings without thinking about reasons were more similar to those of the experts than rankings of subjects who had been asked to deliberate (Wilson & Schooler, 1991).

In another study, subjects looked at five art posters and rated the extent to which they liked each. Again, some subjects were asked to give reasons for their preferences, while others were not. At the end of the rating procedure, subjects were allowed to choose a poster to take home. A few weeks later, the experimenters contacted the subjects to ask how satisfied they were with their choice. Subjects who had analyzed the reasons for their preferences were significantly less satisfied with their choice of poster than subjects who had chosen without reflection (Wilson et al., 1993). Conscious thinking appears to have overridden unconscious judgment, with negative results.

Rarely do psychoanalysts and behaviorists agree, but most behaviorists are similarly skeptical about the centrality of consciousness in decision making. From a behaviorist perspective, the pros and cons of different courses of action—their environmental consequences—determine the decisions people make, whether or not they think about these consequences. People learn, generalize, and discriminate stimuli all the time without conscious thought. One study showed how conditioning without awareness can affect the way people categorize others and behave toward them. Subjects who had a single brief, unfriendly encounter with an experimenter subsequently avoided a confederate who physically resembled the experimenter (Lewicki, 1985). In other words, they generalized a conditioned emotional response, and this emotion in turn motivated avoidance behavior. Control subjects, who did not have an unfriendly encounter with the experimenter, did not avoid the confederate. Perhaps most telling, when the investigators asked subjects who avoided the confederate why they made the choice they did, almost all replied that their choice was random.

An advocate of information-processing models might respond to all this that models of problem solving and decision making were never intended to describe what people actually do, only what they should do if they want to behave rationally. But the studies of jam preference and art posters suggest that even that is not the case: Rational, conscious thought is not always the best guide to action. From an evolutionary perspective, conscious thought is a relatively new invention, superimposed on a cognitive system that worked well for other species for millions of years (Reber, 1992). Much of the time people categorize, solve problems, and make decisions without awareness, and these cognitive processes are often highly adaptive, since they are based on unconscious recognition of regularities in the environment (Holyoak & Spellman, 1993). Increased attention to these unconscious processes is likely to refine cognitive models considerably. Whether and how models of problem solving and decision making predicated on the metaphor of the mind as a computer will accommodate emotional and motivational factors remains to be seen.

LANGUAGE

This chapter is devoted to the way people think, but so much of thinking is done with words that understanding thought is impossible without understanding language. Try, for instance, to solve an arithmetic problem without thinking with words or the symbols we call numbers, or try thinking about the concept *justice* without relying on words.

Beyond its role in thinking, the use of language is fundamental to one of the most central activities of people in literate societies: reading. Without the ability to manipulate and comprehend the written word, we would be unable to carry out the most basic activities, from selecting items from a menu, to filling out a form. And nothing is as potent as language in bridging our separateness from one another, for language permits us to share our most intimate thoughts. Conversely, the lack of a shared language can be frustrating and alienating, contributing to the perception of "otherness" that fuels ethnic strife.

The remainder of this chapter discusses **language**, the system of symbols, sounds, meanings, and rules for their combination that constitutes the primary mode of communication among humans. We begin by considering the ways language and thought shape each other. We then examine the elements of language and the way children acquire the capacity to think and communicate with words. In so doing, we enter into one of the most intriguing debates in all of psychology, the question of whether the capacity to acquire language is innate. We conclude by discussing nonverbal communication and the linguistic capabilities of our simian relatives.

Language and Thought

The Hanunoo people of the Philippines have 92 names for rice (Anderson, 1985). If concepts are the building blocks of thought and each of these names represents a concept, then are the Hanunoo equipped to think about rice in ways that are unavailable to North Americans with a more limited language repertoire? This line of reasoning led Benjamin Whorf and others to formulate what came to be called the **Whorfian hypothesis of linguistic relativity**, the hypothesis that language shapes thought (Hunt & Agnoli, 1991; Whorf, 1956). According to the Whorfian hypothesis, people whose language provides a diversity of terms for distinguishing subtypes within a particular category must perceive their world differently from those who have only one word (or none).

Different languages also call attention to different information. The English language draws attention to a person's gender; one cannot avoid specifying gender when using pronouns such as "his" or "her." Many languages have different words for "you," indicating the relative status of the person being addressed. The more polite, formal form is *usted* in Spanish, *vous* in French, and *Sie* in German. The Japanese have many more gradations of respect, and Japanese professionals often exchange business cards immediately upon meeting so that they will use the correct term (Triandis, 1994). Whorf argued that the Hopi do not have the same conception of time as English speakers because their language has neither terms nor grammatical constructions that refer to time, unlike English, with its tenses.

Considerable research, however, questions the extent to which language structures thought. Cross-cultural research on the perception of color suggests that language has only a minimal role, at least at the sensory-perceptual end of the information-processing continuum. Color is universal in all cultures, but the number of words for colors is not constant. The English language uses at least 11 words to describe commonly perceived colors, such as blue, red, yellow, black, white, gray, green, brown, orange, pink, and purple. Yet the Dani people of New Guinea have only two basic color words: *mola* for bright, warm shades, and *mili* for dark, cold hues (Anderson, 1985). To what extent does the presence or absence of linguistic labels affect the way people perceive or think about colors?

A series of experiments with Dani and English-speaking subjects explored this question (Rosch, 1973). In one experimental design, researchers showed subjects a color chip for a short period of time (Figure 7.12) and then 30 seconds later asked them to select that color from an array of 160 chips. The hypothesis was that English-speaking subjects would perform better if the chip were one of the basic colors for which their language provides a primary name (for instance, a clear, bright red) than if it were an in-between shade, such as magenta or taupe—and indeed they did. What of the Dani subjects? Contrary to the Whorfian hypothesis, they, too, correctly selected basic colors more often than less distinctive shades, even though their language had no names for them. (Dani subjects were, however, outperformed overall by the Westerners.)

Findings such as these challenge the Whorfian hypothesis in its most extreme form. With complex concepts, however, language does appear to play a more central role in shaping thought. Indeed, even *having* certain thoughts, such as *freedom*, would seem impossible without language, so to some extent linguistic representations must shape our understanding. If we could not construct propositions verbally—"All men are mortal" and "Socrates is a man"—could we reason as well deductively?

The converse of the Whorfian hypothesis—that thought shapes language—appears to have some validity as well. Because rice is critically important to the Hanunoo, one would expect their language to provide words to describe distinctions in appearance, texture, use, and so forth. The same evolution in vocabulary can be seen in our own culture, where words such as *yuppie* and *VCR* have emerged

FIGURE 7.12

Language and color. Although the Dani can remember the hue of different colored chips, they would call the first three chips mola *and the last three* mili.

to describe what previously did not exist. Conversely, words describing phenomena that are no longer part of everyday life (such as *flapper, speakeasy, hippie,* and *flower child*) fall into disuse.

The interactions of thought and language are readily apparent in political discourse. At times, language signals that a change in thinking has occurred. Politicians no longer use the plural to refer to "these United States"; the nation was originally founded as a confederation of relatively independent states, but the increasing role of the federal government and the U.S. position as a major power internationally have rendered that usage obsolete. People with political agendas clearly appear to believe that language can influence thinking. In the 1960s and 1970s, feminists attempted to raise consciousness about condescending attitudes toward women by objecting to the use of the word *girl* to describe an adult female. Accepted names for ethnic minority groups have changed in the United States (e.g., from *colored people* and *Negroes* to *blacks, African Americans,* and *people of color*) as the previous names became associated with negative stereotypes. Groups for and against abortion rights have tried to take the moral high ground by referring to themselves as *pro choice* and *pro life.*

Although language is an important medium for thought and appears at times to influence it, thought can certainly occur independent of language. Patients with strokes that damage left-hemisphere language centers often show considerable frustration in trying to get ideas and intentions across without words, as do young toddlers. Further, consider the reasoning processes involved when a person reads familiar instructions, "Wet hair, apply shampoo, lather, rinse, repeat" (Pinker, 1995). If the person did not think beyond the words, she would wet her hair again after each rinse cycle and repeat endlessly (since the instructions never say to stop). While thought probably determines language more than the other way around, in most cases the two are intertwined.

Transforming Sounds and Symbols into Meaning

The symbols of language are arbitrary; the English language could just as easily have called cats *dogs* and vice versa. In this next section, we examine the way sounds and symbols are transformed into meaningful sentences, beginning with the elements of language: phonemes, morphemes, sentences, constituents, and grammar (Table 7.5).

Elements of Language

When people speak, they make many sounds (sighing, licking their lips, and so forth) that are not part of language. The smallest unit of speech that distinguishes one linguistic utterance from another is called a **phoneme**. In the English language, phonemes include not only vowels and consonants but also the different ways of pronouncing them. For instance, the two pronunciations of the letter *a* in *at* and *ate* are both phonemes. A string of randomly connected phonemes, however, does not convey any message; the basic units of meaning are **morphemes**. Words, suffixes, and prefixes are morphemes because they carry meaning. Thus, words such as *pillow, horse,* and *the,* as well as prefixes and suffixes like *pre-* or *-ing,* are morphemes. The word *antediluvian* (which means very old, or literally "before the flood") consists of three morphemes: *ante-*, meaning "before"; the root *diluvi-*, from the Latin *diluvium*, or "flood"; and *-an*, meaning "relating to."

Words are combined into **sentences**, units of language that join a subject and predicate to express a thought or meaning. Propositions, described earlier, are sentences. Within a sentence, morphemes are combined into **phrases**, groups of words that act as a unit and convey a meaning. In the sentence, *When people speak, they make many sounds,* the words *when people speak* and *many sounds* are phrases, both of which convey a meaning.

TABLE 7.5 ELEMENTS OF LANGUAGE

ELEMENT	DEFINITION	EXAMPLES
Phonemes	Smallest units of speech that distinguish utterances	th, s, ē, ĕ
Morphemes	Basic units of meaning	anti-, house, the, -ing
Sentences	Smallest units of language possessing a truth value	the house is old, the lion ate
Phrases	Group of words that act as a unit and convey a meaning	in the den, the rain in Spain, ate the candy
Grammar	System for generating acceptable utterances and identifying unacceptable utterances	the ball landed over the fence

Grammar provides a set of rules for combining these elements of language. It is a system for generating acceptable language utterances and identifying unacceptable ones. Thus, the sentence *The rain in Spain falls mainly on the plain* makes sense, whereas the sentence *Spain falls rain plain on in mainly the* does not. The term **syntax** refers to the rules that govern the placement of specific words or phrases within a sentence.

Slips of the Tongue: Misplacing the Elements of Language

Speech is a prime example of parallel processing, as the speaker simultaneously combines phonemes, assembles units of meaning according to rules of grammar and syntax, and even gauges the perspective and abilities of the listener (which is why

"Good morning, beheaded—uh, I mean beloved."

Drawing by D. Fradon; © 1979, The New Yorker Magazine, Inc.

most people do not talk the same way to toddlers and adults). This multilevel production is mostly unavailable to consciousness, but evidence of it can be seen in slips of the tongue (Dell, 1986; Jaeger, 1992). Errors known as Spoonerisms (after the English clergyman William A. Spooner, to whom many such slips of the tongue were attributed) involve the inadvertent exchange of phonemes, as when an usher greets a woman at church, "May I sew you to your sheet?" Slips of the tongue may also involve morphemes ("thinly sliced" to "slicely thinned," or "sun is in the sky" to "sky is in the sun").

Psychodynamic and cognitive psychologists offer different explanations for slips of the tongue. The psychodynamic perspective considers them evidence of unconscious thoughts, wishes, or feelings that slip past conscious censorship. For example, a woman in her late thirties who was dating a man several years her junior was asked about the age difference. She replied, "Oh, I don't think it really mothers." Apparently, a part of her was not so sure.

From a cognitive perspective, constructing a sentence requires the activation of various morphemes and phonemes. If activation spreads too quickly to a similar element of language or one needed later in the sentence, a slip of the tongue may occur (Dell, 1986). Thus, a person who is trying to tell a joke may accidentally use a word from the punch line.

These psychodynamic and cognitive explanations may actually be more complementary than contradictory, as illustrated in a series of studies that experimentally induced slips of the tongue (Motley, 1980, 1985). In one study, male subjects saw word pairs, such as *worst cottage*, *past fashion*, *brood nests*, and *sham dock*, flashed quickly on a screen. When a buzzer sounded, they read the words aloud. One group of subjects was led to believe they would receive random shocks during the experiment; a second group was sexually stimulated through the behavior and provocative attire of a female experimenter. Subjects in the first condition produced more slips of the tongue related to fear of being shocked (for example, "worst cottage" became "cursed wattage"), whereas subjects in the second condition produced more sexual slips (e.g., "past fashion" became "fast passion").

How can one explain these findings? If fears, wishes, and fantasies are all located along networks of association, then these more emotion-laden phenomena emphasized by psychoanalysis should interfere with conscious word choice just as other thoughts, morphemes, or phonemes do. Activation can spread to fears of being shocked or thoughts and feelings about sex, allowing these mental contents to slip through conscious control into speech when the person is least expecting it.

Surface and Deep Structure

Until the 1950s, the study of language consisted primarily of classifying and quantifying the elements of language, and linguists paid little attention to what sentences mean or how people use them (Searle, 1974). But a linguistic revolution took place four decades ago with the publication of Noam Chomsky's *Syntactic Structures* (1957). Chomsky, a linguist, argued that the meaning of a sentence is much more than the sum of its parts and is not a property of the way the sentence happens to be organized. A person could use many possible combinations of phonemes, morphemes, and phrases to express the same underlying meaning. For example, to communicate a particular sentiment about Chomsky, I might write that "Chomsky is a brilliant thinker," or "As a thinker, Chomsky is brilliant," or "Chomsky's thinking is brilliant." Conversely, the way a sentence happens to be constructed can lead to multiple possible interpretations of its meaning, as in the sentence from *TV Guide*, "On tonight's show Dr. Ruth will discuss sex with Dick Cavett" (Pinker, 1995). Each morpheme in this sentence is clear and unambiguous, yet the sentence can be construed either to mean that Dr. Ruth will discuss sex *in general* as she talks with a talk show host or that she will discuss her experience of having sex *with him*.

Noam Chomsky

According to Chomsky, then, language does not consist simply of structural elements such as phonemes, morphemes, and grammar. The way people happen to combine these elements in a sentence to express a meaning is only the **surface structure** of language. More important than the superficial organization of words is the underlying meaning conveyed by the structures within a sentence, or its **deep structure**. Underlying the surface structure of a sentence such as *My old dog has fleas* are three propositions whose meaning is implicit: that I have a dog, that my dog is old, and that my dog has fleas. Chomsky observed that people transform the surface structure of a sentence into its deep structure automatically or unconsciously.

The importance of deep structure in language is demonstrated by the fact that deep structure, rather than surface structure, is what people tend to store in memory. For instance, subjects given the two sentences, *Jennifer watered the plants* and *The plants were watered by Jennifer*, will later have difficulty remembering which sentence they saw, but they are likely to remember the point (Anderson, 1972).

Transformational Grammar

That people can understand meaning when so many wordings can mean the same thing is truly incredible. The area of linguistic study called **transformational grammar** attempts to define the rules people use in converting (transforming) surface to deep structure and vice versa (Chomsky, 1957). In transforming the sentence *The plants were watered by Jennifer* into its deep structure *Jennifer watered the plants*, people follow the rule of placing the noun that performs the action (Jennifer) at the beginning of the sentence, changing the verb (were watered) from passive to active voice, and changing the apparent subject (the plants) into a direct object.

Similar "grammars" exist in many areas of cognition, providing rules for transforming representations in expected and understandable ways. Learning to compose music involves the acquisition of multiple grammars, such as a grammar of harmony for transforming a single tone into a rich collection of tones that do not produce a dissonant sound. Another musical grammar guides the construction of an overall musical structure. In popular music, this format typically includes a refrain, verses, a bridge or break that diverges from the expected pattern, and a return to the refrain and/or more verses. As with linguistic grammars, people typically apply these musical grammars without any conscious knowledge of their existence. Acquiring conscious declarative knowledge can, however, enhance the automatic use of these grammars. Students of music composition learn to create more complex harmonic structures by studying music theory, just as school children improve their use of language by explicitly learning the rules of grammar.

Context and Meaning

Understanding meaning is not simply a matter of transforming surface to deep structure. Meaning also depends on context. When a communication is unclear, people automatically try to fill in the blanks to make sense of it, and their choice of letters or words is based on context. For example, readers fill in the missing letters to understand the message *ATTN: Joan Sullivan*, just as perceivers tend to see wholes and to perceive what they expect (Chapter 4).

One experiment showed how automatic this process of filling in the blanks is (Warren, 1970). Twenty subjects listened to a tape recording of a sentence in which a cough completely replaced one phoneme. In the sentence, "The state governors met with their respective legislatures convening in the capital city," the first *s* in legislatures was obliterated. The subjects were forewarned that they would be asked where in the sentence the cough occurred, yet most of them reported that no sounds had been obliterated, and the one subject who did think a phoneme had been lost identified the wrong one. **Phonemic restoration**—the process by which listeners replace a sound that has been obliterated by background noise—occurs so automatically that people are not aware of it. People use contextual knowledge more broadly in interpreting the meaning of spoken or written communications. They have little difficulty distinguishing the meaning of the word *sentence* when spoken by a judge rather than a linguist, for example.

FROM MIND TO BRAIN

NATURE AND NURTURE IN THE DEVELOPMENT OF LANGUAGE

The ability to use and comprehend language is a remarkable achievement—and one that children develop with astonishing rapidity. Within five or six years of life, children have mastered the basics of verbal communication. To explain this, some theorists have turned to principles of learning, whereas others have argued that the capacity to use language is an innate potentiality built into the human brain. The behaviorist B. F. Skinner explained verbal behavior using the same conditioning principles that apply to other forms of behavior, notably reward, punishment, generalization, and discrimination (Skinner, 1957; see also MacCorquodale, 1969, 1970; Moerck, 1986, 1992). According to Skinner and other behaviorists, verbal behavior, like any other behavior, is the result of an individual's history of reinforcement and current stimulus conditions. A baby who happens to gurgle *Muh* after his mother says "Say Mommy" will receive tremendous positive reinforcement from his delighted mother. Consequently, the baby will be more likely to say *Muh* in the future and to imitate the sounds his mother produces and subsequently reinforces. Later, his mother will be pickier about what she reinforces, shaping the baby's verbal responses to approximate adult speech more closely. She and other adults will also reinforce the child for grammatical constructions, which he will then generalize to create new sentences. He will also learn to respond appropriately to the verbal behavior of others. According to behaviorists, the most complex linguistic achievements result from these relatively simple principles.

The behaviorist perspective focuses on the nurture side of the nature-nurture controversy in language acquisition. The nature (or sometimes called "nativist") approach challenges the behaviorist perspective on a number of grounds (Chomsky, 1959, 1986; see also Stemmer, 1990). First, research shows that the emphasis on shaping in language acquisition is misplaced; mothers rarely provide negative feedback when their children make grammatical errors, and even when they do, children usually pay little attention (Brown & Hanlon, 1970; Morgan & Travis, 1989). In fact, mothers tend to focus on the *content* of their young children's speech rather than the grammar, providing negative feedback largely when they are entirely unable to understand their children's utterances. Thus, negative feedback typically follows only the grossest errors and is not a significant factor in learning the fine points of grammar (Gordon, 1990; Hoff-Ginsberg & Shatz, 1982).

Second and more importantly, the speed with which children learn language and the fact that children in different cultures go through very similar stages of language acquisition suggest that humans have an innate propensity for language wired into the brain (Caplan & Chomsky, 1980; Chomsky, 1986; Markman, 1992; Nelson, 1991). The presence of specialized centers for processing grammar and word meaning in the left frontal and temporal lobes, respectively, further suggests that language is innate (Chapter 3). According to Chomsky, children could not possibly learn the rules of grammar and thousands of words within such a few short years simply through reinforcement mechanisms. Rather, he argues, humans are born with what he calls a **Language Acquisition Device (LAD)** that allows them to understand the deep structure of language as their brains develop in early childhood. Thus, from an evolutionary perspective, the brain evolved modules to process specialized linguistic information just as the visual system developed specialized cells in the occipital cortex that respond to particular features of the physical world such as angles (Tooby & Cosmides, 1992). The brain adapted to regular features of the linguistic environment, just as it gradually changed its structure to match the structure of nature. The only difference is that the evolution of language capacities fed its own development, as increasing linguistic capacities allowed progressively more complex communication, which required further neural adaptation.

A third argument against the behaviorist position is that children routinely follow unconscious rules of grammar to produce utterances they have never heard before. Most English-speaking 4 year olds use the reflexive pronoun "hisself" instead of "himself," even though they have clearly never had this usage reinforced (Brown, 1973). Children essentially invent "hisself" by applying a general rule of English grammar.

Indeed, children exposed to language without proper grammar will infuse their language with grammatical rules they have never been taught. This has been demonstrated in research with deaf children exposed to sign language by their parents, whose ability to sign is often very limited (Pinker, 1994; Newport, 1990). These children typically become much better speakers than their parents even before they enter school, using grammatical constructions that their parents do not know. Again, this suggests that the tendency to order language using certain rules is innate.

Language acquisition, like most universal psychological attributes, obviously reflects cultural and biological influences, but nature has undoubtedly provided nurture with a stong headstart (Bruner, 1981, 1983; Moerck, 1992; Morgan, 1990). This becomes all the more apparent when examining the universal stages of language development.

From Babbling to Bantering

Long before they begin speaking, human infants display a sensitivity to distinctions between the phonemes that comprise human languages (Cohen et al., 1992). Researchers have documented this ability by measuring the rate at which one- and four-month-old infants suck on a pacifier as they listen to various sounds (Eimas et al., 1971, 1985). Infants will suck faster on a specially wired pacifier to look at a novel stimulus, which allows psychologists to learn how infants think and perceive (Chapter 13). One study investigated whether infants would respond differently to novel linguistic sounds, such as the phonemic change between *bah* and *pah*, than to other novel sounds (Eimas, 1985). In fact, a change in phonemic sound produced a much greater increase in sucking rate than a similar change that carried no potential meaning (Figure 7.13). This predisposition to perceive phonemic sounds provides support for Chomsky's assertion that natural selection has prewired the human brain for language.

Babies begin **babbling** (making utterances such as "lalala" or "baba") sometime between 6 months and 1 year. During this period—even before they speak their first words—their language development bears the imprint of their culture. The baby's innate attention to phonemic distinctions becomes markedly limited during this period, so that infants are soon sensitive only to phonemes in the language to which they are habitually exposed (Eimas, 1985; Kuhl, et al., 1992). One study showed that at

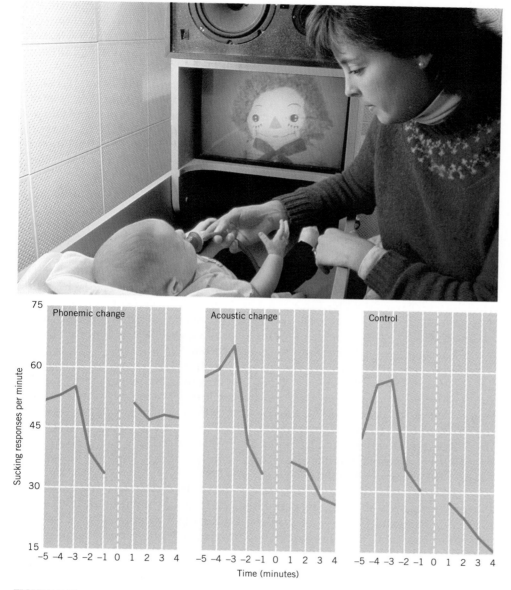

FIGURE 7.13

Infant response to phonemic change. A 4-month-old infant sucks on a pacifier connected to recording instruments while synthetic speech syllables are played through a loudspeaker. The graphs show the mean sucking rate under three conditions: phonemic change (e.g., bah to pah), acoustic change (new sound but same consonant), and control (no change). Sucking rate increases with the presentation of a syllable and then decreases as the stimulus becomes familiar (time -5 to -1). The sucking rate for infants in the phonemic change group increased sharply when the change occurred (Time 0), whereas the sucking rate for infants in the acoustic change group increased only slightly. SOURCE: Eimas, 1985.

the age of 6 months, infants of English-speaking families could discern phonemic distinctions typical of both the Hindi language and a Native American language called Salish. By 12 months, however, their ability to discriminate phonemes from these foreign languages had virtually disappeared (Werker & Tees, 1984).

Sometime between the ages of about 1 and 1-1/2 years, babbling gives way to a stage in which children utter one word at a time (although they may show frustration trying to use a single word to express a more complete idea or desire).

Sometime after the first year of life, children utter a single word at a time, often pointing to things.

Children's first words refer to concrete things or action, such as "mama," "ball," or "go." At about 18 to 20 months, they begin to form two-word phrases. From that point, the number of morphemes they combine in their utterances steadily increases. The use of grammatical niceties such as articles, prepositions, and auxiliary verbs expands as well.

Young children characteristically use **telegraphic speech**, leaving out all but the essential words (as in a telegram), producing phrases such as "Dog out" for "The dog is outside." By the age of 5 or 6, however, both their language comprehension and spontaneous speech reflect most of the rules of grammar (Brown, 1973). Table 7.6 illustrates the progression from telegraphic to grammatical speech in five children.

Influences on Language Development

Although the stages of language development are virtually universal, children acquire language at widely different rates (Goldfield & Snow, 1989; Richards, 1990). These differences in part stem from genetic predispositions, but they also reflect environmental influences. Probably the most important environmental factor is the day-to-day input and feedback that children get from their caregivers. One way caregivers facilitate infants' language development is by speaking "Motherese." Everyone is familiar with the dialect, as it is nearly irresistible when talking to a baby. Motherese is characterized by exaggerated intonation, a slow rate of speech, and high pitch (Fernald & Kuhl, 1987). The exaggerated style of Motherese may help infants recognize where phrases and sentences begin and end, a skill essential for future language learning (Gleitman et al., 1988; Morgan, 1986).

The content of the primary caregiver's speech is also important in language acquisition. When mothers repeat themselves ("Shall we go to the store? Let's go to the store") and expand on their children's telegraphic utterances (for instance, responding to "dog out" with "Is the dog out?"), their children tend to develop earlier in their ability to use verbs correctly. In contrast, merely acknowledging what the child has said without adding any new information ("That's right") is associated with delayed syntax development (Hoff-Ginsberg, 1986, 1990; Hoff-Ginsberg & Shatz, 1982; Newport et al., 1977).

Studies of children who do not receive normal feedback offer insight into the role of experience in shaping language development. One study investigated the language development of 3 and 4 year olds whose hearing was normal but whose parents were deaf and therefore could not provide normal feedback (Murphy & Slorach, 1983). Tape recordings of these children's speech indicated that their language development was well behind other aspects of their cognitive development, with incorrect syntax and poor vocabulary. Other research demonstrates that hearing-impaired children lag both in their repertoire of consonants and the number of syllables they use in each utterance (Geers & Schick, 1988; Stoel-Gammon, 1988; Stoel-Gammon & Otomo, 1986). Still other studies link child neglect to impaired speech comprehension and slow development of verbal expression (Allen & Oliver, 1982; Culp et al., 1991). Thus, while language development follows a universal schedule, the precise timing and course depends on many environmental factors.

A Critical Period for Language Development?

The interplay of nature and nurture in language development has led to a hotly debated question among psychologists and linguists: Does a critical period (Chapter 13) exist for language learning? In other words, is the brain maximally sensitive to language acquisition at a certain point in development (Lenneberg, 1967)? Children before age 12 seem to have an easy time learning languages, even acquiring a correct accent. Readers who have tried to learn a foreign language as teenagers or young adults have probably found that language acquisition is not so easy at later stages of life. As we have seen (Chapter 3), the development of the brain depends

TABLE 7.6 PROGRESSION FROM TELEGRAPHIC SPEECH TO COMPLETE SENTENCES IN CHILDREN AGES 25-1/2 TO 35-1/2 MONTHS

IMITATIONS OF SPOKEN SENTENCES

Model Sentence	Eve, 25-1/2	Adam, 28-1/2	Helen, 30	Ian, 31-1/2	June, 35-1/2
1. I showed you the book.	I show the book.	I show book.	C	I show you the book.	Show you the book.
2. I am very tall.	My tall.	I very tall.	I very tall.	I'm very tall.	I very tall.
3. It goes in a big box.	Big box.	Big box.	In big box.	It goes in the box.	C
4. Read the book.	Read book.	Read book.	—	Read a book.	C
5. I am drawing a dog.	Drawing dog.	I draw dog.	I drawing dog.	Dog.	C
6. I will read the book.	Read book.	I will read book.	I read the book.	I read the book.	C
7. I can see a cow.	See cow.	I want see cow.	C	Cow.	C
8. I will not do that again.	Do again.	I will that again.	I do that.	I again.	C
9. I do not want an apple.	I do apple.	I do a apple.		I do not want apple.	C
10. Do I like to read books?	To read book?	I read books?	I read books?	I read book?	I don't want apple.
11. Is it a car?	't car?	Is it car?	Car?	That a car?	C
12. Where does it go?	Where go?	Go?	Does it go?	Where do it go?	C
13. Where shall I go?	Go?	—	—	C	C

Source: Brown and Fraser, 1963.

— indicates no intelligible imitation was obtained
C indicates imitation was correct

on certain kinds of environmental enrichment, and neurons and neuronal connections not used at age-appropriate times may die or disappear (Cowan, 1979). Exposure to language may be necessary for lateralization of linguistic processes to the left hemisphere, which is typically completed between ages 2 and 5 (Kalat, 1988; Kinsbourne & Smith, 1974).

The language development of children raised in extreme isolation also provides some evidence for the critical period hypothesis. A child known as Genie, found at the age of 13, had lived in a tiny room tied to a chair from the time she was 20 months. She was rarely spoken to, although her father occasionally barked at her. After she was discovered, linguists and psychologists worked with her intensively. Genie acquired a reasonable vocabulary and learned to combine words into meaningful phrases, but she never progressed beyond telegraphic speech (Curtiss, 1977; Fromkin et al., 1974; Rymer, 1992a, b). Other research, however, is less supportive of the critical period hypothesis. Children have been known to recover completely from aphasia that resulted from brain damage after the age of 11 (Prakash, 1984), suggesting that the brain can still rewire itself for language, at least in some cases, after that time.

Nonverbal Communication

People communicate verbally through language, but they also communicate nonverbally. When a parent calls a child by her whole name, it may be to chastise or to praise, depending on the inflection and intonation. ("Jennifer Marie Simp*son* [rising tone on last syllable]? *Stop teasing your brother*," versus "Jennifer Marie Simp*son* [lowering tone on last syllable]. You are *so smart*.") Even when no words are spoken, clenched fists and a tense look convey a clear message.

The grammar of nonverbal communication differs by culture. What feels uncomfortably close in one culture may signal friendship in another.

Nonverbal communication includes a variety of signals: intonation (tone of voice), body language, gestures, physical distance, auditory signals (nonverbal vocalizations), facial expressions, and even touch and smell (Dil, 1984). Being conversant in the grammars of nonverbal communication can be just as important in interpersonal relations as understanding the grammar of verbal language. When a person sits too close to you on a bus or holds his face too close to yours when talking, the effect can be very unsettling. Like other grammars, this one is largely unconscious, encoded as procedural knowledge.

Just how important is nonverbal communication? In a recent study, subjects were shown 30-second video clips of graduate-student teaching assistants and asked to rate them using a number of adjectives, such as accepting, active, competent, and confident. The investigators wanted to know whether these brief ratings from a single lecture would predict student evaluations of the teacher at the end of the term. The investigators added one extra difficulty: They turned off the audio on the videotapes, so that subjects could rely only on nonverbal behavior (Ambady & Rosenthal, 1993).

The findings are extraordinary (Table 7.7). Many of the correlations between initial nonverbal ratings and eventual student evaluations are as near perfect as one finds in psychology, in the range of .75 to .85. Teaching assistants who appeared confident, active, optimistic, and enthusiastic in their nonverbal behavior were much better teachers. Similar findings emerged when the investigators conducted a study of teachers in a high school, correlating ratings of brief nonverbal lecture behavior with the principal's assessment of their effectiveness. Correlations remained substantial (though of course lower) in both samples when judges were asked to rate *two-second* film clips!

TABLE 7.7 NONVERBAL BEHAVIOR AND TEACHER EFFECTIVENESS

VARIABLE	CORRELATION
Accepting	.50
Active	.77
Attentive	.48
Competent	.56
Confident	.82
Enthusiastic	.76
Likable	.73
Low in anxiety	.26
Optimistic	.84
Professional	.53
Warm	.67
Global variable: overall "presence"	.76

Source: Ambady & Rosenthal, 1993, p. 34.

Note. The table shows the correlations between ratings of brief videos of nonverbal behavior and teacher effectiveness ratings at the end of the term.

Is Language Distinct to Humans?

TIM: *Lana want apple.*

LANA: *Yes.* (Thereupon Tim went to the kitchen and got one.)
You give this to Lana.

TIM: *Give what to Lana.*

LANA: *You give this which-is red.*

TIM: *This.* (Tim held up a red piece of plastic as he responded.)

LANA: *You give this apple to Lana.*

TIM: *Yes.* (And gave her the apple.)

(Rumbaugh & Gill, 1977, p. 182)

This conversation is not between two humans but between a human and a chimpanzee named Lana. Apes lack the physiological equipment to speak as humans do, but several chimpanzees have been trained to use nonverbal symbols to communicate with human researchers. Lana learned a computer language called "Yerkish" (named for the Yerkes Regional Primate Research Center in Atlanta where the research took place), which used geometric symbols, or lexigrams, to represent concepts and relationships. Other apes have learned to use signs from American Sign Language or other systems using lexigrams.

The impressive accomplishments of these simian linguists have taught researchers a great deal about the language capabilities of nonhuman primates. One of Ann and David Premack's (1972) chimpanzees, Sarah, learned a vocabulary of about 130 plastic symbols, which she used with 75 to 80 percent accuracy (Figure 7.14). Another chimpanzee, named Nim Chimpsky, has reportedly expressed feelings through signs, saying "angry" or "bite" instead of actually committing those acts (Terrace, 1979). Language-trained chimpanzees have also proven capable of communicating with each other (Figure 7.15), albeit in a very limited fashion, using symbols taught to them by their trainers (Savage-Rumbaugh et al., 1978, 1983). Another chimpanzee who learned to use signs from American Sign Language was observed teaching signs to her son (Fouts et al., 1982).

Do such findings mean that the chimpanzee is, as one researcher put it, "a creature with considerable innate linguistic competence who has, by accident of nature, been trapped inside a body that lacks the proper vocal output modality" (Savage-Rumbaugh et al., 1983)? Although some researchers have compared the linguistic abilities of chimpanzees to human children at the stage of telegraphic speech (Gardner & Gardner, 1975; Nelson, 1987), others do not consider language to be monkey business. After five years of working with Nim Chimpsky, H. S. Terrace (1979) could only report a powerful skepticism about both the ability of chimpanzees to use language and the analogy to child language. While human children combine progressively more words as they get older, the average length of Nim's utterances never rose above 1.1 to 1.6 signs. Furthermore, children frequently use language as an end in itself, to draw attention to objects or events or to announce their intentions. Chimpanzees, Terrace observed, tend to use symbols either for purely pragmatic purposes (to request objects they want) or to imitate their trainers' communications (Seidenberg & Petitto, 1987).

Other psychologists are more convinced by the accomplishments of our primate brethren. Researchers from the Yerkes Regional Primate Research Center have described a chimpanzee named Kanzi who spontaneously began to use symbols to communicate with humans without any special training (Rumbaugh, 1992; Savage-Rumbaugh, 1990; Savage-Rumbaugh et al., 1986). Kanzi was born in captivity at Yerkes and was sent to the Language Research Center at 6 months with his mother.

FIGURE 7.14
Sarah's plastic symbols. Researchers provided Sarah, a chimpanzee, with plastic symbols to serve as language units that varied in color, shape, and size. The symbols were backed with metal so that Sarah could arrange them on a magnetic board. Each symbol stood for a single word or concept. (Sarah preferred to write her sentences vertically from top to bottom.) SOURCE: *Premack & Premack, 1972.*

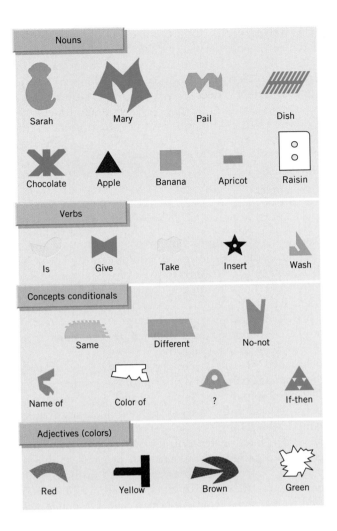

His mother was the subject of language training and was encouraged to communicate by pushing geometric symbols on a keyboard. Kanzi remained with her until he was 2-1/2 years old, observing her training sessions and often interfering by leaping on her or the keyboard, snatching food treats, and generally being a nuisance.

When Kanzi was 2-1/2, his mother was sent to the Yerkes breeding colony. To the researchers' surprise, Kanzi suddenly began using the keyboard to communicate,

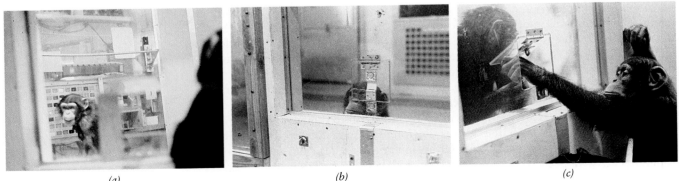

FIGURE 7.15
Two chimpanzees communicating. Sherman and Austin learned to communicate with each other using symbols taught to them by their trainers. In this sequence, Sherman requests M&Ms using his symbol board (a), while Austin watches (b). Austin then hands the M&Ms to Sherman (c).

asking for specific fruits. When presented with apples, bananas, and oranges, he would choose the fruit he had requested, demonstrating that he did indeed know what he was asking. Kanzi's human observers noted many ways in which Kanzi differed from Nim Chimpsky, arguing that Nim may have been a bit dim, so that his limited accomplishments did not adequately reflect the language capacities of apes. Unlike Nim, over 80 percent of Kanzi's communications occurred spontaneously. Kanzi also used language differently than Nim: He pointed out objects to the researchers, and he announced his intentions (for example, by pushing "ball" and then searching for his ball).

Psychologists who study language in nonhuman primates continue to disagree as to whether apes are capable of human language. (On the other hand, no one has definitively shown that humans can be taught to comprehend and use monkeys' communication systems, either.) Chimps apparently have the capacity to use symbolic thought under the right conditions, but are humans the only animals that can actually use language? Linguist Steven Pinker (1994) suggests that the question has actually been badly framed, based on the misconception that humans are the highest and latest rung on an evolutionary ladder that ran from orangutans to gorillas to chimpanzees to *Homo Sapiens*. Rather than a ladder, the proper analogy is a bush, with a common trunk but multiple branches. Gorillas, chimps, humans, and other living primates shared a common ancestor five to ten million years ago, at which point their evolutionary paths began to diverge like branches on a bush. Somewhere after that point, language began to evolve in the now-extinct ancestors of *Homo Sapiens*, such as *Homo erectus*. Natural selection has pruned the bush dramatically—roughly ninety-nine percent of all species become extinct—so that the bush is now quite sparse, leading to the misconception that the species left on the bush are close relatives rather than distant cousins. Pinker's (1995) conclusion to the debate about language in other primates in concise: "Other species undoubtedly have language. Unfortunately, they're all dead."

SOME CONCLUDING THOUGHTS

This chapter began with a conversation with a computer and ended with a conversation with an ape. Both examples show the limits of nonhuman cognition, but they also demonstrate that ours is not the only intelligence in the universe.

It has been said that humankind has suffered four major blows to its exalted conception of itself. First, Copernicus showed that we are not at the center of the universe, that we are just one species on one planet revolving around the sun. When humans persisted in seeing themselves as a privileged species separate from all other animals, Darwin suggested that we are little more than hairless monkeys—remarkable ones, but nonetheless continuous with other species. After Darwin, humans prided themselves on being distinguished from other animals by reason and consciousness—until Freud argued that reason and consciousness are a thin veneer and that below the surface we are primarily motivated by the same drives that direct the behavior of other animals (Freud, 1925). After Freud, what is left to defend as uniquely human? An apologist for the species might argue that the way we *think* still makes us special. Who else can create a syllogism, solve differential equations, or send a vessel into space? No one—except, of course, a computer.

Where the limits of artificial and animal intelligence lie is not entirely clear, but the human capacity for thinking is certainly extraordinary. In the last few chapters, we have focused on the way all people learn, remember, and think. The next chapter turns to differences among individuals in the way they apply thought and knowledge—that is, in their intelligence.

Summary

Units of Thought: Images, Concepts, and Propositions

1. **Thinking** means representing things mentally and operating mentally on these representations.

2. A **concept** is a mental representation of a class of objects, ideas, or events that share common properties. The process of grouping objects or concepts considered equivalent and excluding those that are not is called **categorization**. Concepts that have properties that clearly set them apart from other concepts are relatively **well defined; fuzzy concepts** are not easily defined by a precise set of features. According to some psychologists, when people categorize they often rely less on defining features than on **prototypes**—particularly good or typical examples of a category.

3. In categorizing objects, people naturally tend to use the **basic level,** the most inclusive level at which objects share distinctive common attributes. The way people categorize is partially dependent on culture and expertise.

4. **Proposistions** are the smallest units of meaning that can stand alone and be judged true or false.

Reasoning, Problem Solving, and Decision Making

5. **Reasoning** refers to the process by which people generate and evaluate logical arguments. **Inductive reasoning** means probabilistic reasoning from specific observations to generate propositions. **Deductive reasoning** is logical reasoning that draws conclusions from premises and leads to certainty if the premises are correct.

6. **Problem solving** is the process of transforming one situation into another that meets a goal. **Problem-solving strategies** are techniques that serve as guides for solving a problem.

7. **Decision making** is the process by which people weigh the pros and cons of different alternatives in order to make a choice. Making a rational decision involves a combined assessment of the value and probability of the different options, known as **expected utility.**

8. Whereas information-processing models assume that people are aware of their goals and motives, the psychodynamic perspective maintains that unconscious needs and wishes impinge on decision making. From a behaviorist perspective, people learn, generalize, and discriminate stimuli all the time without conscious thought.

9. Human thinking processes are not flawless. Two **heuristics** (cognitive shortcuts, or rules of thumb) that can lead to errors in information processing are the **representativeness heuristic**, which relies on resemblance of an object to a prototype, and the **availability heuristic**, which makes judgments on the basis of availability to consciousness. Other tendencies that can lead to errors in thinking include the **confirmation bias,** which refers to the tendency for people to believe and search for confirmation of what they already believe, and **functional fixedness,** which refers to the tendency to ignore other possible functions of an object when one has a fixed function in mind.

10. **Parallel distributed processing (PDP)** models propose that many cognitive processes occur simultaneously (in parallel) and are spread (distributed)

throughout a network of interacting neural processing units. PDP models differ from traditional information-processing models in two ways: by minimizing the importance of serial processing and by shifting from the metaphor of mind as computer to mind as brain.

Language

11. **Language** is the system of symbols, sounds, meanings, and rules for their combination that constitutes the primary mode of communication among humans. The basic units of sound are called **phonemes**. **Morphemes** are the basic units of meaning. **Grammar** refers to a system for generating acceptable language utterances and identifying unacceptable utterances. According to the **Whorfian hypothesis**, language shapes thought. The converse—that thought shapes language—is probably more often the case, but separating thought and language is difficult because so much thinking uses words.

12. Noam Chomsky distinguished **surface structure**—the particular way words are combined in a sentence—from **deep structure**, the underlying meaning. **Transformational grammar** attempts to define the rules people use in converting (transforming) surface to deep structure and vice versa. Chomsky argued for the presence of an innate **Language Acquisition Device (LAD)** to account for children's capacity for learning language; Skinner and the behaviorists, in contrast, argued for reinforcement principles. Chomsky was largely right that the brain is constructed to make language learning easy.

13. Cross-culturally, children go through similar stages of language development: **babbling**, **holophrastic speech**, **telegraphic speech**, and **grammatical speech**. However, the precise timing and course of individual language development depends on both nature and nuture.

14. **Nonverbal communication** includes body language, gestures, physical distance, intonation, facial expressions, and even touch and smell.

15. Researchers disagree as to whether chimpanzees can use language, much as they disagree on whether computers really "think."

Todd Siler, "Cerebral Book Form," *1983*

Chapter 8

INTELLIGENCE

*P*eter Franklin, a historian by training, had spent many years of his academic career as the dean of a prestigious liberal arts college. He was also a talented amateur musician and athlete who enjoyed good food and lively conversation. In 1971, while vacationing in Maine, he suffered a stroke. He had been at dinner with a longtime friend, Natalie Hope, and had gone to bed early with a slight headache. He next recalled waking up on the floor with clothing strewn around him, dragging himself outside, and being discovered by Mrs. Hope. He was drooling, disheveled, and confused.

When psychologist Howard Gardner met Mr. Franklin two years later at the hospital where he was being treated, Gardner asked what brought him there. Mr. Franklin replied, "Now, listen here. Now listen here. Well, I'll tell you. I said, sit down, strewn with clothes, sit, sit down, thank you, thank you. Oh goodness gracious, goodness gracious. Mrs. Hope, thank God, Mrs. Hope, going to bed. Sleeping. All right, all right.... And by the way Victoria Hospital, Maine. I said and, by the way. Dead. Dr. Hope, psychiatrist. Brilliant. All right and two days. Sick.... And doctors, doctors. Boys, boys, tip fifty dollars, tip, tip boys." Recognizing this to be a version of what had happened around the time of Mr. Franklin's stroke, Gardner asked, "Could you tell me what's bothering you now?" Mr. Franklin lashed out, shaking his fist, "Now listen here. Irritate. Irritate. Irritate, irritate, irritate, irritate, irritate, irritate! Questions, questions. Stupid doctors. No good, no good. Irritate. Irritate. Dean, dean, yes sir, yes sir.... That's all, that's all, forget it, forget it" (Gardner, 1975, pp. 6–7).

Mr. Franklin's linguistic abilities were impaired in many ways. He could not converse in a straightforward manner, express himself in writing, or follow complex commands. Standard measures of intelligence showed that he had lost much of his mental capacity, yet many of Mr. Franklin's abilities remained intact. He could easily hum familiar tunes and startled Gardner with his renditions of show tunes on the piano. He even maintained a sense of humor. One Saturday afternoon, when Gardner stopped by his office for a few minutes and saw Mr. Franklin in the hall, Mr. Franklin burst out laughing and commented, "Saturday, Saturday, doctor, golf [pantomiming a golf swing], tennis [pantomiming a tennis swing], lazy in the sun, enjoy no work, doctors, doctors.... Only joking, only joking" (Gardner, 1975, p. 11).

Mr. Franklin's case points to a number of questions that are central to understanding intelligence. First, what is intelligence? Can a man who cannot speak coherently but can play show tunes flawlessly be described as intelligent? Second, how accurate are commonly used measures of intelligence?   Mr. Franklin scored very poorly on IQ tests, yet he maintained a sense of humor as well as other capacities reflecting intelligent thinking. Third, is intelligence a general trait, or do people possess different kinds of intelligence, from one that facilitates verbal conversation to another that allows a person's fingers to dance deftly across the ivories?   Finally, to what extent is intelligence biologically or environmentally determined?

This chapter explores each of these questions in turn. We begin by discussing the nature of intelligence and the methods psychologists have devised to assess it, notably IQ tests. Next, we examine theoretical approaches to intelligence, from those that center on the kinds of abilities that best predict school success, to those that expand the concept of intelligence to include aptitudes in domains such as music and sports. We then address the controversial question of the heritability of intelligence—whether differences between people reflect differences in their genetic endowment. We conclude with the extremes of intelligence—mental retardation and giftedness—and exploring the relations among giftedness, creativity, and madness.

THE NATURE OF INTELLIGENCE

The concept of intelligence has so successfully eluded definition that long ago one psychologist somewhat sarcastically defined it as "what intelligence tests measure" (Boring, 1923). When asked what intelligence means, most people emphasize problem-solving abilities and knowledge about the world; they also sometimes distinguish between academic intelligence ("book smarts") and social intelligence or interpersonal skill (Berg, 1992; Sternberg et al., 1981; Sternberg & Wagner, 1993). In recent years, psychologists have come to recognize that intelligence is many-faceted and functional and that it is culturally defined.

The Multifaceted and Functional Nature of Intelligence

Intelligence is multifaceted; that is, aspects of it can be expressed in many domains. Most readers are familiar with people who excel in academic and social tasks and are equally adept at changing spark plugs and concocting an exquisite meal (without a cookbook, of course). Yet other people excel in one realm while impressing those around them with their utter incompetence in other domains. One psychologist with a national reputation in his field is equally well known among his friends and students as the prototypical absent-minded professor. He once drove to a conference out of town, forgot he had driven, and accepted a ride home with a colleague. As we shall see, speaking of "intelligence" may be less useful than speaking of "intelligences."

Intelligence is also functional. Intelligent behavior is always directed toward accomplishing a task or solving a problem. According to one definition, intelligence is "the capacity for goal-directed adaptive behavior" (Sternberg & Salter, 1982, p. 3). From an evolutionary perspective, intelligent behavior solves problems of adaptation and hence facilitates survival and reproduction. From a psychodynamic perspective, people use their intelligence to satisfy wishes and avoid things they fear. From a cognitive perspective, intelligence is applied cognition, using cognitive skills to solve problems or obtain desired ends.

Intelligence comes in different forms.

A GLOBAL VISTA

THE CULTURAL CONTEXT OF INTELLIGENCE

Another characteristic of intelligence is that it is culturally defined. If the function of intelligence is to help people manage the tasks they confront in their lives, then intelligent behavior is likely to vary cross-culturally, since the circumstances that confront members of one society differ markedly from those that face another. Indeed, the kinds of thinking and behavior recognized as intelligent vary considerably. Among the Kipsigi of Kenya, for example, the word *ng'om* is the closest approximation to the English word *intelligent*. The concept of *ng'om*, however, carries a number of connotations that Westerners do not generally associate with intelligence, including obedience and responsibility (Super & Harkness, 1980). Similarly, the Spanish equivalent of *intelligence* is *listura*, but Guatemalan parents who consider children *listo*, or intelligent, use the term to describe attributes such as high physical activity and independence, as well as alertness, good memory, and verbal skills (Klein et al., 1976). The Cree Indians of northern Ontario consider someone a "good thinker" if she is wise and respectful, pays attention, thinks carefully, and has a good sense of direction. The Cree also emphasize taking time (or proceeding slowly and thoroughly) and self-sufficiency (being able to survive without being a burden to others) (Berry & Bennet, 1992).

The attributes a culture considers intelligent are not arbitrary. The personal qualities, skills, and cognitive style a culture values tend to be integrally related to that culture's ecological context, modes of subsistence, and social structure (see Mistry & Rogoff, 1985). Cultures guide their members in efficient ways of solving everyday problems, and these strategies become part of the way individuals think (Vygotsky, 1978; Wertsch & Kanner, 1992). Western views of intelligence emphasize verbal skills (such as the ability to comprehend a written passage) and the kinds of mathematical and spatial abilities useful in engineering or manufacturing, which makes sense in a literate, technologically developed capitalist society. In most African cultures, intelligence tends to be defined in terms of practical abilities and competences (Serpell, 1989). For example, observers have commented on the almost encyclopedic knowledge of animal behavior possessed by some members of the !Kung tribe of Africa's Kalahari Desert, which is adaptive for people who must hunt and avoid dangerous animals (Blurton-Jones & Konner, 1976). Cultural groups who depend on the sea for their livelihood often show an extraordinary ability to remember relevant landmarks or calculate locations in navigating the ocean (Gladwin, 1970). Sir Francis Galton, a pioneer in research on intelligence, described one Eskimo who

> with no aid except his memory...drew a map of a territory whose shores he had but once explored in his kayak. The strip of country was 1100 miles long as the crow flies, but the coast line was at least six times this distance. A comparison of the Eskimo's rude map with an Admiralty chart printed in 1870 revealed a most unexpected agreement. (Werner, 1948, p. 147, in Berry & Irvine, 1986)

Is intelligence, then, a property of individuals, or is it simply a social construction or value judgment? To put it another way, is intelligence solely in the eye of the beholder? Probably not. Some attributes, such as mental quickness or the ability to generate solutions when confronted with novel problems, are valued in any culture. Moreover, among cultures at a similar level of technological development, concepts of intelligence tend to have many shared elements because demands on individuals are similar. An intelligent Norwegian is not very different from an intelligent American, although the Norwegian is like-

Navigational skills are essential for survival and hence highly developed among the Truk Islanders in Micronesia.

ly to know more languages—itself an aspect of intelligence in a small country surrounded by countries with many languages. As the United States increasingly depends on powerful trading partners around the world, particularly to its south, the lack of fluency in other languages characteristic of most people in the United States will probably be increasingly defined as unintelligent.

We can thus provisionally define intelligence as the application of cognitive skills and knowledge to learn, solve problems, and obtain ends that are valued by an individual or culture (see Gardner, 1983). As we will see in the following section, intelligence was not always so broadly defined, and only in recent years has the concept been expanded to include much more than what is measured in intelligence tests.

INTELLIGENCE TESTING

Measuring psychological qualities such as intelligence is not as straightforward as stepping on a bathroom scale. Psychologists use **psychometric instruments**—psychological tests that compare individuals in a population—to determine how people differ on dimensions such as personality attributes or intellectual abilities. Although scientists usually design measures to fit the construct they are trying to quantify (such as scales to measure mass), almost the opposite has occurred with the Western concept of intelligence, which has largely evolved along with the measures devised to assess it. **Intelligence tests** are measures designed to assess an individual's level of cognitive capabilities compared to other people in a population.

Historians credit Sir Francis Galton (1822–1911) of England with the first systematic effort to measure intelligence. A cousin of Charles Darwin and a member

Francis Galton

of his society's aristocracy, Galton set out to evaluate the implications of the theory of evolution for human intelligence (Berg, 1992). He was convinced that intelligence and social preeminence were products of the evolutionary process of "survival of the fittest," so that the upper classes were the most intelligent. Galton also believed that the building blocks of intelligence are simple perceptual, sensory, and motor abilities. Like his German contemporary, the structuralist psychologist Wilhelm Wundt, Galton argued that by studying the "atoms" of thought one could make inferences about the way they combine into larger intellectual "molecules."

To prove his theory, Galton set up a laboratory at London's 1884 International Exposition, where, for threepence, some 10,000 people underwent tests of reaction time, memory, sensory ability, and other intellectual tasks. Galton's findings failed to demonstrate any correlation between social class membership and intelligence as he measured it. Nor did he find any association between the perceptual-motor skills he tested and commonly recognized products of intelligence, such as scientific achievement. Galton is considered the father of mental tests (Boring, 1950), but history will probably remember him more generously as a pioneering statistician who first expressed the relationship between two variables using the correlation coefficient (Chapter 2), which is an important statistical tool in understanding intelligence.

Binet's Scale

The most direct ancestor of today's intelligence tests was developed in 1905 in France by Alfred Binet (1857–1911). Unlike Galton, Binet believed that a true measure of intelligence is an individual's performance on *complex* tasks of memory, judgment, and comprehension (Berg, 1992; Kail & Pellegrino, 1985). Also unlike Galton, Binet was less interested in comparing adults in their intellectual functioning than in measuring intellectual potential in children.

Binet's purpose was quite practical. In 1904, an education commission in France recommended the establishment of special schools for retarded children. This project required some objective way of distinguishing these children from their intellectually normal peers (Kail & Pellegrino, 1985; Tuddenham, 1962). Binet and his associate, Theodore Simon, noted that problem-solving abilities increase with age. They constructed a series of tasks ranging in difficulty from simple to complex, to capture the ability of children at different ages. A 7 year old could explain the difference between paper and cardboard, for instance, whereas this task would be beyond the ability of a typical 5 year old (Peterson, 1925).

To express a child's level of intellectual development, Binet and Simon (1908) introduced the concept of mental age. **Mental age (MA)** is the average age at which children achieve a particular score. A child with a chronological (or actual) age of 5 who can explain the difference between paper and cardboard and answer similar questions at a 7-year-old level has a mental age of 7. A 5 year old who can answer the questions expected for her own age but not for higher age levels is said to have a mental age of 5. Thus, for the average child, mental age and chronological age coincide. From this standpoint, a mentally retarded child is just what the term implies: retarded, or slowed, in cognitive development. A mentally retarded 7 year old might miss questions at the 7- and 6-year-old levels and be able to answer only some of the 5-year-old items.

Intelligence Testing in the United States

Binet's scale was translated and extensively revised by Lewis Terman of Stanford University, whose revision was known as the **Stanford-Binet Scale** (1916). Perhaps the most important modification was the **intelligence quotient**, or **IQ**, a score meant to quantify intellectual functioning in a way that allows comparison

Alfred Binet

among individuals. To arrive at an IQ score, Terman relied on a formula for expressing the relation between an individual's mental age and chronological age that had been developed a few years earlier in Germany. The formula derives a child's IQ by dividing mental age by chronological age and multiplying by 100:

$$IQ = (MA/CA) \times 100.$$

If a child with the chronological age of 8 performs at the level of a 12 year old (in other words, displays a mental age of 12), the child's IQ is 12/8 x 100, or 150. Similarly, a 12-year-old child whose test score is equivalent to that expected of an 8 year old has an IQ of 66; and a 12 year old who performs at the expected level of a 12 year old has an IQ of 100. By definition, then, a person of average intelligence has an IQ of 100.

When intelligence testing crossed the Atlantic, another modification occurred which was at once more subtle, profound, and enduring than the intelligence quotient. Binet had developed intelligence testing for a purpose: to predict school success. For that purpose intelligence testing was, and is, highly successful. But in North America, particularly in the United States, IQ became synonymous with "smarts" rather than "school smarts." People became preoccupied with IQ as a measure of general intellectual ability that could predict their children's ultimate success in life, like a deck of psychological tarot cards.

Group Tests

Terman's adaptation of Binet's scale gained rapid use, for the intelligence test filled a number of pressing needs of U.S. society. One of the most important was military (Weinberg, 1989). At the time of Terman's 1916 revision of his test, the United States was involved in World War I, and the army needed to recruit hundreds of thousands of soldiers from among millions of men, many of them recent immigrants. IQ testing promised a way of determining quickly which men were mentally fit for military service and, of those, which were likely to make good officers.

The army appointed a committee that included Terman to adapt mental testing to these needs. The result was two tests, the Army Alpha for literate adults and the Army Beta for men who either were illiterate or did not speak English (Figure 8.1). Unlike the Stanford-Binet, which required one-on-one administration by trained personnel, the army tests were **group tests**, paper-and-pencil measures that can be administered to a roomful of people at a time. Between September 1917 and January 1919, over 1.7 million men took the Army Alpha test.

Group tests are widely used today to assess IQ and related attributes. A modern group test with which most North American students are familiar is the **Scholastic Aptitude Test**, or **SAT**. As its name implies, the SAT is theoretically designed to measure a person's **aptitude**, or potential for performing well, on scholastic tasks. The name is somewhat misleading, however, for the SAT measures verbal and mathematical reasoning skills that are to a large degree learned (Cohen et al., 1992). Thus, the SAT is as much an **achievement test** (a test of knowledge in a specific area) as it is an aptitude test, which is why test-taking courses can often improve test performance (Kulik et al., 1984; Messick & Jungeblut, 1981; but see Powers, 1993).

The Wechsler Intelligence Scales

Although the Army Beta tried to circumvent the problem of language, the intelligence tests used early in this century were linguistically and culturally biased towards native-born English speakers. David Wechsler attempted to minimize these biases by creating a new instrument, the Wechsler-Bellevue tests (Wechsler, 1939). The latest renditions of these tests are the **Wechsler Adult Intelligence Scale-Revised, or WAIS-R** (1981), and the child version (appropriate through age 16), the **Wechsler Intelligence Scale for Children-Revised, or WISC-R** (1991). IQ as measured by these

FIGURE 8.1
Army Beta test for nonliterate adults. In this set of items, subjects are asked to name the part of each picture that is missing.

tests is a composite score derived from 11 subtests, only 6 of which depend on verbal ability; the other 5 involve nonverbal tasks. The verbal subtests require facility at symbolic thought and language, such as knowledge of general information, arithmetic skills, ability to hold and manipulate numbers in short-term memory, and vocabulary. The nonverbal, or performance subtests present tasks such as object assembly (assembling a jigsaw puzzle) and picture completion (finding missing elements in a picture) that do not depend as heavily on verbal thinking (Table 8.1).

In addition to a single, overall IQ score, the Wechsler scales yield separate scores for each of the 11 subtests and overall scores for verbal and performance intelligence. This feature not only provides a way of evaluating problem-solving capabilities with relatively little dependence on language, but it also allows psychologists to identify specific problem areas or strengths. Peter Franklin, the historian from the opening vignette, would probably not receive an abnormally low Vocabulary score, for he appeared to remember the meaning of many words. On similarities, however, which requires abstract verbal reasoning rather than retrieval of previously stored declarative information, the effects of the stroke would be apparent.

TABLE 8.1 SAMPLE ITEMS SIMILAR TO THOSE ON THE WAIS-R VERBAL AND PERFORMANCE SUBTESTS

VERBAL SUBTESTS		PERFORMANCE SUBTESTS	
Information:	"Who wrote *Silas Marner*?"	Digit Symbol:	Tests speed and accuracy of matching digits with symbols; e.g., putting a "2" in a box above every "~"
Comprehension:	"What does this saying mean: 'A rolling stone gathers no moss'?"	Picture Completion:	Tests speed and accuracy of finding missing parts of pictures; e.g., the laces on a boot
Arithmetic:	"A boy ran 50 yard in 10 seconds. How many yards did he run per second?"	Block Design:	Tests speed and accuracy in matching a design with red and white blocks, e.g.,
Similarities:	"How are fast and slow alike?"	Picture Arrangement:	Tests speed and accuracy in putting cartoon frames in the right order to tell a story; e.g., frames depicting (1) a robber running from a bank, (2) a robber at a teller's window, and (3) a robber in handcuffs should be ordered by the subject 2-1-3
Digit Span:	"Repeat the following numbers backwards: 8-4-2-1-9."		
Vocabulary:	"What does 'tenacious' mean?"	Object Assembly:	Tests speed and accuracy in a task like a jigsaw puzzle; e.g., assembling a hammer

Source: Items similar to those in the Wechsler Adult Intelligence Scale-Revised. Copyright © 1981, 1955 by The Psychological Corporation. Reproduced by permission. All rights reserved.

Frequency Distribution of IQ Scores

Wechsler was responsible for another important innovation in IQ testing. The formula originally devised for deriving IQ (MA/CA × 100) was useful in assessing children's test performance, but it was logically inconsistent when applied to adult test scores. As people grew older, the denominator (chronological age) in the formula grew larger, while the numerator (mental age) remained relatively constant. Thus, subjects seemed to become less intelligent with age. Although this fits with intuitive theories held by many teenagers about their parents, as we will see in Chapter 13, it is not really true. Wechsler remedied the problem by abandoning the concept of mental age and calculating IQ as an individual's position relative to peers of the same age on a frequency distribution (1958).

A frequency distribution (Chapter 2 Supplement) describes the frequency of various scores in a sample of a population. Like the distributions for weight, height, and many other human traits, the distribution for IQ takes the form of a normal, bell-shaped curve (Figure 8.2). A normal curve is a frequency distribution in which

Drawing by Sidney Harris

the vast majority of subjects receive scores close to the mean, leading to the bell-shaped curve. Extremely high IQ scores, such as 150, are relatively rare, as are extremely low scores, such as 50. Most people's scores fall within the average range (between about 85 and 115), while a progressively smaller percentage fall within ranges that deviate farther from the norm.

Limitations of IQ Tests

As we have seen (Chapter 2), the validity of a psychological test refers to its ability to assess the construct it is attempting to assess. If by "intelligence" one means the kind of mental ability that allows people to succeed in school, then intelligence tests have considerable validity. Recall from Chapter 2 that one way of determining a test's validity is to correlate its results with some external measure. IQ, as determined by intelligence tests, is strongly related to school grades, showing a cor-

FIGURE 8.2
Frequency distribution of IQ scores. The frequency distribution for IQ takes the form of a bell-shaped curve. SOURCE: *Anastasi, 1988.*

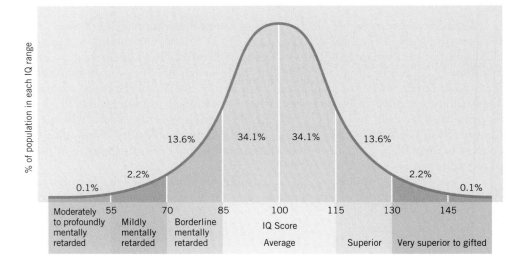

relation coefficient between .60 and .70 (where 1.0 is a perfect correlation coefficient and 0 is no correlation at all) (Brody, 1992; Wilkinson, 1993). In psychological research, this is as robust a correlation as can be found. It is far higher, for example, than the ability of any test of a personality trait (such as conscientiousness) to predict behavior (such as the tendency to come to work or class on time).

Nevertheless, IQ testing has drawn criticism and controversy for many years, largely for two reasons. The first is its lack of a theoretical basis. As one psychologist has noted, "Social needs have seemed to lead, and theoretical developments to follow, the changes in mental tests over the last half century" (Tuddenham, 1962, p. 515). IQ tests have, in many respects, been tests in search of a construct. The question raised by this lack of theoretical clarity is whether the kind of abilities required for academic performance, which IQ assesses with considerable validity, can be equated with general intellectual ability. In contrast to current popular conceptions of IQ, Binet himself never considered his test a measure of native ability but only a means of diagnosing performance deficits (Fass, 1980). Critics argue that the most widely used IQ tests provide little insight into the type of practical intelligence involved in achieving goals in everyday life (Atwater, 1992; Scribner, 1986; Sternberg & Wagner, 1993). Nor do they assess creativity, interpersonal skill, or—as in Mr. Franklin's case—the ability to play a tune.

A second concern frequently raised about IQ tests is their vulnerability to cultural biases. Consider the following questions from the Army Alpha test administered in the early part of this century:

Crisco is a: a) patent medicine, b) disinfectant, c) toothpaste, d) food product.

The number of a Kaffir's legs is: a) 2, b) 4, c) 6, d) 8.

Christy Mathewson is famous as a: a) writer, b) artist, c) baseball player, d) comedian. (Reprinted in Gould, 1981, p. 200)

The knowledge that Crisco is a food product, that a Kaffir (like any other human) has two legs, or that Christy Mathewson was a baseball player demonstrates a familiarity with early twentieth-century U.S. culture more than basic intelligence.

Since the days of the Army Alpha, intelligence tests have undergone considerable revision to eliminate cultural bias. How successful these efforts have been, however, is a matter of debate. Some psychologists argue that intelligence and aptitude tests continue to favor the dominant white middle class (Darou, 1992; Elliott, 1988; Schiele, 1991). Indeed, some opponents of IQ testing contend that IQ tests, like other standardized tests such as the SAT, are *designed* to do so, in order to justify the perpetuation of social inequality (Garcia, 1979; Putnam, 1973; Weinberg, 1989). At issue is the 15-point difference that separates the average IQ scores of white Americans and African Americans (Loehlin et al., 1975). Also at issue is the fact that IQ is strongly correlated with socioeconomic status; that is, poor and working-class people tend to receive lower scores than those who are wealthier. Because educators use scores on IQ and similar tests such as the SAT to place students in different academic tracks throughout their school years and to determine who gets into elite colleges, such tests may legitimize the process of keeping the privileged classes privileged while closing the door to the disadvantaged.

How do these charges hold up against the evidence? Some cultural bias is unavoidable in IQ tests, even when their designers have the best of motives. Tests that may intuitively seem **culture-free** (that is, not dependent on a particular cultural experience) often carry hidden biases. An example is the task of categorizing geometric stimuli according to color or shape, which frequently appears in standardized intelligence tests. At first glance, this task seems culture-free: It requires no language, nor does it seem to depend on familiarity with cultural artifacts that are typically North American. As we saw in the previous chapter, however, this task can be quite confusing to nonliterate people, such as the Liberians, who have no experience with abstract geometrical figures taken out of context and reproduced on paper (Irwin & McGlaughlin, 1970). When the shoe is on the other foot, cultural

Drawing by Sidney Harris

bias becomes readily apparent. North American undergraduates asked to categorize leaves according to whether they come from vines or trees perform much more poorly than nonliterate Liberians (Cole et al., 1971).

Other seemingly culture-free elements of intelligence tests may also carry hidden biases, such as the use of timed tests. IQ and achievement tests impose strict time limits in answering questions. Although this may in part tap a universal feature of intelligence, namely, how quickly a person can think, it also reflects the cultural emphasis on speed characteristic of the advanced capitalist societies that created intelligence testing. The ability to work quickly is essential to a manufacturing economy, where sluggish workers hold up an assembly line and profit margins depend on rapid production. In contrast, many traditional cultures place less value on quick and independent thinking and instead prefer slow deliberation and collective decision making (see Berry et al., 1992).

IQ tests may be equally problematic in assessing subcultures within multicultural societies such as the United States and Canada, in part because many questions rely on knowledge that is more familiar to some groups than to others. For instance, one WISC-R Information subtest asks questions such as "Who wrote *Macbeth*?" and "On what continent is France?" Psychologists have raised particular concerns about the validity of IQ tests in assessing African Americans, many of whom are raised in low-income neighborhoods and have little exposure to Shakespeare or travel. Further, the Black English spoken in many of these homes differs substantially from the language assessed in standardized intelligence tests (see Stewart, 1969).

A case in point was African-American psychologist Robert L. Williams, who was advised to become a bricklayer after receiving an IQ score of 82 at the age of 15. He declined the advice and later illustrated the linguistic bias in IQ tests—after receiving his Ph.D.—by developing the Black Intelligence Test of Cultural Homogeneity. The test drew from a vocabulary more familiar to American blacks than to whites (Figure 8.3), and not surprisingly, blacks tended to outperform whites on it (Williams, 1974). Williams's test and ones similar to it are not offered

1. "To get down" means the same as
   a) to dominate   b) to travel   c) to lower a position
   d) to have sexual intercourse

2. "Boogie Jugie" means the same as
   a) tired   b) worthless   c) old   d) well put together

3. "The bump" means
   a) a condition caused by a forceful blow   b) a suit
   c) a car   d) a dance

4. "Leg" means
   a) it has a sexual meaning   b) a lower limb
   c) a white person   d) food

5. "Black Draught" means
   a) a cold winter wind   b) a laxative   c) a black soldier
   d) a dark beer

6. To "cop an attitude" means to
   a) leave   b) become angry   c) sit down
   d) protect a neighborhood

7. "Running a game" means
   a) writing a bad check   b) looking at something   c) directing a
   contest   d) getting what one wants from another person or system

8. A "boot" is
   a) a cotton farmer   b) a black person   c) an Indian
   d) a Vietnamese citizen

9. An "alley apple" is
   a) a brick   b) a piece of fruit   c) a dog   d) a horse

Answers: 1.d, 2.b, 3.d, 4.a, 5.b, 6.b, 7.d, 8.b, 9.a

FIGURE 8.3
Sample questions from the Black Intelligence Test for Cultural Homogeneity. This test drew from a vocabulary more familiar to blacks than to whites. Not surprisingly, whites tend to perform poorly on such tests. SOURCE: *Adapted from Williams, 1972, 1974.*

as serious alternatives to standard IQ tests, but they certainly make their point (see Elliott, 1988).

Are IQ tests, then, invalid, useless, and dangerous? The answer is not black-or-white: IQ tests are some of the most valid, highly predictive tests psychologists have ever devised, and they can be useful in targeting children on both ends of the bell curve who require special attention. Comparing members of markedly different cultures or subcultures can be problematic, but IQ tests *do* tend to be valid when comparing two people with similar backgrounds. IQ and SAT scores are just as predictive of school success within African-American samples as within white samples; that is, an African-American student with a high IQ is likely to fare much better in school than one with a low IQ (Anastasi, 1988).

Furthermore, despite their biases, IQ tests do evaluate areas of intelligence that are important in a literate industrial society, such as the ability to think abstractly, to reason with words, and to perceive spatial relations quickly and accurately. For many years, psychologists accepted the conclusion that intelligence tests predicted very little outside of the classroom, but a more recent evaluation of the evidence suggests that intelligence tests can be powerful predictors of job performance and occupational achievement (Barrett & Depinet, 1991). All ideology and academic controversies aside, few critics of IQ testing would probably choose a doctor with a low IQ if they needed treatment for heart disease.

APPROACHES TO INTELLIGENCE

IQ tests place individuals on a continuum of intelligence, but they do not explain what intelligence is. Three approaches to understanding the nature of intelligence are the psychometric approach, the information-processing approach, and a theory of multiple intelligences.

The Psychometric Approach

The **psychometric approach** tries to identify clusters of variables that correlate highly with each other and hence to reveal the structure or organization of the underlying skills or abilities. If subjects perform multiple tasks, strong performance on some of these tasks is likely to predict strong performance in other areas. Subjects who have good vocabularies, for example, usually have strong verbal reasoning skills as well. Because vocabulary and verbal reasoning are highly correlated, most of the time a subject's score on one will predict her score on the other.

The primary tool of the psychometric approach is **factor analysis**, a statistical procedure for identifying common elements or factors (in this case, primary mental abilities) that underlie performance on a wide variety of measures. Using factor analysis, researchers set up a table or matrix to show how scores on tests of different abilities correlate with one another (Table 8.2). Their aim is to reduce 10, 50, or 100 scores to a few aggregate or combined variables (factors). Once they identify a factor empirically, they examine the various items that comprise it in order to infer the underlying attribute it is measuring, such as verbal intelligence or arithmetical ability.

Spearman's Two-Factor Theory

The English psychologist Charles Spearman (1863–1945) was the first to apply factor analysis to intelligence tests. Spearman (1904, 1927) set up a matrix of correlations to see how children's test scores on various measures were related to their academic ranking at a village school in England. His analysis formed the basis for his **two-factor theory,** so named because Spearman believed the correlations he found were the result of two types of factors or abilities.

Spearman called the first factor the **g-factor,** or **general intelligence.** Children with the highest academic ranking tended to score well on such measures as arithmetic ability, general knowledge, and vocabulary, suggesting a general intelligence factor. Spearman believed that the g-factor explained why "almost any set of mental tests, no matter how different, will tend to exhibit positive intercorrelations" (Carroll, 1982, p. 38).

Yet Spearman also noted that subjects who performed well or poorly on math tests did not necessarily score equally well or poorly on other measures, such as vocabulary or general knowledge. The correlations among different subtests on a correlation matrix were far from uniform, just as the correlation between weightlifting and number of pullups was far higher than the correlation between weightlifting and sprinting speed in Table 8.2. Spearman therefore proposed another type of factor, an s-factor, to explain the differences in correlations between different pairs of measures. According to Spearman, **s-factors** reveal specific abilities unique to certain tests or shared only by a subset of tests. Individuals vary in overall intellectual acuity (the g-factor), but some people are adept at some kinds of reasoning (such as mathematical, spatial, or verbal) but mediocre at others.

Other Factor Theories

Factor analysis has proven useful in identifying common factors among the profusion of statistical data produced by intelligence tests. However, both the number of factors and the types of mental abilities revealed through factor analysis can vary depending on who is doing the analyzing. To illustrate why this happens, return to the matrix of correlations of physical skills presented in Table 8.2. We noted a somewhat stronger correlation between weightlifting and pullups and suggested that the factor common to the two might be muscle strength. Alternatively, however, one might have concluded that upper-body strength is the s-factor, or perhaps motivation to develop strong upper-body muscles. Factor analysis can yield many varying interpretations of the same findings, and it cannot rule out the possibility that different factors might have emerged if different questions had been asked.

TABLE 8.2 IDENTIFYING A COMMON FACTOR

	SPRINT	WEIGHTS	PULLUPS	PULSE
Sprint	—	.35	.45	.63
Weights		—	.70	.52
Pullups			—	.57
Pulse				—

Note. If a diverse sample were tested on these four measures, and the scores for each measure were correlated, the result might look something like this matrix. The correlations between each pair are moderate to strong: People who are good sprinters tend to be good at weightlifting (a correlation of +.35), and so forth. A common factor shared by all these variables that accounts for the positive correlations may be physical conditioning. The extremely high correlation between weightlifting ability and number of pullups probably reflects a more specific factor, muscle strength.

In fact, when others applied Spearman's factor analysis technique, they arrived at different interpretations. For example, L. L. Thurstone (1938, 1962) argued against the existence of an overriding g-factor, finding instead seven primary factors in intelligence: word fluency, comprehension, numerical computation, spatial skills, associative memory, reasoning, and perceptual speed. Wechsler's WAIS-R produces slightly different factors.

Limitations of the Psychometric Approach

The psychometric approach provides a set of measures that can accurately predict school performance from as early as the preschool years and can show how different abilities correlate with each other. Because psychometrics is purely a descriptive tool, however, it cannot *explain* the way people think intelligently. Even as a descriptive tool, factor analysis has drawn criticism. One problem is the proliferation of factors identified. One psychologist distinguished 120 types of intelligence (Guilford, 1956, 1992)—and these are just the factors that emerge from studying functioning on relatively brief tests related to scholastic abilities. How many thousands of additional factors might one find in everyday life?

The psychometric approach in many ways illustrates the problem of studying a domain without adopting a theoretical perspective. In trying simply to let the facts speak for themselves, and hence to describe intelligence objectively, psychometricians are actually forced to organize their data in highly subjective ways and to decide arbitrarily whether they have even collected the relevant data in the first place. This limits their ability to explain or even adequately describe intelligence, but their measures are still useful for predicting performance at school and work.

The Information-Processing Approach

In contrast to the psychometric approach, which tries to quantify basic abilities, the information-processing approach tries to understand the *processes* that underlie intelligent behavior (Sternberg, 1985). In other words, the information-processing approach looks at the "how" of intelligence instead of the "how much." It defines intelligence as a process rather than a measurable quantity, and it posits that individual differences in intelligence reflect differences in the cognitive operations people use in thinking (Brody, 1992; Ceci, 1990).

In principle, a cognitive psychologist interested in intelligence would test the abilities of subjects at every step of the information-processing sequence—from efficiency of sensory registration, to short-term memory capacity, to efficiency of various long-term memory systems, and ultimately to application of strategies for manipulating mental representations to solve problems and make decisions. He would present subjects with tasks such as repeating digits to measure short-term memory, or memorizing word lists to test explicit memory. For each process, a subject's score would be plotted on a frequency distribution (Figure 8.4). The cognitive psychologist would then examine how functioning on each variable interacted with functioning on the others and might determine which of the many bell curves best predicted some criterion of achievement such as academic performance.

Researchers have studied the cognitive processes that underlie performance on intelligence tests. They have found that three variables are particularly important in explaining individual differences: speed of processing, knowledge base, and ability to acquire and apply mental strategies.

Speed of Processing

We commonly apply the adjective "slow" to people who perform poorly in school or on similar tasks, and we describe more skilled performers as "quick." Several studies have examined the correlation between measures of intelligence and measures of processing speed (Buckhalt, 1991; Vernon & Mori, 1992; Vernon &

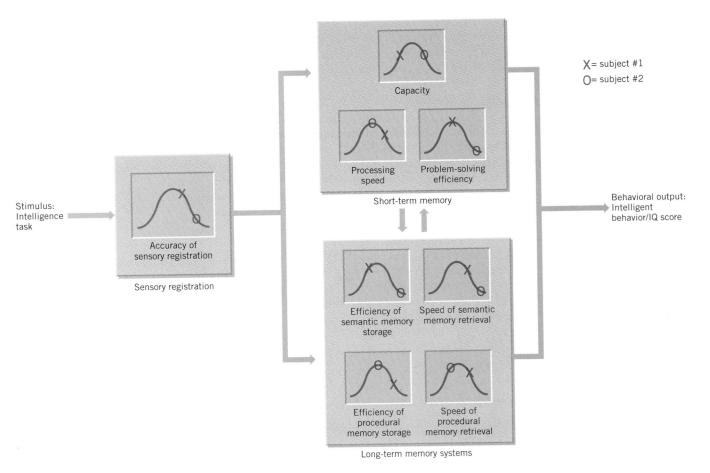

FIGURE 8.4
Multiple components of information processing. People have different degrees of ability and hence fall on different points of a bell-shaped curve on various components of information processing. Subject #2 is generally superior to subject #1 in problem-solving ability and verbal information processing (semantic memory), although the first subject is quicker in manipulating information in short-term memory and has a faster and more efficient procedural memory.

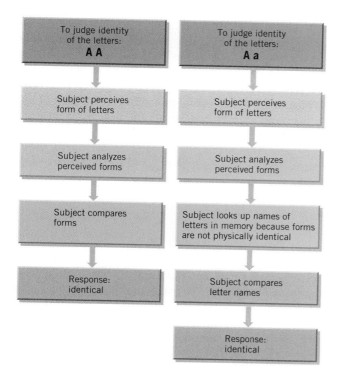

FIGURE 8.5
Speed of processing. In this study of speed of processing, investigators measured the time subjects took to decide whether pairs of letters were physically identical (AA) or identical in name (Aa). Judging name identity when physical identity is absent (b) requires an extra processing step and hence takes longer. SOURCE: *Based on Posner et al., 1969.*

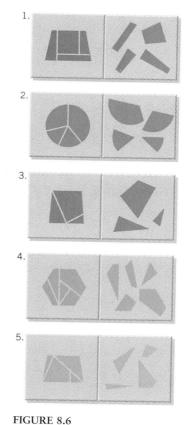

Weese, 1993). One experimental design presents subjects with pairs of letters and measures the amount of time they take to decide whether the letters are identical physically (as are the letters *AA* in Figure 8.5) or identical in name (as is the pair *Aa*). Judging name identity when physical identity is absent is the more complicated of the two tasks. To judge whether two letters have the same name even though they do not look alike, the subject must perform an additional step, searching long-term memory for the name of each letter form before comparing the two symbols. The difference in response times between these two types of task reflects the speed of memory search (Posner et al., 1969).

Research shows that differences in response time in tasks such as this correlate with measures of academic achievement (Campione et al., 1982). Children with above-average scholastic abilities tend to perform this kind of task more rapidly than average-ability children (Keating & Bobbitt, 1978), as do college students with higher IQs than their peers (Lindley & Smith, 1992). Studies using geometric figures (Figure 8.6) document a similar correlation between performance and visual processing speed (Kail & Pellegrino, 1985; Mumaw & Pellegrino, 1984).

Knowledge Base

Variation among individuals in intellectual functioning also reflects variation in their **knowledge base**—the information stored in long-term memory. Differences in knowledge base that affect performance include not only the amount of knowledge a person has but the way it is organized and its accessibility for retrieval (Glaser & Schauble, 1990). People who have expertise in a particular knowledge domain have well-developed schemas that facilitate encoding, retrieval, and mental manipulation of relevant information. Florists, for example, can generally recognize and classify flowers more quickly than people with less exposure to (and interest in) flowers (see Chi et al., 1982). A person with a broad knowledge base is likely to appear more intelligent in many domains simply by virtue of having a ready way of categorizing and retrieving information, like the baseball afficionado who can rattle off World Series scores from decades earlier.

FIGURE 8.6
Spatial transformation problems. Can the figure on the left be constructed from the pieces on the right?
Answers: 1—yes; 2—no; 3—yes; 4—yes; 5—no.
SOURCE: *Mumaw & Pellegrino, 1984.*

Ability to Acquire and Apply Cognitive Strategies

A third variable that correlates with many measures of intelligence is the ability to acquire mental strategies (such as mnemonic devices and formulas for solving math problems) and apply them to new situations. Cognitive strategies are essential for many everyday tasks, from remembering grocery lists to calculating a server's tip. Their efficient use distinguishes children from adults and individuals from their peers. Children are less likely than adults to apply mnemonic strategies such as rehearsal in memorizing information (Flavell & Wellman, 1976), although their performance improves considerably when they are taught and encouraged to use them (Best, 1993). In contrast to their peers, retarded children require more explicit instruction in mnemonic and problem-solving strategies. Moreover, once they have learned a strategy, they remain less able to apply it to different memory tasks than children of average ability (Campione et al., 1982; Niedalman, 1991).

Limitations of the Information-Processing Approach

Unlike the psychometric approach, the information-processing approach begins with a theory as well as a set of observations and uses the theory to explain the data. Although some researchers have started to explore the way people apply cognitive processes to real-world problems (Sternberg, 1985; Wagner, 1987), the major limitation of information-processing approaches is that many remain tied to the kind of intelligence used in academic situations and measured on IQ tests. As the study of intelligence moves into areas such as leadership ability or musical composition, however, traditional models and tasks may require revision. This is particularly true of domains of intelligence such as interpersonal skill because qualities like empathy may be difficult to model using information-processing concepts and methods.

A Theory of Multiple Intelligences

A third view of intelligence is Howard Gardner's **theory of multiple intelligences** (1983; Kornhaber et al., 1990). Gardner views intelligence as "an ability or set of abilities that is used to solve problems or fashion products that are of consequence in a particular cultural setting" (Walters & Gardner, 1986, p. 165). He identifies not one, but seven intelligences: musical, bodily/kinesthetic (such as the control over the body and movement that distinguishes great athletes and dancers), spatial (the use of mental maps), linguistic or verbal, logical/mathematical, intrapersonal (self-understanding), and interpersonal (social skills). Gardner would map a person's intelligence on seven different bell curves, one for each type of intelligence, rather than on a single IQ curve. Someone could be a brilliant mathematician but inhabit the lowest percentiles of musical or interpersonal intelligence.

Some of the intelligences on Gardner's list may surprise readers accustomed to equating intelligence with the logical and linguistic abilities assessed by IQ tests, but Gardner argues that defining intelligence only by the abilities assessed on IQ tests is problematic for several reasons. Although conventional IQ tests have some capacity to predict later occupational success, they are much better at predicting grades in school. A person with high interpersonal intelligence may become a superb salesperson despite having only average logical/mathematical abilities, or a brilliant composer may have poor linguistic skills. Furthermore, the emphasis on verbal and logical/mathematical intelligence in IQ measures reflects a bias toward skills valued in technologically advanced societies. Over the broad sweep of human history, musical, spatial, and bodily intelligences have tended to be more valued.

Selecting Intelligences

Gardner himself acknowledges that one can never develop "a single irrefutable and universally acceptable list of human intelligences" (1983, p. 60). On what basis, then, did he choose each of his seven intelligences? One criterion was whether

Jazz great Miles Davis and Ukrainian figure skater Oksana Baiul display forms of intelligence not measured on standard tests.

an intelligence could be isolated neuropsychologically. According to Gardner's view, people have multiple intelligences because they have multiple neural modules. Each module has its own modes of representation, its own rules or procedures, and its own memory systems. As in the case of Mr. Franklin in the opening vignette, brain damage may impair one system without necessarily damaging others. An intellectual skill that can be specifically affected or spared by brain damage qualifies as an independent intelligence. The modularity of intelligences means that a person's ability in one area does not predict ability in another (Gardner, 1983).

Another criterion emerged from savant and prodigy studies. **Savants** are individuals with extraordinary ability in one area but comparatively low functioning in others. For example, a young man with an IQ in the mentally retarded range was able to memorize lengthy and complex piano pieces in only a few hearings (Sloboda et al., 1985). The existence of **prodigies**—individuals with extraordinary and generally early-developing genius in one area but normal abilities in others—also supports the notion of separate, modular intelligence systems. Indeed, creative geniuses in fields such as music generally require strikingly little time to master their fields. This suggests that an important component of even a specific intelligence like musical ability may be mental quickness or ease of processing (Simonton, 1991).

A third criterion for selecting an intelligence is its distinctive developmental course from childhood to adulthood. The fact that one domain may develop more quickly or slowly than others supports the notion of multiple intelligences. Children learn language and mathematics at very different paces. The existence of prodigies is again instructive. If a Mozart could write music before he could even read, then the neural systems involved in musical intelligence must be separate from those involved in processing language.

Limitations of the Theory of Multiple Intelligences

Gardner presents a refreshing view of intelligence that draws on a far broader range of data than other approaches. It takes into account dimensions of behavior that are not commonly assessed in IQ tests but clearly require intelligence, from writing music to managing a crew of workers. His theory also firmly grounds intelligence in both its neurological and cultural context.

Nevertheless, like all theories, Gardner's has its limitations. One is that it underestimates the possibility of some kinds of general intelligence that are not domain-specific, such as the quickness across different domains that characterizes highly intelligent people. A second limitation of Gardner's theory is that it lacks measures of most of the intelligences, such as intrapersonal and musical, that would allow it to be tested empirically.

A third problem is the potential proliferation of intelligences. If bodily intelligence is a distinct domain of intellectual functioning, can one similarly distinguish dance intelligence, football intelligence, and tennis intelligence? If not, can one assume that someone with a talent for football could equally have turned that talent to ballet? Similarly, the concept of musical intelligence conceals differences between the intelligence required to write a symphony and that required to play pre-

TABLE 8.3 MULTIPLE MUSICAL INTELLIGENCES?

PLAYING LEAD MARIMBA IN AN AFRICAN MARIMBA BAND	PLAYING VIOLIN IN A SYMPHONY ORCHESTRA
Listen to the band and coordinate with it, especially rhythmically.	Listen to the orchestra and coordinate with it, especially on intonation and dynamics.
Maintain and manipulate tempo.	Follow the conductor.
Remember and produce the patterns and structure of the piece.	Read the music.
Plan and play variations.	Minimize variations.
Alter the piece according to the performance of the other players and the response of the crowd.	Ignore the audience—accept coordination from the conductor and the score.
Maintain excitement (through facial expression, body movement, whistling, shouting, singing).	Maintain decorum (modest body language).

Source: Adapted from Judd, 1988.

Note. The ability to perform on these two different instruments clearly reflects different kinds of musical expertise. To play the African marimba requires spontaneity, improvisation, and almost perpetual give-and-take with the audience and other musicians. The violin demands a highly controlled performance, an ability to read musical scores, and an ability to follow a conductor's cues.

cisely or expressively from a musical score. Differences even exist between the ability to perform on various instruments, such as the African marimba and the concert violin (Table 8.3). The marimba requires considerable spontaneity, with musical improvisations and almost perpetual give-and-take with both the audience and other musicians. The violin demands an ability to read a musical score and a highly controlled performance cued by the conductor (Judd, 1988).

HEREDITY AND INTELLIGENCE

Having some concept of what intelligence is and how to measure it, we are now prepared to address the most controversial issue surrounding the concept of intelligence: its origins. The question of the degree to which intelligence is inherited or learned is another incarnation of the nature-nurture controversy, and one that is emotionally loaded. We begin by examining research on the roots of differences among individuals in IQ and then turn to the thorny issue of differences among groups.

Individual Differences in IQ

The influence of both genetic and environmental variables on individual differences in intelligence is well established. On the environmental side, early malnutrition or a pregnant mother's exposure to a disease such as rubella (German measles) can impair a child's mental functioning (see McKeown & Record, 1976; Singh & Agrawal, 1987). These are purely biochemical factors, but environment contributes to intelligence in many other ways. One study found that mother-infant interaction and such factors as the general quality of the home environment are among the best predictors of a child's performance on IQ and language tests four years later (Bee, 1982). Subsequent research has produced similar findings (Beckwith et al., 1992; Hart & Risley, 1992; Landau & Weissler, 1993).

Further evidence of the role of environmental factors comes from a **longitudinal study** (a study following individuals over time) that examined the relation between a child's IQ at age 4 and 13 and the number of risk factors to which the child was exposed. Among these risk factors were maternal level of education, maternal mental illness, minority status (associated with, among other things, low standard of living and inferior schools), and family size. As can be seen from Figure 8.7, the child's IQ varied inversely with the number of risk factors: the more risk factors, the lower the child's IQ. Maternal IQ and multiple risks at age 4 were both highly predictive of IQ at age 13, with each correlation exceeding -.60, which is extraordinarily large.

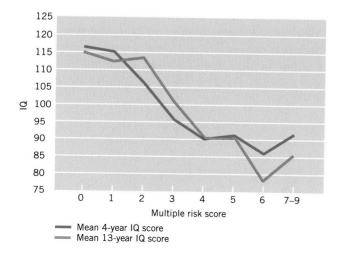

Mean 4-year IQ score
Mean 13-year IQ score

FIGURE 8.7

The impact of the environment on IQ. The figure shows the correlation between number of risk factors and child IQ at ages 4 and 13. By and large, each of several risk factors was highly predictive of IQ on its own, but the combination predicted IQ with a correlation near −.70 at both age 4 and 13. SOURCE: Sameroff et al., 1993, p. 89.

Children reared in unstimulating institutional environments, such as this Rumanian orphanage during the reign of the dictator Nicolai Ceaucescu, often suffer permanent intellectual damage.

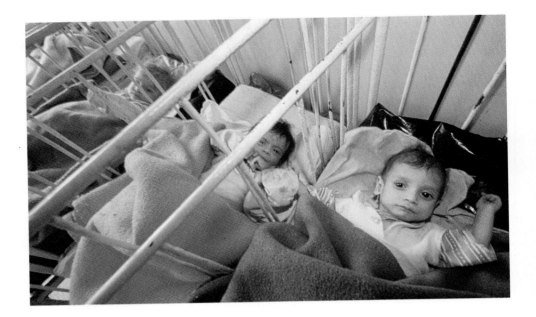

The results of this study are striking, but they cannot definitively tease apart the relative contributions of heredity and environment. Maternal IQ could influence the child's IQ genetically or environmentally, and it could indirectly influence some of the other environmental risk factors, such as low maternal education level. Other methods—notably twin, family, and adoption studies—can, however, distinguish the impact of nature and nurture. The logic of twin, family, and adoption studies is to examine subjects whose approximate degree of genetic relatedness is known and then to correlate degree of genetic relatedness with measured IQ. If the two correlate, this is evidence for a genetic effect. As described in Chapter 3, siblings, dizygotic (DZ) twins, and parent-offspring pairs are all related by .50. Monozygotic (MZ) twins are genetically identical (degree of relatedness = 1.0), whereas adoptive relatives are unrelated (degree of relatedness = 0). Thus, if genetic factors are important in IQ, MZ twins should be more alike than DZ twins, siblings, and parents and their offspring, and biological relatives should be more alike than children and their adoptive parents or siblings.

By and large, the data across dozens of studies show a substantial hereditary effect (Table 8.4). MZ twins are almost identical in IQ. As Table 8.4 shows, the environment also has a considerable impact on IQ. Being born at the same time (and presumably being treated more alike than nontwin siblings) produces a substantially higher correlation between DZ twins (.62) than between siblings (.41), even though both are related by .50. The higher correlation between MZ than DZ twins could reflect either an environmental variable—that parents treat identical twins more similarly than fraternal twins (Beckwith et al., 1991; Kamin, 1974)—or genetic influence; however, most data suggest that the genetic difference is more important (Bouchard et al., 1990; Kendler et al., 1993; Plomin et al., 1976; Scarr & Carter-Saltzman, 1982). Indeed, identical twins reared apart show an average IQ correlation of about .75, which is even stronger than DZ twins reared together (Bouchard et al., 1990; Newman et al., 1937; Plomin & DeFries, 1980; Shields, 1962).

Adoption studies provide a useful source of information on the relative roles of heredity and environment in the intergenerational transmission of IQ. Most of these studies compare the IQs of adopted children with those of other members of the adoptive family, the biological family, and a control group matched for the child's age, sex, socioeconomic status, and ethnic background. From the earliest adoption studies conducted in the first half of this century (Burks, 1928, 1938; Leahy, 1935; Skodak & Skeels, 1949), the results have pointed to genetics as the major influence

TABLE 8.4 CORRELATIONS IN INTELLIGENCE BETWEEN PAIRS OF PEOPLE WITH VARYING DEGREES OF RELATEDNESS REARED TOGETHER OR APART

RELATIONSHIP	REARING	DEGREE OF RELATEDNESS	CORRELATION	NUMBER OF PAIRS
Same individual		1.0	.87	456
Monozygotic twins	Together	1.0	.86	1417
Dizygotic twins	Together	.50	.62	1329
Siblings	Together	.50	.41	5350
Siblings	Apart	.50	.24	203
Parent-child	Together	.50	.35	3973
Parent-child	Apart	.50	.31	345
Adoptive parent-child	Together	0	.16	1594
Unrelated children	Together	0	.25	601
Spouses	Apart	0	.29	5318

> Interestingly, the IQ of adoptive parents has little association with the IQ of their adopted children.

> The environment appears to have a substantial impact, as dizygotic twins and siblings have the same degree of relatedness but different IQ correlations.

> Identical twins score as similarly as the same person taking the test on two occasions.

Source: Adapted from Henderson, 1982.

Note. The table summarizes the results from family studies comparing IQ among multiple pairs of individuals, contrasting the degree of relatedness with correlation of intelligence scores.

on IQ, with environmental circumstances substantially limiting or augmenting the effects of native ability (Cardon et al., 1992; Coon et al., 1990; Loehlin et al., 1989; Scarr & Carter-Saltzman, 1982; Turkheimer, 1991; Weiss, 1992).

In a classic study, researchers tested the IQ of each biological mother in the sample at the time of delivery, finding an average IQ of 86 (Skodak & Skeels, 1949). Years later, they tested the children, who were reared by adoptive parents (often of higher socioeconomic status), using the same test (the Stanford-Binet). At age 13, these children scored an average of 107, over 20 points higher than their biological mothers, providing strong evidence for the environmental component of intelligence. Subsequent French studies have similarly shown increases in both IQ scores and school performance among children adopted into families of higher socioeconomic status (Dumaret, 1985; Schiff et al., 1982), and another large study found IQ differences between twin pairs strongly correlated with the quality of the schools they attended (Dudley, 1991).

At the same time, however, in this classic adoption study as in others, the correlation between IQ of adopted children and their biological parents was considerably larger than the correlation with their adoptive parents' IQ. In other words, blood runs thicker than adoption papers in predicting IQ. For reasons that are not well understood, the correlation between the IQ of children and their adoptive parents also in this study diminished over the years. Other studies have found a similar

Studies of monozygotic (identical) and dizygotic (fraternal) twins provide a way of studying the impact of genetics on intelligence.

TABLE 8.5 CORRELATIONS AMONG IQS OF PARENTS AND CHILDREN IN THE TEXAS ADOPTION PROJECT

	INITIAL ASSESSMENT	FOLLOWUP
Adoptive father/Adopted child	.19	.10
Adoptive mother/Adopted child	.13	.05
Adoptive father/Biological child[a]	.29	.32
Adoptive mother/Biological child	.04	.14
Biological mother[b]/Adopted child	.23	.26
Adopted child/Biological child	.20	.05
Biological child/Biological sibling	.27	.24

[a] Biological child of parents who adopted other children
[b] Biological mother of child who was adopted out

Source: Adapted from Loehlin et al., 1990.

Note. The initial assessment data provide evidence for substantial contributions to IQ by both family environment and heredity. The 10-year followup data, however, suggest that the impact of the family environment decreases with age, as the only substantial correlations at followup were between biological relatives.

decrease over time in the correlation between IQ of adopted children and their adoptive siblings (Scarr & Weinberg, 1974, 1976; Scarr & Yee, 1980), with older adolescents resembling one another "only if they share genes" (Scarr & Weinberg, 1983).

Another large adoption study is the Texas Adoption Project (Horn et al., 1979, 1982). The investigators administered IQ and other tests to 1230 members of 300 Texas families that adopted one or more children from a home for unwed mothers. Researchers tested the adopted child, the adoptive parents, and other adopted or biological children in the family. Many of the birth mothers had taken IQ tests while at the home during their pregnancy, and the researchers had access to these scores. At the time the project began, the adopted children were between 3 and 14 years old. At this initial assessment, the correlations between the IQ of the adoptive parents and their adopted children were similar to the correlations between the IQ of the adoptive parents and their biological children (Table 8.5), suggesting substantial and similar contributions of heredity and environment. Approximately 10 years later, the researchers located and retested many of the subjects (Loehlin et al., 1989). This time the data presented a different picture of genetic and environmental influences. As Table 8.5 shows, the only correlations that remained above .20 were between biological relatives. The results of the Texas Adoption Project thus support the findings of other studies that both genes and environment influence IQ in childhood but the impact of the family environment decreases with age. Similarities among the IQs of family members are apparently a greater reflection of their shared genes than their shared environment (Brody, 1992).

Group Differences: Race and Intelligence

The 15-point discrepancy between the average IQ scores of blacks and whites in the United States has raised the question of the extent to which IQ differences among *groups* reflect genetic or environmental factors. Arthur Jensen created a storm of controversy over two decades ago when he concluded, based on the available data, that "between one-half and three-fourths of the average IQ difference between American Negroes and whites is attributable to genetic factors" (1973, p. 363; see also 1969; Jensen & Reynolds, 1982). Many denounced Jensen's interpretation of the data as blatantly racist, arguing that the conclusion leads inevitably to the implication that African Americans are genetically inferior and destined by their genes to second-class status. Putting aside for a moment the scientific credibility of his conclusion, lost in the furor were Jensen's own assertions that no such implication was warranted. He advocated equal opportunities for blacks and whites, arguing that racial differences in IQ

> should not be permitted to influence the treatment accorded to individuals of any race—in education, employment, legal justice, and political and civil rights. The well-established findings of a wide range of individual differences in IQ and other abilities within all major racial populations and the great amount of overlap of their frequency distributions, absolutely contradicts the racist philosophy that persons of different races should be treated differently, one and all, only by reasons of their racial origins. (Jensen, 1980, pp. 737–738)

Nevertheless, the potential implications of Jensen's hypothesis made it among the most passionately debated in the history of psychology. In the 1970s, psychologists put Jensen's hypothesis to the test in the Minnesota Adoption Study, examining the IQ of children of various races adopted by white middle-class families (Scarr & Weinberg, 1976, 1983). Black children who had been adopted in the first year of life scored an average IQ of 110, at least 20 points higher than comparable children raised in the black community, where economic deprivation is more common. When the researchers retested as many of the adoptees as they could locate 10 years later, the IQ scores of black adoptees remained above the average IQ of blacks raised in the black community, suggesting a substantial environmental effect, although their mean IQ was somewhat below the mean IQ for whites in the sample (Weinberg et al., 1992).

Another study (Scarr et al., 1977) used an entirely different approach to test Jensen's hypothesis. Because a substantial proportion of American blacks have mixed ancestry, one of the measures the researchers used was the chemical composition of blood samples. If a substantial portion of racial IQ differences are attributable to genetics, then IQ levels should rise and fall in direct proportion to the degrees of African and European ancestry in a subject's blood. In fact, the researchers found no correlation between IQ and racial ancestry, refuting the genetic hypothesis.

Still other research supports the influence of the environment. One study of black children whose families had moved north to Philadelphia between World Wars I and II found that subjects gained between 0.5 and 0.7 IQ points for each year they were enrolled in Philadelphia schools (Lee, 1951). Together, these various lines of research suggest that IQ is malleable and that, as a leading authority concludes, "it is highly unlikely that genetic differences between the races could account for the major portion of the usually observed differences in the performance levels of [blacks and whites]" (Scarr & Carter-Saltzman, 1982, p. 864).

How can individual differences in intelligence be largely genetic, while group differences are largely environmental (see Gould, 1981, 1994)? The answer becomes clear through an analogy. Anyone who has ever visited a war museum notices immediately how small the uniforms were even a century ago. If researchers were to measure skeletal remains, they might find that most men who fought in the civil war ranged from 5'2" to 5'6", with an average of 5'4", and that tall fathers tended to beget tall sons. Were they to assess men who fought in the Vietnam War one hundred years later, they would similarly find high heritability, but the average height would be several inches taller. In both samples—from the same country, a mere century apart—heritability is high, but the difference between the average height in 1865 and 1965 is entirely environmental, largely resulting from nutritional differences. Similarly, genetic differences could account for many of the observed differences between individuals in IQ, while environmental effects could account for observed differences between groups.

Commentary: The Science and Politics of Intelligence

It is tempting to conclude, then, that group differences in intelligence can be explained in terms of environmental differences, such as social disadvantage, nutrition, and quality of education. Although research projects such as the Minnesota and racial ancestry studies seem to refute genetic explanations for racial differences in intelligence, a few words of caution are in order.

The question of genetic versus environmental components of intelligence is a highly emotional issue, particularly with respect to racial differences. The notion that a mental attribute as highly valued in our society as intelligence could be genetically determined goes against the grain of many of our most fundamental beliefs and values, including the view that we are all created equal (see Fletcher, 1990). Furthermore, claims of racial superiority have a long and sordid history in human affairs, certainly in our own century. Hence, any psychologist who argues for a genetic basis to any racial differences is immediately suspect, and the psychological community has, by and large, been much less critical of studies that purport to refute genetic or racial differences.

A case in point concerns published reports of an intervention program that took place in the late 1960s and early 1970s. This program, known as the Milwaukee Project, provided an intellectually enriched environment for children who were at high risk for mental retardation. The program's results seemed impressive. The investigators reported an average difference of 24 IQ points between the program's children and a control group. The findings were described in every introductory psychology textbook for nearly two decades to illustrate the decisive impact of environment, as opposed to heredity, on IQ. Unfortunately, the study had never been published by a journal, which means it had never been subjected to normal peer review processes and examined for its scientific merit (Sommer & Sommer, 1983). We have no idea whether or not the study had any validity.

From the other end of the political spectrum, Richard Herrnstein and Charles Murray (1994) recently created a political storm rivaling Jensen's with their publication of *The Bell Curve*. Most of their argument is not about race: They argue that as the United States increasingly approximates a meritocracy, in which people rise in their professions because of their merits, a great divide is emerging between the intellectual "haves" and "have nots." Because individual differences reflect to some large measure variation in genetic endowment and because people of similar intellectual levels tend to marry, the result, they argue, is an increasing concentration of cognitive resources in a small elite and a concentration of low intellect in a rapidly expanding underclass. People with low IQ are disproportionately represented among welfare recipients, prison inmates, mothers of illegitimate babies, drug abusers, and high school dropouts; this finding emerges whether including only white subjects, who share racial background, or members of different races.

Herrnstein and Murray draw some incendiary conclusions—notably the view that IQ differences are immutable, so that spending on social programs such as Head Start is a waste of resources—and the book has drawn wide criticism (e.g., Gould, 1994). For example, the authors provide no new data beyond Jensen's to support their most controversial and least credible thesis, that racial differences, like individual differences, are largely genetic. Further, some of the data they do cite have been criticized as distorted or highly selective (leaving out studies reaching opposing conclusions). Nevertheless, as other commentators have pointed out (e.g., Winship, 1994), some of their arguments deserve serious consideration, such as the possibility of the development of an increasingly large group of people who are cognitively, socially, and economically disenfranchised.

According to Herrnstein and Murray, people with low IQ are overrepresented among pregnant teenagers, prison inmates, and other antisocial elements of society, regardless of race.

In response to *The Bell Curve*, a group of 50 leading professors in the fields of cognition, intelligence, behavioral genetics, and individual differences (such as Thomas Bouchard, Raymond Cattell, John Loehlin, and Sandra Scarr) drafted a document offering a series of propositions they consider now well established by scientifically rigorous studies (Arvey et al., 1994). Among these propositions are several worth noting here. First, they conclude that intelligence is indeed a general capacity to reason, which can be measured, and which intelligence tests measure well. Second, IQ is more strongly related to many valued educational, economic, and occupational outcomes than any other trait ever studied and is so important because nearly every activity requires some reasoning, problem solving, and decision making. Third, intelligence tests are not biased against African Americans or any other native English speakers in the United States since they predict performance in other domains (such as school or work) equally well regardless of race. Fourth, members of different racial and ethnic groups are found at every point on the IQ distribution. Nonetheless, mean scores for Jews and East Asians are somewhat higher than those for other whites, whites' mean scores are higher than Hispanics', and Hispanics' are higher than blacks'. Racial and ethnic differences in IQ are smaller among people from similar socioeconomic backgrounds, but they remain substantial. Finally, heritability for individual differences, which has been estimated in the range of .4 and .8, does not imply that group differences are either heritable or immutable.

So what can we conclude about group differences in intelligence? The 15-point IQ difference between African Americans and white Americans is probably in large part an artifact of social class. But the definitive study will probably have to wait until psychologists can assess African Americans whose families have been middle or upper class for four or five generations and who have attended schools comparable to those of whites of similar socioeconomic status. Such a study is many years away.

Another conclusion, however, is perhaps equally important and is reflected in my own struggle to write this commentary. I rewrote this section many times. I would come upon a new article and suddenly decide that the position I had taken in the last draft was badly flawed. With each new revision, I would wonder whether or not my ideological biases were interfering with my attempt to provide a dispassionate discussion of the topic. My training as a scientist reminded me at every step to look at the data. But my training as a clinician equally reminded me to look at myself, for data are always interpreted by a mind with motives, attitudes, and ideological commitments. No position is the final word on any important issue in psychology. However, the only way to get closer to the truth is to respect the scientific method—and the impediments to it imposed by our own imperfect and passionate intellects.

THE EXTREMES OF INTELLIGENCE

Having explored the nature of intelligence and the factors that contribute to it, we now turn to the extremes of intelligence—mental retardation and giftedness—and to the relationship between creativity and intelligence.

Mental Retardation

Roughly 2 percent of the American population is **mentally retarded**—that is, significantly subaverage in general intellectual functioning, with deficits in adaptive behavior evident during childhood (American Association on Mental Deficiency, cited in Grossman, 1977, p. 11). In practice, significantly subaverage intellectual functioning translates to an IQ below 65 or 70, or about 30 to 35 points below the mean. Adaptive behavior is more difficult to quantify but encompasses a broad range of skills, including social judgment, self-care abilities, and communication skills. It also includes academic skills during the school years and vocational aptitude in adulthood (Landesman-Dwyer & Butterfield, 1983). Adaptation is not easy to define or assess, but most experts now recognize that IQ scores alone are not enough to diagnose retardation (Greenspan & Granfield, 1992).

This definition encompasses a wide spectrum of disabilities, ranging from mild to moderate retardation (IQ between 50 and 70) to more severe conditions with IQ below 50. As Table 8.6 shows, by far the largest group (about 75 to 90 percent) of people classified as retarded falls into the mild to moderate category. Individuals in this range can learn academic skills at an elementary school level, and as adults they are capable of self-supporting activities, although often in special supervised environments (Tyler, 1965). Only about 10 percent of retarded individuals are classified as severely to profoundly retarded; in these cases, retardation is often accompanied by physiological handicaps and a mortality rate three or more times the norm.

Causes of Mental Retardation

Table 8.6 also presents some of the causes of retardation. Many individuals, particularly in the "severe to profound" category, are diagnosed early because of obvious neurological or medical symptoms. Wide-set eyes, flattened facial features, and stunted body shape characterize individuals with **Down syndrome**, a disorder caused by the presence of an extra twenty-first chromosome. Doctors can now diagnose Down syndrome during pregnancy through genetic testing of the amniotic fluid that surrounds the fetus.

Severe forms of retardation are often related to a genetic abnormality, as with Down syndrome and **phenylketonuria** (**PKU**). The cause of phenylketonuria is a single recessive gene that leads to insufficient quantities of the enzyme that converts the amino acid phenylalanine into another amino acid. (Amino acids are building blocks of proteins.) Without the appropriate enzyme, phenylalanine is converted instead into a toxin that damages the infant's developing central nervous system, resulting in severe mental retardation. PKU is treatable, if detected early, by minimizing phenylalanine in the child's diet (Pavone et al., 1993; Wurtman & Ritter-Walker, 1988).

Retardation may also have environmental causes, including brain damage before birth (for instance, as a result of the mother's exposure to diseases), during delivery (as when oxygen to the brain is cut off by the umbilical cord), or after birth (through injury, disease, or other environmental insult). Retardation may also result from exposure in utero to alcohol and other drugs, such as cocaine (Jacobson et al., 1993; McCance-Katz, 1991; Miller, 1992).

Although hundreds of biological factors have been linked to mental retardation, most cases cannot be tied to any specific biological cause (Bregman & Hodapp, 1991). As a result, the vast majority of cases—more than 70 percent—are not diagnosed at birth (Scott & Carran, 1987). The term "sociocultural retardation" is sometimes applied to this group of typically mildly to moderately retarded individuals (Landesman-Dwyer & Butterfield, 1983). Unlike severely or profoundly retarded individuals, children in this group often have parents and siblings with low IQs, and they come disproportionately from families who live in poverty (Abramowicz & Richardson, 1975).

The incidence of more severe forms of retardation is fairly constant in all populations, whereas rates of mild retardation vary considerably from country to country (Grunewald, 1979; Stein & Susser, 1975). Whereas about 1 to 2 percent of the U.S. population is mildly retarded, this condition is unknown in the People's Republic of China (Robinson, 1978). There, intellectually "slow" individuals tend to be more productively engaged and integrated into extended family networks

Children with Down syndrome have characteristic facial features alongside their mental retardation.

TABLE 8.6 CHARACTERISTICS OF MILDER VERSUS MORE SEVERE MENTAL RETARDATION

	LEVEL OF MENTAL RETARDATION	
	Mild to Moderate	**Severe to Profound**
Prevalence	1% or less of population	.25% of population
Proportion of retarded population	75%–90%	10%–25%
IQ range	50–70	below 50
Mortality during childhood	Normal	Three or more times normal rate
Age at diagnosis	School-age	Prior to school-age
Out of home placement rates	Low	High
Physical size	Normal to slightly below average	Much below average
Medical/neurological signs and symptoms	Usually absent	Often present
Primary environmental influences	Inadequate social and/or environmental stimulation, childhood cerebral disease	Cerebral disease or injury in very early life (pre- and post-natal)
Parents' intelligence	Often low IQ	Normal IQ
Siblings' intelligence	Often low IQ	Usually normal, but sometimes similarly retarded, as when recessive genes are expressed in two siblings
Social class	Lower social classes over-represented	All classes

Source: From Landesman-Dwyer & Butterfield, 1983, p. 485.

(Landesman-Dwyer & Butterfield, 1983). Thus, cultural factors alter not only the social conditions that predispose some individuals to retardation but also the way people define and respond to retardation.

Treating Mental Retardation

Some forms of retardation, such as those caused by nutritional or other environmental deficits, may be ameliorated if diagnosed in time. However, most forms

In China, people considered mild-ly mentally retarded in the West are integrated into the community.

are not curable in the sense of restoring the person to normality. Nevertheless, recent decades have seen an emphasis on **normalization** of mentally retarded individuals, taking them out of institutions whenever possible and providing either home care or living arrangements in small community-based centers (Birenbaum & Cohen, 1993; Zigler et al., 1990). In 1967, nearly 200,000 mentally retarded people lived in institutions in the United States. By 1984, this number had been reduced by more than half (Landesman & Butterfield, 1987). Another aspect of normalization is "mainstreaming" children, enrolling them in public schools in regular or special education classes (Gottlieb, 1990; Ittenbach et al., 1993).

Normalization policies have been highly controversial. Supporters consider institutional care degrading and stress the enrichment that comes from living in less restrictive environments. The reality of normalization, however, is often very different from the ideal. Mainstreaming has placed extra strain on schools, which have not always been prepared to handle the special needs of mentally handicapped children (Schroeder et al., 1987). Mentally retarded children are frequently teased and ridiculed by "normal" peers; they may not be socially accepted even after years of mainstreaming (Brewer & Smith, 1989). The discrepancy between the goals and realities of normalization shows why changes in social policy based on theory or prior data should always be accompanied by research on outcome, to see whether the change is really beneficial.

Giftedness

Mental retardation occupies the extreme left-hand side of the bell-shaped IQ distribution. Persons whose IQs fall on the extreme right-hand side are generally classified as **gifted**. Like definitions of intelligence, definitions of giftedness vary, since it refers to whatever skills or talents a particular society labels as gifts (Becker, 1978; Goodnow, 1976; Mistry & Rogoff, 1985). Balinese culture emphasizes artistic expression in music and visual symbolism (Belo, 1955), whereas Eastern European Jewish communities traditionally emphasized literary analysis in studying the scriptures (Zborowski & Herzog, 1952). In our own society, with its emphasis on academic aptitude as measured by psychometric tests, giftedness is often equated with an IQ exceeding 130. Like traditional concepts of intelligence, this definition of giftedness probably focuses too much on only one aspect and measure of intelligent functioning. Indeed, several studies have found little correlation between the IQ scores of students and later recognition in such areas as science, creative writing, or performing arts (Walberg, 1971, 1985).

A broader definition of giftedness proposed by psychologist Robert Sternberg identifies domains areas of special talent: intellectual skills (such as verbal, mathematical, spatial, and memory skills); artistic skills (such as dance, drama, musicianship, and painting); niche-fitting skills (the ability to select, adapt to, and shape physical and interpersonal environments); and physical skills (including survival skills and athletic talents) (Sternberg & Davidson, 1985). As this list suggests, definitions of giftedness depend on definitions of intelligence: Having extraordinary talent in one area confers intellectual giftedness only if that area is considered an aspect of intelligence. Being an expert in discriminating good from bad chocolate does not make a person highly intelligent, important as this ability may be. Rather than defining giftedness unidimensionally as having exceptional g-factor intelligence, many now consider giftedness at least partially domain-specific or limited to particular abilities (Read, 1982). The prodigy who can mentally multiply two 3-digit numbers in 30 seconds may be gifted in mathematics but have only normal abilities in other areas (Smith, 1988).

Are Gifted People Maladjusted?

However giftedness is defined, people of unusual intelligence have been viewed with a mixture of awe and suspicion over the centuries. The early civilizations of Greece and Rome associated uncommon intelligence with divine power, but the Roman philosopher Seneca postulated that "there is no great genius without a touch of madness." Indeed, for much of the history of Western civilization, at least until the Renaissance, giftedness was seen as an aberration that was unhealthy at best and heretical at worst. (From a statistical point of view, of course, gifted people *are* abnormal; that is, they are outside the norm as defined by the middle region of the bell curve.) The common notion persists that extreme intelligence is associated with unhappiness or social maladjustment.

Is this simply wishful thinking on the part of the rest of us? In 1921, Lewis Terman began a longitudinal study of over 1000 California children with IQs above 140, which still continues today (Terman, 1925; Terman & Oden, 1947; Tomlinson-Keasey & Little, 1990; Vaillant & Vaillant, 1990). The primary finding is that gifted individuals tend to have average or above average personality adjustment, slightly better chances of marital success, and far greater likelihood of achieving vocational success than the general population (Terman & Oden, 1947). Numerous other studies have supported these findings (Janos & Robinson, 1985). Only one subset of the gifted population, children with very high IQs in the range of 180, have higher than normal rates of adjustment difficulties (Hollingworth, 1926, 1931, 1942).

Creativity and Intelligence

A quality related to both intelligence and giftedness is **creativity**, which can be defined as the ability to produce valued outcomes in a novel way. Creativity is related to intelligence, but the correlation is far from perfect. In general, intelligence in a particular area seems to be a necessary condition for creativity but not a sufficient one. A person who has little ability in mathematics or architecture would be hard pressed to solve problems in those fields creatively, but many competent mathematicians and architects have no flare for innovation. Individuals with IQs below 120 are less likely to display creative thinking than those with a higher IQ, but above 120, the correlation between intelligence and creativity is essentially zero (Feldman, 1980; Keating, 1983; Wallach, 1970, 1985). Interestingly, in the 40-year followup of Terman's study of children with superior levels of intelligence, none of the subjects had produced highly creative works (Terman & Oden, 1959).

Because people do not express creativity in any uniform way (otherwise, they would not be creative) creativity is extremely difficult to measure. One strategy for assessing creativity is to measure divergent thinking. **Divergent thinking** involves generating multiple possibilities from a given situation, such as describing all the possible uses of a paper clip. At face value, divergent thinking seems to be related to creativity because it involves finding unusual or unconventional ways of solving a problem. Whether Mozart or Einstein would have distinguished themselves in finding uses for a paper clip will, however, never be known.

The best-known creativity tests measure either the thought processes involved in creativity or the personality characteristics of creative people (Khatena, 1982; Torrance, 1966; Wakefield, 1991). Evaluating creativity by examining attributes of the person instead of the process reflects the view that creativity is as much a personality trait as a cognitive trait or aspect of intelligence (Eysenck, 1983). Indeed, research has linked creativity to such personality traits as high energy, intuitiveness, independence, and self-acceptance (Barron & Harrington, 1981).

FROM MIND TO BRAIN

CREATIVITY AND MENTAL DISORDERS

Writers since the time of Plato have postulated an association between creativity and madness. Many famous creative geniuses—including Vincent Van Gogh, Isaac Newton, Michelangelo, and William Blake—have had some form of mental disorder (Karlsson, 1978; Prentky, 1980). An association between creativity and abnormality may not be incidental. The ability to suspend one's normal cognitive structures momentarily and to associate concepts and categories in novel ways is basic to creativity. In their extreme form, these tendencies also characterize severe mental disorders.

Research on creativity and mental illness has recently focused on bipolar disorder, otherwise known as manic-depression (Chapter 15). Bipolar disorder is marked by extreme mood swings from euphoria and grandiosity to paralyzing depression. Heritability of the disorder is high, and although environmental factors appear to influence its course and development, virtually no one develops the illness who does not have a family history of it.

A number of studies have examined the association between bipolar disorder and creativity in writers, especially poets (Andreasen & Glick, 1988; Holden, 1987; Jamison, 1989, 1994). These studies have found similarities between the intense creative episodes during which writers accomplish some of their best work and the highly energized manic phase of bipolar disorder (Richards & Kinney, 1990; Richards et al., 1992). Prominent among twentieth-century American poets with bipolar disorder are Theodore Roethke, Robert Lowell, and Sylvia Plath (who committed suicide in her early 30s).

Composer Cole Porter, writer Virginia Woolf, and writer Ernest Hemingway all appear to have suffered from bipolar disorder, cyclothymia, or a related condition.

One study of 47 of the top writers and artists in England found that fully 38 percent had sought treatment for mood disorders (including bipolar disorder), with poets and writers reporting the highest rates of psychiatric intervention (Jamison, 1989). Other investigations have taken the reverse approach, studying creativity in bipolar patients and their relatives. The relatives of bipolar patients, and patients with a mild form of the disorder (called cyclothymia, meaning cycles of shifting moods that do not reach psychotic levels), appear to have unusually high rates of creativity and occupational achievement (Coryell et al., 1989; Richards et al., 1988). The findings of one such study are depicted in Figure 8.8. As the figure shows, cyclothymic individuals and first-degree relatives of bipolar and cyclothymic patients manifest higher rates of creativity than bipolars, normals, or other people with psychiatric disorders.

Why relatives of bipolar patients and people with a mild version of the disorder show high rates of creativity is a mystery. As we will see (Chapter 15), relatives of schizophrenic patients are more prone than other people to show peculiarities of thinking, but these are not linked to creativity. They are more

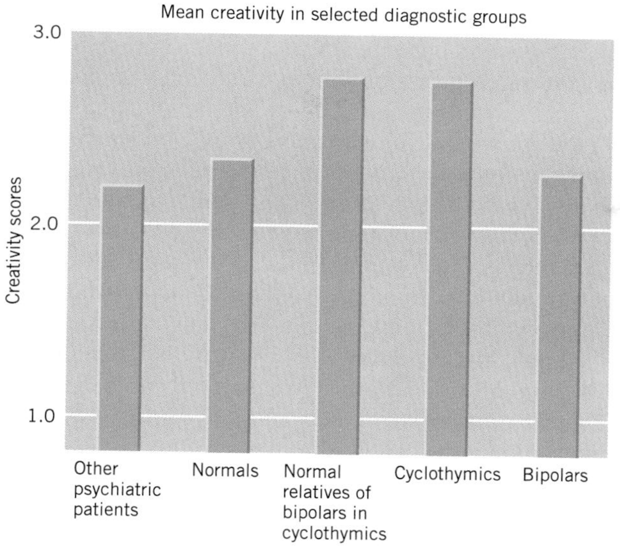

Mean creativity in selected diagnostic groups

FIGURE 8.8
Creativity and mental illness. The highest rates of creativity occurred in cyclothymic individuals and relatives of cyclothymic or bipolar individuals. SOURCE: *Richards et al., 1988, p. 286.*

likely to report odd perceptual experiences and magical ideas, and they frequently have idiosyncratic associations to words (Meehl, 1962, 1989). On questionnaires they tend to endorse items such as, "Sometimes I have had a passing thought that my body was rotting away," "It has seemed at times as if my body was melting into my surroundings," and "I have occasionally had the silly feeling that a TV or radio broadcaster knew I was listening to him" (Chapman & Chapman, 1980; Chapman et al., 1993). We usually assume that a "close cousin" of a disorder must be dysfunctional, as in the milder syndromes genetically related to schizophrenia. This may not always be the case, however. People who receive the gene that causes sickle cell anemia from both parents develop the fatal disease, but individuals who receive the gene from only one parent are immune to malaria. In fact, the sickle cell gene appears to have been favored by natural selection in regions of Africa in which malaria is common. Something similar may be true of the genes that produce a vulnerability to bipolar disorder, which may predispose their bearers either to madness or to creativity, depending on their other genes and the environmental circumstances that activate genetic proclivities.

SOME CONCLUDING THOUGHTS

All the approaches to intelligence explored in this chapter have been, broadly speaking, cognitive. Intelligence is, after all, applied cognition. Yet intelligence cannot be defined entirely without reference to the uses to which individuals put it. Consider the case of a sociopath or antisocial personality, who lacks a mature sense of right and wrong. Many psychologists now argue that **social intelligence**—the ability to store, retrieve, and understand social information—is an important form of intelligence (Bye & Jussim, 1993; Cantor & Kihlstrom, 1987; Gardner, 1983; Ruisel, 1992; Taylor, 1990). Is a sociopath defective in social intelligence?

In some cases, decidedly not. Many sociopaths are extremely successful con artists, with an extraordinary capacity to lie convincingly and manipulate people to achieve their goals. The words "successful" and "convincingly" convey the *intelligent* aspects of the sociopath's behavior. Sociopaths may thus be quite socially intelligent, at least in certain respects, but their social motivation is clearly defective. They may *know* social rules; they just lack the desire to obey them. The question, then, is whether intelligence and motivation can be so clearly distinguished, especially if intelligence is defined in terms of meeting culturally accepted standards.

Intelligence is always at the service of goals, which means that it is embedded in a psychological context that includes motivation and emotion. A person's IQ score reflects not only her intellectual abilities but also her motivation to achieve and her ability to manage anxiety and frustration. The IQ score of a person who is distracted by intense anxiety while taking the test may reflect emotional factors as much as cognitive ability, and a person with a history of learning disabilities or failures in school may give up quickly on items that he could answer if he were not afraid to make the effort and risk failing.

The next three chapters explore this broader context of cognition. We turn first to consciousness, which has loomed increasingly large over the last decade in studies of cognition. We then examine the motives and emotions that give purpose and meaning to our most elegant cognitive processes.

Summary

The Nature of Intelligence

1. **Intelligence** is the application of cognitive skills and knowledge to learn, solve problems, and obtain ends that are valued by an individual or culture. Intelligence is multifaceted, functional, and culturally defined. Some aspects of intelligence, such as mental quickness, are universal, whereas others depend on the tasks of adaptation in a particular society.

Intelligence Testing

2. **Intelligence tests** represent a type of psychometric instrument designed to assess an individual's cognitive capabilities compared to others in a population. The ancestor of modern IQ tests was invented by Binet for the specific purpose of identifying retarded children. Binet developed the concept of **mental age (MA)**, the average age at which children can be expected to achieve a particular score.

3. **The intelligence quotient**, or IQ, is a score meant to represent an individual's intellectual ability, which permits comparison with other individuals. It was initially calculated by dividing mental age by chronological age and multiplying by 100.

4. Wechsler abandoned the concept of mental age and calculated IQ as an individual's position relative to peers of the same age by using a frequency distribution. The Wechsler scales (the **WAIS-R** and the **WISC-R** for children) include six verbal and five nonverbal performance tests.

5. Intelligence tests are highly predictive of scholastic success, and they also predict occupational success. Critics argue that they lack a theoretical basis, are culturally biased, and fail to capture other kinds of intelligence.

Approaches to Intelligence

6. The **psychometric approach** derives the components and structure of intelligence empirically from statistical analysis of psychometric test findings. The primary tool of the psychometric approach is **factor analysis**, a statistical technique for identifying common **factors** that underlie performance on a wide variety of measures. Spearman's **two-factor theory** distinguishes the **g-factor**, or general intelligence, from **s-factors**, or specific abilities. The psychometric approach is useful for predicting performance at school or work but cannot *explain* the way people think intelligently.

7. The information-processing approach tries to understand the specific cognitive processes that underlie intelligent behavior. Three of the most important variables on which people differ are speed of processing, knowledge base, and the ability to learn and apply mental strategies. Unlike the psychometric approach, the information-processing approach is theory-driven, although it remains tied to the kind of intelligence measured by IQ tests.

8. Gardner's theory of **multiple intelligences** distinguishes seven kinds of intelligence that are relatively independent, neurologically distinct, and show different courses of development. Gardner's theory grounds intelligence in its neurological and cultural contexts, but it probably underestimates non-domain-specific intelligence, and most of the intelligences it defines have not yet been empirically tested.

Heredity and Intelligence

9. A central question in the study of intelligence is the extent to which environment and heredity each shape intelligence. To examine the heritability of IQ, studies have correlated the IQ scores of subjects with differing degrees of genetic relatedness, and of biological and adoptive family members. Twin, family, and adoption studies suggest that heredity, environment, and their interaction all contribute to IQ but that individual differences in IQ are highly heritable. Research does not, however, support the hypothesis that differences among racial or ethnic groups are primarily genetic.

The Extremes of Intelligence

10. **Mental retardation** refers to significantly subaverage general intellectual functioning with deficits in adaptive behavior manifested during childhood. **Giftedness** refers to the other extreme of the intellectual spectrum, although theorists differ in the extent to which they limit this concept to the kind of intelligence assessed by IQ tests.

11. **Creativity** is the ability to produce valued outcomes in a novel way; it is only imperfectly correlated with IQ. Highly intelligent people do not tend to be maladjusted, although creativity seems to be particularly high in relatives of people with bipolar disorder (manic-depression) and people with a mild variant of the disorder.

Man Ray, "Repainted Mask," 1941

Chapter 9

CONSCIOUSNESS

lmost a century ago, a Swiss psychologist named Claparede shook hands with a patient suffering from Korsakoff's disorder. Claparede had concealed a pin between his fingers, which pricked the patient as their hands clasped. At their next meeting, the patient had no memory of having met Claparede (Korsakoff's disorder produces amnesia for recent events), but she found herself inexplicably unwilling to shake his hand (Cowey, 1991). What the patient knew (that the good doctor was not so good) and what she knew consciously (that she was meeting a doctor, whom she need not fear) were two very different things.

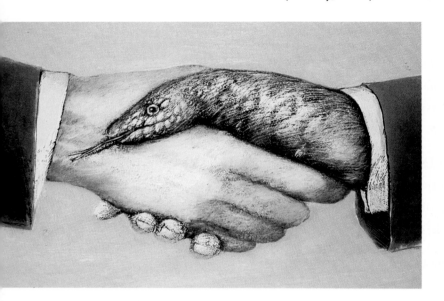

Amnesics are not the only people who may respond to a stimulus at different levels of consciousness. As we shall see, we all do, but the signs are often more subtle. Interest in consciousness has blossomed in the last 10 years, as researchers have begun exploring the relation between conscious and unconscious ways of knowing.

We begin this chapter by discussing the nature and functions of consciousness, examining the way attention focuses consciousness at any given time on a narrow subset of the thoughts and feelings of which a person is aware. Next, we explore perspectives on consciousness, contrasting in particular the psychodynamic focus on unconscious motives and emotions with the "cognitive unconscious." We then address the relation between consciousness and the neural circuits that regulate it. The remainder of the chapter is devoted to **states of consciousness**—qualitatively different patterns of subjective experience and orientations to internal and external events. We start with the most basic distinction, between waking and sleeping, exploring the stages of sleep and the nature of dreaming. We conclude by examining several altered states of consciousness—deviations in subjective experience (and typically in patterns of brain activity) from the normal waking state—including meditation, religious experiences, hypnosis, and drug-induced states.

THE NATURE OF CONSCIOUSNESS

Consciousness, the subjective awareness of mental events, may be easier to describe than to define. William James (1890) viewed consciousness as a constantly moving stream of thoughts, feelings, and perceptions. Shutting off consciousness in this sense is probably impossible, as anyone knows who has ever tried to "stop thinking" to escape insomnia. Following in the footsteps of the French philosopher Rene Descartes, who offered the famous proposition, "*Cogito ergo sum*" (I think, therefore I am), James also emphasized a second aspect of consciousness, the consciousness of self. James argued that part of being conscious of any thought in particular is a simultaneous awareness of oneself as the author or owner of it.

Why do people have consciousness at all? Two of its functions are readily apparent: Consciousness monitors the self and the environment, and it controls thought and behavior (Kihlstrom, 1987). Consciousness as a monitor is analogous to a continuously moving video camera, surveying potentially significant perceptions, thoughts, emotions, goals, and problem-solving strategies. The control function of consciousness allows people to initiate and terminate thought and behavior adaptively in order to attain goals. People often rehearse scenarios before carrying out behavior, as when they ask for a raise or confront a disloyal friend. Consciousness is frequently engaged when people choose between competing strategies (Mandler & Nakamura, 1987) or when standard operating procedures or automatized processes are not successful. Consciousness catches mistakes when automatic or procedural knowledge goes awry, functioning "like the inspector in a garment factory: It does not make a product, but it checks to make sure a product is perfect. If an imperfection is found, it institutes a remedy" (Gilbert, 1989, p. 206). In typing this sentence, for example, I paid no conscious attention to the keys on my terminal, but when I made a mistake—hitting an "m" instead of a comma, the adjacent key—I looked at the keys and corrected the error.

These two functions of consciousness—monitoring and controlling—are intertwined, since consciousness monitors inner and outer experience for the purpose of preventing and solving problems. From an evolutionary standpoint, consciousness probably evolved as a mechanism for directing behavior in adaptive ways, which became superimposed on more primitive psychological processes such as conditioning (Reber, 1992). Consciousness is often "grabbed" by things that are unexpected, unusual, or contrary to expectations—precisely the things that could affect well-being or survival. Much of the time people respond automatically to the environment, learning and processing information without conscious awareness. Important choices, however, require more consideration, and consciousness permits heightened reflection on the adaptive significance of events and potential actions. Consciousness thus serves adaptation by devoting extra cognitive resources to information that may be particularly meaningful or significant.

Consciousness, Awareness, and Attention

At any given time, people are aware of much more than what is conscious. **Awareness** refers to all the current perceptions, thoughts, motives, and feelings that *could* be available to consciousness if attention were turned to them. Awareness is a continuum, ranging from conscious awareness to events at the dim periphery (Figure 9.1). While reading the newspaper, a person may be aware of the radiator clanking, voices in the next room, and the smell of breakfast cooking, none of which is at the center of awareness or consciousness. At some critical point, however, a pattern of olfactory sensations is unconsciously given perceptual meaning (smoke or danger), and attention shifts. (Paradoxically, the monitoring and controlling functions of consciousness are thus to a considerable degree regulated outside of consciousness.) **Attention** refers to the process of focusing consciousness, providing heightened sensitivity to a limited range of experience requiring more extensive information processing. Some psychologists liken attention to a filtering process, through which only more important information passes—as through a cognitive filter (Broadbent, 1958).

The contents of consciousness, then, are a subset of the contents of awareness, namely, the subset to which the person is attending. Conscious awareness is thus a specific form of awareness with specialized functions—monitoring and controlling. Sometimes, however, people divert attention from information that may be relevant but emotionally upsetting, a process called **selective inattention**. They may ignore

FIGURE 9.1
Consciousness, awareness, and attention. Attention focuses consciousness on a narrow range of phenomena available to awareness. Consciousness is a specialized form of awareness.

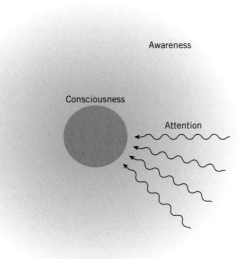

things as small as a darkening birthmark on the arm or as global as nuclear proliferation and hence fail to devote adequate cognitive resources to them (Lifton, 1980). Selective inattention can also be used adaptively, however, as when students divert their attention from the anxiety of taking a test to the task itself.

Information that is out of conscious sight is not always out of mind. People frequently become so engrossed in conversation with one person that they tune out all the other conversations in the room, but if they hear their name spoken across the room, they notice and become oriented to it immediately. This phenomenon is sometimes called the "cocktail party phenomenon" (Cherry, 1953). Precisely how people do this is unclear. If attention focuses consciousness, it may also prioritize information outside of awareness, continuously screening information for potential admission into consciousness.

Psychologists have tried to ascertain precisely how much information people can process outside of awareness and whether they can carry out two complex tasks, such as following two conversations, simultaneously. Splitting attention between two or more tasks is known as **divided attention**. Researchers study divided attention using **dichotic listening** tasks (Figure 9.2): Subjects are fitted with earphones, and different information is directed into each ear simultaneously. They are instructed to attend only to the information from one ear or channel. To make sure they do this, they repeat aloud what they hear in that ear for a period of time, a process called shadowing. Attending to one channel or the other is difficult at first, but it is easier if the two channels differ in topic, voice pitch, and so forth (Hirst, 1986).

Subjects can become so adept at shadowing that they show no ability to recall or recognize information in the unattended channel. For example, they may perform no better than chance when asked whether a word presented in the unattended channel had been presented. Nevertheless, the information does appear to be processed to some degree, much as the smell of smoke is processed while reading the newspaper. This has been clearly demonstrated in research on **priming**, which refers to the influence of recent exposure on performance, such as exposure to semantically related stimuli (Nisbett & Wilson, 1977; Schacter, 1992). For example, a subject who hears "New York" in the unattended channel may have no recollection of having heard the name of any state, but compared to a control subject who has not been similarly primed, the subject is more likely to say "Albany" if asked to name a state capital. Similarly, he will more quickly fill in the missing letters when asked for the name of a city when presented with

    AL———Y.

The data from many dichotic listening studies of divided attention actually suggest that subjects are not dividing their attention at all: Failing to show recognition memory for the prime suggests that subjects never consciously attended to it. On other tasks, however, people do appear to divide their attention, performing two complex tasks simultaneously, both of which require substantial attentional resources. In listening to a lecture while taking notes, a student is hearing and processing one idea while simultaneously writing—and even paraphrasing—a previous idea or sentence. This is remarkable because both tasks are verbal and the content of each is highly similar; hence, one would expect heavy interference between the two. Psychologists have even trained subjects to take dictation while reading (Spelke et al., 1976).

One way people accomplish such feats is by automatizing them. Automatization develops through practice, as actions previously performed with deliberate conscious effort are eventually processed automatically. While students listen to a lecture, their primary focus of consciousness is on the lecturer's current words, while a largely automatic process, perhaps drawing on some subset of attentional processes, allows note-taking. Precisely how much consciousness is involved in what is called divided attention is not well understood. It may be that we should speak of "divided awareness" or "parallel awareness" rather than divided attention, if attention implies consciousness. Or perhaps attentional processes distribute activation widely throughout the various associative and cognitive networks activated at any given time. Those mental contents that receive the most excitation and the least inhibition (as in selective inattention) might then enter into consciousness.

FIGURE 9.2
A dichotic listening task. Subjects are fitted with earphones, and different information is transmitted into each ear simultaneously. Subjects often show awareness of information in the unattended channel, even when they have no conscious recognition of it.

The Normal Flow of Consciousness

Psychologists study the normal flow of consciousness through **experience-sampling** techniques (Klinger & Cox, 1987–1988; Singer & Kolligian, 1987; Wong & Csikszentmihalyi, 1991). In one design, subjects talk aloud, sometimes while performing a task, simply reporting the contents of their consciousness. Researchers then code their verbalizations into categories, such as emotional tone, relevance to the task at hand, or content.

Another experience-sampling technique has provided a window to the flow of consciousness in everyday life: beeper studies. In these studies, subjects carry pagers and report their experience at various points during the day. In one of the most important studies of this type, researchers sampled the experience of 75 adolescents from a Chicago high school (Csikszentmihalyi & Larson, 1984). They randomly selected students within each of several categories, including sex, grade, and social class (a stratified random sample, described in Chapter 2). For one week, subjects were beeped at some point during every two-hour period (except at night) and filled out a brief form reporting what they were doing, with whom, what they were thinking and feeling, and how intensely they were feeling it.

Some of the results were quite unexpected. When subjects were with their families, their negative thoughts outnumbered their positive thoughts by about 10 to 1. When they were asked, "As you were beeped, what were you thinking about?" their responses included, "My aunt talks too much" or "How incompetent my mom is" (p. 139). Using this beeper method, the investigators were also able to explore the subjective experience of individual subjects. Figure 9.3 presents the flow of consciousness in a subject called Katherine over the course of a week.

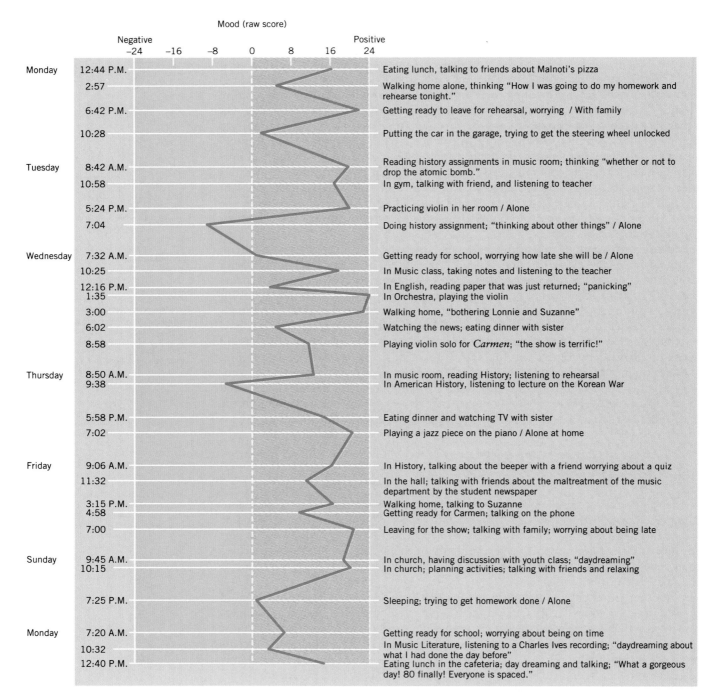

FIGURE 9.3
A week in the life of Katherine. In this experience-sampling study, Katherine reported what she was doing and thinking about whenever she was paged by a beeper. SOURCE: *Csikszentmihalyi & Larson, 1984, p. 117.*

A major component of the normal flow of consciousness is **daydreaming**—turning attention away from external stimuli to internal thoughts and imagined scenarios. Some daydreams are pleasurable fantasies, whereas others involve planning for future actions, particularly involving people in important relationships. Daydreams typically include vivid images of people, objects, and imagined activities. In one large-scale study of daydreaming, all subjects reported daydreaming daily (Singer,

1975). Using the beeper method, another research team found that college students daydream about half the time, if daydreaming includes thoughts about something other than what is currently happening in the person's environment. For example, a student will think about a paper that needs to be written while watching a basketball game (Klinger, 1992).

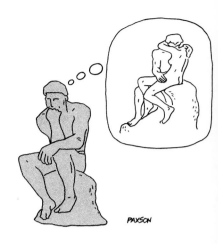

A GLOBAL VISTA

CONSCIOUSNESS AMONG THE IFALUK OF MICRONESIA

We are accustomed to thinking of consciousness as a realm of experience that is uniquely private, but consciousness is in part culturally constructed. According to psychological anthropologist A. Irving Hallowell (1955), people live not only in their actual environment but also in a behavioral environment. The **behavioral environment** refers to mental representations of the environment that orient people to dimensions such as time, space, and the interpersonal world. The behavioral environment is fundamentally shaped by cultural beliefs and practices. Among the Ojibwa Indians studied by Hallowell, for example, the behavioral environment includes not only the self and other people but also deities and ancestors. Thus, when considering an action with moral or interpersonal consequences, the Ojibwa take into account the impact on spirits and on nonliving as well as living relatives. In preindustrial cultures such as the Ojibwa, consciousness is also not segregated into such small units of time as in cultures ruled by the clock.

Anthropologist Catherine Lutz (1992) contends that consciousness among the Ifaluk of Micronesia differs in certain basic respects from the Western experience of consciousness. The contents of Ifaluk consciousness reflect the way their culture organizes reality and the fact that their livelihood depends on navigating the vast surrounding ocean. Lutz describes an incident in which an islander took his only excursion outside of his native land, to Hawaii. He became panicked and disoriented while taking a taxi at night because he could not follow the stars in the closed car and lost all track of direction: "I tried to

Ifaluk consciousness, like consciousness in Western societies, is influenced by culture and ecology.

keep track, but soon I didn't know which way was east, which way was west" (p. 69). The Ifaluk's attentional mechanisms routinely direct consciousness to the heavens.

The focus of Ifaluk consciousness also tends to be less on inner experience than on social interactions. Westerners attend carefully to people's words and actions when they wish to assess their sincerity. In contrast, the Ifaluk are not generally concerned with the inner meanings of social actions. Their moral code revolves around harmony within the group, which is essential for people who must live together on a small island. When people are behaving in ways that maintain this harmony, no one is concerned about whether or not they mean it, since the Ifaluk assume that people behave morally because that is the right thing to do.

When in conflict with each other, however, the Ifaluk practice a particular form of introspection called "dividing the mind." The aim is to look inward to separate thoughts and feelings that are good and moral from those that are bad and unfair, and to adjust one's behavior accordingly. However, the kind of introspection valued in many segments of contemporary Western culture, which involves self-reflection for the purpose of self-knowledge, is perceived by the Ifaluk as a sign of self-absorption. Whereas Westerners since Freud have generally viewed self-reflection as a path to psychological health, the Ifaluk perceive it as a road to illness.

PERSPECTIVES ON CONSCIOUSNESS

Consciousness occupied a central role in the first textbook on psychology, written by William James in 1890. Consciousness also figured prominently in the work of Freud, who, like several philosophers in the nineteenth century, expanded the purview of psychology to include unconscious processes as well. When behaviorism came into ascendance, however, consciousness—not to mention unconsciousness—receded from the consciousness of the scientific community and remained that way until the 1980s. The behaviorists shared a view of unconscious processes offered by William James early in his career, before the advent of psychoanalysis. James commented rather snidely, "The 'unconscious' is the sovereign means of believing whatever one likes in psychology and of turning what might become a science into a tumbling ground for whimsies" (1890, p. 163). According to Skinner (1974), to explain a person's action on the basis of an unconscious process is simply to admit that we have not yet observed the environmental stimuli controlling the behavior. Unlike James, however, behaviorists were equally disinterested in discussions of consciousness: Behaviorism "rejects the conscious mind as an agent, too" (Skinner, 1974, p. 169). Organisms as primitive as snails respond to environmental contingencies, yet no one would propose that snails therefore have consciousness. For the behaviorist, consciousness is not, and cannot be, a scientific concern. For many years, cognitive psychologists, too, paid little attention to consciousness, although their attitude was more one of disinterest than disbelief in its significance.

Thus, only a decade ago, issues of consciousness and unconsciousness were largely the province of psychoanalysis. Recently, however, experimental psychologists have turned their attention to consciousness and to the conditions under which complex thought can occur without conscious awareness. In this section we examine psychodynamic and cognitive perspectives on consciousness and then consider what can be learned about normal consciousness by observing neuropsychological patients like Claparede's, who manifest a dissociation between what they know consciously and unconsciously. As will become apparent, these various points of view on the nature of conscious and unconscious processes are beginning to converge.

Psychodynamic Perspective

Freud (1900) defined consciousness as one of three mental systems which he called the conscious, preconscious, and unconscious (Figure 9.4). **Conscious** mental processes are those of which a person is subjectively and centrally aware. **Preconscious** mental processes are not presently conscious but could be readily brought to consciousness if the need arose. For example, if you were asked what part of the brain is most involved in complex thinking, you would probably say, "the cerebral cortex." A moment ago that information was preconscious; it was not in the center of awareness, but it could be.

Freud recognized that many psychological processes are inherently unconscious, like the activation of hunger by depletion of glucose levels in the blood. He focused, however, on **unconscious processes** that are inaccessible to consciousness because they have been repressed, that is, kept from conscious awareness because they are too anxiety-provoking to acknowledge. Freud likened repression to a censor: Just as a repressive government censors ideas or wishes it considers threatening, so, too, does consciousness censor threatening thoughts (Figure 9.4). Thus, a person may remember an abusive father with love and admiration and have no access to unhappy memories because admitting the truth is too painful.

In the 1940s and 1950s, as part of the New Look in perception (Chapter 4), researchers tested hypotheses derived from Freud's theory of consciousness. Studies of **subliminal perception** (the perception of stimuli below the threshold of consciousness) used a device called a tachistoscope to flash images slowly enough to be perceived but too fast for conscious recognition (Dixon, 1971, 1981). One of these studies used the stimuli shown in Figure 9.5 (Eagle, 1959). After establishing the speed of presentation below which subjects could not report what they had seen, the experimenter flashed one of two pictures subliminally. The first depicted a boy behaving aggressively toward a man; the second depicted the boy presenting a man with a birthday cake. Subjects were then shown a neutral picture of the boy and asked to judge the boy's personality. Subjects exposed to the aggressive picture tended to judge the boy negatively, whereas those who had been flashed the other rated him positively.

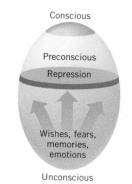

FIGURE 9.4
Freud's model of consciousness. Conscious mental processes are those of which a person is subjectively aware. Preconscious mental processes are not presently conscious but could readily be brought to consciousness. Unconscious mental processes are inaccessible to consciousness because they have been repressed.

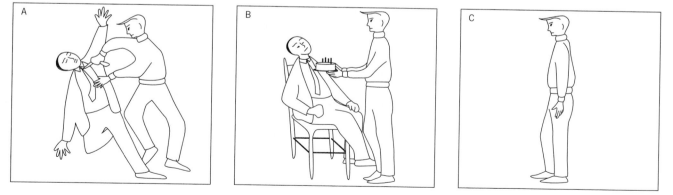

FIGURE 9.5
Subliminal perception. Subjects were presented subliminally with either slide A, a boy behaving aggressively, or B, a boy behaving altruistically. Subjects were then shown a neutral picture of the boy and asked to judge his personality. Subjects who had seen slide A described the boy as aggressive, whereas those who had seen slide B described him as altruistic. SOURCE: Eagle, 1959.

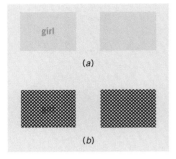

FIGURE 9.6
Subliminal priming. Subjects were presented with either a word or a blank field (a). This stimulus was followed by a mask, a stimulus that would prevent the word or blank field from lingering as a visual memory (b). Subjects were then asked to indicate whether a word or a blank had been flashed. Results showed that subliminally presented stimuli can influence thought. SOURCE: Marcel, 1983.

Ideas about subliminal influence have often captured the popular imagination.

This line of research drew considerable fire (Ericksen, 1962), in part because of its methodology, but also because the discipline at that time was largely hostile to psychodynamic ideas. The weight of the evidence today, particularly from investigations conducted by cognitive researchers, suggests that subliminal presentation of stimuli can indeed influence thought and emotion (Bowers, 1984; Dixon, 1981; Erdelyi, 1985; Neidenthal & Cantor, 1986; Weinberger & Hardaway, 1990). For instance, presenting a happy or sad face directly prior to exposure to a novel stimulus (a Chinese ideograph) affects subjects' liking or disliking of the ideograph but only if the presentation of the face is so brief that subjects cannot consciously perceive it (Murphy & Zajonc, 1993). Subliminal presentation of the face seems to "tag" the ideograph with an emotional connotation.

A highly influential series of studies documented that subjects who cannot detect a stimulus consciously can nevertheless be influenced by it (Marcel, 1983). In one experimental design (Figure 9.6), the investigator subliminally presented subjects with either a word or a blank field. The stimulus was followed immediately by a mask, another stimulus that would prevent the original one from lingering as a visual memory. Subjects were then given one of two tasks. One task was to indicate whether a word or a blank had been flashed. On this task, subjects were wrong half the time, demonstrating that they were never conscious of the stimulus. The second task was to identify a string of letters as either a word or a nonword. Some of the words were semantically related to the original word presented subliminally (the prime). The dependent variable was reaction time, that is, how quickly subjects could decide whether the letters formed a word. The results documented the influence of the subliminal prime on thought: Subjects more quickly recognized words that were semantically related to the prime, even though they had never consciously registered it.

Subliminal processing has drawn interest outside psychology as well. Several years ago, rumors flew that movie theaters were manipulating consumers by subliminally presenting messages like "eat popcorn" and "buy Coke." More recently, parents have expressed fears about subliminal messages in rock music, such as backward messages that encourage violence. The bulk of the evidence suggests that subliminal messages of this sort are usually either ineffective or only minimally effective in motivating consumer behavior and that backward messages have no impact whatsoever, as they cannot be perceived (Vokey & Read, 1985). A person who is already thirsty may become slightly more likely to buy a soft drink after a subliminal message, but a person whose stomach is full is unlikely to make a run for the popcorn. A teenager who hears a subliminal message embedded in a song is equally unlikely to commit a homicide.

Although the proposition that unconscious cognitive and perceptual processes can influence behavior has become less controversial in psychology, what continues to distinguish psychodynamic from other perspectives on consciousness is the contention that emotional and motivational processes can be unconscious. As we shall see in the next two chapters, this view is now gaining experimental support. Research on motivation suggests a distinction between conscious and unconscious motive systems similar to the distinction between implicit and explicit memory in cognitive science (McClelland et al., 1989). Experimental data also show that emotional processes can influence thought and behavior without being conscious. Several research groups, for example, have found that people who are unaware of their emotions or prone to repressing their feelings tend to suffer ill health (Asendorph & Sherer, 1983; Newton & Contrada, 1992; Pennebaker, 1992; Shedler et al., 1993; Singer, 1990; D. Weinberger, 1990). Other research finds that "gut level" feelings that emerge spontaneously often direct people's behavior even when their conscious beliefs lead them in other directions (Epstein, 1994). Like Claparede's patient, people find themselves behaving in ways that do not make sense to their own consciousness.

Cognitive Perspective

Initially, cognitive psychologists paid little attention to whether information processing occurred in or out of conscious awareness. By the mid-1980s, however, this began to change (Kihlstrom, 1987). Information-processing models generally equate consciousness with working memory or short-term memory. Consciousness is thus seen as a repository for current perceptions and retrieved memories. Most models also distinguish between explicit (conscious) and implicit (unconscious) memory, and priming studies have shown, as we have seen, that information never registered consciously can nonetheless be remembered implicitly. Subjects have even shown priming effects for words learned under surgical amnesia, even though they could not recognize them (Kihlstrom et al., 1990). Parallel distributed processing models (Chapter 7) further propose that information processing occurs in relatively separate modules, most of which are unconscious. The brain synthesizes a unitary conscious experience from the various activated unconscious modules (Baars, 1988; Mandler & Nakamura, 1987).

Cognitive scientists have now documented a vast array of cognitive processes that occur without conscious awareness, many of which not only are quite complex but also may be learned without ever being conscious (Holyoak & Spellman, 1993; Kihlstrom, 1987; Uleman & Bargh, 1989). When people construct sentences as they speak, they access semantic memory as they choose the contents of their speech and they apply rules of grammar to organize the words. Probably nothing would be as terrifying to people delivering a speech than the realization that they actually have no idea what will come out of their mouths next. Consciousness issues general "commands" about what to say next, but those commands are executed unconsciously.

Many other everyday cognitive processes are unconscious. For example, people have no difficulty making instantaneous judgments about the age, sex, physical attractiveness, and social class of people they meet, and they can even do so from a photograph of a face. Ask them how they made those judgments, however, or to recall the features of the face they used as guides, and they will often be at a loss (Lewicki, 1986).

Observations such as these have led some cognitive psychologists to propose a distinction similar to that made by memory researchers, between implicit and explicit thinking—that is, unconscious thinking governed by hands-on experience with the environment, versus conscious, rational thought (Holyoak & Spellman, 1993; Reber, 1992). In one study, subjects were asked to compose a ballad after hearing a series of ballads (Rubin et al., 1993, cited in Holyoak & Spellman, 1993). Subjects could readily do so by following certain rules of composition, but they followed roughly twice as many rules as they could consciously describe. In another study, subjects viewed a computer screen divided into four quadrants (Greenwald, 1992). A target stimulus appeared in one of the four quadrants, and its location varied over a number of trials. Although the rules guiding its location were very complicated and subjects could not articulate the way they discovered the target's location, with practice the subjects' ability to locate it improved. Comparable findings appear in numerous other domains, converging on the proposition that if people learn information by doing rather than through instruction, they are likely to follow procedural rules of which they have no consciousness.

John Kihlstrom (1987), a cognitive theorist of consciousness, distinguishes unconscious from preconscious cognitive processes, both of which occur outside of awareness. Unconscious cognitive processes are skills or procedures that operate without awareness and are not accessible to consciousness under any circumstance, any more than regulation of temperature by the hypothalamus is subject to conscious awareness. Preconscious cognitive processes refer to declarative knowledge activated below the threshold of consciousness that influences conscious thought and behavior. This process occurs experimentally in subliminal priming procedures, as well as in everyday life, as when a thought keeps recurring over the course of a day because it is preconsciously activated.

FROM MIND TO BRAIN

THE NEUROPSYCHOLOGY OF CONSCIOUSNESS

Experientially, consciousness is the seat of who we are; to lose consciousness permanently is to lose existence as a psychological being. So what neural structures confer conscious awareness and regulate states of consciousness? The answer to this question depends in part on which meaning of consciousness one has in mind. If one means simply the state of being conscious (rather than being unconscious or asleep), then hindbrain and midbrain structures such as the reticular formation appear to be particularly important (Franklin et al., 1988; Szymusiak et al., 1989). Damage to the reticular formation through head injury in humans or lesioning in animals can lead to coma or loss of consciousness. The pons and medulla are also involved in regulating states of conscious arousal (Figure 9.7).

Isolating neural structures involved in consciousness becomes much more difficult when consciousness is viewed more broadly as the center of subjective awareness. Some theorists who emphasize the importance of verbal thought

FIGURE 9.7
The neuropsychological basis of consciousness. (a) The hindbrain and midbrain structures involved in conscious arousal and shifts from waking to sleep include the reticular formation, the pons, and the medulla. (b) In blindsight, the neural pathway from the lateral geniculate nucleus in the thalamus to the striate cortex, which allows consciousness of visual images, is inoperative. However, a second, evolutionarily older pathway through the midbrain remains intact, permitting the implicit ability to locate visual stimuli.

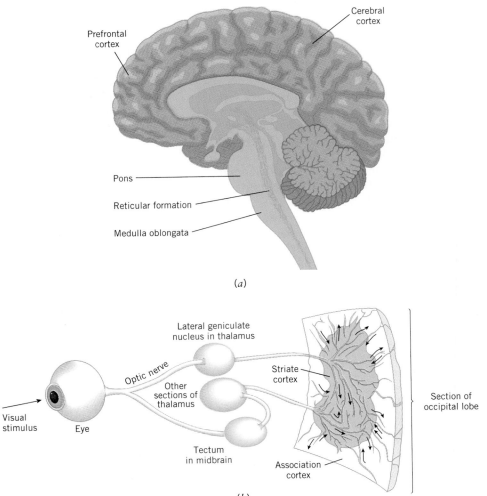

in consciousness consider consciousness primarily a function of the left cerebral hemisphere (Gazzaniga, 1985), although people are conscious of many things they cannot verbalize, such as images or smells. A region of particular importance is the prefrontal cortex (Goldman-Rakic, 1995), which is involved in momentarily storing, manipulating, or calling up information from various sensory modalities into working memory (Chapter 6).

One way to learn about the neural pathways involved in consciousness is to examine neurological disorders that disrupt it, such as split brain, blindsight, and amnesia. People with split brains, whose two hemispheres function independently following severing of the corpus callosum, provide one window to the neuropsychology of consciousness. An instructive case described in Chapter 3 was a 10-year-old boy who could only answer written questions verbally when inquiries were made to the left hemisphere but whose right hemisphere could answer by spelling words with letter tiles with the left hand (LeDoux et al., 1977). The feelings spelled by his nonverbal right hemisphere were consistently more negative than those of his left hemisphere, suggesting that two very different centers of consciousness were inhabiting the same skull.

A second phenomenon that bears on the neural underpinnings of consciousness is blindsight. Pursuing observations made by neurologists in the early part of this century, researchers have examined patients about whom Hamlet might have asked, "To see or not to see?" These patients are, in one sense, totally blind. They have lesions to the striate cortex, the primary cortical region in the occipital lobes responsible for visual sensation. If shown an object, they deny that they have seen it. Yet if asked to describe its geometrical form (e.g., triangle or square) or give its location in space (to the right or left, up or down), they do so with accuracy far better than chance—frequently protesting all the while that they cannot do the task because they cannot see. Researchers call this phenomenon **blindsight** (Weiskrantz et al., 1974).

Although the neural basis for blindsight is not entirely clear, one hypothesis, derived in part from animal research, points to the presence in the visual system of two neural pathways involved in visual processing (Figure 9.7*b*). In the evolutionarily more recent pathway, neurons of the optic nerve carrying sensory information project to the thalamus via the optic tract; the information is subsequently transmitted to the striate cortex in the occipital lobes. This pathway is responsible for conscious visual perception and for determining the precise nature of stimuli. The other pathway is evolutionarily older: Neurons carrying information from the retina project to a midbrain structure responsible for vision in simpler animals such as frogs and birds that lack the highly specialized visual cortex of humans. From there the information passes through the thalamus and eventually on to the cortex. In blindsight, this second pathway appears to allow some visual processing at the midbrain level, even though the first pathway is rendered inoperative by damage to the striate cortex. Thalamic processing may also permit some recognition of what an object is even though this thalamic knowledge cannot be consciously accessed.

Other neurological conditions involving visual processing provide equally intriguing clues to the neurological basis of consciousness (Edelman, 1989). For example, individuals with prosopagnosia have right temporal-parietal damage that leaves them unable to recognize even familiar faces (Chapter 3). People with this disorder may nonetheless demonstrate implicit face recognition to familiar people: They respond differently emotionally and physiologically (measured by heart rate or skin conductance) to familiar and unfamiliar faces (Bruyer, 1991).

Studies with amnesics, like studies of priming in normal subjects, have shown that people can remember things implicitly even while lacking explicit memory. In one series of studies (Squire, 1986), amnesic and normal subjects were shown a word list and asked to recall the words with and without cues.

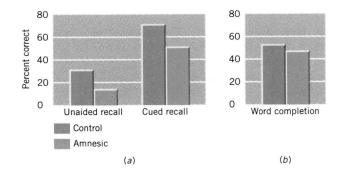

FIGURE 9.8
Priming effects in amnesia. Subjects were shown word lists including words like "absent," "income," and "motel" and asked to recall the words. Amnesic patients were impaired on both unaided recall and cued recall (where the first three letters of the word were given) (a). However, amnesic patients exhibited normal priming effects when they completed three-letter fragments (e.g., ABS—) with the first word that came to mind (b). SOURCE: Squire, 1986.

When later tested for conscious (explicit) memory, amnesic subjects were considerably impaired on both free recall (without cues) and cued recall tasks using word fragments (in which the first three letters of the word were presented) (Figure 9.8). However, amnesics were as likely as neurologically intact subjects to use words from the list when shown word fragments and asked to complete them with the first words that came to mind. Thus, although the amnesic subjects had no recollection of seeing the list of words, priming effects were just as pronounced as for normal subjects.

Priming studies like these suggest that some forms of amnesia may represent less a failure of memory than a failure of *consciousness* of memories: The information has been encoded and stored but cannot be consciously accessed. For example, a graduate research assistant told a joke to a Korsakoff's patient, whose ability to remember new experiences was virtually nonexistent (Jacoby & Kelley, 1987). Predictably, the man laughed, but the next time he heard the joke, he was stone-faced. He had no recollection of having heard it before but thought the joke was "dumb." The patient had apparently anticipated the punch line unconsciously, even though he had no conscious recollection of it.

What, then, are the implications of neurological disorders for understanding consciousness? As with other complex psychological functions, consciousness is not located in a single structure but is distributed across a number of neural pathways. Like amnesics and patients with blindsight, those of us without neurological impairment process information consciously as well as unconsciously, and our actions and conscious beliefs are continuously influenced by discriminations and judgments of which we have no conscious awareness. We are as blind as patients with blindsight to a host of processes, many of them quite primitive in an evolutionary sense, that affect the way we think, feel, and behave.

SLEEP AND DREAMING

Having examined the nature of consciousness, we are prepared to discuss the major change that regularly occurs in normal consciousness: the sleep and waking cycle. Those who lament that life is too short would be horrified to realize that they will sleep away roughly a third of their time on the earth, about 25 years. Infants

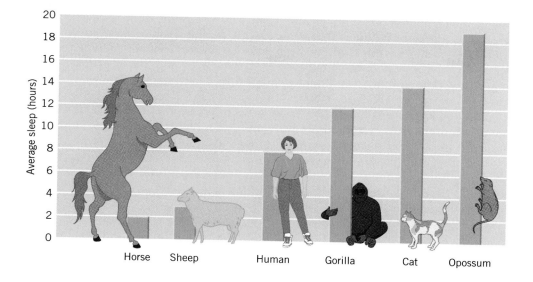

FIGURE 9.9
Average hours of sleep per night. Animals vary according to the amount of sleep they need, with humans somewhere in the middle.

sleep two-thirds of the time, and elderly people, about one-fourth. Sleep is apparently an ancient evolutionary development, of which different animals require varying amounts (Figure 9.9).

Individuals differ widely in the amount of sleep they need and actually get; most people report sleeping eight to nine hours a night (Figure 9.10). Rare cases have been documented of people who require minimal sleep, such as a 70-year-old English nurse who was observed to sleep only one hour every night with no adverse consequences (Borbély, 1986). The number of hours people sleep is related to mortality rates, although the reasons for this are unclear. People who report sleeping for unusually long *or* unusually short durations are prone to die earlier than people whose reported sleep is in the middle of the bell curve (Figure 9.11).

The cycle of sleep and waking in humans and other animals, like the ebb and flow of body temperature and other life support processes, is a circadian rhythm. A **circadian rhythm** (from the Latin, *circa*, meaning "about," and *diem*, meaning "day") is a cyclical biological process that evolved around the daily cycles of light and dark. Circadian rhythms account for the difficulties people experience with jet lag and changing work shifts. Nurses, medical residents on call, police, pilots, and

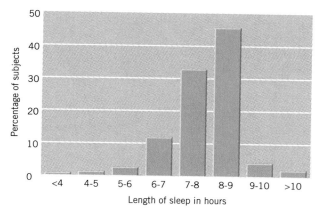

FIGURE 9.10
The number of hours people report sleeping. Most people report sleeping from seven to nine hours a night. Very few report that they sleep less than five or more than ten hours.
SOURCE: *Adapted from Kripke et al., 1979.*

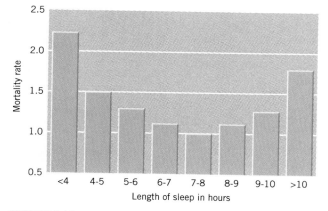

FIGURE 9.11
Sleep duration and mortality. Mortality rates are highest among those at the extremes, who report sleeping less than five or more than ten hours per night. (Mortality rate is scaled against the group with the lowest mortality rate, those who sleep 8 hours.)
SOURCE: *Adapted from Kripke et al., 1979.*

Sleep cycles evolved to match the rotations of the earth around the sun.

flight attendants, whose shifts change from day to day or week to week, suffer greater incidence of health problems because of disrupted circadian rhythms (Tan, 1991). Circadian rhythms akin to sleep-wake cycles may exist in daytime as well. Research supports the distinction between "day people" and "night people," finding that people peak in their alertness, arousal, and even hypnotizability at different times of the day (Wallace, 1993).

No one knows precisely what function sleep serves, although it seems to play some role in the daily restoration of body and mind. People deprived of sleep, like students during examination periods, often have difficulty concentrating and become more susceptible to illness because of diminished immune functioning. Not surprisingly, the time required to fall asleep is dramatically lowered after a sleepless night (Carskadon & Dement, 1982), likely reflecting an evolved mechanism to promote adaptation.

People have known of the ill effects of extreme sleep deprivation for over 2000 years. In Roman times and during the Middle Ages, sleep deprivation was used as a form of torture. About a century ago psychologists published a study of three men deprived of sleep for 90 hours, or about four days (Patrick & Gilbert, 1896). After their second sleepless night, the subjects began to experience disturbances in perception, including hallucinations. The hallucinations disappeared once the subjects were able to sleep. Earlier in this century, Soviet and Chinese experts in thought reform (brainwashing) discovered that depriving people of sleep makes them more susceptible to major alterations in belief and value systems (Lifton, 1963).

In 1959, a New York disk jockey, Peter Tripp, stayed awake for 200 hours, or about eight days, as part of a "wakeathon" for charity (Luce, 1966). As time went on, Tripp deteriorated considerably, developing hallucinations (such as the belief that his bureau drawer was on fire), delusions, and paranoid thinking, until he finally got some sleep. Extreme sleep deprivation does not always produce symptoms such as these, however, leaving researchers to wonder what other factors contribute to, or prevent, the kind of deterioration that Tripp experienced (Gulevich et al., 1966).

Stages of Sleep

Sleep proceeds through a series of stages (Dement & Kleitman, 1957). To study these stages, researchers use an electroencephalograph (EEG), attaching electrodes to subjects' heads to measure brain waves. (They also use electrodes at the corners of the eyes to track eye movements.) In general, as people move from a waking state

As part of a "wakeathon" for the March of Dimes, disc jockey Peter Tripp stayed awake for almost 4 days. By the end of that time, he was hallucinating and delirious, though he returned to normal after a long, sound sleep.

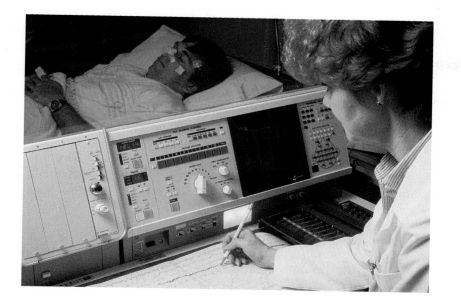

A subject in a sleep laboratory is outfitted with electrodes on the forehead and scalp for the EEG to measure brain waves. Electrodes are applied next to the eyes for a similar instrument, an electro-oculogram, to measure eye movements.

through deeper stages of sleep, their brain waves become slower and more rhythmic, decreasing from over 14 cycles per second in the waking state to as little as one-half cycle per second in deep sleep. (The number of cycles per second is a gross measure of rate of neural firing and hence of mental activity.)

As Figure 9.12 shows, normal waking brain activity has an irregular pattern with a high mental activity level, evidenced in a large number of cycles per second (known as beta waves). As people close their eyes and relax in bed, alpha waves (8 to 12 cycles per second) emerge, signaling a slowing of mental activity and a transition into sleep. Stage 1 sleep is brief (only a few minutes), marked by the appear-

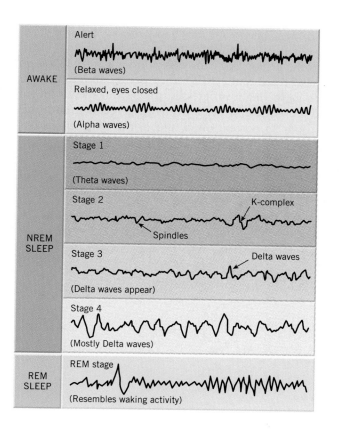

FIGURE 9.12

The stages of sleep. As people move from a waking state through deeper stages of sleep, their brain waves become slower and more rhythmic, decreasing from over 14 cycles per second in the waking state to as little as one-half cycle per second in deep sleep.

ance of slower theta waves (3 to 7 cycles per second). Physiological changes accompany this shift from drowsiness into sleep as eye movements slow, muscles relax, and blood pressure drops, bringing the body into a calm, quiet state.

Stage 2 sleep is marked by an EEG pattern of slightly larger waves interrupted by bursts of low-amplitude activity (called sleep spindles) and slow, high-amplitude waves called K complexes (Halasz, 1993). During Stage 2, sleep deepens, as alpha activity disappears. Stage 3 sleep is marked by the emergence of large, slow, rhythmic delta waves (less than 1 cycle per second). When delta waves comprise more than 50 percent of recorded brain activity, the person has entered Stage 4 sleep. Together, Stages 3 and 4 constitute what is called **delta sleep**. Delta sleep is a deep sleep characterized by relaxation of muscles and decreased rate of respiration and body temperature. People aroused from delta sleep are groggy and disoriented. During delta sleep, muscles apparently rest and rejuvenate, since people deprived of it frequently complain of muscle aches and tension.

Following this descent into Stage 4, the person ascends the stages again, through Stages 3 and 2. Instead of returning to Stage 1, however, a new stage emerges called **rapid eye movement** (or **REM**) **sleep**. REM sleep is qualitatively so different that the other stages are often collectively called simply **non-REM** (or **NREM**) **sleep**. REM sleep is named for the bursts of darting eye movements that occur during this period. In REM sleep, autonomic activity increases: Pulse and blood pressure quicken, respiration becomes faster and irregular, and both males and females evidence signs of sexual arousal that may last for several minutes. The EEG during REM sleep resembles the irregular, faster pattern of waking life, suggesting that, although the body is not moving, the brain is quite active. In addition, people aroused from REM sleep become alert very quickly, unlike those aroused from deep sleep. No one is entirely sure what the function of REM sleep is, but if repeatedly awakened from it, the brain will return to it with increasing persistence.

The mental activity that occurs during REM sleep is dreaming. Roughly 80 percent of the time when people are awakened from REM sleep, they report dream activity. Although many people believe they do not dream, everyone dreams several times a night. Dreams are occasionally reported during NREM sleep, but they are typically simple and lack a story line, such as, "I dreamed I smelled fish" (Antrobus, 1991).

After a period of REM sleep, the person descends again through Stage 2 and on to delta sleep. A complete cycle of REM and NREM sleep occurs about every 90 minutes (Figure 9.13). However, as the night progresses, the person spends less of the 90 minutes in delta sleep and more in REM sleep. REM sleep recurs four or five times a night and accounts for about 25 percent of all time asleep (on the average,

FIGURE 9.13
REM sleep. The stages of sleep follow a cyclical pattern that occurs about every 90 minutes, from Stage 1 through delta sleep and back again. As the night progresses, the person spends less time in deeper sleep and more time in REM sleep. SOURCE: *Cartwright, 1978.*

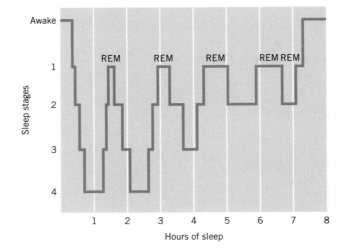

two hours per night). Thus, over the course of a lifetime, the average person spends an estimated 50,000 hours—2000 days, or six full years—dreaming (Hobson, 1988).

Perhaps the most paradoxical aspect of REM sleep is that the mind is quite active but the body is immobile; the only motor activity that typically occurs during REM sleep is occasional twitching. Brain damage, however, can change this. Cats with damage to midbrain structures involved in sleep and consciousness thrash around violently and perform seemingly meaningful behaviors, such as attacking imaginary prey, during REM sleep (Henley & Morrison, 1974). The midbrain in intact animals appears to have a mechanism for inhibiting voluntary muscle movement during REM sleep—which is a good thing, as otherwise people (and presumably cats) would literally act out their dreams. Actually, a small number of people suffer from a syndrome called REM Behavior Disorder: Their motor behavior is not inhibited during REM sleep, and they are dangerous to both themselves and their bed partners, whom they may attack (Mahowald & Schenck, 1989).

During sleep, responsiveness to external, and particularly visual, stimulation is diminished, but it is not entirely absent (see Antrobus, 1991). From an evolutionary perspective, some degree of responsiveness during sleep is essential for survival, as when a person wakes upon hearing a loud noise. The processing of external sensory information is sometimes apparent because of its impact on dreams, which may incorporate elements of sensory experience into the ongoing story. Sleep researchers who sprayed a mist of cold water on subjects during REM sleep received dream reports such as the following:

> Children came into the room and came over to me asking for water. I had a glass of ice water and I tipped the glass to give it to them. I was sitting, and I spilled the water on myself.... Then I got out of the chair and was going to change my pants. (Dement & Wolpert, 1958, p. 550)

Three Views of Dreaming

Since the dawn of human existence, humans have speculated about the nature and significance of dreams. Some cultures view dreams as actions carried out by the dreamer's soul. Others regard dreams as indices of the dreamer's deepest desires, revelations from the spiritual world, or sources of supernatural power (Bourgignon, 1979).

In the late nineteenth century, dream interpretation was considered the realm of "primitives" and charlatans. Freud, however, argued that dream interpretation is a legitimate scientific and psychological pursuit. His psychodynamic theory remains one of the major approaches to dreaming. The other approaches are cognitive and biological.

A Psychodynamic View

Freud (1900) believed that dreams, like all mental events, have meaning but must be deciphered by someone skilled in dream interpretation. As communications spoken in the language of the unconscious, which is irrational and wishful, dreams are often vague, illogical, or bizarre, and thus require translation into the language of rational waking consciousness. For example, in dreams two people are often condensed into one, or thoughts about one person are displaced onto someone else (that is, ascribed to the wrong person). Unconscious processes, according to Freud, are associative processes; thus, ideas are connected by their relationship to each other along networks of association, not by logic. During sleep, a person is not using conscious, rational processes to create or monitor the story, so one thought or image can easily be activated in place of another.

In this sense, Freud saw dreams as "the insanity of the night," where associative thinking replaces logical thought. For example, a man who was angry at his

At night, we are all Ingmar Bergman.

father had a dream of murdering his father's best friend, presumably because anger and murder were associatively linked, as were his father and his father's friend. According to Freud, people often rapidly forget their dreams upon awakening because dreams contain elements of unconscious mental life that would be anxiety-provoking to acknowledge and are repressed during normal waking consciousness.

Freud distinguished between the **manifest content**, or story line of the dream, and the **latent content**, or its underlying meaning. He proposed that the underlying meaning of every dream is an unconscious wish, typically a forbidden sexual or aggressive desire. Today, most psychodynamic psychologists believe, rather, that the latent content can be a wish, a fear, or anything else that is emotionally pressing. To uncover the latent content of a dream, the dreamer free-associates (that is, simply says aloud whatever thoughts come to mind), while the dream analyst tries to trace the networks of association involved in the dream's construction.

A Cognitive View

An alternative viewpoint that shares many points with Freud's theory is a cognitive view proposed by dream researcher David Foulkes (1978). Foulkes, like many contemporary psychodynamic psychologists, takes issue with the contention that the latent meaning of every dream is an unconscious wish. He proposes instead that dreams simply express current concerns of one sort or another, in a language with its own peculiar grammar. The manifest content is constructed from the latent content through rules of transformation, just as a transformational grammar transforms surface structure into deep structure in language (Chapter 7). In everyday language, the sentence "The boy threw the ball" can be transformed into "The ball was thrown by the boy." In dream language, the thought "I am worried about my upcoming exam" can be translated into a dream about falling off a cliff.

Evidence that dreams are related to current concerns—whether wishes, fears, or preoccupations of other sorts—comes not only from the clinic but also from empirical research. In one investigation, researchers studied the dreams of 293 smokers enrolled in a smoking cessation program (Hajek & Belcher, 1991). Having observed that former smokers often report awakening with feelings of panic after dreaming they had been smoking, the investigators studied the incidence of what they called dreams of absent-minded transgression (or DAMITs, for short). In these dreams, indulgence in the forbidden behavior is followed by panic or guilt. Most subjects reported dreaming about smoking over the course of treatment and for a year thereafter, and the majority of these dreams were DAMITs. Perhaps even more interesting, dreaming about smoking (and feeling bad about it in the dream) was predictive of successful outcome. The more such dreams occurred, the more likely the person remained abstinent.

A Biological View

Some dream researchers argue that dreams are biological phenomena with no meaning at all (e.g., Crick & Mitchison, 1983). According to one such theory (Hobson, 1985), dreams reflect cortical interpretations of random neural signals initiated in the midbrain during sleep (Figure 9.14). These signals are relayed through the thalamus to the visual and association cortex, which tries to understand this information in its usual way, namely, by using existing knowledge structures (schemas) to process the information. Because the initial signals are essentially random, however, the interpretations proposed by the cortex rarely make logical sense.

Are these three models of dreaming really incompatible? The psychodynamic and cognitive views converge on the notion that dreams express current concerns or ideas in a highly symbolic language that requires decoding. They differ over the extent to which those concerns involve deep-seated or repressed wishes and fears. In reality, dreams probably express motives (wishes and fears) as well as ideas. Many motives have cognitive components, such as representations of wished-for or feared states (Chapter 10). Thus, a fear of failing an examination includes a representation of the feared scenario and its possible consequences. What applies to cognition, then, probably applies to many aspects of motivation as well.

Moreover, although the biological explanation of dreaming was proposed as an alternative to Freud's theory, it is not necessarily incompatible with either the psychodynamic or the cognitive view. The interpretive processes that occur at the cortical level involve the same structures of meaning—schemas, associational networks, and emotional processes—posited by Freud and Foulkes. Hence, even random activation of these structures would produce dreams that reveal something about the organization of thoughts and feelings in the person's mind, particularly those that have received chronic or recent activation.

You would wish to be responsible for everything except your dreams! What miserable weakness, what lack of logical courage! Nothing contains more of your own work than your dreams! Nothing belongs to you so much! Substance, form, duration, actor, spectator—in these comedies you act as your complete selves!

Nietzsche, Thus Spake Zarathustra

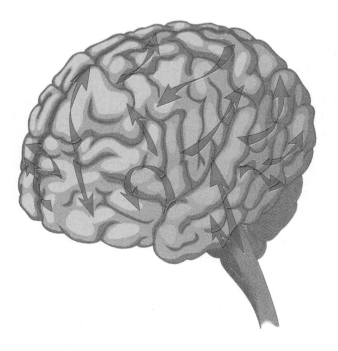

FIGURE 9.14
According to one biological hypothesis, dreams simply reflect cortical rendering of essentially meaningless signals sent by lower brain structures.

Sleep Disorders

Most people have experienced **insomnia** (inability to sleep) of a transient sort, tossing and turning from anxiety or excitement. More enduring sleep disturbances, or **sleep disorders**, result from a number of causes, both biological and psychosocial. On the biological side, insomnia and **hypersomnia** (sleeping too much) are frequent symptoms of depression, since the neurotransmitter systems that mediate mood are also involved in the regulation of circadian rhythms. On the psychosocial side, trauma victims show an elevated incidence of sleep disorders, including nightmares and insomnia (Ross et al., 1989). Following the massive earthquake that struck San Francisco in 1989, the incidence of nightmares in general, as well as nightmares about earthquakes, rose dramatically (Wood et al., 1992). Sleep disturbances may persist for years, even decades after the traumatic experience, particularly if the trauma was prolonged. Survivors of the Nazi Holocaust, now primarily in their 60s and 70s, continue to have significantly more sleep disturbances than normal comparison subjects—over five decades after the experience (Rosen et al., 1991). The longer subjects spent in the camps, the more sleep disturbance they currently report.

The most common sleep disorder is insomnia, which may take one of several forms: initial insomnia (difficulty falling asleep), middle insomnia (typically, frequent awakenings during the night), and early morning insomnia (waking up consistently around four o'clock and being unable to return to sleep) (Reynolds et al., 1991). As prevalent as insomnia is, researchers often find a substantial discrepancy between patients' self-reports of insomnia and their actual sleep patterns when assessed in the laboratory. People who claim to have severe insomnia frequently do sleep several hours, but they think they have not slept.

Insomnia can create a vicious cycle, in which the insomniac starts to worry that she will not be able to sleep as soon as she gets into bed. Essentially, the bed becomes a conditioned stimulus that elicits anxiety, which in turn fuels the insomnia. Using sleeping pills can exacerbate the sleep disturbance by interfering with natural sleep processes (Hindmarch, 1991). A better strategy is to establish a regular bedtime, avoid activities that activate the sympathetic nervous system before bedtime (such as exercising or drinking beverages containing caffeine), and get up rather than roll around restlessly in bed.

Other sleep disorders include nightmares, night terrors, sleep apnea, and narcolepsy. **Nightmares** are vivid, frightening dreams typically associated with fears like falling, death, or calamity (see Bearden, 1994). About 5 percent of the general population suffers from chronic nightmares (Bixler et al., 1979); not surprisingly, chronic nightmare sufferers tend to have other emotional problems (Berquier & Ashton, 1992). Nightmares typically occur during REM sleep and thus can take place at any time during the night. In contrast, **night terrors**, dramatic experiences of intense terror or panic during sleep, typically occur during delta sleep and hence tend to take place in the first two or three hours of sleep. Unlike nightmares, which people usually vividly recall, individuals seldom remember the contents of night terrors upon wakening. Instead, they may scream and awaken, feeling very confused.

Another disorder is **sleep apnea**, which usually produces symptoms of chronic sleepiness because the person is awakened as many as several hundred times during the night. In sleep apnea, breathing typically stops for more than 10 seconds at a time, leaving the person gasping for air. People with sleep apnea often do not know the cause of their distress; they are aware only of feeling as if they have not slept. Their bed partners, however, may be quite aware of their loud snoring and restless sleep. Sleep apnea typically occurs in overweight men.

Narcolepsy is a sleep disorder of the day rather than the night. Narcoleptics are subject to sudden sleep attacks, falling into REM sleep in the middle of talking, driving, laughing, or other activities. Narcolepsy is genetically transmitted, although the incidence varies cross-culturally. In Japan, 1 in 600 people suffers from the disorder, whereas in North America the prevalence is more on the order of 1 in 10,000 (Aldrich, 1990). Narcoleptics often find themselves continuously battling the urge to sleep and hence experience a constant state of fatigue and sleepiness.

ALTERED STATES OF CONSCIOUSNESS

Sleep is the most dramatic example of a psychological state in which normal waking consciousness is suspended, but it is not the only such state. **Altered states of consciousness**—in which the usual conscious ways of perceiving, thinking, and feeling are disrupted—are culturally patterned and occur through meditation, religious experiences, hypnosis, and chemical induction.

Meditation

In **meditation**, which is part of the practice of many religions, the meditator develops a deep state of tranquility by altering the normal flow of conscious thoughts. Many religions, such as Buddhism, believe that meditation leads to a deepened understanding of reality (Ornstein, 1986). Either by focusing attention on a simple stimulus or concentrating on stimuli that are usually in the background of awareness (such as one's breathing), meditation shuts down the normal flow of self-conscious inner dialogue (J. Weinberger, personal communication, 1992). In all types of meditation, the usual goal-directed flow of consciousness is disrupted as the procedures that normally direct conscious attention are de-automatized. Meditators and theologians often describe the experience as leading to a liberation from the self or an expansion of conscious awareness.

Meditation can produce a state of serenity that is reflected in altered brain wave activity. Some forms of meditation facilitate the alpha waves characteristic of the relaxed state of falling into sleep, whereas others even produce theta waves, which are rarely observed except in subjects who are fully asleep (Jangid et al., 1988; Matsuoka, 1990). The result is that some experienced meditators in the East can perform remarkable feats, such as meditating for hours in the bitter cold. Meditation can be highly therapeutic, leading to decreased stress and physiological symptoms (Collings, 1989).

Religious Experiences

Religious experiences are altered states of consciousness in which a person feels at one with nature or the supernatural. In his classic work, *The Varieties of Religious Experience* (1902), William James described the ultimate state of contact with the divine that characterizes the religious experience. During this state, the person experiences a sense of peace and inner harmony, perceives the world and self as having changed dramatically in some way, and has "the sense of perceiving truths not known before" (p. 199). James quotes the manuscript of a clergyman:

> I remember the night, and almost the very spot on the hilltop where my soul opened out, as it were, into the Infinite, and there was a rushing together of the two worlds, the inner and the outer.... The ordinary sense of things around me faded.... It was like the effect of some great orchestra when all the separate notes have melted into one swelling harmony. (James, 1902, p. 67)

In most societies, religious experiences such as this emerge from ritualized religious practices. In possession trances, the soul is believed to be entered by another person or a supernatural being. The person is typically induced into an altered state

Young Buddist monks meditating in a Thai monastery.

Humans seem predisposed to be moved by collective experiences. Left, a Balinese ritual; right, a concert in North America.

through drumming, singing, dancing, and crowd participation (Bourgignon, 1979). Many born-again Christian churches include possession trances as part of their regular religious practices (see, e.g., Griffith et al., 1984).

The use of ritualized altered states dates back at least to the time of the Neanderthals. Pollen found near prehistoric human remains in northern Iraq contains medicinal material that is still used to induce trancelike states in Europe and Asia. The "vision quest" of some Native American tribes frequently included religious trance states during which a young person being initiated into adulthood would come in contact with ancestors or a personal guardian and emerge as a full member of adult society (Bourgignon, 1979). John Lame Deer, a Sioux medicine man, describes an experience that in certain respects resembles that of the Western clergyman quoted by James:

> I was still lightheaded and dizzy from my first sweatbath in which I had purified myself before going up the hill. Even now, an hour later, my skin still tingled. But it seemed to have made my brain empty.... Blackness was wrapped around me like a velvet cloth. It seemed to cut me off from the outside world, even from my own body. It made me listen to voices within me. I thought of my forefathers, who had crouched on this hill before me.... I thought I could sense their presence.... I trembled and my bones turned to ice. (Lame Deer & Erdoes, 1972, pp. 14–15)

Ritualized religious experiences are simultaneously cultural and psychological phenomena. For the individual, they offer a sense of security, enlightenment, and oneness with something greater than themselves. For the group, they provide a sense of solidarity, cohesiveness, and certainty in shared values and beliefs. The individual is typically swept away in the experience, losing the self-reflective component of consciousness and experiencing a dissolution of the boundaries between self and nonself. The French sociologist Emile Durkheim (1915) described this phenomenon as "collective effervescence," in which the individual's consciousness seems dominated by the "collective consciousness". Most readers have probably experienced collective effervescence, either during religious ceremonies or in less profound circumstances, such as rock concerts and sporting events. Collective events of this sort, many of which involve chanting or rhythmic movement and speech, seem to tap into a basic human proclivity for this kind of altered state.

Hypnosis

Another type of altered state, hypnosis, was named after Hypnos, the Greek god of sleep, because of the superficial resemblance between the hypnotic state and sleep. **Hypnosis** is an altered state characterized by deep relaxation and suggestibility (proneness to follow the suggestions of the hypnotist). The subject is like-

A subject responds to a hypnotic suggestion that his hand is tied to a helium-filled balloon.

ly to experience a number of changes in consciousness, including an altered sense of time, self, volition (voluntary control over actions or muscle movements), and perception of the external world. For instance, if the hypnotist directs the subject's arm to float in the air, the individual may have no sensation that she herself is causing the arm to rise; she may feel as if the arm has a mind of its own or as if it is filled with helium (Bowers, 1976). Not everyone, however, can be hypnotized. People differ in their **hypnotic susceptibility**, or capacity to enter into deep hypnotic states (Hilgard, 1965, 1986).

Hypnosis can produce an array of unusual effects, although, as we shall see, many of these are controversial. It can generate amnesia or its opposite, **hypermnesia** (the recall of forgotten memories). A hypnotist can induce **age regression**, leading the subject apparently to relive an incident he experienced at a prior age or speak a language he cannot consciously remember but which was spoken in his home when he was a very young child (Nash, 1988). Hypnotized subjects often demonstrate **hypnotic analgesia**, an apparent lack of pain despite pain-inducing stimulation. For example, if told they are about to smell a beautiful flower, subjects will smile blithely rather than reflexively turning their heads when ammonia is placed under their noses. Some hypnotic subjects have undergone surgery without anesthesia and manifested no sign of conscious pain. Hypnotized subjects have been able to rid themselves of warts (Noll, 1994; Sinclair-Gieben & Chalmers, 1959; Surman et al., 1983) and even to stop blood from flowing profusely from lacerated skin (Bowers, 1976; Kihlstrom, 1985; Ornstein, 1986).

The Hidden Observer

Ernest Hilgard (1986) has experimented extensively with hypnotic phenomena, including hypnotic analgesia and hypnotically induced deafness. In one class demonstration, he hypnotized a subject to become deaf, telling him he could hear nothing until his instructor touched his right shoulder. To prove the extent of the subject's deafness, Hilgard banged together large wooden blocks near the subject's ears and even fired off a starter pistol, to which the subject did not respond. A student in the room wondered whether "some part" of the subject could still hear him, so Hilgard, confident this was not the case, told the subject, "Perhaps there is some part of you that is hearing my voice... If there is, I should like the index finger of your right hand to rise." To the surprise of both instructor and students, the finger rose. The subject then asked Hilgard to restore his hearing to tell him what had just happened, explaining, "I felt my finger rise in a way that was not a spontaneous twitch, so you must have done something to make it rise, and I want to know what you did" (Hilgard, 1986, p. 186). Hilgard then instructed the subject, "When I place my hand on your arm... I can be in touch with that part of you that listened to me before and made your finger rise.... But this hypnotized part of you, to whom I am now talking, will not know what you are saying." The hidden observer—the part of the subject's consciousness that raised the finger—then fully described what had happened, including hearing the slamming wooden blocks. When Hilgard lifted his hand and asked what had happened in the last few minutes, the subject had no idea (pp. 187–188).

Hilgard's discovery of the hidden observer led him to conduct some fascinating experiments on hypnotic analgesia. In the basic design, the subject places her hand and forearm in ice water and reports the degree of pain produced, from 0 (no pain) to 10 (pain so severe that she wants to pull out her hand). In a normal waking state, the person usually hits 10 in less than a minute. When given a suggestion for hypnotic analgesia, subjects often report no pain and in fact keep their arm in the water indefinitely. However, when given the suggestion to have the hidden observer rate the pain (writing with the other hand kept out of sight) using the same 0–10 scale, subjects report steadily increasing pain (Figure 9.15).

Hypnosis and Memory

A controversial claim made by advocates of hypnosis is that hypnosis can restore forgotten memories. In the late 1970s, for example, a busload of children and their driver were kidnapped at gunpoint. Later, under hypnosis, the driver relived the experience from beginning to end and was able to recall the kidnappers' license plate number with enough clarity to lead to their apprehension. Police detectives have used hypnosis to solve other cases as well (Geiselman et al., 1985).

One researcher found that subjects under hypnosis could recall events that occurred under anesthesia (Levinson, 1965). While a surgeon was removing a small lump from the lower lip of a patient, the doctor made the comment, "Good gra-

FIGURE 9.15
The hidden observer. The figure shows overt and covert pain following hypnotic suggestion for analgesia, as compared with normal waking pain, when the hand is immersed in ice water. SOURCE: *Hilgard, 1986, p. 190.*

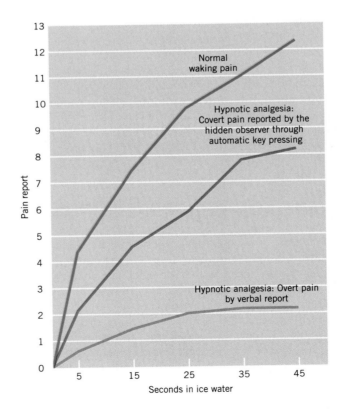

cious... it may be a cancer!" For the next three weeks, the patient was inexplicably depressed. The investigator then hypnotized the woman and induced hypnotic regression to the day of the operation. She remembered the exclamation "Good gracious" and then, crying profusely, recalled, "He is saying this may be malignant" (p. 201). The researcher subsequently demonstrated the capacity for recall of similar events experimentally with a sample of dental patients.

Although these examples show that hypnosis can sometimes be useful in retrieving forgotten memories, many psychologists have expressed concern about its over-enthusiastic use to retrieve memories of sexual abuse or crime scenes. The limits of hypnosis are significant enough that many states now outlaw the use of hypnotically induced memories in court testimony. One of the major problems is that people under hypnosis are highly suggestible and hence are likely to report more than they actually know (Wagstaff, 1984). A subtle inflection or leading question can lead a hypnotized eyewitness to believe he remembers things that simply are not true, although this is applicable, to a lesser degree, to nonhypnotized subjects as well (Chapter 6). Controversy continues as to the conditions under which hypnosis leads to genuine or distorted memories (Barnier & McConkey, 1992).

Commentary: Is Hypnosis Real?

Hypnosis has drawn considerable skepticism since the earliest scientific attention paid to it in the nineteenth century, in part because of a history of charlatans using stage hypnosis mixed with liberal doses of deception (such as planting subjects). A substantial number of scientists remain unconvinced that hypnosis is a real phenomenon at all. Hypnotic effects, they contend, stem primarily from subjects' desires to produce the behavior they think the investigator wants to see. As we shall see in Chapter 17, research over many decades has demonstrated that social pressures can lead people to perform peculiar, deviant, or destructive behavior, even in a normal state of consciousness. Several researchers have produced evidence to suggest that hypnotic subjects are simply playing the role they believe they are expected to play (Murrey et al., 1992; Spanos et al., 1992). Others contend that aspects of hypnotic suggestion not unique to hypnosis, such as heavy reliance on imagery, actually account for hypnotic effects. People instructed to use vivid visual images can often accomplish the same feats as hypnotized subjects, such as eliminating warts (Spanos et al., 1988).

The validity of hypnosis, however, is bolstered by findings from studies in which subjects are given **posthypnotic suggestions**—commands to perform a behavior on demand once they are out of the hypnotic trance. In a study designed to test the hypothesis that hypnotized subjects are simply role-playing, the investigators compared the behavior of subjects instructed to act *as if* they were hypnotized with the behavior of true hypnotized subjects (Orne et al., 1968). When both groups of subjects were distracted from assigned tasks and thus diverted from thinking about what they were supposed to do, hypnotized subjects were three times as likely to carry out the posthypnotic suggestion as simulators.

Some psychologists seem reluctant to accept the validity of hypnosis as an altered state of consciousness because of the same kinds of ideological commitments and temperamental predilections that led researchers in the early 1960s to conclude that subliminal perception and other unconscious processes do not exist. Skeptics claim that patients given only hypnotic suggestions during surgery must be "faking it," but it is difficult to imagine undergoing an operation without anesthesia simply to please an experimenter (Bowers, 1976). Perhaps the safest conclusion at this juncture is that hypnosis is indeed an altered state with its own properties but that many of the phenomena produced under this condition can be produced under other conditions, such as use of imagery or social pressure.

Painting of a peyote ritual of the Delaware Indians of Oklahoma.

Drug-Induced States of Consciousness

The most common way people alter their state of consciousness is by ingesting **psychoactive substances**—drugs that operate on the nervous system to alter mental activity. The substance most frequently used for this purpose throughout the world is alcohol. In the West, people use many psychoactive substances, ranging from caffeine in coffee and nicotine in tobacco to drugs that seriously impair functioning, such as cocaine and heroin. Some psychoactive drugs resemble the molecular structure of naturally occurring neurotransmitters and thus have similar effects at synapses. Others alter the normal processes of synthesis, release, reuptake, or breakdown of neurotransmitters (Chapter 3) and consequently affect the rate of neural firing in various regions of the brain.

The action of psychoactive substances cannot be reduced entirely to their chemical properties, however, because their impact also depends on cultural beliefs and expectations. Native Americans who use peyote (a potent consciousness-altering drug) in religious rituals typically experience visions congruent with their religious beliefs, feelings of reverence, and relief from physical ailments. In contrast, Anglo-Americans using the same drug experience disconcerting visions, extreme mood states, and a breakdown in normal social inhibitions (Wallace, 1959b).

In moderate doses—wine with dinner or a drink after work—alcohol can enhance experience, but the social costs of substance abuse are staggering. In the United States, approximately one in seven people abuse alcohol, and another one in twenty misuse other psychoactive substances. The number of people killed in alcohol-related accidents in the United States every year surpasses the total number killed in the entire Vietnam War (GAP, 1991). The major types of psychoactive substances in widespread use include alcohol and other depressants, stimulants, hallucinogens, and marijuana (Ray & Ksir, 1987).

Alcohol and Other Depressants

Depressants are substances that depress, or slow down, the nervous system. Common depressants include **barbiturates** (often called "downers") and benzodiazepines such as Valium and Xanax, two common tranquilizers. These drugs provide a sedative or calming effect, and higher doses can be used as sleeping pills. Unfortunately, they can also produce both psychological and physical dependence.

Contrary to what many people who rely on alcohol to elevate their mood believe, alcohol is a sedative. The precise neural mechanisms by which it slows down central nervous system activity are unclear, but like other sedatives, alcohol appears to enhance the activity of the neurotransmitter GABA (gamma-aminobutyric acid). GABA normally inhibits transmission of neural impulses (Zorumski & Isenberg, 1991); for example, it is known to inhibit norepinephrine, which is involved in anxiety. Thus, by increasing the neural inhibition of anxiety reactions, alcohol can reduce anxiety. People seem to figure this out, as some use alcohol to escape anxiety or stress (see Cooper et al., 1992).

As with psychoactive substances in general, expectations about alcohol's effects, shaped by culture and personal experience, have as much impact on behavior as the drug's direct effects on the nervous system (see Collins et al., 1990; Leigh & Stacy, 1991). Several studies have sought to distinguish the causal roles of two independent variables: whether subjects are drinking alcohol and whether they *think* they are drinking alcohol. Subjects are placed in one of four groups. In one, they drink an alcoholic beverage and are told they are drinking alcohol; in another, they drink alcohol but are told they are not. (The flavor of the drink makes alcohol detection impossible.) In the other two groups, subjects drink a nonalcoholic beverage and are either informed or misinformed about what they are drinking.

The results of these investigations elucidate the relative contributions of biology and beliefs to the effects of alcohol. For example, male subjects who think they are drinking report greater sexual arousal and less guilt when exposed to sexually arousing stimuli, whether or not they have actually been drinking alcohol. This is even more likely to be the case if they have strong beliefs about the impact of alcohol on arousal (see Abrams & Wilson, 1983; Hull & Bond, 1986). More generally, people are more likely to behave in ways that may be deviant, dangerous, or antisocial if they can attribute their behavior to alcohol.

Alcohol abuse is involved in many violent crimes, including assault, rape, spouse abuse, and murder; the majority of murders appear to be committed by people who have been drinking (Bushman & Cooper, 1990). Precisely how alcohol contributes to aggression is unclear. One theory suggests that the substance disengages normal prohibitions; that is, it contributes to aggression "not by 'stepping on the gas' but rather by paralyzing the brakes" (Muehlberger, 1956, cited in Bushman & Cooper, 1990, p. 342). A related theory suggests that alcohol facilitates aggression by derailing other psychological processes that normally decrease the likelihood of aggression, such as the ability to assess risks accurately. Still another theory suggests that violence-prone individuals drink so that they can have an excuse for aggression (Bushman & Cooper, 1990).

Long-term ingestion of alcohol produces physical changes in the brain that can seriously affect cognitive functioning, sometimes to the point of dementia (confusion and disorientation) or Korsakoff's syndrome. Radiological techniques such as CT scans reveal that roughly half of alcoholics show cerebral atrophy, and many show subcortical damage as well. Some of the behavioral changes associated with these physiological changes appear to be reversible, however, if the person stops drinking (Bowden, 1990).

Stimulants

Stimulants are drugs that increase alertness, energy, and autonomic reactivity (such as heart rate and blood pressure). These drugs range from commonly used substances like nicotine and caffeine to more potent ones such as amphetamines and cocaine. Nicotine increases heart rate and blood pressure while often decreasing emotional reactivity. Thus, cigarette smokers often report that smoking increases their arousal and alertness while also providing a soothing effect. Caffeine is found

O God, that men should put an enemy in their mouths to steal away their brains; that we should, with joy, pleasance, revel and applause, transform ourselves into beasts!

Shakespeare, Othello (II, iii)

In the nineteenth century, cocaine was an ingredient of many elixirs, including Coca-Cola.

in coffee, tea, chocolate, soft drinks, and some nonprescription drugs such as aspirin products, decongestants, and sleep suppressants. Whereas moderate amounts of caffeine can help a person stay awake, high doses can produce symptoms indistinguishable from anxiety disorders, such as "the jitters" or even panic.

Amphetamines (sometimes called "uppers" or "speed") lead to hyperarousal and a feeling of "speeding," or everything moving quickly. The molecular structure of amphetamines is similar to that of the neurotransmitters dopamine and norepinephrine. Stimulation of the norepinephrine receptor sites appears to produce alertness, while stimulation of the dopamine receptors produces euphoria and increased motor activity (Ray & Ksir, 1987). Amphetamines can produce psychosis in vulnerable individuals, death by overdose, or ill health in chronic users, who essentially circumvent the normal signals sent by the brain to protect the body from fatigue and overuse.

Cocaine has held an attraction for people since about 500 A.D., when it was used by the Inca in Peru. The coca leaf, which contains cocaine, was used in religious ceremonies and even treated as money to compensate laborers. In the late 1800s, physicians discovered cocaine's anesthetic properties; soon many medicines and elixirs were laced with cocaine, as was Coca-Cola. Like other stimulants, cocaine appears to increase the activity of norepinephrine and dopamine, leading to a "rush" that can last a few minutes to two or three hours, depending on the form of ingestion and the potency of the drug. Chronic use depletes these neurotransmitters and can cause chronic depression similar to the crash that occurs when the initial high is over (GAP, 1991). Cocaine is one of the most potent pleasure-inducing substances—as well as one of the most addictive—ever discovered. Experimental animals will press a lever thousands of times to receive a single dose (Siegel, 1990).

Cocaine produces momentary distortions in thinking, such as diminished judgment and an inflated sense of one's own abilities. Regular cocaine use commonly produces paranoid thinking, which is often transient but can become more severe and chronic with continued use. One study found that 68 percent of cocaine-dependent men admitted to a rehabilitation program reported paranoid experiences on cocaine that lasted several hours, long after the cocaine high was over (Satel et al., 1991). Moreover, 38 percent of the patients who reported paranoia actually responded by arming themselves with guns or knives.

Hallucinogens

Hallucinogens derive their name from their capacity to create **hallucinations**, in which sensations and perceptions occur in the absence of any external stimulation. While under the influence of hallucinogens, people may experience time slowing down or speeding up, colors bursting from the sky, walls moving, or ants crawling under the skin.

Humans have used hallucinogens for thousands of years, but their impact and cultural meaning differ dramatically. In many areas, hallucinogens have been used largely during cultural rituals, as when Australian aboriginal boys ingest hallucinogenic plants during ceremonies initiating them into manhood (Grob & Dobkin de Rios, 1992). In these settings, the meaning of hallucinations is established by the elders, who consider the drugs essential to bringing the young into the community of adults. In the contemporary West, individuals ingest these substances for recreation and with minimal social control, so the effects are more variable.

Hallucinogenic drug use in Europe and North America dramatically increased in the 1960s with the discovery of the synthetic hallucinogen, **lysergic acid diethylamide (LSD)**. By the late 1970s, concern over the abuse of LSD and other hallucinogens, such as PCP ("angel dust") and hallucinogenic mushrooms ("shrooms"), intensified, and with good scientific reason. Chronic use of LSD, for example, is associated with psychotic symptoms, depression, paranoia, lack of motivation, and changes in brain physiology (Kaminer & Hrecznyj, 1991; King & Ellison, 1989).

The long-term effects of even occasional use are not entirely clear, although tragic events have occurred with LSD use, such as people walking out of windows and falling to their death.

Marijuana

The use of **marijuana** has drawn considerable controversy. Marijuana use between the ages of 18 and 25 peaked in 1979 in the United States at 35 percent (Pope et al., 1990; Schuster, 1987) (see Figure 9.16). Marijuana produces a state of being high, or stoned during which the individual may feel euphoric, giddy, unself-conscious, or contemplative. During a marijuana high, judgment is moderately impaired, problem solving becomes less focused and efficient, and attention is more difficult to direct; some people report paranoia or panic symptoms.

For decades, people have speculated about the detrimental effects of marijuana. Its use has been said to lead to moral depravity, impotence, the development of breasts in males, and an inevitable progression to harder drugs. By and large, these concerns reflect political and ideological agendas, not scientifically credible evidence. No credible scientific studies have documented the negative effects of occasional or recreational use of the drug (Massachusetts General Hospital Bulletin, 1986), and recent research does not support previously alleged long-term negative effects on reproductive functioning (Block et al., 1991). As discussed in Chapter 15 on mental disorders, the most definitive study in this area, a longitudinal followup of young adults observed since early childhood, actually found occasional marijuana users and experimenters to be healthier psychologically than either abusers *or*

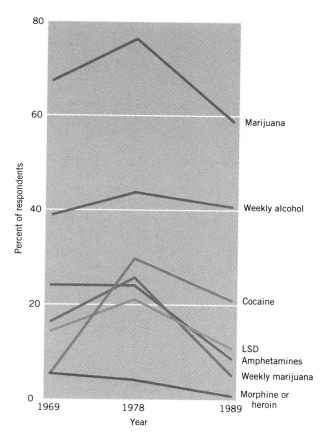

FIGURE 9.16

Drug use among college seniors in 1969, 1978, and 1989. Rates represent the percentage of students who report ever having used a particular drug, except for weekly marijuana and alcohol, where the numbers reflect the percentage of students reporting current weekly use. SOURCE: Pope et al., 1990.

abstainers (Shedler & Block, 1990). Nevertheless, marijuana can produce some unwanted consequences. Memory for incidents that occur under the influence of the drug can be impaired, as reflected in temporary decreases in hippocampal functioning while high (see Heyser et al., 1993), and people drive less safely while stoned on marijuana. Chronic or heavy use, particularly beyond adolescence, is also a symptom of psychological disturbance (Chapter 15), which can contribute to deficits in social and occupational functioning. As with other drugs, smoking during pregnancy should also be avoided, as studies have produced conflicting results on the impact of prenatal exposure (Day et al., 1994; Szeto et al., 1991). In sum, like alcohol, the extent to which marijuana has negative psychological consequences depends on whether or not it is abused.

SOME CONCLUDING THOUGHTS

Like the attentional mechanisms that direct the consciousness of individuals, scientific communities have mechanisms that bring phenomena in and out of focus at various times. In the heyday of behaviorism, consciousness was relegated to the periphery of psychological awareness. The dominance of the cognitive perspective led initially to a continued disinterest in consciousness, but recent developments in cognitive science have generated renewed interest in the roles of conscious and unconscious processes in human information processing. As the computer metaphor has begun to wane, two other neglected topics have begun once again to capture the attention of the psychological community: motivation and emotion. To these we now turn.

Summary

The Nature of Consciousness

1. **Consciousness** refers to the subjective awareness of percepts, thoughts, feelings, and behavior. It performs two functions: monitoring the self and environment, and controlling thought and behavior. **Awareness** refers to all the current thoughts, feelings, and perceptions that *could* be available to consciousness at a given time if attention were turned to them. **Attention** is the process of focusing consciousness, providing heightened sensitivity to a limited range of experience requiring more extensive information processing. **Divided attention** means splitting attention between two or more stimuli or tasks.

2. Psychologists study the flow of consciousness through **experience sampling** techniques. Even such a private experience as consciousness is in part shaped by culture.

Perspectives on Consciousness

3. Freud distinguished among conscious, preconscious, and unconscious processes. **Preconscious** mental processes are not presently conscious but could be readily brought to consciousness if the need arose. Many **unconscious** mental processes are inaccessible to consciousness because they have been repressed, kept from conscious awareness because they are too threatening or anxiety-provoking to

acknowledge. Research supports the hypothesis that subliminal presentation of stimuli can influence the contents of consciousness, but its ability to motivate people to run to the popcorn stand is minimal. Backwards messages on albums have no impact because they cannot be perceived.

4. Information-processing approaches distinguish conscious from unconscious (procedural) and preconscious (below threshold) cognitive processes. Research documents that a vast array of cognitive processes occur in parallel without conscious awareness.

5. Midbrain structures play a key role in regulating states of wakefulness and arousal, and the prefrontal cortex is implicated in directing attention, but consciousness, like most psychological functions, is distributed across a number of neural pathways. Disorders of consciousness like **blindsight** or prosopagnosia can result from neurological damage.

Sleep and Dreaming

6. The sleep/waking cycle is a **circadian rhythm,** a cyclical biological process that evolved around the daily cycles of light and dark. Sleep proceeds through a series of stages that cycle throughout the night. Most dreaming occurs during **REM** sleep, named for the bursts of darting eye movements that occur during this period.

7. Freud distinguished between the **manifest content,** or story line, and the **latent content,** or underlying meaning, of dreams. Freud believed the latent content is always an unconscious wish, although most contemporary psychodynamic psychologists believe that wishes, fears, and current concerns can underlie dreams. Cognitive theorists suggest that dreams express thoughts in a distinct language with its own rules of transformation. Some biological theorists contend that dreams have no meaning; dreams are cortical interpretations of random neural impulses generated in the midbrain. These three approaches to dreaming are not necessarily incompatible.

8. Common **sleep disorders** include **insomnia, nightmares, night terrors, sleep apnea,** and **narcolepsy.**

Altered States of Consciousness

9. In **altered states of consciousness,** the usual conscious ways of perceiving, thinking, and feeling are changed. **Meditation** is an altered state in which the person narrows consciousness to a single thought or expands consciousness to focus on stimuli that are usually at the periphery of awareness. In **religious experiences,** the person feels at one with nature or the supernatural. **Hypnosis,** characterized by deep relaxation and suggestibility, appears to be an altered state, but many hypnotic phenomena can be produced under other conditions.

10. **Psychoactive substances** are drugs that operate on the nervous system to alter patterns of perception, thought, feeling, and behavior. **Depressants,** the most widely used of which is alcohol, slow down the nervous system. **Stimulants** (such as nicotine, caffeine, **amphetamines,** and **cocaine**) increase alertness, energy, and autonomic reactivity. **Hallucinogens** create **hallucinations,** in which sensations and perceptions occur in the absence of any external stimulation. **Marijuana** leads to a state of being high—euphoric, giddy, unself-conscious, or contemplative. Psychoactive substances alter consciousness biologically, by facilitating or inhibiting neural transmission at the synapse, and psychologically, through expectations shaped by cultural beliefs.

Alex Colville, "Skater," 1964, Museum of Modern Art, New York

Chapter 10

MOTIVATION

Since 1981, when an article in the *New York Times* informed the world of a new "gay cancer," knowledge about AIDS in the general population has increased tremendously. Researchers eventually discovered that heterosexuals were at risk as well. In fact, 75 percent of HIV-positive people in the world were infected through heterosexual transmission (Miller et al., 1993).

Given that AIDS is a deadly, contagious disease and that the risk of contracting the HIV virus is substantially diminished in people who practice safe sex, one would expect the use of condoms to be nearly universal among the sexually active. Condom use has indeed increased since the epidemic, but the number of sexually active people who continue to engage in unsafe sex is astonishing. In one study, only 17 percent of heterosexuals with multiple sexual partners reported using condoms regularly (Catania et al., 1992), and physicians in San Francisco, a city whose gay population has been decimated by the virus, report that condom use among young gay males has returned to pre-AIDS levels.

In light of all the knowledge about AIDS transmission and prevention, why do people continue to engage in unsafe sexual practices? One explanation is cognitive. People simply do not understand the risks. Research has not, however, consistently shown any relation between AIDS knowledge and high risk behavior (Huang, 1995; Winslow et al., 1992). An alternative hypothesis is that the problem may lie less in cognition than in motivation. A person who is afraid of contracting AIDS might cope with the fear by downplaying the probability that he could contract it and hence behave in ways that actually maximize his danger. For someone else, the motivation to please a partner who dislikes condoms, and thereby to avoid rejection, may supersede the goal of avoiding AIDS at a particular moment (Miller et al., 1993), especially as the probability of rejection may seem higher and momentarily more salient than of HIV infection. In fact, research shows that individuals high in sensation-seeking—that is, motivation to experience new and exciting activities—are less likely than others to practice safe sex (Stein et al., 1994).

This is the way many people deal with HIV.

A lot of people don't think they have to worry about HIV. But the truth is, anyone can get HIV infection if they are sharing drug needles and syringes or having sex with an infected person. Call your State or local AIDS hotline. Or call the National AIDS Hotline at 1-800-342-AIDS. Call 1-800-243-7889 (TTY) for deaf access.

U.S. DEPARTMENT OF HEALTH & HUMAN SERVICES   CDC   Public Health Service   HIV is the virus that causes AIDS.   AMERICA RESPONDS TO AIDS

The last few chapters have focused primarily on thought and behavior—how people learn to act as they do, how they think and remember, how they solve problems, and how conscious and unconscious processes interact to produce complex responses. An understanding of these processes explains many of the *hows* of human behavior but few of the *whys*, such as why people ignore what they know about AIDS and risk contracting a fatal infection.

This chapter addresses the whys as it explores motivation. After examining the major perspectives on motivation, we consider some of the most important motives that energize human behavior across cultures. Developing an adequate taxonomy, or scheme, for classifying motives is no easy task, but we follow one of the first and most successful efforts, proposed by Henry Murray (1938). Murray distinguished biological needs from nonbiological, "psychogenic" needs. Psychogenic needs, more commonly called psychosocial motives, are needs for order, dominance, achievement, autonomy, aggression, nurturance, and the like that produce mental or emotional satisfactions. We first examine two major biological motives, eating and sex, and then the major psychosocial needs, notably the needs for relatedness and achievement. Throughout, however, we will see that human nature is not as straightforward as our attempts to describe it, since the most biological of needs are shaped by culture and experience, and the most psychogenic draw on innate proclivities. As Sir Francis Bacon wisely warned, the subtlety of nature is far greater than the subtlety of any mind trying to comprehend and categorize it.

PERSPECTIVES ON MOTIVATION

The word **motivation** derives from the Latin *to move* (*movere*) and refers to the moving force that energizes behavior. Motives cannot be directly observed but are inferred from behavior. Motivation has two components: what people want to do and how strongly they want to do it. The first component refers to the *direction* in which activity is motivated—namely, which goals the person is pursuing or avoiding. The range of goals humans can be motivated to pursue is truly extraordinary—from going to the library, to parachuting out of a plane, to murdering a lover in a fit of rage. Motives also vary in their *strength*. People may have dozens of motives available to them at any given point, but they only act on those that currently "move" them.

Throughout this chapter, several basic issues repeatedly emerge. The first is the extent to which people are driven by internal needs or pulled by external goals or stimuli. Does the presence of a condom in a nearby drawer increase the likelihood of its use, or must the goal be internal to matter in a moment of passion? A second and related issue is the extent to which human motivation is rooted in biology or influenced by culture and environment. Do the motives of a Western corporate executive and a tribal chief in the Sudan differ dramatically, or did both rise to their position out of similar needs for power or achievement? Finally, a third issue is the relative importance of thoughts, feelings, and arousal in motivation. Can a person simply be motivated by a thought or goal? Or must goals be connected with feeling or arousal to be motivating? In other words, what transforms a thought or daydream into an intention that directs behavior? Once again, the ways psychologists answer these questions depend on the perspectives they take.

Evolutionary Perspective

In the early part of this century, psychologists took as axiomatic the notion that humans, like other animals, had **instincts**—relatively fixed patterns of behavior that animals produce without learning (Tinbergen, 1951). An example is the mating ritual of the ring dove, which must perform an elaborate, stereotyped sequence of

Does a common need for power unite a tribal chief from Ghana and the chief of a corporate "tribe"?

behaviors in exactly the right manner to attract a mate. If the male does not bow and coo at the proper point in the ritual, the female will not be receptive (Lehrman, 1956). (Male humans whose dancing is less than elegant may feel some kinship with the poor ring dove.) However, most psychologists eventually abandoned instinct theory, arguing that learning, not instinct, directs human behavior.

Contemporary evolutionary psychologists rarely speak of instinct in humans, but they contend that human motivational systems, like other psychological attributes, have been selected by nature for their ability to maximize reproductive success (survival and reproduction). For some motives, this is an unremarkable claim. Organisms that do not replenish their energy by eating or fail to keep their temperature regulated to preserve their cells do not survive and reproduce. Nature has thus designed humans and other animals with intricate systems for maintaining basic life-support processes.

Some evolutionary explanations, however, are much more controversial. For example, we take for granted that people usually tend to care more about, and do more for, their children, parents, and siblings than for their second cousins or non-relatives. Although any theory of motivation should account for such a widespread phenomenon, only the evolutionary perspective offers a cogent explanation: Individuals who care for others who share their genes will simply have more of their genes in the gene pool generations later. Thus, evolutionary theorists have expanded the concept of reproductive success to encompass **inclusive fitness**, which refers to an individual's own reproductive success as well as his influence on the reproductive success of genetically related individuals (Daly & Wilson, 1983; Hamilton, 1964).

According to the theory of inclusive fitness, natural selection should favor animals whose concern for kin is proportional to their degree of biological relatedness. The reasons for this are strictly mathematical. Imagine you are sailing with your brother or sister and with your cousin and the ship capsizes. Neither your sibling nor your cousin can swim, and you can save only one of them. Whom will you save? Most readers, after perhaps a brief, gleeful flicker of sibling rivalry, will opt for the sibling—because first-degree relatives, such as siblings, share much more genetic material than more distant relatives such as cousins. Siblings share half of their genes, whereas cousins share only one-eighth. In crass evolutionary terms, two siblings are worth eight cousins. What evolution selects are neural mechanisms that make this preference feel natural—so natural that psychologists have rarely even thought to explain it.

Many animals have elaborate courting rituals that precede mating.

The reader might object at this point that the real reason for saving the sibling over the cousin is that you know the sibling better; you grew up together, and you have more bonds of affection. This poses no problem for the evolutionary theorist, since familiarity and bonds of affection are probably the psychological mechanisms selected by nature to help you in your choice. When human genes were evolving, close relatives typically lived together. People who were familiar and loved were more often than not relatives. Humans who protected others based on familiarity and affection would be more prevalent in the gene pool thousands of years later because more of their genes would be available.

The theory of inclusive fitness thus makes mathematical sense. An individual who protects only his own child will have 50 percent of his genes available in the next generation because his child shares half his genes. Someone who instead protects his child plus his niece will have 75 percent of his genes present in the gene pool (one-half from his child and one-fourth from his niece). Over many generations, this difference becomes substantial. If the theory of inclusive fitness is valid, people can be expected to care more for genetically distant relatives in societies and subcultures in which extended families live in closer proximity to one another. This is precisely the situation in many parts of India, Pakistan, and much of the Third World, where numerous members of an extended family live in the same house and hence develop affection based on familiarity. Industrial societies essentially fail to activate a mechanism for maximizing inclusive fitness with which humans were endowed when they evolved in a very different ecological setting.

Recent research suggests that some species are actually endowed with chemical mechanisms (pheromones) for kin recognition. Whether these mechanisms foster their inclusive fitness is unknown, but pheromonal cues do help these species avoid incest, which is biologically harmful and would be detrimental to reproductive success (Blaustein & Waldman, 1992; Simmons, 1990). Pheromones are similar to hormones, except that they allow intercellular communication *between* rather than *within* organisms (Figure 10.1). They are typically detected by specialized neural circuits in the olfactory system (Chapter 4) and have the same effects as hormones (Sorenson et al., 1991). At least one species of cricket can detect pheromones emitted by other members of their species that indicate degree of relatedness. In one study, the experimenter allowed female crickets to choose where they would spend their time (Simmons, 1990). Potential male mates were not present, but the experimenter created four territories, marked with the scent (from droppings) of a male who was a full sibling, a half sibling, a cousin, or an unrelated cricket. Thus, the females could spend time in the territory of male crickets related to them by .5, .25, .125, or 0, respectively. The amount of time the females spent in each territory was inversely proportional to degree of relatedness; that is, the more distant the relation, the more time spent in the neighborhood (Figure 10.2). The mechanism for kin

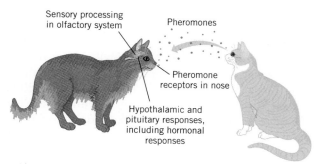

Sensory processing in olfactory system

Pheromones

Pheromone receptors in nose

Hypothalamic and pituitary responses, including hormonal responses

FIGURE 10.1
Pheromonal communication. Pheromones activate sexual and other responses much as hormones do, except that they are secreted by other animals instead of by the animal's own endocrine system.

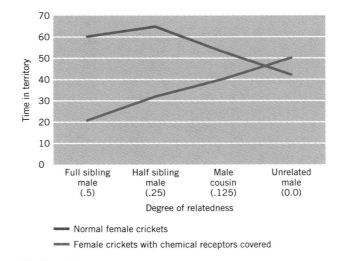

FIGURE 10.2

Pheromonal mechanisms for kin recognition in crickets. In normal females (blue line), the smaller the degree of relatedness, the more time spent in the territory of a male cricket. Females whose pheromone receptors were covered with wax (violet line) did not show the same inverse relationship between degree of relatedness and amount of time in the territory. SOURCE: Adapted from Simmons, 1990, p. 194.

recognition was chemical, since female crickets whose pheromone receptors were covered with wax showed no preference for unrelated males. Humans may not use pheromonal cues of this sort, although some vestiges of pheromonal communication could conceivably persist.

The notion that evolution favors animals that pursue their own and their relatives' survival and reproduction paints a theory of motivation in very broad strokes. Evolutionary psychologists have begun trying to fill in that portrait, distinguishing multiple processes necessary for reproduction and survival that could have independently evolved through natural selection (Buss, 1991, 1993). Reproduction involves many motives. Same-sex members of a species compete for access to desirable partners. This suggests the potential adaptive value of motives for sexual competition, which are certainly observable in humans. At the same time, motives for sexual competition are likely to conflict with motives for coalition building (Tooby & Cosmides, 1990), which allow groups of humans to protect themselves and their kin. Reproduction also involves motives for parental care, which exist in nearly every animal species. The primary motivations that emerge in cross-cultural research are power and love, which is not surprising from an evolutionary perspective (Buss, 1991). Power is related to the ability to dominate potential rivals and protect one's "turf," whereas love is related to caring for offspring, mates, kin, and sometimes alliance partners.

Survival involves such basic motives as eating, drinking, and sleeping. These and other survival motives are regulated by a biological process called homeostasis. **Homeostasis** refers to the body's tendency to maintain an internal equilibrium that permits cells to live and function. Since cells live within a fairly narrow range of conditions, the body monitors such variables as temperature and nutrient levels through specialized receptors. These receptors provide **feedback,** information about a variable in relation to its **set point,** or biologically optimal level (for example, 98.6 degrees Fahrenheit for temperature). The hypothalamus and other central nervous system structures use this feedback to determine whether the nervous system needs to respond with autonomic responses (such as shivering or sweating) or voluntary responses (putting on or taking off a jacket) to prevent body heat from diverging too far in either direction from its set point (Roscoe & Myers, 1991).

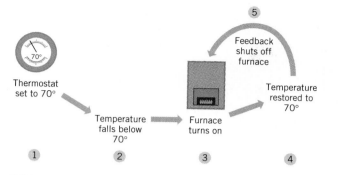

FIGURE 10.3
A homeostatic device. A common homeostatic device is a household thermostat. Temperature is set to a set point (1). If room temperature falls below that point (2), the system's thermometer activates the furnace (3), which restores the temperature to the thermostat setting (4). The system then shuts off until the temperature drops below the set point again (5).

The body's self-regulating systems work much like a thermostat in a house (Figure 10.3). If the thermostat is set at 70 degrees (the set point), the furnace remains off whenever the house temperature meets or exceeds 70 degrees. When the temperature falls below the set point, however, a circuit running from the system's thermometer switches on the furnace long enough to restore the temperature to 70 degrees. Once feedback from the thermostat signals that the goal is attained, the furnace is again deactivated.

Psychodynamic Perspective

The psychodynamic perspective also emphasizes the biological basis of motivation. Humans are animals, and their motives reflect their animal heritage. According to Freud, humans, like other animals, are motivated by internal tension states or **drives**, which build up until they are satisfied. Freud proposed that the basic drives are sex and aggression. The sexual drive includes desires for love, lust, and intimacy, whereas the aggressive drive includes impulses to master other people and the environment. These drives may express themselves in subtle ways; aggression, for example, can underlie sarcastic comments or a preference for violent movies.

Freud initially proposed self-preservation and sex as the two basic drives, much like the contemporary concept of reproductive success. His decision to change from self-preservation to aggression stemmed in part from living through one world war and witnessing the beginning of another. If aggression on such a massive scale kept breaking through in the most apparently "civilized" societies, he reasoned, it must be a basic motivational force. Although few psychologists (or even psychoanalysts) now accept Freud's theory of aggression as an instinct that builds up until discharged, the ethnic warfare in Eastern Europe, the Middle East, and Africa in our own times should perhaps give us pause before we discard the notion of innate mechanisms that fuel a proclivity to behave aggressively (Chapter 18).

Psychodynamic views of motivation have advanced considerably in the half century since Freud's death. In addition to sexual and aggressive desires, psychodynamic theorists now emphasize two other motives: the need for relatedness to others and the need for self-esteem (feeling good about oneself) (Fairbairn, 1954; Kohut, 1977; Mitchell, 1988). Most contemporary psychodynamic theorists and clinicians also focus less on drives than on wishes and fears as the basic units of motivation (Brenner, 1982; Holt, 1976; Westen, 1995). **Wishes** include a representation of a desired state (such as being promoted at work, beating out a rival in a

Observing the immense destruction perpetrated by allegedly civilized nations in one world war and the beginning of another, Freud changed his view of human motivation.

competition, or having a romantic encounter) that is associated with some kind of energy, emotion, or arousal. Once a wish is achieved, it is often temporarily deactivated or becomes less intense. **Fears,** or representations of undesired states, often conflict with wishes.

Perhaps the most distinctive aspect of the psychodynamic theory of motivation is the view that motives can be unconscious. An individual may be tremendously competitive in school or sports but vehemently assert that "I'm only competitive with myself." The child of an abusive alcoholic may desperately want to avoid an alcoholic mate but just keep "finding" herself in relationships with abusive alcoholic men. Until recently, the evidence for unconscious motivation was largely clinical and anecdotal. However, evidence from the laboratory has begun to confirm the distinction between unconscious motives and the conscious motives people can self-report (Koestner et al., 1991; McClelland et al., 1989).

To study unconscious motives, researchers for many years have relied on the **Thematic Apperception Test,** or **TAT** (Murray, 1943). The TAT consists of a series of ambiguous pictures about which subjects make up a story. Researchers then code the stories for motivational themes: Do the stories describe people seeking success or achievement? power? affiliation with other people? intimacy in a close relationship? The motives a subject attributes to characters in stories are highly predictive of long-term behavioral trends. For example, the number of achievement themes a subject produces predicts entrepreneurial success over time, in samples from both the United States and India (McClelland et al., 1989). Similarly, the number of intimacy themes expressed in stories at age 30 predicts the quality of marital adjustment almost 20 years later (McAdams & Vaillant, 1982).

Another way to measure motives is simply to ask people: "Is achievement important to you? is power? is intimacy?" Interestingly, the correlation between conscious, self-reported motives and the motives expressed in TAT stories is typi-

A subject taking the Thematic Apperception Test (TAT)

cally zero. People who demonstrate high achievement motivation in their stories, for example, do not necessarily report high motivation to achieve. Although this could simply mean that one of the two assessment methods is invalid, in fact, each type of measure predicts different kinds of behavior. For instance, achievement motivation assessed by the TAT is far more predictive of long-term entrepreneurial success than is the same motive assessed by self-report. However, if subjects in a laboratory are told they must do well on a task they are about to undertake, self-reported achievement motivation is far more predictive of effort and success than TAT-expressed motivation. How can both types of measure predict achievement behavior but not predict each other?

David McClelland and his colleagues (1989) suggest that the answer lies in a distinction similar to the distinction between implicit and explicit memory. The TAT evokes implicit (unconscious) motives, whereas self-reports activate explicit (conscious) motives. Implicit or unconscious motivation is expressed over time without conscious effort or awareness, whereas explicit or self-reported motivation becomes activated when people focus conscious attention on tasks and goals. Conscious motives, which are more flexible and controllable, can override unconscious motives but often only temporarily, as anyone knows who has ever made—and broken—a New Year's resolution.

The two kinds of motives, implicit and explicit, appear to have different developmental antecedents. One study examined the motives implicit in stories told by 31 year olds whose mothers had been extensively interviewed about their child-rearing practices 26 years earlier (McClelland & Pilon, 1983). The researchers found that several child-rearing variables that predicted implicit motives did not predict self-reported motives, and vice versa. For example, rigidly scheduled feeding in infancy and severe early toilet training correlated with need for achievement assessed by TAT but not by self-report. Thus, parental demands for mastery in early life (in this sample, largely before much language development, since the majority of children were toilet trained by 19 months) appear to shape unconscious needs for achievement but have little effect on conscious motives and values, which are shaped more by later verbal instruction.

Behaviorist Perspective

The behaviorist theory of operant conditioning offers (if only implicitly) one of the clearest and most empirically supported views of motivation, that humans and other animals are motivated to produce behaviors that are rewarded by the environment and to avoid behaviors that are punished. As learning theorists recognized many years ago, however, the internal state of the organism influences reinforcement; a pellet of food will reinforce a hungry rat but not a sated one. Hull (1943, 1952) and other behaviorists dealt with this issue through the concept of drive (Chapter 5). All biological organisms have needs, such as those for food, drink, and sex. Unfulfilled needs lead to drives, defined as states of arousal that motivate behavior. **Drive-reduction theories**, which were popular in the 1940s and 1950s, propose that motivation stems from a combination of drive and reinforcement. Deprivation of basic needs creates an unpleasant state of tension that leads the animal to begin emitting behaviors. If the animal in this state happens to perform an action that reduces the tension (as when a hungry dog finds food on the dinner table), it will associate this behavior with drive reduction. Hence, the behavior will be reinforced (and the family may have to set another plate).

This conditioning process occurs with innate drives, such as hunger, thirst, and sex; these are known as **primary drives**. Most human behaviors, however, are not directed at the fulfillment of primary drives. Especially in cultures with substantial reserves of resources, people spend much of their waking time in activities such as earning a living, playing, or studying. The motives for these behaviors are secondary or acquired drives. **Secondary drives** are learned through classical conditioning and other mechanisms such as modeling. An originally neutral stimulus comes to be associated with drive reduction and thus itself becomes a motivator. In many cultures, the desire for money is a secondary or acquired drive, which ultimately permits the satisfaction of many other primary and secondary drives.

Although drive-reduction theories explain a wide range of behaviors, they leave others unexplained. Why, for instance, do people sometimes stay up until 3:00 A.M. to finish a riveting novel, even though they are exhausted? And why are some people unable to refuse dessert, even after a filling meal? Such behaviors seem motivated more by the presence of an external stimulus or reward—called an **incentive**—than an internal need state. Incentives control much of human behavior, as when a person who was not previously hungry is enticed by the smells of a bakery, or an individual who was not sexually aroused becomes aroused by an attractive, scantily clad body on the beach. In these cases, stimuli activate drive states rather than signal their removal. Furthermore drive-reduction theories have difficulty explaining the motivation to create stimulation, encounter novelty, or avoid boredom, which is present to varying degrees in different individuals (Zuckerman, 1994) and in other animal species (Premack, 1962).

Cognitive Perspective

If evolutionary and biological perspectives on motivation start with nature, cognitive perspectives start with nurture. Cognitive researchers often use **goals** as a motivational construct, viewing them as desired outcomes established through social learning, such as finding a mate or getting good grades (Cantor, 1990). Some theorists use the homeostat or thermostat analogy to describe the way people set goals, monitor their progress, and respond to feedback by adjusting their performance (Miller et al., 1960; Powers, 1973).

Other cognitive theorists employ **expectancy-value theories** to account for motivation. These theories, like theories of decision making (Chapter 7), construe motivation as a joint function of the value people place on an outcome and the extent to which they believe they can attain it. Becoming a rock star may be my wildest dream, but if I know I am tone-deaf and unable to play any instrument, I am unlikely to be motivated to grow my hair and abandon a tenured faculty position. Several factors influence the value of an outcome or goal to a person (Geen, 1985). One factor, of course, is the extent to which the individual needs a goal object for a specific purpose; a student who is not taking organic chemistry is unlikely to buy an organic chemistry text. Another factor is the amount of effort required to attain the goal. In general, goals that are either impossibly difficult or too easy have less attraction than moderately challenging goals.

A cognitive theory of motivation used widely by organizational psychologists interested in worker motivation is **goal-setting theory** (Locke & Latham, 1990). The core proposition of goal-setting theory is that conscious goals regulate much of human behavior, especially performance on work tasks (Locke, 1991, p. 18). People establish goals, which specify desired outcomes that are in some way discrepant from their current situation. A salesperson may set a goal of selling 10 computers next month, which is 10 more than she has currently sold. Goals activate old solutions that have worked before and encourage efforts to create new solutions if the old ones fail.

According to this theory, maximum job performance occurs only under certain conditions (Locke, 1991). The first condition is an undesired discrepancy between what the person wants and currently has. If a salesperson's income is tied to the number of units she sells and she is dissatisfied with her income, she is likely to be motivated to boost her sales figures. Second, the person must have continuing feedback about her progress toward achieving the goal. Goals without feedback have minimal motivational value because people do not know whether they are succeeding or failing, and consequently, they do not know when they need to work harder. Third, the individual must believe she has the ability to attain the goal. Fourth, the person must set a high enough goal. A computer salesperson is not likely to perform optimally if she sets a goal of 10 computers per month when she could reasonably expect to sell 20; when people set their goals too low, they tend to lose their motivation once they have attained the goal. Finally, the person must have a high degree of commitment to the goal. In a work setting, commitment tends to stem from the perception that a legitimate authority values the goal, from peer influence, from the goal being public, and from rewards or punishments that are contingent upon its attainment or nonattainment.

A Different Perspective: A Hierarchy of Needs

An alternative to evolutionary, psychodynamic, behaviorist, and cognitive perspectives on motivation was advanced by Abraham Maslow, who proposed a **hierarchy of needs** (1962, 1970). According to Maslow, some needs are extremely pressing because they are basic to survival, and they energize a person and direct her behavior until they are met. Once these are satisfied, less pressing needs begin to motivate behavior, and so on up the hierarchy.

Figure 10.4 illustrates Maslow's hierarchy of needs. At the most basic level are physiological needs, such as those for water and food. Next activated are safety

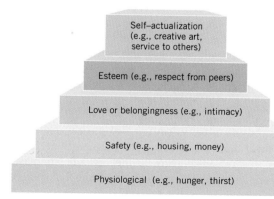

FIGURE 10.4
Maslow's hierarchy of needs. Except for self-actualization, all of Maslow's needs are generated by a lack of something, such as food or shelter.

needs for security and protection. Having satisfied physiological and safety needs to some extent, people are motivated to pursue closeness and affiliation with other people, or what Maslow calls belongingness needs. Next in the hierarchy are esteem needs, including both self-esteem and the esteem of others. Finally, at the highest level are **self-actualization needs**, the need to express oneself and grow, or to actualize one's potential. Self-actualization needs differ from all the previous levels in that they are not **deficiency needs**; that is, they are not generated by a lack of something (food, shelter, closeness, the esteem of others). Rather, they are **growth needs**, motives to expand and develop one's skills and abilities.

According to Maslow, people can spend their lives focused on motives at one level and not develop beyond it. People who are starving are unlikely to think much about art, and people who desperately need the esteem of others may never be motivated for self-expression. In contrast, self-actualized individuals are no longer preoccupied with where they will get their dinner or who will esteem them for their work and are thus free to pursue moral, cultural, or aesthetic concerns. Maslow offered prominent examples of self-actualizers—Gandhi, Martin Luther King, Jr., and Eleanor Roosevelt—but believed that very few people ever reach this level.

Maslow's theory of self-actualization has proven difficult to test (Neher, 1991). However, one organizational psychologist, Clayton Alderfer, refined and applied aspects of Maslow's model to motivation in the workplace (Alderfer, 1972, 1989). Alderfer was a consultant to a small manufacturing company that was having trouble motivating its workers. In interviewing the employees, he noticed that their concerns seemed to fall into three categories: material concerns such as pay, fringe benefits, and physical conditions in the plant; relationships with peers and supervisors; and opportunities to learn and use their skills on the job. His observations led to **ERG theory**, which, among other things, condenses Maslow's hierarchy to three levels of need: existence, relatedness, and growth (hence ERG). According to ERG theory, worker satisfaction and motivation vary with the extent to which a job matches a given worker's needs. Workers whose primary concern is pay are unlikely to appreciate attempts to give them more training to expand their skills. In general, however, the best job is one that provides good pay and working conditions, a chance to interact with other people, and opportunities to develop one's skills, thus satisfying the major needs. This theory offers testable hypotheses, although the empirical evidence for it remains sketchy.

Applying the Perspectives on Motivation

How might the different approaches to motivation explain the puzzling scenario with which this chapter began, that many people show minimal motivation to protect themselves from AIDS in sexual situations? From an evolutionary perspective, the answer lies in the discrepancy between the current environment and the circumstances in which human psychological propensities evolved. AIDS is a new disease (and so, by evolutionary standards, is syphilis, which can also be deadly). Thus, humans have neural programs for sexual arousal that were engineered over millennia, but these programs do not include momentary breaks for safe sex practices. Antipathy for condoms should be particularly high among males, who can lose erections while searching for or wearing condoms, whose reproductive success may be compromised by their application, who face less risk of AIDS transmission than females from heterosexual intercourse, and who in many cultures attract females through apparent bravery ("Nothing scares me, babe").

From a psychodynamic perspective, sex is a basic human motivation, and people are prone to self-deception and wishful thinking; that people frequently deny the risk to themselves of unprotected sex should thus come as no surprise. Furthermore, any sexual encounter reflects multiple motives, and the balance of these motives can lead to ill-advised action. For example, people have sex with casual partners for many reasons beyond biological drive. These include self-esteem motives (to feel desirable), wishes to feel close to someone physically or emotionally, and motives for dominance (the feeling of conquest). Casual, unprotected sex may also reflect blatantly self-destructive motives, as was the case with a suicidal young gay man who regularly attended bath houses at the height of media attention to the epidemic.

From a behaviorist perspective, sexual behavior, like all behavior, is under environmental control. If condom use is punishing (because it breaks the mood, decreases genital sensations, or leads to whining by male partners), it will diminish over time. Partners who consent to unsafe sex may also be negatively reinforced for doing so by the cessation of complaining or cajoling and rewarded by praise or enjoyable sex.

From a cognitive perspective, people's expectancies about the probable outcomes of high-risk behavior can simply be wrong because of misinformation or inattention to media messages. Moreover, because HIV may not lead to symptoms of AIDS for many years, unprotected sexual contact produces no feedback that can deter its continued practice. In fact, the absence of consequences probably bolsters erroneously optimistic expectancies.

Although explaining life-threatening behavior seems difficult from Maslow's perspective, since safety needs come early in the hierarchy, the absence of any obvious negative impact of high-risk behavior for several years presumably gives people a false sense of safety. As a result, they pursue higher level needs, such as belongingness, which may lead them to behave imprudently. As we will see in the next chapter, the mechanism for judging how strongly a need is activated, and hence how much to attend to it, is probably the intensity of feeling it generates. If people do not *feel* scared, they will not focus on their safety needs.

A GLOBAL VISTA

CULTURAL INFLUENCES ON MOTIVATION

Although the major approaches to motivation take the individual as their starting point, cross-cultural work suggests that culture plays a substantial role in shaping motivation (Benedict, 1934). Some societies, such as the United States, view the personal accumulation of material wealth as a worthy end of individual endeavor and even celebrate wealthy people (achievers of the American Dream). In contrast, other cultures disapprove of accumulating material goods for oneself or one's family, considering it a crime against the community or a mark of poor character. The Kapauka Papuans of New Guinea strictly punish individual wealth (Pospisil, 1963). Disapproval or sanctions against individual consumption are common in agricultural or peasant societies, where resources tend to be limited and communalistic sentiments prevail (Foster, 1965).

Psychologist Erich Fromm (1955) argued that a culture's socioeconomic system shapes people's motivations so that they *want* to act in ways that the system *needs* them to act. In other words, for an economic system to work, it must create individuals whose personal needs match the needs of the system. A capitalist economy such as our own depends on workers and consumers to be materialistic. If advertisements for VCRs or the latest compact disk system did not motivate people, entrepreneurs would not create them, and ultimately the economy would stagnate. In contrast, materialism in agricultural societies would only produce frustration because of limits on productivity. In the Third World, rapid technological change can produce sudden increases in expectations, which in turn can dramatically affect motivation. Research from developing countries suggests that when people see the prospect of dramatically higher living standards while continuing to confront roadblocks to achieving these expectations, their political systems are vulnerable to revolution (Huntington, 1968).

In stark contrast to the materialism of contemporary capitalist societies is a ritual called the potlatch, practiced by certain indigenous peoples of the northwest coast of North America, such as the Kwakiutl and the Tlingit. The potlatch is a ceremony of song, dance, and gift-giving that commemorates various occasions, such as a naming, marriage, coming of age, or death. Perhaps the most distinctive feature of the potlatch is that the host typically gives away tremendous quantities of food, possessions, and other resources to his guests. Leaders of neighboring groups may even become caught up in competitive gift-giving "contests," each trying to outshine the other with his generosity.

The potlatch apparently serves a number of functions. Among the most important are maintaining reciprocity and good communal relations among neighbors and redistributing wealth (Cole, 1991; Kan, 1986). These functions are probably similar to the original functions of the lavish events following such Western rituals as marriages, funerals, and bar mitzvahs. Potlatches were outlawed by the Canadian government in 1885, but they have persisted in modified forms into the 1990s (Cole, 1991).

A potlatch among the Kwakiutl.

EATING

The motivation to eat is biologically based, but the story is not that simple. Even as I write these words, I am struggling, as many readers undoubtedly do while writing term papers, to keep my mind from drifting into the refrigerator where ham and cheese are beckoning. In general, however, the function of eating is not to relieve anxiety, frustration, or boredom but to convert what were once the cells of other living organisms into energy. **Metabolism** refers to the processes by which the

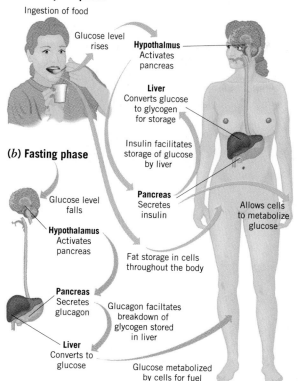

(a) Absorptive phase

Ingestion of food

Glucose level rises

Hypothalmus
Activates pancreas

Liver
Converts glucose to glycogen for storage

Insulin facilitates storage of glucose by liver

Pancreas
Secretes insulin

Allows cells to metabolize glucose

(b) Fasting phase

Glucose level falls

Hypothalamus
Activates pancreas

Fat storage in cells throughout the body

Pancreas
Secretes glucagon

Glucagon faciltates breakdown of glycogen stored in liver

Liver
Converts to glucose

Glucose metabolized by cells for fuel

FIGURE 10.5

Metabolism. During the absorptive phase (a), the person ingests food. The hypothalamus detects rising glucose rates in the bloodstream and activates the pancreas, which secretes insulin. Insulin allows cells to absorb and convert glucose into energy for their use. Insulin also is required for the liver to convert glucose into glycogen to provide a short-term energy reservoir. In the fasting phase (b), when the individual is not eating, the hypothalamus detects falling glucose levels and activates the pancreas. The pancreas now secretes glucagon, which converts the glycogen in the liver into glucose, which the cells in the body can metabolize.

body transforms food into energy for moving muscles, maintaining body heat, operating the nervous system, and building and maintaining organ tissue.

Metabolism has two phases (Figure 10.5): absorptive and fasting. In the **absorptive phase**, the person is ingesting food. A particularly important nutrient is a simple carbohydrate called **glucose** (sugar), which is a primary source of fuel for the body and the nervous system. At the same time that the digestive system is filling short-term reservoirs with glucose and more complex sugars, it is filling a multitude of long-term energy tanks located under the skin and in the abdomen: fat cells. These cells are capable of expanding enormously when reserves are high. From an evolutionary perspective, the ability to store fat served our ancestors well. When winter came and food was scarce, they had both extra reserves of body fuel and an extra layer of warmth. The second phase of metabolism, the **fasting phase**, occurs when a person is not eating, as the body converts its short- and long-term stores into energy.

Hunger and Satiety

Eating is thus part of a complex homeostatic process: Energy reserves become depleted, and a person becomes hungry and eats. As the fuel tanks become full, ingestion stops, and reserves again become depleted. The question is precisely how

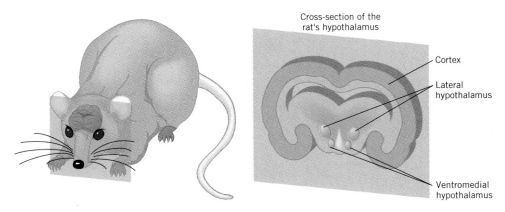

Cross-section of the
rat's hypothalamus

Cortex

Lateral
hypothalamus

Ventromedial
hypothalamus

FIGURE 10.6
The role of the hypothalamus in hunger. This cross-section of a rat's brain shows the lateral and ven-tromedial hypothalamus, which are involved in hunger and satiety.

these biological processes (nutrient depletion and restoration) become translated into a psychological motive (hunger) and how this motive is switched off.

Homeostatic Mechanisms

The hypothalamus plays a key role in homeostatic processes, and hunger is no exception. For several years, psychologists believed the "on" switch for hunger was in the lateral hypothalamus and the "off" switch, signaling satiety, in the ventro-medial hypothalamus (Figure 10.6) (Anand & Brobeck, 1951; Teitelbaum, 1961). This conclusion was based on experiments in which researchers either lesioned or electrically stimulated these two sections of the hypothalamus. Lesioning the later-al hypothalamus in experimental animals led to undereating, sometimes to the point of starvation. In contrast, when the ventromedial hypothalamus was destroyed, the animal would not stop eating and would become obese (Hernandez & Hoebel, 1989; Hetherington & Ransom, 1940). Electrical stimulation of the lateral hypo-thalamus also produced eating even when the animal was satiated, whereas stimu-lation of the ventromedial hypothalamus inhibited eating even if the animal was starved (Wyricka, 1976). Recent research confirms the role of the lateral hypothal-amus in hunger and feeding (Berridge & Valenstein, 1991), but the role of the ven-tromedial hypothalamus is less clear. The brain appears to have multiple mecha-nisms for inhibiting feeding (Rowland, 1991).

The Subjective Experience of Hunger What causes the subjective experience of hunger? The intuitive answer to this question is simple: an empty stomach. A clas-sic experiment performed in the early 1900s by W. B. Cannon and A. L. Washburn supported this notion (1912). Washburn fasted on the days of the experiment and inserted a narrow rubber tube into his esophagus. At the end of the tube was a small balloon that could be inflated in his stomach just enough to register a change in pressure when the stomach walls contracted. (Some people will do almost any-thing to get tenure.) As Figure 10.7 shows, Washburn's reports of hunger pangs occurred consistently toward the end of each measured contraction of the stomach.

Other findings indicate, however, that hunger is more complicated than that. People whose stomachs have been removed because of cancer nonetheless report feeling hunger (Janowitz & Grossman, 1949; Wagensteen & Carlson, 1931). The presence or absence of food in the stomach is only a rough indicator of the biolog-ical need for food because the stomach can be filled with foods or liquids that do not provide the body with energy. Dieters know they can "trick" their stomachs into feeling full by eating quantities of celery and drinking diet cola. The trick does not last very long, however, because the body has a second, and probably more important, measure of the need to eat: the amount of glucose in the bloodstream.

Obese rat after destruction of the ventromedial hypothalamus.

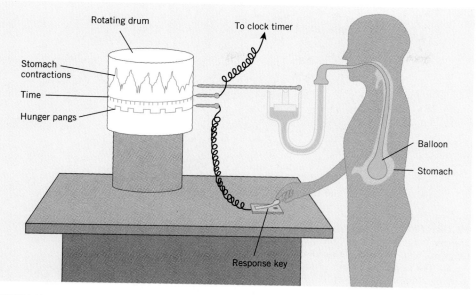

FIGURE 10.7

An early study of hunger. Washburn, deprived of food, inserted a narrow rubber tube with a balloon on one end into his stomach. When inflated, the balloon registered changes in pressure caused by contractions of the stomach walls. At the same time, Washburn tapped a response key to signal hunger pangs. He consistently experienced hunger pangs toward the end of each measured contraction of the stomach. SOURCE: *Adapted from Cannon, 1934.*

The Glucostatic Theory of Hunger The **glucostatic theory** of hunger proposes that hunger arises when glucose "thermostats" in the nervous system (glucostats) detect low levels of glucose in the bloodstream (Hoebel & Teitelbaum, 1966; Mayer, 1955). Both the liver and the hypothalamus contain **glucoreceptors**, cells that monitor glucose levels (Karadi et al., 1990; Russek, 1970; Shimizu et al., 1983). When glucose levels drop, a subjective feeling of hunger arises and initiates eating.

Considerable evidence supports the glucostatic theory. In rats, injecting small amounts of glucose into the bloodstream when glucose levels begin to drop delays feeding behavior (Campfield et al., 1985). In humans, who can report how hungry they feel, hunger is directly related to glucose levels. Figure 10.8 compares the reported sensations of hunger in two groups of well-fed subjects. The experimental group received injections of a drug that suppresses blood glucose levels, while the control group received an inert saline-solution injection (that is, one with no physiological effect). Subjects whose glucose level had been artificially lowered felt hungrier than control subjects, even after a meal (Thompson & Campbell, 1977).

Satiation The processes that terminate eating behavior are similar to those that initiate it. Sensations in the stomach and levels of nutrients in the body, especially glucose, regulate the subjective experience of satiety that causes a person or an animal to leave the table or the trough. The stomach wall has stretch receptors that send emergency messages to the brain signaling that enough is enough, but these receptors probably play less of a role than glucoreceptors in the stomach and liver (Carlson, 1991). Rats will eat more when their stomachs are full of saline solution than of a high-calorie liquid, suggesting that glucoreceptors are involved in feelings of satiety as well as hunger (Angel et al., 1992; Deutsch & Gonzalez, 1980).

External Cues and Eating Behavior

Hunger is the prime motivator for eating, but external factors, such as palatability (the tastiness or appeal of food), also influence the inclination to eat. Palatability plays an important role in eating even in animals not known for their

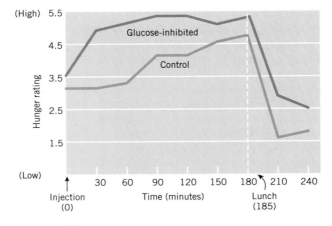

FIGURE 10.8
Hunger and glucose levels. The blue line depicts data from an experimental group, who received injections of a drug that suppresses blood-sugar levels. The violet line illustrates data from the control group, who received a saline-solution injection. As the figure illustrates, subjects whose blood-sugar level had been artificially lowered (the glucose-inhibited group) felt considerably more hunger than the control group, even after a meal.
SOURCE: *Thompson & Campbell, 1977.*

gourmet tastes (Capaldi & VandenBos, 1991; Warwick et al., 1993). Rats, like humans, like variation in their diets, and as pet owners can attest, dogs and cats may grow tired of a brand of food and walk away from a delightful and nutritious bowl of horse meat or tuna innards even if they are hungry. Some taste preferences are inborn, such as the preference of human infants and baby rats for sweet tastes, while others depend on exposure and learning.

Another external factor that influences the motive to eat is the presence of other people. One study gave subjects pocket-sized cards on which they were to record both their food intake and dining companions for seven consecutive days (deCastro & Brewer, 1992). The more people present, the more subjects ate. Meals eaten with a large group of people were 75 percent larger than meals eaten alone.

Obesity

Obesity is defined as body weight of 15 percent or more above the ideal for one's height and age (Metropolitan Life Insurance Co., 1984). By this criterion, about one third of the adult population of the United States is obese, and the percentage is growing. The rates of obesity vary in different races, cultures, subcultures, and social classes. One example is shown in Table 10.1. In industrialized countries, fatness tends to be inversely correlated with socioeconomic status; that is, people in lower social classes tend to be more obese. In developing nations, the direction of the correlation is reversed: the richer, the fatter, at least for women (Sobal & Stunkard, 1989). The situation in the developing world probably approximates the state of affairs through most of human evolution. Particularly for women, whose pregnancies could extend into times of scarcity, larger *internal* food reserves were adaptive in the face of variable *external* reserves.

Cultural Conceptions of Weight and Obesity
Although obesity may sound like an objective phenomenon, it is to some degree culturally relative. When the researchers in the study shown in Table 10.1 asked subjects if they had a weight problem, they found that white women worried about their weight even when they were under their ideal body weight, whereas the other groups did not. A study of black and white undergraduates yielded complementary

	MALE		FEMALE	
CHARACTERISTIC	White	Black	White	Black
Weight (lb)	174.5	175.6	139.9	162.5
Ideal weight	162.1	158.3	138.3	138.2
Pounds overweight (%)				
20 or more	34.2	41.4	22.1	49.2
50 or more	7.0	12.1	8.8	20.0
100 or more	.4	1.4	.6	4.1
Obesity (%)				
Moderate	16.3	27.7	18.2	46.5
Severe	6.2	12.8	5.6	20.1

TABLE 10.1 WEIGHT AND OBESITY CHARACTERISTICS BY RACE AND SEX

Source: Rand & Kuldau, 1990, pp. 333–334.

Note. A recent survey using a stratified random sample of 2115 U.S. adults, aged 18–96, found significant differences in weight and obesity between blacks and whites. The differences likely reflect differences in both social class and culture.

results (Harris et al., 1991). Even though blacks, and especially black females, were heavier than whites, they were more satisfied with their weight and less likely to find weight on other people (particularly women) unattractive. Men were more concerned about the weight of their dates than women were, but black men were less likely to refuse to date a woman because of her weight.

Contemporary North American culture is preoccupied with thinness, particularly for women. Compared to the Rubenesque view of beauty of just a few centuries ago, expressed in the art and culture of that period, the prototypes of feminine beauty portrayed in the mass media today look emaciated. The standards have even changed considerably since the 1950s, when the prototype was the voluptuous beauty of Marilyn Monroe, replete with large breasts and slightly protruding abdomen.

Cultures set standards for body types that are considered attractive and unattractive. In Rubens's time, beautiful meant bountiful. Even in the 1950s and 1960s, the standard of beauty was considerably plumper than it is now. Marilyn Monroe, for example, would probably be considered chubby today— and might well have difficulty making it on television.

A study of *Playboy* centerfolds and Miss America Pageant contestants found a 10 percent decrease in the ratio of weight to height in both groups from the late 1950s to the late 1970s, paralleled by a dramatic increase in the number of articles on dieting in popular women's magazines (Garner et al., 1980, cited in Hsu, 1989).

Ironically, one hypothesis links these changed standards to the women's movement: "As women have moved into previously male-dominated activities, the 'traditional' female body shape has developed negative connotations while the masculine shape has come to symbolize self-discipline and competency" (Garner & Wooley, 1991, p. 731). In fact, curvaceousness went out of fashion in both the 1920s and the 1970s–1980s, periods in which women vigorously sought political and economic equality with men (Silverstein et al., 1986). Whatever the causes, females in our society are obsessed with dieting, and the obsession begins early. At any given moment, two-thirds of high school girls report that they are trying to lose weight (Rosen & Gross, 1987). In contrast to contemporary Western societies, other cultures associate beauty with bulk. This association most often occurs in societies in which food is scarce, where women who are healthy and have more resources tend to be heavier and hence are seen as more attractive (Triandis, 1994).

In Western culture, stereotypes about the obese are extremely negative (Crandall, 1994) and contribute to discrimination in education, jobs, and housing. These stereotypes begin as early as kindergarten (Garner & Wooley, 1991; Hsu, 1989; Rothblum, 1992). Children who are overweight are teased and often develop both lowered self-esteem and negative expectations about the way others will treat them. These expectations and the way others behave toward them may actually contribute to obese people behaving less attractively. In study testing this hypothesis, obese and nonobese women conversed on the phone with other subjects who did not know them and could not see them (Miller et al., 1991). College student raters, unaware of the subjects' weights (or even of what the study was about), then listened to the recorded conversations and rated the women on their social skills, likability, and probable physical attractiveness. Not only did the raters view the obese women more negatively on all dimensions, but the correlations between pounds overweight and each dimension were strongly negative. In other words, the heavier the subject, the less socially skilled, likable, and physically attractive she was perceived to be. Remarkably, coders seemed to be able to judge appearance from purely auditory cues.

Weight and Health

Obesity has physical as well as social costs. It has been linked to cardiovascular disease, hypertension (high blood pressure), some forms of diabetes, and other diseases (Manson et al., 1990; National Research Council, 1989). Overweight, nonsmoking men have mortality rates as much as 3.9 times those of normal-weight nonsmokers, and the rates are similar for women (Foreyt, 1987; Garrison & Castelli, 1985). Many of these risks are well established (Brownell & Rodin, 1994), although some researchers suggest that the health risks may have been exaggerated, in part because health experts share cultural stereotypes about fat people (Garner & Wooley, 1991).

Biology and Obesity

Why are some people obese? The causes of obesity are diverse, but biology plays an important role. The amount of fat in a person's body is highly heritable (Bouchard, 1989). Body weight of adoptees correlates with the weight of their biological parents but not of their adoptive parents (Stunkard et al., 1986). The correlation between the amount of fat in the bodies of monozygotic twins is in the range of .72 to .83, whereas the correlation for dizygotic twins is in the range of .34 to .49 (Brook et al., 1975, summarized in Katahn & McMinn, 1990). Heritability for obesity is estimated to range from .50 to .88, which is extremely high (Borjeson, 1976).

Two physiological factors seem especially important in creating obesity, both of which show substantial heritability. The first is the number and size of fat cells in the body. Obese people have a far greater number of fat cells than average-weight individuals, and the cells they do have tend to be larger (Hirsch & Knittle, 1970). Obese subjects in one study had approximately three times as many fat cells as nonobese subjects, and these fat cells were almost one-third larger. Unfortunately, fat cells that develop early in life do not disappear when a person later attempts to lose weight; they only shrink.

The second physiological factor is the body's tendency to maintain a relatively constant weight, or set point. **Set-point theory** suggests that each person has a natural weight to which the body gravitates, which is regulated by the hypothalamus. If a person starts to gain weight above the set point, his metabolism will increase; thus, even though the person consumes more calories, the body burns these more efficiently than before, making further weight gain difficult. Conversely, if the person starts to lose weight, the body compensates by slowing down metabolism, requiring fewer calories to maintain the same weight (Keesey & Corbett, 1984; Keesey & Powley, 1986; Williams & Thompson, 1993).

Studies of both humans and other animals suggest that metabolism does, in fact, rise and fall with changes in food consumption and body weight. One study examined the metabolism of obese women enrolled in a weight-loss program. Although subjects ate radically less than usual, their bodies compensated by slowing down the metabolic rate disproportionately to the decrease in caloric intake. Conversely, subjects instructed to *overeat* by 1600 calories a day for 10 days in another study showed a 22 percent increase in their metabolic rate by the end of the study, making weight gain harder (Garrow & Warwick, 1978).

The implication of this homeostatic process is by now probably painfully clear to dieters: The more you lose, the harder losing becomes. As weight drops, so, too, does metabolic level, so that even maintaining the loss becomes difficult. Set-point theory may explain why the long-term success rate of almost every diet ever devised—no matter how impressive its advertised short-term gains—is dismal. In the long run, the vast majority of dieters put back every ounce of weight they took off (Garner & Wooley, 1991; Katahn & McMinn, 1990). Those who succeed in keeping it off may need to live with a metabolism rate that has slowed by about 15 percent, requiring food intake forever lower than their previous maintenance-level consumption (see Geissler et al., 1987). Despite many discouraging statistics, how-

Actor-comedian John Candy's obesity appears to have played a role in his untimely death.

ever, studies suggest that weight control through diet and exercise seems to be possible for a subset of people who want to lose weight, but researchers do not yet know who that subset is (Brownell & Rodin, 1994).

Environmental Factors and Obesity

Biological factors do not alone control weight. Environmental factors also influence obesity. The fact that obesity rates in the United States have doubled since 1900 points to the significance of environmental influences and the possibility of reversing them (Brownell & Rodin, 1994). As noted, women of higher socioeconomic status in technologically developed countries are substantially less obese than women of lower socioeconomic status. The difference between the two groups appears to reflect diet, efforts to restrain eating, and trips to the gym (Garner & Wooley, 1991). In fact, the amount of dietary fat is strongly related to the amount of fat that becomes deposited in the body's reserves (Capaldi & VandenBos, 1991; Drewnowski, 1991). Exercise plays a key role in weight control (Katahn & McMinn, 1990) and is strongly linked to decreased mortality (Blair et al., 1989).

Psychological factors also play an important role in obesity, although studies have generally led to conflicting and inconclusive results (Rodin et al., 1989), in part because different people become obese for different reasons (Brownell & Wadden, 1992). One frequent psychological correlate of obesity is low self-esteem (Bruch, 1970; Williams et al., 1993). The extent to which self-esteem problems are a cause or a consequence of obesity is not entirely clear, and the relationship probably runs in both directions.

Another potentially important psychological variable is anxiety. Both clinical and experimental evidence suggests that some people overeat to control anxiety or depression (Ganley, 1989; Leon & Roth, 1977; McKenna, 1972; Slowchower, 1987). People who are morbidly obese—that is, at least 100 pounds or 100 percent over ideal body weight—are more likely than nonobese people to suffer from depressive, anxiety, and personality disorders (Black et al., 1992). Another set of psychological variables that have not been explored systematically are the motivational processes that lead dieters to stay on or go off diet and exercise regimes. Exercising is strongly predictive of weight control, but only 15 percent of dieters continue their exercise regimens after reaching their goal weight (Katahn & McMinn, 1990).

Eating Disorders

Dieters in the United States spend as much per year on weight loss programs and products as the entire federal budget for education, training, employment, and social services (Garner & Wooley, 1991). The obsession with thinness in many Western industrialized countries is no doubt related to the prevalence of two eating disorders, anorexia nervosa and bulimia. Both disorders tend to strike precisely those groups most affected by the cultural preoccupation with thinness; they are most common in young, white females and are rarely reported outside the West, except in Japan (Hsu, 1989; Mumford, 1993).

In **anorexia nervosa** the individual refuses to eat, starving herself until she is less than 85 percent of her ideal body weight. Anorexia is a life-threatening illness that can lead to permanent physiological changes (such as brittle bones) and death, usually through heart attack. Anorexics are frequently terrified of becoming fat and have a distorted image of their bodies as fat, even as they are wasting away. Along with starving themselves, anorexics often exercise excessively. The disorder is about 10 times more prevalent in women than in men (Hsu, 1989), and it typically begins in adolescence or the early adult years. The causes of anorexia are still poorly understood, and the outcome of treatment ranges from complete cure to complete failure.

When people with eating disorders look in the mirror, they often see something very different from what other people see.

Anorexics are often bright, talented, perfectionistic, and preoccupied with feeling in control (Bruch, 1973; Casper et al., 1992). Controlling food intake seems to be a way of maintaining control in general, particularly over impulses (Strauss & Ryan, 1987). Psychotherapists who work with anorexic females commonly report that a wish to avoid becoming a physically mature woman often underlies anorexic symptoms. In this objective, anorexics are successful: Severely restricted food intake can stop the development of secondary sex characteristics such as breasts, halt menstruation, and make the body look like a prepubescent girl's. By restricting food intake, anorexics may be triggering mechanisms that evolved to prevent pregnancy and perhaps to discourage sexual interest from males during famine, when food was scarce and reproduction was secondary to survival.

Bulimia is characterized by a binge-and-purge syndrome in which the person gorges on food (typically massive amounts of carbohydrates such as bags of Oreos or potato chips) and then either induces vomiting or uses laxatives (purging). The typical result is a feeling of relief, but it is often accompanied by depression and a sense of being out of control. Like anorexia, bulimia is almost exclusively a female disorder; some 90 percent of reported cases are female (Halmi et al., 1977; Pyle et al., 1983). About 3 to 5 percent of the female population is bulimic (Hoek, 1993; Kendler et al., 1991).

Unlike anorexics, bulimics are not characterized by any particular or consistent set of personality traits (Striegel-Moore et al., 1986), although studies have linked the disorder to a range of problems, including depression, impulsivity, low self-esteem, poor coping skills, alcoholism, and distorted body image (Hinz & Williamson, 1987; Striegel-Moore et al., 1986). Some research suggests that bulimia may be related genetically to depression (Blouin et al., 1992; Jimmerson et al., 1990; Kendler et al., 1991).

SEXUAL MOTIVATION

Like hunger, sex is a universal drive based in biology, but its expression varies considerably from culture to culture and from person to person. Sexual motivation is even more variable than hunger. Most people eat two or three meals a day, whereas sexual appetites defy generalizations. Sexual behavior is driven as much by fantasies as by hormones; indeed, the primary sexual organ in humans is arguably not the genitals but the brain.

Although psychoanalysis broke down many of the Victorian taboos against discussing sexuality, sex did not become a respectable area of scientific research until Alfred Kinsey and his colleagues published two massive volumes, on the sexual behavior of the human male and female (Kinsey et al., 1948, 1953). Many of Kinsey's findings, based on interviews with thousands of adults, provoked shock and outrage. For instance, some 37 percent of males and 13 percent of women reported having engaged in homosexual activity at some time in their lives. More recent research finds slightly lower rates of male homosexual activity but otherwise paints a similar picture; rates of lesbian contact remain unchanged (Seidman & Reider, 1994). The average sexually active person reports having intercourse between one and three times a week and becomes sexually active between ages 17 and 19 (although many start earlier or later).

Since the time of the Kinsey report, and particularly since the sexual revolution of the 1960s and 1970s, sexual attitudes and practices have become much more liberal. For example, in a recent study that used the original Kinsey data for comparison, both white and black women reported earlier age at first intercourse, a wider range of sexual practices, a larger number of sexual partners, and reduced likelihood of marrying their first lover (Wyatt et al., 1988a, b).

The Sexual Response Cycle

After Kinsey, the next quantum leap forward in the scientific study of sex was William Masters and Virginia Johnson's work, *Human Sexual Response* (1966). Masters and Johnson studied the physiological changes that take place during sexual activity by observing several hundred women and men in the laboratory. Their best known finding is that similar physiological changes take place in both women and men and follow a general pattern that Masters and Johnson called the **sexual response cycle** (Figure 10.9).

The sexual response cycle begins with a phase of **excitement**, characterized by increased muscle tension, engorgement of blood vessels in the genitals causing erection of the penis and lubrication of the vagina, and often a skin flush. Maximum arousal occurs during the second, or **plateau**, phase. During this stage, heart rate, respiration, muscle tension, and blood pressure reach their peak. The third phase, **orgasm**, is characterized by vaginal contractions in females and expulsion of semen in males. During the fourth phase, **resolution**, the person's physiological and psychological functioning gradually returns to normal.

The subjective experience of orgasm is very similar in men and women. When given written descriptions of orgasms, psychologists, medical students, and gyne-

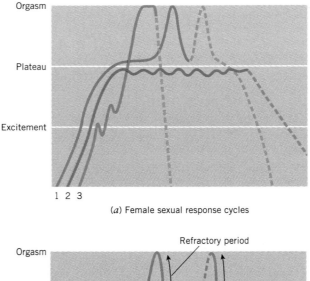

(*a*) Female sexual response cycles

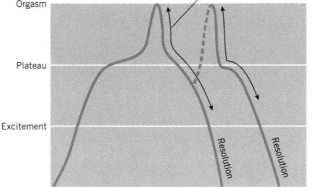

(*b*) Male sexual response cycle

FIGURE 10.9
Sexual response cycles. Part (a) depicts the variations of sensation in women's sexual response. Part (b) illustrates the typical male sexual response cycle. The two are practically indistinguishable, except for the greater variability in women's experience. SOURCE: *Masters & Johnson, 1966, p. 5.*

TABLE 10.2 PERCENTAGES OF WOMEN REPORTING ATTAINING ORGASM FROM SEXUAL RELATIONS

	AGE 29 AND UNDER	AGE 30 AND OVER	TOTAL
Never	10	7	9
Less than 50% of the time	28	21	25
More than 50% of the time but not always	59	48	52
Always	3	24	14

Source: Butler, 1976, p. 42.

cologists are unable to distinguish men's from women's if not told the writer's gender (Vance & Wagner, 1976). However, the female sexual response cycle does seem to be more variable. Women describe a few different types of orgasm, from mild pulsations to a sharp climax to repeated sensations of orgasm (Bardwick, 1971). In addition, many women do not reach orgasm with every sexual encounter (Table 10.2), but they do report a sense of sexual release even without experiencing orgasm (Butler, 1976). Women are capable of experiencing multiple orgasms, although contrary to popular myths and male fantasies, not always or primarily by sexual intercourse (Darling et al., 1991).

Nature and Nurture in Sexual Motivation

In many animal species, females and males are genetically programmed to follow very specific, stereotyped mating rituals, with attraction and mating behavior often controlled by pheromones. In the American cockroach, pheromone detection leads the male to touch its antennae to the female's antennae, spread its wings, and turn

Human sexuality differs substantially from sexuality in other animal species—or does it?

180 degrees in a courtship dance (Seelinger & Schuderer, 1985). Even in species less reliant on pheromonal communication, mating behavior is often rigidly instinctive. Humans do not have the same kinds of genetically based mating rituals or mating seasons as other animals. However, one need only think of the plumage displayed by both sexes at a fraternity mixer, scents with names like "Passion" and "Musk," and the simple fact that most humans choose to mate only with members of their own species to recognize the biological influences on human dating and mating.

Biology and Sexual Motivation

Much of sexual behavior in humans and other animals is under hormonal control. Hormones have two effects on the nervous system and behavior—organizational and activational. **Organizational effects** influence the circuitry or "organization" of the brain. In humans, these effects occur prenatally. All human fetuses begin female and develop into females unless male hormones called androgens are present. Androgens and other substances initiate the development of male genitalia, reproductive systems, and neural circuitry. In rodents, the organizational effects of hormones continue postnatally; thus, psychologists can study them by surgically removing the testes in males (castration) or the ovaries in females (ovariectomy). Male rats castrated at birth and given female hormones in adulthood become sexually receptive to males, manifesting the characteristic female mating behavior of hunching over and exposing the hindquarters (Blaustein & Olster, 1989; Edwards & Einhorn, 1986).

Although researchers cannot similarly experiment on humans, certain natural "experiments" provide insight into the organizational effects of hormones on behavior and sexual orientation (Money, 1987; Money & Ehrhardt, 1972; Money et al., 1984). In **adrenogenital syndrome**, the adrenal glands secrete too much androgen, which masculinizes the genitals in females, producing an enlarged clitoris and labia that may resemble a scrotum. Roughly half of a sample of women with this disorder who would discuss their sexual orientation reported that they were homosexual or bisexual (Money et al., 1984). This suggests that prenatal androgenization organizes neural circuitry for later sexual preference in women.

In **androgen insensitivity syndrome**, androgens are secreted in utero, but a genetic defect leads to an absence of androgen receptors. Thus, even though the hormone is released, the body responds as if no androgen is present. As a result, a genetic male develops female genitalia (and will be reared as a girl, usually leading a perfectly normal life except for sterility). Interestingly, people with this disorder, who are by all outward appearances female, are rarely attracted to other females, even though they have testes instead of ovaries. (Their testicles are not externally visible.) Attraction to females among humans may thus require masculinization of the brain in utero.

As noted earlier, hormones also have **activational effects**; that is, once the brain circuitry is in place, hormones activate these circuits to produce psychobiological changes, such as development of secondary sex characteristics (e.g., breasts in adolescent females and facial hair in males). Hormones also produce fluctuations in sexual arousal in men. One study found a direct association between sexual activity among adolescent boys and testosterone levels in the bloodstream (Udry et al., 1985). Another study found a relation between testosterone levels and sexual desire, arousal, and activity in older men, aged 45 to 74 (Schiavi et al., 1991). Castrated men may continue to become sexually aroused for months or years, but sexual interest gradually declines if testosterone is not administered. Testosterone injections increase arousal in both castrated rats and castrated humans. Figure 10.10 shows the pattern of sexual acts, ejaculations, and sexual thoughts in a 40-year-old man who had been castrated for medical reasons about a year before the study was conducted. The man received testosterone supplements, which were tem-

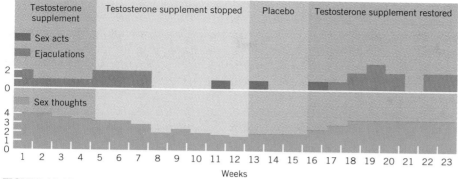

FIGURE 10.10

Testosterone replacement in a castrated man. Sexual activity, ejaculation, and sexual thoughts all decline about three weeks after stopping treatment. There is no response to placebo, but a rapid response occurs shortly after restarting testosterone treatment. SOURCE: *Bancroft, 1984, p. 5.*

porarily interrupted during the study and replaced with a placebo and eventually resumed (Bancroft, 1984). Hormone levels and arousal fluctuate at different points in the menstrual cycle in women, but the relationship between them is unclear.

Culture and Sexual Behavior

Although biology plays an important role in sexual motivation, anthropological studies show enormous cultural diversity in both the ways people carry out sexual acts and the types of behaviors they consider acceptable (Davis & Whitten, 1987). Among the Basongye people of the Congo, for instance, the conventional position for intercourse is for partners to lie facing each other with the woman on her left side and the man on his right; the woman lifts her right leg to allow the man to enter (Merriam, 1971). In many parts of Australia, Melanesia, and India, the woman typically lies on her back as the man squats between her legs (Gebhard, 1971), whereas in Western culture the male lying prone on top of the female is more typical. Cultures also differ in their conceptions of male and female sexuality, with some, such as our own, viewing men as having greater sexual needs, whereas others believe just the opposite (Gordon & Shankweiler, 1971; Griffitt, 1987; Scully & Bart, 1973).

Sexual Orientation

Sexual orientation refers to the direction of a person's enduring sexual attraction—to members of the same sex, the opposite sex, or both. Determining a person's sexual orientation is not as easy as it may seem. Many people report having occasional homosexual fantasies or encounters even though they are not homosexual. Stigma, discrimination, religious values that define homosexuality as sinful, and violence directed against homosexuals lead some people whose sexual motives and fantasies are primarily homosexual to be heterosexual or abstinent in their behavior, to deny their homosexuality to themselves, or to take on the trappings of a heterosexual lifestyle such as marriage to a member of the opposite sex.

An exclusive homosexual orientation is rare among animals, but homosexual behaviors occur frequently among many species, from lizards to langurs (Ellis & Ames, 1987; Money, 1987; Srivastava et al., 1991). The incidence of homosexuality varies substantially among human cultures, largely reflecting cultural attitudes. In some parts of Polynesia, homosexuality is reportedly almost nonexistent

(Marshall, 1971). In contrast, in seventeenth-century Japan, homosexual liaisons among samurai warriors were common (Adams, 1985), as they were among educated men in ancient Greece. In a large part of the world, stretching from Sumatra throughout Melanesia, males almost universally participate in homosexual activities several years before they reach marriageable age (Herdt, 1984; Money & Ehrhardt, 1972).

In contemporary Western societies, approximately 2 to 7 percent of men, and 1 percent of women, consider themselves homosexual, although the numbers vary depending on how researchers phrase the questions (see Ellis & Ames, 1987; Pillard et al., 1981). Until relatively recently, both laypeople and the psychiatric community considered homosexuality a disorder; the official diagnostic manual of the American Psychiatric Association classified it as a disorder until 1973. People harbor many misperceptions about homosexuality, such as the idea that homosexuals are unfit to teach because they will invariably molest children. In fact, homosexuals are no more likely to be child molesters than are heterosexuals. Psychologist John Money (1987), who has conducted some of the best-known research on homosexuality (and on sexuality more generally), points out that one of the most pervasive misconceptions is the notion that homosexuality is a sexual *preference*, which implies voluntary choice. Money argues that people no more choose their sexual orientation than they select their native language or decide to be right-handed.

The best predictor of male homosexuality in adulthood is the presence in childhood of marked behavioral characteristics of the opposite sex, sometimes called "sissy" behavior (Bell et al., 1981; Green, 1987). Although this pattern applies only to a subset of homosexual men, and cross-gender behavior is present in some boys who do not become homosexual, it is a strong predictor nonetheless. An example is described in an interview with the mother of an 8 year old:

> MOTHER: *He acts like a sissy. He has expressed the wish to be a girl. He doesn't play with boys. He's afraid of boys, because he's afraid to play boys' games. He used to like to dress in girls' clothing. He would still like to, only we have absolutely put our foot down. And he talks like a girl, sometimes walks like a girl, acts like a girl.*
>
> INTERVIEWER: *What was the very earliest thing that you noticed?*
>
> MOTHER: *Wanting to put on a blouse of mine, a pink and white blouse which if he'd put it on it would fit him like a dress. And he was very excited about the whole thing, and leaped around and danced around the room. I didn't like it and I just told him to take it off and I put it away. He kept asking for it.*
>
> INTERVIEWER: *You mentioned that he's expressed the wish to be a girl. Has he ever said, "I am a girl"?*
>
> MOTHER: *Playing in front of the mirror, he'll undress for bed, and he's standing in front of the mirror and he took his penis and he folded it under, and he said, "Look, Mommy, I'm a girl."*
>
> *(Green, 1987, pp. 2–3)*

A recent cross-cultural study reported the same finding in females: The distinguishing characteristic between homosexual and heterosexual females in Brazil, Peru, the Philippines, and the United States was cross-gender childhood behavior (Whitam & Mathy, 1991). Lesbians in all four cultures were more interested in "boy things" and less interested in "girl things" than were their heterosexual peers (Table 10.3).

TABLE 10.3 CHILDHOOD CROSS-GENDER BEHAVIOR OF HOMOSEXUAL AND HETEROSEXUAL FEMALES IN FOUR CULTURES

BEHAVIOR	BRAZIL	PERU	PHILIPPINES	UNITED STATES	TOTAL SAMPLE
Interest in boys' toys					
Heterosexual (% "yes")	39.3	39.5	24.4	64.5	47.8
Homosexual (% "yes")	75.4	83.3	87.9	91.9	85.1
Interest in girls' toys					
Heterosexual	78.7	93.6	96.9	86.2	87.3
Homosexual	50.8	51.2	42.3	40.4	46.9
Regarded as "tomboy"					
Heterosexual	1.6	8.5	9.8	39.1	20.1
Homosexual	23.0	16.7	27.3	77.9	43.7
Dressed in men's clothes or pretended with pipes, shaving cream, etc.					
Heterosexual	16.4	4.5	24.4	15.5	15.2
Homosexual	42.6	38.1	75.8	44.2	47.3

Source: Adapted from Whitam & Mathy, 1991.

Note. Being a tomboy as a child is much more common in heterosexual girls in the United States than in the other countries sampled, where it is a stronger predictor of later homosexuality.

FROM MIND TO BRAIN

THE BIOLOGY OF MALE HOMOSEXUALITY

If sexual orientation is not a matter of conscious choice, what are its causes? Homosexuality is probably the end result of many causes, some environmental and some biological; however, most environmental hypotheses (such as absent or weak fathers and dominant mothers in the families of male homosexuals) have received little empirical support (see Bell et al., 1981; Blanchard & Zucker, 1994; Freud, 1922; Friedman & Stern, 1980; Gagnon & Simon, 1973; Lewes, 1988). Researchers who emphasize the nature side of the nature-nurture continuum have had more success, particularly in explaining male homosexuality; the causes of female homosexuality have received much less attention.

Data on the organizing effects of androgens, described earlier, favor a biological explanation for male homosexuality. Androgenization in humans may be necessary for primary sexual attraction to females, just as it is in rats. Another line of intriguing research with humans suggests a possible biochemical factor in sexual orientation (Gladue et al., 1984). In one study, homosexual men, heterosexual men, and heterosexual women received injections of an estrogen preparation called Premarin. Premarin is known to increase concentrations of luteinizing hormone (LH) in women but not in men; LH is responsible for, among other things, stimulating the ovaries in women and producing testosterone in men. As one would expect, Premarin injections led to increases in LH in women but not in heterosexual men. The response of homosexual male sub-

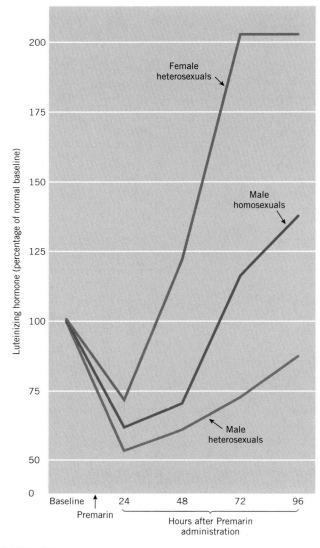

FIGURE 10.11

Hormonal response in male homosexuals. This figure depicts the changes in luteinizing hormone (LH) in response to injections of Premarin in homosexual men, heterosexual men, and heterosexual women. Heterosexual men and women showed very different hormonal responses. The responses of homosexual males, however, were intermediate between the heterosexual men and women. SOURCE: *Gladue et al., 1984, p. 1496.*

jects, however, was intermediate between the two, suggesting some hormonal similarity between homosexual men and heterosexual women (Figure 10.11).

Another study found differences in the neuroanatomy of homosexual and heterosexual men (LeVay, 1991). Based on research with nonhuman primates, the investigator hypothesized that two specific nuclei (sets of neurons) in the anterior hypothalamus (the front portion) would be larger in individuals who are sexually attracted to women than in individuals attracted to men. He compared the brains of homosexual men (who died of AIDS complications) with men and women presumed to be heterosexual and found that one of the two nuclei of interest was twice as large in heterosexual men as in women and homosexual men. Some investigators have criticized the study for design flaws (such as inadequate information on the sexual histories of the heterosexual men and women) and the possible influence of AIDS on the brains of the homosexual men (Byne & Parsons, 1993), but the results are clearly intriguing.

What accounts for physiological differences between homosexuals and heterosexuals? Two biological theories have received attention, one focusing on prenatal maternal stress and the other on genetics. The maternal stress theory stems from the experimental observation that stress during pregnancy in rats leads to more feminine and less masculine sexual behavior, apparently because it interferes with androgenization (Ward, 1984). One researcher studied human males born in Germany over the 20-year period from 1934 to 1953, a time of considerable stress (Dorner et al., 1980). He found a much higher proportion of homosexual males born during World War II and the few years directly after the war than in other years of the study (Dorner et al., 1980). A second study asked homosexual, bisexual, and heterosexual men to report on stresses (such as a death in the family or a divorce) that their mothers experienced while pregnant. Less than 10 percent of mothers of heterosexual sons were reported to have experienced moderate to severe levels of stress, in contrast with two-thirds of the mothers of homosexuals; the bisexual group was intermediate (Dorner et al., 1983). Again, these two studies are suggestive, but neither can rule out alternative explanations. For example, the mothers of homosexuals may have been generally more stress-prone and hence may have interacted differently with their children, or these mothers may have differed genetically in other ways from mothers of heterosexuals. Subsequent research in which mothers directly reported on their stress levels while pregnant has not supported the theory (Bailey et al., 1991).

A second explanation for physiological differences between homosexual and heterosexual men is genetic. Several studies have found a higher incidence of homosexuality among relatives of male homosexuals than in the general population (Buhrich et al., 1991). Whereas rates of homosexuality in the general population are estimated at 2 to 7 percent, nearly 25 percent of brothers of male homosexuals in one study were reportedly homosexual (Pillard et al., 1981, 1982). The most definitive study to date found concordance rates for homosexuality much higher among identical than fraternal twins and adoptive brothers. In other words, if one identical twin is homosexual, the other has a high probability of being homosexual (Bailey & Pillard, 1991). The investigators interviewed homosexual men recruited through advertisements. They asked subjects questions about both their own and their twins' sexual orientation and requested permission to contact the other brother for a second assessment, which they obtained in a number of cases. Although the investigators could not rule out environmental causes, the results closely matched expectations based on a genetic model. Concordance for homosexuality was 52 percent for monozygotic twins, 22 percent for dizygotic twins, and 11 percent for adoptive brothers, with heritability estimated somewhere between .31 and .74. The same research group conducted one of the only studies of heritability of homosexuality in women and found a similar pattern of results. Concordance for homosexuality was 48 percent for monozygotic twins, 16 percent for dizygotic twins, and 6 percent for adoptive sisters, with heritability estimates ranging from .27 to .76 (Bailey et al., 1993).

Can we conclude, then, that homosexuality is genetic? Not yet. First, other research groups studying twins have failed to find convincing genetic effects (Eckert et al., 1986; King & McDonald, 1992). Second, even if heritability is 50 percent, that leaves the rest of the variance in sexual orientation explained by environmental factors. Nevertheless, if sexual orientation is in part a preference exercised by our genes instead of our souls, this would have enormous implications for public policy and attitudes toward homosexuals. No humane person could disparage an individual for his sexual orientation, any more than one would discriminate against someone who is near-sighted.

If homosexuality is substantially influenced by genetics, attacking homosexuality as immoral or unnatural would be as indefensible as persecuting people with blue eyes.

TABLE 10.4 SYMPTOMS AND INCIDENCE OF COMMON SEXUAL DYSFUNCTIONS

DYSFUNCTION	SYMPTOMS	INCIDENCE (%)
Inhibited orgasm (female)	Recurrent delay or absence of orgasm following sexual stimulation and excitement	5–30+
Inhibited orgasm (male)	Retarded ejaculation or inability to achieve ejaculation following sexual stimulation and excitement	3–4
Premature ejaculation (male)	Ejaculation before the individual wishes it	35
Inhibited sexual excitement	Partial or complete failure to attain or maintain erection (in men) or vaginal lubrication (in women)	Unknown (women) 10–20 (men)
Inhibited sexual desire	Persistent and pervasive inhibition of sexual desire	1–35 (women) 1–15 (men)

Source: Adapted from Nathan, 1986.

Sexual Dysfunctions

Sexual dysfunctions are problems that impair sexual functioning. The most common, summarized in Table 10.4, are inhibited orgasm in women, premature ejaculation in men, and inhibited sexual excitement or desire in men and women (Nathan, 1986). Sexual problems are quite common, especially in mild forms or for relatively brief periods in a couple's relationship (Spector & Carey, 1990).

Physiological factors are sometimes involved in sexual dysfunctions. Excessive alcohol use, fatigue, hypertension, and kidney disease all contribute to male difficulties in achieving erection (Shrom et al., 1979). In most cases, however, the causes are primarily psychological, with anxiety a prime culprit (Patterson & O'Gorman, 1989). People often fear they will not perform adequately (Masters & Johnson, 1970), or they are anxious about losing control during intercourse (Kaplan, 1981). Others may not feel comfortable sharing intimacy with another person (Beck & Barlow, 1984) or may have developed anxiety-provoking fantasies, feelings, or ideas about sexuality during childhood. Difficulty in a relationship can also translate into difficulty in bed.

PSYCHOSOCIAL MOTIVES

Unlike sex, **psychosocial motives** (personal and interpersonal motives for such ends as achievement, power, self-esteem, affiliation, and intimacy) are less obviously tied to biology, but they are not independent of it either. Human infants, like the young of other species, have an inborn tendency to form intense social bonds with their primary caretakers, and toddlers spontaneously exhibit joy at their achievements and frustration at their failures. Once again, nature and nurture jointly weave even the most socially constructed fabrics. Two major clusters of goals pursued cross-culturally are communion, or **relatedness,** and **agency** (achievement, autonomy, mastery, power, and other self-oriented goals) (Bakan, 1966; Wiggins, 1990, cited in Buss, 1991).

Needs for Relatedness

Humans have a number of interpersonal needs (Weiss, 1986), which tend to overlap. The earliest to arise in children are related to attachment (Chapter 14). **Attachment motivation** refers to the desire for physical and psychological proximity to another person and for the comfort and positive emotion experienced in the person's presence. Attachment motives form the basis for many aspects of adult love (Hazan & Shaver, 1987, 1994 ; Main, et al., 1985). Adults and older children in some cultures also have needs for **intimacy,** a special kind of closeness characterized by self-disclosure, warmth, and mutual caring (McAdams, 1986; Reis & Shaver, 1988). Intimacy needs are often satisfied in adult attachment relationships and deep friendships.

Another social motive is the need for **affiliation,** or interaction with friends or acquaintances. Most people need to be and communicate with other people, whether that means soliciting support after an upsetting experience, sharing good news, or playing sports together. Unfulfilled affiliative needs, like frustrated desires for attachment or intimacy, lead to loneliness. In one survey of college students, 26 percent reported feeling lonely within the previous two weeks (Stokes, 1985). Individuals differ in the extent to which they seek intimate versus affiliative relationships. Some people have many friends and acquaintances but have little need for intimacy, whereas others desire one or two intimate friends and have little need for a broad social network (Reis & Shaver, 1988; Weiss, 1986).

Social relationships, particularly with people in whom one can confide, are important for both physical and mental health. Women who report having at least one confidante are 10 times less likely to suffer depression following a stressful event than women who do not have someone in whom they can confide (Brown et al., 1975). Lack of supportive relationships is a risk factor for mortality as well. People who feel they have no one to whom they can turn become ill and die earlier than those who report having satisfying relationships (House et al., 1988).

Achievement and Other Agency Motives

Motives for power, personal agency, competence, achievement, and self-esteem form another cluster of motives common to humans throughout the world. The psychoanalyst Robert White (1959) argued that humans have innate impulses to deal competently and effectively with their surroundings. Indeed, as early as the second year of life, infants seem to desire to be competent and effective, even when they are not rewarded by their parents (Kagan et al., 1978); their persistence and pride when they first begin to walk are readily apparent. Some theorists suggest that humans have a related motive to know and understand the world around them (Epstein, 1990). Pleasure in knowing and displeasure in feeling uncertain may have evolved as mechanisms that foster exploration of the environment. Self-esteem motivation refers to the motive to see oneself in a positive light (Wylie, 1979). Theorists of many theoretical persuasions, including psychodynamic (Kohut, 1971), humanistic (Rogers, 1959), and cognitive-social (Higgins, 1990), recognize self-esteem as a central human motive (Chapter 17).

The **need for achievement**—to do well, to succeed, and to avoid failure—is the best researched psychosocial motive. This is not surprising in view of Western cultures' emphasis on personal achievement in school, sports, careers, and many other

The need for achievement was undoubtedly a contributing motive to the success of novelist Toni Morrison, computer magnate Bill Gates, and actress Jodie Foster.

areas. When given a choice, people high in achievement motivation tend to choose moderately difficult tasks (those with about a 50/50 chance of success) over very easy or very difficult tasks (Atkinson, 1977; Slade & Rush, 1991). They enjoy being challenged and take pleasure in accomplishing a difficult task, but they do not want to fail. In one study, subjects played a ring-toss game and were free to choose their own distance from the target (Atkinson & Litwin, 1960). Those who scored high in achievement motivation selected distances that were challenging but not impossible. In contrast, subjects who scored low in achievement motivation and had a high fear of failure stood either very close to the target or impossibly far, which guaranteed either success or a good excuse for failing.

How do these findings about achievement motivation translate into everyday behaviors? People with a high need for achievement tend to work more persistently than others to achieve a goal, and they take pride in their accomplishments when they succeed (Atkinson, 1977). Not surprisingly, this renders them more likely to succeed. They also tend to attribute their past successes to their abilities and their past failures to forces beyond their control, which increases confidence and persistence in the face of adverse feedback (Dweck, 1975; Meece et al., 1990; Weiner, 1974). A student with high achievement motivation is likely to select a major that suits his abilities, commit to a study schedule that is rigorous but not impossible, and work hard to succeed within those limits.

The consequences of achievement motivation extend far beyond the classroom. In an economically depressed area of India, where government programs had been ineffective in raising the standard of living, psychologist David McClelland undertook an interesting experiment. He taught local businessmen to fantasize about high achievement and to problem-solve ways to succeed (McClelland, 1978; McClelland & Winter, 1969). Over time, they began new businesses and employed new workers at a much higher rate than businessmen in a comparable town in the same region.

Components of Achievement Motivation

As with other motives, people may express a need for achievement only in specific domains. For example, an achievement-oriented premedical student may place little value in succeeding in literature courses. From a cognitive perspective, motives may be selectively expressed because they are hierarchically organized, some sections of the hierarchy carrying more motivational weight (Figure 10.12).

The motivation to achieve may also involve a blend of motives. Some children respond to failure by becoming upset and giving up, attributing their failure to lack of ability. Others seem to take failure as a challenge, responding with increased problem-solving efforts, leading to improved performance and heightened interest

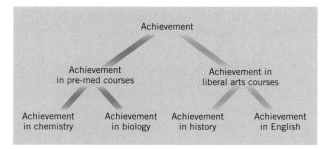

FIGURE 10.12
The cognitive structure of achievement motivation. A premedical student attaches different motivational weight to different section of the hierarchy. Red lines indicate strong motivation; blue lines indicate weaker motivation.

and enjoyment. To understand these starkly contrasting responses requires distinguishing two motives that can underlie the need to achieve: performance goals and learning goals (Elliott & Dweck, 1988). **Performance goals** are motives to achieve at a particular level; the emphasis is on the outcome of a task, namely, the degree to which one succeeds or meets a standard. **Learning goals** are motives to increase one's competence, mastery, or skill. If an individual's motive for achievement is tied to a need to perform well (and be perceived as performing well), failure may lead to giving up because the basic motive has been frustrated. In contrast, if the motive to achieve is tied to learning and mastery, the individual will not be daunted by failure as long as she believes she can continue to learn.

One study found support for this theory by activating either performance or learning goals in a sample of fifth graders. The experimenters placed subjects in one of four conditions by manipulating two variables: type of goal activated (performance vs. learning) and perceived ability at the task (high vs. low) (Figure 10.13). They told subjects in the two performance goal conditions, "In this box we have problems of different levels. Some are hard, some are easier. If you pick this box, although you won't learn new things, it will really show me what kids can do." Subjects in the two learning goal conditions received these instructions: "If you pick the task in this box, you'll probably learn a lot of new things. But you'll probably make a bunch of mistakes, get a little confused, maybe feel a little dumb at times— but eventually, you'll learn some useful things" (Elliott & Dweck, 1988, p. 7). In addition, the investigators led about half the children in each group to believe they were high in ability and the other half, low.

The results corroborated the researchers' hypotheses. Children with performance goals gave up and felt bad if they were led to believe they were low in ability; if they believed they were high in ability, they worked hard and solved problems but avoided tasks on which they could publicly fail, even if they could learn from them. For children given learning goals, beliefs about ability (and hence expectations of failure or success) were irrelevant. These children uniformly persevered at the task and did not avoid difficult tasks at which they might fail.

		Perceived ability	
		High	Low
Goals activated	Performance	Work hard, no unpleasant emotion, avoid tasks that could lead to public failure	Give up, unpleasant emotion, attribute failure to low ability
	Learning	Work hard, no unpleasant emotion, risk public failure if associated with potential to learn	Work hard, no unpleasant emotion, risk public failure if associated with potential to learn

FIGURE 10.13
Perceived ability and achievement-related goals in fifth grade children. Subjects were placed in one of four conditions by manipulating two variables: type of goal activated (performance vs. learning) and perceived ability at the task (high vs. low). SOURCE: *Elliott & Dweck, 1988.*

Research into scholastic achievement in adolescents has produced similar results. Adolescents in North America do not, by and large, find learning enjoyable. When asked to respond to beepers at random intervals during the day, they report feeling sad, passive, bored, and lonely when they are studying. The findings are similar in other cultures, even those in which high achievement motivation characterizes the young, such as South Korea (Wong & Csikszentmihalyi, 1991). Why, then, do any adolescents achieve in school?

A study of gifted high school students found that two independent motive systems influenced their scholastic behavior. The first was work orientation, a belief in the importance of working hard and persevering toward long-term goals (performance goals). Work orientation strongly predicted the amount of time students spent studying and also predicted their grades. The second motive system was **intrinsic motivation**, that is, motivation to perform a behavior for its own sake rather than for some kind of external (or "extrinsic") reward (Deci & Ryan, 1985; Vallerand et al., 1993). Intrinsic motivation includes learning goals as well as other sources of pleasure in a task, such as simple enjoyment. Intrinsic motivation predicted subjects' willingness to take difficult classes. For example, gifted math students who found math problems enjoyable were likely to take difficult math classes regardless of their work orientation. Interestingly, these two sources of motivation were not correlated with each other; that is, students high in intrinsic motivation were not especially likely to show high work orientation, and vice versa.

In real life, motivation to achieve may involve other motives as well, such as interpersonal motives to please one's parents or do better than a sibling. Indeed, a blend of motives probably underlies most behavior. Asking someone out for dinner may reflect multiple motives, including affiliation, attachment, hunger, sex, altruism, and self-esteem.

Parenting, Culture, and Achievement

The need for achievement is primarily a learned motive, and numerous studies have linked it to patterns of child rearing. Parenting practices associated with high achievement motivation include encouraging children to attempt new tasks slightly beyond their reach, praising success when it occurs, encouraging independent thinking, discouraging children from complaining, and prompting children to try new solutions when they fail (McClelland, 1985; Winterbottom, 1953).

Parenting always occurs within a cultural context, however, and motivation for achievement varies considerably across cultures and historical periods. McClelland and his colleagues (1953) have explored some of the links between culture, child rearing, and achievement. In several studies, they rated the extent of achievement imagery in stories and folktales, particularly those told to children, and correlated achievement imagery with child-rearing practices and entrepreneurial activity in each society. They focused on folktales and other stories because these reflect the themes and concerns that members of a society find compelling and transmit to their children. For instance, a prominent children's story in our own achievement-oriented society is *The Little Engine That Could*. From a psychological standpoint, the moral of this story is that those who expect success and strive for it despite adversity will succeed ("I think I can, I think I can. . . .").

In one study, McClelland and his colleagues (1953) collected the folktales of eight Native American cultures and rated them for degree of achievement motivation expressed. Another set of coders independently rated the cultures for independence training, noting the age at which training began and the strength and frequency of punishment for failure to act autonomously. The findings document a clear relationship between achievement motivation and independence training (Table 10.5). Navaho and Central Apache cultures, which stress independence in their child training, show the strongest need for achievement in their folktales.

In another set of studies, McClelland (1961) found that the achievement orientation expressed in children's stories rose dramatically shortly before periods of

When stories told to children become filled with achievement themes, entrepreneurship rises.

TABLE 10.5 RANKING OF CULTURES ON NEED FOR ACHIEVEMENT AND INDEPENDENCE TRAINING		
CULTURE	NEED FOR ACHIEVEMENT MEASURED FROM FOLKTALES	INDEPENDENCE TRAINING (AGE AND SEVERITY)
	Rank	Rank
Navajo	1	1
Central Apache	2	2
Hopi	3	4
Comanche	4	3
Sanpoil	5	5.5
Western Apache	6	5.5
Paiute	7	7
Flatheads	8	8

Source: Adapted from McClelland et al., 1953, p. 294.

rapid economic growth. According to McClelland, as parents in less economically developed countries increasingly value achievement, they transmit this value in the stories they tell their children. Their children, in turn, are more likely to become entrepreneurs, which spurs economic growth.

Western cultures tend to view achievement as a particularly positive motive, but it may not always be the most important motive for success. One intriguing study assessed motivation for power, affiliation, and achievement as reflected in the inaugural addresses of U.S. presidents from George Washington to Ronald Reagan (Spangler & House, 1991). Power motivation, and particularly the motive to use power for institutional rather than personal purposes, was the strongest predictor of presidential success (assessed by historians' ratings). Surprisingly, affiliation and achievement motivation were *inversely* correlated with historians' ratings of presidential greatness. Apparently, needing to be loved and having a burning agenda of goals to achieve ultimately inhibit effective presidential leadership.

SOME CONCLUDING THOUGHTS

Having explored a variety of motives from multiple perspectives, we return to the basic questions with which we began. First, to what extent are people driven by internal needs or pulled by external stimuli? What is clear from examining the most biological of needs—hunger and sex—is that even where a need is undeniably rooted in biology, the strength of a motive depends in part on whether or not appropriate stimuli impinge on the organism—whether the stimulus is a sundae or a sexual partner. A stimulus by itself, however, never motivates behavior unless the person has acquired some motivational tendency toward it. The same hot fudge sundae that calls one person's name will have no effect on another who is indifferent to ice cream.

The second question was whether human motivation is rooted in biology or in culture and experience. As in nearly every other discussion of nature and nurture in this book, the answer is an intellectually unsatisfying "yes." Humans are creatures of biology and culture. Belonging to communities channels their innate motivational proclivities so that their expressed motives fit local social and economic conditions.

The third question pertained to the relative importance of thought, feeling, and arousal in motivation: Do people act on the basis of cognition? emotion? generalized arousal? The most likely answer is that motivation typically requires both cognition and some form of emotional energy or arousal. To put it another way, cognitive representations or thoughts provide the direction or goals of motivation, and feelings provide the strength or force behind motivation, but neither alone is likely to produce a goal-directed action. In neuropsychological terms, the cortex provides the map for life's journeys, but the hypothalamus and limbic system largely provide the fuel. In the next chapter, we continue to examine the fuel as we explore emotion and consider what happens if the vehicle begins to sputter under stress.

Summary

Perspectives on Motivation

1. **Motivation** refers to the moving force that energizes behavior. It includes two components: what people want to do (the direction in which activity is motivated) and how strongly they want to do it (the strength of the motivation). Although some motives (e.g., eating and sex) are more clearly biologically based, and others (e.g., relatedness to others and achievement) are more psychogenic, both types of motives have roots in biology and are shaped by culture and experience.

2. Evolutionary psychologists argue that basic human motives derive from the tasks of survival and reproduction. They have expanded the concept of reproductive success to include **inclusive fitness**, which means that natural selection favors organisms that survive, reproduce, and foster the survival and reproduction of their kin. Natural selection has endowed humans and other animals with motivational mechanisms that lead them to maximize their inclusive fitness.

3. Many survival motives involve **homeostasis**, the body's tendency to maintain an internal equilibrium that permits cells to live and function.

4. Freud believed that humans, like other animals, are motivated by internal tension states, or **drives**, for sex and aggression. Contemporary psychodynamic theorists focus less on drives than on wishes and fears. They emphasize motives for relatedness and self-esteem, as well as sex and aggression, and contend that many human motives are unconscious.

5. Behaviorist theorists use the term "drive" to refer to motivation activated by a need state (such as hunger). According to **drive-reduction theories**, deprivation of basic needs creates an unpleasant state of tension that leads the animal to act. If an action happens to reduce the tension, the behavior is reinforced. Innate drives such as hunger, thirst, and sex are known as **primary drives**; with **secondary drives**, an originally neutral stimulus that comes to be associated with drive reduction itself becomes a motivator.

6. Cognitive theorists often speak of **goals**, valued outcomes established through social learning. **Expectancy-value theories** assert that motivation is a joint function of the value people place on an outcome and the extent to which they believe they can attain it. **Goal-setting theory** proposes that conscious goals regulate much of human action, particularly on work tasks.

7. According to Maslow's **hierarchy of needs**, basic needs must be met before higher-level needs become active. The hierarchy includes physiological, safety, belongingness, esteem, and **self-actualization** needs.

Eating

8. **Metabolism** refers to the processes by which the body transforms food into energy. The **glucostatic theory** of hunger proposes that hunger motivation arises as **glucose** levels drop in the bloodstream. Sensations in the stomach walls also seem to influence hunger motivation, as may levels of other nutrients.

9. **Obesity** is a condition characterized by a body weight over 15 percent above the ideal for one's height and age. The two best predictors of amount of body fat are genetic factors and amount of fat intake in the diet. **Anorexia nervosa** is an eating disorder in which the individual becomes dangerously underweight because of a refusal to eat. **Bulimia** is characterized by a binge-and-purge syndrome.

Sexual Motivation

10. Sexual motivation is driven by both fantasies and hormones and is shaped by culture. Hormones control sexual behavior in humans and other animals through both **organizational effects** (influencing the structure of neural circuitry, largely in utero) and **activational effects** (activating physiological changes that depend on this circuitry).

11. **Sexual orientation** refers to the direction of a person's enduring sexual attraction—to members of the same sex, the opposite sex, or both. Although the data on female homosexuality are scant, accumulating evidence on male homosexuality suggests a heavy biological influence.

12. **Sexual dysfunctions** are problems that impair sexual functioning, such as inhibited orgasm and premature ejaculation.

Psychosocial Motives

13. **Psychosocial motives** are personal and interpersonal motives for such ends as mastery, achievement, power, self-esteem, affiliation, and intimacy. Across cultures, the two major clusters of motives are **agency** (self-oriented goals, such as mastery or power) and communion, or **relatedness** (interpersonal motives for connection with others).

14. The **need for achievement** refers to a motive to succeed and to avoid failure, which is heavily influenced by cultural and economic conditions. Achievement motivation may be linked to performance goals or learning goals; it may also reflect intrinsic (done for its own sake) or extrinsic (done for an external reward) motivation.

15. Even for needs undeniably rooted in biology, such as hunger and sex, the strength of a motive depends in part on whether or not appropriate stimuli impinge on the organism. Motives also often reflect a subtle blend of innate factors (nature) as well as learning and culture (nurture). Motivation usually requires both cognition (representations that provide the direction of motivation) and emotional energy or arousal (providing the "fuel" or strength of motivation).

Jacob Lawrence, "Builders-Red and Green Ball," 1979

Chapter 11

EMOTION, STRESS, AND COPING

*I*n January 1994, a week before the U.S. national figure skating championship competition, a large, burly man entered the rink where one of the country's premier skaters, Nancy Kerrigan, was practicing. With two blows to her right leg, he took her out of the competition, threatening her prospects for the Olympics. Over the next few weeks, a plot against Kerrigan unfolded in the courts and the national media. The assailant turned out to be a bodyguard of Kerrigan's chief rival, Tonya Harding. Attention turned to Harding and her possible involvement in the attack on her competitor, and in an emotional but carefully planned press conference, she finally responded to the accusations.

Surrounded by television cameras and the flash of cameras, Harding revealed that when she returned from the national championship, her husband told her he had masterminded the attack, but that she had waited a week before disclosing the information. Her voice choked with emotion as she apologized to Kerrigan and the nation for withholding this knowledge, and she briefly stopped to compose herself as she denied any prior knowledge of the conspiracy. Commentators described her as a "deer caught in the headlights."

As millions of people watched the press conference, they wrestled with the same questions: Was her impassioned denial of involvement genuine, or was it an impressive display of acting? Was the apparent emotion in her voice real, or was it feigned to elicit sympathy and protect her place on the Olympic team? And if the emotion was truly genuine, did it reflect heartfelt remorse over withholding information, an agonizing realization that people she trusted had betrayed her, or simply fear that instead of a chance at Olympic gold she might be facing penitentiary concrete?

As this example suggests, emotion is a complex phenomenon. It can be authentic or fraudulent. It can involve a blend of feelings. It can be subjectively experienced but hidden from others. Conversely, people can communicate an emotion through body language or vocal tone that they may not even consciously experience, as when someone betrays anxiety with stuttering or tense posture.

This chapter explores the nature of emotion, beginning with components and types of emotion and different perspectives on emotional experience. Throughout, we consider the relative roles of biology and culture in shaping emotion, addressing the question of whether people everywhere experience the same basic emotions. Next, we turn to the related phenomenon of stress, from major stresses like Harding's press conference or Kerrigan's ordeal, to catastrophes like earthquakes, to daily hassles like traffic and sloppy roommates. After examining stress and its effects on health, we explore the strategies people use to cope with stress, as well as the role of culture in patterning responses to experiences ranging from loss and unemployment to discrimination and torture. We conclude by looking back over the last several chapters to consider the interactions of thought, memory, motivation, and emotion as people cope with stressful events.

EMOTION

Everyone has an intuitive sense of what an emotion is, but emotion can be exceedingly difficult to define. Imagine explaining the concept of emotion to someone who has never experienced one (like a tax collector). **Emotion**, or **affect** (a synonym for emotion, pronounced with the accent on the first syllable), is an evaluative response (a positive or negative feeling) that typically includes some combination of physiological arousal, subjective experience, and behavioral or emotional expression. We examine each of the components in turn.

Physiological Components

Over a century ago, William James (1884) argued that emotion is rooted in bodily experience. According to James, an emotion-inducing stimulus elicits visceral, or gut, reactions and voluntary behaviors such as running or gesturing. The physical experience in turn leads the person to feel aroused, and the arousal stimulates the subjective experience of fear. In this view, confronting a bear on a camping trip causes a person to run, and running produces fear.

James thus offered a counterintuitive proposition: We do not run because we are afraid; rather, we become afraid because we run (Figure 11.1a). James's theory is sometimes called the peripheral theory of emotion because it sees the origins of emotion in the peripheral nervous system. Recall that the peripheral nervous system controls both muscle movements and autonomic responses such as racing heart and shortness of breath in the face of fear-eliciting stimuli. Because the Danish physiologist Carl Lange (1885) proposed a similar view at about the same time as James (which no doubt made both of their hearts pound and fists clench, leading them to feel angry), this view of emotion is known as the **James-Lange theory**. As the theory would predict, some emotional experiences—particularly sexual arousal, fear, and anger—do appear to be blunted in individuals with spinal cord lesions that prevent them from moving or experiencing gut feelings (Hohmann, 1966; Jasmos & Hakmiller, 1975). One man with a cervical lesion (a lesion near the neck, which cuts off almost all autonomic signals) compared his feelings of sexual arousal before and after the accident:

> Before I got hurt…I would get a hot, tense feeling all over my body. I've got out and necked a few times since I was hurt, but it doesn't do anything for me. I daydream once in a while about it, and when I'm around a bunch of guys I talk big, but I just don't get worked up anymore. (Hohmann, 1966, p. 148)

Not all evidence on spinal injuries, however, supports the James-Lange theory (Bermond et al., 1991), and the theory was challenged on other grounds over a half century ago by Cannon (1927) and Bard (1934). Cannon and Bard noted that auto-

FIGURE 11.1
The James-Lange and Cannon-Bard theories of emotion. In the James-Lange theory (a), a stimulus leads to a peripheral nervous system response, which in turn is interpreted as an emotion. In the Cannon-Bard theory (b), the stimulus produces simultaneous peripheral responses and subjective experience.

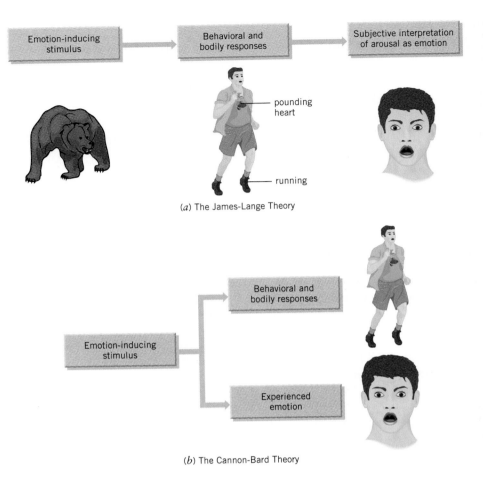

nomic responses are typically slow, occurring about one to two seconds after presentation of a stimulus. In contrast, emotional responses are immediate and often precede both autonomic reactions and behaviors such as running. Cannon and Bard argued further that many different emotional states are linked to the same visceral responses, so that arousal is too generalized to translate directly into discrete emotional experiences. For instance, muscle tension and quickened heart rate accompany sexual arousal, fear, and rage, which people experience as very different emotional states. Cannon and Bard offered the alternative view (known as the **Cannon-Bard theory**) that emotion-inducing stimuli *simultaneously* elicit both an emotional experience, such as fear, and bodily responses, such as sweaty palms (Figure 11.1*b*).

Cannon and Bard's first criticism (about the relative speed of autonomic and emotional responses) continues to be valid. However, their second criticism, that visceral arousal is general, has been challenged by more recent research. In fact, different emotions appear to be associated with distinct patterns of autonomic arousal (Ekman, 1992; Levenson, 1992; Levenson et al., 1990). Different clusters of emotions show modest but consistent differences in variables such as heart rate acceleration, finger temperature, and skin conductance (a measure of sweat on the palms related to arousal or anxiety, also known as galvanic skin response, or GSR). Anger and fear, for example, produce greater heart rate acceleration than happiness. This makes evolutionary sense, because anger and fear are related to fight-or-flight responses, which require the heart to pump more blood to the muscles. Anger and fear are also distinguishable from each other autonomically. The language we use to describe anger ("hot under the collar") appears to be physiologically accurate: People who are angry *do* get "heated" in their surface skin temperatures. Moreover, psychologists have found the same links between emotional experience and physiology among men from the island of Sumatra in Indonesia, suggesting that the connection is wired into the brain (Levenson et al., 1992).

Subjective Experience

The most familiar component of emotion is **subjective experience**, or what it feels like to be happy, sad, angry, or elated. Individuals differ tremendously in the intensity of their emotional states (Larsen & Diener, 1987). At the extreme high end of the bell curve of emotional intensity are people with severe personality disorders (Chapter 15), whose emotions spiral out of control (Linehan, 1987). At the other end of the bell curve are people with a psychological disorder called **alexithymia** (Lindholm et al., 1990; Sifneos, 1973), which literally means "no language for emotions." Alexithymics have difficulty telling one emotion from another and often report what seem to be meaningful, painful, or traumatic experiences with bland indifference. One alexithymic patient told his therapist about a "strange event" that had occurred the previous day. He had found himself shaking and felt his eyes tearing and wondered if he had been crying. The patient showed no recognition that his tears could have been related to frightening news he had received that morning about the results of a biopsy (D. Hulihan, personal communication, 1992).

Acknowledging and examining one's feelings can have a positive impact on health (Berry & Pennebaker, 1993; Pennebaker, 1992). The investigators in one experiment instructed college-student subjects to write for 20 minutes a day for four consecutive days about either traumatic experiences or trivial events. Subjects writing about traumatic experiences made fewer trips to the campus health center in the next several weeks and showed superior functioning of their immune systems (responsible for fighting off disease) than subjects induced to discuss trivial, low-emotion topics (Pennebaker et al., 1988). Another study assessed whether writing about the difficulties of the transition to college would benefit entering students (Pennebaker et al., 1990). The experimenters assigned college freshmen to one of two groups. They asked subjects in the experimental group to write for 20 minutes on three consecutive days about "your very deepest thoughts and feelings about coming to college," including "your emotions and thoughts about leaving your friends or your parents...or even about your feelings of who you are or what you want to become." Subjects in the control group were "to describe in detail what you have done since you woke up this morning" and were instructed not to mention their emotions, feelings, or opinions.

The results were dramatic (Figure 11.2). Subjects in the experimental group made significantly fewer visits to the health service in the following two to three months. As we shall see, considerable evidence suggests that emotions that are not acknowledged may nonetheless eat away at a person physiologically. The experimental effect largely wore off by the fourth month and disappeared thereafter.

Emotional Expression

A third component of emotion is **emotional expression**, the overt behavioral signs of emotion. People express feelings in various ways, including facial expressions, posture, gestures, and tone of voice.

Facial Expression and Emotion

In a twist on William James's peripheral hypothesis of emotion, some theorists argue that the face is the primary center of emotion (Tomkins, 1962, 1980).

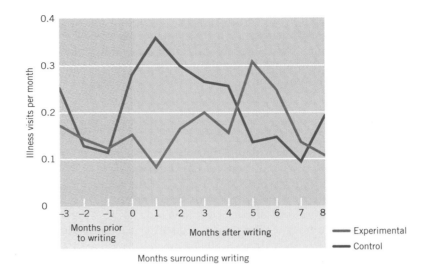

FIGURE 11.2

Emotional expression and health. The figure shows the number of visits to the health service per month for students writing about emotionally meaningful or trivial events. In the three months prior to writing, subjects in the two groups showed no clear differences in number of visits to the health center. Directly following writing (month 0), however, control subjects were much more likely to seek medical attention. Thus, expressing feelings has an impact on health, although without continued attention to emotion, the impact disappears. SOURCE: Adapted from Pennebaker et al., 1990, p. 533.

Then imitate the action of the tiger:

Stiffen the sinews, summon up the blood,

Disguise fair nature with hard-favored rage;

Then lend the eye a terrible aspect;

Let it pry through the portage of the head

Like the brass cannon...

Now set the teeth and stretch the nostril wide,

Hold hard the breath and bend up every spirit

To his full height!

Shakespeare, Henry V, (III. i.)

Whereas James asserted that we feel afraid because we run, these theorists argue that we feel afraid because our face shows fear. In this view, emotion consists of muscular responses located primarily in the face (and secondarily of muscular and glandular responses throughout the body).

Different facial expressions are, in fact, associated with different emotions (Ekman, 1992; Izard, 1971). Terror is marked by eyes that are open wide "in a fixed stare or moving away from the dreaded object to the side" (Tomkins, 1980, p. 142). The relationship between emotion and facial muscle movements is uniform enough across individuals and cultures that electrodes attached to the face to detect muscle movements allow psychologists to assess directly the valence (positive or negative) and intensity of emotion (Tassinary & Cacioppo, 1992).

Facial expressions not only indicate a person's emotional state, but they also influence its physiological and subjective components. In a classic study, researchers gave subjects specific directions to contract their facial muscles in particular ways (Ekman et al., 1983). For instance, as shown in Figure 11.3, they instructed subjects to raise their eyebrows and pull them together, then raise their upper eyelids, and finally stretch their lips horizontally. The result was an expression of fear, even though the subjects (actors) had not been instructed to show a particular emotion.

FIGURE 11.3

Creating fear in the face. Subjects instructed to (a) raise their eyebrows and pull them together, (b) then raise their upper eyelids, and (c) stretch their lips back toward their ears showed physiological changes consistent with fear.

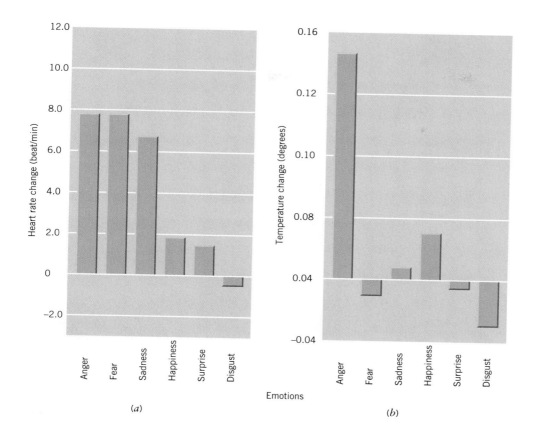

FIGURE 11.4
Facial expression and physiological response. The figure shows changes in heart rate and finger temperature associated with certain emotional expressions. Anger, fear, and sadness elevate heart rate, but of these three emotions, only anger also increases temperature. People presumably learn to distinguish these affects based on subtle physiological cues such as these. SOURCE: *Ekman et al., 1983, p. 1209.*

The experimenters similarly created expressions characteristic of anger, sadness, happiness, surprise, and disgust. Subjects held these expressions for 10 seconds, during which their heart rate and finger temperature were measured.

The researchers found a striking causal relation between the simple act of changing facial expression and patterns of autonomic response (Figure 11.4). Subsequent research documents distinct EEG activity associated with the different posed emotions (Ekman, 1992; Ekman & Davidson, 1993) as well as changes in subjective experience that accompany changes in the face (Izard, 1990; Lanzetta et al., 1976). Whoever wrote the lyric about letting a smile be your umbrella on a rainy day may have been a savvy psychologist. Furthermore, true and fake smiles appear to be physiologically different and rely on different sets of facial muscles (Ekman, 1992). Perhaps an analysis of Tonya Harding's facial expressions during her videotaped press conference will someday reveal whether her emotional pain was genuine.

Culture and Emotional Display Rules

Prior to research documenting the physiological and anatomical differences among emotions, psychologists and sociologists hotly debated whether people across cultures ascribe the same meaning to a smile or a frown. In fact, some facial expressions are universally recognized (see Ekman & Oster, 1979; Frick, 1985; Scherer & Wallbott, 1994). Subjects in one classic study viewed photographs showing the faces of North American actors expressing fear, anger, happiness, and other emotions. Subjects from diverse cultural groups, ranging from Swedes and Kenyans to members of a preliterate tribe in New Guinea with minimal Western contact, all recognized certain emotions (Ekman, 1971). Cross-cultural studies have identified six facial expressions recognized by people of every culture examined (Figure 11.5): surprise, fear, anger, disgust, happiness, and sadness (Ekman & Oster, 1979). Shame and interest also may have universal facial expressions (Izard, 1977). These

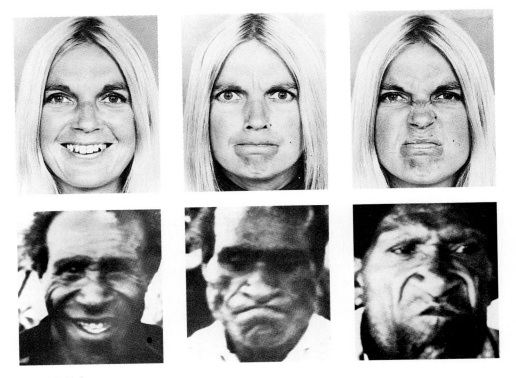

FIGURE 11.5
Universal facial expressions. Members of the remote Fore tribe of New Guinea recognize Western facial expressions, just as Western college students recognize the expressions on Fore faces.

findings suggest that some emotions are biologically linked not only to distinct autonomic states but also to certain facial movements, which people in all cultures can decode.

Not all facial expressions, however, are the same from culture to culture. People learn to control the way they express many emotions, using patterns of emotional expression considered appropriate within their culture or subculture, called **display rules** (Ekman & Friesen, 1975; Ekman et al., 1982b). In a study examining cultural differences in display rules, Japanese and North American subjects viewed a film depicting a painful initiation rite. As long as they were unaware that they were being observed, subjects from the two cultures showed the same facial responses (Figure 11.6). When subjects believed they might be observed, however, their reac-

FIGURE 11.6
Cultural display rules. Japanese and North American viewers watching the same painful initiation rites show very similar emotional reactions—but only when they thought they were not being observed.

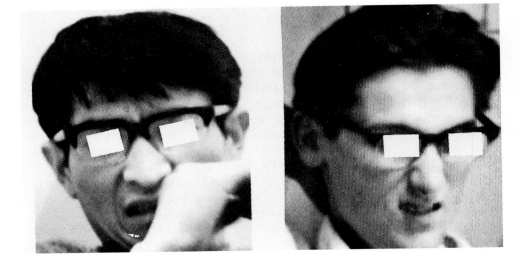

tions were quite different. The North Americans still showed revulsion, but the Japanese, socialized to show far less emotion, masked their expressions (Ekman, 1977). Whether the Japanese *experienced* the emotion differently as a result is unknown.

Since the 1920s, North American culture has seen the emergence of a style of emotional display recognizable to most readers: "cool" (Stearns, 1994). Being cool means "conveying an air of disengagement, or nonchalance" (Stearns, p. 1). The style is expressed in popular culture in characters like "Joe Cool" in the Snoopy cartoon and "the Fonz" in television's *Happy Days*, in Kool cigarettes, and in phrases like, "Be cool," and "Don't blow your cool." Although in some respects this style of emotional expression reflects a continuation of concerns with impulse control inherited from the nineteenth century, it adds elements of restraint not found even in the Victorian era. For example, although the Victorians feared overt sexuality, males were permitted to gush with feelings of deep romantic love in poetry and prose. In contrast, the "cool" male of the late twentieth century attracts a woman by showing romantic interest—but not *too* much, which would be "uncool," that is, over-eager and over-emotional. The emergence of cool as a pattern of emotional display no doubt reflects in part an increased concern in North America, and particularly the United States, with appearance to peers rather than adherence to inner standards or the demands of authority (Reisman, 1966).

1950s actor James Dean, who starred in Rebel Without a Cause, *cornered the market on "cool."*

Gender and Emotional Expression

Display rules differ not only by culture but also by gender. If Tonya Harding had been Thomas Harding, she would clearly not have displayed her emotions in the same way at her press conference. Emotional displays that elicit sympathy for one gender, such as Harding's halting and almost tearful admission that she had withheld information, can elicit discomfort or contempt if produced by the other gender. Whether men and women actually experience their emotions differently is difficult to ascertain, but the best evidence suggests that women probably experience emotion more intensely, are better able to read emotions from other people's faces and nonverbal cues, and express emotion more intensely and openly than men (Brody & Hall, 1993). This is true for all emotions except anger, with which males tend to be more comfortable. From the time they are little, boys receive repeated messages that only "sissies" cry, that feeling scared and showing signs of emotional vulnerability is unmanly, and that intimidating others with displays of anger and aggression, though often discouraged, can also demonstrate status and power. Indeed, children as young as 3 years old recognize that females are more likely to express fear, sadness, and happiness, and males, anger (Birnbaum, 1983).

The reasons for gender differences in emotional expression and recognition of emotion in others are a matter of debate, but they likely reflect adaptation to the roles that men and women have historically tended to occupy. Women are generally more comfortable with emotions such as love, happiness, warmth, shame, guilt, and sympathy, which foster affiliation and caretaking. Men, on the other hand, are socialized to compete and to fight; hence, they avoid "soft" emotions that display their vulnerabilities to competitors and enemies or discourage them from asserting their dominance when the need arises (Brody & Hall, 1993). To what degree gender differences in emotion are changing as gender roles change is as yet unclear.

A Taxonomy of Emotions

Some aspects of emotion, then, are universal, whereas others vary by culture and gender (see Lutz, 1988; Russell, 1994). How many emotions do humans experience, and how many of these are innate? Psychologists have attempted to produce a list of **basic emotions**, emotions common to the human species, similar to primary colors in perception, from which all other emotions and emotional blends are derived. An emotion is basic if it has characteristic physiological, subjective, and expressive components (Izard & Buechler, 1980).

Although theorists generate slightly different lists, and some even argue against the existence of basic emotions (Ortony & Turner, 1990), most classifications include five to nine emotions (Russell, 1991). All theorists of basic emotions list anger, fear, happiness, sadness, and disgust. Surprise, contempt, interest, shame, guilt, joy, trust, and anticipation sometimes make the roster (Plutchik, 1980; Russell, 1991; Shaver et al., 1987; Tomkins, 1980). Similar lists of basic emotions have been compiled in India (Lynch, 1990) and in China, where an encyclopedia from the first century B.C. contained the following entry:

> What are the feelings of men? They are joy, anger, sadness, fear, love, disliking, and liking. These seven feelings belong to men without their learning them. (*The Li Chi*, cited in Russell, 1991, p. 426)

Beyond these basic emotions, cultures vary in the extent to which they elaborate and distinguish emotional states (Kitayama & Markus, 1994; Russell, 1991). The Tahitian language has 46 different words for anger (much as English has several terms, such as annoyance, frustration, and rage) but no word for sadness. The Tahitians do not even have a word for *emotion*. In some African languages, the same word denotes both anger and sadness; members of these cultures seldom seem to distinguish between the two.

Perhaps a distinction even more fundamental than differences among the basic emotions is between **positive affect** (pleasant emotions) and **negative affect** (unpleasant emotions). Factor analysis of data from several cultures suggests that these two factors underlie people's self-reported emotions (see Watson & Clark, 1992; Watson & Tellegen, 1985). (Recall from Chapter 8 that factor analysis combines variables that are highly correlated with each other into superordinate variables, or factors.) Within these two factors, emotions are substantially intercorrelated. In other words, people who frequently experience one negative emotion, such as guilt, also tend to experience others, such as anxiety and sadness. Positive and negative affect are negatively correlated with one another but surprisingly modestly; that is, people who often feel anxious or guilty may also frequently feel happy.

The distinction between positive and negative affect is congruent with behaviorist research and neuropsychological data establishing the existence of a pleasure-seeking, approach-oriented behavioral system driven by positive affect and an aversive or avoidance-oriented system driven by negative affect (Chapter 5; see also Davidson, 1992; Fox, 1991; Gray, 1990; Lang et al., 1992). The tendency to experience positive and negative emotions also appears to some degree heritable, or reducible to genetic factors. For positive affectivity, estimated heritability based on studies of twins reared together and apart is .40; for negative affectivity, heritability is even higher, at .55 (Tellegen, cited in Gabbay, 1992; Watson & Tellegen, 1985).

How can the various views of emotion be reconciled, with their competing claims about the number of emotions and the relative importance of biology and culture? One solution (Figure 11.7) is to organize emotions hierarchically (Fischer et al., 1990). The most universal categories are positive and negative affect. All cultures make this distinction, and it is the first drawn by young children, who use words such as *nice, mean, good, bad, like,* and *don't like.* The basic emotions at the next level of the hierarchy also apply across cultures. Below this level, however, most emotion concepts are culturally constructed. Western culture, for example, distinguishes different forms of love, such as infatuation, fondness, sexual love, nonsexual love, and puppy love. Indian culture, in contrast, distinguishes only two forms of love: *vatsalya bhava,* a mother's love for her child, and *madhurya bhava,* erotic love (Lynch, 1990). Children recognize these culture-specific distinctions much later than the basic emotions.

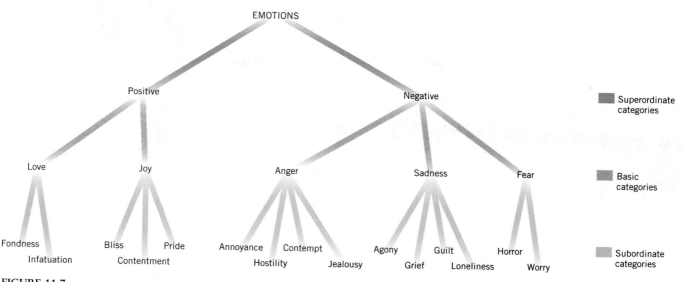

FIGURE 11.7

An emotion hierarchy. Emotions may be arranged hierarchically, with universal categories at the superordinate and basic levels, and categories that vary by culture at the subordinate level. SOURCE: *Fischer et al., 1990, p. 90.*

FROM MIND TO BRAIN

THE NEUROPSYCHOLOGY OF EMOTION

Poets often locate emotion in the heart, whereas theorists with a less romantic bent of mind locate it in the face or the peripheral nervous system. Still other researchers have searched for the neural circuits underlying emotion in the central nervous system. They have found that affects, like cognitions, are distributed throughout the nervous system and are not located in any particular region (Derryberry & Tucker, 1992). Three areas of the brain, however, are particularly important: the hypothalamus, the limbic system, and the cortex.

Since the 1930s, psychologists have recognized the role of the hypothalamus in emotion. Electrical stimulation of this region can produce attack, defense, or flight reactions, with corresponding emotions of rage or terror. Papez (1937) considered the hypothalamus a crucial component of a circuit or "loop" involved in the generation of emotion. Figure 11.8*a* shows a modified version of the Papez circuit.

Papez argued that when the hypothalamus receives emotionally relevant sensory information from the thalamus (which functions as a sensory relay station), it instigates activity in a circuit of neurons higher up in the brain. These neurons, which include what is now referred to as the limbic system as well as the cortex, process the information more deeply to assess its emotional significance. Once the circuit is completed, it feeds back to the hypothalamus, which in turn activates autonomic and endocrine responses.

Many aspects of Papez's theory have turned out to be anatomically correct, although contemporary theories (LeDoux, 1989, 1995) probably place more emphasis on the limbic system (Figure 11.8). In some species, motivation is largely controlled by the hypothalamus, and hence by instinct.

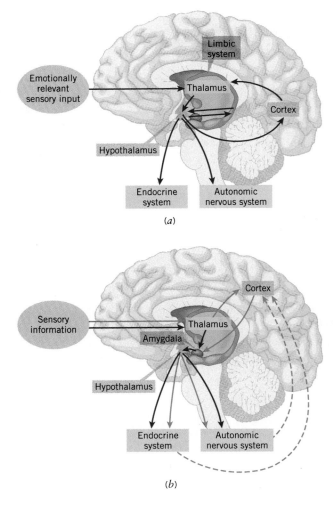

FIGURE 11.8

Neural and endocrine pathways involved in emotion. (a) A modified version of the Papez circuit. According to Papez, sensory information is transmitted from the thalamus to the hypothalamus. If that information is emotionally relevant, it activates the cortex and limbic system, which in turn assess the emotional relevance of the information and influence subsequent hypothalamic response. (b) Two circuits for emotion processing in the brain. Emotionally relevant information is relayed from the thalamus simultaneously to the amygdala and the cortex. The initial emotional response from the amygdala may produce autonomic and endocrine changes (such as those indicative of fear and anger), which the cortex must interpret. The second (cortical) pathway allows the person to evaluate the stimulus on the basis of stored knowledge and goals. SOURCE: Adapted from LeDoux, 1986, p. 329.

However, the evolution of the limbic system meant that in other species, especially humans, behavior is controlled less by instinct than by learning, and particularly by emotional responses to stimuli.

Perhaps the most important limbic structure for emotion is the amygdala. The amygdala is the brain's "emotional computer" for calculating the emotional significance of a stimulus (LeDoux, 1989). In 1937, researchers discovered that lesioning a large temporal region (which later turned out primarily to involve the amygdala) produced a peculiar syndrome in monkeys (Kluver & Bucy, 1939). The monkeys no longer seemed to understand the emotional significance of objects in their environment, even though they had no trouble recognizing or identifying them. The animals showed no fear of previously feared stimuli and were generally unable to use their emotions to guide behavior. They would, for example, eat feces or other inedible objects that normally elicited disgust or indifference. Researchers have subsequently found that lesioning the neurons connecting the amygdala with a specific sense, such as vision or hearing, makes the monkey unable to register the emotional significance of objects perceived by that sense (LeDoux, 1989). In other words, the amygdala (together with the hippocampus, which is involved in memory) plays a crucial role in associating sensory and other information with pleasant and unpleasant feelings (see Derryberry & Tucker, 1992). This allows humans and other animals to adjust their behavior based on positive and negative emotional reactions to objects or situations they encounter.

The amygdala is in many respects the neuronal hub of emotion because of its connections with both the cortex and the hypothalamus. The amygdala also receives some sensory information directly from the thalamus. This information is relatively simple, based on neurons in the thalamus that process primitive sensory patterns (Chapter 4), but it can elicit an immediate emotional response (such as to a snake approaching). Conditioning can also occur through this thalamo-limbic circuit even when links between the amygdala and the cortex have been severed, as long as the neural connections between the amygdala and the hippocampus are intact. (The reason is that the hippocampus allows memory of associations between stimuli and emotional reactions.) For primitive vertebrates, this simple circuit was probably the sole basis of emotional reaction.

In primates such as humans and chimpanzees, however, the amygdala is also connected to higher processing centers in the cortex. Thus, when the thalamus sends sensory information to the amygdala, it simultaneously routes information to the cortex for more thorough examination. Once the cortex has processed the information, it transmits information down to the amygdala. A second emotional response may then occur, based on this more complex information processing.

The emotional reaction to a stimulus, then, may pass through two stages (LeDoux, 1992, 1995), reflecting two somewhat independent processes (Figure 11.8b). One is a quick response based on a cursory reaction to gross stimulus features, involving a circuit running from the thalamus to the amygdala. (A dark shadow in the water frightens a bather.) The second process is slower, based on a more thorough cognitive appraisal, involving a thalamus-to-cortex-to-amygdala circuit. (The bather realizes that the dark shadow is a buoy.) The initial thalamus-to-amygdala process typically occurs faster because it involves fewer synaptic connections; that is, the circuit is shorter. The endocrine and autonomic responses it triggers will in turn produce sensations that are processed by the cortex, which must interpret their significance.

The existence of two circuits for emotional processing raises fascinating questions about what happens when the affective reactions generated by these two circuits are in conflict. For example, a cancer patient may have an immediate aversive conditioned response to the room in which she receives chemotherapy but also recognize that what happens in this room may be key to her survival. She therefore overrides the avoidance behavior that would ordinarily be elicited by the conditioned emotional response and keeps appearing for her treatments.

The cortex plays several roles with respect to emotion. As noted above, it allows people to consider the implications of a stimulus for adaptation or well-being. It is also involved in interpreting the meaning of peripheral responses, as when a person's experience of shaky knees and a dry throat while speaking in front of a group shows her that she is anxious (Pribram, 1980). In addition,

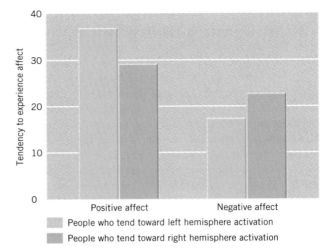

FIGURE 11.9
Emotional experience and hemisphere activation. The figure shows mean positive and negative affect scores for subjects with a strong tendency toward left versus right midfrontal activation. As can be seen, subjects with a bias toward left hemisphere activation reported more positive and less negative affect than those with a right hemisphere bias.
SOURCE: *Adapted from Tomarken et al., 1992, p. 681.*

the frontal cortex plays an important part in the social regulation of the face (Rinn, 1984), such as the ability to amplify, minimize, or feign an emotion.

Finally, the right and left hemispheres appear to be specialized, with the right hemisphere dominant in processing emotional cues from others and producing facial displays of emotion (Borod, 1992). Current research also suggests that pleasant, approach-related emotions are associated with activation of the left frontal cortex, whereas unpleasant, avoidance-related emotions are associated with activation of the right frontal lobe (Davidson, 1992; Fox, 1991). People who show strong asymmetries in activation of regions of the left versus the right hemisphere tend to report corresponding asymmetries in their experience of positive and negative affect (Figure 11.9). In other words, subjects who tend toward left hemisphere activation report that they experience more positive than negative affect.

Perspectives on Emotion

We have now examined the components of emotion and its basis in the nervous system. As we have seen, behaviorist research points to approach and avoidance systems associated with positive and negative affect, respectively. Behaviorist researchers have studied conditioned emotional responses in classical conditioning as well, such as fear upon seeing a doctor approaching with a hypodermic needle. The psychodynamic, cognitive, and evolutionary perspectives offer additional insights into the nature and function of emotion.

Psychodynamic Perspectives on Emotion

A growing body of evidence supports a central, and somewhat counterintuitive, contention of psychodynamic theory: that people can be unconscious of their own emotional experience and that unconscious emotional processes can influence thought, behavior, and even health (Singer, 1990; Westen, 1985, 1990). In one study (see Moray, 1969), the experimenter repeatedly paired previously neutral words with electric shock in a classical conditioning procedure, eventually producing a conditioned emotional response to them (anxiety or fear). The experimenter then exposed subjects to the fear-inducing words using a dichotic listening procedure, presenting the words in the unattended channel, and measured subjects' anxious arousal physiologically by assessing their skin conductance. The conditioned stimuli elicited physiological reactivity (a GSR), even though subjects had no conscious awareness of their presentation. Thus, subjects reacted emotionally to stimuli perceived unconsciously.

Psychodynamic theory asserts that people regularly delude themselves about their own abilities and personality attributes as a way of avoiding unpleasant emotion, and a considerable body of experimental data supports this view (see Epstein, 1992; Greenwald & Pratkanis, 1984). A recent set of studies tested the hypothesis that such defensive self-deception about emotions takes its toll physiologically (Shedler et al., 1993). The experiments focused on subjects who are prone to disavowing negative thoughts and feelings about themselves. Subjects were asked to fill out a questionnaire about their mental health and were then asked to describe in detail their earliest memories (a common procedure used by clinicians to assess degree of psychological health or disturbance; Mayman, 1968). Subjects who self-reported themselves as happy and healthy on the questionnaire but who were judged by a clinician (in one study) or a team of undergraduates (in another) as emotionally troubled were categorized as having "illusory mental health." All subjects then underwent a potentially anxiety-provoking task, such as making up TAT stories or answering items from an IQ test.

During the task, subjects with illusory mental health could be distinguished from other subjects on numerous physiological indices of psychological distress. Notably, they had elevated heart rate and blood pressure, which are related to heart disease. These subjects also consistently scored highest on various indirect measures of anxiety, such as sighing and stammering, during the experimental procedure. All the while, however, they consciously reported the *least* anxiety, suggesting the presence of unconscious anxiety (Figure 11.10). Several other research groups have pre-

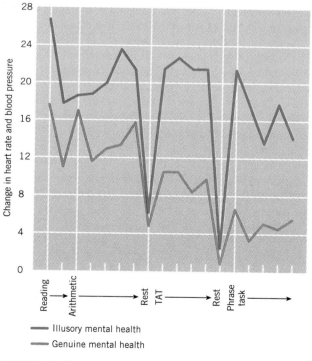

FIGURE 11.10

Illusory mental health. Subjects judged high, but who self-reported themselves low in distress showed substantially larger heart rate and blood pressure increases while performing such mildly stressful tasks as solving arithmetic questions and making up stories in response to TAT cards. Note, however, that during resting periods subjects who deluded themselves showed as little reactivity as genuinely healthy subjects, suggesting that their unconscious anxiety comes out only when performing a potentially threatening task. SOURCE: *Shedler et al., 1993.*

sented similar data on subjects who tend to keep themselves unaware of their emotions (see Asendorph & Sherer, 1983; Newton & Contrada, 1992; Singer, 1990; D. Weinberger, 1990).

Cognitive Perspectives on Emotion

Throughout much of the history of Western culture, beginning at least with Plato in the 5th century B.C., emotion has been viewed as a disruptive force in human affairs. Plato asserted that reason must rein in the passions, which otherwise distort rational thinking. Today cognitive theorists empirically study the impact of feelings on cognitive processes such as memory and judgment (e.g., Mathews & Macleod, 1994) and also the reciprocal influence of cognition on emotion.

Interpretation and Emotion   You have just climbed four flights of stairs to your apartment on a frigid day, to be confronted by a roommate complaining about dirty dishes in the sink. Your heart is racing, and your face feels flushed. Are you angry? Or is your body simply registering the impact of four flights of stairs and a sudden change in temperature? The way you react may well depend on the **attributions** (inferences about causes) you make about these bodily sensations.

In a classic paper, Stanley Schachter and Jerome Singer (1962) argued that a cognitive judgment or attribution is crucial to emotional experience. That is, when people experience a state of nonspecific physiological arousal, which could be anger, happiness, or any other feeling, they try to figure out what the arousal means. If situational cues suggest that they should be afraid, they interpret the arousal as fear; if the cues suggest excitement, they interpret their arousal as excitement. Thus, according to the **Schachter-Singer theory**, emotion involves two factors: physiological arousal and cognitive interpretation (Figure 11.11).

To test their hypothesis, Schachter and Singer injected subjects with either adrenalin or an inert placebo and then placed them in a waiting room. Subjects were either correctly informed, misinformed, or told nothing about the possible effects of the injection, in order to see whether their emotional state would be influenced by knowing they had been physiologically aroused. Next, subjects in each condition were joined by a presumed subject (actually a confederate of the experimenter), who either behaved angrily and stormed out of the room (designed to elicit anger) or assumed a playful and euphoric attitude, throwing paper wads into the wastebasket, flying paper airplanes, and generally enjoying himself (designed to elicit euphoria).

Schachter and Singer predicted that subjects who knew they had been injected with an arousing drug would attribute their arousal to the drug, whereas those who became aroused but did not know why would think they were either angry or euphoric, depending on the condition. The results were as predicted, suggesting that emotional experience is not simply the subjective awareness of arousal. Rather, it is a complex cognitive-affective state that includes inferences about the meaning of the arousal.

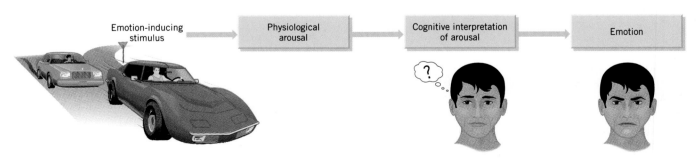

FIGURE 11.11
The Schachter-Singer theory of emotion. According to Schachter and Singer, people must interpret their arousal (for example, when cut off by a speeding car) in order to experience a specific emotion.

Schachter and Singer's conclusions have drawn criticism on a number of grounds (see Leventhal & Tomarken, 1986). For example, people can experience emotions without arousal. Even when physiological arousal is inhibited pharmacologically, subjects sometimes report feeling as anxious or angry as control subjects (Cleghorn et al., 1970; Erdmann & van Lindern, 1980). Thus, while arousal may intensify emotional experience, it may not be necessary for an emotion to occur (Reisenzein, 1983). Moreover, as the research reviewed earlier suggests, different emotions do, in fact, have distinct physiological correlates; thus, emotion is not simply the interpretation of general arousal. Finally, studies using experimental designs similar to Schachter and Singer's have often failed to replicate the original findings (Marshall & Zimbardo, 1979; Maslach, 1979). Nevertheless, intuitive experience as well as experimental data support the view that some degree of interpretation is involved in the experience of many emotional states. For instance, distinguishing between being tired or fatigued and being depressed requires interpretation because the two physiological states share many common features.

Cognition and Appraisal In Schachter and Singer's study, subjects initially became aroused by a shot of adrenalin. In normal life, however, people typically become aroused by their experiences rather than by injection. According to many cognitive theorists, people's emotions reflect their judgments and appraisals of the situations or stimuli that confront them (Lazarus, 1991, 1993; Smith & Ellsworth, 1985; Smith & Lazarus, 1993; Weiner, 1985). Anger results from a judgment that a perceived punishment is caused by another person and is unfair (Roseman et al., 1990). An event that affects a person's well-being in the present leads to joy or distress, whereas an event that influences the person's potential well-being in the future leads to hope or fear (Ortony et al., 1988).

Many of these cognitive principles operate the same way cross-culturally. The cognitive antecedents of anger described above, for instance, appear to be universal (Mauro, Sato, & Tucker, 1992). Judgments underlying emotion may, however, take some very different twists, depending on cultural conceptions of causality. Some preliterate societies believe that prolonged illness is the result of sorcery (Whiting & Child, 1958). Hence, the ill person or his loved ones may direct anger about the illness toward an accused sorcerer. The increased incidence in the United States of malpractice suits against physicians may reflect a similar process, as people respond to their anger and frustration by finding a doctor negligent or incompetent.

Although cognitive appraisals often underlie emotions, they do not always do so. Indeed, emotional responses can sometimes precede complex cognitive evaluations of a stimulus—or as psychologist Robert Zajonc (1980) has put it, "preferences need no inferences." Basing their research on the **mere exposure effect**, which shows that people become more positive about stimuli the more times they are exposed to them, Zajonc and his colleagues briefly exposed subjects several times to Japanese ideographs (written characters). When later asked about their preferences for particular characters, subjects preferred characters they had previously seen, *even when they did not consciously recognize having seen them.* Zajonc concluded that the subjective sense of liking or disliking a stimulus may occur independently of cognitions about that stimulus. At the very least, affect may precede the *conscious* cognitive appraisals proposed by many theorists.

The Influence of Emotion and Mood on Cognition Just as cognition can influence emotion, so, too, can emotion and mood influence ongoing thought and memory. **Mood** refers to relatively extended emotional states that, unlike emotions, typically do not shift attention or disrupt ongoing activities (Oatley & Jenkins, 1992). Investigators studying the effects of mood on thought and memory use various mood-induction techniques, such as exposure to frustrating or demoralizing situations (e.g., rigged intelligence tests that make the subject feel incompetent).

Mood and emotion affect both encoding and retrieval of information in memory, and they also influence thinking (Bower, 1989; Isen, 1984; Isen & Diamond,

1989; Kuiken, 1991; Mathews & Macleod, 1994; Mayer et al., 1992). Individuals in a positive mood tend both to store and to retrieve more positive information (Isen, 1984). Thus, subjects exposed to a list of words are more likely to remember positive words from that list a week later if they were in a positive mood during encoding *or* if they are in a positive mood during retrieval. Negative mood at retrieval often facilitates recall of negative words; however, people actively fight negative moods because they are aversive, so they try to retrieve more positive information. Thus, a motivational process (regulating a negative mood) may counteract an automatic cognitive process (recall of information congruent with current thought and mood). Mood can also influence the way people make judgments, inferences, or predictions (see Basso et al., 1994; Mayer et al., 1992). People who are depressed, for example, tend to underestimate the probability of their own success and overestimate the probability of bad events occurring in the future (Beck, 1976, 1991).

The Evolutionary Perspective

The evolutionary perspective on emotion derives from Charles Darwin's (1872) view that emotions serve an adaptive purpose. Darwin stressed their communicative function: Animals, including humans, signal their readiness to fight, run, or attend to each other's needs through a variety of postural, facial, and other nonverbal communications (see Buck, 1986). A baby's cry and a dog's raised hackles send signals to other members of the species. These communications regulate social behavior and increase the individual's chances of survival. The expression people display when angry—bared teeth and clenched jaws—shares the same evolutionary roots as the expression of other animals prepared to attack and bite an adversary. Darwin's theory explains why basic emotional expressions are wired into the organism and recognized cross-culturally.

Evolutionary theorists also view emotion as a powerful source of motivation—an *internal* communication that something must be done (Izard, 1977, 1978; Izard & Buechler, 1980; Plutchik, 1980, 1991; Tomkins, 1962, 1970). In fact, the words "motivation" and "emotion" share the same Latin root, *movere*, which means to move. For example, when people are threatened, they feel fear, which in turn leads them to deal with the threatening situation through either fight or flight. Table 11.1 shows how emotional reactions motivate behaviors that promote survival and reproduction (Plutchik, 1980). Emotions and drives may also operate in tandem to motivate action, as when excitement accompanies sexual arousal (Tomkins, 1986). From an evolutionary perspective, different emotions serve different functions. Fear facilitates flight in the face of danger; disgust prevents ingestion of potentially toxic substances such as rotting meat.

An emotion that is less well understood is jealousy. Why do people become jealous in intimate sexual relationships? One series of studies tested evolutionary

The similarities of facial expressions of emotions such as anger show their common evolutionary roots.

TABLE 11.1 EVOLUTIONARY LINKS BETWEEN EMOTION AND BEHAVIOR IN HUMANS AND OTHER ANIMALS		
STIMULUS EVENT	EMOTION	BEHAVIOR
Threat	Fear, terror, anxiety	Fight, flight
Obstacle	Anger, rage	Biting, hitting
Potential mate	Joy, ecstasy, excitement	Courtship, mating
Loss of valued person	Sadness, grief	Crying for help
Group member	Acceptance, trust	Grooming, sharing
New territory	Anticipation	Examining, mapping
Sudden novel object	Surprise	Stopping, attending

Source: Adapted from Plutchik, 1980, p. 16.

hypotheses about differences in the concerns men and women have about their partners' fidelity (Buss et al., 1992). Since females can have only a limited number of children during their lifetimes, to maximize their reproductive success they should be motivated to form relationships with males who have resources and will contribute them to their offspring. Indeed, cross-cultural evidence demonstrates that one of the main mate selection criteria used by females around the world is male resources, whether cattle or Corvettes (Chapter 18). From a female's point of view, then, infidelity accompanied by emotional commitment to the other woman is a major threat to resources. A man is unlikely to divert resources from his mate and her offspring to a casual fling, but the risk increases dramatically if he becomes emotionally involved and perhaps considers switching long-term partners. Hence, a woman's jealousy would be expected to focus on her mate's emotional commitment to another female.

For males, the situation is different. If a male commits himself to an exclusive relationship with a female, he must be certain that the offspring in whom he is investing are his own. Since he cannot be sure of paternity, the best he can do is prevent his mate from copulating with any other males. In males, then, jealousy would be expected to focus less on the female's emotional commitment or resources and more on her tendency to give other males sexual access. Indeed, in species ranging from insects to humans, males take extreme measures to prevent other males from inseminating their mates (Hasselquist & Bensch, 1991). Male birds in some species refuse to let a female out of their sight for days after insemination. In humans, male sexual jealousy is the leading cause of homicides and of spouse battering cross-culturally (Daly & Wilson, 1988).

To test the evolutionary hypothesis that males and females differ in their reasons for jealousy, male and female college students were asked to "Imagine that you discover that the person with whom you've been seriously involved became interested in someone else" (Buss et al., 1992). In the first study, subjects were to choose which of two related scenarios would upset them more: "Imagining your partner forming a deep emotional attachment to that person," or "Imagining your partner enjoying passionate sexual intercourse with that person." They were then asked a second question involving similar scenarios contrasting love and sex: "Imagining your partner falling in love with that other person," or "Imagining your partner try-

FIGURE 11.12
Jealousy in males and females. The figure shows the percentage of subjects reporting more distress to the sexual infidelity scenario than to either imagining their lover becoming deeply attached to someone else (left) or falling in love with someone else (right). Men are more concerned than women with sexual infidelity, and this is particularly true of those who have actually been in a committed sexual relationship.
SOURCE: *Buss et al., 1992.*

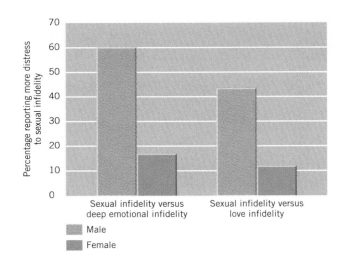

ing different sexual positions with that other person." As Figure 11.12 shows, 60 percent of males reported greater distress at the thought of sexual infidelity in response to the first question, compared to only 17 percent of the females, who were more concerned about emotional attachment. The second question yielded similar results.

In a second study, the investigators tested male and female students' physiological reactions to these questions, to see whether these large gender differences would similarly appear if they assessed people's gut reactions rather than simply their words. Physiological distress was assessed using indices such as pulse rate and electronic detection of subtle facial muscle movements, particularly furrowing the brow, which is associated with unpleasant emotion. The findings were striking: Men showed increased distress as measured by multiple indices when imagining sexual infidelity, whereas females reacted more strongly to the emotional attachment scenario. A third study, recognizing that many college students may not have had intimate sexual relationships, employed the same design as the first study but asked subjects whether or not they had had a physical relationship. Males who had actually had a sexual relationship, who were not just imagining an abstract scenario, were particularly concerned about sexual infidelity. The investigators theorized that having sexual experiences activates or amplifies an innate sexual jealousy mechanism in males. Cultural explanations cannot be ruled out on the basis of these studies, since they were conducted in a single culture, but the results are highly suggestive.

A Different Perspective: Integrating the Perspectives on Emotion

The various perspectives on emotion clearly focus on different parts of the fabled elephant (Chapter 1), and one would hope that ultimately a more fully elephantine portrait might emerge. As a step in that direction, we briefly explore a model of emotion that attempts to integrate aspects of the evolutionary, behavioral, psychodynamic, and cognitive perspectives (Westen, 1985, 1994). According to this model, feelings—including both emotions and sensory experiences of pleasure and pain caused by tactile stimulation—are mechanisms for selecting behavioral and mental responses. In other words, feelings regulate thought and behavior.

From an evolutionary perspective, the model suggests that emotions perform a central function in animals whose behavior is not rigidly controlled by instinct: They select behavior that enhances survival and reproduction. From a behaviorist perspective, the model proposes that the consequences of an action determine whether or not it is maintained or produced again. Those consequences typically involve feelings (Bolles, 1975; Rachman, 1978). When a baby discovers that crying brings its caretaker and alleviates physical or emotional discomfort, crying behavior is reinforced; that is, crying behavior is selected for continued use out of all the baby's other past and potential behaviors. Similarly, when a rat is punished with an electric shock each time it presses a lever, it is motivated to avoid pressing the lever by fear (Chapter 5). Behavior is also influenced by expectancies about the likely positive or negative impact of an action or event, as in expectancy-value theories of motivation (Chapter 10).

From a psychodynamic perspective, mental processes, like behaviors, can also be conditioned—that is, selectively retained—by their association with emotion. Dollard and Miller (1950) argued many years ago that repression is essentially an internal flight mechanism—flight from a thought that would bring on an unpleasant feeling. Integrating behaviorist and psychodynamic thinking, Miller published an ingenious study showing that a conditioned emotional response could be transferred from a stimulus to a thought (see Miller, 1951, 1992). Subjects initially underwent several trials in which they saw a 4 and a T. Presentation of the T was followed by an electric shock. Not surprisingly, this led to a large GSR (indicating anxious arousal) upon presentation of the T, even when it was no longer followed by a shock. Subjects were then shown a series of dots and asked to think of a 4 on the first dot, a T on the second, a 4 on the third, and so on. The thought became a conditioned stimulus: Merely thinking of a T led to measurable anxiety (Figure 11.13). In real life, avoiding consciousness of thoughts associated with unpleasant emotions is reinforced by the elimination of the aversive emotion.

From a cognitive perspective, emotions often reflect a person's judgment about the extent to which current or potential realities match representations of desired states (wishes) or feared states (fears). For example, an individual may worry that his lover is going to leave. Discrepancies between cognitions about reality (his lover's presence is comforting) and desired or feared states (his lover might leave) produce emotional feedback (anxiety, sadness, guilt, shame, and so forth), much as in homeostatic models of motivation (see also Bowlby, 1969; Carver & Scheier, 1981; Menninger et al., 1963; Miller et al., 1960). These emotional signals in turn activate behavioral and mental responses (such as pleading, or convincing himself that the relationship really does not matter) designed to minimize negative feelings and maximize positive ones.

Any number of goal-states can energize human thought and behavior, such as desired closeness to a loved one (Bowlby, 1969), values and ideals (e.g., fighting poverty), ideals for oneself such as behaving morally or competently in some

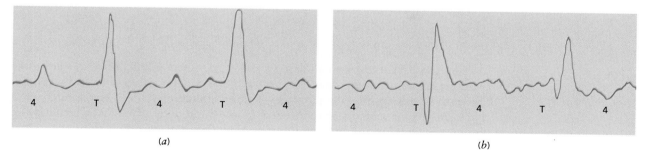

(a)   (b)

FIGURE 11.13
Classical conditioning of a thought. Part (a) shows the GSR of a subject to electric shock presented along with the letter T. Part (b) shows the GSR that occurred each time the subject thought about a T following acquisition of the conditioned response. SOURCE: *Miller, 1992.*

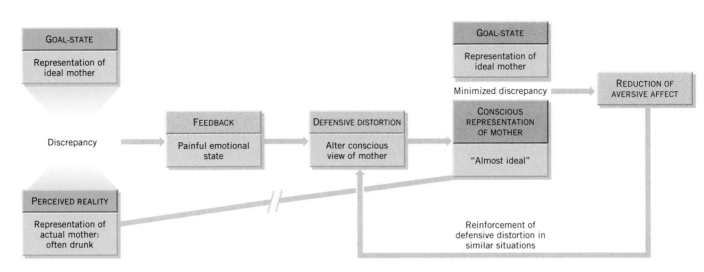

FIGURE 11.14

An integrated model of emotion. In this application of the model, the discrepancy between the son's view of his ideal and real mother produces a painful emotional state that elicits a defensive distortion. The result is that his real view of his mother, which is now unconscious (mother as often drunk), is cut off from his conscious view of his mother (mother as "almost ideal"), as shown by the break in the line. SOURCE: *Adapted from Westen, 1991.*

domain (see Higgins, 1990; Rogers, 1959), or hoping for snow during an upcoming ski trip. Over the long run, the goal-states people pursue tend to promote survival and reproduction, and they are influenced by innate preferences (such as worries about infidelity). Violation of goal-states produces unpleasant emotions and can initiate either mental or behavioral responses. A student who arrives at college and feels lonely (violation of goal-states regarding affiliation or intimacy) may respond behaviorally (joining organizations) or mentally (telling herself that things will get better). If these responses reduce the loneliness, they will be reinforced; that is, they will be maintained and more likely used in similar situations in the future.

Figure 11.14 illustrates how this integrated model might account for the behavior of a teenage boy with an alcoholic mother. The mother had often been grossly negligent in her caretaking, yet the son claimed he did not resent her "little drinking problem" and described her as "almost an ideal mother." According to the model, confronted with the painful discrepancy between his wished-for or ideal mother and the mother he really had, the boy distorted his view of his mother in a positive direction. His conscious view (mother as "almost ideal") then became cognitively cut off from more realistic memories of her.

STRESS

The conflict faced by an adolescent trying to respect his alcoholic mother—like the situation confronting a person worried about a relationship potentially ending, or Tonya Harding's press conference—is an example of stress. **Stress** refers to a challenge to a person's capacity to adapt to inner and outer demands, which may be physiologically arousing and emotionally taxing and call for cognitive or behavioral responses. This definition points to two important aspects of stress: that stress is a psychobiological process and that stress entails a transaction between people and their environments. We begin by discussing these two aspects of stress and then consider the major sources of stress and the impact of stress on health. Afterwards, we explore the cognitive and behavioral strategies people use to cope with stress.

Stress as a Psychobiological Process

Stress is a psychobiological process, with both physiological and psychological components and consequences. An early contribution to the understanding of stress was the physiologist Walter Cannon's (1932) description of the fight-or-flight response (Chapter 3), in which the organism prepares for danger with sympathetic and endocrine activation. If the danger does not abate, however, the organism remains perpetually aroused, which leads to deteriorating health as the body continues to divert its resources away from everyday maintenance and toward emergency readiness.

Another major contribution to the study of stress occurred several decades ago when a young Canadian scientist made an accidental discovery (Selye, 1936, 1976). Hoping to discover a new sex hormone, Hans Selye injected rats with extracts of ovarian tissue. At first he thought he had discovered a new substance because the injections consistently produced specific effects: bleeding ulcers, an enlarged adrenal cortex, and a shrinking thymus gland (which contains white blood cells responsible for fighting disease). However, when he injected tissue from other parts of the body, it produced exactly the same syndrome, suggesting that the effects were not caused by a sex hormone.

At first, the reaction baffled Selye, but eventually he realized he had uncovered something very important about the physiology of stress. Experiments with a wide range of stressful events, from injections to fatigue to extreme cold, revealed that the body responds to stressful conditions with a **general adaptation syndrome** consisting of three stages: alarm, resistance, and exhaustion. The first stage, alarm, involves the release of adrenalin and other hormones such as cortisol, and activation of the sympathetic nervous system. This is what occurs biologically in fight-or-flight responses. Blood pressure, heart rate, respiration, and blood sugar rise as blood is diverted from the gastrointestinal tract to muscles and other parts of the body that may be called upon for an emergency response.

The alarm stage cannot last indefinitely, however, and the parasympathetic nervous system soon comes into play, returning levels of respiration and heart rate to normal. This second stage is what Selye calls the resistance stage. At this stage, all systems may appear to have returned to normal. However, the blood still has elevated levels of glucose (for energy) and some hormones (including adrenalin and the pituitary hormone ACTH), and the body continues to use its resources at an accelerated rate. Essentially, the organism remains on red alert, with heightened energy and arousal, but it has begun to adapt to a higher level of stress. Remaining on red alert, however, is not without its costs. During this stage the organism is especially vulnerable to illness, which is why Selye's rats developed many of their symptoms. It is also why overworked college students become susceptible to influenza, mononucleosis, and whatever garden-variety colds happen to be making the rounds. The situation is analogous to a country that deploys all its military troops to one border to protect against an invasion, leaving its other borders unprotected.

If the resistance phase lasts long enough, the body eventually wears down, and the organism enters a third stage, exhaustion. In this stage, physiological defenses break down, resulting in greatly increased vulnerability to serious or even life-threatening disease. Organs such as the heart that are vulnerable genetically or environmentally (from smoking, too much lifelong cholesterol intake, etc.) are the first to go during the exhaustion stage.

Stress as a Transactional Process

In daily life, injection of ovarian tissue is not a major source of stress, and people do not respond to the same events with uniform stress responses. Richard Lazarus, who developed the most widely used model of stress, views normally occurring stress as a transaction between the individual and the environment rather than a property of either the person or the environment alone (Lazarus, 1981, 1991, 1993). Just as the amount of stress on a rope is jointly determined by the quality of the rope and the amount of weight pulling on it, so, too, is the amount of stress a person experiences a joint function of the individual's internal resources and the external situations "tugging" at the person.

Stress entails an individual's perception that demands of the environment tax or exceed her available psychosocial resources. Thus, in this view, stress depends on the meaning of an event to the individual: An event that fills one person with excitement, such as a new business opportunity, can make another feel overwhelmed and anxious. The extent to which an event is experienced as stressful therefore depends on the person's appraisal of both the situation and her ability to cope with it.

Lazarus's model identifies two stages in the process of stress and coping, neither of which is entirely conscious. In a **primary appraisal** of the situation, the person decides whether the situation is benign, stressful, or irrelevant. If the situation is appraised as stressful, she must determine what to do about it. This second stage, during which the person evaluates the options and decides how to respond, is called **secondary appraisal**. For instance, when Tonya Harding learned that she might be implicated in the assault on Nancy Kerrigan, her primary appraisal was probably that this could destroy her career and even send her to jail, likely leading to extreme anxiety. She then presumably reappraised the situation in light of possible coping strategies, such as getting support from friends, hiring a lawyer, and calling a press conference.

Lazarus distinguishes three types of stress: harm or loss, as when a person loses a loved one or something greatly valued, such as a job; threat, which refers to perceived anticipated harm; and challenge, which refers to opportunities for growth that may nonetheless be fraught with disruption and uncertainty. Stress, then, is not always negative. Positive forms of stress, or challenges, include events such as getting married or entering college. These events can be exceedingly stressful—that is, psychologically and physiologically taxing—because of all the changes and adjustments they entail. Thus, while stress is often associated with anxiety, sadness, and anger, it can also entail pleasure, excitement, and interest.

Researchers study stress in individuals, but stress is often related to broader social and economic forces. Stress levels rise as unemployment levels rise; so, too, do rates of child abuse, violence against spouses, alcoholism, and disease (Hoffman et al., 1991; Jones, 1990). With every 1 percent increase in the unemployment rate, deaths from heart disease and cirrhosis of the liver (associated with drinking) increase approximately 2 percent, suicides increase 4 percent, and first-time mental hospital admissions increase 2 to 4 percent (see Taylor, 1991). Lower social status is also associated with stress and illness. One study found higher rates of cardiovascular disease in low-ranking civil servants, as compared with their higher status co-workers (Kessler, 1979, cited in Taylor, 1991). Other sources of chronic severe stress are institutionalized, such as homelessness in the United States (Goodman et al., 1991).

Sources of Stress

Stress is an unavoidable part of life. Events that often lead to stress are called **stressors**, and they range from the infrequent, such as the death of a parent, to the commonplace, such as a demanding job or a noisy neighbor. Research on stressors has focused on life events, catastrophes, and daily hassles.

Life Events

One of the most significant sources of stress is *change*. Virtually any event that requires someone to make a readjustment can be a stressor. Over 25 years ago, researchers devised a scale to measure the stress of various **life events** that require change and adaptation (Holmes & Rahe, 1967). To create the scale, they asked 394 subjects to complete a questionnaire that listed 43 life events drawn from earlier clinical work. Subjects rated the extent to which each event would require readjustment in their lives. By taking the mean score for each item, the investigators produced a life events rating scale that has been used in thousands of studies (Table 11.2). An individual's total stress score is the sum of all the life change units experienced within a period of 12 months. Although this scale offers a good rough estimate of the amount of stress a person is encountering, it does not take into

TABLE 11.2 THE HOLMES-RAHE LIFE EVENTS RATING SCALE

RANK	LIFE EVENT	MEAN VALUE
1	Death of spouse	100
2	Divorce	73
3	Marital separation	65
4	Jail term	63
5	Death of a close family member	63
6	Personal injury or illness	53
7	Marriage	50
8	Fired at work	47
9	Marital reconciliation	45
10	Retirement	45
11	Change in health in family member	44
12	Pregnancy	40
13	Sex difficulties	39
14	Gain of new family member	39
15	Business readjustment	39
16	Change in financial state	38
17	Death of close friend	37
18	Change to different line of work	36
19	Change in number of arguments with spouse	35
20	Mortgage over $10,000 (1964 dollars)	31
21	Foreclosure of mortgage or loan	30
22	Change in responsibilities at work	29
23	Son or daughter leaving home	29
24	Trouble with in-laws	29
25	Outstanding personal achievement	28
26	Wife begin or stop work	26
27	Begin or end school	26
28	Change in living conditions	25
29	Revision of personal habits	24
30	Trouble with boss	23
31	Change in work hours or conditions	20
32	Change in residence	20
33	Change in schools	20
34	Change in recreation	19
35	Change in church activities	18
36	Change in social activities	18
37	Mortgage or loan less than $10,000	17
38	Change in sleeping habits	16
39	Change in number of family get-togethers	15
40	Change in eating habits	15
41	Vacation	13
42	Christmas	12
43	Minor violations of the law	11

Source: Holmes & Rahe, 1967.

account the different meanings of various experiences for different individuals. Consequently, some researchers have turned, instead, to measures of **perceived stress**—that is, the extent to which subjects consider the experiences they have undergone stressful.

One of the most stressful events any individual can experience is the death of a spouse or child. Some early studies suggested that the effects of such a loss were relatively transitory and that the grieving process could take as little as four to six months (Clayton et al., 1968, 1972). However, the weight of research now points toward longer-lasting effects. One study examined adults 45 years old and younger who had been widowed an average of 14 months. Subjects showed increased illness, appetite disturbance, emotional problems such as depression, difficulty making decisions, and a general sense of strain (Parkes & Brown, 1972). Another study of people who had lost a spouse or child in a car accident indicated that, for many bereaved persons, distress lasts as long as four to seven years after a sudden loss. Symptoms of prolonged distress included depression, sleep disturbances, fatigue, panic attacks, loneliness, and higher mortality rate. Among parents who had unexpectedly lost a child, divorce rates were also higher than among a comparison group (Lehman et al., 1987). Recent research confirms that parents who lose a child suddenly (giving them no time to prepare for the loss) grieve intensely for several years (Hazzard et al., 1992).

Major stressors, such as loss or unemployment, actually include many specific sources of stress, and the effect of major life events on a given person depends on the individual's vulnerabilities to these specific stressors (Monroe & Simons, 1991). A case in point is unemployment, which has been linked to anxiety, depression, and illness (Jahoda, 1988; Kessler et al., 1987). Unemployment can be devastating because of the financial strain on an individual or family. It can also produce other forms of stress, including marital strain, forced relocation, and loss of social contact with friends from work (Atkinson et al., 1983; Bolton & Oakley, 1986; Kessler et al., 1989). Even a person who has other sources of income, such as unemployment compensation or savings, may nevertheless experience lowered self-esteem, loneliness, or anxiety.

A severe form of life stress that is increasingly confronting people throughout the world is acculturative stress (Berry, 1989; Rogler et al., 1991; Williams & Berry, 1991). Acculturation means coming into contact with a new, typically dominant culture. Thus, **acculturative stress** refers to the stress people experience in trying to adapt to a new culture, whether they willingly emigrate for better opportunities or flee as refugees from persecution. Acculturative stress is associated with anxiety, depression, uncertainty and conflict about ethnic identity, and alcohol abuse, although individual responses vary widely.

The stressful effects of loss are initially intense, but less obvious effects may actually last several years, especially if the loss was sudden and unexpected.

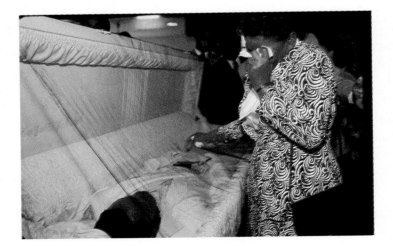

A refugee camp in Mogadishu, during the Somali civil war.

Like other major life stresses, acculturative stress includes many specific stresses. People entering new cultures frequently encounter difficulty communicating (because of language differences), racial or ethnic prejudice, lower socioeconomic status than they enjoyed at home (such as Russian doctors working in North America as paramedics because of licensing requirements), separation from loved ones, total disruption of familiar routines, loss of familiar surroundings, and new values and beliefs. Many refugees must also come to terms with the torture or murder of loved ones back home and may themselves have encountered political repression or inhuman experiences en route to their new lands. The "boat people" who fled Vietnam, for example, not only suffered from lack of food and water, but they also faced robbery, kidnapping, rape, and murder at the hands of pirates (Gong-Guy et al., 1991). Immigrants also typically face tremendous conflicts over the extent to which they preserve their old values or adopt the values of their new culture. Such conflicts are often played out across the generations, as children of immigrants shun their parents' Old World attitudes.

Catastrophes

Catastrophes are stressors of massive proportions—rare, unexpected disasters such as earthquakes, floods, or other traumatic events that affect many people. Catastrophes may be caused by nature, but they may also be caused by humans, as were the Holocaust, the bombing of London during World War II, the exodus of the Vietnamese boat people, the civil wars in Rwanda and Somalia, and the terrorist bombing attack that left nearly two hundred dead in an Oklahoma City building in 1995.

Catastrophes sometimes lead to post-traumatic stress disorder (PTSD), which includes symptoms such as nightmares, flashbacks to the traumatic event, depression, anxiety, and intrusive thoughts about the experience (Chapter 15). Most severe life events, including losses, do not elicit PTSD. The major exception is rape, which leads to PTSD 80 percent of the time (Breslau et al., 1991).

One natural catastrophe studied by psychologists was the 1980 eruption of the Mount St. Helens volcano, which spewed a heavy covering of ash over a large area of Washington State (Adams & Adams, 1984). Unlike most natural disasters, the Mount St. Helens ash fall was predictable, which enabled researchers to compare people's predisaster and postdisaster functioning. Among residents of the small agricultural town of Othello, for example, reactions included significant increases in emergency room visits, court cases, crisis hotline calls, and mental health appoint-

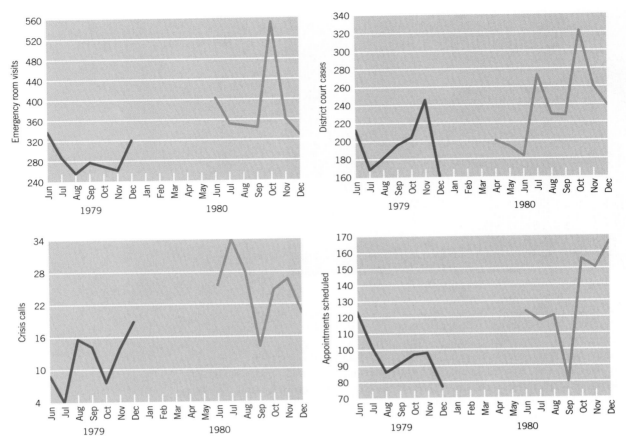

FIGURE 11.15
Impact of catastrophic stress. The number of emergency room visits, court cases, crisis calls, and mental health appointments jumped dramatically after the Mount St. Helens eruption, demonstrating the powerful effects of catastrophic stress. SOURCE: *Adams & Adams, 1984, p. 257.*

ments for months after the eruption (Figure 11.15). The research also documented an 18.6 percent increase in the death rate, a 198 percent increase in stress-aggravated illness, and a 235 percent increase in diagnoses of mental illness in the local mental health clinic.

A catastrophe of particularly horrifying proportions was the Holocaust. Victims in the concentration camps suffered such physical stresses as malnutrition, crowding, sleeplessness, exposure, inadequate clothing, forced labor, beatings, rape, injury, torture, exhaustion, disease, and medical experimentation. Psychological stresses included the ever-present danger to life, separation from family members, and humiliation. Even after the camps were liberated, survivors had to cope with a host of new stresses, such as discovering that many loved ones were dead, not knowing the whereabouts or fate of spouses or family members, and relocating to a foreign country. Another common experience was **survivors' guilt**, a feeling of intense anguish at the seeming unfairness of having survived when others had perished. Many Holocaust survivors today continue to suffer recurrent nightmares, difficulties in close relationships, and proneness to anxiety and depression (Chodoff, 1986; Nadler & Ben-Shushan, 1989).

A man-made (and seldom woman-made) stress of catastrophic proportions, practiced by dozens of countries, is torture (Allodi, 1991; Herman, 1992). A study of torture victims in Turkey found that years later nearly half the survivors continued to suffer from nightmares and other symptoms of post-traumatic stress (Basoglu et al., 1994). The average subject was tortured 291 times over four years in cap-

An Iranian torture victim.

tivity, with forms of torture including beating, electric shock, being stripped naked, prevention of urination or defecation, hanging by the wrists, rape, and twisting of the testicles. Perhaps the most remarkable finding, however, was how many victims did *not* suffer emotional distress years later. Less than 20 percent actually met the criteria for post-traumatic stress disorder, and the mean ratings of anxiety and depression were only slightly higher than for a matched group of people with similar backgrounds who had not been subjected to torture. The low rate of PTSD in this group may perhaps be explained by the fact that the torture victims were political activists, many of whom knew their actions could lead to imprisonment and torture. The researchers speculated, as others have, about survivors of the Holocaust, that people with particularly strong political or religious convictions show the most resilience to torture.

Daily Hassles

Although the concept of stressors tends to bring to mind major events such as death, unemployment, and catastrophes, more mundane but nonetheless potent sources of stress are **daily hassles**, "the irritating, frustrating, distressing demands that to some degree characterize everyday transactions with the environment" (Kanner et al., 1981, p. 3). Daily hassles range from interpersonal conflicts to commuting during rush hour; the most common daily hassles are listed in Table 11.3. Daily hassles can have a substantial impact on health and well-being (Affleck et al., 1994; deBenedittis & Lorenzetti, 1992). In fact, a study of middle-aged adults found hassles to be a considerably better predictor of psychological stress symptoms than life events (Kanner et al., 1981). More recent research finds that hassles do influence distress as well as health, but the findings are not as dramatic (Kohn et al., 1991).

Stress and Health

Stress has a considerable impact not only on psychological well-being but also on health and mortality (Adler & Matthews, 1994). People under stress often suffer from headaches, depression, and other health problems such as influenza, sore throat, and backache (Clover et al., 1989; Cohen et al., 1991; DeLongis et al., 1988; Kessler et al., 1985). Research linking stress to cancer has produced mixed results, although studies show that psychotherapy can substantially increase life expectancies in some cancer patients (Forsen, 1991; Jacobs & Charles, 1980; Levenson & Bemis, 1991).

Stress can have a direct effect on health by decreasing the body's capacity to fight illness. It can also affect health indirectly by instigating behaviors and coping

It's not the large things that send a man to the madhouse....
no, it's the continuing series of small tragedies that send a man to the madhouse...
not the death of his love but a shoelace that snaps with no time left...

C. Bukowski, "The Shoelace," 1980

TABLE 11.3 TEN MOST COMMON DAILY HASSLES

ITEM	PERCENTAGE OF TIMES CHECKED
1. Concerns about weight	52.4
2. Health of a family member	48.1
3. Rising prices of common goods	43.7
4. Home maintenance	42.8
5. Too many things to do	38.6
6. Misplacing or losing things	38.1
7. Yard work or outside home maintenance	38.1
8. Property, investment, or taxes	37.6
9. Crime	37.1
10. Physical appearance	35.9

Source: Kanner et al., 1981, p. 14.

Note. The numbers represent the mean percentage of people checking the item each month averaged over nine monthly administrations.

responses that weaken the body's defenses or lead to exposure to **pathogens**, toxic agents that can produce physical illness (Figure 11.16). People under stress tend to drink more alcohol, smoke more, sleep less, and exercise less than their peers (Cohen & Williamson, 1991; O'Leary, 1992).

Other variables can exacerbate or minimize the impact of stress on health. Stress is more likely to affect people's health, for example, if they do not have adequate social support (Baron et al., 1990; Cohen & Williamson, 1991). Similarly, exercise can moderate the impact of stress on health. One study compared the number of visits to the health clinic of college students who were either high or low in physical fitness (Brown, 1991). Physically fit subjects made fewer visits to the health clinic even when reporting many negative life events, whereas subjects who were less physically fit became ill when stressed (Figure 11.17).

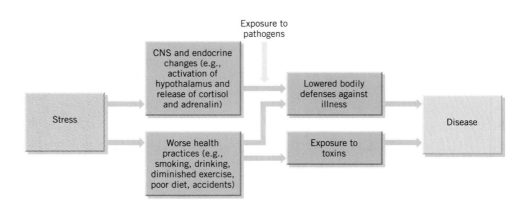

FIGURE 11.16
Pathways linking stress to infectious diseases. Stress can influence the onset of infectious disease in a number of ways. It can lead to CNS (central nervous system) and endocrine responses that diminish immune system functioning, leaving the person vulnerable to infection and illness from random exposure to pathogens such as airborne viruses. Alternatively, stress can lead to nonrandom exposure to toxins through poor health practices such as smoking. SOURCE: Adapted from Cohen & Williamson, 1991, p. 8.

Exercise is an example of a preventive measure that can directly reduce both stress and illness. Unfortunately, people frequently fail to carry out health-promoting behaviors for a variety of reasons (Taylor, 1991). They may, for example, lack the knowledge or resources, or be unrealistically optimistic about their chances for avoiding major health problems (such as believing that others, not themselves, will develop heart disease from smoking). They may also face institutional incentives for waiting until the machinery is broken before fixing anything, such as health plans that cover visits to the doctor but not to the nutritionist, the gym, or the smoking clinic.

Stress and the Immune System

The **immune system** is the body's surveillance and security system, responsible for detecting and eliminating disease-causing agents in the body such as bacteria and viruses (Jemmott & Locke, 1984). Three important types of cells in the immune system are **B cells**, **T cells**, and **natural killer cells**. B cells produce **antibodies**, protein molecules that attach themselves to foreign invaders and mark them for destruction. Some T cells search out and directly destroy invaders, while others (T-helper cells) stimulate immunological activity. T-helper cells are the primary target of HIV, the virus that causes AIDS. Natural killer cells fight viruses and tumors (Weisse, 1992). Both acute and chronic stress can affect the efficiency and availability of cells in the immune system and hence the body's capacity to fight off disease (O'Leary, 1990).

When a group of people are exposed to an infectious disease, such as respiratory illness, only some of them actually become sick. Consequently, one way to explore the effects of stress on the immune system is to see whether people under stress are more likely to suffer from infectious diseases. The evidence suggests that they are (Dorian & Garfunkel, 1987; Jemmott & Locke, 1984; Kiecolt-Glaser et al., 1987; Miller, 1983). An early study of telephone company employees found that subjects who reported greater dissatisfaction with life tended to have more acute respiratory illnesses (Hinkle & Plummer, 1952). A later study of 1400 West Point cadets similarly implicated stress in the susceptibility to mononucleosis (Kasl et al., 1979).

Another study (Jemmott et al., 1983) investigated the relationship between academic pressure and immunologic functioning (specifically, the secretion of an antibody called Immunoglobin A, or IgA). During periods of the academic calendar rated by both the researchers and subjects as most stressful, the secretion rate of IgA was lower—that is, the immune response was reduced. Other research with medical student subjects found that antibody levels produced in response to a vaccine were lower for subjects who were stressed (Benschop et al., 1993). Chronic stress can also lower immune functioning (McKinnon et al., 1989; O'Leary, 1990), as can depression (Evans et al., 1992; Herbert & Cohen, 1993). Perhaps the most conclusive study yet of the influence of stress on both immune functioning and illness assessed 394 healthy subjects for degree of life stress and then administered nasal drops containing one of five different viruses (Cohen et al., 1991). Subjects reporting higher stress showed greater rates of infection for all five viruses (Figure 11.18).

Stress, Health, and Personality

Whether a person under stress remains healthy or becomes ill also depends on the person's enduring personality dispositions (DeLongis et al., 1988; Rodin & Salovey, 1989). Personality can influence stress and health through the motives the person pursues, the way the individual chronically appraises circumstances (for example, easily becoming angry or sad), or the way the person characteristically copes with stress (such as through drinking, cigarette smoking, avoiding doctors, suppressing emotions, and so forth).

One of the most thoroughly researched links between personality and health is between heart disease and the **Type A behavior pattern**. Type A individuals, first identified by two cardiologists (Friedman & Rosenman, 1959), are impatient, hard-driving, ambitious, competitive, and hostile. Type B individuals are more relaxed, easy-

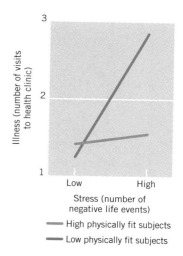

FIGURE 11.17
Interaction between stress and physical fitness. Students who were physically fit did not become sick when confronted with stress. Less fit subjects, however, became ill when confronted with negative life events. SOURCE: *Brown, 1991, p. 559.*

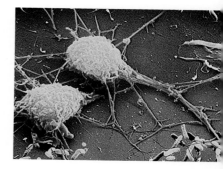

Cells in the immune system attacking E. coli bacteria.

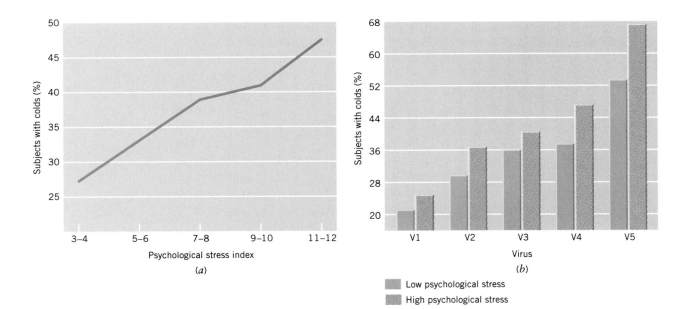

FIGURE 11.18
The relation between stress and illness following viral exposure. Part (a) shows the relation between amount of self-reported psychological stress and the percentage of subjects judged by a physician to have a clinical cold after exposure to a virus. The association was linear: The more stress, the more colds. Part (b) presents data from a biological test of subjects' blood for presence of infection. For each of five viruses, subjects reporting higher stress showed higher rates of infection. SOURCE: *Cohen et al., 1991, pp. 609–610.*

going, and less easily angered. One psychologist illustrated the differences between Type A and Type B behavior in describing a fishing trip he took with a colleague:

> I baited the hook and dropped the line over in a relaxed fashion, watched the gulls, and swayed with the swells. But what really struck [my colleague] was my talking to the fish when they bit the hook: "That's nice" or "Take your time, I'm in no rush." (Schwartz, 1987, p. 136)

In contrast to his own Type B pattern, a man fishing in a boat nearby exhibited Type A behavior:

> He was fishing with two poles, racing back and forth between them, and tangling his lines while cursing the fish that happened to be on the line beyond his reach. If the fish eluded him while others caught them, he would pull up the anchor in frustration, start the engine with a roar, and race to another part of the bay. (p. 136)

A comparison of bus drivers in North America and India suggests that these behavioral patterns occur cross-culturally, at least in some form (Evans et al., 1987). In both samples, Type A bus drivers reported greater job stress, had more accidents, and had more absences per month than Type B drivers. In addition, in India, Type A bus drivers braked, blew their horns, and passed more frequently than Type B drivers.

More recent research suggests that the Type A pattern has subcomponents that may be differentially related to heart disease (Dembroski & Costa, 1987; Rodin & Salovey, 1989; Rosenman, 1990). In particular, hostility, or the combination of defensiveness, negative affect, and disavowed hostility, has been implicated in coronary atherosclerosis, or narrowing of the arteries leading to the heart (Contrada et al., 1990; Dembroski & Costa, 1987). Family experiences in childhood apparently predispose some people to this personality style (Woodall & Matthews, 1993).

Psychologists have linked other personality traits to immune functioning and health outcomes as well. One of these is power motivation (McClelland, 1993).

Subjects high in power motivation, and particularly those who tend to inhibit its expression, are more likely than other subjects to suffer from hypertension (high blood pressure). Another personality dimension that may be related to both stress and health is **hardiness**, which includes three components: commitment (a tendency to involve oneself heavily in one's undertakings), a belief in one's own control (as opposed to powerlessness), and a tendency to treat difficult tasks as a challenge (rather than a threat) (Kobasa, 1979; Kobasa et al., 1985). Studies of managers and executives have found hardy subjects to be less physiologically reactive in the face of high levels of stress and less likely to become ill (Kobasa et al., 1981, 1985; Maddi & Kobasa, 1984), although more recent studies have produced equivocal findings (Alfred & Smith, 1989; Lee, 1991; Wiebe, 1991), probably because some seemingly hardy individuals are actually out of touch with their emotions.

Another personality dimension related to immune functioning and health is optimism/pessimism. One study found that coronary artery bypass patients who reported higher levels of optimism on a questionnaire recovered more quickly and returned to normal life more easily than pessimistic subjects (Scheier et al., 1989). Another study found that college students with a pessimistic explanatory style (a tendency to explain bad events in negative, self-blaming ways; see Chapter 5) experienced more days of illness and visited physicians more frequently than other students (Peterson, 1988). Even more striking results emerged in a 35-year longitudinal study of 99 graduates of Harvard University. Subjects with a pessimistic explanatory style at age 25 were more likely to be in poor health or dead at ages 45–50, even when controlling statistically for physical and mental health at age 25 (Peterson et al., 1988). People who are pessimistic do not take as good care of themselves, do not cope as well, and appear to have depressed immune functioning, all of which lead to greater illness (Kamen & Seligman, 1987; Peterson, 1988; Lin & Peterson, 1990).

COPING

That people get sick or experience unpleasant emotions in response to stress should come as no surprise. What may seem more surprising is that most people who experience life crises remain healthy (Moos & Schaefer, 1986). This resiliency in the face of stress reflects the ways people deal with stressful situations, or ways of **coping**. Many coping strategies are consciously selected, whereas others, known as defense mechanisms, are largely unconscious. A study of women hospitalized while awaiting biopsies to determine whether they had breast cancer shows how variable coping responses can be (Katz et al., 1977). All 30 women were in the same potentially life-threatening situation, but their emotional responses and ability to function despite their anxiety varied considerably. One woman denied she had a problem, blaming the lump on a fall in the bathtub. Another complained that her husband, not she, was the one who required medical attention. Still others drew on their religious faith to cope with their illness.

Coping Mechanisms

Researchers often distinguish three types of coping strategies: efforts to change the situation, efforts to alter one's cognition about the situation, and efforts to alter the unpleasant emotional consequences of stress (Moos & Billings, 1982). In other words, if a person cannot change a stressful situation directly, he can try to change his perception of it or the emotions it engenders.

Efforts to cope by changing the situation typically involve problem solving (Chapter 7). The individual may try to remove the stressor, plan ways of resolving the situation, or seek advice or assistance from others in changing the situation

Type A behavior appears to contribute to the blocking of arteries. The top photo shows a normal artery. The remaining photos show arteries blocked partially (middle) and completely (bottom) by fatty deposits.

(Carver et al., 1989). People high in problem-solving ability and who have a problem-solving orientation (a tendency to define potential problems as challenging and to confront them directly) tend to report less stress and fewer psychological symptoms than other subjects (D'Zurilla & Sheedy, 1991; Epstein & Katz, 1992). Individuals with a problem-focused orientation tend to endorse questionnaire statements such as, "I am the kind of person who takes action rather than just thinks or complains about a situation" (Epstein, 1992, p. 828).

Coping by changing one's cognition or appraisal of the situation often involves reframing an event mentally to make it seem less threatening. For example, a person who is anxious about giving a speech may say to himself, "Come on now, this is ridiculous. You are just talking to a bunch of people who are interested in what you have to say." An example of reframing a more tragic situation is the way a man dying of AIDS combined cognitive restructuring with a sense of humor: "I made a list of all the other diseases I would rather not have than AIDS. Lou Gehrig's disease, being in a wheelchair; rheumatoid arthritis, when you are in knots and in terrible pain. So I said, you've got to get some perspective on this, and where you are on the Great Nasty Disease List" (Reed, 1989, in Taylor, 1991, p. 243).

A third way people cope with stressful situations is by trying to relieve the associated emotional state, as when a person smiles nervously to try to regulate anxiety. Alcohol and drug use are common mechanisms for escaping emotional distress, as is distraction. Another AIDS patient, in describing his efforts to cope with distressing emotions, confided, "I used to depend on drugs a lot to change my mood. Once in a while, I still find that if I can't feel better any other way, I will take a puff of grass or have a glass of wine, or I use music. There are certain recordings that can really change my mood drastically. I play it [music] loud and I dance around and try to clear my head" (Reed in Taylor, p. 242).

Defense Mechanisms

Although many of the coping strategies described thus far are conscious or could readily be made conscious if attention were called to them, other coping strategies, known as defense mechanisms, are unconscious and involve greater self-deception. **Defense mechanisms**, first described by psychodynamic psychologists, are unconscious mental processes aimed at protecting the person from experiencing unpleasant emotions (particularly anxiety) or bolstering positive affect (see Cramer, 1991, 1995; A. Freud, 1936; Perry & Cooper, 1987; Vaillant, 1977, 1990). The most widely used defense is **repression**, an unconscious mechanism that keeps thoughts or memories that would be too threatening to acknowledge from awareness. A similar mechanism is **denial**, in which the person refuses to acknowledge external realities (such as having cancer) or emotions (such as anxiety), rather than thoughts. Denial is at work when an individual notices a peculiar skin growth but concludes that "it's nothing." Much of the time it *is* nothing, but this defense can lead to lack of treatment or death (see Strauss et al., 1990; Zervas et al., 1993).

In **projection**, a person attributes his own unacknowledged feelings or impulses to others. The hard-driving businessman who thinks his competitors, suppliers, and customers are always trying to cheat him may in fact be the one with questionable ethics. To recognize his own greed and lack of concern for others would conflict with his conscience, so he sees these traits instead in others. In **reaction formation**, the person turns unacceptable feelings or impulses into their opposites. For example, at the same time that televangelist Jimmy Swaggart was preaching the evils of sex to millions, he was regularly seeing a prostitute. His conscious repulsion toward sexuality, and particularly illicit sexuality, apparently masked a tremendous need for it.

Sublimation involves converting sexual or aggressive impulses into socially acceptable activities. A young boy may turn his feelings of competition with his father or brother into a desire to excel in competitive sports or to achieve success in business when he is older. **Rationalization** means explaining away actions in a seemingly logical way to avoid uncomfortable feelings, especially guilt or shame. A student who plagiarizes her term paper and justifies her actions by saying that passing the course will help her earn her public policy degree and serve the community is using rationalization to justify her dishonesty. **Passive aggression** is the indirect expression of anger toward others. One administrator frustrated everyone around her by "sitting on" important documents that required a fast turnaround. To be actively aggressive would run afoul of her moral standards and potentially lead to reprimand from her boss, so she accomplished the same goal—frustrating co-workers and thus satisfying her aggressive impulses—in a way that allowed her to disavow any intention or responsibility.

Just as people tailor their problem-solving efforts to specific situations, so too do people typically use defense mechanisms flexibly and creatively. Thus, any taxonomy of defenses is by definition incomplete and overly schematic. Using defenses is neither abnormal nor unhealthy. In fact, some degree of defensive distortion may be useful, such as the tendency for people to see themselves more positively than is warranted by reality (Taylor & Brown, 1988). A bit of denial can also be essential to surmounting seemingly insurmountable odds, as when an aspiring novelist persists despite repeated rejection and suddenly gets a break. Defenses become dysfunctional when they inhibit adaptive functioning rather than foster it.

Defense mechanisms are generally considered properties of individuals, but they often require collusion from other people. An alcoholic who denies his alcoholism will have a much easier time maintaining his defense if his wife and children follow a code of silence. Some defenses are even patterned at a cultural level (Spiro, 1965). In the Kerala province of India, where cows are considered sacred and cannot be killed, an anthropologist observed that the mortality rate for male cows was twice as high as for females (Harris, 1979). Although all the farmers espoused the Hindu prohibition against slaughtering cattle, they were essentially starving the males to death because males cannot give milk and were a drain on scarce economic resources. A single whistle-blower would have challenged this collective denial.

Reaction formation was apparently a primary defense mechanism used by televangelist Jimmy Swaggart, here shown confessing his sins to his faithful after his misdeeds were exposed.

As the example of collective denial suggests, the way people respond to stress, as well as the situations they consider stressful, are in part culturally patterned. One study found significant cultural differences in the coping styles of children in the United States and Mexico, with U.S. subjects more likely to attempt to master stressful situations actively (Diaz-Guerrero, 1979). Mexican children are socialized to adopt a more passive style of coping with events, modifying themselves rather than confronting obstacles in the environment, while U.S. children are encouraged to take an active approach, modifying their physical, social, and interpersonal environments. Mexican children, for example, were more likely to be compliant and to work slowly than U.S. children when given tasks to perform.

This cultural difference is not surprising in the light of psychological and anthropological research on value orientations in different cultures (Kluckhohn & Strodtbeck, 1961). The emphasis on mastering the environment characteristic of highly technologically developed societies is an anomaly in human history. Most cultures instead believe humans should live harmoniously with nature and recognize their place in the natural order. These value differences may limit the applicability of Western theories and research which argue that a sense of personal control or efficacy is important for mental health (Bandura, 1977) and that active coping styles are preferable to passive ones. In a society based on entrepreneurship, technological development, wage labor, and individual productivity, active mastery and a strong belief in one's own ability are highly adaptive traits. In a society organized around family, community, or tribal ties, in which development of new technologies is neither expected nor particularly encouraged, such traits may be unrelated to mental and physical health. Coping is always relative to its cultural context, and coping strategies considered useful in one society (such as wailing at a funeral) may engender disapproval, and hence additional stress, in another.

Understanding patterns of culture and coping may also lead to a better understanding of the dilemmas facing African-American and other minority adolescents in North America, particularly in regard to achievement (Ogbu, 1991). For years educators, social scientists, and policymakers have wrestled with the question of why a large gap exists between the educational performance of whites and some minority groups, such as African and Mexican Americans, while no such gap exists for other immigrant groups, such as Arabs, Chinese, and West Indian blacks. John Ogbu (1991) argues that, throughout the world, minority groups who for generations experience a ceiling on their economic prospects because of job discrimination develop a **low effort syndrome** that is not present in new immigrants who voluntarily move to a culture in search of a better life. The school performance of Koreans in Japan, who have been an underclass there for many years, is very poor, whereas Korean immigrants to North America tend to excel. When social barriers make effort and achievement fruitless, low effort syndrome is an adaptive coping strategy because hard work and academic success would only increase frustration and anger.

Cultural patterns of coping that may be adaptive for one generation may not be adaptive for the next. A low-effort syndrome that helps one generation cope with frustration may create frustration in the next. Cultural coping patterns tend to change gradually as the conditions that create and maintain them change.

Low effort syndrome is an example of a coping strategy that solves one problem (minimizing frustration in the face of racism and barriers to success) but creates another, particularly if opportunities and social attitudes toward race change faster than coping styles developed over several generations. Because African Americans for years faced impassable barriers to upward mobility, scholastic achievement became defined in many black communities as white behavior. Thus, for many black adolescents today the fear of being ridiculed for "acting white," together with a subcultural ambivalence toward achievement, inhibits scholastic achievement. Even high-achieving African-American students from disadvantaged areas may respond with low effort when they enter college and their prior schooling places them at a sudden disadvantage. Although increased effort would actually be the most useful strategy at that point, effort can ironically threaten self-esteem: If increased effort does not bring immediate success, the lack of success cannot be attributed to lack of effort. African Americans also face many of the same kinds of acculturative stresses faced by other ethnic groups (Anderson, 1991), who must wrestle with the question of how much of the dominant culture to assimilate and integrate into their own attitudes, behavior, and identity.

Social Support

An important resource for coping with stress is **social support,** the presence of others in whom one can confide and from whom one can expect help and concern. Social support is as important for maintaining physical as mental health (Pilisuk et al., 1993; Schradle & Dougher, 1985). A high level of social support is associated with protection against a range of illnesses, from hypertension and heart disease to herpes (Bland et al., 1991; Markovitz & Matthews, 1991; Taylor, 1991). In rhesus monkeys, immune functioning is suppressed when adult monkeys are separated from their social group but not if they are given a companion (Gust et al., 1994). In humans, the number of social relationships a person has, and the extent to which the individual feels close to other people, is a powerful predictor of mortality (House et al., 1988). In fact, the evidence supporting the beneficial effects of social relationships on health is as strong as the evidence for the negative relationship between smoking and health in the Surgeon General's 1964 report (House et al., 1988).

Two hypotheses have been advanced to explain the beneficial effects of social support, both of which have received empirical support (Cohn & Wills, 1985; Taylor, 1991). The buffering hypothesis proposes that social support is a buffer or protective factor against the harmful effects of stress during high-stress periods. In a classic study, urban women who experienced significant life stress were much less likely to become depressed if they had an intimate, confiding relationship with a boyfriend or husband (Brown & Harris, 1978). The alternative hypothesis views social support as a continuously positive force that makes the person less susceptible to stress in the first place. In this view, people with supportive relationships are less likely to make a primary appraisal of situations as stressful, and they are more likely to perceive themselves as able to cope. Taking a new job is much more threatening to a person who has no one in whom to confide and no one to tell her, "Don't worry, you'll do well at it." Unfortunately, stress can erode social support, leading to a vicious cycle, particularly if the person under stress responds with anger or helplessness (Lane & Hobfoll, 1992).

Commentary: A Caveat about Research on Stress and Coping

Research on stress and coping has burgeoned over the past two decades, vastly increasing our understanding of the links between psychological processes and disease. Nevertheless, some caveats are in order about the gap between theory on the one hand, and measures and methods on the other. First, most studies of stress and coping have relied largely or exclusively on self-report questionnaires. The use of questionnaires, however, makes two implicit assumptions that violate most stress and coping models. The first is that everyone experiences the same events as stressful to the same degree. In other words, when researchers operationalize life events or hassles with a checklist of events or experiences, they assume that stress is located in objective events that have roughly the same ramifications for all individuals. Yet stress and coping theories emphasize that stress emerges from the meaning of a potential stressor to an individual (see Kessler et al., 1985). A second implicit assumption is that people know what is stressful to them and can report the mech-

Social support protects against stress and illness in humans and other animals.

anisms they use to cope with them. As we have seen (Chapter 9), however, people neither have access to, nor can report accurately on, many of their own cognitive processes, so one has little reason to assume they have greater access to, or accuracy with coping processes, which are a form of procedural knowledge (skills that do not involve conscious retrieval).

Another caveat is that many apparent findings in stress and coping research are really artifacts of correlating variables that are not independent of each other. That is, too frequently the same items appear in both measures being correlated, as when a measure of coping includes the item, "I often find myself venting anger," and a measure of stress includes the item, "I often feel upset or angry." Finding a correlation between two variables that overlap in content is like showing that people's age in years is an excellent predictor of their age in months.

A similar problem arises for researchers studying the influence of coping skills in moderating (increasing or reducing) the impact of stressful life events; the number of stressful events people experience is not independent of their coping skills. People who cope well confront fewer negative events because they do not get themselves in as much trouble in the first place (Epstein & Katz, 1992). Even the ability of social support to buffer stress, an intuitively appealing notion, has come under fire as a potentially spurious finding. Social support may be associated with fewer negative events, less psychological distress, and better health because the kinds of people who are able to develop good relationships are also simply healthier psychologically (Kessler et al., 1992).

SOME CONCLUDING THOUGHTS

Since our picture of psychological processes in normal adults is now almost complete, it is time to take stock of where we stand. Earlier chapters were dominated by "cold" cognitive models of thought and memory. The last three chapters, in contrast, have emphasized "hot" processes—emotions, motives, states of consciousness, and personal meaning—that direct and make use of our capacity for information processing. How, then, does one reconcile cold cognitive models, which apply equally to humans and computers, with hot affective and motivational models, which apply to sophisticated two-legged animals who are driven by a hypothalamus and a limbic system rather than by electricity and software?

Figure 11.19 presents a preliminary integrated information-processing model that incorporates emotional and motivational processes with cognitive processes. In this model, as in the standard cognitive model, the person first perceives a stimulus and then briefly holds a representation of it in sensory registers (a). Some of this information drops out of the system, some is selected for attention, and some is unconsciously processed and stored in long-term memory without ever attaining consciousness. Information selected for attention, usually because of its adaptive significance, is sent to consciousness for further processing (b). The contents of consciousness include current sensory information and information momentarily stored or retrieved into working memory, as well as goals and motives, efforts to solve problems posed by these motives, and emotions and feelings. At the same time that information is being consciously processed, considerable cognitive, affective, and motivational processing is occurring unconsciously, which can influence conscious thought, emotion, and behavior (c). Among the unconscious processes active at any moment, which constitute an "unconscious working memory," are activated schemas, networks of association, motives, components of emotion, and procedural knowledge (such as grammar, which unconsciously organizes language).

Consider how this model might apply to Tonya Harding when she first began to realize her husband was involved in the attack on Nancy Kerrigan (presuming that Harding herself was not involved). According to this model, when the news broke of the attack, Harding started to piece together the meaning of comments her hus-

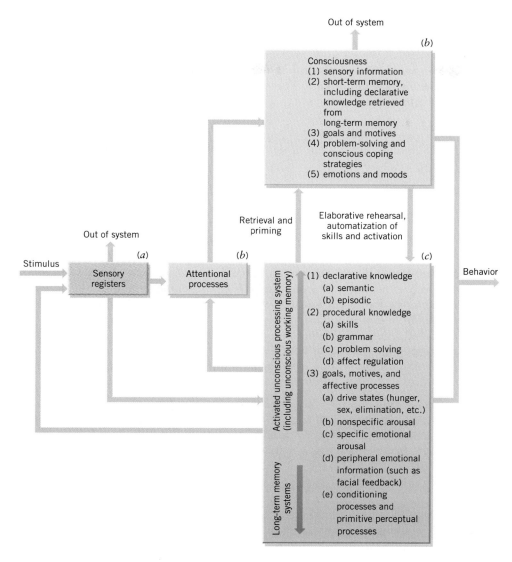

FIGURE 11.19
A modified information-processing model. This substantially modified information-processing model incorporates emotion, motivation, stress, and consciousness. Sensory information or feedback from ongoing behavior leads to subsequent information processing. Attentional processes select some information for consciousness, while other information is processed unconsciously. Conscious and unconscious mental activity involves not only cognitions but also motives, goals, emotions, problem-solving strategies, conditioning processes (which link cognitive representations, affects, and behaviors), and ways of coping with stressful situations and emotions.

band had made, which were retrieved from long-term memory. However, the idea that he might be involved was so discrepant from the way she wanted to see him— and the ramifications of the attack being tied to someone close to her were so severe—that she experienced tremendous anxiety. This anxiety, in turn, activated unconscious defensive processes that distorted her conscious judgment about the likelihood of her husband's complicity. Consciously, she denied that he could have been involved, but she began to worry about the impact of the incident on her career (a dominant conscious motive system), leading to conscious consideration of various problem-solving strategies. To cope with her distress, she consciously told herself she had done nothing wrong, so nothing could happen to her. Unconsciously, however, the situation activated a schema forged in childhood—being helpless in the face of wrongful attack—that developed in her relationship with her apparently sometimes abusive mother and now seemed to be reconfirmed by the media and the public.

This scenario is, of course, filled with conjecture and is meant only as an example of the way "hot" and "cold" processes might interact, at both conscious and unconscious levels. We are now, however, a step closer to understanding the whole person, a person who perceives, learns, thinks, pursues goals, feels, and responds to challenging environmental events. Our next task is to consider how these pieces fit together to form a personality.

Summary

Emotion

1. **Emotion**, or **affect,** is an evaluative response (a positive or negative feeling state) that typically includes subjective experience, physiological arousal, and behavioral expression.

2. The **James-Lange theory** asserts that the subjective experience of emotion results from bodily experience induced by an emotion-eliciting stimulus. According to this theory, we do not run because we are afraid; we become afraid because we run (and our hearts pound). In contrast, the **Cannon-Bard theory** proposes that emotion-inducing stimuli simultaneously elicit both emotional experience and bodily responses. Although both theories have their strengths and limitations, recent research suggests that different emotions are, as James believed, associated with distinct, innate patterns of autonomic nervous system arousal.

3. **Emotional expression** refers to facial and other outward indications of emotion, such as body language and tone of voice. Many aspects of emotional expression, particularly facial expression, are innate and cross-culturally universal. Culturally variable patterns of regulating and displaying emotion are called **display rules**.

4. Psychologists have attempted to produce a list of **basic emotions**, emotions common to the human species from which all other emotions and emotional blends can be derived. Anger, fear, happiness, sadness, and disgust are listed by all theorists as basic. An even more fundamental distinction is between **positive affect** and **negative affect**.

5. Emotions are controlled by neural pathways distributed throughout the nervous system. The hypothalamus activates sympathetic and endocrine responses related to emotion. The limbic system, and particularly the amygdala, is part of an emotional circuit that includes the hypothalamus. The amygdala is the brain's "emotional computer" for calculating the affective significance of a stimulus. The cortex plays several roles with respect to emotion, particularly in the appraisal of events.

6. The behaviorist perspective on emotion points to approach and avoidance systems associated with positive and negative affect, respectively. According to the psychodynamic perspective, people can be unconscious of their own emotional experience, which can nonetheless influence thought, behavior, and even health.

7. From a cognitive perspective, the way people respond emotionally depends on the **attributions** they make—that is, their inferences about causes of the emotion and their own bodily sensations. According to the **Schachter-Singer theory**, emotion involves two factors: physiological arousal and cognitive interpretation of the arousal. Emotion and **mood** (relatively extended emotional states which, unlike emotions, typically do not disrupt ongoing activities) have an impact on encoding, retrieval, judgment, and decision making.

8. The evolutionary perspective on emotion derives from Charles Darwin's view that emotions serve an adaptive purpose. Emotion has both communicative and motivational functions.

9. An integrated model suggests that emotions and other feelings are mechanisms for selecting behavioral and mental responses. Emotion relies on homeostatic principles similar to those that regulate drive-based behavior such as eating, with discrepancies between goal-states and cognitions about reality producing emotional feedback, which in turn instigates action.

Stress

10. **Stress** refers to a challenge to a person's capacity to adapt to inner and outer demands, which may be physiologically arousing and emotionally taxing and call for cognitive and behavioral responses. Stress is a psychobiological process that entails a transaction between a person and her environment. Selye proposed that the body responds to stressful conditions with a **general adaptation syndrome** consisting of three stages: alarm, resistance, and exhaustion.

11. From a psychological standpoint, stress entails a person's perception that demands of the environment tax or exceed his available psychosocial resources. Stress, in this view, depends on the meaning of an event to the individual. Lazarus's model identifies two stages in the process of stress and coping: **primary appraisal**, in which the person decides whether the situation is benign, stressful, or irrelevant; and **secondary appraisal**, in which the person evaluates the options and decides how to respond.

12. Events that often lead to stress are called **stressors**. Stressors include life events, catastrophes, and daily hassles.

13. Stress has a considerable impact on health and mortality, particularly through its effects on the **immune system**. Whether a person under stress remains healthy or becomes ill also depends in part on the person's enduring personality dispositions. **Type A behavior pattern**, and particularly its hostility component, has been linked to heart disease. Power motivation, hardiness, and optimism/pessimism are other personality traits linked to stress and health.

Coping

14. People cope by trying to change the situation directly, changing their perception of it, or changing the emotions it engenders. The ways people deal with stressful situations are known as strategies for **coping**; coping mechanisms are in part culturally patterned.

15. Unconscious strategies for coping aimed at minimizing unpleasant emotions or maximizing pleasant emotions are called **defense mechanisms**. Common defense mechanisms include **repression, denial, projection, reaction formation, sublimation, rationalization,** and **passive aggression**.

16. A major resource for coping with stress is **social support**, which is related to health and longevity.

Some Concluding Thoughts

17. Psychological models often deal with either "cold" cognitive processes or "hot" motivational and affective processes, but both are part of an integrated information-processing system, designed by evolution to maximize adaptation, which consciously and unconsciously processes information relevant to a person's motives, goals, and emotions.

Face Mask, "Haida," Prince of Wales Island

Chapter 12

PERSONALITY

Oskar and Jack were identical twins who shared dozens of idiosyncrasies. They dressed alike (both wore wire-rimmed glasses and two-pocket shirts with epaulets), read magazines from back to front, and wrapped rubber bands around their wrists. Their personalities were similar, from their basic "tempo" or speed of activity to the way they responded to stress, their sense of well-being, and their style of interacting socially. None of this may seem unusual; they were, after all, identical twins. What makes this remarkable, however, is that Oskar Stohr was raised as a Catholic and a Nazi by his mother in Germany, while his twin brother Jack Yufe was raised as a Jew by his father and lived part of his life on an Israeli kibbutz. Separated shortly after birth, the men did not meet again until they were adults, when they participated in a study of twins (Holden, 1980).

The term *personality* is a part of everyday speech. When people make statements such as "Jim isn't the best-looking, but he has a nice personality," they typically use the term to

denote the manner in which a person acts across a variety of situations. Psychologists use the term to describe not only an individual's *reputation*—the way the person acts and is known socially—but also the *internal processes* that create that reputation (Hogan, 1983, 1987). **Personality** refers to the enduring patterns of thought, feeling, and behavior that are expressed in different circumstances.

Personality psychologists have two aims. The first is to construct theories that describe the **structure of personality**, that is, the organization of enduring patterns of thought, feeling, and behavior in the mind. The second task is to study the way people resemble and differ from one another, that is, their **individual differences**. Ideally, these two aims should dovetail, as researchers use their theories to select the relevent personality dimensions on which people can be expected to differ.

The approach psychologists use to carry out this dual mission depends, once again, on their theoretical perspective. We begin by exploring Freud's models of the mind and the evolution of psychodynamic thinking about personality since Freud's time. We then consider cognitive-social approaches, which integrate behaviorist and cognitive principles, and portray humans as more rational in their motives than do psychodynamic theories. Next, we examine trait theories, which use everyday language to describe personality, and humanistic theories, which focus on the way people wrestle with fundamental human concerns, such as mortality and meaning in life. In the process, we examine the extent to which personality characteristics are inherited, as suggested by the case of Jack and Oskar, and conclude by considering the extent to which personality differs across cultures.

PSYCHODYNAMIC THEORIES

Sigmund Freud developed the first comprehensive theory of personality. As a neurologist practicing in the 1880s before the advent of psychology and psychiatry, Freud encountered patients with a wide range of psychological disturbances. A particularly perplexing disorder was hysteria, in which patients (mostly females) suffered from symptoms such as paralysis, numbness, and fainting spells, with no apparent biological origin. In seeking a method of treating hysteria, Freud was particularly influenced by the work of Jean Martin Charcot, a French neurologist who demonstrated that hysterical symptoms could be produced—and alleviated, at least temporarily—through hypnosis. Patients with paralyzed legs could walk again under the influence of a hypnotic suggestion, although the symptoms usually returned before long. These patients wanted to walk, but something seemed to override their conscious determination or will, much as contemporary bulimics cannot stop binging and purging. Freud deduced that if a symptom is not of physiological origin and the patient is consciously trying to stop it but cannot, then opposing the conscious will must be an unconscious counter-will of equal or greater magnitude.

This basic assumption was the centerpiece of Freud's theory of psychodynamics, analogous to dynamics among physical forces. According to Freud, psychological forces such as wishes, fears, and intentions have a direction and an intensity. When several of these motives collide and conflict, the balance of these forces determines the person's behavior, as in the case of a patient suffering from a hysterical paralysis, whose will to move her leg is unconsciously overridden (Figure 12.1).

Why would a counter-will be unconscious? And what balance of unconscious forces could lead to paralysis or to a need to starve or drink oneself to death? Freud

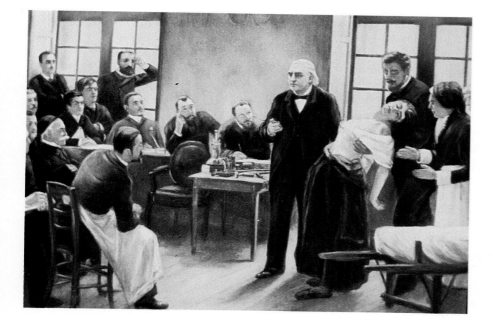

Charcot "mesmerized" his fellow physicians, among them Sigmund Freud, with his demonstrations of hypnotically induced hysterical symptoms.

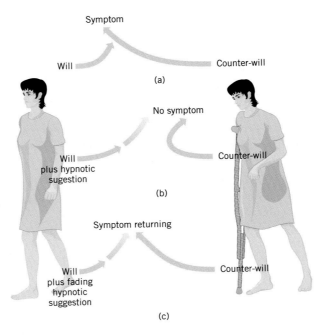

Symptom

Will

Counter-will

(a)

No symptom

Will
plus hypnotic
sugestion

Counter-will

(b)

Symptom returning

Will
plus fading
hypnotic
suggestion

Counter-will

(c)

FIGURE 12.1
Psychodynamics. This figure depicts the conflicting forces involved before, during, and after treatment of hysterical symptoms (such as paralysis) with hypnosis. Originally (a), the conscious will ("I will be able to walk") is overpowered by the stronger unconscious counter-will ("I will not be able to walk"). With hypnosis (b), the conscious desire is strengthened and "bends back" the unconscious counter-will. Note that the counter-will is not lessened; it is simply temporarily overpowered by the extra force added by hypnosis. Eventually, as the hypnotic suggestion begins to wear off (c), the counter-will, which was dormant during the period of maximal hypnotic action, once again begins to overpower the will.

tried to answer these questions throughout his career by developing a series of models, which he never entirely reconciled with each other. We first examine these models, known as the topographic, drive, developmental, and structural, and then explore subsequent developments in the psychodynamic approach to personality.

Before turning to Freud's models, a brief comment about method is in order. The data presented in the next several pages are not the same kind of laboratory data to which the reader is by now accustomed. Although we will explore some of the laboratory evidence for psychodynamic theories, the basis for these theories has largely been observations during clinical sessions with patients. Many critics have rightfully pointed to the problems with case study data of this sort: They cannot easily be observed by other scientists, they are filtered through the biases of the investigator, and they do not easily permit generalization from one subject to another. Nevertheless, clinical observation has led to the discovery of many important phenomena—such as unconscious processes and the self-concept—whose existence many researchers ignored or rejected for up to a century for want of reliable methods to study them (Chapter 2).

The Topographic Model

Freud's first model, the **topographic model** (1900), used a spatial metaphor that divided mental processes into three types: conscious, preconscious, and unconscious (Chapter 9). **Conscious mental processes** are rational, goal-directed thoughts at the center of awareness. **Preconscious mental processes** are not conscious but could become conscious at any point, such as the knowledge of color of robins. Finally, **unconscious mental processes** are irrational, organized along associative lines rather than by logic. They are inaccessible to consciousness because they have been repressed, that is, kept from consciousness to avoid emotional distress.

Unconscious processes, while barred from consciousness, are not inert. Because they are not consciously acknowledged, they may leak into consciousness and behavior in unexpected and often unwelcome ways. Consider the schoolyard bully whose father is physically or verbally abusive. Conscious rage toward his father may be frightening or intolerable to him because he fears that in his anger he might hurt his father, drive him away, or provoke further abuse. The bully thus displaces his feelings toward his father, expressing his anger instead toward schoolmates.

Freud used the topographic model to understand dreams, distinguishing between their story line—the manifest content—and their underlying message—the latent content (Chapter 9). For example, a 30-year-old male virgin considering having his first sexual encounter had a recurring dream of dipping his feet into a polluted river. From a psychodynamic perspective, the dream appeared to express conflicting feelings and wishes about sexuality—will and counter-will. He wanted to get his feet wet, so to speak, but he was reluctant because he considered sex to be unclean. The connection of sexuality, wetness, and pollution, in this view, is not accidental and was supported by many statements the patient made in this and other sessions. Freud postulated that such **ambivalence**—conflicting feelings or intentions—is the rule, rather than the exception in human experience. The reason is simple: From childhood on, we constantly interact with people who are important to us, but those interactions contain both pleasant and unpleasant experiences. We learn to love where we learn to hate.

For example, a patient named Bill was terrified that he would someday marry a woman who would treat him in the same harsh and belittling way that he felt his mother had treated his father. Unfortunately, Bill's most ingrained (and unconscious) models of femininity and of marital interaction were profoundly shaped by observing his parents as a child. Years later, Bill and his friend Pete were in a bar, where they noticed two attractively dressed women. Pete thought they looked somewhat severe, that their gestures and facial expressions seemed harsh or angry, and that they were sending clear signals that they had no interest in being disturbed. Bill laughingly disagreed and insisted that he and Pete introduce themselves. Within ten minutes, both men felt, in Bill's words, like "bananas in a blender"; the women spoke to them with sarcasm and barely veiled hostility for about five minutes and then simply turned back to each other and ignored them. Shortly afterward, Bill asked his friend, "How could you tell they'd treat us that way?" Pete replied, "The more interesting question is, how could you *not* tell?"

Bill's behavior reflects a classic psychodynamic **conflict**, that is, a battle between opposing motives. On the one hand, he is consciously determined to avoid women like his mother; on the other, he is unconsciously compelled to provoke hostility or to pursue hostile women, which he did on many occasions. Bill may not recall incidents from his childhood in which he came to associate excitement, love, sensuality, and sexuality with a woman's scorn, but his behavior nonetheless reflects those unconscious associations.

According to Freud, a single behavior, or a complex pattern of thought and action as in Bill's case, typically reflects compromises among multiple, and often conflicting, forces. The solutions people develop to maximize fulfillment of conflicting motives simultaneously, such as Bill's unconscious pursuit of difficult women while consciously failing to recognize his motive, are called **compromise formations** (Brenner, 1982). Compromise formations occur in normal as well as abnormal functioning. No one, in this view, is entirely normal or abnormal (neurotic); the issue is the extent to which an individual is able to meet needs in a way that is personally satisfying and socially acceptable.

A scene from the erotic thriller Basic Instinct. *Freud would not have been surprised by the symbolism, since he believed our basic instincts, sex and aggression, go hand in hand.*

Conflicts among competing motives may, however, exact a toll in negative emotion and even ill health. One study had students list 15 of their "personal strivings" or goals, defined to subjects as objectives "that you are typically trying to accomplish." Subjects then rated the extent to which each striving conflicted with every other striving; that is, they examined every pair of strivings and rated them for conflict, allowing the researchers to take an average level of conflict score for each subject. Subjects also reported how *unhappy* they would be if they were successful at the striving (a measure of ambivalence). Dependent variables included subjects' daily mood reports taken twice a day over 21 consecutive days; reports of somatic complaints such as headaches, coughing, and acne; and visits to the health service (Table 12.1). The results show that conflict and ambivalence are related to emotion and illness (Emmons & King, 1988).

The Drive or Instinct Model

Freud's topographic model addressed conflict between conscious and unconscious motives. His second model, the **drive** or **instinct model**, tried to explain why people pursue the motives they do. Influenced by the work of Charles Darwin, Freud stressed the continuity of human and nonhuman behavior. He hypothesized that humans are motivated by drives, or instincts, like other animals. Freud proposed two basic drives: sex and aggression. He defined the sexual drive, or **libido**, more broadly than its colloquial usage. Libido refers as much to pleasure seeking, sensuality, and love as it does to the actual act of sexual intercourse. Expressions of libido may be as varied as daydreaming about sex or romance, dressing to attract romantic partners, or selecting a career likely to attract a potential spouse because of its status or income potential.

People also express aggression in various ways, some socially acceptable and others not. We see aggression on the sports field, in the corporate boardroom, and in just about every video game on the market. Freud would not have been surprised by the two criteria used to determine whether television shows and movies are acceptable for general viewing—the amount of sex and the amount of aggression—because these are the same things that individuals regulate and censor in themselves.

TABLE 12.1   THE RELATIONS AMONG PHYSICAL AND MENTAL WELL-BEING, CONFLICT, AND AMBIVALENCE

WELL-BEING	CONFLICT	AMBIVALENCE
Positive affect	−.11	−.34
Negative affect	.21	.18
Anxiety	.17	.27
Depression	.19	**.34**
Somatic complaints	.24	.19
Health center visits	.27	.12
Number of illnesses	.31	.21

Source: Adapted from Emmons & King, 1988, p. 1044.

Note. Conflict and ambivalence in personal strivings are related to emotional and physical indices of well-being. Statistically significant correlations are in bold.

The Developmental Model

Freud (1905) considered the development of the libidinal drive the key to personality development, and hence proposed a **developmental model**, or theory of **psychosexual stages** (Table 12.2). The psychosexual stages reflect the child's evolving quest for pleasure and her growing realization of the social limitations on this quest. To understand these stages, one must view them both concretely and metaphorically. That is, the stages describe specific bodily experiences, but they also represent broader psychological and psychosocial conflicts and concerns (Erikson, 1963). Freud's psychosexual stages may sound preposterous at first, but if you try to imagine yourself a child at each stage—sucking your mother's breast for nourishment, fighting with your parents about toilet training (a fight that can go on for a year), or sobbing and shrieking as your parents leave you alone in your room at night—the broader issues may seem less absurd than at first glance.

The Oral Stage

During the **oral stage** (roughly the first eighteen months of life), children explore the world through their mouths. Many parents are aghast to observe that their infants literally put anything that is not nailed down into their mouths. During the oral stage, sucking the breast or bottle is the means by which infants gain nourishment but it is also a prime avenue for *social* nourishment, that is, warmth and closeness.

From a broader standpoint, in the oral stage children develop wishes and expectations about *dependence* because they are totally dependent on their caretakers. Difficulties (such as feeling chronically unsatisfied or uncomfortable) during the oral stage—or any of the stages—can lead to **fixations**, prominent conflicts and concerns focused on wishes from a developmental period. People with fixations at the oral stage may be extremely clingy and dependent, with an exaggerated need for approval, nurturance, and love. More concretely, the soothing and pleasure associated with mouthing and sucking during this stage may lead to fixated behavior such as thumb sucking and cigarette smoking.

TABLE 12.2 Freud's Psychosexual Stages

Stage	Age	Prominent Conflicts
Oral	0–18 months	Dependency
Anal	2–3 years	Orderliness, cleanliness, control, compliance
Phallic	4–6 years	Identification with parents (especially same-sex) and others, Oedipus complex, castration complex (males) and penis envy (females), establishment of conscience
Latency	7–11 years	Sublimation of sexual and aggressive impulses
Genital	12+ years	Mature sexuality and relationships

An infant in the oral stage (and perhaps a future Olympic gymnast).

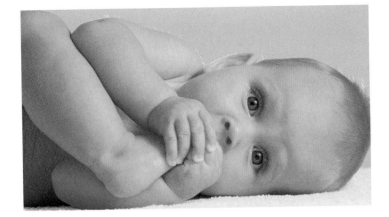

The Anal Stage

The **anal stage** (roughly ages 2–3) is characterized by conflicts with parents about compliance and defiance, which Freud linked to conflicts over toilet training. Freud argued that these conflicts form the basis of attitudes toward order and disorder, giving and withholding, and messiness and cleanliness. Imagine a toddler, who has scarcely been told "no" to anything, who finds himself barraged by rules during his second year, with the ultimate insult of being told to control his own body. This is the age during which the child learns to do unto others what they are now constantly doing unto him: saying *no*.

More concretely, Freud proposed that in the anal stage the child discovers that the anus can be a source of pleasurable excitation. If this seems preposterous, ask any child-care worker or parent about the way young children seem to enjoy this part of the body and its warm, squishy contents. Within a few short years the anal region is experienced as so disgusting that we cannot even touch it without the intervention of a piece of paper. Paradoxically, however, anal elements often enter into adult sexual interest and arousal ("Nice buns!"), foreplay (looking at or touching the buttocks or anus), and intercourse. Freud would suggest that apparent contradictions of this sort—is it disgusting or erotically arousing?—point to the presence of intrapsychic conflict, a conflict between impulses for pleasure and prohibitions against them.

People with anal fixations manifest a variety of different behavioral tendencies. On the one hand, they may be overly orderly, neat, and punctual, or, on the other, extremely messy, stubborn, or constantly late. They may have conflicts about giving and receiving or about compliance versus noncompliance with other people's demands. Children can also regress to anal issues, particularly in times of stress. **Regression** means reverting to conflicts or modes of managing emotion characteristic of an earlier stage, as when young children whose parents are undergoing a divorce suddenly start soiling themselves again (an anal regression) or sucking their thumbs (a regression to the oral stage).

The Phallic Stage

During the **phallic stage** (roughly ages 4–6), children discover that they can get pleasure from touching their genitals and even from masturbating. Adults typically retain little or no memory of these thoughts and feelings, but preschool teachers can attest that children commonly masturbate while rocking themselves to sleep at naptime, and during bathroom visits little boys can be seen comparing the size of their penises. During this stage children also become very aware of differences between boys and girls and mommies and daddies.

More broadly, during the phallic stage the child identifies with significant others, especially the same-sex parent. **Identification** means making another person

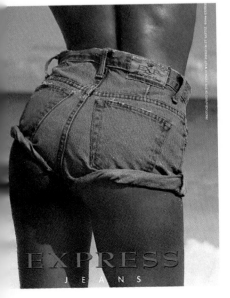

Although many people at first doubt Freud's depiction of the anal region as an erogenous zone, the buttocks are clearly an object of desire, at least in our culture.

part of oneself: imitating the person's behavior, changing the self-concept to see one-self as more like the person, and trying to become more like the person by adopting his or her values and attitudes. Much of adult personality is built through identification, as the child internalizes motives, behaviors, beliefs, and ideals—from the importance of achieving in school to the proper way to hold a fork. A longitudinal study of children's attitudes toward themselves provides empirical support for Freud's theory of identification (Koestner et al., 1991). The extent to which girls were self-critical at age 12 correlated with observer ratings of their mothers as restrictive and rejecting at age 5. For boys, self-criticism correlated with these same behaviors manifested by their fathers, not their mothers, suggesting that boys' and girls' attitudes toward themselves reflect differential identification with the same-sex parent (although, of course, children identify with both parents).

Identification has many roots. Freud emphasized its link to the **Oedipus complex**, named after the character in Greek tragedy who unknowingly slept with his mother. According to Freud, little boys want an exclusive relationship with their mothers, and little girls want an exclusive relationship with their fathers. From a young boy's perspective, for example, "Why should Mommy spend the night alone with Daddy? Why can't I go in there instead?" (Many children manage a compromise by finding ways to spend the night in the middle.) Children sometimes make astoundingly Oedipal comments. A colleague's 3-year-old boy recently exclaimed, "Daddy, I'm going to have to eat you all up so I can have Mommy to myself!"

Freud argued that because people learn about love and sensual gratification from their parents, the ultimate fantasy of the child is to have a sexual relationship with the parent of the opposite sex. At the same time, this wish is so threatening that it is quickly repressed. Boys unconsciously fear that their father, their ultimate rival, will castrate them because of their desires for their mother (the **castration complex**). The fear is so threatening that they repress their Oedipal wishes and identify with their father. In other words, they internalize a moral prohibition against incest as a way of preventing themselves from acting on their wishes, which would be dangerous, and they instead become like their father in the hopes of some-day obtaining someone like their mother. Girls, too, renounce their secret wishes toward their fathers and identify with their mothers because they fear losing her love.

So be sweet and kind to mother, now and then have a chat Buy her candy and some flowers or a brand new hat But maybe you had better let it go at that

—Tom Lehrer, "Oedipus Rex"

During the phallic stage, according to Freud, **penis envy** emerges in girls, who feel that because they lack a penis they are inferior to boys. Taken on a metaphorical level (Horney, 1955), penis envy refers to the envy a girl develops in a society in which men's activities seem more interesting and valued. Given the concreteness of childhood cognition, that a 5 year old might symbolize this in terms of having or not having a penis would not be surprising. Parents often report that their daughters cry when bathing with brothers, who have "one of those things." Therapists working with women frequently hear stories about the way male children were preferentially treated in their families, which is hardly unusual in our culture (or almost any other, for that matter). Clinically, this may lead to deep-seated rage at men, but it may also lead to underlying fears and unconscious attitudes about male superiority, which may conflict with conscious beliefs. An avowedly feminist patient, for instance, refused to work with female mentors because she did not respect them. Hearing female patients describe childhood ideas of their vaginas as wounds or physical defects is also not uncommon.

Some of the more sexual aspects of Freud's theory may seem dubious, and as we shall see, one may reasonably question the extent of his focus on sexuality in personality, or the ubiquity of the castration complex or penis envy. Nevertheless, Freud's psychosexual theory suggests explanations for a number of perplexing phenomena that are not easily explained by other theories. Some men and women *do* recurrently seem to "find" themselves in love triangles involving "another man" or "another woman," which psychodynamic psychologists explain as a fixation on wishes and conflicts from the Oedipal period (the phallic stage). Therapists often see prominent dynamics of this sort in adults whose parents divorced when they were children, whose relationship with the opposite-sex parent seemed to them almost illicit because the other parent envied or detested it. Most readers will also know women who seem to be attracted only to much older men, drawing such casual remarks as, "She's looking for a daddy."

Even the notion of castration anxiety, perhaps Freud's most seemingly outlandish concept, may account for certain observations. In the men's dressing room of a department store, two boys around age 5 were struggling with a curtain that would not quite close—pulling the curtain one way only seemed to open up the other side—when one of them was overheard saying, "You've got to make sure it closes so no one can come in and steal your ding." Surely no one had warned the child to protect his "ding" at J. C. Penney's. Similarly, running down a list of obscenities—verbally taboo words—one will find that most of them reflect one or another of Freud's stages. Indeed, perhaps the most vulgar thing someone can call another person in our society has a distinctly Oedipal ring (you can figure this one out on your own), and its originators were surely not psychoanalysts. How did these terms acquire such strong connotations?

The Latency Stage

During the **latency stage** (roughly ages 6–11), children repress their sexual impulses and continue to identify with the same-sex parent. They also learn to channel their sexual and aggressive drives into socially acceptable activities such as school, sports, and art. Whereas people fixated at the phallic stage may be preoccupied with attracting mates or take on stereotypical characteristics of their own or the opposite gender, individuals fixated at the latency stage may seem totally asexual.

The Genital Stage

During the **genital stage** (approximately age 12 and beyond), conscious sexuality resurfaces after years of repression. Genital sex becomes the primary end of sexual activity, and people become capable of relating to and loving others on a mature level. They also become capable of carrying out adult responsibilities such as work and parenting. Prior elements of sexuality do not disappear—foreplay tends to have decidedly oral and anal components—but these pregenital elements become integrated into patterns of sexual activity involving genital satisfaction. This stage was probably least elaborated by Freud, who believed that the major aspects of personality become firmly established in childhood and may require considerable effort to change thereafter.

The Structural Model

The final model Freud developed was his **structural model** (Freud, 1923, 1933). In it, he shifted his understanding of conflict, from conflict between conscious and unconscious forces, to conflict between one's desires and the dictates of conscience or the constraints of reality. The structural model posits three sets of mental forces, or structures: id, ego, and superego.

The **id** is the reservoir of sexual and aggressive energy. It is driven by impulses and, like the unconscious of the topographic model, is characterized by wishful, illogical, and associative thought (called **primary process**). To counterbalance the "untamed passions" of the id (Freud, 1933, p. 76), the **superego** acts as a conscience and source of ideals. The superego is the parental voice within the person, established through identification. The **ego** is the structure that must somehow balance desire, reality, and morality, a task Freud described in terms of serving three masters: the id, the external world, and the superego. The ego, unlike the id, is capable of secondary process thought. **Secondary process** thinking is rational, logical, and goal directed. The ego is thus responsible for cognition and problem solving (Hartmann, 1939). It is also responsible for managing emotions through coping and defense mechanisms (Chapter 11) and finding compromises among competing demands.

To demonstrate how conflict among these forces plays out, consider an example taken from the therapy of an angry, somewhat insecure junior partner at a law firm who felt threatened by a promising young associate. The partner decided to give the associate a poor job performance evaluation, even though the associate was one of the best the firm ever had. The partner convinced himself that he was justified because the associate could be working harder, and he wanted to send a message that laziness would get the young barrister nowhere—an admirable goal indeed! From the perspective of the structural model (Figure 12.2), the perceived threat activated aggressive wishes (id) to hurt the associate (give him a poor evaluation). The partner's conscience (superego), on the other hand, would not permit such a blatant display of aggression and unfairness. Hence, he unconsciously forged a compromise (ego): He satisfied his aggression by giving the poor evaluation, but he cloaked his action in the language of the superego, claiming really to be helping the young associate by discouraging his laziness, and hence satisfying his conscience.

Neo-Freudians and Early Dissenters

From the start, Freud's theories drew a wide range of responses, from admiration to repulsion and derision. A group who came to be known as **neo-Freudians** accepted the notion of unconscious processes and conflicts among psychological forces but rejected Freud's drive theory, particularly the central role of sexuality. Swiss psychiatrist Carl Jung (1875–1961) and Austrian psychiatrist Alfred Adler (1870–1937) were the first psychodynamic theorists to defect from the Freudian camp. Jung split with Freud over Freud's emphasis on libido because he felt that Freud viewed the brain as "an appendage of the genital glands" (Jung, 1961, p. 213). Furthermore, although Jung accepted the existence of unconscious processes, he proposed that people also have a **collective unconscious**, a repository of ideas, feelings, and symbols shared by all humans and passed genetically from one generation to another. Jung

Superego
(behave morally)

Ego
(hurt associate
but justify it on
moral grounds)

Id
(hurt associate)

FIGURE 12.2
Freud's structural model. Conflict among various forces leads to a compromise forged by the ego.

According to Jung, many symbols are universal, such as the personified sun in this Northwest Coast Indian sun mask.

labeled the basic symbols contained in the collective unconscious **archetypes**, mythological motifs that emerge in dreams and cultural practices and that express basic human needs, such as the image of a mother or a wise elder (Jung, 1923, 1968). Within all men, he argued, is a feminine archetype or **anima**, just as women possess an unconscious masculine side or **animus**.   Adler also took issue with Freud's libido theory, eventually replacing it with a theory based on the "will to power."   Adler maintained that people are motivated by a lifelong need for superiority in order to overcome feelings of inferiority developed in childhood (Adler, 1929).   He also paid more attention to people's conscious goals and values than did Freud, who emphasized unconscious determinants of behavior.

Many neo-Freudians focused on the role of culture, along with biology and childhood experience, in shaping psychodynamics and basic human strivings.   Erich Fromm (1947, 1955) proposed that competitiveness, materialism, and self-involvement are common personality traits in capitalist societies because of economic and social pressures to compete, buy, and focus on oneself (Chapter 10).   According to Karen Horney (1937), the neurotic patterns one sees in a society, such as endless striving after material goods or difficulty committing to intimate relationships, are similarly shaped by cultural forces.   Harry Stack Sullivan (1953) argued that the ways people relate to others, and their deepest views of themselves, are shaped by both cultural norms and their interactions with caregivers during infancy and childhood.   Children will do whatever they must to maintain closeness with their parents and to avoid interpersonal anxiety.   Abused children often cling to abusive parents and see *themselves* as bad and unworthy in order to maintain even a tenuous tie. Erik Erikson (1963) proposed a psychosocial model of development, which stressed the interpersonal nature of human development, to complement Freud's psychosexual theory (Chapter 14).

Object Relations Theories

Perhaps the most important theoretical development in psychoanalysis since Freud's death has been the emergence of object relations theories.   When once asked what the healthy person should be able to do, Freud responded, "to love and to work."   **Object relations theories** attempt to account for the difficulties of people who are highly impaired in both domains, who may show an extreme inability to

The competitiveness and materialism of contemporary Western capitalist societies would have been incomprehensible to people in most cultures in human history. Here, in New Guinea, Dani men participate in a ceremony to divide a dead man's wealth.

maintain commitment or trust in relationships, a disavowal of any wish for intimate human contact at all, or an inability to sustain employment because of chronic interpersonal conflicts with co-workers and employers.

Object relations refers both to enduring patterns of behavior in intimate relationships and to the motivational, cognitive, and affective processes that produce those patterns. (The term came originally from Freud's view that an instinct has an aim, which is some kind of gratification, and an object, which is usually a person. Thus, object relations theories are about people's relationships with others.) Of particular importance are representations of self, significant others, and relationships (Bowlby, 1982; Jacobson, 1964; Sandler & Rosenblatt, 1962). People who have difficulty maintaining relationships tend to represent themselves and others mentally in more negative ways, frequently expecting abuse or malevolence in relationships (Nigg et al., 1992). They also have trouble maintaining *constancy* of their representations; that is, they have difficulty holding in mind positive representations of people they love during the inevitable interpersonal conflicts that friends, family members, and lovers experience (Kernberg, 1984). As a result, they may break off or irreparably damage their relationships while angry.

Instead of explaining such behavior in terms of neurotic compromise solutions to unconscious conflicts, object relations theorists explain severe interpersonal problems in terms of maladaptive interpersonal patterns laid down in the first few years of life. Whereas Freud described development as a sequence of psychosexual stages, object relations theorists describe it as a progressive movement toward more mature relatedness to others. Unlike much of psychodynamic theory, many aspects of object relations theory have been tested and corroborated empirically, such as the relation between childhood experiences and adult representations (Hadley et al., 1993; Porcerelli et al., 1995; Stricker & Healey, 1990; Westen, 1991).

Psychodynamic Assessment

A core assumption of all psychodynamic approaches—that many personality processes are unconscious—raises a difficult question: How can one assess what one cannot *access*? This dilemma led to a number of methods of personality assessment, including life history methods, indirect methods called projective tests, and experimental investigations.

Life History Methods

Life history methods aim to understand the whole person in the context of his life experience and environment (see Alexander, 1990; McAdams, 1988, 1992; Runyan, 1984). They are the bread and butter of psychodynamic investigation, typically involving case studies in which the psychologist studies an individual in depth over an extended time. Information may be gathered through psychotherapy, historical or biographical sources, or research interviews.

Projective Tests

Projective tests present subjects with an ambiguous stimulus to which they are to give some kind of definition, or to "project" a meaning into it. The assumption underlying projective tests is that the different ways people respond to an unstructured, undefined stimulus reflect their characteristic patterns of thinking and feeling—that is, aspects of their personalities.

In the **Rorschach inkblot test**, developed by Swiss psychiatrist Hermann Rorschach in 1921, a subject views a set of inkblots and tells the tester what each inkblot resembles. For example, a teenager whose parents were divorcing and battling for custody of her was shown the inkblot reproduced in Figure 12.3. The subject saw a girl being torn apart down the middle, "with feelings on each side," just as she felt torn by her parents' conflict.

FIGURE 12.3
The Rorschach inkblot test. Subject's responses provide insight into their unconscious perceptual, congnitive, and emotional processes. Reproduced with permission.

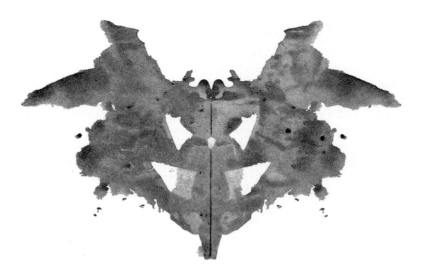

In the Thematic Apperception Test, or TAT (Chapter 10), the subject is asked to make up a story about each of a series of ambiguous drawings, most of which depict people interacting. The assumption is that the individual will fill in the ambiguity with details that reflect her own recurring wishes, fears, and ways of experiencing relationships. Consider the response of a subject with a borderline personality disorder, a disorder that typically manifests itself in tremendously unstable relationships, repeated suicide attempts, and difficulty controlling rage, anxiety, and sadness (Chapter 15). When shown a TAT card depicting a man and woman similiar to Figure 12.4, the subject responded:

> This guy looks a lot like my father—my father going off the handle, ready to beat one of us kids. My mother was trying to control him; she'd get beaten along with the rest of us. Did you choose these pictures by what I told you? The woman in the picture is feeling fear for her kids, thinking of ways to stop him—thinking and feeling fear for herself. What this man is thinking or feeling is beyond me. I don't like this picture—as you can tell—it bothers me bad. (She flips the card over.) The resemblance between this and pictures of my father and me when I was younger is uncanny.

The subject brings in themes of abuse, which is typical of the stories of borderline patients, many of whom were abused as children (Herman et al., 1989; Ogata et al., 1989; Wagner & Linehan, 1994). Further, while most people report stories that are independent of themselves, this subject cannot keep herself out of the cards, a sign of egocentricism or self-preoccupation characteristic of the TAT responses of patients with this disorder (Westen et al., 1990). After another card also reminded her of herself, the subject later wondered whether these cards were chosen just for her, demonstrating a degree of paranoia consistent with her personality disorder.

Psychologists have criticized projective tests for years, citing various inadequacies (Mischel, 1968). Projective tests are often less useful in predicting behavior than simple demographic data such as the subject's age, sex, and social class (Garb, 1984); they are frequently used idiosyncratically by clinicians, who may offer very different interpretations of the same response; and they can be misused to make predictions about behaviors for which the tests are not valid, such as potential job performance. More recent evidence, however, suggests that projective tests can be reliable and valid for assessing disturbances in thinking and in object relations and can effectively distinguish patients with different diagnoses from each other (see Blatt & Lerner, 1983; Coleman et al., 1993; Loevinger, 1976, 1985; Stricker & Healey, 1990; Tuber, 1992). The TAT is also useful for assessing needs that subjects cannot accurately self-report.

FIGURE 12.4
Thematic Apperception Test (TAT). Psychodynamic psychologists often use projective tests like the TAT to assess object relations and personality dynamics. (This is an artist's rendering of a TAT-like image. The actual card is not reproduced to protect the valid use of the test.)

Laboratory Investigations

Although psychodynamic psychologists rely primarily on case study and projective methods, literally hundreds of experimental investigations have tested psychodynamic hypotheses (Dixon, 1981; Erdelyi, 1985; Fisher & Greenberg, 1977; Perry & Cooper, 1987; Vaillant, 1977; Weinberger & Silverman, 1988; Weinberger, 1995). For example, the subliminal presentation of psychodynamically significant messages consistently influences behavior (Hardaway, 1990). In a study attempting to activate Oedipal conflict, a group of male college students received the subliminal message "Beating dad is OK." At a subsequent competitive dart game, they outperformed both subjects who received the message "Beating dad is wrong" and control subjects who received an irrelevant message (see Weinberger & Silverman, 1988). Research on unconscious repression, a major psychodynamic concept, is difficult to conduct; however, studies of *conscious* efforts to suppress thoughts show that the material people try to avoid thinking about constantly slips into consciousness, particularly when they momentarily stop focusing attention on suppressing it (Wegner, 1989; Wegner & Erber, 1992). This corroborates Freud's claim that censoring material from consciousness does not eliminate it but only drives it underground.

Contributions and Limitations of Psychodynamic Theories

The psychodynamic perspective on personality has contributed a number of fundamental insights about unconscious processes, defenses, mental representations of the self and relationships, psychic conflict, and the impact of childhood experiences on adult personality. Perhaps most importantly, psychodynamic approaches offer a way of interpreting what people mean by their communications and actions. Proponents maintain that 30-minute experiments on college students that constitute the bulk of research in personality cannot compare to the richness of clinical observation or lead to the generation of sophisticated theories about personality functioning in complex real-life events.

Perhaps the major limitation of psychodynamic theory is its inadequate basis in scientifically sound observation (see Mischel, 1973; Grunbaum, 1984; Wallerstein,

1988). Some aspects of the theory seem particularly problematic, such as Freud's theory of female development (and especially the concept of penis envy). Indeed, many feminist scholars reject Freud's thought entirely as misogynist, or derogatory toward women. Although Freud's thinking on women was certainly influenced by the gender stereotypes of his time, the charge of misogyny is actually not well founded. Psychoanalysis was one of the only disciplines that elevated women to positions of prominence in the early twentieth century, and it arguably remained more progressive in this respect than the rest of psychology until the 1960s. The most recurrent criticism of psychodynamic theory regards Freud's theory of drives (Holt, 1985). Aggression does not appear to be a bodily need in the same way as sex or hunger, and the theory generally overemphasizes sexual motivation. Still other critics charge that psychodynamic theory pays too much attention to childhood experiences and not enough to adult learning.

In evaluating psychodynamic theory, the reader should keep in mind what it is not. Psychodynamic theory is no longer a single theory forged by a single thinker, Sigmund Freud. Most contemporary psychodynamic psychologists think about motivation in terms of wishes and fears, not sexual and aggressive drives, although they agree with Freud that many motives, such as sex and love, are biologically rooted and fundamentally shaped in childhood. Contemporary psychodynamic psychologists also tend to rely on concepts like conflict, compromise, mental representation, and self-esteem, rather than id, ego, and superego.

Furthermore, psychodynamic theory is not a theory aimed at prediction of behavior. It is a theory aimed at interpretation of behavior that has already occurred, such as the repeated lateness to class of a college student with authority problems. Prediction and interpretation should be central aims of any approach to personality. To the extent that psychodynamic theory fails to generate testable hypotheses, it will probably remain as inadequate as most alternative theories of personality, which do not facilitate the interpretative understanding of behavior.

COGNITIVE-SOCIAL THEORIES

Cognitive-social theories offered the first comprehensive alternative to psychodynamic theories of personality. First developed in the 1960s, these theories go by several names, including social learning theory, cognitive-social learning theory, and social cognitive theory (Chapter 5). Cognitive-social theories developed from behaviorist and cognitive roots (Chapter 1). From a behaviorist perspective, personality consists of learned behaviors and emotional reactions that are relatively specific and tied to particular environmental stimuli. These behaviors are selected through operant conditioning on the basis of their rewarding or aversive consequences.

Cognitive-social theories share the behaviorist belief that learning (rather than instinct, conflict, or defense) is the basis of personality and that personality dispositions tend to be relatively specific and shaped by their consequences. However, they also focus on beliefs, expectations, and information processing. According to this approach, personality reflects a constant interplay between environmental demands and the way the individual processes information about the self and the world. As Albert Bandura (1986) argues, people are not driven by inner forces, as in psychodynamic theory, nor are they automatically shaped and controlled by external stimuli, as asserted by radical behaviorists such as B. F. Skinner. Rather, people's actions reflect the schemas they use in understanding the world, their expectations of what will happen if they act in particular ways, and the degree to which they believe they can attain their goals. Whereas psychodynamic theory centers on the irrational, cognitive-social theories are eminently rational; and whereas behaviorists eschew thinking, cognitive-social theorists celebrate it.

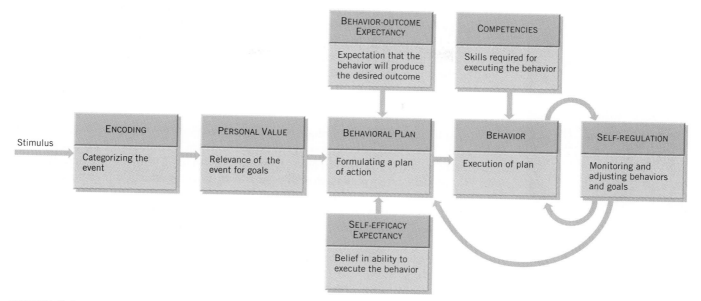

FIGURE 12.5

A cognitive-social model of behavior. This figure depicts the conditions that must be met for a behavior to occur according to cognitive-social theories.

According to cognitive-social theories (Bandura 1977b, 1986; Mischel, 1990), several conditions must be met for a behavior to occur. As can be seen in Figure 12.5, the person must encode the current situation as relevant to her goals or current concerns, and the situation must have enough personal meaning or value to initiate goal-driven behavior. The individual must believe that performing the behavior will lead to the desired outcome and that she has the ability to perform it. She must also actually have the ability to carry out the behavior, or it cannot occur. Finally, the person must be able to regulate her ongoing activity in a way that leads toward fulfilling the goal. This may mean monitoring her behavior at each step of the way until the goal is fulfilled, as in decision-making theories, or changing the goal if she cannot fully achieve it. If any of these conditions is not met, the behavior will not occur.

Before briefly examining each of these stages in turn, imagine that you have just been stood up for a date (the stimulus). When you realize what has happened (encoding as personally relevant), your self-esteem plummets, you see that your plans for the evening are ruined, and you would like to make the person feel bad and think twice before doing that again (personal value). You therefore decide to confront your date (behavioral plan). In formulating a behavioral plan, however, you must decide whether any action you can take will actually achieve the desired result (expectation of link between behavior and outcome). Will your date simply ignore you and make up an excuse? On top of that, your expectations and beliefs must be accurate: You must actually be able to respond quickly (competence), or you will emit the wrong behavior, such as saying, "Oh, that's OK. I found something else to do. Do you want to set up another date?" Finally, as you begin to execute the action, you will need to monitor progress toward your goal—is your "date" squirming enough yet?—as you go along.

Encoding and Personal Relevance

For people to respond to a situation, they must first encode it as relevant to them. If a delinquent or maladjusted boy is accidentally bumped by a peer, he may punch his unwitting assailant because he encoded the bump as deliberate (Dodge et

According to cognitive-social theorist, the way people conceive of themselves and others is a central aspect of personality.

al., 1990). George Kelly (1955) developed an early cognitive approach to personality that focused on personal constructs. **Personal constructs** are mental representations of the people, places, things, and events that are significant to a person. According to Kelly, people can construe the world in many different ways, which define their personality. Kelly looked for the roots of behavior not in motivation, as in psychodynamic theory, but in cognition. For example, an individual who believes someone will always step in to take care of him may act in a manner that appears dependent.

People are not always able to articulate their personal constructs when asked directly. Thus, Kelly and his colleagues developed a technique for assessing them indirectly, called the **repertory grid technique** (Brown & Chiesa, 1990; Sewell et al., 1992). Subjects are asked to describe the dimensions on which important people in their lives differ (e.g., "How does your father differ from your mother? from your sister?"). By eliciting enough comparisons, the psychologist can discern the constructs that the subject implicitly uses in thinking about people. Experimental research using very different methods confirms that the idiosyncratic categories individuals characteristically use to describe themselves and others influence their behavior (Higgins, 1990).

Nancy Cantor and John Kihlstrom (1987) combined Kelly's emphasis on personal constructs with information-processing theory to create a cognitive theory of personality. They argue that the way people conceive of themselves and others and encode, interpret, and remember social information defines both their personality and their social intelligence. In this view, individuals who have more accurate and well-organized schemas about people and relationships have greater social intelligence and should be more effective in accomplishing their interpersonal goals, such as making friends and getting desirable jobs.

Individuals have elaborate schemas about people and situations that have relevance or personal value to them. **Personal value** refers to the importance individuals attach to various outcomes or potential outcomes (Mischel, 1979). Whether a situation or anticipated action has a positive or negative value for an individual often depends on the person's goals. Cantor and Kihlstrom (1987) define motivation in terms of **life tasks**, the conscious, self-defined problems people attempt to solve. For a college student, salient life tasks may involve establishing independence from parents, getting good grades, or making and keeping friends (Cantor, 1990; Harlow & Cantor, 1994).

Expectancies and Competences

Whether people carry out various actions depends substantially on their **expectancies,** or expectations relevant to desired outcomes (Chapter 5). Of particular importance are behavior-outcome expectancies and self-efficacy expectancies. A **behavior-outcome expectancy** is a belief that a certain behavior will lead to a particular outcome. A **self-efficacy expectancy** is a person's conviction that she can perform the actions necessary to produce the desired outcome. For example, a person will not start a new business unless she believes both that starting the business is likely to lead to desired results (such as wealth or satisfaction) and that she has the ability to get a new business off the ground.

Bandura (1977a, 1982, 1991) argues that self-efficacy expectancies are generally the most important determinant of successful task performance. Research in a number of areas clearly documents that people who are confident in their abilities are more likely to act, and ultimately to succeed, than those plagued by self-doubts. James Joyce weathered 22 rejections when trying to publish *Dubliners*, and a prominent psychologist was once told that "one is no more likely to find the phenomenon [that he eventually discovered and documented] than bird droppings in a cuckoo clock" (Bandura, 1989, p. 1176).

Believing in one's abilities is one thing, but truly having them is another. Thus, another variable with a crucial impact on behavior is **competences**, that is, skills and abilities used for solving problems. Social intelligence includes a variety of competences that help people navigate interpersonal waters that can sometimes be turbulent, such as social skills that allow them to talk comfortably with strangers at a cocktail party, or the ability to end an argument to maintain a friendship (see Cantor & Kihlstrom, 1987; Kosmitzki & John, 1993; Mischel, 1990). Individuals develop highly specific skills for handling particular tasks through operant conditioning, observational learning, practice, and deliberate conscious effort.

Self-Regulation

The final variable required for successful execution of a behavior is self-regulation. **Self-regulation** refers to setting goals, evaluating one's performance, and adjusting one's behavior to achieve these goals in the context of ongoing feedback (Bandura, 1986, 1991; Mischel, 1990). Cognitive-social theorists take a problem-solving or decision-making approach to personality, much like information-processing approaches to cognition (Chapter 7) and goal-setting and expectancy-value theories of motivation (Chapter 10). In other words, people are constantly setting goals, applying their skills to achieve them, and monitoring their thoughts and actions until their goals are reached or modified. Personality, in this view, is nothing more or less than the problem-solving efforts of people trying to fulfill their life tasks (Harlow & Cantor, 1994).

One study applied this goal-setting, problem-solving approach to organizational decision making (Wood & Bandura, 1989). Using a computer simulation, graduate business students were asked to allocate workers and resources to maximize efficient production. The simulation involved 18 decision-making trials, with each trial followed by performance feedback useful for the next. Half of the subjects (the acquirable skill group) were told that in "acquiring a new skill, people do not begin with faultless performance. However, the more they practice, the more capable they become." Essentially, these subjects were encouraged to use the task to develop their skills rather than to evaluate their ability. The other half (the fixed ability group) were led to believe that the simulation would test their underlying ability as a manager, a basic competence they either did or did not have.

The researchers wanted to know how this manipulation would affect subjects' perceived self-efficacy, goal setting, efficiency in problem solving, and managerial success at running the simulated company. Self-efficacy was assessed by regularly asking subjects how confident they were of achieving production goals following feedback on their performance. Performance goals were assessed by asking subjects after each trial what performance level they were striving for on the next trial. The researchers also measured the efficiency of subjects' problem-solving strategies as well as their actual level of performance on the task (Figure 12.6). Subjects who believed they could learn from the task showed consistent increases in perceived self-efficacy, unlike subjects who believed their ability was fixed. The fixed ability group showed a steady decline in self-efficacy performance goals, efficiency of problem solving, and actual performance. Essentially, in confronting a difficult task, the group who believed their skills were fixed steadily lowered their estimates of their efficacy and their level of aspiration, and they steadily declined in performance. Statistical analysis showed that the declines in self-efficacy expectancies particularly affected performance. In other words, managers are much more likely to be successful if they *believe* they can be successful.

FIGURE 12.6
An experimental study of self-regulation. Subjects who believed they could learn from the task showed consistent increases in perceived self-efficacy, unlike subjects who believed their ability to be fixed (a). The latter showed a steady decline in performance goals (b), efficiency of problem solving (c), and actual performance (d). SOURCE: *Wood & Bandura, 1989, pp. 411–413.*

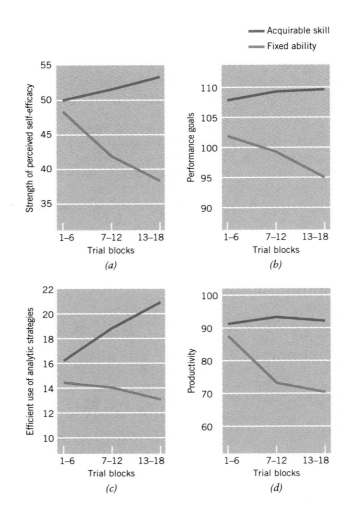

Contributions and Limitations of Cognitive-Social Theories

Cognitive-social theories have contributed substantially to the study of personality. With a few basic principles, a wide spectrum of behavior becomes comprehensible. The approach also makes intuitive sense. It seems reasonable to suppose, for example, that people who believe studying hard will lead to good grades are likely to study hard, especially if they perceive some value in good grades, think they have the capacity to excel, and have the skills to do so. Furthermore, unlike psychodynamic theory, which is difficult to test, cognitive-social theory is readily testable through experimentation.

Cognitive-social approaches are limited, however, in two respects. First, they overemphasize the rational side of life and underemphasize the emotional, motivational, and irrational. If personality is really reducible to cognitive processes (Cantor, 1990), one would have difficulty accounting for the psychological abnormalities of a man like Adolph Hitler. Because Hitler was tremendously adept at getting people to follow him and had an extraordinary sense of self-efficacy, one would have to rate him high on several dimensions of social intelligence. Yet his social motives, and his ways of dealing with his emotions, were clearly disturbed.

Indeed, one might never know from reading cognitive-social accounts of personality that people get jealous, have sexual fantasies, rebel against their parents, sometimes enjoy watching other people suffer, or have genitals (let alone sex).

These are important omissions. If the image one gets from reading Freud is of people who do little more than find sublimated ways to satisfy their sexual urges, the image one gets from reading cognitive-social theory is of individuals who spend their days reading and thinking. Jung once said that every psychology is the personal confession of the psychologist, and he might have argued that cognitive-social theories too heavily reflect their academic roots.

A related problem stems from the attempt of cognitive-social theorists to avoid explanations that resemble anything psychodynamic, such as defenses. Rather, they tend to assume that people consciously know what they want and hence can report it. But would most of us accept Hitler's self-report of his life task of bettering the world and creating a master race? Or would we suspect that his dreams of world domination and his program of genocide reflected thoughts, feelings, and motivations that he could not easily have described? As we have seen (Chapter 9), much of human mental life is not accessible to consciousness, and this is equally true of research subjects as of führers.

TRAIT THEORIES

Trait theories of personality have been largely derived from the words people use to classify themselves and others in their everyday lives—adjectives like shy, devious, manipulative, open, or friendly. **Traits** are emotional, cognitive, and behavioral tendencies that constitute underlying dimensions of personality on which individuals vary. According to Gordon Allport (1937; Allport & Odbert, 1936), who developed the trait approach to personality, the concept of trait has two separate but complementary meanings. On the one hand, a trait is an observed tendency to behave in a particular way. On the other, a trait is an inferred underlying personality disposition that generates this behavioral tendency. Presumably, a tendency to be cheerful (an observed trait) stems from an enduring pattern of internal processes, such as a tendency to experience positive affect, to think positive thoughts, or to wish to be perceived as happy (an inferred disposition).

How does one measure traits? The most straightforward way is the same way people intuitively assess other people's personalities: Observe their behavior over time and in different situations. Because extensive observation of this sort can be very cumbersome and time-consuming, psychologists often use two other methods. One is to ask people who know the subject well to fill out questionnaires about the person's personality. The second, and more commonly used method is to ask subjects themselves to answer self-report questionnaires.

To describe personality from a trait perspective, one must know not only how to measure traits but also which ones to measure. Oskar and Jack, the twins who opened this chapter, dressed alike and were similar in their sense of well-being. Are these central personality traits?

With literally thousands of different ways to classify people, choosing a set of traits that definitively describes personality seems like a Herculean task. Allport and Odbert (1936) began by compiling a list of some 18,000 words from Webster's unabridged dictionary that could be used to distinguish one person from another. Many of these words denote similar characteristics, however, so over the years trait psychologists have collapsed the list into fewer and fewer traits. Raymond Cattell (1957, 1990) reduced these to just 16 traits, such as warm, emotionally stable, intelligent, cheerful, suspicious, imaginative, sensitive, and tense. To select these key traits, Cattell relied on factor analysis (Chapter 8) to group the adjectives on Allport's and Odbert's list that were highly correlated with each other. Cattell then named each of the overarching, or superordinate, factors.

FIGURE 12.7
Eysenck's model of personality. Extroversion-introversion is a type, or a group of correlated traits. Persistence, rigidity, and so forth are traits, groups of correlated behavioral tendencies (habits). Habits are abstractions from observing specific instances of behavior. SOURCE: *Eysenck, 1953, p. 13.*

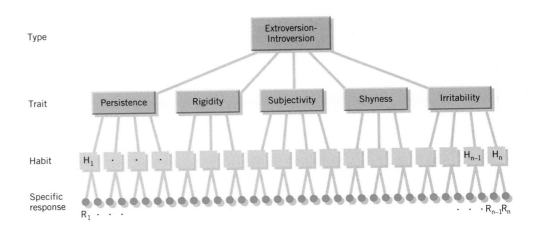

Eysenck's Theory

One of the best-researched trait theories was developed by Hans Eysenck (1953, 1990). Eysenck distinguishes traits and types, with types representing a higher-order organization of personality (Figure 12.7). In his view, individuals produce specific behaviors, some of which are frequent or habitual (that is, they are habits). A trait is a group of correlated habits. For example, avoiding attention, not initiating conversation, and avoiding large social gatherings are habitual behaviors of people with the trait of shyness. A type is a group of correlated traits. People who are shy, rigid, and inwardlooking are introverts.

On the basis of thousands of studies conducted over the last half century, Eysenck identified three overarching psychological types: extroversion-introversion, neuroticism-emotional stability, and psychoticism-impulse control. **Extroversion** refers to a tendency to be sociable, active, and willing to take risks. Introverts, who score at the low end of the extroversion scale, are characterized by social inhibition, seriousness, and caution. **Neuroticism** defines a continuum from emotional stability to instability. It is closely related to the construct of negative affect (Chapter 11). People high on neuroticism report feeling anxious, guilty, tense, and moody, and they tend to have low self-esteem. **Psychoticism** is an oddly named scale whose opposite pole is impulse control. People high on psychoticism are aggressive, egocentric, impulsive, and antisocial. People low on psychoticism are empathic and able to control their impulses.

The "Big Five" Personality Factors

Most theorists who have used factor analysis to arrive at a taxonomy of traits have found that their classifications boil down to five superordinate traits, known as the **Big Five** factors (Goldberg, 1981, 1993; John, 1990; McCrae & Costa, 1990; Norman, 1963). Different studies yield slightly different factors, and theorists label them in different ways, but the lists are strikingly consistent (Church & Burke, 1994). Costa & McCrae (1987, 1990) use the labels extroversion, agreeableness, conscientiousness, neuroticism, and openness to experience. As Table 12.3 shows, people high on extroversion tend to be affectionate rather than reserved, talkative rather than quiet, and so forth. The Big Five taxonomy provides a comprehensive assessment of the personality traits that most people perceive in themselves and others. (To demonstrate this for yourself, rate yourself or someone you know well on each of these factors, including the lower-order traits, and see if the profiles that emerge leave out anything important.)

TABLE 12.3 THE "BIG FIVE" PERSONALITY TRAITS

I. EXTROVERSION

Reserved–affectionate
Loner–joiner
Quiet–talkative
Passive–active
Sober–funloving
Unfeeling–passionate

II. AGREEABLENESS

Ruthless–soft-hearted
Suspicious–trusting
Stingy–generous
Antagonistic–acquiescent
Critical–lenient
Irritable–good-natured

III. CONSCIENTIOUSNESS

Negligent–conscientious
Lazy–hard-working
Disorganized–well-organized
Late–punctual
Aimless–ambitious
Quitting–persevering

IV. NEUROTICISM

Calm–worrying
Even-tempered–temperamental
Self-satisfied–self-pitying
Comfortable–self-conscious
Unemotional–emotional
Hardy–vulnerable

V. OPENNESS TO EXPERIENCE

Down-to-earth–imaginative
Uncreative–creative
Conventional–original
Prefer routine–prefer variety
Uncurious–curious
Conservative–liberal

Source: Adapted from McCrae & Costa, 1990, p. 3.

Note. These are the higher-order and lower-order traits that constitute the Big Five. Within each factor, traits are highly correlated; across factors, they are not.

The delineation of basic factors in personality initially arose from the assumption that important individual differences are likely to show up in language, so that classifying hundreds of adjectives into a small group of higher-order trait descriptions would generate an adequate taxonomy of traits (Goldberg, 1981). Interestingly, the same five factors seem to appear almost regardless of the specific data used, including adjectives, antonym pairs, or statements such as "I often feel that...." (Goldberg, 1993; John, 1990). The five factors even emerged in a cross-cultural study using a *nonverbal* personality test (Paunonen et al., 1992). Subjects in Canada, Finland, Poland, and Germany viewed drawings of people engaged in behaviors related to various traits and rated how often they engage in similar behaviors. Once again, five traits seemed to encompass the spectrum of personality dispositions that they ascribed to themselves.

Are the Big Five factors cross-culturally universal? Research in Europe and North America, as well as in other cultures using Western lists of adjectives, has produced remarkably similar results (see John, 1990; Stumpf, 1993). A study of university students in Taiwan, however, suggests limits to the universality of the Big Five (Kuo-shu & Bond, 1990). The investigators asked subjects to describe several people they knew, using two sets of adjectives. One set was drawn from Cattell's inventory, whereas another was drawn from adjectives culled from Chinese newspapers, designed to represent indigenous (that is, native) conceptions of personality. The researchers then used factor analysis to see which adjectives clustered together. The Big Five factors clearly emerged from the Cattell inventory data, suggesting that when people in a very different culture rate these Western-derived adjectives (translated into their native language, of course), they cluster them in ways similar to Westerners. However, when they rated adjectives that are normally used by Chinese to describe people, a very different factor structure emerged. The first factor, social orientation, appears similar to extroversion. Self-control also resembles conscientiousness, and optimism-neuroticism resembles the Big Five neuroticism factor. Statistical analysis did not, however, produce a particularly strong one-to-one correspondence between the Western and Chinese factors.

FROM MIND TO BRAIN

THE GENETICS OF PERSONALITY

Criminality runs in families—as in the legendary outlaw family of Jesse and Frank James.

Why is one person extroverted and another introverted? While few would doubt the substantial influence of learning and environment on behavioral dispositions of this sort, a considerable body of evidence supports the somewhat counterintuitive position that a substantial part of personality is inherited, an idea first proposed by the Greek physician Galen 2,000 years ago.

The case of Oskar and Jack is not unusual in finding strong similarities among people with shared genes (Bergman et al., 1993; Lykken et al., 1993; McGue et al., 1993; Plomin et al., 1990). Studies comparing the personality characteristics of adopted children with their biological and adoptive families show that many traits are highly heritable (Plomin et al., 1990). Despite the fact that adopted children may have lived with their adoptive family from birth, biological relatives tend to be more similar than adoptive relatives, even if they have had no contact with one another (Loehlin et al., 1987, 1988). Similar results emerged in a study of the role of heredity and environment in criminality (Mednick et al., 1984). In comparing the court convictions of 14,427 adoptees, researchers found the conviction rates of the adopted children related to the conviction rates of their biological, rather than their adoptive parents. Some heritable personality traits emerge quite early in development. Extroversion, task orientation, and activity level already show high heritability in one- and two-year-olds (Braungart et al., 1992).

The most definitive studies in this area compare twins reared together and twins reared apart, a procedure that can distinguish cleanly between genetic and environmental influences. Two studies have yielded somewhat discrepant findings. A Minnesota study (Tellegen et al., 1988) examined 217 monozygotic (MZ) and 114 dizygotic (DZ) adult twin pairs who had been reared together, and 44 MZ and 27 DZ adult twin pairs who had been reared apart (average age 22). Table 12.4 displays the correlations between MZ and DZ twins reared together and apart on a personality test measuring such traits as well-being, achievement, aggression, and traditionalism. MZ twins showed substantially higher correlations than DZ twins on almost every trait, even when they were reared apart. The differences in the correlations between MZ twins reared together and MZ twins reared apart were also not particularly large, suggesting that heredity accounts for more of the variance in personality than environment.

A series of studies of Swedish adoptees with a much larger sample but a higher mean age of subjects (in their fifties rather than their twenties) also found considerable evidence for genetic influences but yielded much lower heritability estimates, averaging about .27 (see Plomin et al., 1990). As Table 12.5 shows, the correlations for MZ twins reared together are considerably larger than those reared apart, demonstrating substantial environmental influences on personality. Some traits show greater genetic effects, while others show stronger environmental influence. For example, two Big Five factors, agreeableness and conscientiousness, appear to have minimal heritability (low correlations for MZ twins reared apart) but substantial environmental influence (contrastingly high correlations for MZ twins reared together). Openness is largely heritable, while extroversion and neuroticism show substantial genetic *and* environmental impact (see also Viken et al., 1994).

The evidence thus points to heritability estimates in the range of .15 to .40 for most personality traits, with the balance attributable to the environment.

TABLE 12.4   CORRELATIONS BETWEEN MINNESOTA TWINS REARED TOGETHER AND APART ON A MULTIDIMENSIONAL PERSONALITY MEASURE

	REARED APART		REARED TOGETHER		
	MZ	DZ	MZ	DZ	
Primary traits					
Well-being	.48	.18	.58	.23	
Social potency	.56	.27	.65	.08	Substantial differences between MZ and DZ twins suggest a genetic effect
Achievement	.36	.07	.51	.13	
Social closeness	.29	.30	.57	.24	
Stress reaction	.61	.27	.52	.24	
Alienation	.48	.18	.55	.38	
Aggression	.46	.06	.43	.14	
Control	.50	.03	.41	–.06	Substantial differences between MZ twins reared apart and together suggest an environmental effect
Harm avoidance	.49	.24	.55	.17	
Traditionalism	.53	.39	.50	.47	
Absorption in fantasy	.61	.21	.49	.41	
Higher-order traits					
Positive emotionality	.34	–.07	.63	.18	
Negative emotionality	.61	.29	.54	.41	
Constraint	.57	.04	.58	.25	

Source: Tellegen et al., 1988, p. 1035.

TABLE 12.5 CORRELATIONS BETWEEN SWEDISH TWINS REARED TOGETHER AND APART

	REARED APART		REARED TOGETHER	
	MZ	DZ	MZ	DZ
Scale				
Extroversion	.30	.04	.54	.06
Neuroticism	.25	.28	.41	.24
Openness	.43	.23	.51	.14
Conscientiousness	.15	−.03	.41	.23
Agreeableness	.19	.10	.47	.11
Emotionality-distress	.30	.26	.52	.16
Emotionality-fear	.37	.04	.49	.08
Emotionality-anger	.33	.09	.37	.08
Type A-hard driving	.39	.10	.47	.00
Type A-hostility	.21	.21	.33	.40

Substantial differences between MZ twins reared together and apart suggest an environmental effect

Substantial differences between MZ and DZ twins suggest a genetic effect

Source: Adapted from Plomin et al., 1990, p. 231.

Interestingly, despite this strong environmental influence, the same family does not necessarily produce children with similar personalities. Adoptive siblings, for example, tend to share few personality traits, and even natural siblings show great variations. While this may be surprising in one sense, in another, it may simply attest to the flexibility with which human beings can respond to similar circumstances. In a family with erratic alcoholic parents, one sibling may cope by turning inward, becoming introverted and studious, while another may cope by becoming wild, poorly controlled, and eventually alcoholic. In both cases, their personalities have been shaped by a similar environment, but for reasons that can only be understood by examining their individual life histories, they took different roads. Each sibling in a family also has different experiences within that family and outside of it, and these unshared experiences can be as important in shaping personality as shared environment.

Is Personality Consistent?

The concept of personality traits described thus far implies that personality has some degree of consistency. If John is an honest person, one assumes he is likely to behave honestly in various situations and to be honest two years from now. No one is honest all the time, however, and people do change. Thus, two questions arise: Is personality consistent from one situation to another? And is personality consistent over time?

Consistency across Situations

A business owner might admit to his mother or minister, but not to an IRS agent, that he cheated on his income taxes. In Walter Mischel's (1968) view, **situational variables**—that is, characteristics of the particular circumstance in which people find themselves—are more important in determining the way they act than broad personality dispositions. In 1968, Mischel published a book that had a tremendous impact on the field for over two decades. In it, he marshaled considerable evidence that people do not act consistently—that they do not possess generalized traits. Rather, much of the consistency we perceive in other people reflects our constructs or schemas of them; once I decide that John is honest, he can get away with a lot of slippery behavior before I reinterpret his behavior.

Mischel almost single-handedly slew the mighty field of personality. If personality is not consistent, one has nothing to measure, so one might as well pack up one's questionnaires and go home. Indeed, the field of personality languished for years after Mischel's critique. Several psychologists, however, challenged Mischel's arguments. Seymour Epstein (1979, 1986) criticized Mischel for looking at too few behaviors in too few situations to overcome measurement errors inherent in experiments:

> The fact that people read in a library and swim in a swimming pool does not establish that there is no generality, or "cross-situational stability," in either swimming or in reading behavior. More to the point is that some people are more prone to swim than others when there is a reasonable opportunity to do so, and this may include swimming in pools, in lakes, and in oceans. Further, one cannot test such a cross-situational proclivity to swim by observing a person once in the vicinity of a swimming pool and once in the vicinity of a lake, as there may be many reasons for that person to forego swimming on a particular occasion. (Epstein, 1979, pp. 1122–1123)

To support his point, Epstein referred to a classic series of studies on honesty, which Mischel had used as evidence that people do not have broad traits (Hartshorne & May, 1928, 1929). Over a 6-year period, the investigators assessed the behavior of a national sample of over 8,000 children with measures of dishonesty such as cheating in class, cheating on take-home exams, and stealing. After conducting a series of tests, the researchers concluded that honesty in one situation has little predictive value for honesty in other situations; the correlation between the scores on several subtests was only .23. Epstein noted, however, that when the investigators combined several tests of honesty into a single score, the reliability coefficient (which assesses consistency) increased to a whopping .73. Thus, by aggregating, or combining measures, the researchers could reliably predict responses from one situation to another.

Bem and Allen (1974) argued further, against Mischel's point of view, that psychologists cannot predict all of the people all of the time, but they can predict some of the people some of the time. The key is to find traits that are especially relevant for particular people or traits on which they tend to behave consistently. Bem and Allen found that subjects who report that they tend to behave consistently on a particular trait do, in fact, show consistency on that trait but not necessarily on others (see also Kenrick & Stringfield, 1980). A subsequent study (Zuckerman et al., 1988) found that correlations between self-reports and peer reports are strongest not only for traits on which subjects judge themselves to be consistent but especially for traits they deem relevant or central to their personality (Table 12.6). Further, some people are more open, more easily "read," and hence easier for people who know them well to predict (Colvin, 1993).

Consistency over Time

Researchers who have investigated whether personality traits endure over time have found considerable evidence to suggest that they do (Wiggins & Pincus, 1992). One research program has been studying a cluster of attributes in children, which includes shyness and anxiety in the face of novelty, called inhibition to the unfamiliar (Kagan, 1989; Kagan & Snidman, 1991). Inhibition to the unfamiliar appears to be an aspect of **temperament**, that is, a basic personality disposition heavily influenced by genes (Chess & Thomas, 1987). Infants who are inhibited (roughly 10

An infant in Kagan's lab shows little inhibition to the unfamiliar.

TABLE 12.6   INFLUENCE OF CONSISTENCY AND RELEVANCE OF TRAITS ON THE CORRELATIONS BETWEEN SELF-REPORTS AND PEER REPORTS

TRAIT	SELF-REPORTED CONSISTENCY		SELF-REPORTED RELEVANCE	
	HIGH	LOW	HIGH	LOW
Emotional–calm	.44	.25	.47	.24
Reserved–outgoing	.48	.47	.60	.34
Assertive–mild-mannered	.37	.34	.45	.25
Self-assured–worrying	.41	.13	.38	.16

The influence of self-reported consistency primarily occurred for this variable.

Note how much higher the correlations are for subjects reporting high rather than low relevance.

Source: Adapted from Zuckerman et al., 1988, pp. 1013–1014.

percent of the population) show a distinct pattern of crying and motor behavior as early as 4 months when confronted with unfamiliar stimuli. In fact, infants classified as inhibited at 4 months show more fear responses than uninhibited children at 9, 14, and 21 months when confronted with novel stimuli (such as an unfamiliar room, application of painless electrodes to the skin, or application of liquid through a dropper to the mouth or eye) (Figure 12.8). At 7-1/2 years of age, inhibited children also have significantly more fears outside the laboratory, about attending summer camp, public speaking, remaining alone at home, and so forth.

Psychologists have also documented consistency from childhood through early adulthood and throughout the adult years. One group of investigators reanalyzed data from a longitudinal project that assessed every third birth in Berkeley, California, in 1928–1929 (Caspi et al., 1990). The most striking finding was that

FIGURE 12.8
Inhibition to the unfamiliar. Subjects classified as inhibited to the unfamiliar in infancy (dark triangles) show considerably more fears at 14 and 21 months. Note how the data points are shifted upward and to the right (that is, higher at both ages) for the high-inhibited children. SOURCE: *Kagan & Snidman, 1991, p. 859.*

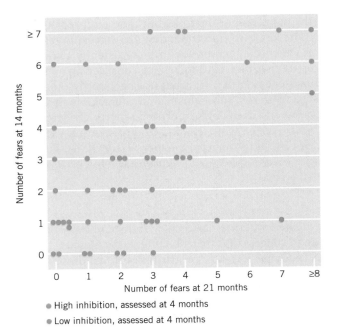

● High inhibition, assessed at 4 months

● Low inhibition, assessed at 4 months

TABLE 12.7 STABILITY OF THE BIG FIVE TRAITS IN ADULTHOOD

SCALE	TEST–RETEST CORRELATION
Extroversion	.82
Agreeableness	.63
Conscientiousness	.79
Neuroticism	.83
Openness	.83

Source: Adapted from Costa & McCrae, 1990, p. 88.

Note. This table reports test–retest correlations, that is, correlations between subjects' scores on each of the Big Five factors assessed 3–6 years apart.

8-, 9-, and 10-year-old boys characterized as ill-tempered, who had repeated temper tantrums, were characterized at age 30 by maladaptive personality traits, poor occupational performance, and disrupted marriages. As adults they were also rated as undercontrolled, irritable, moody, unethical, and undependable. A Swedish study similarly found that children (particularly boys) rated as aggressive at ages 10 and 13 by their teachers were disproportionately represented among criminals (especially perpetrators of violent crime) at age 26 (Stattin & Magnusson, 1989). Personality also manifests considerable stability throughout adulthood (Block, 1977; Conley, 1985; Costa and McCrae, 1990). A study of the stability of the Big Five factors in a sample of adults ages 30 to 96 (Costa & McCrae, 1988, 1990) found that personality stabilizes by age 30 and remains consistent thereafter (Table 12.7).

Commentary: Beyond the Consistency Debate

In retrospect, Mischel's counterintuitive argument that people do not really have broad and stable dispositions was probably counterintuitive for a good reason: It was wrong. In fact, Mischel (1990) now concludes that several important dimensions of personality—including skills, some expectancies, constructs of the self and others, ability to respond flexibly to the environment, ability to self-regulate, and goals—do indeed demonstrate consistency over time and situations. While his original hypothesis has gradually been abandoned, it has led to more sophisticated thinking about the interplay between individuals and situations and to much more caution in attempting to predict behavior by assessing personality without simultaneously looking at situational demands. Today, personality psychologists widely acknowledge the importance of **person by situation interactions**; that is, some personality dispositions are activated only in particular situations.

Recent research has begun to move beyond the consistency debate. Two studies, one examining personality across situations and the other examining personality across years, exemplify sophisticated contemporary approaches to the consistency of personality. The first, by David Funder and C. Randall Colvin (1991), videotaped subjects in three sessions. In session 1, the experimenters placed subjects in a room with another subject of the opposite sex and simply instructed them to get acquainted for five minutes. Approximately four weeks later (session 2), they placed subjects in the same situation with a different person. Shortly after the conclusion of session 2, subjects were asked to debate each other on the topic of capital punishment (session 3). Coders then rated the way subjects behaved in each videotaped session on a number of dimensions.

The investigators reasoned that behaviors and traits exhibited in sessions 1 and 2 should be highly correlated because the situations, though separated by a month, were highly similar. Less consistency should be shown with session 3, which was much more highly structured and unlike the first two sessions. Results were as predicted (Table 12.8). By and large, subjects evidenced considerable consistency between sessions 1 and 2, less consistency between sessions 2 and 3, and even less consistency between sessions 1 and 3, which were not only quite different but separated by several weeks. The researchers also found that certain qualities (such as timidity) show high consistency across situations, while others do not.

This study, then, supports a crucial postulate of early trait theorists that seems to have been forgotten: Consistency is most likely to emerge in similar situations (Allport, 1937; Rotter, 1990). Like Spearman's distinction between s-factors and g-factors in intelligence (Chapter 8), some personality traits are specific to particular situations, whereas other traits are probably general or global in some individuals. A person who is generally quite low on neuroticism may nevertheless tend to become extremely distressed after a loss. Her difficulty in coping with loss is just as much a part of her personality as her generally placid nature; the only difference is that the circumstances that activate neurotic behavior are much more specific than those that activate its opposite.

A second study, by Jack Block, Per Gjerde, and Jean Block (1991), examined the childhood personality antecedents of depressive tendencies in 18-year-olds. They assessed personality using a **Q-sort** technique: Raters are given a stack of cards with relatively concrete personality descriptions on them (such as "tries to be the center of attention" or "is eager to please") and asked to sort them in order of their descriptiveness of the person. Thus, a child who is hostile toward peers, lies frequently, and tends to disobey adults would have items such as "teases other children" in the top pile (rated 9) and items such as "is obedient and compliant" in the bottom (rated 1). Using the Q-sort procedure, several preschool teachers rated the children at ages 3 and 4, and various teachers and psychologists who observed them in depth rated the same subjects at ages 7, 11, 14, and 18. (No observer rated any subject at more than one age to insure against biases from a previous assessment.) Subjects at age 18 were also given an extensive self-report questionnaire, including a measure of their tendency to experience depression.

The investigators wanted to find out whether childhood personality dimensions could predict depressive tendencies at age 18. Their previous research suggested

TABLE 12.8 CROSS-SITUATIONAL CONSISTENCY CORRELATIONS FOR TRAITS RATED FROM THREE VIDEOTAPED SESSIONS			
	CORRELATION		
TRAIT	SESSION 1/ SESSION 2	SESSION 2/ SESSION 3	SESSION 1/ SESSION 3
Awkward interpersonal style	.60	.31	.28
Seems fearful and timid	.65	.60	.45
Cheerful	.60	.41	.28
Tense or anxious	.45	.46	.28
Seems to regard self as physically attractive	.55	.42	.43

Source: Adapted from Funder & Colvin, 1991, pp. 780–782.

that an important variable that could influence the results was gender: Based on their knowledge of research on the way boys and girls are socialized (boys to be autonomous and girls to be more attuned to social demands), they hypothesized that the personality antecedents of depression in males and females might be quite different. The results supported their hypothesis. Boys who later showed depressive tendencies were characterized when young as aggressive, self-aggrandizing, and unable to control their impulses. Girls who later became depressed, in contrast, showed almost the opposite attributes in childhood: They were shy, obedient, conscientious, and unassuming. Boys who were less bright were also more prone to depression at age 18, whereas girls who were less intelligent were *less* likely to report depression at age 18. Some of the differences in childhood personality antecedents of depression in boys and girls are reproduced in Table 12.9. Although

TABLE 12.9   GENDER DIFFERENCES IN SELECTED ITEMS THAT CORRELATE WITH DEPRESSIVE SYMPTOMS AT AGE 18

ITEM	CORRELATION	
	FOR BOYS	FOR GIRLS
Ages 3–4		
Can admit to own negative feelings	−.34	.28
Tends to be judgmental of others	−.26	.26
Is attentive and able to concentrate	−.04	.37
High intellectual capacity	−.14	.25
Age 7		
Characteristically stretches limits	.37	−.22
Seeks physical contact with others	.28	−.44
Has unusual thought processes	.29	−.28
Teases other children	.25	−.32
Tries to be center of attention	.30	.29
Is empathic	−.30	.29
Can be trusted; is dependable	−.37	.20
Is obedient and compliant	−.22	.30
Age 11		
Is stubborn	.34	−.19
Characteristically stretches limits	.29	−.27
Is unable to delay gratification	.19	−.37
Has high intellectual capacity	−.19	.24
Is eager to please	−.37	.00
High standards of performance	−.33	.24
Age 14		
Is self-indulgent	.37	−.09
Is power oriented	.37	.02
Bodily manifestations of anxiety	−.18	.21

Source: Adapted from Block et al., 1991.

Note. The table reports the correlations between personality dimensions assessed at ages 3–4, 7, 11, and 14 with degree of depression reported at age 18. As can be seen, on many dimensions, what predicted depression in males and females differed considerably.

the pattern is not consistent at ages 3–4, by age 7 a clear picture emerges of the kind of boy or girl who is likely to be depressed in late adolescence.

Taken together, these two studies of consistency in personality lead to two conclusions. First, what you get out of research is only as good as what you put into it. That two of the best-designed studies in this area demonstrate considerable consistency to personality is probably no accident. If previous research failed to find consistency, this was probably because the methods were not subtle enough to detect it (Block, 1971).

Second, personality is complex. We should not assume that for personality to be consistent, an individual who manifests a trait at one time must show precisely the same trait at another. As the study by Block and colleagues demonstrates, a much more complex kind of continuity may occur when a trait (such as the tendency to become depressed) is a natural outgrowth of a broader personality style (such as the tendency to be over- or undercontrolled). Consistency of personality does not mean that people behave the same way no matter what the circumstance and that they show this kind of rigidity from the time they are young. It means only that they are likely to respond similarly to similar situations over time and that their current dispositions can be understood in the context of who they were in the past.

Contributions and Limitations of Trait Theories

The trait approach to personality has several advantages. Traits lend themselves to measurement and hence to empirical investigation through questionnaires. Without the trait approach, we would not have been able to assess the heritability or consistency of personality. Further, trait theories are not committed to theoretical assumptions that may be valid for some people but not for others. Psychodynamic and cognitive-social theory offer universal answers to questions such as, "Are humans basically aggressive?" or "Are people basically rational?" Trait theories, in contrast, offer a very different answer: "Some people are, some aren't, and some are in between" (see McCrae & Costa, 1990, pp. 20–21).

Trait approaches, however, have three limitations. First, they often rely uncritically on self-reports, and subjects sometimes cannot or will not give an accurate assessment of themselves. For example, people who consider themselves psychologically healthy may deny statements about themselves that are true but threaten their self-concept (Shedler et al., 1993). Correlations between self-reports and peer reports tend to be in the range of .40 to .50 (Costa & McCrae, 1990; McCrae, 1993). These are substantial correlations, but for a hefty percentage of subjects, either their peers do not know them very well or they do not know themselves.

Second, trait theories can be no more sophisticated than the theories of personality held by lay people and particularly by college students, who serve as subjects for most studies, because the basic terms of trait theory come from everyday language (see Block, 1995). Trait theory in some respects is less a theory of personality than a theory of the way *everyday people* think about personality. Where do concepts developed by experts such as defenses, unconscious processes, and expectancies fit in? One could argue that relying almost exclusively on the self-reports of undergraduates is like asking a physicist to depend on the observations of untrained observers who report, "Yeah, I think that apple fell pretty fast."

Finally, traits are simply descriptive and provide little insight into the how and why of personality (Block, 1995). They may describe and even predict behavior, but they cannot explain it. A person may rank high in aggressiveness, but this says little about the internal processes that occur when the person is behaving aggressively or why he behaves aggressively in some circumstances but not in others.

HUMANISTIC THEORIES

During the 1950s and especially during the 1960s, an approach to personality emerged known as **humanistic psychology**, which developed as an alternative to psychoanalysis and behaviorism. Humanistic psychology asserts the importance of free will, abandons the view that environmental and genetic variables determine all behavior, and questions the applicability of scientific methods to human psychology. Humanistic approaches to personality hold that within each individual is an active, creative force or "self" that seeks expression, development, and growth. Thus, the aim of the psychologist should not be to search for unconscious processes or environmental contingencies but to understand how individuals experience themselves, others, and the world and to help them actualize their potential.

That this emphasis on individual potential occurred during the 1960s—a decade that challenged traditional values—is no accident. People were tired of fitting into roles others set for them and instead sought ways to be true to themselves and their personal values. Humanistic psychology was, like all psychological movements, a product of its times, although many of its concepts remain relevant today, in what many view as an era of renewed conformity (see Smith, 1978, 1988, 1994). We will examine two humanistic theories: the person-centered approach of Carl Rogers and existential theories of personality.

Rogers's Person-Centered Approach

The most widely used humanistic theory of personality is Carl Rogers's **person-centered approach** (1951, 1959). Philosophically, Rogers descended from the French philosopher Jean-Jacques Rousseau, who two centuries earlier wrote that "Man is born free but everywhere he is in chains." Rousseau meant that people are innately free and compassionate to their fellows, but somehow in the course of growing up, they become mean-spirited, selfish, and fettered by convention. Rogers similarly believed that human beings are basically good but their personalities become distorted by interpersonal experiences, especially in childhood. In his view, psychology should try to understand individuals' **phenomenal experience**—that is, the way they conceive of reality and experience themselves and their world. The fundamental tool of the psychologist is not a projective test, an experiment, or a questionnaire, but **empathy**, the capacity to understand another person's experience cognitively and emotionally.

Rogers, like other humanistic theorists, postulated that individuals have a **true self**—a core aspect of being, untainted by the demands of those around them—but that they often distort this into a **false self**—a mask they wear and ultimately mistake to be their true psychological "face." According to Rogers, the false self emerges because of people's natural desire to gain the positive regard of other people. As children develop, they learn that to be loved they must meet certain standards. In the process of internalizing these **conditions of worth**, they distort themselves into being what significant others want them to be.

Rogers defines the self or **self-concept** as an organized pattern of thought and perception about oneself. When the self-concept diverges too much from the **ideal self** (the person's view of what she *should* be like), the individual may distort her behavior or the way she sees herself to avoid this painful state. Thus, people's internalized expectations of what others want them to be may lead them to abandon their own talents or inclinations and ignore their own needs and feelings. The artistic student who becomes an accountant because that is what his father always wanted him to be is, in Rogers's view, sacrificing his true self to meet internalized conditions of worth.

Carl Rogers developed an approach to personality that emphasizes authenticity and empathy.

...No one of us can help the things life has done to us. They're done before you realize it, and once they're done, they make you do other things until at last everything comes between you and what you'd like to be, and you've lost your true self forever.

—Eugene O'Neill, Long Day's Journey into Night

Rogers proposed that the primary motivation in humans is an **actualizing tendency**, a desire to fulfill the range of needs that humans experience, from the basic needs for food and drink to the needs to be open to experience and to express one's true self. These needs were similarly described by Maslow, another humanistic psychologist (Chapter 10). Opposing the actualizing tendency, however, are the needs for positive regard from others and for positive self-regard, which often require distorting the self to meet imposed standards.

Existential Approaches to Personality

Existentialism is a school of modern philosophy that focuses, like Rogers's theory, on subjective existence. According to many existentialist philosophers, the individual is alone throughout life and must confront what it means to be human and what values to embrace. In other words, unlike other animals and physical objects, people have no fixed nature and must essentially *create themselves.*

Existentialist philosopher Jean-Paul Sartre (1971) argued that the meaning we find in life is essentially our own invention and dies along with us. The paradox inherent in the human condition is that we must find meaning in our lives by committing ourselves to values, ideals, people, and courses of action while simultaneously recognizing that these things are finite and have no intrinsic meaning—that we have simply endowed them with meaning in order to make our lives seem worthwhile. Sartre further argued that people make choices every day with complete freedom, but they may want to think otherwise to avoid the anxiety that accompanies this enormous freedom to choose who they are and will become. Someone who works for the same company for 20 years makes a new decision every day to go to work, although he may not conceptualize this as a choice. People who act as if they are not making these continuous choices are practicing what Sartre termed **bad faith**. **Bad faith** is a form of self-deception in which people convince themselves that their actions are determined—that they must stay with a job or in an unfulfilling marriage—even when doing so feels stifling or false.

According to existential psychologists, the dilemmas at the heart of existential philosophy are central to personality. Although many different theoretical perspectives have emerged within existential psychology (Frankl, 1959; May, 1953; May, Angel, & Ellenberger, 1958), they converge on several key issues: the importance of subjective experience; the centrality of the human quest for meaning in life; the dangers of losing touch with one's own inner feelings; and the hazards of conceiving of oneself as thinglike, rather than as a changing, ever-forming, creative source of will and action. Chief among the problems humans face is **existential dread**, the

A central function of culture is to help people cope with the inevitability of death. Here, an Aztec mask with stone tiles set on an actual skull gives cultural meaning to death.

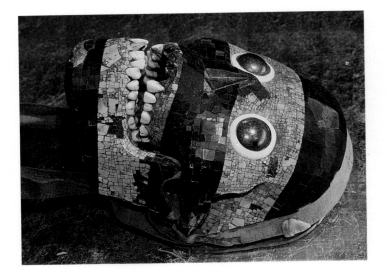

recognition that life has no absolute value or meaning and that, ultimately, we all face death. People spend their lives denying their mortality and the nothingness hidden behind their values and pursuits (Brown, 1959; Becker, 1973).

Existential psychologists, like other humanistic psychologists, have often avoided testing their hypotheses or developing methods of personality assessment, distrusting psychological techniques that turn people into objects to be studied rather than subjects to be understood. Nevertheless, a team of researchers has been systematically testing Ernest Becker's (1973) theory that cultural beliefs and values serve to protect people from facing the reality of their mortality. According to Becker's theory, an unfortunate by-product of the evolution of human intelligence is that people can imagine possible futures, including those that are painful and tragic. To avoid the potentially debilitating anxiety that could result, they create and embrace cultural beliefs and values that symbolically deny death and allow hope in the face of mortality and meaninglessness. Cultural values and worldviews thus "imbue the world with meaning, order, stability, and permanence, and by so doing, buffer the anxiety that results from living in a terrifying and largely uncontrollable universe in which death is the only certainty" (Solomon et al., 1991, p. 96).

The researchers testing Becker's theory have demonstrated across a series of studies that when confronted with experimental procedures designed to stimulate death anxiety (such as a questionnaire asking subjects to think about their own death), subjects cling more tenaciously to their cultural values (Solomon et al., 1991; Greenberg et al., 1994). In one study, actual municipal court judges served as subjects (Rosenblatt et al., 1989). Half the judges received the mortality salience manipulation (the death questionnaire), whereas the other half (the control group) did not. The experimenters then asked the judges to set bond for a prostitute in a hypothetical case. Prostitution was chosen as the crime because of its culturally defined moral overtones. As predicted, judges who filled out the mortality questionnaire were significantly more punitive, setting bond substantially higher than judges in the control group whose death anxiety had not been activated.

In another study, the experimenters presented Christian college students with information on two people, one identified as Christian and the other as Jewish (Greenberg et al., 1990). The researchers hypothesized that inducing death anxiety would lead subjects to prefer people who share their cultural beliefs, in this case, other Christians. As predicted, subjects exposed to a mortality salience procedure evaluated the Christian more favorably than the Jew, while subjects in the control condition showed no preference for the Christian or the Jew.

Sartre argued that to be human means to create meaning from nothingness and to commit to personal goals and values while admitting their objective meaninglessness.

Contributions and Limitations of Humanistic Theories

Humanistic psychology has made two major contributions to the study of personality. First, its unique focus on the way humans strive to find meaning in life has added a dimension that other approaches have failed to address. In day-to-day life this need may not be readily observable because culture confers meaning on activities, relationships, and values. The salience of this aspect of personality emerges, however, in times of personal crisis or loss (Janoff-Bulman, 1992), when life may seem capricious and meaningless. The search for meaning also becomes apparent in times of rapid cultural change (Wallace, 1956), when a culture's values and worldview are breaking down and no longer fulfill their function of making life predictable and meaningful (see also Baumeister, 1990).

The second contribution of humanistic psychology lies in the distinction it makes between true and false self. Psychodynamic accounts of identification and cognitive-social theories of modeling do not do justice to the feelings of unease and even fraudulence that people may feel when they are essentially living their lives as others would have them live—going through the motions, mouthing the words, but never feeling as if they are really themselves.

The quest for meaning is most apparent when cultural values and beliefs no longer feel satisfying. The photo depicts an aging "hippie" at a 1960s "love in."

The humanistic approach has two major limitations. One is that it does not offer a comprehensive theory of personality in the same way that psychodynamic and cognitive-social theory do. It does not, for example, offer a general theory of cognition, emotion, behavior, and psychological disorder, although different theorists at times address many of these. Second, with some notable exceptions (Rogers, 1959), humanistic psychology has largely failed to develop a body of testable hypotheses and research, although this reflects its rejection of empiricism as a philosophy of science.

PERSONALITY AND CULTURE

The theories we have explored in this chapter represent our own culture's most sophisticated attempts to understand personality. Other cultures, however, have alternative views. In fact, every culture has some implicit, common-sense conception of personality. The Cheyenne people of North America, for example, distinguish several aspects of personhood (Straus, 1977). The individual's basic nature and identity reside in the heart. The person's power, called *omotome*, is distinguished from spirit, which is the storehouse of learning, experience, and memory. To some degree the Cheyenne believe in behavioral genetics, holding that certain behaviors run in families and that children are born predisposed to behave in particular ways. They are also somewhat psychodynamic in their view of childhood as an extremely important period of life, crucial for learning and spiritual development. Unlike contemporary Western theories, however, the Cheyenne do not believe personality resides entirely or even primarily in individuals. Rather, they believe, like many preliterate societies, that the innermost parts of the soul or personality are in part communal, shared by kin and community (see Geertz, 1973; Markus & Kitayama, 1991; Shweder & Bourne, 1982; Triandis et al., 1989; Westen, 1985).

Linking Personality and Culture

Although most Western theories of personality have been constructed with Western subjects in mind, the complex interactions of personality and culture have intrigued psychologists and anthropologists since the early part of the century. Do cultures with harsh child-rearing practices create hostile or paranoid personalities? And how do cultural practices help individuals satisfy psychological needs, such as escaping from death anxiety? We briefly consider four approaches to culture and personality: Marx's, Freud's, the culture pattern approach, and interactionist approaches.

Marx's Approach

One of the earliest theories of personality and culture was proposed by the social philosopher Karl Marx. Marx disputed the idea of a common human nature and instead proposed that people's needs, wishes, beliefs, and values are products of the conditions under which they live and work. According to Marx, the materialistic, competitive, individualistic personality style of people in Western, industrialized, capitalist nations reflects underlying economic realities, such as competition of workers for scarce jobs and the breakdown of extended family work units (such as family farms) that occurred with the rise of capitalism.

An orientation toward individual liberty, materialism, and achievement seems like human nature to us, but Marx was indeed correct that human nature looks very different in other societies. Research has consistently shown that individualism and competitiveness are highly correlated with the extent of industrialization of the economy. For example, the personality trait of Machiavellianism (the belief that manipulating other people is acceptable and even desirable) is highly correlated with

Among the Cheyenne, the community, not the individual, is the center of much of personality.

degree of technological development (Christie & Geis, 1980; Geis, 1978). People in industrial societies tend to rear their children to compete and achieve, whereas those in less technologically advanced societies stress the virtues of obedience and cooperation (see Werner, 1979). Marx further argued that the conditions under which individuals labor play a fundamental role in shaping the kind of people they are. He would not have been surprised to find high rates of drug abuse among automobile factory workers in America, who may spend much of their day performing tasks that have no personal meaning and provide little personal satisfaction.

Freud's Approach

Whereas Marx essentially reduced personality and culture to economic factors, Freud reduced culture to personality, seeing cultural phenomena as reflections of individual psychodynamics. The Freudian method of analyzing cultures is the same method applied to dreams, neurotic symptoms, and conscious beliefs in individuals: Look beneath manifest content to find latent content. Freud viewed cultural phenomena such as myths, moral and religious beliefs, and games as expressions of the needs and conflicts of individuals. For example, my friends are all aghast to find that I am a devotee of boxing. Because I do not appear to be a very aggressive person, they cannot understand how I could enjoy watching two grown men dancing around on a piece of canvas, trying to destroy each other's cerebellum with flurries of punches. The function of boxing for me, no doubt, is to express aggressive impulses that I would not permit myself in my daily life.

Freud (1928) similarly argued that institutions such as religion can be understood in terms of their functions for individuals. Should one be surprised, he asked, to find representations in Western culture of a Holy Father and a sacred Mother? The monotheistic concept of God in many religions is remarkably similar to a young child's conception of his father: a strong, masculine, frightening figure who can be both loving and vengeful. A Freudian might also note that the virgin mother of Christian theology is a perfect resolution of Oedipal conflict: No child wants to think that his parents have sex, and the best way of keeping mother pure is to imagine that she could have had an immaculate conception.

The Culture Pattern Approach

A third approach asserts that individual psychology reflects cultural practices, not the other way around. The **culture pattern approach** sees culture as an organized set of beliefs, rituals, and institutions that shapes individuals to fit its patterns. Some cultures stress community and pursuit of the common good, and their mem-

A holy mother is a motif that recurs in religious imagery throughout the world.

bers generally internalize these values. Others foster a paranoid attitude, which individuals express in their relations with neighbors or outsiders, such as the Nuer of the Sudan (Evans-Pritchard, 1956) or the Aymaya of South America (LaBarre, 1966). As Ruth Benedict put it, "The life history of the individual is first and foremost an accommodation to the patterns and standards traditionally handed down in the community" (1934, p. 2).

From the standpoint of the culture pattern approach, culture is like a great sculptor that chisels the raw biological material of an individual from infancy on until it conforms to the sculptor's aesthetic ideal. Some slabs of humanity, however, are very difficult to chisel and are labeled as deviants or thrown back into the quarry after being deformed by the hand of the frustrated artist. Those whose temperament and personality patterns do not readily conform to culture patterns may thus find themselves ostracized or incarcerated, viewed in various societies as sinners, criminals, dissidents, or mentally ill.

A GLOBAL VISTA

INTERACTIONIST APPROACHES TO PERSONALITY AND CULTURE

Each of the approaches described thus far essentially reduces one broad set of variables to another: personality to economics, culture to personality, or personality to culture. While each has considerable merit, more complex interactionist approaches, which view causality as multidirectional, combine many of their virtues (Whiting & Child, 1953; Whiting & Whiting, 1975; LeVine, 1982). Personality must certainly accommodate to economic and cultural demands, but cultural and economic processes themselves are in part created to fulfill psychological needs. These in turn are shaped by cultural and economic practices, so that causality runs in more than one direction (Figure 12.9).

For example, societies that treat children more abusively tend to have more aggressive myths and religious beliefs (Rohner, 1975). From an interactionist perspective, this should not be surprising. On the one hand, the schemas or representations that children develop about relationships in childhood color their understanding of supernatural relationships. Thus, children with hostile or abusive parents are likely to respond emotionally to images of evil or sadistic gods when they grow older. Indeed, one could argue that in the West, as child-rearing practices considered acceptable have become less harsh since the Middle Ages, the image of God has shifted from a vengeful, angry father to a loving, nurturant one.

FIGURE 12.9
An interactionist approach to personality and culture. Interactionist models attempt to address the mutual influences of culture, personality, and economics, rather than reducing one to another. In this view, cultural beliefs and economic forces shape individual needs, which in turn give rise to new economic and cultural forces.

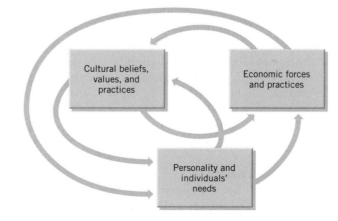

On the other hand, causality runs in the opposite direction as well, from aggressive myths to abusive child-rearing practices. Societies use myths and religious beliefs to train people to behave in ways valued by the culture. People reared on a steady diet of myths depicting aggressive interactions are likely to treat their children more aggressively—which in turn produces children who resonate with the aggression in the myths they will teach their own children.

Other interactionist approaches have considered historical as well as cultural factors. The psychoanalyst Erik Erikson (1969) examined the life of powerful leaders like Gandhi and Hitler and explored the intersection of their personality dynamics, the needs of their followers, and cultural and historical circumstances. Erikson argued, for example, that Hitler's strong need for power and his grandiosity, sensitivity to humiliation, and disgust for anyone he saw as weak contributed to the development of Nazi ideology, which stressed the greatness of Germany (with which Hitler identified) and the need to destroy groups Hitler perceived as either powerful (and hence threatening) or powerless. This ideology appealed to a nation that had been humiliated in World War I and forced to pay reparations to its adversaries, as well as to members of a culture whose child-rearing patterns left them vulnerable to feeling humiliated and unable to express their rage (Chapter 17).

The Western conception of God was once much more frightening and judgmental, as in Michelangelo's depiction of God creating the world (from the Sistine Chapel).

SOME CONCLUDING THOUGHTS

We began with Oskar and Jack, whose shared genes seemed to contribute to some remarkable similarities in their personalities, and end with the powerful impact of culture. Had Oskar and Jack grown up among the Nuer of the Sudan, they would likely have shared fierceness and hostility as personality traits, but this would have little to do with their genes. How, then, do we understand the complex forces that produce an individual personality? Some aspects of personality are clearly heritable, others reflect the conflicts and concerns of childhood, while still others reflect the daily impact of social interaction. A person is the handiwork of both nature and nurture, of chromosomes and culture.

Precisely how do biology, culture, and experience interact to produce a person? To this question we now turn, as we explore the nature of human development.

Summary

1. **Personality** refers to the enduring patterns of thought, feeling, and behavior that are expressed in different circumstances. Personality psychologists study both the **structure of personality** (the organization or patterning of thoughts, feelings, and behaviors) and **individual differences** in dimensions of personality.

Psychodynamic Theories

2. Freud's theory of **psychodynamics** holds that psychological forces such as wishes, fears, and intentions determine behavior. His **topographic model** distinguished among **conscious, preconscious, and unconscious mental processes.** Freud argued that mental **conflict** is ubiquitous and that **ambivalence**—conflicting feelings or intentions—is the rule rather than the exception in human experience. The solutions people develop in an effort to maximize fulfillment of conflicting motives simultaneously are called **compromise formations.**

3. Freud's **drive** or **instinct model** views sex (**libido**) and aggression as the basic human motives. His **developmental model** proposed a series of **psychosexual stages**—stages in the development of personality and sexuality. These include the **oral, anal, phallic, latency,** and **genital stages.** Problematic experiences during a stage can lead to **fixations**—prominent conflicts and concerns that are focused on wishes from a particular period—or **regressions,** in which issues from a past stage resurface. During the phallic stage, the child undergoes the **Oedipus complex,** desiring an exclusive, sensual/sexual relationship with the opposite-sex parent.

4. Freud's **structural model** distinguished among **id** (the reservoir of sexual and aggressive energy), **superego** (conscience), and **ego** (the rational part of the mind that must somehow balance desire, reality, and morality).

5. The **neo-Freudians** accepted the influence of unconscious processes and conflicts among psychological forces but tended to reject Freud's drive theory and to focus more on the role of culture. **Object relations theories** stress the role of representations of self and others in interpersonal functioning and the role of early experience in shaping the capacity for intimacy and chart the development of the capacity for mature love.

6. Psychodynamic approaches usually assess personality using life history and projective methods, such as the **Rorschach inkblot test** and Thematic Apperception Test (TAT), though they also use experimental procedures to test hypotheses.

7. The psychodynamic perspective has contributed a number of fundamental insights about unconscious processes, defenses, conflict, and so forth; however, it is weaker in its empirical base than are other theories.

Cognitive-Social Theories

8. Cognitive-social theories argue for the importance of encoding, personal value, expectancies, competencies, and self-regulation in personality. The schemas people use to encode and retrieve social information play an important role in personality. **Personal value** refers to the importance individuals attach to various outcomes or potential outcomes. **Expectancies** are expectations relevant to desired outcomes. A **behavior-outcome expectancy** is a belief that a certain behavior will lead to a particular outcome. **Self-efficacy expectancies** are people's beliefs about their ability to perform actions necessary for producing a desired outcome. **Competences** are skills and abilities used for solving problems. **Self-regulation** means setting goals, evaluating one's own performance, and adjusting one's behaviors flexibly to achieve these goals in the context of

ongoing feedback. Cognitive-social theories view personality as problem solving to attain goals.

9. Cognitive-social theory can explain a wide spectrum of behavior and has considerable empirical support; however, it tends to be overly rational and to assume that people can report on the most important aspects of their personality.

Trait Theories

10. Trait theories are based on the concept of **traits**, emotional, cognitive, and behavioral tendencies that constitute underlying dimensions of personality on which individuals vary. Using factor analysis, different theorists have proposed different theories of the major factors that constitute personality. Eysenck considers the major factors, which he calls types, to be extroversion, neuroticism, and psychoticism. The current consensus among trait psychologists is that personality consists of five traits, known as the **Big Five factors** (extroversion, agreeableness, conscientiousness, neuroticism, and openness to experience).

11. The heritability of personality traits varies considerably, with most influenced by nature and nurture but some highly heritable. A debate about the consistency of personality has raged for the past 25 years, sparked by Mischel's arguments against consistency in personality. Although his argument has not weathered the test of time, it has sensitized researchers to the complexities of **person-by-situation interactions,** in which personality processes become activated in only particular situations.

12. Trait theories lend themselves to empirical measurement and heritability studies; however, they tend to describe, rather than explain, personality.

Humanistic Theories

13. **Humanistic** theories of personality suggest that within each individual is an active, creative force or "self" seeking expression, development, and growth. Rogers's **person-centered approach** aims at understanding individuals' **phenomenal experience**—that is, how they conceive of reality and experience themselves and their world. According to Rogers, individuals have a **true self** (a core aspect of being, untainted by the demands of those around them), which is often distorted into a **false self** by the desire to conform to social demands. When the self-concept diverges too much from the individual's **ideal self** (the person's view of what she should be like), she may distort the way she behaves or the way she sees herself to avoid this painful state of affairs. Psychological understanding requires **empathy.**

14. **Existential personality theories** stress the importance of subjective experience and the individual's quest for meaning in life. Chief among the problems human beings face is **existential dread,** the recognition that life has no absolute value or meaning and that death is inevitable. The ways people handle issues of meaning, mortality, and existential dread are central aspects of personality.

15. Humanistic theories contribute to the understanding of some fundamental aspects of personality, like the quest for meaning; however, they tend not to be as comprehensive as other approaches.

Personality and Culture

16. Some aspects of personality are probably universal, whereas others are culturally specific. Marx's theory reduces personality to economics, while Freud's reduces culture to personality. The culture pattern approach sees personality primarily as an accommodation to culture. According to interactionist approaches, personality is shaped by economic and cultural demands, but cultural and economic processes themselves are in part created to fulfill psychological needs.

Romare Bearden, "Morning: Grandma and Grandaughter," 1985

Chapter 13

PHYSICAL AND COGNITIVE DEVELOPMENT

Dear God,

I saw Saint Patrick's Church last week when we went to New York. You live in a nice house.

Frank

Frank is a young child who wrote this letter as part of a research project studying children's developing conceptions of God (Heller, 1986, p. 16). As Frank's letter suggests, young children translate cultural concepts like God into their own "language." Frank converted the idea of the church as God's home into his own concrete notion of what constitutes a "nice house." Children's drawings similarly reveal the way they translate adult spiritual beliefs into "childese" (Figure 13.1).

In the area of religious belief, as in other areas, children frequently wrestle with concepts beyond their conceptual grasp, and their efforts reveal much about childish thought. Consider the mighty task faced by a 6 year old trying to make sense of the relation between Jesus and God in Christian theology: "Well, I know Jesus was a president and God is not...sort of like David was a king and God is not" (p. 40). In thinking about God and religion, children also deal with broader issues on their minds, as in the following letter:

Dear God,

Are boys better than girls? I know you are one (a boy), but try to be fair.

Sylvia (p. 57)

Whether children are reared Jewish, Baptist, Catholic, or Hindu, their views of God, like their understanding of most objects of thought, begin as quite concrete and gradually grow more abstract (Heller, 1986). By the time they move into adolescence, they are likely to offer abstract conceptions, such as "God is a force within us all." If cultural conditions permit, they may also express considerable skepticism about religious notions, since they are able to imagine and reflect on a variety of possible realities.

Changes in the way children comprehend reality and cultural constructs (like God) are a central focus of **developmental psychology**, which studies the way humans develop and change over time. For years, psychologists focused largely on childhood and adolescence and tended to consider development complete by the teenage years. More recently, however, psychologists have adopted a lifespan developmental perspective, considering both constancy and change, and gains and losses in functioning, that occur at different points over the entire human life cycle (Baltes, 1987).

In this chapter, we first consider some basic issues in developmental psychology. Then we examine physical development insofar as it bears on psychological functioning throughout the lifespan: How does an individual adapt to a changing body during puberty, menopause, or old age? Next, we describe cognitive development, from the time infants first begin to observe regularities in the world, such as the relation between their mother's smell and comfort or nurturance, through the growing capacity for abstract thinking that allows adolescents to question social institutions and contemplate concepts like God in a new light. We conclude by describing cognitive changes in adulthood, addressing myths and realities of aging, such as the view that "senility" is the inevitable endpoint of development. The next chapter continues our discussion of developmental psychology by exploring changes in personality and social functioning throughout the lifespan.

BASIC ISSUES IN DEVELOPMENTAL PSYCHOLOGY

Throughout this chapter and the next, three major issues repeatedly emerge: How do genetic and environmental influences interact to shape development? To what extent do capacities such as language or morality depend on early experiences? And is development characterized by leaps and plateaus or by continuous growth? We consider each issue in turn and then describe the methods psychologists use to try to answer specific developmental questions, such as how much infants really know or how sibling relationships change throughout the lifespan.

Nature and Nurture

For almost as many years as psychologists have been interested in development, they have wrestled with the extent to which changes in individuals over time reflect the influence of genetically programmed maturation or of experience—that is, of nature or nurture. **Maturation** refers to biologically based changes that follow an orderly sequence, each step setting the stage for the next step according to an age-related timetable (Wesley & Sullivan, 1986). Infants crawl before they walk, and they utter single syllables and words before they talk in complete sentences. Unless reared in a profoundly deprived environment, virtually all human infants follow these developmental patterns in the same sequence and at roughly the same age, give or take a few months.

Most contemporary psychologists believe that development, like intelligence or personality, reflects the interaction of genes and environment and of biology and culture (Plomin, 1990; Plomin et al., 1994). Nature may provide a rich and fertile field, but without cultivation, the harvest may be meager. Thus, the question is not *which* is more important, nature or nurture, or even *how much* each contributes, but rather, *how* nature and nurture contribute interactively to development (Anastasi, 1958).

The Relative Importance of Early Experience

Before dawn on January 9, 1800, a remarkable creature came out of the woods near the village of Saint-Sernin in southern France.... He was human in bodily form and walked erect. Everything else about him suggested an animal. He was naked except for the tatters of a shirt and showed... no awareness of himself as a human person.... He could not speak and made only weird, meaning-

FIGURE 13.1
Drawing of God by a six-year-old girl. Children translate cultural beliefs into their own "language." In this picture, God is a man with a halo wearing a white smock. Another child, a preschooler, attributed the origins of the universe to "God, Mother Nature, and Mother Goose."

less cries. Though very short, he appeared to be a boy of about eleven or twelve, with a round face under dark matted hair. (Shattuck, 1980, p. 5)

The "Wild Boy of Aveyron" created an immediate sensation in Europe. To scientists, the child was a unique laboratory for exploring the question of **critical periods** in human development, periods of special sensitivity to specific types of learning that shape the capacity for future development. Would a boy who was raised, at best, by wolves be able to develop language, interact with other people, and develop a conscience? A young doctor named Jean-Marie Itard became the boy's tutor. Itard's efforts met with limited but nonetheless substantial success: The boy became affectionate and learned to respond to some verbal instructions, but he never learned to talk.

Critical periods have been demonstrated in many animal species. The first few hours after hatching are a critical period during which goslings are biologically prepared to follow whatever moving object they see, which is usually their mother (Lorenz, 1935). The concept of critical periods in humans is more controversial. Can a child who does not experience nurturant caretaking in the first five years of life ever develop the capacity to love?

Human development is more flexible than development in other animals, but the brain is particularly sensitive to certain kinds of environmental input at certain times (see Bornstein, 1989). We saw in Chapter 7 that language learning is more difficult in adulthood than childhood and that the language spoken in a culture shapes an infant's sensitivity to particular linguistic sounds even before the end of the first year of life (Eimas, 1985; Werker & Lalonde, 1988). Similarly, Chapter 10 discussed the organizational effects of prenatal hormones, which appear to shape psychological characteristics such as sexual motives and behavior as well as physical characteristics.

The neuropsychological basis for critical periods of development probably lies in the connections among neurons. During some periods, the nervous system is maximally sensitive to sprouting particular connections among neurons, given the right environmental stimulus. Furthermore, infants are born with an abundance of neural connections, and those that are not used or activated by the environment are gradually lost (Greenough, 1991; Greenough et al., 1987).

Research on nonhuman animals has documented the importance of early environmental experience on the developing brain. In one study, newborn monkeys were deprived of visual experience for their first 12 months by having their eyelids surgically closed (S. Carlson, 1990). Then, over the following 12 months, they were tested on a number of visual tasks. Although the monkeys were able to perform some tasks, including following a large object with their eyes, they showed a number of abnormal behaviors in trying to explore their environment, for example, relying heavily on their hands to compensate for visual deficits (Figure 13.2).

Early experience is not lost on human infants either, despite their cognitive immaturity. Infants can remember linguistic information from the time they are born, and these memories can influence later learning. Newborns can remember hearing particular words (such as "beagle" or "tinder") 24 hours later, responding differently to them (with more interest) a day later than infants who did not hear them, suggesting implicit memory (Chapter 6) for semantic information (Swain et al., 1993). Although most people lack explicit memory for events from early childhood, such as memories of having their diapers changed, the absence of explicit memory does not mean that experiences in the first two or three years are forgotten. In one study, 2-1/2 year olds who had been exposed once to a stimulus at age 6 months responded faster to it than peers who were not previously exposed to it, demonstrating implicit memory for a single event that occurred in infancy (Perris et al., 1990). If a brief, relatively meaningless early experience can affect later learning, what about the impact of experiences such as abandonment or abuse in early childhood on subsequent development?

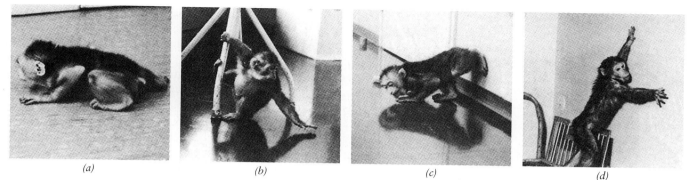

(a)   *(b)*   *(c)*   *(d)*

FIGURE 13.2

The importance of early environmental experience. Visually deprived monkeys showed a number of peculiarities in the way they explored their environments in the year following deprivation. Photo (a) shows a monkey carefully moving about the floor, in a "spider walk"; (b) shows a monkey anchoring himself to a chair while exploring with one hand; (c) shows similar anchoring to the wall; and (d) shows a monkey exploring the wall with his hands. Lacking early perceptual experience, these monkeys could not navigate their world visually.

Indeed, many psychologists view studies of children who have experienced extreme deprivation in their early years as evidence for critical periods in humans. In one famous case, a girl named Genie received no exposure to language after the age of 1 or 2 (Fromkin et al., 1974; Rymer, 1993). Genie's father was emotionally ill and locked her in a small room, where she was frequently bound and unable to move. She was discovered at age 13. Like the Wild Boy of Aveyron, Genie was subsequently able to learn some aspects of language; however, her use of syntax never reached normal levels, and she remained severely handicapped socially (Fromkin et al., 1974; Sroufe et al., 1992).

Other psychologists, however, question whether the impact of early deprivation is so indelible (Kagan, 1984; Lerner, 1991). In one study, children who spent their first 19 months in an overcrowded and understaffed orphanage experienced average IQ gains of 28.5 points after being moved to an environment in which they received individual care (Skeels, 1966). Even the case of Genie can be used to counter the notion of critical periods, since she demonstrated remarkable, though still limited, progress in social and intellectual skills in a few short years (Kagan, 1984).

Does the evidence, then, support the notion of critical periods in humans? The conservative answer is that humans have **sensitive periods**—times that are more important to subsequent development than others but do not necessarily serve as absolute gatekeepers for future psychological growth. In some domains, such as language, these sensitive periods may actually be critical; appropriate environmental input at certain points may be required, or further development is permanently impaired. In most domains, however, sensitive periods are simply sensitive—particularly important but not decisive. This is likely to be the case for most aspects of social development (Sroufe et al., 1992).

Stages or Continuous Change?

The third basic issue in development concerns the nature of developmental change, whether it is stagelike or continuous. According to one view, development occurs in **stages**, relatively discrete steps through which everyone progresses in the same sequence. Behavior in one stage is not just *quantitatively* different from the next, involving a little less or more of something, such as more rebelliousness at age 13 than at 11. Rather, stages are *qualitatively* different from one another. A stage theorist would suggest that adolescent rebelliousness is qualitatively different because it rests on a rejection of parental authority and a new way of experiencing the self. The point is not that the 13 year old breaks the rules 20 or 30 percent more than the 11 year old but that he has passed from one stage of life to another and his old assumptions and values have changed.

An alternative perspective sees development as **continuous**, characterized less by major transformations than by steady and gradual change. From this point of view, what may look like a massive change, such as becoming literate between the ages of 5 and 8, or rebellious at 13, may actually reflect a slow and steady process of learning at school or increased reinforcement for independent behavior. Actually, many theorists suggest that development involves both stages and continuous processes (Fischer, 1992; Piaget, 1972). Stagelike phenomena are much more obvious in childhood, when the nervous system is maturing. As individuals move into adulthood, they are likely to develop in a number of alternative directions, and stages become especially difficult to discern across cultures.

Studying Development

Developmental psychologists primarily use three types of research designs: cross-sectional, longitudinal, and sequential. **Cross-sectional studies** compare groups of different-aged subjects at a single time to see whether differences exist among them. For example, a research group in Georgia is currently studying centenarians—people who have reached 100 years of age—to compare them on a number of dimensions with people in their 60s and 80s (Poon et al., 1992). Cross-sectional studies are useful for providing a snapshot of **age differences**, that is, variations among people of different ages.

The major limitation of cross-sectional studies is that they do not directly assess **age changes**, the ways *individuals change* over time. As a result, they are vulnerable to confounding variables such as cultural changes. For example, the centenarian researchers note that one of their groups of subjects grew up in the early years of Reconstruction in the South following the Civil War, another during World War I, and the third during the Great Depression and World War II. The groups' different historical experiences could profoundly influence observed differences between the three **cohorts** (that is, groups of people born around the same time). Cultural changes in education, mass communication, and nutrition could also have a profound impact on subjects' later ways of thinking and acting. Cross-sectional studies are most useful when **cohort effects**, differences among age groups associated with differences in the culture, are minimal, as when assessing differences in the self-concept between contemporary 4 and 6 year olds.

Longitudinal studies follow the same individuals over time and thus can directly assess age changes rather than age differences. The advantage of longitudinal over cross-sectional studies is that they reveal differences among individuals as well as changes within individuals over time. Like cross-sectional designs, however, longitudinal designs are vulnerable to cohort effects. Because they investigate only one cohort, they cannot rule out the possibility that people born at a different time might show different life trajectories. For example, the data from four longitudinal studies of gifted women at midlife showed that gifted women born after 1940 were higher on all measures of psychological well-being than gifted women born before that time (Schuster, 1990). The impact of giftedness on women's well-being appears to depend in part on cultural attitudes toward women's intelligence and on opportunities for achievement.

Sequential studies minimize cohort effects by studying multiple cohorts longitudinally. In an ideal sequential design, a group of people at one age is studied and followed up over time. As the study progresses, a new, younger cohort is added to the study, beginning at the same age at which the first cohort began. Essentially, a sequential design combines cross-sectional and longitudinal comparisons, allowing

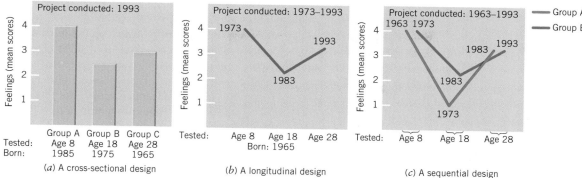

FIGURE 13.3

Cross-sectional, longitudinal, and sequential designs. The figure illustrates the way three designs might assess feelings toward parents at three ages. In these hypothetical studies, feelings are rated on a 1–5 scale, where 1 = "terrible" and 5 = "wonderful." Results from the cross-sectional study (a) suggest that between ages 8 and 18, feelings become more negative (from 4.0 to 2.5) and then improve again (to 3.0) at age 28. The longitudinal study (b) finds a slightly larger drop at age 18 (to 2.0). The sequential study suggests an interaction between age effects and cohort effects: Children begin with very positive attitudes toward their parents at age 8 and become relatively positive again by age 28. They also tend to become more negative in adolescence, but the extent to which they do so depends on their cohort. Eighteen year olds in 1973 grew up during the social upheaval of the 1960s and were thus more negative toward their parents than children who grew up in the next decade. (All data are hypothetical.)

researchers to distinguish between age effects (differences associated with age) and cohort effects.

Figure 13.3 illustrates the differences among the three designs in hypothetical studies of attitudes toward parents at ages 8, 18, and 28. The sequential design yields the most useful and precise information but takes 30 years to yield its returns. The moral of the story is that, ideally, psychologists should live a long time, find successors to carry on their research after they are dead, and do sequential studies—preferably in several cultures. Short of that, researchers should, and do, try to use the best methods at their disposal and to be aware that methodological limitations affect the generalizability of their results.

PHYSICAL DEVELOPMENT AND ITS PSYCHOLOGICAL CONSEQUENCES

Having examined some of the basic issues and methods of developmental psychology, we turn now to one particular area, physical development and its impact on psychological functioning. From an evolutionary perspective, the timing of physical changes has evolved as a series of adaptations that maximize survival and reproduction. Humans have much to learn before taking on the responsibilities of parenthood; not surprisingly, then, humans have longer childhoods than any other animal, and their physical capacity to reproduce occurs only in the second decade of life, after inculcation of cultural knowledge.

Many changes associated with physical development are obvious even to the untrained eye. Children develop rapidly during the early years, outgrowing clothes before wearing them out. Some of the most dramatic aspects of physical development, however, cannot be observed directly, for they take place before birth.

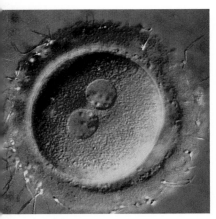

(a)

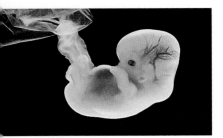

(b)

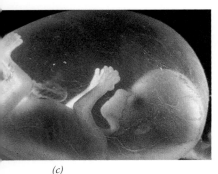

(c)

The rapidity of prenatal development is truly astonishing. The photo in (a) shows a fertilized egg surrounded by sperm. Photo (b) shows a six-week-old embryo. Only 8 weeks later (c), the fetus is recognizably human.

Prenatal Development

One of the most remarkable aspects of development is that a single cell, forged by the union of a sperm and an egg, contains the blueprint for an organism that will emerge—with billions of specialized cells—several months later. Substantial development occurs during the interim period of **gestation** (between conception and birth). This **prenatal** (before birth) period is divided into three stages. During the **germinal period** (approximately the first two weeks after conception), the fertilized egg becomes implanted in the uterus. The second stage, the **embryonic period** (from the beginning of the third week to about the eighth week of gestation), is the most important period in the development of the central nervous system and of the organs. By the end of this stage, the features of the embryo become recognizably human, the rudiments of most organs have formed, and the heart has begun to beat. During the third or **fetal period** (from about 9 weeks to birth), muscular development is rapid. By about 28 weeks, the fetus is capable of sustaining life on its own. (The term *fetus* is often used, more broadly, to refer to the organism between conception and birth.) Birth usually occurs at 38 weeks, or 9 months.

Environmental Influences on Prenatal Development

The stages of prenatal development provide perhaps the clearest example in humans of the process of maturation. They follow a timetable so closely that a doctor can tell when the child was conceived and predict within a matter of days when a fetus's heartbeat will be audible. At the same time, prenatal development provides a dramatic example of the influence of environment—and particularly hazardous environmental toxins—on the developing psyche. The embryonic stage is the period of greatest vulnerability to **teratogens**, harmful environmental agents such as drugs, radiation, and viruses that cause maternal illness such as rubella (German measles) (Figure 13.4).

Some of the most widespread environmental contaminants that affect development through prenatal exposure are polychlorinated biphenyls (PCBs), chemical compounds once used in many industrial products, such as carbonless copy paper, various electrical components, and hydraulic fluids (Jacobson et al., 1992). PCBs were banned in the United States in the 1970s, but by then they had contaminated a number of bodies of water, most notably Lake Michigan, where they entered the food chain through fish. Residues persist in the air, water, and soil and can be found in the body tissue of most people living in industrialized countries (Jacobson et al., 1990). Children whose mothers ate fish from Lake Michigan have shown cognitive deficits from birth through age 4, with longitudinal research on later effects still pending (Jacobson et al., 1990, 1992). Postnatal exposure through breastmilk had no effect on cognitive functioning, suggesting that the chemicals affected the nervous system during a critical period of prenatal development.

Another widespread teratogen is alcohol. In the 1970s researchers identified **fetal alcohol syndrome**, a serious condition affecting up to half of the babies born to alcoholic mothers (Jones et al., 1973). Fetal alcohol syndrome babies are born with numerous physical defects: deformed limbs, faces, ears, and genitals. They also show a wide range of mental abnormalities, including learning disabilities, behavior problems, and attention difficulties (Larsson et al., 1985; Rosett, 1980; Steinhausen et al., 1993; Streissguth et al., 1985, 1989). Precisely when the damage occurs to the fetus is unclear, but the syndrome has been observed in the offspring of mothers who had occasional binges as well as mothers who chronically abused the drug.

Whether *any* amount of maternal alcohol ingestion is dangerous, or whether the hazard only arises from crossing some threshold of consumption, is a matter of controversy (see Knupfer, 1991). Research suggests, however, that women who are try-

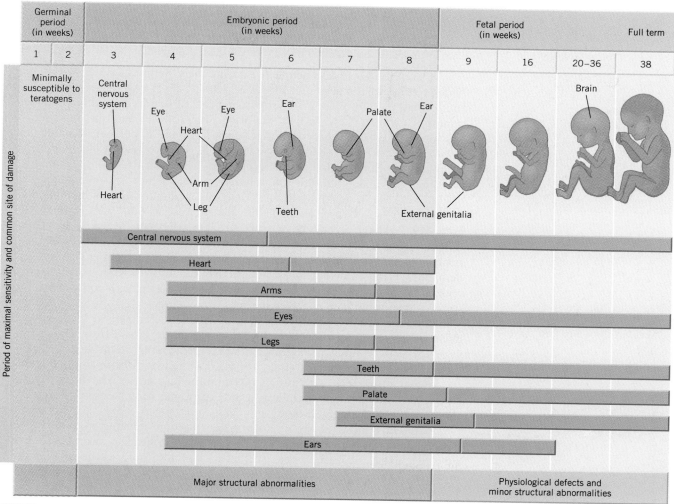

FIGURE 13.4
Sensitivity to teratogens during prenatal development. The figure shows the periods during which different systems and body parts develop and the impact of teratogens at different stages. The mauve lines show maximal periods of vulnerability for different systems, and the green lines show continued vulnerable periods. The embryonic stage is the period of greatest vulnerability to environmental insult.
SOURCE: *Adapted from Moore, 1993.*

ing to get pregnant should probably minimize their alcohol consumption, because the teratogenic effect appears to be maximal in the early weeks of pregnancy (before the woman knows she is pregnant), and it increases with greater consumption (Barr et al., 1990).

Another increasingly prevalent teratogen is crack cocaine. Prenatal cocaine exposure carries risk of premature birth, malformed internal organs, withdrawal symptoms, respiratory problems, delayed motor development, and death (Bingol et al., 1987; Chasnoff, 1988; Griffith et al., 1994; Lester et al., 1991; MacGregor et al., 1987; Oro & Dixon, 1987; Smith, 1988). "Crack babies" tend to be triply exposed: to cocaine prenatally (the teratogenic effect of the drug), to neglectful parenting postnatally, and to poverty and environmental hazards throughout childhood.

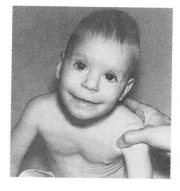

A child born with fetal alcohol syndrome. Facial and other physical abnormalities often occur alongside intellectual deficits.

FROM MIND TO BRAIN

THE DEVELOPMENT OF THE NERVOUS SYSTEM

Most of the nerve cells people use during their lifetimes develop within the first seven months of gestation (Rallison, 1986). What this means is that neuron formation takes place at the staggering rate of hundreds of thousands per minute (Cowan, 1979). In fact, the brain overproduces neurons by as much as a factor of two and then trims them back by about 50 percent, weeding out those that are not used (Kolb, 1989). Thus, the environment is like a building contractor working with a genetic blueprint: The contractor follows the general plan but makes modifications based on experience and availability of materials. The physical brain itself is therefore a collaboration of heredity and environment (see Myhrer et al., 1992; Rosenzweig, 1966, 1984; Rosenzweig et al., 1972; Shapiro & Vukovich, 1970). The process of weeding and trimming continues through adolescence (Barnes, 1990; Siegler, 1989) and contributes to the flexibility, or **plasticity**, of the brain in meeting environmental demands. From an evolutionary perspective, the brain is wired to adapt to a wide array of environmental circumstances and is prepared to compensate for some degree of damage or faulty wiring.

Although the formation of neurons is virtually complete at birth, neural development continues for several years. The brain grows from about 350 grams at birth to about 1250 grams at 4 years, which represents nearly 80 percent of its adult size (Spreen et al., 1984). The increase in size is due primarily to two processes: continuing myelination (growth of the fatty myelin sheath that surrounds neural axons) and sprouting of new synaptic connections between existing neurons.

Different regions of the nervous system become myelinated at different periods of development. Some neurons involved in hearing and balance are fully myelinated at birth, whereas others, especially those in the association areas that govern higher cortical functions like abstract thinking, may not become myelinated for months or years (Benes, 1989; Björklund & Harnishfeger, 1990). Some myelination even continues in adulthood (Benes et al., 1994; Cotman, 1990).

Another important aspect of neural development after birth involves the formation of new dendrites (the branchlike projections that reach from the cell body to the terminal buttons of another neuron to form synapses) and dendritic connections between neurons. The ability to create new dendritic connections appears to underlie the brain's ability to compensate in the face of injury in adulthood (Bondareff, 1985; Cotman, 1990; Kolb & Gibb, 1991; O'Leary et al., 1994).

Infancy

At birth, an infant possesses many adaptive reflexes. For example, the **rooting reflex** helps ensure that the infant will get nourishment; when touched on the cheek, an infant will turn her head and open her mouth, ready to suck. The **sucking reflex** is similarly adaptive; infants suck rhythmically in response to stimulation 3 or 4 centimeters inside their mouths. Many early reflexes disappear within the first six or seven months, as infants gain more control over their movements. In general, motor skills progress from head to toe. Infants master movements of the head, then those of the trunk and arms, and finally those of the legs (Rallison, 1986).

Motor development in infancy follows a universal maturational sequence, from smiling, turning the head, and rolling over, to creeping, walking with support, and

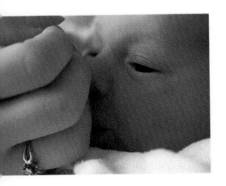

A newborn infant reflexively sucks on its mother's finger.

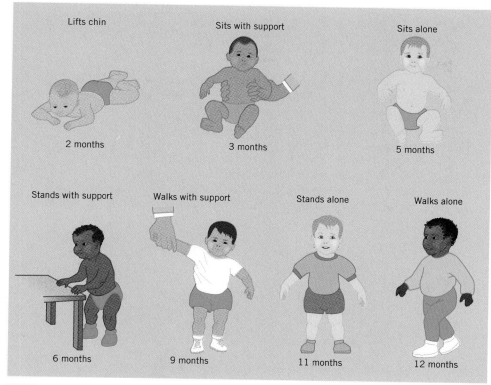

FIGURE 13.5
Milestones in infant motor development. The maturational sequence of motor development is universal, although the age at which skills are acquired varies. This figure shows average ages at which children reach these milestones. SOURCE: *Adapted from Frankenburg & Dodds, 1967.*

ultimately standing alone and walking unaided (Figure 13.5). Nevertheless, cross-cultural evidence suggests that environmental stimulation can affect the *pace* of development. The Kipsigis of Kenya teach their infants to sit, stand, and walk at an early age. At 5 or 6 months, infants are placed in a specially constructed hole in the ground that supports them while they sit upright, and at 7 or 8 months, their mothers hold them either under the arms or by the hands to give them walking practice. As a result, Kipsigi infants walk at a considerably earlier age than North American infants (Super, 1981). This does not mean, however, that infants under the right conditions could be crawling off the delivery table. As will be seen throughout the chapter, environmental inputs can hasten or delay the maturation of the brain and behavior, but only within limits.

Childhood and Adolescence

Growth rates for girls and boys are roughly equal until about age 10. At that point, girls begin a growth spurt that usually peaks at age 12, and boys typically follow suit about two or three years later. As Figure 13.6 illustrates, girls and boys usually grow very little after the ages of 16 and 18, respectively, although in some cases, growth may actually continue for a decade (Garn, 1980).

Individuals vary in the age at which they enter **puberty**, the stage during which they become capable of reproduction. Girls usually experience the onset of menstruation (known as menarche) at about age 11 to 13, preceded by the growth of breasts and the appearance of pubic hair (Frisch et al., 1980). For boys, enlargement of the genitals begins at about 11 to 13-1/2 years, with the first ejaculations of live sperm occurring somewhat later at about 14-1/2 years (Rallison, 1986). The onset of menarche or ejaculation often precedes the presence of eggs or live sperm

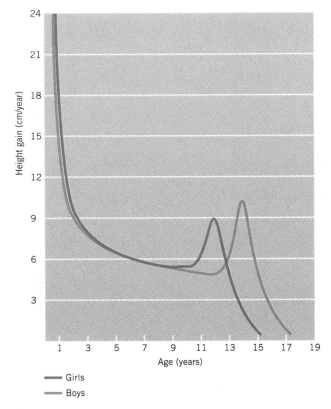

FIGURE 13.6
The adolescent growth spurt. Growth rates in height for girls and boys fol-
low a similar course until about age 10. At that point, girls begin a growth
spurt that usually peaks at about age 12. Boys typically follow suit about
two or three years later. SOURCE: *Adapted from Tanner et al., 1966.*

by a few months (Tanner, 1978). Girls under 15 still have immature reproductive systems, putting their infants at risk for prematurity and low birth weight (Garn, 1980). Most teenagers rank the onset of puberty very high among important life events (Eme et al., 1979). Adolescents tend to be acutely concerned with their physical appearance and are more dissatisfied with their bodies during puberty than in later adolescence (Wright, 1989).

The effects of unusually early or late maturation tend to be different for boys and girls (Gross & Duke, 1980; Jones & Mussen, 1958; Simmons & Blythe, 1987). Boys whose growth spurt comes early are more likely to excel at athletics, be more popular, and appear more poised and relaxed than late-maturing boys. For girls, early onset of puberty tends to be more stressful than later maturation. A study from New Zealand found that girls with early menarche were more likely to be delinquent than their on-time or late-maturing peers, but only if they attended mixed-sex schools (Caspi et al., 1993). Parents report more conflict with early-maturing than late-maturing daughters but *less* conflict with early-maturing than late-maturing sons (see Savin-Williams & Small, 1986; Steinberg, 1988). Presumably, this gender difference in parent-child conflict reflects, in part, a different level of parental concern about their teenagers' sexuality.

Adulthood and Aging

By the end of adolescence, physical growth is virtually complete, and the physical changes that occur thereafter tend to be gradual and less dramatic. People often gain a few centimeters in height and several more centimeters in fat between ages 18 and 28 (Garn, 1980), and many more centimeters in fat with middle age. Indeed, someone once described middle age as the period during which a person's broad mind and narrow waist trade places—although, as we shall see, maturity may broaden the mind as well.

With aging comes a gradual decline in physical abilities (see Spence, 1989; Spirduso & MacRae, 1990). Muscular strength, sensory acuity, and reaction time all peak by the 20s or early 30s. Lung capacity and cardiac output also begin to decline in the 30s, although many people do not feel a change until their 40s, 50s, or 60s, when the rate of decline accelerates. Individuals differ tremendously in the extent and pace of these changes, ranging from the frail elderly person in a nursing home who cannot dress herself or walk without assistance, to the 80 year old who lives independently and runs marathons in seniors' track meets (Spirduso & MacRae, 1990). Whether the variable is muscle strength, intellectual ability, or sexual functioning, the rule of thumb is *use it or lose it*: Mental and physical capacities atrophy with disuse.

A profile of middle age?

Menopause

For women, the most dramatic physical change of middle adulthood is **menopause**, the cessation of the menstrual cycle. Menopause usually occurs in the 40s or 50s; in Western cultures the average age is 51 (Riley, 1991). With most women now living into their 70s or 80s, the postmenopausal period encompasses roughly a third of their lives. Until recently, menopause was considered traumatic for women because of the psychological loss of the capacity for childbearing (Deutsch, 1945) and symptoms such as "hot flashes," joint aches, and irritability. However, research over the last three decades suggests that most women neither expect nor experience menopause to be traumatic (Matthews, 1992). Many women enjoy the increased freedom of no longer having monthly periods and not having to worry about birth control. Moreover, most of the uncomfortable symptoms of menopause can be alleviated medically with hormone replacement therapy, which compensates for the ovaries' reduced estrogen production (Buchsbaum, 1983; Sherwin, 1993).

Sexuality does not end following menopause (Frock & Money, 1992), although it does change. Decreased vaginal lubrication, for example, can indirectly affect sexual desire and interest because women may gauge their own arousal from the amount of lubrication and mistakenly conclude they are not aroused. The evidence on whether a woman's sexual interest declines during menopause is conflicting, but several studies across cultures ranging from the United States to Nigeria have documented decreases in both interest and sensory sensitivity (Hallstrom, 1973; Riley, 1991).

A GLOBAL VISTA

MENOPAUSE IN A MAYAN VILLAGE

Because menopause is both a physiological and a psychological event, its impact on a woman reflects an interaction of biological processes and personal expectations. Women who expect menopause to be very distressing tend to have more symptoms (Matthews, 1992). Many of these expectations depend on culture. In our own culture, which values youth and beauty, menopause tends to be viewed as a negative event, a milestone along the path to aging, diminished sexuality, and ultimately death.

Cultures with different beliefs and values about aging, menstruation, and the role of older women view the psychological experience of menopause differently. Many societies consider menstruation unclean and contaminating and hence impose strict taboos and sanctions on menstruating women

Mayan women have a very different experience of menopause than many of their North American neighbors.

(Douglas, 1966). Consequently, cessation of menstruation means greater freedom for women in these cultures. In fact, in some Islamic and African cultures with strict taboos on menstruating women, women do not appear to manifest many of the physical and psychological symptoms associated with menopause in our society (Beyenne, 1986).

One researcher studied one hundred pre-, peri- (that is, during), and postmenopausal women in a rural Mayan Indian village in Yucatan, Mexico (Beyenne, 1986). In addition to interviewing the women themselves, the investigator interviewed local physicians, midwives, and traditional healers to explore more fully the psychological and cultural aspects of menopause. Mayan women marry and begin having children in their teens. They are frequently grandmothers in their 30s, and the onset of menopause is typically in the thirties or early forties. As in many traditional societies, old age is a period of power and respect, particularly for women, who become the head of the extended family households of their married sons.

The Mayans believe that menstruating women carry danger. Women therefore stay home during their menstrual periods to avoid contaminating other people, particularly newborn babies. Not surprisingly, Mayan women report being pleased to gain freedom from restrictions and taboos that comes with the cessation of menstruation. Premenopausal women reported looking forward to menopause and did not expect any adverse physical or psychological effects. Peri- and postmenopausal women, like others in the community, were unfamiliar with the concept of hot flashes and denied ever experiencing anything of the sort. This was corroborated by medical personnel, who had never treated any of the women of the village for menopause-related symptoms.

The absence of the most cross-culturally universal physical symptom of menopause, hot flashes, may be related to diet or to physiological processes, such as bearing a large number of babies and early onset of menopause. Nevertheless, the dramatically different experience of menopause among the Mayans underscores the role of culture in shaping what, to us, may have seemed a universal stage driven by biological maturation.

Midlife Changes in Men

The term *male menopause* is part of the American vernacular, although male reproductive ability does not undergo any dramatic, circumscribed period of physical change. Healthy men can produce sperm and engage in sexual activity as long as they live, although male sexuality does change gradually with age. One study found strong negative correlations between age and a number of sexual variables in a sample of healthy married men aged 45 to 74. For example, age correlated -.61 with frequency of sexual thoughts and -.49 with number of orgasms per month. These results suggest that, at least in terms of quantity, sexual functioning in males declines substantially from midlife to later life, although individuals differ considerably in the extent to which they experience such declines (Schiavi et al., 1990). Decreasing sexual interest in men appears in part to reflect lower levels of testosterone in the bloodstream (Chapter 10). The ability to sense touch and vibration in the penis also diminishes with age and is correlated with decline in sexual activity. Research with rats suggests that diminished sensitivity of the tactile receptors in the penis may cause diminished penile sensitivity (Johnson & Murray, 1992).

Later Life

Beyond the middle years, among the more obvious changes associated with advanced aging in men and women are declines in sensory-perceptual functioning. Older adults have a reduced sensitivity to contrasts, as when climbing stairs (see Scialfa et al., 1992), and their ability to see at night declines (Fozard, 1990). They take longer to adapt to the dark, which can cause problems driving at night, as oncoming headlights may create temporary flashes of brightness (AARP News Bulletin, 1989; Perlmutter, 1983). Hearing loss is also common; many older people experience **presbycusis,** the inability to hear high-frequency sounds (Fozard, 1990; Spence, 1989). Presbycusis can make hearing the telephone ring or understanding high-pitched voices more difficult. In addition, some consonant sounds (such as *f, s,* and *z*) are harder to distinguish, which can make speech slightly less intelligible (Perlmutter, 1983; Spence, 1989).

The inability to understand what others are saying can have disturbing psychological consequences. People often lose patience with older people who constantly ask them to repeat what they have said. Younger people may also inadvertently treat older individuals with hearing loss condescendingly, simplifying their communications instead of speaking more loudly or distinctly. Declines in hearing may even foster paranoia among the impaired because seeing people talk without being able to hear what they are saying can be misunderstood as whispering or keeping secrets (Zimbardo et al., 1981).

Aging inevitably brings with it deterioration in certain areas of functioning, but development throughout the lifespan is characterized by gains as well as losses. Many Western images of the elderly stem from negative cultural myths and stereotypes, such as the idea that sexuality ends in the 40s or 50s or that senility is inevitable. **Gerontologists,** scientists who study the elderly, refer to such images as examples of **ageism,** or prejudice against old people (Butler, 1969; Schaie, 1988; Whitbourne & Hulicka, 1990). Ageism can lead not only to condescending treatment of the elderly ("How are *we* today, Mrs. Jones?") but also to discrimination in employment and access to medical care.

Experimental evidence suggests that people in the West process information about the aged in a negatively biased way automatically, without conscious awareness (Perdue & Gurtman, 1990). Using a priming procedure (Chapter 6), investigators in one study presented subjects (college students) with 18 positive adjectives (such as skillful and helpful) and 18 negative adjectives (such as clumsy and impolite) on a computer screen. Immediately prior to presenting each adjective, the computer screen randomly flashed the word *old* or *young* briefly enough to register but too briefly to be recognized consciously. The investigators measured subjects' reaction time (in milliseconds) in identifying whether each word was positive or negative.

If subjects differentially associated old and young with positive and negative traits, then flashing "young" should have facilitated responding about positive words, while "old" should have reduced reaction time in identifying negative words. In fact, subjects were slightly quicker to identify negative traits when presented with

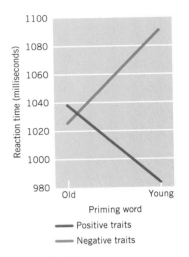

FIGURE 13.7
Automatic elicitation of ageism in cognitive processing. The figure shows mean reaction times to recognize positive and negative traits as a function of priming. Priming subjects with "old" led to slightly decreased reaction time in identifying negative words. In contrast, priming with "young" markedly facilitated identification of positive traits in comparison to negative ones. SOURCE: *Perdue & Gurtman, 1990, p. 21.*

"old," and substantially faster in identifying positive traits when presented with "young" (Figure 13.7). Apparently, people (or at least college students) are prejudiced in favor of the young without a moment's thought.

In another study, six groups of subjects (old and young Chinese, North American deaf, and North Americans with intact hearing) completed various memory tasks (Levy & Langer, 1994). The investigators hypothesized that Chinese and North American deaf subjects, whose cultures have fewer negative stereotypes about the elderly than the North American hearing culture, would perform better in old age than nondeaf North Americans. The results supported the hypothesis. The three young groups did not differ, but among the old groups, the Chinese performed the best, followed by deaf and then by hearing North Americans. In fact, older Chinese subjects performed similarly to young Chinese subjects. If older people become physically, cognitively, or sexually inactive, the causes may lie in cultural beliefs that amplify biological declines.

COGNITIVE DEVELOPMENT IN INFANCY, CHILDHOOD, AND ADOLESCENCE

In a study performed in the 1960s, 3- and 6-year-old children were allowed to pet an unusually docile cat named Maynard (DeVries, 1969). When asked what kind of animal Maynard was, each child responded correctly that he was a cat. In plain sight of the children, the researcher then put a dog mask on Maynard and again asked whether Maynard was a dog or a cat. The 6 year olds knew that Maynard was still a cat, but the 3 year olds were not so sure; most of them said that Maynard was now a dog! How do children learn that physical entities—such as their pets or their parents—remain constant over time? How do they learn to distinguish objects that do rapidly change their form, such as clouds, from those that do not? These are the kinds of questions explored by psychologists who study cognitive development. We begin by describing perceptual and cognitive development in infancy and then examine three approaches to cognitive development through adolescence: Piagetian, information-processing, and integrative.

Perceptual and Cognitive Development in Infancy

For many years, psychologists underestimated the cognitive capacities of infants (Bower, 1982). William James wrote in 1890 that infants are born into a "blooming, buzzing confusion" of sights and sounds. A few decades later, behaviorist John Watson (1925) described the infant as "a lively, squirming bit of flesh, capable of making a few simple responses." These were logical assumptions. With neither motor control nor the ability to describe what they are thinking, newborn infants do not appear to be a particularly impressive lot. In addition, infants have notoriously short attention spans, falling asleep so frequently that a researcher must schedule two hours of laboratory time for every five minutes of useful experimental time (Butterworth, 1978).

New Methods, New Discoveries

A very different picture of infancy has emerged, however, as the methods to study it have become more sophisticated. Three decades ago, psychologists discovered that they could learn about infant perception and cognition by taking advantage of the **orienting reflex**, the tendency of humans, even from birth, to pay more attention to novel stimuli than to stimuli to which they have become habituated, or grown accustomed (Fantz, 1966; Fantz et al., 1975). Thus, even though a picture of a face might hold an infant's attention at first, after repeated exposures the infant will no longer show interest in it. What makes this finding useful to researchers is that they can tell when an infant is discriminating between two stimuli, such as the face of its mother and the face of another woman of the same age. If the infant is presented with a photograph of its mother's face, it will gradually habituate to it. Suppose now that the photograph is switched to the other woman's face. If the infant shows renewed interest in the photograph, then the experimenter can tell that the infant knows the difference.

The orienting reflex allows psychologists to study infant perception and cognition because it produces behavioral and physiological responses that can be measured in the laboratory. Researchers can measure a primary behavioral response, the amount of time an infant looks at each of several visual stimuli (called fixation time), by using special equipment to observe the reflection in the infant's cornea. Another behavioral response frequently measured is sucking. Infants prefer novelty, and they can be operantly conditioned to suck in response to novel stimuli. An infant's sucking rate thus tends to decrease as it habituates to a stimulus and increase with the presentation of a new stimulus. Physiological responses that can be measured include heart rate and brain wave patterns.

Measuring behavioral and physiological responses associated with the orienting reflex has enabled researchers to answer some very subtle questions about cognition, such as whether infants can form abstractions of concepts such as "ball": Will they habituate to a red ball they have never seen if they have previously habituated to a blue ball and a green ball? In general, studies of infant cognitive development have asked two questions: What are infants capable of sensing, and to what extent do infants perceive meaning in the stimuli they sense (Flavell, 1985)?

What Are Infants Capable of Sensing?

Infants are born with many sensory capabilities, some of which are better developed than others. The sense of hearing is in working order quite early. Even before birth, fetal heart rate and movements increase in response to loud sounds. By a few days after birth, infants can hear soft tones, especially in the frequency range of the human voice (1000 to 3000 Hz). They also show greater response to complex sounds that contain a range of frequencies (again, like the human voice) than to pure tones with a single frequency. As early as three days after birth, infants can discriminate the sound of their mother's voice from that of another woman (De Caspar & Fifer, 1982; Mills & Melhuish, 1974; Spence & DeCasper, 1987). Such discrimination may reflect prenatal experience. Since myelination of the neurons involved in hearing is complete before birth, the mother's voice is audible to the fetus.

Vision is not as well developed at birth as hearing; the visual cortex, retina, and some other structures are still immature. At birth, visual acuity is estimated to be approximately 20/500 (that is, an object 20 feet away looks as clear as an object 500 feet away would look to an adult), but it improves to about 20/100 by six months (Banks & Salapatek, 1983; Dobson & Teller, 1978). Infants focus best on objects between 7 and 8 inches away—approximately the distance between a nursing infant and its mother's face. As early as one week after birth, infants can discriminate colors, although their color perception is very limited (Adams, 1989, 1994).

The attention infants pay to various objects in their environment is not arbitrary. They pay particular attention to human faces and to objects with qualities similar to faces, which move, are complex, are of similar color, and produce sounds (Siegler, 1991). This tendency is innate and likely evolved because of the important emotional information carried by the face. Infants prefer progressively more complex visual stimuli as they develop, which reflects and stimulates their growing cognitive capacities (Banks & Salapatek, 1983). Whereas 3 week olds prefer to look at simple checkerboards with only four squares, 14 week olds prefer 8-by-8 boards (Brennan et al., 1966).

Intermodal Understanding

Processing of visual, auditory, and other forms of sensory information occurs in anatomically discrete neural modules (Chapter 4). To what extent can infants integrate information across these different neural systems? When they see their mothers talking, do they connect the sound with the visual image, or is the world like a dubbed movie, with lips moving and people talking out of sync? And do infants *learn* to make connections across different modes or between what they observe and what they do, or are these capacities innate?

Intermodal (also called cross-modal) **processing** allows infants to associate sensations of an object from different senses or to match their own actions to behaviors they have observed visually. Psychologists have known for some time that infants show *some* recognition of the relation between sights and sounds even minutes after birth, turning their eyes toward the direction of a sound (Bower, 1982; Wertheimer, 1961). By 10 to 16 weeks, they attend more to an experimenter if the sound of her speech is in synchrony with her lip movements than if it is not (Dodd, 1979; Kuhl & Meltzoff, 1988). By 18 weeks, they follow a conversation by shifting visual attention between two adults as they speak to one another (Horner & Chethik, 1986). Research also suggests an innate coordination between vision and reaching (von Hofsten, 1982).

Over the last 20 years, however, Andrew Meltzoff and his colleagues have demonstrated that infants are capable of much more intermodal integration than anyone had expected. In an initial study, Meltzoff and Moore (1977) found that newborns between 12 and 21 days old were able to imitate the facial gestures of an adult. Infants who observed an adult sticking out his tongue were more likely to stick out their own tongues, while those who observed other facial movements, such as opening the mouth, were more likely to perform those behaviors (Figure 13.8). Although this may not seem to be a remarkable achievement to an adult, how does an infant—who has no idea what a tongue is—recognize that she can move her own as an adult model does? Such capacities appear to be innate, having been demonstrated in children as young as 42 *minutes* old.

FIGURE 13.8
Imitation in infants. These photographs, published in 1977, show 2- to 3-week-old infants imitating the facial gestures of an adult. Infants are capable of considerably more intermodal integration than early researchers suspected.

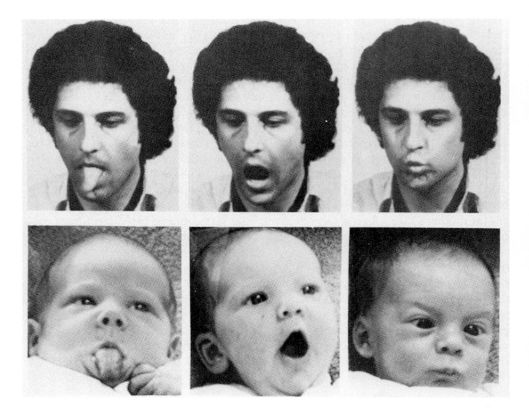

Subsequent research documents that infants can also match information across visual and tactile modes; that is, they know something by sight when they have explored it by touch (Meltzoff, 1990; see also Meltzoff & Moore, 1994). Getting young infants to explore an object with their hands is no easy trick because they tend to grasp it rigidly. The researchers therefore designed an experiment in which infants could explore an object with their mouths. One-month-old infants sucked on one of two pacifiers, exploring them with their lips and tongues (Figure 13.9). One of the pacifiers was a sphere and the other a sphere-with-nubs. To test whether infants could recognize these shapes visually, they were simultaneously presented with similar objects constructed out of orange styrofoam. The investigators reasoned that if the infants visually recognized the shape they had been sucking, they would fixate on the two visual stimuli for different lengths of time. In fact, of 32 infants tested, 24 stared longer at the shape they had sucked, demonstrating that they knew with their eyes what they had felt with their mouths. Later research also found that 4-month-old infants can actually imitate different vowel sounds by listening to an adult produce them (Meltzoff, 1990).

The findings of these studies are not intuitively obvious. How can infants make connections between senses they have barely used? And how can an infant 42 minutes old know how to make a facial gesture she has just observed for the first time? We come, once again, to what philosophers call the doctrine of innate ideas: Like the linguist Noam Chomsky and many philosophers before him, Meltzoff suggests that humans are born with some types of knowledge, in this case, about the equivalence of certain forms of stimulation. How such a cross-modal connection could be wired neurologically remains a mystery.

Do Infants Perceive Meaning in Their Environment?

The research described thus far suggests that infants perceive more than psychologists, and probably most laypeople, ever imagined. But do they recognize the meaning of the objects they perceive? According to ecological theorists, they do. Psychologists who take an **ecological approach** to the development of perception attempt to understand perception in its environmental, adaptive context (Gibson, 1984; Gibson & Gibson, 1966, 1969). They are therefore interested in infants' and children's understanding of the personal implications (called **affordances**) of objects or events; a nipple affords the pleasant sensation of a full stomach, while the receding figure of a parent means the infant is being left alone. Ecological theorists argue that the nervous system is wired to recognize certain dangers and to perceive the potential utility of some stimuli without prior learning, as in the visual cliff (Chapter 4).

Ecological researchers have used looming object studies (Gibson, 1969) to demonstrate that infants can attach meaning to their perceptions (Figure 13.10). As an alert infant sits in a seat, an object suddenly begins moving directly toward the

FIGURE 13.9
Stimuli used for tactile exploration. One-month-old infants sucked on one of two pacifiers like those depicted above. Later, they explored similar objects with their eyes. Most stared longer at the shape they had sucked, demonstrating that they knew with their eyes what they had felt with their mouths. SOURCE: *From Meltzoff, A. N., & Borton, R. W. (1979). Intermodal matching by human neonates.* Nature, 282, 403-404.

FIGURE 13.10
The looming object. Infants show distress and defensive responses to looming objects as early as 2 weeks of age. Since they would not yet have had the opportunity to associate a looming object with being hit, many psychologists consider their response evidence of innate knowledge. SOURCE: *Adapted from Bower, 1971.*

infant at a constant rate. The object may be real, such as the box shown in the figure, or it may be an expanding shadow. As early as two weeks after birth, infants show a defensive response to the looming object, drawing their heads back, jerking their hands in front of their faces, and showing distress (Bower, 1971). Since most 2-week-old infants have not yet had the opportunity to learn to associate looming objects with being hit, their response would seem to be another form of innate knowledge.

Piaget's Theory of Cognitive Development

Cognitive development begins in infancy, but it proceeds at a rapid pace through adolescence. The first theorist to trace cognitive development systematically was the Swiss psychologist Jean Piaget (1896–1980). The philosopher of science Thomas Kuhn (1970) suggests that major innovations often come from outsiders to a field who have not yet been indoctrinated into the discipline, and this was the case with Piaget. Piaget began his career as a biologist, publishing his first paper at the age of 11. He was offered the curatorship of a Geneva museum's mollusk collection while still in high school (the offer was rescinded when the museum realized he was a child) and received his doctorate in biology at the age of 21. How, then, did a biologist become a world-famous psychologist by age 30?

Piaget also had a keen interest in epistemology, the branch of philosophy concerned with the nature of knowledge. The empiricist philosophers, such as John Locke, argued that all knowledge comes from experience. To know what a dog is like, a person has to examine a number of dogs, experience them with the senses, and come to some conclusions about their common properties. In contrast, the German philosopher Immanuel Kant argued that some forms of knowledge do *not* come from observation. People impose certain categories of thought—such as space, time, and causality—on the data of their senses, but these categories are not derived from experience. Similarly, the rules of logic and mathematics seem to work in the world, yet they are not mere summaries of sensory information: No one has ever seen the square root of 2 or pi, but these concepts have real-world applications, as any engineer or architect can attest. Kant argued that the human propensity for mathematical thinking, like the tendency to use certain categories of thought, is innate.

Kant's ideas were the starting point for Piaget's life's work. His hunch was that Kant was both right and wrong: Kant was right that people's understanding of time, space, and logic is not simply derived from experience but wrong that people are born with this knowledge. Piaget therefore decided to look into the way children develop an understanding of these categories of thought—a "temporary" intellectual foray that occupied the next 60 years of his life.

Piaget began his study in Paris, working in Alfred Binet's intelligence-testing laboratory. There he noticed that children of the same age tended to make the same types of mistakes. They not only gave the same kinds of wrong answers, but when questioned about their reasoning, they provided similar explanations. This suggested to Piaget that children of different ages think in qualitatively different ways and that understanding these differences might hold the key to understanding the origins of knowledge. This led him to a stage theory of cognitive development.

Piaget (1970) proposed that children develop knowledge by inventing or *constructing* reality out of their own experience, mixing what they observe with their own ideas about how the world works. Thus, the preschooler who sees a dog's mask placed on Maynard the cat applies her own rules of logic—"When things look different, they are different"—to conclude that Maynard is a dog. Similarly, a toddler who notices that a shadow is attached to his feet no matter where he is on a sunny playground may use his own logic to conclude that the shadow is following him.

Assimilation and Accommodation

Piaget viewed intelligence as the individual's way of adapting to new information about the world and argued that children cognitively adapt to their environment through two interrelated processes, called assimilation and accommodation (Piaget & Inhelder, 1969). **Assimilation** means interpreting actions or events in terms of one's present schemas—that is, fitting reality into one's existing structures of knowledge. A schema, for Piaget, is an organized, repeatedly exercised pattern of thought or behavior (Flavell, 1985). An example of a behavioral schema is an infant's propensity to suck anything that will fit into its mouth—a nipple, a finger, or a pacifier. All of these objects can be assimilated—taken in without modifying the existing schema or pattern—by sucking, just as a person with a cognitive schema about "police" can drive into a crowded intersection and immediately understand the role of the person directing traffic.

If humans only assimilated information into existing schemas, no cognitive development would take place. The second adaptational process, **accommodation**, is the modification of schemas to fit reality. At the behavioral level, accommodation takes place when an infant with a sucking schema is presented with a cup: She must modify her existing schema to drink from this new device. At the thought level, accommodation is likely to occur if the reader looks carefully at the spelling of *accommodation*—it has two *c*'s and two *m*'s, which is highly unusual. The word "accommodation" requires revision of the implicit schema most people hold that would lead them to double only one consonant or the other.

For Piaget, the driving force behind cognitive development is **equilibration**, which means balancing assimilation and accommodation to adapt to the world. When a child comes across something she does not understand, she finds herself in a state of cognitive disequilibrium, or lack of adjustment, which motivates her to try to make sense of what she has encountered. She may attempt to fit it into existing schemas (assimilation), or she may combine schemas or construct a new schema to fit the new reality (accommodation). This process of disequilibrium and readjustment is what Piaget means by equilibration, and it occurs throughout the lifespan.

Stages of Cognitive Development

According to Piaget, people assimilate and accommodate when confronted with new information throughout their lives, but at each stage of development children use a distinct underlying logic, or **structure of thought**, to guide their thinking. The same four stages—sensorimotor, preoperational, concrete operational, and formal operational—occur in the same sequence for everyone, although the ages may vary somewhat (Table 13.1).

Sensorimotor Stage The concept of an operation is basic to Piaget's notion of the development of knowledge, for to know an object is to operate or act on it. **Operations** are internalized, or mental, actions that the individual can use to manipulate, transform, and return an object of knowledge to its original state (Piaget, 1972). Alphabetizing a list of names is an operation, as is imagining what one could have said to someone who behaved rudely.

According to Piaget, such mental operations are beyond the capability of very young, preverbal children, who are in the **sensorimotor stage**. The sensorimotor stage lasts from birth to about 2 years of age, when toddlers become more thoroughly verbal. Sensorimotor thought primarily takes the form of action, as infants learn about the world by mouthing, grasping, watching, and manipulating objects. According to Piaget, the practical knowledge infants develop during this period forms the basis for their later ability to represent things mentally. He calls this period "sensorimotor" to emphasize that infants are bound by their sensations and actions and are capable of very little reasoning beyond what they are sensing and doing.

During the sensorimotor stage, children learn through doing.

TABLE 13.1 PIAGET'S STAGES OF COGNITIVE DEVELOPMENT

STAGE	APPROXIMATE AGES	CHARACTERISTICS
Sensorimotor	0–2	Thought and action are virtually identical, as the infant explores the world with its senses and behaviors; object permanence develops; the child is completely egocentric.
Preoperational	2–7	Symbolic thought develops; object permanence is firmly established; the child cannot coordinate different physical attributes of an object or different perspectives.
Concrete operational	7–12	The child is able to perform reversible mental operations on representations of objects; understanding of conservation develops; the child can apply logic to concrete situations.
Formal operational	12 +	The adolescent (or adult) can apply logic more abstractly; hypothetical thinking develops.

A major achievement of the sensorimotor stage is the development of **object permanence**, the recognition that objects exist in time and space independent of one's actions on, or observation of them. According to Piaget, before the age of about 8 to 12 months, an object such as a ball exists for an infant only when it is in sight. If it is hidden from view, it no longer exists, as illustrated by Piaget's description of his own son, Laurent:

> At age 7 months, 28 days, I offer him a little bell behind a cushion. So long as he sees the little bell, however small it may be, he tries to grasp it. But if the little bell disappears completely, he stops all searching.... I then resume the experiment, using my hand as a screen. Laurent's arm is outstretched and about to grasp the little bell at the moment I make it disappear behind my hand.... He immediately withdraws his arm, as though the little bell no longer existed. I then shake my hand.... Laurent watches attentively, greatly surprised to rediscover the sound of the little bell, but he does not try to grasp it. I turn my hand over and he sees the little bell: he then stretches his hand toward it. (Piaget, 1954, p. 39)

A few months later, when Laurent has acquired object permanence, he will look for the bell even when it is hidden from view and will be delighted to find it. Once infants recognize the permanence of objects in this way, they have a seemingly endless fascination for games such as peek-a-boo, which affirm their newfound understanding. Subsequent research suggests that children acquire *aspects* of object permanence much earlier than Piaget supposed (Baillargeon & DeVos, 1991), even by 4 or 5 months, but a comprehensive understanding of the permanence of objects evolves gradually during infancy (Halford, 1989).

Sensorimotor children are extremely **egocentric**; that is, they are thoroughly embedded in their own point of view. When an infant closes her eyes, the world becomes dark; when a bell is no longer in Laurent's view, it ceases to exist. For Piaget, development entails a gradual process of moving away from egocentrism and recognizing alternative points of view (see Flavell, 1985; Selman, 1980).

Preoperational Stage   The **preoperational stage** begins roughly around age 2 and lasts until ages 5 to 7. It is characterized by the emergence of symbolic thought. During this stage, children develop the ability to use symbols to represent events and objects, as they learn to use language, mental imagery, and categories. In this way, thought becomes detachable from action.

Symbolic thought is an impressive accomplishment that allows preschool children to enter into dialogue with those around them and to imagine solutions to problems before actually performing any actions. Preoperational thought continues, however, to have a number of limitations. Preschool children remain egocentric in many respects; they still tend to think about the external world primarily from their own point of view. A classic demonstration of egocentrism at this stage occurs in the **three-mountain task**. Here, a child is seated at a table displaying three model mountains, as depicted in Figure 13.11, with a teddy bear or doll seated at another chair at the same table. The child is shown a number of pictures of the table from different perspectives and is asked which view the teddy bear would see.

Preschool children often answer that the bear would see their own view of the table (Piaget & Inhelder, 1956). Preoperational children are not egocentric in every situation (Ford, 1979; Lempers et al., 1977) and can even solve variants of the three-mountain task that are perceptually less complex (Burke, 1975). Nevertheless, they are much more likely to make egocentric cognitive errors than older children, like the 3 year old who covers her eyes and declares, "You can't see me!"

Another limitation of preoperational thought is the tendency to focus, or center, on one perceptually striking feature of an object without considering other features that might be relevant. Piaget calls this process **centration**. When asked which of two candy bars is bigger, a long, thin one or a short, thick one, the preschooler is likely to pick the longer one and ignore thickness, even though the amount of chocolate is identical.

Preoperational thinking also tends to be fairly literal. The mother of a 3 year old tried to teach her son the meaning of "compromise" when he wanted her to read him three bedtime stories instead of the usual one, suggesting that they compromise on two. A few days later, they were debating his bedtime, and the mother asked, "Billy, do you remember what 'compromise' means?" "Yes," he replied, earnestly, "*two*."

THE FAMILY CIRCUS.   **By Bil Keane**

"Look what I can do, Grandma!"

Reprinted with special permission of King Features Syndicate.

FIGURE 13.11
The three-mountain task. Preoperational children tend not to recognize that the stuffed animal "sees" the mountain from a perspective different from their own, although they can do so if the stimulus is very simple.

Concrete Operational Stage Piaget called the third stage **concrete operational** because at this point (roughly ages 7 to 12) children are capable of operating on, or mentally manipulating, internal representations of concrete objects in ways that are reversible. In other words, children can imagine performing mental manipulations (operations) on a set of objects and then mentally put them back the way they found them (Piaget, 1972).

This achievement of the concrete operational stage is demonstrated in Piaget's classic experiments with conservation problems. According to Piaget, only when children reach this third stage are they able to understand the concept of **conservation**—that basic properties of an object or situation remain stable (or are conserved) even though superficial properties may be changed. For example, if preoperational children are shown the three beakers in part *(a)* of Figure 13.12, they easily recognize that the two same-sized beakers contain the same amount of liquid. They will not realize, however, that the tall and short beakers contain the same amount of liquid even if they watch the experimenter pour the liquid from the short to the tall beaker. In contrast, concrete operational children understand that the amount of liquid remains unchanged even though it has been poured into a beaker of a different shape. If asked to justify their answers, they usually say something like, "You just poured it from one container to another!"

Two other types of conservation problems, conservation of number and conservation of mass, are shown in parts *(b)* and *(c)*, respectively, of Figure 13.12. Children typically master different kinds of conservation at slightly different ages. Many children understand conservation of number by age 6 but do not understand conservation of mass until about age 8 (Elkind, 1981; Katz & Beilin, 1976).

Concrete operational children also understand transitivity—that if $a < b$ and $b < c$, then $a < c$. Although preoperational children can be trained to make some transitive

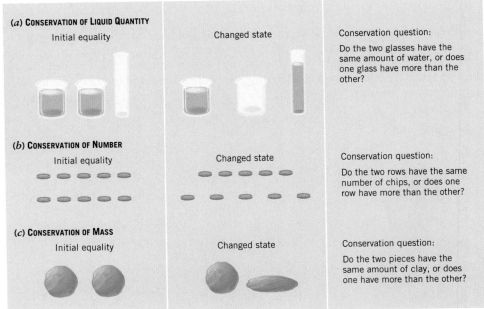

FIGURE 13.12

Conservation. (a) Conservation of liquid quantity: Unlike preoperational children, concrete operational children understand that the amount of liquid remains unchanged even though it has been poured into a beaker of a different shape. (b) Conservation of number: Preoperational children believe that altering the physical configuration changes the number of objects present. (c) Conservation of mass: Preoperational children fail to realize that mass is conserved despite changing the shape of a ball of clay.

inferences (Bryant & Trabasso, 1971), by and large they have difficulty keeping enough information in mind to solve transitive thinking problems. One transitivity problem asks, "If Henry is taller than Jack, and Jack is taller than Claude, which boy is the shortest?" Preschoolers are equally likely to pick Jack or Claude because each one is shorter than someone else; they fail to put together the two pieces of information about relative height into a single transitive proposition.

Formal Operational Stage   Piaget's fourth stage, formal operations, begins at about ages 12 to 15, when children start to think more abstractly. The **formal operational stage** is characterized by the ability to manipulate abstract as well as concrete objects, events, and ideas mentally—that is, to reason about formal propositions rather than concrete events. Teenagers are less likely to argue that the two beakers in the conservation task contain the same amount because they saw the liquid being poured back and forth. They may instead discuss the law of conservation, or present the argument that surface appearances do not always reflect the underlying reality.

This new ability to reason with abstractions is commonly recognized by school systems in planning curricula. Curriculum planners typically wait until the eighth or ninth grade to teach algebra, which requires abstract reasoning. Another hallmark of formal operational reasoning, commonly used in high school chemistry classes, is the ability to frame hypotheses and figure out how to test them systematically (Inhelder & Piaget, 1958).

Putting Piaget in Perspective

Piaget's theory literally defined cognitive development for several decades, and it continues to exercise a profound influence. In recent years, however, it has come under fire. One criticism is that Piaget focused too heavily on the kind of thinking most evident in scientific or philosophical pursuits. Whereas Piaget saw the methodical, systematic thinking of formal operations as the pinnacle of development, much of what people actually think about—food, television programs, and social encounters (Csikszentmihalyi, 1982)—has little to do with science or logic, so the theory may apply only to a subset of thought processes. Indeed, Piaget viewed the formal operational teenager as "infinitely rational"; however, even well-educated adults do not meet this ideal much of the time (Cohen, 1983; see Wason & Johnson-Laird, 1972).

Another criticism concerns Piaget's assumption that as children progress through the stages of cognitive development, they apply the same underlying logic to every task at roughly the same age. To the contrary, evidence suggests that cognitive development often progresses unevenly and may be domain-specific (Case, 1992; Flavell, 1982). Just as people have varying intellectual abilities in different domains (Chapter 8), children progress differently in different areas depending on their abilities and their familiarity with the domain.

Piaget also underestimated the capacities of infants and preschool children (Gelman & Baillargeon, 1983). For example, although Piaget held that object permanence does not begin to develop until about 8 months, subsequent research suggests that even by the age of 20 days infants are aware, at least for a few seconds, that a hidden object is still there, and by 2 months they can distinguish between objects going out of sight and ceasing to exist (Breuer, 1985). Numerous studies also suggest that children can sometimes accomplish conservation tasks by age 5 rather than 7. In fact, preschoolers may have some understanding of conservation, as indicated by research asking young children to make judgments about dissolving substances such as sugar. They understand, for example, that poisonous substances may remain poisonous despite changes in their form. By age 5, children recognize that some substances may dissolve into tiny pieces that can no longer be seen but that still preserve their qualities, such as sweet taste (Rosen & Rozin, 1993).

Still another criticism is that Piaget underestimated the role of culture in development. A number of cross-cultural studies have found that the stages of develop-

Children in nomadic cultures learn early how to organize their world spatially, since they must adapt rapidly to changing locales.

ment occur in the sequence described by Piaget but that the age at which children attain particular stages often varies greatly and depends on the task assessed (Modgil & Modgil, 1982; Price-Williams, 1981). By and large, these studies have observed slower cognitive development in preliterate societies, except when a cultural group has particular familiarity with the task materials used in cognitive tests. For instance, although Mexican children of potters show delayed development on the conservation task using beakers, they demonstrate a relatively early understanding of conservation when asked if a ball of clay has the same volume when it is stretched into an oblong shape (Price-Williams et al., 1969). Similarly, farm children from the Punjab region in India who help their parents weigh corn, rice, and other products demonstrate an early understanding of conservation of weight (Ghuman, 1982). An investigation comparing children from three continents (North America, Australia, and Africa) found that children excelled in tasks that were important to their culture and its mode of subsistence (Dasen, 1975; Dasen & Heron, 1981). For example, children in nomadic societies, which travel from location to location for their survival, outperformed other children on spatial tasks.

The bulk of research thus suggests that Piaget was correct in many of the broad strokes he used to describe cognitive development (Halford, 1989), such as decreasing egocentrism, increasing capacity to think symbolically and without reference to concrete sensory and motor experience, increasing capacity to reason abstractly, and growing understanding of logic and causality. At the same time, many of the specific strokes, hues, and textures of his portrait require revision. His timetables are not entirely accurate, and he underestimated the extent to which children can learn to use more advanced modes of thought in very limited domains (Halford, 1989). Infants and young children appear to be more competent, and adults less competent, than Piaget believed (Flavell, 1992). Finally, he underestimated the role of culture in cognitive development.

The Information-Processing Approach to Cognitive Development

The information-processing approach is well suited to the task of sketching the finer details of cognitive development. This approach examines the component processes involved in thinking, from sensory registration and attention, through maintaining and manipulating information in working memory, encoding it in long-term memory systems, and retrieving it (Chapter 6). Developmental psychologists who take this perspective want to discover how each stage of processing changes with age.

The information-processing perspective thus focuses on continuous, quantitative changes rather than the broad, qualitative stages studied by Piaget. For example, speed of processing across a wide array of tasks increases throughout childhood and levels off around age 15 (Kail, 1991). An information-processing approach is not, however, necessarily at odds with Piagetian theory; the gradual development of several component processes can lead to a global change, such as diminished egocentrism. Information-processing researchers, however, work at a much narrower level of analysis, studying several factors responsible for cognitive development, notably children's knowledge base, automaticity of processing, ability to use strategies, and metacognitive abilities (their ability to understand their own thinking processes) (Kail & Bisanz, 1992; Sternberg, 1984).

Knowledge Base

One factor that influences children's cognitive efficiency is the accumulated knowledge already in long-term storage, or their **knowledge base**. Compared to adults, children's knowledge bases are obviously limited because of their comparative inexperience with life (Chi 1976, 1978). To what extent, then, does the size of children's knowledge base, rather than some other factor such as smaller memory capacity, account for their comparative cognitive inefficiency? This question was explored in a study that reversed the usual state of affairs by selecting children who were more knowledgeable than adult subjects (Chi, 1978). The cognitive task was to remember chessboard arrangements. Child subjects (averaging age 10) were recruited from a local chess tournament, while adult subjects had no particular skill at chess. The children easily outperformed the adults at remembering the arrangement of pieces on the board, thereby demonstrating that knowledge base was more important than age-related factors in this cognitive task. Other studies have corroborated this finding, using stimuli such as cartoon characters with which children are more familiar than adults (Lindberg, 1980).

Automatic Processing

A second factor that influences children's cognitive skill is their increasing ability to perform cognitive tasks automatically (Anderson, 1985; Sternberg, 1984). **Automatization** refers to the process of executing mental processes with increasing efficiency, so that they require less and less attention. Because automatic information processing makes few demands on conscious attentional processes, individuals can devote more attention to other tasks and therefore handle multiple problems simultaneously.

In many tasks, from performing addition problems to driving a car, increased competence involves shifting from conscious, controlled processing to automatic processing (Chapter 6). Age and experience again give older children and adults an edge over younger children. Simply living longer provides the practice necessary to increase automatization of processing.

Cognitive Strategies

Children's ability to use cognitive strategies also increases throughout childhood and adolescence. In memory tasks, young children tend to use simple strategies such as rote repetition; older children learn to use increasingly sophisticated, elaborative rehearsal strategies (Chapter 6), such as arranging lists into categories or using imagery (see Alexander & Schwanenflugel, 1994; Brown et al., 1983; Hasselhorn, 1990). One early study demonstrated differences in the way children of various ages spontaneously use memory strategies (Flavell et al., 1966). The experimenter

Children can remember the names and personalities of dozens of cartoon characters who "all look alike" to their parents.

showed 5-, 7-, and 10-year-old children seven pictures and pointed to three they should remember. Between the time the children saw the pictures and the next phase, when their memory was tested, the experimenter carefully watched them to see whether they used any verbalizations to "think aloud" as an aid to memory. (The researcher was trained at lip-reading.) Whereas only 10 percent of the 5 year olds talked to themselves to help remember the pictures, 60 percent of the 7 year olds and 85 percent of the 10 year olds did so.

Metacognitive Abilities

A fourth variable influencing cognitive development is metacognition—thinking about thinking. **Metacognition** refers to people's understanding of the way they perform cognitive tasks such as remembering, learning, and solving problems. Considerable evidence suggests that metacognitive abilities increase with age and that children's growing ability to control and consciously regulate their own thinking is a fundamental aspect of cognitive development (Reeve & Brown, 1985). For instance, simply knowing what one does and does not know can be crucial for accurate performance of a variety of skills. Knowing something involves a *feeling* of knowing, which may or may not be accurate (Costermans et al., 1992; Reder & Ritter, 1992). When young children are asked if they understand things, they typically have difficulty discriminating whether they do or not, so they may fail to ask other people or seek information that could inform them (Brown, 1983).

An incident in which a friend and I struggled to recall the name of a famous maker of fine crystal provides a good example of metacognitive processing. My friend suggested that the name was something like "Stanford." Somehow "feeling" that she was on the right track, I at first guessed—based, presumably, on my intuitive knowledge of the way memory works—that the name must begin with "St," but then suddenly changed my mind, concluding that the name ended with "-ford." She said it had a British sound to it, I said it had three syllables like "Rutherford," and then she retrieved the name—Waterford. Although our exchange may sound more like an example of senile dementia, it illustrates the complex processes involved in knowing what one does and does not know, processes that develop with age.

As children mature, they develop a better understanding of their own memory, of the difficulty level of various tasks, and of the types of strategies useful for approaching different kinds of tasks (Flavell, 1985; Flavell & Wellman, 1977; Schneider & Pressley, 1989; Yussen & Levy, 1975). In one study, researchers showed pictures to younger and older children and asked them to predict how many they could remember. The older children's predictions were much more accurate than those of younger children, who often predicted total recall (Flavell et al., 1970).

Integrative Theories of Cognitive Development

Piaget's theory views cognitive development as a progression through qualitatively different stages, whereas the information-processing perspective focuses on small-scale, quantitative refinements in the child's ability to encode, remember, and process different kinds of information. As different as these viewpoints are, they are not mutually exclusive: Development may be characterized by both qualitative and quantitative changes and general and specific processes (Fischer, 1980).

Theorists who attempt to integrate these views (sometimes called **neo-Piagetian** theorists) tend to focus more heavily than either perspective on the roles of emotion and motivation in shaping thought (Berg, 1992), but they agree with several fundamental tenets of Piagetian theory: that children are active in structuring their understanding, that knowledge progresses from a pre-concrete to a concrete and then to an abstract stage, and that this all occurs in roughly the order and at the ages reported by Piaget (Bidell & Fischer, 1992; Case, 1992; Fischer, 1980). Like information-processing theorists, however, the neo-Piagetians pay more attention to discrete components of cognitive processing than did Piaget, and they stress the way cognition develops within specific domains.

One theory that attempts to wed Piagetian and information-processing models was developed by Robbie Case. Case (1978, 1985, 1992) holds that cognitive development progresses within a general stage framework similar to Piaget's, from a sensorimotor period to an abstract, complex, highly symbolic, formal operational stage. Each stage is qualitatively different from the others in the way children represent problems and strategies for solving them (Case, 1984). Unlike Piaget, Case believes that cognitive progress within each stage is possible because humans are innately motivated to engage in certain types of behaviors, including problem solving, exploration, imitation, and social interaction. Cognitive development occurs within each stage as children set goals, formulate problem-solving strategies, and evaluate the results of those strategies. They then integrate existing problem-solving strategies into more elaborate strategies as new situations arise, and they practice those new strategies until these become automatic.

Development from one stage to another depends on cultural input, but the factor most responsible for qualitative changes in cognitive development is an increasing capacity for working memory—that is, for devoting conscious attention to the processing of new information. Working memory expands with increased automaticity and more efficient use of cognitive strategies, allowing children to keep progressively more things in mind simultaneously and to coordinate previously separate actions and ideas. Case uses the development of artistic skills in children as an example. Between ages 2 and 5, children become capable of coordinating the image of an object, such as a person, with the image they are drawing, which allows them to go beyond mere scribbling. By age 8 to 10, children in Western cultures incorporate artistic conventions developed over the past several centuries in the West for depicting perspective (Chapter 4). For example, they represent closer objects as larger, and they occlude (that is, block) distant objects with closer ones.

In one study, children ages 10 to 18 were asked to draw a picture of a mother looking out the window of her home to see her son playing peek-a-boo with her in the park across the street (Dennis, 1992, cited in Case, 1992). The youngest subjects could not simultaneously coordinate the two scenes. They could keep in mind the image of the mother in the house and the image of the boy in the park, but they could not integrate the two images—that is, they lacked the cognitive "workspace" to keep the interrelation of the two in mind. Figure 13.13 shows the drawing of a 10-year-old subject, who drew each scene accurately but drew the mother and son facing the artist instead of each other.

The two-scene study illustrates the advantages of Case's neo-Piagetian model over classical Piagetian theory. Certain broad processes, notably limitations in working memory, *constrain* the thinking of the child, providing an upper limit on what a child within a given age range can achieve. This leads to qualitative differences in thought at different stages that appear across a variety of domains (such as art, language, and mathematics), just as Piaget postulated. At the same time, the neo-Piagetian model, like similar theories about the way children acquire and coordinate skills (Fischer, 1980), recognizes that development occurs in specific domains and is influenced by culture and experience. A person who attends art class is more likely to master certain skills than someone who does not, but a 4 year old with a crayon is unlikely to outperform an adult regardless of training.

An important question that remains is why development follows any broad stages at all, particularly if learning always occurs in specific situations. Why, for example, are children constrained by working memory capacity, particularly when they have extensive experience in a domain? Cross-cultural research shows that certain stages are, indeed, universal. From North American suburbs to villages in West Africa, children develop basic skills such as counting at approximately the same age,

FIGURE 13.13
Artistic skill and working memory. Subjects ages 10 to 18 were asked to draw a picture of a mother looking out the window to see her son playing peek-a-boo with her in the park. The youngest subjects could keep in mind the image of the mother in the house and the image of the boy in the park, but they could not integrate the two, as this 10 year old's drawing shows. According to Case's neo-Piagetian model, the amount of cognitive "workspace" available to a child at different developmental stages limits what he can achieve.

despite wide variations in experience (Case, 1985). At the same time, studies show that even with extensive practice in counting, young children seem to reach a ceiling level of efficiency beyond which they cannot progress at their stage of development (Kurland, 1981).

Case proposes a maturational explanation: the myelination of the brain, particularly of the frontal lobes. The frontal lobes are, in fact, involved in attention, including both the capacity to hold multiple ideas in working memory and the ability to inhibit irrelevant thoughts from consciousness (see Björklund & Harnishfeger, 1989; Goldman-Rakic, 1995). The association areas of the frontal cortex also mediate abstract thought, and their maturation could account for the emergence of this capacity during adolescence.

COGNITIVE DEVELOPMENT AND CHANGE IN ADULTHOOD

All cultures consider adolescents and adults better decision makers than children, but cultures differ dramatically in their beliefs about cognition and aging. Many cultures associate age with wisdom; our own associates it with decline. Contemporary Western culture is ambiguous about when this decline begins and whether middle age confers cognitive advantages over youth. In the United States, for example, people can vote at 18, but the minimum ages required to run for the House of Representatives, the Senate, and the presidency are 21, 25, and 35, respectively. Apparently, the framers of the Constitution held some implicit theory of cognitive development in adulthood, even though most contemporary North Americans believe that some cognitive functions, such as memory, decline by the 40s (see Ryan, 1992).

Experimental data are as ambiguous about cognition in middle age as our cultural beliefs. Many measures of memory show steady declines in adulthood, with

John Kennedy and Bill Clinton were "youngsters" when they assumed the United States presidency—in their fifth decade.

young adults performing better than both middle-aged and older adults. Figure 13.14 shows the results of a study of Belgian and American subjects on a task requiring them to associate names with faces, much as one might at a party. In both cultures, memory drops dramatically between young adulthood and middle age and continues to decline thereafter. On other measures, however, people in their early 20s and 40s perform equally well, with both groups outperforming their elders (Lavigne & Finley, 1990).

Unlike cultural concepts of intelligence in middle age, views of cognition in the elderly in contemporary Western societies are unambiguously negative. In part, the stereotype of the slow, forgetful senior citizen reflects real changes in speed of pro-

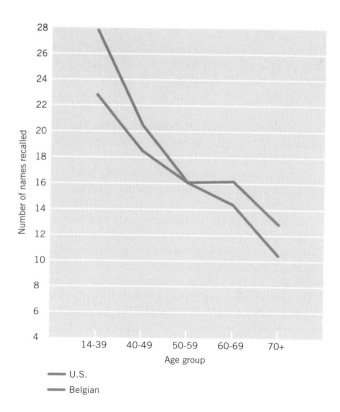

FIGURE 13.14
Age differences in recall in the United States and Belgium. The experimenters presented subjects with faces and names in a task approximating learning at a party. They subsequently showed subjects pictures of the faces and asked them to retrieve the names. In both societies, performance showed steady decline with increased age. SOURCE: Crook et al., 1992, p. 133.

cessing and capacity for learning and memory that occur cross-culturally (see Crook et al., 1992). In other respects, however, the negative view of cognition in later life is idiosyncratic and culture-specific. Unlike most periods in human history, in times of rapid technological change such as the twentieth century, the knowledge and strategies used by one generation may be irrelevant or even unproductive 20 or 30 years later. To younger individuals, an older person's reliance on accumulated wisdom may thus look like a sign of cognitive rigidity or failure to accommodate, rather than maturity. As we shall see, the extent to which cognition declines in old age varies not only across cultures but also across individuals within a single culture.

Studying Cognition and Aging: Some Cautions

Almost any method of studying cognition and aging has its limitations. Cohort effects render cross-sectional data problematic. Older people have generally had less exposure to experiences such as higher education, computers, and television, and younger adults have had more experience with psychometric tests than the elderly, who may never have taken an IQ test or an SAT. These factors could clearly influence findings on measures of cognitive functioning. In contrast, longitudinal and sequential designs suffer from subject attrition. Wittingly or unwittingly, elderly subjects do not always return for the final assessments.

Another methodological problem is that the psychometric tests used to measure intelligence were developed to predict school performance. Some researchers question whether these youth-oriented tests are appropriate measures of intelligence in older people (Labouvie-Vief, 1985; Willis & Baltes, 1980). For example, older people may simply not be as motivated to jump through cognitive hoops as younger people, who are likely either to be in school or recently out of it (Kausler, 1990). Lack of motivation could easily affect performance, particularly on timed tests that require vigilant attention.

An additional problem in studying aging and cognition is that both factors, aging and cognition, are multifaceted. The body ages, the brain ages, social roles shift, the social environment changes, and beliefs about the self alter. Understanding how aging affects cognitive capabilities requires determining precisely *which* aspects of aging are responsible for any changes observed. Anyone who has taken an important examination while feeling ill knows that poor health interferes with cognitive performance. Because older people are more likely than the general population to be in poor health, cognitive studies that use random samples may show declines with age simply because a greater proportion of their older subjects are ill (see Perlmutter & Nyquist, 1990).

To further complicate matters, different aspects of aging may produce gains or losses in different cognitive processes. Most people would trust their legal work more readily to a senior partner in a law firm than to a young associate, even though the senior partner may, at 60, suffer some of the memory declines illustrated in Figure 13.14. Despite aging neural hardware, years of experience enable the older lawyer to solve problems more efficiently—enough, at times, to justify the cost difference between a senior partner at $300 an hour and an associate at $150.

Intelligence has many facets, and different aspects of intelligence change in different ways as people age. As the legal example suggests, an important distinction with respect to aging is between fluid and crystallized intelligence (Cattell, 1941; Horn & Cattell, 1967; Horn & Hofer, 1992). **Fluid intelligence** refers to intellectual capacities that have no specific content but are used in processing information, particularly novel information. Measures of fluid intelligence assess speed of processing, the capacity to spot missing elements in a picture, the ability to solve analogies or form concepts quickly, and similar abilities. Fluid intelligence peaks in young adulthood and then levels off and begins declining by mid-adulthood, largely because of reduced speed of processing.

The second type of intelligence, **crystallized intelligence**, refers to people's store of knowledge, including vocabulary, general world knowledge or cultural information, and knowledge about reasoning strategies. Unlike fluid intelligence, crystallized intelligence increases throughout most of life, showing declines only in very old age (Horn, 1979, in Labouvie-Vief, 1985). These declines appear to occur, if at all, only when the "machinery" for processing information breaks down to such a degree that new memories, strategies, and ways of categorizing information can no longer be processed by an aging neural assembly line. Figure 13.15 shows the different developmental trajectories of fluid and crystallized intelligence in adulthood.

Another methodological issue in studying the relationship between aging and cognition involves ecological validity; that is, to what extent do cognitive tests tap dimensions that are meaningful in everyday life? Experimental research has documented several areas in which cognition declines in adulthood, such as speed of processing, which would lead one to expect older workers to be less productive than their younger colleagues. However, an analysis of nearly one hundred studies with a combined total of more than 38,000 subjects found that the correlation between worker productivity and age is essentially zero (McEvoy & Cascio, 1989); job performance does not decline with age. Most workers probably compensate for declines in fluid intelligence with gains in crystallized intelligence and with alternative strategies for carrying out tasks (see Baltes, 1987; Perlmutter et al., 1990; Salthouse, 1985). Some researchers have begun developing more ecologically valid measures, such as grocery list memory tasks or telephone dialing tasks that tap short-term memory as used in daily life (Crook et al., 1992).

A final problem in considering the relationship between aging and cognition is that culturally constructed beliefs about lifespan development affect the way people actually think and remember. Researchers studying an aspect of metacognition called **metamemory** (people's cognition about their own memory) have documented that what people believe about their capacity to remember influences both the strategies they use and their ultimate ability to retrieve information (Devolder & Pressley, 1989; Hertzog et al., 1990). Because the elderly in our culture tend to hold unrealistically negative views of memory in old age (Perlmutter, 1978), they often fail to make the effort that would allow them to remember, leading to a self-fulfilling prophecy.

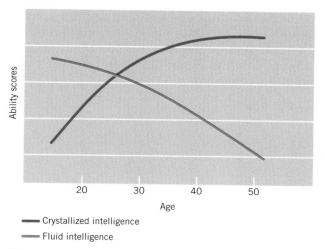

■— Crystallized intelligence
— Fluid intelligence

FIGURE 13.15
Fluid and crystallized intelligence throughout the lifespan. Unlike fluid intelligence, which shows a steady decline with age, crystallized intelligence increases through at least the 40s and 50s and then levels off. SOURCE: *Horn & Hofer, 1992, p. 79.*

Cognitive Changes Associated with Aging

Within these methodological constraints, experimental investigations suggest that cognition does change as people age. The most prominent changes are in psychomotor speed and memory.

Changes in Psychomotor Speed

One of the clearest changes that accompanies aging is **psychomotor slowing**, an increase in the time between sensory input and motor output, and a general increase in time required for processing. This slowing actually begins early, around the mid-20s. Psychomotor slowing can be observed both on tasks of simple reaction time, such as pushing a button in response to a flash of a light, and on more complex reaction-time tasks, such as typing or writing (Era et al., 1986; Spirduso & McCrae, 1990; Welford, 1984; Wilkinson & Allison, 1989). Semantic information processing, assessed by priming studies, takes approximately 1.5 times as long in adults in their 60s and 70s as in younger adults (Lima et al., 1991; Myerson et al., 1992).

Increases in skill and efficiency often compensate for slowing in more complex tasks, but they cannot compensate for increases in simple reaction time (Baron & Mattila, 1989; Era et al., 1986). Psychomotor slowing varies considerably from one individual to another. Factors that seem to be associated with faster reaction times at all ages are good health, high activity level, and higher level of education (Era et al., 1986).

For most people, psychomotor slowing is so gradual that it escapes notice until they are in their 50s or 60s. However, for professional athletes, like tennis players, who make their living responding deftly to balls coming at them in rapid succession, increased reaction time can be a devastating problem—and explains why most athletes are considered has-beens by their early 30s. The way people think of athletes' age is a good example of the relativity of conceptions of aging, as words normally reserved for the elderly, like "old" and "ready to retire," are applied to individuals who would otherwise be considered youthful. Middle-aged athletes such as George Foreman, who shocked the world in 1994 by winning back the heavyweight championship in his late 40s, know their days are numbered, but they can stage temporary comebacks through extra practice and reliance on increased skill and compensatory strategies.

Why psychomotor processes take longer as people age is not entirely clear. A parallel distributed processing model (Chapter 7) suggests that if a mental process or representation is distributed across a number of neurons that form a circuit, any small break that occurs with aging will require additional steps to re-complete the circuit (Cerella, 1990). Because every synaptic connection adds processing time, the more broken connections that amass over the years, the more time will be required to find alternative routes to carry out psychological processes (Figure 13.16).

FIGURE 13.16
Parallel distributed processing model of psychomotor slowing with aging. This figure illustrates a neural circuit that is broken with aging, forcing a detour that adds an extra step and hence increased reaction time. Progressive breaks in neural circuits add up to steady increases in reaction time. Source: *Adapted from Cerella, 1990, p. 203.*

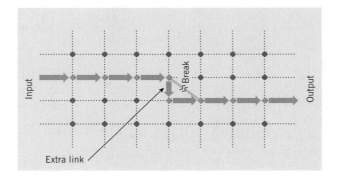

Changes in Memory

A common stereotype is that older people are constantly forgetting things—names of people they have just met, what they did yesterday, and where they put their house keys. This stereotype has grains of truth, but it is far too sweeping. The information-processing model specifies several stages and types of memory, which are differentially affected by aging processes. Older people show minimal impairment on sensory registration or simple short-term memory tasks (Hultsch & Dixon, 1990; Labouvie-Vief & Schell, 1982). However, if short-term memory tasks include more complex processing (as when subjects must repeat lists *backwards*), the performance of older subjects is appreciably inferior to that of younger subjects (Bromley, 1958).

Some information-processing theorists believe that the root of most memory problems in old age is a diminished ability to control multiple pieces of information in working memory simultaneously (Salthouse, 1992, 1994). Elderly people tend to have difficulty on divided attention tasks (Ponds et al., 1988), such as keeping the actions of multiple cars in mind at an intersection with a four-way stop. If neo-Piagetian theorists such as Robbie Case are right that the key to cognitive development in childhood is increased processing capacity in working memory, then advanced aging means development in reverse.

As for long-term memory, some aspects remain intact throughout the lifespan, whereas others show clear decline. Long-term memory requires encoding, storage, and retrieval (Chapter 6). On the encoding end of the process, older people tend to take more time to learn new information than younger people; however, when given ample encoding time on tasks such as learning a series of word pairs, their performance level approaches that of younger subjects (Perlmutter, 1983). Older subjects seem to have more difficulty with complex learning or encoding tasks that involve divided attention than with simple memory tasks (McDowd & Craik, 1988).

Long-term memory storage, on the other hand, seems to give older people little difficulty. Healthy people continue to add to their crystallized intelligence until the day they die (Horn & Hofer, 1992; Light, 1990; Salthouse, 1992). One way researchers know that the memory losses of later life do not reflect problems with storage is that older subjects show few declines in recognition memory. For example, if shown a list of words and subsequently asked which words in a new list were in the old one, older subjects are as likely as younger subjects to recognize words they had previously seen. Similarly, implicit memory, as assessed by tasks such as the tendency to complete a word stem (e.g., PER—) with a previously primed word (e.g., perfume), is not impaired with age; the information has apparently been stored without difficulty (see Schacter et al., 1992).

The problem older people have with long-term memory appears to lie in retrieval rather than in storage. Compared to their unimpaired performance on recognition tasks ("Did you see the word *dove*?"), older people show relative deficits in free recall ("What words did you see?") and cued recall ("Did you see the name of a bird?"). As people age, they have more difficulty with such tests of explicit memory than with implicit memory tasks.

In part, declines in retrieval and in the kinds of complex encoding that facilitate retrieval reflect changes in the use of cognitive strategies. Although older subjects still have the capacity to use chunking, imagery, and deep processing strategies (Chapter 6), they tend not to employ these strategies spontaneously (Perlmutter, 1983). When trained to use mnemonic devices and encouraged to organize learning materials, they show significant improvements in memory performance (Greenberg & Powers, 1987). However, older subjects often do not transfer these skills to other situations and do not continue to apply them months later (Baltes et al., 1986; Labouvie-Vief & Gonda, 1976).

Older people also have difficulty with some forms of problem solving, such as the strategic questioning required in the game "Twenty Questions," which laboratory researchers have adapted to assess problem-solving ability. The subject is shown several pictures and told that the researcher is thinking of one of them. The subject then asks the researcher questions to narrow the field and eliminate all but the selected picture. Older subjects tend to ask many more redundant and unnecessary questions than younger ones (Denney & Denney, 1973; Denney & Palmer, 1981). In contrast, when presented with more familiar everyday problems, older people appear to make better use of their cognitive "software" (such as making grocery lists rather than relying strictly on memory) to compensate for deteriorating neural "hardware" (see Martin, 1986).

Commentary: Intelligence and Aging

The picture painted thus far of intelligence in adulthood is one of selective decline. Recent research suggests, however, that this is only part of the picture—the gloomier part. First, many studies have used timed tests. To the extent that psychomotor speed decreases with aging, older people will show deficits compared with younger subjects on a host of variables, such as memory (because they take longer to encode and retrieve) and problem solving (because selecting strategies takes time). Whether timed tests have any ecological validity—that is, whether they translate to real-life deficits—depends on the subjects and their occupations. If their jobs require rapid performance, they will either show declines or have to find ways to compensate; if they have time to think and work at their own pace, then they are unlikely to show declines.

Second, most of the studies showing declines with aging have been cross-sectional, which means the findings are vulnerable to cohort effects. Perhaps more importantly, what cross-sectional studies do not show is the *proportion* of people who manifest declines. Statistically, if a sizable minority of older people evidence substantial cognitive deterioration, mean scores for their age group will be lower than for younger groups, leading to the apparent conclusion that intelligence declines with age. But longitudinal studies can ask a different question: What *percentage* of people in different age groups shows deterioration?

The most extensive longitudinal study, the Seattle Longitudinal Study (Schaie, 1990), provides an important corrective to the view of inexorable cognitive decline through middle and old age. The investigators followed a large sample of subjects ranging in age from 25 to 81 over a seven-year interval. They administered a battery of tests of mental abilities such as verbal meaning (vocabulary) and facility with numbers (arithmetic). The findings are striking (Figure 13.17): Most people do not

FIGURE 13.17

Cognitive stability over seven years. On five tests of mental ability, less than 25 percent of subjects tested at seven-year intervals showed any declines prior to age 60. Even by age 81, over 60 percent of all subjects showed stable cognitive functioning rather than decline.
Source: *Adapted from Schaie, 1990, p. 297.*

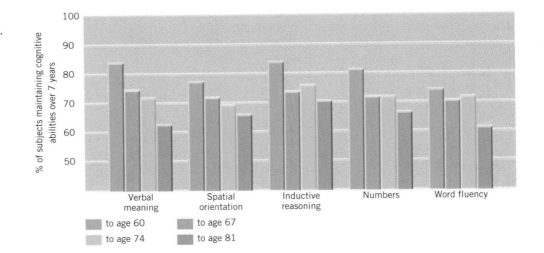

show significant mental declines. Even on the average, intellectual functioning does not decline until the 60s and 70s.

The Seattle study shows that people differ tremendously in the way they age. People who are healthy and mentally active experience fewer mental declines than those who are not (Diamond, 1978; Horn & Meer, 1987). The "use it or lose it" theory applies to mental functioning as much as to physical domains. People like B. F. Skinner, Pablo Picasso, Sigmund Freud, Eleanor Roosevelt, Jean Piaget, Thurgood Marshall, and a host of other septuagenarians and octogenarians have shown remarkable cognitive longevity in diverse fields.

Third, teaching strategies for memory or problem solving can dramatically increase people's functioning, so that skilled older people can outperform less-skilled younger people. Both the promise of such training and the limitations imposed by an aging nervous system are illustrated in a study that taught old and young adults mnemonic strategies for remembering words and numbers (Baltes, 1987). Older subjects improved dramatically, outperforming untrained younger subjects, but younger subjects with training were far superior to their trained elders (Figure 13.18).

Finally, the tests used to assess cognitive functioning may mask some ways in which the cognition of older people is actually superior to that of their children and grandchildren. Most memory tests assess the kind of rote memory—for lists of words, numbers, or propositions in an essay—that is frequently required of students but less relevant for complex thought and decision making throughout the lifespan. One researcher examined the way four groups of subjects recalled the events of a story: early adolescents (aged 12 to 15), late adolescents (aged 16 to 19), middle-aged adults (aged 39 to 56), and older adults (aged 60 to 78) (Adams, 1991). Whereas the younger subjects were somewhat more likely to recall the details of the story, the older subjects were more likely to "get it"—to elaborate on the underlying meaning of the story. In summarizing the story, only 15 to 20 percent of early and late adolescents offered an interpretation of its main theme or moral, compared with 70 percent of middle-aged and 60 percent of older subjects. Thus, at least until middle age, changes in cognition probably involve both gains and losses (Baltes, 1987).

Clearly, then, cognition is not all downhill after college. People continue to accrue knowledge until the day they die, so that their expertise in particular domains should expand as long as they are active and healthy. When the data are in, I suspect we will also find that the *subtlety* of mind, such as the ability to inte-

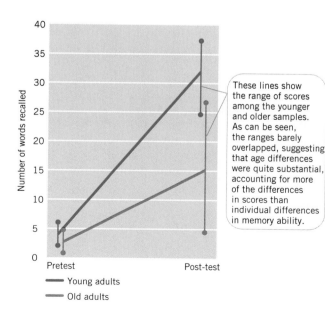

These lines show the range of scores among the younger and older samples. As can be seen, the ranges barely overlapped, suggesting that age differences were quite substantial, accounting for more of the differences in scores than individual differences in memory ability.

Young adults

Old adults

FIGURE 13.18

The impact of training on memory. Older and young adult subjects participated in an extensive training program to increase their memory. After 30 sessions, both groups performed substantially better, but almost no older adult outperformed even the least successful performers among the trained younger adult group. SOURCE: *Baltes, 1987, p. 619.*

The first forty years of life furnish the text, while the remaining thirty supply the commentary; without the commentary we are unable to understand aright the true sense and coherence of the text, together with the moral it contains.

Schopenhauer (cited in Adams, 1991, p. 323)

grate information across various domains, or to see long-term implications, increases through at least the 40s, even as the speed of thought begins to decline. On the other hand, youth has its cognitive advantages, which stem from a combination of mental quickness, youthful energy, less investment in existing ways of doing things, and lack of encumbrance by precisely the expert schemas that normally facilitate efficient thinking in a domain. Their youthful attitudes and mental flexibility may allow younger adults to see solutions their elders would not recognize. Perhaps we would do well to put fewer of our older people out to pasture and fewer of our younger people under harness.

Aging and "Senility"

One of the most pervasive myths about aging is that in old age people lose their memory, their intellectual capacity, and their ability to think and reason—or, to use the vernacular, they become "senile" (Butler, 1975, 1984). In fact, only about 5 percent of the population suffer progressive and incurable **dementia**, a disorder marked by global disturbance of higher mental functions (Morris & Baddeley, 1988). Another 10 to 15 percent experience mild to moderate memory loss, whereas the majority of people retain sharp mental functioning even through old age (Butler, 1984; Schaie, 1990). Although organic brain disease, or what people often call senility, is far more prevalent among people in their 80s and 90s than among those in their 60s and 70s, even in the ninth decade, only about 20 percent of people are affected by senile dementia (Roth, 1978).

Senile dementia has a variety of causes, such as vascular problems that reduce blood supplies to the brain, or neurological syndromes brought on by exposure to toxins such as alcohol. Roughly 10 to 20 percent of dementias are curable by diagnosing and eliminating an environmental toxin (Elias et al., 1990). Well over half the cases, however, are caused by **Alzheimer's disease**, a progressive and incurable illness that destroys neurons in the brain, causing severe impairment of memory, reasoning, perception, language, and behavior. Although onset can occur in middle adulthood, as early as a person's 40s, Alzheimer's disease most commonly occurs later in life.

Characteristic changes in brain tissue include tangled neurons and protein deposits on cortical cells, which destroy their functioning. Alzheimer's patients also have abnormally low levels of several neurotransmitters (Winblad et al., 1985), most importantly acetylcholine, which plays a central role in memory functioning. The acetylcholine deficit is linked to an insufficient quantity of an enzyme necessary for its production (Price et al., 1985); levels of this enzyme are 60 to 90 percent lower in patients with Alzheimer's disease than in the normal population of the same age (Coyle et al., 1983).

PET scans of a brain with Alzheimer's (left) and a normal brain (right). Note the comparative inactivity of the Alzheimer's brain.

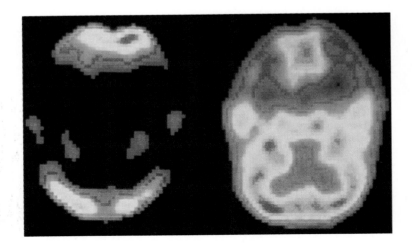

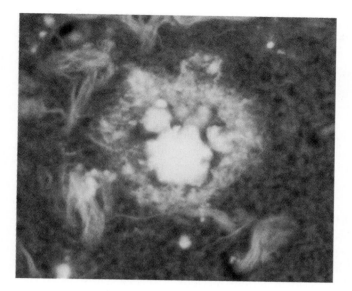

The brains of Alzheimer's patients show abnormal chemical deposits (called plaques) and tangled neural fibers.

Alzheimer's disease may have several different causes, some of them viral, but at least one major form of the disorder is genetic (Coyle, 1991). Researchers have isolated genes on at least three chromosomes that are implicated in the genetic transmission of Alzheimer's. One form of the disease has been linked to a defect on chromosome 21 (St. George-Hyslop et al., 1987), the chromosome implicated in Down syndrome, a form of mental retardation (Chapter 8). Down syndrome patients who live into late middle age often develop symptoms and neurological changes similar to Alzheimer's disease (Anderton, 1987; Price et al., 1985).

Whether the pathological processes involved in Alzheimer's are unique to the disease or are present to some extent in normal aging is a subject of debate (see Dixon et al., 1992; Muller et al., 1991; Von Dras & Blumenthal, 1992). Some of the abnormalities seen in Alzheimer's patients, such as acetylcholine deficits and protein deposits, are found, to a lesser degree, in normal aged humans and other animals, but the extent of their presence does not predict degree of cognitive impairment, as it does in Alzheimer's patients (see Bondareff 1985; Bondareff et al., 1990; Pearlson et al., 1992).

SOME CONCLUDING THOUGHTS

This chapter began with three questions about development: What are the relative contributions of nature and nurture? To what extent is development characterized by critical or sensitive periods? And to what extent is development stagelike or continuous? All three questions address the way maturational, cultural, and environmental forces interact over time to create an organism capable of responding adaptively to its social and physical environment.

Maturational factors provide both the potentialities and limits of physical and cognitive development. Young children cannot think in the abstract ways that adolescents can about justice, God, or conservation of matter, and old people cannot think as quickly as their younger compatriots. In both cases, the nervous system determines the range within which people can function. Except in cases of congenital mental retardation or neural degeneration, however, that range is extraordinarily large. Moreover, the nervous system that establishes the parameters of cognitive functioning is itself partially a product of its environment. Experience can enrich the developing brain, increasing the connections among neurons that underlie the capacity for complex thought, or it can constrain psychological functioning by limiting the processing power of the brain.

Understanding development thus means living with ambiguities. Perhaps that is a developmental achievement in itself.

Summary

1. **Developmental psychology** studies the way humans develop and change over time. A lifespan developmental perspective examines both constancy and change, and gains and losses in functioning, that occur at different points over the human life cycle.

Basic Issues in Developmental Psychology

2. Three basic issues confront developmental psychologists. The first concerns the relative roles of nature (genetically programmed **maturation**) and nurture. The second is the relative importance of early experience and whether human development is characterized by **critical periods** (periods of special sensitivity to specific types of learning that shape the capacity for future development) or **sensitive periods** (periods of special, but not definitive, importance). The third issue is whether development occurs in **stages**—relatively discrete steps through which everyone progresses in the same sequence—or whether it is **continuous**, or gradual.

3. Developmental psychologists rely on three types of research designs. **Cross-sectional studies** compare groups of different-aged subjects at a single time to see whether differences exist among them. **Longitudinal studies** follow the same individuals over time and thus can directly assess age changes rather than age differences. **Sequential studies** minimize the confounding variable of cohort by studying multiple cohorts longitudinally.

Physical Development and Its Psychological Consequences

4. **Prenatal** (before birth) development is divided into three stages: the **germinal**, **embryonic**, and **fetal periods**. Prenatal development can be disrupted by harmful environmental agents known as **teratogens**, such as PCBs, alcohol, and cocaine.

5. Neural development, both prenatally and throughout childhood, proceeds through progressive myelination, trimming back of neurons, and increasing dendritic connections. Throughout life the brain demonstrates considerable **plasticity**, or flexibility, in meeting environmental demands.

6. Physical and psychological development are intertwined. At birth, an infant possesses many adaptive reflexes. Motor development follows a universal maturational sequence, although cross-cultural research indicates that the environment can affect the pace of development. By the end of adolescence, physical growth is virtually complete, but with aging comes a gradual decline in physical and sensory abilities with which people must cope psychologically. Women experience a dramatic physical change in middle adulthood during **menopause**, the cessation of the menstrual cycle.

Cognitive Development in Infancy, Childhood, and Adolescence

7. For many years psychologists underestimated the substantial abilities of infants; researchers now know they are capable of **intermodal** understanding—the ability to associate sensations about an object from different senses, and to match their own actions to behaviors they observe visually in the earliest days of life.

8. Piaget proposed that children develop knowledge by inventing or constructing reality out of their own experience. According to Piaget, people cognitively adapt to their environment through two interrelated processes. **Assimilation** means interpreting actions or events in terms of one's present schemas—that is, fitting reality into one's previous structures of knowledge. **Accommodation** is the modification of schemas to fit reality.

9. Piaget proposed a stage theory of cognitive development. During the **sensorimotor stage**, thought primarily takes the form of perception and action. Gradually, children acquire **object permanence**, recognizing that objects exist in time and space independent of their actions on, or observation of them. Sensorimotor children are extremely **egocentric**, being thoroughly embedded in their own point of view. The **preoperational stage** is characterized by the emergence of symbolic thought. **Operations** are internalized or mental actions the individual can use to manipulate, transform, and return an object of knowledge to its original state. Piaget called the third stage the **concrete operational stage** because at this point children are capable of operating on, or mentally manipulating, internal representations of concrete objects in ways that are reversible. The concrete operational child understands **conservation**—the idea that basic properties of an object or situation remain stable even though superficial properties may be changed. The **formal operational stage** is characterized by the ability to reason about formal propositions rather than concrete events.

10. In its broadest outlines—such as the movement from concrete, egocentric thought to abstract thought—Piaget's theory appears to be accurate. Psychologists have, however, criticized Piaget for underestimating the capacities of younger children, assuming too much consistency across domains, and downplaying the influence of culture.

11. The information-processing approach to cognitive development focuses on the development of different components of cognition. Several variables that develop over time are children's **knowledge base**, their **automatization** of processing, their ability to use cognitive strategies, and their **metacognitive abilities** (understanding of their own thinking processes).

12. Integrative or **neo-Piagetian theories** attempt to wed stage conceptions with research on information processing and domain-specific knowledge; they also focus more heavily than either perspective on the roles of emotion and motivation in shaping thought.

Cognitive Development and Change in Adulthood

13. Whether the variable is muscle strength, intellectual ability, or sexual functioning, the rule of thumb is *use it or lose it*: Mental and physical capacities atrophy with disuse.

14. **Fluid intelligence** (intellectual capacities that have no specific content but are used in processing information) begins to decline gradually in mid-life, whereas **crystallized intelligence** (a person's store of knowledge) continues to expand over the lifespan. One of the clearest changes that accompanies aging is a general **psychomotor slowing**. Only in a minority of people does substantial intellectual decline occur.

15. **Senile dementia** is a disorder marked by global disturbance of higher mental functions. Well over half the cases of senile dementia result from **Alzheimer's disease**, a progressive and incurable illness that destroys neurons in the brain, causing severe impairments of memory, reasoning, perception, language, and behavior.

Lincoln Perry, **"All in a Summer's Day,"** *1989*

Chapter 14

SOCIAL DEVELOPMENT

*K*ate was 2-1/2 years old when her mother was hospitalized for 27 days with a complicated delivery. Long hospital stays for mothers giving birth were not unusual in the 1960s, and fathers often felt unable to care for young children. Thus, her parents placed Kate temporarily in the home of psychologists James and Joyce Robertson (1971), who were studying the way infants and young children respond to prolonged separation from their mothers. Kate was well prepared for the event: Her parents had discussed it with her for weeks and had taken her for several long visits to the Robertsons' home. Kate knew her parents loved her and would be taking her back home and that her father would visit regularly.

On the day her mother was to be hospitalized, Kate left home with the words, "Kate come back soon." During the first week in her new home, she was cooperative and cheerful but in an exaggerated, somewhat unnatural way, as if to reassure herself and her caretakers that she felt safe and happy. At one point she said, "Look, I'm a good girl, I'm laughing." She would sometimes repeat to herself her parents' instructions: "Be a good girl, don't cry," "Eat up your potatoes," and "Don't make a mess."

During the second week, the Robertsons began to observe a paradoxical combination of behaviors. On the one hand, Kate seemed more natural and spontaneous; on the other, she showed growing signs of sadness and listlessness. When Kate's mother came up in conversation, the child would sometimes point to her psychologist surrogate mother and insist, "*You* are my Mummy." After her first visit with her real "Mummy" in the hospital, her behavior changed markedly. She became negative and aggressive, difficult to console, and readily flew into tears or tantrums.

When Kate returned home, she generally reverted to her good-natured self, but she slept restlessly, wet her bed, and was much more defiant than prior to the separation. Two weeks after returning home, Kate's mother took her to register for nursery school. That night Kate screamed, presumably from nightmares, and awoke with an acute asthma attack, a symptom seen more frequently in children whose bonding with their mothers is problematic (Madrid & Schwartz, 1991). When the doctor inquired about recent stresses, the mother realized that she and a school official had talked that day about Kate being "taken"—meaning "accepted"—but Kate had apparently misunderstood what they meant.

Children react to separation very differently at different ages. At age 2-1/2, separation can be devastating for a child; by age 6, a few weeks away may lead only to occasional homesickness. The difference reflects **social development**, predictable changes in interpersonal thought, feeling, and behavior throughout the lifespan. In exploring social development, we begin with the earliest relationship between an infant and her caregivers and examine its lasting effects on later relationships. Next, we examine the way children learn the ways of their culture, considering what happens to children when their parents are harsh and rejecting and how and when children take on the attributes expected of their gender. Then we explore children's relationships with siblings and peers, their changing conceptions of themselves and others, and their developing moral sense. We conclude with a discussion of lifespan development, studying the changing nature of human nature from infancy to the final days of life.

ATTACHMENT

In the middle of this century, psychoanalysts observed that children reared in large institutional homes, with minimal stimulation and no consistent contact with a loving caretaker, often became emotionally unstable, lacking in conscience, or mentally retarded (see Bowlby, 1969). These observations led to recognition of the importance of **attachment**, the enduring affectional ties that children form with their primary caregivers (Ainsworth & Bell, 1970; Ainsworth & Bowlby, 1991; Bowlby, 1969). Attachment includes a desire for proximity to an attachment figure, a sense of security derived from the person's presence, and feelings of distress when the person is absent. Attachment is not unilateral; rather, it involves an interaction between two people who react to each other's signals.

For many years, psychoanalysts and behaviorists were in rare agreement on the origins of attachment behavior, both linking it to feeding. For the psychoanalyst, the gratification of oral needs led infants to become attached to people who satisfy those needs; for the behaviorist, mothers became secondary reinforcers through their association with food, which is a primary (innate) reinforcer. Both theories, however, proved to be wrong. Definitive evidence came from a series of classic experiments performed by Harry Harlow (Harlow & Zimmerman, 1959).

As described in Chapter 2, Harlow reared infant rhesus monkeys in isolation from their mothers for several months and then placed them in a cage with two inanimate surrogate mothers (Chapter 2). One, a wire monkey that provided no warmth or softness, held a bottle from which the infant could nurse. The other was covered with terrycloth to provide softness, but it had no bottle, so it could not provide food. Baby monkeys spent much of their time clinging to the softer mother, to which they would also run when they were frightened, but they virtually ignored the wire surrogate except when hungry. Harlow's findings established that security, not food, is the crucial element in forming attachment relationships.

John Bowlby (1969, 1973, 1983), who developed attachment theory, provided the link between these findings and the psychodynamic literature on children reared in institutional settings. Although Bowlby was a psychoanalyst, he was also an ethologist (a psychologist interested in comparative animal behavior), and he proposed an evolutionary theory of attachment. He argued that attachment behavior is prewired into humans, as similar behavior is in many other animal species, to keep immature animals close to their parents. Bowlby noted the relation between human attachment behavior and a phenomenon studied by the ethologist Konrad Lorenz (1935) called imprinting. **Imprinting** is the tendency of young animals of certain species to follow an animal to which they were exposed during a period of

FIGURE 14.1
*Imprinting. Normally, imprinting
leads young animals to follow an
adult member of their species.
At times, however, Mother Nature
may lead her children astray.
Here, geese trail Lorenz, on
whom they imprinted when
young.*

sensitivity early in their lives (Figure 14.1). Lorenz postulated that imprinting confers an evolutionary advantage: A gosling that stays close to its mother or father is
more likely to be fed, protected from predators, and taught skills useful for survival
and reproduction than a gosling that strays from its parents (Hess, 1959; Lorenz,
1937). Bowlby argued that attachment behavior in human infants, such as staying
close to parents and crying loudly in their absence, evolved for the same reasons.

Bowlby proposed a model of attachment that relies on the concept of homeostasis (Chapters 10 and 11). The child's goal is to maintain physical proximity to the
attachment figure. When the goal is threatened, as when a toddler's mother leaves
the room for a few minutes, the child experiences a feedback signal, distress. Distress
motivates such behaviors as crying or searching for her, which, if successful, shut off
the feedback and deactivate the attachment system, temporarily switching off attachment-related motives and thoughts. This leaves the child free for other goals and
tasks, such as exploring the environment.

The attachment figure thus becomes a safe base from which the child can
explore (Ainsworth, 1979) and to whom he can periodically return for "emotional
refueling" (Mahler et al., 1975). Toddlers who are playing happily often suddenly
look around to establish the whereabouts of their attachment figures. Once they
locate their caregiver or even run to a comforting lap, they return to play, refueled
for the next period of time. Later in life, a college student's telephone call home may
serve a similar function.

Attachment behavior emerges gradually over the first several months of life,
peaking some time during the second year and then diminishing in intensity as children become more confident in their independence (Ainsworth, 1967). Among the
first precursors of attachment is a general preference for social stimuli over other
objects in the environment. Visual recognition of mother (the primary caregiver
studied in most research) occurs at about 3 months (Olson, 1981), and by 5 or 6
months, infants recognize and greet their mothers and other attachment figures
from across the room.

At about 6 months, infants begin to show distress at separation from attachment figures, or **separation anxiety**. In 9 month olds, a 30-minute separation from
the mother leads to hormonal as well as behavioral changes such as crying and fret-
ting (Gunnar et al., 1992). Separation anxiety emerges at about the same time in
children of different cultures (Figure 14.2), despite widely different child-rearing
practices (Kagan, 1976). Blind children show a comparable pattern (although a few
months later in onset), becoming anxious when they no longer hear the familiar
sounds of their mother's voice or movements (Adelson & Fraiberg, 1974; Fraiberg,

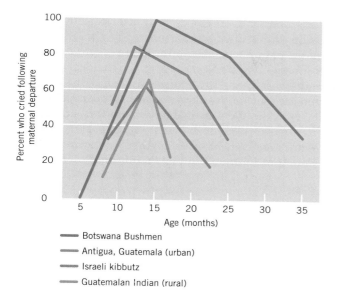

FIGURE 14.2
Separation anxiety in various cultures. Separation anxiety (as measured by the percentage of children who cry following separation from the mother) tends to peak at approximately the same time across various cultures. SOURCE: Kagan, 1983, p. 198.

1975). These data suggest a maturational basis for separation anxiety. In fact, separation anxiety emerges about the same time infants begin to crawl, which is probably not accidental from an evolutionary perspective. As one anthropologist noted, "When a child knows it *can* [physically] get away, then it is afraid it *could* get away" (Konner, in Greenberg, 1977, p. 75).

Individual Differences in Attachment Patterns

Bowlby observed that young children typically respond to separations from their attachment figures with a sequence of behaviors. Like 2-1/2-year-old Kate, they initially protest with crying or tantrums, but unlike Kate, they may ultimately become detached and indifferent to the attachment figure if she is gone too long. Mary Ainsworth, a student of Bowlby's, recognized that children vary in their responses to separation: While some seem secure in their relationship with their attachment figure, others seem perpetually stuck in protest or detachment. Ainsworth demonstrated these differences among infants using an experimental procedure called the **Strange Situation**. In the Strange Situation, the mother leaves her young child (aged 12 to 18 months) alone in a room of toys. The child is joined for a brief time by a friendly stranger, after which the mother returns and greets the child (Ainsworth, 1973, 1979, 1991).

Ainsworth found that children respond to their mothers leaving and returning in three basic ways. Some infants (called securely attached) welcome the mother's return and seek closeness to her. Others, characterized as insecurely attached, either ignore her (an avoidant style) or show a combination of anger and rejection, simultaneous with a clear desire to be close to her (an ambivalent or anxious-ambivalent style). Avoidant children often seem relatively unfazed by their mother's departure, whereas ambivalent children become very upset.

More recent research with infants in high-risk samples, such as those who have been maltreated, has uncovered a fourth style of attachment, a variant of insecure attachment called disorganized (Main & Solomon, 1986). Disorganized children perform contradictory actions, such as approaching the mother while simultaneously gazing away. They also appear disoriented, a response manifested in stereotyped rocking and dazed facial expressions. Surprisingly, an infant's pattern of attachment to its mother is not highly predictive of its attachment to its father; children can be secure with one parent but insecure with another. Infants apparently form specific expectations of different attachment relationships.

Secure attachment is the most commonly observed attachment pattern around the world, and individual differences within any given culture tend to be larger than differences between the norm in one culture and the norm in any other (see Main, 1990; von IJzendoorn & Kroonenberg, 1988). Nevertheless, the frequency of different styles of attachment does differ substantially across cultures. For example, infants reared on Israeli kibbutzim are much more likely to have ambivalent attachments to their mothers than infants in the West, probably because they are reared by day along with other children by another woman (Sagi, 1990; Sagi et al., 1994). Interestingly, the quality of an infant's attachment to its daytime mother surrogate, not to its parents, predicts later social adjustment in childhood, unlike in Europe and North America.

FROM MIND TO BRAIN

TEMPERAMENT AND EXPERIENCE IN ATTACHMENT STYLE

Why do infants differ in their patterns of attachment? The answer appears to lie in the temperament of the child, the behaviors and personality of the parent, and the fit between the two (Belsky & Isabella, 1988; Goldsmith & Harman, 1994; Rosen & Rothbaum, 1993).

Attachment, like all psychological processes, can be understood in part at a psychobiological level. Attachment-related behavior such as protest at separation probably does not occur in the first half of the first year of life because myelination of neurons has not sufficiently progressed in limbic structures that regulate emotional distress, particularly fear and anxiety (Konner, 1991). Protest, distress, and despair at separation after that time appear mediated by several neurotransmitter systems, notably norepinephrine, dopamine, and serotonin, which are involved in arousal, anxiety, and depression (Kraemer, 1992). For example, monkeys separated from their mothers show elevated norepinephrine levels when isolated from them, which is consistent with behavioral responses indicating distress. These normal neurotransmitter responses to separation can be altered in monkeys either pharmacologically, using chemicals that disrupt neural transmission, or through abnormal rearing, in which the infant is removed from the mother at birth and reared in isolation or with peers. Abnormal rearing conditions alter neuronal development in the cortex, cerebellum, and limbic system in monkeys, suggesting that even environmental events can produce lasting biological changes in the systems that mediate attachment behavior. These monkeys are particularly vulnerable upon later separations to despair responses.

The relation between attachment style and temperament is a matter of some controversy. In humans, researchers have identified three infant temperaments—easy, difficult, and slow-to-warm-up—which correspond in certain respects to secure, ambivalent, and avoidant attachment styles (Chess & Thomas, 1986). Some researchers have, therefore, argued that attachment security largely reflects temperament (see Kagan, 1984; Manglesdorf et al., 1990). An inborn proclivity toward timidity or fearfulness, for example, could produce anxious behavior in the Strange Situation (Goldsmith & Alansky, 1987). The temperamental variable most highly predictive of attachment status across several studies is negative affect, although the correlation is only .30 (Vaughn et al., 1992). This suggests that temperament is only one determinant of attachment style.

The variable that appears to have the biggest impact on security of attachment is environmental: the mother's sensitivity to her baby's signals (Ainsworth, 1979; Bowlby, 1969; Sroufe & Fleeson, 1986; Sroufe & Waters,

1977). When mothers are responsive to their children's communications, are psychologically accessible, and convey a sense of acceptance and enjoyment, infants are more likely to feel secure. In contrast, infants whose mothers do not respond to their needs form less secure attachment bonds and display more anger, fear, and avoidance (Bretherton, 1985; Erickson et al., 1985; Pederson et al., 1990; Ricks, 1985). Similarly, the extent to which fathers feel positive about their infant and their role in its development at 3 months strongly correlates ($r = .54$) with the later attachment security of the infant toward its father (Cox et al., 1992).

Personality characteristics, such as warmth and empathy, can heavily influence maternal responsiveness, but so can environmental factors. Even seemingly innocuous variables can affect attachment status. In a study of infants of poor inner-city mothers, whose children are at risk for insecure attachment, mothers in the experimental condition were given a soft baby carrier that permitted close physical contact with their infants (Anisfeld et al., 1990). Control mothers received plastic seats that minimized direct contact. The results were startling. The vast majority of infants in the experimental group were securely attached at age 13 months, whereas the majority in the control group were insecurely (avoidantly or ambivalently) attached (Figure 14.3). (This study was conducted before the "disorganized" category became widely used in research.)

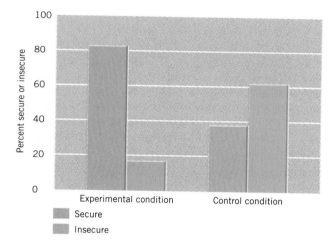

FIGURE 14.3
Maternal physical contact and attachment. At age 13 months, children in the experimental condition, who had closer physical contact with their mothers, were much more likely to be securely attached. SOURCE: *Adapted from Anisfeld et al., 1990, p. 1623.*

Cultural factors substantially influence maternal responsiveness as well. Mothers of 10 month olds in the United States tend to talk to and look at their infants, particularly when the infants vocalize, look at them, or cry. In contrast, among the Gusii of East Africa, mothers generally avert their gaze when they hold their infants (Richman et al., 1992). Differences exist not only between but within cultures. Within a society, more educated mothers tend to be more responsive to their infants (Richman et al., 1992).

Although both biology and experience play a role in creating individual differences in attachment, the interaction of the two—that is, the match between the proclivities of children and their caregivers—is equally important. For example, infants who are temperamentally prone to distress may be more likely to become insecurely attached if their caretakers are rigid and emotionally controlled (Mangelsdorf et al., 1990). Thus, the relation between temperament and attachment is complex, far less direct than the association between a characteristic such as eye color and an underlying genotype.

Implications of Attachment for Later Development

Attachment patterns developed in infancy tend to persist and find expression in a wide range of social behaviors throughout the lifespan. Children rated avoidant in infancy tend to be described by their teachers as relatively insecure and detached in nursery school and to have difficulty discussing their feelings about separation at age 6. In contrast, securely attached preschoolers studied in longitudinal research have higher self-esteem, are more socially competent, show greater sensitivity to the needs of their peers, and are more popular (Jacobson et al., 1986; LaFreniere & Sroufe, 1985; Main et al., 1985; Sroufe, 1983; Waters et al., 1979). More recent longitudinal studies find that security of attachment in infancy predicts a range of behaviors in the elementary-school years, from self-control and peer acceptance to competent behavior in the classroom (Bretherton, 1990; Olson et al., 1989; Urban et al., 1991).

Adult Attachment

Although no infants assessed in longitudinal Strange Situation research studies have yet reached adulthood, other evidence suggests that early attachment patterns continue to be influential much later in life. Researchers studying **adult attachment** have examined the way subjects describe and recall their relationships with their parents (Main et al., 1985). Adults with secure adult attachment styles speak freely and openly about their relationships with their parents. People with ambivalent styles appear preoccupied with, and ambivalent about, their parents. Avoidant adults dismiss the importance of attachment relationships or offer idealized generalizations about their parents, while being unable to back them up with specific examples.

Avoidant adults, like avoidant infants, apparently shut off attachment feelings to avoid distress. Physiological evidence of this deactivating process comes from a study that monitored electrodermal response (a measure of anxiety or conflict) as subjects recalled memories involving separation, rejection, and threat from their parents (Dozier & Kobak, 1992). As can be seen in Table 14.1, more secure subjects are slightly less reactive. The picture is quite different with avoidance: The more avoidance, the more physiological reactivity. This is particularly striking given that avoidance was measured, among other things, by subjects' claims during these interviews that they were not at all distressed by separations, rejections, or parental threats.

Other research has compared parents' adult attachment styles (as measured by interviews) with their children's attachment styles. The match is remarkably close.

TABLE 14.1 CORRELATONS BETWEEN ATTACHMENT AND PHYSIOLOGICAL REACTIVITY

INTERVIEW QUESTION	SECURITY OF ATTACHMENT	TENDENCY TO USE AVOIDANT (DEACTIVATING) STRATEGIES
1. Background information	.11	−.07
2. Memories of separation from parents	−.27	.43
3. Memories of parental rejection	−.18	.34
4. Memories of parental threat	−.28	.39

Note that avoidant subjects were only physiologically reactive during threatening questions—precisely the questions they claimed to find nonthreatening.

Source: Dozier & Koback, 1992.

Note. The table shows the correlations between physiological reactivity (assessed by increases in electrodermal activity) and two dimensions of attachment (security and use of avoidant strategies).

For example, mothers who are uncomfortable or avoidant in describing their own attachment to *their* mothers tend to have avoidant infants and children (Fonagy et al., 1991; Main et al., 1985). Considerable evidence suggests that mothers whose early attachment experiences were disrupted—through death of a parent, divorce, abuse or neglect, or long-term separation from their parents—are more likely to have difficulty forming close attachment relationships with their own infants (Ricks, 1985; Rutter et al., 1983; Zeanah & Zeanah, 1989). Mothers who have insecure attachment relationships with their own mothers are less responsive and have more difficulty maintaining physical proximity to their infants and young children (Crowell & Feldman, 1991). Other studies find a continuity between relationship patterns of college students and the security of their attachment to their parents (Kobak & Sceery, 1988).

Why should early attachments have such a powerful effect on later relationships? Bowlby proposed that an infant develops an **internal working model,** or mental representation of the attachment relationship, which forms the basis for expectations in close relationships (Bowlby, 1969, 1982; Bretherton, 1985, 1990; Main, 1990; Main et al., 1985). For example, a child whose early attachment to her mother is marked by extreme anxiety resulting from inconsistent or abusive caretaking may form a working model of herself as unlovable or unworthy. She may also see significant others as hostile or unpredictable and generalize some of those feelings and expectations, carrying them into later relationships. Bowlby's theory explains not only why security of attachment to the mother remains quite consistent through infancy and toddlerhood but also why infants and toddlers who are secure with one caretaker may not be secure with another (Howes & Hamilton, 1992). A child's experience with one person, such as the mother, may feel secure, while another relationship (such as with a father or preschool teacher) may feel less comfortable or predictable because the child has different internal working models of the relationships.

Stability of Early Attachment Patterns

Is history destiny? Can a person ever overcome a bad start in childhood or infancy? Research certainly suggests that problematic early attachments substantially increase vulnerability to subsequent difficulties. Disturbances in childhood attachment relationships predict later difficulties in childhood and adolescence (Bowlby, 1969; Ricks, 1985; Spitz, 1945). Disrupted attachments are associated with severe personality disturbances (Ludolph et al., 1990; Zanarini et al., 1989), depression (Brown et al., 1986), antisocial behavior and adjustment problems (Tizard & Hodges, 1978), and difficulty behaving appropriately as a parent (Ricks, 1985).

Early severe attachment problems and dysfunctional parenting frequently lead to poor social functioning. Some people, however, like poet Maya Angelou, are resilient in the face of even highly traumatic childhood experiences.

Nevertheless, early attachment style is not the only determinant of later functioning. Some children are remarkably resilient in the face of neglectful or abusive life experiences (Anthony & Cohler, 1987). Furthermore, as circumstances change, so may patterns of attachment. Internal working models, like the schemas described in previous chapters, are inherently conservative, but they are not immutable (see Belsky & Nezworski, 1987; Lamb, 1987). Many forms of psychotherapy are predicated on the notion that exploring experiences and feelings in a therapeutic relationship can help people change basic patterns of relatedness (Chapter 16). Indeed, some of Harlow's monkeys who had been raised in isolation and were extremely socially maladapted showed marked improvement in social interactions after developing a close relationship with a normal monkey who served as a simian "therapist" (Novak & Harlow, 1975).

One recent study provides dramatic evidence of the possibilities for altering problematic patterns of attachment. The investigators provided a group of high-risk infants and mothers with a weekly home visitor. The mothers were poor, often depressed, and exhibited enough signs of inadequate caretaking to warrant referrals from health, educational, or social service professionals (Lyons-Ruth et al., 1990). The home visitor offered support and advice, modeled positive and active interactions with the infant, and provided a trusting relationship for the mother. The results were compelling: In comparison to an untreated control group, infants in the intervention group scored 10 points higher on an infant IQ measure and were twice as likely (roughly 60 versus 30 percent) to be classified as securely attached at 18 months.

Effects of Maternal Employment

If early attachment experiences shape later emotional health, does a working mother's daily routine of leaving her child with surrogate caregivers adversely affect the child's emotional and cognitive development? In the United States, the number of women with children under age 6 who are employed has doubled over the last two decades and tripled over the last three. Roughly two-thirds of mothers with infants and toddlers are now employed outside the home (see Silverstein, 1991). We have essentially embarked on a massive social experiment, the outcome of which we are just beginning to observe. Predictably, at this early stage, the impact of full-time maternal employment on infants' well-being is a matter of considerable debate (see Clarke-Stewart, 1989; Collins & Gunnar, 1990).

One large-scale study found maternal employment in the first year of life associated with relatively poor intellectual functioning and greater behavioral problems when the child is in preschool (ages 3 to 4). This was true across race, gender, and social class. Delaying maternal employment until even the fourth quarter of the first year, and involving a grandmother in childcare, proved to be highly advantageous, particularly for poor children (Baydar & Brooks-Gunn, 1991). Similarly, other studies find that infants whose mothers work full-time outside the home have a greater incidence of insecure attachment in the Strange Situation, are less compliant toward their parents as young children, and are more aggressive with peers than infants whose mothers work part-time or stay home (see Belsky & Rovine, 1988; Blehar, 1974). Yet other research finds just the opposite, that children in daycare are more popular and assertive and less aggressive with their peers (e.g., Field, 1991; Scarr & Eisenberg, 1993).

Researchers are beginning to tease apart the factors that determine whether daycare leads to positive or negative outcomes. One of the most important factors is socioeconomic status. For children of poor families, daycare is generally associated with more positive cognitive, social, and emotional outcomes than maternal care at home. Equally important are parents' attitudes about parenthood, the amount of time they spend with their children, and the quality of that time (Campos et al.,

1983; Easterbrooks & Goldberg, 1985). Women who stay at home to care for their infants when they want to be working outside the home may not be doing their children any favors (Farel, 1980). These mothers report higher levels of depression than mothers who experience a better fit between reality and their preferences (Hock & DeMeis, 1990). Depression, in turn, is related to poorer child outcomes.

Quality of daycare—whether meals are nutritious, curricula are carefully designed, staff turnover is low, and so forth—is also crucial (Scarr & Eisenberg, 1993). Early entry into low-quality daycare is particularly detrimental to children's later adaptation in kindergarten (Bates et al., 1994; Howes, 1990), whereas early entry into high-quality daycare may confer advantages that last many years (Andersson, 1992; Howes et al., 1992; McCartney et al., 1982). Unfortunately, the children most likely to benefit from quality daycare—poor children—are most likely to get low-quality care.

SOCIALIZATION

Attachment relationships provide the child's first social experiences and a model for many future relationships, but they are only one avenue for initiating the child into the social world. To function as adults, children must learn the rules, beliefs, values, skills, attitudes, and behavior patterns of their society, a process called **socialization**. Children learn from a variety of **socialization agents** (individuals and groups that transmit social knowledge and values to the child).

Before describing research on socialization, three caveats are in order. First, socialization is not a unidirectional process in which adults fill children's minds with values and beliefs. Rather, it is interactive, or transactional. Children are active participants in their own socialization, who must construct an understanding of social rules and gradually come to experience cultural beliefs and values as their own (Maccoby, 1980, 1992; Sapir, 1949). Children also have innate temperamental dispositions that influence attempts to shape them. Second, although our focus is on socialization during childhood, socialization is a lifelong process. People are socialized throughout their lives to play different roles, such as student, parent, friend, wage-earner, or retiree, and these roles change from one phase of life to the next. A third caveat is that socialization always occurs within a broader social and economic context (Bronfenbrenner, 1986; Garbarino et al., 1991; McLoyd, 1989). Adults who are economically stressed, for example, are less likely to parent effectively than financially secure parents (Conger et al., 1993). Similarly, low-income African-American mothers who parent children without the help of the child's father are more likely to use controlling, harsh, and less child-centered disciplinary techniques than their counterparts in intact families (Kelley et al., 1992).

The Role of Parents

Parents are particularly important socialization agents, and their methods vary widely. Diana Baumrind (1967, 1971, 1991) discovered three styles of parenting, distinguished by the extent to which parents control their children's actions and respond to their feelings. Authoritarian parents place high value on obedience and respect for authority. They do not encourage discussion of why particular behaviors are important or listen to the child's point of view. Rather, authoritarian parents impose a rigid set of standards to which they expect their children to adhere; they are likely to punish their children frequently and to use physical means. Permissive parents, in contrast, impose virtually no controls on their children, allowing them to make their own decisions whenever possible. Permissive parents tend to accept their children's impulsive behaviors, including angry or aggressive ones, and rarely dole out punishments. Authoritative parents, the third group, set standards for their children and firmly enforce them, but they also encourage verbal give-and-take, explaining their views and showing respect for their children's opinions.

Each parenting style tends to produce children with different characteristics. Preschool studies have found that the most self-controlled, independent, inquisitive, and sociable children usually have authoritative parents. Studies of grade school children and adolescents have similarly found authoritative parenting associated with social, intellectual, and academic competence (Baumrind, 1987; Dornbush et al., 1987; Sternberg et al., 1994). Authoritarian parenting, on the other hand, has been linked to low independence, vulnerability to stress, low self-esteem, and an external locus of control (a sense that one has little control over what happens in life) (Buri et al., 1988; Loeb et al., 1980; Steinberg et al., 1994). Children with permissive parents tend to be low in self-reliance and control over their aggressive impulses (Olweus, 1980; Maccoby & Martin, 1983; Yarrow et al., 1971) and to have more trouble with substance abuse in adolescence (Baumrind, 1991).

The Role of Culture

Over two decades of research on parenting styles thus indicate that the authoritative style most effectively produces traits valued in Anglo-European culture. However, this parenting style is rare or nonexistent in many cultures and is probably not the most adaptive pattern everywhere (Whiting & Whiting, 1973, 1975). Agricultural societies usually consider obedience a far more important value than autonomy or independence. Among the Mayan Zinacanteco Indians of Mexico, for example, an entire family shares a single-room, 20-square-foot hut, and every member contributes to the family's survival by farming (Brazelton, 1972). In this culture, where people have no real choice in the roles they will fill, socialization for independence and free choice would be counterproductive.

Training for independence or for embeddedness in kin or clan begins in the first days of life. Infants in most cultures sleep in the same beds, or at least the same rooms, as their mothers (Whiting, 1964). In contrast, North American pediatricians recommend against bringing the child into the parental bed, and most middle-class parents give infants their own rooms by 3 to 6 months at the latest, fostering independence from the start. In a study comparing the sleeping patterns of Mayan and North American infants, Mayan infants tended simply to fall asleep when they were tired, whereas American families had elaborate bedtime rituals that might begin with a bath and toothbrushing and include reading bedtime stories, singing lullabies, and providing the baby with a special object (Morelli et al., 1992). One North American mother jokingly reported, "When my friends hear that it is time for my son to go to bed, they teasingly say, 'See you in an hour.'" Mayan parents were generally aghast to hear that parents could separate infants from their mothers at night and seemed to consider it tantamount to child neglect. One horrified Mayan mother asked, "But there's someone else with them there, isn't there?" The Mayan children typically slept with their mothers until another child was born, at which time they joined their fathers or siblings.

A Mayan mother and her children.

A GLOBAL VISTA

PARENTAL ACCEPTANCE AND REJECTION IN CROSS-CULTURAL PERSPECTIVE

One of the most important ways in which parents vary across and within cultures is parental warmth—the extent to which they are accepting or rejecting of their children (Rohner, 1975, 1986). Parents can express acceptance verbally through praise, compliments, or support, or nonverbally through hugging, approving glances, smiling, and caressing. Like acceptance, rejection can be expressed verbally (bullying or derision) or nonverbally (hitting, beating, shaking, or simply neglecting). Although parental warmth can be measured from parental behaviors, equally important is the subjective experience of the child. A child who construes occasionally abusive parents as basically loving may suffer few ill effects of his mistreatment.

Whether a specific behavior is accepting or rejecting depends in part on shared cultural meanings. Parents in India do not praise their children openly, particularly in front of other people. Instead, a mother may express positive feelings by peeling an orange for her child and removing the seeds. A North American child who received no praise from his mother but plenty of seedless oranges would likely look on the oranges much differently than would his Indian counterpart (Rohner, 1986). An important empirical question, however, is whether behavior experienced throughout the world as accepting or rejecting has similar effects on personality development. A body of research suggests that it does, at least within limits.

Findings both within the West and across cultures show that parental acceptance is quite consistently associated with high self-esteem, independence, and emotional stability. Parental rejection, on the other hand, is associated with a wide range of problems, including delinquency, difficulty maintaining intimate relationships, poorly controlled aggression, unpredictable mood, and lower intelligence (Rohner, 1986). A longitudinal study in the West found that people who have a warm or affectionate mother or father are more likely, 35 years later, to have a long and happy marriage, children, and close friendships in middle age (Franz et al., 1991). Research using Western samples of child-abuse victims shows that abused children and adults are more likely than their nonabused peers to have a malevolent worldview, poor self-esteem, and difficulty maintaining close relationships (see Finkelhor, 1994; Gelinas, 1983; Nigg et al., 1992). A large cross-cultural study correlating parental acceptance–rejection with personality traits in children and adults demonstrated that these patterns are indeed universal (Rohner, 1975): Cultures in which parents were rated from anthropological reports as rejecting produced children who were more hostile and dependent, and adults who were less emotionally stable, than cultures with more benign parenting practices (Table 14.2).

TABLE 14.2 PARENTAL ACCEPTANCE-REJECTION AND PERSONALITY CHARACTERISTICS

PERSONALITY CHARACTERISTIC IN A CULTURE	CORRELATION WITH DEGREE OF ACCEPTANCE IN PARENTING	
	Children	Adults
Hostility	−.48	−.31
Dependence	−.30	−.39
Self-esteem	.72	.38
Emotional stability	—	.62
Generosity	—	.41
Nurturance	—	.39

The more accepting the parents in a culture are, the less dependent and higher in self-esteem their children tend to be.

Source: Adapted from Rohner, 1975, p. 260.

Note. Dashes indicate missing data.

Alorese children are fed at their parents' convenience and frequently have temper tantrums when they are frustrated.

The Alorese, who inhabit a Pacific island off Java, exemplify a culture with highly rejecting parenting practices (see DuBois, 1944; Rohner, 1975). Alorese women return to the fields within two weeks of childbirth—if they have not had an abortion, which is common since they tend to find children intensely burdensome. After a brief initial period of benign and playful caretaking, Alorese infants receive very inconsistent care, such as sporadic feeding. Alorese children are constantly teased, ridiculed, and frightened for sport by older children and adults. Mothers may tease young children they are weaning by nursing the neighbor's baby. Parents threaten children with abandonment and send them to live with relatives if they are too difficult. As young children, the Alorese are left for the day without food unless they can get some by begging or screaming at their elders.

Generalizations about an entire people are, of course, always overgeneralizations, for individual differences exist in all cultures. Nevertheless, anthropologists have described Alorese adults as hostile, aggressive, and distrustful, characteristics that make sense in the context of Alorese child-rearing. Children are prone to tantrums and hitting other children, and adults frequently burst into rages, utter curses, ridicule each other, and hit younger kinsmen on the head with weapons. The Alorese are intensely sensitive to insults and humiliation. Relationships between adults in Alor are fraught with discord. Males strive to amass as much wealth as they can, always expecting others to cheat and deceive them. Marital affairs are common in both sexes, divorce is rampant, and men often beat their wives in jealousy or anger. Direct aggression between males is strongly discouraged, although women at times may openly brawl. Even the supernatural world of the Alorese is hostile and unstable, with the Good Beings under constant attack in their myths. In Alor, as elsewhere, patterns of child-rearing reflect cultural beliefs and values, and parents tend to harvest what they sow.

Socialization of Gender

Among the most powerful roles into which people are socialized are **gender roles**, which specify the range of behaviors considered appropriate for males and females. Unlike sex (a biological categorization based on genetic and anatomical differences), **gender** (the psychological meaning of being male or female) is influenced by learning. When a new baby is born, people greet its arrival with one of two announcements: "It's a girl!" or "It's a boy!" The immediacy and strength of this response rests on a relatively small anatomical feature, but it has important consequences for the way the person will come to think, feel, and behave (Archer & Lloyd, 1985). The process by which children acquire personality traits, emotional responses, skills, behaviors, and preferences that are culturally considered appropriate to their sex is called **sex typing** (Perry & Bussey, 1979).

Differential treatment of boys and girls begins at the very beginning. In one study, first-time mothers of young infants were asked to play with a 6-month-old baby (not their own) for 10 minutes (Smith & Lloyd, 1978). Several toys were available. Some, like a squeaky hammer and a stuffed rabbit wearing a bow-tie and trousers, were typical masculine toys; others, like a doll and a squeaky Bambi, were more feminine. The mothers did not know the babies were cross-dressed—that the 6 month old in the little boy's outfit was actually a little girl, and the baby in the pink dress, a boy. The mothers tended to offer the infants "gender-appropriate" toys and to encourage more physical activity in the "boys."

Similar findings emerge from studies of socialization in slightly older children. In experimental settings, adults tend to compliment and encourage girls more, particularly in nurturance play, such as taking care of dolls. They hold higher expectations for boys and provide them with more goal-directed reinforcements (Day, cited in Block 1979; Frisch, 1977). Naturalistic investigations of parents' behavior with their own children indicate that sons and daughters receive different treatment, especially after the first year of life, as children's activities become more sex-typed (O'Brien & Huston, 1983). Throughout early childhood, parents (especially fathers) tend to encourage traditional sex-typed behavior, discouraging play with toys that are typical of the opposite gender (Langlois & Downs, 1980). Throughout childhood and adolescence, boys in Europe and North America receive more encouragement to compete, more punishment, and more pressure not to cry or express feelings; girls receive more warmth, affection, and trust, although they are kept under closer surveillance (presumably for their protection) than boys (Block, 1978). Peers, too, enforce gender roles and become distressed and often ridiculing when others violate them (Etaugh et al., 1975; Fagot & Patterson, 1969; Lamb & Roopnarine, 1979).

Childern are reinforced early for sex-typed behavior.

RELATIONSHIPS WITH SIBLINGS AND PEERS

Parents and other caregivers are thus not the only significant figures in a child's life. Siblings and peers figure prominently as well.

Sibling Relationships

Until the 1980s, relationships with siblings received almost no attention from researchers. This is rather remarkable, since many children spend as much time with siblings as with parents. Sibling relationships involve rivalry and conflict as well as warmth and companionship (Collins & Gunnar, 1992). From an evolutionary perspective, one would expect both conflict and love between siblings. On the one hand, siblings are genetically related by half, so the welfare of each influences the inclusive fitness of the other. Thus, natural selection should have selected mechanisms leading humans and other animals to care for their siblings. On the other hand, particularly in childhood, siblings compete for precious parental resources, which can mean the difference between life and death in conditions of scarcity (see Trivers, 1972). As they mature, they may compete for familial resources that attract mates; squabbling over an estate is, in fact, a major source of conflict among adult siblings.

Sibling competition for resources often destroys family relations when estates are divided and can lead to substantial suffering. Here, England's King John begs forgiveness from his brother Richard, whom he betrayed for power and wealth.

The birth of a sibling can be a difficult event. Parents report a wide range of behavioral disturbances in their children when a new child is born, such as increased dependency, anxiety, bedwetting, toilet "accidents," and aggressiveness (Dunn & McGuire, 1992). The younger the child's age at the birth, the more difficulty the child has with being displaced (Kramer & Gottman, 1992). Not knowing whether to express hostility or nurturance, the young child may alternate between the two. Parents commonly report the heartwarming experience of watching their child happily sidle up to the crib to play with the baby—only to find their hearts beating faster and less warmly as their ambivalent offspring tries to tip the crib.

Closeness is as integral a part of the sibling relationship as conflict and rivalry. Childhood experiences as playmates, confidantes, nurturers, or objects of nurturance plant the seeds for adult sibling relationships that may be warm and intimate. The majority of Western adults report being close to their siblings, with pairs of sis-

Sibling relationships have both loving and aggressive elements.

ters the closest and pairs of brothers the least close (Cicirelli, 1991). Only 20 percent report apathy or hostility toward their adult siblings.

Peer Relationships

Relationships with peers can be as important as relationships with siblings. Researchers have examined the development of children's friendships, and they have focused, as well, on children who are rejected by their peers.

The Development of Friendship

Children's friendships are almost exclusively same-sex friendships; children simply like same-sex peers better (Bukowski et al., 1994). Cross-sex relationships account for only about 5 percent of friends in childhood (Hartup, 1989). Friendships begin to emerge around the third year of life and are marked by the same kind of commitment, reciprocity (sharing and mutuality), and relative equality that characterize friendships throughout the lifespan (see Hartup, 1989). Even preschool friendships have some stability. Young children tend to maintain their friendships unless one member of the pair moves away (see Collins & Gunnar, 1990).

The meaning of friendship, however, changes throughout childhood (Damon, 1977; Selman, 1980). Young children focus on the gratification they expect from relationships, describing friends as people who give them things or let them play with their toys. By middle childhood, children recognize the longer-term payoffs of specific friendships. When asked why one girl was her friend, an 8 year old responded, "Because she helps when I'm getting beat up, she cheers me up when I'm sad, and she shares.... I share so she'll share" (Damon, 1977, pp. 159–160). Adolescents are more concerned than children with intimacy in friendships, that is, mutual self-disclosure and feeling understood (Buhrmester, 1990). Girls tend to self-disclose more than boys; when boys self-disclose, they generally do so with girls (Youniss & Haynie, 1992).

The role of friends, siblings, and parents changes over the course of social development. Between the fifth and ninth grades, the amount of time North American children spend with their families drops roughly in half (Larson & Richards, 1991). By mid-adolescence (roughly ages 14 to 16) peer conformity is at its peak, but it diminishes by late adolescence (ages 17 to 22) (Youniss & Haynie, 1992). The experience of relationships as sources of conflict and support also changes during this period (Blos, 1967; Sullivan, 1953). Table 14.3 presents the results of a cross-sectional study that asked children, adolescents, and college students to rate the degree of support and conflict they experienced in several relationships (Furman & Buhrmester, 1992). For fourth graders, mothers and fathers are the primary sources of support, but this wanes during the adolescent years, when conflict with parents is at a peak. Friends loom much larger as sources of support in seventh grade but are gradually replaced by romantic partners by college age. Romantic relationships, like relationships with parents, are emotionally intense. They are experienced as most supportive at the same time as they are most conflictual, suggesting that they represent a battleground for both love and hate, as psychodynamic theory asserts.

The way children experience their parents, siblings, and peers at different times in their lives varies from culture to culture. In less individualistic, more collectivistic cultures, such as Costa Rica, elementary school children report higher satisfaction across the board with their families (and their teachers, who do not change from year to year as they do in the United States). The shift toward greater satisfaction and intimacy with friends occurs later, if at all, in Costa Rica, perhaps because the task of becoming separate and autonomous from one's family is not central, as in the United States and much of the West (DeRosier & Kupersmidt, 1991).

TABLE 14.3 SUPPORT AND CONFLICT IN RELATIONSHIPS

		GRADE			
		4	**7**	**10**	**COLLEGE**
RELATIONSHIP		**AMOUNT OF SUPPORT**			
Mother	The relationship with the mother takes a dip in the teenage years but begins to rise again as a source of support in college. The same is true for the relationship with the father.	3.90	3.51	3.32	3.42
Father		3.89	3.34	2.98	3.16
Sibling		3.43	2.99	3.11	3.22
Same-sex friend		3.41	3.61	3.57	3.37
Romantic relationship	Romantic relationships steadily increase in perceived support.	2.77	3.08	3.19	3.50
RELATIONSHIP		**AMOUNT OF CONFLICT**			
Mother		1.98	2.37	2.30	2.07
Father		1.94	2.26	2.30	1.98
Sibling		3.01	3.36	2.69	1.94
Same-sex friend		2.01	1.94	1.66	1.54
Romantic friend		1.68	1.47	1.74	1.88

Source: Furman & Buhrmester, 1992, p. 107.

Note. Subjects rated support and conflict on a 1-5 scale.

Peer Rejection

For some children, friendship comes less easily. Children who are disliked by their peers, called **rejected children**, are scapegoated, teased, and ostracized. **Neglected children**, on the other hand, are friendless and ignored. Researchers study peer acceptance by using peer nomination methods: They ask students in a class, for example, to write down the names of children they really like and dislike. Rejected children are those whose names frequently show up on the "disliked" list; neglected children receive no mention at all. Most research to date has focused on rejected boys.

Children develop reputations among their peers even in preschool, and these reputations affect the way other children behave toward them (Denham & Holt, 1993). Not all children who develop early negative reputations maintain this status throughout the rest of their school careers, but boys who are aggressive and impulsive by kindergarten and first grade have a much harder time "growing out of" their rejected status than other rejected boys (Cillessen et al., 1992). Being disliked by peers is associated with low self-esteem and difficulties later in life, such as higher incidence of school dropout and delinquency (Dunn & McGuire, 1992; Parker & Asher, 1987).

Why do some children have trouble forming friendships? Neglected children tend to be shy and lacking in social skills, but they are not hostile or aggressive.

Rejected children are less responsive than their socially accepted peers and make more irrelevant comments when entering a new peer group. Once they have a reputation as disliked, their behavior becomes more negative, which compounds the problem (Black & Hazen, 1990). Making matters worse, their peers often interpret even their appropriate social initiatives as negative or neutral (Coie & Dodge, 1983), preventing operant conditioning of more adaptive behavior. Rejected boys tend to come from families characterized by less effective and appropriate discipline practices, more family stress, and lower socioeconomic status (Dishion, 1990). Not surprisingly, secure attachment lays the groundwork for positive peer relationships.

DEVELOPMENT OF SOCIAL COGNITION

The changing nature of children's friendships partly results from children's emotional and motivational development, such as an increasing concern with intimacy and an expanding capacity to commit to relationships despite momentary ups and downs. Children's friendships also change as their understanding of themselves, others, and relationships—that is, their **social cognition**—develops.

The Evolving Self-Concept

One of the initial tasks of social-cognitive development is acquiring a sense of self as a distinct entity, with its own physical qualities and psychological processes (Stern, 1985). As adults, we tend to assume that we have always had a **self-concept,** an organized view of ourselves or way of representing information about the self. However, children are not born knowing that other people have thoughts and feelings or that their own experience is not the center of the universe.

Since infants cannot talk about themselves, researchers have had to devise indirect methods to learn how the self-concept develops in the first few years. One of the most reliable methods is to assess visual self-recognition, by putting rouge on the child's nose (Amsterdam, 1972; Asendorpf & Baudonniere, 1993; Lewis & Brooks-Gunn, 1979). Infants of different ages respond very differently to the image they

By two years, children clearly recognize their own image, demonstrating the existence of a visual self-concept.

FIGURE 14.4
Self-concept in childhood and adolescence. The cognitive structure of the self-concept changes substantially as children develop. School-age children most frequently mention activities, significant others, and attitudes when describing themselves, as in this excerpt from an interview with a 9-year-old boy. With age, the self-concept becomes more abstract and complex, as in the response by a 17-year-old girl. Source: Montemayor & Eisen, 1977, pp. 317–318.

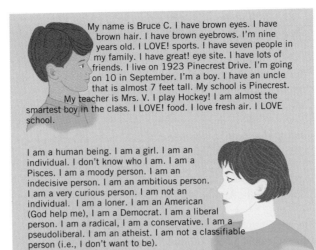

see. Children younger than 15 months rarely touch their noses, unlike the vast majority of 2 year olds, who recognize a discrepancy between the way they look and the way they should look. Thus, infants appear to develop a visual self-concept between 15 and 24 months.

During the toddler years, children begin to categorize themselves on various dimensions, especially age and gender (Daman & Hart, 1988; Lewis & Brooks-Gunn, 1979). Throughout early childhood, the categories they use are largely concrete. When asked to describe themselves, they will offer information such as their membership in groups ("I live with my mommy and my daddy and my sister Jenny and my cat, Sneakers"), material possessions ("I have a pretty room"), things they can do ("I can tie my shoes"), and appearance. That is not to say the self-concept of young children is entirely devoid of subtlety; even preschoolers can sometimes observe consistencies in their own behaviors that resemble adult categories of personality like extroversion ("I usually play with my friends" versus "I usually play by myself"). However, they have difficulty making generalizations about their enduring feelings, such as "I get mad a lot" versus "I don't usually get mad," or "I like myself" versus "I don't like myself" (Eder, 1990).

Around age 8, children begin to define themselves based on internal, psychological attributes as much as on the obviously perceptible qualities or appearances

FIGURE 14.5
Changing self-concepts in adolescents. Researchers asked seventh, ninth, and eleventh graders to describe themselves with their parents, their friends, and at school. The figure shows the percentage of qualities attributed to the self that overlapped across role relationships. Roughly a third of the attributes seventh graders use to describe themselves in their relationship with their parents they also use to describe themselves with peers and at school. Eleventh graders, in contrast, have a much more differentiated and situation-specific view of themselves. Source: Adapted from Harter & Monsour, 1992, p. 253.

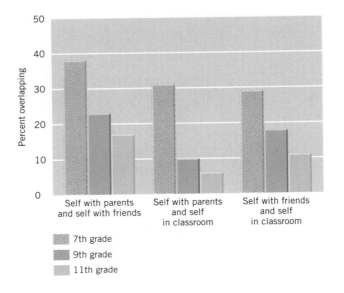

that dominate all cognition in early childhood (Broughton, 1978; Damon & Hart, 1988). In other words, they start to think about their aptitudes, their likes and dislikes, and the ways they tend to feel and think—namely, their personality. Conceiving the self at this point often involves comparisons with other children ("I'm good at math," or "I'm the best skateboarder in my school").

In adolescence, representations of the self become much more subtle (Harter, 1983) (Figure 14.4). For example, a 17-year-old research subject described herself, "I seem really shy on the outside, but *inside* I'm really involved when I'm with people, thinking a lot about what they are saying and doing; and with people I'm comfortable with, I probably don't seem shy at all" (Westen, unpublished data). As children move into adolescence, they also recognize that they are not the same kind of person with everyone or in every situation (Harter & Monsour, 1992) (Figure 14.5).

Concepts of Others

Coming to understand other people, like coming to understand the self, is a lengthy developmental process. An accomplishment of infancy is recognizing that social interactions are reciprocal—that other people's actions are contingent on one's own. Infants learn, for instance, that smiling brings playful responses from caregivers, whereas crying usually means being picked up and held. Infants also come to read emotions in people's faces. As early as 12 months of age, infants "consult" their mothers by looking to them for reassurance when introduced to a new toy. If their mother's face shows concern, infants approach their mother rather than the toy (Klinnert et al., 1983). If they receive a smile from one parent but a fearful look from the other, infants become confused and distressed (Hirshberg & Svejda, 1990).

From early childhood until about age 8, children tend to focus on relatively simple, concrete attributes of other people, such as the way they look or the roles they perform (Shantz, 1983). For instance, a typical 7 year old described a neighbor she liked as follows: "She is very nice because she gives my friends and me toffee. She lives by the main road.... She sometimes gives us flowers" (Livesley & Bromley, 1973, p. 214). Around age 8, however, children's schemas about others begin to change. Figure 14.6 illustrates the changes that occur in children's understanding of people and relationships between ninth and twelfth grades.

Perspective-Taking

An important social-cognitive skill that develops throughout childhood and adolescence, and probably beyond, is **perspective-taking**, the ability to understand other people's viewpoints or perspectives. One ingenious technique researchers have devised for assessing perspective-taking involves observing the way children play games of strategy (Flavell et al., 1968; Selman, 1980). In a game called "Decoy and Defender" (Selman, 1980), which is played on a checkerboard, each player has two "flag carriers" as well as several less valuable tokens. The object is to move one's flag carriers to the opponent's side of the board. From the opposite side of the table, all the pieces look alike, so players must figure out which pieces to block by observing their opponents' moves.

The strategies used by children of different ages illustrate the stagelike development of perspective-taking ability. Children aged 3 to 6 have an egocentric perspective, totally failing to take their opponent's perspective into account. Typical of this age is the "rush for glory" strategy: The child simply moves her flag carrier as quickly as possible across the board. By ages 6 to 8, children become craftier but in a transparent fashion: They often announce, "I'm moving my *flag carrier* now" while moving an unimportant token. (They may even clear their throat first for effect.) They are beginning to recognize that to win they must influence the *beliefs*

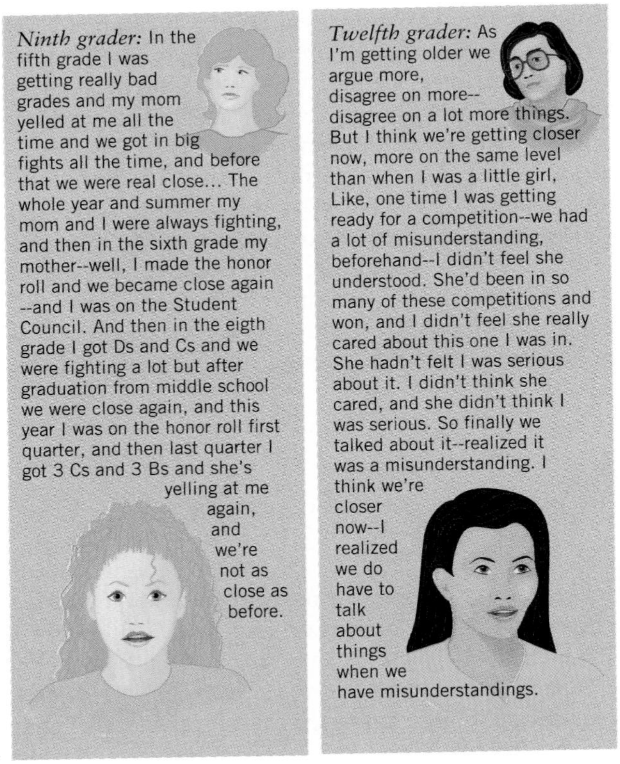

FIGURE 14.6
The development of views of relationships in adolescence. These are excerpts from interviews with a ninth and a twelfth grader who were asked to describe their relationship with their mothers. The twelfth grader provided a rich account of a developing relationship, pointing out the different perspectives she and her mother held. The ninth grader, in contrast, saw her mother just as "mom," who scolds or praises, not as a separate person with whom she is involved in an ongoing relationship. SOURCE: *Westen et al., 1991.*

Ninth grader: In the fifth grade I was getting really bad grades and my mom yelled at me all the time and we got in big fights all the time, and before that we were real close... The whole year and summer my mom and I were always fighting, and then in the sixth grade my mother—well, I made the honor roll and we became close again—and I was on the Student Council. And then in the eigth grade I got Ds and Cs and we were fighting a lot but after graduation from middle school we were close again, and this year I was on the honor roll first quarter, and then last quarter I got 3 Cs and 3 Bs and she's yelling at me again, and we're not as close as before.

Twelfth grader: As I'm getting older we argue more, disagree on more—disagree on a lot more things. But I think we're getting closer now, more on the same level than when I was a little girl, Like, one time I was getting ready for a competition—we had a lot of misunderstanding, beforehand—I didn't feel she understood. She'd been in so many of these competitions and won, and I didn't feel she really cared about this one I was in. She hadn't felt I was serious about it. I didn't think she cared, and she didn't think I was serious. So finally we talked about it—realized it was a misunderstanding. I think we're closer now—I realized we do have to talk about things when we have misunderstandings.

of their opponents. Other research similarly indicates that by age 5 children start to recognize the value of trying to influence others' mental states in order to alter their behavior (Peskin, 1992).

By ages 8 to 10, children show more sophistication. For example, in the "double take" strategy, they might advance their flag carrier with considerable fanfare, with the expectation that the other player would not think they would be so stupid. Behind this strategy is a more complex perspective-taking process: "He's thinking that I'm thinking...." The subtlety and complexity of this kind of recursive (back and forth) thinking expands throughout adolescence.

Children's Understanding of Gender

Children's social cognition thus develops in complexity and abstractness, much as cognition does in nonsocial domains (Chapter 13). The same is true of children's understanding of what gender is and how it applies to them, which changes dramatically over the first several years of life and continues to evolve throughout the lifespan. One cognitive-developmental theory proposes that children progress through three stages in understanding gender (Kohlberg, 1966). First, they acquire **gender identity**, categorizing themselves as either male or female. Usually by age 2 they can correctly label themselves as a boy or girl and identify other children of the same sex (Slaby & Frey, 1975).

In the second stage, **gender stability**, children come to understand that their gender remains constant over time. Girls learn that they will never grow up to be Batman, Superman, or even a garden-variety father, and boys learn that they will not become Wonder Woman, Madonna, or a mommy. Even after they recognize that they will never change their sex, however, children are not absolutely certain that this is also beyond the reach of other people. Before age 6 or 7, some children believe that boys who wear dresses may eventually become girls and girls may metamorphose into boys if they do enough boyish things (Marcus & Overton, 1978; McConaghy, 1979; Slaby & Frey, 1975). For example, when a 4 year old saw his father dressed as a woman for Halloween, he exclaimed, "Two mommies!"

Thus, in the third stage, **gender constancy**, children learn that a person's gender cannot be altered by changes in appearance or activities (except, of course, in exceptional circumstances). This last stage is related to a major cognitive achievement of this age, understanding conservation of physical properties such as mass (Chapter 13). Gender constancy may seem a simple achievement to us, but it does not necessarily come easily. One psychologist tells the story of a 4-year-old boy who wore a barrette to nursery school. When another little boy called him a girl, the first child pulled down his pants to demonstrate that he was indeed still a boy. The other child, however, found this unconvincing. In a you-can't-fool-me tone of voice, he responded, "Everyone has a penis; only girls wear barrettes" (Bem, 1983, p. 607).

Gender Schemas

While cognitive developmentalists focus on the cognitive *structure* of children's thinking about gender (that is, on properties such as the conservation or constancy of gender), other researchers have turned their attention to the *content* of children's knowledge. Cross-culturally, children begin to show an awareness of their culture's beliefs about gender by the age of 5, and by middle childhood they share many of the stereotypes common in their society (Best et al., 1977; Huston, 1983). They encode and organize information about their culture's definitions of maleness and femaleness in **gender schemas,** mental representations that associate psychological characteristics with one sex or the other (Bem, 1985). Children form coherent schemas of their own gender before doing so for the opposite gender (Martin et al., 1990). Throughout the school years, they continue to be more attuned to, and have a better memory for, information relevant to their own gender (see Liben & Signorella, 1993).

Gender schemas can be quite persistent across the lifespan. Consider the following scenario, familiar to any woman doctor, reported by a colleague:

"Is Dr. Williams in?"

"Yes, speaking."

"I'm calling regarding one of the doctor's patients. May I speak with the doctor please?"

"This is the doctor."

"No, I need to speak with the doctor, Dr. Williams."

"This is Dr. Williams."

Because the caller's gender schema associates doctors with masculinity, the person has difficulty recognizing that the doctor is, indeed, on the phone. (Interestingly, my colleagues uniformly report that callers who do this are usually female.)

Gender schemas across the globe show remarkable similarities as well as considerable differences. One team of researchers gave an adjective checklist with three hundred items (e.g., aggressive, arrogant, artistic, bossy) to university students in 25 countries and asked them to rate whether the words were more characteristic of men, women, or neither (Best & Williams, in press; Williams & Best, 1982). Although many adjectives were categorized differently in different countries, a number were almost universally associated with men or with women. Broadly speaking, people everywhere consider men more active, strong, dominant, and aggressive, and perceive women as more passive, weak, and nurturant (Table 14.4).

Although the consistency of these findings is striking, two qualifications are in order. First, technological change is reducing the distinctions between the sexes. In a followup to their initial investigation (1990), the researchers examined **sex-role ideology** (beliefs about appropriate behaviors of the sexes) in 14 countries using a

TABLE 14.4 ADJECTIVES ASSOCIATED WITH MALES AND FEMALES ACROSS CULTURES

MALE	FEMALE
Active (23)	Affectionate (24)
Adventurous (25)	Attractive (23)
Aggressive (24)	Charming (20)
Clear-thinking (21)	Dependent (23)
Coarse (21)	Emotional (23)
Courageous (23)	Fearful (23)
Cruel (21)	Gentle (21)
Dominant (25)	Sensitive (24)
Egotistical (21)	Sentimental (25)
Forceful (25)	Sexy (22)
Hardhearted (21)	Submissive (25)
Lazy (21)	Weak (23)
Rational (20)	
Self-confident (21)	
Unemotional (23)	
Wise (23)	

Source: Williams & Best, 1982, p. 77.

Note. The numbers in parentheses represent the number of countries sharing the stereotype, out of a sample of 25 cultures.

TABLE 14.5 EGALITARIAN SEX-ROLE IDEOLOGY AND CULTURAL CHARACTERISTICS

CULTURAL VARIABLE	CORRELATION WITH EGALITARIAN IDEOLOGY
Economic-social development	.75
Religion	
% Catholic	.46
% Protestant	.62
% Muslim	−.69
Status of women	
% employed outside home	.50
% women in university populations	.46
Urban/rural	.67
Individualistic values	.57

Source: Williams & Best, 1990, p. 93.

similar adjective checklist method. Technologically developed, urban, individualistic societies tended to have more egalitarian sex roles, with less divergent views of the appropriate behaviors of men and women (Table 14.5). Protestant countries were also more likely to be egalitarian, while people in predominantly Muslim countries tended to believe men should be dominant and women, submissive. In more traditional, less economically developed societies, men's concepts of themselves tended to be more favorable, strong, and active than women's self-concepts.

A second qualification is that gender differences are only *average* differences (Williams, 1983). The only differences that are absolute—on which males categorically differ from females—are primary and secondary sex characteristics, such as the genitals or breasts. For most traits, such as aggressiveness or sensitivity, the bell-shaped curves for males and females overlap substantially, so that within a culture, some women score higher than some men even on "masculine" traits and vice versa (Figure 14.7).

Cross-Cultural Gender Stereotypes

Why are gender stereotypes so similar cross-culturally? As early as age 2, Western boys prefer blocks and transportation toys such as trucks and cars, and girls prefer dolls and soft toys. Boys play more actively at manipulating objects and are more likely to engage in forbidden activities (Fagot, 1985; Smith & Daglish, 1977), whereas girls are more likely to play dress-up and dance. Girls also tend to talk earlier than boys (Schachter et al., 1978). Do these differences between boys and girls entirely reflect differences in socialization? Cross-cultural research with a large sample of preindustrial societies shows that the vast majority socialize boys from early childhood to be brave and self-reliant and girls to be responsible, self-restrained, obedient, and sexually restrained (Low, 1989). Why do so many cultures socialize children in similar ways?

As we saw in exploring the links between gender differences and brain structures in Chapter 3, where nature lays a foundation, culture tends to adorn, embellish, and reshape it. This is likely to be the case with the most well-documented difference between the sexes, that males are more aggressive, and females, more nurturant (see Archer & Lloyd, 1985; Hyde, 1984; Jacklin, 1989; Maccoby & Jacklin, 1974, 1980). These differences occur across cultures and species and are evident well before children begin school. Boys display higher rates of aggression in virtually every society and are far more likely to engage in rough-and-tumble play (Edwards & Whiting, 1983; Omark et al., 1975; Whiting & Edwards, 1973; Whiting & Pope, 1973). In no societies have girls ever been found to be more prone to initiate aggressive encounters (Maccoby & Jacklin, 1980).

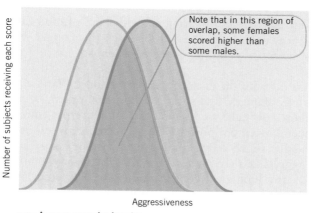

Aggressiveness

— Average score for females
— Average score for males

FIGURE 14.7

Aggressiveness in men and women. In this hypothetical distribution of scores on a measure of aggressiveness, one for men and one for women, the male curve is shifted to the right, signifying that most men are more aggressive than most women. Note the significant region of overlap, however, in which many women's scores are higher than many men's.

The male hormone testosterone appears to be related to aggression in both males and females (Chapter 18). Highly suggestive data come from studies of girls with a malfunction of the adrenal glands called **adrenogenital syndrome (AGS)**, which exposes the female fetus to unusually high levels of male hormones (Erhardt & Baker, 1974; Money & Erhardt, 1972). The result is not only an increase in aggressiveness but also a general increase in "tomboy" behavior during childhood.

According to the evolutionary perspective, sex differences in aggression and nurturance are products of natural selection. In many species, including most primates, males compete for sexual access to females, often physically establishing dominance over other males by fighting. Hence, males' greater tendency to exhibit aggressive behavior and to practice such behavior in childhood would optimize reproductive success. Behavioral differences would likely have been selected alongside physical differences such as greater body mass in males of most species, including humans. Females, in contrast, had no choice but to invest their resources heavily in their offspring, since they carry the fetus for nine months. In the context of these sex differences, a division of labor may have evolved in which males fight for status and protect the group and females care for infants and young children.

The most stridently biological version of this hypothesis about sex differences is difficult to sustain, since research finds that males are quite capable of nurturant behavior but are often discouraged from it by socialization practices (Fogel et al., 1986; Williams, 1983). In fact, changing gender roles now allow fathers to care for infants and young children in ways that would have been considered "unnatural" decades ago. A social learning interpretation of sex differences holds that most behavioral differences observed between women and men result not from innate differences but from expectancies, which in turn reflect social structure (Eagly, 1983). Women and men consistently find themselves in hierarchical relationships in which men are in positions of power and status and women are subordinate (e.g., doctor/nurse, executive/secretary). Because this occurs so frequently, people see it as natural and generalize to other situations, even where status is presumably equal, such as dinner-table discussions of politics.

Although the social learning theory is compelling and can certainly help explain the maintenance of gender stereotypes, it does not account for the fact that such similar social structures have emerged throughout history and across cultures. Perhaps a more balanced account would consider the interaction among biological evolution, cultural evolution, and the learned expectations described by social learning theory. In this view, biological evolution produced motivational proclivities that diverge somewhat for the two sexes, such as a tendency toward aggressive behavior in males and toward nurturant behavior in females, along with physical differences such as body size and strength. These biological differences led nearly all cultures to create a division of labor between the sexes and to amplify innate proclivities through socialization that maximizes safety of offspring and efficiency of food gathering. Simply noting the differences in size and strength between the average man and woman, for example, most cultures would be expected to enlist men and not women in warfare.

As ecological conditions shift (as with the disappearance of hand-to-hand combat, for example), cultural ideology changes, and so do socialization practices (and ultimately the personality attributes of males and females). In fact, cross-cultural data document that where women have more power (where they control resources such as property), girls are taught to be less submissive and more aggressive, although they still remain less aggressive than males (Low, 1989). Many feminist scholars reject the possibility of any biological contribution to sex differences in behavior, fearing that such acknowledgment inherently implies that the subordination of women is natural and unchangeable. Perhaps, however, the problem lies less

Fathers are much more capable of nurturance toward infants and children than was once believed.

in acknowledging biological differences between women and men than in devaluing those functions typically associated with femaleness, such as caring for infants, and overvaluing those functions typically associated with maleness, such as warfare (Korfine, 1994, personal communication).

MORAL DEVELOPMENT

> INTERVIEWER: *Should boys get more? Why should they get more?*
> FOUR-YEAR-OLD BOY: *Because they always need more.*
> INTERVIEWER: *Why do they need more?*
> BOY: *Because that's how I want it.*
>
> (Damon, 1977, p. 121)

Thankfully, children's thinking about what is fair (and why) changes dramatically over the years, so that older children and adults do not operate at the same level of morality as the 4 year old above. The development of **morality**—the set of rules people use for balancing or adjudicating the conflicting interests of themselves and others—is a richly researched area (see Rest, 1983). One of the central questions concerns the relative roles of cognition and emotion in the child's evolving sense of right and wrong.

The Role of Cognition

Several theories focus on the role of cognition in moral development. These include cognitive-social, cognitive-developmental, and information-processing theories.

Cognitive-Social Theories

Behaviorist and cognitive-social theories hold that moral behaviors, like other behaviors, are learned through processes such as conditioning and modeling (Bandura, 1977; Mischel & Mischel, 1976). Cognitive-social approaches measure moral development in terms of **prosocial behavior**, that is, behavior that benefits other individuals or groups (Mischel & Mischel, 1976). Morality develops as children come to discover through trial and error, as well as through deliberate instruction, that certain actions are reinforced and others, punished. Thus, children learn that stealing is wrong because they are punished for it, they see someone else punished (vicarious conditioning), or they are told they will be punished (direct tutelage). They acquire expectancies about the outcome of their behaviors under different circumstances (whether they will, or will not, be punished), and they develop conditioned emotional responses (such as anxiety) to behaviors that are regularly punished. They also generalize from one situation to the next, recognizing, for example, that talking in the library is no more acceptable than talking while a teacher is speaking.

Cognitive-Developmental Theories

The cognitive-developmental models of Jean Piaget and his student, Lawrence Kohlberg, focus less on moral behavior than on moral reasoning. These models propose that moral development proceeds through a series of stages that reflect cognitive development.

Piaget observed moral principles as they emerged in simple games of marbles.

Piaget's Theory   Piaget observed a simple occasion—games of marbles among children—and noted important differences in the way younger and older children thought about the rules (Piaget 1932/65). The youngest children, who were essentially pre-moral, arbitrarily altered the rules so they could win. Once children had accepted the notion of rules, however, they would stick staunchly to them, and if asked where the rules of marbles came from, they would reply with answers like, "They just are," "From Daddy," or "From God!" This stage of moral judgment, which Piaget called the **morality of constraint**, is typical of school children before the age of 9 or 10. Piaget described this morality as one "of duty pure and simple," of conformity to societal rules, which are viewed as unchanging and immutable (1932/65, p. 335).

Older children and adults, in contrast, view rules as instruments created by individuals for coordinating social interaction. In this **morality of cooperation**, moral rules can be changed if they are not appropriate to the occasion, as long as the people involved agree to do so. Older children playing marbles may thus endorse rule changes by mutual consent without believing they are violating something sacred.

Kohlberg's Theory   Kohlberg shared two of Piaget's central convictions about moral development. The first is that changes in moral reasoning result from basic changes in cognitive structures—that is, changes in ways of thinking. For example, as children's thinking becomes more abstract, so, too, does their moral reasoning. Second, Kohlberg conceptualized children as active constructors of their own moral reality, not passive recipients of social rules.

Kohlberg (1976; Kohlberg & Kramer, 1969) proposed a sequence of three levels of moral development, each comprised of two stages. He assessed moral development by presenting subjects with hypothetical dilemmas and asking them how these dilemmas should be resolved and why. An example is the dilemma of Heinz and the druggist:

> In Europe a woman was near death from a special kind of cancer. There was one drug that the doctors thought might save her. It was a form of radium that a druggist in the same town had recently discovered. The drug was expensive to make, but the druggist was charging ten times what the drug cost him to make. He paid $200 for the radium and charged $2,000 for a small dose of the drug. The sick woman's husband, Heinz, went to everyone he knew to borrow the money, but he could only get together about $1,000, which is half of what it cost. He told the druggist that his wife was dying and asked him to sell it cheaper or let him pay later. But the druggist said, "No, I discovered the drug and I'm going to make money from it." So Heinz got desperate and broke into the man's store to steal the drug for his wife. Should the husband have done that? (Kohlberg, 1963, p. 19)

The level of moral development a person shows in answering this question depends not on the particular answer (to steal or not to steal) but on the reasoning behind the response (Table 14.6). At the first level, **preconventional morality**, children follow moral rules either to avoid punishment (Stage 1) or to obtain reward (Stage 2). A preconventional child might conclude that Heinz should steal the drug "if he likes having his wife around." At the second level, **conventional morality**, individuals define what is right by the standards they have learned from other people, particularly respected authorities. People with conventional morality justify their choice of moral actions on the basis of their desire to gain the approval or avoid the disapproval of others (Stage 3), or on the need to maintain law and order (e.g., "if everyone stole whenever he wanted to, what would this world come to?") (Stage 4).

The third level, **postconventional morality**, is a morality of abstract, self-defined principles that may or may not accord with the dominant morals of the times. A

TABLE 14.6 Kohlberg's Stages of Moral Development

Level	Reasons to Steal the Drug	Reasons Not to Steal the Drug
Preconventional: Morality centers on avoiding punishment and obtaining reward.	"He should steal it if he likes her a lot"; "If he gets caught, he won't get much of a jail term, so he'll get to see her when he gets out."	"He'll get caught"; "He shouldn't have to pay with jail time for his wife's problem."
Conventional: Morality centers on meeting moral standards learned from others, avoiding their disapproval, and maintaining law and order.	"If he doesn't steal it, everyone will think he's a terrible person"; "It's his duty to care for his wife."	"If he steals it, everyone will think he's a criminal"; "He can't just go stealing things whenever he wants to—it isn't right."
Postconventional: Morality centers on abstract, carefully considered principles.	"If he has to run from the police, at least he'll know he did the right thing"; "Sometimes people have to break the law if the law is unjust."	"If he steals it, he'll lose all respect for himself"; "Other people might say it was okay, but he'll have to live with his conscience, knowing he's stolen from the druggist."

Source: Adapted from Kohlberg, 1969.

postconventional adult, like a preconventional child, might condone stealing the drug but for a very different reason, such as, "The value of a human life far exceeds any rights of ownership or property." Kohlberg developed his theory during the 1960s, a time of social turbulence in which people questioned the norms and values of their parents and the larger society. He argued that people who never question their parents' moral beliefs are less developed in their moral reasoning than people who consider alternative ways of thinking about morality. (Distinctions between the two postconventional stages originally outlined by Kohlberg have not proven useful and will thus not be described here.)

The basic logic of Kohlberg's theory is that at the preconventional level, the person accepts moral standards only insofar as doing so is personally advantageous; this is an ethic of hedonism or self-interest. The child is preconventional in the sense that he has not yet come to accept society's conventions in their own right as rules that good people should follow. At the conventional level, the individual believes in the moral rules he has learned. The person with postconventional morality, in contrast, views the values of the time as conventions—rules established by social contract rather than by any absolute or divine power—and hence as both potentially fallible and changeable.

Virtually all normal children progress to Stage 3 by the age of 13. Beyond stages 3 and 4, however, the development of moral reasoning is not related to age and is more a matter of individual differences. Only about 5 percent reach the postconventional level (Colby & Kohlberg, 1984). Cross-cultural studies largely support the general sequence Kohlberg discovered in Western subjects (Chiu, 1990; Kuhn, 1976; Rest, 1983; White et al., 1978).

Information-Processing Theories

An alternative cognitive view of moral development is an information-processing approach (Darley & Schultz, 1990; Grusec & Goodnow, 1994). Information-processing theories do not postulate broad stages of moral development; rather, like information-processing approaches to cognitive development, they break moral thinking down into component processes and examine the way each changes during childhood.

According to one such view (Schultz & Schliefer, 1983), when adults make decisions about whether an act is immoral and whether it deserves punishment, as in jury deliberations, they make a series of sequential judgments (Figure 14.8). The first question concerns cause: Did the person cause the damage? If so, the next question is whether the individual was morally responsible. Did the person intend to do harm? Should the person have foreseen the results of his actions? Was the person grossly negligent in not taking measures to prevent the harm?

If the individual is morally responsible, the next question is whether he is blameworthy. Did someone else suffer significant harm from his action? If so, did the perpetrator have reasonable justification for his actions? Finally, if the person is to blame, the last judgment involves assigning appropriate punishment. In our culture, people make determinations about appropriate punishment, whether in a jury trial or in the discipline of their children, according to three criteria: the extent of the damage, whether the perpetrator has already made appropriate restitution (e.g., by apologizing), and whether the perpetrator has suffered as a result of his actions.

From an information-processing view, then, understanding moral development means understanding changes in the way children answer these multiple questions. For example, when do children come to understand the difference between directly causing someone to suffer (e.g., taking something from them) as opposed to taking an action which, combined with what someone else has done, produces suffering (forgetting to lock a door, which contributed to a theft)? From an information-processing view, global stage theories cannot capture developmental changes in multiple components of moral reasoning that may vary independently of each other.

FIGURE 14.8

An information-processing model of moral decision making. According to this model, when people make decisions about whether an act is immoral and whether it deserves punishment, they make a series of sequential judgments, such as whether the person caused the event, was morally responsible, is blameworthy, and deserves punishment. SOURCE: *Adapted from Darley & Schultz, 1990, p. 532.*

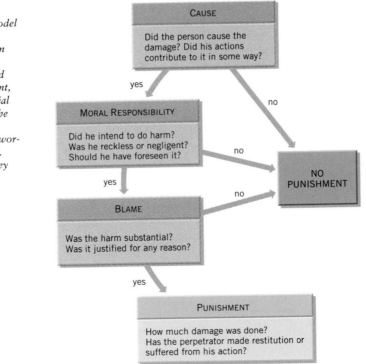

The Role of Emotion

The theories of moral development discussed thus far emphasize the role of cognition—judgment and decision making—in moral development. Other approaches, however, focus on the emotional side. Prominent among these are psychodynamic theories and research on childhood empathy.

Psychodynamic Theories

The psychodynamic view of moral development proposes that children start out relatively **narcissistic** (self-centered and interested in gratifying their own needs), as when the young child who wants an extra piece of cake simply grabs it. This need-gratifying orientation begins to change with the development of a conscience or superego between ages 2 and 5. Moral development thus stems from identification, or internalization: Children take in the values of their parents, which are at first external, and gradually make them internal by adopting them as their own. The way very young children begin to internalize their parents' values and edicts was illustrated by Kate, who opened this chapter, as she repeated her parents' commands in their absence ("Be a good girl, don't cry," or "Eat up your potatoes"). Empirically, parents and their children do tend to think similarly about moral questions (Speicher, 1994).

From a psychodynamic perspective, guilt is the primary moral emotion and the mechanism that motivates people to obey their conscience. Guilt arises from discrepancies between what people feel they should do and what they contemplate or observe themselves doing. When toddlers are learning about morals, as their parents instruct them in what they should and should not do, they may feel anxious or ashamed at being caught. Yet they do not experience genuine guilt until they actually internalize their parents' values as their own—that is, until they not only know them but also believe in them. Little children's moral beliefs are very concrete, specific, and often tied directly to a mental image or representation of a parent. Toddlers may thus be observed telling themselves, "No!" even as they follow a forbidden impulse, or, as in the opening vignette, repeat their parents' admonitions as a way of stopping themselves from doing something they have been told is wrong ("Don't make a mess"). As children get older, they rely less on an internalized parent "sitting on their shoulder" than on more abstract moral demands integrated from their parents and the wider culture (see Williams & Bybee, 1994).

Research on Empathy

Unpleasant emotions such as guilt, anxiety, and shame are not the only emotions involved in moral behavior. Some theorists emphasize the motivational role of **empathy**, or feeling for another person who is hurting. Empathy has both a cognitive component (understanding what the person is experiencing) and an emotional component (experiencing a similar feeling). Research supports the view that empathy contributes to prosocial behavior, although empathizing too much in an emotional way can actually make people self-focused and hence less helpful (Strayer, 1993).

According to one theorist (Hoffman, 1978, 1990), the ability to respond empathically changes considerably over the course of development. (For empirical support, see Strayer, 1993.) During the first year, infants experience global empathy; that is, they feel the same distress as the other person but cannot separate whose distress is whose. An 11 month old who witnesses another child fall and cry may put her thumb in her mouth and bury her head in her mother's lap as if she were hurt herself. Infants show primitive signs of empathy in the first days of life; one baby crying in a nursery can trigger a cacophony of crying.

As children become better able to distinguish their own thoughts and feelings from those of others, they begin to experience genuine **empathic distress**—that is,

By adolescence, people often feel empathy for others in need whom they have never met. These students from West Virginia came to Miami in 1992 to help rebuild homes after Hurricane Andrew.

feeling upset for another person—which motivates moral or prosocial behavior. As early as the second year of life, children can recognize when someone is hurting, feel bad for them, and try to take action to make them feel better (Zahn-Waxler et al., 1992). The response may nonetheless be egocentric: A 13 month old may give a sad-looking adult his own favorite stuffed animal or bring his own mother over to comfort a crying playmate. This behavior reflects the immature perspective-taking ability of the young child. As children get older, they respond more accurately to cues about what other people are feeling. By adolescence, a more mature form of empathy emerges, as individuals begin to think about suffering that exists beyond the immediate moment and hence become concerned about broader issues such as poverty or famine.

Commentary: Making Sense of Moral Development

Cognitive and emotional approaches to moral development each present part of the picture, but none alone covers the entire landscape. The strength of the cognitive-social approach is its emphasis on precisely what is missing from most other approaches, namely, moral or prosocial *behavior*. People may think as abstractly about moral questions as they like, but thinking is irrelevant if it does not affect their actions. Research does not, in fact, show particularly strong correlations between moral reasoning and prosocial behavior; nor are the correlations between empathy and prosocial behavior very large (e.g., Eisenberg et al., 1991).

On the other hand, the cognitive-social approach assumes that certain behaviors are moral or prosocial and offers little insight into situations that require choosing between imperfect options—which is the essence of moral decision making. A German citizen who "pitched in" to help bring about Hitler's Final Solution might have behaved "morally" if one judges morality by the act of contributing to a larger cause or following social rules; however, if one considers the cause itself, his actions were anything but moral. What constituted prosocial behavior during the Vietnam War? Answering the draft, even though many considered the war immoral or nonsensical? Evading the draft and letting other people die instead? Protesting the war? These kinds of questions are what moral decision making is about.

Cognitive-developmental models have their advantages and disadvantages as well. Kohlberg's theory highlights a significant phenomenon that no other theory addresses—that moral development may go beyond the internalization of society's rules through identification, conditioning, schema formation, or social learning. This was the message of Sophocles' tragedy *Antigone*, whose heroine defied the king's laws in the name of higher principles, and it has been the principle of many moral leaders, from Jesus to Gandhi and Martin Luther King, Jr.

At the same time, Kohlberg's theory has drawn considerable criticism. People at the higher stages of moral reasoning do not necessarily behave any differently from people who are conventional in their moral reasoning. The philosopher Martin Heidegger, who reflected deeply and abstractly on a range of human experiences, found ways to rationalize cooperation with the Nazi regime, which many more "ordinary" Europeans did not. Other critics, including Carol Gilligan (1982), contend that Kohlberg's theory is biased against women. In Kohlberg's studies, women rarely transcend Stage 3 morality, in which goodness is equated with pleasing or helping others; men more often reach Stage 4, which is oriented toward maintaining the social order. Does this mean women are morally inferior? Gilligan thinks not—and a glance around the globe at the perpetrators of violence supports her view. According to Gilligan, women and men follow divergent developmental paths, with one no less mature than the other. Women's moral concerns, she argues, are more likely to center on care and responsibility for specific individuals. Men, on the other hand, are more concerned with duty, law and order, and formal procedures for resolving moral and legal questions. Gilligan's arguments have strong intuitive appeal, although they have not, by and large, been supported by empirical research (e.g., Crow et al., 1991; Walker, 1989). Both Gilligan's and Kohlberg's theories may also require modification when applied to other cultures, since research shows, for example, that concepts of duty and caring are different among Hindus in India than in North American samples (Miller, 1994).

As for the information-processing approach to moral development, its greatest contribution is that, like similar approaches to cognitive development, it fills in and clarifies many of the broad strokes painted by stage theories. Nevertheless, an information-processing account leaves many central questions unanswered, particularly about the way motivation influences moral reasoning and behavior. Why do children accept values in the first place, when doing so produces guilt, and why are they willing to control their impulses at all? Why do children make excuses when they have committed a transgression? How do they adjudicate conflicts between their own needs and those of others, and how do their judgments about their own culpability differ from their judgments about others'? Asking people to make judgments about what other people have done is very different from understanding their own struggles to remain faithful to their lover, to report their income honestly to the Internal Revenue Service, or to resist saying something unkind behind a friend's back.

Perspectives that focus on the emotional side of morality fare better in answering these questions. Because morality so often requires self-sacrifice and self-restraint, an emotional counterweight such as anxiety or guilt seems essential to balance out the net losses in gratification. Empathy adds a further source of motivation for moral behavior: Helping other people leads to a sense of satisfaction as well as to the reduction of the empathic distress that comes from observing someone else's suffering (Chapter 18).

Affective approaches, however, also have their pitfalls. Why children internalize moral values is unclear. Freud linked identification with the father to the fear of castration in boys, which seems a rather unlikely impetus for the development of morality and cannot account for moral development in females. Moreover, research indicates that mothers are largely responsible for moral training in most Western families (Hoffman & Saltzstein, 1967). Therefore, identification with the father is probably not as central as Freud supposed, although research on moral reasoning does show particularly strong links between fathers' level of moral reasoning and the moral reasoning of both their sons and daughters (Speicher, 1994). Research on empathy challenges the psychodynamic view of infants as "totally id" (Chapter 12) by documenting their loving and compassionate sides as well.

Empathy theories, however, do not provide insight into specifically moral questions, which arise when people's needs are in conflict. Prosocial responses are common by 18 to 20 months when infants witness other people's distress but *not* when they cause the distress themselves (Zahn-Waxler et al., 1992). Prosocial responses aimed at making up for a transgression emerge at around 2 years, precisely when psychodynamic and other theorists argue for the beginnings of moral conscience fueled by guilt. Infants as young as 12 to 18 months often share toys with other children or with their parents, but by age 2 they are less likely to do so if this means they have to give them up (Hay et al., 1991). Perhaps not incidentally, by this age most children have mastered the word "mine."

An integrated account of moral development would need to spell out more carefully the interactions of cognition, affect, and motivation involved when children and adults wrestle with moral questions. Infants and toddlers have many selfish impulses, but they also have prosocial impulses based on their innate capacity for empathy. When self-centered and other-centered motives clash, young children tend to opt for the most gratifying course of action. This probably changes over time for a number of reasons. Children mature in their capacity to love and care about other people, and they develop a heightened ability to understand the perspective of others. They also become more able to regulate their impulses as neural circuits in the frontal lobes mature and as expanding cognitive abilities allow them to transform situations in their minds. Furthermore, through social learning, children come to associate actions such as sharing with positive reinforcement, and hitting and lying with punishment. By identifying with people they fear and admire, children's fear of punishment gradually becomes transformed into fear of their own internal monitor of right and wrong—and hence into guilt. Eventually, they reflect more abstractly about moral questions and try to integrate the moral feelings and beliefs they have accrued over the course of their development.

LIFESPAN DEVELOPMENT

In discussing social development, we have thus far focused on the first quarter of the lifespan. Like physical and cognitive development, however, social development continues throughout life. The most widely known theory of lifespan development was formulated by Erik Erikson (1963). We use Erikson's theory as the basis for organizing our discussion of lifespan development in the remainder of the chapter. Erikson's is not the only model of adult development, but it is unique in two respects. First, it is culturally sensitive, emerging not only from Erikson's experience as a psychoanalyst but also from his having lived among, and observed, several cultures, from Denmark and Germany to a Sioux reservation. Second, Erikson's theory integrates biology, psychological experience, and culture by grounding development simultaneously in biological maturation and changing social demands. For example, like his mentor, Anna Freud (1958), Erikson notes the connection between adolescents' questions about who they are and what they believe with the surge of new feelings and impulses they experience as they wrestle with puberty and emerging sexuality. Reconstituting a self-concept that now includes the self as a sexual being is a major task spurred by biological maturation, but the extent to which adolescents find this conflictual depends on the beliefs, values, rituals, and sexual practices of their culture (Mead, 1928). Aspects of Erikson's developmental model have also received empirical support in cross-sectional, longitudinal, and sequential studies (Kowza & Marcia, 1991; Marcia, 1987; McAdams & de St. Aubin, 1992; Whitbourne et al., 1992).

Erikson intended his model of **psychosocial stages**—stages in the development of the person as a social being—to supplement Freud's psychosexual stages. At each of eight stages, the individual faces a **developmental task**, or challenge that is normative for that period of life (Table 14.7). Each successive task provides a crisis, an opportunity for steaming ahead or a danger point for psychological derailment, that influences subsequent development. These alternative "tracks" at each juncture are not, of course, absolute. No infant, for example, ever feels *totally* trusting or mistrusting, and people have many opportunities over the course of development to backtrack or take a new route.

The Stages of Childhood

Four of the eight stages in Erikson's theory take place in childhood. During the first stage, **basic trust versus mistrust**, infants come to trust others or to perceive the social world as hostile or unreliable. This stage comprises roughly the first 18 months of life and is the period during which infants develop their earliest internal working models of relationships.

The second stage, **autonomy versus shame and doubt**, occurs during the second and third years as maturation allows children to walk and talk and hence to experience themselves as independent sources of will and power. Toddlers learn to feel secure in their independence, or they doubt their newfound skills and feel shame at their failures. During the second year, children spontaneously set standards for

TABLE 14.7 ERIKSON'S PSYCHOSOCIAL STAGES IN RELATION TO OTHER MODELS OF DEVELOPMENT

LIFE PERIOD	ERIKSON'S PSYCHOSOCIAL STAGE	FREUD'S PSYCHOSEXUAL STAGE	PIAGET'S COGNITIVE STAGE
Infancy	*Basic trust versus mistrust:* Development of interpersonal expectations and hope	Oral	Sensorimotor
Toddlerhood	*Autonomy versus shame and doubt:* Development of will and self-control	Anal	Preoperational
Preschool and early school years	*Initiative versus guilt:* Development of conscience and purpose	Phallic	
Late childhood	*Industry versus inferiority:* Development of competence	Latency	Concrete operational
Adolescence	*Identity versus identity confusion:* Development of commitment and sense of integration	Genital	Formal operational
Young adulthood	*Intimacy versus isolation:* Development of adult love		
Midlife	*Generativity versus stagnation:* Development of care for the next generation and one's legacy		
Old age	*Integrity versus despair:* Development of wisdom		

Note. Erikson's model describes psychosocial development, which is not independent of either the development of pleasure-seeking motives, as described by Freud, or cognition, as described by Piaget. Among the major theories we have discussed, however, Erikson's is the only one that posits development through adulthood.

themselves and experience pride in their accomplishments (Kagan, 1984). This is also the time of the "terrible twos," in which toddlers regularly assert their authority. A danger of this stage is that the child may be afraid to explore and challenge, and never develop a secure sense of autonomous selfhood. Long or repeated separations from attachment figures during this period can threaten the child's growing autonomy, as temporarily occurred with 2-1/2-year-old Kate, who became somewhat clinging and fearful for a while after separation from her parents.

In the third stage, roughly between 3 and 6, children struggle with **initiative versus guilt.** Initiative refers to a sense of planfulness and responsibility that enables a child to follow through with ideas and goals. Initiative adds purpose to the will-fulness of the toddler years. The opposite pole is the guilt that accompanies the emergence of a conscience and of heightened control over impulses. Children who have difficulty with this stage may develop a tyrannical conscience that is always berating them, or they may become rigid and constricted as a way of dealing with impulses they have come to view as bad.

The next stage, which occurs roughly between ages 7 and 11, is **industry versus inferiority**. Children develop a sense of industry or competence as they begin to practice skills they will use for a lifetime in productive work. During this period, **social comparison** processes become salient, as children size themselves and others up on intelligence, athletic ability, popularity, and so on. The vulnerability of this stage reflects the dangers inherent in learning and in social comparison: feelings of incompetence or inferiority. In literate cultures, children enter school during this age, and their experiences of academic and social success or failure shape both their self-concepts and the strategies they use to protect their self-esteem. Some children become caught in a vicious cycle, in which a sense of inferiority leads them to give up quickly on tasks, which, in turn, increases the probability of further failure. In nonliterate societies this is a time children learn such skills as hunting, gathering, and caring for infants that prepare them for adulthood.

Adolescence

According to Erikson, the developmental crisis of adolescence is **identity versus identity confusion**. **Identity** refers to a stable sense of knowing who one is and what one's values and ideals are (Erikson, 1968). **Identity confusion** occurs when the individual fails to develop a coherent and enduring sense of self and has difficulty committing to roles, values, people, or occupational choices. Empirically, individuals differ in the extent to which they explore and maintain commitments to ideologies, occupational choices, and interpersonal values (Marcia, 1987). Whereas some establish an identity after a period of soul-searching, others commit early without exploration, foreclosing identity development. Still others remain perpetually confused or put off identity consolidation for many years while trying on various roles throughout their 20s. These different paths to identity are heavily dependent on culture. Many traditional cultures have **rites of passage** in adolescence, ceremonies that initiate the child into adulthood and impose a socially bestowed identity. A period of identity confusion occurs primarily in technologically more advanced societies or in cultures that are undergoing rapid changes, as in much of the contemporary world.

Sometimes adolescents have trouble establishing a positive identity; they may be doing poorly in school or lack models of successful adulthood with whom to identify. As a result, they may develop a **negative identity**, taking on a role society defines as bad but that nevertheless provides them with a sense that they are *something*. This is a path often taken by gang members and chronic delinquents, who may seemingly revel in their "badness." Failure to form a cohesive identity beyond adolescence can augur problems later on. Girls who have difficulty forming an identity in late adolescence are more likely than their peers to experience marital disruption at midlife, and boys with late-adolescent identity problems are more likely to remain single and be unsatisfied with their lives in middle age (Kahn et al., 1985).

As adolescents grow less dependent on their parents and try out new values and roles, they may become rebellious and moody, shifting from compliance one moment to defiance the next. According to the **conflict model** put forth at the turn of the century (Hall, 1904) and later elaborated by psychodynamic theorists (Blos, 1962; A. Freud, 1958), conflict and crisis are normal in adolescence. Indeed, conflict theorists argue that adolescents *need* to go through a period of crisis to separate themselves psychologically from their parents and carve out their own identity.

An initiation ritual among the Ituri tribe of Zaire.

Beeper studies (Chapter 9) show that adolescents do, in fact, experience a wider range of moods over a shorter period of time than adults (Csikszentmihalyi & Larson, 1984; Larson et al., 1980). Longitudinal studies find decreases in hostility and negative emotionality and increases in diligence, self-control, and congeniality as teenagers move into early adulthood (see McGue et al., 1993).

Other theorists argue, however, that the stormy, moody, conflict-ridden adolescent is the exception rather than the rule (Douvan & Adelson, 1966; Offer et al., 1990; Petersen, 1988). According to the **continuity model,** adolescence for most individuals is essentially continuous with childhood and adulthood, undistinguished by turbulence. Research supporting this view finds that roughly 80 percent of adolescents show no signs of severe storm and stress and that some of the remaining 20 percent are emotionally troubled (Offer & Offer, 1975; Offer et al., 1981). Probably the most accurate conclusion is that adolescence is a time of enormous individual differences, with many alternative paths that vary according to the individual, culture, and historical epoch.

Early Adulthood

Erikson was one of the first theorists to take seriously the notion of development after adolescence. While his stages of childhood and adolescence correspond loosely to Freud's psychosexual stages (Table 14.7), Freud's have no parallel in adulthood. Erikson describes the developmental task confronting young adults as **intimacy versus isolation. Intimacy** for Erikson means establishing enduring, committed relationships, including friendships and romantic relationships. The danger of this period is isolation—withdrawing from relationships or avoiding commitment.

Establishing intimacy does not mean simply getting married. In Western cultures, marital distress actually increases over the first three years of marriage, whether or not the couple has children. This is particularly true for families lower in socioeconomic status (Kurdek, 1991). Maintaining intimate relationships in the face of conflict and disillusionment is a challenge that requires continuous negotiation and compromise.

With the establishment of intimacy often comes the transition to parenthood, which is one of the most abrupt and dramatic transitions in the lives of men and women (Miller & Sollie, 1986). Although most parents report tremendous satisfaction with the birth of a new child, parenthood is not without substantial costs. At the most concrete level, the birth of the first child typically doubles housework (Peskin, 1982). With the transition to parenthood, household division of labor generally becomes more traditional, couples report less time for shared leisure activities, marital satisfaction declines, and couples experience more conflict and fewer positive interchanges (Belsky & Pensky, 1988; Berman & Pedersen, 1987). For women, motherhood usually involves a redefinition of roles and reallocation of time. For men, fatherhood means that they are no longer the primary recipients of their wives' attention and love at the same time that they incur new financial and domestic responsibilities (Lamb, 1987). The stresses of early parenthood are lessened when the marital relationship is supportive and when the couple is financially comfortable (Schaie & Willis, 1986).

Middle Age

Erikson describes the crisis of midlife as **generativity versus stagnation**. **Generativity** means concern for the next generation as well as an interest in producing (generating) something of lasting value to society. People express their generative impulses through rearing children, participating in culturally meaningful institutions such as churches or civic organizations, mentoring younger workers, or creating something that will last beyond them, such as a work of art. The opposite of generativity is stagnation, which may be expressed as dissatisfaction with a marital partner, alienation from one's children, or a feeling that the promise of one's youth has gone unfulfilled. Empirically, people in midlife do express more generative themes than younger adults when describing their lives, and they report more generative activities (McAdams & de St. Aubins, 1992; McAdams et al., 1993).

Some observers have described this period as a time of **midlife crisis** (Jacques, 1965; Levinson et al., 1978; Sheehy, 1976). One researcher found roughly 80 percent of the men he interviewed were in a state of crisis around age 40, as they began to think of themselves as middle-aged instead of young and to question the basic structure of their lives (Levinson, 1978). In Western culture, people are frequently at the apex of their careers in their 40s and 50s, enjoying leadership positions at work or in the community. At the same time, however, the death of parents, the occasional jarring death of siblings or contemporaries, and an aging body inevitably lead people to confront their mortality consciously or unconsciously and to consider how they will live their remaining years.

As is the case with adolescence, some psychologists challenge the view of midlife as a time of crisis. Only a minority of people report experiencing a midlife crisis, and in these cases, the crisis usually occurs along with a specific interruption in the normal rhythm of life, such as job loss or divorce (Neugarten, 1968, 1977). Research on the degree of stress people experience at different points in the lifespan does not point to midlife as a time of particular crisis (Brim, 1976; Lazarus & DeLongis, 1981), and epidemiological studies show fewer divorces and suicides at midlife than in young adulthood and old age (Kramer et al., 1983). Longitudinal studies indicate that women's sense of psychological well-being remains stable and often improves from age 40 to 50 (Livson, 1976, 1981). Women also report feeling more independent, more competent, more generative, and better about themselves in midlife than they did at age 30 (Table 14.8) (Helson & Moane, 1987). For men, both in our society and across many cultures, the 50s and 60s often bring a gradual toning down of aggressiveness and a blossoming of nurturant impulses (Guttman, 1974; Hyde et al., 1991; Neugarten, 1972). For many people the changes of midlife are thus gradual, not cataclysmic.

TABLE 14.8 CHANGES IN WOMEN'S SELF-CONCEPT IN ADULTHOOD	
AGE	**STATEMENTS**
Early 30s	Feeling I will never get myself together Doing for others and then feeling exploited Feeling depressed, resentful, or disillusioned Feeling very much alone Feeling weak, incompetent, or not as strong as other people Wishing I had a wider scope to my life
Early 40s	Having a sense of being my own person Feeling more confident Having a wider perspective Focusing on reality; meeting the needs of the day and not being too emotional about them Having influence in my community or area of interest Feeling my life is moving well Feeling secure and committed Feeling a new level of productivity or effectiveness Having interest in things beyond my own family Feeling powerful Appreciating and being aware of older people Making an effort to ensure that young people get their chance to develop Being more involved with parents and siblings Feeling a new level of intimacy Feeling women are more important to me than they used to be Having an interest in my family tree or ancestral culture Having an intense interest in inner life Having religious and philosophical interests Discovering new parts of myself

Source: Adapted from Helson & Moane, p. 181.

Note. The table shows the statements women in their early 30s and early 40s rated higher at either one age or the other.

Old Age

The meaning of old age has changed dramatically over the course of the twentieth century. The average lifespan has increased 26 years (Labouvie-Vief, 1985), and the proportion of people over age 65 in North America has grown from 1 in 30 in 1900 to a projected 1 in 5 by the year 2020 (Eisdorfer, 1983). People over 85 currently account for nearly 10 percent of the population and are expected to constitute roughly 20 percent by 2040 (Verbrugge, 1989, cited in Von Dras & Blumenthal, 1992). These demographic shifts have produced substantial changes in perceptions of old age. Even three decades ago, people were considered "old" in their 60s; today, no one is surprised to play tennis next to a courtful of active 70 year olds.

In Erikson's final stage, **integrity versus despair**, individuals look back on their lives with a sense of satisfaction that they have lived it well or with despair, regret, and loss for loved ones who have died. In many respects, the balance between integrity and despair is fluid, as individuals must inevitably cope with losing people who have made their lives meaningful. Although some evidence suggests that older people are generally more resilient in the face of losses and other life crises than

Shakespeare would be surprised by the popularity of seniors' tennis tournaments.

younger people (Rodeheaver & Datan, 1988), our own culture tends to devalue the elderly and hence to emphasize the despairing end of the continuum. William Shakespeare's characterization of old age, from *As You Like It*, presents a grim picture that is not far from the contemporary Western conception of life's final phase:

> *Last scene of all,*
> *That ends this strange eventful history,*
> *Is second childishness and mere oblivion,*
> *Sans teeth, sans eyes, sans taste, sans every thing.*

> II. vii.

Fortunately, Shakespeare took some poetic license; reality is nowhere near this bleak. For example, contrary to stereotypes, only about 5 percent of the population over 65 have physical or mental impairments serious enough to require continuous nursing care (Tolliver, 1983). Why, then, are our stereotypes so negative? A prime culprit appears to be technological development. Paradoxically, the same factor that has prolonged life by decades has undermined the status of the aged by making their jobs obsolete, limiting the applicability of their beliefs and values in a radically changed social and cultural milieu, and eroding the traditional structure of the extended family. Furthermore, the geographical mobility associated with economic development means that children may live hundreds of miles from their aging parents. In contrast, in more traditional societies, the aged are by definition the most knowledgeable because they have lived the longest and accumulated the most information, and mutual ties of affection between the generations are reinforced by daily interaction.

In the face of physical decline, negative stereotypes, and the loss of spouse, friends, and social roles, what allows an individual to find satisfaction, or what Erikson describes as integrity, in the final years of life? In one study of 1000 people aged 65 to 72, several variables predicted life satisfaction: close relationships, an active social and community life, continuing recreation, good health, and sufficient income (Flanagan, 1981). Longitudinal studies point to earlier factors that predict happiness and physical and mental health in later life, including marital and career fulfillment as a younger adult, sustained family relationships, and long-lived ancestors; risk factors from young and middle adulthood include defense mechanisms such as projection that grossly distort reality, alcoholism, and depression before age 50 (Sears, 1977; Vaillant & Vaillant, 1990). The quality of old age thus appears to depend to a substantial degree on the quality of youth.

SOME CONCLUDING THOUGHTS

This chapter and the last have focused on pathways through development. Psychological development through the lifespan involves continuous adaptation to a changing brain and body within a social and cultural context. A toddler upset by the absence of her mother, an adolescent trying to make sense of a body that looks and feels increasingly unfamiliar, a person whose spouse has died and whose time on life's stage is drawing to an end—in each case, psychological experience reflects a social animal wrestling with biological givens.

In the next chapter we examine what happens when development goes awry, as we explore psychological disorders. Then, in the following chapter, we consider approaches to helping people return to more satisfying pathways through psychological treatment.

Summary

1. **Social development** refers to predictable changes in interpersonal thought, feeling, and behavior over the lifespan.

Attachment

2. **Attachment** refers to the enduring affectional ties that children form with their primary caregivers. **Separation anxiety**, distress at separation from attachment figures, occurs around the same time in all human cultures and peaks in the second year. Harlow's experiments with monkeys showed that security, not food, is the basis for attachment. Integrating psychodynamic and evolutionary theory, Bowlby proposed that attachment is a mechanism to keep immature animals close to their parents.

3. Researchers using a procedure called the **Strange Situation** have identified four styles of attachment: secure, avoidant, ambivalent, and disorganized. Early attachment patterns have a powerful impact on later social functioning and form the basis of **adult attachment** styles. Infants develop **internal working models**, or mental representations of attachment relationships, which form the basis for their expectations in later close relationships.

Socialization

4. **Socialization** refers to the processes through which individuals come to learn the rules, beliefs, values, skills, attitudes, and behavior patterns of their society. Socialization is transactional (interactive), lifelong, and occurs within a broader economic and social context.

5. Parents are particularly important **socialization agents**. Research distinguishes authoritarian, permissive, and authoritative parenting styles. Each parenting style tends to produce children with different characteristics. An important dimension on which parents vary across and within cultures is parental warmth, that is, the extent to which they are accepting or rejecting of their children. Parental acceptance is associated with self-esteem, independence, and emotional stability.

6. Among the most powerful roles into which people are socialized are **gender roles**, the range of behaviors considered appropriate for males and females. Unlike sex (a biologically based categorization), **gender** (the psychological meaning of being male or female) is influenced by learning. Gender socialization begins in the first days of life.

Relationships with Siblings and Peers

7. Sibling relationships have many dimensions, including both rivalry and closeness. Friendships with other children begin to emerge around the third year. Some children suffer the fate of being disliked by their peers: Rejected children are scapegoated, teased, and ostracized, while neglected children find themselves friendless and ignored.

Development of Social Cognition

8. As with cognitive development in nonsocial domains, children develop in their **social cognition**—the way they conceptualize themselves, others, and relationships. The **self-concept** refers to a person's organized way of representing infor-

mation about the self. Initially, children lack a distinct concept of self; gradually, concrete views develop, and by adolescence the self-concept is more abstract and based more on internal psychological processes such as feelings and personality traits. An important social-cognitive skill that develops gradually is **perspective-taking**, the ability to understand other people's viewpoints.

9. Children's understanding of what gender is and how it applies to them develops substantially throughout the first several years of life. Children develop **gender schemas**, mental representations that associate psychological characteristics with one sex or the other, by integrating cultural beliefs with their personal experiences. Gender schemas share striking similarities across cultures, which appear to reflect an interaction between biology and social learning.

Moral Development

10. Researchers have concentrated considerable effort on **moral development**, the acquisition of values and rules for balancing the potentially conflicting interests of the self and others. Behaviorist and cognitive-social theories assert that **prosocial behavior** (behavior that benefits others), like other behaviors, is learned through processes such as conditioning and modeling. Cognitive-developmental models focus less on moral behaviors than on moral reasoning. Kohlberg's stage theory distinguishes three levels of moral reasoning: **preconventional** (following moral rules to avoid punishment or obtain reward), **conventional** (defining right and wrong according to learned cultural standards), and **postconventional** (applying abstract, self-defined principles). Information-processing approaches break moral development down into component processes and examine the way each changes during childhood.

11. According to psychodymanic theories, a child internalizes the parents' values, and guilt motivates people to obey their conscience. Other theorists emphasize the role of **empathy** (feeling for someone who is hurting) in motivating prosocial behavior. Undoubtedly, moral development reflects an interaction of cognitive and emotional development.

Lifespan Development

12. The most widely known theory of lifespan development is Erik Erikson's eight psychosocial stages: **basic trust versus mistrust, autonomy versus shame and doubt, initiative versus guilt,** and **industry versus inferiority** in childhood; **identity versus identity confusion** in adolescence; and **intimacy versus isolation, generativity versus stagnation,** and **integrity versus despair** during adulthood. Psychologists disagree on the extent to which adolescents and people in midlife experience crises, but in general, there does not appear to be any single path to "successful aging."

Susan Grabel, "Rachael," *1992*

Chapter 15

PSYCHOLOGICAL DISORDERS

*L*ate on a blustery February night, a woman we shall call Mary was crying in the corner of a shelter for battered women. Her eyes blackened, her ribs badly bruised, and sobbing with pain and betrayal, she told a staff member her story: Her boyfriend of two years, drunk and enraged, had kicked and beaten her.

This was not the first time Mary had told this story. Twice before she had sought the safe confines of the shelter because of her boyfriend. Each time, over the objections of shelter staff, she returned home, seduced by his promises that he would change. Her ex-husband had also abused her, as had her father when she was a child.

This vignette challenges our notions of normality and abnormality, sickness and sin. Until very recently, police officers intervened only minimally in cases of domestic violence, doctors treated broken noses and ribs in obviously battered women without addressing their equally broken spirits, and laws allowed angry, jealous men to stalk and terrorize their ex-lovers under the guise of civil liberties. Apparently, our society has not considered battering abnormal. Rather, violence against women has been "a domestic affair."

Yet few readers would disagree that something is wrong with the violent men in Mary's life. They are bad or mad, criminal or disturbed. They are unlikely, however, ever to serve time for their crimes or to receive psychiatric diagnoses. And what about Mary? Is she simply a victim of circumstance, accidentally finding herself over and over again at the mercy of abusive men? Or does the abuse she suffered at her father's hands influence her choice of partners and the choices she makes when they become abusive?

As this vignette suggests, whether to consider a particular pattern of psychological functioning as disordered is not always clear and is influenced by cultural values and beliefs. In this chapter, we examine **psychopathology** (literally, sickness, or pathology, of the mind), which refers to problematic patterns of thought, feeling, or behavior that disrupt an individual's sense of well-being or social or occupational functioning. We begin with the cultural context of psychopathology, considering how people like Mary and the men in her life become classified as normal or disordered. Next we examine the often starkly contrasting ways psychodynamic, cognitive-behavioral, biological, and systems theorists understand psychopathology as well as a descriptive approach that centers on diagnosis. Then we describe the major psychopathological syndromes, from those that first manifest themselves in childhood, to those characterized by specific symptoms such as depression and anxiety, to disorders of the entire personality. We conclude by asking whether mental disorders really fit into discrete categories as medical syndromes do, whether we have identified the right syndromes, and whether their causes can be neatly categorized as either nature or nurture.

THE CULTURAL CONTEXT OF PSYCHOPATHOLOGY

Every society has its concept of "madness," and what a society considers normal or abnormal is constantly changing. One hundred years ago many doctors and laypeople alike considered a person who engaged in various forms of sexual behavior such as oral sex perverse. Today a person who finds oral sex disgusting might seek treatment for a sexual phobia, perhaps at the urging of a partner.

Some of the psychopathological syndromes clinicians encounter today were identified and classified as early as 2500 BC by the ancient Sumerians and Egyptians. However, Western culture at various times has attributed mental illness to demon possession, supernatural forces, witches, Satan, and wandering uteruses. To what extent does culture shape and define mental illness? And are diagnoses anything but labels a culture uses to brand its deviants?

Culture and Psychopathology

Cultures differ in both the disorders they spawn and the ways they categorize mental illness (see Kleinman, 1988; Leff, 1988). Jamaican culture produces many fewer children with disorders characterized by undercontrol (such as fighting and stealing) than the United States (Lambert et al., 1989). One Alaskan Eskimo group's concept of "being crazy" is somewhat similar to our own, including talking to oneself, screaming at people who do not exist, or making peculiar grimaces. Their concept of mental illness, however, also includes some symptoms unusual in the rest of North America, such as believing that a loved one was murdered by witchcraft when no one else thought so, believing oneself to be an animal, drinking urine, or

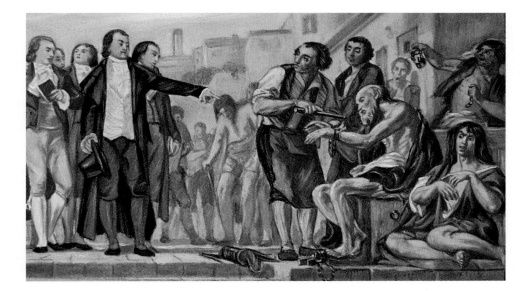

Philippe Pinel, a French physician, challenged the prevailing treatment of the mentally ill in the eighteenth century and ordered the removal of the chains in a Paris hospital.

TABLE 15.1 Culture and Mental Illness

	PERCENT OF SAMPLE WITH THE DISORDER		
COMMUNITY	Alcoholism	Schizophrenia	Major Depression
Metropolitan Taipei	5.17	.34	.94
Small Taiwan towns	9.96	.23	1.61
Rural Taiwan villages	7.58	.17	1.01
Urban North Carolina	8.97	1.36	5.13
Rural North Carolina	9.60	1.21	2.44
West Los Angeles	14.37	.46	7.03

Source: Adapted from Compton et al., 1991, pp. 1700–1701.

killing dogs (Murphy, 1976). In rural Ireland, which is almost uniformly Catholic, people with schizophrenia are more likely than North American schizophrenics to have bizarre religious beliefs, such as the conviction that their body has become inhabited by the Virgin Mary (Scheper-Hughes, 1979). In other words, when people fall ill psychologically, they tend to do so in a cultural idiom (see Fabrega, 1989, 1994).

Psychopathology differs within as well as across cultures (Table 15.1). For example, prevalence rates of alcoholism, schizophrenia, and severe depression vary depending on cultural and demographic factors (such as city size), although the reasons for these variations are not entirely clear (Compton et al., 1991). Conceptions of psychopathology also differ within cultures, especially in multicultural societies. The Amish, who value humility and frugality, consider a person who races a horse too hard, treats livestock too harshly, or buys and consumes in excess to have an emotional disturbance (Draguns, 1986). Cuban Americans who practice a religion called *santeria* believe that people can be possessed by spirits and communicate with deceased ancestors. Individuals who report this belief to clinicians unfamiliar with their religious beliefs can be misdiagnosed as psychotic (Alonso & Jeffrey, 1988). Thus, diagnosis of psychiatric illness always requires knowledge of the patient's culture or subculture.

Cultural shifts can also lead to changes in prevalent forms of psychopathology. In times of rapid social change, when people do not know what norms to follow and have lost the sense of meaning in life that an intact culture provides, drug abuse, suicide, and aggressive behavior tend to rise dramatically (Berry, 1989; Wallace, 1956). The extended family may buffer children against some of the negative effects of rapid social change. In Khartoum, the capital of the Sudan, children reared in extended families have considerably fewer emotional problems than those reared in nuclear families; children with a grandmother involved in parenting are especially likely to be psychologically healthy (El Hassan Al Awad & Sonuga-Barke, 1992).

Is Mental Illness Nothing But a Cultural Construction?

If definitions of abnormality vary by culture, can one really speak of mental illness at all? Or is mental illness simply a construct used by a society to brand and punish those who fail to respect its norms? In the 1960s and 1970s, several prominent researchers and social critics suggested that this is the case. Psychiatrist Thomas

Szasz (1974, 1989) proposed that mental illness is a myth used to make people conform to society's standards of normality. In his view, which was highly influential in changing laws regarding commitment to mental institutions, people should only be treated for mental illness if they regard their symptoms as a problem.

A variation of this view, called labeling theory, focuses on the disadvantages of categorizing mental disorders at all (Scheff, 1970). According to **labeling theory**, diagnosis is simply a way of labeling individuals whom a society considers deviant. Labeling can be dangerous because it stigmatizes and stereotypes "patients," whose subsequent actions will be interpreted as part of their "craziness" and who may face discrimination based on their diagnoses. Individuals who have been labeled may also take on the role of a sick or crazy person and hence actually begin to play the part into which they have been cast.

A classic study raised some of these issues in a dramatic way. David Rosenhan had himself and seven other normal persons around the United States admitted to various psychiatric hospitals by feigning symptoms of schizophrenia, complaining of hearing voices that said "empty," "hollow," or "thud" (Rosenhan, 1973). All but one of these "patients" was subsequently diagnosed schizophrenic. Once on the psychiatric wards, however, the pseudo-patients behaved as they normally would and told staff they no longer heard voices. Psychiatric staff nonetheless interpreted their behavior as evidence of disturbance. For example, when the pseudo-patients took copious notes while on the unit, hospital personnel commented in their psychiatric records about their peculiar "note-taking behavior." When these pseudo-patients were finally discharged, which took an average of 19 days, they were given the label, "schizophrenia, in remission." (The pseudo-patients also experienced neglect and depersonalizing treatment in the hospital, receiving contact with psychologists, psychiatrists, or physicians only an average of 6.8 minutes a day.)

Rosenhan's study set off a wave of controversy, for it appeared to demonstrate that psychiatric illness is in the eye of the beholder and that even trained eyes are not very acute. Others argued, however, that the study led to some very dramatic but largely incorrect conclusions (see Spitzer, 1985). Behavior is meaningful only when it is understood in context. Singing is both normal and expected in a chorus, but singing during a lecture would be very peculiar. Similarly, in a psychiatric hos-

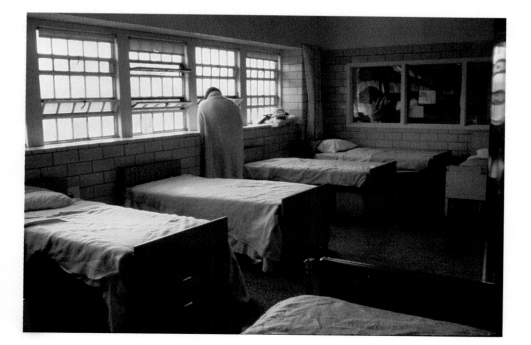

According to labeling theory, once people take on the label of "patient," they may be forced into the role by others and may assume the identity of someone who is helpless and dysfunctional.

pital, taking notes does appear to be abnormal behavior for a person complaining of hallucinations, and had the pseudo-patients not lied about their initial symptoms, this would have been an appropriate inference. Furthermore, in medical parlance, "in remission" means simply that a patient has previously reported symptoms that are no longer present. One critic concluded that the study did little more than illustrate that people can fool a clinician if they try hard enough (Spitzer, 1985)—just as they can trick a neurologist by complaining of all the symptoms of stroke, or a potential employer by creating a false resume.

Empirical investigations have not supported labeling theory either, at least in its more sweeping forms (see Gove, 1982; Phillips & Dinitz, 1982). Many disorders occur and are recognized as problems cross-culturally, suggesting that they are not just ways of labeling deviants (Draguns, 1990). This is the case, for example, with schizophrenia, in which people lose touch with reality and may hold bizarre beliefs (for example, that their thoughts are being broadcast on the radio). The negative consequences of labeling can indeed be profound, but without diagnosis, mental health professionals would be in the same helpless and confused position as physicians in the early 1980s were when confronted with patients exhibiting the strange set of symptoms that turned out to be AIDS. One cannot research and treat a problem without distinguishing those who have it from those who do not.

The idea that psychopathology is a myth or an arbitrary label also tends to romanticize illness. Would anyone in his "right mind" really want to take on the problems that accompany schizophrenia, such as loss of contact with reality and the profound sense of aloneness that arises from chronically misunderstanding and feeling misunderstood if not shunned? In light of the tremendous suffering that accompanies this illness, the view that schizophrenia is simply an alternative way of seeing the world appears rather naive. It is also contradicted by an accumulating body of evidence documenting that schizophrenia is an illness of the brain, much like Alzheimer's disease, which no one would similarly describe as an alternative way of seeing the world.

Contemporary Approaches to Psychopathology

Although few contemporary psychologists view mental illness as a myth or ascribe its causes to demon possession, they differ considerably in the way they conceptualize the nature and causes of psychological disorders. Consider the case of Charlie, a 24-year-old business-school student with an intense fear of being in groups. Whenever Charlie is at a party, he feels tremendously anxious and usually ends up leaving shortly after he arrives. He worries that people will laugh at and ostracize him and that he will be mortally embarrassed. His mouth becomes dry, his hands become clammy, and his stomach knots. Paradoxically, he feels most anxious when he should feel most confident, as when he has expertise in the topic being discussed. Charlie's problem has intensified since he began business school. His father, who never attended college, ridiculed him for his decision to enter graduate school ("Why don't you just get a job?"), and his schoolwork requires him to participate in many group situations.

The way a psychologist would understand Charlie's anxiety depends on the psychologist's theoretical orientation. We first examine psychodynamic and cognitive-behavioral perspectives. Next we consider two very different approaches: biological and systems. Then we present a descriptive approach aimed at categorizing and diagnosing psychopathological syndromes.

Psychodynamic Perspective

Psychodynamic theorists distinguish among three broad classes of psychopathology: neuroses, personality disorders, and psychoses. **Neuroses** are problems in living, such as phobias, chronic self-doubts, and repetitive interpersonal problems (for example, trouble with authority figures). They occur in most if not all people at different points in their lives and usually do not stop them from functioning reasonably well. **Personality disorders** are chronic and severe disturbances that substantially inhibit the capacity to love and to work. People with personality disorders often have difficulty maintaining meaningful relationships, show substantial distortions in their interpretations of interpersonal events, are chronically vulnerable to depression or despair, and have difficulty maintaining employment. **Psychoses** are gross disturbances involving a loss of touch with reality, as when a person hears voices telling him to kill himself or believes (without good reason) that the CIA is trying to assassinate him.

By and large, psychodynamic clinicians view these three broad classes of disorders as a continuum of functioning (Figure 15.1), reflecting the maturity and solidity of the person's underlying personality structure (Kernberg, 1984). The three classes of pathology also represent a continuum in terms of **etiology** (origins).

LEVEL OF DISTURBANCE	CAPACITIES		
	Love	Work	Relation to Reality
Normal to neurotic	Able to maintain relationships.	Able to maintain employment.	Able to see reality clearly.
	May have minor difficulties such as conflicts with significant others or tendency to be competitive with same or opposite sex.	May have difficulties such as rigidity, defensiveness, underconfidence, workaholism, overambition, or underachievement.	May have minor defensive distortions, such as seeing the self and significant others as better than they really are.
Personality disordered	Unable to maintain relationships consistently.	Difficulty maintaining employment.	Generally able to see reality with clarity (i.e., with no hallucinations or delusions).
	May avoid relationships, jump into them too quickly, or end them abruptly.	May be grossly underemployed, extremely unable to get along with bosses, or have a tendency to terminate employment abruptly. (A subset of these patients can work successfully, for example, in occupations that allow work in total isolation or that permit or encourage grandiosity.)	Prone to gross misinterpretations in interpersonal affairs. (A subset has chronically idiosyncratic thinking.)
Psychotic	Tremendous difficulty maintaining relationships; may be socially isolated.	Unable to maintain employment anywhere near intellectual level.	Unable to distinguish clearly between what is real and what is not.
	Socially peculiar.	Large percentage are chronically unemployed.	Has delusions, hallucinations, or other psychotic thought processes.

FIGURE 15.1

Continuum of psychopathology. Psychodynamic theorists place disorders on a continuum of functioning, reflecting the maturity and strength of the person's underlying personality structure.

Psychoses result primarily from biological abnormalities with some environmental input, whereas neuroses and personality disorders stem more from environmental (particularly childhood) experiences, sometimes interacting with biological vulnerabilities (Figure 15.2). People tend to function consistently at one level or another. However, neurotic symptoms (such as phobias) also occur in more severely disturbed patients, and psychotic states can occur episodically in people who are otherwise healthier, such as patients with bipolar disorder (manic-depression), who may be relatively unimpaired between episodes.

To assess psychopathology, a psychodynamic psychologist gathers information about the patient's current level of functioning and life stresses, the origins and course of the symptom, and salient events in the person's developmental history. Taking a thorough developmental history is particularly important from a psychodynamic perspective because the patient's recounting of childhood experiences may hold clues to the origins and meanings of the symptom.

The clinician uses all of this information to make a **psychodynamic formulation**, a set of hypotheses about the patient's personality structure and the meaning of the symptom. This formulation attempts to answer three questions: What does the patient wish for and fear? What psychological resources does the person have at his disposal? And how does he experience himself and others (Westen, 1995)? The first question focuses on the person's dominant motives and conflicts. Psychodynamic clinicians view neurotic symptoms as expressions of, or compromises among, various motives. In this view, symptoms typically reflect unconscious conflicts among wishes and fears and the defensive efforts used to resolve these. The second question is about ego functioning—the person's ability to function autonomously, make sound decisions, think clearly, and regulate impulses and emotions (see Bellack et al., 1973). The third question regards the patient's object relations (Chapter 12), notably the ability to form meaningful relationships with other people and to maintain self-esteem.

Like clinicians of all perspectives, a psychodynamic psychologist would require more data before arriving at a formulation of Charlie's case. Nevertheless, he might hypothesize that Charlie's symptoms reflect a conflict over success, for his anxiety is strongest when he is in a position to shine and is exacerbated as he gets closer to achieving his goals. Charlie wants to be successful and display his abilities, but this desire evokes old feelings of ridicule by his father. To be successful might also unconsciously mean outdoing his father, who had minimal education; hence he feels anxious and guilty. A psychodynamic psychologist assessing Charlie would also want to assess whether Charlie's functioning is impaired in other ways or whether

FIGURE 15.2

Biology and experience in psychopathology. From a psychodynamic point of view, neuroses are primarily environmental in origin, although they may reflect some biological vulnerabilities. Personality disorders stem either from extreme childhood experiences or from an interaction of genetic and environmental vulnerabilities. Psychoses are primarily biological in origin, although childhood and adult experiences shape their expression.

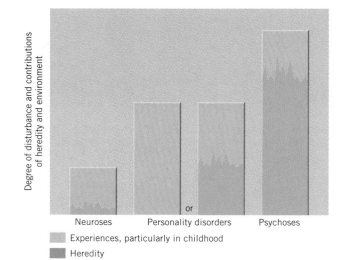

the impairment is limited to this phobia (that is, to assess ego functioning). The clinician would also assess whether his social phobia is specific to groups or is part of a more serious underlying difficulty in forming and maintaining relationships (object relations).

Cognitive-Behavioral Perspective

In clinical psychology, many practitioners consider themselves cognitive-behavioral, integrating an understanding of classical and operant conditioning with a cognitive-social perspective (Turner et al., 1992). They focus not on a hypothesized underlying personality structure but on discrete processes, such as thoughts that precede an anxiety reaction or physiological symptoms (e.g., racing heart) that accompany it. From a more behavioral perspective, the clinician carefully assesses the conditions under which symptoms such as anxiety arise and tries to discover the stimuli that elicit them (see Hersen, 1988). From a more cognitive perspective, the clinician focuses on irrational beliefs that maintain dysfunctional behaviors and emotions (Beck, 1976, 1991).

From a behavioral point of view, Charlie's phobia is a conditioned emotional response (anxiety) that may first have occurred while he was with one group of people but has now generalized to many other group situations. Avoidance behavior is being negatively reinforced the more he avoids the phobic situation. In other words, avoidance reduces anxiety, which reinforces avoidance. Making matters worse, Charlie's anxiety may actually make him less socially competent, leading others to respond less positively to him, which in turn makes him more anxious and avoidant. To try to disentangle the conditions eliciting his anxiety, the behaviorally oriented clinician would ask precisely where and when Charlie becomes anxious. Are there group situations in which he does not become anxious? Does he become anxious only when he is expected to talk or even when he can remain silent?

Working more cognitively, the cognitive-behavioral clinician would assess the thoughts that run through Charlie's mind as his anxiety mounts. For instance, Charlie may erroneously believe that if people laugh at him, he will "die" of embarrassment or that some other calamity will befall him. The clinician would examine the way such irrational ideas maintain the phobia. For example, Charlie might disclose that he feels anxious in any situation that requires him to speak articulately because he does not believe he can do so effectively. Alternatively, he may hold the irrational belief that he must excel in all situations if people are to like and respect him and consequently becomes terrified at the possibility of failure.

Biological Approach

To understand psychopathology, mental health professionals often move from a psychological to a biological level of analysis. Practitioners from all theoretical perspectives operate at this level of analysis when they evaluate patients for potential biological contributions to their symptoms, as when they take a family history to assess possible genetic contributions. However, some practitioners, mainly psychiatrists (medical doctors trained in psychiatry), believe a biological approach can explain all or most psychopathology. The biological approach looks for the roots of mental disorders in problems with the circuitry of the brain. For example, overactive or underactive neurotransmitters that disrupt normal patterns of neural firing may cause a person to behave in dysfunctional ways, feel depressed, or lose contact with reality.

Aside from family history, clinicians considering biological contributions to mental disorders often assess the patient's mental status. **Mental status** refers to the intactness of memory, orientation to reality (whether the patient knows who he is, what day of the week it is, and so forth), state of consciousness (whether the person is clear and alert), reasoning ability, and ability to think abstractly. For example, if the patient tended to use words idiosyncratically, the clinician might suspect psychosis. The clinician might then inquire whether she ever hears voices or sees things that are not there or ask her to explain the meaning of a proverb like "A stitch in time saves nine." A patient whose thinking is disordered may produce a very concrete response such as, "You have to sew things now or they will fall apart again" or a response filled with idiosyncratic elaborations such as, "A stitch now could save your life—nine lives, like a cat." A clinician suspecting organic disturbance might also order laboratory tests or brain scans to rule out hormonal disturbances (such as thyroid dysfunction) or brain abnormalities.

The biological approach is not incompatible with the perspectives described thus far. Charlie's anxiety may indeed be associated with his conflicts about achieving success, or he may be caught in a spiral of negatively reinforced avoidance of social situations. Nevertheless, his propensity to become anxious in the first place could reflect a biological predisposition. Theorists of various persuasions adopt a **diathesis-stress model**, which proposes that people with an underlying vulnerability (called a diathesis) may become symptomatic under stressful circumstances. The diathesis may be biological, such as a genetic propensity for anxiety symptoms caused by overactivity of epinephrine and norepinephrine (which underlie normal anxiety reactions). Alternatively, the diathesis can be environmental, stemming from events such as a history of neglect, excessive parental criticism, or loss in childhood. Upsetting events in adulthood, such as the loss of a lover or a failure at work, might then activate the vulnerability.

Systems Approach

A social systems approach looks for the roots of psychopathology not in cells but in the broader social context in which they are embedded, which is quite a different level of analysis. A **systems approach** explains an individual's behavior in the context of a social group, such as a couple, family, or larger group. An individual is part of a **system**, a group with interdependent parts, and what happens in one part of the system influences what happens in others. From this standpoint, diagnosing a problem in an individual without considering the systems in which he is embedded is like trying to figure out why a car is getting poor gas mileage but refusing to consider traffic conditions.

Like the biological approach, a systems approach is not incompatible with other perspectives, since it operates at another level of analysis. For example, a child whose parents inadvertently contribute to his tendency to behave aggressively at school, by modeling aggression at home and failing to reinforce alternative behaviors, is part of a broader family system that may be dysfunctional. Nevertheless, in clinical practice, practitioners who take a systems approach frequently consider it their primary theoretical orientation, much as biological psychiatrists consider theirs a comprehensive approach to psychopathology.

Most systems clinicians adopt a **family systems model**, which proposes that the symptoms of an individual are really symptoms of dysfunction in a family (Hoffman, 1981, 1991). In other words, the **identified patient** (the person identified as the one who needs help) is the **symptom bearer** (the person displaying the family's difficulties), but the problem lies in the family, not primarily in the individual. For instance, a couple brought their child to see a therapist because he was very disruptive at school and punishing him had been ineffective. The psychologist inquired about the parents' marriage and found that it had been very shaky until the child began having difficulties at school. Once the child became symptomatic, the parents worked together to help him, and their marital problems subsided. Thus, the problem was not so much a disruptive child as a disruptive marriage. The child not only *expressed* his parents' marital problems through his symptom but also helped preserve their marriage by becoming symptomatic.

Systems theorists refer to the methods family members use to preserve equilibrium in a family (such as a tolerable level of tension or the preservation of a marriage) as **family homeostatic mechanisms**. These mechanisms operate much like the homeostatic mechanisms discussed in Chapter 10 on motivation. In the case above, marital tension evoked a set of behaviors by the child, which in turn reduced the marital tension, much as a furnace turns on until the temperature in a room reaches the temperature set on the thermostat. Thus, psychological symptoms are actually dysfunctional efforts to cope with a disturbance in the family (Stanton, 1981).

Family systems theorists also focus on the ways families are organized, including family roles, boundaries, and alliances (see Boszormenyi-Nagy & Spark, 1973; Elizur & Minuchin, 1989; Haley, 1976; Minuchin, 1974; Ryder & Bartle, 1991). **Family roles** are parts individuals play in repetitive family "dramas" or interaction patterns among family members, much like actors in a play. Playing roles is not in itself pathological and occurs in every social group (Chapter 18); for example, one child in a family may take on the role of mediator between two siblings who are often in conflict. In some families, however, a child may become a **scapegoat**, a lightning rod for anger in the family who is blamed for anything bad that happens (Bermann, 1973). In other families, a child and parent may switch roles, a phenomenon known as **role reversal**: The child's role becomes that of taking care of the parent, attending to the parent's needs, and taking on the parent's responsibilities (see Alexander, 1992; Burkett, 1991).

In assessing a family, a psychologist with a systems orientation wants to know about the status of the marital subsystem (the relationship between the parents) and the roles people play. The clinician may want to assess the **boundaries**, or physical and psychological limits, of the family system and its subsystems (see Finkelhor, 1984; Friedman et al., 1987; Goldstein, 1988; Ryder & Bartle, 1991). Some families are enmeshed, that is, too involved with each other's business, so that privacy and autonomy are impossible. Others are disengaged, with minimal contact among family members (see Olson, 1985). Some families have rigid boundaries with the outside world, punishing their members if they disclose too many family secrets or spend too much time away from home, whereas others seem to lack internal boundaries, as when a parent refuses to allow a child any privacy.

The systems-oriented psychologist also assesses **family alliances**—that is, who is typically on whose side in conflicts—and other interaction patterns. A child who begins abusing drugs may, for example, be expressing frustration at feeling excluded from, or consistently attacked by, an alliance between a parent and sibling who is seen as the "good" child. The clinician also looks for problematic **communication patterns**, as when a couple communicates primarily by fighting.

THE DYSFUNCTIONAL FAMILY ROBINSON

CALLAHAN

A psychologist working from a systems approach might evaluate Charlie first in one session by himself and then in another with his father or family. Although systems theorists differ considerably in their specific approaches, the clinician might assess the extent to which Charlie is bringing issues from his family of origin into his new relationships (Bowen, 1978, 1991). The systems clinician would likely observe the way Charlie and his father communicate, looking for mutually unsatisfying patterns in their interactions. The clinician might also understand these patterns in the context of the family's subculture, which may have particular ways of regulating emotional expression and intergenerational communication.

Descriptive Approach to Diagnosis: DSM-IV

Another approach to psychopathology is descriptive. In **descriptive diagnosis,** mental disorders are classified in terms of **clinical syndromes,** or constellations of symptoms that tend to occur together. For example, in a depressive syndrome, depressed mood is often accompanied by loss of interest in pleasurable activities, insomnia, loss of appetite, poor concentration, and decreased self-esteem. The American Psychiatric Association publishes a manual of clinical syndromes that clinicians use to make diagnoses, called *The Diagnostic and Statistical Manual of Mental Disorders-IV,* (1994), which is now in its fourth edition (**DSM-IV**). DSM-IV aims to identify mental disorders on the basis of readily observable signs or symptoms to minimize idiosyncratic diagnoses.

The descriptive approach attempts to be atheoretical, that is, not wedded to any particular theoretical perspective on etiology. In reality, descriptive diagnosis is frequently allied with a **medical model** of psychopathology, which presumes that psychological disorders fall into discrete categories like medical disorders such as tuberculosis or melanoma. Not surprisingly, then, an emphasis on descriptive diagnosis is more characteristic of psychiatrists than psychologists, although nearly all mental health professionals use descriptive diagnoses when initially evaluating a patient. The advantage of descriptive diagnosis is that researchers and clinicians in many different settings can use it to diagnose patients in a similar manner, regardless of their theoretical orientation (see Spitzer et al., 1992; Williams et al., 1992).

DSM-IV uses a **multiaxial system of diagnosis,** placing symptoms in their biological and social context, by evaluating patients along five axes (Table 15.2). These

TABLE 15.2 THE AXES OF DSM-IV

AXIS	DESCRIPTION
Axis I	Symptoms that cause distress or significantly impair social or occupational functioning
Axis II	Personality disorders—personality patterns that are so pervasive, inflexible, and maladaptive that they impair interpersonal or occupational functioning
Axis III	Medical conditions that may be relevant to the understanding or treatment of a psychological disorder
Axis IV	Psychosocial and environmental problems (such as negative life events and interpersonal stressors) that may affect the diagnosis, treatment, and prognosis of psychological disorders
Axis V	Global assessment of functioning—the individual's overall level of functioning in social, occupational, and leisure activities

Source: Adapted from *Diagnostic and Statistical Manual of Mental Disorders, Fourth Edition,* American Psychiatric Association, 1994.

axes cover not only symptoms and personality disturbances but also variables such as medical conditions and environmental stressors. Axis I lists the clinical syndromes for which a patient seeks treatment, such as depression or schizophrenia, whereas Axis II lists personality disorders. On Axis III, the clinician lists any general medical conditions that may be relevant (such as diabetes or hypothyroidism, which can affect mood). Axis IV is reserved for psychosocial and environmental stressors (life events such as death of a family member that could be contributing to emotional problems). On Axis V, the clinician rates on a scale of 0 to 100 the patient's current level of functioning and the highest level of functioning the patient has maintained during the past year.

PSYCHOPATHOLOGICAL SYNDROMES

In this section, we examine some of the major clinical syndromes, starting with disorders that usually become evident in childhood and working our way through substance-related disorders, schizophrenia, mood disorders, anxiety disorders, dissociative disorders, and personality disorders. The major diagnostic categories of DSM-IV are listed in Table 15.3. First, however, a brief warning is in order. You may have experienced some of these symptoms at one time or another and may start to worry that you have one (or all) of the disorders. This reaction is similar to the first-year medical syndrome experienced by many beginning medical students, who imagine they have whichever disease they are currently studying. Thus, while you may think you recognize yourself in one of the disorders, bear in mind that only when symptoms disrupt a person's functioning or sense of well-being would a trained mental health professional actually diagnose a disorder and that most forms of psychopathology can be treated (Chapter 16).

Disorders Usually First Diagnosed in Infancy, Childhood, or Adolescence

Several mental disorders arise during infancy, childhood, or adolescence. This section focuses on two common disorders: attention-deficit hyperactivity disorder and conduct disorder.

Attention-Deficit Hyperactivity Disorder

Many children and adolescents are brought to mental health professionals because of behavioral difficulties at school or at home. Consider the case of Jimmy, a 6 year old whose teacher reports that he cannot sit still, does not pay attention, and is constantly disturbing his classmates. Jimmy fidgets in his chair, and when his teacher directs him to do work, he can only concentrate for a few seconds before becoming disruptive, making noises or throwing paper wads across the room. Jimmy's teacher may suspect that he has **attention-deficit hyperactivity disorder** (**ADHD**). ADHD is characterized by inattention, impulsiveness, and hyperactivity that are not appropriate for the child's age. Children with this disorder have disturbances in each of these areas to differing degrees. In the extreme case, a child may be in perpetual motion—running, jumping, disrupting activities, or picking fights with other children.

Although children with ADHD may exhibit symptoms by age 4, frequently the disorder is not recognized until they enter school, since children are not usually required to comply with stringent social demands before that time (Campbell, 1985). Furthermore, to set a standard for hyperactive behavior in preschoolers is difficult because, as one study found, as many as 50 percent of mothers of 4-year-old boys believe their son is hyperactive (Varley, 1984). The prevalence of ADHD is estimat-

TABLE 15.3 MAJOR DIAGNOSTIC CATEGORIES OF THE **DSM-IV**

CATEGORY	DESCRIPTION
Disorders usually first diagnosed in infancy, childhood, or adolescence	Disorders involving deviations from normal development, such as mental retardation, attention deficit/hyperactivity disorder, and conduct disorder
Delirium, dementia, amnesic, and other cognitive disorders	Disorders in which the primary disturbance is severe cognitive deficits caused by aging, degenerative diseases of the nervous system, a general medical condition, or a substance
Mental disorders due to a general medical condition not elsewhere classified	Disorders in which psychiatric symptoms (such as depression) other than cognitive deficits are clearly the direct result of a medical condition
Substance-related disorders	Disorders associated with abusing drugs (including alcohol), as well as side effects of medication and toxin exposure
Schizophrenia and other psychotic disorders	Disorders characterized by loss of contact with reality, marked disturbances of thought and perception, and bizarre behavior
Mood disorders	Disorders characterized by disturbances of normal mood, notably depression, mania (elation), or alternation between periods of both
Anxiety disorders	Disorders in which anxiety is the main symptom (such as generalized anxiety, panic, phobic, post-traumatic stress disorders, and obsessive-compulsive disorder)
Somatoform disorders	Disorders involving physical symptoms that lack an organic basis, such as hypochondriasis (excessive preoccupation with health and fear of disease without a realistic basis for concern)
Factitious disorders	Disorders characterized by physical or psychological symptoms that are intentionally produced or feigned in order to assume the role of sick person
Dissociative disorders	Disorders characterized by temporary alterations or disruptions in consciousness, memory, identity, or perception, such as psychologically induced amnesia
Sexual and gender identity disorders	Disorders of sexuality and gender identity, including sexual dysfunctions, paraphilias (sexual urges, fantasies, or behaviors involving unusual objects, nonconsenting partners, or pain or humiliation, which cause significant distress or dysfunction), and gen der identity disorders (such as cross-dressing that leads to considerable distress or impairment in functioning)
Eating disorders	Disorders characterized by severe disturbance in eating behavior, including anorexia nervosa and bulimia nervosa
Sleep disorders	Disorders characterized by abnormalities in sleep or dreaming
Impulse-control disorders not elsewhere classified	Disorders in which an individual fails to resist the impulse to perform an act that may be harmful to the self or others, such as pyromania or kleptomania
Adjustment disorders	Disorders that are usually relatively mild and transient, in which clinically significant emotional or behavioral symptoms develop as a consequence of some identifiable stressor
Personality disorders	Disorders characterized by long-standing patterns of maladaptive behavior that deviate from cultural expectations and are pervasive and inflexible, such as borderline and antisocial personality disorders

Source: Adapted from *Diagnostic and Statistical Manual of Mental Disorders, Fourth Edition*, American Psychiatric Association, 1994.

A frustrated hyperactive child.

ed at 3 to 5 percent of school-aged children (see Cantwell, 1976; Whalen & Henker, 1991). The disorder is four to nine times more prevalent in males than females.

ADHD runs in families. As many as 20 to 30 percent of children with ADHD have a parent or sibling with a history of the disorder (Brunstetter & Silver, 1985), and families of children with ADHD have a higher incidence of alcoholism and personality disorders in both parents, especially fathers (Cantwell, 1972; Morrison & Stewart, 1971; Pihl et al., 1990). Although many cases probably stem from central nervous system dysfunction, the families of children with ADHD are frequently characterized by abuse, neglect, and disinterest in academic performance, all of which can contribute to hyperactivity and poor concentration.

Recent evidence contradicts the traditional wisdom that children "grow out of" this disorder. Roughly half of adults who were hyperactive as children exhibit residual signs of the disorder in adulthood, such as difficulty sustaining attention (Weiss et al., 1985). Adolescents and adults who were hyperactive as children also have higher rates of antisocial behavior and substance abuse than the general population (Fischer et al., 1990; Mannuzza et al., 1991; Weiss et al., 1985).

Conduct Disorder

Another commonly observed disturbance of childhood is **conduct disorder**, in which a child persistently violates societal norms and the rights of others. Symptoms include physical aggression toward people or animals, chronic fighting, vandalism, persistent lying, and stealing. Such children are obstinate, resent taking direction, lack empathy and compassion, and seldom express remorse for their destructive behavior. Roughly 6 to 16 percent of boys and 2 to 9 percent of girls have this disorder.

Researchers offer varying explanations for conduct disorders. Neuropsychological and behavioral research suggests that some children with conduct disorders are difficult to condition—that is, they have trouble learning from their experience—because they are physiologically less responsive to rewards and especially punishments (Kruesi et al., 1992; Quay et al., 1987; Raine & Venables, 1984). Their autonomic nervous system is less reactive, so they lack the anxiety that motivates other children to adjust their behavior to avoid threatening consequences. The extent to which this reflects biological abnormalities is unclear, since parents who are either ineffectively lax or excessively punitive tend to rear poorly socialized children (see Binder, 1988; Eysenck, 1983; Patterson & Bank, 1986; Reid & Kavanaugh, 1986).

The relative roles of heredity and environment in conduct disorder vary depending on the population and provide a good example of the need for caution in generalizing about heritability from any given sample. Biological factors may be less important in explaining individual differences in antisocial behavior in boys from violent, chaotic homes, which strongly predispose boys to behavior problems, because such environmental influences far outweigh genetic endowment. Some research, for example, finds that boys from intact homes who later commit violent or sexual offenses do show less autonomic responsivity to anxiety-provoking events and are hence less likely to be conditioned to avoid actions associated with punishment. For boys from broken homes, however, who had higher rates of delinquency, autonomic reactivity was not predictive of later criminality (Lytton, 1990).

Substance-Related Disorders

The disorders discussed thus far begin in childhood and often continue in one form or another into adulthood. One set of adult disorders to which both ADHD and conduct disorders predispose individuals are **substance-related disorders**, characterized by continued use of a substance (such as alcohol or cocaine) that negatively affects psychological and social functioning.

Alcoholism

The most common substance disorder is **alcoholism**. An estimated 13 million people in the United States are alcoholics (Kaplan & Sadock, 1988). Alcoholism is the third largest health problem in the country today, following heart disease and cancer, and the most common psychiatric problem in males (Kessler et al., 1994).

Why would someone use and abuse drugs such as alcohol when the effects are clearly destructive to relationships, professional ambitions, and health? As in much research on psychopathology, the major controversy concerns the relative contributions of genetics and environment. Perhaps the best predictor of whether someone will develop alcoholism is a family history of alcoholism (Bohman, 1978; Cadoret et al., 1985; Goodwin et al., 1973; Marlatt & Baer, 1988; Pickens et al., 1991; Russell et al., 1985). Children of alcoholics are four times as likely to develop alcoholism as children of nonalcoholics (Murray et al., 1983; Peele, 1986; Schuckit, 1987). Family history, however, supports both genetic and environmental hypotheses.

On the biological side, children whose biological parents are alcoholic may be predisposed to respond differently to alcohol physiologically than children of nonalcoholic parents (O'Malley & Maisto, 1985; Schuckit, 1984, 1994). Alternatively,

Alcoholism occurs in all social classes and can produce different degrees of social dysfunction.

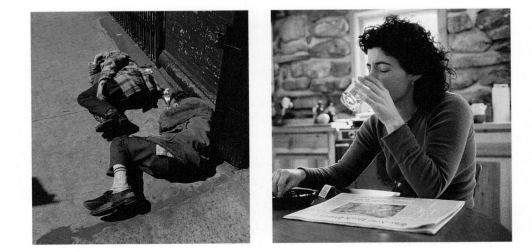

children could inherit a predisposition to other emotional disorders, which indirectly leads to alcoholism. For example, an inherited vulnerability to depression or anxiety could lead them, like their parents, to medicate themselves with alcohol. In this case, a predisposition to alcoholism per se is not what is inherited, but the effect is the same. Similarly, offspring of alcoholic parents could inherit a predisposition to impulsivity, emotional lability (ups and downs), and antisocial behavior, which could also predispose them to alcoholism (see Phillips et al., 1990; Winokur et al., 1973).

A growing body of evidence suggests that one type of alcoholism is highly heritable but that environmental factors play a substantial role in most or all cases of alcoholism. Several studies, relying on different methods, have distinguished two types of alcoholism. One is a severe, early-onset alcoholism associated with delinquency, antisocial personality disorder, and other forms of substance abuse. This form appears to be heritable in males; if it is heritable in females, its heritability is quite low (Kendler et al., 1994; McGue et al., 1992). The more common form of alcoholism, which is less severe and not associated with such significant psychopathology, shows no evidence of heritability and appears to stem largely from environmental factors shared by family members, such as parents who model alcoholic behavior or who damage their children's self-esteem and hence leave them vulnerable to use alcohol as self-medication for depression (Babor et al., 1992; Cloninger et al., 1981; McGue et al., 1992; Pickens et al., 1991).

When Substance Use Is Pathological

Substance abuse can be a crippling psychological disorder, but the relation between substance use and abuse is not always clear. Most people drink alcohol, but this does not mean that most people are alcoholics. Similarly, is minor, occasional, or experimental use of drugs such as marijuana a sign of mental disorder?

Contrary to popular wisdom, the most definitive study in the area found that teenagers (age 18) who experimented with marijuana in moderate amounts actually tended to be healthier psychologically than those who either used marijuana frequently or abstained (Shedler & Block, 1990). Abstaining subjects were more anxious, emotionally inhibited, and lacking in social skills than "experimenters" (defined as subjects who used marijuana no more than once a month and had tried no more than one other illicit drug). Conversely, frequent users were more impulsive and alienated than experimenters (see Figure 15.3). The study suggests that experimentation

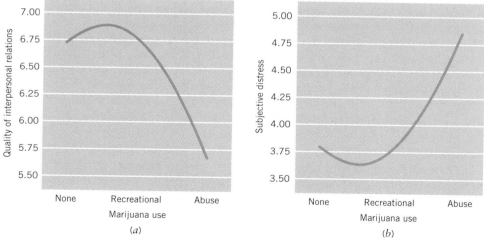

FIGURE 15.3

Relation between marijuana use and adjustment. The two graphs show the relations between level of marijuana use and two composite variables of psychological adjustment, quality of interpersonal relations (a) and subjective distress (b). The relation between marijuana use and these variables is clearly not linear; that is, more marijuana use (e.g., from 0 to 2) does not predict worse mental health. Abstention, mild use, and frequent use are qualitatively different, not on a continuum of abuse. SOURCE: Shedler & Block, 1990, p. 624.

may be a relatively normal expression of adolescent rebellion and the desire to try new experiences.

Another finding of the study was that future substance use could be predicted from interactions between subjects and their mothers when subjects were 5 years old. The most positive, mutually pleasurable mother-child interactions occurred in the group who later experimented with marijuana but did not abuse it. The mother-child interactions of both abstainers and frequent users at age 5 were rated as more hostile, more critical, less spontaneous, less relaxed, and less enjoyable to the child than those of the experimenters.

These findings have important implications for the potential effectiveness of anti-substance abuse campaigns that encourage teenagers and young adults to "Just Say No." As the investigators point out, such campaigns may unnecessarily frighten parents of normal teenagers who experiment with marijuana and underplay the deep-seated personality disturbances that give rise to substance abuse in heavy users. With marijuana as with alcohol, substance use and abuse are not synonymous, although for vulnerable individuals, use will lead to abuse, which can in turn grossly disrupt functioning. An important caveat of this study is that the findings did not apply to use of hard drugs. Marijuana use and hard drug use in this sample appeared to mean very different things (Block et al., 1988). In girls, for example, marijuana use was not correlated with depression, but hard drug use was. Hard drug use also correlated with mood swings and with confusion about identity.

Schizophrenia

Of all the mental disorders that can afflict a human being, schizophrenia is probably the most tragic. **Schizophrenia** is an umbrella term for a number of psychotic disorders that involve disturbances in nearly every dimension of human psychology, including thought, perception, behavior, language, communication, and emotion (see Lehmann & Cancro, 1985). Most forms of schizophrenia begin in the late teens and early 20s. Although estimates vary, only 10 to 20 percent of individuals with schizophrenia ever fully recover (Breier et al., 1991; Carone et al., 1991), and less than half show even moderate improvement after falling ill with the disease (Hegarty et al., 1994). Most schizophrenic patients periodically experience acute phases of the illness and otherwise suffer residual impairment in social and occupational functioning throughout life. This pattern appears to hold true cross-culturally (Marengo et al., 1991), although relapse rates and severity of the illness tend to be higher in the industrialized West (Jenkins & Karno, 1992).

Epidemiological studies find that between 1.2 and 6 million Americans suffer from schizophrenia, or 0.6 to 3 percent of the population. Some studies in the United States have found the rate of schizophrenia to be higher among black and economically impoverished populations. The higher incidence among the poor may reflect the detrimental effect of poverty on people vulnerable to the illness, a tendency of schizophrenics and their offspring to plummet socioeconomically, or both.

Symptoms

Perhaps the most distinctive feature of schizophrenia is a disturbance of thought, perception, and language. Schizophrenics often suffer from **delusions**, false beliefs firmly held despite evidence to the contrary. The person may believe the CIA is trying to kidnap him, that he is Jesus, or that his thoughts are being broadcast on the radio so that others can hear them. **Hallucinations**—sensory perceptions that occur without an external stimulus—are also common; auditory hallucinations (hearing voices) are the most frequent kind of hallucinations in schizophrenia.

Schizophrenic thinking is also frequently characterized by a **loosening of associations**, the tendency of conscious thought to move along associative lines rather than to be controlled, logical, and purposeful. One schizophrenic patient, talking

Disorganized thoughts and perceptions are apparent in the artwork of many schizophrenic patients–though in much of contemporary art as well.

about her sister April, said, "She came in last night from Denver, in like a lion, she's the king of beasts." Whereas a poet might use a similar metaphor deliberately to express the sentiment that a person is angry or hostile, the schizophrenic patient has minimal control over associative thinking and intersperses it with rational thought. In this example, the patient's associations apparently ran from April to March, to an aphorism about March coming in like a lion, and then to another network of associations linked to lions. Schizophrenic patients may thus speak what sounds like gibberish, as they substitute one word for another associatively connected to it or simply follow a train of associations wherever it takes them.

Individuals suffering from schizophrenia also have difficulty maintaining focused attention (Cornblatt & Kelip, 1994; Elkins et al., 1992). In many respects, schizophrenia is a disorder of consciousness, in which the normal monitor and control functions of consciousness (Chapter 9) are suspended. Brain scan (MRI) research, in fact, shows abnormalities in the prefrontal cortex of schizophrenic patients, a region involved in attention and regulation of working memory (Park & Holzman, 1993; Weinberger et al., 1992).

Schizophrenic symptoms can be categorized into positive and negative symptoms (Crow, 1980; McGlashan & Fenton, 1992; Strauss et al., 1974). **Positive symptoms**, such as delusions and hallucinations, are most apparent in acute phases of the illness and are often treatable by antipsychotic medications. They are called positive symptoms because they reflect the presence of something not usually or previously there, such as delusions. **Negative symptoms**, so named because they signal something missing (like normal emotions), are relatively chronic and unresponsive to medication. Negative symptoms include **flat affect** (blunted emotional response), socially inappropriate behavior, and intellectual impairments such as **impoverished thought** (lack of complex thought in response to environmental events).

Types of Schizophrenia

DSM-IV delineates three main subtypes of schizophrenia: paranoid, catatonic, and disorganized (Table 15.4). It also adds an "undifferentiated" category to describe mixed cases, and a "residual" category to refer to people who have had at least one episode but currently experience primarily negative symptoms.

TABLE 15.4 MAJOR SUBTYPES OF SCHIZOPHRENIA

TYPE OF SCHIZOPHRENIA	MAJOR SYMPTOMS
Paranoid	Delusions or auditory hallucinations
Catatonic	Motor immobility, rigid posture, or excessive motor activity, including parrotlike repetition of what someone else says or does
Disorganized	Disorganized speech, bizarre behavior, and flat or inappropriate affect
Undifferentiated	Mixed symptoms not meeting criteria for any of the above subtypes
Residual	Primarily negative symptoms, such as lack of affect, poverty of speech (nothing to say), or lack of motivation

Source: Adapted from *Diagnostic and Statistical Manual of Mental Disorders, Fourth Edition*, American Psychiatric Association, 1994.

...THE GOOD NEWS IS: YOU'RE NOT PARANOID!
...THE BAD NEWS IS THAT EVERYONE REALLY IS OUT TO GET YOU!!.

© 1992, Ziggy and Friends, Inc. Distributed by Universal Press Syndicate

Paranoid schizophrenia is marked by delusions of persecution. People with paranoid schizophrenia are tense, suspicious, and guarded. They may believe people are trying to harm them or are plotting against them, as the following example illustrates:

> Well, I started for my sister's home and on the streetcar again there were two women talking. I did not know them at all. They were looking in my direction and one woman said to the other, "She is always looking for a fight." They changed their seats to the same side as I was on, and I heard one of them say, "He will never marry her." One of the women followed me into the grocery store. The man at the counter said, "Maybe they will put your heart on a platter." Saying that out loud to no one in particular... I seemed to be known wherever I went. (Lehmann & Cancro, 1985)

Paranoid schizophrenia has a much better prognosis (that is, a better likely outcome) than other kinds of schizophrenia, as well as a substantially later age of onset, usually the late 20s (Fenton & McGlashan, 1991).

Catatonic schizophrenia is marked by peculiar motor behavior, such as an extended period of frozen movement and stupor, in which the individual is minimally responsive to the external world. Catatonic patients may assume peculiar poses for long periods of time (Figure 15.4), or they may sometimes echo or mirror the words or actions of people in their company.

In **disorganized schizophrenia**, the person has extremely poor contact with reality, looks disheveled, and exhibits bizarre behavior such as breaking into explosive laughter at inappropriate times. One schizophrenic 17-year-old girl described the futility of continuing to live and her sense of emotional isolation in a monotone, occasionally looking up and chuckling. Another woman with disorganized schizophrenia stated that she heard voices, that a popular singer was chasing her with a knife, and that she was pregnant because she hugged a psychiatrist.

Theories of Schizophrenia

Over the last century, several theories have been offered to explain the causes of schizophrenia. Most contemporary theorists adopt a diathesis-stress model, hypothesizing that people with an underlying genetic vulnerability develop the disorder or fall into an episode under stress (Fowles, 1992; Goldstein, 1988; Rosenthal, 1970; Zubin & Spring, 1977). Some individuals are probably geneti-

FIGURE 15.4
A group of catatonic patients, photographed in 1896.

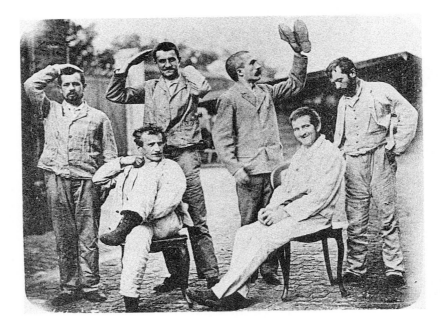

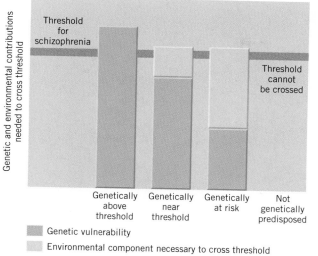

FIGURE 15.5
Diathesis-stress model of schizophrenia. Some individuals probably have a genetic makeup above threshold for schizophrenia. For others, differing degrees of environmental stress activate the vulnerability or diathesis. People not biologically at risk will not develop the disorder, regardless of environmental circumstances.

cally above threshold for the illness, meaning that they will become schizophrenic regardless of environmental circumstances (Figure 15.5). Others are near threshold, requiring only a small environmental contribution. Still others, simply at risk, will not develop the disorder without exposure to substantial pathogenic (that is, disease-causing) experiences (Fowles, 1992). Whether the vulnerability to schizophrenia reflects a single gene or multiple genes is a matter of considerable controversy, although the disorder may be the end result of multiple disruptions in neural functioning, carried on several genes, which different individuals with the disorder may have to varying degrees (see Carpenter, 1992).

Genetics   Genetics undoubtedly play a primary role in the etiology of schizophrenia (Gottesman, 1991; Gottesman et al., 1987; Heston, 1966; Kendler & Diehl, 1993; Weiner, 1985). Table 15.5 shows the risk of developing schizophrenia in people with differing degrees of relatedness to a person with schizophrenia, based on data pooled across over 40 studies conducted over nearly 60 years (Gottesman, 1991). As one would expect for a disorder with a genetic basis, concordance rates between schizophrenic subjects and their relatives increase with their degree of relatedness; that is, people who share more genes are more likely to share the diagnosis (Table 15.5). For monozygotic twins, the concordance rate is roughly 48 percent,

TABLE 15.5 RISK OF SCHIZOPHRENIA AND DEGREE OF GENETIC RELATEDNESS

RELATIONSHIP	DEGREE OF RELATEDNESS	RISK (%)
Identical twin	1.0	48
Fraternal twin	.5	17
Sibling	.5	9
Parent	.5	6
Child	.5	13
Second-degree relatives	.25	2–6

Source: Adapted from Gottesman, 1991, p. 96.

Each of these identical quadruplets later developed schizophrenia.

which means that a person whose identical twin has schizophrenia has about a 50–50 chance of having the disorder. In contrast, the concordance rate for first-degree relatives such as siblings or parent-offspring pairs, who share about half their genes, is 9 to 14 percent, and only 3 to 6 percent for second-degree relatives such as aunts and uncles (Fowles, 1992; Gottesman, 1991; Gottesman et al., 1987; Nicol & Gottesman, 1983). The offspring of the healthy twin in a discordant pair of monozygotic twins are also just as likely as the offspring of the schizophrenic twin to become schizophrenic (Gottesman & Bertelsen, 1989). By most estimates, heritability for this disorder is above 50 percent (Fowles, 1992).

Dopamine   Precisely how a genetic defect produces schizophrenia is not entirely clear. The most widely held view, called the **dopamine hypothesis**, proposes that the nervous system of schizophrenics produces too much of the neurotransmitter dopamine or is overly reactive along dopamine pathways. Evidence for this hypothesis comes from several quarters (Davis et al., 1991). Amphetamines increase dopamine activity, and high doses of amphetamines induce psychotic-like symptoms such as paranoia and hallucinations in normal people (Angrist et al., 1974; Kleven & Seiden, 1991). An amphetamine-induced psychosis is even more likely to occur in individuals with a predisposition to schizophrenia.

The strongest evidence for the dopamine hypothesis, however, is the response of schizophrenic patients to medications known to decrease dopamine activity in the brain (Pickar, 1988; Seeman & Lee, 1975; Snyder, 1976). These so-called antipsychotic medications block dopamine from binding with postsynaptic receptors, thus preventing neural transmission. The result is a reduction or elimination of positive symptoms such as hallucinations, suggesting that overactivity of neurons excited by dopamine is related to psychotic symptoms. The dopamine hypothesis is, however, too simple to account for all the data (Breier et al., 1990). Not all patients respond to medicines that block dopamine activity, different types of dopamine receptors control different psychological processes, and other neurotransmitters, particularly serotonin, appear to be involved in ways that are not yet well understood (perhaps in modulating the effects of dopamine).

The most current formulation of the dopamine hypothesis suggests that two different neural circuits underlie the positive and negative symptoms of schizophrenia (Breier et al., 1991; Davis et al., 1991; Tamminga et al., 1992). One set of neurons that projects from the midbrain to the limbic system has excess dopamine and seems to be responsible for positive symptoms. Another circuit that projects from the midbrain to the frontal cortex seems to be characterized by too *little* dopamine transmission. This circuit is thought to be responsible for negative symptoms of schizophrenia, since frontal activation is necessary for emotion, attention, and social judgment. The association of negative symptoms with low levels of dopamine transmission in a neural pathway leading to the frontal lobes may explain why antipsychotic medications, which reduce positive symptoms by diminishing the action of dopamine, do not alleviate negative symptoms and may even exacerbate them.

Ventricular Enlargement   Another biological theory of schizophrenia points to brain atrophy or neuronal loss, reflected in enlargement of the fluid-filled cavities in the brain called **ventricles**. Enlargement of the ventricles means that the neural regions surrounding them have atrophied or degenerated. Ventricular enlargement is measured by using brain scanning techniques such as CT or MRI. After death, ventricular size and weight can also be assessed at autopsy. Chronic schizophrenic patients often have enlarged ventricles when compared with normal subjects (Lieberman et al., 1992), as Figure 15.6 shows. Ventricular enlargement may not, however, be exclusive to schizophrenia, as it has been observed in patients with other psychotic disorders (Andreason et al., 1990; Weiner, 1985). Interestingly, severity of schizophrenic symptoms (particularly auditory hallucinations) is strongly correlated with the degree of atrophy of a region of the left temporal cortex specialized for auditory processing of language (Barta et al., 1990).

Environmental Contributions   Although a genetic predisposition is probably essential for the development of schizophrenia, environmental variables play an important role in the onset and course of the disorder. A large body of research focuses on patterns of communication and expression of emotion within the families of schizophrenics (Doane et al., 1981; Goldstein, 1985; Hooley, 1985; Hooley et al., in press; Miklowitz et al., 1991; Mirsky & Duncan, 1986; Wynne et al., 1963). Adoption studies show that biological children of schizophrenics adopted away are likely to become schizophrenic if their adoptive families have hostile or confusing communication patterns that involve many mixed messages but not if the adoptive family functions normally (Kety et al., 1975; Tienari, 1991).

Other researchers have looked at **expressed emotion**, a family interaction style characterized by criticism, hostile interchanges, and emotional overinvolvement or intrusiveness by family members. Several studies have found that roughly three-fourths of schizophrenic patients who return to homes high in expressed emotion relapse relatively quickly, compared to only one-fourth of those whose homes are

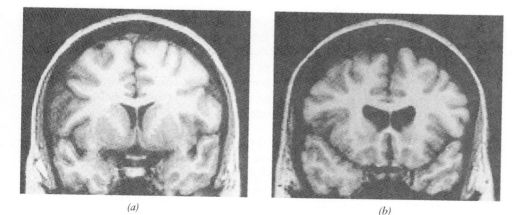

(a)   *(b)*

FIGURE 15.6
Ventricular enlargement in schizophrenic patients. Magnetic resonance imaging (MRI) demonstrates a biological basis for schizophrenia: (a) shows the brain of a 30-year-old woman with normal ventricles, whereas (b) shows the enlarged ventricles of a 36-year-old schizophrenic woman.

characterized by less intense and negative emotional climates (Brown, 1962, 1985; Falloon, 1986; Jenkins et al., 1986). These findings have been replicated cross-culturally, particularly the link between criticism and relapse. High expressed emotion, however, is much less common in families of schizophrenics outside the West (Jenkins & Karno, 1992). Although the incidence of schizophrenia is similar across cultures (Jablensky, 1989), the relapse rate tends to be lower, and the course of the illness more benign, in cultures low in expressed emotion (such as India).

One explanation for the more benign course of the illness in many Third World countries is that their cultures are less committed to concepts of personal responsibility and hence assign less blame to schizophrenics for their actions. Research in North America finds that family members high in expressed emotion tend to have an internal locus of control; that is, they believe they control their own destiny. They also tend to believe that their schizophrenic relatives could fight their symptoms better if they exercised more willpower (Hooley et al., in press). Cultures that do not stress personal control may be less likely to blame schizophrenics for their condition. Although theorists in our culture generally view an internal locus of control as a sign of positive adjustment, this view is not universal and probably understates the negative side-effects of an individualistic worldview. Believing that people can control their destiny may be destructive when it is not true.

Although the term *environmental* typically connotes something nonbiological, researchers have considered other possible environmental causes of schizophrenia such as birth complications and viruses. Perinatal (at birth) complications are more common among individuals who develop schizophrenia (Cannon et al., 1993; Cannon & Marco, 1994), and some of the brain abnormalities discovered in schizophrenic patients are similar to changes in the brain resulting from viral infections (Mirsky & Duncan, 1986; Weinberger et al., 1983). Thus, schizophrenia may actually be a heterogeneous category that includes several syndromes with various causes.

Mood Disorders

Whereas the most striking feature of schizophrenic disorders is disordered thinking, **mood disorders** are characterized by disturbances in emotion and mood. In most cases the mood disturbance is negative, marked by persistent or severe feelings of sadness and hopelessness, but a mood disturbance can also be dangerously positive, as in manic states. Individuals who are **manic** feel excessively happy or euphoric and believe they can do anything. As a consequence, they may undertake unrealistic ventures such as starting a new business on a grandiose scale.

Types of Mood Disorders

Depression has been recorded as far back as ancient Egypt, when the condition was called melancholia and treated by priests. Occasional blue periods are a common response to life events such as loss of a job, ending of a relationship, or death of a loved one. In a depressive disorder, however, the sadness may emerge without a clear precipitant, continue long after one would reasonably expect, and include intense feelings of worthlessness (or even delusions).

Major Depressive Disorder   The most severe form of depression is **major depressive disorder,** characterized by depressed mood and loss of interest in pleasurable activities (**anhedonia**). It also includes disturbances in appetite, sleep, energy level, and concentration. People in a major depressive episode may be so fatigued that they sleep day and night or cannot go to work or do household chores because of intense sadness and lethargy. They often feel worthless, shoulder excessive guilt, and are preoccupied with thoughts of suicide.

At any given moment, 2 to 3 percent of males and 5 to 9 percent of females suffer from major depression. The lifetime risk for major depressive disorder is 5 to 12 percent in men and 10 to 26 percent in women (APA, 1994). Research suggests that major depression is a progressive disorder, with episodes gradually increasing in severity. Roughly 75 percent of patients who experience a major depressive episode will have a recurrence within five years (Maj et al., 1992).

Dysthymia A less severe type of depression is dysthymia. **Dysthymia** refers to a chronic low-level depression of more than two years duration, with intervals of normal moods that never last more than a few weeks or months. Dysthymia includes symptoms found in major depression (such as disturbances in sleep, energy, and self-esteem), but they are not debilitating. The effects of dysthymia on functioning are more subtle, as when people who are chronically depressed choose professions that underutilize their talents because of a lack of confidence, self-esteem, or motivation. Others, like Mary, whose case opened this chapter, remain in unpleasant or abusive relationships and lack the energy or self-esteem to pull themselves out of them.

Bipolar Disorder A manic episode, or **mania**, is characterized by a period of abnormally elevated or expansive mood. While manic, a person usually has an inflated sense of self that reaches grandiose proportions. During a manic episode people generally require less sleep, experience their thoughts as racing, and feel a constant need to talk. Individuals with **bipolar disorder** experience both emotional "poles," depression and mania (in contrast with **unipolar depression**, which involves only depression). About 15 to 20 percent of patients who have manic episodes also develop psychotic delusions and hallucinations (Lehmann, 1985).

Bipolar disorder is relatively uncommon, with a lifetime risk in the general population of less than 1 percent (Weissman & Boyd, 1985). The disorder appears to occur more frequently in the upper social classes. Bipolar patients and their relatives tend to achieve higher levels of education and are disproportionately represented among creative writers and other professionals (Chapter 8).

Suicide

An estimated 30,000 people commit suicide annually in the United States, 40 to 50 percent of whom suffer from major depression (see Robins & Kulbok, 1988). Women attempt suicide more than men, but men complete suicide more than

(a)   *(b)*   *(c)*

People commit suicide for many reasons. Most, like Kurt Cobain of the rock group Nirvana (a), do so after struggling for years with psychological pain. Others, like Japanese Kamikaze pilots in World War II (b), do so in ways consistent with cultural values. Still others try to make a rational choice in the face of terminal illness about when their quality of life has dropped below an acceptable level (c).

women (Earls et al., 1990). Often the most dangerous period for depressed patients occurs when they are beginning to come out of their depression, for the lethargy or emotional paralysis has begun to subside but the suicidal impulses have not yet diminished. Several studies have found low levels of the neurotransmitters serotonin and dopamine in suicidal patients, suggesting that suicidality has biological correlates as well (Coccaro et al., 1989; Mann et al., 1992; Roy et al., 1992). To what degree these biological phenomena cause or reflect suicidal states is unclear.

Suicide is not limited to patients with a primary diagnosis of depression. It is the leading cause of premature death in schizophrenics (Cohen et al., 1990), which is not surprising, since these individuals frequently confront social alienation, ostracism, homelessness (in the United States), and a sense of tragic loss of the possibilities that seemed open to them before they were stricken with the disease. A Swedish study of over 3000 inpatients diagnosed with anxiety disorders (without depression or other diagnoses) found that a third of the deaths before age 70 in this group were also from suicide, suggesting that anxiety disorders may predispose people to suicide as well (Allgulander & Lavori, 1991). Suicide is also a frequent cause of death in patients with some personality disorders, who experience chronic chaos and social disruption and whose lives may be an emotional rollercoaster.

Theories of Depression

Depression can arise for many different reasons. As in schizophrenia, biological and psychological processes often interact, with environmental events frequently triggering a biologically based vulnerability. However, unlike schizophrenia, in which a genetic predisposition is almost a prerequisite for development of the illness, depression can occur in people with no genetic vulnerability.

Genetics Heredity clearly plays a major role in some cases of depression, particularly severe forms of major depression, although heritability is still substantially lower than in schizophrenia (Gershon et al., 1985; Katz & McGuffin, 1993; Kendler et al., 1986, 1992). A family history of depression doubles or triples an individual's risk of a mood disorder (Weissman & Boyd, 1985). An estimated 50 percent of individuals with unipolar depression have a family history of depression (Winokur et al., 1978).

Bipolar disorder, like schizophrenia, probably requires a genetic predisposition (Andreasen et al., 1987). Roughly 80 to 90 percent of individuals with bipolar disorder have a family history of some mood disorder (Winokur et al., 1969). First-degree relatives of bipolar patients have an 11.5 percent risk of developing the disease, which is 15 to 30 times higher than that in the general population (Schlesser & Alshuler, 1983). Twin studies provide strong support for the role of genetic factors in the development of bipolar disorder. In one sample of 110 twin pairs, the concordance rate for monozygotic twins was 67 percent, compared with 20 percent for dizygotic twins (Bertelson, 1979).

Serotonin and Norepinephrine Serotonin and norepinephrine have been implicated in both major depression and bipolar disorders. This makes neurobiological sense because these same neurotransmitters are involved in reward centers in the brain, in the capacity to be aroused or energized, and in the control of other functions affected by depression such as sleep cycles and hunger (Delgado et al., 1990; Price et al., 1991; Stokes et al., 1987). Drugs that alter the activity of these neurotransmitters decrease the symptoms of depression (and hence are called antidepressants).

Environmental Factors Early childhood and familial experiences also play an important role in the etiology of depression (Weissman & Boyd, 1985; see also Kendler et al., 1992). Depressed adults are more likely than other people to have been raised in disruptive, hostile, and negative home environments (Brown &

Harris, 1989). Depressed children report a greater incidence of negative life events (such as family deaths and divorce) than their nondepressed peers (Nolen-Hoeksema et al., 1992). Children of depressed mothers who themselves become severely depressed tend to do so shortly after the onset of their mother's depression (Hammen et al., 1991).

Adult experiences also play a significant role. Severe stressors such as loss of a significant other tend to occur within the nine months prior to the onset of depression in roughly 90 percent of people who become depressed (Brown & Harris, 1978, 1989). The family life of adult depressed patients tends to be problematic (Keitner & Miller, 1990), with high levels of expressed emotion (especially criticism) predicting relapse in major depression, much as it does in schizophrenia (Hooley & Teasdale, 1989). This finding has been replicated cross-culturally (Okasha et al., 1994). Lack of involvement in an intimate relationship is also a high-risk factor for depression, particularly in women (Brown & Harris, 1989). Adult experiences influence the course of bipolar illness as well. In one study, bipolar patients with high life stress were over four times more likely to relapse than those with few significant stressors (Ellicott et al., 1990).

The negative environments of depressed people are not always independent of their actions. A lack of intimate relationships is often a byproduct of personality patterns that also generate depression, and depression itself can be hard for another person to tolerate day after day. Remarkably, experimental research also finds that depressed people seek out partners who view them negatively, and they prefer negative to positive feedback (Swann et al., 1992). In one study, depressed, mildly dysphoric (unhappy), and nondepressed college students were allowed to choose whether they wanted to interact with someone they were led to believe viewed them in a negative, neutral, or positive manner. Depressed subjects, unlike the others, preferred the partner who perceived them negatively (Figure 15.7). Depressed individuals apparently share with their nondepressed peers a need to have others verify their self-concept (Chapter 17), but for people who are depressed, this means being surrounded by others who view them negatively instead of positively. Preliminary evidence suggests that patients who do not like themselves even evoke subtly negative blaming behavior from their psychotherapists (Henry et al., 1990).

Cognitive Theories Cognitive theories look for the roots of depression in dysfunctional patterns of thinking. Learned helplessness theory ties depression to expectancies of helplessness in the face of unpleasant events (Chapter 5). According to helplessness theorists, the way people feel depends on the way they explain events or outcomes to themselves, particularly aversive events (Abramson et al., 1978;

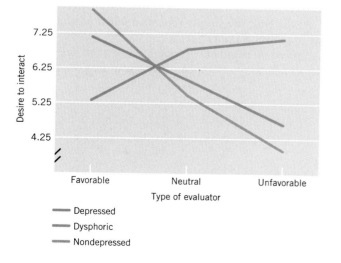

FIGURE 15.7
Partner choice in depression. The figure graphs the desire to interact with people believed to hold positive, neutral, and negative views of self. Depressed subjects, unlike mildly dysphoric and nondepressed subjects, preferred to interact with people who viewed them negatively. SOURCE: *Swann et al., 1992, p. 296.*

Peterson & Seligman, 1984). People with a pessimistic explanatory style, who interpret the causes of bad occurrences as internal (their own fault), stable (unchanging), and global (far-reaching), are more likely to become depressed. A person who is vulnerable to depression may conclude, upon being jilted by a lover, that he is inherently unloveable. Some theorists have reformulated helplessness theory, focusing on the way feelings of *hopelessness* in the face of unpleasant events lead to depression. They argue that learned helplessness theory may describe a particular subtype of depression rather than all depressive disorders (Abramson et al., 1988; Alloy & Clements, 1992).

Depressed people differ both in the *content* of their thinking—how negative their ideas about themselves and the world are—and in their cognitive *processes*—the ways they manipulate and use information (Hollon, 1988). Aaron Beck (1976, 1991), who developed the most prominent cognitive theory of depression, proposes that depressed people interpret events unfavorably, do not like themselves, and regard the future pessimistically. Beck calls this negative outlook on the world, the self, and the future the **negative triad** (Figure 15.8). Research suggests that depressed individuals automatically process information about themselves in a negative way—that is, they do so unconsciously and without much effort—so that they perceive even neutral or positive information negatively (Bargh & Tota, 1988; Mineka & Sutton, 1992). Beck calls the cognitive mechanisms by which a depressed person transforms neutral or positive information in a depressive direction **cognitive distortions** (Beck, 1976). Consider the following interaction between a therapist and a highly intelligent patient who was afraid to go back to school to pursue a career in law:

PATIENT: *I can't go back to school. I'm just not smart enough.*

THERAPIST: *How did you do the last time you were in school?*

PATIENT: *Um... I got mostly As. But that was a long time ago. And what have I ever done career-wise that suggests I could handle being a lawyer?*

THERAPIST: *That's not really a fair question is it? Don't you think your low image of yourself has something to do with why you haven't done anything "spectacular" career-wise?*

PATIENT: *I guess you're right. I'm as smart as my sister, and she's a lawyer.*

THERAPIST: *Right.*

PATIENT: *But what have I ever done career-wise that says I could handle being a lawyer?*

The patient repeatedly doubts herself, ignores her past successes, and generalizes in ways that do not fit the "data." At the end, she simply repeats a self-doubting question that she has just admitted is based on a faulty premise.

Beck (1976, 1985) has identified a number of cognitive errors typical of depressed patients. For example, in arbitrary inference, the person draws a conclu-

FIGURE 15.8
Beck's negative triad. Beck believes that a negative outlook on the world, the self, and the future—the negative triad—affects mood, motivation, and behavior.
SOURCE: *Beck, 1976, p. 256.*

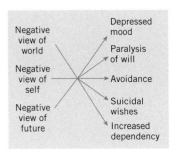

sion in the absence of supporting evidence or in the presence of contradictory evidence. The patient above used arbitrary inference when she concluded with little reason that she could not succeed at school despite prior success. Similarly, when faced with contradictory evidence (her prior grades), she arbitrarily dismissed that as "a long time ago." Magnification and minimization are biases in evaluating the relative importance of events, as when a man reacted to storm damage to his house by thinking, "The side of the house is wrecked.... It will cost a fortune to fix it." In fact, the damage was minor and cost only about fifty dollars to fix (Beck, 1976). Personalization occurs when depressed people relate external events to themselves without a basis for doing so, as when a student with the highest grades in a class assumed the teacher had a low opinion of him whenever she called on or complimented another student. Overgeneralization occurs as a person draws a general conclusion on the basis of a single incident. One depressed patient, for example, concluded after a disagreement with his parents, "I can't get along with anybody" (Beck, 1985).

Psychodynamic Theories Psychodynamic theorists argue that depression may have a number of roots, such as identification with a depressed or belittling parent. For instance, Mr. B, whose father was very critical of him, never allowed himself to feel pleasure when he accomplished something. Instead, he would say to himself, much as his father had said to him when he was a child, "You could have done better." Unlike cognitive theories, which focus on faulty cognition, psychodynamic explanations focus on motivation. Mr. B may have had a number of motivations to deny the reality of his successes. Acknowledging a success might get his hopes up that he could succeed and win other people's esteem in the future, but because that wish had been frustrated so often in childhood, he may have been motivated to avoid putting himself in that position again. If one does not wish, one cannot be disappointed.

From a psychodynamic perspective, depression cannot be isolated from the personality structure in which it is embedded (see Kernberg, 1984). A person who has poor object relations, that is, who has difficulty investing in relationships and ideals, may experience depression because he is prone to feeling abandoned, empty, and alone. Such patients frequently report feeling that they are totally evil and not just helpless or incompetent. In contrast, a person with a greater capacity for relationships is likely to have a depression characterized by feeling that he is a failure at

From a psychodynamic perspective, the meaning and quality of depression can differ substantially, depending on the person's underlying personality structure.

meeting standards (Blatt & Zuroff, 1992; Gunderson, 1984; Westen et al., 1992; Wixom et al., 1993). Cognitive theorists have recently posed a similar distinction and have found that people whose depression focuses on interpersonal issues tend to develop depression in the face of rejection or loss, whereas people whose depression focuses on autonomy and achievement issues tend to become depressed by failures (Hammen et al., 1989; Peselow et al., 1992).

A Global Vista

Depression on a Hopi Reservation

Depression, like most mental disorders, has equivalents in every culture, but the way people view and experience depression varies considerably. Shiite Muslims in Iran consider the ability to feel depressed at tragedy and injustice a sign of personal depth. Buddhists believe that pleasure is the basis of all suffering and hence view a willful dysphoria as a step toward salvation (Kleinman & Good, 1985).

People from diverse cultures describe depression in very different terms. Depressed Nigerians complain that "ants keep creeping in parts of my brain," while Chinese complain that they feel "exhaustion of their nerves" and that their hearts are being "squeezed and weighed down" (Kleinman & Good, 1985, p. 4). While people in Western society tend to view depression as originating within themselves, the Maori believe that distressing emotional states such as sadness are inflicted from the outside, often by angry spirits (Smith, 1981).

Do these differences in the way members of different cultures describe depression imply that the actual subjective experience of depression differs cross-culturally? The answer appears to be yes. Members of less individualistic societies tend to focus more on the behavioral dimensions of depression (such as lethargy, fatigue, loss of appetite, and slowness of movement) than on the subjective experience. In contrast, contemporary Westerners are far more attuned to their internal psychological states than people in most cultures in human history. When they suffer from depression, they typically focus on their inner sense of helplessness, hopelessness, and low self-esteem.

Guilt is also a common component of depression in the contemporary West, unlike much of the Third World (Kleinman & Good, 1985) or the West of previous epochs. When the Greek physician Hippocrates described the syndrome of depression 2500 years ago, he listed symptoms such as irritability, sleeplessness, and despondency. Not until the sixteenth to seventeenth centuries did physicians note a relationship between depression and guilt (Jackson, 1985). That this occurred at the same time as the beginning of the Industrial Revolution is probably no accident, since technological development brings with it social changes that lead to increased individualism and a premium on personal responsibility (Chapter 18). The shift to urban living may also have played a role in heightening vulnerability to guilt. As people moved to cities and lost the constant interpersonal surveillance of smaller groups, parents began to socialize their children to monitor themselves more closely—to bring significant others *inside* themselves psychologically to watch over their behavior (Piers & Singer, 1953).

Spero Manson and his colleagues studied the Hopi of northeastern Arizona (Manson et al., 1985), whose culture was disrupted by the conquest of white settlers in the nineteenth century. Like many contemporary Native American peoples who live on reservations, the Hopi suffer from disproportionate rates of depression, alcoholism, suicide, and antisocial behavior. Instead of assuming that Western categories apply to the Hopi, the investigators began by asking their Hopi informants, "What are the sicknesses or things

A Hopi reservation, where depression, alcoholism, and suicide are common emotional problems.

that can be wrong with people's minds or spirits?" With further probing, the researchers identified several categories of illness recognized by their subjects: worry sickness, unhappiness, heartbrokenness, drunkenlike craziness with or without alcohol, and disappointment or "turning one's face to the wall" (pouting). When the subjects, who were bilingual, were asked if they knew of any Hopi word or phrase that corresponds to the English term "depression," 93 percent indicated that they did not. The nearest equivalent seems to be "heartbrokenness" the illness ascribed to most Hopi subjects diagnosed in Western terms with major depression. Thus, the Western concept of depression can be translated into Hopi culture, but doing so may lose some of the nuances of experience that depressed Hopi verbalize.

Another finding of Manson's study was an alarmingly high incidence of depression in the Hopi community. Indeed, depression appears to be on the rise cross-culturally, as documented by a recent study of 39,000 subjects across the world, in societies from North America and Western Europe to Puerto Rico, Asia, and the Middle East (Cross-National Collaborative Group, 1992). Depression increases in periods of crisis such as civil wars, but it has apparently been steadily increasing and afflicting people at an earlier age in this century. The causes of this trend are unclear, but it likely relates to the enormous social changes that have occurred in the modern era. These changes include disruption of family, social relationships, cultural values, and ways of understanding the world that have, throughout human history, allowed people to experience the world and their lives as meaningful.

Anxiety Disorders

Anxiety, like sadness, is a normal feeling. Anxiety is normally useful as an internal alarm bell that warns of potential danger, but in **anxiety disorders**, the individual is subject to false alarms that may be intense, frequent, or even continuous. These false alarms may lead to dysfunctional avoidance behavior, as when a person refuses to leave the house for fear of a panic attack.

Anxiety disorders are the most frequently occurring category of mental disorders in the general population (American Psychiatric Association, 1994). An estimated 5 percent of the population suffers from acute or chronic anxiety, with women twice as likely as men to be afflicted (Nemiah, 1985a; Reich, 1986). Researchers estimate that up to a third of North Americans have at least one irrational fear or **phobia** (Myers et al., 1984; Robins et al., 1984). Over 2 percent have a **generalized anxiety disorder**, characterized by persistent anxiety at a moderate but disturbing level and excessive and unrealistic worry about life circumstances (Rapee, 1991; Weissman et al., 1978). Although patients with generalized anxiety disorders often have phobias, their anxiety is less circumscribed and less tied to specific triggers.

Types of Anxiety Disorders

In this section we review the symptoms of some other common anxiety disorders. Although we discuss them separately, people with one anxiety disorder often have others (Kendler et al., 1992; Schneier et al., 1992).

Panic Disorders

I was 25 when I had my first attack. It was a few weeks after I'd come home from the hospital. I had had my appendix out. The surgery had gone well, and I wasn't in any danger, which is why I don't understand what happened. But one night I went to sleep and I woke up a few hours later…with this vague feeling of apprehension. Mostly I remember how my heart started pounding. And my chest hurt; it felt like someone was standing on my chest. I was so scared, I was sure that I was dying…. (Patient cited in Barlow, 1988)

Panic disorders are distinguished by attacks of intense fear and feelings of doom or terror not justified by the situation. The attacks typically include physiological symptoms such as shortness of breath, dizziness, heart palpitations, trembling, and chest pains (Barlow, 1988). Psychological symptoms include fear of dying or going crazy.

Agoraphobia A related disorder is **agoraphobia**, a fear of being in places or situations from which escape might be difficult, such as crowded grocery stores or elevators (Reich, 1986). Agoraphobia can be extremely debilitating. An agoraphobic may not leave the house because of intense fears of being outside alone, being in a crowd, being on a bridge, or traveling in a train, car, or bus. Agoraphobia is often instigated by a fear of having a panic attack and may ultimately lead people to avoid leaving home because they fear having a panic attack in a public place.

Obsessive-Compulsive Disorder

Mrs. C is a 47-year-old mother of six children who are named in alphabetical order. For 10 years she had been suffering with a compulsion to wash excessively, sometimes 25 to 30 times a day for five- to ten-minute intervals. Her daily morning shower lasts two hours, with rituals involving each part of her body…. If she loses track of her ritual, she must start at the beginning. Mrs. C's compulsions affect her family as well. She does not let family members wear a pair of underwear more than once and prohibits washing them. The family spends large sums of money buying new underwear for daily use. Mrs. C has hoarded various items such as towels, sheets, earrings, and her own clothes for the past two decades. (Prochaska, 1984)

An **obsessive-compulsive disorder** is marked by recurrent obsessions and compulsions that cause severe distress and significantly interfere with an individual's life. **Obsessions** are persistent thoughts or ideas, such as the notion that a terrible accident is about to occur to a loved one or that underwear is filled with germs. **Compulsions** are intentional behaviors or mental acts performed in response to an obsession in a stereotyped fashion, often as a magical way of warding off the obsessive thought, such as washing every part of the body over and over in the shower in a prescribed order. People with obsessive-compulsive disorder experience their compulsions as irresistible acts that must be performed even though they generally recognize them as irrational (Insel, 1985).

Common compulsions include counting, hand-washing, and touching, while common obsessions are repetitive thoughts of contamination, violence, or doubt (Jenike, 1983). Typically, obsessive-compulsive people experience intense anxiety or even panic if they are prevented from performing their rituals. Obsessive-compulsive disorders typically begin during childhood, adolescence, or early adulthood (Goodwin, 1969; Lo, 1967; Swedo et al., 1992).

Many Vietnam veterans with untreated post-traumatic stress disorder cannot extricate themselves from the past.

Post-Traumatic Stress Disorder　An anxiety disorder that began receiving wide attention following the Vietnam War is **post-traumatic stress disorder (PTSD)**. PTSD is marked by flashbacks and recurrent thoughts of a psychologically distressing event outside the range of usual human experience. Typically, the traumatic event is of horrific proportions, such as seeing someone murdered, surviving torture or imprisonment in a concentration camp, being raped, or losing one's home in an earthquake or some other natural disaster. In Vietnam veterans, exposure to human brutality and atrocities, rather than to possible death in combat, tends to predict PTSD symptoms and their severity (Green et al., 1990; Yehuda et al., 1992). One study examined Cambodian refugees, who escaped massive genocide during the 1980s but experienced multiple losses, uprooting from their homes, torture, rape, and immigration to a new country with a new language. Over 80 percent were diagnosable with PTSD as well as clinical depression (Carlson & Rosser-Hogan, 1991).

PTSD has a number of symptoms: nightmares, flashbacks, deliberate efforts to avoid thoughts or feelings about the traumatic event, diminished responsiveness to the external world, and psychological numbness. Other symptoms that may occur are hypervigilance (constant scanning of the environment), an exaggerated startle response (such as screaming when tapped on the shoulder), and autonomic activation when exposed to stimuli associated with the traumatic event (see Brett et al., 1988). PTSD can last a lifetime, as many combat veterans, prisoners of war, and Holocaust survivors report (see Basoglu et al., 1994; Sutker et al., 1991).

Theories of Anxiety Disorders

Like depression, anxiety disorders have many roots. As in depression, genetic vulnerability is a contributing, but probably not an essential, factor (Kendler et al, 1992). Twin and family studies show that genetics contribute to many anxiety syndromes, such as panic, simple phobia, and obsessive-compulsive disorder (Fyer et al., 1990; Gabbard, 1992; Torgersen, 1983). In fact, patients with anxiety disorders tend to have both anxiety and mood disorders in their families. The mechanism that translates a genetic vulnerability into most anxiety disorders probably involves the neurotransmitters epinephrine and norepinephrine (Judd et al., 1985; Ley, 1988). In the case of obsessive-compulsive syndromes, an imbalance among several neurotransmitter systems may be at fault (Altemus et al., 1992; Swedo et al., 1992).

Caution is in order, however, in interpreting research on the biology of anxiety disorders, since both genetic and environmental hypotheses could explain the results of many family history studies. Growing up in a home with a pathologically anxious parent—or parents—poses significant environmental risk even if no genetic risk is present. Even studies showing that medications ameliorate specific symptoms do not necessarily demonstrate the role of biology in *causing* a disorder. Giving a sedative to someone who has just discovered she has cancer and finding that it allays her anxiety does not prove that her anxiety was genetic. Anxiety is mediated by neurotransmitters, so anxious people should demonstrate overactivity of those neurotransmitters, but this overactivity could reflect learning, heredity, or both. Once again we see the potential danger of mistaking correlation for causation.

Environmental Factors and Stress Stressful life events have been implicated in the development or exacerbation of many anxiety disorders (Zal, 1987). Roughly 80 percent of patients suffering from panic attacks describe a negative life event that coincided with their first attack (Finaly-Jones & Brown, 1981; Mathews et al., 1981), and panic patients report a higher incidence of stressful life events in the months preceding the onset of their symptoms than comparison subjects (Faravelli & Pallanti, 1989). Stressful events occurring in childhood, such as loss of a parent, also predispose people to anxiety disorders in adulthood (Hafner & Roder, 1987).

Cognitive-Behavioral Theories Cognitive-behavioral theories focus on the learning of anxiety reactions and on the dysfunctional cognitive patterns that generate and maintain them. From a behaviorist perspective, pathological anxiety, like normal anxiety, typically arises through classical conditioning (Chapter 5). People who are afraid of dogs, for example, may develop the phobia after being frightened by a dog. The emotional response is then elicited each time they see a dog. The anxiety may in turn evoke avoidance behavior, which is negatively reinforced: By avoiding dogs, the person avoids the anxiety associated with them. Unfortunately, avoiding dogs also prevents the emotional response from being extinguished because extinction in classical conditioning requires exposure to the conditioned stimulus (dogs) without the unconditioned stimulus (the original experience that initially made the individual afraid, such as a dog attacking them).

Cognitive theorists add that negative biases in thinking (such as a tendency to fear the worst) and low self-efficacy expectancies ("I can't do it") contribute to the origin and maintenance of anxiety disorders (Mineka & Sutton, 1992). Anxiety, like depression, leads people to see things in a negative light, but unlike depression, it also focuses their attention on threatening stimuli. For example, when presented with pairs of threatening and nonthreatening homophones (words that sound the same but have different spellings), anxious people are likely to select the threatening spelling (e.g., die vs. dye) (Mathews et al., 1989).

David Barlow (1988a, 1988b; Zinbarg et al, 1992) has proposed an integrated cognitive-behavioral model of anxiety disorders (Figure 15.9). In Barlow's view, biological vulnerabilities, environmental stresses, or their interaction lead to an initial panic attack. The attack includes autonomic responses such as quickened pulse, pounding heart, difficulty breathing, dry mouth, and sweaty palms. These responses then become associated with the panic state through classical conditioning, so that whenever the person starts to experience them, she becomes frightened that a panic attack will occur. To put it another way, the individual develops a fear of fear (Goldstein & Chambless, 1978; Kenardy et al., 1992). Thus people with panic disorders become especially aware of their autonomic activity, constantly on the lookout for signals of arousal. Panic patients show heightened awareness of cardiac changes such as rapid heartbeat and palpitations (Ehlers & Breuer, 1992), and they are more likely to panic when exposed to air that contains slightly more carbon dioxide than normal (Figure 15.10, p. 610), presumably because they start to feel short of breath (Rapee et al., 1992). The fear of their own autonomic responses, in turn, magnifies the anxiety of panic-prone individuals and may trigger an actual attack. Repeated experiences of this sort may lead them to avoid situations associated with panic attacks or physiological arousal. People with panic disorders may, for example, give up jogging because it produces autonomic responses such as racing pulse and sweating that they have come to associate with panic attacks. Such avoidance behavior may ultimately lead to agoraphobia.

Psychodynamic Theories Psychodynamic approaches similarly assert that anxiety disorders stem from the way thoughts and feelings are associated with each other mentally, but they do not assume that actual events, such as being bitten by a dog,

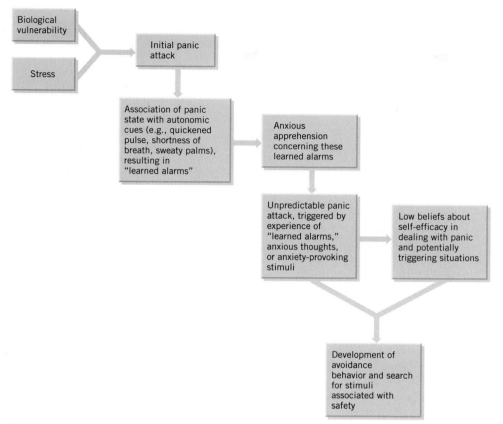

FIGURE 15.9

A cognitive-behavioral view of the development of panic symptoms. From a cognitive-behavioral perspective, biological vulnerabilities, environmental stresses, or their interaction lead to an initial panic attack. The attack includes autonomic responses that then become associated through classical conditioning with the panic state, so whenever the person starts to experience them, she becomes frightened that a panic attack will occur. SOURCE: *Adapted from Barlow, 1988.*

necessarily underlie phobias or other recurrent anxieties. Often, they assert, the phobic object is a source of anxiety because of its unconscious connection to something that is *really* feared, as in the following example. Mr. P sought therapy for a fear of driving. Exploring the thoughts, memories, and fantasies connected with driving uncovered an incident in which he felt an uncontrollable urge to hit a pedestrian who cavalierly walked across the street in front of his car. He became furious and on several other occasions felt the urge to hit pedestrians he thought were "being arrogant" in the way they walked across the street or failed to acknowledge his right of way. Mr. P was a chronically angry person who had long-standing concerns about people not taking him seriously, beginning with his relationships with his parents as a child. From a psychodynamic perspective, Mr. P's phobia reflected a fear of his own aggressive impulses to hurt pedestrians who do not "take him seriously." What he feared was not really driving but the impulses and fantasies stirred up while driving.

From a psychodynamic perspective, anxiety, like depression, always occurs in the context of a personality structure. Anxiety in severe personality disorders often reflects tremendous fears of abandonment by attachment figures, whereas neurotic anxiety is frequently a residue of unresolved conflict or unconscious activation of childhood fears and beliefs. For example, one man became extremely anxious on dates with women, particularly when they made clear their romantic interest. Although he consciously wanted a relationship, the closer he came to it, the more

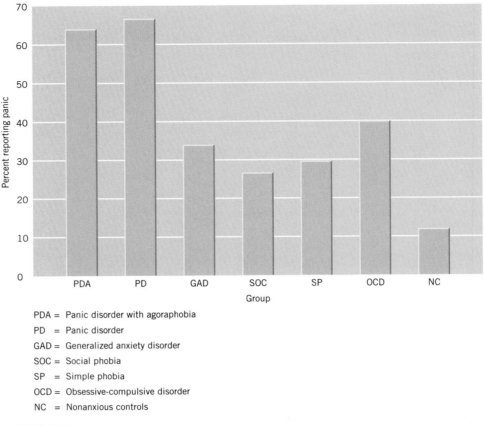

PDA = Panic disorder with agoraphobia

PD = Panic disorder

GAD = Generalized anxiety disorder

SOC = Social phobia

SP = Simple phobia

OCD = Obsessive-compulsive disorder

NC = Nonanxious controls

FIGURE 15.10
Precipitation of panic episodes by exposure to carbon dioxide-enriched air. Subjects with various anxiety disorders were exposed to air with a slightly elevated carbon dioxide content (5.5 percent elevation), which makes the air feel harder to breathe. All anxiety-disorder patients were more likely to panic than normal subjects, with panic patients particularly prone to experience panic symptoms.
Source: *Rapee et al., 1992, p. 545.*

anxious he became. Exploring his networks of association related to dating, sex, and closeness with women led to childhood memories of feeling controlled by his mother and feeling anxious and uncomfortable when she would touch him. Adult romantic relationships were thus fraught with anxiety because they were associated with being controlled and with conflicts about his mother's touch, all of which were activated without awareness.

Psychodynamic and cognitive-behavioral views of anxiety may not be entirely incompatible. From both perspectives, anxiety emerges when a contemporary situation (a phobic stimulus, a quickened pulse, or an interpersonal involvement) resembles a past situation and activates the attendant feeling. This activation may be relatively straightforward, as when the presence of a dog activates a conditioned response and conscious fears ("I can't get away," or "What if it bites me?"). Alternatively, a seemingly innocuous event may activate a network of associations that includes thoughts or memories associated with anxiety, or it may simultaneously evoke conflicting motives, one or more of which may be threatening and hence repressed, so that the anxiety emerges without the cognition.

Dissociative Disorders

A class of disorders akin to PTSD and usually created by repeated exposure to situations evoking intense anxiety is dissociative disorders. **Dissociative disorders** are characterized by disruptions in consciousness, memory, sense of identity, or perception. The patient may have significant periods of amnesia, may find herself in a new city with no recollection of her old life, or may feel as if she is separated from her emotions and experience, as if her mind and body are in two different places. The primary feature is **dissociation**, a disturbance in which significant aspects of experience are kept separate and distinct (that is, *dis-associated*) in memory and consciousness. Dissociation is usually a response to overwhelming psychic pain, as when victims of severe physical abuse or rape mentally separate themselves from the situation by experiencing themselves and their feelings outside of their bodies.

The most severe dissociative disorder is **dissociative identity disorder**, otherwise known as multiple personality disorder, in which at least two separate and distinct personalities exist within the same person. People with multiple personalities are frequently unaware that they have these alter-selves, as in the following case report:

> Irene, a 29-year-old suicidal woman, told her psychotherapist that she avoided most people because she felt that they were not trustworthy. She was puzzled by the fact that her husband told her that she physically abused their children, since she had no recollection of doing so. Shirley is a young woman who is abusive to other women but sexually provocative with men. She was physically abused by her mother as a young girl and sexually molested by her brother and uncle between the ages of 10 and 17. (Herzog, 1984)

Irene and Shirley are part of the same woman; a third personality is "The Man," who surfaces whenever the two women need protection. At the start of her psychotherapy, Irene was aware of neither Shirley nor The Man. Another patient with this disorder had two lives—including two addresses, two sets of doctors, and two lovers who did not understand why she was so often unavailable. Some intriguing, but preliminary, data suggest that the different personalities in cases such as these may be both psychologically and physiologically distinct: Not only do they have access to different memories and look strikingly different on personality tests, but they may also differ in physiological qualities such as muscle tension, heart rate, and even allergies (Putnam, 1991).

In dissociative disorders, the patient cordons off parts of experience that are too painful to integrate into a conscious sense of herself and her history. Individuals with dissociative disorders typically come from chaotic home environments and have suffered physical and sexual abuse in childhood (Bliss, 1984; Chu & Dill, 1990; Gelinas, 1983). In fact, a history of extreme trauma, usually sexual abuse, is found in nearly all cases of dissociative disorder (Ross et al., 1990). The vast majority of cases are female, probably because of the greater incidence of sexual abuse in females. The prevalence of dissociative identity disorder is a matter of controversy. The disorder appears to be quite rare (see Modestin, 1992; Ross et al., 1991), despite the attention it has drawn by gripping accounts such as *Sybil* (Schreiber, 1973) and *The Three Faces of Eve* (Thigpen & Cleckly, 1954).

Personality Disorders

Personality disorders are characterized by enduring maladaptive ways of thinking, feeling, and behaving, which are basic to the person's personality and lead to chronic disturbances in interpersonal and occupational functioning. For example, a person with **narcissistic personality disorder** has severe trouble in relationships because of a tendency to use people, to devalue or totally dismiss them when they "get in the way," to be hypersensitive to criticism, to feel entitled to special privileges, and to become rageful. Individuals with this disorder show little empathy for other people, as in the callous remark of one patient who was asked about the feelings of a woman he had just rejected: "What do I care? What can she do for me anymore? Hey, that's the breaks of the game—sometimes you dump, sometimes you get dumped. Nobody would be crying if this had happened to me."

TABLE 15.6 DSM-IV PERSONALITY DISORDERS

PERSONALITY DISORDER	DESCRIPTION
Paranoid	Distrust and suspiciousness
Schizoid	Detachment from social relationships and restricted range of emotional expression
Schizotypal	Acute discomfort in close relationships, cognitive or perceptual distortions, and eccentricity
Antisocial	Disregard for, and violation of the rights of others
Borderline	Impulsivity and instability in interpersonal relationships, self-concept, and emotion
Histrionic	Excessive emotionality and attention seeking
Narcissistic	Grandiosity, need for admiration, and lack of empathy
Avoidant	Social inhibition and avoidance, feelings of inadequacy, and hypersensitivity to negative evaluation
Dependent	Submissive and clinging behavior and excessive need to be taken care of
Obsessive-compulsive	Preoccupation with orderliness, perfectionism, and neeed for control (fixed obsessions or compulsions need not be present as in the anxiety disorder on Axis I)
Personality disorder not otherwise specified	Enduring, pervasive, and dysfunctional personality patterns not described by any other personality disorder

Source: Adapted from *Diagnostic and Statistical Manual of Mental Disorders, Fourth Edition,* American Psychiatric Association, 1994, p. 629.

Table 15.6 shows the personality disorders delineated in DSM-IV. We examine two of them here, borderline personality disorder, which is more prevalent in women, and antisocial personality disorder, which is more prevalent in men.

Borderline Personality Disorder

The popular movie *Fatal Attraction* portrayed a disturbed woman who took revenge on a married man with whom she had had an affair. This character, with her dramatic suicide gestures and extreme mood swings, would likely be diagnosed with a severe borderline personality disorder. **Borderline personality disorder** is marked by extremely unstable interpersonal relationships, dramatic mood swings, an unstable sense of identity, intense fears of separation and abandonment, manipulativeness, and impulsive behavior. Also characteristic of this disorder is self-mutilating behavior, such as wrist-slashing, carving words on the arm, or burning the skin with cigarettes (see Gunderson, 1984; Winchel & Stanley, 1991; Yeomans et al., 1994).

Although patients with borderline personality disorder may seem superficially normal, in intimate relationships the volatility and insecurity of their attachments become clear. In part, this reflects the ways they form mental representations of people and relationships. Their representations are often simplistic, one-sided, and influenced by their moods and needs (Kernberg, 1975; Kernberg et al., 1989;

Masterson, 1976; Westen et al., 1990). Borderline patients are particulary noted for "splitting" their representations, so that at any moment a given person may be seen as totally good or totally bad (Baker et al., 1992; Kernberg et al., 1989). The tendency to split makes maintaining relationships extremely difficult. One woman with a borderline personality disorder had been involved with a man for only three weeks before deciding he was "the only man in the world who could love me." She began calling him incessantly and suggested they live together. He became concerned about the intensity of her feelings and suggested they see each other only on weekends so they could get to know each other a little more slowly. She was furious and accused him of leading her on and using her. Whereas hours before he was a knight in shining armor, now he was a demon incarnate. Several studies document that borderline patients are also extremely prone to attribute negative or malevolent intentions to other people and to expect abuse and rejection (Bell et al., 1989; Nigg et al., 1992).

In Fatal Attraction, *Glenn Close played Alex Forrest, a woman with many features of borderline personality disorder.*

Antisocial Personality Disorder

Antisocial personality disorder is marked by irresponsible and socially disruptive behavior in a variety of areas. Symptoms include stealing, destroying property, lack of empathy, and lack of remorse for misdeeds. Also characteristic of these individuals is an inability to maintain jobs because of unexplained absences and harassment of co-workers, lying, stealing, vandalism, impulsivity, and recklessness. People with antisocial personality disorders can be exceedingly charming, leading those who have been fooled by them to see them ultimately as con artists.

Typically, an antisocial personality disorder is evident by age 15. The characteristic behaviors are similar to those of childhood conduct disorder. In fact, nearly all adult antisocial personality disorders were conduct-disordered as children, although only 40 to 50 percent of conduct-disordered children become antisocial adults (Lytton, 1990). The syndrome is more prevalent in men (3 percent of adult males) than women (less than 1 percent). It is also more commonly found in poor urban areas (Kaplan & Sadock, 1988).

Antisocial individuals rarely take the initiative to seek treatment; rather, they are most commonly seen in courts, prisons, and welfare departments (Vaillant & Perry, 1985). When they do seek psychiatric treatment, it is usually to avoid some legal repercussion. For example, Mr. C was a tall, muscular man with a scruffy beard and steely blue eyes. He came to a clinic complaining of depression and lack of direction in life. He presented a very moving description of a childhood filled with abuse at the hands of his father and neglect by his severely mentally ill mother, which may well have been accurate. He talked about wanting to come to understand why his life was not going well and wanting to work hard to change. He also described chronic dysphoria and feelings of boredom and worthlessness that are common in antisocial personalities.

By the end of the first session, however, Mr. C disclosed a troubling history of violence, in which he had escalated several bar brawls by hitting people in the face with empty bottles or pool cues. His casual response when asked about whether they were seriously hurt was, "You think I stuck around to pick their face up off the floor?" He also had a history of carrying weapons and spoke of a time in his life during which he had his finger on the trigger "if anybody even looked at me wrong." When asked why he had finally come in for help now, he admitted that he had been "falsely accused" of breaking someone's nose at a bar and that his lawyer thought "seeing a shrink" would help his case—but that this, of course, had nothing to do with his genuine desire to turn his life around.

People with antisocial personality disorder frequently appear in prisons rather than in psychiatric facilities.

Theories of Personality Disorders

Once again, both genetic and environmental factors play a role in the genesis of many personality disorders (Nigg & Goldsmith, 1994; Reid, 1985; Seiver & Davis, 1991). For borderline personality disorder, the evidence for biological contributions is not well established, although some recent data are more promising (Hollander et al., 1994). According to psychodynamic theorists, borderline personality disorder originates in pathological attachment relationships in early childhood, which lead to attachment problems later in life (Adler & Buie, 1979; Kernberg, 1975; Masterson & Rinsley, 1975), and empirical research has begun to bear this out (Ludolph et al., 1990). Recent research also implicates sexual abuse in the etiology of this disorder, perhaps accounting for its prevalence in females (Herman et al., 1989; Ogata et al., 1990; Westen et al., 1990; Zanarini, in press; Zanarini et al., 1989). The best available evidence suggests that a chaotic homelife (Golomb et al., 1994), a mother with a troubled attachment history, a male relative who is sexually abusive, and a family history of impulsivity and difficulty regulating emotions provide fertile ground for the development of this syndrome.

The etiology of antisocial personality disorder in many respects resembles the etiology of borderline personality disorder, except that physical abuse is more common than sexual abuse (see Pollock et al., 1990). Both social learning and psychodynamic approaches implicate physical abuse, neglect, and absent or criminal male role models. Biological researchers point to the elevated rates of substance abuse in the families of antisocial personalities and suggest that, like conduct disorders, patients with antisocial personality disorder may be genetically unresponsive to punishment.

RETHINKING PSYCHOPATHOLOGY

In this chapter, we have examined several psychopathological syndromes from multiple perspectives and have discussed the interactions of heredity and environment that produce them. Before concluding, however, we should take a step back to ask three questions about the relation between psychopathology and the categories we use to understand it. First, can disorders really be so neatly taxonomized? Second, to what degree have cultural and political processes shaped the diagnostic categories included in, and excluded from, DSM-IV? And, finally, can biology and learning be so readily distinguished in the etiology of psychological disorders?

Are Mental Disorders Really Distinct?

Although we have followed DSM-IV in describing discrete disorders, most practicing clinicians question whether psychopathology can be so neatly categorized. For instance, does major depression really exist as a distinct condition, or is it on a continuum with dysthymia? The most clearly demarcated syndromes are the psychotic disorders, schizophrenia and bipolar disorder. Genetic evidence typically taken as conclusive for the distinction between the two disorders documents that bipolar disorder in a first-degree relative (mother, father, brother, or sister) does not elevate a person's risk for schizophrenia, and vice versa. Yet some researchers have produced evidence suggesting that the psychoses actually form a continuum, from schizophrenic to depressive psychoses (Crow, 1986, 1990). Studies show a high rate of bipolar disorder among the twins of schizophrenics, while other studies indicate that over several generations, bipolar disorders do predispose individuals to schizophrenia. Thus, the two disorders may be variants of a common psychotic syndrome, perhaps reflecting various combinations of defective genes carried on different chromosomes.

Distinguishing between manic and paranoid schizophrenic episodes can also be difficult. People who are manic often have a delusional belief in their own importance, which can lead them to think people are trying to get them because of their elevated position. Conversely, paranoids often have grandiose delusions (Garvey et al., 1980; Zigler & Glick, 1988). Another DSM-IV diagnostic category, **schizoaf-**

fective disorder, is used for individuals who seem to have attributes of both schizophrenia and psychotic depression and may not easily fit the criteria for just one or the other (see Grossman et al., 1991).

To make matters even more complicated, patients often have symptoms indicative of multiple disorders. Depression tends to co-occur with numerous other syndromes (Hudson & Pope, 1990), including anxiety, eating, and substance-related disorders (Coryell et al., 1992; Hendren, 1983; King et al., 1991; Schneier et al., 1992; Shuckit, 1987; Swift et al., 1986). Cross-cultural evidence suggests that most nonpsychotic disorders involve some mixture of anxiety and depression (Kleinman, 1988), which is consistent with data showing that people who tend to experience one unpleasant emotion tend to experience others (Chapter 11).

Perhaps the most complex questions along these lines pertain to the relationship between Axis I disorders and personality disorders (Axis II). Most patients with severe Axis I disorders of all sorts—anxiety, mood, eating, substance use—have concurrent personality disorders (Green & Curtis, 1988; Shea et al., 1987), and the majority of schizophrenic patients experience chronic patterns of interpersonal and occupational instability, which are the defining features of personality disorders. Trying to distinguish enduring aspects of personality from specific episodes of illness may be futile when the personality itself is the wellspring of diverse symptoms. For example, anyone who cannot maintain relationships and jobs is going to be vulnerable to depression and anxiety, so putting borderline personality disorder on one axis and depression and anxiety on another may be artificial.

Commentary: The Politics of Diagnosis

Beyond the question of whether psychopathology falls neatly into discrete syndromes is the question of whether DSM-IV identifies the right syndromes. As we have seen, cultural beliefs and values influence conceptions of mental illness, and this is true of Western scientific conceptions as well. A case in point is homosexuality, which was once considered a mental disorder. As a result of shifting cultural norms, homosexuality was dropped from the DSMs in the 1980s and is no longer considered pathological. The inclusion and exclusion of syndromes in DSM-IV is a political as well as scientific process.

Even more recently, politics have played a part in a proposed diagnostic category called self-defeating personality disorder (see Caplan, 1991; Frances et al., 1991). A self-defeating personality disorder is characterized by a pervasive pattern of self-damaging behavior. The name understates the seriousness of the disorder: People with this disorder are typically involved in relationships that are physically and emotionally abusive, as in the case of Mary at the beginning of this chapter, and they often do not follow through with treatment recommendations.

The controversy surrounding this disorder stems from its relative prevalence in women. Some feminist critics argue that adding self-defeating personality disorder to the DSM is little more than a medical version of victim-blaming, a common psychological mechanism for dealing with injustice or victimization. Advocates of the diagnosis counter that such people clearly exist and typically move from one abusive relationship to another. Thus, staying in an abusive relationship cannot solely reflect economic dependence on a particular man, a common explanation offered by opponents. Furthermore, argue proponents, pretending that self-defeating individuals either do not exist or do not suffer from an emotional disturbance is actually harmful because it prevents them from being treated appropriately and from obtaining insurance coverage for their treatment, which requires a diagnosable disorder.

Both sides clearly have merit. On the one hand, mental health professionals were quicker to find a label for the women who seek out or remain in abusive relationships than the men who abuse them. On the other hand, few would deny that boys who are physically or sexually abused may develop disturbances that lead them to abuse others. The parallel assertion, however—that women who have been abused may find themselves psychologically compelled to repeat the abuse as victims—seems politically unacceptable. In fact, it has proven so unacceptable that the diagnosis of self-defeating personality disorder was only included in the prior edition of the DSM in an appendix as a diagnosis under consideration, and it has been deleted entirely from DSM-IV. Thus, neither Mary, who chronically entered into abusive relationships, nor the men who chronically abused her, would receive a psychiatric diagnosis. Why males who are disturbed tend to hurt other people, whereas females who are disturbed tend to hurt themselves, is an open question. So, too, is the issue of why neither is officially considered pathological.

FROM MIND TO BRAIN

WHEN NURTURE BECOMES NATURE

Just as the gods of abnormality did not create six discrete disorders and rest on the seventh day, they were not particularly careful to separate nature and nurture. Thus, efforts to reduce the causes of disorders to genetics or environment may be problematic.

Pathogenic experiences—unfortunate life events—can create changes in the brain that become part of an individual's "nature." Monkeys separated from their mothers for prolonged periods show neuropsychological changes, permanent alterations in the number and sensitivity of receptors for neurotransmitters in the postsynaptic membrane (Gabbard, 1992). Similarly, people who undergo traumatic experiences and develop post-traumatic stress disorder also develop abnormalities in hypothalamic and pituitary functioning (Mason et al., 1994; Yehuda et al., 1991). These symptoms may then be amenable to biological treatments such as antidepressant medication, even though the causes were initially environmental. To speak of the causes as completely environmental, however, is not entirely accurate either. The environmental event of repeated separation from attachment figures only produces biological abnormalities because the brain has evolved to be innately sensitive to attachment-related stimulation. Environmental causes presuppose a nervous system that makes them relevant.

Environmental factors can also activate biological vulnerabilities, so that neither heredity nor environment can alone bear the blame. For example, the amount of sunlight to which people are exposed has an impact on circadian rhythms, mood, eating, and sleep. For some people, the lack of sunlight in the winter months triggers seasonal affective disorder (SAD), a depressive syndrome that occurs in the winter (see Cohen et al., 1992). Binging increases for some bulimics in winter months as well (Blouin et al., 1992). As we have seen, environmental events may also take biologically vulnerable individuals above the threshold for schizophrenic, mood, or anxiety disorders to which they would otherwise not succumb.

Once a disorder has emerged, biology and experience may weave an even more tangled web. Research suggests that environmentally triggered episodes seem to lay down neural "tracks" that subsequent episodes employ, much as repeated use gradually blazes a trail in the woods. First episodes of mood disorders tend to have a clear precipitant, but later episodes, especially of bipolar disorder, occur after progressively shorter periods of remission and with less input from environmental stressors (Post, 1992). Although schizophrenia may not require an environmental trigger, the longer the interval between development of symptoms and treatment for first-episode schizophrenic patients, the worse the prognosis (Loebel et al., 1992), presumably because the more the disease is able to blaze a trail, the less able the brain is to cover the tracks.

SOME CONCLUDING THOUGHTS

We have learned a great deal about psychopathology over the last century. Research has finally dispelled explanations based on demons and spirit possession and replaced them with scientifically grounded theories. Yet it is clear that our categories of thought do not adequately mirror the categories of nature. If the role of science is progressively to narrow the discrepancy between reality and appearance—between the world and our representations of it—we have come a long way, but we have a long way to go. And we probably always will.

Having examined the major disorders that afflict the human psyche, in the next chapter we turn to their treatment.

Summary

1. **Psychopathology** refers to patterns of thought, feeling, or behavior that disrupt a person's sense of well-being or social or occupational functioning.

The Cultural Context of Psychopathology

2. The concept of mental illness varies historically and cross-culturally. Cultures differ in the ways they describe and pattern psychopathology, but "mentally ill" is not simply an arbitrary label applied to deviants, as was the claim of labeling theory.

Contemporary Approaches to Psychopathology

3. Psychodynamic theorists make a general distinction among **neuroses, personality disorders**, and **psychoses**, which form a continuum of disturbance. Making a **psychodynamic formulation** means assessing the person's wishes and fears, cognitive and emotional resources, and experience of the self and others.

4. The cognitive-behavioral perspective integrates aspects of classical and operant conditioning with a cognitive-social perspective. Dysfunctional behavior results from environmental contingencies and faulty cognitions.

5. Understanding psychopathology often requires shifting to a biological level of analysis. The biological approach proposes that psychopathology stems from faulty wiring in the brain, particularly in the abundance, overreactivity, or underreactivity of specific neurotransmitters. **Diathesis-stress models** of psychopathology propose that people with an underlying vulnerability may become symptomatic under stressful circumstances.

6. A **systems approach** attempts to explain an individual's behavior in the context of a social group with which he or she is involved, such as a couple, a family, or

618 CHAPTER 15 PSYCHOLOGICAL DISORDERS

a larger social system. A **family systems model** suggests that the symptoms of any individual are really symptoms of dysfunction in a family.

7. The *Diagnostic and Statistical Manual of Mental Disorders-IV*, or **DSM-IV**, is the official manual of mental illnesses published by the American Psychiatric Association, which is the basis for **descriptive diagnosis**.

Psychopathological Syndromes

8. One disorder that is usually first diagnosed in childhood or adolescence is **attention-deficit hyperactivity disorder**, characterized by age-inappropriate inattention, impulsiveness, and hyperactivity. Another is **conduct disorder**, a disturbance in which a child persistently violates the rights of others as well as societal norms.

9. **Substance-related disorders** refer to continued use of substances that negatively affect psychological and social functioning. Worldwide, alcoholism is the most common substance use disorder. As with most psychological disorders, the roots of alcoholism lie in genetics, environment, and their interaction.

10. **Schizophrenia** is a disorder in which people lose touch with reality, experiencing both **positive symptoms** such as **hallucinations**, **delusions**, and **loosening of associations**, and **negative symptoms**, such as **flat affect** and poor social skills. Types of schizophrenia include **paranoid**, **catatonic**, **disorganized**, **undifferentiated**, and **residual**. Schizophrenia is a highly heritable disease of the brain, although environmental circumstances such as a critical family environment can trigger or exacerbate the disorder in vulnerable individuals.

11. **Mood disorders** are characterized by disturbances in emotion and mood. In **manic** states, people feel excessively happy and believe they can do anything. The most severe form of depression is **major depressive disorder**. **Dysthymia** refers to a long-standing, less acute depression of more than two years. A **bipolar disorder** is a mood disturbance marked by alternating manic and major depressive episodes. Suicide does not occur exclusively in mood disorders, but suicidal thoughts are a common component of depression.

12. Genetics contribute to the etiology of mood disorders, but except for bipolar disorder, which generally requires a biological vulnerability (like schizophrenia), environmental events alone can precipitate depression. Cognitive theories look for the roots of depression in dysfunctional thoughts. Psychodynamic theories suggest that the nature of, and triggers for, depression depend on an individual's personality structure.

13. **Anxiety disorders** are characterized by intense, frequent, or continuous anxiety that is not warranted by the situation. **Panic disorders** are distinguished by attacks of intense fear and feelings of doom or terror not justified by the situation. **Agoraphobia** refers to a fear of being in places or situations from which escape might be difficult. **Obsessive-compulsive disorder** is marked by recurrent **obsessions** (persistent thoughts or ideas) and **compulsions** (intentional behaviors performed in response to an obsession in a stereotyped fashion). **Post-traumatic stress disorder** is marked by flashbacks and recurrent thoughts of a psychologically distressing event that was outside the range of usual human experience.

14. Anxiety disorders, like depression, show substantial heritability but do not require a genetic predisposition. Cognitive-behavioral theories link them to conditioned emotional responses and dysfunctional cognitions. Psychodynamic theories link anxiety disorders to conflict and to childhood beliefs, fears, and wishes.

15. **Dissociative disorders** are characterized by disruptions in consciousness, memory, sense of identity, or perception of the environment. The primary feature is **dissociation**, a disturbance in which significant aspects of experience are kept separate and distinct in consciousness. The most severe type is **dissociative personality disorder**, also called multiple personality disorder.

16. **Personality disorders** are characterized by maladaptive personality patterns that lead to chronic disturbances in interpersonal and occupational functioning. **Borderline personality disorder** is marked by extremely unstable interpersonal relationships, dramatic mood swings, an unstable sense of identity, intense fears of separation and abandonment, manipulativeness, impulsive behavior, and self-mutilating behavior. **Antisocial personality disorder** is marked by a pattern of irresponsible and socially disruptive behavior in a variety of areas. Genetics play a role in many personality disorders, as do childhood experiences such as abuse and neglect.

Rethinking Psychopathology

17. Diagnostic categories overstate the discreteness of disorders and understate their cultural and political bases. Nature and nurture are so intertwined in the etiology of many syndromes that they cannot be readily distinguished.

Mike Green, "Two Chairs," *1989*

Chapter 16

TREATMENT OF PSYCHOLOGICAL DISORDERS

*J*enny was a frail, bright, obstinate 19 year old from a working-class neighborhood in Boston. She came to the hospital under duress: Her parents threatened that if she did not, they would try to have her committed. They had a good case. Jenny was 5'3" and 72 pounds, suffering from anorexia nervosa, and would likely have been dead two weeks later.

During her 10 weeks in the hospital, Jenny was not the easiest of patients. Like many hospitalized anorexics, she regularly played cat-and-mouse games with her nurses. When weigh-in time came each morning, she had to wear a hospital gown because otherwise she would fill her pockets with coins to fool the scales. The nurses even had to monitor her first trip to the bathroom each morning before weigh-in so she would not drink huge quantities of water to increase her apparent weight. Jenny also required a watchful eye at mealtime to make certain she did not find venues for her food other than her mouth.

In the hospital, Jenny received several forms of treatment. She met with a psychotherapist three times a week to try to uncover the roots of her need to starve herself. The therapist also set up a behavior plan to reward Jenny for weight gain with increased privileges (beginning with walks on the hospital grounds, and eventually trips to the movies) and punish weight loss with increased restrictions. Jenny and her family met twice weekly with a family therapist, who explored the role of family dynamics in her disorder, which was considerable. Her mother, a very anxious woman with a severe personality disorder, was dependent on Jenny in many ways. Jenny was completely enmeshed with her mother, taking care of her and sometimes missing school to stay home with her when her mother was anxious. Jenny's mother was especially anxious about Jenny's sexuality and would regularly cut out articles from the newspaper about rapes and leave them on Jenny's bed. Jenny eliminated any hint of her own sexuality by losing so much weight that she stopped menstruating and lost her female shape. Jenny's father was preoccupied with her physically frail, severely mentally retarded sister, whom Jenny always resented for consuming his attention. By becoming so frail herself, Jenny finally caught her father's eye. In addition to individual and family therapy, Jenny participated in a therapy group for eating-disordered patients, where her peers confronted her rationalizations about her eating behavior and where she could clearly see her own psychopathology in them.

Once Jenny left the hospital, with her weight stabilized, she spent the next four years in psychotherapy. The therapy focused primarily on the way her anorexic symptoms reflected her fear of her sexuality, her rage at her sister (which she could not acknowledge to either herself or her parents), and her desperate wish to have her father notice her. At one point in the treatment, when she moved out of her family's home for the first time, she became so anxious at being away from her mother that her therapist also referred her to a psychiatrist who prescribed a brief regimen of medication for her anxiety.

By the end of her treatment, Jenny's life-threatening disorder had not returned, and she was no longer preoccupied with food. She was now able to deal more appropriately with her mother, was openly able to acknowledge her mixed feelings toward her sister, had a much more satisfying relationship with her father, and was happily ensconced in a romantic relationship (something she could not even imagine at the beginning of treatment).

Jenny's case is unusual, because rarely do people receive so many different forms of treatment. The more typical case is that they find themselves in the office of a clinician who believes their disorder reflects a chemical imbalance and prescribes medication, or that their problem lies in their childhood relationships with their parents and suggests long-term psychotherapy, or that the real problem is their irrational thoughts about themselves and suggests exploration of their cognitive distortions, and so forth. In fact, the variety of psychotherapies is astounding—over 400 different types at last count (see Bergin & Garfield, 1994)—and the treatment people receive generally depends less on the nature of the disorder than on the theoretical perspective of the therapist.

In this chapter, we focus on the most widely practiced treatments for psychological disorders: psychodynamic, cognitive-behavioral, humanistic, group, family, and biological (Table 16.1). Each approach has its own theory of etiology and consequently its own prescriptions for treatment. After exploring each of these treatments in turn, we examine the evidence for the effectiveness of each, the possibility of integrating therapeutic strategies (as in Jenny's treatment), and the role of culture in psychological healing. We conclude with a discussion of who gets—and does not get—treatment in our society and the way treatment is evolving in the context of economic pressures.

PSYCHODYNAMIC THERAPIES

Modern psychotherapy developed in the late nineteenth century out of the work of Sigmund Freud. Most contemporary psychotherapists report that they rely to some extent on psychodynamic theory and technique although to differing degrees (Pope et al., 1987). The psychodynamic approach to therapeutic change rests on two principles: the role of insight and the role of the therapist-patient relationship.

Insight refers to the understanding of one's own psychological processes. According to psychodynamic theory, symptoms reflect unconscious conflicts and compromises among competing wishes and fears and maladaptive ways of coping and defending against unpleasant emotions. Therapeutic change requires that patients come to understand the internal workings of their mind and hence, as one adolescent patient put it, to become "the captain of my own ship." Becoming the

TABLE 16.1 VARIETIES OF PSYCHOLOGICAL TREATMENT

THERAPY	DESCRIPTION
Psychodynamic	Attempts to change personality patterns through insight (using free association and interpretation) and the therapist-patient relationship (analysis of transference).
Psychoanalysis	The patient lies on a couch and free associates three to five times a week.
Psychodynamic psychotherapy	The patient sits face to face with the therapist once to three times a week.
Short-term psychodynamic psychotherapy	Lasts 12 to 50 sessions, usually once a week, with a more active stance by the therapist.
Cognitive-behavioral	Attempts to change problematic behaviors and cognitive processes.
Systematic desensitization	Classical conditioning technique in which the therapist induces the patient to approach a phobic stimulus gradually in imagination.
Exposure techniques	Classical conditioning techniques in which the therapist presents the patient with the phobic stimulus in real life, either all at once (flooding) or gradually (graded exposure).
Operant techniques	Therapist alters operant behaviors by redesigning rewards and punishments, as in a token economy.
Participatory modeling	Cognitive-social technique in which the therapist models behavior and induces the patient to participate in it.
Skills training	Cognitive-social technique in which the therapist teaches behaviors necessary to accomplish goals, as in social skills or assertiveness training.
Cognitive therapy	Aimed at altering problematic thought patterns that underlie dysfunctional feelings and behavior.
Humanistic	Attempts to restore a sense of genuineness and attunement with inner feelings.
Gestalt	Focuses on the "here and now" and brings out disavowed feelings.
Client-centered	Uses empathy and unconditional positive regard to help patients experience themselves as they really are.
Family and marital	Attempts to change problematic family or marital patterns, such as communication patterns, boundaries, and alliances.
Group	Attempts to use group process and group interaction to help people change problematic patterns, either with the help of a therapist or through self-help.
Biological	Attempts to change problematic brain physiology responsible for psychological symptoms.

captain of one's own ship means gaining the capacity to make conscious, rational choices as an adult about wishes, fears, and defensive strategies that may have been forged in childhood. Insight is not, however, a cold cognitive act. Psychodynamic clinicians often speak of "emotional insight," stressing that knowing intellectually about one's problems is not the same as really confronting intense feelings and fears (such as Jenny's fear that if she did not take care of her mother something terrible might happen).

A second principle of psychodynamic treatment is that the relationship between the patient and therapist is crucial for therapeutic change. A patient has to feel comfortable with the therapist in order to speak about emotionally significant experiences, a phenomenon called the **therapeutic alliance**. Beyond this, many psychodynamic therapists argue, as do some humanistic therapists, that being with someone who listens nonjudgmentally and empathically, rather than critically, is inherently therapeutic. Furthermore, as we explore below, psychodynamic therapists assume that patients often bring enduring and troubling interpersonal patterns into the relationship with the therapist, which can then be more readily explored and changed.

Therapeutic Techniques

To bring about therapeutic change, psychodynamic psychotherapies rely on three techniques: free association, interpretation, and analysis of transference. We examine each in turn.

Free Association

If a person becomes anxious without knowing why or starves herself despite knowledge of the dangers of malnutrition, then an important goal is to understand the unconscious events guiding behavior—or, as Freud put it, "to make the unconscious conscious." The patient and her therapist must find a way to map her unconscious mind, to see what fears or wishes are associatively linked to her symptom. Free association is a technique for exploring associational networks and unconscious processes involved in symptom formation. In **free association**, the therapist instructs the patient to say whatever comes to mind—thoughts, feelings, images, fantasies, memories, or wishes—and to try to censor nothing. The patient and therapist then collaborate to solve the mystery of the symptom, piecing together the connections in what has been said and noting what has *not* been said (that is, what the patient may be defending against). As in any good detective story, the most important clues are often those that are concealed, and only by examining gaps in the suspect's account does one find hidden motives and concealed data. The only difference is that in psychotherapy the patient is both the co-detective and the prime suspect.

Interpretation

Although the patient may work hard to understand her associations, the therapist has two advantages in solving the mystery: The therapist is trained in making psychological inferences and is not personally embroiled in the patient's conflicts and ways of seeing reality. For example, Jenny's aversion to sexuality seemed natural to her until she discovered how she had learned to associate sex and danger from her mother. Thus, a central element of psychodynamic technique is the **interpretation** of conflicts, defenses, and compromise-formations (Chapter 12), whereby the therapist helps the patient understand her experiences in a new light.

One patient, for example, repeatedly had affairs with married men. As she talked about sneaking around the wife of one man in order to see him, her associations led to her parents' divorce. At one point, her mother had refused to allow her to see her father, so the patient arranged secret meetings with him. The therapist interpreted the connection between the patient's pattern of seeking out married men

Freud's office in Vienna.

and sneaking around her mother's back to see her father. Apparently, the rage she felt toward her mother for not letting her see her father was now directed toward the wives of the men with whom she had affairs, which allowed her to rationalize sleeping with their husbands.

An important kind of interpretation is the interpretation of **resistance**, barriers to free association or to the treatment more generally that the patient creates. As both sleuth and suspect, the patient is consciously on the trail of mental processes that she is unconsciously covering up. Resistance emerges because the patient originally developed her symptoms to reduce anxiety, and the closer she comes to its source, the more she is motivated to run from it. Jenny, for example, insisted for two years that her attitudes toward sexuality were totally realistic and refused to discuss the matter further.

Analysis of Transference

The relationship between the patient and therapist provides a particularly useful source of information in psychotherapy (Freud, 1912; Gill, 1982; Luborsky & Crits-Christoph, 1990). Freud observed that patients tend to play out with their therapists many of the same interpersonal scenarios that give them trouble in their lives. For example, a man who recently came to therapy complaining of problems getting along with people in positions of authority immediately added, "By the way, I don't believe in this psychotherapy crap." Within this first session, the man had already replicated his symptom with a new authority figure—the therapist. The therapy relationship is a very intimate relationship in which the patient communicates personal experiences to someone commonly perceived as an authority. As research documents, this relationship consequently tends to become a magnet for experiences from prior relationships involving intimacy and authority, particularly parental relationships (Luborsky et al., 1990).

Transference refers to the displacement (or transfer) of thoughts, feelings, fears, wishes, and conflicts from past relationships, particularly from childhood, onto new relationships, especially with the therapist. For example, one patient had experienced his father as extremely critical and impossible to please. In therapy, the patient tended to interpret even neutral comments from the therapist as severe criticism and would then respond by doing things (like missing appointments without calling) that would in most relationships elicit criticism and hostility. By examining such transferential processes, the patient and therapist can learn about the patient's dynamics directly without relying on his self-reports. The intensity of transference can also be a potent force in developing emotional insight. Freud wrote that the relationship between the patient and therapist creates "new editions of the old conflicts" (1917, p. 454). The aim of working with transference is to rewrite the new edition in light of new information.

Recent experimental research from a cognitive perspective documents transference processes in everyday relationships (Andersen & Cole, 1991). The investigators asked subjects to describe significant others and then embedded pieces of those descriptions in descriptions of fictional characters. Thus, if a subject described his mother as gentle, intelligent, feminine, and courageous, the investigators would create a fictional character who was described, among other things, as gentle. The investigators then exposed subjects to these descriptions and later asked them to remember them. Upon recall, subjects attributed qualities of the significant other (such as courage) to these characters, even though these qualities had not been part of the characters' initial description. Essentially, subjects transferred aspects of one representation to another.

A Case Study

The following case study illustrates the principles of psychodynamic psychotherapy. A woman in her early 30s went to a clinic suffering from tremendous anxiety and inexplicable depression. She was developing a relationship with a somewhat older man that was beginning to become physical, and she had never been sexually intimate with anyone as an adult. Although this case occurred several years before the recent publicity given to repressed memories, the therapist suspected a history of sexual abuse. He noticed a flicker of fear cross her face when he flipped the "Do not disturb" sign on the door. Her response, of which she seemed unaware, could have had many possible meanings; however, the therapist hypothesized that something about being alone with a man who indicated that he did not want to be disturbed might have triggered the fear. The patient was also flirtatious in the sessions and would sit inappropriately in a relatively short skirt. This combination of seductiveness and fear sometimes characterizes sexually abused patients, who may be sexually promiscuous, fearful of men, or both simultaneously.

Ultimately, the patient did recall a history of sexual abuse, in part through dream analysis, another technique used in psychodynamic psychotherapies. In one recurring dream, her mother was selling her as a prostitute. Exploring her associations suggested that this symbolized her belief that her mother had looked the other way when two of her mother's boyfriends sexually molested the patient and her sister, fearing that her boyfriends would leave her if she did not allow it. As the memories began to return, however, the patient was reluctant to disclose them. The therapist wondered aloud whether by discussing something sexual with him the patient felt that something sexual was happening between the two of them and whether that might not be frightening in light of her history. This interpretation made the patient more comfortable in disclosing what she had remembered; it indicated that the therapist was not about to reenact with her a previous trauma. Later in the treatment, she was also able to see how the conflicting signals she sent the therapist in the first session—fear plus flirtatiousness—stemmed from her abuse history and contributed to some confusing and unpleasant experiences with men as an adult.

One important feature of this case was that the therapist had to handle many sensitive issues, particularly around the transference (see Herman, 1992). He needed to help the patient remember what had happened to her so she could begin to control her actions and cope with her emotions. At the same time, he could not move too quickly or she might feel sexually intruded on by "demands" for her to disclose, reenacting her experience of helplessness and vulnerability. Working with such intense experiences exerts a pressure on the therapist known as **countertransference**, in which interaction with the patient, and particularly becoming the object of her transference reactions, triggers emotional responses in the therapist. To learn to detect and appropriately handle countertransference, psychodynamic psychotherapists must themselves undergo psychodynamic treatment to explore their own psychological processes.

Varieties of Psychodynamic Therapy

The main contemporary forms of psychodynamic treatment are psychoanalysis, psychodynamic psychotherapy, and short-term therapy. These forms may be viewed along a continuum, ranging from the most long-term and broad-ranging (psychoanalysis) to the briefest and most focused (short-term therapy).

Psychoanalysis

The first variety of psychodynamic therapy, developed by Freud, was **psychoanalysis**. The patient lies on a couch, and the analyst sits behind him. The purpose of the couch is to create an environment in which people can set aside many of their defenses, simply letting associations come to mind. This arrangement can also make disclosing sensitive material easier because the person does not have to look the therapist in the eye. Patients usually undergo psychoanalysis three to five times a week for several years, making it a very intensive, extensive, and expensive form of therapy.

Psychodynamic Psychotherapy

In **psychodynamic psychotherapy**, the patient and therapist sit face-to-face, with the patient in a chair rather than on the couch. The therapy is more conversational than psychoanalysis, with patients typically instructed at the beginning of the treatment to talk about whatever is on their mind on a given day. The therapy makes use of free association, but the patient is usually more goal-directed than in psychoanalysis, where the primary aim is to relax conscious control in order to explore unconscious associations.

Psychodynamic psychotherapy is particularly appropriate for addressing repetitive interpersonal patterns or difficulties in relationships, such as consistently choosing the wrong kind of lover or fearing vulnerability in close relationships. For Jenny, who initially had trouble maintaining an appropriate weight after she left the hospital, this kind of treatment proved crucial in keeping her alive by allowing her to confront her feelings about herself, her retarded sister, her parents, and her sexuality that contributed to creating a life-threatening symptom. Psychodynamic ther-

Psychodynamic psychotherapy.

apy takes place one to three times a week and, like psychoanalysis, can last several years. Versions of psychodynamic therapy are probably the most widely practiced form of therapy (see Svartberg & Stiles, 1991).

Short-term Psychodynamic Psychotherapy

In recent years, a number of psychodynamically oriented therapists have developed systems of short-term therapy (see Crits-Christoph, 1992; Strupp & Blackwood, 1985). Short-term dynamic psychotherapies rely on the same principles as other forms of psychodynamic therapy (Horvath & Luborsky, 1993; Luborsky et al., 1993), but they last only 12 to 50 sessions, usually once a week. A brief transcript from a short-term psychodynamic therapy is reproduced in Figure 16.1.

Unlike more intensive psychodynamic treatments, short-term therapies tend to have a specific focus, which is formulated in the first few sessions. Formulating the focus usually entails linking the patient's symptom or initial complaint with a hypothesized conflict or dynamic issue, such as unresolved grief, repressed anger, or authority conflicts (Davanloo, 1985; Mann, 1982; Sifneos, 1987). For example, one patient experienced intermittent depression after his parents' divorce and his father's subsequent departure. The focus of the therapy was thus grieving, using the ultimate loss of the therapist and the patient's responses to it as points of entry into emotion-laden material. The time limit and specific focus of short-term therapy require that the therapist be much more active and directive, although the aim is still to explore psychodynamics. Compared to other psychodynamic therapies, short-term therapies are very cost-effective, although they are not appropriate for most personality disorders and cannot be expected to effect broad personality change.

MACBETH: *Canst thou not minister to a mind diseas'd, Pluck from the memory a rooted sorrow, Raze out the written troubles of the brain, And with some sweet oblivious antidote Cleanse the stuff'd bosom of that perilous stuff Which weighs upon the heart?*

DOCTOR: *Therein the patient must minister to himself.*

—Shakespeare, Macbeth, *V.iii*

Loretta was a woman in her late thirties who sought treatment for long-standing problems with anxiety and depression and an unsatisfying sexual relationship with her husband. Loretta came from a very conservative religious family and described her father as aloof and her mother as extremely critical. In the excerpt below, she describes feeling more relaxed with men, an exciting but still unsettling feeling:

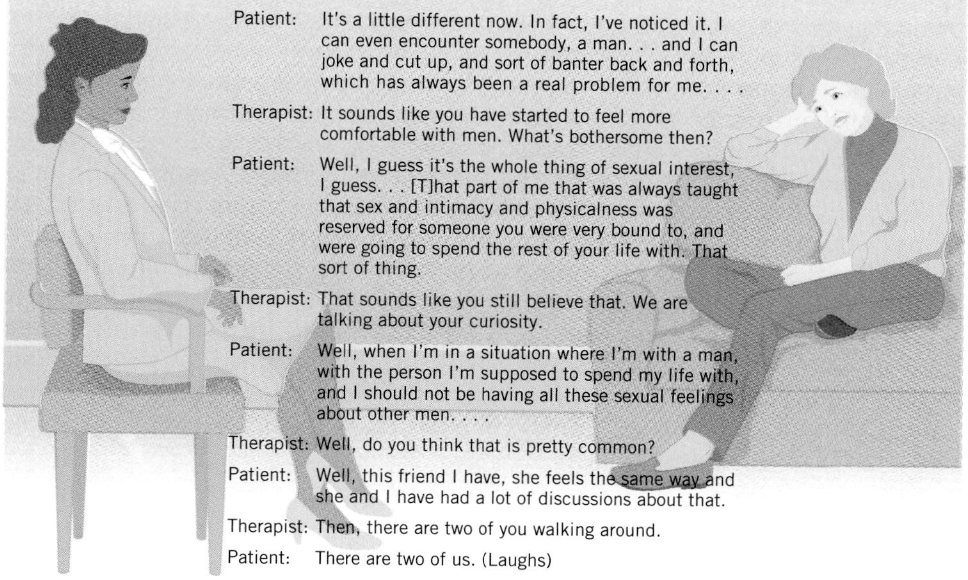

Therapist: How would you experience men before you started feeling this way?

Patient: Sort of avoidance. I didn't—difficulty relating to them. . . .

Therapist: Is that different now?

Patient: It's a little different now. In fact, I've noticed it. I can even encounter somebody, a man. . . and I can joke and cut up, and sort of banter back and forth, which has always been a real problem for me. . . .

Therapist: It sounds like you have started to feel more comfortable with men. What's bothersome then?

Patient: Well, I guess it's the whole thing of sexual interest, I guess. . . [T]hat part of me that was always taught that sex and intimacy and physicalness was reserved for someone you were very bound to, and were going to spend the rest of your life with. That sort of thing.

Therapist: That sounds like you still believe that. We are talking about your curiosity.

Patient: Well, when I'm in a situation where I'm with a man, with the person I'm supposed to spend my life with, and I should not be having all these sexual feelings about other men. . . .

Therapist: Well, do you think that is pretty common?

Patient: Well, this friend I have, she feels the same way and she and I have had a lot of discussions about that.

Therapist: Then, there are two of you walking around.

Patient: There are two of us. (Laughs)

FIGURE 16.1

Transcript from a short-term psychodynamic psychotherapy. In this excerpt, the therapist helps the patient distinguish between fantasies, for which one need not feel guilty, and actions. The therapist is nonjudgmental and helps Loretta understand that her feelings are normal, through the joke about "two of you walking around." SOURCE: *Strupp & Binder, 1984.*

COGNITIVE-BEHAVIORAL THERAPIES

In the late 1950s and early 1960s, an increasing number of psychologists rejected psychoanalysis as a form of treatment, arguing that it was based on unproven principles and techniques that had not been scientifically validated. They turned to behaviorism and learning theory, viewing psychological problems as maladaptive learned behavior patterns (Wolpe, 1964). The majority of clinical psychology faculty members at U.S. universities today are behavioral or **cognitive-behavioral** in their orientation (Sayette & Mayne, 1990), using methods derived from behaviorist and cognitive approaches to learning.

Cognitive-behavioral therapies are typically short-term. Unlike psychodynamic therapies, they are not concerned with exploring and altering underlying personality patterns or unconscious processes (see Eysenck, 1965, 1987; Goldfried & Davison, 1994; Turner et al., 1992). The focus is on the individual's behavior in the present, not on childhood experiences or inferred motives. Cognitive-behavioral therapists are far more directive than their psychodynamic counterparts, suggesting specific ways patients should change their thinking and behavior, assigning homework, and structuring sessions with questions and strategies. Whereas the role of the psychodynamic psychotherapist is like that of an English professor interpreting layers of meaning in a passage of poetry, the cognitive-behavioral therapist is more like an engineer trying to design solutions for mechanical problems.

Cognitive-behavioral therapists begin with a careful **behavioral analysis**, examining the symptom and the stimuli or thoughts associated with it. They then tailor procedures to address problematic behaviors, cognitions, and emotional responses. The effectiveness of cognitive-behavioral therapies lies in their ability to target specific psychological processes. Panic attacks, for example, include physiological arousal, a subjective experience of terror, anxious thoughts, and a tendency to avoid stimuli associated with anxiety. Panic patients come to associate autonomic reactions such as a racing heart and a feeling of suffocation with an impending panic attack, leading them to panic whenever they have these experiences (Chapter 15). They also develop expectancies of helplessness in the face of impending panic and may have catastrophic cognitions such as "I am about to die," or "Everyone will be able to see that I am helpless and incompetent." The therapist addresses different components of the problem with different techniques. These may include paced breathing exercises to deal with feelings of breathlessness (Salkovskis et al., 1986), repeated exposure to the experience of a racing heart (for example, through climbing up and down stairs) so that the emotional response is eventually extinguished, and rational analysis of the accuracy of catastrophic beliefs (Barlow, 1988; Zinbarg et al., 1992). This kind of multifaceted treatment is effective for 80 to 90 percent of panic patients (see Clum et al., 1993; Klosko et al., 1990; Zinbarg et al., 1992).

Cognitive-behavioral therapies all focus on symptoms rather than insight, and they take a rational problem-solving approach, but their techniques vary considerably. Most therapists who practice **behavior therapy** (treatment based primarily on behaviorist learning principles) also use strategies targeted at cognition, although some behavior therapists consider cognitive interventions unscientific and unproductive and rely strictly on techniques based on classical and operant conditioning. In this section, we examine a range of cognitive-behavioral techniques, from those based on classical and operant conditioning to those that rely on cognitive-social and more strictly cognitive principles.

Classical Conditioning Techniques

Some behavioral procedures use classical conditioning to alter emotional responses that have become triggered by particular stimuli. Prominent among these techniques are desensitization and exposure techniques.

Systematic Desensitization

One of the earliest and still most widely used cognitive-behavioral techniques is **systematic desensitization**, in which the patient mentally confronts a phobic stimulus gradually while in a state that inhibits anxiety (Wolpe, 1958). The assumption behind desensitization is that through classical conditioning phobics have learned to fear what should be a neutral stimulus. In classical conditioning of emotional responses (Chapter 5), a previously neutral stimulus comes to elicit an emotion by being paired with a stimulus that already elicits the emotion. For example, a person who has an automobile accident feels afraid to drive afterward because being behind the wheel of a car (conditioned stimulus) is associated with a terrifying experience (unconditioned stimulus). Normally, future encounters with the conditioned stimulus (driving) without it being paired with the stimulus that elicited the fear (the accident) will lead to extinction of the response (fear). (Whoever penned the proverb about the need to get back on a horse as soon as one has fallen off was a latent behavior therapist.) However, if the person starts walking instead of driving, this short-circuits an adaptive learning process: She avoids the fear by not driving, but this prevents extinction from occurring, so the fear will remain. Thus, phobic responses, like all avoidance responses, become particularly resistant to extinction.

If patients are to extinguish irrational fear responses, then, they must confront the feared stimulus. This is the aim of systematic desensitization, which takes place in four steps. First, the therapist teaches the patient relaxation techniques, such as tensing and then relaxing muscle groups throughout the body or breathing from the diaphragm. Then the therapist questions the patient about his fears and uses this information to construct a hierarchy of feared imagined stimuli, from scenes that provoke mild anxiety to those that induce intense fear. For the patient who is afraid of driving, the scenes might range from sitting behind the wheel of a nonmoving car to driving on a crowded expressway on a rainy night (Figure 16.2). The third step,

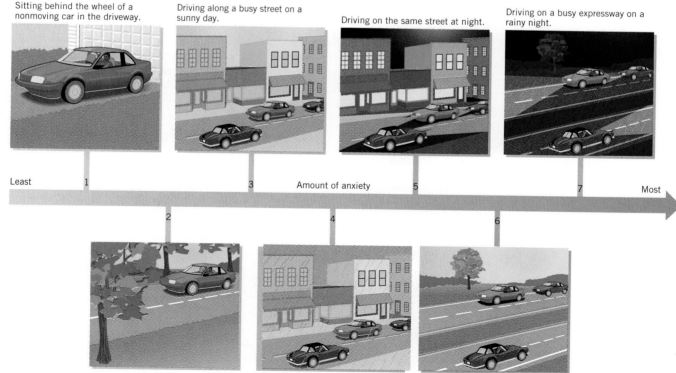

FIGURE 16.2 *Systemic desensitization. The patient exposes himself to progressively more threatening imagined approximations of the phobic stimulus.*

which usually begins in the third or fourth session, is desensitization proper. The patient relaxes, using the techniques he has learned, and is then instructed to imagine vividly the first, least threatening scene in the hierarchy. When the patient can imagine this scene comfortably, perhaps with additional relaxation instructions, he then imagines the next scene, and so on up the hierarchy. In the fourth step, the therapist encourages the patient to confront his fears in real life and monitors his progress as he does so, desensitizing additional scenes as needed to eliminate anxiety and avoidance.

Desensitization has been used with a long list of anxiety-related disorders, among them phobias, impotence, nightmares, obsessive-compulsive disorders, social anxiety, and even fears of death or authority figures (McGlynn et al., 1981; O'Sullivan et al., 1991). In one striking case, desensitization was used to help a 20-year-old woman overcome a fear of babies (Free & Beekhuis, 1985). Whereas initially the patient was unable even to look at photographs of babies long enough to establish a hierarchy, by the end of treatment and at a one-year followup, she could approach babies without discomfort. This form of therapy is markedly different from a psychodynamic therapy, which would instead have explored what babies meant to her: Was she feeling guilty about an abortion she had had? Was she a victim of incest whose anxiety reflected an unconscious association of babies with her childhood fear that she was pregnant? In contrast, the cognitive-behavioral therapist aims to extinguish the fear response, not to search for insight into its origins.

Desensitization works, but the basis for its success is a matter of some dispute (see Levin & Gross, 1985; McGlynn et al., 1981). One theory proposes that desensitization is a **counterconditioning** process; that is, it runs opposite, or counter, to previous conditioning that created the symptom (Wolpe, 1958). Thus, if the person was conditioned to experience anxiety, the therapist tries to create muscular and parasympathetic responses (such as steady breathing) incompatible with anxiety. Another hypothesis is a simple extinction hypothesis: Because the patient's repeated exposure to a stimulus is unaccompanied by a feared outcome, the fear response is extinguished.

Exposure Techniques

Another type of cognitive-behavioral procedure based on classical conditioning is called exposure (or in vivo exposure). **Exposure techniques**, unlike desensitization procedures, present the patient with the actual phobic stimulus in real life (*in vivo*), rather than having the patient merely imagine it. In **flooding**, the patient confronts the phobic stimulus all at once. The theory behind flooding is that

Exposure techniques confront the patient with the feared stimulus directly.

inescapable exposure to the conditioned stimulus eventually desensitizes the patient through extinction or related mechanisms. Flooding, like desensitization, prevents the person from escaping onset of the conditioned stimulus (such as sitting in the driver's seat of a running car).

One therapist used flooding to treat a young woman with an intense fear of escalators (Nesbitt, 1973). With considerable coaxing from the therapist, the patient rode the escalators in a large department store for hours, first with the therapist and then alone, until the symptom abated. Some research has found flooding more effective in treating social phobias than antianxiety medication (Turner et al., 1994). The release of endorphins (natural pain killers or opiates) in response to intense anxiety may partially account for the efficacy of exposure techniques (Merluzzi et al., 1991). From a more cognitive perspective, inescapable exposure eventually leads patients to recognize that the situation is not really catastrophic and that they have the self-efficacy to confront it.

From the patient's point of view, flooding can be a very frightening procedure. A modification of the technique that is less difficult to endure is graded exposure. Like flooding, **graded exposure** uses real stimuli, but like desensitization, the stimuli are graduated in intensity. One psychologist used graded exposure with a 70-year-old woman who had developed a fear of dogs after having been savagely bitten by one (Thyer, 1980). During the first two sessions, she was exposed to a small dog, first at the other end of the room and then gradually closer until she let it lick her hand. During the third session, she made an hour-long visit to the humane society, where she was exposed to the barking of dozens of dogs. During the fourth and fifth sessions, she repeated the earlier treatments but with large dogs. After five sessions, her symptom disappeared.

Go to the heart of danger, for there you will find safety.

Ancient Chinese proverb, cited in Goldfried & Davison, 1994

THE FAR SIDE   By GARY LARSON

Professor Gallagher and his controversial technique of simultaneously confronting the fear of heights, snakes and the dark.

Operant Conditioning Techniques

In operant conditioning, behavior is controlled by its rewarding or punishing consequences (Chapter 5). Therapies based on operant conditioning therefore use reward and punishment to modify unwanted behavior, as when Jenny was rewarded for gaining weight with increased privileges. Operant conditioning is the principle behind the **token economy** procedure, in which points or tokens can be cashed in for rewards such as food, privileges, or cigarettes. Token economies were first used systematically with psychotic patients, who received tokens for socially acceptable behaviors and were fined tokens when they were obstreperous, assaultive, or physically destructive (Ayllon & Azrin, 1968). Psychologists have since applied this approach in a number of settings (Hurley and Sovner, 1985; Rimmerman et al., 1992), including institutions for mentally retarded people, who tend to respond well to structured settings and tangible rewards.

Operant techniques can be particularly effective in working with children and their parents, since parents often intuitively apply rewards and punishments in ineffective or counterproductive ways (see Kendall, 1993). Deliberately altering contingencies of reinforcement can bring unwanted behaviors under control, as in the treatment of a 12-year-old girl who repeatedly scratched herself raw and then picked at the scabs (Latimer, 1979). The girl received points for clipping her fingernails and for each half hour in which she did not scratch or pick at herself. She could exchange the points for privileges such as reading, watching television, or going on outings.

Modeling and Skills Training

Because people learn not only through their own experiences but also by observing the behavior of others, some cognitive-behavioral therapists rely on modeling procedures. In **participatory modeling**, which tends to be more effective than modeling alone, the therapist models the desired behavior and gradually induces the patient to participate in it. Bandura and his colleagues (1969) demonstrated the effectiveness of participatory modeling in treating patients with snake phobias. In this procedure, the therapist first handles snakes without showing anxiety and without being harmed. (This, of course, presumes fearless therapists and cooperative reptiles.) Then the therapist coaxes the patient to handle the snakes. By watching the therapist, the patient begins to be desensitized vicariously, enabling him to approach the phobic stimulus. Participatory modeling alters self-efficacy expectancies as well, since observing the model safely approach the feared stimulus suggests to the patient that he can, too. Participating with the therapist in snake handling then leads to even more radical revisions of his expectancies.

Even if self-efficacy expectancies are high, however, people cannot emit a behavior they lack the competence to perform (Chapter 12). Bandura (cited in Goldfried & Davison, 1994) warns that desensitizing people who are socially phobic but who actually *do* lack the ability to interact in socially competent ways produces little more than "relaxed incompetents." Hence, another cognitive-behavioral technique is **skills training**, which means teaching the behaviors necessary to accomplish relevant goals. Skills are a form of procedural knowledge and are typically carried out automatically (Chapter 6). Acquiring new skills, however, usually requires that the individual focus conscious awareness on a set of procedures until they gradually become routinized (Meichenbaum, 1977, 1990).

Skills training procedures often draw on theories of problem solving and self-regulation. For example, skills training with impulsive and hyperactive children teaches them to decide what the problem is, divide it into components, develop ways to solve each component part, and use performance feedback to determine whether each part (and eventually the entire problem) has been successfully handled. For example, impulsive children might be taught to ask themselves a series of questions:

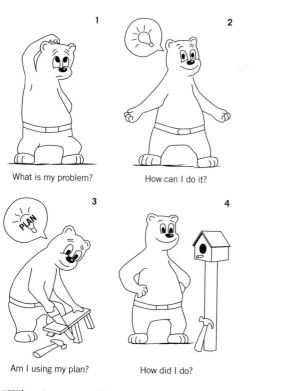

FIGURE 16.3
Skills training for children. This approach was designed to treat impulsive children. It teaches them how to solve a problem, from framing the problem to self-monitoring and attending to feedback. Source: Camp & Bash, 1981.

1. What is my problem?
2. How can I do it?
3. Am I using my plan?
4. How did I do?

"What is my problem?"; "What can I do about it?"; "Am I using my plan?"; "How did I do?" (Figure 16.3). In several studies, this approach has led to improved academic and social skills, at least in the short term (Camp et al., 1976, cited in Meichenbaum, 1977; Palkes et al., 1968). Skills training has similarly been used with adult alcoholics to help them cope with urges to drink (Monti et al., 1993).

Clinicians use a technique called **social skills training** for people with specific interpersonal deficits, such as shyness or lack of assertiveness. Following assessment, treatment usually begins with direct teaching of skills or modeling of behavior on film, videotape, or in person. The next stage is rehearsal of the new skills—practicing gestures, imagining responses, role-playing various scenarios, and so forth. Patients then receive feedback through observation of themselves or others (Ladd & Mize, 1983). Social skills training often integrates other behavioral and cognitive techniques, such as desensitizing social anxiety through group interactions, altering contingencies of reinforcement, and examining irrational expectancies (such as "No one will like me if I ask for what I want"). Social skills training has been used effectively with various groups, such as aggressive and rejected children (Bierman et al., 1987; Lochman et al., 1993) and mentally retarded children and adults (Foxx & Faw, 1992). It has also been used extensively with schizophrenics (Benton & Schroeder, 1990), who frequently suffer from social isolation, although its long-term efficacy and generalization to behaviors outside of very specific settings is unclear (see Bellack & Mueser, 1992; Halford & Hayes, 1991).

Cognitive Therapy

Whereas most cognitive-behavioral techniques try to alter behavior, cognitive therapies focus primarily on changing the dysfunctional cognitions presumed to underlie psychological disorders. Cognitive therapies target the things individuals spontaneously say to themselves and the assumptions they make (Ellis, 1962), or what Aaron Beck calls **automatic thoughts** (Beck, 1976, 1993). Only secondarily do cognitive therapies rely on behavioral techniques, largely to induce patients to implement therapeutic suggestions (see Ellis, 1984).

The cognitive therapist takes an active role. By questioning the patient's assumptions and beliefs and asking her to identify the data underlying them, the therapist engages the patient in empirical hypothesis testing (Hollon & Beck, 1985). A patient who says, "I never enjoy anything anymore" might receive an assignment to keep a record of each day's events and to rate them according to the degree of satisfaction they evoke (Beck, 1989). Two approaches to combating cognitive distortions are Ellis's rational-emotive therapy and Beck's cognitive therapy.

Ellis's Rational-Emotive Therapy

Albert Ellis began as a psychoanalyst but came to believe that psychodynamic treatments take too long and are too often ineffective (Ellis, 1962, 1989). According to Ellis, what people think and say to themselves about a situation affects the way they respond to it. He proposed the **ABC theory of psychopathology**, where *A* refers to activating conditions, *B* to belief systems, and *C* to emotional consequences (Ellis, 1977; Muran, 1991; Yankura & Dryden, 1990). Activating conditions such as loss of a job (*A*) do not lead directly to consequences such as depression (*C*). The process that turns unpleasant events into depressive symptoms involves dysfunctional belief systems, often expressed in a person's self-talk, such as, "I am not a worthy person unless I am very successful" (*B*).

Ellis thus developed **rational-emotive therapy**, which proposes that the patient "can rid himself of most of his emotional or mental unhappiness, ineffectuality, and disturbance if he learns to maximize his rational and minimize his irrational thinking" (Ellis, 1962, p. 36). The therapist continually brings the patient's illogical or self-defeating thoughts to her attention, shows her how they are causing problems, demonstrates their illogic, and teaches alternative ways of thinking (Ellis, 1962, 1977, 1987). If the source of psychological distress is irrational thinking, then the path to eliminating symptoms is increased rationality.

Beck's Cognitive Therapy

Like Ellis, Aaron Beck was a disenchanted psychoanalyst. Also like Ellis, Beck views cognitive therapy as a process of "collaborative empiricism," in which the patient and therapist work together like scientists testing hypotheses (Beck, 1989, 1991). In therapy sessions, which typically number only 12 to 20, the therapist and patient focus on the present, not the past, devising strategies for changing maladaptive patterns of thought and behavior. The sessions are highly structured, beginning with setting an agenda. The therapist teaches the patient the theory behind the treatment, often assigning books or articles to read, and trains the patient to fill in the cognitive link between the stimulus that leads to depressed or anxious feelings and the feelings that get generated in the situation. For example, a patient who felt sad whenever he made a mistake was instructed to focus on his thoughts the next time he made a mistake. At his next session, he reported that he would think, "I'm a dope," or "I never do anything right" (Beck, 1976).

The core of Beck's therapy, like Ellis's, is the testing of cognitive distortions. The therapist questions the data on which the patient's assumptions are based and identifies errors in thinking. A woman who was suicidal believed she had nothing to look forward to because her husband was unfaithful. The beliefs underlying her suicidality seemed to be that she was nothing without her husband and that she could not save her marriage. The dialogue between the therapist and this patient included the following exchange:

> THERAPIST: *You say that you can't be happy without Raymond.... Have you found yourself happy when you are with Raymond?*
>
> PATIENT: *No, we fight all the time and I feel worse.*
>
> THERAPIST: *You say you are nothing without Raymond. Before you met Raymond, did you feel you were nothing?*

> PATIENT: *No, I felt I was somebody.*
>
> THERAPIST: *If you were somebody before you knew Raymond, why do you need him to be somebody now?*
>
> PATIENT: [Puzzled] *Hmmm....*

(Beck, 1976)

Eventually, this patient concluded that her happiness did not, in fact, depend on her husband and divorced him, enjoying a more stable life.

Cognitive therapy began as a treatment for depression, but more recently therapists have applied cognitive techniques to other disorders, such as anxiety and eating disorders (Beck, 1991, 1992; Borkovec & Costell, 1993; Chambless & Gillis, 1993; Wilson & Fairburn, 1993). In extending his work to anxiety, Beck has incorporated research on stress, notably Lazarus's (1966, 1991) view that what makes an event stressful is the way the person interprets it (Chapter 11). According to Beck (1985), people with anxiety disorders tend to overestimate the probability and severity of the feared event and underestimate their coping resources. Thus, anxiety disorders are seen as extreme reactions to threat (Shaw & Segal, 1988).

HUMANISTIC, GROUP, AND FAMILY THERAPIES

Although psychodynamic and cognitive-behavioral psychotherapies are the most widely practiced, clinicians have many other alternatives. The most common are humanistic, group, and family therapies.

Humanistic Therapies

Particularly in the 1960s, a number of therapists took issue with what they perceived as mechanistic and dehumanizing aspects of psychoanalysis and behaviorism. **Humanistic therapies**, like humanistic personality theories, focus on the phenomenology of the patient, that is, on the way each person consciously experiences the self, relationships, and the world. The aim of humanistic therapies is to help people get in touch with their feelings, with their "true selves," and with a sense of meaning in life.

Humanistic therapies come in dozens of varieties. **Gestalt therapy** developed in response to the belief that people had become too socialized—controlling their thoughts, behaviors, and even their feelings in order to conform to social expectations. According to Gestalt therapists, losing touch with one's emotions and one's authentic inner "voice" leads to psychological problems such as depression and anxiety.

Although the practice of many Gestalt therapists resembles psychodynamic psychotherapy, others avoid focusing on childhood antecedents of current difficulties, believing this leads further away from emotions, not toward them (Perls, 1969, 1990). In this view, understanding *why* one feels a certain way is far less important than recognizing *that* one feels that way. Gestalt therapy thus focuses on the "here and now" rather than the "then and there." The best known method associated with Gestalt therapy is the **empty chair technique**, in which the therapist places an empty chair near the client and asks him to imagine that the person to whom he would like to express his feelings (such as a dead parent) is in the chair. The client can then safely express his feelings and learn what authentic communication and self-understanding mean, by "talking" with the person without consequences.

The most widely practiced humanistic therapy is Carl Rogers's **client-centered therapy**. Rogers was among the first to refer to people who seek treatment as *clients* rather than *patients*. He rejected the medical model and suggested that people come to therapy seeking help in solving problems, not cures for disorders. Client-centered therapy is based on Rogers's view that people experience psychological difficulties when their concept of self is not congruent with their actual experience (Chapter 12). For example, a man who thought of himself as someone who loved his father came to realize through therapy that he also felt a great deal of rage toward him. He had denied his negative feelings because he learned as a child that he should always be loving and obedient and that feeling otherwise was "bad." The aim of client-centered therapy is to help clients experience themselves as they actually are—in this case, for the man to accept himself as a person who can feel both love and rage toward his father and thus to alleviate tension and anxiety, particularly with his father (Rogers, 1961; Rogers & Sanford, 1985).

Rogerian therapy assumes that the basic nature of human beings is to grow and mature. Hence, the goal is to provide a supportive environment in which clients can start again where they left off years ago when they denied their true feelings in order to feel worthy and esteemed by significant others. The therapist creates a supportive environment by demonstrating **unconditional positive regard** for the client—that is, expressing an attitude of fundamental acceptance toward the client, without any requirements or conditions (Rogers, 1961, 1980)—and by listening empathically. Rogers stressed the curative value of empathy, by which he meant becoming emotionally in tune with, and understanding the patient's phenomenal experience without judging it. Therapeutic change occurs as the client hears his own thoughts and feelings reflected by a caring, empathic, nonjudgmental listener (Rogers, 1961, 1980). The Rogerian therapist, often called a counselor, evaluates clients' thoughts and feelings only for their authenticity, not for their unconscious meanings or their rationality.

Group Therapies

The therapies described thus far all consider the individual as the unit of analysis and treatment. In contrast, group and family therapies treat multiple individuals simultaneously, although they often apply psychodynamic, cognitive-behavioral, or humanistic principles.

In group therapy, typically eight to ten people meet with a therapist on a regular basis, usually once a week for two hours (Vinogravdov & Yalom, 1989; Yalom, 1975). As in individual therapy, members of the group talk about problems in their own lives, but they also gain from exploring **group process**, or the way members of

In group therapy, people discuss their own lives as well as the process of interacting in the group itself.

the group interact with each other. Some cognitive-behavioral therapy also takes place in groups, particularly where the aim is to teach skills that do not require individual instruction, such as stress management.

Group therapy is designed to produce benefits that may not arise from individual therapy (Dies, 1992; Yalom, 1975). For example, for newcomers to a group, the presence of other members who have made demonstrable progress can instill a therapeutic sense of hope. Discovering that others have problems similar to their own may also relieve shame, anxiety, and guilt. In addition, the group provides possibilities for members to repeat, examine, and alter the types of relationships they experienced with their own families, which they may bring with them to many social situations (see Sadock, 1985).

Groups assembled for therapy may be more or less heterogeneous. Heterogeneous therapy groups work on the same kinds of problems each person would address in individual therapy, such as anxiety, depression, or trouble finding and maintaining satisfying intimate relationships. The members of the group typically vary not only in symptoms but also in age, socioeconomic status, and gender. In contrast, homogeneous groups usually focus on a common issue or disorder, such as incest, bulimia, or even borderline personality disorder (Linehan, 1987, 1991). Groups can be quite helpful (Wilflely et al., 1993), in part because members can see and confront in other members what they cannot acknowledge in themselves, as when Jenny, whose case opened this chapter, observed other obviously emaciated anorexics complain that they were fat. Children and adolescents also benefit from group therapy for issues such as coping with divorce (Kalter, 1987).

A variation on group therapy is the **self-help group**, which is generally not guided by a professional (see Dies, 1992; Walker et al., 1992). Self-help groups tend to have a larger membership than other therapy groups. The goal is to help members cope with a specific problem rather than explore individual psychodynamics or make major changes in personality (Riordan & Beggs, 1988; Sadock, 1985). One of the oldest and best known self-help groups is Alcoholics Anonymous. Other widely attended groups include Adult Children of Alcoholics, Weight Watchers, Gamblers Anonymous, Recovery Inc. (an organization of former mental patients), and groups for cancer patients or parents who have lost a child. Psychotherapists frequently refer patients to self-help groups to supplement individual therapy, particularly if the patient has a problem such as overeating or alcoholism (see Frustaci, 1988; Kurtz & Powell, 1987). Although evidence exists that self-help groups can be effective for many people with alcoholism (Baer et al., 1992), eating disorders (Jones, 1992), and smoking (Curry, 1993), some controversy remains (see Emrick, 1987; Peele, 1990; Saunders, 1989). Their main limitation, particularly when used alone, is that they often oversimplify the problem and its causes, leading their members to believe that all their difficulties can be reduced to being "co-dependent," an "adult child of an alcoholic," and so forth.

An Alcoholics Anonymous meeting.

Family Therapies

Family therapies are predicated on the view that a family is a system of interdependent parts, so that the problem lies in the structure of the system itself rather than in the family member who is merely expressing the symptom (Haley, 1971; Simon, 1985; Wynne, 1961) (Chapter 15). The aim of **family therapy**, then, is to change maladaptive family interaction patterns. As in group and psychodynamic therapy, the focus of family therapy is on *process* rather than simply on *content*. In other words, the process that unfolds in the therapy hour—whether a transference reaction to a therapist, a sibling-like competitive relationship in a group, or a round of accusations and counteraccusations between a husband and wife—is as important as the content of what the patient says. In family therapy the therapist takes a relatively active role, including assigning the family tasks to carry out between sessions.

Family therapists view the roots of psychopathology less in individuals than in dysfunctional family patterns. Thus, they often treat the whole family rather than the person who happens to be expressing its symptoms.

Family therapy has many schools of thought. **Structural and strategic approaches** share a focus on the organization (structure) of the family system and use active interventions (strategies) to disrupt dysfunctional patterns. Structural and strategic therapists attend to boundaries between generations, alliances and schisms between family members, the hierarchy of power in the family, and family homeostatic mechanisms (Aponte & VanDeusen, 1981; Elizur & Minuchin, 1989; Minuchin, 1974; Richardson, 1991). In one family with an anorexic daughter, the therapist discovered that the father forbade his children to close the doors to their rooms and felt more intimate with his daughter than his wife. Hypothesizing that the father-daughter relationship might underlie the girl's refusal to eat (particularly since the symptom postponed physical maturation and puberty), the therapist prescribed as a first step that the daughter be allowed to keep her door closed for two hours a day and that the parents spend an hour each evening together in their room with the door closed (Hoffman, 1981).

Another approach to family therapy is the **intergenerational approach** of Murray Bowen (1978; Kerr & Bowen, 1988). Bowen argues that people have difficulty maintaining satisfying relationships when they have not successfully resolved issues from their family of origin. Typically, these issues involve either overdependence or a total break, in which the person is cut off emotionally or physically from important people from the past. Being emotionally caught up with unsettled scores from the past can make satisfying involvement with a spouse or child difficult. Bowen developed an assessment technique called a **genogram**, a map of a family over three or four generations (Figure 16.4). The clinician supplements this bare-bones picture of the family by adding the patient's comments about each person or relationship depicted in the genogram, looking for possible similarities between current difficulties and the family's past. Unlike other family therapies, intergenerational family therapy can be conducted with a single family member without actually bringing in everyone.

A variant of family therapy, called **marital** or **couples therapy**, focuses on a smaller system, the marital unit or couple. The therapist may see the spouses individually, together, or some combination of the two. Many marital therapists take

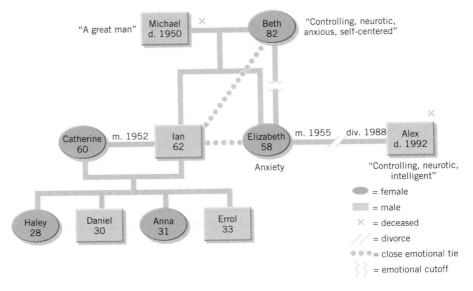

FIGURE 16.4
A genogram. The patient, Elizabeth, sought treatment for anxiety. From the genogram, the therapist could see that she was cut off from her mother, who remained close to her brother, which left her feeling left out. She also appeared to have married a man somewhat like her mother, and to be anxious like her mother.

primarily a family systems approach, looking for problematic communication or interaction patterns. For example, one couple was trapped in a cycle in which the husband did something, the wife criticized it, and the husband felt angry and helpless and tried to defend himself (Haley, 1971, pp. 275–276). When the therapist pointed out the pattern, the wife responded, "I have to criticize, because he never does what he should," to which the husband replied, "Well, I try"—which was precisely the pattern repeating itself again.

Marital therapists may also adopt psychodynamic or cognitive-behavioral perspectives. The goal of psychodynamic marital therapy is to help both people discover the ways their wishes, fears, and expectations of their partners reflect patterns from the past. A man who complained that his wife was unsupportive repeatedly changed the subject or criticized his wife during therapy sessions every time she was about to do or say something supportive. He appeared to be replaying his experience of his parents' highly critical relationship, which unconsciously guided his expectations of his wife and their interactions.

Behavioral marital therapy addresses the ways spouses often control each other's behavior in inefficient and punishing ways. Cognitive-behavioral therapists use techniques such as building communication skills, assertiveness training, and "good faith" contracts in which each spouse takes responsibility for changing something that is bothering the other (Goldfried & Davidson, 1994). Cognitive marital therapy techniques focus on irrational beliefs spouses hold about themselves and one another. Teaching couples conflict management strategies before they even encounter difficulties can also be an effective preventative measure (Markman et al., 1993).

BIOLOGICAL TREATMENTS

The approaches we have examined thus far are all, broadly speaking, psychosocial, using experiential and interpersonal interventions to address psychological problems. A very different type of treatment emerges from the view that psychological disorders reflect pathology of the brain, particularly of the neurotransmitters that carry messages from one neuron to another. Biological treatments use medication to restore the brain to as normal functioning as possible (pharmacotherapy), or if medications are ineffective, they use electroconvulsive (shock) therapy or psychosurgery. (Unlike psychotherapy, which can be administered by a variety of clinicians, such as psychologists and clinical social workers, biological treatments can only be administered by physicians.)

FROM MIND TO BRAIN

PSYCHOTROPIC MEDICATIONS

For many years, patients with severe mental illness were sent to state mental hospitals, which provided little more than custodial care in overcrowded wards. But with the discovery of **psychotropic medications**, drugs that act on the brain to affect mental processes (Table 16.2), care of psychiatric patients changed dramatically. In 1956, chlorpromazine (trade name Thorazine) was introduced to treat schizophrenia, and the population of state mental institutions dropped rapidly thereafter (Figure 16.5). Patients who did remain hospitalized were less likely to require physical restraint or isolation (see Berger, 1976, 1978; Davis, 1985; Simpson & May, 1985). The recent discovery of a new chemical agent, clozapine (trade name Clozaril), has led to substantial improvement in an additional 30 percent of psychotic patients who have not

TABLE 16.2 PSYCHOTROPIC MEDICATIONS

SYMPTOM	TYPE OF MEDICATION	EXAMPLES
Psychosis	Antipsychotics	chlorpromazine (Thorazine) clozapine (Clozaril)
Depression	Tricyclic antidepressants	trazodone (Desyrel) amitriptyline (Elavil) desipramine (Nopramin)
	MAO inhibitors	phenelzine (Nardil)
	Selective serotonin reuptake inhibitors	fluoxetine (Prozac)
Mania	Mood stabilizers	lithium (Lithonate)
Anxiety	Anxiolitics	benzodiazepines (Valium, Xanax)
	Antidepressants	(see medications for depression, above)

responded to chlorpromazine or other medications (Kane et al., 1988; Perry et al., 1991; Pickar et al., 1992) and may prove more effective for less chronically disturbed schizophrenic patients as well (Breier et al., 1994).

Many of the first drugs for treating mental illness were discovered serendipitously, when physicians and researchers using them to treat one medical condition noticed that they altered another (Davis, 1985). For example, when J. F. Cade, an Australian researcher, gave animals a lithium salt as part of his research into animal metabolism and behavior, he noticed that the animals became calm and quiet. Further investigation showed that lithium was an effective treatment for bipolar disorder (Baldessarini, 1985), although researchers still do not fully understand the mechanisms by which it works (Bunney et al., 1992; Matsui-Yuasas & Otani, 1992; McCance et al., 1992).

Psychotropic medications act at neurotransmitter sites (Figure 16.6). Different drugs act in different ways, although as with lithium, our understanding of their mechanisms is still speculative (see Cooper et al., 1991; Grabowski & VandenBos, 1992). Some drugs inhibit overactive neurotransmitters or receptors that are overly sensitive, which lead to too-frequent firing. One way they can do this is by "locking up" the postsynaptic membrane, binding with receptors that would naturally bind with the neurotransmitter (part *a* of Figure 16.6). This renders the postsynaptic receptors unable to fire as frequently or at all.

FIGURE 16.5
Impact of chlorpromazine on institutionalization. The populations of state and county psychiatric hospitals declined rapidly after the introduction of the antipsychotic medication, chlorpromazine. SOURCE: *Adapted from Davis, 1985.*

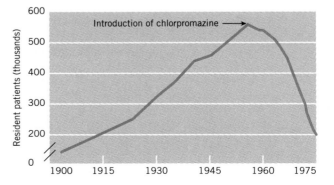

(*a*) Decreases neural transmission

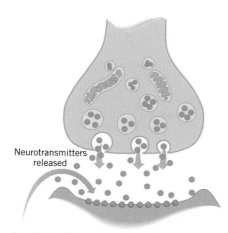

(*b*) Increases neural transmission by blocking reuptake

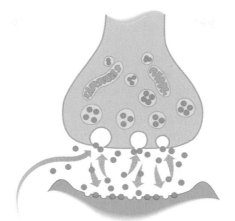

(*c*) Increases neural transmission by blocking breakdown of neurotransmitters in synaptic vesicles

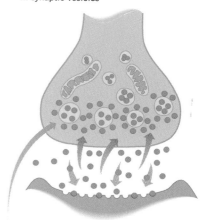

Neurotransmitters released

Drug binds with receptors to prevent them from being activated by the neurotransmitters in the synapse.

Drug blocks neurotransmitters from being taken back into the presynaptic membrane, leaving the neurotransmitters in the synapse longer.

Drug prevents the neurotransmitter returning from the synapse from being broken down for storage, making it readily available at the synapse.

FIGURE 16.6

The therapeutic action of psychotropic medications. This figure depicts three neural mechanisms by which psychotropic medications can reduce symptoms. Psychotropics can decrease neural transmission of overactive neurotransmitters (a), or increase neural transmission where neurotransmitters are depleted (b and c).

Other medications have the opposite effect, increasing the action of neurotransmitters that are underactive or in short supply. They may do this in various ways. Some medications prevent the neurotransmitter from being taken back into the presynaptic membrane, causing the neurotransmitter to remain in the synapse and hence to facilitate further firing (part *b* of Figure 16.6). Others prevent the neurotransmitter from being broken down once it has returned to the presynaptic neuron, leading to more ready release of the chemical from the vesicles that store neurotransmitters (part *c*).

Not all the beneficial effects of psychotropic medications stem from their molecular structure. Their psychological and cultural "composition" also influence their efficacy. Both Western and non-Western cultures have long known the healing power of the placebo. Since a patient's expectation of cure is influenced by cultural beliefs about the causes of mental illness, even drugs or herbal remedies that have no known physiological action can be health-promoting simply because the person has faith that they will work (Torrey, 1986). In the same way, placebo effects can boost the power of medications that are biologically efficacious. Thus, chemical agents can affect the mind via the brain, or they can affect the brain via the mind.

Antipsychotic Medications

The drugs used to treat schizophrenia and other acute psychotic states are called **antipsychotic medications**. They are also sometimes called major tranquilizers because many are highly sedating, but their efficacy is not reducible to their tranquilizing effect.

The most widely accepted biological hypothesis about the positive symptoms (of schizophrenia, such as delusions and hallucinations) is that they result from too much dopamine (Chapter 15). Antipsychotic medications, which inhibit the action of dopamine, reduce precisely these symptoms. Unfortunately, antipsychotics typically have far less effect on negative symptoms such as flattened affect and interpersonal difficulties (Carpenter, 1992).

Few competent clinicians doubt the enormous utility of antipsychotic medications for treating schizophrenia, which has been documented in thousands of studies (see Davidson et al., 1991; Volavka et al., 1992). These medications can, however, have significant side effects, some of which are almost as debilitating and socially devastating as the disorder itself. Because dopamine is found in many regions of the brain and serves many functions, blocking its overactivity in one region may have the unwanted effect of inhibiting its normal functions in another. The most serious side effect is a movement disorder called **tardive dyskinesia** (*tardive*, meaning late or tardy in onset, and *dyskinesia*, meaning disorder of movement), in which the patient develops involuntary twitching, typically involving the tongue, face, and neck. Tardive dyskinesia does not occur in all patients, and it usually only arises with prolonged use, but it is unpredictable, can occur at any point during the treatment, and is largely irreversible. Of patients in a chronic ward of a Montreal hospital who had received antipsychotics on the average of 20 years, 30 to 40 percent showed symptoms of tardive dyskinesia (Yassa et al., 1990). Because the side effects of prolonged administration can be so severe and because antipsychotics are often ineffective for treating the more chronic negative symptoms, they are usually prescribed in high doses during acute phases and lower doses between episodes.

Antidepressant and Mood-Stabilizing Medications

Psychosis is not the only condition amenable to psychotropic drugs. For some patients, particularly those with severe depressions that include physiological symptoms such as sleep disturbance or loss of appetite, **antidepressant medications** can be very effective (Maj et al., 1992; Montgomery, 1994). Antidepressants increase the amount of norepinephrine, serotonin, or both available in synapses; these neurotransmitters are depleted in many cases of depression. Contrary to some popular misconceptions, antidepressants are not "uppers" like amphetamines; they do not make normal people feel euphoric (Davis, 1985).

Several different types of antidepressant medications have proven effective in treating depression. The **tricyclic antidepressants,** so named for their molecular structure, act by blocking reuptake of serotonin and norepinephrine into the presynaptic membrane (Baldessarini, 1985; Davis, 1985; Grabowski & VandenBos, 1992). In other words, they cause the neurotransmitter to stay in the synapse longer and hence compensate for depleted neurotransmitters. Trycyclics can be extremely effective. Double-blind studies (in which neither the patient nor the physician knows whether the patient is taking the drug or an inert placebo) have found improvement rates of 70 to 80 percent compared to 20 to 40 percent for placebo (Maj et al., 1992; Prien, 1988). Frequently prescribed tricyclics include trazadone (trade name Desyrel), amitriptyline (Elavil), and desipramine (Norpramin).

Some patients who do not respond well to tricyclics do respond to **monoamine oxidase (MAO) inhibitors** (Prien, 1988; Quitkin et al., 1991). MAO inhibitors keep the chemical MAO from breaking down neurotransmitter substances in the presynaptic neuron, which makes more neurotransmitter available for release into the synapse. MAO inhibitors are more effective than tricyclics in the treatment of many depressed patients with personality disorders, particularly borderline personality disorders (Gardner & Cowdry, 1988; Gunderson, 1986; Quitkin et al., 1991).

The third and most recently developed class of antidepressants, **selective serotonin reuptake inhibitors (SSRIs),** target serotonin rather than norepinephrine. SSRIs have fewer side effects than other antidepressants and are better tolerated over prolonged periods (Leonard, 1993). The best known SSRI is fluoxetine (Prozac), which has vastly expanded the patient population for whom antidepressants are prescribed since its approval for use in the United States in 1988. No longer are people with severe depression the only candidates for antidepressants. SSRIs have helped people with chronic mild depression significantly improve their overall mood as well as their social functioning (Kramer, 1993). However, the use of psychotropic medications for people who are not seriously depressed is somewhat controversial. Detractors, who refer to the practice as "cosmetic psychopharmacology," see this as the first step down the road to Aldous Huxley's *Brave New World*, in which everyone takes a pill called "soma" to avoid any psychological distress.

For bipolar depression, **lithium** is the treatment of choice, although other medications are sometimes effective for manic patients who are not responsive to it (Calabrese & Delucchi, 1990; Cooper et al., 1991). Improvement rates in the range of 70 to 80 percent are common for patients with acute mania or hypomania (a milder form of mania) who receive lithium (Baldessarini, 1985; Grabowski & VandenBos, 1992; Keller et al., 1992). Lithium acts relatively slowly, often taking three or four weeks to begin having an effect, so in the acute phases of mania patients are usually treated simultaneously with antipsychotics to clear their thinking until the lithium "kicks in."

Perhaps the most serious side effect of medications for both unipolar and bipolar depression is that they can be lethal if used for suicide attempts. Prescribing potentially toxic drugs to depressed people obviously carries risks of overdose. Antidepressants can also have minor side effects, including weight gain, dry mouth, sweating, or blurred vision. Patients on MAO inhibitors may experience restlessness, hyperactivity, or agitation, and they must restrict their diets, cutting out certain foods, including cheese and red wine, that interact dangerously with the drug (Davis, 1985). The side effects of lithium are usually mild compared to the potentially disastrous effects of the disorder or the side effects of antipsychotic medications; patients may experience a fine tremor, weight gain, nausea, and lightheadedness.

Antianxiety Medications

Antianxiety medications called **benzodiazepines** can be useful for short-term treatment of anxiety symptoms, as with Jenny, who experienced a brief period of intense anxiety. The earliest drug of this class that was widely prescribed was diazepam (Valium), but it has since been supplanted by other medications such as alprazolam (Xanax), which are more effective in treating panic symptoms. These medications increase the activity of GABA (Chapter 3), a neurotransmitter that inhibits activation throughout the nervous system. Thus, by increasing the activity of an inhibitory neurotransmitter, they reduce anxiety. Unfortunately, anxiety symptoms, particularly panic, tend to recur as soon as medication is discontinued (Noyes et al., 1991).

Psychiatrists have more recently been prescribing antidepressants rather than benzodiazepines for anxiety, particularly for panic disorder (Fyer & Sandberg, 1988; Liebowitz et al., 1992; Mavissakalian & Perel, 1992). While the impact of antidepressants on depression generally takes three to four weeks, anxiety symptoms usually respond within a week. The notion of prescribing antidepressants to treat anxiety seems counterintuitive; however, many neurotransmitters have multiple functions, and neurotransmitter systems are interdependent, so that altering one can lead to widespread effects on others. Some neurotransmitters are even used in the synthesis of others; norepinephrine, for example, is synthesized from dopamine. Controlled comparisons show that both antidepressants and antianxiety medications are more effective than placebo in relieving anxiety symptoms (Rickels et al., 1994).

Antianxiety medications are not without their drawbacks. Patients can become both physiologically and psychologically dependent on them. Many fear that if they get off the medications they will become crippled with panic again. They may in fact be right: The relapse rate after discontinuing antianxiety drugs is very high (see

Mavissakalian & Perel, 1992; O'Sullivan, 1991). Nevertheless, some anxiety symptoms such as recurrent panics can be so unpleasant or debilitating that medications are clearly in order, particularly in combination with psychotherapy.

Electroconvulsive Therapy and Psychosurgery

Two other biological treatments that were more widely used in previous eras are electroconvulsive therapy and psychosurgery. **Electroconvulsive therapy (ECT)**, also known as electroshock therapy, is currently used as a last resort in the treatment of severe depression (see Weiner & Krystal, 1994). Patients lie on an insulated cart or bed and are anesthetized, and electrodes are placed on their heads to administer an electric shock strong enough to induce a seizure. The mechanisms by which ECT works are not known, but its efficacy seems to depend on eliciting a seizure (Frankel, 1984).

The horrifying idea of deliberately shocking a person conjures up images of unscrupulous or overworked mental health professionals using technology to control unruly patients. But ECT can in fact be the only hope for some patients with crippling depression, and it can be remarkably effective in those cases. Studies have found that ECT is more effective than antidepressant drugs in the treatment of many severe depressions, particularly **delusional depressions**, which have psychotic features (Buchan et al., 1992; Goodwin & Roy-Byrne, 1987). As with other therapies for depression, however, relapse rates are high, sometimes requiring readministration a few months later (Weiner & Coffey, 1988). ECT can also sometimes be useful in treating mania (Hanin et al., 1993), but it is ineffective for schizophrenia, for which it was once widely used and abused. Recent research suggests that ECT can also be effective in treating obsessive-compulsive disorder (Maletzky et al., 1994).

The main side effect of ECT is memory loss; however, this has been ameliorated by the discovery that applying electrodes to only one hemisphere is virtually as effective as the bilateral procedures once common. Figure 16.7 demonstrates the dramatic recovery of severely depressed patients treated with ECT applied either to the right or the left hemisphere. After three to six treatments, their depression was eliminated (Abrams et al., 1989).

Those who think that "shock therapy" is a brutal invention of technologically developed Western societies are incorrect in another respect. Hieroglyphics on the walls of Egyptian tombs depict the use of electrical fish (such as eels) to numb emo-

ECT may seem barbaric, but for some severely depressed individuals it is the only hope.

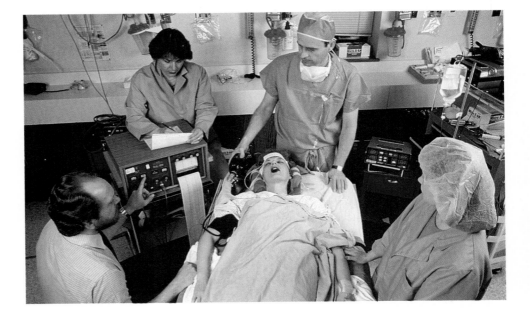

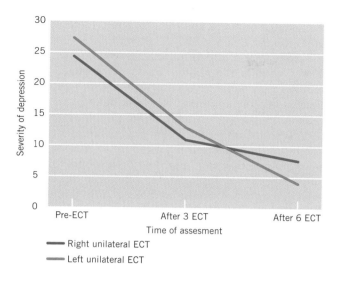

FIGURE 16.7
The effects of unilateral ECT on depressed patients. Applying ECT to either the right or left hemisphere dramatically reduces depressive symptoms. SOURCE: *Abrams et al., 1989.*

tional states, and a number of Greek writers, including Aristotle, make reference to the practice. A medieval priest living in Ethiopia observed the use of electrical catfish to drive the devil out of the human body. Today, the San Blas Indians, who live off the coast of Panama and have been relatively untouched by Western culture, use a potion that induces convulsions to quell psychotic states (Torrey, 1986).

Another procedure that was once widely practiced is **psychosurgery**, brain surgery to reduce psychological symptoms. Like ECT, psychosurgery is an ancient practice. Fossilized remains from thousands of years ago show holes bored in the skulls, presumably to allow demons to escape from the heads of mentally ill individuals, much as in some preliterate cultures studied by anthropologists. The most widely practiced Western psychosurgery technique was the **lobotomy**, which involved severing tissue in a cerebral lobe, usually the frontal (Valenstein, 1988). Before the development of psychotropic drugs, some clinicians, frustrated in trying to treat the mentally ill patients who jammed the state institutions, embraced psychosurgery as a way of calming patients who were violent or otherwise difficult to manage. Two leaders in psychosurgery were Egas Moniz, a Portuguese neurologist who introduced the frontal lobotomy in 1935 and received the Nobel Prize for his work, and Walter Freeman, an American neurologist and psychiatrist who popularized the use of lobotomies. Freeman traveled throughout the United States performing his technique, termed a transorbital lobotomy. The procedure involved

In One Flew Over the Cuckoo's Nest, *Jack Nicholson's character lost his aggressiveness—but also his personality—following a frontal lobotomy.*

inserting a cutting tool into the socket of each eye and then rotating the tool to cut the fibers at the base of the frontal lobes.

Lobotomy reached its peak between 1949 and 1952, during which time neurosurgeons performed about 5000 a year in the United States (Valenstein, 1986, 1988). Unfortunately, the procedure rarely cured psychosis (Robin, 1958) and often had devastating side effects. Patients became apathetic, lost self-control, and could no longer think abstractly (Freeman, 1959), as portrayed in the popular book and film, *One Flew over the Cuckoo's Nest*. More recently, however, psychiatrists have been experimenting with a much more limited surgical procedure to treat severely debilitating cases of obsessive-compulsive disorder that do not respond to other forms of treatment (Goodman et al., 1993; Insel, 1992; Jenike et al., 1991). Psychosurgery is also the only effective treatment for intractable seizures that do not respond to medication.

EVALUATING PSYCHOLOGICAL TREATMENTS

One of the most difficult issues facing researchers trying to evaluate the effectiveness of various treatments for psychological disorders is that symptoms tend to diminish over time regardless of any therapeutic intervention. Roughly 30 to 40 percent of patients spontaneously improve without treatment because people seek treatment when they are most distressed and symptomatic and they develop ways of coping with their problems on their own. But what of those individuals who receive treatment? How effective are the various approaches? And can they be combined to maximize their efficacy?

Pharmacotherapy

The utility of pharmacotherapy for several disorders is well established. Antipsychotic medication is essential in the treatment of schizophrenia (see Davidson et al., 1991; Volavka et al., 1992), although full recovery is unusual. Lithium and other mood-stabilizing drugs are similarly indispensable for bipolar disorder (Keller et al., 1992; Pope et al., 1991), although some bipolar patients remain chronically unstable. In addition, as we have seen, medication can also be useful in treating some anxiety and mood disorders. Medication has proven useful for disorders ranging from obsessive-compulsive disorder (Clomipramine Collaborative Study Group, 1991; Goodman et al., 1990; Rapoport et al., 1992) to bulimia (Mitchell et al., 1990).

A major problem associated with biological treatments, however, is the high relapse rate when pharmacotherapy is terminated. One way to minimize this drawback is to continue the medication for a considerable length of time after the treatment has succeeded, usually at a lower dosage (see Montgomery, 1994). As shown in Figure 16.8, most people who experience a major depressive episode will experience another within five years, but continued preventive use of antidepressants can somewhat temper the tendency to relapse (Maj et al., 1992). Similarly, treating bulimia with antidepressants can lessen the symptoms substantially but rarely completely, and relapse is common (Walsh et al., 1991). Psychopharmacological interventions can also have serious side effects.

Psychotherapy

People who enter into psychotherapy also fare considerably better than those who try to heal themselves (Lambert et al., 1986; Parloff et al., 1986). Researchers have demonstrated this using a statistical technique called **meta-analysis**, which

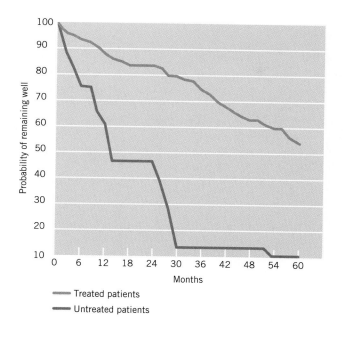

FIGURE 16.8
Relapse rates with and without medication. The figure shows the effects of prophylactic (preventive) use of antidepressant medication or lithium. Virtually all untreated patients relapsed within three years. Prophylactic use of medication was clearly helpful, although the majority of patients (65 percent) nevertheless relapsed by five years. SOURCE: *Maj et al., 1992.*

Treated patients

Untreated patients

allows them to aggregate, or combine, the findings of diverse studies, yielding a measure of the average effect of psychotherapy. Beginning with a pioneering study in the late 1970s (Smith & Glass, 1977), meta-analyses have shown that the average patient who receives psychotherapy is essentially 25 percent better off than the average control subject, as shown in Figure 16.9 (see Andrews & Harvey, 1981; Landman & Dawes, 1982). In other words, the bell-shaped curve for subjects who have been treated is shifted in the direction of mental health, so that a person in the fiftieth percentile of mental health in the group receiving treatment would be in the seventy-fifth percentile of subjects if now placed in the control group. This is a substantial shift, equivalent to the difference in reading skill between a third-grader who goes to school and one who stays home and gets no instruction for a year (Lambert et al., 1986). The success of treatment is also directly related to its duration (Howard et al., 1986). Longer treatments are generally associated with more successful outcomes (Figure 16.10).

How effective are the specific psychotherapies we have examined? The answer is more complicated than it seems because many criteria enter into the concept of "successful" treatment. For example, a researcher could measure average improvement, percentage of patients who improve, or relapse rate. One treatment might lead to 90 percent improvement but in only 50 percent of patients, whereas another could reduce symptoms by only 50 percent but do so in 90 percent of patients. Furthermore, one treatment might be very effective but slow and costly; is this, then,

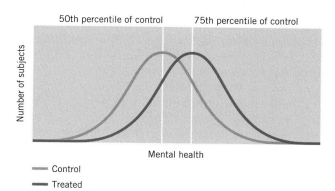

Control

Treated

FIGURE 16.9
Effectiveness of psychotherapy. Researchers aggregated the findings of 375 studies to assess the effectiveness of psychotherapy. Subjects treated with psychotherapy were, on the average, substantially better off than untreated control subjects. SOURCE: *Adapted from Smith & Glass, 1977.*

FIGURE 16.10
Length and efficacy of psychotherapy. The graph shows the relation between the number of sessions of psychotherapy and the percentage of patients improved, according to observer reports (blue line) and self-reports (red line). The more sessions, the more patients improved. Improvement leveled off between 50 and 100 sessions (usually one to two years at once per week). SOURCE: *Howard et al., 1986.*

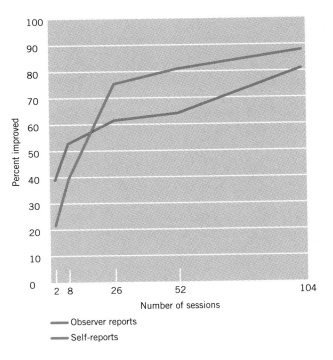

a more effective treatment than one that is less ambitious but faster and cheaper? The results of outcome studies also vary depending on who rates improvement: the therapist, an outside observer, or the patient (Lambert et al., 1986).

Each of the major approaches has evidence for its efficacy, though to widely varying degrees. The effectiveness of cognitive-behavioral therapy is much better established than any other form of psychotherapy, especially for anxiety disorders (Chambless & Gillis, 1993; Laberge et al., 1993; Michelson & Marchione, 1991; Zinbarg et al., 1992). For example, one study (Beck et al., 1992) compared a cognitive-behavioral with a Rogerian therapy for panic disorder (Table 16.3). Subjects in the cognitive-behavioral treatment, which addressed patients' fears about panic-related bodily sensations, showed a substantial decrease in panic symptoms, and at one-year followup, 87 percent were free of panic attacks. An 87 percent improvement rate is probably the best of any treatment for any disorder. Cognitive-behavioral therapy is also useful for treating common maladies such as performance anxiety in musicians (Clark & Agras, 1991).

Considerable research has also demonstrated the usefulness of cognitive therapy for depression (Hollon et al., 1993; Scogin & McElreath, 1994; Thase et al., 1991). Many studies have, however, screened out patients with personality disorders, who typically do not respond to treatment. Furthermore, relapse rates are extremely high, even among patients who appear at first to have successful outcomes. For example, a project that has been studying cognitive therapy patients over time screened over 130 depressed patients, of whom only 76 were deemed suitable for the treatment plan. Of these, 23 fully recovered and 27 partially recovered by the end of treatment. Within a year, 16 of these 50 successful cases had fully relapsed (Thase et al., 1992). Thus, at one year, the success rate was really only 34 out of 130, or roughly 20 percent of the depressed patients who walked into the clinic.

Psychodynamic, humanistic, group, and marital therapies have not been subjected to as much empirical scrutiny as cognitive-behavioral treatments. Only in recent years have psychodynamic clinicians shown much interest in demonstrating the effectiveness of their techniques (see Blatt, 1992; Blatt et al., 1994; Piper, 1993; Wallerstein, 1989). Empirically sound studies of long-term psychodynamic treatments are very rare, in part because psychoanalysts have long held that the value of their techniques is self-evident, and in part because funding agencies have been

TABLE 16.3 EFFECTIVENESS OF TWO KINDS OF THERAPY FOR PANIC

MEASURE	MEAN NUMBER OF ATTACKS		
	Before Treatment	After 4 Weeks of Treatment	After 8 Weeks of Treatment
Clinician rating			
Cognitive-behavioral	5.6	1.4	.4
Rogerian	4.4	3.2	3.1
Self-rating			
Cognitive-behavioral	5.2	2.0	.8
Rogerian	5.5	3.7	2.5

Source: Adapted from Beck et al., 1992.

Note. Both therapies were effective for treating panic attacks; however, according to both clinician- and self-reports, the cognitive-behavioral was more effective.

reluctant to support studies of treatments lasting longer than six months—which are the most widespread treatments in clinical practice.

Studies of short-term psychodynamic psychotherapies are much more common and demonstrate a clear advantage over no treatment (Crits-Christoph, 1992). Psychodynamic therapy has also proven useful in treating medical conditions that can be affected by psychological factors. For example, psychodynamic therapy stabilized the physical condition of children with life-threatening cases of diabetes who had not responded to medical treatment (Fonagy & Moran, 1990). The only study of marital therapy that has followed patients beyond two years after termination found insight-oriented psychodynamic treatment more beneficial than behavioral marital therapy (Snyder et al., 1991). At four-year followup, only 3 percent of couples treated psychodynamically were divorced, compared with 38 percent of those treated with behavioral techniques.

Humanistic and other treatments are, like psychodynamic psychotherapies, less grounded in solid empirical work. Where evidence exists, however, they are generally as effective as other psychotherapies. For example, in a study of Hispanic children and their families, both psychodynamic and family therapy were superior to a control condition in reducing a range of symptoms, but family therapy was superior in improving family interactions (Szapocznik et al., 1989). A promising new humanistic therapy (called experiential therapy), which integrates Gestalt and Rogerian principles with careful scientific investigation of therapy process and outcome, has also demonstrated considerable efficacy (Greenberg, 1990; Greenberg et al., 1993).

Commentary: Are All Treatments Created Equal?

Although advocates of different treatments typically argue for the superiority of their own brand, most research suggests that different therapies yield comparable effects (Smith & Glass, 1977). This is certainly counterintuitive. How could a treatment predicated on the view that psychopathology stems from unconscious conflicts have the same effect as one that denies their existence or importance?

In addressing this question, one must bear in mind that studies comparing different treatments have some serious methodological limitations. The therapies offered to patients for research purposes frequently bear little resemblance to the way therapy is actually practiced (Persons, 1992). For example, psychodynamic treatments often last three to five years, yet nearly every study ever done has assessed treatments averaging five to fifteen total *sessions*. Perhaps the greatest complication in comparing different therapies is experimenter bias: One of the best predictors of the relative efficacy of one treatment over another in any given study is the strength of the investigator's commitment to that treatment (Smith et al., 1980).

Making matters more complicated still, patients differ in their response to different treatments (Beutler, 1991). Even patients who share a diagnosis, such as depression, differ substantially in other respects, so that comparing mean outcome scores across treatment groups may obscure the fact that different treatments are successful with different patients. For example, panic disorders probably best respond to cognitive-behavioral treatments. Many panic patients, however, also have personality disorders that influence the success of cognitive-behavioral interventions and may require long-term psychotherapy. Effective treatment for alcoholics may also depend on whether or not they have broader personality disturbances. In one study, alcoholic patients received either a cognitive-behavioral group therapy with coping skills training or a less structured, psychodynamically oriented group therapy. An important interaction between patient type and therapy type emerged: The healthier group of alcoholics had better outcome (less relapse) with a psychodynamic treatment focusing on insight into their interpersonal dynamics, whereas the more severe group profited more from the structured coping-focused group (Litt et al., 1992).

The most definitive evidence yet collected about the relative effectiveness of different treatments comes from a nonpartisan study of depression conducted by the National Institutes of Mental Health (NIMH) (Elkin et al., 1989). The NIMH study compared three treatments for patients with major depression: cognitive therapy, interpersonal therapy (a short-term offshoot of psychodynamic psychotherapy), and imipramine (an antidepressant) combined with supportive clinical management (regular meetings with a concerned physician). A fourth group of control subjects received a placebo with supportive clinical management. The purpose of giving supportive management to the latter two groups, particularly the placebo group, was to determine whether the effectiveness of psychotherapy is reducible simply to giving patients regular and kind attention. The study was conducted at several treatment sites, with collaborators from different perspectives administering treatments according to standardized treatment manuals. Biases imposed by investigator allegiances could thus be minimized and assessed. Finally, a total of 250 subjects participated in the study, a very large number compared to previous studies.

For all intents and purposes, the three treatments fared equally well. Initial results found both imipramine and interpersonal therapy significantly better than placebo, while the difference between cognitive therapy and placebo fell just short of statistical significance. None of the three treatment approaches worked significantly better than the others, except that cognitive therapy proved ineffective for more severe depressions. Thus, at least for short-term treatments, all treatments have relatively similar outcomes. Longer-term followup evaluation of the subjects who participated in this study revealed that most continued to show improvement (Shea et al., 1992); only a minority, however, met the criteria for full recovery.

One possible explanation for different treatments having similar outcomes is that, despite their specific mechanisms (such as altering compromise-formations or inhibiting negative automatic thoughts), they share **common factors**—that is, shared elements that produce positive outcomes (Arnkoff et al., 1993; Frank, 1978; Lambert et al., 1986; Weinberger, 1994). Such factors include empathy, a warm relationship between therapist and client, and instilling a sense of hope or efficacy in coping with the problem (Grencavage & Norcross, 1990). Recent evidence suggests, in fact, that patients' perceptions of therapeutic empathy play a crucial role even in cognitive therapy, which is highly structured and technical (Burns & Nolan-Hoeksema, 1992). A positive therapeutic alliance with the therapist also predicts positive outcome in the treatment of schizophrenics, who are then more likely to take their medication regularly (Frank & Gunderson, 1990).

A Different Perspective: Psychotherapy Integration

All the treatments described in this chapter have their limitations, and each is likely to be effective with only a subset of patients. For example, psychodynamic psychotherapy tends to be time-consuming, expensive, and inefficient for treating some disorders. Cognitive-behavioral therapy frequently lacks the depth to treat enduring interpersonal pathologies such as personality disorders, where motivational and emotional disturbances are as or more central than cognitive distortions (though see Beck, 1993; Beck & Freeman, 1990; Linehan, 1991). Biological treatments are appropriate for treating disorders with a genetic or organic basis but are inappropriate for treating many disorders for which the symptoms reflect a person's learning history, conflicts, or interpersonal concerns. Since no therapy is effective across the board, some mental health professionals argue that the best strategy is **psychotherapy integration**, either choosing techniques selectively to suit the individual case (sometimes called eclectic therapy) or relying on theory that cuts across different perspectives (sometimes called integrative psychotherapy) (Beitman et al., 1989; Clarkin et al., 1993).

As noted earlier, Jenny's therapists used many forms of therapy in treating her anorexia. Her individual psychotherapy integrated behavioral and psychodynamic principles. As an outpatient, Jenny's weight was at first precarious, so her therapist required her to weigh in at her doctor's office and bring a slip each week to therapy reporting her weight. Jenny found this acutely embarrassing, so her therapist made a behavioral contract with her: If she maintained her weight for several weeks, he would stop asking to see her weight unless she obviously appeared to be losing again. Aside from reinforcing appropriate behavior, this arrangement led to exploration of Jenny's need to be in control, her anger at feeling controlled by her therapist, and ultimately to her longstanding ambivalence about her mother's dependence on her that left her feeling both controlled and controlling. Thus, a behavioral intervention generated a transference reaction that led to discovery of repressed ambivalence toward her mother and a problematic family dynamic of role reversal between mother and daughter.

Although the notion of therapeutic integration is intuitively appealing, it is difficult to practice because the assumptions, methods, and techniques of the various approaches are so different (Arkowitz & Messer, 1984; Messer & Winokur, 1980). How can a clinician integrate principles of therapy derived from a theory that emphasizes unconscious conflict and compromise with one that focuses instead on conditioning?

Perhaps the best example of an integrative approach comes from Paul Wachtel (1977, 1987, 1994). Wachtel, who was originally trained psychodynamically, contends that insight into the dynamics of a problem, though often essential to treatment, is not enough: Behavioral techniques can be invaluable in encouraging the patient to confront the problem and developing the necessary skills to master it. For example, a patient who is afraid of his own and other people's anger, and hence avoids confrontations at all costs, may develop a psychodynamic understanding of the ways he runs from anger in many areas of his life and may link this pattern to a fearful relationship with his father as a child. Yet he may remain unable to confront people because the anxiety associated with confrontation is a conditioned emotional response that motivates avoidance and needs to be extinguished. The therapist may thus need to take a more active stance, encouraging the patient, applying operant techniques (such as rewarding confrontive behavior with praise), or role-playing confrontations to desensitize him to real-life confrontations. At the same time, the patient may benefit from examining the way he avoids confrontations with the therapist (examining transference) when he feels the therapist has misunderstood him or made a mistake.

Wachtel has also proposed ways of integrating psychodynamic and family systems therapy, based on the notion that maladaptive interpersonal strategies are maintained through both internal psychodynamic processes and the behavior of significant others, who serve as "accomplices" (Wachtel & Wachtel, 1984). A patient who is depressed and self-hating is often part of a larger family or marital system, and other people in the system may have vested interests in the symptom. The husband of a patient who seeks treatment for low self-esteem may have a need to degrade or dominate his wife, based on a problematic relationship with his own mother, so that he may actively resist his wife's efforts to get better unless he is included in the treatment. Thus, a single mode of treatment—such as treating the wife's self-esteem with cognitive therapy—may fail because it leaves other important factors that caused or maintain the problem untouched. Helping the husband develop insight into his conflicts with his mother and altering the way the couple communicates may be equally important parts of a treatment plan.

THE BROADER CONTEXT OF PSYCHOLOGICAL TREATMENT

What clinicians consider therapeutic depends on their perspective, but their views of appropriate treatment also reflect cultural values, beliefs, and economic pressures. In the West, attitudes toward treatment have changed along with attitudes toward psychological distress and disorder. Until recently, the popular assumption was that only "crazy" people sought psychiatric treatment. Although this stigma remains in some quarters, matters have changed dramatically. People today seek treatment for a wide range of problems, from panic attacks to trouble with intimacy. The kind of treatment they receive, however, depends as much on economics as on the nature of the problem or the perspective of the practitioner. In this final section, we explore the cultural and economic contexts of treatment.

A GLOBAL VISTA

CULTURE AND PSYCHOTHERAPY

In the industrialized nations of the West, which are highly individualistic by cross-cultural standards, most therapies assume that problems lie in individuals. This is particularly true in the United States (Jansen, 1986), with its historical tradition of rugged individualism. Both psychodynamic and cognitive therapies are predicated on the idea of restoring rational control where unreason has prevailed. The role played by the cognitive-behavioral therapist—who acts in many respects like a mechanic repairing malfunctioning behavioral machinery—is readily understood and embraced by people in a technologically developed society. When, during the 1960s, a segment of the culture rebelled against individualism and rationalism, other treatments emerged, notably group and humanistic therapies that advocated healing through communion with others and experiencing one's emotions (Strupp & Blackwood, 1985).

Cross-culturally, methods of treatment similarly depend on cultural value systems and beliefs about personality and psychopathology (Kleinman, 1988). Many cultures treat psychological disturbances by bringing the community together in healing rituals (Boesch, 1982; Turner, 1969). These rituals give the ill person a sense of social support and solidarity, similar to the healing properties of empathic relationships in many Western therapies. At the same time, by uniting families or extended kin whose conflicts may be contributing to the individual's symptoms, community healing rituals perform functions similar to family systems therapy.

Among the Ndembu of northwestern Zambia, a ritual doctor thoroughly "researches" the social situation of a person afflicted with illness, mental or physical (Turner, 1967). He listens to gossip and to the patient's dreams and persuades community members to confess any grudges. In one case, the patient held a position of power in the community but was greatly disliked. During the curing ritual, the patient was required to shed some blood, and members of the community were required to confess their hostilities. In this way, the ritual appeased all parties: The patient paid for his character defects with his blood, and the confession repaired social relationships. At the end of the ritual, the mood was jubilant, and people who had been estranged for years joined hands warmly.

A healing ritual among the San of Botswana. Are psychotherapists the witch doctors of the twentieth century West?

To the extent that successful treatment requires faith in the possibility of help, all psychotherapy—if not all medicine—is to some degree "faith healing." The factors that confer faith, however, differ dramatically from culture to culture (Torrey, 1986). Western cultures value academic achievement, and patients tend to respect therapists whose walls are filled with advanced degrees. In non-Western cultures, such as Nigeria, where witch doctors have practiced medicine for generations, family lineage and claims to supernatural powers are more likely to enhance a "therapist's" prestige. One could argue that neither academic achievement nor familial descent has any obvious influence on the degree to which a person can empathize with another, although the ability to convey warmth, genuineness, and empathy—which contributes to therapeutic success—is observed in healers throughout the world (see Triandis, 1994).

The Economics of Mental Health Care

In the West, economic pressures have probably exerted as much impact on treatment as cultural values and beliefs. The development of antipsychotic medications dramatically decreased the warehousing of mental patients, but what seemed the solution to one problem created another—deinstitutionalization.

Deinstitutionalization

Spurred by the efficacy of antipsychotic medications and by outrage at the conditions in many state mental hospitals, the **deinstitutionalization** movement sought to integrate patients whose severe disturbances could be treated with medication into the community. Unfortunately, in the United States, what began as an effort to increase the autonomy of patients gradually evolved into a program of dumping patients onto the street to trim federal and state budgets. The result has been both an abundance of homeless schizophrenic panhandlers (Lamb & Lamb, 1990) and a "criminalization" of mental illness, in which psychotic patients who cannot care for themselves are incarcerated when their disorders lead to acts that are illegal, such as disturbing the peace (Abram & Teplin, 1991; Teplin, 1984).

The problems of homelessness, lack of treatment, and criminalization of the mentally ill have been exacerbated by laws originally designed to protect people from being locked away without due process. Legal changes in the 1960s often arose from celebrated cases of people who were committed to mental institutions inappropriately. To hospitalize mentally ill people against their will in most states today requires not only that they be psychotic—that is, grossly out of touch with reality—but also that they be demonstrably dangerous to themselves or others. Unfortunately, this means that patients who could be treated for their disorders (such as mania, which is usually responsive to medication) and who could be presumed to want treatment if they were able to weigh their options rationally, too often become street people because no one has the authority to hospitalize or treat them if they refuse. For paranoid patients, who by definition are distrustful, or manic patients, who may destroy their relationships or spend their life savings while feeling euphoric, these changes in the law have often proven disastrous. Under the guise of civil liberties, municipalities often pass statutes that shield them from the responsibility of caring for deinstitutionalized patients. In one major American city, for example, a person suspected by mental health professionals of being dangerous or suicidal is sent a letter asking him to appear in court for a commitment hearing. If he does not appear, or if he is homeless and has no address, the police do not have the authority to pick him up until he commits a violent crime.

Managed Care

Even for people who seek help for much less disabling conditions, economic pressures are increasingly shaping the kind of treatment they receive. Mental health care, like all health care, costs money. In the United States, people with more money

The deinstitutionalization movement integrated the severely mentally ill into the community—but certainly not in the way initially intended.

generally receive more and better treatment, although many clinicians and practitioners see some patients on a sliding scale according to ability to pay. To contain spiraling costs, employers and public health programs such as Medicaid are increasingly turning to "managed care" and health maintenance organizations (HMOs). The most effective way for these for-profit health care companies to reduce costs, at least in the short run, is to offer only short-term treatments, such as medication and extremely brief psychotherapies. Thus, HMOs have been criticized for providing the least possible, rather than the best possible, care (Sederer, 1992; Shulman, 1988). At many HMOs, mental health coverage consists of five sessions per year, and case reviewers, some of whom may lack appropriate training in mental health, frequently decide how long patients stay in the hospital.

Although cost-containment is admittedly a major concern throughout the health care system and not just in mental health, HMOs and insurance companies commonly pay tens of thousands of dollars per patient for costly long-term medical treatments for diseases such as cancer, asthma, or emphysema. The policy difference between treatment for mental and physical disorders appears to reflect public attitudes of fear, prejudice, and neglect toward emotional problems (see Melton, 1987). Because unacceptable behaviors, rather than chest pains, may be the symptoms of a severe mental disorder, people have difficulty recognizing that a person suffering from a brain disease like schizophrenia is no more blameworthy or deserving of a life on the street than someone with heart disease. Disparities between coverage for mental and physical disorders are much less prevalent in Canada and other countries where health benefits are nationalized.

The Ascent of Biological Treatments

In an environment that sometimes subordinates care to cost, medication is an appealing treatment for mental illness. Medication can be cost-effective and fast-acting, and it is often the most appropriate treatment. On the other hand, financial incentives can lead to overuse of medication, since a psychiatrist can treat five or six medication patients in an hour, versus the one person per hour seen by a psychotherapist. Medical doctors with no training in psychiatry also routinely prescribe psychotropic medications, especially for anxiety and depression. Moreover, pharmaceutical companies fund dozens of studies on every new drug, providing vastly more scientific attention than ever devoted to psychological treatments. Thus, biological treatments are better tested and hence preferred by many insurance companies and practitioners.

SOME CONCLUDING THOUGHTS

In this chapter, we have explored a wide variety of techniques devised for alleviating psychological distress. Yet all of these approaches treat disorders that have already taken hold. One of the positive outcomes of the interest in cost-effective health care is the increasing recognition that one can often save money—and misery—by preventing illness rather than treating it. Just as exercising, avoiding a high-fat diet, and minimizing stress can promote physical health (Chapter 11), psychologists have long argued that addressing social problems such as poverty, malnutrition, physical and sexual abuse, and some of the factors that influence child and marital abuse (e.g., unemployment) could promote psychological health (Albee, 1986; Fitzpatrick, 1993; Masten et al., 1993; Zigler & Berman, 1983). Of course, these efforts cannot eradicate all forms of mental illness any more than exercising will keep a person from eventually dying, but **primary prevention** (preventative mental health measures) can reduce the incidence of mental illness among those whose problems stem at least in part from environmental sources.

Psychological health and illness, then, exist within a social context. The remaining chapters explore that larger context as we examine the way our social nature shapes, and is shaped by, our psychological nature.

Summary

Psychodynamic Therapies

1. Psychodynamic therapy is predicated on the notion that **insight**—understanding one's own psychological processes—is important for therapeutic change, as is the therapeutic relationship.

2. **Free association** is a technique designed to explore associational networks and unconscious processes involved in symptom formation. Another central element of psychodynamic therapy is the **interpretation** of conflicts, defenses, compromise formations, and transference reactions. **Transference** refers to the displacement of thoughts, feelings, fears, wishes, and conflicts from past relationships, particularly from childhood, onto the therapist. Therapists must also keep a watchful eye on their own **countertransference**, emotional reactions triggered by interactions with the patient, and particularly by the patient's transference to them.

3. The main contemporary forms of psychodynamic treatment are psychoanalysis (which is very intensive and long-term), psychodynamic psychotherapy (which relies on the same principles but is more conversational), and short-term psychodynamic psychotherapy (which is also based on the same principles but which has a specific focus and circumscribed number of sessions).

Cognitive-Behavioral Therapies

4. **Cognitive-behavioral therapies** are relatively short term, directive, and focused on specific symptoms. They rely on operant and classical conditioning as well as cognitive-social and more strictly cognitive interventions.

5. In **systematic desensitization** (a classical conditioning technique), the patient gradually approaches feared stimuli mentally while in a relaxed state. **Exposure techniques**, like desensitization, rely on classical conditioning, but they present the patient with the actual phobic stimulus in real life rather than having the patient merely imagine it. Therapies based on operant conditioning apply rewards and punishments to modify unwanted behavior, as in token economies.

6. In **participatory modeling**, the therapist not only models the desired behavior but also gradually induces the patient to participate in it. **Skills training** teaches the procedures necessary to accomplish relevant goals; **social skills training** helps people with specific deficits in interpersonal competence.

7. Cognitive therapy attempts to replace dysfunctional cognitions with more useful and accurate ones. Ellis, who developed **rational-emotive therapy**, proposed an **ABC theory** of psychopathology, where A refers to activating conditions, B to belief systems, and C to emotional consequences. Beck's cognitive therapy similarly proposes that altering distorted cognition is the key to therapeutic change.

Humanistic, Group, and Family Therapies

8. **Humanistic therapies** focus on the phenomenal (experiential) world of the patient. Rogers' **client-centered therapy** aims at helping individuals experience themselves as they really are, through therapeutic empathy and **unconditional positive regard**.

9. Group, family, and marital therapies involve the treatment of multiple individ-

uals simultaneously. **Group therapy** focuses on both individual dynamics and group process. A variation on group therapy is the **self-help group**, which is not guided by a professional. **Family therapy** presumes that the roots of symptoms lie in the structure of the family system, so that therapy should target family interaction patterns. A variant of family therapy, **marital** or **couples therapy**, treats the couple as a unit and may utilize systems, psychodynamic, or cognitive-behavioral techniques.

Biological Treatments

10. The aim of **biological treatments** is to alter the functioning of the brain to restore as normal functioning as possible. **Pharmacotherapy** is the major type of biological treatment; it refers to the use of drugs to treat psychological disorders. **Psychotropic medications** affect mental processes by acting at neurotransmitter sites. **Antipsychotic medications** are useful in the treatment of psychotic symptoms, particularly the positive symptoms of schizophrenia. **Tricyclic antidepressants, MAO inhibitors,** and **selective serotonin reuptake inhibitors** can be useful in the treatment of depression, while **lithium** is the treatment of choice for bipolar disorder. Both antidepressants and **benzodiazepines** (antianxiety medications) can be useful in the treatment of anxiety.

11. **Electroconvulsive therapy (ECT)**, or shock therapy, is currently used as a last resort in the treatment of severe depression. At one time, **psychosurgery**, brain surgery to reduce psychological symptoms, was widely practiced.

Evaluating Psychological Treatment

12. **Pharmacotherapy** is well established as an effective treatment for schizophrenia, bipolar disorder, and many other forms of psychopathology. The two major problems of pharmacotherapy are relapse rates and side effects.

13. Researchers have found all psychotherapies to be relatively effective and none to be generally more effective than others, although comparisons among different treatments are methodologically quite difficult. Cognitive-behavioral and biological treatments have received the most empirical attention and support, but the most important study yet conducted did not find them superior to a variant of short-term psychodynamic psychotherapy.

14. Each form of treatment has limitations, which has led some psychotherapists to advocate **psychotherapy integration**, either by selecting techniques to suit individual patients' needs or by using integrative theories to devise techniques that synthesize insights from different perspectives.

The Broader Context of Psychological Treatment

15. Cross-culturally, methods of treatment depend on cultural value systems and beliefs about personality and psychopathology. In the West, economic conditions often play a part in determining who gets mental health care and what kind.

16. The **deinstitutionalization** movement, designed to maximize the autonomy and community integration of patients whose severe disturbances could be treated with medication, has led to widespread homelessness and lack of care for the severely mentally ill in the United States. Today, in the United States, economic factors make managed health care more appealing; policies for treating physical and mental problems differ greatly, however, so that mental health coverage is becoming progressively less adequate.

17. **Primary prevention** refers to preventative measures that can reduce the incidence of mental illness.

Randy Stevens, "They're Here!," 1995

Chapter 17

ATTITUDES AND SOCIAL COGNITION

*I*n the 1960s, Stanley Milgram (1965) conducted a series of classic studies at Yale University that took many people, including psychologists, by surprise. The basic design of the studies was as follows. The experimenter told subjects they were participating in an experiment to examine the effect of punishment on learning. Subjects were instructed to punish a "learner" (actually a confederate of the researcher) in the next room whenever the learner made an error. They administered punishment using an instrument they believed to be a shock generator. Panel switches were labeled from 15 volts (SLIGHT SHOCK) to 450 volts (DANGER: SEVERE SHOCK). The experimenter instructed the subjects to begin by administering a slight shock and increase the voltage each time the learner made an

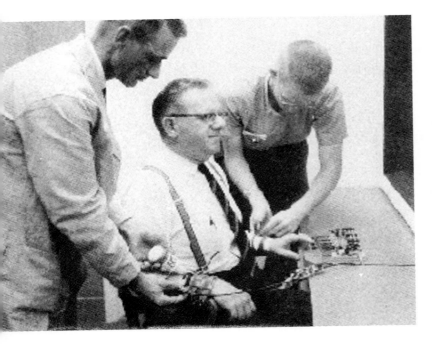

error. The learner actually received no shocks, but subjects had no reason to question what they were told, for they heard protests and later screaming from the next room as they increased the punishment.

Milgram was not actually studying the impact of punishment on learning; rather, he wanted to determine how far people would go in obeying orders. A team of psychiatrists predicted that only one-tenth of 1 percent of subjects would continue with the experiment all the way to 450 volts.

They were wrong. Two-thirds of the subjects administered the full 450 volts, even though the learner had by that point stopped screaming and was apparently either unconscious or dead. The subjects were torn between wanting to obey the experimenter and not wanting to hurt the learner. Each time they asked to discontinue the experiment, however, the researcher admonished them that the experiment must go on, that they had no choice. In the end, most chose obedience.

Milgram's experiments drew storms of controversy from psychologists concerned that he did not safeguard the rights of his subjects, who were often manifestly distressed by the experience. Following the experiment, he did discuss with them any negative feelings they had, and his subjects did not ultimately express regret about their participation. Whether the knowledge generated by Milgram's extraordinary results outweighs the possible costs to his subjects remains a matter of debate, and with contemporary ethics standards, such studies could not be conducted today. Nevertheless, the Milgram studies are probably the most widely known psychological studies ever conducted, and a classic in social psychology. **Social psychology** examines the way thought, feeling, and behavior are influenced by the actual, imagined, or implied presence of others (Allport, 1968, p. 3). In other words, social psychology examines not only the manner in which people interact but also the influence of their beliefs about themselves and others on their actions.

Because almost everything people do is social, the subject matter is enormous and varied. Researchers often choose topics because of their social or political significance (see Allport, 1985; Jones, 1985). For example, during World War II, many European psychologists who fled the Nazis turned their attention to propaganda, styles of leadership, obedience to authority, and conformity—inspiring one psychologist to credit Adolf Hitler as the person who most influenced the history of social psychology (Cartwright, 1979). In later decades, concern over urban alienation and apathy led to research into why bystanders frequently fail to intervene in a crisis.

In this chapter we focus on the first component of social psychology, interpersonal thinking. We begin with a discussion of attitudes and how they change. This topic is of central concern to advertisers, who try to shape attitudes toward their products. It is also an important area of research for understanding political questions, such as how Yassir Arafat, long considered a terrorist, eventually came to share a Nobel Peace Prize with Israeli leaders Yitzhak Rabin and Shimon Peres. Next we examine the process by which people make sense of each other, from the first impressions they form to enduring beliefs. Among these enduring beliefs are stereotypes, which can lead to prejudice, discrimination, and bloodshed. We conclude by considering the way people think about one of the major actors in their social worlds, themselves. Perhaps surprisingly, the nature of the self-concept differs dramatically across cultures, and individuals' views of themselves can have biological repercussions, affecting the functioning of their immune systems. The next chapter focuses on the other components of social psychology, interpersonal feelings and actions, particularly altruism, love, and aggression, and on the influence of group processes on individual behavior.

ATTITUDES

One of the major areas of social-psychological research from the start has been attitudes. Some of the first social psychologists studied the adaptation of immigrants from small Eastern European towns to the vastly different culture of the United States and how their attitudes toward people, work, and family influenced their adjustment (Thomas & Znaniecki, 1927). An **attitude** is an association between an act or object and an evaluation (Eagly & Chaiken, 1992; Fazio, 1986). To say that alcohol (object) leads to major social problems (evaluation) is to express an attitude. Social psychologists actually distinguish three components of an attitude: a cognitive component, or belief (alcohol leads to major social problems); an emotional or evaluative charge, or valence (alcohol is bad); and a behavioral disposition (alcohol should be avoided).

These three components seem like they should be mutually consistent, but they are often surprisingly at odds. Most people believe that alcohol is a major social problem, since drinking is involved in the majority of fatal car accidents and murders. Yet many people also have positive feelings associated with various drinks and brands, recall with humor and gusto incidents in which they were intoxicated, and drink with some regularity, sometimes to excess. Logic suggests that the cognitive and emotional aspects of attitudes would be congruent because an emotional evaluation of an object should reflect a cognitive appraisal of its qualities. In fact, however, the beliefs and feelings comprising an attitude frequently develop separately and can change independently (see Petty & Cacioppo, 1981, 1986; Edwards, 1991). A classic example occurred during Ronald Reagan's tenure in the White House, when opinion polls consistently showed that a majority of voters disagreed with many of Reagan's policy positions, such as his opposition to abortion, but they maintained a highly favorable attitude toward him anyway. As political consultants well understand, the emotional component of a political attitude—which can be decisive in voting behavior—rests as much on an unconscious assessment of nonverbal gestures, likability, and apparent sincerity as on the issues (see Epstein, 1994).

Attitudes and Behavior

People with favorable attitudes toward environmentalism should presumably recycle their garbage. Once again, however, the empirical David is mightier than the logical Goliath: Attitudes predict behavior—but not very well (Fishbein & Ajzen, 1974). Students' attitudes toward cheating are not very useful predictors of the probability that they will cheat, and their religious attitudes bear only a modest relation to their church attendance (Wicker, 1969). A striking early demonstration of the incongruence between attitudes and behavior was a study published in 1934, in which a psychologist interested in prejudice wrote to 251 hotels and restaurants to see if they would serve Chinese patrons (LaPiere, 1934). Nearly all said no—yet nearly all of them had actually served the investigator and a young Chinese couple traveling with him several months earlier.

People's attitudes predict their actions if the attitude and action are at the same level of generality, particularly if both are circumscribed (Ajzen & Fishbein, 1977). In other words, asking people their attitude toward environmental concerns does not predict whether they will recycle, but asking their attitude toward recycling does (Oskamp, 1991). But this observation is not very revealing; it simply means that people often do what they intend.

The tenuous link between expressed attitudes and behavior—such as the drinking behavior of people who think drinking is a problem—reflects several factors. One is that people's attitudes are only one of many influences on what they do (Ajzen & Fishbein, 1977). From a behaviorist perspective, behavior is under the control of rewards and punishments. An ecologically minded person who buys one small bag of groceries a week might use her own canvas shopping bag and thus contribute to the longevity of tropical rain forests. An equally environmentally conscious person who totes groceries for her family up six flights of stairs might find the convenience of plastic bags such overwhelming reinforcement that she contributes instead to the longevity of landfills.

Another factor that affects the link between expressed attitudes and behavior is the strength and accessibility of the attitude (Olson & Zanna, 1993). An attitude is *strong* if it is emotionally powerful, important to the person, and held with considerable certainty (Petty & Krosnick, 1994). An attitude is *accessible* if it readily comes to mind; the speed with which an attitude can be retrieved from memory predicts its likely impact on behavior (Fazio, 1990). As with motives and cognitions, psychologists are increasingly recognizing the importance of distinguishing between conscious attitudes and those that regulate thought and behavior unconsciously and automatically. Someone who has just attended a lecture on alcohol-related fatalities is unlikely to stop at the bar on the way home, but he may well overindulge at a happy hour a few days later. Apparently, this person has two sets of attitudes toward alcohol, and the one that is more salient at the time will control his behavior.

The manner in which an individual acquires a particular attitude also affects its impact on behavior. Attitudes shaped by personal experience are especially likely to influence action (Fazio & Zanna, 1981; Smith & Swinyard, 1983). Thus, a parent whose child died of AIDS is much more likely to become an AIDS activist than someone whose compassion developed vicariously. One study examined students' attitudes when a housing shortage on campus left several students sleeping on cots in makeshift quarters for weeks (Regan & Fazio, 1977). Both the affected students and their more comfortably housed peers had negative attitudes toward the situation and the university's handling of it, but those who were personally affected were much more likely to act in accordance with their attitudes by writing a letter, signing a petition, and the like. Emotional arousal can affect the expression of attitudes in behavior as well. A person who opposes capital punishment in principle because he does not believe government has the right to take a life may nevertheless be so horrified by a news report of a brutal murder that he avows that this particular murderer should be put to death.

The link between attitudes and behavior is in many respects analogous to the link between personality traits and behavior (Chapter 12). Internal dispositions are important, whether attitudes or traits, but they are just one of many variables that influence an action. Furthermore, just as personality traits can be situation-specific, so can some attitudes (such as voting in a particular election). Other attitudes are more general and can be seen to express themselves across situations, providing the psychologist measures enough situations to get a reliable estimate of the person's behavioral tendencies.

Attitude Change

People often have a vested interest in changing others' attitudes, whether in selling products, running for political office, or convincing a lover to reconcile one more time. Social psychologists have focused on two avenues of attitude change: change through persuasion and change resulting from a discrepancy between an existing attitude and new information.

Persuasion

Persuasion refers to deliberate efforts to induce attitude change, and it can take one of two forms. The first is to induce the recipient of a message to think carefully and weigh the arguments. This is likely to occur only if the receiver of the information has the motivation and time to think about the issues. The second form of

All men who wear Calvins will, no doubt, develop the looks and popularity of rapper Marky Mark.

persuasion is to encourage emotional and other less carefully considered responses that bypass the belief component of the attitude (Petty & Cacioppo, 1981, 1986; Eagly & Chaiken, 1992; Petty, 1995). Most beer commercials, for example, have little to offer in terms of rational persuasion. Were weekends *really* made for Michelob? When you say "Bud," have you *really* said it all? Advertisers use a catchy slogan and humor to lead people to associate their product with a positive feeling, or they populate their commercials with beautiful women and virile men, implying that using their product or drinking their beer leads to an increase in reproductive success (rather than a beer gut). This kind of classical conditioning of an object with an emotional response can occur unconsciously. In one study, the experimenters showed subjects slides of a young woman, which were preceded immediately by subliminal presentation of either a positive or negative emotion-arousing photograph. When asked their attitudes toward the woman, subjects exposed to the positive subliminal pictures were more positive than those exposed to the negative (Krosnick et al., 1992).

Other nonrational appeals can also be persuasive. Simply repeating a message enough times can lead people to believe it (Arkes et al., 1991). Indeed, one cue for credibility of a message is the number of times one hears it. This idea will come as no revelation to managers of political campaigns, who often repeat false messages about opposing candidates—and in highly emotional terms—in order to bias public opinion.

To change someone's attitude, then, requires attention to several variables. If the attitude really matters to the person, if the recipient of the message is knowledgeable about the subject, and if the attitude was initially generated rationally by weighing costs and benefits, the best appeal is to the head. In this case, the persuader should avoid distractions (glitzy campaigns, jingles, and hoopla) that impede conscious, rational processing and annoy the receiver. If, however, the attitude is not strongly held and is based on minimal knowledge, the best route is to the heart or the gut.

Interest in persuasion actually has a venerable past. Long before modern psychology, Aristotle described rhetoric—the art of persuasive speaking—as a combination of ethos (characteristics of the speaker), pathos (the message), and logos (the logic of the argument). Psychologists have expanded Aristotle's view to distinguish five components of persuasion (Figure 17.1): the source, the message, the channel (the medium in which the message is delivered), the receiver, and the target behavior at which the message is directed (Lasswell, 1948; McGuire, 1985). Attending to each of these aspects is central to the success of a persuasive appeal, whether the goal is to sell a car or to ask someone out on a date.

Source and Message Characteristics of the source that play an important role in the success of a persuasive appeal include the speaker's credibility, attractiveness,

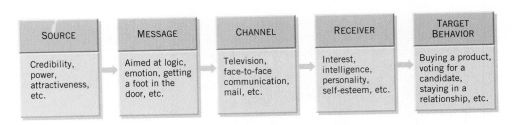

FIGURE 17.1
Components of the persuasion process. The components of persuasion include the source of the message, the message itself, the channel or medium, the receiver, and the target behavior or goal of persuasion. SOURCE: *Adapted from McGuire, 1985, p. 259.*

and power (see Chaiken, 1980; Simons et al., 1970). In Milgram's studies, the prestige of the Yale name and the matter-of-fact, scientific presence of the experimenter enhanced the persuasive appeal of the message—that the experiment must continue. The type of appeal and the way it is delivered also affect attitude change. When the message is subtle rather than obvious (Cohen, 1957; Katz et al., 1956; McGuire, 1960) and when the appeal uses a low rather than a high level of fear (Insko et al., 1965), attitude change is more likely to occur and persist. Too much fear can lead people to stop attending to the message and to focus instead on managing their anxiety, as when students in a driving class watching a gory movie about traffic fatalities laugh and deny its applicability to them. Fear is useful primarily if the recipients of the message believe the danger applies to them and that they can do something to avoid it (see Olson & Zanna, 1993). Otherwise, they are likely to react defensively.

As advertisers know, the first step in getting a message across is delivering it in a way that people will attend to it. This often takes considerable ingenuity, since, for example, people receive hundreds of direct mailings every year and read only a fraction of them. One strategy is the **foot-in-the-door technique**, which is based on the principle that once people comply with a small request, they are likely to comply with a bigger one (Beaman et al., 1983). In one classic study, experimenters posed as representatives of the Community Committee for Traffic Safety or the Keep California Beautiful Committee (Freedman & Fraser, 1966). They visited over 100 homes in Palo Alto, California and asked residents to comply with a small request —to sign a petition or post a small, unimposing sign on their lawns reading, "Be a safe driver" or "Keep California Beautiful." About two weeks later, the investigators visited the same and several additional homes with a larger request—asking residents to install a large "Drive Carefully" sign on their front lawn. Less than 20 percent of those who received the large request only consented, but over 55 percent of the subjects who had granted the small request agreed to the large one. The same principle works in dating: If a potential date seems uncertain or ambivalent, suggest lunch (a much smaller investment) before proposing an entire evening out.

Channel   The channel of persuasion is the means by which a message is sent: visually or aurally, verbally or nonverbally, in person or through media such as telephone or television. Choosing the right channel can be as important as selecting the right message. Turning someone down for a date is much more difficult face to face than on the telephone, so suitors whose targets seem reluctant should make their pitch in person. Emotional appeals to contribute to emergency relief funds are similarly more effective when the target of the communication can see starving children with distended stomachs rather than simply hear about their plight.

Receiver   Receiver characteristics—qualities of the person the communicator is trying to persuade—also affect the persuasiveness of a communication. People bias their processing of information in order to preserve attitudes they do not want to change. Coffee drinkers, for example, discount messages about the dangers of caffeine (Liberman & Chaiken, 1992). Prior attitude strength also influences the impact of an appeal; people with weaker opinions are obviously easier to persuade. Moreover, some individuals are simply more resistant to attitude change in general (see Haugtvedt & Petty, 1992; Hovland & Janis, 1959). Intelligence and high self-esteem render people less persuasible (Rhodes & Wood, 1992).

Behavioral Change The final component of persuasion, behavioral change, is ultimately the only component that really counts. If a persuasive appeal does not lead to a purchase, a vote, a date, or some other target behavior, it is ineffective. Changing behavior through persuasion is often complicated by the fact that someone else has a vested interest in the opposite outcome; Reebok's loss is Nike's gain. Psychologists and advertisers have devised many methods to increase resistance to contrary appeals. Simply being the first one to make a pitch—being the first of two opposing messages—renders a persuasive appeal more likely to succeed and persist (Insko, 1964; Miller & Campbell, 1959; Wilson & Miller, 1968).

One method for countering an opposing appeal, called **attitude inoculation**, involves building up the receiver's resistance to an appeal. The speaker does this by presenting weak and easily assailable arguments for the other point of view or forewarning of a strong attack, much as a vaccine builds the body's defenses through exposure to small, inert amounts of a virus (McGuire, 1961; McGuire & Papegeorgis, 1962). Salespeople frequently use this technique when they know a customer is about to visit a competitor ("He'll tell you that the Escort has a better safety record, but don't believe him").

Another way to maximize behavioral change and ward off opposing appeals is to ask people to state their position publicly, which puts pressure on them to maintain the appearance of consistency, or to have them carry out an onerous action on the basis of an attitude so they feel they have an investment in it (Bennett, 1955; Halverson & Pallak, 1978; Hovland et al., 1957; Janis & Mann, 1977; Kiesler, 1971; Wicklund & Brehm, 1976). Someone who has been convinced by a friend to canvass or stuff envelopes for a political candidate is unlikely to vote for the opposition.

Cognitive Dissonance

Inducing a person to carry out a difficult, tedious, or even morally questionable action in order to foster resistance to contrary persuasive appeals relies on a mechanism known as cognitive dissonance. **Cognitive dissonance** occurs when a person experiences a discrepancy between an attitude and a behavior or between an attitude and a new piece of information. This discrepancy leads to a state of tension (dissonance) akin to anxiety. The tension, in turn, motivates the individual to change the attitude, the behavior, or the perception of the anomalous information in order to eliminate the discrepancy and with it, the tension (Festinger, 1957, 1962).

Cognitive dissonance theory is essentially a drive-reduction theory (Chapter 10), in which an attitude change is reinforced by reduction of a painful emotional state (a drive). Suppose, for example, a person succumbs to a skilled salesperson and buys a motorcycle instead of a car. He subsequently reads about the high death and injury rates for motorcyclists. The tension he experiences may lead him to convince himself that these drivers, unlike himself, were just careless. Alternatively, he may begin buying motorcycle magazines that preach the virtues of cycling to bolster his conviction that he did the right thing. These are examples of post-decision dissonance reduction.

Cognitive dissonance can also arise when people carry out an act contrary to their attitudes, which frequently leads to attitude change. In a classic test, Festinger and Carlsmith (1959) had subjects perform monotonous tasks for an hour. The experimenters told the subjects that the aim of this procedure was to test their performance, but the actual purpose was to create a negative attitude toward the tasks. The investigators then instructed some subjects to tell the next "subject" (actually a confederate of the experimenter) that the experiment was enjoyable. They paid subjects either $1 or $20 for their compliance.

One might expect that subjects who received $20 for hyping a boring task would feel more positive toward the task than those paid only $1. In fact, just the opposite occurred. Subjects who received only $1 rated the experimental tasks more enjoyable, and they more frequently agreed to participate in a similar experiment again. While these results seem counterintuitive, they exquisitely matched the predictions of dissonance theory: To say that a boring task is interesting, and to do so for a meager payment, creates considerable dissonance. Subjects who received only $1 either had to change their attitude toward the task or acknowledge that they had sold their souls rather cheaply, like a low-budget Faust. In contrast, subjects who received $20 experienced minimal dissonance because their behavior was readily explicable in terms of the payment, a considerable amount in the late 1950s.

Two variables that influence the extent to which dissonance arises and requires resolution are the perception of choice and the size of rewards and punishments. A person with a gun to his head will not feel much pressure to cling to attitudes he publicly professed at the time. Coerced statements create little dissonance because they are uttered with minimal choice. Similarly, as in Festinger and Carlsmith's study, the smaller the reward or punishment, the greater the attitude change because larger incentives minimize dissonance. This paradoxical finding, that a smaller reward leads to greater attitude change, has obvious implications for teaching children, who must often be induced to perform tasks that do not at first appear intrinsically compelling, such as practicing multiplication tables. Rewarding children too generously for activities they might come to enjoy spontaneously can actually lead them to attribute their enjoyment to the rewards and hence to find the task itself intrinsically unrewarding (Lepper, 1978), although this is much more likely to occur with simple, routine tasks than with more complex or creative ones (Eisenberger & Selbst, 1994).

Cognitive dissonance theory received tremendous interest from social psychologists for many years, but it is not without its critics. An alternative explanation of dissonance phenomena, derived from behaviorism, is self-perception theory. **Self-perception theory** holds that individuals infer their attitudes, emotions, and other internal states by observing their own behavior (Bem, 1967, 1972). Thus, if they see themselves telling someone that they like a task and they have only received $1 for doing so, they conclude that they must have liked it or they would not be doing it. If they slander their country at gunpoint, they conclude that they did so to avoid dying, not because they dislike their country. According to self-perception theory, the attitudes people report depend on their behavior, and as their behavior changes (because of changes in reinforcement contingencies), so again will their attitude. No motivation, tension, or perceived inconsistency is involved.

Self-perception theory thus offers a nonmotivational explanation for dissonance phenomena. Other theories, however, point to motives other than dissonance reduction to explain the findings of dissonance experiments. A **self-presentation** explanation focuses on the way people try to present themselves to others. According to this view, what appear to be changes in attitudes in dissonance studies are really changes in *reported* attitudes. Because subjects do not want to look foolish to the experimenter by behaving inconsistently, they report attitudes they do not really hold. Another motivational explanation, which might be called a self-esteem theory of dissonance, is that people feel guilty or ashamed after doing something that conflicts with their values, such as lying about a task. Thus, they change their attitudes to minimize their discomfort and preserve their self-esteem (see Abelson, 1983; Scher & Cooper, 1989).

Most likely, each of these explanations is applicable at various times. Studies measuring physiological responses do suggest that encountering conflicting information can produce emotional arousal (see Croyle & Cooper, 1983; Pallak & Pittman, 1972; Zanna & Cooper, 1974), that people experience this arousal as uncomfortable, and that this discomfort is alleviated when they use a dissonance-reducing strategy such as changing a belief (Elliott & Devine, 1994). When the discrepant information makes the person feel foolish, ashamed, or guilty, however, this tension is as likely related to self-presentation or self-esteem motivation as to dissonance aroused by cognitive inconsistency.

SOCIAL COGNITION

A friend has just told you she has the "perfect person" for you. She describes the individual as intelligent, witty, engaging, and articulate, and thinks the two of you would make a great pair. You immediately form an impression of this person, which probably includes traits such as attractive, kind, outgoing, and generous. Now suppose instead your friend describes a potential date with precisely the same words—intelligent, witty, engaging, and articulate—but first warns that this person is a "real con artist." This time your impression probably includes less favorable traits, such as selfish, cold, and ruthless. How does a simple phrase ("perfect for you" versus a "real con artist") change the meaning of a series of adjectives and lead to an entirely different impression? The anwer lies in **social cognition**, the processes by which people make sense of others, themselves, social interactions, and relationships (see Fiske, 1993, 1995; Fiske & Taylor, 1991).

Social versus Nonsocial Cognition

The study of social cognition emerged as psychologists began to extend models and metaphors from cognitive psychology into the realm of social information processing. Most researchers assumed that social cognition was similar to nonsocial cognition and therefore adapted cognitive-experimental methods to study the way people think about themselves and others (see, for example, Srull & Wyer, 1989; Wyer & Srull, 1986). Thus, if an investigator in a cognitive experiment presented subjects with a list of words or phrases and later tested their recall, a social-cognitive experimenter might substitute adjectives or paragraphs describing personality traits or features of social situations but otherwise follow the same design. Over time, however, psychologists came to recognize that social cognition differs from nonsocial cognition in several ways (see Fiske, 1993; Fiske & Taylor, 1991; Markus & Zajonc, 1985).

First, human action and interaction are ambiguous. A person with relatively good eyesight and some knowledge of horticulture can judge from the condition of the ground and vegetation whether a garden needs watering. In contrast, an individual who perceives a social interaction as a participant or as a bystander is missing some of the most crucial and relevant data: the unspoken intentions, thoughts, and feelings of the people involved. Because observers of a social interaction have access only to behaviors, they must infer what those behaviors mean. Ambiguity is thus the rule in social cognition, leaving substantial opportunities for error, bias, and idiosyncratic interpretation.

A second difference between social and nonsocial cognition involves emotion.

Unlike cognition about plants, social cognition is inherently intertwined with emotion. People either like or dislike their roommate; their psychology professor is either interesting or boring; the clerk is either courteous or rude.

Third, although culture influences many cognitive processes such as categorization, it plays a particularly important role in social cognition. Cultural beliefs, norms, and values influence the dimensions on which people categorize each other. Some concepts are cross-culturally invariant (Chapter 12); people in all cultures use categories such as extroversion and agreeableness (Zebrowitz-McArthur, 1988). Others, however, are more variable. An individual who is competitive and driven to accumulate wealth may appear perfectly normal in Western culture but be classified as antisocial, self-centered, or even dangerous in an agrarian society, where resources are limited. Social cognition is inherently infused with cultural value judgments because categories (such as men, nurses, or students) carry with them implications of how people who fit them *should* behave (Shweder, 1980).

Culture also influences the way people interpret interpersonal events, by providing intuitive theories of personality and causality. When children and adults in the West explain their successes and failures, they refer to such concepts as skill, effort, and luck (Weiner, 1980). In contrast, Buddhist children from Sri Lanka sometimes attribute achievement and failure to good and bad deeds in past lives. Good deeds from another life lead to good karma, a positive moral force that guides one's fate (Little, 1988).

Finally, social cognition is reciprocal. The "object" being perceived in social cognition responds to the perceiver—and changes its actions based on how it believes it is being perceived. Getting annoyed at a textbook for being obtuse and boring does not change it. Getting annoyed at a professor for the same reasons, however, may well influence the way he lectures. Trying to understand another person is like shooting at a moving target—and one that is shooting back.

People as Intuitive Scientists

Many social psychologists have suggested that, in trying to understand the social world, people act like **intuitive scientists**, or intuitive psychologists; that is, they use intuitive theories, frame hypotheses, collect data about themselves and others, and examine the impact of various "experimental" manipulations on dependent variables that are relevant to them (Heider, 1958; Ross, 1977). They also try to discover the ways different social variables are associated with each other so they can better predict and control the social environment, as when they learn that certain behaviors are appropriate in specific situations.

For example, a woman we shall call Nancy meets a man she finds interesting at a party. While they are carrying on small talk, she is busy trying to assess whether the interest is mutual. For most people, blurting out, "Do you want to go out with me?" is not very easy, so, like Nancy, they employ a variety of experimental or quasi-experimental procedures to test the hypothesis that their potential date is interested. Nancy begins by observing that "there are a lot of good movies out these days, aren't there?" and carefully attends to the reaction to this experimental manipulation. Like a good experimentalist, she relies on multiple measures: his words, his gestures, the amount of hemming and hawing he does in answering, and other nonverbal cues such as whether he continues to make eye contact with her. She also gauges the reaction time between her statement and his answer; a long reaction time could indicate that he is looking for a way to respond tactfully despite his disinterest. These measures are remarkably similar to measures employed by psychologists in laboratory experiments (Chapter 2).

Suppose that Brett (her partner in this interaction) says he is not really interested in movies. Nancy now faces the dilemma posed by an ambiguous message. Brett might simply dislike movies, or he might be trying to signal that he is not interested in going out with her. If she is self-confident, Nancy will, like a good experimenter, set up a second experiment. She makes a comment about pizza, on the assumption that only a highly deviant individual would dislike both movies and pizza. Brett fails the pizza test but explains that he is allergic to cheese. A few minutes later he yawns and says he is thinking of calling it a night, and Nancy concludes that he is not interested.

Note the complex nature of such a simple and commonplace scenario. The interaction is driven by motivation. Nancy has a question she wants answered, but she also wants to preserve her self-esteem and avoid being openly rejected. Brett is the subject in her experiment, but he never signed a consent form, and he may be too dense to realize what is going on. If he does recognize what is happening, he, too, may have conflicting motivations. Perhaps he wants to indicate his disinterest, but he does not want to hurt her feelings. Or he may be interested but may himself be afraid of being rejected. Thus, each utterance by each partner in the exchange may combine multiple subtle and conflicting messages that the two must somehow decode. That anyone ever enters into a relationship is truly a wonder.

First Impressions

Before computer models and cognitive science spawned the field of social cognition, psychologists interested in interpersonal perception studied **first impressions**. These initial perceptions of another person can have remarkably powerful effects. For example, subjects in one study read the two passages shown in Figure 17.2 (Luchins, 1957). Half the subjects read the top paragraph first, and the other half read the bottom paragraph first. The order of the material substantially influenced subjects' evaluations of the person described. Of subjects who read paragraph A first, 78 percent considered Jim friendly, whereas only 18 percent of those who read paragraph B first did so. A first impression creates a mental representation that influences the way subsequent information is processed.

One salient piece of information people consider, particularly on first impression, is attractiveness. Individuals who are physically attractive benefit from the tendency to assume that positive qualities cluster together, a phenomenon known as the **halo effect**. Researchers have found halo effects for physical attractiveness across a wide array of situations: in experiments measuring the way people evaluate the transgressions of attractive versus unattractive children (Dion, 1972), the sentences recommended by simulated jurors for crimes involving attractive and unattractive criminals and victims (Landy & Aronson, 1969), and the traits ascribed to political and media figures (Lachman & Bass, 1985). The positive glow of beauty, of course, has its limits (see Eagly et al., 1991; Feingold, 1992). It is most powerful on first impression when people have minimal information about each other. It also extends more to some traits than to others. People attribute greater sociability and social competence to attractive people, but they do not expect them to have more integrity, modesty, or concern for others.

Is the perceived correlation between physical and emotional beauty entirely illusory? Actually, some of the beliefs people hold about the relation between physical attractiveness and other qualities are true. Subjects rated by panels of judges as more physically attractive tend to self-report being more socially comfortable and less lonely than less attractive subjects. An even more important variable than physical attractiveness, however, may be *perceived* physical attractiveness. Individuals who perceive themselves as physically attractive report being more extroverted, socially comfortable, and mentally healthy than those less comfortable with their appearance (Feingold, 1992). Seeing oneself as attractive likely produces a self-fulfilling prophe-

Paragraph A

Jim left the house to get some stationery. He walked out into the sun-filled street with two of his friends, basking in the sun as he walked. Jim entered the stationery store, which was full of people. Jim talked with an acquaintance while he waited for the clerk to catch his eye. On his way out, he stopped to chat with a school friend who was just coming into the store. Leaving the store, he walked toward school. On his way out he met the girl to whom he had been introduced the night before. They talked for a short while, and then Jim left for school.

Paragraph B

After school Jim left the classroom alone. Leaving the school, he started on his long walk home. The street was brilliantly filled with sunshine. Jim walked down the street on the shady side. Coming down the street toward him, he saw the pretty girl whom he had met on the previous evening. Jim crossed the street and entered a candy store. The store was crowded with students, and he noticed a few familiar faces. Jim waited quietly until the counterman caught his eye and then gave his order. Taking his drink, he sat down at a side table. When he had finished his drink he went home.

FIGURE 17.2
First impressions. In this classic study, the order of presentation of two paragraphs had a substantial influence on the impression subjects formed of Jim. Source: *Luchins, 1957, pp. 34–35.*

cy (Chapter 2), as many readers will recognize from confident periods in their own lives: When people feel and act attractive, others are more likely to see them that way.

Schemas and Social Cognition

First impressions are essentially the schemas people form when they encounter someone for the first time. Schemas, the patterns of thought that organize human experience, apply in the social realm as in other areas of life (see Fiske, 1993, 1995; Taylor & Crocker, 1980). **Person schemas** represent information about specific people or types of people. Individuals develop schemas about broad categories (extroverts, librarians, Hispanics, and women) as well as about specific others (one's father, neighbor, or taxi driver).

Situation schemas represent information about different kinds of social situations, including what to expect and how to act. People know how to behave in a classroom, in a library, or in a restaurant because they have schemas for each of these situations. Situation schemas undoubtedly contributed to the obedience of Milgram's subjects, who encoded the situation as one calling for compliance with an authority's demand. Situation schemas often include **scripts**, which specify how to do something socially, such as ordering a meal or handling a disagreement with a friend (Abelson, 1981). Like other schemas, situation schemas can be organized hierarchically. Within a broad category (such as "parties"), several subcategories may be nested (formal and informal, fun and boring). At the lowest level of the hierarchy are episodic memories of specific social encounters ("the party at my neighbor's house last New Year's Eve"). Closely related to situation schemas are culturally constructed **role schemas**, which represent information about what is expected of people in particular social positions or roles, such as student, professor, or parent.

Relationship schemas tend to be more idiosyncratic and personal than role schemas. They encode expectations about how the self and others interact in different kinds of relationships (Baldwin, 1992; Horowitz, 1988). Relationship schemas are like internal working models of relationships (Chapter 14), although they are not all about attachment relationships (they can be about friends or strangers). Many relationship schemas are also hierarchically organized. An individual may have information organized around *authority relationships* but more specific information stored about *interactions with male authorities* or *interactions with male authorities who resemble my father*. Research on relationship schemas has been influenced by the psychodynamic perspective and emphasizes that these schemas, like all schemas, are usually activated unconsciously. Thus, a student may bristle at a comment by a professor and not realize that the professor's remark triggered a reaction shaped in his relationship with his father.

As in other cognitive domains, social schemas guide information processing. They specify what information is likely to be relevant, they direct attention, they organize encoding, and they influence retrieval. An employer who suspects that a job candidate may be overly generous in describing his accomplishments is likely to scrutinize his resume with special care and inquire about details that would normally not catch her eye. If later asked about the candidate, the thing she may remember first is that he described a part-time job as a courier at a radio station as a "communications consultant." People are especially prone to recall **schema-relevant** social information, that is, behaviors or aspects of a situation related to an activated schema (Higgins & Bargh, 1987). For example, subjects presented with a vignette about a librarian are likely a week later to remember information congruent with their librarian schema, such as a bun hairstyle and glasses. They are also prone to remember highly discrepant information, such as her tendency to go out dancing every night. If a librarian schema is active during encoding or retrieval, what people are *least* likely to remember are details irrelevant to the schema, such as her hair color.

Stereotypes and Prejudice

Schemas are essential for social cognition. Without them, people would walk into every new situation without knowing how to behave or how others are likely to act. Schematic processing can go awry, however, when schemas are so rigidly or automatically applied that they preclude the processing of new information. This often occurs with **stereotypes**, schemas about the personal attributes of a group of people that are typically overgeneralized, inaccurate, and resistant to new information (see Myers, 1993). Stereotypes, like other schemas, save cognitive "energy" (Gilbert & Hixon, 1991; Macrae et al., 1994). In other words, they simplify experience and allow individuals to categorize others quickly and effortlessly (Allport, 1954; Hamilton & Sherman, 1994), which frees their conscious attention for other things that seem more relevant.

The problem with stereotypes is that they can lead to automatic activation of prejudicial thoughts and behaviors toward people based on their race, ethnicity, gender, or other attributes rather than on their actions or achievements. **Prejudice**, which literally means prejudgment, means judging people based on negative stereotypes. Racial, ethnic, and religious prejudice has contributed to more bloodshed over the past 50 years than perhaps any other force in human history. Its path of destruction can be traced through the violence and institutionalized discrimination carried out against blacks in the United States and South Africa, to the Holocaust, the Arab-Israeli conflict, the tension between Anglophones and Francophones in Quebec, the carnage in Northern Ireland, the tribal warfare and genocide that has occurred in Rwanda and other African countries, the civil war and atrocities carried out in Bosnia, and the other civil wars that erupted after the breakup of the Soviet Union. This is, indeed, a long and grim list. Can social-psychological research contribute to the understanding of prejudice?

(a)

(b)

(c)

Prejudice has a grim history, from the Nazi concentration camps (a), to the cross-burnings and lynchings of the Klu Klux Klan (b), to the more recent camps created by the Bosnian Serbs (c).

Since the 1930s, psychologists have proposed a number of explanations for prejudice, based on their answers to two central questions: Do the roots of prejudice lie in individual psychology (such as personality dynamics or cognition) or in social dynamics (the oppression of one group by another)? And are the causes of prejudice to be found in cognition or motivation—in the way people think or in the way they *want* to think? As we shall see, the absence of a single widely accepted theory of prejudice probably reflects the fact that researchers have tried to choose among these options rather than to recognize the influence of both individual and collective factors and cognitive and motivational ones (see Duckitt, 1992).

Psychodynamic Perspectives on Prejudice

Around the time of World War II, psychologists turned to psychodynamic theory to explain the racism that was devouring Europe and eating away at the United States. They noted that acts of racial violence tend to increase in times of economic recession, as people search for scapegoats, or targets for displaced anger (Dollard et al., 1939). Scapegoats bolster the self-esteem of prejudiced individuals by providing a rationalization for their unemployment or low status. In this view, prejudice is a defense mechanism motivated by anger, anxiety, or feelings of low self-worth.

A second psychodynamically informed view tried to explain why some people are attracted to racist ideology while others are not. In *The Authoritarian Personality*, Theodore Adorno and his colleagues (1950) isolated a particular character style, called the **authoritarian personality**, which is prone to hate people who are different or downtrodden. They found this character type most prevalent in families with a dominant, stern, and often sadistic father and a submissive mother—a common pattern in many German homes at that time, including Adolf Hitler's family of origin. The children in such families fear and hate their fathers, but these feelings are unacceptable to them and would be brutally punished if exposed, so they repress them. As adults, authoritarian individuals displace or project their rage onto groups such as Jews, blacks, homosexuals, or others who do not conform to social norms. Adorno and later researchers found that these personality dynamics were not limited to Nazi Germany but were present in every society studied. Despite criticism of Adorno's methodology, more recent work has supported many of the original findings (Christie, 1978; Snyder & Ickes, 1985), such as the link between this personality style and harsh parenting demanding strict obedience.

Psychodynamic concepts of conflict and defense underlie a third, more recent approach to understanding racial prejudice. This approach emerged from the observation that racism has changed in the last three decades, particularly in the United States. Overt racial discrimination against ethnic minorities no longer receives institutional support and is generally met with public disapproval; gone are the days of separate buses, drinking fountains, and bathrooms for whites and blacks. Many theorists and researchers contend, however, that a new, more subtle kind of racism exists in its wake (see Allport, 1954; Devine, 1995; Devine et al., 1991; Dovidio & Gaertner, 1993; Katz & Hass, 1988; McConahay & Hough, 1976; Sears, 1988). Although some people remain overtly racist, most struggle with unconscious negative stereotypes that conflict with their conscious values and beliefs. These individuals often express nonbigoted views, but when they act or respond without much conscious attention, their unconscious stereotypes prevail. For example, their reactions to black criminals seen on television may be more severe than to whites who commit the same acts, even though they feel no conscious animosity toward people of color.

In part, this discrepancy between saying and doing reflects a simple cognitive process. When people process information without much conscious thought, they are more likely to rely on stereotypes, to treat people as an instance of a category rather than as a specific individual (see Olson & Zanna, 1993). Racist sentiments, like other attitudes, may thus be activated without awareness, as when a white man automatically checks his wallet after standing next to a young black man on the subway. Emotional arousal also renders people more susceptible to stereotypic think-

"...it required years of labor and billions of dollars to uncover the secret of the atom. It will take still a greater investment to gain the secrets of man's irrational nature. It is easier...to smash an atom than a prejudice...."

Gordon Allport (1954, p. xi)

Scenes like this were commonplace in the American South less than 40 years ago.

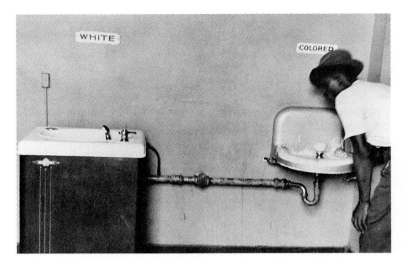

ing because, among other things, it draws limited attentional resources away from conscious reflection (Bodenhausen, 1993). The less people make conscious attributions, the more their unreflective, unconscious attitudes prevail (see Gilbert, 1995).

When conscious beliefs and values conflict with deep-seated, automatic negative stereotypes, people tend to oscillate between extreme positions or to defend against any vulnerability to racist thinking. They may thus respond with particular harshness toward members of minority groups who break the law, and justify their behavior on principle. Alternatively, they may employ reaction-formation as a defense against their discomfort (Chapter 11) and not hold members of minority groups responsible for committing violent or destructive acts. Other people learn to recognize their unconscious tendencies toward racist thinking and perpetually monitor their reactions to prevent racist attitudes from coloring their actions.

Prejudice and Social Conditions

In the late 1950s and 1960s, the civil rights movement in the United States was at its peak, and social scientists were optimistic about eradicating social evils such as poverty and racism. A view emerged among researchers at that time that the roots of prejudice lay less in personality dynamics than social dynamics, and particularly in socialization practices that teach children racist attitudes (Duckitt, 1992; Pettigrew, 1958). Prejudice is indeed transmitted from one generation to the next, and it takes hold very early in a child's socialization. In India, which has seen continued violence between Muslims and Hindus, children show signs of prejudice by age 4 or 5 (Saraswathi & Dutta, 1988). By the preschool years in multiethnic societies such as our own, children from both minority and majority subcultures tend to express preferences toward the majority culture, presumably reflecting internalization of social norms and attitudes (see Spencer & Markstrom-Adams, 1990). Internalization of prejudice makes later identity formation difficult for adolescent members of devalued groups, who must somehow integrate a positive view of themselves with negative attitudes and stereotypes of their group.

The roots of prejudice may lie in social conditions in yet another way. Many theorists, from Karl Marx to contemporary sociologists, have argued that prejudiced social attitudes serve the function of preserving the interests of the dominant classes. Promulgating the view that blacks are inferior justifies a social order in which whites hold disproportionate power, and teaching black children to devalue themselves gives them less confidence to challenge white authority and persevere in the face of adversity. Disparities in wealth and property ownership often provide the fault lines around which societies crumble with ethnic strife, since the haves and have-nots frequently differ in color, religion, or ethnicity.

Ingroups and Outgroups

Prejudice requires a distinction between **ingroups** and **outgroups**—that is, people who belong to the group and those who do not. Human beings make these distinctions with astonishing rapidity, on even the most arbitrary bases (Brewer, 1979; Tajfel, 1981). The impact of ingroups and outgroups was demonstrated in a remarkable classroom experiment in a rural, all-white community conducted by a third-grade teacher named Jane Elliott (1977). To demonstrate what prejudice and discrimination feel like, Elliott one day announced that the brown-eyed children in her class were superior and the blue-eyed children, inferior. Within a brief period, the brown-eyed children refused to play with their blue-eyed classmates and became vicious in the way they excluded them from activities. Friendships dissolved as children internalized their labels. The blue-eyed children began to think of themselves as stupid and bad, and their schoolwork deteriorated. When Elliott switched the group labels, placing the blue-eyed children in the superior ingroup and the brown-eyed children in the inferior outgroup, she observed the same type of behavior. Like the Milgram obedience studies, of course, this classroom experiment raises ethical questions about the extent to which the findings might outweigh potential adverse effects on the subjects, but the results were clearly striking.

Similar ingroup-outgroup behavior occurs with adults and is amplified in naturally occurring groups such as families, clans, or communities. It is manifestly apparent at sporting events, where taunting and physical violence may erupt between opposing fans, whose only commonality lies in their identification with a city, school, or team. People tend to perceive members of outgroups as much more homogeneous than they really are and to emphasize the individuality of ingroup members (Judd & Park, 1988; Moreland, 1985; Mullen & Hu, 1989). Thus, people of other races "all look alike," and members of other fraternities or sororities are perceived as sharing many core traits, which is highly unlikely, given the tremendous individual differences in personality that exist within any group of people.

Interpretations of other people's behavior also depend on their ingroup/outgroup status. One set of studies examined the way Hindu and Muslim students in Bangladesh explained the causes of helpful or unhelpful behavior presented in vignettes (Islam & Hewstone, 1993). Subjects tended to explain the helpful behavior of ingroup members in terms of their goodness as a person and unhelpful behaviors as a result of environmental circumstances. The reverse pattern applied to outgroup members, whose positive acts were explained away and whose negative behaviors were seen to reflect enduring personality attributes. Interestingly, these findings were much stronger for the majority Muslims than for the minority Hindus, who are socially disadvantaged as well as numerically outnumbered in Bangladesh. This is not an uncommon finding cross-culturally: Minority groups tend to show conflicting responses, with one tendency to favor their ingroup and another to favor the majority culture, which is more socially valued in the broader society (see Fletcher & Ward, 1988).

The readiness to create and act on ingroup/outgroup distinctions probably rests on both motivational and cognitive processes. From a motivational point of view, casting ingroup members in a positive light gives oneself a positive glow as a member of the group (Tajfel, 1981). From a cognitive perspective, ingroup effects reflect the mind's continuous efforts to categorize and schematize information—and may even be rooted in the language people use to describe themselves and others (Perdue et al., 1990). Words denoting an ingroup automatically trigger more positive feelings than words related to an outgroup. One study found that briefly flashing the word "us" facilitated recognition of positive words. "Us" is associatively connected to positive feelings and events stored in memory; thus, flashing this word primes positive words, making them more accessible. Subjects also feel more positive toward nonsense syllables paired unobtrusively with words such as "we" and "us" than those paired with "they" and "them." From an evolutionary perspective, preference for ingroup members and fear or distrust of outgroups may have evolved as a mechanism for minimizing threats from outside the group and maximizing cooperation among people who are likely to be genetically related and to rely on each other for mutual security.

Reducing Group Antagonisms

Research on ingroups and outgroups inevitably led to interest in techniques for reducing group antagonisms. In a classic experiment, researchers first created friction between two groups of boys, dubbed the Rattlers and the Eagles, at a Boy Scout summer camp (Sherif et al., 1961). The experimenters fostered the formation of strong ingroup sentiments by having the children in each group give their group a name, wear special clothes, and so forth; they encouraged rivalries through competitive activities. Within a short time, the competition became so heated that it degenerated into physical aggression.

Initial attempts to defuse the hostility, such as bringing the groups together for pleasant activities, failed. Another approach, however, was more successful: The experimenters contrived situations that created **superordinate goals**, that is, goals requiring the groups to cooperate for the benefit of all (see also Gaertner et al., 1990). In one instance, the experimenters arranged for a truck transporting food for an overnight trip to stall. Eventually, members of both groups cooperated in pulling the truck with a rope. Similar positive interactions occurred when the camp's water supply stopped and the boys from both groups were asked to help solve the problem.

The researchers concluded that contact alone is not enough to reduce conflict. The contact must also involve cooperation (see Sherif & Sherif, 1979). This finding has important implications for social policies such as school desegregation, since it suggests that simply placing children from two different races in the same school may not minimize animosities and may in fact exacerbate them (see Devine, 1995). For desegregation to work, whites and nonwhites must share enough common goals, such as playing on the same sports teams, to feel they have a common fate. They also need to have enough shared values, beliefs, culture, and skills that their interactions dissolve stereotypes rather than confirm them. Unfortunately, shared beliefs and culture are precisely the variables on which members of various cultures and subcultures differ.

Commentary: Are Stereotypes Arbitrary?

We have seen that the schemas or stereotypes people hold of groups other than their own contribute to prejudice, discrimination, and ethnic and racial hatred. Stereotypes tend to be the least accurate of schemas, but are they completely arbitrary?

Probably not, at least when they first arise. When people initially form stereotypes, they do not generate them without data. Like other schemas, stereotypes reflect people's attempts to make sense of and categorize their experience. The central features encoded in stereotypes are those that people find most characteristic of people of different groups (Ford & Stangor, 1992). When Southerners travel to New York City, one of the first things they typically observe is that New Yorkers are cold and unfriendly—*by Southern standards*. They note a salient difference in behavior (people avoid eye contact, do not spontaneously offer directions to people who look lost, smile less to strangers, and so forth), and they categorize this difference in a way that is meaningful to them (cold and unfriendly).

Similarly, when Europeans first described Latin Americans and Africans as "lazy," their error probably resulted less from inaccurate observations of behavior than from imposing their own values and categories of thought on the behavior of people who were following very different cultural rules. In our own century,

Western entrepreneurs with factories in Third World countries have repeatedly reported frustration that their employees do not observe Western standards of punctuality and do not consider hard work a moral value, as do people in the West (Inkeles & Smith, 1974). By twentieth-century Western standards, nearly every human being who has ever lived outside the contemporary West is lazy, passive, and lacking in industriousness. In contrast, by the standards of most cultures in human history, most Westerners are self-centered and frenetic. Both viewpoints partake of some reality, but they impose radically different meanings on the same behavior.

Herein lies a significant problem for self-consciously multicultural societies such as our own. Social categorization is inherently evaluative. Try as we might, we cannot suspend our repugnance at the gross subordination of women in cultures throughout the world, regardless of what the behavior means to them, when we are striving for equality at home. And if we could suspend our moral judgment, should we not then extend the same tolerance to classes and subcultures within our own society in which wife-beating is condoned or accepted as a man's prerogative?

We are all members of races, ethnic groups, and socioeconomic classes that cherish their values and deliberately display the signs of their social identities. Perhaps to be a person in an era of multiculturalism means brushing up against one of the givens of human nature—that what is different, what is "other," what speaks a different language and partakes of different rituals, is frightening. This automatically elicited fear, unchecked by knowledge and self-reflection, tends to elicit fight or flight. We are also all members of social groups that enjoy privilege or suffer disadvantages. Thus, we can never address matters of race and prejudice without an underlying agenda of assuaging our guilt, justifying our privilege, or voicing our outrage.

These tensions provide the emotional undergirding of every public policy debate remotely related to race or ethnicity, whether the issue is welfare, crime, or affirmative action. We are torn between the values we cherish and those we must somehow accept in others, between a conscious toleration or celebration of diversity and an unconscious fear of it. The most dangerous thing we can do, however, is to deny these conflicts within ourselves and remain unaware of the profound ambivalence all of us have about people of different colors, ethnicities, and cultures. When we see a disproportionate number of violent crimes committed by people of color, we tend either to lay the blame on these "hoodlums" or on a society that relegates 20 percent of its population to poverty and calls itself civilized. Each response alone is a half-truth that resolves conflict and ambiguity at the expense of reality. To deny our ambivalence is to lead us inevitably and unknowingly to continue to judge people, as Martin Luther King so eloquently decried, by the color of their skin—or to fail to judge others who deserve our condemnation for the content of their character.

Maintaining an open mind toward what is foreign may require constant, conscious vigilance against bigotry, hatred, and fear of the unfamiliar.

Attribution

Whether trying to understand the causes of inner-city violence or a terse response from a boss, people are constantly thinking about the "whys" of social interaction. The process of inferring the causes of one's own and others' mental states and behaviors is called **attribution** (Harvey & Weary, 1981). Attribution plays a central role in social behavior. Whether a judge attributes the actions of a defendant charged with murder to malevolent intent, accidental mishandling of a gun, or a deprived childhood will have a tremendous impact on the sentence he hands down. Similarly, the inferences a person makes about her boss's terseness can influence her feelings about her boss and ultimately her behavior, such as whether she begins looking for new employment.

People attribute causes by observing the **covariation** of different social events (such as situations or behaviors)—that is, by assessing the extent to which the presence of one variable implies the presence of another (Heider, 1958; Kelley, 1973,

1992). The employee who receives a terse reponse to a question may have observed that her boss is always brusque when he is stressed by approaching deadlines. In so doing, she is acting like an intuitive scientist trying to understand the relations among different variables and looking for correlations and interactions among them, much as a researcher does.

Making Inferences

Understanding others' behavior requires that the perceiver try to discern when people's actions reflect demands of the situation, aspects of their personalities, or interactions between the two (that is, ways specific people behave in particular situations). Thus, people make **external attributions**, or attributions to the situation, and **internal attributions**, attributions to the person (Chapter 5). Often they combine the two, as when the employee concludes that her boss has a tendency to become tense and brusque (internal attribution) when he is stressed by deadlines (external attribution). When Milgram found that most subjects obeyed, he made the attribution that the behavior of individual subjects was less a reflection of their personalities than of the situation. People make similar judgments in everyday life, as when they hear from several friends that a movie is excellent and infer that the movie is probably good rather than that their friends uniformly have bad taste. Alternatively, they might make the more complex attribution that this movie is enjoyable to people like their friends—an interaction between a type of person (their friends, who may be intellectual and like foreign flicks) and a situation (the movie).

In making attributions to the person or the situation, people rely on three types of information: consensus, consistency, and distinctiveness (Kelley, 1973, 1979). If everyone in the organization responds tersely to her questions, the employee attributes her boss's brusque behavior to something situational (such as the organizational culture, or atmosphere of the company) because her boss's behavior is a normative, or **consensus** response. **Consistency** refers to the extent to which the person always responds in the same way to the same stimulus. If her boss is frequently brusque, the employee will make an internal attribution. The **distinctiveness** of a person's action refers to whether the individual responds this way to many different stimuli. Does her boss treat other people this way? If so, she is likely to conclude that brusqueness is an enduring aspect of his personality. Consistency and distinctiveness are the intuitive scientist's versions of the concepts of consistency across time and consistency over situations debated by personality psychologists (Chapter 12).

Part of the difficulty in making accurate attributions is that most actions have multiple causes, some of them situational and some based on personal dispositions. In deciding how much to credit or blame a person, people generally adjust for the strength of situational demands through processes called discounting and augmentation. **Discounting** occurs when people downplay (discount) the role of one variable (such as personality, intelligence, or skill) because they know that another may be contributing to the behavior in question. A judge may discount the responsibility of a defendant accused of murder because he had a bad childhood, or the employee may discount her boss's bad manners because he is under the strain of an approaching deadline. The opposite situation occurs with **augmentation**, which means increasing, or augmenting, an internal attribution for behavior that has occurred *despite* situational pressures. The judge may perceive the defendant as particularly morally deficient because he continued to shoot the person repeatedly after he already appeared dead, or the employee may attribute particular coldness to her boss when he continues to respond tersely to her questions when the workload is low.

When people make inferences about other people's behavior, they typically go through a three-step process (Gilbert, 1995; Gilbert et al., 1988). First, they categorize the behavior. (They look at a facial expression and decide that it is angry, or they hear a comment and conclude that it is provocative.) Next, they categorize the actor based on the way they have interpreted the behavior. (An aggressive comment implies a hostile person.) Finally, they correct their inference if the situation calls for a particular response. (They may discount the attribution of hostility when they recognize that the comment was provoked by something another person said.) Interestingly, once people have identified an action, they are likely to make internal attributions automatically and unconsciously and only correct them with conscious effort. Subjects who are distracted while making attributions tend to make internal attributions even when situational variables call for discounting because they have no time to reflect and correct their initial impression (Gilbert, 1995).

Self-Attribution

Not only do people make inferences about the causes of other people's actions; they also attribute causes to their own psychological processes, a process called **self-attribution**. The notion of self-attribution may seem counterintuitive because we tend to assume that we have direct access to our own psychological processes. However, people are only conscious of a subset of the events that occur in their minds (Chapter 9) and hence must make educated guesses about their own personalities or the causes of their own actions.

In one study, male subjects were asked to rate the attractiveness of photos of nude women while hearing what they believed were their own heartbeats (Valins, 1966). Subjects rated the photos at which they were looking when the heartbeat accelerated as more attractive. Apparently, they thought that if their heart was beating faster, they must be aroused and assumed the photos were the cause. In another experiment, male subjects crossed either a wobbly suspension bridge high over a canyon, which tended to generate anxiety, or a solid bridge only 10 feet above a brook (Dutton & Aron, 1974). As each subject crossed the bridge, an attractive female research assistant approached and asked him to complete a short questionnaire pertaining to pictures of people. Afterward, she gave the subject her phone number in case he had questions about the study or its results. As predicted, the subjects on the suspension bridge not only found more sexual themes in the pictures, but they were also much more likely to call the woman. The arousal that occurred on the wobbly suspension bridge was fear, but subjects misattributed it to sexual arousal because of the presence of the attractive research assistant.

Surprisingly, people apply the discounting and augmentation principles to themselves as well. In a study exploring the self-perception of humor, subjects listened to two sets of jokes, with a laugh track accompanying one set (Olson, 1992). In one condition, the experimenter told subjects that canned laughter increases laughter. He told another group that canned laughter actually *decreases* the perceived humor of jokes, and he told the control group that canned laughter has no effect whatsoever. The logic of the experiment was that people who believe canned laughter enhances the comic appeal should discount the humor of the jokes accompanied by laugh tracks. The opposite should be the case for subjects who are led to believe that canned laughter diminishes enjoyment; that is, they should augment for jokes accompanied by the laugh track.

After subjects listened to the two sets of jokes, the experimenter left the room, encouraging them to read either of two books from which the jokes had been extracted. The results were as predicted (Table 17.1). Subjects who were led to believe that the laugh track inflated their enjoyment of jokes spent twice as much time reading jokes from the book that had been presented without the laugh track. Subjects who believed the laugh track had diminished their mirth spent twice as much time with the joke book that had been "ruined" by the laugh track. Subjects in the control condition were as likely to read one book as the other.

Individual Differences in Attributions

People differ considerably in the way they make attributions. Some people attribute the causes of unfortunate events to stable and global attributes of them-

BOOK	AVERAGE NUMBER OF SECONDS WITH EACH BOOK		
	Told That Canned Laughter Increases Perceived Humor	Told That Canned Laughter Decreases Perceived Humor	Told That Canned Laughter Has No Effect
With laugh track	54.5	117.6	88.3
Without laugh track	107.2	48.1	90.0

TABLE 17.1 SELF-ATTRIBUTION

Source: Adapted from Olson, 1992, p. 373.

selves, as when they explain their failure on a math exam in terms of lack of ability; others find the causes of their misfortunes elsewhere, as when they attribute the failure to a difficult exam (Chapter 5). People also differ in the complexity of their attributions (Fletcher et al., 1986). Some reflect carefully on the causes of their own and other people's behaviors ("I think she got angry because she knew she was wrong, and being angry prevented her from feeling guilty"), whereas others make more superficial inferences ("Something must have made her mad, I guess").

Individuals also vary in the hostility or malevolence of their attributions, which in turn influences the way they respond to people. Several studies have examined the attributional processes of boys with conduct problems (Crick & Dodge, 1994; Dodge & Somberg, 1987). In these studies, delinquent and nondelinquent boys view videotaped scenes that are ambiguous as to whether one boy intentionally or unintentionally caused harm to another. Boys with conduct problems tend to assume the action was intentional, not accidental. Other researchers have found that partners in distressed marriages make more hostile attributions about each other's behavior than nondistressed couples (Bradbury & Fincham, 1990; Fincham & Bradbury, 1993) and that abusive mothers tend to make hostile inferences about the intentions of their own children as well as children depicted in vignettes (Larrance & Twentyman, 1983). Several studies have also documented, through interviews and projective tests such as the TAT, a propensity toward malevolent attributions in patients with borderline personality disorders (Westen, 1991).

Biases in Social Information Processing

Although individuals often act as intuitive scientists, their "studies" are not generally suitable for publication because of methodological shortcomings. Indeed, one reason why rigorous application of scientific method is so important in social psychology is to prevent researchers from making the same kinds of intuitive errors people make in daily life. Social psychologists have identified several biases in social information processing and have explored their causes.

Common Biases in Social Cognition

One common bias is the false confirmation of schemas and hypotheses: People tend to look for information that confirms their beliefs and ignore information that does not (Chapter 7). False confirmation is one of the cognitive roots of stereotyping. Other research suggests that people overestimate the causal role of internal factors and underestimate situational causes (Heider, 1958), a bias called the **fundamental attribution error** (Ross, 1977). In one series of experiments, subjects read or listened to a discourse in support of, or against, Fidel Castro's regime in Cuba (Jones & Harris, 1967). The experimenters led half the subjects to believe the attitude was the author's and told the other half that the author had been instructed which position to take (Figure 17.3). Being informed or misinformed had no effect on attributions about the anti-Castro speech; listeners assumed it was the speaker's point of view whether he was told to take that viewpoint or not because nearly everyone in the United States at that time was anti-Castro. Yet subjects tended to overestimate the pro-Castro position of the speaker even when they had been informed that the author had been assigned a point of view. In other words, they attributed the speaker's behavior to internal dispositions even though they knew otherwise.

The concept of the fundamental attribution error was in many respects predicated on Walter Mischel's argument that behavior reflects situations, not personality—a view that has turned out to be largely incorrect (Chapter 12). Subsequent theory and research have similarly questioned whether the fundamental attribution error is so fundamental or so erroneous. Calling this bias fundamental may itself reflect a cultural bias in the research, all of which was all conducted in the West. Because contemporary Western culture is individualistic, Western subjects tend to emphasize individual responsibility when they make attributions. People outside Western technologically developed societies are more likely to believe that external factors control their lives. For example, one study asked subjects from India and the United States to explain why someone might have carried out various socially acceptable and deviant acts (Miller, 1984). Indian subjects were far less likely to make internal attributions and more likely to explain behavior in terms of social roles and responsibilities. Their responses may reflect not only different cultural explanatory systems but also differences in reality: Indians may well be more heavily influenced or constrained in their behavior by role demands and social obligations (see Fletcher & Ward, 1988).

A third bias in social cognition is that people tend to see themselves in a more positive light than they deserve, known as the **self-serving bias** (Epstein, 1992; Greenwald, 1980; Snyder & Higgins, 1988). The self-serving bias takes a number of forms. A majority of people rate themselves above average on most dimensions, which is, of course, statistically impossible (Taylor & Brown, 1988). People are more likely to recall positive than negative information about themselves (Kuiper &

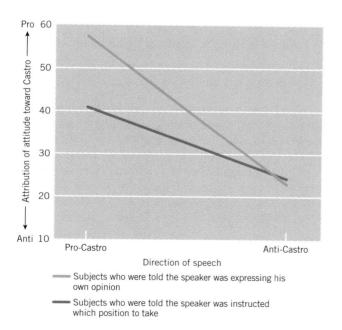

FIGURE 17.3
The fundamental attribution error. Subjects attributed pro-Castro sentiment to speakers who spoke positively of the Castro regime even when informed that the speaker had to take a pro-Castro position. SOURCE: Adapted from Jones, 1976, p. 301.

Derry, 1982; Kuiper et al., 1985), to see their talents as more striking and unusual than their deficiencies (Campbell, 1986; Marks, 1984), and to attribute to themselves greater responsibility for a group product than other group members attribute to them (Ross & Sicoly, 1979). A study of divorced couples similarly found that each divorced partner tended to rate him- or herself as less responsible for the breakup, as more willing to reconcile, and as the victim rather than the cause of the breakup (Gray & Silver, 1990).

Self-serving biases are not without their limits. Most people will not totally ignore reality to perceive themselves in the best possible light. Extroverts who are induced to believe that extroversion is not conducive to academic success come to see themselves as less extroverted, but they do not completely deny their extroversion (see Kunda, 1990). Individuals also differ tremendously in the extent to which they allow their wishes about themselves to interfere with their objectivity. One study observed MBA-student subjects interacting over a weekend (John & Robins, 1994). Groups of six subjects each participated in simulated corporate decision-making meetings. At the end of the weekend, subjects ranked themselves and their peers as to who had done the best, second best, and so on, from one to six. Eleven psychologist observers also ranked each subject.

Subjects' rankings of peers in their groups were remarkably consistent with the rankings of disinterested observers; peer and psychologist rankings correlated at about .50. Thus, subjects were fairly objective in ranking their peers' performance, but they were much less objective about themselves. Their self-rankings correlated with peer and psychologist rankings of them at only about .30. Sixty percent overestimated their own performance, suggesting a self-serving bias.

Does this mean that people routinely ignore the data to make themselves feel better? Perhaps, but with two substantial qualifications (Table 17.2). First, roughly 50 percent of subjects ranked themselves (from 1 to 6) within one rank of the way psychologists and their peers ranked them. This suggests that, within bounds, half of all subjects were reasonably accurate in their self-perceptions. Second, the one-third who overestimated themselves by two or more ranks had a distinguishing characteristic: They were more narcissistic by both observer- and self-report. The tendency to self-enhance in this study correlated around .50 with objective observers' ratings of subjects' narcissism. Narcissistic people are self-aggrandizing and self-centered. Clinicians suggest that narcissists are prone to distort their accomplishments in order to compensate for underlying feelings of worthlessness or self-doubt (Kernberg, 1975). This study thus suggests that most people wear mildly rose-tinted glasses when they look in the mirror, but people who are narcissistic keep a pair of opaque spectacles on hand in case the spotlight shines too brightly on their flaws.

Causes of Biases

Why do people have so many biases in processing social information? The answer lies in both cognition and motivation. Some of the errors people make result from the same kinds of cognitive biases people display in nonsocial cognition, such as false confirmation of schemas (Chapter 7). People also frequently lack the information they need to make accurate attributions. They are more likely, for example, to recognize situational influences on their own behavior than on others' behavior because they have more information about themselves (Jones & Nisbett, 1971). Other biases reflect motivation (Bruner & Tagiuri, 1954; Fiske, 1992; Kunda, 1990; Westen, 1991). Schemas and attributions are influenced by wishes, needs, and goals. One study, for example, found that subjects who were currently in romantic relationships tended to perceive opposite-sex peers as less attractive and sexually desirable than subjects who were uninvolved (Simpson et al., 1990). This bias is useful because it makes maintaining a monogamous relationship easier.

Motivation can also influence the extent to which people think complexly about themselves and others, as documented in a study comparing subjects high in need

TABLE 17.2 SELF-SERVING BIASES AND NARCISSISM

(a) COMPARISON

Self-Rankings	Peer Rankings	Psychologist Rankings
Overestimate > one rank	31%	32%
Within one rank	54%	53%
Underestimate > one rank	15%	15%

(b) SELF-ENHANCEMENT

Narcissism	Compared with Peer Rankings	Compared with Psychologist Rankings
Observer rating	.55	.49
Self-report	.34	.38

Source: Adapted from John & Robins, 1994.

Note. Part *(a)* shows the relative accuracy of subjects' self-rankings compared to the way their peers and neutral observers ranked them. Part *(b)* shows the correlations between narcissism scores and the extent to which subjects' self-rankings were inflated when compared to the way they were ranked by peers and psychologists.

for intimacy with those high in need for power (Woike & Aronoff, 1992). Subjects were asked to evaluate potential research assistants by watching them interact with each other on videotape. In one condition, the investigators emphasized the need to be sensitive and empathic toward the applicant. In the other condition, the investigators stressed the importance of taking control of the situation and exercising decision-making power.

After watching the videotapes, subjects described the candidates, and the researchers coded their responses for the complexity of their social cognition. The investigators reasoned that subjects motivated by power would think more deeply and complexly when their power motives were activated, just as those high in intimacy motivation would think more complexly when motivated by instructions emphasizing intimacy. These findings were strongly confirmed (Figure 17.4), suggesting that the extent to which people think deeply about others depends on their motivation to do so.

Motivated biases can occur at the societal or national level as well as the personal. Nations on the verge of war systematically distort their attributions about the motives of the other side, often portraying the enemy—but not themselves, of course—as interested in little else but power (Winter, 1987, 1993). Even Abraham Lincoln, not a person known for biased thinking, declared in his Second Inaugural Address, "Both parties depreciated war, but one of them would *make* war rather than let the nation survive, and the other would *accept* war rather than let it perish, and the war came."

Lincoln's biased attributions were shared by his countrymen, as demonstrated in a study of motives attributed by Northern and Southern newspapers to Lincoln and his Confederate counterpart, Jefferson Davis, following a series of

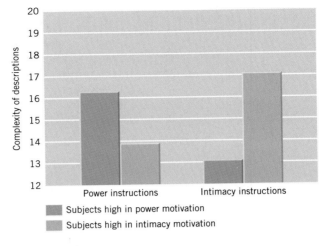

FIGURE 17.4
Motivation and the complexity of social cognition. When the instructions stressed power, subjects high in power motivation showed cognitive complexity in describing potential research assistants. When the instructions stressed intimacy, subjects high in intimacy motivation thought more complexly. SOURCE: *Woike & Aronoff, 1992, p. 102.*

speeches in 1861 (Winter, 1987). The Northern media exaggerated Davis's power motivation, whereas the Southern media diminished Lincoln's motives for affiliation (Figure 17.5). Similar biases have been documented in British and German newspapers from World War I (Winter, 1993) and were apparent in more recent international conflicts, such as the confrontation between George Bush and Saddam Hussein in 1991.

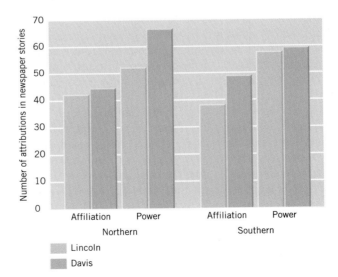

FIGURE 17.5
Motives attributed to Lincoln and Davis by Northern and Southern newspapers. Northern newspapers saw Davis as power hungry, whereas Southern newspapers saw Lincoln as unaffiliative (rather ironically, since he was trying to keep the South from disaffiliating). SOURCE: *Adapted from Winter, 1987, p. 44.*

Research thus shows that if people behave like intuitive scientists, they are not very good ones and could use some basic courses in research design. Social perceivers have many goals besides the scientific objective of seeking truth, and these other agendas influence their "findings." They are interested in looking good, maintaining positive feelings about themselves, believing good things will happen to them, protecting their idealized views of people they care about, and maintaining negative schemas of people (or groups) they dislike. Since motives play a fundamental role in attention, encoding, retrieval, and problem solving, social cognition is inherently intertwined with social motivation (see Fiske, 1993; Fiske & Taylor, 1991).

THE SELF

Thus far, we have paid little attention to the social stimulus to which people attend more than any other: the self (James, 1890; Markus, 1980). The concept of self has a long and rather serpentine history in psychology, slithering in and out of vogue. In some eras, such as the present, psychologists have viewed the self as a central aspect of psychological functioning (Epstein, 1990; Markus & Cross, 1990). In others, particularly during the heyday of behaviorism, psychologists viewed the self as a fuzzy, mushy concept, unobservable and hence scientifically unknowable.

One of the greatest challenges in describing the self seems to be defining it. Behaviorists complain, with considerable justification, that psychologists have used the same word to denote dozens of discrete phenomena and hence have failed to provide a coherent, empirically valid view of the self. For years, theorists of nearly every persuasion have defined the self as the self-concept—that is, as the way people see themselves. The problem with this definition is that it is logically impossible: If the self-concept is a concept of something, it must be a concept of the self. The self, then, cannot be a self-concept, or the self-concept becomes a person's concept of her self-concept. This is analogous to saying that a person's lamp and her concept of the lamp are the same thing.

The only logically sensible definition, then, is that the **self** is the person, including mental processes, body, and personality characteristics. From this definition several others logically follow. The **self-concept** is the person's concept of himself; it is a concept like any other (Chapter 7), such as squirrel, tree, or hairdresser. **Self-esteem** refers to the degree to which the person likes, respects, or esteems the self; and so forth.

Approaches to the Self

William James (1890) proposed a fundamental distinction between self as subject and self as object. The **self as subject** refers to the person's experience of self as thinker, feeler, and actor. When I feel an emotion or think a thought, it is "I"—the self as subject—who is doing the feeling or thinking. When I take an action, I have a sense that it is I who has made a choice about how to behave. In contrast, the **self as object** is the person's view of the self. This is the self-concept on which people reflect when they take the self as an object of thought. (The difference between self as subject and as object can be easily remembered grammatically. The self as subject, which James called the "I," is the subject who is capable of thinking about the self as object, the "me." Thus, the statement, "I am thinking about me," contains both elements of self.)

Although the self as described by James seems eminently private, numerous theorists have emphasized the role of significant others in shaping it, particularly in childhood. The **symbolic interactionists**, a school of sociological theorists, argued that the way people perceive themselves, and even their ability to recognize and label their own emotions, are heavily influenced by those around them. A child who frequently hears from his parents that he is bad is likely to come to see himself as bad, just as a child whose anger makes his parents uncomfortable may eventually fail to acknowledge even to himself when he is angry (Sullivan, 1953). In this view, children learn who they are by looking at themselves in the reflection of other people's eyes.

Carl Rogers (1959) defined the self-concept as a Gestalt or integrated view of the self (Chapter 12). People strive to actualize their ideal self—their view of the way they ideally should be—as well as the conditions of worth (standards required for esteeming the self) learned from their parents. In so doing, they may distort both the way they see themselves and the way they actually behave. Like other humanistic and existential psychologists (Laing, 1959; Smith, 1978), Rogers also argued that individuals may develop a false self, molding themselves to other people's expectations and to the demands of the roles they play, so that they no longer know who they are underneath the masks they wear.

Two contemporary perspectives have given increasing prominence to the self: the psychodynamic and the cognitive (see Curtis, 1991; Tesser, 1991; Westen, 1992).

Psychodynamic Perspective

Contemporary psychodynamic thinking focuses on **self-representations**, mental models or representations of the self. Object relations theories assert that people's representations of themselves and others play a key role in personality and psychopathology (Chapter 12). Patients with borderline personality disorders, for example, often view themselves as totally unlovable or evil to the core (Gunderson, 1984; Kernberg, 1975; Wixom et al., 1993), which can make them vulnerable to suicide. They tend to see themselves as either totally good or totally bad and are prone to attributing to other people motives or feelings (such as aggressive impulses) that they really fear in themselves (Kernberg, 1975).

From a psychodynamic perspective, self-representations, like representations of significant others, are compromise-formations: They reflect not only attempts at accurate perception but a host of other motives as well (Chapter 12). Prominent among these goals are maintaining self-esteem and avoiding anxiety and guilt. In this view, the self-serving bias stems from a defensive effort to ward off unpleasant feelings and maximize positive feelings about the self.

Self-representations can be conscious or unconscious, and the two are often at odds. One patient with a narcissistic personality disorder was furious and deeply depressed when he was passed over for a supervisory position. At some level he worried that his own failings were the cause, but he convinced himself that the only reason he was passed over was because "mediocrity" (like his boss) "cannot appreciate true genius." This consciously grandiose representation seemed to mask a very different unconscious view of himself. Research on subjects with avoidant attachment styles, who steadfastly deny their tender and angry feelings despite electrophysiological evidence showing otherwise, provides empirical evidence of conscious self-representations that contradict unconscious experience (Chapter 14).

Cognitive Perspective

Although cognitive theorists are paying increasing attention to motivation related to the self (Showers & Cantor, 1985; Higgins, 1990; Markus & Wurf, 1987; Swann, 1990; Erber & Tesser, 1994), they have focused primarily on the way the self-concept shapes thought and memory (see Greenwald & Pratkanis, 1984; Markus & Cross, 1990). Arguing that people are intuitive scientists even when examining themselves, Seymour Epstein (1973, 1990) has proposed that the self-

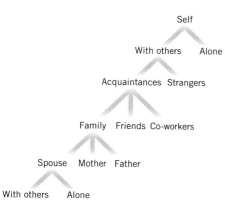

FIGURE 17.6
Hierarchical organization of a self-schema. Self-schemas may be organized hierarchically with multiple components, many defined by relationships, such as self with family, friends, and co-workers.
SOURCE: *Kihlstrom & Cantor, 1983.*

concept is like a theory of oneself. A good self-theory should have the virtues of a good scientific theory, such as accuracy and internal consistency.

Other cognitive theorists propose that the self-concept is a **self-schema** (a schema or pattern of thought about the self) that organizes and guides the processing of self-related information (Kuiper & Rogers, 1977; Markus, 1977; Markus & Wurf, 1987). Self-schemas may be hierarchically organized (Kihlstrom & Cantor, 1983). At the core of the broader self-schema are fundamental attributes of the self, such as one's name, sex, physical appearance, relationships to family members, and salient personality traits. Below this general level in the hierarchy are schemas of the self in different situations or relationships (Figure 17.6). Each subschema is associated with its own attributes; a person may see herself as annoyed and anxious with her mother but comfortable with friends.

Discerning precisely where people's self-schemas leave off and their schemas of other people, groups, or even inanimate objects begin is not as easy as it might seem. William James asserted that people's material possessions are part of the self, and recent research confirms that people display self-enhancing biases toward their possessions: They like them more than others' possessions, simply by virtue of being their own (Beggan, 1992). Significant others and groups also play a role in the self-concept. A person may conceive of herself as a Canadian, David's wife, or Elaine's daughter. People gain self-esteem through their association with esteemed others, as when the parent of an athlete beams with pride (Tesser, 1990). Biases thus arise that are analogous to self-serving biases, except that the object is a significant other rather than the self. Parents show the same bias toward overestimating their children's abilities as adults do for their own abilities (Miller et al., 1991); children overestimate the strength of peers they like and underestimate their disliked peers (Boulton & Smith, 1990); and adults show biased thinking that is favorable to their own versus other groups (Schaller, 1992).

FROM MIND TO BRAIN

PHYSICAL HEALTH AND VIEWS OF THE SELF

People have schemas not only about the way they are but also about the way they wish they were or fear becoming (Markus & Nurius, 1986; Niedenthal et al., 1992). One theory distinguishes three kinds of self-concepts: actual, ideal, and ought (Higgins, 1987, 1990). The actual self refers to people's views of how they actually are; the ideal self refers to the hopes, aspirations, and wishes that define the way the person would like to be; and the ought self includes the duties, obligations, and responsibilities that define the way the person should be. Thus, a person may see himself as a moderately successful businessman (actual self) but hope to become the chief executive officer of a company (ideal self). At the same time, he may volunteer at a soup kitchen on Thanksgiving to satisfy a nagging sense that he is not contributing enough to his community (ought self). People have actual, ideal, and ought selves from a number of points of view, including their own and those of significant others. A person may feel she is meeting her "ought" standards for herself but that she has failed to meet her mother's expectations.

Discrepancies between these various self-schemas are associated with particular types of emotion (Higgins, 1987; Strauman, 1992). When people perceive their actual self as varying from their ideal self, they tend to feel dejection-related emotions such as disappointment, dissatisfaction, shame, and embarrassment (Table 17.3). These are characteristic feelings of individuals who are depressed, who feel their wishes and hopes are unfulfilled. People who experience a discrepancy between actual self and ought self feel agitation-related emotions such as fear, resentment, guilt, self-contempt, or uneasiness. These feelings are characteristic of anxious individuals, who believe they have failed to meet their obligations and hence may be punished.

Research suggests that these schemas may influence not only mood but physical health as well. As we have seen (Chapter 11), emotional distress can depress immune-system functioning, making a person vulnerable to ill health. Enduring ways of perceiving the self may thus lead to chronic feeling states that increase vulnerability to illness. One remarkable study demonstrated this by comparing subjects who were anxious, depressed, or neither (Strauman et al., 1993). The investigators asked subjects to describe their actual, ideal, and ought selves, thanked them for their participation, and told them the experiment was over. Six weeks later, a group of their research assistants, allegedly conducting a different experiment, primed discrepancies between actual and ideal self in the depressed subjects and between actual and ought self in the anxious subjects. They did this by exposing them to words they had previously mentioned that were related to these discrepancies. For example, the investigators might ask an anxious subject who described his actual self as shy but his ought self as confident to think about the importance of being confident. (They also included words that were irrelevant to the person so that subjects would not figure out what was happening.) A week later, the experimenters exposed the subject to a set of entirely irrelevant words (actually, taken from other subjects), in order to compare against the results of the previous session. Control subjects were similarly exposed one day to self-referential words and another day to words that were irrelevant. After each session, the investigators took blood samples to ascertain levels of natural killer cells, a rough index of immune response.

The main findings are reproduced in Figure 17.7. The killer cell activity of control subjects, who were neither depressed nor anxious, went up slightly

---

TABLE 17.3 EMOTIONS ASSOCIATED WITH SELF-CONCEPT DISCREPANCIES

DISCREPANCY	EMOTION TYPE	EXAMPLES
Actual self ≠ ideal self	Dejection-related	Disappointment, dissatisfaction, shame, embarrassment, depression
Actual self ≠ ought self	Agitation-related	Fear, resentment, guilt, self-contempt, uneasiness, anxiety

Source: Adapted from Higgins, 1987, pp. 319–340.

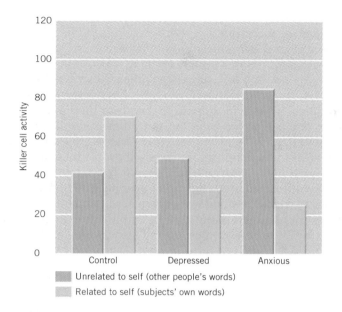

FIGURE 17.7
*Self-schemas and immune functioning. Exposing nondepressed, nonanx-
ious subjects to words related to their ideal and ought selves led to a slight
increase in killer cell activity—that is, to heightened immune functioning.
For depressed and especially for anxious subjects, in contrast, exposure led
to diminished immune functioning.* SOURCE: *Adapted from Strauman et
al., 1993, p. 1049.*

when they were exposed to self-referential words. Depressed subjects showed
a slight decrease in killer cell activity when exposed to words related to their
ideal-self discrepancies, although this was not statistically significant. The
most striking finding was for anxious subjects, whose killer cell levels were significantly lower after being exposed to words related to their self-perceived
failings (actual/ought discrepancies). Thinking about their unfulfilled obligations or unmet standards made them momentarily more vulnerable to illness.
These findings are preliminary, but they strongly suggest that chronic discrepancies between the way one believes one is and the way one ought or ideally
should be might have a lasting impact on health.

Self-Esteem

Self-esteem refers to a person's feelings toward the self. Just as individuals can
conjure up a typical or prototypical self-concept, they have a core or global sense of
self-esteem (Rosenberg, 1979), a usual way they feel about themselves. They also
experience momentary fluctuations in self-esteem, depending on which self-schemas
are currently active. An athlete who wins a competition sees herself as a winner and
enjoys a momentary boost in self-esteem, regardless of whether being a winner is
part of her prototypical self-concept.

Research with Western subjects suggests that self-esteem is hierarchically organized, presumably tied to a hierarchically organized view of the self. Thus, nested
below a general level of self-esteem, people have feelings about themselves along
specific dimensions, such as their morality, physical appearance, and competence
(Coopersmith, 1967; Harter 1983). A person with generally low esteem for his athletic prowess may nevertheless recognize himself to be a decent tennis player. People

generally maintain positive self-esteem by giving greater emotional weight to areas in which they are more successful.

Most people regulate their self-esteem so that it does not fall too low or become unrealistically high or grandiose (Kohut, 1971; Reich, 1960). People with positive self-esteem obviously do this more successfully than those with negative self-esteem (or narcissists, who alternate between feelings of superiority and worthlessness). Individuals with high self-esteem respond to threats to their self-esteem by comparing themselves to others who are worse on some dimension than they are (Gibbons & McCoy, 1991; Wills, 1981). They use other strategies as well, such as compensating for weak areas. One set of studies exposed people to an alleged test of intelligence that was rigged so they would fail (Brown & Smart, 1991). Subjects with high self-esteem compensated by exaggerating their positive social traits (rather than intellectual traits, at which they had just experienced failure). Since they could not deny the feedback they had just received, they simply distorted information in a different domain in order to restore their overall self-esteem. Unlike other subjects, they were also especially helpful after failure, which contributed to a positive appraisal of their social or moral self, adding extra positive weight to balance the emotional scales.

Men and women appear to differ in the way they derive self-esteem. Men tend to gain esteem by emphasizing their distinctiveness in comparison to others—particularly their superiority—whereas women tend to derive more of their esteem from their capacity to connect with other people (Josephs et al., 1992). To what degree this is changing as gender roles converge is an open question, as women gain more self-esteem from their feelings of competence at work and men increasingly appreciate their ability to nurture and connect with others.

Self-Consistency

That people bias their cognitions to enhance their self-esteem is not surprising, but a less obvious motivation regarding the self is **self-consistency**. People are motivated to interpret information to fit the way they already see themselves, and they prefer people who verify rather than challenge their views of themselves (Lecky, 1945; Swann, 1990). Most of the time, self-consistency and self-esteem motives produce similar effects. Since most people hold relatively favorable views of themselves, they prefer positive information because it enhances self-esteem and bolsters their existing self-concept.

For people who do not like themselves, however, these two motives can lead them in opposite directions. They want to feel better about themselves, but they also dislike evidence that conflicts with their self-concept. Depressed people actually prefer to interact with others—including marital partners—who have a negative view of them (Chapter 15). Individuals who perceive themselves negatively appear to avoid people who give them feedback to the contrary for several reasons. They consider the feedback untrue, they feel that the relationship will be smoother and more predictable if the other person understands them, and they believe people who view them positively are less perceptive (Swann et al., 1992).

A GLOBAL VISTA

CULTURE AND SELF

The notion that people have a self-concept and some core of selfhood that distinguishes them from others seems intuitively obvious to people living in twentieth-century Western societies. This view would not, however, be commonsensical to people in most cultures in most historical epochs (Geertz, 1974; Markus & Kitayama, 1991; Shweder & Bourne, 1982). That the phrase, "the individual" is synonymous with "the person" in contemporary usage demonstrates how the individualism of our culture is reflected in its language. Indeed, the prefix "self-," as in "self-esteem" or "self-representation," did not evolve in the English language until around the time of the Industrial Revolution, a co-occurrence that is not coincidental.

The contemporary Western view of the person is of a bounded individual, distinct from others, who is defined by more or less idiosyncratic attributes. In contrast, most cultures, particularly the nonliterate tribal societies in which people lived throughout the vast expanse of human history, view the person in her social and familial context, so that the self-concept is far less distinctly bounded. When the Wintu Indians of North America described being with another person who was closely related or intimate with them, they would not use a phrase such as "John and I," but rather, "John we." They reserved "and" to signify distance between people with minimal relation. When anthropologist Dorothy Lee (1950) tried to elicit an autobiography from a Wintu woman, she received an extensive account of the lives of the woman's ancestors. Only with considerable prompting did the woman eventually discuss "that which was in my mother's womb." Cheyenne autobiographies similarly tend to begin with "My grandfather..." (Straus, 1982).

This relational view of selfhood is not confined to North American tribes. It is common among many African groups, such as the Tshidi of Southern Africa (Comaroff, 1980). It has also been observed among traditional Hindus in India (De Vos et al., 1985), who frequently give their caste and village along with their name when they are asked to identify themselves.

Two factors seem to explain the differences between contemporary Western and other views of the self. First, some cultures are simply more group-centered, and others, more individualistic (Markus & Kitayama, 1991; Triandis, 1989). Because Japanese culture emphasizes cooperation rather than the Western ideal of autonomy, the Japanese experience the self less in terms of internal states than in terms of social relationships (Cousins, 1989; DeVos et al., 1985). Thus, for the Japanese, sincerity describes behavior that conforms to a person's role expectations (carrying out one's duties), whereas for North Americans it means behaving in accordance with one's inner feelings (DeVos et al., 1985). Sincere behavior in Japan may thus be very insincere to an American. Similarly, Japanese students more readily link their personality traits to situations than their American counterparts (Cousins, 1989), emphasizing the social context ("I am shy in school" rather than "I am shy").

A second factor that has played a key role in producing differences between contemporary Western and other forms of selfhood is technological development (Westen, 1985, 1991). Careful examination of historical documents suggests that only a few centuries ago the Western concept of self was much closer to the non-Western, group-centered view (see Baumeister, 1986). The values, attitudes, and self-concepts of people in rural Greece, for example, resemble the collectivistic orientation one finds in China more than the individualism of contemporary Athens (see Triandis, 1989).

Ten thousand years ago, before the advent of agriculture, humans lived in bands (small groups) that were not altogether different from the band societies discovered by anthropologists in this century and the last. In these groups, individualism is rarely developed, a concept of self distinct from other people and nature is generally absent, and moral values focus on the interests of the clan or band. With the rise of agriculture, which allowed accumulation of personal resources and stratification into social classes, people became more aware of individuality, but it was countered by cultural proscriptions against it. As one anthropologist observed, in these societies, made up largely of poor peasants, "individual progress is seen as—and in the context of the traditional society in fact is—the supreme threat to community stability" (Foster, 1965, p. 310). Around the time of the Industrial Revolution, something remarkable

In the nineteenth century, Americans thought nothing of lending neighbors a hand for days or weeks to build a barn. This seems inconceivable just a century later, with the highly individualized sense of self produced by industrialization.

happened: The concept of the individual, shorn of attachments and duties, was born. And the individual has been born again wherever technological development has taken hold.

Technological development seems to facilitate individualism, and with it a more individuated sense of selfhood, for several reasons. The first is geographical mobility. People who remain throughout their lives in a small community with parents, grandparents, and extended kin are likely to view themselves in a very different context than people who can expect to leave home and relocate hundreds or thousands of miles away. In addition, changing work conditions, such as wage labor and work that is not performed communally with kin or clan, leads to a sense of individual competence. Furthermore, in technologically developed societies people earn much of their status through their actions rather than their family affiliations. They also frequently take up occupations different from those of their parents. When a man is no longer a hunter or farmer like his father, his representations of self and father diverge. Literacy and education also personalize skills and competences, which are no longer experienced as collective knowledge and may be learned through individual study. In addition, increased lifespan and higher standard of living make personal pleasures, desires, and interests more important. Factors such as family size and whether children have their own rooms probably have a subtle influence as well.

All of these factors foster a sense of individuality, which in turn spurs technological development by creating entrepreneurs, people with highly specialized expertise, and individuals willing to challenge received wisdom. Whether cultural differences such as those that divide Japan and the West will remain despite the pressures of industrialization is a profound psychological question, one that will probably be resolved over the course of the next century.

SOME CONCLUDING THOUGHTS

If culture and social interaction can shape something so private as the experience of self, what can it do to more public or interpersonal experiences, like love or aggression? These are the questions we examine in the final chapter, as we explore the influence of social experience on emotion, motivation, and behavior.

Summary

1. **Social psychology** examines the way thought, feeling, and behavior are influenced by the actual, imagined, or implied presence of others.

Attitudes

2. An **attitude** is an association between an object and an evaluation, which usually includes cognitive, evaluative, and behavioral components. These three components can, however, vary independently. Attitudes are not always good predictors of behavior.

3. Social psychologists have focused on two avenues of attitude change: persuasion and cognitive dissonance. **Persuasion** refers to deliberate efforts to induce attitude change. Optimal persuasion requires attending to all the components of a persuasive communication, including the source of the communication, the message, the channel (the means by which a message is sent), the receiver, and the target behavior at which the message is directed. **Cognitive dissonance** occurs when a person experiences a discrepancy between an attitude and a behavior or between an attitude and a new piece of information that does not fit with it.

Social Cognition

4. **Social cognition** refers to the processes by which people make sense of others, themselves, social interactions, and relationships. Social cognition differs from nonsocial cognition in several ways: Human actions are ambiguous and involve emotion, culture plays a much bigger role in social cognition, and social cognition is reciprocal. Many social psychologists have suggested that, in trying to understand the social world, people act like **intuitive scientists**, framing hypotheses, collecting data, and manipulating variables.

5. **First impressions** are the initial schemas people form when they encounter someone for the first time. Schemas, the patterns of thought that organize human experience, apply in the social realm as in other areas of life. **Person schemas** represent information about specific people or types of people. **Situation schemas** represent information about different kinds of social situations and often include **scripts**, which are schemas that specify how to do something socially. **Role schemas** represent culturally patterned information expected of people in particular social positions. **Relationship schemas** encode more idiosyncratic, personal expectations about how the self and others interact.

6. **Stereotypes** are overgeneralized schemas about characteristics ascribed to a group of people based on qualities such as race, ethnicity, or gender. **Prejudice** refers to judging an individual based on a negative stereotype. Racial and ethnic prejudice has roots both in motivation and cognition, and in personality and social dynamics. Prejudice typically requires the distinction between **ingroups** and **outgroups**, people who belong to the group and those who do not. People are remarkably quick to categorize this way and to respond on the basis of even an arbitrary categorization. Contact alone is not enough to reduce conflict between ingroups and outgroups; the contact must involve cooperation as well.

7. The process of making inferences about the causes of one's own and others' thoughts, feelings, and behavior is called **attribution**. One of the most important distinctions people make in their attributions is between **external attribu-**

tions—attributions to the situation—and **internal attributions**—attributions to the person. In making these attributions, people rely on three types of information: **consensus** (how everyone acts in that situation), **consistency** (how this person typically reacts in that situation), and **distinctiveness** (how this person usually reacts in different situations). **Discounting** occurs when people downplay the role of one variable because they know another may be contributing to the behavior in question. The opposite situation occurs with **augmentation**, which means increasing or augmenting an internal attribution for behavior that has occurred *despite* situational pressures.

8. Social cognition is biased in a number of ways, including the false confirmation of schemas and hypotheses, the tendency (at least, some argue, in the West) to overestimate the role of internal causes of behavior and underestimate situational causes (the **fundamental attribution error**), and the propensity to see oneself in a more positive light than one deserves (the **self-serving bias**).

The Self

9. The **self** refers to the person. The **self as subject** refers to the individual's experience of self as thinker, feeler, and actor. The **self as object**, in contrast, is the person's view of the self. **Symbolic interactionists** argue that the way people perceive themselves, and even their ability to recognize and label their own emotions, are heavily influenced by those around them.

10. Contemporary psychodynamic thinking focuses on mental representations of the self or **self-representations**, which can be conscious or unconscious. From a cognitive perspective, the self-concept is a **self-schema**, which guides thought, attention, and memory. **Self-esteem** refers to a person's feelings toward the self. People are also motivated by the need for **self-consistency**, interpreting information to fit the way they already see themselves.

11. The contemporary Western view of the person is of a bounded individual, distinct from significant others, who is defined by more or less idiosyncratic attributes. In contrast, most cultures, particularly the nonliterate tribal and band societies in which people lived throughout the vast expanse of human history, have understood the person in social and familial context. Technological development has fostered individualism and taken the self-concept out of its social context.

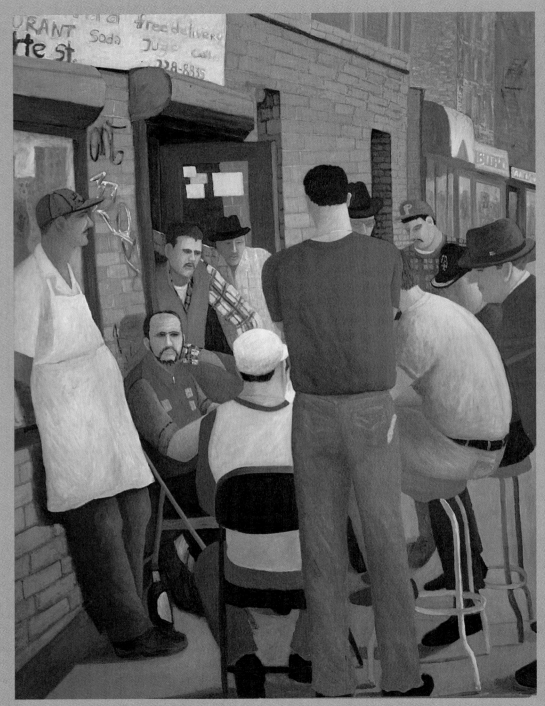

INTERPERSONAL PROCESSES

*S*amuel Oliner was a boy of 12 when the Nazis invaded the Jewish ghetto in Poland where he lived. His entire family was killed, but he managed to escape. After two days of hiding, during which he witnessed a child bayoneted and a baby shot with a pistol, he found his way to the home of a Christian woman with whom his father had done business. She fed him and taught him how to pass for a Christian peasant, and he survived the war.

Years later, Oliner wrote a book about the small number of people who risked their lives and the lives of their families to protect Jews during the Holocaust (Oliner & Oliner, 1988). He and his research team interviewed over 400 rescuers and compared them with 72 individuals who neither helped nor hindered the Nazis. They sought to answer a simple question: What made the rescuers perform such extraordinary acts of **altruism** (helping another person with no apparent gain, and even potential cost, to oneself)?

The altruism of these individuals seems to defy theories of moral development (Chapter 14). For example, according to cognitive-social theories, reward, punishment, and expectancies control behavior. Everyone in Germany and the occupied countries during the war faced the same contingencies of reinforcement—to rescue and be caught meant certain execution— but several thousand people rescued Jews in Europe nonetheless. According to cognitive-developmental theories, moral heroism should occur only among people with a high level of moral reasoning. Yet only about half of Oliner's rescuers referred to complex or abstract principles. In fact, several offered strikingly conventional reasons for their actions, such as, "I am an obedient Christian; the Lord wanted us to rescue those people and we did" (p. 155).

Rescuers differed from nonrescuers on both situational and dispositional variables, that is, in both their circumstances and their personality and attitudes. Perhaps surprisingly, one of the variables that distinguished the two groups was completely situational: Rescuers had more available rooms in their houses and were more likely to have a cellar. Rescuers also reported having come from closer-knit families and having had parents who sometimes reasoned with them as a mode of discipline (rather than simply punishing them). Overwhelmingly, they reported being taught to treat people fairly regardless of their race, color, or class.

Understanding why some people risked their lives while others did nothing—and why still others used ultranationalist ideology as an excuse to steal, rape, and murder, much as in Serbian "ethnic cleansing" in our own times—is the work of social psychologists. The previous chapter focused on the cognitive processes people use to try to understand themselves and others. This chapter addresses interpersonal motives, emotions, and behaviors that emerge in social interaction. We begin by examining interpersonal attraction and relationships, from brief encounters through long-term love relationships. We then turn to two very different forms of social interaction, which Oliner encountered in his childhood odyssey: altruism and aggression. Next we investigate the influence of other people on the way individuals behave, as they obey and conform, and consider what happens as individuals participate in groups. We conclude by placing the psychology of our era in its social and historical context and returning to some of the central themes with which we began in the opening chapter.

INTERPERSONAL ATTRACTION AND RELATIONSHIPS

People affiliate, or seek out and spend time with others, for many reasons. Sometimes they interact to accomplish instrumental goals, such as raising money for a charity or meeting over dinner to discuss a business deal. Other interactions reflect familial ties, shared interests, desires for companionship, or sexual interest. Social psychologists have devoted considerable attention to why people choose to spend time with other people, or **interpersonal attraction.** One line of research examines factors that lead people to become attracted to each other. Another focuses on a particular kind of attraction in enduring relationships, love.

Factors Leading to Interpersonal Attraction

Why are we attracted to some people but not to others? Sometimes the answer is as simple as proximity. Numerous studies have documented that people tend to choose their friends and lovers from individuals close at hand. Interviews of 270 residents of a New York City housing project found that nearly 88 percent of their friends in the seven-building project lived in the same building as the respondent (Nahemow & Lawton, 1975). Almost half lived on the same floor. Another study surveyed 44 male Maryland State Police trainees who had been assigned rooms and classroom seats by the alphabetical order of their surnames (Segal, 1974). When the trainees were asked to name their three closest friends on the force, the closer together their surnames, the more likely they were to be close friends. Proximity plays an equally important role in romantic relationships. As one observer wryly commented, "Cherished notions about romantic love notwithstanding, the chances are about 50–50 that the 'one and only' lives within walking distance"(Eckland, cited in Buss & Schmitt, 1993, p. 205). Social-psychological research has repeatedly shown that situational influences such as proximity (or merely having a spare room, as in the opening vignette) have a remarkably strong impact on behavior.

A second factor that influences attraction is similarity. Contrary to folk wisdom, opposites generally do not attract. In fact, people tend to choose casual acquaintances, as well as mates and best friends, on the basis of shared attitudes, values, and interests. One study periodically assessed the attitudes and patterns of affiliation of incoming male college transfer students assigned to the same dormitory (Newcomb, 1961). Over the course of the semester, as the students had a chance to learn one another's attitudes, friendship patterns began to match initial attitude profiles. The more accurate aphorism, then, is that birds of a feather flock together.

A third factor that influences interpersonal attraction is the degree to which interaction with another person is rewarding. From a behaviorist point of view, the more people associate a relationship with reward, the more they are likely to affiliate (Byrne & Murnen, 1988; Clark & Pataki, 1995; Newcomb, 1956). One ingenious experiment tested a classical conditioning theory of attraction: Children should prefer other children they meet under more enjoyable conditions (Lott & Lott, 1974). The investigators placed first and third graders in groups of three, giving some subjects a chance to succeed on a task and rewarding them for it, while rigging the task so that others would fail. Later, the experimenters asked the children to name someone from the class who they would like to take on a family vacation. One-fourth of the children who succeeded on the task chose one of the children who shared the experience with them. Only 1 in 20 children who failed made a similar choice.

Social exchange theories, based on behaviorist principles, hold that the foundation of relationships is reciprocal reward (Homans, 1961). Choosing a relationship is like trying to get the best "bang for the buck"; as in economic exchange, people try to maximize the value they can obtain with their resources (Kenrick et al., 1993). The resources in social relationships are personal assets: physical attractiveness, wit, charm, intelligence, material goods, and the like. These same assets are the "values" sought in others as well, as any glance at the Personals will attest. In romantic relationships, people tend to choose others of similar value (as culturally defined) because both partners are trying to maximize the value of their mate.

A final factor that influences interpersonal attraction is physical attractiveness (Chapter 17). Even in nonsexual relationships, physically attractive people are magnets. Attractive children are more popular among their peers and are treated more leniently by adults (Adams & LaVoie, 1974; Clifford & Walster, 1973; Dion, 1972; Dion & Berscheid, 1974; Kleck et al., 1974). Attractive adults receive more cooperation and assistance from others (Benson et al., 1976; Sigall et al., 1971), get better job recommendations (Cash et al., 1977), and have others self-disclose to them more (Brundage et al., 1977).

With romantic attraction, of course, the impact of physical attractiveness is even greater. Numerous studies show physical attractiveness to be a major, if not the major, criterion college students use in judging initial attraction (e.g., Curran & Lippold, 1975; Walster et al., 1966). One study asked students to indicate whether they were attracted to strangers pictured in photographs. The experimenters gave another group the same photographs but stapled them to surveys showing the strangers' attitudes. Information about the strangers' attitudes did not affect the subjects' choices of who most attracted them (Byrne et al., 1968).

In real life, people tend to choose partners they perceive to be equally attractive to themselves, not necessarily the most beautiful or handsome (Berscheid et al., 1971). However, when the investigators in one experiment assured male subjects that a number of different women would gladly date them, the subjects chose more physically attractive women than men who were given no such assurance. By choosing a less attractive partner, members of the latter group were apparently trying to maximize the beauty of their partner while minimizing their risk of rejection (see Huston, 1973).

Standards of physical attractiveness vary tremendously from culture to culture (and from individual to individual). Nevertheless, views of beauty are not entirely culture-specific. People across the world—even infants—tend to rate facial attractiveness in similar ways (Langlois et al., 1991). Cross-cultural studies have found remarkable consistency in judgments of the attractiveness of faces of different races; correlations between raters across cultures generally exceed .60. Several studies have also found that infants in our own culture, who have not yet been socialized to norms of physical beauty, gaze longer at faces rated attractive by adults than those rated unattractive. This occurs whether the faces are of adults or infants,

Conceptions of beauty differ by culture. Pictured here are three women considered beautiful in their native lands: a Tuareg nomad from Northern Africa, the Western model Claudia Schiffer, and a woman from India.

males or females, or blacks or whites. The mechanisms accounting for these preferences remain unknown.

The research on interpersonal attractiveness described thus far suggests that we humans are a shallow lot indeed. What we most desire is someone a few doors down, who brings us a beer on a warm afternoon, reminds us of ourselves, and looks like Michelle Pfeiffer or Tom Cruise. We may be shallow creatures, but probably not quite that shallow. An important caveat about this body of research is that most studies were conducted in brief laboratory encounters between college students who did not know each other. While all the factors identified are probably important, the extent to which each influences interpersonal attraction outside this special circumstance is largely unknown. The late teens and early twenties are a life stage during which people emphasize physical attractiveness more than during any other stage. Concerns about identity in late adolescence also probably promote a preference for peers who are similar because they reinforce the individual's sense of identity (Sears, 1986). More generally, the reliance of social-psychological research on college student samples should be borne in mind whenever generalizing the findings to other populations (Table 18.1).

College students may not be representative subjects for research on relationships for another reason: Few have had long-term relationships, simply by virtue of their age. The importance of various dimensions of attraction waxes and wanes at different points in a relationship, which cannot be observed in first encounters of students brought together in a laboratory or in relationships that typically last only a few months. Studies using broader community samples find that marital satisfaction is typically high initially, lower during child-rearing years (especially when children are toddlers), and higher again once the children leave, particularly during retirement (Sillars & Zietlow, 1993). Such trends cannot be assessed with college samples.

The Nature of Love

Researchers aware of these limitations have turned their attention to long-term adult love relationships, attempting to convert this enigmatic experience from sonnets to statistics, from poetry to *p*-values.

Classifying Love

Some researchers have tried to classify types or components of love (Henrick & Henrick, 1986; Lee, 1988). A basic distinction is between passionate and companionate love (Walster & Walster, 1978). **Passionate love** is the stuff of Hollywood movies, sleepless nights, and daytime fantasies; it is a wildly emotional condition,

TABLE 18.1   SUBJECTS IN JOURNAL ARTICLES IN SOCIAL PSYCHOLOGY

SUBJECTS	JOURNAL OF PERSONALITY AND SOCIAL PSYCHOLOGY	PERSONALITY AND SOCIAL PSYCHOLOGY BULLETIN	JOURNAL OF EXPERIMENTAL SOCIAL PSYCHOLOGY	TOTAL
1980 Articles				
North American college students	82%	81%	81%	81%
Other students	5%	0%	8%	4%
Nonstudents	13%	19%	11%	15%
1985 Articles				
North American college students	71%	79%	82%	74%
Other students	8%	6%	12%	8%
Nonstudents	21%	16%	6%	17%

Source: Adapted from Sears, 1986, pp. 515-530.

Note. The table shows subjects sampled in the three major social psychology journals in two years, 1980 and 1985. The vast majority were college students in their late teens—the age of most college freshmen and sophomores. Some of these conclusions may be true of people generally, but the only way to know is to use a variety of samples.

marked by intense physiological arousal and absorption in another person. In contrast, **companionate love** involves deep affection, friendship, and emotional intimacy. It grows over time and increasingly takes the place of passionate love—which, alas, does not last forever, despite the fantasies of young lovers who swear their passion will never wane. Companionate love develops over time through shared experiences, emotions, and daily life routines. The two kinds of love often coexist, and people experience resurgences of passionate love at different points in a long relationship (Figure 18.1).

Another taxonomy of love, proposed by Robert Sternberg (1988), is a triangular theory of love. Sternberg and his colleagues administered questionnaires to a community sample, inquiring about subjects' experiences in love relationships (see Sternberg & Grajek, 1984). Using factor analysis, they found that most responses fell into three categories: intimacy, passion, and decision/commitment. The intimacy component includes feelings of closeness, connection, and bonding that provide the warmth of a loving relationship. The passion component describes the physical and sexual feelings that attract one person to another sexually. The decision/commitment component refers to the decision that one loves the person and is committed to the relationship. Considering all the possible combinations of these three components produces a classification of eight basic types of love (Figure 18.2), ranging from infatuation (passion only) to consummate love (all three components combined).

An Evolutionary Perspective on Love

Taxonomies undoubtedly take some of the romance out of love. The same can probably be said about evolutionary views of this quixotic human passion, which offer an explanation for the existence of romantic love (in its popular sense, referring to the relatively enduring bond between lovers, rather than Sternberg's particular definition). From an evolutionary perspective, romantic love, like any human

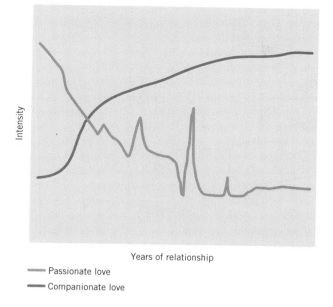

FIGURE 18.1
Passionate and companionate love in a long-term relationship. Passionate love, marked by intense emotion, arousal, and absorption in another person, is high at the beginning of a relationship but tends to diminish over time. Companionate love, which involves deep affection, friendship, and emotional intensity, grows over time.

Intensity

Years of relationship

— Passionate love
— Companionate love

attribute, is an adaptation that fostered the reproductive success of our ancestors—in this case by bonding two people who would "likely become parents of an infant who would need their reliable care" (Hazan & Shaver, 1987, p. 523). Neither love nor lust, however, inevitably leads to monogamous marriage, which is just one mating strategy among many that occur across species. Even among humans, 80 percent of societies practice polygyny, in which men are permitted multiple wives or mistresses. In our own culture, premarital sex is virtually ubiquitous, and roughly half of married people at some point have extramarital affairs (Buss & Schmitt, 1993).

Evolutionary psychologists have studied the **sexual strategies** (tactics used in selecting mates) people use in different kinds of relationships, from brief romantic liaisons to marriages (Buss & Schmitt, 1993). Unlike most researchers studying

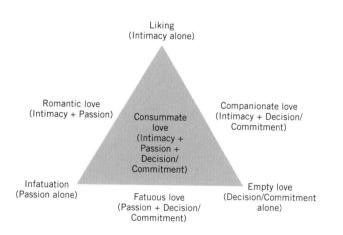

FIGURE 18.2
Sternberg's triangular theory of love. Sternberg's theory proposes three components of love: intimacy, passion, and decision/commitment. The combinations of these components produce eight types of relationships: liking (intimacy only), infatuation (passion only), empty love (commitment only, as when a couple stays together for the sake of their children), romantic love (intimacy plus passion), companionate love (intimacy plus commitment), fatuous love (passion plus commitment, as in a whirlwind courtship), and consummate love (in which all three components are present). The eighth type, nonlove, is characteristic of most casual acquaintanceships. SOURCE: *Adapted from Sternberg, 1988, p. 122.*

"I dreamt I had a Harem, but they all wanted to talk about the relationship."

interpersonal attraction and relationships, who often generalize across genders, evolutionary theorists argue that males and females face different selection pressures and have thus evolved different sexual strategies. Because males can have an infinite number of offspring, they can maximize their reproductive success by spreading their seed widely, inseminating as many fertile females as possible. In contrast, women can bear only a limited number of children, and they make an enormous initial investment in their offspring during nine months of gestation. As a result, according to the theory, women should be choosier about their mating partners, selecting those who can and will commit resources to them and their offspring.

From these basic differences ensues a battle of the sexes. Females maximize their reproductive success by forcing males with resources to commit to them in return for sexual access. Short-term and long-term mating strategies are similar for females; they use short-term liaisons to assess and attract potential long-term mates. Women should be especially concerned with a man's resources. For males, short-term and long-term sexual strategies are very different. In the short term, the female with the greatest reproductive value is one who is both fertile (young) and readily available for copulation. In the long run, committed relationships bring exclusive sexual access to a female, which allows the male to contribute resources to offspring without worrying about paternity. Long-term relationships also bring potential alliances and resources from the female's family. Thus, males should prefer less promiscuous long-term partners who are young enough to produce many offspring and attractive enough to elicit arousal over time and increase the man's status. Men should also be choosier in long-term than in short-term encounters, since this female will provide half the genes of the offspring in whom they invest.

Aspects of this portrait of male and female sexual strategies probably sound familiar to anyone who has ever dated. Consider the Casanova who professes commitment and then turns out a few months later not to be ready for it; the man who gladly sleeps with a woman on a first date but then does not want to see her again, certainly not for a long-term relationship; or the woman who only dates men of high status and earning potential. From an evolutionary perspective, these are well-known figures because they exemplify common mating strategies. Like other mechanisms for adaptation, sexual strategies were selected in an environment very different from our own, tens or hundreds of thousands of years ago. Their expression should be apparent over the long run, but only under particular environmental circumstances; they are not rigidly instinctive behaviors like the mating dance of a ring dove.

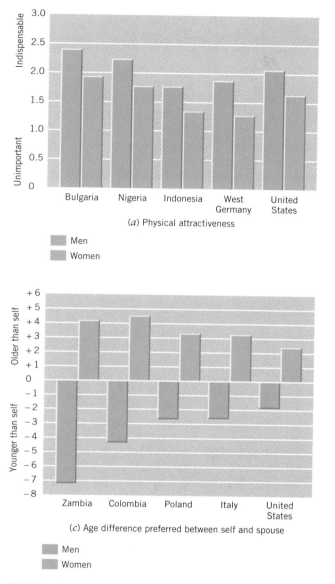

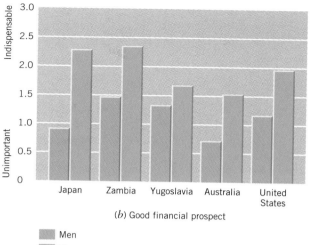

FIGURE 18.3

Preferred characteristics of mates across cultures. Across cultures, males show a stronger preference for physically attractive mates than females (a). Financial prospects are more important to females than males in choosing a mate (b). Nearly everywhere, males prefer females who are younger, while females prefer males who are older (c). SOURCE: *Buss & Schmitt, 1993, pp. 204–232.*

How well do the data support evolutionary theory? Although the differences between the sexes are not always enormous, they tend to be consistent. For example, a study of 37 cultures found that in all but one, males tended to value the physical attractiveness of their mates more than females, whereas females were more concerned than males about the resources a spouse could provide (Buss, 1989). Males also consistently prefer females who are younger, and hence have greater reproductive potential; females prefer males who are older and hence are more likely to command resources (Buss & Schmitt, 1993; Kenrick & Keefe, 1992; Kenrick et al., 1993). Figure 18.3 shows the results of some tests of evolutionary hypotheses in several cultures.

SWF, 29, slim, brown hair, green eyes, beautiful, sexy, professional, seeks intelligent, financially independent, professional man for committed relationship. Box 8734.

Anyone interested in testing evolutionary hypotheses need look no further than the Personals, where male and female sexual strategies, while showing some overlap (no one advertises for an unattractive, irresponsible partner), show considerable divergences.

Studies of North American undergraduates also corroborate many evolutionary predictions about sexual strategies. For example, when males are asked about desired characteristics of potential partners, they respond that they prefer good-looking, promiscuous women for the short run but dislike promiscuity and pay somewhat less attention to physical appearance in the long run. In general, men report a desire for a greater number of short-term sexual partners, a greater number of sexual partners in a lifetime, and a willingness to engage in intercourse after less time has elapsed, compared with women (Buss & Schmitt, 1993). In one study, attractive male and female confederates of the experimenter approached opposite-sex students on campus and told them, "I have been noticing you around campus. I find you very attractive." They then asked, among other things, if the student would sleep with them that night (Clark & Hatfield, 1989). Seventy-five percent of men approached agreed, whereas none of the women accepted the invitation. If the results seem obvious, consider for a moment whether any other theory could have predicted them.

Research examining the content of personal advertisements in newspapers provides intriguing confirmation of the view of "men as success objects and women as sex objects" (Davis, 1990; Mills, 1995). Women tend to advertise their physical beauty and request men who are high in status, prestige, or wealth, and men do the opposite. Men tend to prefer women who are younger, and women are more likely to emphasize that they are seeking a committed long-term relationship. Further, in newspapers read by people of lower socioeconomic status, males tend to be overrepresented among advertisers in the Personals, presumably because low-resource males have more trouble finding mates.

These evolutionary hypotheses are, of course, controversial, particularly since they could be used to justify a double standard ("Honey, I couldn't help it, it's just in my genes"). They also do not adequately explain the large numbers of extramarital affairs among females, the choice to limit family size or remain childless among couples with plenty of resources in cultures like our own, or homosexuality. They do, however, offer some very challenging explanations for phenomena that are not otherwise easily explained.

Romantic Love as Attachment

Another theory of love based on evolutionary principles comes from attachment theory. Romantic love relationships have several features in common with attachment relationships in infancy and childhood (Hazan & Shaver, 1987, 1994). Adults feel security in their lover's arms, desire physical proximity, and experience distress when their lover is away for a considerable period or cannot be located (Shaver et al., 1988). Adults respond to wartime and job-related marital separations with much the same pattern of depression, anger, and anxiety observed in childhood separations; this finding suggests that attachment processes continue into adulthood (Vormbrock, 1993). Like the satisfaction of an infant in its mother's arms, romantic love also brings security, contentment, and joy. The bond between lovers does, of course, differ from infant attachment, in that it involves sexual attraction between people who may have approximately equal power and status, including the power to end the relationship. Care for offspring and sexuality are components of adult romantic love absent from infant attachment. Nevertheless, the love between an infant and mother and between two lovers may have more in common than may first appear.

Attachment theorists argue that people pattern their love relationships on the mental models they constructed of earlier attachment relationships. Thus, the way individuals love as adults tends to reflect the way they loved and were loved as children—that is, whether their attachment style was secure or insecure (Chapter 14). Early childhood attachment styles may be especially evident in adults when they are under stress, since the attachment system is activated by threats to security. Striking evidence comes from an experiment on the relation between attachment style and the way members of college-student couples give and receive support (Simpson et al., 1992). After administering attachment style questionnaires to both members of a couple, the investigator told the woman she would shortly be exposed to an experimental procedure that arouses "considerable anxiety and distress in most people" but that he could not explain further (p. 437). Then the experimenter took her to a room that looked like an isolation chamber filled with psychophysiological equipment, told her that the apparatus was not yet ready, and escorted her to a waiting room to sit with her boyfriend for five minutes. While the couple waited for the experiment to begin, their behavior was videotaped and coded for the types of support given and received by each member of the couple. The female's behavior was also rated for level of anxiety.

As predicted, securely attached women sought support from their boyfriends when they were anxious. The opposite was the case for avoidantly attached women, who feel uncomfortable being emotionally close to others and tend to shut off attachment needs when stressed. The more anxious they appeared, the less they sought support (Figure 18.4). Also as predicted, securely attached men gave more support, and avoidant men gave less support. No consistent results held for subjects classified as anxiously attached (who crave security but tend to be vulnerable to anxiety and depression).

Similar findings emerged in a study of coping mechanisms among Israeli college students during the Gulf War, when Iraq was bombarding civilian areas of Israel (Mikulincer et al., 1993). Subjects who lived in areas directly threatened by SCUD

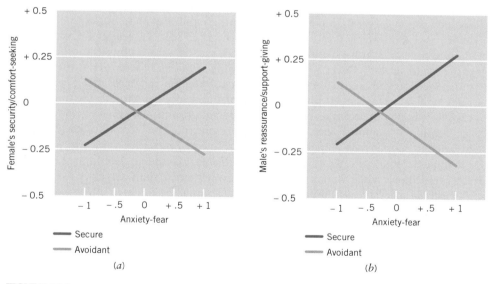

FIGURE 18.4
Relation between attachment style and giving and receiving support. In (a), among securely attached women, those who felt more anxious correspondingly sought more comfort from their partners. Precisely the opposite pattern held for avoidantly attached women. In (b), the same pattern emerged for support-giving from their male partners. Secure males responded with increased support when their girlfriends were more anxious, while avoidant males withdrew as their girlfriends' anxiety increased. SOURCE: *Simpson et al., 1992, p. 440.*

missile attacks differed from each other in the ways they coped with the danger. Securely attached subjects tended to seek support from others and generally experienced less distress from the bombings. Avoidantly attached people used distancing strategies (such as, "I tried to forget about the whole thing"). Their distress was manifested primarily in physical symptoms, as might be expected since they tend to be unwilling to feel emotional distress consciously. Ambivalently attached subjects used coping strategies aimed at calming themselves and quelling their emotions, which makes sense given their high level of conscious distress.

A GLOBAL VISTA

LOVE IN CROSS-CULTURAL PERSPECTIVE

Western theorists were not the first to recognize a link between infant and adult love. The Japanese have a concept of love that combines the experience of attachment and dependence, called *amae*, derived from the word for "sweet" (Doi, 1992). *Amae* is both what infants desire with their mothers and what adults feel in the presence of their beloved.

Although adult romantic love may have its origins in the biological proclivity of infants to form attachments, by the time people have participated in relationships for 15 to 20 years, their manner of loving as adults is highly influenced by their culture. Many societies have arranged marriages, which are as much economic bonds linking families or clans as personal and sexual bonds between lovers. Chinese culture has historically expected couples to consider their obligations to family in choosing a marriage partner: "An American asks, 'How does my heart feel?' A Chinese asks, 'What will other people say?'" (Hsu, 1981, p. 50). Indeed, in Chinese culture, love is so secondary to family obligations that the term *love* does not refer to a legitimate, socially sanctioned relationship between a man and a woman but connotes an illicit, shameful affair (see also Dion & Dion, 1988). In feudal China, passionate love was more likely to constitute a reason why a couple should not, rather than should, marry. The female protagonist in Chinese love stories was more likely to be a concubine than a woman eligible for marriage. The marriage contract was signed by the fathers of the bride and groom; the engaged couple was not required to endorse the contract (Lang, 1946).

Similarly, in many parts of India, where marriages have traditionally been arranged, people may experience passionate love, but they typically hide it (Traiwick, 1990). Public displays of affection are avoided, although they are tolerated more when they are between an unmarried than a married couple. Patterns of marriage and intimacy also vary among castes. In one Untouchable caste, the Chuhras, even private expressions of affection and desire are limited, and spouses do not share sleeping quarters. A study using data from 42

The experience of love differs cross-culturally, but the sentiments of these 18th century Japanese lovers are not difficult to recognize today.

hunter-gatherer societies from across the globe (gathered by anthropologists over the last century) found evidence of romantic love in 26 of them, or about 60 percent (Harris, 1995). Only 6 cultures allowed pure individual choice of marital partners, however, with the other 36 requiring some degree of parental control, either in the form of veto power over the union of two lovers or arranged marriages.

In the United States, the meaning of marriage has changed substantially over the last three centuries. As in other societies prior to industrialization, marriage was once primarily an arrangement for procreating and managing property and financial unions between families, not a vessel for emotional and sexual intimacy. Based on evidence from diaries and letters written in the nineteenth century, some historians argue that for women, passion and romance were not absent, but they were often separate from sex and more likely experienced in nonsexual relationships. One mother wrote her daughter, "All the day I muse away, since the sound of your voice no longer rouses me to sympathy.... You cannot know how much I miss your affectionate demonstrations" (Smith-Rosenberg, 1975, p. 16). Teenage girls wrote of their pleasure in hugging and sleeping together while speaking in much more muted tones of their male suitors, as in this young woman's dispassionate mention of the man she would marry: "The last week I received the unexpected intelligence of the arrival of a friend in Boston" (Smith-Rosenberg, 1974, p. 20).

Historians have also tracked changes in the meaning of love, sex, and marriage during the nineteenth century from a survey of middle-class women conducted by a female physician, Clelia Mosher, who inquired about her patients' sexual and reproductive lives. Although her sample was small and vulnerable to a number of biases, subjects born in the middle of the century tended to describe sexual intercourse in utilitarian, almost neutral terms; it was necessary for reproduction and neither particularly pleasurable nor unpleasurable. Subjects who came of age toward the end of the century were more prone to describe experiences of "absolute physical harmony" with their husbands during intercourse and to consider sex inextricably linked with passionate love (D'Emilio & Freedman, 1988, p. 56).

As the country industrialized and people began focusing more on their own needs and individuality, patterns of courtship and dating changed. By the late nineteenth century, romance and emotional bonding between lovers had become a value (D'Emilio & Freedman, 1988). Rather than courting in public places such as church gatherings, middle-class men and women began to spend more time alone. A number of factors facilitated privacy, some as seemingly insignificant as changes in architecture. Colonial homes, for example, had larger but fewer rooms than Victorian homes and were designed to accommodate family gatherings. Victorian homes, in contrast, had many rooms with various functions. Parlors, sitting rooms, and dining rooms provided places for young couples to visit with each other apart from the company of supervising adults and therefore to share more of their inner lives (D'Emilio & Freedman, 1988).

The contemporary emphasis on passionate, romantic, intimate love portrayed daily on movie screens and in novels may be predicated on some degree of individualism. As noted in previous chapters, cultures differ in the extent to which they cultivate personal emotional experience. Contemporary Western culture is unique in its focus on individual satisfaction as a valued end. This orientation extends into relationships, which are viewed as vehicles for personal gratification and are terminated when they are no longer satisfying. The nature and experience of long-term adult love relationships, then, differs not only cross-culturally but even within a single culture over time.

Did you never see little dogs caressing and playing with one another, so that you might say there is nothing more friendly? But that you may know what friendship is, throw a bit of flesh among them, and you will learn. Throw between yourself and your son a little estate, then you will know how soon he will wish to bury you and how soon you wish your son to die…. For universally, be not deceived, every animal is attached to nothing so much as to its own interest…. For where the I and Mine are placed, to that place of necessity the animal inclines.

Epictetus

ALTRUISM

Thus far, we have focused on the ties that bind. In this section, we examine another interpersonal process that brings people together, altruism. A person who undergoes a painful operation to donate bone marrow to a dying stranger or risks death by hiding Jews from the Nazis is displaying altruism (presuming the intention is primarily to help the other person). Some altruistic behavior is so common that we take it for granted—holding open a door, giving a stranger directions, or trying to make someone feel comfortable during a conversation. Charitable contributions in the United States alone exceed $50 billion a year (Batson, 1995). We begin this section by examining theories of altruism and then consider experimental research on a particular form of altruism, bystander intervention.

Theories of Altruism

For centuries, philosophers have debated whether any prosocial act—no matter how generous or unselfish it may appear on the surface—is truly altruistic. When people offer money to a homeless person on the subway, is their action motivated by a pure desire to help, or are they primarily alleviating their own discomfort? Many philosophers argue for **ethical hedonism,** the doctrine that all behavior, no matter how apparently altruistic, is—and should be—designed to increase one's own pleasure or reduce one's own pain. As one observer put it, "Scratch an 'altruist' and watch a 'hypocrite' bleed (Gheslin, cited in Batson, 1995).

Indeed, people have many selfish reasons to behave selflessly (Batson, 1991). People are frequently motivated by their emotions (Chapter 11), and behaving altruistically can produce positive emotions and diminish negative ones. The overwhelming majority of Oliner's subjects who saved Jews from the Nazis reported that their emotions—pity, compassion, concern, or affection—drove them to help (Oliner & Oliner, 1988). Prosocial acts can also lead to material and social rewards (gifts, thanks, and the esteem of others) as well as to positive feelings about oneself that come from meeting one's ideal-self standards. Behaving prosocially can also reduce negative feelings. Some theorists explain the motivation to act on another's behalf in terms of empathic distress: Helping relieves the negative affect state aroused through empathy with a person in distress (Hoffman, 1982).

Empathizing with others apparently does involve actually feeling some of the things they feel. In one experiment, subjects watched videotaped interactions between spouses and were asked to rate the degree of positive or negative affect one of the spouses was feeling at each instant (Levenson & Ruef, 1992). To assess subjects' accuracy, their ratings were correlated with the spouses' own ratings of how they felt at each point. Subjects who accurately gauged these feelings showed a similar pattern of physiology to the person with whom they were empathizing, such as a similar level of skin conductance, but this was true only for unpleasant emotions. In other words, when people "feel for" another's pain, they do just that—feel something similar, if less intensely—and use this feeling to gauge the other person's feeling. With positive emotions, people apparently use their head instead of their gut.

An alternative philosophical position to ethical hedonism is that people can be genuinely altruistic. Jean-Jacques Rousseau, the French Romantic philosopher, proposed that human beings have a natural compassion for one another and that the only reason they do not always behave compassionately is that society beats it out of them. Adam Smith, an early capitalist economist, argued that people are generally self-interested but have a natural empathy for one another that leads them to behave altruistically at times. Some experimental evidence suggests that Rousseau and Smith may have been right. Empathic people who have the opportunity to escape empathic distress by walking away, or who are offered rewards for doing so,

How selfish soever man may be supposed, there are evidently some principles in his nature, which interest him in the fortune of others, and render their happiness necessary to him, though he derives nothing from it except the pleasure of seeing it. Of this kind is pity or compassion, the emotion which we feel for the misery of others, when we either see it, or are made to conceive it in a very lively manner.

Adam Smith, 1759, A Theory of Moral Sentiments

still frequently choose instead to help someone in distress (Batson, 1991). In addition, people at times behave altruistically for the benefit of a group, usually one with which they identify themselves.

Evolutionary psychologists have taken the debate about altruism a step further by redefining self-interest as reproductive success. By this definition, protecting oneself and one's offspring is in an organism's evolutionary "interest." Evidence of this type of altruistic behavior abounds in the animal kingdom. Some mother birds will feign a broken wing to draw a predator away from their nest, at considerable potential cost to themselves (Wilson, 1975). Chimpanzees "adopt" orphaned chimps, particularly if they are close relatives (Batson, 1995). If reproductive success is expanded to encompass inclusive fitness (Chapter 10), one would expect humans and other animals to care preferentially for themselves, their offspring, and their relatives. Organisms that paid little attention to the survival of related others, or animals that indiscriminately invested in kin and nonkin alike, would be less represented in the gene pool with each successive generation.

Why, then, do people sometimes behave altruistically toward others who are not even their relatives? Is Mother Teresa an evolutionary anomaly? And why does a flock of black jackdaws swarm to attack a potential predator carrying a black object that resembles a jackdaw, when some of the attacking birds may be risking their feathers for a bird to which they are genetically unrelated? To answer such questions, evolutionary theorists invoke the concept of **reciprocal altruism**—that is, natural selection favors animals that behave altruistically if the likely benefit to each individual over time exceeds the likely cost (Trivers, 1971). In other words, if the dangers are small but the gains in survival and reproduction are large, altruism is an adaptive strategy.

For example, a jackdaw takes a slight risk of injury or predation when it screeches or attacks a predator, but its action may save the lives of many other birds in the flock. If most birds in the flock warn each other, they will all be more likely to survive than if they wander in solitude through the woods like the Transcendentalist philosopher Henry David Thoreau. Thus, altruism can sometimes be more adaptive than "selfishness" (Simon, 1990). The same argument applies to humans. Social organization for mutual protection, food gathering, and so forth permits far greater reproductive success for each member on the average than a completely individualistic approach that loses the safety of numbers and the advantages of shared knowledge and culture.

Bystander Intervention

Although philosophers and evolutionists may question the roots of altruism, apparent acts of altruism are so prevalent that their absence can be shocking. A case in point was the brutal 1964 murder in Queens, New York City, of Kitty Genovese. Arriving home from work at 3:00 A.M., Genovese was attacked over a half-hour period by a knife-wielding assailant. Although her screams and cries brought 38 of her neighbors to their windows, not one came to her assistance or even called the police. These bystanders put on their lights, opened their windows, and watched while Genovese was repeatedly stabbed and ultimately murdered.

To understand how a group of law-abiding citizens could fail to help someone who was being murdered, social psychologists John Darley and Bibb Latane (1968) designed several experiments to investigate **bystander intervention**—helping a stranger in distress. Darley and Latane were particularly interested in whether being part of a group of onlookers affects individuals' sense of responsibility to take action. In one experiment, they invited male college students to what was billed as an interview (Darley & Latane, 1968). While the students waited to be interviewed either individually or in groups of three, the investigators pumped smoke into the room through an air vent. Students who were alone reported the smoke 75 percent

This quiet street in New York was the scene of a brutal murder—and the impetus for research attempting to understand why Kitty Genovese's neighbors did nothing to help.

of the time. In contrast, only 38 percent of the students in groups of three acted, and only 10 percent acted when in the presence of two confederates who behaved as if they were indifferent to the smoke.

In another experiment (Latane & Rodin, 1969), college students waited, alone or with one other person, purportedly to participate in a market research study. While waiting, they heard a tape of what sounded like a woman falling and injuring herself in the next room. Seventy percent of the students who were alone or with a friend tried to help, but only 7 percent of those with a nonresponsive confederate did so. In a third experiment (see Latane & Darley, 1970), students were seated in separate rooms to participate, via an intercom system, in what they believed was an anonymous discussion of personal problems faced by college students. During the staged discussion, one of the participants appeared to have an epileptic seizure. The most frequent and fastest efforts to seek help came when the subject and victim were the only members of the discussion group. As in the previous studies—and Kitty Genovese's murder—the presence of other people inhibited action on another's behalf.

Based on these experiments, Darley and Latane developed a three-stage model of the decision-making process that underlies bystander intervention (Figure 18.5). First, bystanders must notice the emergency. Second, they must interpret the incident as an emergency. Finally, they must assume personal responsibility for intervention. At any point during these three stages, a bystander may make a decision that leads to inaction.

The presence of others has a substantial impact on the bystander's decision-making process. If other people are paying little or no attention to the emergency during stage one, the bystander may conclude that nothing significant has happened. Similarly, a bystander is unlikely to interpret an event as an emergency during stage two if other people do not seem to take it seriously. This is especially true if the situation is at all ambiguous (see Clark & Ward, 1972, 1974). The presence of others during these two initial stages acts not only as an informational source ("Is there a crisis here or isn't there?") but also as a source of reassurance. Hence, the mere presence of other people lowers the likelihood of intervention, particularly if the others do not appear to be distressed. During stage three, the presence of others leads to a **diffusion of responsibility**, that is, a diminished sense of personal

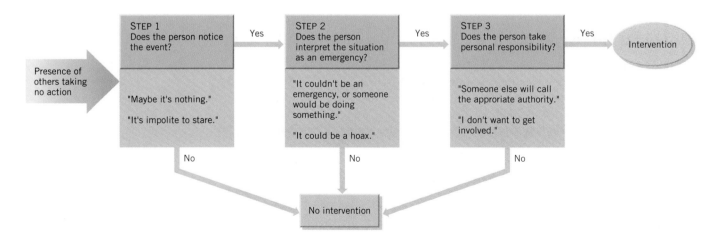

FIGURE 18.5

Bystander intervention. In the first stage of this decision-making model, the bystander must notice the emergency. In stage two, the bystander must interpret the incident as an emergency. In stage three, the bystander must assume responsibility. SOURCE: *Adapted from Darley & Latane, 1968, pp. 70–71.*

responsibility to act because others are seen as equally responsible. During this third stage, people also consider the consequences of acting. Clearly, people are less willing to intervene if taking action jeopardizes their own safety. Individuals are also less willing to act if they fear they might turn out to be goats instead of heroes; what if the event is really a hoax or they are misinterpreting the situation?

Other factors influence bystander intervention, such as the attractiveness of the victim (Pilliavin et al., 1975). The bystander's perceived similarity to the victim further increases the likelihood of action, apparently because it maximizes empathy (Graf & Riddle, 1972). Bystanders who are anonymous, like Kitty Genovese's neighbors and most German citizens during the reign of Nazism, are less likely to help. Sociologists have long argued that the anonymity of city life reduces individuals' sense of personal responsibility for the welfare of others. Research comparing the responses of urban and rural subjects largely supports this view (see Solomon et al., 1982). Population density—the number of people crammed into a small urban space—is also highly predictive of helping. The more densely populated a city, the less people help (Levine et al., 1994), which supports Darley and Latane's contention that people are less likely to intervene when responsibility is diffused.

Most of the bystander studies described so far involved simulated emergencies in laboratory settings. Under different experimental conditions, the results are sometimes quite different. One study examined whether bystanders are more likely to respond to an emergency in a natural setting where their compatriots are friends rather than strangers. The investigators staged a rape in a campus parking lot (Harari et al., 1985). When unsuspecting male bystanders observed the female victim struggling with her attacker and heard her cries for help, 85 percent of those walking in groups of two or three responded, versus 65 percent of those walking alone. In this study, the presence of several people increased, rather than decreased, bystander intervention. According to the investigators, the naturalistic setting of the rape, the clarity of the victim's plight, and the ability of group members to see and talk to one another made intervention more likely. The rapist's lack of a weapon was surely important as well.

One variable that investigators have not examined in bystander studies is fascination with, or titillation over the suffering of others. An element of vicarious enjoyment may have led Kitty Genovese's neighbors to watch but not intervene; in fact, one couple shut off the lights so they could see better. The manifest enjoyment of another per-

People living in different parts of a single state—in this case, New York—respond differently to the needs of their neighbors.

son's suffering and degradation was even more apparent in a New Bedford, Massachusetts, bar several years after the Kitty Genovese incident: A woman was gang raped while bystanders watched and cheered. Crowds of onlookers have similarly been known to encourage potential suicide victims to jump off buildings.

AGGRESSION

Charitable contributions may exceed $50 billion in the United States, but that is less than half the military budget. **Aggression**—verbal or physical behavior aimed at harming another person or living being—is at least as characteristic of human interaction as altruism. Aggression is often elicited by anger, as when someone lashes out at a perceived injustice, but it can also be carried out for practical purposes without anger, as when a driver leans on the horn to protest reckless lane-changing that could cause an accident. Calm, pragmatic aggression is called **instrumental aggression** and is often used by institutions such as the judicial system to punish wrongdoers (Geen, 1990). Aggressive acts are also frequently alloyed with other motives. The behavior of kamikaze pilots during World War II, terrorists who carry out suicide bombings, and many soldiers in wartime involve blends of aggression and altruism, depending upon one's point of view.

The prevalence and forms of aggression vary by culture and gender. Among technologically developed countries, the United States has the highest rates of aggression. Indeed, violence has overtaken communicable diseases as the leading cause of death among the young and continues to grow steadily. Homicide rates are up to 10 times higher in the United States than in Europe (see Lore & Schultz, 1993), and the murder rate in some major U.S. cities dwarfs the number of annual murders in all of Canada. In Canada, roughly 600 people a year die from homicides, compared with 24,000 in the United States, which outstrips by a factor of 5 the relative difference in population size.

Gender differences in aggression are highly consistent across cultures. In most societies, males commit the majority of criminal and aggressive acts. Male adolescents are particularly likely to be the perpetrators; in fact, fluctuations in crime rates in the United States and most other countries can be predicted simply from the proportion of adolescent males in the population (see Segall, 1988).

Violence perpetrated by men against men is so universal that it scarcely seems to draw attention. Recently, however, psychologists have come to recognize the extent of male violence perpetrated against women (Goodman et al., 1993). The number of women battered by their male partners is unknown because many women do not report domestic violence, but the U.S. Department of Justice estimates that approximately 2.1 million women are battered each year in the United States (Frieze & Browne, 1989). Most batterers do not begin abusing their partners until the woman has made an emotional commitment to them, and attacks are most likely during pregnancy or upon separation or divorce (Russell, 1991).

Sexual aggression against women is as old as the species. Men have traditionally viewed rape as one of the spoils of war. Because most women do not report rape to the police, legal records are not a valid index of its prevalence. Some studies suggest that as many as 14 to 25 percent of women have been forced into sex by strangers, acquaintances, husbands, or boyfriends at some point in their lives (Goodman et al., 1993; Koss, 1993). A substantial percentage of women (27 percent) also report histories of childhood sexual abuse (as do 16 percent of men) (Finkelhor et al., 1990).

Rapists vary in their personalities, motives, and modus operandi. Roy Hazelwood (1993), a counseling psychologist, was a special investigator for many years with the FBI who tracked serial rapists (those who commit many rapes, and account for the majority of stranger rapes). According to Hazelwood, rapists vary in the extent to which they are motivated by power over their victim or by anger and sadism. The most common and least violent of rapists are usually solitary, socially inadequate men with low self-esteem, whose primary aim is to reassure themselves of their sexual adequacy and masculinity by exercising power over their victim. When interviewed months or years later, they typically report the fantasy that the women they rape will fall in love with them, and their behavior during the rape reflects this fantasy: They tend to kiss and fondle their victims, to compliment them on their beauty, to avoid violence, and to become distressed if the woman becomes too manifestly upset or struggles too much. Prior to being apprehended for a series of rapes, one such man received commendation from his city for heroically subduing an attacker who was brutally raping a woman. When later apprehended himself and asked why he had rescued the woman, he indignantly responded that *he* would never "hurt" a woman (Hazelwood & Harpold, 1986).

The most dangerous type of rapist is the sexual sadist, who is excited by the woman's suffering. These rapists tend to be extremely intelligent and active, often raping dozens of women before being apprehended. They torture their victims and often create their own violent pornography by photographing, videotaping, or audiotaping their crimes. Unlike other rapists, they are typically cool and calm when committing and recounting their crimes, which they carry out with precision and forethought. They often kidnap and torture their victims for days and weeks, work with partners (sometimes their girlfriends or spouses), force their victims to say and do degrading things, and penetrate their victims as violently as possible (usually anally). These men generally do not appear odd or peculiar to the people who know them in daily life (Dietz et al., 1990).

One study examined 41 incarcerated serial rapists, who had raped at least 10 women each, accounting as a group for over 800 sexual assaults and another 400 attempted rapes (Hazelwood & Warren, 1989). The men ranged in occupation, from professionals to blue-collar workers, with most holding steady employment. Most had a history of prior sexual offenses, such as voyeurism (being a "peeping tom") or making obscene phone calls, if not prior rapes. Many also had a general history of antisocial behavior; half of those who had been in the military were discharged other than honorably, and over half reported being physically assaultive from the time they were children. Only 33 percent collected pornography. Perhaps the most consistent finding was a history of sexual abuse: 76 percent reported being sexually abused or witnessing sexual abuse in childhood or adolescence. One subject was initiated into rape by his father, who took him out with him while he raped women and initially had to force the boy to participate.

The universality of aggression, as well as individual differences in aggressive behavior, have led to considerable controversy about its origins. Some theories maintain that the roots of aggression lie in biology and evolution, whereas others look to the environment and social learning. In this section we explore psychodynamic, evolutionary, and cognitive-behavioral perspectives (which tend to be integrated in approaching aggression). We also examine the biopsychological processes that underlie aggressive behavior and offer a tentative integration of multiple standpoints.

A Psychodynamic Perspective

Freud viewed aggression as a basic instinct in humans, a drive that builds in intensity over time if not discharged, analogous to hunger and sex (Chapter 10). Most psychodynamic psychologists no longer accept this model; instead, they view aggression as an inborn behavioral potential that is usually activated by frustration and anger. Infants and toddlers bite, scratch, and kick when they are not comfortable or do not get what they want. In every human society ever observed, socialization to control aggressive impulses is one of the most basic tasks of parenting (see

Whiting & Child, 1953). This suggests that aggression is a class of behavior that societies inhibit rather than implant through social learning. As children grow older and become increasingly socialized, they do, in fact, tend to use less physical violence against one another (Hartup, 1977).

Psychodynamic theory, unlike other perspectives, argues that aggressive fantasies and behavior can be pleasurable and that humans are inherently capable of sadism, regardless of their upbringing (Sandler, personal communication, 1993). Although the enjoyment of aggression is perhaps most obvious in sexual sadists, delinquents, and antisocial personalities, psychodynamic psychologists contend that all people enjoy aggression to some degree, if only in very controlled circumstances. Crowds flock to boxing matches and attend hockey games in hopeful anticipation of fistfights. Many people's sexual behavior includes mildly aggressive acts such as squeezing, biting that leaves "passion marks," scratching, pulling skin, light bondage such as holding a partner's arms down, or fantasies of tying up or being tied. Although most men as well as women would find the actual experience of rape traumatic and repulsive, research documents that both men and women report being sexually aroused by stories of sexual coercion (Malamuth et al., 1980). This fact is obviously known to script writers, who frequently pepper motion pictures with aggressive sex.

Another basic tenet of psychodynamic theory is that aggression frequently finds indirect expression. Aggressive impulses are often expressed in sublimated, less overtly hostile forms. A prominent lawyer who was badly abused as a child appeared mild-mannered in all contexts except one—the courtroom—where she "took no prisoners." Aggression is often only one of several motives influencing behavior. Parents who beat their children generally intend to teach the child a lesson, but they are also expressing frustrations and hostilities they cannot safely—or legally—visit upon another adult. Aggression may also be expressed through passive resistance rather than overt action—passive aggression (Chapter 10)—as when a husband "forgets" to pick up the dry cleaning after an argument with his wife.

An Evolutionary Perspective

Aggression, including killing members of one's own species, occurs in all animals; hence, the capacity for aggression presumably evolved because of its value for survival and reproduction (Lore & Schultz, 1993). Males typically attack other males to obtain access to females and to keep or supplant territory. In many animal species, including some lions and monkeys, males who take over a "harem" from another male kill all the infants so that the females will breed with him and devote their resources only to his progeny, maximizing his reproductive success. Females often try to fight back in these circumstances. Across species, overt female aggression is elicited largely by attacks on their young. As noted earlier, contemporary evolutionary psychologists do not consider aggression a drive that builds up and requires discharge. Rather, many believe that humans, like other animals, have evolved aggressive mechanisms that can be activated when circumstances threaten their survival, reproduction, the reproductive success of their kin, or the survival of alliance partners.

Although aggression is common to all animal species, the degree of violence toward members of their own species is remarkable in humans, who slaughter each other on a scale unimaginable to even the cruelest of beasts (see Lorenz, 1966). Other animals have evolved inhibitory mechanisms that stop them from ravaging their own. Wolves can call off a potential battle simply by rolling over. In the midst of a vicious fight for territory or status, a wolf whose competitor rolls over and exposes his jugular will immediately halt his attack; a biologically-based inhibitory mechanism is activated, and the victor scores a technical knockout. Such mechanisms are particularly prevalent in animals with built-in weaponry, such as powerful jaws, which can kill each other with ease.

Wolves, unlike humans, know how to stop a confrontation from becoming too dangerous.

Primates, including humans, have a variety of appeasement gestures to avoid violence, notably facial expressions, vocalizations, and gestures (Krebs & Miller, 1985). Unfortunately, however, humans are unique in their capacity to override evolved mechanisms for inhibiting aggression, particularly when divided by nationality, ethnicity, or ideology. Furthermore, as Konrad Lorenz noted, humans have developed the ability to kill one another from a distance. Not seeing our victims suffer prevents activation of natural inhibitions against killing members of the species, such as empathic distress responses, which are probably involved in both inhibiting aggression and promoting altruism. We are not, sadly, as civilized as wolves.

FROM MIND TO BRAIN

THE BIOLOGICAL BASIS OF AGGRESSION

The psychodynamic and evolutionary perspectives presume that aggression is built into the human behavioral repertoire. If a tendency to behave aggressively is innate, it must be rooted in the nervous system and perhaps in the endocrine system as well. Mounting evidence in animals and humans suggests that this is, in fact, the case (see Albert & Walsh, 1984; Carlson, 1991; Moyer, 1983).

The neural systems that control aggression, like those involved in other forms of behavior, are hierarchically organized (Figure 18.6). Sensory information (such as the sight of a threatening gesture) transmitted by the thalamus to the amygdala and hypothalamus can instigate aggression, since the hypothalamus and amygdala are specialized for drive states and emotional reactions (Chapter 3). Lesioning parts of the midbrain can also eliminate an animal's ability to respond with species-typical aggressive motor movements, such as hissing and bared teeth in cats (Carlson, 1991). More sophisticated processing at the cortical level can either inhibit or facilitate aggression instigated at lower levels. A threatening gesture, for example, can be interpreted as an attack or a joke.

Research with humans and other animals documents the role of the hypothalamus and amygdala in aggression. When researchers electrically stimulate the lateral hypothalamus of a normally nonpredatory cat, the animal immediately attacks (Egger & Flynn, 1963). The same phenomenon occurs with rhe-

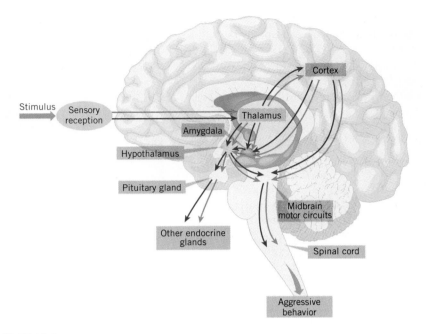

FIGURE 18.6

Areas of the brain involved in aggressive behavior. The neural circuitry for aggression, like other complex psychological functions, is hierarchically organized. Stimulus information (e.g., a threatening gesture) is relayed via the thalamus to the amygdala and hypothalamus for immediate action. The information is also relayed from the thalamus to the cortex for more careful consideration. One or both of these pathways can generate an aggressive response, which requires coordinating motor cortex, midbrain motor mechanisms specialized for species-specific aggressive responses, and other structures involved in control of movement (such as the basal ganglia and cerebellum, not shown here). Information about the emotional significance of the stimulus calculated by the amygdala is transmitted to the hypothalamus, which activates endocrine responses, which in turn affect arousal and readiness for fight or flight.

sus monkeys (see Robinson et al., 1969). In humans, a study of 1800 tumor patients found increased irritability associated with tumors in regions of the hypothalamus (Sano, 1962).

Similar results occur when electrodes are implanted in the amygdala during surgery. With electrical stimulation, a normally submissive, mild-mannered woman became so hostile and aggressive that she tried to strike the experimenter—who was able to control the outburst by switching off the current (King, 1961). Conversely, numerous animal studies show that destroying the amygdala can make extremely wild, hostile animals so docile they can be picked up and petted (Schreiner & Kling, 1953; Woods, 1956). Neurosurgeons who performed essentially the same operation (a partial or complete amygdalectomy) on extremely violent human patients reported a success rate of 85 to 92 percent in reducing violent behavior (Heimburger et al., 1966; Narabayashi et al., 1963). Unfortunately, this type of surgery also produced unpredictable and permanent damage, such as loss of emotion (see Valenstein, 1988).

Outside the central nervous system, gonadal hormones, especially androgens (testosterone), appear to be involved in aggression. In species after species, males are more aggressive, starting in childhood. Such differences have been linked to the action of androgens on the brain both before birth and during development (Archer & Lloyd, 1985). Recall that hormones both organize and activate neural circuits (Chapter 10). Thus, stressing pregnant mice produces male offspring that show less species-typical male behavior as adults, presumably because it reduces prenatal androgen secretion that normally organizes male brains (Carlson, 1991). These male offspring are less aggressive toward male competitors in adulthood (Kinsley & Svare, 1986). Similarly, when female rats and monkeys receive testosterone *in utero*, the result is often an increase in play fighting after birth (Goy, 1968; Meaney & McEwen, 1986; Meaney et al., 1981). Other research has investigated whether prenatal exposure to synthetic hormones such as progestins is associated with heightened aggression years later. Millions of women take progestins to prevent miscarriage. One researcher administered a questionnaire to males and females ranging in age from 6 to 17 that asked how they would respond to a variety of hypothetical situations (Reinisch, 1981). Subjects exposed to progestins during gestation reported a higher potential for physical aggression than the control group.

As for activational effects of hormones on neural circuits, studies with rats show definitively that the amount of aggressive behavior displayed by males and females correlates with circulating blood testosterone levels, with additional hormones involved in females (Albert et al., 1991). The impact of hormones, however, depends on the presence of environmental events that activate aggression, such as competition with members of the same sex or repeated exposure to unfamiliar members of the same species. Without environmental triggers, hormonal levels are relatively unimportant. The data in humans are less definitive, largely because they rely on correlational designs. Correlational studies show that higher levels of testosterone are associated with aggression, but they cannot distinguish the relative contributions of prenatal and circulating testosterone or the possibility that aggression increases testosterone levels and does not simply reflect them (Archer, 1991).

Nevertheless, several studies are suggestive. One examined the relation between physical and verbal aggression and levels of testosterone in adolescent boys (Olweus et al., 1980). Subjects with higher levels of testosterone tended to be more impatient and irritable. Investigations have also found that men convicted of violent crimes have higher testosterone levels than nonviolent offenders and nonoffenders (see Archer, 1991). The dramatic increase in male aggression that occurs at sexual maturation (puberty) in many species and cultures is also likely related to a surge in testosterone levels (see Segall, 1988).

Genetic factors contribute to individual differences in aggressive behavior. Successful attempts to breed highly aggressive strains of rats, mice, and rabbits suggest that among these animals, some individuals inherit a more aggressive temperament than others (see Cologer-Clifford et al., 1992; Moyer, 1983). Questionnaire studies comparing monozygotic and dizygotic twin pairs find aggressive behavior to be heritable in humans, like other personality dimensions (Rushton, 1986). The evidence seems clear that humans are constructed with a potential for aggression and that innate differences exist between the two sexes and among individuals.

A Cognitive-Behavioral Perspective

Although a proclivity for aggression appears to be innate, the activation and inhibition of aggression depends on culture and learning. Harsh parental discipline, for example, produces children who are more aggressive than those whose parents spare the rod (Weiss et al., 1992). As one psychologist put it simply, "You can make a dog mean by breeding, or you can make him mean by beating him" (Dinklage, 1993, personal communication).

According to cognitive-behavioral theories of social learning, children and adults learn to behave aggressively through observational learning such as modeling and through social rewards and punishments. As Bandura (1977) demonstrated, when children watch adults abusing Bobo dolls, they are much more likely to do so themselves (Chapter 5). Such findings have fueled public debates—and psychological research—on the influence of television violence.

To estimate the long-term effects of television violence on behavior is very difficult because people who are aggressive tend to seek out aggressive shows, and they do this from the time they are young. In the short run, experimental data show that children and adolescents are slightly more likely to behave aggressively immediately after viewing violent television shows (Singer & Singer, 1981; Wood et al., 1991). This could occur because watching television violence increases arousal, decreases inhibition, provides aggressive models, or desensitizes children to violence by making violent acts seem commonplace (Gunter & McAleer, 1990). As for long-term effects, the data are inconclusive (see Gadow & Sprafkin, 1993; McGuire, 1986). However, the effect of violence on the screen pales as a predictor of aggressive behavior in comparison with violence witnessed at home, in schools, or on the streets (Gunter & McAleer, 1990).

Similar results emerge from research assessing the effects of pornography on sexual violence. Viewing pornography does not cause sexual violence, but viewing pornographic *aggression* appears to desensitize men to the brutality of rape and other sexual crimes against women (see Malamuth & Donnerstein, 1982). As with television violence, pornographic aggression may affect people's emotional response to violence or slightly weaken inhibitions in deviant individuals with poor internal controls. Nonetheless, most people will not kill or rape after watching a violent or pornographic movie.

The results of 30 years of research on television violence are not without policy implications. In the United States, politicians periodically browbeat network executives during televised hearings and threaten them with governmental controls. (Televised aggression apparently begets televised aggression.) The relatively weak and contradictory findings on television violence suggest, however, that lawmakers might better spend their time addressing the abundance of *real* weapons in the nation's cities rather than demonstrating their fierce determination to keep fictional handguns off make-believe streets.

Toward an Integrated View of Aggression

In 1939, John Dollard, Neal Miller, and their colleagues at Yale University presented the **frustration-aggression hypothesis**, which states that when people are frustrated in achieving a goal, they may become aggressive. The child who wants a cookie and is told to wait until after dinner may throw a tantrum, or the college student who had her heart set on a particular graduate school and was rejected may become not only sad but furious. This model is simple and intuitively appealing and was initially hailed as a significant advance toward a comprehensive theory because it tied aggression to environmental events rather than solely to instincts. However, researchers soon realized that not all aggression results from frustration and not all frustration leads to aggression. Physical pain may cause aggression, and frustrated goals can lead one person to become aggressive, another to become depressed, and still another to become more determined.

A reformulated frustration-aggression hypothesis suggests that frustration breeds aggression to the extent that a frustrating event elicits unpleasant affect (Berkowitz, 1989). Blocked goals can be frustrating, as Dollard and his colleagues emphasized, but so can innumerable other unpleasant experiences. Air pollution, tobacco smoke, and other noxious odors have all been linked to increases in aggressive behavior (Rotton et al., 1979; Zillman et al., 1981).

The relation between heat and aggression is particularly well documented (Anderson, 1989). As temperature rises, so does temper. One study found a strong correlation between temperature and the incidence of riots in U.S. cities between 1967 and 1971 (Carlsmith & Anderson, 1979). Rape, murder, assault, and prison unrest all vary with the time of the year, peaking in the hot summer months (Figure 18.7). Within countries as diverse as Spain, Italy, France, and the United States, the southern regions typically have the highest rates of violent crime (Anderson, 1989). Even the number of batters hit by pitches in professional baseball varies with the temperature (Reifman et al., 1991).

Other research implicates crowding as an environmental factor contributing to aggression (Schmitt, 1966). One team of investigators found a correlation between the extent of prison overcrowding and the rates of suicide, death, disciplinary problems, and psychiatric problems among inmates (Paulus et al., 1988). Overcrowding of "inmates" in college dormitories can similarly have many negative consequences (Glassman et al., 1978; Karlin et al., 1979). Overcrowding increases physiological arousal, blood pressure, and subjective experience of distress (Epstein et al., 1981).

The reformulated frustration-aggression hypothesis may point the way toward an integrative perspective on aggression, which takes seriously both the role of biology and the influence of culture and experience. Although humans do not appear driven to aggression like they are driven to eat, children spontaneously behave aggressively, and humans are endowed with hormonal and neural mechanisms that mediate aggressive responses. Moreover, like other animals, humans, and particularly males, compete for territorial resources and sexual partners, and they are omnivores who hunt prey. That natural selection would have failed to endow them

I pray thee, good Mercutio, let's retire:
The day is hot, the Capulets abroad,
And, if we meet, we shall not 'scape a brawl;
For now, these hot days, is the mad blood stirring.

Shakespeare, Romeo and Juliet *(III, i)*

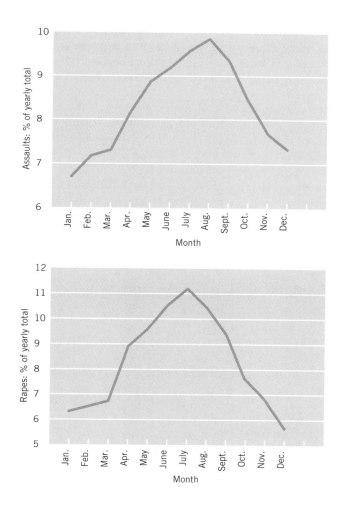

FIGURE 18.7
Aggression and time of year. The number of assaults (a) and rapes (b) committed varies by the time of year and is highest in the hottest months. Data were averaged across studies from North America and Europe over the last hundred years. SOURCE: *Anderson, 1989, pp. 85–86.*

with emotional and behavioral mechanisms that produce aggression under certain circumstances therefore seems inconceivable.

Culture and learning, however, largely define those circumstances. Humans appear biologically constructed to behave aggressively when they feel hurt, deprived, or blocked from reaching their goals, but many goals, as well as strategies for dealing with frustration, reflect culture and learning. Prior experiences with aggressive behavior and its consequences, both direct and vicarious, also influence future tendencies to behave aggressively. Wife-beaters who are arrested for their crimes re-victimize their wives at a much lower rate than those who are not arrested, just as children who get a clear message that violence will not be tolerated tend to develop other ways of regulating conflicts (Lore & Schultz, 1993). Because aggression is rooted in our biology, then, does not mean it is uncontrollable. Finally, cognitive processes, especially the attributions people make for the causes of their misfortunes, play a role in eliciting and controlling aggression as well. Individuals are more likely to become aggressive, for example, if they believe someone has willfully and knowingly inflicted harm (see Geen, 1995).

SOCIAL INFLUENCE

In 1991, a nation and world were shocked by a home video of Los Angeles police officers beating black motorist Rodney King after a high-speed chase. Equally shocking, on April 29 of the following year, a jury acquitted the officers, convinced after repeatedly viewing the tape in slow motion that King's continued resistance justified the officers' actions. When news of the acquittal hit the streets, the African-American community erupted. Angry mobs looted stores, pulled people from their vehicles and beat them senseless, set buildings and cars on fire, and attacked anyone whose race placed him in the wrong neighborhood at the wrong time. The riots left 54 people dead, over 2000 injured, and racial tensions burning like the streets of the city.

By the late nineteenth century, sociologists and philosophers had recognized that people behave differently in crowds than they do as individuals and that a crowd is more than the mere sum of its parts. In his classic 1895 study, *The Crowd*, Gustave Le Bon argued that people in a crowd may lose their personal identities and ability to judge right and wrong. They become anonymous and no longer consider themselves accountable for their behavior. Le Bon had in mind events of the eighteenth and nineteenth centuries, such as the frenzied mobs of the French

The Los Angeles riots in April 1992 exemplify the urban mob behavior that worried Le Bon and other philosophers and sociologists a century earlier.

Revolution, but his reflections could equally apply to the behavior of the police officers who beat Rodney King or the rioters who rampaged through Los Angeles after the jury found the officers not guilty.

Since Le Bon's time, social psychologists have examined a number of forms of **social influence**, or effects of the presence of others on the way people think, feel, and behave. In one of the earliest social-psychological experiments, Norman Triplett (1897) investigated how the mere presence of other people affects performance. When he asked 40 adolescents to wind a fishing reel as quickly as possible, he found that they wound it faster when competing with others than when racing solely against the clock. Psychologists call the performance-enhancing effect of the presence of others **social facilitation** and have observed the phenomenon in a wide variety of species, from humans to cockroaches (Buck et al., 1992; Zajonc, 1965). In this section we cast aside the cockroaches to explore three forms of social influence in humans: obedience, conformity, and group processes.

Obedience

In the small South Vietnamese village of My Lai on March 16, 1968, at the height of the Vietnam War, three platoons of American soldiers massacred several hundred unarmed civilians, including children, women, and the elderly. The platoons had arrived in Vietnam only a month before but in that short time had sustained heavy casualties, leaving the survivors scared and vengeful. Any inhibitions the soldiers might have had against killing innocent civilians disappeared when their commander ordered them to shoot the villagers, whom he suspected of being enemy sympathizers. Tremendous controversy ensued: Do soldiers relinquish their duty to judge right and wrong upon receiving an order? And if soldiers remain morally responsible actors who must make their own independent decisions, what happens to the chain of command?

Such tragic consequences of **obedience**, or compliance with authority, are not limited to warfare. In 1978, in the small community of Jonestown, located in a Guyana jungle, over 900 members of the People's Temple cult drank cyanide-laced Kool Aid to commit mass suicide. The cult's leader, Jim Jones, told his people that a "revolutionary suicide" would dramatize their dedication. According to the few survivors, some people resisted, but most took their lives willingly, with mothers giving cyanide to their children and then drinking it themselves. The more recent inferno in Waco, Texas, in which many Branch Davidian cult members lit their own compound ablaze under the leadership of David Koresh, and a similar scene of carnage in Switzerland under the direction of a Canadian cult leader, are equally grizzly examples of misplaced obedience.

Efforts to understand the conditions under which people obey or disobey began after the collapse of the Third Reich in 1945. Many social psychologists were refugees from the Nazis who presumed that the blind obedience they had witnessed was an aberration caused by flaws in the German character or by the political, social, and economic upheaval that left Germany in ruin after the First World War. Subsequent research on authoritarian personality dynamics (Chapter 17) in their new land led instead to a disquieting conclusion: Many people in the United States were also attracted to ideology glorifying blind obedience (Adorno et al., 1950).

This was the context in which Stanley Milgram (1963, 1974) began his classic work on obedience, in which two-thirds of subjects delivered the maximum shock to subjects (who had even stopped screaming) simply because the experimenter asserted his authority (Chapter 17). The implications of Milgram's study are painfully clear: People will obey, without limitations of conscience, when they believe an order comes from a legitimate authority (Milgram, 1974).

By varying the experimental conditions, Milgram discovered several factors that influence obedience. One is the proximity of the victim to the subject. Obedience

Still saluting after his conviction for mass murder in the town of My Lai, Lt. William Calley began a life prison term in a case that drew controversy about the limits of military obedience.

FIGURE 18.8
Effects of proximity on maximum shock delivered. Subjects in the Milgram experiments generally obeyed, but the closer the subject was to the victim, the less the subject obeyed. SOURCE: *Milgram, 1965, p. 63.*

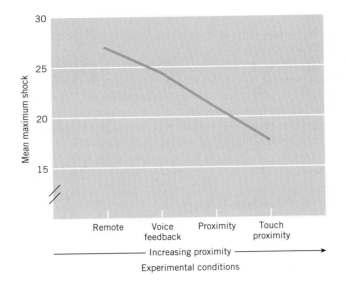

declines substantially if the victim is moved from a separate room into the subject's room, if the sound of his voice replaces pounding on the wall, and if the subject has to force the victim's hand onto a shockplate to administer further punishments (see Figure 18.8). Proximity to the experimenter also affects the subject's decision to obey. The closer the subject is to the experimenter, the more difficult is disobedience; when the experimenter sits in another room, obedience drops sharply. Another factor that influences obedience is a countervailing form of social influence. In the presence of dissenters who refuse to proceed, subjects more readily refuse to continue. Subsequent research shows that personality variables such as authoritarianism and hostility can also influence the likelihood of obedience (Blass, 1991). Nevertheless, the philosopher Hannah Arendt may have been right when she said that the horrifying thing about the Nazis was not that they were so deviant but that they were "terrifyingly normal."

Conformity

Whereas obedience refers to compliance with the demands of an authority, **conformity** means changing attitudes or behavior to accommodate the standards of peers or groups. The pressure to conform can be immense, even if subtle. Consider how fads and fancies change with the times. Real estate agents can date the interior of a house by the colors and patterns in the kitchen and bathrooms. The loud green and orange wallpaper designs that excited decorators and consumers in the 1960s make contemporary home buyers wince. Wearing a thin tie when wide is in vogue makes many men intensely uncomfortable, as does wearing the wrong brand of tennis shoes for many teenagers.

A series of classic studies by Solomon Asch (1955, 1956) documented the power of conformity, much as Milgram's studies established the power of obedience. Asch assembled groups of seven to nine college students and told them they were participating in an experiment on visual judgment. All but one of the students were actually confederates, so their responses were planned in advance. The experimenter asked the "subjects" to match the lines on two white cards (Figure 18.9). On one card was a line, and on the other were three vertical lines of varying length. One of these three lines was the same length as the line on the other card, while the others were substantially different. The experimenter asked each student to choose which of the three lines matched the line on the other card.

Conformity can take many forms.

On the first and second trials, everyone—subject and confederates alike—gave the right answer. On subsequent trials, however, the confederates (who went first) unanimously chose a line that was obviously incorrect. Their answers placed the subject in the uncomfortable position of having to choose between publicly opposing the view of the group or giving an answer that was clearly incorrect.

Without peer pressure to conform, subjects chose the wrong line less than 1 percent of the time. However, with the opinions of others weighing heavily upon them, subjects made incorrect choices 36.8 percent of the time. Not surprisingly, the degree of unanimity affected the tendency to conform. If only one confederate gave

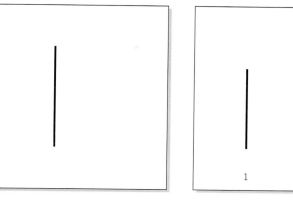

FIGURE 18.9
The Asch conformity experiments. Subjects in Asch's experiments on conformity were asked which of the three lines on the right matched the one on the left. Pressure to conform swayed their responses. SOURCE: *Asch, 1955, p. 193 (3).*

an incorrect answer, subjects continued to follow their own judgment in almost all cases. When three or more confederates dissented, however, roughly one-third of subjects conformed to the majority (Figure 18.10). If even one of the confederates allied himself with the subject, on the other hand, the subject made significantly fewer errors than when forced to face the majority alone.

The Asch studies powerfully demonstrate the power of situations to influence behavior and attitudes. Personality factors, however, also influence the tendency to conform. Individuals with low self-esteem and those who are especially motivated by a need for social approval are more likely to conform (Crown & Marlowe, 1964; Dittes, 1959; Moeller & Applezweig, 1957; Strang, 1972). To what extent subjects actually alter their beliefs in the Asch studies rather than simply comply with situational demands to avoid disapproval is a matter of debate, but when asked, Asch's subjects generally reported that they believed their answers, perhaps because of cognitive dissonance (see Chapter 17).

Conformity varies by culture and appears to be linked to the way people earn their livelihood (Price-Williams, 1985). People in hunter-gatherer societies exercise more independent judgments than people in agricultural societies (Berry, 1979). Agricultural societies depend heavily on communal organization and coordinated action; too much independent judgment can be counterproductive during planting and harvest times, when work needs to be done. Agricultural societies also have much higher population density, whereas hunter-gatherer societies are often highly dispersed across a territory and may thus require less compliance with social norms (see Barry et al., 1957).

Conformity also varies within cultures. In both North America and Australia, low-income and rural parents tend to emphasize obedience and conformity in their child-rearing practices compared with urban and middle-class parents (Cashmore & Goodnow, 1986; Peterson & Peters, 1985). This finding, too, makes adaptive sense, since parents typically prepare their children for work similar to their own (LeVine, 1982), and laborers have less autonomy than professionals. Within a single culture over time, conformity appears to wax and wane as well, depending on broader social currents (Larsen, 1990).

FIGURE 18.10
Effect of number of confederates on performance. Subjects in Asch's experiments tended to conform when three or more confederates chose the wrong line.
SOURCE: *Asch, 1955, p. 193 (6).*

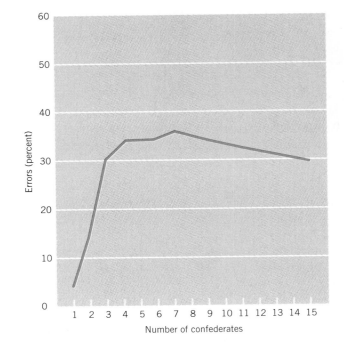

Group Processes

The Asch conformity experiments illustrate just how powerful group processes can be. A **group** is a collection of people whose actions affect the other group members. When a collection of people congregate for even relatively short periods of time, their interactions tend to become patterned in various ways. In fact, many similar patterns emerge in informal groups that come together on the spur of the moment and in enduring institutions such as families and corporations. Features common to groups include norms, roles, and leadership.

Norms

All groups develop **norms**, or standards for behavior. Norms guide thought, feeling, and behavior, from the way people dress to their attitudes about sex, Republicans, and lawyers. Different groups have different norms, and particularly in complex societies, people must pick and choose the norms to obey because they belong to many groups, which may have conflicting norms. Adolescents, for example, frequently find themselves choosing between the norms of adults and peers.

The way people respond to norms depends on their attitude toward the groups with which the norms are associated. Groups whose norms matter to an individual, and hence have an impact on the individual's behavior, are known as **reference groups**, since these are the groups to which a person refers when taking action. A reference group can be positive or negative. A reference group is considered positive if the person tries to emulate its members and meet their standards. When a teenage boy gets drunk on weekends because his friends do, his friends are a positive reference group (but not necessarily a positive influence). A reference group is negative if a person rejects its members and disavows their standards. If a teenager gets drunk every weekend to establish his independence from his teetotaling parents, his parents are a negative reference group. In both cases, the reference group is influencing the teenager's behavior (which he might be loath to admit), but the direction of influence is different.

Roles

Not all norms apply equally to everyone in a group or society. A **role** is a position in a group that has norms specifying appropriate behavior for its occupants (see Merton, 1957; Parsons, 1951). Roles tend to be flexible, letting the individual make decisions about specific actions, much like roles do in improvisational theater. A mother can decide how she will care for her child in a given circumstance, but her culture provides general guidelines for acceptable maternal behavior, such as whether she should stay home with her child or what forms of discipline she should employ. Role theorists often use a dramaturgical metaphor: Roles are parts individuals play in life's drama; society directs them until their time on the stage is no more and another actor takes their place. Individuals internalize roles as role schemas (Chapter 17), which direct their behavior and lead them to expect certain responses from people with complementary roles (such as husband and wife, teacher and student).

Several roles routinely emerge in groups, even in brief, unstructured ones (see Bales, 1953). When strangers enter into groups in the laboratory and are asked to solve problems, some group members usually take responsibility for seeing that the group completes its tasks; these are called **task leaders**, or instrumental leaders. Others, called **social-emotional leaders**, try to keep the group working cohesively and with minimal animosity. Sometimes a group member takes on a **tension-release role**, making jokes to relieve the pressure that builds as the group tries to accomplish its tasks. Although people in this role may appear at times to interfere with the group's progress, their presence in a jury room or corporate meeting can actually help the group function. Another role that sometimes arises in small groups, families, organizations, or nations is the scapegoat, the person blamed for problems.

Zimbardo's prison study showed how powerful the demands of roles and situations can be on individual behavior.

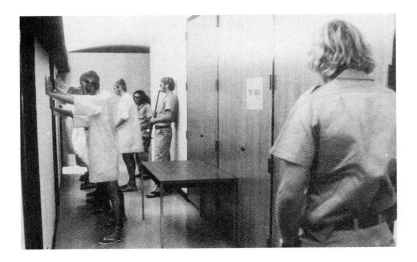

Group members focus their anger and project their feelings of personal responsibility for failure onto the scapegoat, who becomes a common enemy (even if subtly, through annoyed glances or rolling eyes).

Because people often define themselves by their roles, roles can have a profound impact on attitudes. One classic study examined the way workers' attitudes change as a result of job promotions (Lieberman, 1956). The researcher measured the attitudes of plant workers and then reassessed them after some were promoted to foreman (a management position) or shop steward (a union position). Not surprisingly, after their promotions, the foremen were more pro-company than they had been as workers, whereas the shop stewards had become more pro-union. More interestingly, however, when the company later experienced financial problems and had to demote some of the foremen to their previous rank-and-file positions, they returned to their original attitudes.

One of the most dramatic illustrations of the influence of roles on social behavior occurred in a study by Philip Zimbardo (1972, 1975). Twenty-two male college student volunteers played the roles of prisoners and guards in a simulated prison. To make the experiment as realistic as possible, students designated as prisoners were arrested at their homes and searched, handcuffed, fingerprinted, and booked at a police station. They were then blindfolded and driven to the simulated prison where they were stripped, sprayed with a delousing preparation (actually a deodorant spray), and told to stand alone naked in the cell yard. After a short time, they were given a uniform and placed in a cell with two other "prisoners." The guards received minimal instructions and were free to devise their own rules. The only prohibition was against physical punishment.

Soon after the experiment began, Zimbardo noted marked differences between the behavior of the guards and prisoners (Figure 18.11). The guards became increasingly aggressive, treating the prisoners as less than human, seldom using their names (instead calling them by number, if referring to them as individuals at all), and subjecting them to roll calls that could last for hours. Many acted with clear sadistic pleasure.

The prisoners, for their part, initiated progressively fewer actions and appeared increasingly depressed. Half the prisoners (five subjects) suffered such extreme depression, anxiety, or psychosomatic illness that they had to leave. The prisoners talked almost exclusively about prison life, maintaining the illusion of their roles. By the fifth day, those who remained were brought before a mock parole board, which would determine whether they would be released. Most were willing to forfeit all the money they had earned in the experiment if they could be released. When their requests for parole were denied, they obediently returned to their cells.

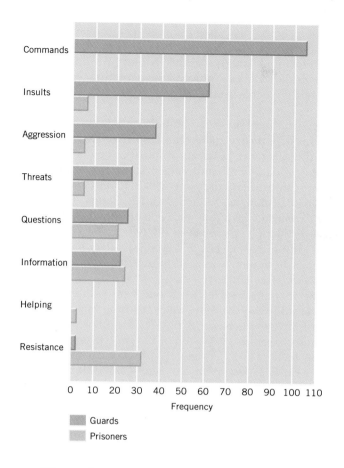

Guards
Prisoners

FIGURE 18.11
Behavior of guards and prisoners in the Zimbardo experiment. As time passed, the guards became more authoritarian and the prisoners, helpless. The figure shows the differences in behavior between guards and prisoners as coded from videotapes of their interactions over the six days in the simulated prison. SOURCE: *Zimbardo, 1975, p. 45.*

The study was originally designed to last two weeks, but the shocking results led Zimbardo to abort it after only six days. The study provides a powerful demonstration of the way roles structure people's behavior and ultimately their emotions, attitudes, and even their identities. Although the subjects were, in reality, college students randomly assigned to be prisoners or guards, within days they had *become* their roles, in action, thought, and feeling.

Leadership

As we have seen, groups tend to have formal or informal **leaders**, people who exercise greater influence than the average member. A major initial impetus to research on leadership was Adolf Hitler. Social scientists were astonished that an individual so manifestly disturbed and filled with rage could arouse such popular sentiment and create such a well-oiled war machine. Could democratic forms of leadership be as efficent?

Leadership Styles   In a classic study, Kurt Lewin and his colleagues (1939) randomly assigned 10-year-old boys to one of three groups for craft activities after school. Each group had an adult leader who took one of three leadership styles: He made all the decisions (an autocratic leadership style); involved himself in the group and encouraged members to come to decisions themselves (a democratic style); or simply let things happen, intervening as little as possible (a laissez-faire style). Boys with an autocratic leader produced more crafts, but they were more likely to stray from the task when the leader left the room, and their products were judged inferior to those produced in the democratic condition. Boys in the democratic group expressed greater satisfaction and displayed less aggression than comparison subjects. Laissez-faire leadership led to neither satisfaction nor efficiency. Lewin and his colleagues concluded that autocratic leadership breeds discontent among group members but can be efficient. In contrast, democratic leadership seems to be both efficient and motivating. Lewin's leadership categories largely parallel Baumrind's findings on parenting styles (Chapter 14), which showed that authoritative parenting (equivalent to democratic leadership) is more effective than authoritarian (autocratic) or permissive (laissez faire).

In recent years, industrial/organizational (I/O) psychologists have taken the lead in studying leadership, trying to translate theory and research on effective leadership into interventions to make organizations more efficient. Implicit in Lewin's typology of leaders are two factors emphasized by contemporary organizational psychologists: task orientation and relationship orientation (see Blake & Mouton, 1964; Hersey & Blanchard, 1982; Misumi & Peterson, 1985; Stogdill & Coons, 1957). In other words, leaders differ in the extent to which they focus on efficiency and on the feelings of their employees. The distinction is similar to the two major clusters of psychosocial motives found cross-culturally—agency and communion (Chapter 10). Leaders can be high or low on one or both dimensions, although the extent to which the two correlate is a matter of debate (see Dipboye et al., 1994).

Intuitively, one would assume that the best leader is one who is interested in both the product and the producer and who therefore takes a strong but democratic leadership style, but this is not always the case. A physician cannot effectively perform delicate surgery by seeking consensus every step of the way, any more than a company in a rapidly changing field such as computer software can encourage innovative thinking with an autocratic leadership style. Many situational factors influence the effectiveness of a particular management style, such as the motivation and ability of employees, the extent to which tasks require autonomy and creativity, the leader's position in the organizational hierarchy, the degree of pressure to produce, the type of organization, and the extent to which the environment is competitive (Dipboye et al., 1994).

Cultural values and norms also guide leadership styles (see Gerstner & Day, 1994). Managers in traditional societies like Greece and India tend to prefer autocratic leadership styles with passive subordinates, whereas leaders in technologically developed societies like Japan, the United States, Canada, and England prefer subordinates who are active and participatory (Barrett & Franke, 1969; Negandhi, 1973). A study of managers in the United States, Hong Kong, and China found American managers more concerned with worker productivity and Chinese managers more concerned with maintaining a harmonious work environment (Ralston et al., 1992). Hong Kong managers expressed moderate concerns about both productivity and harmony, presumably reflecting Hong Kong's economic similarity to the United States and cultural similarity to China.

North American executives are now trying to adapt some of the more participatory, less hierarchical forms of management that have made Japanese organizations so productive (Deming, 1986; Sahney et al., 1991). Some companies, for example, have tried variants of the Japanese *ringi* procedure, in which work groups at lower levels draft a plan, which is then circulated up the organizational ladder (Berry et al., 1992). The result is that employees, from the lowest levels up, can see their influence on company decisions and feel responsible for them.

Leadership style and effectiveness also depend on the leader's personality (Hogan et al., 1994). Research on the Big Five factors and similar dimensions of personality (Chapter 12) finds that successful leaders tend to be high on extroversion (including dominance, energy, and orientation toward status), agreeableness, and conscientiousness. Thus, effective leaders tend to be outgoing, energetic, powerful, kind, hard-working, and attentive to the task at hand. Ineffective leaders tend to be perceived as arrogant, untrustworthy, selfish, insensitive, and overambitious—in a word, narcissistic. These generalizations, however, require the same caveat as all generalizations about personality traits: They are more likely to apply in some situations than in others (Chapter 12).

Charismatic Leaders   A type of leader prevalent today in much of the Third World, and in most periods of rapid social change, is the charismatic leader. A **charismatic leader** is one who inspires obedience by the force of his personality (House, 1977; Weber, 1924). This century has witnessed charismatic leaders from Martin Luther King, Jr., Mahatma Gandhi, and John Kennedy to Adolf Hitler, Jim Jones, and David Koresh. As this list suggests, leaders can harness charisma for good or for ill.

Charismatic leadership generally reflects the interaction of a singular personality and a singular time. According to Erik Erikson, charismatic leaders are often motivated to greatness or infamy by their own inner turmoil, yet their actions simultaneously answer the needs of their followers. In Erikson's artful words, "Now and again... an individual is called upon (called by whom, only the theologians claim to know, and by what, only bad psychologists) to lift his individual patienthood to the level of a universal one and to try to solve for all what he could not solve for himself alone" (1958, p. 67). For example, Hitler felt controlled and persecuted by an autocratic father (Erikson, 1963). His resulting fantasies of rebellion and domination touched a sympathetic chord in many Germans, who had suffered as children at the hands of autocratic parents and who as a nation had suffered humiliating defeat in World War I.

Charismatic leaders offer their followers a vision of a better life and often redemption from suffering (House & Singh, 1987), which is particularly appealing to people who feel oppressed, humiliated, confused by rapid cultural change, or conflicted about their identity. Charismatic leaders capture the hearts of their followers because their political message is not merely pragmatic but infused with cultural or spiritual meaning. This infusion was especially evident in Gandhi's leadership of the Indian independence movement (Erikson, 1969). Gandhi's success as a leader lay in developing a strategy for political action—passive resistance—that was compatible with traditional Indian collectivistic and nonviolent values while fostering independence from British colonialism.

Gandhi was one of the most powerful charismatic leaders of the twentieth century.

SOME CONCLUDING THOUGHTS

Our psychological odyssey is rapidly coming to an end, after traveling through the hills and valleys of the brain and traversing the seemingly impenetrable jungles of culture. In the process, we have encountered four soothsayers, each offering a different perspective on the psychological terrain that lies between brain and culture. One implores us to remember that humans are fundamentally animals, whose reason is always at the service of their motivation, and whose motivation is only partially available for conscious inspection. A second exhorts us to remember that human behavior, like that of other animals, is first and foremost a response to environmental events, and that what may look like freely chosen behavior is always controlled by its consequences. A third perspective reminds us of the power of human thought, of the capacity to transform simple sensations into complex ideas and to call them up moments or even years later to solve problems. The fourth reminds us that people think, feel, and behave for a reason, and that the method behind the mind's madness is the handiwork of millions of adaptations to an environment that is always one step ahead of us.

So is the mind a battleground for warring internal forces, a machine, a computer, or an instrument for maximizing adaptation? The human mind is no doubt all of these and none of these. We will surely someday encounter other soothsayers bearing new metaphors, but they will have to save their sooth for another book and another time.

As psychologists, we view human nature from a scientific standpoint but cannot escape our own historical and cultural vista. Our knowledge of mental life and behavior is the knowledge of a particular people at a particular time. The only way

Never in human history has the engine of change moved so quickly as in contemporary Indonesia (shown here) and throughout the Third World.

to catch a glimpse of what lies beyond this limited vista is to train our eyes on the observer—ourselves—as we study the observed. This means examining our idiosyncratic reactions as we try to comprehend our nature (or what psychodynamic theorists call countertransference), as well as recognizing our own cultural and historical context.

These are very special times to study psychology. In this century, we will have witnessed the most momentous period of social change in human history, as the vast majority of the world's people shift from agricultural, nomadic, or hunter-gatherer societies to industrial nation-states. Not since the rise of agriculture thousands of years ago has the structure of human society changed so dramatically, and never as rapidly as in the present epoch. A century ago, most people lived with their extended families and believed in the values of their parents and ancestors. Within a few brief generations, traditional values and beliefs have broken down, and technology has advanced beyond anyone's wildest predictions.

People cope with social change in many ways. Some embrace new ideologies, technologies, and values. Others, coping with spiritual unease and often with feelings of envy, inferiority, and hatred of the dominant cultures that swept away their traditions, search for the future in the past, embracing fundamentalist ideologies that rigidly define good and evil, eliminate ambiguity, and offer a blueprint for how to live (Lifton, 1963). Another route to personal meaning lies in transferring loyalties from family and clan to large nation-states (see Geertz, 1963). Unfortunately, this process can produce the kind of fervent nationalism that has left so many dead in this century, from Nazi Germany to the civil wars that engulfed Eastern Europe after the demise of the Soviet Union. Yet still another strategy for coping with social change is to synthesize the old and the new, to preserve a continuity with the past while somehow mooring one's identity in the future, as was Gandhi's path.

These psychological responses to the social and political realities of our age lie at the intersection of mind, brain, and culture. The aggression that fuels conflicts between nations, like the powerful feelings of kinship and solidarity that unite people and give their lives meaning, springs from a brain constructed to make possible the passions that divide and unite. We all share a core of human nature rooted in biology. But the way that nature develops and expresses itself is as diverse as the cultures and individuals who populate the globe.

Summary

Interpersonal Attraction and Relationships

1. Several factors lead to **interpersonal attraction**, including proximity, similarity, rewards, and physical attractiveness. **Social exchange theory** holds that the foundation of relationships is reciprocal rewards.

2. Psychologists have proposed various taxonomies of love. One contrasts **passionate love** (marked by intense physiological arousal and absorption in another person) with **companionate love** (love that involves deep affection, friendship, and emotional intimacy). Sternberg divides love into three components—intimacy, passion, and decision/commitment. Other theorists argue that romantic love is a continuation of infant attachment mechanisms. Evolutionary theorists emphasize **sexual strategies**, tactics used in selecting mates, which vary by gender and reflect the different evolutionary selection pressures on males and females.

3. The capacity for love is rooted in biology, but its nature is shaped by culture, as many cultures do not consider romantic love necessary or even important in marriage relationships.

Altruism

4. **Altruism** means behaving in a way that helps another person, with no apparent gain, or with potential cost, to oneself. Philosophers and psychologists disagree as to whether any act can be genuinely altruistic, or whether all apparent altruism is really aimed at making the apparent altruist feel better (**ethical hedonism**). Altruistic behavior probably reflects a blend of selfish and unselfish motives. Evolutionary psychologists propose that people act in ways that maximize their inclusive fitness and hence are most likely to behave altruistically toward their relatives. Natural selection favors animals that behave altruistically toward unrelated members of the species if the likely benefit to each individual over time exceeds the likely cost, a phenomenon known as **reciprocal altruism**.

5. Researchers studying **bystander intervention** have found that in the presence of other people who do not take action, people often do not help in a crisis. In part this reflects a **diffusion of responsibility** (a diminished sense of personal responsibility to act).

Aggression

6. **Aggression** refers to verbal or physical behavior aimed at harming another person or living being. Across cultures and species, males tend to be more aggressive than females. Researchers are increasingly recognizing the prevalence of male violence perpetrated against females, including battering and rape.

7. Psychodynamic and evolutionary psychologists view aggression as rooted in biology. The neural control of aggression is hierarchically organized, with the amygdala and hypothalamus playing prominent roles. Aggression is also partially controlled by hormones, particularly testosterone. The cognitive-behavioral perspective explains aggressive behavior as a result of social learning (such as modeling) and rewards and punishments.

8. The **frustration-aggression hypothesis** asserts that aggressive behavior arises from frustrated desires or needs. A reformulated hypothesis suggests that frustrating or unpleasant circumstances are likely to evoke aggression if they elicit unpleasant emotion.

Social Influence

9. **Social influence** refers to the ways in which the presence of other people influences thought, feeling, and behavior. **Obedience** is a social influence process whereby individuals follow the dictates of an authority. The Milgram studies demonstrated that most people will obey without limitations of conscience if they believe the authority is legitimate.

10. **Conformity** is the process whereby people change their attitudes or behavior to accommodate the standards of peers or groups. Asch's studies demonstrated that a substantial number of people will conform when confronted by a group with a consensus opinion, even if the opinion is manifestly wrong. Conformity is highest in agricultural societies with dense population, where independence can be maladaptive.

11. A **group** is a collection of people whose actions affect the other group members. Naturally occurring groups routinely have **norms** (standards for the behavior of group members), **roles** (socially patterned positions within a group that define appropriate behavior for the people occupying them), and **leaders** (people who exercise greater influence than the average member).

12. The massive social changes in our century, such as rapid technological development and the breakdown of traditional family structures and values, create profound psychological changes and present dilemmas for coping.

GLOSSARY

The page number following each glossary term indicates the page on which the term appears.

A

ABC theory Albert Ellis's theory of psychopathology, in which A refers to activating conditions, B to belief systems, and C to emotional consequences (p. 636).

absolute threshold The minimum amount of physical energy (stimulation) needed for an observer to notice a stimulus (p. 121).

absorptive phase Phase of metabolism during which the person is ingesting food (p. 379).

accommodation In vision, the changes in the shape of the lens that focus light rays (p. 157); in Piaget's theory, the modification of schemas to fit reality (p. 509).

acculturative stress The stress people experience while trying to adapt to a new culture (p. 430).

acetylcholine (ACh) A neurotransmitter involved in muscle contractions, learning, and memory (p. 82).

achievement test A test of knowledge in a specific area (p. 301).

acquisition Initial learning of a conditioned response (p. 179).

action potential A temporary shift in the polarity of the cell membrane, which leads to the firing of a neuron (p. 78).

activational effects Effects of hormones activating brain circuitry to produce psychobiological changes (p. 390).

actualizing tendency The primary motivation in humans, according to Carl Rogers, which includes a range of needs that humans experience, from the basic needs for food and drink to the needs to be open to experience and express one's true self (p. 480).

adaptive A term applied to traits that help organisms adjust to their environment (p. 20).

additive color mixture The color that results when light of differing wavelengths simultaneously strikes the retina; the perception is the result of adding or combining the wavelengths (p. 135).

adrenal glands Endocrine glands located above the kidneys that secrete epinephrine and other hormones during emergency situations (p. 85).

Adrenalin A hormone that leads to arousal (p. 83).

adrenogenital syndrome A condition in which the adrenal glands secrete too much androgen, leading to the masculinization of the genitals in females (p. 390).

adult attachment Patterns of mental representation, emotion, and proximity-seeking in adults related to childhood attachment patterns (p. 538).

aerial perspective A monocular cue for depth perception, in which objects farther away appear fuzzier and more bluish than those nearby because of reduction and filtering of light by the atmosphere (p. 158).

affect A positive or negative feeling state that typically includes arousal, subjective experience, and behavioral expression (p. 407).

afferent neuron Neuron that carries sensory information to the brain or spinal cord, also called sensory neuron (p. 75).

affiliation motive A need for some kind of satisfying interaction with others (p. 397).

affordance Personal implication of objects or events (p. 507).

afterimage Visual image that persists after a stimulus has been removed (p. 136).

age changes Changes in functioning associated with age (p. 494).

age differences Differences among people of different ages (p. 494).

age regression Reliving an experience from a prior age under hypnosis (p. 355).

ageism A form of prejudice against old people comparable to racism and sexism (p. 503).

agency motives Motives for achievement, mastery, power, autonomy, and other self-oriented goals (p. 397).

aggression Verbal or physical behavior aimed at harming another person or living being (p. 716).

agoraphobia Fear of being in places or situations from which escape might be difficult (p. 606).

alarm stage The first stage of the general adaptation syndrome that involves the release of epinephrine and other hormones such as cortisol (p. 472).

alcoholism Tendency to use or abuse alcohol to a degree that leads to social or occupational dysfunction (p. 590).

alexithymia Psychological disorder in which individuals are unable to describe their emotional experience (p. 409).

algorithm Systematic problem-solving procedure that inevitably produces a solution (p. 269).

all-or-none The quality characteristic of the depolarization of an axon membrane; an action potential either occurs, or it does not (p. 78).

altered states of consciousness Deviations in subjective experience from a normal waking state (p. 353).

altruism Behaving in a way that helps another person with no apparent gain, or with potential cost, to oneself (p. 700).

Alzheimer's disease A progressive and incurable illness that destroys neurons in the brain, causing severe impairment of memory, reasoning, perception, language, and behavior (p. 526).

ambivalence Conflicting feelings or intentions (p. 451).

amnesia Memory loss (p. 214).

amphetamine Drug that leads to hyperarousal and a feeling of "speeding" (p. 360).

amplitude The difference between the minimum and maximum pressure levels in a sound wave, measured in decibels; amplitude corresponds to the psychological property of loudness (p. 139).

amygdala Brain structure associated with the expression of rage, fear, and calculation of the emotional significance of a stimulus (p. 94).

anal stage Psychosexual phase occurring roughly around ages 2 to 3, which is characterized by conflicts with parents over compliance and defiance (p. 454).

analysis of variance (ANOVA) Statistic that assesses the likelihood that mean differences between groups occurred by chance (p. 71).

androgen insensitivity syndrome A condition in which androgens are secreted in utero, but a genetic defect leads to an absence of androgen receptors, so that a genetic male develops female genitalia (p. 390).

anhedonia Lack of any pleasure in life (p. 598).

anima In Jungian theory, an unconscious feminine archetype that exists in all men (p. 458).

animus In Jungian theory, an unconscious masculine archetype that exists in all women (p. 458).

anorexia nervosa Eating disorder in which a person refuses to eat, starving herself to the point that physical complications and sometimes death may occur (p. 386).

anterograde amnesia A loss of memory

for events since the damage to the brain (p. 214).

antibodies Protein molecules that attach themselves to foreign agents in the body, marking them for destruction (p. 435).

antidepressant medication Biological treatment of depression that increases the amount of norepinephrine and/or serotonin available in synapses (p. 644).

antipsychotic medication Medication used to treat schizophrenia and other psychotic states, which has sedating effects and reduces positive symptoms such as hallucinations and delusions (p. 643).

antisocial personality disorder A personality disorder marked by irresponsible and socially disruptive behavior in a variety of areas (p. 613).

anxiety disorder A disorder characterized by intense, frequent, or continuous anxiety, which may lead to disruptive avoidance behavior (p. 605).

aphasia Language disorders (p. 4).

aplysia A marine snail with very large cells that are easy to study (p. 185).

aptitude Potential for performing well (p. 301).

aqueous humor Clear fluid filling the space between the cornea and lens of the eye (p. 127).

archetypes According to Jung, mythological motifs that emerge in dreams and cultural practices, express basic human needs, and are represented by symbols in the collective unconscious (p. 458).

artificial intelligence The use of computers to perform tasks that require intelligence when performed by humans (p. 275).

assimilation The interpretation of actions or events in terms of one's present schemas (p. 509).

association areas Areas of cortex involved in putting together perceptions, ideas, and plans (p. 96).

associationism The school of philosophy that focused on the way thoughts and ideas become associated with each other in the mind (p. 184).

attachment Enduring affectional ties that children form with their primary caregivers and become the basis for later love relationships (p. 533).

attachment motivation The desire for physical and psychological proximity to an attachment figure (p. 397).

attention The process of focusing consciousness on a limited range of experience (p. 333).

attention-deficit/hyperactivity disorder (ADHD) A disorder characterized by age-inappropriate inattention, impulsiveness, and hyperactivity (p. 587).

attitude An association between an action or object and an evaluation (p. 663).

attitude innoculation Building up a receiver's resistance to an opposing attitude by presenting weak arguments for it or forewarning of a strong opposing persuasive appeal (p. 668).

attribution The process of making inferences about the causes of one's own and others' thoughts, feelings, and behavior (pp. 420, 679).

audition Hearing (p. 138).

auditory canal Part of the outer ear, an inch-long passageway just inside the skull in which sound waves resonate and are amplified (p. 140).

auditory nerve The bundle of sensory neurons that transmit auditory information from the ear to the brain (p. 141).

augmentation Attributional phenomenon in which people emphasize an internal explanation for a behavior because it occurred despite situational pressures (p. 680).

authoritarian personality Personality type that is prone to hate people who are different or downtrodden (p. 675).

autocratic A leadership style identified in which the leader makes all the decisions (p. 731).

automatic thoughts The things people say spontaneously to themselves, which can lead to irrational feelings and behaviors (p. 635).

automatization The process of executing mental processes with increasing efficiency, so that they require less and less attention (p. 515).

autonomic nervous system (ANS) The part of the peripheral nervous system that serves visceral or internal bodily structures connected with basic life processes, such as the beating of the heart and breathing. It consists of two parts: the sympathetic nervous system and the parasympathetic nervous system (p. 86).

autonomy versus shame and doubt In Erikson's theory, the stage in which children begin to walk, talk, and get a sense of themselves as independent sources of will and power (p. 564).

availability heuristic A strategy that leads people to judge the frequency of a class of events or the likelihood of something happening on the basis of how easy it is to retrieve from explicit memory (p. 272).

avoidance learning Negative reinforcement procedure in which the behavior of an organism is reinforced by the prevention of an expected aversive event (p. 187).

awareness A continuum of experience that ranges from consciousness to peripheral awareness (p. 333).

axon The extension from the cell body of a neuron through which electrical impulses pass (p. 76).

axon hillock The juncture of the axon and the cell body, the site of the action potential that adds up the total voltage change from all the graded potentials sent along the dendrites and cell body (p. 78).

B

B cells Cells in the immune system that produce antibodies (p. 435).

babbling A child's earliest language utterances that are spontaneous and incomprehensible (p. 248).

backward conditioning Classical conditioning procedure in which the conditioned stimulus is presented after the unconditioned stimulus has occurred (p. 182).

barbiturate Drug that depresses the action of the nervous system (p. 358).

basal ganglia A set of structures involved in the control of movement (p. 95).

basic emotions Feeling states common to the human species from which other feeling states are derived (p. 413).

basic level The level of categorization to which people naturally go; the level at which objects share distinctive common attributes (p. 260).

basic trust versus mistrust In Erikson's theory, the stage in which infants come to trust others or to perceive the social world as unfriendly or unreliable (p. 564).

basilar membrane Membrane that separates two of the cochlea's chambers and is flexed by pressure waves in the cochlear fluid, leading to transduction of sound (p. 141).

behavioral analysis In cognitive–behavioral therapy, the process of assessing the symptom and the stimuli or thoughts associated with it (p. 630).

behavior therapy Treatment based on behaviorist learning principles of classical and operant conditioning (p. 630).

behavior-outcome expectancy Belief that a certain behavior will lead to a particular outcome (p. 464).

behavioral approach system (BAS) The anatomical system that is associated with pleasurable emotional states and is responsible for approach-oriented operant behavior (p. 201).

behavioral environment the environment as mentally represented within the individual that orients the person to time, space, and people (p. 337).

behavioral inhibition system (BIS) The anatomical system that is associated with anxiety and avoidance behavior (p. 201).

behaviorism Perspective pioneered by John Watson and B. F. Skinner that focuses on the relation between observable behaviors and environmental events or stimuli (p. 13).

benzodiazepines Antianxiety medications that indirectly affect the action of norepinephrine (p. 645).

Big Five factors Five superordinate personality traits: extroversion, agreeableness, conscientiousness, neuroticism, and openness to experience (p. 468).

binocular cells Neurons that receive information from both eyes (p. 157).

binocular cues Visual input integrated from two eyes that provides perception of depth (p. 157).

biofeedback A procedure for monitoring autonomic physiological processes and learning to alter them at will (p. 197).

biopsychology The field that examines the physical basis of psychological phenomena such as motivation, emotion, and stress (p. 4).

bipolar cells Neurons in the retina that combine information from many receptors and excite ganglion cells (p. 128).

bipolar disorder A psychological disorder marked by extreme mood swings; also called manic-depression (p. 599).

bleaching Process by which photoreceptors lose their characteristic color when exposed to light (p. 130).

blind spot The point on the retina where the optic nerve leaves the eye and which contain no receptor cells; also called optic disk (p. 129).

blind studies Studies in which subjects are kept unaware of or "blind" to important aspects of the research (p. 43).

blindsight A phenomenon in which individuals with cortical lesions have no conscious visual awareness but can make discriminations about objects placed in front of them (p. 343).

blocking When a stimulus fails to elicit a conditioned response because it is combined with another stimulus that already elicits the response (p. 182).

borderline personality disorder A personality disorder characterized by extremely unstable interpersonal relationships, dramatic mood swings, an unstable sense of identity, intense fears of abandonment, manipulativeness, and impulsive behavior (p. 612).

bottom-up processing Perceptual processing that starts with raw sensory data that feed "up" to the brain; what is perceived is determined largely by the features of the stimuli reaching the sense organs (p. 165).

boundaries In family systems theory, the physical and psychological limits of a family or system (p. 585).

brain grafting Neural tissue transplants (p. 82).

brightness Sensory counterpart of visual stimulus intensity (p. 134).

Broca's aphasia Language disorder caused by damage to Broca's area of the left frontal cortex, in which a person has difficulty speaking, putting together grammatical sentences, understanding complex sentences, and articulating words (p. 99).

Broca's area Brain structure located in the left frontal lobe at the base of the motor strip, involved in the ability to talk and use grammar (p. 99).

buffering hypothesis The view that social support acts as a protective factor against the harmful effects of stress (p. 441).

bulimia A disorder characterized by a binge-and-purge syndrome in which the person binges on food and then either induces vomiting or uses laxatives to purge (p. 387).

bystander intervention A form of altruism involving helping a person in need (p. 713).

C

Cannon-Bard theory A theory of emotion that asserts that emotion-inducing stimuli elicit both emotional experience and bodily response (p. 408).

case study In-depth observation of one subject or a small group of subjects (p. 46).

castration complex In Freud's theory, the fear the boy has in the phallic stage that his father will castrate him for his wishes toward his mother (p. 455).

catastrophes Rare, unexpected disasters such as earthquakes, floods, and other traumatic events that affect a group of people (p. 431).

catatonic schizophrenia Type of schizophrenia marked by peculiar motor behavior, such as an extended period of frozen movement and stupor (p. 594).

categorical variable A variable comprised of groupings, classifications, or categories (p. 36).

categorization The process of grouping objects considered equivalent and excluding those that are not (p. 258).

cell body (soma) Part of the neuron which includes a nucleus containing the genetic material of the cell (the chromosomes) as well as other microstructures vital to cell functioning (p. 75).

central fissure The deep divide in cortical tissue that separates the primary motor and somatosensory cortex (p. 97).

central nervous system The brain and spinal cord (p. 86).

centration The tendency to focus or center on one perceptually striking feature of an object without considering other features that might be relevant (p. 511).

cerebellum A large bulge in the dorsal or back area of the brain, responsible for the coordination of smooth, well-sequenced movements as well as maintaining equilibrium and regulating postural reflexes (p. 92).

cerebrum The "thinking" center of the brain, which includes the cortex and subcortical structures such as the basal ganglia and limbic system (p. 90).

chaining Process of learning in which a sequence of already established behaviors is reinforced step by step (p. 188).

charismatic leader A leader who inspires obedience by the force of his or her personality (p. 733).

chi-square (X^2) test Inferential statistic that compares the observed data with the results one would expect by chance and tests the likelihood the differences between observed and expected are accidental (p. 70).

childhood amnesia The inability to recall early childhood memories (p. 244).

chromosomes Strands of DNA arranged in pairs (p. 108).

chunking The process of organizing information into small, meaningful bits to aid memory (p. 222).

cilia Dendrite-like projections from olfactory receptor cells that extend through the mucous layer into the nasal cavity (p. 141).

circadian rhythms Biological rhythms that evolved around the daily cycles of light and dark (p. 345).

classical conditioning A procedure by which a previously neutral stimulus comes to elicit a response after it is paired with a stimulus that automatically elicits that response (p. 177).

client-centered therapy Therapeutic approach developed by Carl Rogers, based on the assumption that psychological difficulties result from incongruence between one's concept of self and one's actual experience, and that empathy is curative (p. 637).

clinical psychology The field that studies the nature and treatment of psychopathology (p. 26).

clinical syndrome A constellation of symptoms that tend to occur together (p. 586).

closure A Gestalt rule of perception which states that people tend to perceive incomplete figures as complete (p. 156).

cocaine A stimulant that increases the activity of norepinephrine and dopamine (p. 360).

cochlea Three-chambered tube in the inner ear in which sound is transduced (p. 141).

cognition Thought and memory (p. 16).

cognitive dissonance Phenomenon in which a person experiences a discrepancy between an attitude and a behavior or between an attitude and a new piece of information incongruent with it, which leads to a state of tension and a subsequent change in attitude, behavior, or perception (p. 668).

cognitive distortions Cognitive mechanisms by which a depressed person transforms neutral or positive information in a depressive direction (p. 602).

cognitive maps Mental representations of visual space (p. 202).

cognitive social theory A theory of learning that emphasizes the role of thought and social learning in behavior (p. 202).

cognitive therapy A psychological treatment that focuses on the thought processes that underlie psychological symptoms (p. 635).

cognitive-behavioral therapy Psychotherapy that uses methods derived from behaviorist and cognitive learning theories (p. 630).

cohort Age group born around the same time (p. 494).

cohort effects Differences among age groups associated with differences in the culture (p. 494).

collective unconscious A repository of ideas, feelings, and symbols that are shared by all humans and passed genetically from one generation to another, according to Jung (p. 457).

color constancy The tendency to perceive the color of objects as stable despite changing illumination (p. 160).

color-opponent cells Neurons excited by wavelengths that produce one color but inhibited by those that produce another (p. 136).

companionate love Love that involves deep affection, friendship, and emotional intimacy (p. 704).

competence An ability to perform a behavior even if never performed in the past (p. 203).

competencies Skills and abilities used for solving problems (p. 465).

complex cells Feature detectors in the visual cortex that respond when a stimulus of the right orientation falls anywhere within their receptive field; the cells respond most vigorously to lines of a specific orientation moving in a particular direction (p. 133).

complexity The extent to which a sound wave is composed of multiple frequencies (p. 139).

compromise formations A single behavior, or a complex pattern of thought and action, which typically reflects compromises among multiple (and often conflicting) forces (p. 451).

compulsion An intentional behavior or mental act performed in a stereotyped fashion (p. 606).

computerized axial tomography (CT scan) Brain scanning technique used to detect lesions (p. 52).

concepts Mental representations of a class of objects, ideas, or events that share common properties (p. 257).

concrete operational stage Piaget's third stage of cognitive development, in which children are capable of mentally manipulating internal representations of concrete objects in ways that are reversible (p. 512).

conditioned emotional response An emotional response that is learned by pairing an unconditioned stimulus or previously conditioned stimulus with a formerly neutral stimulus (p. 179).

conditioned response In classical conditioning, a response that has been learned (p. 178).

conditioned stimulus A stimulus that the organism has learned to associate with the unconditioned stimulus (p. 178).

conditioning trial Each pairing of the conditioned stimulus and the unconditioned stimulus during the acquisition of the conditioned response (p. 181).

conditions Values or versions of the independent variable that vary across experimental groups (p. 40).

conditions of worth In Carl Rogers' theory, standards children internalize that they must meet in order to esteem themselves (p. 479).

conduct disorder A childhood disorder in which a child persistently violates the rights of others as well as societal norms (p. 589).

conduction loss Type of hearing defect in which the outer or middle ear fails to conduct sound to the hair cells (p. 142).

cones One of two types of photoreceptors, which are specialized for color vision and allow perception of fine detail (p. 128).

confederates Individuals posing as subjects, who assist an experimenter, in a deception experiment (p. 708).

confirmation bias The tendency for people to search for information that confirms their expectations (p. 272).

conflict A battle between opposing motives (p. 451).

conflict model Theoretical model of adolescence that holds that conflict and crisis are normal in adolescence (p. 566).

conformity The process of changing attitudes or behavior to accommodate the standards of a group (p. 726).

confounding variable A variable that produces effects that are confused with the effects of independent variables (p. 44).

conscious mental processes In psychoanalytic theory, mental processes of which people are aware (p. 450).

consciousness The subjective awareness of mental events (p. 331).

consensus In attribution theory, a normative response in a social group (p. 680).

conservation Recognition that basic properties of an object remain stable even though superficial properties may change (p. 512).

consistency In attribution theory, the extent to which a person always responds in the same way to the same stimulus (p. 680).

consolidation The processes by which knowledge becomes stored in long-term memory systems (p. 225).

context of discovery Part of scientific process in which phenomena are observed, hypotheses are framed, and theories are built (p. 60).

context of justification Part of scientific process in which hypotheses are tested (p. 60).

continuity model Theoretical model that holds that adolescence for most individuals is essentially continuous with childhood and adulthood and not distinguished by turbulence (p. 567).

continuous development Steady and gradual change, as opposed to major qualitative transformations; see also **stages** (p. 494).

continuous schedule of reinforcement When the environmental consequences are the same each time an organism emits a behavior (p. 192).

continuous variable A variable that can be placed on a continuum, from none or little to much (p. 36).

control group Subjects in an experiment who receive a relatively neutral condition to serve as a comparison group (p. 43).

conventional morality Level of morality in which individuals define what is right by the standards they have learned from other people, particularly respected authorities (p. 558).

convergence The turning inward of the eyes as an object gets closer; a binocular cue for depth perception (p. 157).

coping Ways people deal with stressful situations (p. 437).

core feature Aspect of a concept not shared by other concepts that clearly distinguishes the concept from others (p. 258).

cornea Tough, transparent tissue covering the front of the eyeball (p. 127).

corpus callosum A band of fibers that connect the two hemispheres of the brain (p. 96).

correlation coefficient An index of the extent to which two variables are related (p. 50).

correlation matrix A table presenting the correlations among several variables (p. 51).

correlational research Research that assesses the degree to which two variables are related, so that knowing the value of one can lead to prediction of the other (p. 50).

cortex The many-layered surface of the cerebrum that allows complex movement and information processing (p. 90).

counterconditioning A technique by which the patient learns physiological and muscular processes that are the opposite of a previously conditioned anxiety response (p. 632).

countertransference The phenomenon in which transference reactions of the patient trigger emotional responses in the therapist (p. 627).

couples therapy Psychotherapy that treats a couple (p. 640).

covariation The extent to which the presence of one variable implies the presence of another (p. 679).

creativity The ability to produce valued outcomes in a novel way (p. 325).

critical period A period of special sensitivity to specific types of learning that shapes the capacity for future development (p. 492).

cross-cultural psychology The field that attempts to test psychological hypotheses in different cultures (p. 7).

cross-sectional studies Type of research that compares groups of different-aged subjects at a single time to see whether differences exist among them (p. 494).

crystallized intelligence People's store of knowledge (p. 521).

culture pattern approach Approach to personality and culture that views culture as an organized set of beliefs, rituals, and institutions that shape individuals to fit its patterns (p. 483).

culture-free Not dependent on a particular cultural experience (p. 305).

cycle A single round of expansion and contraction of the distance between molecules of air in a sound wave (p. 138).

D

daily hassles The small, but irritating demands that characterize daily life (p. 433).

dark adaptation The eyes' adjustment to dim light (p. 130).

daydreaming Part of the flow of consciousness in which attention turns from external stimuli to internal thoughts (p. 336).

decay theory of forgetting The notion that memories are lost as a result of a fading of the memory trace (p. 244).

decibels (dB) Unit of measure of amplitude (loudness) of a sound wave (p. 139).

decision criterion In signal detection theory, the subject's readiness to report detecting a signal when uncertain; also called response bias (p. 122).

decision making The process by which people weigh the pros and cons of different alternatives in order to make a choice among two or more options (p. 269).

declarative memory Knowledge that can be consciously retrieved and "declared" (p. 225).

deductive reasoning The process of reasoning that draws logical conclusions from premises (p. 264).

deep structure The underlying meaning conveyed by a sentence (p. 282).

default value Standard information that fills in for missing data in schematic processing (p. 238).

defense mechanisms Unconscious mental processes aimed at protecting a person from experiencing unpleasant emotions, especially anxiety (p. 438).

deficiency needs In Maslow's hierarchy of needs, motives generated by a lack of something (p. 376).

degree of relatedness The probability that two people share any particular gene (p. 108).

deinstitutionalization A movement to increase the autonomy of severely psychiatrically impaired people and to integrate them in community life (p. 656).

delta sleep A deep sleep characterized by relaxation of muscles and a reduction in biological processes such as rate of respiration and body temperature (p. 348).

delusion A false belief firmly held despite evidence to the contrary (p. 592).

delusional depression Severe depression with psychotic features (p. 464).

demand characteristics The influence of subjects' perception of the researchers' goals on subjects' behavior (p. 43).

dementia A disorder marked by global disturbance of higher mental functions (p. 526).

demographic characteristics Subject characteristics such as age, sex, and race (p. 49).

dendrites Branch-like extensions of the cell body, which receive information from other cells (p. 76).

denial A defense mechanism in which the person refuses to acknowledge external realities or emotions (p. 438).

dependent variables Subjects' responses in a study, hypothesized to depend on the influence of the independent variables (p. 40).

depolarization Process by which the inside of the cell membrane of a neuron becomes less negative (a decrease in polarization) resulting from the stimulation of a neuron's dendrites or cell body by impulses from other neurons (p. 78).

depressant Drug that slows down the nervous system (p. 358).

depth of processing The degree to which information is processed in a meaningful way (p. 230).

depth perception The organization of perception in three dimensions (p. 155).

descriptive diagnosis Classification of mental disorders in terms of clinical syndromes (p. 586).

descriptive research Research methods that cannot unambiguously demonstrate cause and effect, including case studies, naturalistic observation, survey research, and correlational methods (p. 46).

descriptive statistics Numbers that describe the data from a study in a way that summarizes their essential features (p. 44).

developmental model In Freud's theory, the model of psychosexual stages (p. 453).

developmental psychology The field that studies the way thought, feeling, and behavior develop through the lifespan (pp. 26, 490).

developmental task Challenge that is normative for a particular period of life (p. 564).

Diagnostic and Statistical Manual of Mental Disorders-IV (DSM-IV) Manual of clinical syndromes published by the American Psychiatric Association and used for descriptive diagnosis (p. 586).

diathesis-stress model Model of psychopathology which proposes that people with an underlying vulnerability (also called a diathesis) may develop a disorder under stressful circumstances (p. 584).

dichotic listening A procedure in which different information is presented to the left and right ears simultaneously (p. 334).

difference threshold The smallest difference in intensity between two stimuli that a person can detect (p. 122).

diffusion of responsibility The phenomenon in which the presence of other people leads to a diminished sense of personal responsibility to act (p. 714).

direct perception A theory which states that sensory information intrinsically carries meaning (p. 163).

discounting Attributional phenomenon in which people downplay the role of one variable that might explain a behavior because they know another may be contributing (p. 680).

discriminative stimulus A stimulus that signals to an organism that particular contingencies of reinforcement are in effect (p. 196).

disorganized schizophrenia Type of schizophrenia marked by extremely poor contact with reality and bizarre behavior (p. 594).

display rules Patterns of emotional expression that are considered acceptable in a given culture (p. 412).

dissociation A disturbance in memory and consciousness in which significant aspects of experience are kept separate and distinct (or dis-associated) (p. 611).

dissociative disorders Disorders characterized by disruptions in consciousness, memory, sense of identity, or perception of the environment (p. 610).

dissociative identity disorder The most severe dissociative disorder, also known as multiple personality disorder (p. 611).

distinctiveness In attribution theory, the extent to which an individual responds in a particular way to many different stimuli (p. 680).

divergent thinking Generating multiple possibilities from a given situation (p. 325).

divided attention The process by which attention is split between two or more sets of stimuli (p. 334).

dizygotic (DZ) twins Fraternal twins who, like other siblings, share only about half of their genes (p. 109).

doctrine of specific nerve energies Formulated by Johannes Müller in 1826; states that whether a neural message is experienced as light, sound, or some other sensation results less from differences in stimuli than from the particular neural pathways excited by them (p. 120).

dominant Cortical hemisphere more involved in certain functions than the other (p. 101).

dopamine A neurotransmitter with wide-ranging effects, involved in movement, thought, and emotion (p. 79).

double-blind study Study in which both subjects and researchers are blind to the status of subjects (p. 43).

Down syndrome Disorder caused by an extra 21st chromosome, resulting in severe mental retardation (p. 322).

drive According to Freud, an internal tension state that builds up until satisfied; according to behaviorist theory, an unpleasant tention state that motivates behavior, classified as either primary or secondary (acquired) (p. 371).

drive model Freud's theory of motivation, which held that people are motivated by sexual and aggressive instincts or drives (p. 452).

drive-reduction theories Mid-twentieth century behaviorist theories which proposed that motivation stems from a combination of drive and reinforcement, in which stimuli become reinforcing because they are associated with reduction of a state of biological deficit (pp. 199, 374).

dysthmymia Chronic low-level depression of more than two years' duration, with intervals of normal moods that never last more than a few weeks or months (p. 599).

E

eardrum Thin, flexible membrane that marks the outer boundary of the middle ear; the eardrum is set in motion by sound waves and in turn sets in motion the ossicles; also called the tympanic membrane (p. 140).

early memories Memories of events that took place early in one's life (p. 225).

echoic storage An auditory sensory registration process by which people retain an echo or brief auditory representation of a sound to which they have been exposed (p. 218).

echolocation Process used by bats and other animals to sense objects by emitting waves of sounds and sensing the echoes as these waves bounce off the objects (p. 120).

ecological approach Approach to the development of perception which attempts to understand perception in its environmental, adaptive context (p. 507).

educational psychology Field that studies psychological processes in learning and applies psychological knowledge to practical problems in educational settings (p. 26).

efferent neuron (motor neuron) Neuron that transmits commands from the brain to the glands or musculature of the body, typically through the spinal cord (p. 75).

ego The structure that must somehow balance desire, reality, and morality (p. 457).

ego functioning The person's ability to function autonomously, make sound decisions, think clearly, and regulate impulses and emotions (p. 582).

egocentrism Being thoroughly embedded in one's own point of view (p. 510).

eidetic imagery A kind of visual representation that is of photographic accuracy (p. 220).

elaborative rehearsal An aid to long-term memory storage that involves thinking about the meaning of information in order to process it with more depth; see also **depth of processing** (p. 222).

electroconvulsive therapy (ECT) A last-resort treatment for severe depression, in which an electric shock to the brain is used to induce a seizure (p. 646).

electroencephalograph (EEG) Instrument that assesses electrical activity in the brain, used especially in sleep research and diagnosis of epilepsy (p. 52).

elevation Monocular depth cue in which distant objects are higher on the person's plane of view (p. 158).

embryonic period Second phase of prenatal development that extends from the beginning of the third week to about the eighth week of gestation (p. 496).

emotional expression The variety of modes (e.g., facial expression, posture, hand gestures, voice tone) through which people express feelings (p. 410).

empathic distress Feeling upset for another person (p. 561).

empathy Feeling for another person who is hurting, which includes a cognitive component (understanding what the person is experiencing) and an emotional component (experiencing a feeling of empathic distress or discomfort) (p. 561); in Rogers's theory of personality, the capacity to understand another person's experience cognitively and emotionally (p. 479).

empty chair technique A technique associated with Gestalt therapy, in which clients practice emotional expression by imagining that the person to whom they would like to speak is seated in the chair (p. 637).

encoding The process by which information is put into a representational form that can be stored and accessed from memory (p. 229).

encoding specificity principle The notion that the match between the way information is encoded and the way it is retrieved is important to remembering (p. 243).

endocrine system Collection of ductless glands that secrete hormones into the bloodstream and control various bodily and psychological functions (p. 83).

endogenous Produced within the body (p. 83).

endorphins Chemicals in the brain similar to morphine that act as analgesics (p. 83).

environmental psychology Area of psychology that applies psychological knowledge to the design of buildings and landscapes (p. 152).

epinephrine Hormone secreted by the adrenal glands (p. 83).

episodic memory Memories of particular episodes or events from personal experience (p. 225).

equilibration According to Piaget, a balancing of assimilation and accommodation in trying to adapt to the world (p. 509).

ERG theory A theory of worker motivation distinguishing existence, relatedness, and growth needs (p. 376).

error That part of a subject's score on a test that is unrelated to the true score (p. 40).

escape learning Negative reinforcement procedure in which the behavior of an organism is reinforced by the cessation of an aversive event that already exists (p. 187).

estrogens Hormones produced by the female gonads, the ovaries, which control sex drive as well as the development of secondary sex characteristics (p. 85).

ethical hedonism School of philosophical thought that asserts that all behavior, no matter how apparently altruistic, is and should be designed to increase one's own pleasure or reduce one's own pain (p. 712).

ethology Field that studies animal behavior from a biological and evolutionary perspective (p. 21).

etiology Causes of a disorder (p. 581).

Eustachian tube Passage that connects the middle ear to the throat and allows release of pressure (p. 140).

evolutionary perspective Viewpoint built on Darwin's principle of natural selection; argues that human behavioral proclivities must be understood in the context of their evolutionary and adaptive significance (p. 10).

excitatory neurotransmitters Chemicals that depolarize the postsynaptic cell membrane, making an action potential more likely (p. 79).

excitement phase First phase of the sexual response cycle, characterized by increased muscle tension, engorgement of blood vessels in the genitals, and often a skin flush (p. 388).

exhaustion stage The third stage of the general adaptation syndrome in which the body's physiological defenses break down (p. 472).

existential dread The recognition that life has no absolute value or meaning, that any meaning that does exist we create for ourselves, and that ultimately, we all face death (p. 480).

existentialism A school of modern philosophy that focuses on each individual's subjective existence or phenomenology and on the way the individual comes to terms with basic issues such as meaning in life and mortality (p. 480).

expectancies Expectations relevant to desired outcomes (p. 203).

expectancy-value theories Theories which assert that motivation is a joint function of the value people place on an outcome and the extent to which they believe they can attain it (p. 374).

expected utility A combined assessment of the value and probability of different options (p. 270).

experience sampling Technique designed to study the flow of consciousness in which subjects may talk through a task or report their thoughts when beeped on a pager (p. 335).

experimental research Research design in which investigators manipulate some aspect of a situation and examine the impact of this manipulation on the way subjects respond (p. 40).

explanatory style The way people make sense of events or outcomes, particularly aversive ones (p. 204).

explicit memory Conscious memory for facts and events (p. 225).

exposure techniques Behavior therapy techniques based on classical conditioning in which the patient is confronted with the actual phobic stimulus (p. 632).

expressed emotion A family climate that includes criticism, hostile interchanges, and emotional overinvolvement or intrusiveness on the part of family members, which predicts relapse in schizophrenia and other forms of psychopathology (p. 597).

external attribution Explanation of behavior that attributes it to the situation rather than the person (p. 680).

external validity The extent to which the findings of a study can be generalized to situations outside the laboratory (p. 37).

extinction In classical conditioning, the process by which a conditioned response is weakened by presentation of the conditioned stimulus without the unconditioned stimulus; in operant conditioning, the process by which the connection between an operant and a reinforcer or punishment is similarly broken (p. 182).

extroversion Tendency to be sociable, active, and willing to take risks (p. 468).

F

factor analysis A statistical technique for identifying common factors that underlie performance on a wide variety of measures (p. 308).

false confirmation The tendency to look for information that confirms beliefs and to ignore information that does not (p. 682).

false self Condition in which people mold themselves to other people's expectations and to the demands of the roles they play (p. 479).

familiar size A monocular cue for depth perception in which familiar objects are assumed to be their usual size, so that if they appear small they are perceived as farther away (p. 159).

family alliances Patterns of taking sides in family conflicts (p. 585).

family homeostatic mechanisms Methods members use to preserve equilibrium in a family (p. 585).

family roles Parts individuals play in repetitive family interaction patterns (p. 585).

family systems model Model of psychopathology which suggests that an individual's symptoms are really symptoms of dysfunction in a family (p. 584).

family therapy A psychological treatment that attempts to change maladaptive interaction patterns among members of a family (p. 639).

farsightedness Condition in which the eye focuses light on a point beyond the retina, leading to decreased acuity at close range; also called hyperopia (p. 127).

fasting phase The second stage of metabolism, when the body converts glucose and fat into energy (p. 379).

feature detector Neuron that fires only when stimulation in its receptive field matches a particular pattern or orientation (p. 133).

Fechner's law Law of psychophysics proposed by Gustav Fechner, that the subjective magnitude of a sensation grows as a proportion of the logarithm of the stimulus (p. 124).

feedback Information about the extent to which a system is meeting a goal (p. 370).

fetal alcohol syndrome A condition affecting up to half of babies born to alcoholic mothers, which leads to birth defects (p. 496).

fetal period The third phase of prenatal development, from about 9 weeks to birth (p. 496).

fight/flight system Anatomical system associated with unconditioned escape and defensive aggression and the emotions of terror and rage (p. 201).

figure-ground perception A fundamental rule of perception described by Gestalt psychology which states that people inherently differentiate between figure (the object they are viewing, sound to which they are listening, etc.) and ground (background) (p. 155).

firing When a neuron is activated enough to send information to other neurons (p. 77).

first impressions Initial perceptions of another person that can be powerful in shaping future beliefs about the person (p. 672).

fixations In psychoanalytic theory, prominent conflicts and concerns focused on wishes from a particular period (p. 453).

fixed interval schedules When the organism receives rewards for its responses only after a fixed amount of time (p. 194).

fixed ratio schedules When the organism receives reinforcement at a fixed rate, according to the number of responses emitted (p. 194).

flashbulb memories Vivid memories of exciting or highly consequential events (p. 236).

flat affect Blunted emotional response, often found in schizophrenic patients (p. 593).

flooding Cognitive-behavioral technique designed to eliminate phobias, in which the patient confronts the real phobic stimulus all at once (p. 632).

fluid intelligence Intellectual capacities that have no specific content but are used in processing information (p. 520).

foot-in-the-door technique Persuasive technique often used by salespeople, which involves getting people to comply with a small request in order to induce compliance with a larger one (p. 667).

forebrain In humans, the most evolutionary recent part of the brain, which allows complex emotional reactions, thought processes, and movement patterns (p. 94).

forgetting Inability to retrieve memories (p. 244).

form perception The organization of sensations into meaningful shapes and patterns (p. 155).

formal operational stage Piaget's fourth stage of cognitive development, which begins at about age 12 to 15, and is characterized by the ability to manipulate abstract as well as concrete objects, events, and ideas mentally (p. 513).

forward conditioning When the conditioned stimulus precedes the unconditioned stimulus (p. 182).

fovea The central region of the retina, where light is most directly focused by the lens (p. 128).

free association Therapeutic technique for exploring associational networks and unconscious processes involved in symptom formation (p. 625).

free nerve endings Receptors in the skin that appear sensitive to pain (p. 150).

free will versus determinism The philosophical question of whether people act on the basis of their freely chosen intentions, or whether their actions are caused or determined by physical processes in their bodies or the environment (p. 8).

frequency In a sound wave, the number of cycles per second, expressed in hertz and responsible for subjective experience of pitch (p. 138).

frequency distribution A way of organizing data to show how frequently subjects received each of the many possible scores (p. 63).

frequency theory Theory of pitch which asserts that perceived pitch reflects the rate of vibration of the basilar membrane (p. 143).

frontal lobes Brain structures involved in coordination of movement, attention, planning, social skills, conscience, abstract thinking, and aspects of personality (p. 97).

frustration-aggression hypothesis Hypothesis that when people are frustrated in achieving a goal, they may become aggressive (p. 722).

functional fixedness The tendency to ignore other possible functions of an object when one already has a function in mind (p. 273).

fundamental attribution error Hypothesized attributional bias in which people overestimate the role of internal causes of behavior and underestimate situational causes (p. 682).

fuzzy concept Concept that is not reliably understood but rather has different meanings in different contexts (p. 258).

G

g-factor The general intelligence factor that emerges through factor analysis of IQ tests (p. 308).

galvanic skin response An electrical measure of the amount of sweat on the skin that is produced during states of anxiety or arousal; also called skin conductance or electrodermal activity (EDA) (p. 118).

ganglion cells Nerve cells in the retina that integrate information from multiple bipolar cells, the axons of which bundle together to form the optic nerve (p. 128).

gate control theory Theory of pain perception which proposes that cells in the spinal cord act as neurological "gates," allowing some pain signals through while blocking others (p. 151).

gender The psychological meaning of being male or female (p. 544).

gender constancy The recognition that people's gender cannot be altered by changes in appearance or activities (p. 553).

gender identity Categorization of oneself as either male or a female (p. 552).

gender roles The range of behaviors considered appropriate by society for males and females (p. 544).

gender schemas Representations that associate psychological characteristics with one sex or the other (p. 553).

gender stability The understanding that one's gender remains constant over time (p. 552).

gene The unit of hereditary transmission (p. 108).

general adaptation syndrome The three-stage process (alarm, resistance, exhaustion) by which a person responds to stressful conditions (p. 427).

general intelligence The general quickness and efficiency of solving problems that differs among individuals (p. 308).

generalizability Applicability of a study's finding to the entire population of interest (p. 37).

generalized anxiety disorder Persistent anxiety at a moderate but disturbing level (p. 606).

generativity Concern for the next generation as well as an interest producing something of lasting value to society (p. 568).

generativity versus stagnation In Erikson's theory, the stage in which people in mid-adulthood experience concern for the next generation as well as an interest in producing something of lasting value to society (p. 568).

genital stage In Freudian theory, psychosexual stage that occurs at approximately age 12 and beyond, when conscious sexuality resurfaces after years of repression (p. 456).

genogram A map of a family over three or four generations, drawn by a therapist to explore possible similarities between current difficulties and the family's past (p. 640).

genotype Genetic blueprints underlying phenotypic variance (p. 108).

germinal period First two weeks of prenatal development, when the fertilized egg becomes implanted in the uterus (p. 496).

gerontologist Scientist who studies the elderly (p. 503).

Gestalt therapy A psychological treatment based on the assumption that psychological distress results from losing touch with one's emotions and one's authentic inner voice, and that focusing on the "here and now" is curative (p. 637).

gestation Period of prenatal development (p. 496).

giftedness The high extreme of the intellectual spectrum (p. 324).

glucoreceptors Neurons that monitor glucose levels (p. 381).

glucose A simple carbohydrate or sugar that is a source of energy for humans and other animals (p. 379).

glucostatic theory A theory of hunger which proposes that hunger arises when glucose "thermostats" in the nervous system—or "glucostats"—detect low levels of glucose in the bloodstream (p. 381).

goal state The final stage of problem solving in which the problem is solved (p. 267).

goal-setting theory Theory of motivation which suggests that conscious goals regulate much human action, particularly performance tasks (p. 375).

gonads Endocrine glands that control much of sexual development and behavior (p. 85).

good continuation A Gestalt rule of perception which states that, if possible, the brain organizes stimuli into continuous lines or patterns rather than discontinuous elements (p. 155).

graded exposure A modified version of the behaviorist flooding technique for treating anxiety, in which stimuli are real but are presented to the patient in a gradual manner (p. 633).

graded potential Spreading voltage change that occurs when the neural membrane receives a signal from another cell (p. 78).

grammar A system of rules for generating understandable and acceptable language utterances (p. 280).

group A collection of people whose actions affect the other group members (p. 729).

group process The interactions among members of a group (p. 638).

group test A pencil-and-paper measure of intelligence or similar qualities that can be administered simultaneously to a roomful of people (p. 301).

growth needs Motives to expand and develop one's skills and potential (p. 379).

gustation Taste (p. 147).

gyrus Cortical "hill" (p. 96).

H

hair cells Receptors for sound attached to the basilar membrane (p. 141).

hallucination Sensation and perception that occurs in the absence of any external stimulation (p. 360).

hallucinogen Drug that produces hallucinations (p. 360).

halo effect A tendency to attribute additional positive characteristics to someone who has one salient quality, such as physical attractiveness (p. 672).

health psychology Field that lies at the intersection of psychology and medicine, looking at psychological factors involved in health and disease (p. 26).

heritability The extent to which individual differences in phenotype are determined by genetic factors or genotype (p. 110).

heritability coefficient Statistic that quantifies the degree to which a trait is heritable (p. 110).

hermeneutic Interpretive approach to methodology which proposes that a science of human action should aim to understand personal meaning, not predict behavior (p. 45).

hertz (Hz) Unit of measurement of frequency of sound waves (p. 138).

heuristics In problem solving, cognitive shortcuts or rules of thumb (p. 272).

hierarchical organization of memory When information is organized first by broad, general categories which are in turn comprised of narrower subcategories, and ultimately of representations of specific information (p. 236).

hierarchy of needs Maslow's theory that needs are arranged hierarchically, from physiological needs, safety needs, belongingness needs, and esteem needs, through self-actualization needs (p. 375).

hindbrain Part of the brain above the spinal cord that includes the medulla, cerebellum, and parts of the reticular formation (p. 92).

hippocampus A structure in the limbic system involved in the acquisition and consolidation of new information in memory (p. 94).

histogram A graph that plots ranges of scores along the x axis and the frequency of scores in each range on the y axis (p. 63).

homeostasis Regulation of vital processes such as body temperature, blood-sugar level, and metabolism, so that they do not diverge too much from a constant rate or value (p. 370).

hormone Chemical secreted directly into the bloodstream by the endocrine glands (p. 83).

hue The sensory quality people normally consider color (p. 134).

humanistic psychology Branch of psychology that asserts the importance of free will, abandons the view that environmental and genetic variables determine all behavior, and thus questions the applicability of scientific methods to human psychology (p. 479).

humanistic therapies Psychological treatments that focus on the patient's conscious or lived experience and on the way each person uniquely experiences relationships and the world (p. 637).

hyper-complex cells A type of feature detector in the visual cortex that responds to moving lines of a specific length and to moving angles of a specific size (p. 133).

hypermnesia Recalling forgotten memories during hypnosis (p. 355).

hyperopia Condition in which the eye focuses light on a point beyond the retina, leading to decreased acuity at close range. Also called farsightedness (p. 127).

hyperpolarization Process by which the inside of the cell membrane of a neuron becomes more negative (increasing the polarization), decreasing the likelihood that the neuron will fire (p. 78).

hypersomnia Sleep disorder in which the individual sleeps too much (p. 352).

hypnosis Altered state of consciousness characterized by deep relaxation and suggestibility which a person voluntarily enters through the efforts of a hypnotist (p. 354).

hypnotic analgesia Under hypnosis, an apparent lack of pain despite pain-inducing stimulation (p. 355).

hypnotic susceptibility The capacity to enter into a deep hypnotic state (p. 355).

hypothalamus Brain structure situated directly below the thalamus, involved in the regulation of eating, sleeping, sexual activity, movement, and emotion (p. 94).

hypothesis A tentative belief or educated guess that purports to predict or explain the relationship between two or more variables (p. 36).

hypothesis testing In problem solving, a strategy that involves pursuing an educated guess (p. 269).

hypothyroidism Disorder in which the thyroid gland is underactive (p. 85).

I

iconic storage A visual sensory registration process by which people retain an afterimage of a visual stimulus (p. 217).

id In Freudian theory, the reservoir of sexual and aggressive energy, which is driven by impulses and is characterized by primary process thinking (p. 457).

ideal self A person's view of what she/he should be like (p. 479).

identification Making another person part of oneself by imitating the person's behavior, changing the self-concept to see oneself as more like that person, and attempting to become more like the person by accepting his or her values and attitudes (p. 454).

identified patient In a family system model of psychopathology, the person identified as needing help, or the symptom bearer (p. 548).

identity confusion Condition in which the individual fails to develop a coherent and enduring sense of self, and has difficulty committing to roles, values, people, and occupational choices (p. 566).

identity A stable sense of knowing who one is and what one's values and ideals are (p. 566).

identity versus identity confusion In Erikson's theory, stage in which adolescents develop a stable sense of who they are and a stable set of values and ideals (p. 566).

ill-defined problem A situation in which both the information needed to solve a problem and the criteria that determine whether the goals are attained are vague (p. 267).

immune system A system of cells throughout the body that fights disease (pp. 179, 435).

implicit memory Memory that cannot be brought to mind consciously but can be expressed in behavior (p. 226).

impoverished thought Negative symptom of schizophrenia, characterized by lack of complex thought in response to environmental stimuli (p. 593).

incentive An external motivating stimulus (as opposed to an internal need state) (p. 374).

inclusive fitness The notion that natural selection favors organisms that survive, reproduce, and foster the survival and reproduction of their kin (p. 368).

independent variable The variable an experimenter manipulates, or whose effects the experimenter assesses (p. 40).

individual differences The way people resemble and differ from one another in personality or intelligence (p. 448).

inductive reasoning The process of reasoning from specific observations to generate propositions (p. 264).

industry versus inferiority In Erikson's theory, the stage in which children develop a sense of competence as they begin to practice skills they will use in productive work (p. 566).

inferential statistics Procedures for assessing whether the results obtained with a sample are likely to reflect characteristics of the population as a whole (p. 44).

information processing The transformation, storage, and retrieval of environmental inputs through thought and memory (p. 17).

informed consent Subject's ability to agree to participate in a study in an informed manner (p. 58).

ingroup People perceived as belonging to a valued group (p. 677).

inhibition to the unfamiliar A temperamental variable involving shyness and fear of novel stimuli (p. 473).

inhibitory neurotransmitter Neurotransmitter that hyperpolarizes the membrane, reducing the likelihood that the postsynaptic neuron will fire (p. 79).

initial state The first stage of problem solving that involves the recognition that a problem exists (p. 267).

initiative versus guilt In Erikson's theory, the stage in which children develop a sense of planfulness and responsibility (p. 565).

insight In learning theory; the ability to perceive a connection between a problem and its solution; in psychodynamic treatments, the understanding of one's own psychological processes (p. 623).

insomnia The inability to sleep (p. 352).

instinct Relatively fixed pattern of behavior that animals produce without learning (p. 368).

instinct model Freud's theory of motivation, which held that people are motivated by sexual and aggressive instincts or drives (p. 451).

instrumental aggression Calm, pragmatic aggression that may or may not be accompanied by anger (p. 716).

instrumental conditioning Learning that results when an organism associates a response that occurs spontaneously with a particular effect; also called operant conditioning (p. 185).

instrumental leader See task leader (p. 729).

integrity versus despair In Erikson's theory, stage in which older people look back on their lives with a sense of satisfaction that they have lived it well, or with despair, regret, and loss for loved ones who have died (p. 569).

intelligence The application of cognitive skills and knowledge to learn, solve problems, and obtain ends that are valued by an individual or culture (p. 299).

intelligence quotient (IQ) A score originally derived by dividing mental age and chronological age and multiplying by 100, but now generally established by comparing the individual's performance to norms of people his or her own age (p. 300).

intelligence test measure designed to assess an individual's level of cognitive capabilities compared to other people in a population (p. 299).

intensity In sensation, the strength of a stimulus (p. 120).

inter-rater reliability A measure of the similarity with which different raters apply a measure (p. 39).

intergenerational approach Approach to family therapy that examines the ways in which problems are repeated across generations of a family (p. 640).

intermittent schedule of reinforcement Operant procedure in which an organism is reinforced only some of the time it emits a behavior (p. 193).

intermodal processing The capacity to associate sensations of an object from different senses, or to match one's own actions to behaviors that are observed visually; also called cross-modal processing (p. 506).

internal attribution Explanation of behavior that attributes it to the person rather than the situation (p. 680).

internal consistency A type of reliability that assesses whether the items in a test measure the same construct (p. 39).

internal validity The extent to which a study is methodologically adequate (p. 37).

internal working model Mental representation of the attachment relationship, which forms the basis for expectations in close relationships (p. 539).

interneuron Neuron that connects other neurons to each other, found only in the brain and spinal cord (p. 75).

interpersonal attraction The factors that lead people to choose to spend time with other people (p. 701).

interposition Monocular depth cue in which one object blocks part of another, leading to perception of the occluded (blocked) object as more distant (p. 158).

interpretation A therapeutic technique whereby the therapist helps the patient understand his or her experiences in a new light (p. 625).

interstimulus interval The duration of time between presentation of the conditioned stimulus and the unconditioned stimulus (p. 182).

interval schedules of reinforcement Operant conditioning procedures in which rewards are delivered according to intervals of time (p. 193).

interview Research tool in which the investigator asks the subject questions (p. 49).

intimacy A kind of closeness characterized by self-disclosure, warmth, and mutual caring (p. 567).

intimacy versus isolation In Erikson's theory, the stage in which young adults establish enduring, committed friendships and romantic relationships (p. 567).

intrinsic motivation Motivation to perform a behavior for its own sake, rather than for some kind of external (or extrinsic) reward (p. 400).

introspection Method used by Wundt and other structuralists in which trained subjects verbally reported everything that went through their minds when presented with a stimulus or task; more generally, refers to the process of looking inward at one's own mental contents or processes (p. 15).

intuitive scientist Conception of people as lay scientists who use intuitive theories, frame hypotheses, collect data about themselves and others, and examine the impact of various experimental manipulations when trying to understand themselves and others; also called intuitive psychologist (p. 671).

iris The ring of pigmented tissue that gives the eye its blue, green, or brown color; its muscle fibers cause the pupil to constrict or dilate (p. 127).

J

James-Lange theory A theory of emotion that asserts that emotion originates with peripheral arousal, which people then label as an emotional state (p. 407).

just noticeable difference (jnd) The smallest difference in intensity between two stimuli that a person can detect (p. 122).

K

kinesthesia Sense that provides information about the movement and position of the limbs and other parts of the body; receptors in joints transduce information about the position of the bones, and receptors in the tendons and muscles transmit messages about muscular tension (p. 153).

knowledge base Accumulated information stored in long-term memory (p. 515).

Korsakoff's syndrome Disorder related to chronic alcoholism that impairs the ability to acquire and consolidate new information in memory (p. 214).

L

labeling theory Theory that psychiatric diagnosis is a way of labeling individuals a society considers deviant (p. 579).

laissez-faire A leadership style in which the leader intervenes as little as possible (p. 731).

language The system of symbols, sounds, meanings, and rules for their combination that constitutes the primary mode of communication among humans (p. 277).

Language Acquisition Device (LAD) The prewired, innate mechanism that allows for the acquisition of language hypothesized by Noam Chomsky (p. 283).

latency stage Psychosexual phase that occurs roughly around age 6 to 11, when children repress their sexual impulses (p. 456).

latent content According to Freud's dream theory, the meaning that underlies the symbolism in a dream (p. 350).

latent learning Learning that has occurred but is not currently manifest in behavior (p. 203).

lateral geniculate nucleus Group of neurons in the thalamus that transmit information from the eye to the visual cortex (p. 132).

lateralized Localized on one or the other side of the brain (p. 101).

law of effect Law proposed by Thorndike which states that the tendency of an organsim to produce a behavior depends on the effect the behavior has on the environment (p. 185).

laws of learning Invariant causal connections between environmental events and the way individuals behave (p. 177).

leader A person who exercises greater influence than the average member of a group (p. 731).

learned helplessness The expectancy that one cannot escape from aversive events (p. 204).

learning Any relatively permanent change in the way an organism responds based on its experience (p. 176).

learning goals Motives to increase one's competence, mastery, or skill (p. 399).

left hemisphere Left half of the cerebrum (p. 96).

lens Disc-shaped, elastic structure of the eye that focuses light (p. 127).

libido In Freudian theory, the human sexual drive, which refers as much to pleasure-seeking and love as to sexual intercourse (p. 451).

life events Stressful experiences that require change and adaptation (p. 428).

life history method Method of personality assessment whose aim is to understand the whole person in the context of his or her life experience and environment (p. 459).

life tasks The conscious, self-defined problems people attempt to solve (p. 464).

light The form of electromagnetic radiation to which the eye is sensitive (p. 126).

light adaptation The eyes' adjustment to bright light after exposure to darkness (p. 130).

limbic system Subcortical structures responsible for emotional reactions, many motivational processes, and aspects of memory (p. 94).

linear perspective A monocular cue for depth perception in which parallel lines appear to converge as they recede into the distance (p. 162).

lithium The drug treatment of choice for bipolar disorder (p. 645).

lobe Section of the cortex (p. 96).

lobotomy A surgical treatment no longer practiced involving removal of part of the brain (usually the frontal lobes) to try to treat schizophrenia (p. 647).

localization of functioning The extent to which different parts of the brain control different aspects of functioning (p. 4).

locus of control Generalized expectancies people hold about whether or not their own behavior will bring about the outcomes they seek (p. 203).

long-term memory (LTM) Memory for facts, images, thoughts, feelings, skills, and experiences that may last as long as a lifetime (p. 215).

longitudinal fissure Deep sulcus or valley in the brain that divides the cortex down the middle from front to back (p. 96).

longitudinal study Type of research that follows the same individuals over time (pp. 315, 494).

loosening of associations A tendency common in individuals with schizophrenia, in which conscious thought is directed along associative lines rather than by controlled, logical, purposeful processes (p. 592).

loudness The psychological property corresponding to a sound wave's amplitude (p. 139).

low-effort syndrome Phenomenon in which members of a racial or ethnic group experience an upper limit, or ceiling, on their ability to succeed as a result of repeated exposure to situations in which effort and academic success are thwarted, producing frustration, anger and decreased effort (p. 440).

lysergic acid diethylamide (LSD) Synthetic hallucinogenic drug (p. 360).

M

magnetic resonance imaging (MRI) Brain scanning technique (p. 53).

maintenance rehearsal The process of repeating information over and over to maintain it momentarily in STM (p. 222).

major depressive disorder Form of psychopathology characterized by depressed mood, loss of interest in pleasurable activities, and disturbances in appetite, sleep, energy level, and concentration (p. 598).

major tranquilizers Another name for antipsychotic medications (p. 643).

mania An excessively euphoric, elevated, or expansive mood (p. 599).

manifest content The obvious story line of a dream (p. 350).

marijuana Drug that leads to a state of feeling high (euphoric, giddy, unself-conscious, or contemplative) (p. 361).

marital therapy A psychological treatment that focuses on maladaptive interaction patterns between a couple (p. 640).

maturation Biologically based development (p. 491).

mean The statistical average of the scores of all subjects on a measure (p. 64).

measure A concrete way of assessing a variable (p. 38).

measures of central tendency Statistical concepts that provide an index of the way a "typical" subject responded on a measure (p. 64).

mechanoreceptors Pressure receptors that transduce mechanical energy in the skin (p. 149).

median The score that falls in the middle of the distribution of scores, with half of subjects scoring below it and half above it (p. 65).

medical model A model of psychopathology that assumes that mental disorders fall into discrete categories like other medical illnesses (p. 586).

meditation A relaxation practice, often associated with religion, characterized by a state of tranquility (p. 353).

medulla oblongata An extension of the spinal cord, essential to life, controlling such vital physiological functions as heartbeat, circulation, and respiration (p. 92).

memory scanning Combing or scanning long-term memory to find information (p. 243).

memory systems Discrete but interdependent processing units responsible for different kinds of remembering (p. 216).

menopause The cessation of the menstrual cycle (p. 501).

mental age (MA) The average age at which children can be expected to achieve a particular score on an intelligence test (p. 300).

mental image A visual representation of a stimulus (p. 257).

mental models Representations of systems that enable people to describe, explain, and predict the way things work (p. 257).

mental representation A mental model of a stimulus or category of stimuli (p. 218).

mental retardation Significantly subaver-age general intellectual functioning, existing concurrently with deficits in adaptive behavior and manifested during childhood (p. 321).

mental status The intactness of memory, orientation to reality, state of consciousness, reasoning ability, and ability to think abstractly (p. 583).

mere exposure effect The phenomenon in which people feel more positively toward stimuli as their exposure to the stimuli increases (p. 421).

meta-analysis Statistical technique that allows researchers to combine findings from various studies and make comparisons between the effects of treatment and no treatment (p. 648).

metabolism The processes by which the body transforms food into energy (p. 378).

metacognition People's understanding of the way they perform cognitive tasks such as remembering, learning, or solving problems (p. 516).

metamemory People's cognition about their own memory (p. 521).

method of loci A memory aid or mnemonic device in which images are remembered by fitting them into an orderly arrangement of locations (p. 231).

midbrain Section of the brain above the hindbrain that is involved in some auditory and visual functions, movement, and conscious arousal and activation (p. 93).

mind-body dualism The view that the mind and body are two distinct realms, with different principles explaining each realm (p. 8).

mind-body problem The question of how mental and physical events interact (p. 8).

mnemonic devices Memory aids or procedures that aid retrieval from long-term memory (p. 231).

mode The most common or most frequent score or value of a variable observed in a sample (p. 65).

modeling Social learning procedure in which a person learns to reproduce behavior exhibited by a model (p. 206).

modules Independently functioning systems of neurons (p. 216).

monamine oxidase inhibitor (MAOI) A class of medications for depression that prevents monoamine oxidase from breaking down neurotransmitters, thus increasing neurotransmitter availability in the synapse (p. 644).

monocular cues Visual input from a single eye alone that contributes to depth perception (p. 157).

monozygotic (MZ) twins Twins identical in their genetic makeup (p. 109).

mood Relatively extended emotional states that usually do not shift attention or disrupt ongoing activities (p. 421).

mood disorder Disorder characterized by disturbances in emotion and mood (p. 598).

moral development Development of the values and rules a person uses for balancing or adjudicating the conflicting interests of the self and others (p. 557).

morpheme In language, basic unit of meaning (p. 279).

motion parallax A monocular depth cue involving the relative movements of retinal images of objects; nearby objects appear to speed across the field of vision, whereas distant objects barely seem to move (p. 159).

motivation The moving force that energizes behavior (p. 367).

motor cortex The primary zone of the frontal lobes responsible for control of motor behavior (p. 97).

motor neuron Neuron that transmits commands from the brain to the glands or musculature of the body, typically through the spinal cord; also called efferent neuron (p. 75).

Müller-Lyer illusion Perceptual illusion in which two lines of equal length appear different in size (p. 161).

multiaxial system of diagnosis System used in DSM-IV that places mental disorders in their social and biological context, assessing the patient on five axes (p. 586).

multiple measures The use of several ways of assessing a variable to minimize the impact of measurement error (p. 40).

myelin sheath A coat of cells composed primarily of lipids, which serves to insulate the axon from chemical or physical stimuli that might interfere with the transmission of nerve impulses and speeds neural transmission (p. 77).

myopia Condition in which light waves from distant objects converge in front of the retina rather than on it, leading to decreased acuity for distant objects; also called nearsightedness (p. 127).

N

nanometer (nm) One-billionth of a meter, used to measure wavelengths (p. 126).

narcissism Tendency to be self-centered and focused on gratifying one's own needs (p. 561).

narcissistic personality disorder A personality disorder characterized by feelings of entitlement, tendencies to use or devalue others, and a lack of empathy (p. 611).

narcolepsy A disorder in which people are prone to sudden sleep attacks and fall into rapid eye movement sleep during daytime activities (p. 352).

nasal cavity Region hollowed out of bone in the skull that contains smell receptors (p. 146).

natural killer cells Cells that fight viruses and tumors (p. 435).

natural selection Theory proposed by Darwin, which states that natural forces select traits in organisms that help them adapt to their environment (p. 20).

naturalistic observation The in-depth observation of a phenomenon in its natural setting (p. 48).

nature-nurture controversy The question of degree to which inborn biological processes or environmental events determine human behavior (p. 19).

nearsightedness Condition in which light waves from distant objects converge in front of the retina rather than on it, leading to decreased acuity for distant objects; also called myopia (p. 127).

need for achievement A motive to do well, to succeed, and to avoid failure (p. 397).

negative affect A general category of emotions related to feeling bad (p. 414).

negative correlation Relation between two variables in which the higher one is, the lower the other tends to be (p. 50).

negative identity Taking on a role that society defines as bad but that nevertheless provides one with a sense of being something (p. 566).

negative reinforcement The process whereby a behavior is made more likely because it is followed by the removal of an aversive stimulus (p. 187).

negative reinforcer Aversive or unpleasant stimulus that strengthens a behavior by its removal (p. 187).

negative symptoms Symptoms of schizophrenia such as flat affect, socially inappropriate behavior, and intellectual impairments that relect a deficit or a loss of something that was once present or should be present (p. 593).

negative triad In Beck's cognitive theory of depression, negative outlook on the world, the self, and the future (p. 602).

neo-Freudians Theorists who accepted the influence of unconscious processes and conflicts among psychological forces but rejected Freud's instinct theory, particularly his insistence on the centrality of sexuality in psychological functioning (p. 457).

neo-Piagetian theories Theories that attempt to wed a stage model of cognitive development with research on information processing and domain-specific knowledge (p. 516).

nerves Bundles of neurons (p. 92).

nervous system The interacting network of nerve cells that underlies all psychological activity (p. 74).

network of association A cluster of interconnected information stored in long-term memory (p. 233).

neurons Cells in the nervous system (p. 75).

neuroses Problems in living, such as phobias, chronic self-doubts, and repetitive interpersonal problems (p. 581).

neuroticism A continuum from emotional stability to emotional instability (p. 468).

neurotransmitter Chemical substance that transmits information from one neuron to another (p. 79).

New Look An approach to perception that integrated perceptual research with personality theory and focused on the influence of motives on perception (p. 168).

niche The particular environmental circumstance to which an organism adapts (p. 20).

night terrors Dramatic experiences during sleep of intense terror or panic, in which the sufferer can rarely recall the dream content associated with the panic (p. 352).

nightmare A vivid bad dream, often associated with fears of falling, calamity, or death (p. 352).

node A cluster or piece of information along a network of association (p. 233).

nodes of Ranvier Small spaces between the cells that form the myelin sheath (p. 77).

noise Irrelevant, distracting information in any sensory modality (p. 121).

normalization The movement to take mentally retarded individuals out of institutions and place them, as much as possible, within the community (p. 324).

non-REM (NREM) sleep Stages of sleep in which rapid eye movements (REM sleep) are not present (p. 348).

nonverbal communication Mode of communication that relies on gestures, expressions, intonation, body language, and other unspoken signals (p. 288).

normal distribution A frequency distribution in which most subjects' scores fall in the middle of the bell-shaped distribution, and progressively fewer subjects have scores at either extreme (p. 66).

norms Standards for the behavior of group members (p. 729).

O

obedience Overt compliance with authority (p. 725).

obesity Condition characterized by a body weight over 15 percent above the ideal for one's height and age (p. 382).

object permanence In Piaget's theory, the recognition that objects exist in time and space independent of one's actions on, or observation of, them (p. 510).

object relations Behavioral patterns in intimate relationships and the motivational, cognitive, and affective processes that produce them (p. 459).

object relations theories Theories that attempt to account for the capacity for intimacy or the lack thereof in individuals with severe personality disorders (p. 148).

observational learning Learning that occurs by observing the behavior of others (p. 206).

obsession Persistent unwanted thought or idea (p. 606).

obsessive-compulsive disorder Disorder characterized by recurrent obsessions and compulsions that cause distress and significantly interfere with an individual's life (p. 606).

occipital lobes Brain structures located in the rear portion of the cortex involved in vision (p. 97).

Oedipus complex In Freudian theory, process that occurs during the phallic stage of development when the child desires an exclusive, sensual/sexual relationship with the opposite sex parent (p. 455).

olfaction Smell (p. 145).

olfactory bulb Multilayered structure that combines information from the olfactory nerve (p. 147).

olfactory epithelium Thin pair of structures in which transduction of smell occurs (p. 146).

olfactory nerve The bundle of axons from sensory receptor cells that transmits information from the nose to the brain (p. 147).

operant A behavior that is emitted by the organism rather than elicited by the environment (p. 185).

operant conditioning Learning that results when an organism associates a response that occurs spontaneously with a particular environmental effect (p. 185).

operation In Piagetian theory, a mental action that the individual can use to manipulate, transform, and return an object of thought to its original state (p. 509).

operationalizing Turning an abstract concept or variable into a concrete form that can be defined by some set of operations or actions (p. 41).

operator In problem solving, mental and behavioral process aimed at transforming the initial state into the goal state (p. 267).

opponent-process theory A theory of color vision that proposes the existence of three antagonistic color systems: a blue-yellow system, a red-green system, and a black-white system; according to this theory, the blue-yellow and red-green systems are responsible for hue, while the black-white system contributes to perception of brightness and saturation (p. 136).

optic chiasm The point at which the optic nerve splits (p. 132).

optic disk The point on the retina where the optic nerve leaves the eye and which contain no receptor cells; also called blind spot (p. 129).

optic nerve The bundle of axons of ganglion cells that carries information from the retina to the brain (p. 128).

optic tract The bundle of neurons that carries combined information from the two eyes to higher centers in the brain (p. 132).

oral stage In Freudian theory, the psychosexual phase occurring roughly in the first year of life, when children explore the world through their mouths (p. 453).

organizational effects Effects of hormones that influence the structure of the brain (p. 390).

orgasm The third phase of the sexual response cycle characterized by a release of built-up tension (p. 388).

orienting reflex The tendency of humans, even from birth, to pay more attention to novel stimuli than to stimuli to which they have grown accustomed (p. 504).

ossicles Three tiny bones in the middle ear (the malleus, incus, and stapes) that amplify sound through mechanical leverage when set in motion by the vibration of the eardrum (p. 140).

outcome expectancy An expectation about the type of consequence that will be produced by a given behavior (p. 203).

outgroup People perceived as not belonging to a valued group (p. 677).

oval window Membrane covering the cochlea that vibrates when struck by the stirrup, causing pressure waves in the fluid filling the cochlea (p. 140).

ovaries The female gonads (p. 85).

P

p-value The probability that obtained findings were accidental or just a matter of chance (p. 68).

painful neuropathy Neurological disorder in which normal touch sensations are experienced as excruciating pain (p. 116).

pancreas Endocrine gland located near the stomach, which produces various hormones that control blood-sugar level (p. 85).

panic disorder Disorder characterized by attacks of intense fear and feelings of doom or terror not justified by the situation (p. 606).

papillae Small bumps on the surface of the tongue in which taste buds are located (p. 148).

paradigm A broad system of theoretical assumptions employed by a scientific community to make sense out of a domain of experience (p. 10).

paradoxical conditioning Classical conditioning process in which the conditioned response represents an effort by the organism to counteract the effects of a stimulus that is about to occur (p. 184).

parallel distributed processing (PDP) Model of human cognitive processes in which many cognitive processes occur simultaneously (i.e., in parallel), so that a representation is spread out (i.e., distributed) throughout a network of interacting processing units (p. 274).

paranoid schizophrenia Type of schizophrenia marked by preoccupation with delusions of persecution (p. 594).

parasympathetic nervous system The part of the autonomic nervous system involved in conserving and maintaining the body's energy resources (p. 88).

parietal lobes Brain structures located in front of the occipital lobes and involved in a number of functions, including sense of touch and the experience of one's own body in space and in movement (p. 97).

Parkinson's disease Disorder characterized by uncontrollable tremors, repetitive movements, and difficulty initiating movements (p. 80).

participatory modeling A cognitive-behavioral technique in which the therapist models desired behavior and gradually induces the patient to participate in it (p. 634).

passionate love A highly emotional form of love marked by intense physiological arousal and absorption in another person (p. 703).

passive aggression The indirect expression of anger toward others (p. 439).

pathogens Agents that cause physical illness (p. 434).

peg method A memory aid or mnemonic device in which information to be remembered is imagined or visualized to hang on mental pegs (p. 231).

penis envy In Freudian theory, feeling of envy that emerges in girls, who feel that because they lack a penis they are inferior to boys (p. 456).

perceived stress The extent to which a person himself regards an experience as stressful (p. 430).

percentile scores A method of representing subjects' scores on a variable that shows the percentage of scores that fall below a score (p. 67).

perception The process by which the brain selects, organizes, and interprets sensations (p. 117).

percepts Meaningful perceptual units, such as images of particular objects (p. 155).

perceptual constancy The organization of changing sensations into percepts that are relatively stable in size, shape, and color (p. 159).

perceptual defense The unconscious tendency of people to resist perceiving anxiety-provoking stimuli (p. 168).

perceptual illusions Perceptual misinterpretations produced in the course of normal perceptual processes (p. 156).

perceptual interpretation The process of generating meaning from sensory experience (p. 163).

perceptual organization The process of integrating sensations into meaningful perceptual units (p. 155).

perceptual set The expectations an observer brings to a situation which influence what is perceived, notably context and schemas (p. 166).

performance goals Motives to achieve at a particular level (p. 399).

peripheral nervous system (PNS) Component of the nervous system that includes neurons that travel to and from the central nervous system; includes the somatic nervous system and the autonomic nervous system (p. 86).

person schemas Knowledge structures that represent information about specific people or types of people (p. 673).

person-by-situation interaction Process by which some personality dispositions are activated only under certain circumstances (p. 457).

person-centered approach Carl Rogers' theory of personality, which focuses on understanding the individual's phenomenal world (p. 479).

personal constructs Mental representations of the people, places, things, and events that are significant in a person's life (p. 464).

personal value The importance individuals attach to various stimuli and to the outcomes they expect as a result of their behavior (p. 464).

personality The enduring patterns of thought, feeling, and behavior that are expressed in different circumstances (p. 448).

personality disorder Chronic and severe disorder that substantially inhibits the capacity to love and to work (p. 611).

perspective taking The ability to understand other people's viewpoints or perspectives (p. 552).

persuasion Deliberate efforts to induce attitude change (p. 665).

pessimistic explanatory style A tendency to explain bad events that happen in a self-blaming manner, viewing their causes as global and stable (p. 204).

phallic stage In Freudian theory, the psychosexual phase occurring roughly around ages 4 to 6, when children discover that they can get pleasure from touching their genitals (p. 454).

phantom limb pain Pain felt in an amputated limb (p. 151).

pharmacotherapy Drug therapy for mental illness (659).

phenomenal experience The way individuals conceive of reality and experience themselves and their world (p. 479).

phenomenological Having to do with subjective experience (p. 118).

phenotype Observable psychological attributes that reflect genetic variation (p. 108).

phenylketonuria (PKU) Disorder produced by a single recessive gene which causes a deficiency in the enzyme responsible for converting the amino acid phenylalanine into another amino acid, resulting in severe mental retardation (p. 322).

pheromone Chemical secreted by organisms in some species that allow communication between organisms (p. 145).

phobia Irrational fear of a specific object or situation (p. 606).

phoneme The smallest unit of speech that distinguishes one linguistic utterance from another (p. 279).

phonemic restoration Process by which listeners replace a sound that has been obliterated by background noise (p. 282).

photoreceptors Light receptors located at the back of the retina (p. 128).

phrase Group of words that act as a unit and convey a meaning (p. 279)

pinna The projecting external portion of the ear (p. 140).

pitch The psychological property corresponding to the frequency of a sound wave; the quality of a tone from low to high (p. 138).

pituitary gland Often referred to as the "master gland" of the endocrine system because some of the hormones it releases stimulate and thus regulate the hormonal action of other endocrine glands (p. 84).

place theory A theory of pitch which proposes that different areas of the basilar membrane are maximally sensitive to different frequencies (p. 142).

placebo effect Phenomenon in which an experimental intervention produces an effect because subjects believe it will produce an effect (p. 43).

plasticity Flexibility of the brain to adapt to changing circumstances or damage (p. 498).

plateau phase Second phase of the sexual response cycle during which maximum arousal occurs (p. 388).

polysensory association area Cortical region that receives information from more than one sensory system (p. 97).

population Group of people or animals of interest to a research from which a sample is drawn (p. 37).

position correlation Relation between two variables in which the higher one is, the higher the other tends to be (p. 50).

positive affect A general category of emotions related to feeling good (p. 414).

positive reinforcement The process by which a behavior is made more likely because of the presentation of a rewarding stimulus (p. 186).

positive reinforcer A rewarding stimulus that strengthens a behavior when it is presented (p. 186).

positive symptoms Symptoms of schizophrenia such as delusions and hallucinations that reflect the presence of something that was not there previously and is not normally present (p. 593).

positron emission tomography (PET) Computerized brain scanning technique that allows observation of the brain in action (p. 53).

possession trance A type of religiously patterned altered state that involves the alleged possession of the soul by a spirit (Ch. 9).

post-traumatic stress disorder (PTSD) An anxiety disorder characterized by symptoms such as flashbacks and recurrent thoughts of a psychologically distressing event outside the normal range of experience (p. 607).

postconventional morality In Kohlberg's theory, the level of morality in which individuals follow abstract, self-defined principles which may or may not accord with the dominant mores or morals of the times (p. 558).

posthypnotic suggestion A suggestion to perform a behavior on demand once out of the hypnotic trance (p. 357).

postsynaptic neuron The cell receiving a neural impulse as neurotransmitters are released across the synapse (p. 79).

preconscious mental processes Thoughts that are not conscious but could become conscious at any point, much like information stored in long-term semantic memory (p. 451).

preconventional morality In Kohlberg's theory, the level of morality in which children follow moral rules either to avoid punishment or to obtain reward (p. 558).

prefrontal cortex Anterior (front) section of frontal lobes, implicated, among other functions, in attention and working memory (p. 227).

prejudice Judging people based on negative stereotypes (p. 674).

prenatal Before birth (p. 469).

preoperational stage Piaget's second stage of cognitive development, beginning roughly around age 2 and lasting until age 5 to 7, characterized by the emergence of symbolic thought (p. 511).

prepared learning Responses to which an organism is predisposed because they were selected through natural selection (p. 183).

presbycusis The inability to hear high-frequency sounds, which usually occurs with aging (p. 503).

presynaptic neuron The cell that is sending an impulse and releasing neurotransmitters (p. 79).

primacy effect The superiority of memory for words presented at the beginning of a list than for words presented later (p. 224).

primary appraisal The first stage in the process of stress and coping in which the person decides whether the situation is benign, stressful, or irrelevant (p. 428).

primary area Area of the cortex involved in sensory functions and in the direct control of motor movements (p. 96).

primary drive Innate drive such as hunger, thirst, and sex (p. 374).

primary prevention Preventative mental health measures (p. 657).

primary process thought Associative thinking described by Freud, in which ideas connected in people's minds through experience come to mind automatically when they think about related ideas; primary process thought is also wishful and unrealistic (p. 234).

primary reinforcer Stimulus that is innately rewarding to an organism (p. 199).

priming The process by which a person's performance is influenced by recent exposure to associatively connected stimuli (p. 334).

priming effects The processing of specific information is facilitated by prior exposure to the same or similar information (p. 226).

proactive interference Phenomenon in which old memories that have already been stored interfere with the retrieval of new information (p. 244).

probability value The probability that obtained findings were accidental or just a matter of chance; also called *p*-value (p. 68).

problem solving The process of transforming one situation into another that meets a goal (p. 267).

problem solving strategy Technique used to solve problems (p. 269).

procedural memory Knowledge of procedures or skills that emerges when people engage in activities that require them (p. 226).

prodigy An individual with early-developing genius in one area and normal abilities otherwise (p. 313).

programmed learning Learning that proceeds at the learner's own rate, with reinforcement received upon mastery of each task (p. 208).

projection Defense mechanism in which a person attributes his own unacknowledged feelings or impulses to others (p. 438).

projective test Personality assessment method in which subjects are confronted with an ambiguous stimulus and asked to define it in some way; the assumption underlying these tests is that when people are faced with an unstructured, undefined stimulus, they will project their own thoughts, feelings, and wishes into their responses (p. 459).

proposition The smallest unit of meaning that can stand alone as an assertion and can be judged to be true or false (p. 263).

proprioceptive senses Senses that provide information about body position and movement; the two proprioceptive senses are kinesthesia and vestibular sense (p. 153).

prosocial behavior Behavior that benefits either specific individuals or society as a whole (p. 557).

prosopagnosia Neurological disorder involving an inability to recognize different people's faces (p. 102).

prototype Particularly good example of a category (p. 258).

proximity A Gestalt rule of perception which states that, other things being equal, the brain groups objects together that are close to each other (p. 155).

psychoactive substance Any drug that operates on the nervous system to alter patterns of mental activity (p. 358).

psychoanalysis An intensive therapeutic process in which the patient meets with the therapist three to five times in a week, lies on a couch, and uses free association, interpretation, and transference (p. 628).

psychodynamic formulation A set of hypotheses about the patient's personality structure and the meaning of a symptom (p. 582).

psychodynamic perspective The perspective initiated by Sigmund Freud that focuses on the dynamic interplay of mental forces (p. 10).

psychodynamic psychotherapy A form of psychotherapy based on psychodynamic principles, in which the patient meets the therapist somewhat less frequently than in psychoanalysis and sits face to face with the therapist (p. 628).

psychodynamics A view analogous to dynamics among physical forces in which psychological forces such as wishes, fears, and intentions have a direction and an intensity (p. 582).

psychological anthropology Field that studies psychological phenomena in other cultures by observing the way the natives behave in their daily lives (p. 6).

psychological perspectives Broad ways of understanding psychological phenomena, including theoretical propositions, shared metaphors, and accepted methods of observation (p. 10).

psychology The systematic study of mental processes and behavior (p. 3).

psychometric approach Approach to the study of intelligence, personality, and psychopathology which tries to derive some kind of theoretical meaning empirically from statistical analysis of psychometric test findings (p. 308).

psychometric instruments Psychological "yardsticks" that compare individuals (p. 299).

psychomotor slowing A slowing in the time between sensory input and cognitive and motor output that occurs with aging (p. 522).

psychopathology Problematic patterns of thought, feeling, or behavior that disrupt an individual's sense of well-being or social or occupational functioning (p. 576).

psychophysics Branch of psychology that studies the relationship between attributes of the physical world and the psychological experience of them (p. 118).

psychosexual stages In Freudian theory, the developmental phases that represent the child's evolving quest for pleasure and growing realization of the social limitations of this quest (p. 564).

psychosis Gross disturbance involving a loss of touch with reality (p. 581).

psychosocial motives Personal and interpersonal motives that lead people to strive for such ends as mastery, achievement, power, self-esteem, affiliation, and intimacy with other people (p. 396).

psychosocial stages In Erikson's theory, the stages in the development of the person as a social being (p. 564).

psychosurgery Brain surgery to reduce psychological symptoms (p. 647).

psychotherapy integration Choosing therapeutic techniques from different treatment approaches selectively or integrating across perspectives (p. 653).

psychoticism A dimension whose low end is defined by people who display empathy and impulse control and the high end is defined by people who are aggressive, egocentric, impulsive, and antisocial (p. 468).

psychotropic medications Drugs that act on the brain to affect mental processes (p. 641).

puberty The stage at which individuals become capable of reproduction (p. 499).

punishment Conditioning process that decreases the probability that a behavior will occur (p. 186).

pupil The opening in the center of the iris that constricts or dilates to regulate the amount of light entering the eye (p. 127).

Q

Q-sort A procedure for assessing personality (or other domains) in which a rater sorts items into piles, depending on how much the items describe a person (p. 476).

quality In sensation, the nature of the stimulus sensed (e.g., color, pitch, taste, etc.) (p. 120).

quasi-experimental design A research design that employs the logic of experimental methods but lacks absolute control over variables (p. 45).

questionnaire Research tool in which the investigator asks subjects to respond to a written list of questions or items (p. 49).

R

random sample Sample of subjects selected from the population in a relatively arbitrary manner (p. 49).

range A measure of variability that represents the difference between the highest and the lowest value on a variable obtained in a sample (p. 66).

rapid eye movement (REM) sleep Period of sleep during which darting eye movements occur, autonomic activity increases, and patterns of brain activity resemble those observed in waking states (p. 348).

ratio schedules of reinforcement Operant conditioning procedures in which an organism is reinforced for some proportion of responses (p. 193).

rational-emotive psychotherapy A psychological treatment in which the therapist helps uncover and alter the illogical thoughts that provoke psychological distress (p. 636).

rationalist philosophy School of philosophical thought that emphasizes the role of reason in creating knowledge (p. 17).

rationalization Defense mechanism that involves explaining away actions in a seemingly logical way to avoid uncomfortable feelings (p. 438).

reaction formation Defense mechanism in which the person turns unacceptable feelings or impulses into their opposites (p. 438).

reasoning The process by which people generate and evaluate logical arguments (p. 264).

recall The spontaneous retrieval of information from long-term memory (p. 243).

recency effect The superiority of memory for items presented at the end of a list (p. 225).

receptive field A region within which a neuron responds to appropriate stimulation (p. 130).

receptors In neurons, protein molecules in the postsynaptic membrane that pick up neurotransmitters (p. 79); in sensation, specialized cells of the sensory systems that respond to environmental stimuli and typically activate sensory neurons (p. 120).

reciprocal altruism Theory that natural selection favors animals that behave altruistically if the likely benefit to each individual over time exceeds the likely cost to reproductive success (p. 713).

recognition memory The explicit knowledge of whether something has been previously encountered or learned (p. 243).

reference group Group to which a person refers when taking action (p. 729).

regression Reverting to conflicts or modes of managing emotion characteristic of an earlier particular stage (p. 454).

rehearsal Repeating or studying information to retain it in memory (p. 222).

reinforcer An environmental consequence that increases the probability that a behavior will occur (p. 186).

relatedness motives Interpersonal motives for connectedness with other people; also called communion motives (p. 397).

relationship schemas Knowledge structures that encode expectations about how the self and others interact in different kinds of relationships (p. 673).

relative size A monocular cue for depth perception in which looking at two objects known to be of similar size leads to the perception of the smaller object as farther away (p. 159).

reliability A measure's ability to produce consistent results (p. 38).

religious experience Altered state of consciousness in which the individual feels at one with nature or the supernatural (p. 353).

repertory grid techinique A technique for assessing personal constructs indirectly (p. 464).

replicate To repeat a study to see if the same findings are obtained (p. 45).

representative A sample that reflects characteristics of the population as a whole (p. 37).

representativeness heuristic A cognitive shortcut used to assess whether an object or incident belongs in a particular class (p. 272).

repression Defense mechanism in which thoughts that are too anxiety-provoking to acknowledge are kept from conscious awareness (pp. 13, 438).

reproductive success The capacity to survive and reproduce offspring (p. 22).

resistance Barriers to psychotherapy created by the patient in an effort to reduce anxiety (p. 626).

resistance stage The second stage of the general adaption syndrome, in which blood glucose levels are elevated and the body uses its resources at an accelerated rate (p. 472).

resolution The fourth phase of the sexual response cycle when the body gradually returns to normal physiological functioning, and psychological arousal is also reduced (p. 388).

response bias In signal detection theory, the readiness of an observer to report detecting a stimulus when uncertain; also called decision criterion (p. 122).

resting potential Condition in which the neuron is not firing (p. 77).

reticular formation A network of neural nuclei and axons in the brainstem that maintains consciousness and regulates activity states throughout the central nervous system (p. 93).

retina The light-sensitive layer of tissue at the back of the eye that transduces light into neural impulses (p. 127).

retinal disparity The slight difference between the retinal images of the right and left eyes; the degree of disparity is greater for close objects and diminishes as objects move away (p. 157).

retrieval Bringing information from long-term memory into short-term, or working, memory (p. 216).

retrieval cues Stimuli or thoughts that can be used to stimulate retrieval (p. 243).

retroactive interference Interference of new information with the retrieval of old information (p. 244).

retrograde amnesia Loss of memory for events prior to brain damage (p. 214).

right hemisphere Right half of the cerebrum (p. 96).

rites of passage Ceremonies that initiate the child into adulthood or other major life transitions and impose a socially bestowed identity (p. 566).

rods One of two types of photoreceptors; allow vision in dim light (p. 128).

role A position within a group that defines appropriate behavior for the person occupying it (p. 729).

role reversal Situation in which a child and parent switch roles and the child's role is to take care of the parent (p. 585).

role schemas Knowledge structures that represent information about what is expected of people in particular social positions or roles (p. 673).

rooting reflex Reflex that helps ensure infants will get the nourishment they need; when touched on the cheek, the infant turns its head and opens its mouth to suck (p. 498).

Rorschach inkblot test A projective personality test in which a subject views a set of inkblots and tells the tester what each inkblot resembles (p. 459).

S

s-factors Specific cognitive abilities (p. 308).

sample A subgroup of a population likely to be representative of the population as a whole (p. 37).

saturation Purity of sensed color (p. 134).

savant Individual with extraordinary ability in one area who has comparatively low functioning in other areas (p. 313).

scapegoat A role that may emerge in a group in which a person is blamed for the group's problems (p. 730).

scatterplot graph A graph that charts subjects' scores on two variables showing correlations (p. 50).

Schacter-Singer theory Theory which asserts that emotion involves cognitive interpretation of general physiological arousal (p. 420).

schema Integrated pattern of knowledge stored in memory that organizes information and guides the acquisition of new information (p. 167).

schema-relevant information Information about behaviors or aspects of a situation related to an activated schema (p. 673).

schizoaffective disorder A disorder characterized by both schizophrenia symptoms and psychotic depression (p. 614).

schizophrenia Psychotic disorders characterized by disturbances in thought, perception, behavior, language, communication, and emotion (p. 592).

scripts Schemas that specify how to do something socially (p. 673).

secondary appraisal The second stage in the process of stress and coping during which the person evaluates the options and decides how to respond (p. 428).

secondary drive Motive learned through classical conditioning and other learning mechanisms such as modeling; also called acquired drive (p. 374).

secondary process thought Rational, logical, goal-directed thinking (p. 457).

secondary reinforcer A stimulus that acquires reinforcement value after an organism learns to associate it with stimuli that are innately reinforcing (p. 199).

selective inattention The process by which important information is ignored (p. 333).

selective serotonin reuptake inhibitor (SSRI) A class of antidepressant medications, including Prozac, that blocks the presynaptic membrane from taking back serotonin, and hence leaves it acting longer in the synapse (p. 644).

self The person, including mental processes, body, and attributes (p. 687).

self as object The person's view of the self (p. 687).

self as subject The person's experience of self as a thinker, feeler, and actor (p. 687).

self-actualization needs In Maslow's theory, the needs to express oneself, grow, and actualize or attain one's potential (p. 376).

self-attribution Phenomenon in which people attribute causes to their own psychological processes (p. 681).

self-concept a person's view of him/herself (pp. 479, 549).

self-consistency The motivation to interpret information to fit the self-concept and to prefer people who verify rather than challenge it (p. 692).

self-efficacy expectancy A person's conviction that he can perform the actions necessary to produce an intended behavior (p. 464).

self-esteem The degree to which a person likes, respects, or esteems the self (p. 687).

self-esteem motivation The desire to feel good about oneself (p. 397).

self-fulfilling prophecy A false definition of a situation that evokes a new behavior, which makes the originally false conception come true (p. 34).

self-help groups Groups that are leaderless or guided by a nonprofessional, in which members assist each other in coping with a specific problem, as in Alcoholics Anonymous (p. 639).

self-perception theory Alternative explanation of cognitive dissonance phenomena which holds that individuals become aware of their attitudes, emotions, and other internal states by observing their own behavior (p. 669).

self-presentation Ways individuals try to make themselves appear to others; an alternative explanation for cognitive dissonance phenomena (p. 669).

self-regulation Setting goals, evaluating one's own performance, and adjusting one's behaviors flexibly to achieve these goals in the context of ongoing feedback (p. 465).

self-representations Mental models of the self (p. 688).

self-schema A schema or pattern of thought about the self (p. 689).

self-serving bias Phenomenon in which people tend to see themselves in a more positive light than they deserve (p. 683).

semantic memory General world knowledge or facts (p. 225).

semicircular canals Vestibular organs that sense acceleration and deceleration (p. 154).

sensation The process by which the sense organs gather information about the environment (p. 117).

sensitive period Developmental period during which environmental input is especially important, but not absolutely required, for future development in a domain (p. 493).

sensorimotor stage Piaget's first stage of cognitive development, from birth to about 18 months of age, with thinking primarily characterized by action (p. 509).

sensorineural loss Form of deafness involving failure of receptors in the inner ear or of neurons in any auditory pathway in the brain (p. 142).

sensory adaptation The tendency of sensory systems to respond less to stimuli that continue without change (p. 125).

sensory modalities Senses that provide ways of knowing about stimuli (p. 117).

sensory neuron Neuron that carries sensory information to the brain or spinal cord; also called afferent neuron (p. 75).

sensory process According to signal detection theory, the first of two processes occurring when an observer detects a stimulus; the sensory process involves sensation and reflects the observer's sensitivity to the stimulus (p. 119).

sensory registers Memory systems that hold information for a very brief period of time (p. 215).

sensory representation Information that is represented in one of the sense modalities (p. 219).

sentence A unit of language that combines a subject and predicate and expresses a thought or meaning (p. 280).

separation anxiety Distress at separation from attachment figures (p. 534).

septal area Limbic structure of unknown function, possibly involved in the sensation of pleasure (p. 94).

sequential study Type of research in which multiple cohorts are studied over time (p. 494).

serial position effect The phenomenon that people are more likely to remember information that appears first and last in a list than information in the middle of the list (p. 224).

serotonin Neurotransmitter involved in the regulation of mood, sleep, eating, arousal, and pain (p. 82).

set point The value of some variable that the body is trying to maintain, such as temperature (p. 370).

sex typing The process by which children come to acquire personality traits, emotional responses, skills, behaviors, and preferences that are culturally considered to be appropriate to their sex (p. 545).

sex-role ideology Beliefs about appropriate behaviors of the sexes (p. 553).

sexual dysfunction Problem that impairs sexual functioning (p. 396).

sexual orientation The direction of a person's enduring sexual attraction—to members of the same sex, the opposite sex, or both (p. 391).

sexual response cycle Pattern of physiological changes during sexual stimulation consisting of four phases excitement, plateau, orgasm, and resolution (p. 388).

sexual strategies Tactics used in selecting mates (p. 705).

shading Monocular depth cue that uses shadows to indicate depth or distance (p. 158).

shape constancy The perception that an object's shape remains constant despite the changing shape of the retinal image as the object is viewed from varying perspectives (p. 159).

shaping The process of teaching a new behavior by reinforcing closer and closer approximations of the desired response (p. 187).

short-term memory (STM) Memory for information that is available to consciousness for roughly 20 to 30 seconds (p. 215).

signal detection theory A theory which asserts that the ability to detect a stimulus depends on both sensitivity to the stimulus (a sensory process) and response bias (a decision process) (p. 121).

similarity A Gestalt rule of perception which states that the brain tends to group similar elements within a perceptual field (p. 155).

simple cells Feature detectors in the visual cortex that respond most vigorously to lines of a specific orientation (p. 133).

simplicity A Gestalt rule of perception which states that people tend to perceive the simplest pattern possible (p. 156).

simultaneous conditioning Conditioning procedure in which the conditioned stimulus and the unconditioned stimulus are presented simultaneously (p. 182).

single-blind study Study in which subjects are kept blind to crucial information, notably about the experimental condition in which they have been placed (p. 43).

single-cell recording Procedure in which researchers insert a tiny electrode into an animal's brain and map the response of specific cells in response to stimulation (p. 130).

situation schemas Knowledge structures that represent information about different kinds of social situations, including what to expect and how to act (p. 673).

situational variables Aspects of the situation that interact with aspects of the person to produce behavior (p. 472).

size constancy The perception that an object's size remains constant despite the changing size of the retinal image as the object is seen from different distances (p. 160).

skills training A technique that involves teaching behaviors or procedures for accomplishing specific goals (p. 634).

skin conductance An electrical measure of the amount of sweat on the skin that is provided during states of anxiety or arousal (p. 181). also called galvanic skin response (GSR) or electrical activity (EDA).

sleep apnea A disorder in which a person's breathing is interrupted during sleep and the person is awakened gasping for air (p. 352).

sleep disorder Chronic syndrome of disrupted sleep (p. 352).

social cognition The processes by which people make sense of others, themselves, social interactions, and relationships (pp. 549, 670).

social comparison Process that becomes prominent in children's thinking in middle childhood, in which children size themselves and others up on various dimensions such as intelligence, athletic ability, and popularity (p. 566).

social development Predictable changes in interpersonal thought, feeling, and behavior (p. 533).

social exchange theories Theories based on behaviorist principles that suggest the foundation of relationships is reciprocal reward (p. 702).

social facilitation The phenomenon in which the presence of other people facilitates performance (p. 725).

social influence The ways in which the presence of other people influences a person's thought, feeling, or behavior (p. 725).

social intelligence The ability to store, retrieve, and understand social information (p. 327).

social psychology Field of psychology that examines the way thought, feeling, and behavior are influenced by the actual, imagined, or implied presence of others (p. 662).

social skills training Cognitive-behavioral technique that involves instruction and modeling, and was designed to help people develop interpersonal competence (p. 653).

social support Relationships with others that provide resources for coping with stress (p. 441).

social-emotional leader A role that may emerge in a group in which that member seeks to maximize group cohesion and minimize hostility (p. 729).

socialization Process by which children and adults learn the rules, beliefs, values, skills, attitudes, and patterns of behavior of their society (p. 541).

socialization agents Individuals, groups, and organizations that transmit social values (p. 541).

sociobiology Field that explores evolutionary and biological bases of human social behavior (p. 22).

soma (cell body) Part of the neuron which includes a nucleus containing the genetic material of the cell (the chromosomes) as well as other microstructures vital to cell functioning (p. 75).

somatic nervous system Division of the peripheral nervous system that consists of sensory and motor neurons that transmit sensory information and control intentional actions (p. 86).

somatosensory cortex Primary area of the parietal lobes, behind the central fissue, which receives sensory information from different sections of the body (p. 97).

sound wave Pulsation of acoustic energy (p. 138).

spacing of rehearsal The interval between rehearsal sessions, which influences memory retention (p. 230).

spinal cord Part of the central nervous system that transmits information

from sensory neurons to the brain, and from the brain to motor neurons that initiate movement; also capable of reflex actions (p. 91).

spinal nerves Bundles of axons to and from the spinal cord to the periphery that carry sensory and motor information (p. 91).

split-brain Condition that results when the corpus callosum has been surgically cut, blocking communication between the two cerebral hemispheres (p. 102).

spontaneous recovery The spontaneous re-emergence of a response or an operant that has been extinguished (p. 182).

spreading activation The theory that the presentation of a stimulus triggers activation of closely related nodes (p. 234).

stages Relatively discrete steps through which everyone progresses in the same sequence (p. 493).

standard deviation (SD) The amount that the average subject deviates from the mean of the sample on a measure (p. 66).

standardized procedures Procedures applied uniformly to subjects to minimize unintended variation (p. 36).

Stanford-Binet Scale IQ test initially devised in the early part of the twentieth century, which introduced the intelligence quotient, or IQ (p. 300).

state-dependent memory The phenomenon in which information encoded in a particular state can better be recalled when the person is again in that state (p. 243).

states of consciousness Different ways of orienting to internal and external events, such as awake states and sleep states (p. 332).

statistical significance The degree to which the results of a study are likely to have occurred simply by chance (p. 68).

stereotypes Schemas about characteristics ascribed to a group of people based on qualities such as race, ethnicity, or gender rather than achievements or actions (p. 674).

Stevens's power law Law of sensation proposed by S. S. Stevens, which states that the subjective intensity of a stimulus grows as a proportion of the actual intensity raised to some power (p. 124).

stimulant Drug that increases alertness, energy, and autonomic reactivity (p. 359).

stimulus An object or event in the environment that elicits a response in an organism (p. 177).

stimulus control When behavior emitted by an organism is under the control of the stimulus, as in discriminative stimuli (p. 196).

stimulus discrimination The tendency for an organism to respond to a very restricted range of stimuli (p. 181).

stimulus generalization The tendency for learned behavior to occur in response to stimuli that were not present during conditioning but that are similar to the conditioned stimulus (p. 180).

stimulus substitution The explanation of classical conditioning that focuses on the way in which the conditioned stimulus acts as substitute for the unconditioned stimulus (p. 184).

Strange Situation Research design for studying attachment, in which the mother leaves her child alone in a room of toys; the child is joined for a brief time by a friendly stranger, after which the mother returns and greets the child, and coders observe the child's response (p. 535).

strategic therapy Family therapy that tries to change the organization of the family (p. 640).

stratified random sample Sample selected to represent subpopulations proportionately, randomizing only within groups (such as age or race) (p. 49).

stress A challenge to a person's capacity to adapt to inner and outer demands, which may be physiologically arousing, emotionally taxing, and cognitively and behaviorally activating (p. 426).

stressors Situations that often lead to stress, including life events, catastrophes, and daily hassles (p. 428).

stroke Condition that occurs when blood flow to parts of the brain is cut off by disease of the blood vessels, leading to brain damage (p. 107).

structural model Freud's model of conflict between desires and the dictates of conscience or the constraints of reality, which posits three sets of mental forces or structures: id, ego, and superego (p. 457).

structural therapy Family therapy that tries to change the organization of the family (p. 640).

structuralism A school of psychological thought in the early twentieth century that attempted to understand the way conscious sensations, feelings, and images fit together (p. 15).

structure of personality The way enduring patterns of thought, feeling, and behavior are organized within an individual (p. 448).

structure of thought In Piaget's theory, a distinct underlying logic used by a child at a given stage (p. 509).

subcortical Below the cortex (p. 94).

subjects The individuals whom a researcher observes in a study (p. 34).

sublimation Defense mechanism that involves converting sexual or aggressive impulses into socially acceptable activities (p. 438).

subliminal perception The perception of stimuli below the threshold of consciousness (p. 438).

subordinate level A level of categorization below the basic level in which more specific attributes are shared by members of a category (p. 260).

substance P A chemical believed to be released by damaged cells that activates pain receptors (p. 150).

substance-related disorders Disorders involving continued use of a substance (such as alcohol or cocaine) that negatively affects psychological and social functioning (p. 590).

subtractive color mixing The process by which pigments are combined before reaching the eye, so that each pigment absorbs, or subtracts, a portion of the visual spectrum, leaving only the remaining wavelengths to perceive (p. 135).

sucking reflex Infant reflex of rhythmic sucking in response to stimulation three or four centimeters inside the mouth (p. 498).

sulcus Cortical "valley" (p. 96).

superego In Freudian theory, the structure that acts as conscience and source of ideals, or the parental voice within the person, established through identification (p. 457).

superior colliculus A clump of neurons in the midbrain involved in controlling eye movements, detecting the position of objects in space, and integrating sensory input from the eyes and ears (p. 132).

superordinate goals Goals requiring groups to cooperate for the benefit of all (p. 678).

superordinate level The most abstract level of categorization in which members of a category share few common features (p. 260).

surface structure The particular way that words are combined in a sentence to express meaning (p. 282).

survey research Research asking a large sample of subjects questions, often about attitudes or behaviors, using questionnaires or interviews (p. 49).

survivors' guilt A feeling of intense guilt at the seeming unfairness of having survived when others have been harmed or killed in traumatic circumstances (p. 432).

syllogism A formal statement of deductive reasoning, which consists of two premises that lead to a logical conclusion (p. 266).

symbolic interactionists Sociological theorists who argue that the way people see themselves depends heavily on the way others see them (p. 688).

sympathetic nervous system Branch of the autonomic nervous system typically activated in response to threats to the organism, which readies the body for "fight-or-flight" reactions (p. 87).

symptom bearer In a family systems model of psychopathology, the person identified as needing help, or the symptom bearer; also called identified patient (p. 548).

synapse Place at which transmission of information between neurons occurs (p. 77).

synaptic cleft Space between two neurons (p. 77).

synaptic vesicles Small sacs in the terminal buttons of a neuron that contain neurotransmitters (p. 79).

syntax Rules that govern the placement of specific words or phrases within a sentence (p. 280).

systematic desensitization A cognitive-behavioral procedure in which the patient is induced to approach feared stimuli gradually, in a state that inhibits anxiety (p. 631).

T

T cells Cells in the immune system that directly attack foreign agents in the body or that stimulate other immunologic activity (p. 435).

t-test Inferential statistic that compares the mean scores of two groups (p. 71).

tardive dyskinesia A serious, unpredictable, irreversible side effect of prolonged use of antipsychotic medications, in which a patient develops involuntary or semivoluntary twitching, usually of the tongue, face, and neck (p. 644).

task leader Group member who takes responsibility for seeing that the group completes its tasks (p. 729)

taste buds Structures that line the walls of the papillae of the tongue (and elsewhere in the mouth) that contain taste receptors (p. 147).

tectorial membrane Membrane in the inner ear that flexes when sound waves pass through the cochlear fluid, contributing to movement of hair cells, which trigger action potentials in the sensory neurons forming the auditory nerve (p. 141).

tectum Midbrain structure involved in vision and hearing (p. 93).

tegmentum Midbrain structure that includes a variety of neural structures, related mostly to movement and conscious arousal and activation (p. 93).

telegraphic speech Speech used by young children that leaves out all but the essential words in a sentence (p. 286).

temperament Basic personality dispositions heavily influenced by genes (p. 473).

temporal lobes Brain structures located in the lower side portion of the cortex that are important in audition (hearing) and language (p. 99).

tension-release role Group member who makes jokes to relieve the pressure that builds as the group tries to accomplish its tasks (p. 729).

teratogen Harmful environmental agent, such as drugs, irradiation, and viruses that cause maternal illness, which can produce fetal abnormalities or death (p. 496).

terminal buttons Structures at the end of the neuron that receive nerve impulses from the axon and transmit signals to adjacent cells (p. 77).

test-retest reliability A measure of the tendency of a psychometric instrument to yield relatively similar scores for the same individual over time (p. 39).

testes The male gonads (p. 85).

testosterone Hormone produced by the testes (p. 85).

texture gradient A monocular cue for depth perception, in which the pattern of textured surfaces appears coarser at closer range and finer and more densely packed at greater distances (p. 158).

thalamus Structure located deep in the center of the brain which acts as a relay station for sensory information (p. 94).

Thematic Apperception Test (TAT) A projective test consisting of a series of ambiguous pictures about which subjects are asked to make up a story (p. 373).

theory A systematic way of organizing and explaining observations (p. 36).

theory of multiple intelligences Howard Gardner's theory of seven intelligences used to solve problems or produce culturally significant products (p. 312).

therapeutic alliance The patient's degree of comfort with the therapist, which allows him or her to speak about emotionally significant experiences (p. 625).

thinking The ability to represent things mentally and to operate mentally on these representations (p. 257).

three-mountain task Piagetian procedure for assessing egocentrism, in which a child must describe the view of three mountains from a perspective other than her own (p. 511).

thyroid gland Endocrine structure located next to the trachea and larynx in the neck, which releases hormones that control growth and metabolism (p. 85).

timbre The psychological property corresponding to a sound wave's complexity; the texture of a sound (p. 139).

token economy An operant conditioning technique used to modify undesirable behavior, in which points or tokens that can be exchanged for rewards (e.g., candy) are given or taken away (p. 634).

top-down processing Perceptual processing that starts with the observer's expectations and knowledge (p. 165).

topographic model Freud's model of conscious, preconscious, and unconscious processes (p. 450).

traits Emotional, cognitive, and behavioral tendencies that constitute underlying dimensions of personality on which individuals vary (p. 467).

transduction The process of converting physical energy into neural impulses (p. 120).

transference The phenomenon in which the patient displaces thoughts, feelings, fears, wishes, and conflicts from past relationships, especially childhood relationships, onto the therapist (p. 626).

transformational grammar A field of study that attempts to describe and define the conversion from surface to deep structure and vice versa (p. 282).

trichromatic theory of color A theory of color vision initially proposed by Thomas Young and modified by Herman Von Helmholtz that proposes that the eye contains three types of receptors, each sensitive to wavelengths of light that produce sensations of blue, green, and red; by this theory, the colors that humans see reflect blends of the three colors to which the retina is sensitive; also called the Young-Helmholtz theory (p. 135).

tricyclic antidepressant A class of medications for depression that compensates for depleted neurotransmitters (p. 644).

true self A core aspect of being, untainted by the demands of others (p. 479).

tumor Abnormal tissue growth (p. 107).

tutelage The teaching of concepts or procedures primarily through verbal explanation or instruction (p. 208).

two-factor theory Theory derived by Charles Spearman which holds that two types of factors or abilities underlie intelligence (p. 308).

tympanic membrane Eardrum (p. 140).

Type A behavior pattern A pattern of behavior and emotions that includes ambition, competitiveness, impatience, and hostility (p. 435).

U

unconditional positive regard An attitude of total acceptance expressed by the therapist toward the client in client-centered therapy (p. 638).

unconditioned reflex A reflex that occurs naturally, without any prior learning (p. 177).

unconditioned response An organism's unlearned, automatic response to a stimulus (p. 177).

unconditioned stimulus A stimulus that produces a reflexive response without any prior learning (p. 177).

unconscious Mental processes that are not conscious; in Freud's topographic model, mental processes that are inaccessible to consciousness because they are too anxiety-provoking to acknowledge (p. 339).

unconscious mental processes In Freud's theory, mental processes that are inaccessible to consciousness, many of which are repressed (p. 451).

unipolar depression Mood disorder involving only depression; see also bipolar disorder (p. 591).

utility In expectancy value theories, the value of alternatives that are considered in decision making (p. 269).

V

validation Demonstrating the validity of a measure by showing that it consistently relates to other phenomena in theoretically expected ways (p. 39).

validity The extent to which a test measures the construct it attempts to assess, or a study adequately addresses the hypothesis it attempts to assess (pp. 37, 39).

variability The extent to which subjects tend to vary from each other in their scores on a measure (p. 66).

variable Phenomenon that changes across circumstances or varies among individuals (p. 36).

variable interval schedule of reinforcement Operant conditioning procedure in which an organism receives a reward for its responses after an amount of time that is not constant (p. 194).

variable ratio schedule of reinforcement An organism receives a reward for a certain percentage of behaviors that are emitted, but this percentage is not fixed (p. 194).

ventricles Fluid-filled cavities of the brain that are enlarged in schizophrenics, suggesting neuronal atrophy (p. 597).

verbal representations Information represented in words (p. 220).

vertebrate Animal with a spinal cord (p. 91).

vestibular sacs Organs located in the inner ear at the base of the semicircular canals that sense gravity and the position of the head in space (p. 154).

vestibular sense Sense that provides information about the position of the body in space by sensing gravity and movement (p. 153).

vicarious conditioning The process by which an individual learns the consequences of an action by observing its consequences for someone else (p. 206).

visual acuity Sharpness of vision (p. 127).

vitreous humor The clear, gelatinous liquid that fills the space between the lens and the retina (p. 127).

W

wavelength The distance over which a wave of energy completes a full oscillation (p. 126).

Weber fraction The proportion by which two stimuli must differ for a person to detect a just noticeable difference (p. 123).

Weber's law Perceptual law described by Ernst Weber which states that for two stimuli to be perceived as differing in intensity, the second must differ from the first by a constant proportion (p. 123).

Wechsler Adult Intelligence Scale-Revised (WAIS-R) Intelligence test for adults that yields scores for both verbal and nonverbal (performance) IQ scores (p. 301).

Wechsler Intelligence Scale for Children-Revised (WISC-R) Intelligence test for children up to age 16 that yields verbal and nonverbal (performance) IQ scores (p. 301).

weighted utility In expectancy value theory, a combined measure of the importance of an attribute and how well a given option satisfies it (p. 269).

well-defined concept Concept that has properties clearly setting it apart from other concepts (p. 258).

well-defined problem Problems in which there is adequate information to solve the problem and clear criteria by which to determine whether the problem has been solved (p. 267).

Wernicke's aphasia Language disorder caused by damage to Wernicke's area, in which the individual has difficulty understanding language (p. 99).

Wernicke's area Brain structure located in the left temporal lobe, involved in language comprehension (p. 99).

Whorfian hypothesis of linguistic relativity The notion that language shapes thought (p. 278).

working memory Conscious "workspace" used for retrieving and manipulating information, maintained through maintenance rehearsal; also called short-term memory (p. 215).

Y

Young-Helmholtz theory A theory of color vision initially proposed by Young and modified by Helmholtz which proposes that the eye contains three types of receptors, each sensitive to wavelengths of light that produce sensations of blue, green, and red; by this theory, the colors that humans see reflect blends of the three colors to which the retina is sensitive; also called trichromatic theory (p. 135).

REFERENCES

AARP News Bulletin. (January 1989). New study finds older drivers "capable, safe." *30*, 14.

Abelson, R. P. (1981). Psychological status of the script concept. *American Psychologist, 36*, 715–729.

Abelson, R. P. (1983). Whatever became of consistency theory? *Personality and Social Psychology Bulletin, 9*, 37–54.

Abram, K. M., & Teplin, L. (1991). Co-occurring disorders among mentally ill jail detainees: Implications for public policy. *American Psychologist, 46*, 1036–1045.

Abramov, I., & Gordon, J. (1994). Color appearance: On seeing red—or yellow, or green, or blue. *Annual Review of Psychology, 45*, 451–485.

Abrams, D. B., & Wilson, G. T. (1983). Alcohol, sexual arousal, and self control. *Journal of Personality and Social Psychology, 45*, 188–198.

Abrams, R., Swartz, C. M., & Vedak, C. (1989). Antidepressant effects of right versus left unilateral ECT and the lateralization theory of ECT action. *American Journal of Psychiatry, 146*, 1190–1192.

Abramson, L. Y., Seligman, M.E.P., & Teasdale, J. D. (1978). Learned helplessness in humans: Critique and reformulation. *Journal of Abnormal Psychology, 87*, 49–74.

Adams, B. D. (1985). Age, structure, and sexuality. *Journal of Homosexuality, 11*, 19–33.

Adams, C. (1991). Qualitative age differences in memory for text: A life–span developmental perspective. *Psychology and Aging, 6*, 323–336.

Adams, G. R., & Lavoie, J. C. (1974). The effect of sex of child, conduct, and facial attractiveness on teacher expectancy. *Education, 95*, 76–83.

Adams, P. R. & Adams, G. R. (1984). Mount Saint Helens's Ashfall: Evidence for a disaster stress reaction. *American Psychologist, 39*, 252–260.

Adams, R., Courage, M., & Mercer, M. (1994). Systematic measurement of human neonatal color vision. *Vision Research, 34*, 1691–1701.

Adams, R. J. (1989). Newborns' discrimination among mid– and long–wavelength stimuli. *Journal of Experimental Child Psychology, 47*, 130–141.

Adelson, E., & Fraiberg, S. (1974). Gross motor development in infants blind from birth. *Child Development, 45*, 114–26.

Ader, R., & Cohen, N. (1985). CNS immune system interactions: Conditioning phenomena. *Behavioral and Brain Sciences, 8*, 379–426.

Ader, R., & Cohen, N. (1993). Psychoneuroimmunology: Conditioning and stress. *Annual Review of Psychology, 44*, 53–85

Adler, A. (1929). *The practice and theory of individual psychology.* (2nd ed.). London: Routledge & Kegan Paul.

Adler, M. (1975). Interpreting Peanuts cartoons. In J.A.M. Howe & B. Meltzer (Eds.), *Computer simulation of perceptual processes.* Edinburgh: University of Edinburgh, Department of Computer Science.

Adler, N., & Matthews, K. (1994). Health psychology: Why do some people get sick and some stay well? *Annual Review of Psychology, 45*, 229–259.

Adorno, T. W., Frenkel–Brunswik, E., Levinson, D., & Sanford, R.N. (1950). *The authoritarian personality.* New York: W.W. Norton.

Affleck, G., Tennen, H., Urrows. S., & Higgins, P. (1994). Person and contextual features of daily stress reactivity: Individual differences in relations of undesirable daily events with mood disturbance and chronic pain intensity. *Journal of Personality and Social Psychology, 66*, 329–340.

Ainsworth, M.D.S. (1967). (1967). *Infancy in Uganda.* Baltimore, Md.: Johns Hopkins University.

Ainsworth, M.D.S. (1973). The development of infant–mother attachment. In B. Caldwell & H. Ricciuti (Eds.), *Review of Child Development Research*, Vol. 3. Chicago: University of Chicago Press.

Ainsworth, M.D.S. (1979). Infant–mother attachment. *American Psychologist, 34*, 932–937.

Ainsworth, M.D.S., & Bell, S. M. (1970). Attachment, exploration, and separation: Illustrated by the behavior of one–year–olds in a strange situation. *Child Development, 41*, 49–67.

Ainsworth, M. S., & Bowlby, J. (1991). An ethological approach to personality development. *American Psychologist, 46*, 333–341.

Ajzen, I., & Fishbein, M. (1977). Attitude–behavior relations: A theoretical analysis and review of empirical research. *Psychological Bulletin, 84*, 888–918.

al–Absi, M., & Rokke, P. D. (1991). Can anxiety help us tolerate pain? *Pain, 46*, 43–51.

Alba, J. W. & Hasher, L. (1983). Is memory schematic? *Psychological Bulletin, 93*, 203–231.

Albee, G. W. (1986). Toward a just society: Lessons from observations on the primary prevention of psychopathology. *American Psychology, 41*, 891–898.

Albert, D. J., Jonik, R. H., & Walsh, M. (1991). Hormone–dependent aggression in the female rat: Testosterone plus estradiol implants prevent the decline in aggression following ovariectomy. *Physiology & Behavior, 49*, 673–677.

Albert, D. J., & Walsh, M. L. (1984). Neural systems and the inhibitory modulation of agonistic behavior: A comparison of mammalian species. *Neuroscience and Behavioral Review, 8*, 5–24.

Albert, M. K. (1993). Parallelism and the perception of illusory contours. *Perception, 22*, 589–595.

Aldag, R., & Fuller, S.R. (1993). Beyond fiasco: A reappraisal of the groupthink phenomenon and a new model of group decision processes. *Psychological Bulletin, 113*, 533–552.

Alderfer, C. (1972). Existence, relatedness, and growth: *Human needs in organizational settings.* New York: Free Press.

Alderfer, C. P. (1989). Theories reflecting my personal experience and life development. *Journal of Applied Behavioral Science, 25*, 351–365.

Aldrich, M. S. (1990). Narcolepsy. *New England Journal of Medicine, 323*, 389–394.

Alexander, I. (1990). *Personology: Method and content in personality assessment and psychobiography.* Durham, NC: Duke University Press.

Alexander, J. M., & Schwanenflugel, P.J. (1994). Strategy regulation: The role of intelligence, metacognitive attributions, and knowledge base. *Developmental Psychology, 30*, 709–723.

Alexander, P. C. (1992). Application of attachment theory to the study of sexual abuse. *Journal of Consulting and Clinical Psychology, 60*, 185–195.

Alfred, K., & Smith, T. W. (1989). The hardy personality: Cognitive and physiological responses to evaluative threat. *Journal of Personality and Social Psychology, 56*, 357–366.

Allee, W. C. (1938). *The social life of animals.* New York: W. W. Norton.

Allen, N., Panian, S., & Lotz, R. (1979). Managerial succession and organizational performance: A recalcitrant problem revisited. *Administrative Science Quarterly, 24*, 167–180.

Allen, R. E. & Oliver, J. M. (1982). The effects of child maltreatment on language development. *Child Abuse and Neglect, 6*, 299–305.

Allen, V. L. & Wilder, D. A. (1975). Categorization, belief similarity, and intergroup discrimination. *Journal of Personality and Social Psychology, 32*, 971–977.

Alley, T. R. (1981). Head shape and the perception of cuteness. *Developmental Psychology, 17*, 650–654.

Allgulander, C., & Lavori, P. (1991). Excess mortality among 3302 patients with "pure" anxiety neurosis. *Archives of General Psychiatry, 48*, 599–602.

Allodi, F. A. (1991). Assessment and treatment of torture victims. *The Journal of Nervous and Mental Disorders, 179,* 4–11.

Alloy, L. B. & Clements, C. M. (1992). Illusion of control: Invulnerability to negative affect and depressing symptoms after laboratory and natural stressors. *Journal of Abnormal Psychology, 101,* 234–245.

Allport, G. (1937). *Personality: A psychological interpretation.* New York: Henry Holt & Co.

Allport, G. (1954). *The nature of prejudice.* Cambridge, MA: Addison–Wesley.

Allport, G. (1968). The historical background of modern social psychology. In G. Lindzey & E. Aronson (Eds.), *Handbook of social psychology,* Vol. I. Reading, MA: Addison–Wesley.

Allport, G. & Odbert, H. (1936). *Trait–names: A Psycho–lexical study.* Psychological Monographs, Vol. 47, No. 1. Princeton, NJ: Psychological Review Co.

Alnaes, R., & Torgersen, S. (1990). DSM–III personality disorders among patients with major depression, anxiety disorders, and mixed conditions. *Journal of Nervous and Mental Disease, 178,* 693–698.

Alonso, L., & Jeffrey, W. D. (1988). Mental illness complicated by the santeria belief in spirit possession. *Hospital and Community Psychiatry, 39,* 1188–1191.

Altemus, M., Pigott, T., Kalogeras, K., Demitrack, M., Dubbert, B., & Gold, P. W. (1992). Abnormalities in the regulation of vasopressin and corticotropin releasing factor secretion in obsessive–compulsive disorder. *Archives of General Psychiatry, 49,* 9–20.

Alty, J. L. (1989). Machine expertise. In K.J. Gilhooly (Ed.), *Human & machine problem solving.* New York: Plenum Press.

Ambady, N., & Rosenthal, R. (1993). Half a minute: Predicting teacher evaluations from thin slices of nonverbal behavior and physical attractiveness. *Journal of Personality and Social Psychology, 64,* 431–441.

American Psychological Association, Committee for the Protection of Human Participants in Research. (1973). *Ethical principles in the conduct of research with human subjects.* Washington, DC.

American Psychological Association, Committee for the Protection of Human Participants in Research. (1982). *Ethical principles in the conduct of research with human subjects.* (2nd ed.). Washington, DC.

American Psychological Association, Committee for the Protection of Human Participants in Research. (1990). *Ethical principles in the conduct of research with human subjects.* (3rd ed.). Washington, DC.

Amoore, J. E. (1970). *Molecular basis of odor.* Springfield, Ill.: Charles C. Thomas.

Amoore, J. E., Johnston, J. W., Jr., & Rubin, M. (1964). The stereochemical theory of odor. *Scientific American,* 42–49.

Amsterdam, B. (1972). Mirror self–image reactions before age two. *Developmental Psychology, 5,* 297–305.

Anand, B., & Brobeck, J. (1951). Hypothalamic control of food intake in rats and cats. *Yale Journal of Biological Medicine, 24,* 123–140.

Anastasi, A. (1958). Heredity, environment, and the question "How?" *Psychological Review, 65,* 197–208.

Anastasi, A. (1988). *Psychological testing.* (6th ed.). New York: Macmillan.

Andersen, S., & Cole, S. (1991). Do I know you? The role of significant others in general social perception. *Journal of Personality and Social Psychology, 59,* 384–399.

Anderson, C. (1989). Temperature and aggression: Ubiquitous effects of heat on occurrence of human violence. *Psychological Bulletin, 106,* 74–96.

Anderson, C. A., & Anderson, D. C. (1984). Ambient temperature and violent crime: Tests of the linear and curvilinear hypotheses. *Journal of Personality and Social Psychology, 46,* 91–97.

Anderson, J. (1983). *The architecture of cognition.* Cambridge, MA: Harvard University Press.

Anderson, J. R. (1972). Recognition confusions in sentence memory. Unpublished manuscript.

Anderson, J. R. (1985). *Cognitive psychology and its implications.* (2nd ed.). New York: Freeman.

Anderson, J. R. (1991). The adaptive nature of human categorization. *Psychological Review, 98,* 409–429.

Anderson, J. R. (1993). Problem solving and learning. *American Psychologist, 48,* 35–44.

Anderson, J. R. (1995). *Learning and memory: An integrated approach.* New York: John Wiley.

Anderson, L. P. (1991). Acculturative stress: A theory of relevance to black Americans. *Clinical Psychology Review, 11,* 685–702.

Anderson, N. H. (1971). Integration theory and attitude change. *Psychological Review, 78,* 171–206.

Anderson, R. A., Baron, R.S., & Logan, H. (1991). Distraction, control, and dental stress. *Journal of Applied Social Psychology, 21,* 156–171.

Anderson, V. E. (1972). Discussion. In L. Ehrman, G. S. Omenn, & E.Caspari (Eds.), *Genetics, environment, and behavior.* New York: Academic Press.

Andersson, B. (1992). Effects of day–care on cognitive and socioemotional competence of thirteen–year–old Swedish schoolchildren. *Child Development, 63,* 20–36.

Anderton, B. (1987). Alzheimer's disease: Progress in molecular pathology. *Nature, 325,* 658–59.

Andreasen, N., & Glick, I. (1988). Bipolar affective disorder and creativity: Implications and clinical management. *Comprehensive Psychiatry, 29,* 207–217.

Andreasen, N. C., Rice, J., Endicott, J., Coryell, W., Grove, W. M., & Reich, T. (1987). Familial rates of affective disorder: A report from the National Institute of Mental Health collaborative study. *Archives of General Psychiatry, 44,* 461–469.

Andreason, N., Swayze, V., Flaum, M., Alliger, R., & Cohen, G. (1990). Ventricular abnormalities in affective disorder: Clinical and demographic correlates. *American Journal of Psychiatry, 147,* 893–900.

Andrews, G., & Harvey, R. (1981). Does psychotherapy benefit neurotic patients? *Archives of General Psychiatry, 38,* 1203–1208.

Angel, I., Hauger, R., Giblin, B., & Paul, S. (1992). Regulation of the anorectic drug recognition site during glucoprovic feeding. *Brain Research Bulletin, 28,* 201–207.

Angrist, B., Sathananthan, G., Wilk, S., & Gershon, S. (1974). Amphetamine psychosis: Behavioral and biochemical aspects. *Journal of Psychiatric Research, 11,* 13–23.

Anisfeld, E., Casper, V., Nozyee, M., & Cunningham, N. (1990). Does infant carrying promote attachment? An experimental study of the effects of increased physical contact on the development of attachment. *Child Development, 61,* 1617–1627.

Anthony, E., & Cohler, B. (Eds.) (1987). *The invulnerable child.* New York: Guilford Press.

Antrobus, J. (1991). Dreaming: Cognitive processes during cortical activation and high afferent thresholds. *Psychological Review, 98,* 96–121.

Aponte, H. J., & VanDeusen, J. M. (1981). Structural family therapy. In A. S. Gurman and D. P. Kniskern (Eds.), *Handbook of family therapy.* New York: Brunner/Mazel.

Archer, D., & Gartner, R. (1976). Violent acts and violent times: A comparative approach to postwar homicide rates. *American Sociological Review, 41,* 937–963.

Archer, D., & Gartner, R. (1984). *Violence and crime in cross–national perspective.* New Haven, Conn.: Yale University Press.

Archer, J. (1991). The influence of testosterone on human aggression. *British Journal of Psychology, 82,* 1–28.

Archer, J., & Lloyd, B. (1985). *Sex and gender.* (2nd ed.). New York: Cambridge University Press.

Ardila, A., Montanes, P., & Gempeler, J. (1986). Echoic memory and language perception. *Brain and Language, 29,* 134–140.

Arkes, H., Boehm, L., & Xu, G. (1991). Determinants of judged validity. *Journal of Experimental Social Psychology, 27,* 576–605.

Arkowitz, H., & Messer, S. B., (Eds.) (1984). *Psychodynamic therapy and behavior therapy: Is integration possible?* New York: Plenum Press.

Arnkoff, D., Victor, B., & Glass, C. (1993). Empirical research on factors in psychotherapeutic change. In G. Stricker & J. Gold (Eds.), *Comprehensive handbook of psychotherapy integration* (pp. 27–42). New York: Plenum Press.

Aronson, E. (1978). *The jigsaw classroom.* Beverly Hills, CA: Sage.

Aronson, E. (1978). The theory of cognitive dissonance: A current perspective. In L. Berkowitz (Ed.), *Cognitive theories in social psychology.* New York: Academic Press.

Aronson, E., & Carlsmith, J. M. (1963). Effect of severity of threat on the valuation of forbidden behavior. *Journal of Abnormal and Social Psychology, 66,* 584–588.

Aronson, E., & Cope, V. (1968). My enemy's enemy is my friend. *Journal of Personality and Social Psychology, 8,* 8–12.

Asch, S. E. (1955). Opinions and social pressure. *Scientific American, 193,* 31–35.

Asch, S. E. (1956). Studies of independence and conformity: A minority of one against unanimous majority. *Psychological Monographs: General and Applied, 70,* 1–69.

Asendorph, J., & Baudonniere, P. (1993). Self–awareness and other–awareness: Mirror self–recognition and synchronic imitation among unfamiliar peers. *Developmental Psychology, 29,* 88–95.

Asendorph, J., & Scherer, K. (1983). The discrepant repressor: Differentiation between low anxiety, high anxiety, and repression of anxiety by autonomic–facial–verbal patterns of behavior. *Journal of Personality and Social Psychology, 45,* 1334–1346.

Atkinson, J. W. (1977). Motivation for achievement. In Blass, T. (Ed.), *Personality Variables in Social Behavior.* Hillsdale, NJ: Erlbaum.

Atkinson, J. W., & Litwin, G. H. (1960). Achievement motive land test anxiety conceived as motive to approach success and motive to avoid failure. *Journal of Abnormal and Social Psychology, 60,* 52–63.

Atkinson, R. C., & Shiffrin, R. N. (1968). Human memory: A proposed system and its control processes. In K.W. Spence and J.T. Spense (Eds.), *The psychology of learning and motivation,* Vol. 2. New York: Academic Press.

Attneave, F. (1954). Some information aspects of visual perception. *Psychological Review, 61,* 183–193.

Atwater, L. E. (1992). Beyond cognitive ability: Improving the prediction of performance. *Journal of Business and Psychology, 7,* 27–44.

Ax, A. F. (1990–1991). Individual differences in autonomic learning: A quarter century of reflection. *International Journal of Psychophysiology, 10,* 1–9.

Ayllon, T., & Azrin, N. H. (1968). *The token economy: A motivational system for therapy and rehabilitation.* New York: Appleton–Century–Crofts.

Baars, B. J. (1988). Momentary forgetting as a "resetting" of a conscious global workspace due to competition between incompatible contexts. In M. J. Horowitz (Ed.), *Psychodynamics and cognition* (pp. 269–293). University of California.

Babor, T., Hoffman, M., DelBoca, F., Hesselbrock, V., Meyer, R. E., Dolinsky, Z., & Rounsaville, B. (1992). Types of alcoholics, I: Evidence for an empirically derived typology based on indicators of vulnerability and severity. *Archives of General Psychiatry, 49,* 599–608.

Backhaus, W. (1992). Vision in honeybees. *Neuroscience and Biobehavioral Reviews, 16,* 1–2.

Baddeley, A. D., & Patterson, K. (1971). The relation between long–term and short–term memory. *British Medical Bulletin, 27,* 237–242.

Baer, J. S., Marlatt, G., Kivlahan, D., & Fromme, K. (1992). An experimental test of three methods of alcohol risk reduction with young adults. *Journal of Consulting and Clinical Psychology, 60,* 974–979.

Bahrick, H. P. (1984). Semantic memory content in permastore: Fifty years of memory for Spanish learned in school. *Journal of Experimental Psychology General, 113,* 1–29.

Bailey, J. M., & Pillard, R. (1991). A genetic study of male sexual orientation. *Archives of General Psychiatry, 48,* 1089–1096.

Bailey, J. M., Pillard, R. C., Neale, M. C., & Agyei, Y. (1993). Heritable factors influence sexual orientation in women. *Archives of General Psychiatry, 50,* 217–223.

Bailey, J. M., Willerman, L., & Parks, C. (1991). A test of the maternal stress theory of human homosexuality. *Archives of Sexual Behavior, 20,* 277–293.

Baillargeon, R., & DeVos, J. (1991). Object permanence in young infants: Further evidence. *Child Development, 62,* 1227–1246.

Baldessarini, R. J. (1985). *Chemotherapy in psychiatry.* (Rev. ed.). Cambridge, MA: Harvard University Press.

Baldwin, M. (1992). Relational schemas and the processing of social information. *Psychological Bulletin, 112,* 461–484.

Bales, R. F. (1953). The equilibrium problem in small groups. In T. Parsons, R. F. Bales, & E. A. Shils (Eds.), *Working papers in the theory of action.* Glencoe, Ill: Free Press.

Ballantyne, J. (1985). The results varies from various viewpoints. In R. I. Gray (Ed.), *Cochlear implants.* San Diego, CA: College–Hill Press.

Baltes, P. (1987). Theoretical propositions of life–span developmental psychology: On the dynamics between growth and decline. *Developmental Psychology, 23,* 611–626.

Baltes, P. B., Dittmann–Kohli, F., & Kliegl, R. (1986). Reserve capacity of the elderly in aging–sensitive tests of fluid intelligence: Replication and extension. *Psychology and Aging, 1,* 172–77.

Banaji, M. R., & Crowder, R. G. (1989). The bankruptcy of everyday memory. *American Psychologist, 44,* 1185–1193.

Bancroft, J. (1984). Hormones and human sexual behavior. *Journal of Sex and Marital Therapy, 10,* 3–21.

Bandler, R. (1982). Identification of neuronal cell bodies mediating components of biting attack behavior in the cat: Induction of jaw opening following microinjections of glutamate into hypothalamus. *Brain Research, 245,* 192–197.

Bandler, R. J., Jr., Madaras, G. R., & Bem, D. J. (1968). Self–observation as a source of pain perception. *Journal of Personality and Social Psychology, 9,* 205–209.

Bandura, A. (1967). The role of modeling personality development. In C. Lavatelli & F. Stendler (Eds.)., *Readings in childhood and development* (pp. 334–343). New York: Harcourt Brace Jovanovich.

Bandura, A. (1977). Self–efficacy: Toward a unifying theory of behavioral change. *Psychological Review, 84,* 191–215.

Bandura, A. (1977). *Social learning theory.* Englewood Cliffs, NJ: Prentice–Hall.

Bandura, A. (1982). Self–efficacy mechanisms in human agency. *American Psychologist, 37,* 122–147.

Bandura, A. (1986). *Social foundations of thought and action: A social cognitive theory,* Englewood Cliffs, NJ: Prentice–Hall.

Bandura, A. (1989). Human agency in social cognitive theory. *American Psychologist, 44,* 1175–1184.

Bandura, A. (1991). Social cognitive theory of self–regulation. *Organizational Behavior and Human Decision Processes, 50,* 248–287.

Bandura, A., Blanchard, E. B., & Ritter, B. (1969). Relative efficacy of desensitization and modeling approaches for inducing behavioral, affective, and attitudinal changes. *Journal of Personality and Social Psychology, 13,* 173–199.

Bandura, A., Ross, D., & Ross, S. (1961). Transmission of aggression through imitation of aggressive models. *Journal of Abnormal and Social Psychology, 66,* 3–11.

Bandura, A., Ross, D., & Ross, S. (1963). Vicarious reinforcement and imitative learning. *Journal of Abnormal and Social Psychology, 67,* 601–607.

Banks, M. S. & Salapatek, P. (1983). Infant visual perception. In M.M. Haith & J. J. Campos (Eds.), *Handbook of child psychology: Vol. 2, Infancy and developmental psychobiology.* New York: JohnWiley.

Bard, P. (1934). On emotional expression after decortication with some remarks on certain theoretical views. *Psychological Review, 41,* 309–328.

Bardwick, J. (1971). *Psychology of women.* New York: Harper & Row.

Barends, A., Westen, D., Byers, B., Leigh, J., & Silbert, D. (1990). Assessing affect–tone of relationship paradigms from TAT and interview data. *Psychological Assessment: A Journal of Consulting and Clinical Psychology, 2,* 329–332.

Bargh, J., Chaiken, S., Govender, R., & Pratto, F. (1992). The generality of the automatic attitude activation effect. *Journal of Personality and Social Psychology, 62,* 893–912.

Bargh, J. A. (1989). Conditional automaticity: Varieties of automatic influence in social perception and cognition. In J. S. Uleman & J. A. Bargh (Eds.), *Unintended thought* (pp.3–51). New York.: Guilford Press.

Bargh, J. A., & Tota, M. E. (1988). Context–dependent automatic depression: Accessibility of negative constructs with regard to self but not others. *Journal of Personality and Social Psychology, 54,* 925–939.

Barlow, D. H. (1988). *Anxiety and its disorders.* New York: Guilford Press.

Barlow, D. H. (1988). Current models of panic disorder and a view from emotion theory. In A. J. Frances & R. E. Hales (Eds.), *Review of psychiatry,* Vol. 7. Washington, DC: American Psychiatric Press.

Barnes, D. M. (1990). Silver Spring monkeys yield unexpected data on brain reorganization. *Journal of NIH, 2,* 19–20.

Barnier, A., & McConkey, K. (1992). Reports of real and false memories: The relevance of hypnosis, hypnotizability, and context of memory test. *Journal ofAbnormal Psychology, 101,* 521–527.

Baron, A. & Mattila, W. (1989). Response slowing of older adults: Effects of time–limit contingencies on single– and dual–task performances. *Psychology and Aging, 4.*

Baron, R. A. (1985). In H. I. Kaplan, & B. J. Sadock (Eds.), *Comprehensive textbook of psychiatry.* (4th ed.). Baltimore, MD: Williams & Wilkins.

Baron, R. S., Cutrona, C. E., Hicklin, D., Russell, D. W., & Lubaroff, D. M. (1990). Social support and immune function among spouses of cancer patients. *Journal of Personality and Social Psychology, 59,* 344–352.

Barr, H., Pytkowicz, Streissguth, Darby, B., & Sampson, P. (1990). Prenatal exposure to alcohol, caffeine, tobacco, and aspirin: Effects on fine and gross motor performance in 4–year–old children. *Developmental Psychology, 26,* 339–348.

Barrett, G. V., & Depinet, R. L. (1991). A reconsideration of testing for competence rather than for intelligence. *American Psychologist, 46,* 1012–1024.

Barrett, G. V., & Franke, R. H. (1969). Communication preference and performance: A cross–cultural comparison. *Proceedings of the 77th Annual American Psychological Association Convention,* 597–598.

Barron, F., & Harrington, D. M. (1981). Creativity, intelligence, and personality. *Annual Review of Psychology, 32,* 439–476.

Barry, H. M., et al. (1957). A cross–cultural survey of some sex differences in socialization. *Journal of Abnormal Social Psychology, 55,* 327–332.

Barta, P., Pearlson, G., Powers, R. E., Richards, S. S., & Tune, L. (1990). Auditory hallucinations and smaller superior temporal gyral volume in schizophrenia. *American Journal of Psychiatry, 147,* 1457–1462.

Bartlett, F. C. (1932). *Remembering: A study in experimental and social psychology.* Cambridge: Cambridge University Press.

Bartoshuk, L. M. (1980). Separate worlds of taste. *Psychology Today, 14,* 48–63.

Bartoshuk, L. M., & Beauchamp, G. K. (1994). Chemical senses. *Annual Review of Psychology, 45,* 419–449.

Bashford, J. A., Riener, K. R., & Warren, R. M. (1992). Increasing the intelligibility of speech through multiple phonemic restorations. *Perception and Psychophysics, 51,* 211–217.

Basoglu, M., Paker, M., Paker, O., Ozmen, E., Marks, I., Sahin, D., & Sarimurat, N. (1994). Psychological effects of torture: A comparison of tortured with nontortured political activists in Turkey. *American Journal of Psychiatry, 151,* 6–81.

Basso, M. R., Schefft, B., & Hoffmann, R. G. (1994). Mood–moderating effects of affect intensity on cognition: Sometimes euphoria is not beneficial and dysphyoria is not detrimental. *Journal of Personality and Social Psychology, 66,* 363–368.

Bates, J. E., Marvinney, D., Kelly, T., Dodge, K. E., Bennett, D. S., & Pettit, G. S. (1994). Child–care history and kindergarten adjustment. *Developmental Psychology, 39,* 690–700.

Bates, M. E., & Tracy, J. I. (1990). Cognitive functioning in young "social drinkers": Is there impairment to detect? *Journal of Abnormal Psychology, 99,* 242–249.

Bates, M. S. (1987). Ethnicity and pain: A biocultural model. *Social Science and Medicine, 24,* 47–50.

Batson, C. D. (1991). Evidence for altruism: Toward a pluralism of prosocial motives. *Psychological Inquiry, 2,* 107–122.

Batson, C. D. (1995). Altruism. In A. Tesser (Ed.), *Advanced social psychology.* New York: McGraw–Hill.

Battacchi, M. W., Pelamatti, G., Umilta, C., & Michelotti, E. (1981). On the acoustic information stored in echoic memory. *International Journal of Psycholonguistics,8,* 17–29.

Batteau, D. W. (1967). The role of the pinna in human localization. Proceedings of the *Royal Society of London, Series, B, 168,* 158–180.

Batuev, A. S., & Gafurov, B. G. (1993). The chemical nature of the hypothalamocortical activation underlying drinking behavior. *Neuroscience of Behavioral Psychology, 23,* 35–41.

Baumeister, R. (1987). How the self became a problem: A psychological review of historical research. *Journal of Personality and Social Psychology, 52,* 163–176.

Baumeister, R. F. (1990). Item variances and median splits: Some encouraging and reassuring findings. *Journal of Personality, 58,* 588–594.

Baumeister, R. F. (1991). *Meanings of life.* New York: Guilford Press.

Baumeister, R. F., & Jones, E. E. (1978). When self–presentation is constrained by the target's knowledge: Consistency and compensation. *Journal of Personality and Social Psychology, 36,* 608–618.

Baumrind, D. (1967). Child care practices anteceding three patterns of preschool behavior. *Genetic Psychology Monographs, 75,* 43–88.

Baumrind, D. (1971). Current patterns of parental authority. *Developmental Psychology Monograph, 4,* 1–103.

Baumrind, D. (1985). Research using intentional deception: Ethical issues revisited. *American Psychologist, 40,* 165–174.

Baumrind, D. (1987). A developmental perspective on adolescent risk taking in contemporary America. *New Directions for Child Development, 37,* 93–125.

Baumrind, D. (1991). The influence of parenting style on adolescent competence and substance use. *Journal of Early Adolescence, 11,* 56–95.

Baxter, D. W., & Olszewski, J. (1960). Congenital universal insensitivity to pain. *Brain, 83,* 381–393.

Baydar, N., & Brooks–Gunn, J. (1991). Effects of maternal employment and child–care arrangements on preschoolers' cognitive and behavioral outcomes: Evidence from the children of the National Longitudinal Survey of Youth. *Developmental Psychology, 27,* 932–945.

Bazler, J., & Simonis, D. (1991). Are high school chemistry textbooks gender fair? *Journal of Research in Science Teaching, 28,* 353–362.

Beaman, A. L., Barnes, P. J., Klentz, B., & McQuirk, B. (1978). Increasing helping rates through information dissemination: Teaching pays. *Personality and Social Psychology Bulletin, 4,* 406–411.

Beaman, A. L., Cole, C. M., Preston, M., Klentz, B., & Steblay, N. M. (1983). Fifteen years of foot–in–the–door research: A meta–analysis. *Personality and Social Psychology Bulletin, 9,* 181–196.

Bearden, C. (1994). The nightmare: Biological and psychological origins. *Dreaming, 4,* 139–152.

Beck, A. (1985). *Anxiety disorders and phobias: A cognitive perspective.* New York: Basic Books.

Beck, A. (1989). *Cognitive therapy in clinical practice: An illustrative casebook.* New York: Routledge.

Beck, A. (1991). Cognitive therapy: A 30–year retrospective. *American Psychologist, 46,* 368–375.

Beck, A., & Freeman, A. (1990). *Cognitive therapy of personality disorders.* New York: Guilford Press.

Beck, A. T. (1976). *Cognitive therapy and the emotional disorders.* New York: International Universities Press.

Beck, A. T. (1993). Cognitive therapy: Past, present, and future. *Journal of Consulting and Clinical Psychology, 61,* 194–198.

Beck, A. T., & Emery, G. (1985). *Anxiety disorders and phobias: A cognitive perspective.* New York: Basic Books.

Beck, A. T., Sokol, L., Clark, D. A., Berchick, R., & Wright, R. (1992). A crossover study of focused cognitive therapy for panic disorder. *American Journal of Psychiatry, 149,* 778–783.

Beck, J. G., & Barlow, D. H. (1984). Current conceptualizations of sexual dysfunction: A review and an alternative perspective. *Clinical Psychology Review, 4,* 363–78.

Becker, E. (1973). *The denial of death.* New York: Free Press.

Becker, G. (1978). *The mad genius controversy.* Beverly Hills, Calif: Sage.

Beckwith, J., Geller, L. & Sarkar, S. (1991). Sources of human psychological differences: The Minnesota Study of Twins Reared Apart: Comment. *Science, 252,* 191.

Beckwith, L, Rodning, C., & Cohen, S. (1992). Preterm children at early adolescence and continuity and discontinuity in maternal responsiveness from infancy. *Child Development, 63,* 1198–1208.

Bee, H. (1982). Prediction of IQ and language skill from perinatal status, child performance, family characteristics, and mother–infant interaction. *Child Development, 53,* 1134–1156.

Beets, J.G.T. (1978). Odor and stimulant structure. In E.C. Carterette & M.P. Friedman (Eds.), *Handbook of perception.* New York: Academic Press.

Beggan, J. (1992). On the social nature of nonsocial perception: The mere ownership effect. *Journal of Personality and Social Psychology, 62,* 229–237.

Beitman, B. D., Goldfried, M. R., & Norcross, J. C. (1989). The movement toward integrating the psychotherapies: An overview. *American Journal of Psychiatry, 146,* 138–147.

Bekesy, G. von. (1959). Synchronism of neural discharges and their demultiplication in pitch perception on the skin and in learning. *Journal of the Acoustical Society of America, 31,* 338–349.

Bekesy, G. von. (1960). *Experiments in hearing.* New York: McGraw–Hill.

Bekesy, G. von, & Rosenblith, W. A. (1951). The mechanical properties of the ear. In S.S. Stevens (Ed.), *Handbook of experimental psychology.* New York: John Wiley & Sons.

Bell, A. P., Weinberg, M. S., & Hammersmith, S. (1981). *Sexual preference: Its development in men and women.* Bloomington: Univeristy of Indiana Press.

Bell, B. D. (1978). Disaster impact and response: Overcoming the thousand natural shocks. *The Gerontologist, 18,* 531–540.

Bell, P. (1992). In defense of the negative affect escape model of heat and aggression. *Psychological Bulletin, 111,* 342–346.

Bellack, A., & Hersen, M., (Eds.). *Behavioral assessment: A practical handbook* (3rd ed.). Elmsford, NY: Pergamon.

Bellack, A., & Mueser, K. (1992). Social skills training for schizophrenia? *Archives of General Psychiatry, 49.*

Bellack, L., Hurvich, M., & Gediman, H. (1973). *Ego functions in schizophrenics, neurotics, and normals.* New York: John Wiley.

Bellah, R. N., et al. (1985). *Habits of the heart: Individualism and commitment in American life.* Berkeley: University of California Press.

Belo, J. (1955). Balinese children's drawing. In M. Mead & M. Wolfenstein (Eds.), *Childhood in Contemporary Cultures* (pp. 52–69). Chicago: University of Chicago Press.

Belsky, J., & Isabella, R. (1988). Maternal, infant, and social–contextual determinants of attachment security. In J. Belsky & T. Nezworsky (Eds.), *Clinical implications of attachment* (pp. 41–94). Hillsdale, N J: Erlbaum.

Belsky, J., & Nezworski, T. (Eds.). (1987). *Clinical implications of attachment theory.* Hillsdale, NJ: Erlbaum.

Belsky, J., & Pensky, E. (1988). Marital change across the transition to parenthood. *Marriage and Family Review, 12,* 133–156.

Belsky, J., & Rovine, M. J. (1988). Nonmaternal care in the first year of life and the security of infant–parent attachment. *Child Development, 59,* 157–167.

Bem, D. J. (1967). Self perception: An alternative interpretation of cognitive dissonance phenomena. *Psychological Review, 74,* 183–200.

Bem, D. J. (1972). Self–perception theory. In L. Berkowitz (Ed.), *Advances in experimental social psychology* (Vol. 6). New York: Academic Press.

Bem, D. J., & Allen, A. (1974). On predicting some of the people some of the time: The search for cross–situational consistencies in behavior. *Psychological Review, 81,* 506–520.

Bem, S. L. (1983). Gender schema theory and its implications for child development: Raising gender–aschematic children in a gender–schematic society. *Signs, Journal of Women in Culture and Society, 8,* 354–64.

Bem, S. L. (1985). Androgyny and gender schema theory: A conceptual and empirical integration. In T. B. Sonderegger (Ed.), *Nebraska symposium on motivation: Psychology and gender,* Vol. 32. Lincoln: University of Nebraska Press.

Benbow, C., & Stanley, J. (1983). Sex differences in mathematical reasoning ability: More facts. *Science, 222,* 1029–103O.

Bench C. J., Dolan, R. J., Raymond, J., Friston, K. J., & Frackowiack, R. S. (1990). Positron emission tomography in the study of brain metabolism in psychiatric and neuropsychiatric disorders. *British Journal of Psychiatry, 157,* 82–95.

Benedict, R. (1934). *Patterns of culture.* New York: Mentor/New American Library.

Benes, F. (1989). Myelination of cortical–hippocampal relays during late adolescence. *Schizophrenia Bulletin, 15,* 585–593.

Benes, F., Turtle, M., Khan, Y., & Farol, P. (1994). Myelination of a key relay zone in the hippocampal formation occurs in the human brain during childhood, adolescence, and adulthood. *Archives of General Psychiatry, 51,* 477–484.

Bennett, E. (1955). Discussion, decision, commitment and consensus in 'group decisions.' *Human Relations, 8,* 251–274.

Benschop, R. J., Jabaaij, L., Oostveen, F., & Vingerhoets, A. J. (1993). Psychobiological factors related to human natural killer cell activity and hormonal modulation of NK cells in vitro. *Life Sciences, 52,* 1825–1834.

Benson, D., Charlton, C., & Goodhart, F. (1992). Acquaintance rape on campus: A literature review. *Journal of American College Health, 40,* 157–165.

Benson, P. L., Karabenick, S. A., & Lerner, R. M. (1976). Pretty pleases: The effects of physical attractiveness, race, and sex on receiving help. *Journal of Experimental Social Psychology, 12,* 409–415.

Benton, M. K., & Schroeder, H. E. (1990). Social skills training with schizophrenics: A meta–analytic evaluation. *Journal of Consulting and Clinical Psychology, 58,* 741–747.

Berg, C. (1992). Perspectives for viewing intellectual development throughout the life course. In R. J. Sternberg & C. A. Berg (Eds.), *Intellectual development* (pp.1–15). New York: Cambridge University Press.

Berger, C. R. (1980). Power and the family. In M.E. Roloff and G.E. Miller (Eds.), *Persuasion: New directions in theory and research.* Beverly Hills, CA: Sage.

Berger, P. A. (1978). Medical treatment of mental illness. *Science, 200,* 974–981.

Bergin, A., & Garfield, S., (Eds.). (1994). *Handbook of psychotherapy and behavior change,* (4th ed.). New York: John Wiley.

Bergman, C. S., Chipuer, H. M., Plomin, R., Pedersen, N. L., et al. (1993). Genetic and environmental effects on openness to experience, aggreeableness, and conscientiousness: An adoption/twin study. *Journal of Personality, 61,* 159–179.

Berkowitz, L. (1972). Social norms, feelings, and other factors affecting helping and altruism. In L. Berkowitz (Ed.), *Advances in experimental social psychology,* Vol. 6. New York: Academic Press.

Berkowitz, L. (1982). Aversive conditions as stimuli to aggression. *Advances in Experimental Social Psychology, 15,* 249–289.

Berkowitz, L. (1989). Frustration–aggression hypothesis: Examination and reformulation. *Psychological Bulletin, 106,* 59–73.

Berkowitz, L., & Connor, W. H. (1966). Success, failure, and social responsibility. *Journal of Personality and Social Psychology, 4,* 664–669.

Berman, P. W., & Pedersen, F. A. (1987). Research on men's transitions to parenthood: An integrative discussion. In P.W. Berman & F.A. Pederson (Eds.), *Men's transitions to parenthood: Longitudinal studies of early family experience.* Hillsdale, NJ: Erlbaum.

Bermond, B., Fasotti, L., Nieuwenhuyse, B., & Schuerman, J. (1991). Spinal cord lesions, peripheral feedback and intensities of emotional feelings. *Cognition and Emotion, 5,* 201–220.

Berndt, T. J., & Heller, K. A. (1986). Gender stereotypes and social inferences: A developmental study. *Journal of Personality and Social Psychology, 50,* 889–898.

Bernstein, I. L. (1991). Aversion conditioning in response to cancer and cancer treatment. *Clinical Psychology Review, 11,* 185–191.

Berquier, A., & Ashton, R. (1992). Characteristics of the frequent nightmare sufferer. *Journal of Abnormal Psychology, 101,* 246–250.

Berridge, K., & Valenstein, E. (1991). What psychological process mediates feeding evoked by electrical stimulation of the lateral hypothalamus? *Behavioral Neuroscience, 105,* 3–14.

Berridge, K., & Zajonc, R. (1991). Hypothalamic cooling effects elicit eating: Differential effects on motivation and pleasure. *Psychological Science, 2,* 184–189.

Berry, D. S., & Pennebaker, J. W. (1993). Nonverbal and verbal emotional expression and health. *Psychotherapy and Psychosomatics, 59,* 11–19.

Berry, J. W. (1966). Temne and Eskimo perceptual skills. *International Journal of Psychology, 1,* 207–229.

Berry, J. W. (1979). A cultural ecology of social behavior. In L. Berkowitz (Ed.), *Advances in experimental social psychology,* Vol. 12. New York: Academic Press.

Berry, J. W. (1989). Psychology of acculturation. In J.Berman (Ed.), *Nebraska Symposium on Motivation,* Vol.37 (pp. 201–234). Lincoln: University of Nebraska Press.

Berry, J. W., & Bennet, J. A. (1992). Cree conceptions of cognitive competence. *International Journal of Psychology, 27,* 73–88.

Berry, J. W., & Irvine, S. H. (1986). Bricolage: Savages do it daily. In R. J. Sternberg, & R. K. Wagner (Eds.), *Practical Intelligence: Nature and Origins of Competence in the Everyday World* (pp. 271–305). New York: Cambridge University Press.

Berry, J. W., Poortinga, Y. H., Segall, M. H., & Dasen, P. R. (1992). *Cross–cultural psychology: Research and applications.* New York: Cambridge University Press.

Berscheid, E. (1985). Interpersonal attraction. In G. Lindzey and E. Aronson (Eds.), *Handbook of social psychology.* Reading, MA: Addison–Wesley.

Berscheid, E., Dion, K., Walster, E., & Walster, G. (1971). Physical attractiveness and dating choice: A test of the matching hypothesis. *Journal of Experimental Social Psychology, 7,* 173–189.

Besson, J., & Chaouch, A. (1987). Peripheral and spinal mechanisms of nociception. *Physiological Reviews, 67,* 67–186.

Best, D. L. (1993). Inducing children to generate mnemonic organizational strategies: An examination of long–term retention and materials. *Developmental Psychology, 29,* 324–336.

Best, D. L., & Williams, J. E. (in press). Cross–cultural viewpoint. In A. E. Beall & R. J. Steinberg (Eds.), *Perspectives on the psychology of gender.* New York: Guilford Press.

Best, D. L., Williams, J. E., Cloud, J. M., Davis, S.W., Robertson, L. S., Edwards, J. R., Giles, H., & Fowles, J. (1977). Development of sex–trait stereotypes among young children in the United States, England, and Ireland. *Child Development, 48,* 1375–1384.

Beutler, L. E. (1991). Have all won and must all have prizes? Revisiting Luborsky et al's verdict. *Journal of Consulting and Clinical Psychology, 59,* 226–232.

Beyene, Y. (1986). Cultural significance and physiological manifestations of menopause: A biocultural analysis. *Culture, Medicine, & Psychiatry, 10,* 47–71.

Beyer, C., Caba, M., Banas, C., & Komisaruk, B. R. (1991). Vasoactive intestinal polypeptide (VIP) potentiates the behavioral effect of substance P intrathecal administration. *Pharmacology, Biochemistry and Behavior, 39,* 695–698.

Bidell, T. R. & Fischer, K. W. (1992). Beyond the stage debate: Action, structure, and variability in Piagetian theory and research. In R. Sternberg & C. Berg (Eds.), *Intellectual development* (pp. 100–140). Cambridge: Cambridge University Press.

Biederman, I., Glass, A. L., & Stacy, E. W., Jr. (1973). Searching for objects in real–world scenes. *Journal of Experimental Psychology, 97,* 22–27.

Biederman, I., Mezzanotte, R. J., & Rabinowitz, J. C. (1982). Scene perception: Detecting and judging objects undergoing relational violations. *Cognitive Psychology, 14,* 143–177.

Biederman, I., Mezzanotte, R. J., Rabinowitz, J.C., Francolini, C.M., & Plude, D. (1981). Detecting the unexpected in photointerpretation. *Human Factors, 23,* 153–164.

Biederman, I., Rabinowitz, J.C., Glass, A. L., & Stacy, E. W., Jr. (1974). On the information extracted from a glance at a scene. *Journal of Experimental Psychology, 102,* 597–600.

Bierman, K. L., Miller, C. L., & Stabbo, S. D. (1987). Improving the social behavior and peer acceptance of rejected boys: Effects of social skill training with instructions and prohibitions. *Journal of Consulting and Clinical Psychology, 55,* 194–200.

Binder, A. (1988). Juvenile delinquency. *Annual Review of Psychology, 39,* 253–282.

Binet, A., & Simon, T. (1908). Le developpement de l'intelligence chez les enfants. *L'Annee Psychologique, 14,* 1–94.

Bingol, N., Fuchs, M., Diaz, V., Store, R., & Gromisch, D. (1987). Teratogenicity of cocaine in humans. *Journal of Pediatrics, 110,* 93–96.

Birenbaum, A., & Cohen, H.J. (1993). On the importance of helping families: Policy implications from a national study. *Mental Retardation, 31,* 67–74.

Birnbaum, D.W. (1983). Preschoolers` stereotypes about sex differences in emotinality: A reaffirmation. *Journal of Genetic Psychology, 143,* 139–140.

Bishop, J.A., & Cook, L.M. (1975). Moths, melanism and clean air. *Scientific American, 232,* 90–99.

Bixler, E., Kales, A., Soldatos, C., Kales, J., & Healey, S. (1979). Prevalence of sleep disorders in the Los Angeles metropolitan area. *American Journal of Psychiatry, 136,* 1257–1262.

Bjorklund, A., & Gage, F. (1985). Neural grafting of neurodegenerative diseases in animal models. *Annals of the New York Academy of Sciences, 457,* 53–81.

Bjorklund, D., & Harnishfeger, K. (1990). The resources construct in cognitive development: Diverse sources of evidence and a theory of inefficient inhibition. *Developmental Review, 10,* 48–71.

Black, B., & Hazen, N. (1990). Social status and patterns of communication in acquainted and unacquainted children. *Developmental Psychology, 27,* 379–387.

Black, D.W., Goldstein, R.B., & Mason, E.E. (1992). Prevalence of mental disorder in 88 morbidly obese bariatric clinic patients. *American Journal of Psychiatry, 149,* 227–234.

Blair, S. N., Kohl, H. W., Paffenbarger, R., Clark, D. G., Cooper, K. H., & Gibbons, L. W. (1989). Physical fitness and all–cause mortality: A prospective study of healthy men and women. *Journal of the American Medical Association, 262,* 2395–2401.

Blake, R., & Hirsch, H.V.B. (1975). Deficits in binocular depth perception in cats after alternating monocular deprivation. *Science, 190,* 1114–1116.

Blake, R., & Mouton, J. (1964). *The managerial grid.* Houston, Tex.: Gulf.

Blakemore, C., & Cooper, G.F. (1970). Development of the brain depends on the visual environment. *Nature, 228,* 477–478.

Blanchard, E. B., McCoy, G. C., Musso, A., Gerardi, M. A., Pallmeyer, T. P., Gerardi, R. J., Cotch, P. A., Siracusa, K., & Andrasik, F. (1986). A controlled comparison of thermal biofeedback and relaxation training in the treatment of essential hypertension: I. Short–term and long–term outcome. *Behavior Therapy, 17,* 563–579.

Bland, S. H., Krogh, V., Winkelstein, W., & Trevisan, M. (1991). Social network and blood pressure: A population study. *Journal of Psychosomatic Medicine, 53,* 598–607.

Blass, T. (1991). Understanding behavior in the Milgram obedience experiment: The role of personality, situations, and their interactions. *Journal of Personality and Social Psychology, 60,* 398–413.

Blatt, S. (1992). The differential effect of psychotherapy and psychoanalysis with anaclitic and introjective patients: The Menninger Psychotherapy Research Project revisited. *Journal of the American Psychoanalytic Association, 40,* 691–724.

Blatt, S., Ford, R., Berman, W., Cook. B., Cramer, P., & Robins, C.E. (1994). *Therapeutic change: An object relations perspective.* New York: Plenum Press.

Blatt, S., & Zuroff, D. (1992). Interpersonal relatedness and self–definition: Two prototypes for depression. *Clinical Psychology Review, 12,* 527–562.

Blatt, S. J., & Lerner, H. (1983). Investigations in the psychoanalytic theory of object relations and object representations. In J. Mashling (Ed.), *Empirical studies of psychoanalytic theories,* Vol. 1 pp. 189–249. Hillsdale, NJ: Erlbaum.

Blaustein, A. R., & Waldman, B. (1992). Kin recognition in anuran amphibians. *Animal Behaviour, 44,* 207–221.

Blehar, M. (1974). Anxious attachment and defensive reactions associated with daycare. *Child Development, 45,* 683–692.

Block, J. (1971). *Lives through time.* Berkeley, CA: Bancroft Books.

Block, J. (1977). Advancing the psychology of personality: Paradigmatic shift or improving the quality of research? In D. Magnusson & N. Endler (Eds.), *Psychology at the crossroads: Current issues in interactional psychology* (pp. 37–63). Hillsdale, NJ: Erlbaum.

Block, J., Block, J. H., & Keyes, S. (1988). Longitudinally foretelling drug usage in adolescence: Early childhood personality and environmental precursors. *Child Development, 59,* 336–355.

Block, J. H. (1978). Another look at sex differentiation in the socialization behaviors of mothers and fathers. In J. Sherman & F.L. Denmark (Eds.), *The psychology of women: Future directions of research.* New York: Psychological Dimensions.

Block, R., Farinpour, R., & Schlechte, J. (1991). Effects of chronic marijuana use of testosterone. *Drug and Alcohol Dependence, 28,* 121–128.

Block, R.I., Farinpour, R., & Schlechte, J.A. (1991). Effects of chronic marijuana use on testosterone, luteinizing hormone, follicle stimulating hormone, prolactin and cortisol in men and women. *Drug & Alcohol Dependence, 28,* 121–128.

Block, R., Farnham. S., & Braverman, K., &

Noyes, R. (1990). Long–term marijuana use and subsequent effects on learning and cognitive functions related to school achievement: Preliminary study. *National Institute on Drug Abuse Research Monograph Series,* Research Monograph 101, 96–111.

Blos, P. (1958). The second individuation process of adolescence. *Psychoanalytic Study of the Child, 22,* 162–186.

Blos, P. (1962). *On adolescence: A psychoanalytic interpretation.* New York: Free Press.

Blouin, A., Blouin, J., Aubin, P., Carter, J., Goldstein, C., Boyer, H., & Perez, E. (1992). Seasonal patterns of bulimia nervosa. *American Journal of Psychiatry, 149,* 73–81.

Blumer, D., & Benson, D. (1984). Personality changes with frontal and temporal lesions. In D. F. Benson & F. Blumer (Eds.), *Psychiatric aspects of neurologic disease.* New York: Grune & Stratton.

Blurton–Jones, N. & Konner, M. (1976). !Kung knowledge of animal behavior. In R. B. Lee & I. De Vore (Eds.), *Kalahari hunter–gatherers* (pp.326–348). Cambridge, MA: Harvard University Press.

Bock, P. (1988). *Rethinking psychological anthropology: Continuity and change in the study of human action.* San Francisco: Freeman.

Bodenhausen, G. (1993). Emotions, arousal, and stereotypic judgments: A heuristic model of affect and stereotyping. In D. Mackie & D. Hamilton (Eds.), *Affect, cognition, and stereotyping: Interactive processes in group perception.* New York: Academic.

Boersch, E. E. (1982). Ritual und Psychotherapie. *Zeitschrift fur Klinische Psychologie und Psychotherapie, 30,* 214–234.

Bohman, M. (1978). Some genetic aspects of alcoholism and criminality. *Archives of General Psychiatry, 35,* 269–276.

Bolles, R. C. (1970). Species–specific defense reactions and avoidance learning. *Psychological Review, 77,* 32–48.

Bolles, R. C. (1975). *Learning theory.* New York: Holt, Rinehart & Winston.

Bolton, W. & Oatley, K. (1987). A longitudinal study of social support and depression in unemployed men. *Psychological Medicine, 17,* 453–460.

Bondareff, W. (1985). The neural basis of aging. In J. Birren & K.W. Schaie (Eds.). *Handbook of the psychology of aging.* (2nd ed.). New York: Van Nostrand.

Bondareff, W., Raval, J., Woo, B., Hauser, D., & Colletti, P. (1990). Magnetic resonance imaging and the severity of dementia in older adults. *Archives of General Psychiatry, 47,* 47–51.

Borbely, A. (1986). *Secrets of sleep.* New York: Basic.

Boring, E. (1950). *A history of experimental psychology.* (2nd ed.). New York: Appleton–Century–Crofts.

Boring, E. G. (1930). A new ambiguous figure. *American Journal of Psychology, 42,* 444–445.

Borjeson, M. (1976). The aetiology of obesity in children. *Acta Paediatrica Scandinavica, 65,* 279–287.

Borkovec, T. D., & Costello, E. (1993). Efficacy of applied relaxation and cognitive–behavioral therapy in the treatment of generalized anxiety disorder. *Journal of Consulting and Clinical Psychology, 61,* 611–619.

Bornstein, M. H. (1989). Sensitive periods in development: Structural characteristics and causal interpretations. *Psychological Bulletin, 105,* 179–197.

Borod, J. (1992). Interhemispheric and intra-hemispheric control of emotion: A focus on unilateral brain damage. *Journal of Consulting and Clinical Psychology, 60,* 339–348.

Boszormenyi–Nagy, I., & Sparks, G. (1973). *Invisible loyalties.* New York: Harper & Row.

Bouchard, C. (1989). Genetic factors in obesity. *Medical Clinics of North America, 73,* 67–81.

Bouchard, T. J., Lykken, D. T., McGue, M. & Segal, N. L. (1990). Sources of human psychological differences: The Minnesota study of twins reared apart. *Science, 250,* 223–228.

Bouchard, T. J., Lykken, D. T., McGue, M. & Segal, N. L. (1991). Sources of human psychological differences: Response. *Science, 252,* 191–192.

Boulton, M. J., & Smith, P. K. (1990). Affective bias in children's perceptions of dominance relationships. *Child Development, 61,* 221–229.

Bourguignon, E. (1979). *Psychological anthropology: An introduction to human nature and cultural differences.* New York: Holt, Rinehart & Winston.

Bovbjerg, D., Redd, W. H., Maier, L. A., Holland J. C., Leske, L. M., Niedzwiecki, D., Rubin, S. C., & Herkes, T. B. (1990). Anticipatory immune suppression and nausea in women receiving cyclic chemotherapy for ovarian cancer. *Journal of Consulting and Clinical Psychology, 58,* 153–157.

Bowd, A. D. (1990). A decade of animal research in psychology: room for consensus? *Canadian Psychology, 31,* 74–82.

Bowden, S. C. (1990). Separating cognitive impairment in neurologically asymptomatic alcoholism from Wernicke–Korsakoff syndrome: Is the neuropsychological distinction justified? *Psychological Bulletin, 107,* 355–366.

Bowen, M. (1978). *Family therapy in clinical practice.* New York: Jason Aronson.

Bowen, M. (1991). Alcoholism as viewed through family systems theory and family psychotherapy. *Family Dynamics of Addiction Quarterly, 1,* 94–102.

Bower, B. (1991). Darwin's minds: Psychologists probe the descent of the human psyche. *Science News, 140,* 232–234.

Bower, G. (1975). Cognitive psychology: an introduction. In W.K. Estes, (Ed.), *Handbook of Learning and Cognitive Processes*, Vol. 1, Introduction to concepts and Issues (pp. 25–80). Hillsdale, NJ: Erlbaum.

Bower, G. H. (1970). Analysis of a mnemonic device. *American Scientist, 58,* 496–510.

Bower, G. H. (1981). Mood and memory. *American Psychologist, 36,* 129–148.

Bower, H. (1989). Beethoven's creative illness. *Australian and New Zealand Journal of Psychiatry, 23,* 111–116.

Bower, G. H. (1989). In search of mood–dependent retrieval. *Journal of Social Behavior & Personality, 4,* 121–156.

Bower, T. G. R. (1971). The object in the world of the infant. *Scientific American, 225,* 30–38.

Bower, T. G. R. (1982). *Development in infancy.* (2nd ed.). San Francisco: W. H. Freeman.

Bower, T. G. R., & Patterson, J. G. (1972). Stages in the development of the object concept. *Cognition, 1,* 47–55.

Bowers, J. S. & Schacter, D. L. (1990). Implicit memory and test awareness. *Journal of Experimental Psychology: Learning, Memory, and Cognition, 16,* 404–416.

Bowers, K. (1976). *Hypnosis for the seriously curious.* Monterey, CA: Brooks/Cole Publishing Co.

Bowers, K., & Meichenbaum, D. (1984). *The unconscious reconsidered.* New York: John Wiley.

Bowers, K. S. (1984). On being unconsciously informed and uninformed. In K. S. Bowers & D. Meichenbaum (Eds.), *The unconscious reconsidered.* New York: John Wiley.

Bowlby, J. (1969). *Attachment and loss.* Vol. I. *Attachment.* New York: Basic Books.

Bowlby, J. (1973). *Separation, attachment, and loss: Vol. 2.* New York: Basic Books.

Bowlby, J. (1979). *The making and breaking of affectional bonds.* London: Tavistock.

Bowlby, J. (1988). *A secure base: Parent–child attachment and healthy human development.* New York: Basic Books.

Bradberry, J. S. (1989). Gender differences in mathematical attainment at 16+. *Educational Studies, 15,* 301–314.

Bradbury, T., & Fincham, F. (1990). Attributions in marriage: Review and critique. *Psychological Bulletin, 107,* 3–33.

Brannigan, G., & Merrens, M. (Eds.) (1993). *The undaunted psychologist: Adventures in research.* Philadelphia: Temple University Press.

Bransford, J., & Johnson, M. K. (1972). Contextual prerequisites for understanding: Some investigations of comprehension and recall. *Journal of Verbal Learning and Verbal Behavior, 11,* 717–726.

Bransford, J. D., & Johnson, M. K. (1973). Consideration of some problems of comprehension. In W. Chase (Ed.), *Visual information processing.* New York: Academic Press.

Braungart, J., Plomin, R., DeFries, J., & Fulker, D. (1992). Genetic influence on tester–rated infant temperament as assessed by Bayley's infant behavior record: Nonadoptive and adoptive siblings and twins. *Developmental Psychology, 28,* 40–47.

Brazelton, T.B. (1972). Implications of infant development among the Mayan Indians of Mexico. *Human Development, 15,* 90–111.

Bregman, J. D. and Hodapp, R. M. (1991). Current developments in the understanding of mental retardation. *Journal of the American Academy of Child and Adolescent Psychiatry, 30,* 707–719.

Breier, A., Buchanan, R., Kirkpatrick, B., & Davis, O. (1994). Effects of Clozapine on positive and negative symptoms in outpatients with schizophrenia. *American Journal of Psychiatry, 151,* 20–26.

Breier, A., Schreiber, J. L., Dyer, J., & Pickar, D. (1991). National Institute of Mental Health Longitudinal Study of chronic schizophrenia: Prognosis and predictors of outcome. *Archives of General Psychiatry, 48,* 239–246.

Breier, A., Wolkowitz, O., Roy, A., Potter, W.Z., & Pickar, D. (1990). Plasma norepinephrine in chronic schizophrenia. *American Journal of Psychiatry, 147,* 1467–1470.

Breland, K., & Breland, M. (1961). The misbehavior of organisms. *American Psychologist, 16,* 681–684.

Brennan, W., Ames, E., & Moore, R. (1966). Age differences in infants' attention to patterns of different complexity. *Science, 151,* 354–356.

Brenner, C. (1982) *The mind in conflict.* New York: International Universities Press.

Breslau, N., Davis, G. C., Andreski, P., & Peterson, E. (1991). Traumatic events and posttraumatic stress disorder in an urban population of young adults. *Archives of General Psychiatry, 48,* 216–222.

Bretherton, I. (1985). Attachment theory: Retrospect and prospect. In I. Bretherton & E. Waters (Eds.), Growing points of attachment theory and research. *Monographs of the Society for Research in Child Development, 50* (1–2, serial No. 209), 3–35.

Bretherton, I. (1990). Communication patterns, internal working models, and the intergenerational transmission of attachment relationships. *Infant Mental Health Journal, 11,* 237–257.

Brett, E. A., Spitzer, R. L., & Williams, J.B.W. (1988). DSM–III–R criteria for posttraumatic stress disorder. *American Journal of Psychiatry, 145,* 1232–1236.

Breuer, K. (1985). Intentionality and perception in early infancy. *Human Development, 28,* 71–83.

Brewer, M. (1979). Ingroup bias in the minimal intergroup situation: A cognitive motivational analysis. *Psychological Bulletin, 86,* 307–324.

Brewer, M., & Kramer, R. M. (1985). The psychology of intergroup attitudes and behavior. *Annual Review of Psychology, 36,* 219–243.

Brewer, N. and Smith, J. M. (1989). Social acceptance of mentally retarded children in regular schools in relation to years mainstreamed. *Psychological Reports, 64,* 375–380.

Brewer, W. F., & Treyens, J. C. (1981). Role of schemata in memory for places. *Cognitive Psychology, 13,* 207–230.

Briere, J. & Conte, J. R. (1993). Self–reported amnesia for abuse in adults molested as children. *Journal of Traumatic Stress, 6,* 21–31.

Brim, O. G. (1976). Theories of the male mid–life crisis. *Counseling Psychologist, 6,* 2–9.

Brislin, R. W. (1986). The culture general assimilator: Preparation for various types of sojourns. Special issue: Theories and methods in cross–cultural orientation. *International Journal of Intercultural Relations, 10,* 215–234.

Brislin, R. W. & Keating, C. F. (1976). Cultural differences in the perception of a three–dimensional Ponzo illusion. *Journal of Cross–Cultural Psychology, 7,* 397–412.

Broadbent, D. E. (1958). The hidden preattentive processes. *American Psychologist, 32,* 109–118.

Broberg, A., Lamb, M. E., & Hwang, P. (1990). Inhibition: Its stability and correlates in sixteen– to forty–month–old children. *Child Development, 61,* 1153–1163.

Brodsky, S. L., Esquerre, J., & Jackson, R. R. (1990–1991). *Imagination, Cognition & Personality, 10,* 353–360.

Brody, L., & Hall, J. A. (1993). Gender and emotion. In M. Lewis & J. Haviland (Eds.), *Handbook of emotions* (pp. 447–460). New York: Guilford Press.

Bronfenbrenner, U. (1986). Ecology of the family as a context for human development: Research perspectives. *Developmental Psychology, 20,* 995–1003.

Broughton, J. (1978). Development of concepts of self, mind, reality, and knowledge. *New Directions for Child Development, 1,* 75–100.

Brown, A., Bransford, J., Ferrara, R., Campione, J. (1983). Learning, remembering, and understanding. In E. M. Markman, & J. H. Flavell (Eds.), *Carmichael's Manual of Child Psychology,* Vol. III. New York: John Wiley.

Brown, G., Bhrolchain, M., & Harris, T. (1975). Social class and psychiatric disturbance among women in an urban population. *Sociology, 9,* 225–54.

Brown, G. W., & Harris, T. O. (1978). *Social origins of depression: A study of* psychiatric disorder in women. New York: Free Press.

Brown, G. W., & Harris, T. O. (1989). Depression. In G. W. Brown & T. O. Harris (Eds.), Life events and illnesses. New York: Guilford Press.

Brown, J., & Smart, S. A. (1991). The self and social conduct: Linking self–representations to prosocial behavior. Journal of Personality and Social Psychology, 60, 368–375.

Brown, J. B. (1991). Staying fit and staying well: Physical fitness as a moderator of life stress. Journal of Personality and Social Psychology, 61, 555–561.

Brown, N. O. (1959). Life against death: The psychoanalytic meaning of history. Middleton, Conn.: Wesleyan University Press.

Brown, P. K., & Wald, G. (1964). Visual pigments in single rods and cones in the human retina. Science, 144, 45–52.

Brown, R. (1973). A first language: The early stages. Cambridge, MA: Harvard University Press.

Brown, R., & Chiesa, M. (1990). An introduction to repertory grid theory and technique. British Journal of Psychotherapy, 6, 411–419.

Brown, R., & Fraser, C. (1963). The acquisition of syntax. In C. N. Cofer & B. Musgrave (Eds.), Verbal behavior and learning: Problems and processes (pp. 158–201). New York: McGraw–Hill.

Brown, R., & Hanlon, C. (1970). Derivational complexity and order of acquisition in child speech. In J.R. Hayes (Ed.), Cognition and the development of language. New York: John Wiley.

Brown, R., & Kulik, J., (1977). Flashbulb memories. Cognition, 5, 73–99.

Brown, R.W., & McNeill, D. (1966). The tip–of–the–tongue phenomenon. Journal of Verbal Learning and Verbal Behavior, 5, 325–37.

Brownell, K., & Rodin, J. (1994). The dieting maelstrom: Is it possible and advisable to lose weight? American Psychologist, 49, 781–791.

Brownell, K. D., & Wadden, T. A. (1992). Etiology and treatment of obesity: Understanding a serious, prevalent, and refractory disorder. Journal of Consulting and Clinical Psychology, 60, 505–517.

Bruch, H. (1970). Eating disorders in adolescence. Proceedings of the American Psychopathology Association, 59, 181–202.

Bruch, H. (1973). Eating disorders: Obesity, anorexia nervosa, and the person within. New York: Basic Books.

Bruhn, A. R. (1992). The early memories procedure: A projective test of autobiographical memory: I. Journal of Personality Assessment, 58, 1–15.

Brundage, L. E., Derlega, V. J., & Cash, T. F. (1977). The effects of physical attractiveness and need for approval on self–disclosure. Personality and Social Psychology Bulletin, 3, 63–66.

Bruner, J. S. (1981). The social context of language acquisition. Language and Communication, 1, 155–178.

Bruner, J. S. (1983). Child's talk: Learning to use language. New York: Norton.

Bruner, J. S. (1992). Another look at New Look 1. American Psychologist, 47, 780–783.

Bruner, J. S., & Goodman, C. C. (1947). Value and need as organizing factors in perception. Journal of Abnormal and Social Psychology, 42, 33–44.

Brunstetter, R. W., & Silver, L. B. (1985). Attention deficit disorder. In H. I. Kaplan & B. J. Sadock (Eds.), Comprehensive textbook of psychiatry. (4th ed.). Baltimore, MD: Williams & Wilkins.

Bruyer, R. (1991). Covert face recognition in prosopagnosia: A review. Brain and Cognition, 15, 223–235.

Bruyer, R. et al. (1983). A case of prosopagnosia with some preserved covert remembrance of familiar faces. Brain and Cognition, 2, 257–284.

Buchan, H., Johnstone, E., McPherson, K., & Palmer, R. L. (1992). Who benefits from electroconvulsive therapy? Combined results of the Leicester and Northwick Park trials. British Journal of Psychiatry, 160, 355–359.

Buchsbaum, H.J. (1983). The menopause. New York.: Springer–Verlag.

Buck, R. (1986). The psychology of emotion. In J.E. LeDoux and W. Hirst (Eds.), Mind and brain: Dialogues in cognitive neuroscience. New York: Cambridge University Press.

Buck, R., Losow, J., & Murphy, M. (1992). Social facilitation and inhibition of emotional expression and communication. Journal of Personality and Social Psychology, 63, 962–968.

Buckhalt, J.A. (1991). Reaction time measures of processing speed: Are they yielding new information about intelligence? Personality and Individual Differences, 12, 683–688.

Buglass, D. (1977). A study of agoraphobic housewives. Psychological Medicine, 7, 73–86.

Buhrich, N., Bailey, J. M., Martin, N.G. (1991). Sexual orientation, sexual identity, and sex–dimorphic behaviors in male twins. Behavior Genetics, 21, 75–96.

Buhrmester, D. (1990). Intimacy of friendship, interpersonal competence, and adjustment during preadolescence and adolescence. Child Development, 61, 1101–1111.

Bukowski, W., Gauze, C., Hoza, B., & Newcomb, A. (1994). Differences and consistency between same–sex and other–sex peer relationships during early adolescence. Developmental Psychology, 29, 255–263.

Bunney, W., Goodwin, F., & Murphey, D.L. (1992). Affective illness: Two decades of psychobiological investigations. Pharmacopsychiatry, 25, 10–13.

Bunney, W. E. , Jr. (1981). Current biologic strategies for anxiety. Psychiatric Annals, 11, 21–29.

Burger, J. M. (1981). The low–ball compliance technique: Task or person commitment? Journal of Personality and Social Psychology, 492–500.

Burgess, P. R., & Perl, E. R. (1973). Cutaneous mechanoreceptors and nociceptors. In A. Iggo (Ed.), Handbook of sensory physiology. Berlin: Springer–Verlag.

Buri, J., Louiselle, P., Misukanis, T., & Mueller, R. (1988). Effects of parental authoritarianism on self–esteem. Personality and Social Psychology Bulletin, 14, 271–282.

Burke, W., & Cole, A. M. (1978). Extra–retinal influences on the lateral geniculate nucleus. Review of Physiology, Biochemistry, and Pharmacology, 80, 105–166.

Burkett, L. (1991). Parenting behaviors of women who were sexually abused as children in their families of origin. Family Process, 30, 421–434.

Burks, B. (1938). On the relative contributions of nature and nurture to average group differences in intelligence. Proceedings of the National Academy of Sciences, 24, 276–282.

Burks, B. S. (1928). The relative influence of nature and nurture upon mental development: A comparative study of foster parent–foster child resemblance and true parent–true child resemblance. 27th Yearbook of the National Society for the Study of Education, 27, 219–316.

Burns, D. D., & Nolan–Hoeksema, S. (1992). Therapeutic empathy and recovery from depression in cognitive–behavioral therapy: A structural equation model. Journal of Consulting and Clinical Psychology, 60, 441–449.

Bushman, B. J., & Cooper, H. M. (1990). Effects of alcohol on human aggression: An integrative research review. Psychological Bulletin, 107, 341–354.

Buss, D. (1989). Sex differences in human mate preferences: Evolutionary hypotheses tested in 37 cultures. Behavioral and Brain Sciences, 12, 1–49.

Buss, D. (1992). Manipulation in close relationships: Five personality factors in interactional context. Journal of Personality, 60, 477–499.

Buss, D. M. (1988). The evolution of human intrasexual competition: Tactics of mate attraction. Journal of Personality and Social Psychology, 54, 616–628.

Buss, D. M., & Schmitt, D. P. (1993). Sexual strategies theory: An evolutionary perspective on human mating. Psychological Review, 100, 1–29.

Buss, D.M. (1991). Conflict in married couples: Personality predictors of anger and upset. Journal of Personality, 58, 663–688.

Buss, D. M. (1991). Evolutionary personality psychology. Annual Review of Psychology, 42, 459–492.

Buss, D. M., & Barnes, M. (1986). Attraction as a linear function of proportion of positive reinforcements. Journal of Personality and Social Psychology, 50, 559–570.

Buss, D. M. (1988). Love act: The evolutionary biology of love. In R.J.Sternberg & M. L. Barnes (Eds.), *The anatomy of love*. New Haven, Conn.: Yale University Press.

Buss, D. M., Larsen, R. J., Westen, D., & Semmelroth, J. (1992). Sex differences in jealousy: Evolution, physiology, and psychology. *Psychological Science, 3*, 251–255.

Butler, C. A. (1976). New data about female sexual response. *Journal of Sex and Marital Therapy, 2*, 40–46.

Butler, R. N. (1969). Age–ism: Another form of bigotry. *The Gerontologist, 9*, 243–246.

Butler, R. N. (1975). *Why survive? Being old in America*. New York: Harper & Row.

Butler, R. N. (1984). Senile dementia: Reversible and irreversible. *Counseling Psychology, 12*, 75–79.

Butterworth, A. (1978). A review of a primer of infant development. *Perception, 17*, 363–364.

Bye, L., & Jussim, L. (1993). A proposed model for the acquisition of social knowledge and social competence. *Psychology in the Schools, 30*, 143–161.

Byne, W., & Parsons, B. (1993). Human sexual orientation: The biologic theories reappraised. *Archives of General Psychiatry, 50*, 228–239.

Byrne, D. et al. (1968). The effects of physical attractiveness, sex, and attitude similarity on interpersonal attraction. *Journal of Personality, 36*, 259–271.

Byrne, D., & Murnen, S. (1988). Maintaining loving relationships. In R. Sternberg & M.L. Barnes (Eds.), *The psychology of love* (pp. 293–310). New Haven, Conn.: Yale University Press.

Byrne, D., & Nelson, D. (1965). Attraction as a linear function of proportion of positive reinforcements. *Journal of Personality and Social Psychology, 1*, 659–663.

Cadoret, R., Troughton, E., O'Gorman, T., & Heywood, E. (1986). An adoption study of genetic and environmental factors in drug abuse. *Archives of General Psychiatry, 43*, 1131–1136.

Cadoret, R. J., O'Gorman, T. W., Troughton, E., & Heywood, E. (1985). Alcoholism and antisocial personality. *Archives of General Psychiatry, 42*, 161–167.

Caggiula, A. R., Epstein, L. H., Antelman, S., Seymour, M., & Taylor, S. S. (1991). Conditioned tolerance to the anorectic and corticosterone–elevating effects of nicotine. *Pharmacology, Biochemistry, and Behavior, 40*, 53–59.

Calabrese, J. R., & Delucchi, G. (1990). Spectrum of efficacy of valproate in 55 patients with rapid–cycling bipolar disorder. *American Journal of Psychiatry, 147*, 431–434.

Campbell, D. T. (1965). Ethnocentrism and other altruistic motives. In D. Levine (Ed.), *Nebraska symposium on motivation*, Vol. 13. Lincoln: University of Nebraska Press.

Campbell, D. T., & Stanley, J. C. (1963). *Experimental and quasiexperimental designs for research*. Chicago: Rand McNally.

Campbell, J. D. (1986). Similarity and uniqueness: The effects of attribute type, relevance, and individual differences in self–esteem and depression. *Journal of Personality and Social Psychology, 50*, 281–294.

Campbell, S. B. (1985). Hyperactivity in preschoolers: Correlates and prognostic implications. *Clinical Psychology Review, 5*, 405–428.

Campfield, L., Brandon, P., & Smith, F. J. (1985). On–line continuous measurement of blood glucose and meal pattern in free–feeding rats: The role of glucose in meal initiation. *Brain Research Bulletin, 14*, 605–617.

Campione, J. C., Brown, A. L., & Ferrara, R. A. (1982). Mental retardation and intelligence. In R. J. Sternberg (Ed.), *Handbook of human intelligence* (pp. 393–490). New York: Cambridge University Press.

Campos, J. J., Barrett, K. C., Lamb, M. E., Goldsmith, H. H., & Stenberg, C. (1983). Socioemotional development. In P.H. Mussen (Ed.), *Handbook of Child Psychology: Vol. II. Infancy and Developmental Psychobiology*. New York: John Wiley.

Canfield, R. L., & Ceci, S. J. (1992). Integrating learning into a theory of intellectual development. In R. J. Sternberg & C. A. Berg (Eds.), *Intellectual Development*. New York: Cambridge University Press.

Cannon, T. D., & Marco, E. (1994). Structural brain abnormalities as indicators of vulnerability to schizophrenia. *Schizophrenia Bulletin, 20*, 89–102.

Cannon, T. D., Mednick, S. A., Parnas, J., Schulsinger, F., Praestholm, J., & Vestergaard, A. (1993). Developmental brain abnormalities in the offspring of schizophrenic mothers. *Archives of General Psychiatry, 50*, 551–564.

Cannon, W., & Washburn, A. (1912). An explanation of hunger. *American Journal of Physiology, 29*, 441–454.

Cannon, W. B. (1927). The James–Lange theory of emotions: A critical examination and an alternative theory. *American Journal of Psychiatry, 39*, 106–124.

Cannon, W. B. (1932). *The wisdom of the body*. New York: W. W. Norton.

Cantor, N. (1990). From thought to behavior: Having and doing in the study of personality and cognition. *American Psychologists, 45*, 735–750.

Cantor, N., & Kihlstrom, J. F. (1987). Personality and social intelligence. Englewood Cliffs, NJ: Prentice–Hall.

Cantor, N., & Kihlstrom, J. F. (1989). Social intelligence and cognitive assessments of personality. In R. S. Wyer, Jr. & T. K. Skrull (Eds.), *Social intelligence and cognitive assessments of personality* (pp. 1–59) . Hillsdale, NJ: Erlbaum.

Cantor, N., & Mischel, W. (1979). Prototypes in person perception. In L. Berkowitz (Ed.), *Advances in experimental social psychology*, Vol. 12. New York: Academic Press.

Cantor, N., & Mischel, W. (1982). A prototype analysis of psychological situations. *Cognitive Psychology, 14*, 45–77.

Capaldi, E., & VandenBos, G. (1991). Taste, food exposure, and eating behavior. *Hospital and Community Psychiatry, 42*, 787–789.

Caplan, P. J. (1991). How do they decide who is normal? The bizarre, but true, tale of the DSM process. *Canadian Psychology, 32*, 162–170.

Caplow, T., Bahr, H. M., Chadwick, B. A., Hill, R., & Williamson, M. H. (1982). *Middletown families: Fifty years of change and Continuity*. Minneapolis: University of Minnesota Press.

Carbonell, V., Enrique, J., & Marti–Villalba, C. (1987). The Journal of American Psychology and the American experimental psychology between 1916 and 1945. *Revista de Historia de la Psicologia, 8*, 87–119.

Cardon, L. R., Fulker, D. W., DeFries, J. C., & Plomin, R. (1992). Multivariate genetic analysis of specific cognitive abilities in the Colorado Adoption Program at age 7. *Intelligence, 16*, 383–400.

Carlsmith, J. M., & Anderson, C. A. (1979). Ambient temperature and the occurrence of collective violence: A new analysis. *Journal of Personality and Social Psychology, 37*, 337–344.

Carlsmith, J. M., Ebbesen, E. B., Lepper, M. R., Zanna, M. P., Jonas, A. J., & Abelson, R. P. Dissonance reduction following forced attention to the dissonance. *Proceedings of the American Psychological Association*, 321–322.

Carlson, E. B., & Rosser–Hogan, R. (1991). Trauma experiences, posttraumatic stress, dissociation, and depression in Cambodian refugees. *American Journal of Psychiatry, 148*, 1548–1551.

Carlson, N. R. (1991). *Physiology of behavior*. (4th ed.). New York: Allyn & Bacon.

Carlson, S. (1990). Visually guided behavior of monkeys after early binocular visual deprivation. *International Journal of Neuroscience, 50*, 185–194.

Carone, B. J., Harrow, M., & Westermeyer, J. F. (1991). Posthospital course and outcome in schizophrenia. *Archives of General Psychiatry, 48*, 247–253.

Carpenter, W. T. (1992). The negative symptom challenge. *Archives of General Psychiatry, 49*, 236–237.

Carroll, J. B. (1982). The measurement of intelligence. In R. J. Sternberg, (Ed.), *Handbook of human intelligence* (pp. 29–120).. New York: Cambridge University Press.

Cartwright, D. (1979). Contemporary social psychology in historical perspective. *Social Psychology Quarterly, 42*, 82–93.

Carver, C. S., Scheier, M. F., & Weintraub, J.K. (1989). Assessing coping strategies:

A theoretically based approach. *Journal of Personality and Social Psychology, 56,* 267–283.

Carver, M., & Scheier, H. (1981). *Attention and self–regulation: A control–theory approach to human behavior.* New York: Springer–Verlag.

Case, R. (1978). Intellectual development from birth to adulthood: A neo–Piagetian interpretation. In R.S. Siegler (Ed.), *Children's thinking: What develops?* Hillsdale, NJ: Erlbaum.

Case, R. (1984). The process of stage transition: A neo–Piagetian view. In R. J. Sternberg (Ed.), *Mechanisms of cognitive development.* New York: Freeman.

Case, R. (1985). *Intellectual development: Birth to adulthood.* New York: Academic Press.

Case, R. (1992). Neo–Piagetian theories of child development. In R.J. Sternberg & C.A. Berg, *Intellectual development* (pp. 161–196). New York: Cambridge University Press.

Cash, T. F., Gillen, B., & Burns, D.S. (1977). Sexism and "beautyism" in personnel consultant decision making. *Journal of Applied Psychology, 62,* 301–310.

Casper, R.C., Hedeker, D., & McClough, J. F. (1992). Personality dimensions in eating disorders and their relevance for subtyping. *Journal of the American Academy of Child and Adolescent Psychiatry, 31,* 830–840.

Caspi, A., Elder, G. E., & Herbener, E. (1990). Childhood personality and the prediction of life–course patterns. In L.N. Robins & M. Rutter (Eds.), *Straight and devious pathways from childhood to adulthood* (pp. 13–35). New York: Cambridge University Press.

Caspi, A., Lynam, D., Moffitt, T., & Silva, P. (1993). Unraveling girls' delinquency: Biological, dispositional, and contextual contributions to adolescent misbehavior. *Developmental Psychology, 29,* 19–30.

Catania, J. A., Coates, T. J., Stall., R., Turner, H., Peterson, J., Hearst, N., Dolcini, M. M., Hudes, E., Gagnon, J., Wiley, J., & Groves, R. (1992). Prevalence of AIDS–related risk factors and condom use in the United States. *Science, 258,* 1101–1106.

Cattell, R. B. (1941). Some theoretical issues in adult intelligence testing. *Psychological Bulletin, 38,* 592.

Cattell, R. B. (1957). *Personality and motivation: Structure and measurement.* Yonkers–on–Hudson, NY: World Book Co.

Cattell, R. B. (1990). Advances in Cattellian personality theory. In L. Pervin (Ed.), *Handbook of personality: Theory and research* (pp. 101–110). New York: Guilford Press.

Ceci, S. J. (1990). Framing intellectual assessment in terms of a person–process–context model. *Educational Psychologist, 25,* 269–291.

Ceci, S. J., & Bronfenbrenner, U. (1991). On the demise of veryday memory: "The

rumors of my death are much exaggerated" (Mark Twain). *American Psychologist, 46,* 27–31.

Cerella, J. (1990). Aging and information–processing rate. In J. E. Birren & K. W. Schaie (Eds.), *Handbook of the psychology of aging.* (3rd ed.). New York: Van Nostrand Reinhold.

Cesi, S. J. & Bruck, M. (1993). Suggestibility of the child witness: A historical review and synthesis. *Psychological Bulletin, 113,* 403–439.

Chafel, J. (1992). Funding Head Start: What are the issues? *American Journal of Orthopsychiatry, 62,* 9–21.

Chaiken, S. (1980). Heuristic versus systematic information processing and the use of source versus message cues in persuasion. *Journal of Personality and Social Psychology, 39,* 752–766.

Chaiken, S., & Stangor, C. (1987). Attitudes and attitude change. *Annual Review of Psychology, 38,* 575–630.

Chambless, D. C. & Gillis, M. M. (1993). Cognitive therapy of anxiety disorders. *Journal of Consulting and Clinical Psychology, 61,* 248–260.

Chance, J. E., Turner, A. L., & Goldstein, A. G. (1982). Development of differential recognition for own– and other–race faces. *Journal of Psychology, 112,* 29–37.

Chance, P. (1988). *Learning and behavior,* (2nd ed.). Belmont, CA: Wadsworth.

Chaplin, W. F., John, O. P., & Goldberg, L. R. (1988). Conceptions of states and traits: Dimensional attributes with ideals as prototypes. *Journal of Personality and Social Psychology, 54,* 541–557.

Chapman, L., & Chapman, J. (1980). Scales for rating psychotic and psychotic–like experiences as continua. *Schizophrenia Bulletin, 6,* 476–489.

Chapman, L., Chapman, J., & Fowles, D. (1993). *Progress in experimental personality and psychopathology research,* Vol.16. New York: Springer.

Chase, M. H., & Morales, F. R. (1990). The atonia and myoclonia of active (REM) sleep. *Annual Review of Psychology, 41,* 557–584.

Chasnoff, J. (1988). Newborn infants with drug withdrawal symptoms. *Pediatrics in Review, 9,* 273–277.

Chess, S. & Thomas, A. (1986). *Temperament in clinical practice.* New York: Guilford Press.

Chess, S., & Thomas, A. (1987). *Origins and evolution of behavior disorders: From infancy to early adult life.* Cambridge, MA: Harvard University Press.

Chi, M.T.H. (1976). Short–term memory limitations in children: Capacity or processing deficits? *Memory and Cognition, 4,* 559–72.

Chi, M.T.H. (1978). Knowledge structures and memory development. In R. Siegler (Ed.), *Children's thinking: What deficits?* Hillsdale, NJ: Erlbaum.

Chi, M.T.H., Glaser, R., & Rees, E. (1982). Expertise in problem solving. In R. J.

Sternberg (Ed.), *Advances in the psychology of human intelligence,* Vol. 1 (pp. 7–76). Hillsdale, NJ: Erlbaum.

Chiu, L–H. (1990). A comparison of moral reasoning in American and Chinese school children. *International Journal of Adolescence and Youth, 2,* 185–198.

Chiu, L. (1988). Locus of control differences between American and Chinese adolescents. *Journal of Social Psychology, 128,* 411–413.

Chodoff, P. (1986). Survivors of the Nazi Holocaust. In R. H. Moos and J.A. Schaefer (Eds.), *Coping with life crises: An integrated approach.* New York: Plenum Press.

Chomsky, N. (1957). *Syntactic structures.* The Hague: Mouton.

Chomsky, N. (1959). Review of Skinner's Verbal Behavior. *Language, 35,* 26–58.

Chomsky, N. (1986). *Knowledge of language: Its nature, origins, and use.* New York: Praeger.

Christensen, A. (1988). Deception in psychological research: When is it justified? *Personality & Social Psychology Bulletin, 14,* 663–675.

Christianson, S. A. (1992). Emotional stress and eyewitness memory: A critical review. *Psychological Bulletin, 112(2)Z,* 284–309.

Christie, R., & Geis, F. L., Eds. (1970). *Studies in Machiavellianism.* New York: Academic.

Chu, J. A., & Dill, D. (1990). Dissociative symptoms in relation to childhood physical and sexual abuse. *American Journal of Psychiatry, 147,* 887–892.

Church, A. T., & Burke, P. J. (1994). Exploratory and confirmatory tests of the Big Five and Tellegen's three– and four–dimensional models. *Journal of Personality and Social Psychology, 66,* 93–114.

Cialdini, R. (1984). *Influence: How and why people agree to things.* New York: Morrow.

Cialdini, R. B., Petty, R. E., & Capiopppo, J. T. (1981). Attitude and attitude change. *Annual Review of Psychology, 32,* 357–404.

Cicirelli, V. (1991). Sibling relationships in adulthood. *Marriage and Family Review, 16,* 291–310.

Cillessen, A., van IJzendoorn, H. W. [sic], & van Lieshout, C. (1992). Heterogeneity among peer–rejected boys: Subtypes and stabilities. *Child Development, 63,* 893–905.

Clark, A. S., & Goldman–Rakic, P. (1989). Gonadal hormones influence the emergence of cortical function in nonhuman primates. *Behavioral Neuroscience, 103,* 1287–1295.

Clark, D. B., & Agras, W. S. (1991). The assessment and treatment of performance anxiety in musicians. *American Journal of Psychiatry, 148,* 598–605.

Clark, H. H., & Clark, E. V. (1977). *Psychology and language.* New York: Harcourt Brace Jovanovich.

Clark, M. S., & Pataki, S. (1995). Interpersonal processes influencing attraction and relationships. In A. Tesser (Ed.), *Advanced social psychology*. New York: McGraw–Hill.

Clark, R., & Hatfield, E. (1989). Gender differences in receptivity to sexual offers. *Journal of Psychology & Human Sexuality, 2,* 39–55.

Clark, R. D., III, & Word, L. E. (1972). Why don't bystanders help? Because of ambiguity? *Journal of Personality and Social Psychology, 24,* 392–400.

Clark, R. D., III, & Word, L. E. (1974). Where is the apathetic bystander? Situational characteristics of the emergency. *Journal of Personality and Social Psychology, 29,* 279–287.

Clarkin, J., Frances, A., & Perry, S. (1992). Differential therapeutics: Macro and micro levels of treatment planning. In J. Norcross & M. Goldfried (Eds.), *Handbook of psychotherapy integration* (pp. 463–502). New York: Basic Books.

Clayton, P. J., Desmarais, L. & Winokur, G. (1968). A study of bereavement. *American Journal of Psychiatry, 125,* 168–178.

Clayton, P. J., Halikas, J. A., & Maurice, W. L. (1972). The depression of widowhood. *British Journal of Psychiatry, 120,* 71–78.

Cleghorn, J. M., Peterfy, G., Pinter, E. J., & Pattee, C. J. (1970). Verbal anxiety and the beta adrenergic receptors: A facilitating mechanism? *Journal of Nervous and Mental Disease, 151,* 266–272.

Clifford, M. M., & Walster, E. (1973). The effect of physical attractiveness on teacher expectations. *Sociological Education, 46,* 248–258.

Clomipramine Collaborative Study Group. (1991). Comipramine in the treatment of patients with obsessive–compulsive disorder. *Archives of General Psychiatry, 48,* 730–738.

Cloninger, C. R., Bohman, M., & Sigvardsson, S. (1981). Inheritance of alcohol abuse. *Archives of General Psychiatry, 38,* 861–868.

Clover, R., Abell, T., Becker, L. A., & Crawford, S. (1989). Family functioning and stress as predictors of influenza B infection. *Journal of Family Practice, 28,* 535–539.

Clum, G., Clum, G., & Surls, R. (1993). A meta–analysis of treatments for panic disorder. *Journal of Consulting and Clinical Psychology, 61,* 317–326.

Coccarro, E. F., Siever, L. J., Klar, H. M., Maurer, G., Cochrane, K., Cooper, T. B., Mohs, R.C., & Davis, K. L. (1989). Serotonergic studies on patients with affective and personality disorders: Correlates with suicidal and impulsive aggressive behavior. *Archives of General Psychiatry, 46,* 587–599.

Cohen, A. R. (1957). Need for cognition and order of communication as a determinant of opinion change. In C.I. Hovland (Ed.) *Order of presentation in persuasion.* New Haven, Conn.: Yale University Press.

Cohen, D. (1983). *Piaget: Critique and reassessment.* New York: St. Martin's Press.

Cohen, L. B., Diehl, R. L., Oakes, L. M., & Loehlin, J. L. (1992). Infant perception of /aba/ versus /apa/: Building a quantitative model of infant categorical discrimination. *Developmental Psychology, 28,* 261–272.

Cohen, L. J., Test, M. A., & Brown, R. L. (1990). Suicide and schizophrenia: Data from a prospective community treatment study, *American Journal of Psychiatry, 147,* 602–607.

Cohen, R. M., Gross, M., Nordahl, T., Semple, W., Oren, D., & Rosenthal, N. (1992). Preliminary data on the metabolic brain pattern of patients with Winter seasonal affective disorder. *Archives of General Psychiatry, 49,* 545–552.

Cohen, S., Tyrrell, D.A.J., & Smith, A. P. (1991). Psychological stress and susceptibility to the common cold. *New England Journal of Medicine, 325,* 606–612.

Cohen, S., & Williamson, G.M. (1991). Stress and infectious disease in humans. *Psychological Bulletin, 109,* 5–24.

Cohen, S. & Wills, T. A. (1985). Stress, social support, and the buffering hypothesis. *Psychological Bulletin, 98,* 310–357.

Cohn, L. D. (1991). Sex differences in the course of personality development: A meta–analysis. *Psychological Bulletin, 109,* 252–266.

Cohn, T. E., & Lasley, D. J. (1986). Visual sensitivity. *Annual Review of Psychology, 37,* 495–521.

Coie, J., & Dodge, K. (1983). Continuities and changes in children's social status: A five year longitudinal study. *Merrill–Palmer Quarterly, 29,* 261–282.

Colby, A., & Kohlberg, L. (1984). Invariant sequence and internal consistency in moral judgment stages. In W. M. Kurtines & J.L. Gewirtz (Eds.), *Morality, moral behavior and moral development.* New York: John Wiley.

Cole, D. (1991). Underground potlatch: How the Kwakiutl kept the faith. *Natural History, 100,* 50–53.

Cole, M. (1975). An ethnographic psychology of cognition. In R. Brislin et al. (Eds.), *Cross–cultural Perspectives on Learning.* New York: Sage Publications.

Cole, M., & Bruner, J.S. (1971). Cultural differences and inferences about psychological processes. *American Psychologist, 26,* 867–876.

Cole, M., & Scribner, S. (1974). *Culture and thought: A psychological introduction.* New York: John Wiley.

Cole, M., Gay, J., Glick, J. A., & Sharp, D. W. (1971). *The cultural context of learning and thinking.* New York: Basic Books.

Coleman, E., & Remafedi, G. (1989). Gay, lesbian, and bisexual adolescents: A critical challenge to counselors. *Journal of Counseling & Development, 68,* 36–40. .

Collett, T. S., & Baron, J. (1994). Biological compasses and the coordinate frame of landmark memories in honeybees. *Nature, 368,* 137–140.

Collings, G. (1989). Stress containment through meditation. *Prevention in Human Services, 6,* 141–150.

Collins, A., & Loftus, E. F. (1975). A spreading–activation theory of semantic processing. *Psychological Review, 82,* 407–428.

Collins, R. L., Lapp, W. M., Emmons, K. M., & Isaac, L. M. (1990). Endorsement and strength of alcohol expectancies. *Journal of Studies on Alcohol, 51,* 336–342.

Collins, W. A., & Gunnar, M. R. (1990). Social and personality development. *Annual Review of Psychology, 41,* 387–416.

Cologer–Clifford, A., Simon, N., & Jubilan, B. (1992). Genotype, uterine position, and testosterone sensitivity in older female mice. *Physiology and Behavior, 51,* 1047–1050.

Colvin, C.R. (1993). Judgable people: Personality, behavior, and competing explanations. *Journal of Personality and Social Psychology, 64,* 861–873.

Comaroff, J. (1980). Healing and the cultural order: The case of the Barolong boo Ratshidi of Southern Africa. *American Ethnologist, 7,* 637–657.

Compton, W. M., Helzer, J., Hai–Gwo, H., Eng–Kung, Y., McEvoy, L., Tipp, J., & Spitznagel, E. (1991). New methods in cross–cultural psychiatry: Psychiatric illness in Taiwan and the United States. *American Journal of Psychiatry, 148,* 1697–1704.

Conger, J. J. (1981). Freedom and commitment: Families, youth and social change. *American Psychologist, 36,* 1475–1484.

Conger, R., Conger, K., Elder, G., Lorenz, F., Simons, R., & Whitbeck, L. (1993). Family economic stress and adjustment of early adolescent girls. *Developmental Psychology, 29,* 206–219.

Conley, J. J. (1985). Longitudinal stability of personality traits: A multitrait–multimethod–multioccasion analysis. *Journal of Personality and Social Psychology, 49,* 1266–1282.

Contrada, R., Leventhal, H., & O'Leary, A. (1990). Personality and health. In L. Pervin (Ed.), *Handbook of personality: Theory and research* (pp. 638–669). New York: Guilford Press.

Conway, M. A. (1991). In defense of everyday memory. *American Psychologist, 46,* 19–26.

Cooley, C. H. (1902). *Human nature and the social order.* New York: Scribner's.

Coombs, G. (1980). Decision theory and subsistence strategies: Some theoretical considerations. In T. Earle & A. Christenson (Eds.), *Modeling change in prehistoric subsistence economies.* New York: Academic Press.

Coon, H., Fulker, D. W., DeFries, J.C. & Plomin, R. (1990). Home environment and environmental etiologies. *Developmental Psychology, 26,* 459–468.

Cooper, J., Bloom, F., & Roth, R. (1991). *The biochemical basis of neuropharmacol-*

ogy. (6th ed.). New York: Oxford University Press.

Cooper, J., & Croyle, R. T. (1984). Attitudes and attitude change. *Annual Review of Psychology, 35, 395–426.*

Cooper, L. A. (1975). Mental rotation of random two–dimensional shapes. *Cognitive Psychology, 7, 20–43.*

Cooper, L. A. (1976). Demonstration of a mental analog of an external rotation. *Perception and Psychophysics, 19, 296–302.*

Cooper, L. A., & Shepard, R. N. (1973). Chronometric studies of the rotation of mental images. In W. G. Chase (Ed.), *Visual information processing.* New York: Academic.

Cooper, L. A., & Shepard, R. N. (1973). The time required to prepare for a rotated stimulus. *Memory and Cognition, 1, 246–250.*

Cooper, M. L., Russell, M., Skinner, J. B., Frone, M. R., & Mudar, P. (1992). Stress and alcohol use: Moderating effects of gender, coping, and alcohol expectancies. *Journal of Abnormal Psychology, 101, 139–152.*

Coopersmith, S. (1967). *The antecedents of self–esteem.* San Francisco: Freeman.

Cornblatt, B. A., & Kelip, J. G. (1994). Impaired attention, genetics, and the pathophysiology of schizophrenia. *Schizophrenia Bulletin, 20, 31– 46.*

Corter, J. E. & Gluck, M. A. (1992). Explaining basic categories: Feature predictability and information. *Psychological Bulletin, 111, 291–303.*

Coryell, W., Endicott, J., Keller, M., Andreason, N., Grove, W., Hirschfeld, R., & Scheftner, W. (1989). Bipolar affective disorder and high achievement: A familial association. *American Journal of Psychiatry, 146, 983–988.*

Coryell, W., Endicott, J., & Winokur, G. (1992). Anxiety syndromes as epiphenomena of primary major depression: Outcome and familial psychopathology. *American Journal of Psychiatry, 149, 100–107.*

Cosmides, L. (1989). The logic of social exchange: Has natural selection shaped how humans reason? Studies with the Wason selection task. *Cognition, 31, 187–276.*

Cosmides, L., & Tooby, J. (1992). Cognitive adaptations for social exchange. In J.Barkow, L. Cosmides, & J. Tooby (Eds.), *The adapted mind: Evolutionary psychology and the generation of culture.* (pp. 117–182). New York: Oxford University Press.

Costa, P. T. Jr., & McCrae, R. R. (1987). Neuroticism, somatic complaints, and disease: Is the bark worse than the bite? Special issue: Personality and physical health. *Journal of Personality, 55, 299–316.*

Costa, P. T. Jr., & McCrae, R. R. (1988). Personality in adulthood: A six–year longitudinal study of self–reports and spouse ratings on the NEO Personality Inventory.

Journal of Personality and Social Psychology, 54, 853–863.

Costa, P. T. Jr., & McCrae, R. R. (1990). Personality: Another "hidden factor" in stress research. *Psychological Inquiry, 1, 22–24.*

Costermans, J., Lories, G., & Ansay, C. (1992). Confidence level and feeling of knowing in question answering: The weight of inferential processes. *Journal of Experimental Psychology: Learning, Memory, & Cognition, 18, 142–150.*

Cotman, C. W. (1990). Synaptic plasticity, neurotropic factors, and transplantation in the aged brain. In E. L. Schneider & J. W. Rowe (Eds.), *Handbook of the biology of aging* (3rd ed.). San Diego: Academic Press.

Cousins, S. (1989). Culture and self–perception in Japan and the United States. *Journal of Personality and Social Psychology, 56, 124–131.*

Cowan, N. (1984). On short and long auditory stores. *Psychological Bulletin, 96, 341–370.*

Cowan, W. M. (1979). The development of the brain. *Science American, 241, 112–33.*

Cowey, A. (1991). Grasping the essentials. *Nature, 349, 102–103.*

Cox, J. R. & Griggs, R. A. (1982). The effects of experience on performance in Wason's selection task. *Memory and Cognition, 10, 496–502.*

Cox, M. J., Owen, M. T., Henderson, V.., & Margand, N. (1992). Prediction of infant–father and infant–mother attachment. *Developmental Psychology, 28, 474–483*

Coyle, J. (1991). Molecular biological and neurobiologic contributions to our understanding of Alzheimer's disease. In A. Tasman & S. Goldfinger, (Eds.), *American Psychiatric Press Review of Psychiatry*, Vol. 10 (pp. 515–527). Washington, DC: American Psychiatric Press.

Coyle, J, Oster–Granite, M, Reeves, R, & Gearhart, J. (1988). Down syndrome, Alzheimer's disease and the trisomy 16 mouse. *Trends in Neurosciences, 11, 390–394.*

Coyle, J. Y., Price, D. L., & DeLong, M. R. (1983). Alzheimer's disease: A disorder of cortical cholinergic innervation. *Science, 219, 1184–1190.*

Craik, F.I.M. & Tulving, E. (1975). Depth of processing and the retention of words in episodic memory. *Journal of Experimental Psychology: General, 104, 268–294.*

Cramer, P. (1991). *The development of defense mechanisms: Theory, research, and assessment.* New York: Springer–Verlag.

Cramer, P. (in press). Identity, narcissism, and defense mechanisms in late adolescence. *Journal of Research in Personality.*

Crandall, C. (1994). Prejudice against fat people: Ideology and self–interest. *Journal of Personality and Social Psychology, 66, 882–894.*

Crescimmano, G., Piazza, P., Benigno, A., &

Amato, G. (1986). Effects of substantia nigra stimulation on hypothalamic rage in cats. *Physiology and Behavior, 37, 129–133.*

Crick, F., & Mitchison, G. (1983). The function of dream sleep. *Nature, 304, 111–114.*

Crick, N., & Dodge, K. (1994). A review and reformulation of social information–processing mechanisms in children's social adjustment. *Psychological Bulletin, 115, 74–101.*

Crits–Christoph, P. (1992). The efficacy of brief dynamic psychotherapy: A meta–analysis. *American Journal of Psychiatry, 149, 151–158.*

Crook, T. H., Youngjohn, J., Larrabee, G., & Salama, M. (1992). Aging and everyay memory. *Neuropsychology, 6, 123–136.*

Cross–national Collaborative Group (1992). The changing rate of major depression: Cross–national comparisons. *Journal of the American Medical Association, 268, 3098–3105.*

Crow, S. M., Fok, L., Hartman, S. J., & Payne, D. (1991). Gender and values: What is the impact on decision making? *Sex Roles, 25, 255–268.*

Crow, T. J. (1980). Molecular pathology of schizophrenia: More than one disease process? *British Medical Journal, 280, 66–68.*

Crow, T. J. (1986). The continuum of psychosis and its implication for the structure of the gene. *British Journal of Psychiatry, 149, 419–429.*

Crow, T. J. (1990). The continuum of psychosis and its genetic origins. *British Journal of Psychiatry, 156, 788–797.*

Crowe, S. J., Guild, S. R., & Polvost, C. M. (1934). Observations on the pathology of high–tone deafness. *Bulletin of the Johns Hopkins Hospital, 54, 315–379.*

Crowell, J. A., & Feldman, S. S. (1991). Mothers' working models of attachment relationships and mother and child behavior during separation and reunion. *Developmental Psychology, 27, 597–605.*

Crowne, D. P., & Marlow, D. (1964). *The approval motive: Studies in evaluative dependence.* New York: John Wiley.

Croyle, R., & Cooper, J. (1983). Dissonance arousal: Physiological evidence. *Journal of Personality and Social Psychology, 45, 782–791.*

Csikszentmihalyi, M. (1992). *Validity and reliability of the Experience Sampling Method.* Cambridge: Cambridge University Press.

Csikszentmihalyi, M., & Larson, R. (1984). *Being adolescent: Conflict and growth in the teenage years.* New York: Basic Books.

Culp, R. E., Watkins, R. V., Lawrence, H., & Letts, D. (1991). Maltreated children's language and speech development: Abused, neglected, and abused and neglected. *First Language, 11, 377–389.*

Cummings, J. L. (1992). Depression and Parkinson's disease: A review. *American Journal of Psychiatry, 149, 443–454.*

Cummins, R. A., Livesey, P. J., & Evans, J. G. M. (1977). A developmental theory of environmental enrichment. *Science, 197,* 692–694.

Cunningham, M. R. (1979). Weather, mood, and helping behavior: The sunshine Samaritan. *Journal of Personality and Social Psychology, 37,* 1947–1956.

Curran, J. P., & Lippold, S. (1975). The effects of physical attraction and attitude similarity on attraction in dating dyads. *Journal of Personality and Social Psychology, 43,* 528–539..

Curry, S. J. (1993). Self–help interventions for smoking cessation. *Journal of Consulting and Clinical Psychology, 61,* 790–803.

Curtis, R. C., Ed. (1991). *The relational self: Theoretical convergences in psychoanalysis and social psychology.* New York.: Guilford Press.

Curtiss, S. (1977). *Genie: A psycholinguistic study of a modern–day wild child.* New York: Academic Press.

Cutting, J. E. (1987). Perception and information. *Annual Review of Psychology, 38,* 61–90.

D'Emilio, J., & Freedman, E. (1988). *Intimate matters: A history of sexuality in America.* New York: Harper & Row.

D'Zurilla, T., & Sheedy, C. (1991). Relation between social problem–solving and subsequent level of psychological stress in college students. *Journal of Personality and Social Psychology, 61,* 841–846.

Daiguji, M. (1990). Significance of the affinity of the epileptic to somatesthetic religion. *Psychopathology, 23,* 176–180.

Daly, M., & Wilson, M. (1983). *Sex, evolution, and behavior.* Boston: Willard Grant Press.

Daly, M., & Wilson, M. (1988). Evolutionary social psychology and family homicide. *Science, 242,* 519–524.

Damasio, A. R. (1994). *Descartes' error: Emotion, reason, and the human brain.* New York: Grosset/Putnam.

Damon, W. (1977). *The social world of the child.* San Francisco: Jossey–Bass.

Damon, W., & Hart, D. (1982). The development of self–understanding from infancy through adolescence. *Child Development, 53,* 841–864.

Damon, W., & Hart, D. (1988). Self–understanding in childhood and adolescence. New York: Cambridge University Press.

Darley, J., & Schultz, T. R. (1990). Moral rules: Their content and acquisition. *Annual Review of Psychology, 41,* 525–556.

Darling, C. A., Davidson, J. K., & Jennings, D. A. (1991). The female sexual response revisited: Understanding the multiorgasmic experience in women. *Archives of Sexual Behavior, 20,* 527–540.

Darou, W. G. (1992). Native Canadians and intelligence testing. *Canadian Journal of Counselling, 26,* 96–99.

Dartnall, H.J.A., Bowmaker, J. K., & Mollon, J. D. (1983). Human visual pigments: Microspectrophotometric results from the eyes of seven persons. *Proceedings of the Royal Society of London, 220,* 115–130.

Darwin, C. (1859). *On the origin of species.* New York: New York University Press, 1988.

Darwin, C. (1872). *The expression of the emotions in man and animals.* London: John Murray/Julian Friedmann, 1979.

Darwin, C. J., Turvey, M. T., & Crowder, R.G. (1972). An auditory analogue of the Sperling partial report procedure: Evidence for brief auditory storage. *Cognitive Psychology, 3,* 255–267.

Dasen, P. (1975). Concrete operational development in three cultures. *Journal of Cross–Cultural Psychology, 6,* 156–172.

Dasen, P. & Heron, A. (1981). Cross–cultural tests of Piaget's theory. In H.C. Triandis & A. Heron (Eds.), *Handbook of cross–cultural psychology:* Vol. 4, *Developmental psychology.* Boston: Allyn & Bacon.

Davanloo, H. (1985). Short–term dynamic psychotherapy. In H.I. Kaplan & B.J. Sadock (Eds.), *Comprehensive Textbook of Psychiatry.* (4th ed.). Baltimore, MD: Williams & Wilkins.

Davidson, A. R., & Thomson, E. (1980). Cross–cultural studies of attitudes and beliefs. In H. C. Triandis & R. W. Brislin (Eds.), *Handbook of cross–cultural psychology,* Vol. 5. Boston: Allyn & Bacon.

Davidson, M., Kahn, R., Knott, P., Kaminsky, R., Cooper, M., DuMont, K., Apter, S., & Davis, K. L. (1991). Effects of neuroleptic treatment on symptoms of schizophrenia and plasma homovanillic acid concentrations. *Archives of General Psychiatry, 48,* 910–913.

Davidson, M., Stern, R. G., Bierer, L., & Horvath, T. (1991). Cholinergic strategies in the treatment of Alzheimer's disease. *Acta Psychiatrica Scandinavica, 83* (Supplement), 47–50.

Davidson, R. (1992). Emotion and affective style: Hemispheric substrates. *Psychological Science, 3,* 39–43.

Davidson, R. J. (1992). Emotion and affective style: Hemispheric substrates. *Psychological Science, 3,* 39–43.

Davis, D. L., & Whitten, R. G. (1987). The cross–cultural study of human sexuality. *Annual Review of Anthropology, 16,* 69–98.

Davis, J. M. (1985). Minor tranquilizers, sedatives, and hypnotics. In H. I. Kaplan, & B. J. Sadock (Eds.), *Comprehensive textbook of psychiatry.* (4th ed.). Baltimore, MD: Williams & Wilkins.

Davis, K. L., Kahn, R. S., Ko, G., & Davidson, M. (1991). Dopamine in schizophrenia: A review and reconceptualization. *American Journal of Psychiatry, 148,* 1474–1486.

Davis, M. (1992). The role of the amygdala in fear and anxiety. *Annual Review of Neuroscience, 15,* 353–375.

Davis, S. (1990). Men as success objects and women as sex objects: A study of personals advertisements. *Sex Roles, 23,* 43–50.

Dawson, J. (1975). Socioeconomic differences in size judgments of discs and coins by Chinese primary VI children in Hong Kong. *Perceptual and Motor Skills, 41,* 107–110.

Day, N., Richardson, G., Goldschmidt, L, Robels, N., et al. (1994). Effect of prenatal marijuana exposure on the cognitive development of offspring at age three. *Neurotoxicology and Teratology, 16,* 169–175.

Day, N. L., & Richardson, G. A. (1994). Comparative teratogenicity of alcohol and other drugs. *Alcohol Health and Research World, 18,* 42–48.

De Casper, A., & Fifer, W. (1980). Of human bonding: newborns prefer their mothers'voices. *Science, 208,* 1174–76.

de Castro, J., & Brewer, M. (1992). The amount eaten in meals by humans is a power function of the number of people present. *Physiology and Behavior, 51,* 121–125.

Deaux, K. (1976). Sex: A perspective on the attribution process. In J. H. Harvey, W. J. Ickes, & R. F. Kidd (Eds.), *New directions in attribution research* (Vol. 1). Hillsdale, NJ: Erlbaum.

deBenedittis, G., & Lorenzetti, A. (1992). The role of stressful life events in the persistence of primary headache: Major events vs. daily hassles. *Pain, 51,* 35–42.

Deci, E. L., & Ryan, R.M. (1985). *Intrinsic motivation and self–determination in human behavior.* New York: Plenum Press.

Decker, A., Connor, D., & Thal, L (1991). The role of cholinergic projections from the nucleus basalis in memory. *Neuroscience & Behavioral Reviews, 15,* 299–317.

DeLander, G. E., & Wahl, J. (1991). Descending systems activated by morphine (ICV) inhibit kainic acid (IT)–induced behavior. *Pharmacology, Biochemistry and Behavior, 39,* 155–159.

Delgado, P., Charney, D., Price, L., Aghajanian, G., Landis, H., & Heninger, R. (1990). Serotonin function and the mechanism of antidepressant action. *Archives of General Psychiatry, 47,* 411–418.

Dell, G. S. (1986). A spreading activation theory of retrieval in sentence production. *Psychological Review, 93*(3), 283–321.

DeLongis, A., Folkman, S., & Lazarus, R. S. (1988). The impact of daily stress on health and mood: Psychological and social resources as mediators. *Journal of Personality and Social Psychology, 54*(3), 486–495.

DeLucia, P. R., & Hochberg, J. (1991). Geometrical illusions in solid objects under ordinary viewing conditions. *Perception and Psychophysics, 50,* 547–554.

Dembroski, T. M. & Costa, P. T. (1987). Coronary prone behavior: Components of the Type A pattern and hostility. *Journal of Personality, 55,* 211–235.

Dement, W. C., & Kleitman, N. (1957). The relation of eye movements during sleep to dream activity: An objective method for the study of dreaming. *Journal of Experimental Psychology, 55,* 543–553.

Dement, W. C., & Wolpert, E.A. (1958). The relation of eye movements, body motility, and external stimuli to dream content. *Journal of Experimental Psychology, 55,* 543–553.

Deming, W. (1986). *Out of crisis.* Cambridge, MA: MIT Press.

Demorest, M. E. (1986). Problem solving: Stages, strategies, and stumbling blocks. *Journal of Academic Rehabilitation Audiology, 19,* 13–26.

Denham, S., & Holt, R. W. (1993). Preschoolers' likability as cause or consequence of their social behavior. *Developmental Psychology, 29,* 271–275.

Denney, N. R., & Denney, N. W. (1973). The use of classification for problem solving: A comparison of middle and old age. *Developmental Psychology, 9,* 275–278.

Denney, N. W. & Palmer, A. M. (1981). Adult age differences on traditional and practical problem–solving measures. *Journal of Gerontology, 36,* 323–28.

Denning, P. J. (1986). The science of computing: Expert systems. *American Scientist, 74,* 18–20.

Deregowski, J. B. (1970). Effect of cultural value of time upon recall. *British Journal of Social and Clinical Psychology, 9(11),* 37–41.

Deregowski, J. B. (1980). *Illusions, patterns, and pictures: A cross–cultural perspective.* New York: Academic Press.

DeRosier, M., & Kupersmidt, J. (1991). Costa Rican children's perceptions of their social networks. *Developmental Psychology, 27,* 656–662.

Derryberry, D., & Tucker, D. M. (1992). Neural mechanisms of emotion. *Journal of Consulting and Clinical Psychology, 60,* 329–338.

Deutsch, H. (1945). *Psychology of women: A psychoanalytic interpretation.* New York: Grune & Statton.

Deutsch, J. A., & Gonzalez, M. F. (1980). Gastric nutrient content signals satiety. *Behavioral and Neural Biology, 30,* 113–116.

DeValois, R. L., & DeValois, K. (1975). Neural coding of color. In E. C. Carterette & M. P. Friedman (Eds.), *Handbook of perception.* NewYork: Academic Press.

Devine, P. (1995). Prejudice and outgroup perception. In A. Tesser (Ed.), *Constructing social psychology.* New York: McGraw–Hill.

Devine, P., Monteith, M., Zuwerink, J., & Elliot, A. (1991). Prejudice with and without compunction. *Journal of Personality and Social Psychology, 60,* 817–830.

Devolder, P., & Pressley, M. (1989). Metamemory across the adult lifespan. *Canadian Psychology, 30,* 578–587.

DeVos, G. (1985). Dimensions of the self in Japanese culture. In A. J. Marsella, G. DeVos, & F.L.K. Hsu (Eds.) *Culture and self: Asian and Western perspectives.* New York: Tavistock.

DeVries, R. (19695). Constancy of generic identity in the years three to six.

Monographs of the Society for Research on Child Development, 34 (Whole No. 127).

Dews, P. B. (1959). Some observations on an operant in the octopus. *Journal of the Experimental Analysis of Behavior, 2,* 57–63.

Diamond, I. T., & Hall, W. C. (1969). Evolution of the neocortex. *Science, 164,* 551–562.

Diamond, M. C. (1978). The aging brain: Some enlightening and optimistic results. *American Psychologist, 66,* 66–71.

Diaz–Guerrero, R. (1979). The development of coping style. *Human Development, 2,* 320–331.

Dies, R. (1992). The future of group therapy. *Psychotherapy, 29,* 58–64.

Dietz, P., Hazelwood, R., & Warren, J. (1990). The sexually sadistic criminal and his offenses. *Bulletin of the American Academy of Psychiatry and Law, 18,* 27–2.

Dil, N. (1984). Nonverbal communication in young children. *Topics in Early Childhood Special Education, 4,* 82–99.

Dimberg, U. (1990). Facial electromyography and emotional reactions. *Psychophysiology, 27,* 481–494.

Dion, K. K. (1972). Physical attractiveness and evaluations of children's transgressions. *Journal of Personality and Social Psychology, 24,* 207–213.

Dion, K. K., & Berscheid, E. (1974). Physical attractiveness and peer perception among children. *Sociometry, 37,* 1–12.

Dion, K. L., & Dion, K. K. (1988). Romantic love: Individual and cultural perspectives. In R. Sternberg and M. Barnes (Eds.), *The psychology of love.* New Haven Conn.: Yale University Press.

Dipboye, R., Smith, C. S., & Howell, W. C. (1994). *Understanding industrial and organizational psychology: An integrated approach.* Fort Worth, Tex.: Harcourt Brace.

Dishion, T. (1990). The family ecology of boys' peer relations in middle childhood. *Child Development, 61,* 874–892.

Dittes, J. E. (1959). Effect of changes in self–esteem upon impulsiveness and deliberation in making judgments. *Journal of Abnormal Social Psychology, 53,* 100–107.

Dixon, D.W., Crystal, H. A., Mattiace, L., & Masur, D. M. (1992). Identification of normal and pathological aging in prospectively studied nondemented elderly humans. *Neurobiology of Aging, 13,* 179–189.

Dixon, N. F. (1981). *Preconscious processing.* New York: John Wiley.

Dixon, Norman F. (1971). *Subliminal perception: The nature of a controversy.* New York: McGraw–Hill.

Dobson & Teller (1978). Visual acuity in human infants: A review and comparison of behavioral and electrophysiological studies. *Vision Research, 18,* 1469–1483.

Dodd, B. (1979). Lip reading in infants: Attention to speech presented in–and out–of–synchrony. *Cognitive Psychology, 11,* 478–484.

Dodge, K., Price, J. M., Bachorowski, J., & Newman, J. P. (1990). Hostile attributional biases in severely aggressive adolescents. *Journal of Abnormal Psychology, 99,* 385–392.

Dodge, K., & Somberg, D. (1987). Hostile attributional biases among aggressive boys are exacerbated under conditions of threats to the self. *Child Development, 58,* 213–224.

Doi, T. (1992). On the concept of amae. *Infant Mental Health Journal, 13,* 7–11.

Dolezal, H. (1982). *Living in a world transformed.* New York: Academic Press.

Dollard, J., Doob, L., Miller, N. E., Mowrer, O., & Sears, R. (1939). *Frustration and aggression.* New Haven Conn.: Yale University Press.

Dollard, J., & Miller, N. (1950). *Personality and psychotherapy: An analysis in terms of learning, thinking, and culture.* New York: McGraw–Hill.

Donnerstein, E. (1980). Aggressive erotica and violence against women. *Journal of Personality and Social Psychology, 39,* 269–277.

Donnerstein, E. (1983). Erotica and human aggression. In R. Geen & E. Donnerstein (Eds.), *Aggression: Theoretical and empirical reviews.* New York: Academic Press.

Donnerstein, E., & Wilson, D. W. (1976). Effects of noise and perceived control on ongoing and subsequent aggressive behavior. *Journal of Personality and Social Psychology, 34,* 774–781.

Doob, L. W. (1960). *Becoming more civilized: A psychological exploration.* New Haven, Conn.: Yale University Press.

Dorian, B. & Garfinkel, P. E. (1987). Stress, immunity and illness—a review. *Psychological Medicine, 17,* 393–407.

Dornbusch, S. M., Ritter, P. L., Leiderman, P. H. The relation of parenting style to adolescent school performance. *Child Development, 58,* 1244–57.

Dorner, G., Geier, T., Ahrens, L., Krell, L., Munx, G., Sieler, H., Kittner, E., & Muller, H. (1980). Prenatal stress and possible aetiogenetic factor homosexuality in human males. *Endokrinologie, 75,* 365–368.

Dorner, G., Schenk, B., Schmiedel, B., & Ahrens, L. (1983). Stressful events in prenatal life of bi–and homosexual men. *Experimental and Clinical Endocrinology, 81,* 83–87.

Doty, R. L., Green, P. A., Ram, C., & Tandeil, S. L. (1982). Communication of gender from human breath odors: Relationship to perceived intensity and pleasantness. *Hormones and Behavior, 16,* 13–22.

Dougherty, J.W.D. (1978). Salience and relativity in classification. *American Ethnologist, 5,* 66–80.

Douglas, M. (1966). *Purity and danger: An analysis of concepts of pollution and taboo.* Middlesex: Penguin.

Douvan, E., & Adelson, J. (1966). *The Adolescent Experience.* New York: John Wiley.

Dovidio, J., & Gaertner, S. (1993).

Stereotypes and evaluative intergroup bias. In D. Mackie & D. Hamilton (Eds.), *Affect, cognition, and stereotyping: Interactive processes in group perception.* San Diego: Academic Press.

Dozier, M., & Kobak, R. (1992). Psychophysiology in attachment interviews: Converging evidence for deactivating strategies. *Child Development, 63,* 1473–1480.

Draguns, J. G. (1986). Culture and psychopathology: What is known about their relationship? *American Journal of Psychology, 38,* 329–338.

Draguns, J. G. (1990). Normal and abnormal behavior in cross–cultural perspective: Specifying the nature of their relationship. In J. J. Beeman (Ed.), *Cross–Cultural perspectives. Current theory and research in motivation.*

Drasdo, N. (1977). The neural representation of visual space. *Nature, 266,* 554–556.

Drewnowski, A. (1991). Obesity and eating disorders: Cognitive aspects of food preference and food aversion. *Bulletin of the Psychonomic Society, 29,* 261–264.

Dreyfus, H., & Dreyfus, S. (1986). Why computers may never think like people. *Technology Review, 89,* 42–61.

Dreyfus, H. L. (1979). *What computers can't do: The limits of artificial intelligence* (revised ed.). New York: Harper & Row.

Dreyfus, H. L. (1986). *What machines can't do: A critique of artificial intelligence.* New York: Harper & Row.

Druke, M. A. (1980). The concept of personhood in seventeenth and eighteenth century Iroquois ethnopersonality. In N. Bonvillain (Ed.), *Studies in Iroquoian Culture. Occasional Papers in Northeastern Anthropology,* No. 6.

DuBois, C. (1944). *The people of Alor: A social psychological study of an East Indian.* Minneapolis: University of Minnesota Press.

Duckitt, J. (1992). Psychology and prejudice: A historical analysis and integrative framework. *American Psychologist, 47,* 1882–1197.

Dudley, R. (1991). IQ and heritability. *Science, 252,* 191–192.

Dumaret, A., (1985). I.Q., scholastic performance and behavior of sibs raised in contrasting environments. *Journal of Child Psychology and Psychiatry and Allied Disciplines, 26,* 553–580.

Dumont, L. (1966). *Homo hierarchicus: The caste system and its implications.* Chicago: University of Chicago Press.

Duncker, K. (1946). On problem solving. *Psychological Monographs, 158, 5, #270.*

Dunn, J., & McGuire, S. (1992). Sibling and peer relationships in childhood. *Journal of Child Psychology and Psychiatry, 33,* 67–105.

Dunnett, S. (1991). Cholingeric grafts, memory, and aging. *Trends in Neurosciences, 14,* 371–376.

Durand, R. P., Fincher, R.E., Reigart, J. R.,

& Lancaster, C. J. (1991). Association between third year medical students' abilities to organize hypotheses about patients' problems and to order appropriate diagnostic tests. *Academic Medicine, 66,* 702–704.

Durkheim, E. (1915). *The elementary forms of the religious life.* New York: Free Press.

Dutton, D. G., & Aron, A. P. (1974). Some evidence for heightened sexual arousal under conditions of high anxiety. *Journal of Personality and Social Psychology, 30,* 510–517.

Dwain, I., Zelazo, P., & Clifton, R. (1993). Newborn infants' memory for speech sounds retained over 24 hours. *Developmental Psychology, 29,* 312–323.

Dweck, C. (1975). The role of expectations and attributions in the alleviation of learned helplessness. *Journal of Personality and Social Psychology, 31,* 674–685.

Dworkin, R. H., Hartsetin, G., Rosner, H., Walther, R., Sweeney, E. W., & Brand, L. (1992). A high–risk method for studying psychosocial antecedents of chronic pain: The prospective investigation of herpes zoster. *Journal of Abnormal Psychology, 101,* 200–205.

Dworkin, S.F., Von Korff, M., & LeResche, L. (1990). Multiple pains and psychiatric disturbance. *Archives of General Psychiatry, 47,* 239–244.

Eagle, M. (1959). The effects of subliminal stimuli of aggressive content upon conscious cognition. *Journal of Personality, 27,* 678–688.

Eagly, A., Ashmore, R., Makhijani, M., & Longo, L. (1991). What is beautiful is good, but. . . : A meta–analytic review of research on the physical attractiveness stereotype. *Psychological Bulletin, 110,* 109–128.

Eagly, A., & Chaiken, S. (1992). *The psychology of attitudes.* San Diego: Harcourt, Brace.

Eagly, A. H. (1983). Gender and Social Influence: A social psychological analysis. *American Psychologist, 38,* 971–981.

Earls, F., Escobar, J. I., & Manson, S. M. (1990). Suicide in minority groups: Epidemiologic and cultural perspectives. In S. J. Blumenthal and D. J. Kupfer (Eds.), *Suicide over the life cycle: Risk factors, assessment, and treatment of suicidal patients.* Washington, DC: American Psychiatric Press.

Easterbrooks, M. A., & Goldberg, W.A. (1985). Effects of early maternal employment on toddlers, mothers, and fathers. *Developmental Psychology, 21,* 774–783.

Ebbinghaus, H. (1885). *Memory.* New York: Columbia University/Dover, 1964.

Eckert, E. D., Bouchard, T. J., Bohlen, J., & Heston, L. (1986). Homosexuality in monozygotic twins reared apart. *British Journal of Psychiatry, 148,* 421–425.

Edelman, G. M. (1989). *The remembered present: A biological theory of consciousness.* New York.: Basic Books.

Eder, R. (1990). Uncovering young children's psychological selves: Individual and developmental differences. *Child Development, 61,* 849–863.

Edwards, C. P., & Whiting, B. B. (1983). Differential socialization of girls and boys in light of cross–cultural research. In W. Damon (Ed.), *Social and personality development: Essays on the growth of the child.* New York: W. W. Norton.

Edwards, D. A., & Einhorn, L. C. (1986). Preoptic and midbrain control of sexual motivation. *Physiology and Behavior, 37,* 329– 335.

Edwards, K. (1990). The interplay of affect and cognition in attitude formation and change. *Journal of Personality and Social Psychology, 59,* 202–216.

Edwards, W. (1977). How to use multiattribute utility measurement for social decision making. *IEEE Transactions in Systems Man and Cybernetics, 17,* 326–340.

Egger, M. D., & Flynn, J. P. (1963). Effect of electrical stimulation of the amygdala on hypothalamically elicited attack behavior in cats. *Journal of Neurophysiology, 26,* 705–720.

Ehlers, A., & Breuer, P. (1992). Increased cardiac awareness in panic disorder. *Journal of Abnormal Psychology, 101,* 371–382.

Eich, J. E. (1980). The cue–dependent nature of state–dependent retrieval. *Memory & Cognition, 8,* 157–173.

Eimas, P. (1985). The perception of speech in early infancy. *Scientific American, 252,* 46–52.

Eimas, P. D., Siqueland, E. R., Jusczyk, P., & Vigorito, J. (1971). Speech perception in infants. *Science, 171,* 303–306.

Eisenberg, N., Miller, P. A., Shell, R., McNalley, S., & Shea, C. (1991). Prosocial development in adolescence: A longitudinal study. *Developmental Psychology, 27,* 849–857.

Eisenberger, R. & Selbst, M. (1994). Does reward increase or decrease creativity? *Journal of Personality and Social Psychology, 66,* 1116–1127.

Ekman, P. (1971). Universals and cultural differences in facial expression. In J.K. Cole (Ed.), *Nebraska Symposium on Motivation.* Lincoln: University of Nebraska Press.

Ekman, P. (1977). Biological and cultural contributions to body and facial movement. In J. Blacking (Ed.), *The anthropology of the body.* A.S.A. Monograph 15. London: Academic Press.

Ekman, P. (1992). Facial expressions of emotion: New findings, new questions. *Psychological Science, 3,* 34–38.

Ekman, P. & Davidson, R. (1993). Voluntary smiling changes regional brain activity. *Psychological Science, 4,* 342–345.

Ekman, P., & Friesen,W. V. (1975). *Unmasking the face: A guide to recognizing emotions from facial cues.* Englewood Cliffs, NJ: Prentice–Hall.

Ekman, P., Friesen, W. V., & Ellsworth, P. (1982). What are the similarities and differences in facial behavior across cultures? In P. Ekman (Ed.), *Emotion in the human face* (2nd ed.). New York: Cambridge University Press.

Ekman, P., Levenson, R., & Friesen, W. (1983). Autonomic nervous system activity distinguishes between emotions. *Science, 221,* 1208–1210.

Ekman, P., & Oster, H. (1979). Facial expressions of emotion. *Annual Review of Psychology, 30,* 527–554.

El Hassan Al Awad, A., & Sonuga–Barke, E. (1992). Childhood problems in a Sudanese city: A comparison of extended and nuclear families. *Child Development, 63,* 906–914.

Elias, M., Elias, J., & Elias, P. (1990). Biological and health influences on behavior. In J. Birren & K.W. Schaie (Eds.), *Handbook of the psychology of aging,* (pp. 80–102). (3rd ed.). New York: Academic Press.

Elizur, J., & Minuchin, S. (1989). *Institutionalizing madness: Families, therapy, and society.* New York: Basic Books.

Elkin, I. (1994). The NIMH Treatment of Depression Collaborative Research Program: Where we began and where we are. In A. Bergin & S. Garfield (Eds.), *Handbook of psychotherapy and behavior change* (pp. 114–139). (4th ed.) New York: John Wiley.

Elkin, I., Shea, M. T., Watkins, J., & Imber, S. (1989). National Institute of Mental Health Treatment of Depression Collaborative Research Program: General effectiveness of treatments. *American Journal of Psychiatry, 46,* 971–982.

Elkind, D. (1981). Children's discovery of the conservation of mass, weight, and volume: Piaget replications studies II. *Journal of Genetic Psychology, 98,* 37–46.

Elkins, I. J., Cromwell, R. L., & Asarnow, R. (1992). Span of apprehension in schizophrenic patients as a function of distractor masking and laterality. *Journal of Abnormal Psychology, 101,* 53–60.

Ellicott, A., Hammen, C., Gitlin, M., Brown, G., & Jamison, K. (1990). Life events and the course of bipolar disorder. *American Journal of Psychiatry, 147,* 1194–1198.

Elliot, A., & Devine, P. (1994). On the motivational nature of cognitive dissonance: Dissonance as psychological discomfort. *Journal of Personality and Social Psychology, 67,* 382–394.

Elliot, R. (1988). Tests, abilities, race, and conflict. *Intelligence, 12,* 333–350.

Elliott, A. J., & Devine, P. (1994). On the motivational nature of cognitive dissonance: Dissonance as psychological discomfort. *Journal of Personality and Social Psychology, 67,* 382–394.

Elliott, E. S., & Elliot, C.S. (1988). Goals: An approach to motivation and achievement. *Journal of Personality and Social Psychology, 54,* 5–12.

Elliott, J. (1977). The power and pathology of prejudice. In P.G. Zimbardo and F.L.

Ruch, *Psychology and Life.* (9th ed.). Glenview, Ill: Scott, Foresman.

Elliott, R. (1988). Tests, abilities, race, and conflict. *Intelligence, 12,* 333–350.

Ellis, A. (1962). *Reason and emotion in psychotherapy.* New York: Lyle Stuart.

Ellis, A. (1977). The basic clinical theory of rational–emotive therapy. In A. Ellis and R. Grieger (Eds.), *Handbook of rational–emotive therapy.* New York: Springer.

Ellis, A. (1984). Rational–emotive therapy. In R. J. Corsini (Ed.), *Current psychotherapies.* (2nd ed.). Itasca, Ill: Peacock Publishers.

Ellis, A. (1987). Cognitive therapy and rational–emotive therapy: A dialogue. *Journal of Cognitive Psychotherapy, 1,* 205–255.

Ellis, A. (1989). I*nside rational–emotive therapy: A critical appraisal of the theory and therapy of Albert Ellis.* New York: Academic.

Ellis, L., & Ames, M. A. (1987). Neurohormonal functioning and sexual orientation: A theory of homosexuality–heterosexuality. *Psychological Bulletin, 101,* 233–58.

Ellis, A., Gutsch, K., Wessler, R., & Neimeyer, R., & Mahoney, M. (1990). Cognitive psychotherapy. In J. Zeig & M. Munion (Eds.), *What is psychotherapy? Contemporary perspectives* (pp. 145–168). San Francisco: Jossey–Bass.

Eme, R., Maisiak, R., & Goodale, W. (1979). Seriousness of adolescent problems. *Adolescence, 14,* 93–99.

Emmons, R., & King, L. A. (1988). Conflict among personal strivings: Immediate and long–term implications for psychological and physical well–being. *Journal of Personality and Social Psychology, 54,* 1040–1048.

Emrick, C. D. (1987). Alcoholics Anonymous: Affiliation processes and effectiveness and treatment. *Alcoholism: Clinical and Experimental Research, 11,* 416–423.

Engels, G. I., Garnefski, N., & Diekstra, R.F.W. (1993). Efficacy of rational–emotive therapy: A quantitative analysis. *Journal of Consulting and Clinical Psychology, 61,* 1083–1090.

Engen, T. (1982). *The perception of odors.* New York: Academic.

Epstein, S. (1973). The self–concept revisited, or a theory of a theory. *American Psychologist, 28,* 404–416.

Epstein, S. (1979). The stability of behavior: On predicting most of the people much of the time. *Journal of Personality and Social Psychology, 37,* 1097–1126.

Epstein, S. (1986). Does aggregation produce spuriously high estimates of behavior stability? *Journal of Personality and Social Psychology, 50,* 1199–1210.

Epstein, S. (1990). Cognitive–experiential self theory. In L. Pervin (Ed.)., *Handbook of personality: Theory and research* (pp. 165–192). New York: Guilford.

Epstein, S. (1992). Coping ability, negative

self–evaluation, and overgeneralization: Experiment and theory. *Journal of Personality and Social Psychology, 62,* 826–836.

Epstein, S. (1994). Integration of the cognitive and the psychodynamic unconscious. *American Psychologist, 49,* 709–724.

Epstein, S., & Katz, L. (1992). Coping ability, stress, productive load, and symptoms. *Journal of Personality and Social Psychology, 62,* 813–825.

Epstein, Y. M., Woolfolk, R. L., & Lehrer, P. M. (1981). Physiological, cognitive, and nonverbal responses to repeated exposure to crowding. *Journal of Applied Social Psychology, 11,* 1–13.

Era, P., Jokela, J., & Heikkinen, E. (1986). Reaction and movement times in men of different ages: A population study. *Perceptual and Motor Skills, 63,* 111–130.

Erber, R., & Tesser, A. (1994). Self–evaluation maintenance: A social psychological approach to interpersonal relationships. In R. Erber & R.Gilmour (Eds.), *Theoretical frameworks for personal relationships* (pp. 211–233). Hillsdale, NJ: Erlbaum.

Erdelyi, M. H. (1974). A new look at the New Look: Perceptual defense and vigilance. *Psychological Review, 81,* 1–25.

Erdelyi, M. H. (1985). *Psychoanalysis: Freud's cognitive psychology.* New York: W. H. Freeman.

Erdmann, G. & van Lindern, B. (1980). The effects of beta–adrenergic stimulation and beta–adrenergic blockade on emotional reactions. *Psychophysiology, 17,* 332–338.

Erhardt, A. A., & Baker, S. W. (1974). Fetal androgens, human central nervous system differentiation, and behavior sex differences. In R. C. Friedman, R. M. Richart & R. L. Vande Wiele (Eds.), *Sex differences in behavior.* New York: JohnWiley.

Erhman, R., Ternes, J., O'Brien, C. P., & McLellan, A. T. (1992). Conditioned tolerance in human opiate addicts. *Psychopharmacology, 108,* 218–224.

Ericcson, K., & Chase, W. G. (1982). Exceptional memory. *American Scientist, 70,* 697–614.

Erickson, R. P. (1968). Stimulus coding in topographic and nontopographic afferent modalities: On the significance of the activity of individual sensory neurons. *Psychological Review, 75,* 447–465.

Erickson, R. P., Priolo, C. V., Warwick, Z. S., & Schiffman, S. S. (1990). Synthesis of tastes other than the "primaries": Implications for neural coding theories and the concept of "suppression." *Chemical Senses, 15,* 495–504.

Ericsson, K.A. (1985). Memory skill. *Canadian Journal of Psychology, 39,* 188–231.

Erikson, E. (1963). *Childhood and society.* New York: W. W. Norton.

Erikson, E. (1968). *Identity: Youth and crisis.* New York: W. W. Norton.

Erikson, E. (1969). *Gandhi's truth On the origin of militant nonviolence.* New York: W. W. Norton.

Erikson, E. H. (1958). *Young Man Luther.* New York: W. W. Norton.

Erikson, M. F., Sroufe, L. A.& Egeland, B. (1985). The relationship between quality of attachment and behavior problems in preschool in a high risk sample. In I. Bretherton & E. Waters (Eds.), Growing points of attachment theory and research. *Monographs of the Society for Research in Child Development, 50* (No.1–2), 147–167.

Ernst, B. (1976). *The magic mirror of M.C. Escher.* New York: Random House.

Ernst, G., & Newell, A. (1969). *GPS: A case study in generality and problem solving.* New York: Academic Press.

Etaugh, C., Collins, G., & Gerson, A. (1975). Reinforcement of sex–typed behaviors of two–year–old children in a nursery school setting. *Developmental Psychology, 11,* 255.

Etcoff, N. L. (1984). Selective attention to facial identity and facial emotion. *Neuropsychologia, 22,* 281–295.

Evans, D. L., Folds, J., Petitto, J., Golden, R. N., Pedersen, C., & Corrigan, M. (1992). Circulating natural killer cell phenotypes in men and women with major depression: Relation to cytotoxic activity and severity of depression. *Archives of General Psychiatry, 49,* 388–395.

Evans, G. W., Palsane, M. N., & Carrere, S. (1987). Type A behavior and occupational stress: A cross–cultural study of blue–collar workers. *Journal of Personality and Social Psychology, 52,* 1002–1007.

Evans–Pritchard, E. E. (1956). *Nuer religion.* Oxford: Clarendon Press.

Eysenck, H. (1987). The growth of a unified scientific psychology: Ordeal by quackery. In A. Staats & L. Mos (Eds.), *Annals of theoretical psychology,* Vol. 5 (pp. 91–113). New York: Plenum Press.

Eysenck, H. (1987). *Theoretical foundations of behavior therapy.* New York: Plenum Press.

Eysenck, H. J. (1953). *The structure of human personality.* New York: John Wiley.

Eysenck, H. J. (1967). *The biological basis of personality.* Springfield, Ill.: Charles C. Thomas.

Eysenck, H. J. (1983). Human learning and individual differences: The genetic dimension. *Educational Psychology, 3,* 169–188.

Eysenck, H. J. (1983). The roots of creativity: Cognitive ability or personality trait? *Roeper Review, 5,* 10–12.

Eysenck, H. J. (1990). Biological dimensions of personality. In L.A. Pervin (Ed.), *Handbook of personality: Theory and research* (pp. 244–276). New York: Guilford Press.

Fabrega, H. (1989). On the significance of an anthropological approach to schizophrenia. *Psychiatry, 52,* 45–65.

Fabrega, H. (1994). Personality disorders as medical entities: A cultural interpretation. *Journal of Personality Disorders, 8,* 149–167.

Fagot, B. I. (1978). The influence of sex of child on parental reactions to toddler children. *Child Development, 49,* 459–465.

Fagot, B. I. (1985). Changes in thinking about early sex role development. *Developmental Review, 5,* 83–98.

Fagot, B. I., & Patterson, G. R. (1969). An in vivo analysis of reinforcing contingencies for sex–role behaviors in the preschool child. *Developmental Psychology.*

Fairbairn, W. (1954). *An object–relations theory of personality.* New York: Basic Books.

Falloon, I.R.H. (1986). Family stress and schizophrenia. *Psychiatric Clinics of North America, 9,* 165–182.

Fantz, R.L. (1966). Pattern discrimination and selective attention as determinants of perceptual developmental from birth. In A. H. Kidd & L. J. Rivoire (Eds.), *Perceptual development in children.* New York: International Universities Press.

Fantz, R. L., Fagan, J. F., III, & Miranda, S. B. (1975). Early visual selectivity. In L. B. Cohen & P. Salapatek (Eds.), *Infant perception: From sensation to cognition: Vol I. Basic visual processes.* New York: Academic Press.

Faravelli, C., & Pallanti, S. (1989). Recent life events and panic disorder. *American Journal of Psychiatry, 146,* 622–626.

Farel, A. (1980). Effects of preferred maternal roles, maternal employment, and sociodemographic status on school adjustment and competence. *Child Development, 51,* 1179–1196.

Fass, P. S. (1980). The I.Q.: A cultural and historical framework. *American Journal of Education,* 431–458.

Fazio, R. (1990). Multiple processes by which attitudes guide behavior: The MODE model as an integrative framework. In L. Berkowitz (Ed.), *Advances in Experimental Social Psychology, 23,* 75–109.

Fazio, R., & Cooper, J. (1983). Arousal in the dissonance process. In J. Cacioppo & R. Petty (Eds.), *Social psychophysiology: A sourcebook* (pp.122–152). New York: Guilford.

Fazio, R., Sanbonmatsu. D., Powell, M., & Kardes, F. (1986). On the automatic activation of attitudes. *Journal of Personality and Social Psychology, 50,* 229–238.

Fazio, R., & Zanna, M. (1981). Direct experience and attitude–behavior consistency. In L. Berkowitz (Ed.), *Advances in experimental social psychology,* Vol.14. New York: Academic.

Fazio, R. H. (1986). How do attitudes guide behavior? In R.M. Sorrentino and E.T. Higgins (Eds.), *The handbook of motivation and cognition: Foundations of social behavior.* New York: Guilford Press.

Federoff, J. P., et al. (1992). Depression in patients with acute traumatic brain injury. *American Journal of Psychiatry, 149,* 918–923.

Fehr, B. & Russell, J. A. (1991). The concept of love viewed from a prototype perspective. *Journal of Personality and Social Psychology, 60,* 425–438.

Feingold, A. (1992). Good–looking people are not what we think. *Psychological Bulletin, 111,* 304–341.

Feldman, D. H. (1980). *Beyond universals in cognitive development.* Norwood, NJ: Ablex.

Fenton, W., & McGlashan, T. (1991). Natural history of schizophrenia subtypes, I: Longitudinal study of paranoid, hebephrenic, and undifferentiated schizophrenia. *Archives of General Psychiatry, 48,* 969–977.

Fernald, A. & Kuhl, P. (1987). Acoustic determinants of infant preference for motherese speech. *Infant Behavior and Development, 10,* 279–293.

Ferre, N. S., & Garcia–Sevilla, L. (1987). Conditionability and open field measures. *Personality and Individual Differences, 8,* 193–200.

Ferster, C. B., & Skinner, B. F. (1957). *Schedules of reinforcement.* New York: Appleton–Century–Crofts.

Festinger, L. (1957). *A theory of cognitive dissonance.* New York: Harper & Row.

Festinger, L. (1962). Cognitive dissonance. *Scientific American, 107,* 409–415.

Festinger, L., & Carlsmith, J. M. (1959). Cognitive consequences of forced compliance. *Journal of Abnormal and Social Psychology, 58,* 203–210.

Field, T. (1991). Quality infant day care and grade shcool behavior and performance. *Child Development, 62,* 863–870.

Fincham, F., & Bradbury, T. (1993). Marital satisfaction, depression, and attributions: A longitudinal analysis. *Journal of Personality and Social Psychology, 64,* 442–452.

Finkelhor, D. (1993). Epidemiological factors in the clinical identification of child sexual abuse. Special Issue: Clinical recognition of sexually abused children. *Child Abuse and Neglect, 17,* 67–70.

Finkelhor, D., et al. (1990). Sexual abuse in a national survey of adult men and women: Prevalence, characteristics, and risk factors. *Child Abuse and Neglect, 14,* 19–28.

Finkelhor, D., Hotaling, G., Lewis, I. A., & Smith, C. (1990). Sexual abuse in a national survey of adult men and women: Prevalence, characteristics, and risk factors. *Child Abuse & Neglect, 14,* 19–28.

Finlay, B. L., & Darlington, R. (1995). Linked regularities in the development and evolution of mammalian brains. *Science, 268,* 1578–1583.

Fischer, K. W. (1980). A theory of cogntive development: The control and construction of hierarchies of skills. *Psychological Review, 87,* 477–531.

Fischer, M., Barkley, R. A., Edelbrock, C., & Smallish, L. (1990). The adolescent outcome of hyperactive children diagnosed by research criteria: II. Academic, attentional, and neuropsychological status. *Journal of Consulting and Clinical Psychology, 58,* 580–588.

Fischer, K. W., Shaver, P.R., & Carnochan, P.

(1990). How emotions develop and how they organise development. *Cognition and Emotion, 4*, 81–127.

Fishbein, M., & Ajzen, I. (1974). Attitudes towards objects as predictors of single and multiple behavioral criteria. *Psychological Review, 81*, 59–74.

Fisher, S. (1954). The role of expectancy in the performance of posthypnotic behavior. *Journal of abnormal and social psychology, 49*, 503–507.

Fisher, S., & Greenberg, R. (1985). *The scientific credibility of Freud's theories and therapy.* New York: Columbia University Press.

Fiske, S. (1992). Thinking is for doing: Portraits of social cognition from daguerreotype to laserphoto. *Journal of Personality and Social Psychology, 63*, 877–889.

Fiske, S. (1995). Social cognition. In A. Tesser (Ed.), *Constructing social psychology.* New York: McGraw–Hill.

Fiske, S., & Taylor, S. (1991). *Social cognition.* (2nd ed.). Reading, MA: Addison–Wesley.

Fiske, S. T. (1982). Schema–triggered affect: Applications to social perception. In M. S. Clark and S. T. Fiske (Eds.), *Affect and cognition: The 17th Annual Carnegie Symposium on Cognition.* Hillsdale, NJ: Erlbaum.

Fiske, S. T., & Pavelchak, M. A. (1986). Category–based versus piecemeal–based affective responses: Developments in schema–triggered affect. In R. Sorrentino and E. T. Higgins (Eds.), *Handbook of motivation and cognition: Foundations of social behavior.* New York: Guilford Press.

Fitzpatrick, K. M. (1993). Exposure to violence and presence of depression among low–income African–American youth. *Journal of Consulting and Clinical Psychology*, 528–531.

Flavell, J. (1992). Cognitive development: past, present, and future. *Developmental Psychology, 28*, 998–1005.

Flavell, J. H. (1982). Structures, stages, and sequences in cognitive development. In W. A. Collins (Ed.), *The concept of development:* Vol. 15. Hillsdale, NJ: Erlbaum.

Flavell, J. H., Beach, D. R., & Chinsky, J. M. (1966). Spontaneous verbal rehearsal in a memory task as a function of age. *Child Development, 37*, 283–299.

Flavell, J. H., Botkin, P. T., Fry, C. L. Jr., Wright, J. W., & Jarvis, P. E. (1968). *The development of role–taking and communication skills in children.* New York: John Wiley.

Flavell, J. H., Friedrichs, A. G., & Hoyt, J. D. (1970). Developmental changes in memorization processes. *Cognitive Psychology, 1*, 324–40.

Flavell, J. H., & Wellman, H. M. (1977). Metamemory. In R. V. Kail & J. W. Hagen (Eds.), *Memory in cognitive development.* Hillsdale, NJ: Erlbaum.

Fletcher, G. (1986). Attributional complexity: An individual differences measure. *Journal of Personality and Social Psychology, 51*, 875–884.

Fletcher, G., & Ward, C. (1988). Attribution theory and processes: A cross–cultural perspective. In M. Bond (Ed.), *The cross–cultural challenge to social psychology.* Beverly Hills, CA: Sage.

Flor, H., Haag, G., & Turk, D. C. (1986). Long term efficacy of EMG biofeedback for chronic rheumatic back pain. *Pain, 27*, 195–202.

Fodor, J. (1983). *The modularity of mind.* Cambridge, MA: MIT.

Fogel, A., Melson, G. F., & Mistry, J. (1986). Conceptualizing the determinants of nurturance: A reassessment of sex differences. In A. Fogal & G. F. Melson (Eds.), *Origins of nurturance.* Hillsdale, NJ: Erlbaum.

Foley, R. & Mulhern, G. (1991). Capacity, duration, and position effects in visual memory following a successive field procedure. *Perceptual and Motor Skills, 73*, 195–198.

Fonagy, P., & Moran, G. S. (1990). Studies on the efficacy of child psychoanalysis. *Journal of Consulting and Clinical Psychology, 58*, 684–695.

Fonagy, P., Steele, H., & Steele, M. (1991). Maternal representations of attachment during pregnancy predict the organization of infant–mother attachment at one year of age. *Child Development, 62*, 891–905.

Fong, G. T. & Nisbett, R. E. (1991). Immediate and delayed transfer of training effects in statistical reasoning. *Journal of Experimental Psychology: General, 120*, 34–45.

Ford, M. (1979). The construct validity of egocentrism. *Psychological Bulletin, 86*, 1169–1188.

Ford, T., & Stangor, C. (1992). The role of diagnosticity in stereotype formation: Perceiving group means and variances. *Journal of Personality and Social Psychology, 62*, 356–367.

Foreyt, J. P. (1987). Issues in the assessment and treatment of obesity. *Journal of Consulting and Clinical Psychology, 55*, 677– 84.

Forsen, A. (1991). Psychosocial stress as a risk for breast cancer. *Psychotherapy and Psychosomatics, 55*, 176–185.

Foster, G. (1965). Peasant society and the image of limited good. *American Anthropologist, 67*, 293–315.

Fouts, R. S., Hirsch, A. D., & Fouts, D. H. (1982). Cultural transmission of a human language in a chimpanzee mother–infant relationship. In H. E. Fitzgerald, J. A. Mullins, & P. Gage (Eds.), *Child Nurturance*, Vol. 3. New York: Plenum Press.

Fowles, D.C. (1992). Schizophrenia: Diathesis–stress revisited. *Annual Review of Psychology, 43*, 303–336.

Fox, N. (1991). Hemispheric specialization and attachment behaviors: Developmental processes and individual differences in separation protest. In J. Gewirtz & W. Kurtines (Eds.), *Intersections with attachment* (pp. 147–164). Hillsdale, NJ: Erlbaum.

Fox, N. (1991). If it's not left, it's right:

Electroencephalograph asymmetry and the development of emotion. *American Psychologist, 46*, 863–872.

Foxx, R. M., & Faw, G. (1992). An eight–year followup of three social skills training studies. *Mental Retardation, 30*, 63–66.

Fozard, J. (1990). Vision and hearing in aging. In J. Birren & K.W. Schaie (Eds.), *Handbook of the psychology of aging.* (3rd ed.). New York: Academic Press.

Fraiberg, S. (1975). The development of human attachments in infants blind from birth. *Merrill–Palmer Quarterly, 21*, 315–34.

Frances, A., Widiger, T., First, M. B., & Pincus, H. (1991). DSM–IV: Toward a more empirical diagnostic system. *Canadian Psychology, 32*, 171–173.

Frank, A. F., & Gunderson, J. (1990). The role of the therapeutic alliance in the treatment of schizophrenia: Relationship to course and outcome. *Archives of General Psychiatry, 47*, 226–236.

Frank, J. D., Hoehn–Saric, R., Imber, S. D., Liberman, B. L., & Strong, A. R. (1978). *Effective ingredients of successful psychotherapy.* New York: Brunner/Mazel.

Frankel, F. H. (1984). Electroconvulsive therapy. In American Psychiatric Commission on Psychiatric Therapies, *The psychiatric therapies.* Washington, DC: American Psychiatric Association.

Frankl, V. (1959). *Man's search for meaning: An introduction to logotherapy.* New York: Pocket Books.

Franklin, J., Donohew, L., Dhoundiyal, V., & Cook, P. L. (1988). Attention and our recent past: The scaly thumb of the reptile. *American Behavioral Scientist, 31*, 312–326.

Franz, C., McClelland, D., & Weinberger, J. (1991). Childhood antecedents of conventional social accomplishment in midlife adults: A 36–year prospective study. *Journal of Personality and Social Psychology, 60*, 586–595.

Frazier, J. G. (1922). *The golden bough.* New York: Macmillan.

Frederiksen, N., Glaser, R., & Lesgold, A. (Eds.). *Diagnostic monitoring of skill and knowledge acquisition.* Hillsdale, NJ: Erlbaum.

Free, M., & Beekhuis, M. (1985). A successful adaptation of systematic desensitization in the treatment of a phobia of babies. *Behavior Change, 2*, 59–64.

Freedman, J. L., & Fraser, S. C. (1966). Compliance without pressure: The foot–in–the–door technique. *Journal of Personality and Social Psychology, 4*, 195–202.

Freeman, W. (1959). Psychosurgery. In S. Aneti (Ed.), *American handbook of psychiatry II.* New York: Basic Books.

Freud, A. (1936). *The ego and the mechanisms of defense.* New York: International Universities Press.

Freud, A. (1958). Adolescence, *Psychoanalytic study of the child. 13*, 255–278.

Freud, S. (1895). Project for a scientific psychology. *In The standard edition of the complete psychological works of Sigmund Freud,* J. Strachey (Ed.), Vol. 1. London: Hogarth Press, 1966.

Freud, S. (1900). *The interpretation of dreams.* New York: Avon, 1965.

Freud, S. (1905). *Three contributions to the theory of sexuality.* New York: E. P. Dutton, 1962.

Freud, S. (1912). The dynamics of transference. In J. Strachey (Ed. & Trans.), *The standard edition of the complete psychological works of Sigmund Freud,* Vol. 12 (pp. 97–108). London: Hogarth, 1958.

Freud, S. (1922). Certain neurotic mechanisms in jealousy, paranoia, and homosexuality. In J. Strachey (Ed. & Trans.), *The standard edition of the complete psychological works of Sigmund Freud,* Vol. 1, London: Hogarth Press, 1966.

Freud, S. (1923). *The ego and the id.* New York: W. W. Norton.

Freud, S. (1925). An autobiographical study. J. Strachey (Ed. & Trans.), *The standard edition of the complete psychological works of Sigmund Freud,* Vol. 20. London: Hogarth Press, 1952.

Freud, S. (1933). *New introductory lectures on psychoanalysis.* New York: W. W. Norton, 1965.

Frick, R. W. (1985). Communicating emotion: The role of prosodic features. *Psychological Bulletin, 97,* 412–429.

Friedman, H. R., & Goldman–Rakic, P. (1994). Coactivation of prefrontal cortex and inferior parietal cortex in working memory tasks revealed by 2DG functional mapping in the rhesus monkey. *Journal of Neuroscience, 14,* 2775–2788.

Friedman, M. & Rosenman, R. H. (1959). Association of specific overt behavior pattern with blood and cardiovascular findings—blood cholesterol level, blood clotting time, incidence of arcus senilis, and clinical coronary heart disease. *Journal of the American Medical Association, 162,* 1286–1296.

Friedman, R. C., & Stern, L.O. (1980). Juvenile aggressivity and sissiness in homosexual and heterosexual males. *Journal of American Academy of Psychoanalysis, 8,* 427–440.

Frieze, I. H., & Browne, A. (1989). Violence in marriage. In L. Ohlin & M. Tonry (Eds.), *Family violence.* Chicago: University of Chicago Press.

Frisch, H. L. (1977). Sex stereotypes in adult–infant play. *Child Development, 48,* 1671–1675.

Frisch, R. E., Wyshak, G., & Vincent, L. (1980). Delayed menarch and amenorrhea of ballet dancers. *New England Journal of Medicine, 303,* 17–19.

Frock, J., & Money, J. (1992). Sexuality and the menopause. *Psychotherapy and Psychosomatics, 57,* 29–33.

Fromkin, V., Krashen, S., Curtiss, S., Rigler, D., & Rigler, M. (1974). The development of language in Genie: A case of language acquisition beyond the critical period. *Brain and Language, 1,* 81–107.

Fromm, E. (1947). *Man for himself: An inquiry into the psychology of ethics.* New York: Holt, Rinehart & Winston.

Fromm, E. (1955). *The sane society.* Greenwich, Conn.: Fawcett Books.

Frustaci, J. (1988). A survey of agoraphobics in self–help groups. *Smith College Studies in Social Work, 58,* 193–211.

Fryer, D. (1985). Stages in the psychologial response to unemployment: A (dis)integrative review. *Current Psychological Research and Reviews,* 257–273.

Fukuda, T., Kanada, K., & Saito, S. (1990). An ergonomic evaluation of lens accommodation related to visual circumstances. *Ergonomics, 33,* 811–831.

Fuller, J. L., & Thompson, W. R. (1978). *Foundations of behavior genetics.* New York: John Wiley.

Funder, D., & Colvin, C. R. (1991). Explorations in behavioral consistency: Properties of persons, situations, and behaviors. *Journal of Personality and Social Psychology, 60,* 773–794.

Furman, W., & Buhrmester, D. (1992). Age and sex differences in perceptions of networks of personal relationships. *Child Development, 63,* 103–115.

Fuster, J. (1989). *The prefrontal cortex.* (2nd ed.) New York: Raven.

Fyer, A., Mannuzza, S., Martin, L., Aaronson, C., Gorman, J., Liebowitz, M., & Klein, D. F. (1990). Familial transmission of simple phobias and fears. *Archives of General Psychiatry, 47,* 252–256.

Fyer, A. J., & Sandberg, D. (1988). Pharmacologic treatment of panic disorder. In A.J. Frances and R.E. Hales, *Review of Psychiatry,* Vol. 7. Washington, DC: American Psychiatric Press.

Gabbard, G. (1992). Psychodynamic psychiatry in the "decade of the brain." *American Journal of Psychiatry, 149,* 991–998.

Gabbay, F. (1992). Behavior–genetic strategies in the study of emotion. *Psychological Science, 3,* 50–55.

Gackenbach, J., & Bosveld, J. (1989). Take control of your dreams. *Psychology Today,* 27–32.

Gadow, K., & Sprafkin, J. (1993). Television violence and children with emotional and behavioral disorders. *Journal of Emotional and Behavioral Disorders, 1,* 54–63.

Gaertner, S., Mann, J., Dovidio, J., Murrell, A., & Pomare, M. (1990). How does cooperation reduce intergroup bias? *Journal of Personality and Social Psychology, 59,* 692–704.

Gagnon, J., & Simon, W. (1973). *Sexual conduct.* Chicago: Aldine.

Galanter, E. (1966). *Textbook of elementary psychology.* San Francisco: Holden–Day.

Galotti, K. M., Baron, J., & Sabini, J. P. (1986). Individual differences in syllogistic reasoning: Deduction rules or mental models? *Journal of Experimental Psychology: General, 115,* 16–25.

Gamsa, A. (1990). Is emotional disturbance a precipitator or a consquence of chronic pain? *Pain, 42,* 183–195.

Gandevia, S. C., McCloskey, D. I., & Burke, D. (1992). Kinaesthetic signals and muscle contraction. *Trends in Neurosciences, 15,* 62–65.

Ganley, R. (1989). Emotion and eating in obesity: A review of the literature. *International Journal of Eating Disorders, 8,* 343–361.

Garb, H. N. (1984). The incremental validity of information used in personality assessment. *Clinical Psychology Review, 40,* 641–655.

Garbarino, J., Kostelny, K., & Dubrow, N. (1991). What children can tell us about living in danger. *American Psychologist, 46,* 376–383.

Garcia y Robertson, R., & Garcia, J. (1988). Darwin was a learning theorist. In R. Bolles & M. Beecher, (Eds.), *Evolution and learning* (pp. 17–38). Hillsdale, NJ: Erlbaum.

Garcia, J. (1979). I.Q.: The conspiracy. In J. B. Maas (Ed.), *Readings in psychology today* (pp. 198–202) (4th ed.). New York: Random House.

Garcia, J., & Garcia y Robertson, R. (1985). Evolution of learning mechanisms. In B.L. Hammonds (Ed.), *The Master Lecture Series,* Vol.4. Washington, DC: American Psychological Association.

Garcia, J., & Koelling, R. (1966). Relation of cue to consequence in avoidance learning. *Psychonomic Science, 4,* 123–124.

Garcia, J., Lasiter, P., Bermudez–Rattoni, & Deems, D. (1985). A general theory of aversion learning. *Annals of the New York Academy of Sciences, 443,* 8–21.

Gardner, B. T., & Gardner, R. A. (1975). Evidence for sentence constituents in the early utterances of child and chimpanzee. *Journal of Experimental Psychology: General, 104,* 244–267.

Gardner, H. (1975). *The shattered mind.* New York: Alfred A. Knop.

Gardner, H. (1983). *Frames of mind: The theory of multiple intelligences.* New York: Basic Books.f.

Garn, S. M. (1980). Human growth. *Annual Review of Anthropology, 9,* 275–292.

Garner, D. M., Garfinkel, P. E., Schwartz, D., & Thompson, M. (1980). Cultural expectations of thinness in women. *Psychological Reports, 47,* 483–497.

Garner, D. M., & Wooley, S. (1991). Confronting the failure of behavioral and dietary treatments for obesity. *Clinical Psychology Review, 11,* 729–780.

Garrison, R. J., & Castelli, W. P. (1985). Weight and thirty–year mortality of men in the Framingham study. *Annals of Internal Medicine, 103,* 1006–1009.

Garrow, J. S., & Warwick, P. M. (1978). Diet and obesity. In J. Yudkin, (Ed.), *The Diet of Man: Needs and Wants.* Barking: Applied Science Pub., 127–144.

Garvey, M. J., & Tuason, V. B. (1980). Mania misdiagnosed as schizophrenia. *Journal of Clinical Psychiatry, 41,* 75–78.

Gay, M., Glick, J., & Cole, J. (1968). A cross–cultural investigation of information processing. *International Journal of Psychology, 3*, 93–102.

Gazzaniga, M. (1967). The split brain in man. *Scientific American, 217*, 24–29.

Gazzaniga, M. S. (1985). *The social brain: Discovering the networks of the mind.* New York: Basic Books.

Gazzaniga, M. S. (1989). Organization of the human brain. *Science, 245*, 947–952.

Gebhard, P. H. (1971). Human sexual behavior: A summary statement. In D. S. Marshall, & R. C. Suggs, (Eds.) *Human Sexual Behavior: Variations in the Ethnographic Spectrum.* New York: Basic Books.

Gecas, V. (1982). The self–concept. *Annual Review of Sociology, 8*, 1–33.

Geen, R. (1990). *Human aggression.* Pacific Grove, CA: Brooks–Cole.

Geen, R. G. (1983). Aggression and television violence. In R. Geen & E. Donnerstein (Eds.), *Aggression: Theoretical and empirical reviews.* New York: Academic Press.

Geen, R. G. (1985). Human motivation: New perspectives on old problems. In V. P. Makosky, (Ed.), *G. Stanley Hall Lecture Series, 6.* Washington, DC: American Psychological Association.

Geen, R. G. (1995). Human aggression. In A. Tesser (Ed.), *Advanced social psychology.* New York: McGraw–Hill.

Geers, A. E. & Schick, B. (1988). Acquisition of spoken and signed English by hearing–impaired children of hearing–impaired or hearing parents. *Journal of Speech and Hearing Disorders, 53*, 136–143.

Geertz, C. (1963). The integrative revolution: Primordial sentiments and civil politics in the new states. In C. Geertz (Ed.), *Old societies and new states.* New York: Free Press.

Geertz, C. (1973). *The interpretation of cultures.* New York: Basic Books.

Geertz, C. (1974). From the natives í point of view. *American Academy of Arts and Sciences Bulletin, 28*, 26–43.

Geis, F. (1978). Machiavellianism. In H. London and J.E. Exner (Eds.), *Dimensions of personality.* New York: Wiley.

Geiselman, R. E., Fisher, R. P., MacKinnon, D. P., & Holland, H .L. Eyewitness memory enhancement in the police interview: Cognitive retrieval mnemonics versus hypnosis. *Journal of Applied Psychology, 70*, 401–412.

Gelinas, D. J. (1983). The persisting negative effects of incest. *Psychiatry, 46*, 312–332.

Gelman, R., & Baillargeon, R. (1983). A review of Piagetian concepts. In J. H. Flavell & E. M. Markman (Eds.), *Handbook of child psychology: Cognitive development* (Vol.3). New York: John Wiley.

Geoghehan, W. H. (1976). Polytypy in folk biological taxonomies. *American Ethnologist, 3*, 469–480.

Gerard, H. B. et al. (1968). Conformity and group size. *Journal of Personality and Social Psychology, 8*, 79–82.

Gershon, E. S., Nurnberger, J. I., Berrettini, W. H., & Goldin, L. R. (1985). In H. I. Kaplan, & B. J. Sadock (Eds.), *Comprehensive textbook of psychiatry* (4th ed.). Baltimore, MD: Williams & Wilkins.

Gerstner, C., & Day, D. V. (1994). Cross–cultural comparison of leadership prototypes. *Leadership Quarterly, 5*, 121–134.

Gholson, B., Levine, M., & Phillips, S. (1972). Hypothesis, strategies, and stereotypes in discrimination learning. *Journal of Experimental Child Psychology, 13*, 423–446.

Ghuman, P.A.S. (1982). An evaluation of Piaget's theory from a cross–cultural perspective. In S. Modgil & C. Modgil (Eds.), *Jean Piaget: Consensus and Controversy.* New York: Holt, Rinehart, & Winston.

Gibb, C. A. (1969). Leadership. In G.Lindzey & E.Aronson (Eds.), *Handbook of social psychology*, Vol. 4. (2nd ed.) Reading, MA: Addison–Wesley.

Gibbons, F., & McCoy, S. (1991). Self–esteem, similarity, and reactions to active versus passive downward comparisons. *Journal of Personality and Social Psychology, 60*, 414–424.

Gibson, E. J. (1969). *Principles of perceptual learning and development.* New York: Appleton–Century–Crofts.

Gibson, E. J. (1984). Perceptual development from the ecological approach. In M. E. Lamb, A. L. Brown, & B. Rogoff, *Advances in developmental psychology, Vol. 3.*

Gibson, E. J., & Walk, R. D. (1960). The "visual cliff." *Scientific American, 202*, 64–71.

Gibson, J. J. (1966). *The senses considered as perceptual systems.* Boston: Houghton Mifflin.

Gibson, J. J. (1979). *The ecological approach to visual perception.* Boston: Houghton Mifflin.

Gilbert, D. (1989). Thinking lightly about others: Automatic components of the social inference process. In J. S. Uleman & J. A. Bargh (1989), *Unintended thought* (pp. 189–211). New York: Guilford Press.

Gilbert, D., & Hixon, J. (1991). The trouble of thinking: Activation and application of stereotypic beliefs. *Journal of Personality and Social Psychology, 60*, 509–517.

Gilbert, D., Pelham, B., & Krull, D. (1988). On cognitive busyness: When person perceivers meet persons perceived. *Journal of Personality and Social Psychology, 54*, 733–740.

Gilhooly, K. J. (1989). Human and machine problem solving: Toward a comparative cognitive science. In K. J. Gilhooly (Ed.), *Human and machine problem solving.* New York: Plenum Press.

Gill, M. (1982). *The analysis of transference.*

Vol. 1. *Theory and technique. Psychological Issues, Monograph*, No. 53.

Gilligan, C. (1982). *In a different voice.* Cambridge, MA: Harvard University Press.

Gilligan , S., & Bower, G. (1984). Cognitive consequences of emotional arousal. In C. E. Izard, J. Kagan, & R. B. Zajonc (Eds.), *Emotion, cognition, and behavior* (pp. 547–588). Cambridge: Cambridge University Press.

Gilovich, T. (1991). *How we know what isn't so: The fallibility of human reason in everyday life.* New York: Free Press.

Giray, E. F. (1985). A life span approach to the study of eidetic imagery. *Journal of Mental Imagery, 9*, 21–32.

Gladue, B. A., Green, R., & Hellman, R.E. (1984). Neuroendocrine response to estrogen and sexual orientation. *Science, 225*, 1496– 99.

Gladwin, T. (1970). *East is a big bird.* Cambridge, MA: Belknap Press.

Glaser, R. and Schauble, L. (1989). Scientific thinking in children and adults. *Contributions to Human Development, 21*, 9–27.

Glassman, J. B., Burkhart, B. R., Grant, R. D., & Vallery, G. G. (1978). Density, expectation, and extended task performance: An experiment in the natural environment. *Environment and Behavior, 10*, 299–316.

Gleitman, L. R., Gleitman, H., Landau, B., & Warner, E. (1988). Where learning begins: Initial representations for language learning. In F. Newmeyer (Ed.), *Linguistics: The Cambridge survey.* Vol. III. *Language: Psychological and biological aspects.* Cambridge: Cambridge University Press.

Glenberg, A. (1976). Monotonic and non-monotonic effects in paired–associate and recognition memory paradigms. *Journal of Verbal Learning and Verbal Behavior, 15*, 1–16.

Godden, D. R., & Baddeley, A. D. (1975). Context–dependent memory in two natural environments: On land and underwater. *British Journal of Psychology, 66*, 325–331.

Gold, M. S., & Pearsall, H. R. (1983). Hypothyroidism—or is it depression? *Psychosomatics, 24*, 646–656.

Goldberg, L. R. (1981). Language and individual differences: The search for universals in personality lexicons. In L. Wheeler (Ed.), *Review of Personality and Social Psychology*, Beverly Hills, CA: Sage Publications.

Goldberg, L. R. (1990). An alternative description of personality: The big–five factor structure. *Journal of Personality and Social Psychology, 59*, 1216–1229.

Goldberg, L. R. (1993). The structure of phenotypic personality traits. *American Psychologist, 48*, 26–34.

Golden, R. M., & Rumelhart, D. E. (1993). A parallel distributed processing model of story comprehension and recall. *Discourse Processes, 16*, 203–237.

Goldfield, B. A. & Snow, C. E. (1989). Individual differences in language acquisition. In J. Berko Gleason (Ed.), *The development of language.* (2nd ed.). Columbus, Ohio: Merrill.

Goldfried, M., & Davison, G. (1994). *Clinical behavior therapy.* (2nd ed.). New York: Holt, Rinehart & Winston.

Goldman, H. H., Skodol, A., & Lave, T. (1992). Revising Axis V for DSM–IV: A review of measures of social functioning. *American Journal of Psychiatry, 149,* 1148–1156.

Goldman–Rakic, P. (1995). Cellular basis of working memory. *Neuron, 14,* 477–485.

Goldsmith, H. H., & Alansky, J. A. (1987). Maternal and infant temperamental predictors of attachment: A meta–analytic review. *Journal of Consulting and Clinical Psychology, 55,* 805–816.

Goldsmith, H. H., & Harman, C. (1994). Temperament and attachment: Individuals and relationships. *Current Directions in Psychological Science, 3,* 53–57.

Goldstein, A. J., & Chambless, D. J. (1978). A reanalysis of agoraphobia. *Behavior Therapy, 9,* 47–59.

Goldstein, M. J. (1988). The family and psychopathology. *Annual Review of Psychology 39,* 283–299.

Gong–Guy, E., Cravens, R., & Patterson, T. E. (1991). Clinical issues in mental health service delivery to refugees. *American Psychologist, 46,* 642–648.

Goodman, L., Koss, M., Fitzgerald, L., Russo, N., & Keita, G. (1993). Male violence against women: Current research and future directions. *American Psychologist, 48,* 1054–1058.

Goodman, L., Saxe, L., & Harvey, M. (1991). Homelessness as psychological trauma: Broadening perspectives. *American Psychologist, 46,* 1219–1225.

Goodman, W., McDougle, C., Barr, L., & Aronson, S. (1993). Biological approaches to treatment–resistant obsessive compulsive disorder. *Journal of Clinical Psychiatry, 54,* 6–26.

Goodman, W. K., Price, L., Delgado, P., Palumbo, J., Krystal, J., Nagy, L., Rasmussen, S., Heninger, G., & Charney, D. (1990). Specificity of serotonin reuptake inhibitors in the treatment of obsessive–compulsive disorder. *Archives of General Psychiatry, 47,* 577–585.

Goodnow, J. J. (1976). The nature of intelligent behavior: Questions raised by cross–cultural studies. In L. B. Resnick (Ed.), *The nature of intelligence* (pp. 169–188). Hillsdale, NJ: Erlbaum.

Goodwin, F. K., & Roy–Byrne, P. (1987). Treatment of bipolar disorders. In A. J. Frances and R. E. Hales (Eds.), *Psychiatric Update Annual Review,* Vol. 6.

Goody, J. (1977). *The domestication of the savage mind.* Cambridge: Cambridge University Press.

Gordon, M., & Shankweiler, P. J. (1971). Different equals less: Female sexuality in recent marriage manuals. *Journal of Marriage and the Family, 33,* 459–466.

Gordon, P. (1990). Learnability and feedback. *Developmental Psychology, 26,* 217–220.

Gorski, R. A., & Barraclough, C. A. (1963). Effects of low dosages of androgen on the differentiation of hypothalamic regulatory control of ovulation in the rat. *Endocrinology, 73,* 210–216.

Goto, H. (1971). Auditory perception by normal Japanese adults of the sounds "l" and "r." *Neuropsychologia, 9,* 317–323.

Gottesman, I. I. (1991). *Schizophrenia genesis: The origins of madness.* New York: W. H. Freeman & Co.

Gottesman, I. I., & Bertelsen, A. (1989). Confirming unexpressed genotypes for schizophrenia: Risks in the offspring of Fischer's Danish identical and fraternal discordant twins. *Archives of General Psychiatry, 50,* 527–540.

Gottesman, I. I., McGuffin, P., & Farmer, A. E. (1987). Clnical genetics as clues to the 'real' genetics of schizophrenia. *Schizophrenia Bulletin, 13,* 23–47.

Gottlieb, J. (1990). Mainstreaming and quality education. *American Journal on Mental Retardation, 95,* 16–17.

Gouchie, C., & Kimura, D. (1991). The relationship between testosterone levels and cognitive ability patterns. *Psychoneuroendocrinology, 16,* 323–334.

Gould, S. J. (1981). *The mismeasure of man.* New York: W.W. Norton.

Gove, W. (1982). Labeling theory's explanation of mental illness: An update of recent evidence. *Deviant Behavior, 3,* 307–327.

Grabowski, J., & VandenBos, G. (1992). *Psychopharmacology: Basic mechanisms and applied interventions.* Washington, DC: American Psychological Association.

Gracely, R., Lynch, S., & Bennett, G. J. (1992). Painful neuropathy: Altered central processing maintained dynamically by peripheral input. *Pain, 51,* 175–194.

Graf, R. G., & Riddell, J. C. (1972). Helping behavior as a function of interpersonal perception, *Journal of Social Psychology, 86,* 227–231.

Gralewicz, S. (1983). Relationship between some behavioral and electroencephalographic changes induced by intrahypothalamic injections of carbachol in the cat. *Acta Neurobiologicae Experimentalis, 43,* 311–328.

Gray, C. R., & Gummerman, K. (1975). The enigmatic eidetic image: A critical examination of methods, data, and theories. *Psychological Bulletin, 82,* 383–407.

Gray, J., & Silver, R. (1990). Opposite sides of the same coin: Former spouses' divergent perspectives in coping with their divorce. *Journal of Personality and Social Psychology, 59,* 1180–1191.

Gray, J. A. (1987). *The psychology of fear and stress.* (2nd ed.). New York: Cambridge University Press.

Gray, J.A. (1990). Brain systems that mediate both emotion and cognition. *Cognition and Emotion, 4,* 269–288.

Graziadei, P.P.C. (1969). The ultra–structure of vertebrate taste buds. In C. Pfaffman (Ed.), *Olfaction and taste,* Vol. 3. New York: Rockefeller University Press.

Green, B. L., Grace, M. C., Lindy, J. D., Gleser, G., & Leondard, A. (1990). Risk factors for PTSD and other diagnoses in a general sample of Vietnam veterans. *American Journal of Psychiatry, 147,* 729–733.

Green, D. M. & Swets, J. A. (1966). *Signal detection theory and psychophysics.* New York: John Wiley.

Green, M. A., & Curtis, G. C. (1988). Personality disorders in panic patients: Response to termination of antipanic medication. *Journal of Personality Disorders, 2,* 303–314.

Green, R. (1987). *The 'sissy boy' syndrome and the development of homosexuality.* New Haven, Conn.: Yale University Press.

Greenberg, C., & Powers, S. M. (1987). Memory improvement among adult learners. *Educational Gerontology, 13,* 263–280.

Greenberg, J. (1977). The brain and emotions: Crossing a new frontier. *Science News, 112,* 74–75.

Greenberg, J., Pyszczynski, T., Solomon, S., Rosenblatt, A., Veeder, M., Kirkland, S., & Lyon, D. (1990). Evidence for terror management theory II: The effects of mortality salience on reactions to those who threaten or bolster the cultural worldview. *Journal of Personality and Social Psychology, 58,* 308–318.

Greenberg, L. (1993). Emotion and change processes in psychotherapy. In M. Lewis & J. Haviland (Eds.), *Handbook of emotions* (pp. 499–508). New York: Guilford Press.

Greenberg, L., Rice, L., & Elliott, R. (1993). *Facilitating emotional change: The moment–by–moment process.* New York: Guilford.

Greeno, J. G. (1978). Natures of problem–solving abilities. In W. K. Estes (Ed.), *Handbook of Learning and Cognitive Processes,* Vol. 5. Hillsdale, NJ: Erlbaum.

Greenough, W., Black, J., & Wallace, C. (1987). Experience and brain development. *Child Development, 58,* 539–559.

Greenough, W. T. (1991). Experience as a component of normal development: Evolutionary considerations. *Developmental Psychology, 27,* 14–17.

Greenspan, S. and Granfield, M. (1992). Reconsidering the construct of mental retardation: Implications of a model of social competence. *American Journal on Mental Retardation, 96,* 442–453.

Greenwald, A., Pratkanis, A. R., Leippe, M. R., & Baumgardner, M. H. (1986). Under what conditions does theory obstruct research progress. *Psychological Review, 93,* 216–229.

Greenwald, A. G. (1980). The totalitarian ego: Fabrication and revision of personal history. *American Psychologist, 35,* 603–618.

Greenwald, A. G. (1992). New Look 3: Unconscious cognition reclaimed. *American Psychologist, 47*, 766–779.

Greenwald, A. G., & Brecker, S. J. (1985). To whom is the self presented? In B. R. Schlenker (Ed.), *The self and social life.* New York: McGraw–Hill.

Greenwald, A. G., & Pratkanis, A. R. (1984). The self. In R. S. Wyer & T. K. Srull (Eds.), *Handbook of social cognition*, Vol. 3 (pp. 1129–178). Hillsdale, NJ: Erlbaum.

Greenwood, J. D. (1991). *Relations and representations: An introduction to the philosophy of social psychological science.* New York: Routledge.

Gregory, R. (1970). *The intelligent eye.* New York: McGraw–Hill.

Gregory, R. (1978). *Eye and brain: The psychology of seeing.* (3rd ed.). New York: McGraw–Hill.

Grencavage, L. M., & Norcross, J. C. (1990). Where are the commonalities among the therapeutic common factors? *Professional Psychology: Research and Practice, 21*, 372–378.

Griffin, D. R. (1959). *Echoes of bats and man.* New York: Anchor Books/Doubleday.

Griffith, D. R., Azuma, S. D., & Chasnoff, I. J. (1994). Three–year outcome of children exposed prenatally to drugs. Special Section: Cocaine babies. *Journal of the American Academy of Child and Adolescent Psychiatry, 33*, 20–27.

Griffith, E. E., Young, J. L, & Smith. (1984). An analysis of the therapeutic elements in a Black church service. *Hospital and Community Psychiatry, 35*, 464–469.

Griffitt, W. (1987). Females, males, and sexual responses. In K. Kelley, (Ed.), *Females, males, and sexuality: Theories and research,* Albany: State University of New York Press.

Griggs, R. A. & Cox, J. R. (1982). The elusive thematic–materials effect in Wason's selection task. *British Journal of Psychology, 73*, 407–420.

Grigsby, J. & Schneiders, J. L. (1991). Neuroscience, modularity, and personality theory: Conceptual foundations of a model of complex human functioning. *Psychiatry, 54*, 21–38.

Grob, C., & Dobkin de Rios, M. (1992). Adolescent drug use in cross–cultural perspective. *Journal of Drug Issues, 22*, 121–138.

Grochowicz, P. M., Schedlowski, M., Husband, A .J., & King, M. G. (1991). Behavioral conditioning prolongs heart allograft survival in rats. *Brain, Behavior, and Immunity, 5*, 349–356.

Gross, R. T., & Duke, P. M. (1980). The effect of early versus late physical maturation on adolescent behavior. *Pediatric Clinic of North America, 27*.

Grossman, A. (1985). Endorphins: Opiates for the masses. *Medicine & Science in Sports & Exercise, 17*, 101–105.

Grossman, H.J. (Ed.) (1977). *Manual on terminology and classification in mental retardation.* Washington, DC: American Association of Mental Deficiency.

Grossman, L. S., Harrow, M., Goldberg, J. F., & Fichtner, C. (1991). Outcome of schizoaffective disorder at two long–term follow–ups: Comparisons with outcome of schizophrenia and affective disorders. *American Journal of Psychiatry, 148*, 1359–1365.

Group for the Advancement of Psychiatry (GAP) Committee on Alcoholism and the Addictions (1991). Substance abuse disorders: A psychiatric priority. *American Journal of Psychiatry, 148*, 1291–1300.

Grunbaum, A. (1984). *The foundations of psychoanalysis: A philosophical critique.* Berkeley: University of California Press.

Grunberg, M. M., Morris, P. E., & Sykes, R. N. (1991). The obituary on everyday memory and its practical applications is premature. *American Psychologist, 46*, 74–76.

Grunewald, K. (1979). Mentally retarded children and young people in Sweden. *Acta Paediatrica Scandinavica*, suppl. 275, no. 75, 75–84.

Guerin, B. (1986). Mere presence effects in humans: A review. *Journal of Experimental Social Psychology, 22*, 38–77.

Guerin, B., & Innes, J. M. (1984). Explanations of social facilitation: A review. *Psychological Research and Reviews, 3*, 37–52.

Guilford, J. P. (1956). The structure of intellect. *Psychological Bulletin, 53*, 267–293.

Guilford, J. P. (1954). *Psychometric methods.* (2nd ed.). New York: McGraw–Hill.

Gulevich, G., Dement, W., & Johnson, L. (1966). Psychiatric and EEG observations on a case of prolonged wakfulness. *Archives of General Psychiatry, 15*, 29–35.

Gunnar, M., Larson, M.C., Hertsgaard, L., Harris, M.L., & Brodersen, L. (1992). The stressfulness of separation among nine–month–old infants: Effects of social context variables and infant temperament. *Child Development, 63*, 290–303.

Gunter, B., & McAleer, J. (1990). *Children and television: The one eyed monster?* London: Routledge.

Gur, R.C., Erwin, R., & Gur, R. E. (1992). Neurobehavioral probes for physiological neuroimaging studies. *Archives of General Psychiatry, 49*, 409–414.

Gust, D., Gordon, T., Brodie, A., & McClure, H. (1994). Effect of a preferred companion in modulating stress in adult female rhesus monkeys. *Physiology and Behavior, 4*, 681–684.

Gustavson, C. R., Kelly, D. J., Sweeny, M. & Garcia, J. (1976). Prey–lithium aversions: I: Coyotes and wolves. *Behavioral Biology, 17*, 61–72.

Guttfreund, D. G. (1990). Effects of language usage on the emotional experience of Spanish–English and English–Spanish bilinguals. *Journal of Consulting and Clinical Psychology, 58*, 604–607.

Guttman, D. (1974). The country of old men: Cross cultural studies in the psychology of later life. In R. LeVine (Ed.), *Culture and personality: Contemporary readings.* Chicago: Aldine.

Guze, B., & Barrio, J. (1991). The etiology of depresssion in Parkinson's disease patients. *Psychosomatics, 32*, 390–395.

Haber, R. N. (1979). Twenty years of haunting eidetic imagery: Where's the ghost? *Behavioral and Brain Sciences, 2*, 583–629.

Hadley, J. A., Holloway, E. L., & Mallinckrodt, B. (1993). Common aspects of object relations and self–representations in offspring from disparate dysfunctional families. *Journal of Counseling Psychology, 40*, 348–356.

Hafner, R. J., & Roder, M. J. (1987). Agoraphobia and parental bereavement. *Australian and New Zealand Journal of Psychiatry 21*, 340–344.

Haggerty, J. J., Stern, R., Mason, G., & Beckwith, J. (1993). Subclinical hypothyroidism: A modifiable risk factor for depression? *American Journal of Psychiatry, 150*, 508–510.

Hahn, W. K. (1987). Cerebral lateralizationof function: From infancy through childhood. *Psychological Bulletin, 101*, 376–392.

Haier, R., Siegel, B. V., Neuchterlein, K., & Hazlett, E. (1988). Cortical glucose metabolic rate correlates of abstract reasoning and attention studied with positron emission tomography. *Intelligence, 12*, 199–217.

Hajek, P., & Belcher, M. (1991). Dreams of absent–minded transgresssion: AN empirical study of a cognitive withdrawal symptom. *Journal of Abnormal Psychology, 100*, 487–491.

Halasz, P. (1993). Arousals without awakening: Dynamic aspect of sleep. *Physiology & Behavior, 54*, 795–802.

Haley, J. (1971). Family therapy: A radical change. In J. Haley (Ed.), *Changing families: A family therapy reader.* New York: Grune & Stratton.

Haley, J. (1976). *Problem–solving therapy.* San Francisco: Jossey–Bass.

Halford, G. (1989). Reflections on 25 years of Piagetian cognitive developmental psychology, 1963–1988. *Human Development, 32*, 325–357.

Halford, W., & Hayes, R. (1991). Psychological rehabilitation of chronic schizoprephrenic patients: Recent findings on social skills training and family psychoeducation. *Clinical Psychology Review, 11*, 23–44.

Hall, G. S. (1904). *Adolescence: Its psychology and its relations to physiology, anthropology, sociology, sex, crime, religion, and education.* Vols. 1–2. New York: Appleton–Century–Crofts.

Hallowell, A. I. (1955). *Culture and experience.* Philadelphia: University of Pennsylvania Press.

Hallstrom, T. (1973). *Mental disorder and sexuality in the climacteric.* Gotenborg: Scandinavian University Books.

Halmi, K. A., Goldberg, S., & Cunningham, S. (1977). Perceptual distribution of body image in adolescent girls: Distortion of body image in adolescence. *Psychological Medicine, 7,* 253–257.

Halverson, R. R., & Pallak, M. S. (1978). Commitment, ego–involvement, and resistance to attack. *Journal of Experimental Social Psychology, 14,* 1–12.

Hamilton, D. & Sherman, J. (1994). Stereotypes. In R. S. Wyer, Jr., & T. K. Srull, (Eds.), *Handbook of social cognition,* Vol. 1, *Basic processes,* (pp. 1–68) (2nd ed.). Hillsdale, NJ: Erlbaum.

Hamilton, D. L., Katz, L. B., & Leirer, V. O. Cognitive representation of personality impressions: Organizational processes in first impression formation. *Journal of Personality and Social Psychology, 39,* 1050–1063.

Hamilton, D. L., & Zanna, M. P. (1972). Differential weighting of favorable and unfavorable attributes in impressions of personality. *Journal of Experimental Research in Personality, 6,* 204–212.

Hamilton, W. D. (1964). The genetical theory of social behavior. *Journal of Thoeretical Biology, 6,* 1–52.

Hammen, C., Burge, D., & Adrian, C. (1991).Timing of mother and child depression in a longitudinal study of children at risk. *Journal of Consulting and Clinical Psychology, 59,* 341–345.

Hammen, C., Ellicott, A., Gitlin, M., & Jamison, K. R. (1989). Sociotropy/autonomyh and vulnerability to specific life events in patients with unipolar depression and bipolar disorders. *Journal of Abnormal Psychology, 98,* 154–160.

Hammond, P., & MacKay, D. (1977). Differential responsiveness of simple and complex cells in cat striate cortex to visual texture. *Experimental Brain Research, 30,* 275–296.

Hampson, S. E. (1995). *When is an inconsistency not an inconsistency?* Paper presented at the Nag's Head Conference on Personality and Social Behavior, June, Highland Beach, Florida.

Hanin, B., Sprour, N., Margolin, J., & Braun, P. (1993). Electroconvulsive therapy in mania: Successful outcome despite short duration of convulsions. *Convulsive Therapy, 9,* 50–53.

Harari, H., Harari, O., & White, R. V. (1985). The reaction to rape by American male bystanders. *Journal of Social Psychology, 125,* 653–658.

Hardaway, R. A. (1990). Subliminally activated symbiotic fantasies: Facts and artifacts. *Psychological Bulletin, 107,* 177–195.

Harder, D., Maggio, J., & Whitney, G. (1989). Assessing gustatory detection capabilities using preference procedures. *Chemical Senses, 14,* 547–564.

Harlow, H. F. (1958). The nature of love. *American Psychologist, 13,* 673–685.

Harlow, H. F., & Zimmerman, R. R. (1959). Affectional responses in the infant monkey. *Science, 130,* 421–432.

Harlow, R., & Cantor, N. (1994). Personality as problem solving: A framework for the analysis of change in daily–life behavior. *Journal of Personality Integration, 4,* 355–386.

Harris, A. R. (1982). The social psychology of deviance: Toward a reconciliation with social structure. *Annual Review of Sociology, 8,* 161–186.

Harris, B. (1979). Whatever happened to little Albert? *American Psychologist, 34,* 151–160.

Harris, C. S. (1965). Perceptual adaptation to inverted, reversed, or displaced vision. *Psychological Review, 72,* 419–444.

Harris, M. B., Walters, L. C., & Waschull, S. (191). Gender and ethnic differences in obesity–related behaviors and attitudes in a college sample. *Journal of Applied Social Psychology, 21,* 1545–1566.

Harris, T., Brown, G. W., & Bifulco, A. (1986). The loss of parent in childhood and adult psychiatric disorder: The role of lack of adequate parental care. *Psychological Medicine, 16,* 641–659.

Harris, Y. H. (1995). *The opportunity for romantic love among hunter–gatherers.* Paper presented at the annual convention of the Human Behavior and Evolution Society, June, Santa Barbara, California.

Hart, B., & Risley, T. (1992). American parenting of language–learning children: Persisting differences in family–child interactions observed in natural home environments. *Developmental Psychology, 28,* 1096–1105.

Harter, S. (1983). The development of self–esteem. In M. Hetherington (Ed.), *Handbook of child psychology: Vol. 4. Social and personality development* (pp. 275–386). New York: John Wiley.

Harter, S., & Monsour, A. (1992). Development analysis of conflict caused by opposing attributes in the adolescent self–portrait. *Developmental Psychology, 28,* 251–260.

Harth, E. (1985). Brainstem control of sensory information: A mechanism for perception. *International Journal of Psychophysiology, 3,* 101–119.

Hartline, H. K. (1938). The response of single optic nerve fibers of the vertebrate eye to illuminate of the retina. *American Journal of Physiology, 121,* 400–415.

Hartmann, H. (1939). *Ego psychology and the problem of adaptation.* New York: International Universities Press.

Hartshorne, H., & May, M. A. (1928). *Studies in the nature of character: Vol. 1. Studies in deceit.* New York: Macmillan.

Hartshorne, H., & May, M. A. (1929). *Studies in the nature of character: Vol. 2, Studies in service and self–control.* New York: Macmillan.

Hartup, W. (1989). Social relationships and their developmental significance. *American Psychologist, 44,* 120–126.

Harvey, J. H., & Weary, G. (1981). *Perspectives on attributional processses.* Dubuque, Iowa: William C. Brown.

Hasselhorn, M. (1990). The emergence of strategic knowledge activation in categorical clustering during retrieval. *Journal of Experimental Child Psychology, 50,* 59–80.

Hasselquist, D., & Bensch, S. (1991). Trade–off between mate guarding and mate attraction in the polygynous great reed warbler. *Behavioral Ecology and Sociobiology, 28,* 187–193.

Hatta, T. (1977). Hemispheric differences in a categorization matching task. *Japanese Journal of Psychology, 48,* 141–147.

Haugtvedt, C., & Petty, R. (1992). Personality and persuasion: Need for cognition moderates the persistence and resistance of attitude changes. *Journal of Personality and Social Psychology, 63,* 308–319.

Hay, D. F., Caplan, M., Castle, J., & Stimson, C. A. (1991). Does sharing become increasingly 'rational' in the second year of life? *Developmental Psychology, 27,* 987–993.

Hazan, C., & Shaver, P. (1987). Romantic love conceptualized as an attachment process. *Journal of Personality and Social Psychology, 57,* 731–739.

Hazan, C., & Shaver, P. (1994). Attachment as an organizational framework for research on close relationships. *Psychological Inquiry, 5,* 1–22.

Hazelwood, R. (1993). Analyzing the rape and profiling the offenders. In. R. Hazelwood & A. Burgess (Eds.), *Practical aspects of rape investigation: A multidisciplinary approach.* Boca Raton, Fla: CRC Press.

Hazelwood, R., & Harpold, J. (1986). Rape: The dangers of providing confrontational advice. *FBI Law Enforcement Bulletin.*

Hazelwood, R., & Warren, J. (1989). The serial rapist: His characteristics and victims. *FBI Law Enforcement Bulletin, 58,* 10–17.

Hazzard, A., Weston, J., & Gutterres, C. (1992). After a child's death: Factors related to parental bereavement. *Journal of Developmental & Behavioral Pediatrics, 13,* 24–30.

Heath, R. G. (1955). Correlations between levels of psychological awareness and physiological activity in the central nervous system. *Psychosomatic Medicine, 17,* 383–395.

Hegarty, J., Baldessarini, R., Tohen, M., Waternaux, C., & Oepen, G. (1994). One hundred years of schizophrenia: A meta–analysis of the outcome literature. *American Journal of Psychiatry, 151,* 1409–1416.

Heider, F. (1946). Attitudes and cognitive organization. *Journal of Psychology, 21,* 107–112.

Heider, F. (1958). *The psychology of interpersonal relations.* New York: John Wiley.

Heimburger, R. F. et al. (1966). Stereotaxic amygdalotomy for epilepsy with aggressive behavior. *Journal of American Medical Association, 198,* 165–169.

Held, R., & Hein, A. (1963).

Movement–produced stimulation in the development of visually deprived behavior. *Journal of Comparative and Physiological Psychology, 56*, 872–876.

Heller, D. (1986). *The children's God.* Chicago: University of Chicago Press.

Helmholtz, H. von. (1852). On the theory of compound colors. *Philosophical Magazine, 4*, 519–534.

Helmholtz, H. von. (1863). *Die Lehre von den tonempfindungen als physiolgisdne grundlage fur die theorie der musik.* Brunswick: Vierweg–Verlag.

Helmholtz, H. von. (1909). *Treatise on physiological optics.* New York: Dover, 1962.

Helmholtz, H. von. (1962). *Treatise on physiological optics* (Vol. 3). New York: Dover.

Helson, R., & Moane, G. (1987). Personality change in women from college to midlife. *Journal of Personality and Social Psychology, 53*, 176–86.

Hendrick, C., & Hendrick, S. (1986). A theory and method of love. *Journal of Personality and Social Psychology, 50*, 392–402.

Henley, K., & Morrison, A.R. (1974). A re–evaluation of the effects of lesions of the positive tegmentum and locus coeruleus on phenomena of paradoxical sleep in the cat. *Acta Neurobiologica Experimental, 34*, 215–232.

Henry, W. P., Schacht, T. E., & Strupp, H. (1990). Patient and therapist introject, interpersonal process, and differential psychotherapy outcome. *Journal of Consulting and Clinical Psychology, 58*, 768–774.

Herbert, T. B., & Cohen, S. (1993). Depression and immunity: A meta–analytic review. *Psychological Bulletin, 113*, 472–486.

Herdt, G. H. (Ed.). (1984). *Ritualized Homosexuality in Melanesia.* Berkeley: CA: University of California Press.

Herek, G., Janis, I., & Huth, P. (1987). Decision making during international crises: Is quality of process related to outcome? *Journal of Conflict Resolution, 31*, 203–226.

Herek, G. M., Janis, I. L., & Huth, P. (1987). Decision making during international crises. *Journal of Conflict Resolution, 31*, 203–226.

Hergenhan, B. R. (1976). *An introduction to theories of learning.* Belmont, CA: Wadsworth.

Hering, E. (1878). *Zur lehre vom lichtsinne.* Vienna: Gerold.

Hering, E. (1920). *Grundzuge der Lehr vs. Lichtsinn.* Berlin: Springer–Verlag.

Heritch, A., Henderson, K., & Westfall, T. (1990). Effects of social isolation on brain catecholamines and forced swimming in rats. *Journal of Psychiatric Research, 24*, 251–258.

Herman, J., Perry, J. C., & Van der Kolk, B. A. (1989). Childhood trauma in borderline personality disorder. *American Journal of Psychiatry, 146*, 490–495.

Herman, J. L. (1992). *Trauma and recovery: The aftermath of violence—from domestic violence to political terror.* New York: Basic Books.

Hernandez, A. P. (1990). Artificial intelligence and expert systems in law enforcement: Current and potential uses. *Computers, Environment, and Urban Systems, 14*, 299–306.

Hernandez, L., & Hoevel, B. (1989). Food intake and lateral hypothalamic self–stimulation covary after medial hypothalamic lesions or ventral midbrain 6–hydroxy-dopamine injections that cause obesity. *Behavioral Neuroscience, 103*, 412–422.

Hersen, M. (Ed.). (1988). *Behavioral assessment: A practical handbook.* New York: Pergamon.

Hersey, P., & Blanchard, K. (1982). Management of organizational behavior: *Utilizing human resources.* (2nd ed.). Englewood Cliffs, NJ: Prentice–Hall.

Hertzog, C., Dixon, R., & Hultsch, D. (1990). Relationships between metamemory, memory predictions, and memory task performance in adults. *Psychology and Aging,* 215–227.

Hess, E. H. (1956). Space perception in the chick. *Scientific American,* 71–80.

Hess, E. H. (1959). Imprinting. *Science, 130*, 135–141.

Hess, E. H. (1975). *The tell–tale eye.* Cincinnati: Van Nostrand.

Heston, L. L. (1966). Psychiatric disorders in foster home reared children of schizophrenic mothers. *British Journal of Psychiatry, 112*, 819–825.

Hetherington, A. W., & Ranson, S. W. (1940). Hypothalamic lesions and adiposity in the rat. *The Anatomical Record, 78*, 149–172.

Hetherington, E. M. (1989). Coping with family transitions: Winners, losers, and survivors. *Developmental Psychology, 7*, 313–326.

Hewstone, M., & Jaspars, J. (1987). Covariation and causal attribution: A logical model of the intuitive analysis of variance. *Journal of Personality and Social Psychology, 43*, 663–672.

Heyser, C. T., Hampson, R. E., & Deadwyler, S. A. (1993). Effects of delta–9–tetrahydrocannabinol on delayed match to sample performance in rats: Alterations in short–term memory associated with changes in task specific firing of hippocampal cells. *Journal of Pharmacology and Experimental Therapeutics, 264*, 294–307.

Higgins, E. T. (1987). Self–discrepancy: A theory relating self and affect. *Psychological Review, 94*, 319–340.

Higgins, E. T. (1990). Lay epistemic theory and the relation between motivation and cognition. *Psychological Inquiry, 1*, 209–210.

Higgins, E. T. (1990). Personality, social psychology, and person–situation relations: Standards and knowledge activation as a common language. In L. Pervin (Ed.), *Handbook of personality: Theory and research* (pp. 301–338). New York.: Guilford Press.

Higgins, E. T., & Bargh, J. A. (1987). Social cognition and social perception. *Annual Review of Psychology, 38*, 369–425.

Higgins, E. T., Klein, R., & Strauman, T. (1985). Self–concept discrepancy theory: A psychological model for distinguishing among different aspects of depression and anxiety. *Social Cognition, 3*, 51–76.

Higley, J., Mehlman, P., Taub, D., Higley, S., Suomi, S., Linnoila, M., & Vickers, J. H. (1992). Cerebrospinal fluid momoamine and adrenal correlates of aggression in free–ranging rhesus monkeys. *Archives of General Psychiatry, 49*, 436–441.

Hilgard, E. R. (1965). *Hypnotic susceptibility.* New York: Harcourt Brace Jovanovich.

Hilgard, E. R. (1986). *Divided consciousness: Multiple controls in human thought and action.* New York: John Wiley.

Hilgard, E. R., & Hilgard, J. R. (1975). *Hypnosis in the relief of pain.* Los Altos, CA: William Kaufman.

Hill, J. W. & Bliss, J. C. (1967). Properties of human tactile memory. *Psychonomic Bulletin, 1*, 15.

Hilliard, R. B. (1993). Single–case methodology in psychotherapy process and outcome research. *Journal of Consulting and Clinical Psychology, 61*, 373–380.

Hilts, P. (1980). Bulldozers, bassoons, and silicone chips. *Science, 80*, 77–79.

Himmelweit, H. T., Humphreys P., Jaegers, M., & Katz, M. (1981). *How voters decide: A longitudinal study of political attitudes and voting extended over fifteen years.* London: Academic Press.

Hinde, R. (1982). *Ethology: Its nature and relations with other sciences.* New York: Oxford University Press.

Hindmarch, I. (1991). Residual effects of hypnotics: An update. *Journal of Clinical Psychiatry, 52*(s), 14–15.

Hines, M. (1982). Prenatal gonadal hormones and sex differences in human bahavior. *Psychological Bulletin, 92*, 56–80.

Hinkle, L. E. Jr. & Plummer, N. (1952). Life stress and industrial absenteeism. *Industrial Medicine and Surgery, 21*, 363–375.

Hinz, L. D., & Williamson, D. A. (1987). Bulimia and depression: A review of the affective variant hypothesis. *Psychological Bulletin, 102*, 150–158.

Hirsch, J., & Knittle, J. L. (1970). Cellularity of obese and nonobese human adipose tissue. *Federation Proceedings, 29*, 1516–1521.

Hirst, W. (1986). The psychology of attention. In J. Ledoux & W. Hirst (Eds.), *Mind and brain: Dialogues in cognitive neuroscience* (pp. 105–142). Cambridge: Cambridge University Press.

Hobson, J. A. (1988). *The dreaming brain.* New York: Basic Books.

Hobson, P. R. (1985). Self–representing dreams. *Psychoanalytic Psychotherapy, 1*, 43–53.

Hochberg, J. (1970). Attention, organization, and consciousness. In D. I. Mostofsky

(Ed.), *Attention: Contemporary theory and analysis.* New York: Appleton–Century–Crofts.

Hochberg, J., & Brooks, V. (1978). Art and perception. In E.C. Carterette & H. Freedman (Eds.), *Handbook of perception.* New York: Academic Press.

Hock, E., & DeMeis, D. (1990). Depression in mothers of infants: The role of maternal employment. *Developmental Psychology, 26,* 285–291.

Hoebel, B. G., & Teitelbaum, P. (1966). Weight regulation in normal and hyperphagic rats. *Journal of Comparative and Physiological Psychology, 61,* 189–193.

Hoek, H. W. (1993). Review of the epidemiological studies of eating disorders. *International Review of Psychiatry, 5,* 61–74.

Hoff–Ginsberg, E. (1986). Function and structure in maternal speech: Their relation to the child's development of syntax. *Developmental Psychology, 22,* 155–163.

Hoff–Ginsberg, E. (1990). Maternal speech and the child's development of syntax: A further look. *Journal of Child Language, 17,* 85–99.

Hoff–Ginsberg, E., & Shatz, M. (1982). Linguistic input and the child's acquisition of language. *Psychological Review, 92,* 3–26.

Hoffman, L. (1981). *Foundations of family therapy.* New York: Basic Books.

Hoffman, L. (1991). A reflexive stance for family therapy. *Journal of Strategic and Systemic Therapies, 10,* 4–17.

Hoffman, M. (1990). Empathy and justice motivation. *Motivation and Emotion, 14,* 151–172.

Hoffman, M. L. (1978). Psychological and biological perspectives on altruism. *International Journal of Behavioral Development, 1,* 323–339.

Hoffman, M. L. (1982). Development of prosocial motivation: Empathy and guilt. In N. Eisenberg (Ed.), *The development of prosocial behavior.* New York: Academic Press.

Hoffman, M. L. (1994). Discipline and internalization. *Developmental Psychology, 30,* 26–28.

Hoffman, M. L., & Saltzstein, H. D. (1967). Parent discipline and the child's moral development. *Journal of Personality and Social Psychology, 5,* 45–7.

Hoffman, W. S., Carpentier–Alting, P., Thomas, D., & Hamilton, V. L. (1991). Initial impact of plant closings on automobile workers and their families. *Families in Society, 72,* 103–107.

Hogan, R. (1983). What every student should know about personality psychology. In A. M. Rogers and J. Scheirer (Eds.), *G. Stanley Hall Lecture Series,* vol. 6. Washington, DC: American Psychological Association.

Hogan, R. (1987). Personality psychology: Back to basics. In J.Aronoff et al. (Eds.), *The emergence of personality.* New York: Springer.

Hogan, R., Curphy, G., & Hogan, J. (1994). What we know about leadership: Effectiveness and personality. *American Psychologist, 49,* 493–304.

Hohmann, G. W. (1966). Some effects of spinal cord lesions on experienced emotional feelings. *Psychophysiology, 3,* 143–156.

Holden, C. (1980). Identical twins reared apart. *Science, 207,* 1323–1325.

Holden, C. (1987). Creativity and the troubled mind. *Psychology Today, 21,* 9–10.

Holland, J., Holyoak, K., Nisbett, R., & Thagard, P. (1986). *Induction: Processes of inference, learning, and discovery.* Cambridge, MA: MIT Press.

Hollander, E., Stein, D. J., DeCaria, C. M., Cohen, L., Saoud, J.B., Skodol, A. E., Kellman, D., Rosnick, L., & Oldham, J. M. (1994). Serotonergic sensitivity in borderline personality disorder: Preliminary findings. *American Journal of Psychiatry, 151,* 277–280.

Holldobler, B., & Lumsden, C. J. (1980). Territorial strategies in ants. *Science, 210,* 732–739.

Hollingworth, L. S. (1926). *Gifted children: Their nature and nurture.* New York: Macmillan.

Hollingworth, L. S. (1931). The child of very superior intelligence as a special problem in social development. *Mental Hygiene, 15,* 3–16.

Hollingworth, L. W. (1942). *Children above 180 IQ Stanford–Binet: Origin and development.* Yonkers, NY: World Book.

Hollon, S. Cognitive therapy. In Lyn Y. Abramson (Ed.), *Social cognition and clinical psychology: A synthesis* (pp. 204–253). New York: Guilford Press.

Hollon, S., & Beck, A. T. (1994). Cognitive and cognitive–behavioral therapies. In A.Bergin & S. Garfield (Eds.), *Handbook of psychotherapy and behavior change* (pp. 428–466). (4th ed.). New York: John Wiley.

Hollon, S., Shelton, R. C., & Loosen, P. (1991). Cognitive therapy and pharmacotherapy for depression. *Journal of Consulting and Clinical Psychology, 59,* 88–99.

Holm, J. E., Holroyd, K. A., Hursey, K. G., & Penzien, D. B. (1986). The role of stress in recurrent tension headache. *Headache,* 160–167.

Holmes, D. (1990). The evidence for repression: An examination of sixty years of research. In J. L. Singer, (Ed.), *Repression and dissociation: Implications for personality theory, psychopathology, and health* (pp. 85–102). Chicago, IL: University of Chicago Press.

Holmes, T. H., & Rahe, R. H. (1967). The social readjustment rating scale. *Journal of Psychosomatic Research, 11,* 213–218.

Holroyd, K. A., & Penzien, D. B. (1990). Pharmacological versus non–pharmacological prophylaxis of recurrent migraine headache: A meta–analytic review of clinical trials. *Pain, 42,* 1–13.

Holt, R. (1976). Drive or wish? A reconsideration of the psychoanalytic theory of motivation. In M.Gill & P. Holzman (Eds.), *Psychology vs. metapsychology: Psychoanalytic essays in memory of George Klein. Psychological Issues,* Monograph 36, Vol. 9, No. 4.

Holt, R. R. (1985). The current status of psychoanalytic theory. *Psychoanalytic Psychology, 2,* 289–315.

Holyoak, K. J., & Spellman, B. A. (1993). Thinking. *Annual Review of Psychology, 44,* 265–315.

Homans, G. (1961). *Social behavior: Its elementary forms.* London: Routledge & Kegan Paul.

Honeybourne, C., Matchett, G., & Davey, G. (1993). Expectancy models of laboratory preparedness effects: A UCS–expectancy bias in phylogenetic and ontogenetic fear–relevant stimuli. *Behavior Therapy, 24,* 253–264.

Hooley, J., & Teasdale, J. D. (1989). Predictors of relapse in unipolar depressives: Expressed emotion, marital distress and perceived criticism. *Journal of Abnormal Psychology, 98,* 229–235.

Hooley, J., Rosen, L., & Richters, J. (in press). Expressed emotion: Toward clarification of a critical construct. In G.A.. Miller (Ed.), *The behavioral high–risk paradigm in psychopathology.* New York: Spring–Verlag.

Hooley, J. M. (1985). Expressed emotion: A review of the critical literature. *Clinical Psychology Review, 5,* 119–139.

Hooley, J. M. (1987). The nature and origins of expressed emotion. In K. Hahlweg and M. J. Goldstein (Eds.), *Understanding major mental disorder: The contribution of family interaction research* (pp. 176–194). New York: Family Process Press.

Horn, J. (1992). *Major abilities and development in the adult period.* Cambridge: Cambridge University Press.

Horn, J. M., Loehlin, J. C., & Willerman, L. (1979). Intellectual resemblance among adoptive and biological relatives: The Texas Adoption Project. *Behavior Genetics, 9,* 177–207.

Horn, J. M., Loehlin, J. C., & Willerman, L. (1982). Aspects of the inheritance of intellectual abilities. *Behavior Genetics, 12,* 479–516.

Horn, J. C., & Meer, J. (1987). The vintage years. *Psychology Today, 21,* 76–90.

Horn, J. L., & Cattell, R. B. (1967). Age differences in fluid and crystallized intelligence. *Acta Psychologica, 26,* 107–129.

Horn, J. L., & Hofer, S. M. (Eds.). Major abilities and development in the adult period. In R.J. Sternberg & C.A. Berg (1992), *Intellectual development* (pp.44–99). New York: Cambridge University Press.

Horner, T. M., & Chethik, L. (1986). Conversation attentiveness and following in 12– and 18–week–old infants. *Infant Behavior and Development, 9,* 203–213.

Horney, K. (1937). *The neurotic personality of our time.* New York: W. W. Norton.

Horney, K. (1950). *Neurosis and human growth: The struggle toward self–realization.* New York: W. W. Norton.

Horowitz, M. (1988). *Introduction to psychodynamics: A synthesis.* New York: Basic Books.

Horvath, A. O., & Luborsky, L. (1993). The role of the therapeutic alliance in psychotherapy. *Journal of Consulting and Clinical Psychology, 61,* 561–573.

House, J. S., Landis, K. R., & Umberson, D. (1988). Social relationships and health. *Science, 241,* 540–545.

House, J. S., Umberson, D., & Landis, K. R. (1988). Structures and processes of social support. *American Review of Sociology, 14,* 293–318.

House, R. J. (1977). A 1976 theory of charismatic leadership. In J. G. Hunt & L. L. Larson (Eds.), *Leadership: The cutting edge* (pp. 189–207). Carbondale, IL: Southern Ill. University Press.

House, R. J., & Howell, J. M. (1992). Personality and charismatic leadership. *Leadership Quarterly, 3,* 81–108.

House, R. J., & Singh, J. V. (1987). Organizational behavior: Some new directions for I/O psychology. *Annual Review of Psychology, 38,* 669–718.

Hovland, C. (1937). The generalization of conditioned responses: IV. The effects of varying amounts of reinforcement upon the degree of generalization of conditioned responses. *Journal of General Psychology, 21,* 261–276.

Hovland, C. (1937). The generalization of conditioned responses: The sensory generalization of conditioned responses with varying frequencies of time. *Journal of General Psychology, 21,* 125–148.

Hovland, C. I., Campbell, E. H., & Brock, T. (1957). The effect of "commitment" on opinion change following communication. In C. I. Hovland (Ed.), *Order of presentation in persuasion.* New Haven, Conn.: Yale University Press.

Hovland, C. I., Irving, L. J., & Harold, H. K. (1953). *Communication and persuasion: Psychological studies of opinion changes.* New Haven, Conn.: Yale University Press.

Hovland, C. I., & Janis, I. (Eds.) (1959). *Personality and persuasibility.* New Haven, Conn.: Yale University Press.

Howard, K. I., Kopta, S. M., Krause, M. S., & Orlinsky, D. E. (1986). The dose–effect relationship in psychotherapy. *American Psychologist, 41,* 159–164.

Howard, A., Pion, G., Gottfredson, G., Flattau, P., Oskamp, S., Pfafflin, S., Bray, D., & Burstin, A. (1986). The changing face of American psychology: A report form the Committee on Employment and Human Resources. *American Psychologist, 41,* 1311–1327.

Howes, C. (1990). Can the age of entry into child care and the quality of child care predict adjustment in kindergarten? *Developmental Psychology, 26,* 292–303.

Howes, C., & Hamilton, C. E. (1992). Children's relationships with child care teachers: Stability and concordance with parental attachments. *Child Development, 63,* 867–878.

Howes, C., Phillips, D. A., & Whitebook, M. (1992). Thresholds of quality: Implications for the social development of children in center–based child care. *Child Development,* 449–460.

Hser, Y., Anglin, M. D., & Powers, K. (1993). A 24–year follow–up of California narcotics addicts. *Archives of General Psychiatry, 50,* 577–584.

Hsu, F.L.K. (1981). *Americans and Chinese: Passage to difference.* (3rd ed.). Honolulu: University Press of Hawaii.

Hsu, L.K.G. (1989). The gender gap in eating disorders: Why are the eating disorders more common among women. *Clinical Psychology Review, 9,* 393–407.

Huang, E. (1995). When AIDS education fails: How personality, perceived HIV–risk, and HIV–risk knowledge predict risky behaviors for contracting HIV. Unpublished honors thesis, Harvard University, Cambridge, Massachusetts.

Hubel, D. H., & Wiesel, T. N. (1959). Receptive fields of single neruons in the cat's striate cortex. *Journal of Physiology, 148,* 574–591.

Hubel, D. H., & Wiesel, T. N. (1963). Single–cell responses in striate cortex of kittens deprived of vision in one eye. *Journal of Neuropsychology, 26,* 1003–1009.

Hubel, D. H., & Wiesel, T. N. (1970). Stereoscopic vision in macaque monkey. *Nature, 225,* 41–42.

Hubel, D. H., & Wiesel, T. N. (1979). Brain mechanisms of vision. *Scientific American, 241,* 150–162.

Hudson, J. L., & Pope, H. G. (1990). Affective spectrum disorder: Does antidepressant response identify a family of disorders with a common pathophysiology? *American Journal of Psychiatry, 147,* 552–564.

Hudspeth, A. J. (1985). The cellular basis of hearing: The biophysics of hair cells. *Science, 230,* 745–752.

Hull, C. L. (1943). *Principles of behavior: An introduction to behavior theory.* New York: Oxford University Press.

Hull, C. L. (1951). *Essentials of behavior.* New Haven, Conn.: Yale University Press.

Hull, C. L. (1952). *A behavior system: An introduction to behavior theory concerning the individual organism.* New Haven, Conn.: Yale University Press.

Hull, J. G., & Bond, C. F. (1986). Social and behavioral consequences of alcohol consumption and expectancy: A meta–analysis. *Psychological Bulletin, 99,* 347–360.

Hultsch, D., & Dixon, R. (1990). Learning and memory in aging. In J. Birren & K.W. Schaie (Eds.), *Handbook of the psychology of aging.* (3rd. ed.). New York: Academic Press.

Humphrey, A., & Saul, A. (1992). Action of brain stem reticular afferents on lagged and nonlagged cells in the cat lateral geniculate nucleus. *Journal of Neurophysiology, 68,* 673–691.

Hunt, E., & Agnoli, F. (1991). The Whorfian hypothesis: A cognitive psychology perspective. *Psychological Review, 98,* 377–389.

Huntington, S. P. (1968). *Political order in changing societies.* New Haven, Conn.: Yale University Press.

Hurley, A. D. & Sovner, R. (1985). Behavior modification: III. The token economy. *Psychiatric Aspects of Mental Retardation Reviews, 4,* 1–4.

Hurvich, L. M., & Jameson, D. (1957). An opponent–process theory of color vision. *Psychological Review, 64,* 384–404.

Huston, A. C. (1983). Sex–typing. In M. Hetherington (Ed.), *Handbook of child psychology: Vol. 4. Social and personality develpment.* New York: John Wiley.

Huston, T. L. (1973). Ambiguity of acceptance, social desirability, and dating choice. *Journal of Experimental Social Psychology, 9,* 32–42.

Huttenlocher, J., & Hedges, L. V. (1994). Combining graded categories: Membership and typicality. *Psychological Review, 101,* 157–165.

Hyde, J. S. (1984). How large are gender differences in aggression? A developmental meta–analysis. *Developmental Psychology, 20,* 722–36.

Hyde, J. S. (1990). Meta–analysis and the psychology of gender differences. *Signs, 16,* 55–73.

Hyde, J. S., Krajnik, M., & Skuldt–Niederberger, K. (1991). Androgyny across the life span: A replication and longitudinal follow–up. *Developmental Psychology, 27,* 516–519.

Inhelder, B., & Piaget, J. (1958). *The growth of logical thinking from childhood to adolescence.* New York: Basic Books.

Inkeles, A., & Smith, D. H. (1974). *Becoming modern: Individual change in six developing countries.* Cambridge, MA: Harvard University Press.

Innis, N. K. (1992). Early research on the inheritance of the ability to learn. *American Psychologist, 47,* 190–197.

Insel, T. R. (1985). Obsessive–compulsive disorder. *Psychiatric Clinics of North America 8,* 105–117.

Insel, T. R. (1992). Neurobiology of obsessive compulsive disorder: A review. *Journal of Clinical Psychopharmacology, 7,* 31–33.

Insko, C. A. (1964). Primacy versus recency in persuasion as a function of the timing of arguments and measures. *Journal of Abnormal and Social Psychology, 69,* 381–391.

Insko, C. A. (1985). Conformity and group size: The concern with being right and the concern with being liked. *Personality and Social Psychology Bulletin, 11,* 41–50.

Insko, C. A., Arkoff, A., & Insko, V. M.

(1965). Effects of high and low fear–arousing communications upon opinions toward smoking. *Journal of Experimental Social Psychology, 1,* 156–266.

Irwin, M., Schafer, G., & Feiden, C. (1974). Emic and unfamiliar category sorting of Mano farmers and U.S. undergraduates. *Journal of Cross–Cultural Psychology, 5,* 407–423.

Irwin, M. H., & McLaughlin, D. H. (1970). Ability and preference in category sorting by Mano school children and adults. *Journal of Social Psychology, 82,* 15–24.

Isen, A. (1984). Toward understanding the role of affect in cognition. In R.S. Wyer, Jr. & T.K. Srull (Eds.), *Handbook of social cognition, Vol. 3.* Hillsdale, NJ: Erlbaum.

Isen, A., & Levin, P. F. (1972). Effects of feeling good on helping: cookies and kindness. *Journal of Personality and Social Psychology, 21,* 384–388.

Isen, A., & Diamond, G. (1989). Affect and automaticity. In J. Uleman & J. Bargh (Eds.), *Unintended thought* (pp. 124–152). New York: Guilford Press.

Islam, M. R., & Hewstone, M. (1993). Intergroup attributions and affective consequences in majority and minority groups. *Journal of Personality and Social Psychology, 64,* 936–950.

Ittenbach, R. F., Bruininks, R. H., Thurlow, M. L., & McGrew, K. S. (1993). Community integration of young adults with mental retardation: A multivariate analysis of adjustment. *Research in Developmental Disabilities, 14,* 275–290.

Iwashita, Y., Kawaguchi, S., & Murata, M. (1994). Restoration of function by replacement of spinal cord segments in the rat. *Nature, 367,* 167–169.

Izard, C. (1990). Facial expressions and the regulation of emotions. *Journal of Personality and Social Psychology, 58,* 487–498.

Izard, C. E. (1971). *The face of emotion.* New York: Appleton.

Izard, C. E. (1977). *Human emotions.* New York: Plenum Press.

Izard, C. E. (1978). Emotions in personality and psychopathology: An introduction. In C. E. Izard & R. Zajonc (Eds.), *Emotion in personality and psychopathology.* New York: Plenum Press.

Izard, C. E. & Buechler, S. (1980). Aspects of consciousness and personality in terms of differential emotions theory. In R. Plutchik & H. Kellerman (Eds.), *Emotion: Theory, research, and experience, Vol. I: Theories of emotion.* New York: Academic Press.

Izard, C. E., Libero, C., Putnam, P., & Haynes, O. M. (1993) Stability of emotional experiences and their relations to traits of personality. *Journal of Personality and Social Psychology, 64,* 847–860.

Jablenski, A. (1989). Epidemiology and cross–cultural aspects of schizophrenia. *Psychiatric Annals, 19,* 516–524.

Jacklin, C. (1989). Female and male: Issues of gender. *American Psychologist, 44,*127–133.

Jacob, T., Krahn, G. L., & Leonard, K. (1991). Parent–child interactions in families with alcoholic fathers. *Journal of Consulting and Clinical Psychology, 59,* 176–181.

Jacob, T., & Leonard, K. (1991). Experimental drinking procedures in the study of alcoholics and their families: A consideration of ethical issues. *Journal of Consulting and Clinical Psychology, 59,* 249–255.

Jacobs, J. E., & Eccles, J. (1992). The impact of mothers' gender–role stereotypic beliefs on mothers' and children's ability perceptions. *Journal of Personality and Social Psychology, 63,* 932–944.

Jacobs, T. J., & Charles, E. (1980). Life events and the occurrence of cancer in children. *Psychosomatic Medicine, 42,* 11–24.

Jacobson, E. (1964). The self and the object world. *Psychoanalytic Study of the Child, 9,* 75–127.

Jacobson, J., Jacobson, S., & Humphrey, H. (1990). Effects of exposure to PCB's and related componds on growth and activity in children. *Neurotoxicology and Teratology, 12,* 319–326.

Jacobson, J., Jacobson, S., & Humphrey, H. (1990). Effects of in utero exposure to polychlorinated buphenyls on cogntive functioning in young children. *Journal of Pediatrics, 116,* 38–45.

Jacobson, J., Jacobson, S., Padgett, R., Brumitt, G., & Billings, R. (1992). Effects of prenatal PCB exposure on cogntive processing efficiency and sustained attention. *Developmental Psychology, 28,* 297–307.

Jacobson, J. L., Jacobsen, S. W., Sokol, R. J., Martier, S. S. (1993). Teratogenic effects of alcohol on infant development. *Alcoholism: Clinical and Experimental Research, 17,* 174–183.

Jacoby, L. L., & Kelley, C. M. (1987). Unconscious influences of memory for a prior event. *Personality and Social Psychology Bulletin, 13,* 314–336.

Jacobson, J. L., & Wille, D. E. (1986). The influence of attachment pattern on developmental changes in peer interaction from the toddler to the preschool period. *Child Development, 57,* 338–47.

Jacques, E. (1965). Death and the mid–life crisis. *International Journal of Psychoanalysis, 46,* 502–514.

Jaeger, J. J. (1992). 'Not by the chair of my hinny hin hin': Some general properties of slips of the tongue in young children. *Journal of Child Language, 19,* 335–366.

Jahoda, A., Markova, I., & Cattermole, M. (1988). Stigma and the self concept of people with a mild mental handicap. *Journal of Mental Deficiency Research, 32,* 103–115.

Jahoda, G. Psychology and social change in developing countries. In *Proceedings of the XVIth International Congress of Applied Psychology.* Amsterdam: Swets and Zeitlinger.

James, W. (1884). What is emotion? *Mind, 19,* 188–205.

James, W. (1890). *Principles of psychology,* Vol. 1. New York: Henry Holt.

James, W. (1910). The Self. In *Psychology: The briefer course.* New York: Henry Holt and Co. Reprinted in C. Gordon & K.J. Gergen, *The self in social interaction,* 1968. New York: JohnWiley.

Jamison, K. R. (1989). Mood disorders and patterns of creativity in British writers and artists. *Psychiatry, 52,* 125–134.

Jamison, K. R. (1993). *Touched with fire.* New York: Free Press.

Janal, M. N., Colt, W. D., Clark, W. C., & Glusman, M. (1984). Pain sensitivity, mood and plasma endocrine levels in man following long–distance running: effects of naloxone. *Pain, 19,* 13–25.

Jangid, R. K., Vyas, J. N., & Shukla, T. R. (1988). The effects of the transcendental meditation programme on the normal individuals. *Journal of Personality and Clinical Studies, 4,* 145–149.

Janis, I. (1972). *Victims of groupthink: A psychological study of foreign–policy decisions and fiascos.* Boston: Houghton Mifflin.

Janis, I. (1989). Crucial decisions: *Leadership in policymaking and crisis management.* New York: Free Press.

Janis, I., & Mann, L. (1977). Decision making. New York: Free Press.

Janoff–Bulman, R. (1992). *Shattered assumptions: Towards a new psychology of trauma.* New York: Free Press.

Janos, P. M., & Robinson, N. M. (1985). Psychosocial development in intellectually gifted children. In Horowitz, F. D., & O'Brien, M. (Eds.) The gifted and talented: *Developmental perspectives* (pp. 149–195). Washington, DC: American Psychological Association.

Janowitz, H. D., & Grossman, M. I. (1949). Some factors affecting the food intake of normal dogs and dogs esophagostomy and gastric fistula. *American Journal of Physiology, 159,* 143–48.

Jansen, M. A. (1986). Mental health policy: Observations from Europe. *American Psychologist, 41,* 1273–1278.

Jarmas, A., & Kazak, A. (1992). Young adult children of alcoholic fathers: Depressive experiences, coping styles, and family systems. *Journal of Consulting and Clinical Psychology, 60,* 244–251.

Jasmos, T. M., & Hakmiller, K. I. (1975). Some effects of lesion level, and emotional cues of affective expression in spinal cord patients. *Psychological Reports, 37,* 859–870.

Jelicic, M. & Bonke, B. (1991). Level of processing affects performance on explicit and implicit memory tasks. *Perceptual and Motor Skills, 72(3, Pt.2),* 1263–1266.

Jemmott, J. B. III, Borysenko, J. Z., Borysenko, M., McClelland, D. C., Chapman, R., Meyer, D. & Benson, H. (1983). Academic stress, power motivation, and decrease in salivary secretory immunoglobin A secretion rate. *Lancet, 1,* 1400–1402.

Jemmott, J. B. III & Locke, S. E. (1984). Psychosocial factors, immunologic mediation, and human susceptiility to infectious diseases: How much do we know? *Psychological Bulletin, 95*, 78–108.

Jenike, M., Baer, L., Ballantine, T., & Martuza, R. (1991). Cingulotomy for refractory obsessive–compulsive disorder: A long–term follow–up of 33 patients. *Archives of General Psychiatry, 48*, 548–555.

Jenike, M. A. (1983). Obsessive compulsive disorder. *Comprehensive Psychiatry, 24*, 99–111.

Jenkins, J. H., & Karno, M (1992). The meaning of expressed emotion: Theoretical issues raised by cross–cultural research. *American Journal of Psychiatry, 149*, 9–21.

Jensen, A. R. (1969). How much can we boost IQ and scholastic achievement? *Harvard Educational Review, 39*, 1–123.

Jensen, A. R. (1973). *Educability and group differences*. New York: Harper & Row.

Jensen, A. R. (1980). *Bias in mental testing*. New York: Free Press.

Jensen, A. R., & Reynolds, C. R. (1982). Race, social class and ability patterns on the WISC–R. *Personality and Individual Differences, 3*, 423–438.

Jessop, D. J. (1982). Topic variation in levels of agreement between parents and adolescents. *Public Opinion Quarterly, 46*, 538–559.

Jewesbury, E.C.O. (1951). Insensitivity to pain. *Brain, 74*, 336–353.

Jimmerson, D., Lesem, M., Kaye, W., Hegg, A., & Brewerton, T. (1990). Eating disorders and depression: Is there a serotonin connection? *Biological Psychiatry, 28*, 443–454.

John, O., & Robins, R. (1994). Accuracy and bias in self–perception: Individual differences in self–enhancement and the role of narcissism. *Journal of Personality and Social Psychology, 66*, 206–219.

John, O. P. (1990). The big five factor taxonomy: Dimensions of personality in the natural language and in questionnaires. In L. Pervin (Ed.), *Handbook of personality: Theory and research* (pp. 66–100). New York: Guilford Press.

Johnson, H. H., & Scileppi, J. A. (1969). Effects of ego–involvement conditions on attitude change to high and low credibility communicators. *Journal of Personality and Social Psychology, 13*, 31–36.

Johnson, K. E., Mervis, C. B., & Boster, J. S. (1992). Developmental changes within the structure of the mammal domain. *Developmental Psychology, 28*, 74–83.

Johnson, K. O., & Lamb, G. H. (1981). Neural mechanisms of spatial tactile discrimination: Neural patterns evoked by Braille–like dot patterns in the monkey. *Journal of Physiology, 310*, 117–144.

Johnson, R., & Murray, F. (1992). Reduced sensitivity of penile mechanoreceptors in aging rats with sexual dysfunction. *Brain Research Bulletin, 28*, 61–64.

Johnson–Laird, P. N., Legrenzi, P., & Legrenzi, M. S. (1972). Reasoning and a sense of reality. *British Journal of Psychology, 63*, 395–400.

Jones, A. (1992). Community self–help groups for women with bulimic and compulsive eating problems. *British Review of Bulimia and Anorexia Nervosa, 6*, 63–71.

Jones, E. E. (1976). How do people perceive the causes of behavior? *American Scientist, 64*, 300–305.

Jones, E. E. (1985). Major developments in social psychology during the past five decades. In G. Lindzey and E. Aronson (Eds.), *Handbook of social psychology*. Reading, MA: Addison–Wesley.

Jones, E. E. (1986). Interpreting interpersonal behavior: The effects of expectancies. *Science, 234*, 41–46.

Jones, E. E., & Davis, K. E. (1965). From acts to dispositions: The attribution process in personality perception. In L. Berkowitz (Ed.), *Advances in experimental social psychology*, (Vol. 2). New York: Academic Press.

Jones, E. E., Farina, A., Hastorf, A. H., Markus, H., Miller, D. T., & Scott, R. A. (1984). *Social stigma: The psychology of marked relationships*. New York: Freeman.

Jones, E. E., & Harris, V .A. (1967). The attribution of attitudes. *Journal of Experimental Social Psychology, 3*, 1–24.

Jones, E. E., & Nisbett, R. E. (1971). The actor and the observer: Divergent perceptions of the causes of behavior. In E. E. Jones et al. (Eds.), *Attribution: Perceiving the causes of behavior*. Morristown, NJ: General Learning Press.

Jones, E. E., & Pittman, T. S. (1982). Toward a general theory of strategic self–presentation. In J. Suls (Ed.), *Psychological perspectives on the self*. Hillsdale, NJ: Erlbaum.

Jones, E. E., Wood, & Quattrone, G. A. (1981). Perceived variability of personal characteristics in in–groups and out–groups: The role of knowledge and evaluation. *Personality and Social Psychology Bulletin, 7*, 523–528.

Jones, K. L., Smith, D. W., Ulleland, C. N., & Streissguth, A. (1973). Pattern of malformation in offspring of chronic alcoholic mothers. *Lancet, 1*, 1267–1271.

Jones, L. (1990). Unemployment and child abuse. *Families in Society, 71*, 579–588.

Jones, M., & Mussen, P. (1958). Self–conceptions, motivation and interpersonal attitudes of early– and late–maturing girls. *Child Development, 29*.

Josephs, R., Markus, H., & Tafarodi, R. (1992). *Journal of Personality and Social Psychology, 63*, 391–402.

Josephs, R., & Steele, C. M. (1990). The two faces of alcohol myopia: Attentional mediation of psychological stress. *Journal of Abnormal Psychology, 99*, 115–126.

Judd, C. M., & Park, B. (1988). Out–group homogeneity: Judgments of variability at the individual and group levels. *Journal of Personality and Social Psychology, 54*, 778–788.

Judd, F. K., Burrows, G. D., and Norman, T. R, (1985). The biological basis of anxiety. *Journal of Affective Disorders, 9*, 271–284.

Judd, T. (1988). The varieties of musical talent. In L. K. Obler, & D. Fein (Eds.), *The exceptional brain: Neuropsychology of talent and special abilities* (pp. 127–155). New York: Guilford Press.

Jung, C. G. (1923). *Psychological types*. New York: Pantheon Books.

Jung, C. G. (1961). *Memories, dreams, reflections*. New York: Random House.

Jung, C. G. (1968). *Analytical psychology: Its theory and practice*. New York: Vintage Books, 40–45.

Jussim, L. (1986). Self–fulfilling prophecies: A theoretical and integrative review. *Psychological Review, 93*, 429–445.

Jussim, L., Coleman, L. M., & Lerch, L. (1987). The nature of stereotypes: A comparison and integration of three theories. *Journal of Personality and Social Psychology, 52*, 536–546.

Jussim, L., & Eccles, J. (1992). Teacher expectations II: Construction and reflection of student achievement. *Journal of Personality and Social Psychology, 63*, 947–961.

Kaas, J. H. (1987). Somatosensory cortex. In G. Adelman (Ed.), *Encyclopedia of neuroscience*. Vol. 2. Boston: Birkhauser.

Kagan, J. (1976). Emergent themes in human development. *American Scientist, 64*, 186–96.

Kagan, J. (1983). Stress and coping in early development. In N. Garmezy & M. Rutter (Eds.), *Stress, coping, and development in children*. New York: McGraw–Hill.

Kagan, J. (1984). *The nature of the child*. New York: Basic Books.

Kagan, J. (1989). Temperamental contributions to social behavior. *American Psychologist, 44*, 668–674.

Kagan, J., Kearsley, R. B., & Zelazo, P. R. (1978). *Infancy: Its place in human development*. Cambridge, MA: Harvard University Press.

Kagan, J., & Snidman, N. (1991). Temperamental factors in human development. *American Psychologist, 46*, 856–862.

Kahn, S., Zimmerman, G., Csikszentmihalyi, M., & Getzels, J. (1985). Relations between identity in young adulthood and intimacy at midlife. *Journal of Personality and Social Psychology, 49*, 1316–1322.

Kail, R. (1991). Processing time declines exponentially during childhood and adolescence. *Developmental Psychology, 27*, 259–266.

Kail, R., & Bisanz, J. (1992). The information–processing perspective on cognitive development in childhood and adolescence. In R. J. Sternberg & C. A. Berg (1992), *Intellectual development* (pp.229–260). New York: Cambridge University Press.

Kail, R., & Pellegrino, J. W. (1985). *Human intelligence: Perspectives and prospects*. New York: Freeman.

Kalat, J. W. (1988). *Biological psychology.* (3rd ed.). Belmont, CA: Wadsworth.

Kalter, N. (1987). Long–term effects of divorce on children: A developmental vulnerability model. *American Journal of Orthopsychiatry, 57,* 587–600.

Kalter, N. (1990). *Growing up with divorce: Helping your child avoid immediate and later emotional problems.* New York: Free Press; London: Collier Macmillan, Ltd.

Kamen, L. P., & Seligman, M.E.P. (1987). Explanatory style and health. *Current Psychological Research & Reviews, 6,* 207–218.

Kamin, L. J. (1969). Predictability, surprise, attention, and conditioning. In B. A. Campbell & R. M. Church (Eds.), *Punishment and aversive behavior.* New York: Appleton–Century–Crofts.

Kamin, L. J. (1974). *The science and politics of I.Q.* Hillsdale, NJ: Erlbaum.

Kaminer, Y., & Hrecznyj, B. (1991). Lysergic acid diethylamide–induced chronic visual disturbances in an adolescent. *Journal of Nervous and Mental Disease, 179,* 173–174.

Kan, S. (1986). The 19th century Tlinglit potlatch: A new perspective. *American Ethnologist, 13,* 191–212.

Kandel, E. R. (1989). Genes, nerve cells, and the remembrance of things past. *Journal of Neuropsychiatry and Clinical Neurosciences, 1,* 103–125.

Kandel, E. R., & Schwartz, J. H. (1982). Molecular biology of learning: Modulation of transmitter release. *Science, 218,* 433–44.

Kane, J., Honigfeld, G., Singer, J., et al. (1988). Clozapine for the treatment–resistant schizophrenic: A double–blind comparison with chlorpromazine. *Archives of General Psychiatry, 45,* 489–496.

Kanizsa, G. (1976). Subjective contours. *Scientific American, 234,* 48–52.

Kanner, A. D., Coyne, J. C., Schaefer, C. & Lazarus, R. S. (1981). Comparison of two modes of stress measurement: Daily hassles and uplifts versus major life events. *Journal of Behavioral Medicine, 491,* 1–39.

Kaplan, H. I., & Sadock, B. J. (1985). *Comprehensive group psychotherapy.* (4th ed.). Baltimore, MD: Williams & Wilkins.

Kaplan, H. S. (1981). *The new sex therapy: Active treatment of sexual dysfunctions.* New York: Brunner/Mazel.

Karadi, Z., Oomura, Y., Nishino, H., & Scott, T. R. (1990). Complex attributes of lateral hypothalamic neurons in the regulation of feeding of alert rhesus monkeys. *Brain Research Bulletin, 25,* 933–939.

Kardiner, A. (1945). *The psychological frontiers of society.* New York: Columbia University Press.

Karlin, R. A., Rosen, L.S., & Epstein, Y.M. (1979). Three into two doesn't go: A follow–up on the effects of overcrowding dormitory rooms. *Personality and Social Psychology Bulletin, 5,* 391–395.

Karlins, M., Coffman, T. L., & Walters, G. On the fading of social stereotypes: Studies in three generations of college students. *Journal of Personality and Social Psychology, 13,* 1–16.

Karlsson, J. L. (1978). *Inheritance of creative intelligence.* Chicago: Nelson–Hall.

Kasl, S. V., Evans, A. S. & Neiderman, J. C. (1979). Psychosocial risk factors in the development of infectious mononucleosis. *Psychosomatic Medicine, 41,* 445–466.

Katafuchi, T., Oomura, Y., & Yoshimatsu, H. (1985). Single neuron activity in the rat lateral hypothalamus during 2–deoxy–d–glucose induced and natural feeding behavior. *Brain Research, 359,* 1–9.

Katahn, M., & McMinn, M. (1990). Obesity: A biobehavioral point of view. *Annals of the New York Academy of Arts and Sciences, 602,* 189–204.

Katz, D., Sarnoff, I., & McClintock, C. (1956). Ego–defense and attitude change. *Human Relations, 9,* 27–45.

Katz, H., & Beilin, H. (1976). A test of Bryant's claims concerning the young children's understanding of quantitative invariance. *Child Development, 47,* 877–880.

Katz, I., & Hass, R. (1988). Racial ambivalence and American value conflict: Correlational and priming studies of dual cognitive structures. *Journal of Personality and Social Psychology, 55,* 893–905.

Katz, J. L., Weiner, H., Gallagher, T. F., & Hellman, L. (1977). Stress, distress, and ego defenses: Psychoendocrine response to impending breast tumor biopsy. In A. Monat and R.S. Lazarus (Eds.), *Stress and coping: An anthology.* New York: Columbia University Press.

Katz, R., & McGuffin, P. (1993). The genetics of affective disorders. In L. Chapman, J. Chapman, & D. Fowles (Eds.) *Progress in personality and psychopathology research,* (Vol. 16). New York: Springer Publishing Co.

Kausler, D. (1990). Motivation, human aging, and cognitive performance. In J. Birren & K. W. Schaie (Eds.), *Handbook of the psychology of aging* (3rd ed.). New York: Academic Press.

Keating, D. P. (1983). The creative potential of mathematically precocious boys. In R. S. Albert (Ed.), *Genius and eminence: The social psychology of creativity and exceptional achievement* (pp. 128–138). Elmsford, NY: Pergamon Press.

Keating, D. P., & Bobbitt, B. L. (1978). Individual and developmental differences in cognitive–processing components of mental ability. *Child Development, 49,* 155–167.

Keesey, R. E., & Corbett, S. W. (1984). Metabolic defense of the body weight set–point. In A. J. Stunkard & E. Stellar (Eds.), *Eating and its disorders.* New York: Raven Press.

Keesey, R. E., & Powley, T. L. (1986). The regulation of body weight. *Annual Review of Psychology, 37,* 109–134.

Keitner, G., & Miller, I. W. (1990). Family functioning and major depression: An overview. *American Journal of Psychiatry, 147,* 1128–1137.

Keller, M., Lavori, P., Kane, J., Gelenbert, A., Rosenbaum, J. F., Waltzer, E., & Baker, L. A. (1992). Subsyndromal symptoms in bipolar disorder: A comparison of standard and low serum levels of lithium. *Archives of General Psychiatry, 49,* 371–376.

Kelley, H. H. (1967). Attribution theory in social psychology. In D. L.Vine (Ed.), *Nebraska Symposium on Motivation.* Lincoln: University of Nebraska Press.

Kelley, H. H. (1972). *Causal schemata and the attribution process.* Morristown, NJ: General Learning Press.

Kelley, H. H. (1973). The process of causal attribution. *American Psychologist, 28,* 107–128.

Kelley, H. H. (1979). *Personality relationships.* Hillsdale, NJ: Erlbaum.

Kelley, H. H. (1992). Common–sense psychology and scientific psychology. *Annual Review of Psychology, 43,* 1–23.

Kelley, H. H., & Michela, J. L. (1980). Attribution theory and research. *Annual Review of Psychology, 31,* 457–501.

Kelley, M. L., Power, T. G., & Wimbush, D. (1992). Determinants of disciplinary practices in low–income *Black mothers. Child Development, 63,* 573–582.

Kelling, S. T., & Halpern, B. P. (1983). Taste flashes: Reaction times, intensity, and quality. *Science, 219,* 412–414.

Kelly, G. A. (1955). *Psychology of personal constructs.* New York: W. W. Norton.

Kelman, H. C. (1983). Conversations with Arafat: A social–psychological assessment of the prospects for Israeli–Palestinian peace. *American Psychologist, 3–216.*

Kenardy, J., Evans, L., & Tian, P. (1992). The latent structure of anxiety symptoms in anxiety disorders. *American Journal of Psychiatry, 149,* 1058–1061.

Kendall, P. C. (1993). Treating anxiety disorders in children: Results of a randomized clinical trial. *Journal of Consulting and Clinical Psychology, 62,* 100–110.

Kendler, K., MacLean, C., Neale, M., Kessler, R., Heath, A., & Eaves, L. (1991). The genetic epidemiology of bulimia nervosa. *American Journal of Psychiatry, 148,* 1627–1637.

Kendler, K., Neale, M., Kessler, R., Heath, A., & Eaves, L. (1992). Generalized anxiety disorder in women: A population–based twin study. *Archives of General Psychiatry, 49,* 267–272.

Kendler, K., Neale, M., Kessler, R., Heath, A., & Eaves, L. (1992). The genetic epidemiology of phobias in women: The interrelationship of agoraphobia, social phobia, situational phobia, and simple phobia. *Archives of General Psychiatry, 49,* 273–281.

Kendler, K., Neale, M., Kessler, R., Heath, A., & Eaves, L. (1992). A population–based twin study of major depression in women. *Archives of General Psychiatry, 49,* 257–266.

Kendler, K. S., & Diehl, S. R. (1993). The genetics of schizophrenia: A current, genetic–epidemiologic perspective. *Schizophrenia Bulletin, 19,* 261–285.

Kendler, K. S., Heath, A., Martin, N. G., & Eaves, L. J. (1986). Symptoms of anxiety and depression in a volunteer twin population. *Archives of General Psychiatry, 43,* 213–221.

Kendler, K. S., Neale, M. C., Heath, A. C., Kessler, R. C., & Eaves, L. J. (1994). A twin–family study of alcoholism in women. *American Journal of Psychiatry, 151,* 707–715.

Kendler, K. S., Neale, M. C., Kessler, R. C., & Heath, A. C. (1993). A test of the equal–environment assumption in twin studies of psychiatric illness. *Behavior Genetics, 23,* 21–27.

Kenrick, D., Groth, G., Trost, M., & Sadalla, E. (1993). Integrating evolutionary and social exchange perspectives on relationships: Effects of gender, self–appraisal, and involvement level on mate selection criteria. *Journal of Personality and Social Psychology, 64,* 951–969.

Kenrick, D., & Keefe, R. (1992). Age preferences in mates reflect sex differences in human reproductive strategies. *Behavioral and Brain Sciences, 15,* 75–113.

Kenrick, D. T., & Stringfield, D. O. (1980). Personality traits and the eye of the beholder: Crossing some traditional philosophical boundaries in the search for consistency in all of the people. *Psychological Review, 87,* 88–104.

Kernberg, O. (1975). *Borderline conditions and pathological narcissism.* New York: Aronson.

Kernberg, O. (1984). *Severe personality disorders: Psychotherapeutic strategies.* New Haven, Conn.: Yale University Press.

Kerr, M., & Bowen, M. (1988). *Family evaluation: An approach based on Bowen theory.* New York: Norton.

Kessler, D. C. (1979). Stress, social status, and psychological distress. *Journal of Health and Social Behavior, 20,* 259–272.

Kessler, R. C., House, J. S. & Turner, J. B. (1987). Unemployment and health in a community sample. *Journal of Health and Social Behavior, 28,* 51–59.

Kessler, R. C., Kendler, K., Heath, A., Neale, M. C., & Eaves, L. J. (1992). Social support, depressed mood, and adjustment to stress: A genetic epidemiologic investigation. *Journal of Personality and Social Psychology, 62,* 257–272.

Kessler, R. C., McGonagle, K. A., Zhao, S., Nelson, C. B., Hughes, M., Eshleman, S., Wittchen, H., & Kendler, K. S. (1994). Lifetime and 12–month prevalence of DSM–III–R psychiatric disorders in the United States. *Archives of General Psychiatry, 51,* 8–19.

Kessler, R. C., Price, R. H. & Wortman, C. B. (1985). Social factors in psychopathology: Sress, social support, and coping processes. *Annual Review of Psychology, 36,* 531–572.

Kessler, R. C., Turner, J. B. & House, J. S. (1987). Intervening processes in the rela-

tionship between unemployment and health. *Psychological Medicine, 17,* 949–961.

Kessler, R. C., Turner, J. B., & House, J.S. (1989). Unemployment, reemployment, and emotional functioning in a community sample. *American Sociological Review, 54,* 648–657.

Kety, S. S., Rosenthal, D., Wender, P. H., Schulsinger, F., & Jacobsen, B. (1975). Mental Illness in the biological and adoptive families of adopted individuals who have become schizophrenic: A preliminary report based on psychiatric interviews. In Fieve, Rosenthal, & Brill (Eds.), *Genetic research in psychiatry.* Baltimore, MD: Johns Hopkins University Press.

Keung, H., & Hoosain, R. (1989). Right hemisphere advantage in lexical decision with two–character Chinese words. *Brain and Language, 37,* 606–615.

Khatena, J. (1982). Myth: Creativity is too difficult to measure. *Gifted Child Quarterly, 26,* 21–23.

Kiecolt–Glaser, J. K.,Fisher, L. D., Ogrocki, P., Stout, J., Speicher, C. E., & Glaser,R. (1987). Marital quality, marital disruption, and immune function. *Psychosomatic Medicine, 49,* 13–34.

Kienhorst, I., Diekstra, R., & Wolters, W. (1992). The relationship between adolescent suicidal behavior and life events in childhood and adolescents. *American Journal of Psychiatry, 149,* 45–51.

Kiesler, C. A. (1971). *The psychology of commitment: Experiments linking behavior to belief.* New York: Academic Press.

Kiesler, C. A., & Pallack, M. S. (1976). Arousal properties of dissonance manipulations. *Psychological Bulletin, 83,* 1014–1025.

Kihlstrom, J., Schacter, D., Cork, R., & Hurt, C. (1990). Implicit and explicit memory following surgical anesthesia. *Psychological Science, 1,* 303–306.

Kihlstrom, J. F., & Cantor, N. (1983). Mental representations of the self. In L. Berkowitz (Ed.), *Advances in experimental social psychology,* Vol. 15. New York: Academic Press.

KihlstromJ. F., (1987). The cognitive unconscious. *Science, 237,* 1445–1452.

Kimble, D. P. (1988). *Biological psychology.* New York: Holt, Rinehart, & Winston.

Kimura, D. (1987). Are men's and women's brains really different? *Canadian Psychology, 28,* 133–148.

Kimura, D. & Folb, S. (1968). Neural processing of backwards speech sounds. *Science, 161,* 395–396.

King, H. E. (1961). Psychological effects of excitation in the limbic system. In D.E. Sheer (Ed.) *Electrical stimulation of the brain.* Austin: University of Texas Press.

King, M., & McDonald, E. (1992). Homosexuals who are twins: A study of 46 probands. *British Journal of Psychiatry, 160,* 407–409.

King, N., Ollendick, T., & Gullone, E. (1991). Negative affectivity in children and adolescents: Relations between anxi-

ety and depression. *Clinical Psychology Review, 11,* 441–459.

King, W., & Ellison, G. (1989). Long–lasting alterations in behavior and brain neurochemistry following continuous low–level LSD administration. *Pharmacology, Biochemistry & Behavior, 33,* 69–73.

Kinsbourne, M., & Smith, W. L. (1974). *Hemispheric disconnection and cerebral function.* Springfield, Ill.: Charles C Thomas.

Kinsey, A. C., Pomeroy, W. B., & Martin, C. E. (1948). *Sexual behavior in the human male.* Philadelphia: W.B. Saunders.

Kinsey, A. C., Pomeroy, W. B., Martin, C. E., & Gebhard, P. (1953). *Sexual behavior in the human female.* Philadelphia: W.B. Saunders.

Kinsley, C., & Svare, B. (1986). Prenatal stress reduces intermale aggression in mice. *Physiology and Behavior, 36,* 783–785.

Kintsch, W., & Greeno, J. G. (1985). Understanding and solving word arithmetic problems. *Psychological Review, 92,* 109–129.

Kintsch, W., & van Dijk, T. A. (1978). Toward a model of text comprehension and production. *Psychological Review, 85,* 363–394.

Klatzky, R. L. (1991). Let's be friends. *American Psychologist, 46,* 43–45.

Klayman, J. & Ha, Y. (1989). Hypothesis testing in rule discovery: Strategy, structure, and content. *Journal of Experimental Psychology: Learning, Memory, and Cognition, 15,* 596–604.

Kleck, R. E., Richardson, S. A., & Ronald, L. (1974). Physical appearance cues and interpersonal attraction in children. *Child Development, 45,* 305–310.

Klein, R. E., Freeman, H. E., Spring, B., Nerlove, S. B., & Yarborough, C. (1976). Cognitive test performance and indigenous conceptions of intelligence. *Journal of Psychology, 93,* 273–279.

Kleinman, A. (1985). *Culture and depression.* Berkeley: University of California Press.

Kleinman, A. (1988). *Rethinking psychiatry: From cultural category to personal experience.* New York: Macmillan.

Kleinman, C. C. (1990). Forensic issues arriving from the use of anabolic steroids. *Psychiatric Annals, 20,* 219–221.

Kleven, M., & Seiden, L. (1991). Repeated injection of cocain potentiates methamphetamine–induced toxicity to dopamine–containing neurons in rat striatum. *Brain Research, 557,* 340–343.

Kline, D. (1985). Vision and aging. In J. Birren & K.W. Schaie (Eds.), *Handbook of the psychology of aging* (pp. 296–331). (2nd ed.). New York: Van Nostrand Reinhold.

Klinger, E. (1992). What will they think of next? Understanding daydreaming. In G. Brannigan & M. Merrens (Eds.), *The undaunted psychologist: Adventures in research.* New York.: McGraw-Hill.

Klinger, E., & Cox, W. M. (1987–1988). Dimensions of thought flow in everyday life. *Imagination, Cognition & Personality, 7,* 105–128.

Klinnert, M. D., Campos, J. J., Sorce, J. F., Emde, R. R., & Svejda, M. (1983). Emotions as behavior regulators: Social referencing in infancy. In R. Plutchik & H. Kellerman (Eds.), *Emotion: Theory, research, and experience: Vol. 2, Emotions in early development.* San Diego: Academic Press.

Klosko, J., Barlow, D., Tassinari, Ro., & Cerny, J. (1990). A comparison of alprazolam and behavior therapy in treatment of panic disorder. *Journal of Consulting and Clinical Psychology, 58,* 77–84.

Kluckhohn, F., & Strodtbeck, F. (1961). *Variations in value orientations.* Evanston, Ill.: Row, Peterson.

Kluver, H., & Bucy, P. (1939). Preliminary analysis of functions of the temporal lobe in monkeys. *Archives of Neurology & Psychiatry, 42,* 979–1000.

Knupfer, G. (1991). Abstaining for foetal health: The fiction that even light drinking is dangerous. *British Journal of Addiction, 86,* 1063–1073.

Kobak, R. R., & Sceery, A. (1988). Attachment in late adolescence: Working models, affect regulation, and presentations of self and others. *Child Development, 59,* 135–46.

Kobasa, S. C. (1979). Stressful life events, personality, and health: An inquiry into hardiness. *Journal of Personality and Social Psychology, 37,* 1–11.

Kobasa, S. C., Maddi, S. R., & Courington, S. (1981). Personality and construction as mediators in the stress–illness relationship. *Journal of Health and Social Behavior, 22,* 368–378.

Kobasa, S. C., Maddi, S. R., Puccetti, M. & Zola, M. A. (1985). Effectiveness of hardiness, exercise and social support as resources against illness. *Journal of Psychosomatic Research, 29,* 525–533.

Kochanska, G. 1992). Children's interpersonal influence with mothers and peers. *Developmental Psychology, 28,* 491–499.

Koestner, R., Weinberger, J., & McClelland, D. C. (1991). Task–intrinsic and social–extrinsic sources of arousal for motives assessed in fantasy and self–report. *Journal of Personality, 59,* 57–82.

Koestner, R., Zuroff, D., & Powers, T. (1991). Family origins of adolescent self–criticism and its continuity into adulthood. *Journal of Abnormal Psychology, 100,* 191–197.

Kohlberg, L. (1963). The development of children's orientations toward a moral order. I. Sequence in the development of moral thought. *Vita Humana, 6,* 11–33.

Kohlberg, L. (1969). Stage and sequence: The cognitive–developmental approach to socialization. In D.Goslin (Ed.), *Handbook of socialization and research* (pp. 347–480). Chicago: Rand–McNally.

Kohlberg, L. (1976). Moral stages and moralization: The cognitive–developmental perspective. In T. Lickona (Ed.), *Moral development and behavior:*

Theory, research, and social issues. New York: Holt, Rinehart, & Winston.

Kohlberg, L., & Kramer, R. (1969). Continuities and discontinuities in childhood and adult moral development. *Human Development, 12,* 93–120.

Kohlberg, L. A. (1966). A cognitive–developmental analysis of children's sex–role concepts and attitudes. In E. E. Maccoby (Ed.), *The development of sex differences.* Stanford, CA: Stanford University Press.

Kohler, I. (1962). Experiments with goggles. *Scientific American,* 62–72.

Kohler, W. (1925). *The mentality of apes* (2nd ed.). New York: Liveright, 1973.

Kohn, P. M., Lafreniere, K., & Gurevich, M. (1991). Hassles, health, and personality. *Journal of Personality and Social Psychology, 61,* 478–482.

Kohnken, G. & Maass, A. (1988). Eyewitness testimony: False alarms on biased instructions? *Journal of Applied Psychology, 73,* 363–370.

Kohut, H. (1971). *The analysis of the self: A systematic approach to the treatment of narcissistic personality disorders.* New York: International Universities Press.

Kohut, H. (1977). *The restoration of the self.* New York: International Universities Press.

Kolb, B. (1989). Brain development, plasticity, and behavior. *American Psychologist, 44,* 1203–1212.

Kolb, B., & Gibb, R. (1991). Environmental enrichment and cortical injury: Behavioral and anatomical consequences of frontal cortex lesions. *Cerebral Cortex, 1,* 189–198.

Kolb, F., & Whishaw, I. (1990). *Fundamentals of human neuropsychology* (3rd ed.). New York: Freeman.

Konner, M. (1991). Universals of behavioral development in relation to brain myelination. In K.R.Gibson & A.C. Petersen (Eds.), *Brain maturation and cognitive development: Comparative and cross–cultural perspectives.* New York: Aldine de Gruyter.

Konner, M. (in press). Anthropology and psychiatry. In H.I. Kaplan, & B.J. Sadock (Eds.), *Comprehensive textbook of psychiatry.* (5th ed.). Baltimore, MD: Williams & Wilkins.

Koocher, G. P. (1991). Questionable methods in alcoholism research. *Journal of Consulting and Clinical Psychology, 59,* 246–248.

Korn, J. H., Davis, R., Davis, S. F. (1991). Historians' and chairpersons' judgments of eminence among psychologists. *American Psychologist, 46,* 789–792.

Kornhaber, M., Krechevsky, M. & Gardner, H. (1990). Engaging intelligence. *Educational Psychologist, 25,* 177–199.

Kosmitzki, C., & John, O. (1993). The implicit use of explicit conceptions of social intelligence. *Personality and Individual Differences, 15,* 11–23.

Koss, M. (1993). Rape: Scope, impact, interventions, and public policy responses. *American Psychologist, 48,* 1062–1069.

Koss, M. P., Gidycz, C. A., & Wisniewski, N.

(1987). The scope of rape: Incidence and prevalence of sexual aggression and victimization in a national sample of higher education students. *Journal of Consulting and Clinical Psychology, 55,* 162–170.

Kosslyn, S. M. (1983). *Ghosts in the mind's machine.* New York: Norton.

Kosslyn, S. M., Alpert, N. M., Thompson, W. L., Maljokovic, V., et al. (1993). Visual imagery activates topographically organized visual cortex: PET investigations. *Journal of Cognitive Neuroscience, 5(3),* 263–287.

Kowza, A., & Marcia, J. (1991). Development and validation of a measure of Eriksonian industry. *Journal of Personality and Social Psychology, 60,* 390–397.

Kraemer, G. (1992). A psychobiological theory of attachment. *Behavioral and Brain Sciences, 15,* 493–541.

Kramer, L., & Gottman, J. (1992). Becoming a sibling: "With a little help from my friends." *Developmental Psychology, 28,* 685–699.

Kramer, M., Taube, C., & Redick, R. (1973). Pattern of use of psychiatric facilities by the aged: Past, present, and future. In C. Eisdorfer & M. P. Lawton (Eds.), *The psychology of adult development and aging.* Washington, DC, American Psychological Association.

Kramer, P. (1993). *Listening to Prozac.* New York: Viking Press.

Kripke, D., Simons, R. N., Garfinkel, L., & Hammond, E. C. (1979). Short and long sleep and sleeping pills. *Archives of General Psychiatry, 36,* 103–116.

Krishnan, K. R. (1993). Neuroanatomic substrates of depression in the elderly. *Journal of Geriatric Psychiatry and Neurology, 6,* 39–58.

Krosnick, J. (1992). Subliminal conditioning of attitudes. *Personality & Social Psychology Bulletin, 18,* 152–162.

Krosnick, J., Betz, A., Jussim, L., Lynn, A., & Stephens, L. (1992). Subliminal conditioning of attitudes. *Personality and Social Psychology Bulletin, 18,* 152–162.

Kruesi, M., Hibbs, E., Zahn, T., & Keysor, C. (1992). A 2–year prospective follow–up study of children and adolescents with disruptive behavior disorders: Prediction by cerebrospinal fluid 5–hydroxyindoleacetic acid, homovanillic acid, and autonomic measures? *Archives of General Psychiatry, 49,* 429–435.

Kruglanski, A., & Webster, D. (1991). Group members' reactions to opinion deviates and conformists at varying degrees of proximity to decision deadline and of environmental noise. *Journal of Personality and Social Psychology, 61,* 212–225.

Kuhl, P. K. & Meltzoff, A. N. (1988). Speech and an intermodal object of perception. In A. Tonas (Ed.), *Minnesota symposium on child psychology: Vol. 20. Perceptual development in infancy.* Hillsdale, NJ: Erlbaum.

Kuhl, P. K., Williams, K. A., Lacerda, F., & Stevens, K. N. (1992). Linguistic experience alters phonetic perception in infants by 6 months of age. *Science, 255*(5044), 606–608.

Kuhn, D. (1976). Short-term longitudinal evidence for the sequentiality of Kohlberg's early stages of moral judgment. *Developmental Psychology, 12,* 162–166.

Kuhn, T. S. (1970). *The structure of scientific revolutions.* (2nd Ed.). Chicago: University of Chicago Press.

Kuiken, D., (Ed.) (1991). *Mood and memory: Theory, research, and applications.* Newbury Park, CA: Sage.

Kuiper, N. A., & Derry, P. A. (1982). Depressed and nondepressed content self–reference in mild depression. *Journal of Personality, 50,* 67–79.

Kuiper, N. A., Olinger, L. J., MacDonald, M. R., & Shaw, B. F. (1985). Self–schema processing of depressed and nondepressed content: The effects of vulnerability on depression. *Social Cognition, 3,* 77–93.

Kulik, J. A., Bangert–Downs, R. L., & Kulik, C. C. (1984). Effectiveness of coaching for aptitude tests. *Psychological Bulletin, 95,* 179–188.

Kulik, J. A., Sledge, P., & Mahler, H.I.M. (1986). Self–conformatory attribution, egocentrism, and the perpetuation of self–beliefs. *Journal of Personality and Social Psychology, 50,* 587–594.

Kunda, Z. (1990). The case for motivated reasoning. *Psychological Bulletin, 108,* 480–498.

Kuo–shu, Y., & Bond, M. H. (1990). Exploring implicit personality theories with indigenous or imported constructs: The Chinese case. *Journal of Personality and Social Psychology, 58,* 1087–1095.

Kuperman, S., Gaffney, G. R., Hamden–Allen, G., & Preston, D. F. (1990). Neuroimaging in child and adolescent psychiatry. Journal of the *American Academy of Child and Adolescent Psychiatry, 29,* 159–172.

Kurdek, L. (1991). Predictors of increases in marital distress in newlywed couples: A 3–year prospective longitudinal study. *Developmental Psychology, 27,* 627–636.

Kurtz, L. F., & Powell, T. J. (1987). Three approaches to understanding self–help groups. *Social Work with Groups, 10,* 69–80.

LaBarre, W. (1966). The Aymara: History and world view. *Ethnology,* 130–144.

Laberge, B., et al. (1993). Cognitive–behavioral therapy of panic disorder with secondary major depression: A preliminary investigation. *Journal of Consulting and Clinical Psychology, 61,* 1028–1037.

Labouvie–Vief, G. (1985). Intelligence and cognition. In J. E. Birren & K. W. Schaie (Eds.), *Handbook of the psychology of aging.* (2nd ed.). New York: Van Nostrand.

Labouvie–Vief, G., & Gonda, J. N. (1976). Cognitive strategy training and intellectual performance in the elderly. *Journal of Gerontology, 31,* 327–332.

Labouvie–Vief, G., & Schell, D. A. (1982).

Learning and memory in late life. In B. B. Wolman (Ed.), *Handbook of developmental psychology.* Englewood Cliffs, NJ: Prentice–Hall.

Lachman, S. J., & Bass, A. R. (1985). A direct study of halo effect. *Journal of Psychology, 119,* 535–540.

Ladd, G. W., & Mize, J. (1983). A cognitive–social learning model of social skill training. *Psychological Review, 90,* 127–157.

LaFreniere, P. J., & Sroufe, L. A. (1985). Profiles of peer competence in the preschool: Interrelations between measures, influences of social ecology, and relation to attachment history. *Developmental Psychology, 21,* 56–69.

Laing, D. G., Prescott, J., Bell, G. A., & Gillmore, R. (1993). A cross–cultural study of taste discrimination with Australians and Japanese. *Chemical Senses, 18,* 161–168.

Laing, R. D. (1959). *The divided self.* New York: Penguin.

Lakoff, G. (1985). *Women, fire, and dangerous things.* Chicago: University of Chicago Press.

Lamb, H. R., & Lamb, D. M. (1990). Factors contributing to homelessness among the chronically and severely mentally ill. *Hospital and Community Psychiatry, 41,* 301–305.

Lamb, M. E. (1987). Introduction: The emergent American father. In M.E. Lamb (Ed.), *The father's role: Cross–cultural perspectives.* Hillsdale, NJ: Erlbaum.

Lamb, M. E., & Roopnarine, J. L. (1979). Peer influences on sex–role development in preschoolers. *Child Development, 50,* 1219–22.

Lamb, M. E., Frodi, A. M., Hwang, C. P., & Frodi, M. (1982). Varying degrees of paternal involvement in infant care. In M. D. Lamb (Ed.), *Nontraditional families.* Hillsdale, NJ: Erlbaum.

Lambert, M. C., Weisz, J. R., & Knight, F. (1989). Over– and undercontrolled clinic referral problems of Jamaican and American children and adolescents: The culture general and the culture specific. *Journal of Consulting and Clinical Psychology, 57,* 467–472.

Lambert, M. J., Shapiro, D. A., & Bergin, A. E. (1986). The effectiveness of psychotherapy. In S.L. Garfield and A. E. Bergin, (Eds.), *Handbook of psychotherapy and behavior change.* New York: John Wiley.

Lame Deer, J., & Erdoes, R. (1972). *Lame Deer, seeker of visions.* New York: Simon & Schuster.

Landau, E. & Weissler, K. (1993). Parental environment in families with gifted and nongifted children. *Journal of Psychology, 127,* 129–142.

Landesman, S., & Butterfield, E. C. (1987). Normalization and deinstitutionalization of mentally retarded individuals: Controversy and facts. *American Psychologist, 42,* 809–816.

Landesman–Dwyer, S., & Butterfield, E. C. (1983). Mental retardation: Developmental issues in cognitive and

social adaptation. In M.Lewis (Ed.), *Origins of intelligence: Infancy and early childhood* (2nd ed.). New York: Plenum Press.

Landman, J. T., & Dawes, R. M. (1982). Psychotherapy outcome: Smith and Glass' conclusions stand up under scrutiny. *American Psychologist, 37,* 504–516.

Landy, D., & Johnson, E. (1969). The influence of the character of the criminal and his victim on the decisions of simulated jurors. *Journal of Experimental Social Psychology, 5,* 141–152.

Landy, D., & Sigall, H. (1974). Beauty is talent: Task evaluation as a function of a performer's physical attractiveness. *Journal of Personality and Social Psychology, 29,* 299–304.

Lane, C., & Hobfoll, S. E. (1992). How loss affects anger and alienates potential supporters. *Journal of Consulting and Clinical Psychology, 6,* 935–942.

Lang, P. J., Bradley, M. M., & Cuthbert, B. (1992). A motivational analysis of emotion: *Reflex–cortex connections. Psychological Science, 3,* 44–49.

Lange, C. G. (1885). The emotions: A psychophysiological study, trans. I.A. Haupt. In C. G. Lange & W. James (Eds.), *Psychology classics,* Vol. I. Baltimore, MD: Williams & Wilkins, 1922.

Langlois, J., Ritter, J. M., Roggman, L., & Vaughn, L. S. (1991). Facial diversity and infant preferences for attractive faces. *Developmental Psychology, 27,* 79–84.

Langlois, J. H., & Downs, A. C. (1980). Mothers, fathers, and peers as socialization agents of sex–typed play behaviors in young children. *Child Development, 51,* 1217–1247.

Langs, O. (1946). Chinese family and society. New Haven, Conn.: Yale University Press.

Lanzetta, J. T., Cartwright–Smith, J. & Kleck, R. E. (1976). Effects of nonverbal dissimulation on emotional experience and autonomic arousal. *Journal of Personality and Social Psychology, 33,* 354–370.

Larkin, K., Manuck, S., & Kasprowicz, A. (1990). The effect of feedback–assisted reduction in heart rate reactivity on videogame performance. *Biofeedback & Self Regulation, 15,* 285–303.

Larkin, K. T., Zayfert, C., Abel, J. L., & Veltum, L. G. (1992). Reducing heartrate reactivity to stress with feedback: Generalization across test and time. *Behavior Modification, 16,* 118–131.

Larsen, K. S. (1990). The Asch conformity experiment: Replication and trans-historical comparisons. *Journal of Social Behavior and Personality, 5,* 163–168.

Larsen, R. J., & Diener, E. (1987). Affect intensity as an individual differences characteristic: A review. *Journal of Research in Personality, 21,* 1–39.

Larson, R., Csikszentmihalyi, M., & Graef, R. (1980). Mood variability and the psychosocial adjustment of adolescents. *Journal of Youth and Adolescence, 9,* 469–90.

Larsson, G., Bohlon, A., & Turnell, R. (1985). Prospective study of children exposed to various amounts of alcohol in utero. *Archives of Disease in Childhood*, 60, 306–321.

Larzelere, R. (1986). Moderate spanking: Model or deterrent of children's aggression in the family? *Journal of Family Violence*, 1, 27–36.

Lasswell, H. D. (1948). The structure and function of communication in society. In L. Bryson (Ed.), *Communication of ideas*. New York: HarperCollins.

Latane, B., & Darley, J. M. (1968). Group inhibition of bystander intervention in emergencies. *Journal of Personality and Social Psychology*, 10, 215–221.

Latane, B., & Darley, J. M. (1970). *The unresponsive bystander: Why doesn't he help?* New York: Appleton–Century–Crofts.

Latane, B., & Rodin, J. (1969). A lady in distress: Inhibiting effects of friends and strangers on bystander intervention. *Journal of Experimental Social Psychology*, 5, 189–202.

Latimer, P. R. (1979). The behavioral treatment of self–excoriation in a twelve–year–old girl. *Journal of Behavioral Therapy and Experimental Psychiatry*, 10, 349–352

Lavigne, V., & Finley, G. E. (1990). Memory in middle–aged adults. *Educational Gerontology*, 16, 447–461.

Lavond, D., Kim, J., & Thompson, R. (1993). Mammalian brain substrates of classical conditioning. *Annual Review of Psychology*, 44, 317–342.

Lazarus, R. (1981). The stress and coping paradigm. In C. Eisdorfer, D. Cohen, A. Kleinman & P. Maxim (Eds.), *Models for clinical psychopathology*. New York: Spectrum.

Lazarus, R. S. (1966). *Psychological stress and the coping process.* New York: McGraw–Hill.

Lazarus, R. S. (1991). Cognition and motivation in emotion. *American Psychologist*, 46, 352–367.

Lazarus, R. S. (1993). From psychological stress to the emotions: A history of changing outlooks. *Annual Review of Psychology*, 44, 1–21.

Le Bon, G. (1895). *The crowd.* New York: Balantine, 1969.

Leahy, A. M. (1935). Nature–nurture and intelligence. *Genetic Psychological Monographs*, 237–308.

Lecky, P. (1945). *Self–consistency: A theory of personality.* New York: Island Press.

LeDoux, J. E. (1986). The neurobiology of emotion. In J. E. LeDoux & W. Hirst (Eds.), *Mind and brain: Dialogues in cognitive neuropsychology*. New York: Cambridge University Press.

LeDoux, J. E. (1989). Cognitive–emotional interactions in the brain. *Cognition and Emotion*, 3, 267–289.

LeDoux, J. E. (1992). Emotional memory systems in the brain. *Behavioural Brain Research*, 58, 69–79.

Lee, D. (1950). The conception of the self among the Wintu Indians. In D. Lee, *Freedom and culture*. Englewood Cliffs, N J: Prentice–Hall, 1959.

Lee, E. (1951). Negro intelligence and selective migration: A Philadelphia test of Klineberg's hypothesis. *American Sociological Review*, 61, 227–233.

Lee, H. J. (1991). Relationship of hardiness and current life events to perceived health in rural adults. *Research in Nursing and Health*, 14, 351–359.

Lee, J. A. (1973). *The colors of love: An exploration of the ways of loving.* Don Mills, Ontario: New Press.

Lee, J. A. (1988). Lovestyles. In R.J. Sternberg and M.L. Barnes (Eds.), *The anatomy of love*. New Haven, Conn.: Yale University Press.

Leff, J. (1988). *Psychiatry around the globe: A transcultural view.* (2nd ed.) London: Gaskell.

Lehman, D. R., Lempert, R. O., & Nisbett, R. E. (1988). The effects of graduate training on reasoning: Formal discipline and thinking about everyday–life events. *American Psychologist*, 43, 431–442.

Lehman, D. R. & Nisbett, R. E. (1990). A longitudinal study of the effects of undergraduate training on reasoning. *Developmental Psychology*, 26, 952–960.

Lehman, D. R., Wortman, C. B. & Williams, A. F. (1987). Long–term effects of losing a spouse or child in a motor vehicle crash. *Journal of Personality and Social Psychology*, 52, 218–231.

Lehmann, H. E. (1985). Affective disorders: Clinical features. In H. I. Kaplan & B.J. Sadock (Eds.), *Comprehensive textbook of psychiatry*. (4th ed.). Baltimore, MD: Williams & Wilkins.

Lehmann, H. E., & Cancro, R. (1985). Schizophrenia: Clinical features. In H. Kaplan & B. J. Sadock (Eds.), *Comprehensive textbook of psychiatry* (4th ed.). Baltimore, MD: Williams & Wilkins.

Lehrer, P. M., Saragunaraj, D., & Hochron, S. (1992). Psychological approaches to the treatment of asthma. *Journal of Consulting and Clinical Psychology*, 60, 639–643.

Lehrman, D. S. (1956). On the organization of maternal behavior and the problem of instinct. In *L'instinct dans le Comportement des Animaux et de l'homme*. Paris: Masson et Cie.

Leigh, B. C., & Stacy, A. W. (1991). On the scope of alcohol expectancy research: Remaining issues of measurement and meaning. *Psychological Bulletin*, 110, 147–154.

Lele, P. P., & Weddell, G. (1956). The relationship between neurohistology and corneal sensibility. *Brain*, 79, 119–154.

Lempers, J. D., Flavell, E. R., & Flavell, J. H. (1977). The development in very young children of tacit knowledge concerning visual perception. *Genetic Psychology Monographs*, 95, 3–53.

Lenneberg, E. (1967). *The biological foundations of language.* New York: John Wiley.

Leon, G. R., & Roth, L. (1977). Obesity: Psychological causes, correlations, and speculations. *Psychological Bulletin*, 84, 117– 39.

Leonard, B. (1993). The comparative pharmacology of new antidepressants. *Journal of Clinical Psychiatry*, 54, 3–15.

Lepper, M. R., & Greene, D. (1978). *The hidden costs of reward: New perspectives on the psychology of motivation.* New York: Halstead.

Lepper, M. R., Zanna, M. P., & Abelson, R. P. (1970). Cognitive irreversibility in a dissonance reduction situation. *Journal of Personality and Social Psychology*, 16, 191–198.

Lerner, R. (1991). Changing organism–context relations as the basic process of development: A developmental contextual perspective. *Developmental Psychology*, 27, 27–32.

Lester, B., Corwin, M., Sepkoski, C., Seifer, R., Peucker, M., McLaughlin, S., & Golub, H. (1991). Neurobehavioral syndromes in cocaine–exposed newborn infants. *Child Development*, 62, 694–705.

LeVay, S. (1991). A difference in hypothalamic structure between heterosexual and homosexual men. *Science*, 253, 1034–1037.

Levenson, J. L., & Bemis, C. (1991). The role of psychological factors in cancer onset and progression. *Psychosomatics*, 32, 124–132.

Levenson, R., & Ruef, A. (1992). Empathy: A physiological substrate. *Journal of Personality and Social Psychology*, 63, 234–246.

Levenson, R. W. (1992). Autonomic nervous system differences among emotions. *Psychological Science*, 3, 23–27.

Levenson, R. W., Ekman, P., & Friesen, W. (1990). Voluntary facial action generates emotion–specific autonomic nervous system activity. *Psychophysiology*, 27, 363–385.

Levenson, R., W., Ekman, P., Heider, K., & Friesen, W, V, (1992). Emotion and autonomic nervous system activity in the Minangkabau of West Sumatra. *Journal of Personality and Social Psychology*, 62, 972–988.

Leventhal, E. A., Leventhal, H., Shacham, S., & Easterling, D. V. (1989). Active coping reduces reports of pain from childbirth. *Journal of Consulting and Clinical Psychology*, 57, 365–371.

Leventhal, H. & Tomarken, A. J. (1986). Emotion: Today's problems. *Annual Review of Psychology*, 37, 565–610.

Levin, P. F., & Isen, A. M. (1975). Further studies on the effect of feeling good on helping. *Sociometry*, 38, 141–147.

Levin, R. B. & Gross, A. M. (1985). The role of relaxation in systematic desensitization. *Behavior Research and Therapy*, 23, 187–196.

Levine, J. M., & Moreland, R. L. (1995). Group Processes. In A. Tesser (Ed.), *Advanced Social Psychology*. New York: McGraw–Hill.

LeVine, R. (1982). *Culture, behavior, and personality*. (2nd ed.). Chicago: Aldine.

LeVine, R. A., & LeVine, B. B. (1963). Nyasongo: A Gusii Community in Kenya. In B. Whiting (Ed.), *Six cultures: Studies in child rearing* (pp. 19–202). New York: John Wiley.

Levine, R. V., Martinez, T., Brase, G., & Sorenson, K. (1994). Helping in 36 U.S. cities. *Journal of Personality and Social Psychology*, 67, 69–82.

Levinger, G. (1974). A three–level approach to attraction: Toward an understanding of pair relatedness. In T. L. Huston (Ed.), *Foundations of Interpersonal Attraction*. New York: Academic Press.

Levinson, D. J., Darrow, C. N., Klein, E. B., Levinson, M. H., McKee, B. (1978). *The seasons of a man's life*. New York: Alfred A. Knopf.

Levy, B., & Langer, E. (1994). Aging free from negative stereotypes: Successful memory in China and among the American deaf. *Journal of Personality & Social Psychology* 66, 989–997.

Levy–Bruhl, L. (1923). *Primitive mentality*. (L.A. Clave, Trans.) London: Allen & Unwin.

Lewes, K. (1988). *The psychoanalytic theory of male homosexuality*. New York: Simon & Schuster.

Lewicki, P. (1985). Nonconscious biasing effects of single instances on subsequent judgments. *Journal of Personality and Social Psychology*, 48, 563–574.

Lewicki, P. (1986). *Nonconscious social information processing*. New York: Academic Press.

Lewin, K. (1939). Field theory and experiment in social psychology: Concepts and methods. *American Journal of Sociology*, 44, 868–897.

Lewin, K., Lippitt, R., & White, R. K. (1939). Patterns of aggressive behavior in experimentally created social climates. *Journal of Social Psychology*, 10, 271–301.

Ley, R. (1988). Hyperventilation and lactate infusion in the production of panic attacks. *Clinical Psychology Review, 8*, 1–18.

Lezak, M. D. (1983). *Neuropsychological assessment* (2nd ed.). New York: Oxford University Press.

Liben, L., & Signorella, M. (1993). Gender–schematic processing in children: The role of initial interpretations of stimuli. *Developmental Psychology*, 29, 141–149.

Liberman, A., & Chaiken, S. (1992). Defensive processing of personally relevant health messages. *Journal of Experimental Social Psychology*.

Lieberman, J., Bogerts, B., Degreef, G.,

Ashtari, M., Lantos, G., & Alvir, J. (1992). Qualitative assessment of brain morphology in acute and chronic schizophrenia. *American Journal of Psychiatry*, 149, 784–794.

Lieberman, S. (1956). The effects of changes in roles on the attitudes of role occupants. *Human Relations, 9*, 385–402.

Liebowitz, M. R., Schneier, F., Campeas, R., Hollander, E., Hatterer, J., Fyer, J., Gorman, J., et al. (1992). Phenylzine vs. atenolol in social phobia: A placebo–controlled comparison. *Archives of General Psychiatry*, 49, 290–300.

Lifton, R. J. (1963). *Thought reform and the psychology of totalism: A study of brainwashing in China*. New York: W. W. Norton.

Lifton, R. J. (1980). Nuclearism. *Journal of Clinical Child Psychology*, 9, 119–124.

Light, L. (1990). Interactions between memory and language in old age. In J. E. Birren & K. W. (Schaie, Eds.), *Handbook of the Psychology of Aging*. (3rd ed.). New York: Van Nostrand Reinhold.

Lima, S., Hale, S., & Myerson, J. (1991). How general is general slowing? Evidence from the lexical domain. *Psychology and Aging*, 6, 416–425.

Lin, E., & Peterson, C. (1990). Pessimistic explanatory style and response to illness. *Behaviour Therapy & Research*, 28, 243–248.

Lindberg, M. (1980). Is knowledge base development a necessary and sufficient condition for memory development? *Journal of Experimental Child Psychology*, 30, 401–410.

Lindholm. T., Lehtinen, V., Hyyppa, M., & Puuka, P. (1990). Alexithymic features in relation to the dexamethasone suppression test in a Finnish population sample. *American Journal of Psychiatry*, 147, 1216–1219.

Lindley, R. H., & Smith, W. R. (1992). Coding tests as measures of IQ: Cognitive or motivation? *Personality and Individual Differences*, 13, 25–29.

Lindsay, R. K. (1991). Symbol–processing theories and the SOAR architecture. *Psychological Science*, 2, 294–302.

Lindsley, D. B., Schreiner, L.H., Knowles, W.B., & Magoun, H.W. (1950). Behavioral and EEG changes following chronic brain stem lesions in the cat. *Electroencephalography and Clinical Neurology*, 2, 483–98.

Lindvall, O. (1991). Prospects of transplantation in human neurodegenerative diseases. *Trends in Neurosciences*, 14, 376–384.

Linehan, M. (1987). Dialectical behavior therapy for borderline personality disorder: Theory and method. *Bulletin of the Menninger Clinic*, 51, 261–276.

Linehan, M. (1993). *Cognitive–behavioral treatment of borderline personality disorder*. New York: Guilford Press.

Linehan, M. M. (1987). Dialectical behavioral therapy: A cognitive behavioral

approach to parasuicide. *Journal of Personality Disorders*, 1, 328–333.

Lipman, J., Miller, B.E., Mays, K., & Miller, M. N. (1990). Peak B endorphin concentration in cerebrospinal fluid: Reduced in chronic pain patients and increased during the placebo response. *Psychopharmacology*, 102, 112–116.

Lippert, R. C. (1989). Expert systems: tutors, tools, and tutees. *Journal of Computer–Based Instruction*, 16, 11–19.

Lishman, T., & Lee, D. N. (1975). The autonomy of visual kinesis. *Perception, 2*, 287–294.

Lisspers, J., & Ost, L. (1990). Long–term follow–up of migraine treatment: Do the effects remain up to six years? *Behaviour Therapy and Research*, 28, 313–322.

Litt, M., Babor, T., DelBoca, F., Kadden, R., & Cooney, N. (1992). Types of alcoholics, II: Application of an empirically derived typology to treatment matching. *Archives of General Psychiatry*, 49, 609–614.

Little, A. (1987). Attributions in a cross–cultural context. *Genetic, Social, and General Psychology Monographs*, 113, 61–79.

Livesley, W. J., & Bromley, D. B. (1973). *Person perception in childhood and adolescence*. London: John Wiley.

Livingstone, M., & Hubel, D. H. (1988). Segregation of form, color, movement, and depth: Anatomy, physiology, and perception. *Science*, 240, 740–749.

Livson, F. B. (1976). Patterns of personality development in middle–aged women: A longitudinal study. *International Journal of Aging and Human Development*, 7, 107–15.

Livson, F. B. (1981). Paths to psychological health in the middle years: Sex differences. In D. Eichorn, J. Clausen, N. Haan, M. Honzik & P. Mussen (Eds.), *Present and past in middle life*. New York: Academic Press.

Lochman, J., Coie, J., Underwood, M., & Terry, R. (1993). Effectiveness of a social relations intervention program for aggressive and nonaggressive, rejected children. *Journal of Consulting and Clinical Psychology*, 61, 1053–1058.

Locke, E., & Latham, G. (1990). *A theory of goal–setting and task performance*. Englewood Cliffs, NJ: Prentice–Hall.

Locke, E. A. (1991). Goal theory vs. control theory: Contrasting approaches to understanding work motivation. *Motivation and Emotion*, 15, 9–27.

Locke, J. (1950). *An essay concerning human understanding*. New York: Dover.

Loeb, G. E. (1985). The functional replacement of the ear. *Scientific American*, 252, 104–111.

Loeb, R. C., Horst, L., & Horton, P. J. (1980). Family interaction patterns associated with self–esteem in preadolescent girls and boys. *Merrill–Palmer Quarterly*, 26, 203–217.

Loebel, A., Lieberman, J. A., Alvir, J., Mayerhoff, D., Geisler, S., & Syzmanski,

S. (1992). Duration of psychosis and outcome in first–episode schizophrenia. *American Journal of Psychiatry, 149,* 1183–1188.

Loehlin, J. (1992). *Genes and environment in personality development.* New York: Guilford Press.

Loehlin, J., Horn, J., & Willerman, L. (1990). Modeling IQ change: Evidence from the Texas Adoption Project. *Child Development, 60,* 993–1004.

Loehlin, J. C. (1988). Human behavior genetics. *Annual Review of Psychology, 39,* 101–133.

Loehlin, J. C. (1989). Partitioning environmental and genetic contributions to behavioral development. *American Psychologist, 44,* 1285–1292.

Loehlin, J. C., Horn, J. M. & Willerman, L. (1989). Modeling IQ change: Evidence from the Texas Adoption Project. *Child Development, 60,* 993–1004.

Loehlin, J. C., Lindzeg, G., & Spuhler, J. N. (1975). *Race differences in intelligence.* San Francisco, CA: Freeman.

Loehlin, J. C., Willerman, L., & Horn, J. M. (1987). Personality resemblance in adoptive families: A 10–year follow–up. *Journal of Personality and Social Psychology, 53,* 961–969.

Loehlin, J. C., Willerman, L., & Horn, J. M. (1988). Human behavior genetics. *Annual Review of Psychology, 39,* 101–133.

Loevinger, J. (1976). *Ego development.* San Francisco: Jossey–Bass.

Loevinger, J. (1985). Revision of the sentence completion test for ego development. *Journal of Personality and Social Psychology, 48,* 420–427.

Loewenstein, W. R. (1960). Biological transducers. *Scientific American,* 98–108.

Loftus, E. F. (1993). The reality of repressed memories. *American Psychologist, 48*(5), 518–537.

Loftus, E.F., Levidow, B., & Duensing, S. (1992). Who remembers best? Individual differences in memory for events that occurred in a science museum. *Applied Cognitive Psychology, 6,* 93–107.

Loftus, E. F., & Palmer, J. C. (1974). Reconstruction and automobile destruction. An example of the interaction between language and memory. *Journal of Verbal Learning and Verbal Behavior, 13,* 585–589.

Loftus, E. F., Polonsky, S., & Fullilove, M. T. (1994). Memories of childhood sexual abuse: Remembering and repressing. *Psychology of Women Quarterly, 18,* 67–84.

Loftus, E. F., & Zanni, G. (1975). Eyewitness testimony: the influence of the wording of a question. *Bulletin of the Psychonomic Society, 5,* 86–88.

Lonner, W., & Malpass (Eds.) (1994). *Readings in psychology and culture.* Boston: Allyn & Bacon.

Lore, R., & Schultz, L. A. (1993). Control of human aggression: A comparative perspective. *American Psychologist, 48,* 16–25.

Lorenz, K. (1966). *On aggression.* New York: Harcourt, Brace & World.

Lorenz, K. (1979). King Solomon's ring. New York: HarperCollins.

Lott, A., & Lott, B. (1974). The role of reward in the formation of positive interpersonal attitudes. In T. Huston (Ed.), *Foundations of interpersonal attraction.* New York: Academic.

Low, B. S. (1989). Cross–cultural patterns in the training of children: An evolutionary perspective. *Journal of Comparative Psychology, 103,* 311–319.

Lu, C., Shaikh, M. B., & Siegel, A. (1992). Role of NMDA receptors in hypothalamic facilitation of feline defensive rage elicited from the midbrain pariaqueductal gray. *Brain Research, 581,* 123–132.

Luborsky, L., & Crits–Christoph, P. (1990). *Understanding transference: The core conflictual relationship theme method.* New York: Basic Books.

Luborsky, L., Barber, J. P., & Crits–Christoph, P. (1990). Theory–based research for understanding the process of dynamic psychotherapy. *Journal of Consulting and Clinical Psychology, 58,* 281–287.

Luchins, A. (1957). Primacy–recency in impression formation. In C. Hovland (Ed.), *The order of presentation in persuasion* (pp. 33–61). New Haven, Conn.: Yale University Press.

Lundberg, S. G. (1990). Domestic violence: A psychodynamic approach and implications for treatment. *Psychotherapy, 27,* 243–248.

Luria, A. R. (1973). *The working brain.* Harmondsworth: Penguin.

Lutz, C. (1988). Ethnographic perspectives on the emotion lexicon. In V. Hamilton, G. H. Bower, & N. Frijda (Eds.), *Cognitive perspectives on emotion and motivation* (pp. 399–419). Kluwer: Dordrecht.

Lutz, C. (1992). Culture and consciousness: A problem in the anthropology of knowledge. In F. S. Kessel, P. M. Cole, & D. L. Johnson (Eds)., *Self and consciousness: Multiple perspectives* (pp. 64–87). Hillsdale, NJ: Lawrence Erlbaum.

Lykken, D. T., Bouchard, T. J., McGue, M., & Tellegen, A. (1993). Heritability of interests: A twin study. *Journal of Applied Psychology, 78,* 649–661.

Lykken, D. T., McGue, M., Tellegen, A., & Bouchard, T. J. (1992). Emergenesis: Genetic traits that may not run in families. *American Psychologist, 47,* 1565–1577.

Lynch, O. M. (1990). The social construction of emotion in India. In O. M. Lynch (Ed.), *Divine passions: The social construction of emotion in India* (pp. 3–34). Berkeley: University of California Press.

Lyons, L. C., & Woods, P. J. (1991). The efficacy of rational–emotive therapy: A quantitative review of the outcome research. *Clinical Psychology Review, 11,* 357–370.

Lyons–Ruth, K., Connell, D., Grunebaum, H., & Botein, S. (1990). Infants at social risk: Maternal depression and family support services as mediators of infant development and security of attachment. *Child Development, 61,* 85–98.

Lytton, H. (1990). Child and parent effects in boys' conduct disorder: A reinterpretation. *Developmental Psychology, 26,* 683–697.

Maaney, M., Dodge, A., & Beatty, W. (1981). Sex–dependent effects of amygdaloid lesions on the social play of prepubertal rats. *Physiology and Behavior, 26,* 467–472.

Maccoby, E. (1992). The role of parents in the socialization of children: An historical overview. *Developmental Psychology, 28,* 1006–1017.

Maccoby, E. E., & Jacklin, C. N. (1974). *The psychology of sex differences.* Stanford, CA: Stanford University Press.

Maccoby, E., & Jacklin, C. N. (1980). The "person" characteristics of children and the family as environment. In D. Magnusson & V. Allen (Eds.), *Human development: An interactional perspective.* New York: Academic Press.

Maccoby, E. E., & Jacklin, C. N. (1980). Sex differences in aggression: A rejoinder and reprise. *Child Development, 51,* 964–980.

Maccoby, M. (1980). Work and human development. *Professional Psychology, 11,* 509–519.

MacCorquodale, K. (1970). On Chomsky's review of Skinner's verbal behavior. *Journal of the Experimental Analysis of Behavior, 13,* 83–99.

MacGregor, S. Keith, L., Chasnoff, I., Rosner, M., Chisum, G., Shaw, P., & Minugue, J. (1987). Cocaine use during pregnancy: Adverse perinatal outcome. *American Journal of Obstetrics and Gynecology, 157,* 686–690.

MacLean, P. D. (1982). On the origin and progressive evolution of the triune brain. In E. Armstrong & D. Falk Eds.), *Primate brain evolution.* New York: Plenum Press.

MacLean, P. D. (1985). Evolutionary psychiatry and the triune brain. *Psychological Medicine, 15,* 219–221.

MacLean, P. D. (1993). On the evolution of three mentalities. In J. B. Ashbrook (Ed.), *Brain, culture, & the human spirit: Essays from an emergent evolutionary perspective* (pp. 15–44).

MacLeod, C., & Campbell, L. (1992). Memory accessibility and probability judgments: An experimental evaluation of the availability heuristic. *Journal of Personality and Social Psychology, 63,* 890–902.

Macrae, C. N., Milne, A. B., & Bodenhausen, G. (1994). Stereotypes as energy–saving devices: A peek inside the cognitive toolbox. *Journal of Personality and Social Psychology, 66,* 37–47.

Maddi, S. R., & Kobasa, S. C. (1984). *The hardy executive: Health under stress.* Homewood, Ill.: Dorsey Press.

Madigan, S., & O'Hara, R. (1992). Short–term memory at the turn of the century: Mary Whiton Calkin's memory research. Special Issue: The history of American psychology. *American Psychologist, 47,* 170–174.

Madrazo, I., Drucker–Collin, R., Diaz, V., Martinez, J., Torres, C., & Becerrill, J. (1987). Open microsurgical autograft of adrenal medulla to the right caudate nucleus in two patients with intractable Parkinson's disease. *New England Journal of Medicine, 316,* 831–834.

Madrid, A., & Schwartz, M. (1991). Maternal–infant bonding and pediatric asthma: An initial investigation. *Pre- and Peri-natal Psychology Journal, 5,* 347–358.

Magnavita, J. (1993). The evolution of short–term dynamic psychotherapy: Treatment of the future? *Professional Psychology: Research and Practice, 24,* 360–366.

Mahler, M., Pine, F., & Bergman, A. (1975). *The psychological birth of the human infant: Symbiosis and individuation.* New York: Basic Books.

Mahowald, M. W., & Schenck, C. H. (1989). In M. H. Kryger, T. Roth, & W. C. Dement (Eds.), *Principles and practice of sleep medicine.* Philadelphia: Saunders (pp. 389–401).

Maier, N.R.F. (1931). Reasoning in humans II: The solution of a problem and its appearance in consciousness. *Journal of Comparative Psychology, 12,* 181–194.

Main, M. (1990). Cross–cultural studies of attachment organization: Recent studies, changing methodologies, and the concept of conditional strategies. *Human Development, 33,* 48–61.

Main, M., Kaplan, N., & Cassidy, J. (1985). Security in infancy, childhood, and adulthood: A move to the level of representation. In I. Bretherton & E. Waters (Eds.), Growing points of attachment theory and research. *Monographs of the Society for Research in Child Development, 50* (No. 1–2), 67–104.

Main, M., & Solomon, J. (1986). Discovery of a new, insecure–disorganized/disoriented attachment pattern. In T. Brazelton & M. Yogman (Eds.), *Affective development in infancy* (pp. 95–124). Norwood, NJ: Ablex.

Maj, M., Veltro, F., Pirozzi, R., Lobrace, S., & Magliano, L. (1992). Pattern of recurrence of illness after recovery from an episode of major depression: A prospective study. *American Journal of Psychiatry, 149,* 795–800.

Malamuth, N. M., & Donnerstein, E. (1982). The effects of aggressive–pornographic mass media stimuli. In L. Berkowitz (Ed.) *Advances in Experimental Social Psychology,* Vol. 15. New York: Academic Press.

Malamuth, N. M., Heim, M., & Feshbach, S. (1980). Sexual responsiveness of college students to rape depictions: Inhibitory and disinhibitory effects. *Journal of*

Personality and Social Psychology, 38, 399–408.

Maletsky, B., McFarland, B., & Burt, A. (1994). Refractory obsessive compulsive disorder and ECT. *Convulsive Therapy, 10,* 34–42.

Mandler, G., & Nakamura, Y. (1987). Aspects of consciousness. *Personality and Social Psychology Bulletin, 13,* 299–313.

Mangelsdorf, S. Gunnar, M., Kestenbaum, R., Lang, S, & Andreas, D. (1990). Infant proneness–to–distress temperament, maternal personality, and mother–infant attachment: Associations and goodness of fit. *Child Development, 61,* 820–831.

Manis, M., Nelson, T. E., & Shedler, J. (1988). Stereotypes and social judgment: Extremity, assimilation, and contrast. *Journal of Personality and Social Psychology, 55,* 28–36.

Manis, M., Paskewitz, J., & Cotler, S. (1986). Stereotypes and social judgment. *Journal of Personality and Social Psychology, 50,* 461–473.

Mann, J. (1982). *A casebook in time-limited psychotherapy.* New York: McGraw–Hill.

Mann, J. J., McBridge, P. A., Brown, R. P., Linnoila, M., Leon, A. C., et al. (1992). Relationship between central and peripheral serotonin indexes in depressed and suicidal psychiatric inpatients. *Archives of General Psychiatry, 49,* 442–446.

Mannuzza, S., Klein, R. G., Bonagura, N., Malloy, P., Giampino, T., & Addali, K. (1991). Hyperactive boys almost grown up, V: A replication of psychiatric status. *Archives of General Psychiatry, 48,* 77–83.

Manson, J. E., Colditz, G. A., Stampfer, M. J., Willett, W. C., Rosner, B., Monson, R. R., Speizer, F., & Hennekens, C. (1990). A prospective study of obesity and risk of coronary heart diease in women. *New England Journal of Medicine, 322,* 882–889.

Manstead, A.S.R., Proffitt, C., & Smart, J. L. (1983). Predicting and understanding mothers' infant–feeding intentions and behavior: Testing the theory of reasoned action. *Journal of Personality and Social Psychology, 44,* 657–671.

Marcel, A. J. (1983). Conscious and unconscious perception: Experiments on visual masking and word recognition. *Cognitive Psychology, 15,* 197–237.

Marcia, J. (1987). The identity status approach to the study of ego identity development. In T. Honess & K.Yardley (Eds.), *Self and identity: Perspectives across the lifespan* (pp. 161–171). Boston: Routledge & Kegan Paul.

Marcotte, A., & Morere, D. (1990). Speech lateralization in deaf populations: Evidence for a developmental critical period. *Brain & Language, 39,* 134–152.

Marcus, D. E., & Overton, W. E. (1978). The development of cognitive gender constancy and sex role preferences. *Child Development, 49,* 434–444.

Marengo, J., Harrow, M., Sands, J., &

Galloway, C. (1991). European versus U.S. data on the course of schizophrenia. *American Journal of Psychiatry, 148,* 606–611.

Margolskee, R. (1995). Receptor mechanisms in gustation. In R.L. Doty (Ed.), *Handbook of olfaction and gustation.* New York: Marcel Dekker.

Markman, E. (1992). Constraints on word learning: Speculations about their nature, origins, and domain specificity. In M. R. Gunnar & M. P. Maratsos (Eds.), *Minnesota Symposium on Child Psychology,* Vol. 25 (pp. 59–101). Hillsdale, NJ: Erlbaum.

Markman, H. J., Renick, M., Floyd, F., & Stanley, S. (1993). Preventing marital distress through communication and conflict management training: A 4– and 5–year follow–up. *Journal of Consulting and Clinical Psychology, 61,* 70–77.

Markovitz, J. H., & Matthews, K. A. (1991). Platelets and coronary heart disease: Potential psychophysiologic mechanisms. *Journal of Psychosomatic Medicine, 53,* 643–668.

Marks, G. (1984). Thinking one's abilities are unique and one's opinions are common. *Personality and Social Psychological Bulletin, 10,* 203–208.

Marks, I. M. (1969). *Fears and phobias.* New York: Academic Press.

Markus, H. (1977). Self–schemata and processing information about the self. *Journal of Personality and Social Psychology, 35,* 63–78.

Markus, H. (1980). The self in thought and memory. In D.M. Wegner & R.R. Vallacher (Eds.), *The self in social psychology.* New York: Oxford University Press.

Markus, H., & Cross, S. (1990). The interpersonal self. In L. Pervin (Ed.), *Handbook of personality: Theory and research* (pp. 576–608). N.ew York.: Guilford Press.

Markus, H., & Kitayama, S. (1991). Culture and the self: implications for cognition, emotion, and motivation. *Psychological Review, 98,* 224–253.

Markus, H., & Nurius, P. (1986). Possible selves. *American Psychologist, 41,* 954–969.

Markus, H., & Sentis, K. (1980). The self in social information processing. In J. Suls (Ed.), *Social psychology: Perspectives on the self.* Hillsdale, NJ: Erlbaum.

Markus, H., & Wurf, E. (1987). The dynamic self–concept: A social psychological perspective. *Annual Review of Psychology, 38,* 299–337.

Markus, H., & Zajonc, R. B. (1985). The cognitive perspective in social psychology. In G. Lindzey and E. Aronson (Eds.), *Handbook of social psychology.* Reading, MA: Addison–Wesley.

Marlatt, G. A., & Baer, J. S. (1988). Addictive behaviors: Etiology and treatment. *Annual Review of Psychology, 39,* 223–252.

Marshall, D. S. (1971). Sexual behavior on

Mangaia. In D. S.Marshall, & R. C. Suggs (Eds.) *Human sexual behavior: Variations in the ethnographic spectrum.* New York: Basic Books.

Marshall, G. & Zimbardo, P. G. (1979). Affective consequences of inadequately explained physiological arousal. *Journal of Personality and Social Psychology, 37,* 970–988.

Marshall, J. C., & Halligan, P. W. (1988). Blindsight and insight in visuo–spatial neglect. *Nature, 336,* 766–767.

Martin, C. L., Wood, C. H., & Little, J. K. (1990). The development of gender stereo-type components. *Child Development, 61,* 1891–1904.

Martin, M. (1986). Ageing patterns of change in everyday memory and cognition. *Human Learning Journal of Practical Research and Application, 5,* 63–74.

Martin, M. A. (1985). Students' applications of self–questioning study techniques: An investigation of their efficacy. *Reading Psychology, 6,* 69–83.

Maslach, C. (1979). Negative emotional biasing of unexplained arousal. *Journal of Personality and Social Psychology, 37,* 953–969.

Maslow, A. H. (1962). *Toward a psychology of being.* Princeton, NJ: Van Nostrand.

Maslow, A. H. (1970). *Motivation and personality* (2nd Ed.). New York: Harper & Row.

Mason, J., Southwick, S., Yehuda, R., & Wang, S. (1994). Elevation of serum free triiodothyronine, total triiodothyronine, thyroxine–binding globulin, and total thy-roxine levels in combat–related posttraumatic stress disorder. *Archives of General Psychiatry, 51,* 629–641.

Mason, R. T., Fales, H. M., Jones, T. H., Pannel, L. K., Chinn, J. W., & Crews, D. (1989). Sex pheromones in snakes. *Science, 245,* 290–293.

Masten, A. S., Price, A., Charney, D., & Heninger, G. (1993). Children in homeless families: Risks to mental health and development. *Journal of Consulting and Clinical Psychology, 61,* 335–343.

Masters, W., & Johnson, V. (1966). *Human sexual response.* Boston: Little, Brown.

Masters, W. H., & Johnson, V. E. (1970). *Human sexual inadequacy.* Boston: Little, Brown.

Mathews, A., & Macleod, C. (1994). Cognitive approaches to emotion. *Annual Review of Psychology, 45,* 25–50.

Mathews, A., Richards, A., & Eysenck, M. (1989). Interpretation of homophones related to treament in anxiety states. *Journal of Abnormal Psychology, 98,* 31–34.

Mathews, A., & Ridgeway, V. (1981). Personality and surgical recovery: A review. *British Journal of Clinical Psychology, 20,* 243–260.

Matlin, M. M. (1983). *Perception.* Boston: Allyn & Bacon.

Matsu–Yuassa, I., & Otani, S. (1992). Lithium in polyamine metabolism. *Lithium, 3,* 231–238.

Matsuoka, S. (1990). Theta rhythms: State of consciousness. *Brain Topography, 3,* 203–208.

Matthews, K. A. (1992). Myths and realities of the menopause. *Psychosomatic Medicine, 54,* 1–9.

Matthies, H. (1989). Neurobiological aspects of learning and memory. *Annual Review of Psychology, 40,* 381–404.

Mauro, R., Sato, K., & Tucker, J. (1992). The role of appraisal in human emotions: A cross–cultural study. *Journal of Personality and Social Psychology, 62,* 301–317.

Mavissakalian, M., & Perel, J. (1992). Protective effects of imipramine mainte-nance treatment in panic disorder with agoraphobia. *American Journal of Psychiatry, 149,* 1053–1057.

May, R. (1953). *Man's search for himself.* New York: Signet Books.

May, R., Angel, E. & Ellenberger, H. F. (1958). *Existence: A new dimension in psychiatry and psychology.* New York: Basic Books.

Mayer, J. (1955). Regulation of energy intake and body weight. The glucostatic and the lipostatic hypothesis. *Annals of the New York Academy of Science, 63,* 15–43.

Mayer, J., Gasche, Y., Braverman, D., & Evans, T. (1992). Mood–congruent judg-ment is a general effect. *Journal of Personality and Social Psychology, 63,* 119–132.

Mayer, R. E. (1983). *Thinking, problem solving, cognition.* New York: Freeman.

Mayman, M. (1968). Early memories and character structure. *Journal of Projective Techniques and Personality Assessment, 32,* 303–316.

Mayman, M. & Faris, M. (1960). Early memories as expressions of relationship paradigms. *Journal of Orthopsychiatry, 30,* 507–520.

McAdams, D. (1988). Biography, narrative, and lives: An introduction. *Journal of Personality, 56,* 1–18.

McAdams, D. (1992). The intimacy motive. In C. P. Smith, J. W. Atkinson, D.McClelland, & J. Veroff (Eds.), Motivation and personality: *Handbook of thematic content analysis* (pp. 224–228). Cambridge: Cambridge University Press.

McAdams, D., & de St. Aubin, E. (1992). A theory of generativity and its assessment through self–report, behavioral acts, and narrative themes in autobiography. *Journal of Personality and Social Psychology, 62,* 1003–1015.

McAdams, D., & Vaillant, G. (1982). Intimacy motivation and psychosocial adjustment: A longitudinal study. *Journal of Personality Assessment, 46,* 586–593.

McAdams, D. P., & Constantian, C. A. (1983). Intimacy and affiliation motives in daily living: An experience sampling analysis. *Journal of Personality and Social Psychology, 45,* 851–861.

McAdams, D. P., de St. Aubin, E., & Logan, R. L. (1993). Generativity among young, midlife, and older adults. *Psychology and Aging, 8,* 221–230.

McAdams, J. (1986). Status polarization of social welfare attitudes. *Political Behavior, 8,* 313–334.

McArthur, D. J. (1982). Computer vision and perceptual psychology. *Psychological Bulletin, 92,* 283–309.

McArthur, L. A. (1972). The how and what of why: Some determinants and conse-quences of causal attribution. *Journal of Personality and Social Psychology, 22,* 171–193.

McCance–Katz, E., Price, L., Charney, D., & Henninger, G. (1992). Serotonergic func-tion during lithium augmentation of refractory depression. *Psychopharmacology, 108,* 93–97.

McCann, I. L., & Pearlman, L. (1990). *Psychological trauma and the adult sur-vivor: Theory, therapy, and transforma-tion.* New York: Brunner/Mazel.

McCartney, K., Scarr, S., Phillips, D., Grajek, S., & Schwartz, J. C. (1982). Environmental differences among day care centers and their effect on children's devel-opment. In E. F. Zigler & E. W. Gordon (Eds.), *Day care: scientific and social pol-icy issues.* Boston: Auburn House.

McCaul, K. D., & Malott, J. M. (1984). Distraction and coping with pain. *Psychological Bulletin, 95,* 516–533.

McCauley, C., & Jacques, S. (1979). The popularity of conspiracy theories of presi-dential assassination: A Bayesian analysis. *Journal of Personality and Social Psychology, 37,* 637–644.

McClelland, D. (1993). Motivation. In G. Brannigan, & M. Merrens (Eds.), *The undaunted psychologist: Adventures in research.* Philadelphia, PA: Temple University Press.

McClelland, D. C. (1961). *The achieving society.* Princeton, NJ: D. Van Nostrand.

McClelland, D. C. (1978). Managing moti-vation to expand human freedom. *American Psychologist, 33,* 201–210.

McClelland, D. C. (1985) *Human motiva-tion.* Glenview, Ill: Scott, Foresman.

McClelland, D. C., Atkinson, J. W., Clark, R. A., & Lowell, E. L. (1953). *The achievement motive.* New York: Appleton–Century–Crofts.

McClelland, D. C., Koestner, R., & Weinberger, J. (1989). How do self–attrib-uted and implicit motives differ? *Psychological Review, 96,* 690–792.

McClelland, D. C., & Pilon, D. A. (1983). Sources of adult motives in patterns of parent behavior in early childhood. *Journal of Personality and Social Psychology, 44,* 564–554.

McClelland, D. C., & Winter, D. G. (1969). *Motivating economic achievement.* New York: Free Press.

McClintock, M. K. (1971). Menstrual synchrony and suppression. *Nature, 229,* 244–245.

McCloskey, M. & Egeth, H. E. (1983). Eyewitness identification: What can a psychologist tell a jury? *American Psychologist, 38,* 550–563.

McConaghy, N. (1979). Maternal deprivation: Can its ghost be laid? *Australian and New Zealand Journal of Psychiatry, 13,* 209–217.

McConahay, J., & Hough, J. (1976). Symbolic racism. *Journal of Social Issues, 32,* 23–45.

McConahay, J. B. (1982). Self–interest versus racial attitudes as correlates of anti–busing attitudes in Louisville: Is it the buses or the blacks? *J. Polit., 44,* 692–720.

McConahay, J. B., Hardee, B. B., & Batts, V. (1981). Has racism declined in America? It depends on who is asking and what is asked. *Journal of Conflict Resolution, 25,* 563–579.

McConkey, K. M., Bryant, R. A., Bibb, B. C., & Kihlstrom, J. F. (1991). Trance logic in hypnosis and imagination. *Journal of Abnormal Psychology, 100,* 464–472.

McCrae, R. (1993). Agreement of personality profiles across observers. *Multivariate Behavioral Research, 28,* 25–40.

McCrae, R. R., & Costa, P. T. (1990). *Personality in adulthood.* New York: Guilford Press.

McDowd, J. M., & Craik, F. I. (1988). Effects of aging and task difficulty on divided attention performance. *Journal of Experimental Psychology Human Perception and Performance, 14,* 267–280.

McEvoy, G. M. & Cascio, W. F. (1989). Cumulative evidence of the relationship between employee age and job performance. *Journal of Applied Psychology, 74,* 11–17.

McFarland, S., Ageyev, V., & Abalakina–Paap, M. (1992). Authoritarianism in the former Soviet Union. *Journal of Personality and Social Psychology, 63,* 1004–1010.

McGinnies, E. (1949). Emotionality and perceptual defense. *Psychological Review, 56,* 244–251.

McGlashan, T., & Fenton, W. (1992). The positive–negative distinction in schizophrenia: Review of natural history validators. *Archives of General Psychiatry, 49,* 63–72.

McGlynn, F. D., Mealies, W. L. Jr., & Landau, D. L. (1981). The current status of systematic desensitization. *Clinical Psychology Review, 1,* 149–179.

McGue, M., Bacon, S., & Lykken, D. (1993). Personality stability and change in early adulthood: A behavior genetic analysis. *Developmental Psychology, 29,* 96–109.

McGue, M., Pickens, R. W., & Svikis, D. (1992). Sex and age effects on the inheritance of alcohol problems: A twin study. *Journal of Abnormal Psychology, 101,* 3–17.

McGuire, W. (1986). The myth of massive media impact: Savagings and salvagings. In G. Comstock (Ed.), *Public communication and behavior* (Vol.1). New York: Academic Press.

McGuire, W. J. (1960). A syllogistic analysis of cognitive relationships. In M.J. Rosenberg and C.I. Hovland (Eds.), *Attitude organization and change.* New Haven, Conn.: Yale University Press.

McGuire, W. J. (1961). The effectiveness of supportive and refutational defenses in immunizing and restoring beliefs against persuasion. *Sociometry, 24,* 184–197.

McGuire, W. J. (1985). Attitudes and attitude change. In G. Lindzey and E. Aronson (Eds.), *Handbook of Social Psychology.* Reading, MA: Addison–Wesley.

McGuire, W. J. (1986). The vicissitudes of attitudes and similar representational constructs in twentieth century psychology. *European Journal of Social Psychology, 16,* 89–130.

McGuire, W. J., & Padawer–Singer, A. (1978). Trait salience in the spontaneous self–concept. *Journal of Personality and Social Psychology, 33,* 743–754.

McGuire, W.J., & Papageorgis, D. (1962). Effectiveness of forewarning in developing resistance to persuasion. *Public Opinion Quarterly, 26,* 24–34.

McKantz–Katz, E. F. (1991). The consequences of maternal substance abuse for the child exposed in utero. *Psychosomatics, 32,* 268–274.

McKeachie, W. J. (1976). Psychology in America's bicentennial year. *American Psychologist, 31,* 819–833.

McKelvey, R., Webb, J. A., & Mao, A. (1993). Premigratory risk factors in Vietnamese Amerasians. *American Journal of Psychiatry, 150,* 470–473.

McKenna, R. J. (1972). Some effects of anxiety level and food cues on the eating behavior of obese and normal subjects. *Journal of Personality and Social Psychology, 22,* 311–319.

McKeown, T., & Record, R. G. (1976). Relationship between childhood infections and measured intelligence. *British Journal of Preventative and Social Medecine, 30,* 101–106.

McKinnon, W., Weisse, C. S., Reynolds, C. P., Bowles, C. A., & Baum, A. (1989). Chronic stress, leukocyte subpopulations, and humoral response to latent viruses. *Health Psychology, 8,* 389–402.

McLoyd, V. (1989). Socialization and development in a changing economy: The effects of paternal job and income loss on children. *American Psychologist, 44,* 293–302.

Mead, G. H. (1913). The social self. *Journal of Philosophy, Psychology and Scientific Methods, 10,* 374–380.

Mead, G. H. (1934). *Mind, self, and society.* Chicago: University of Chicago Press.

Mead, M. (1928). *Coming of age in Samoa: A psychological study of primitive youth for Western civilization.* New York: Morrow & Co.

Meaney, M., & McEwen, B. (1986). Testosterone implants into the amygdala during the neonatal period masculinize the social play of juvenile female rats. *Brain Research, 398,* 324–328.

Medin, D. L. (1989). Concepts and conceptual structure. *American Psychologist, 44,* 1469–1481.

Medin, D. L., & Smith, E. E. (1981). Strategies and classification learning. *Journal of Experimental Psychology: Human Learning and Memory, 7,* 241–253.

Medin, D. L., & Smith, E. E. (1985). Concepts and concept formation. *Annual Review of Psychology, 35,* 113–138.

Mednick, S. A., Gabrielli, W. F., & Hutchings, B. (1984). Genetic influences in criminal convictions: Evidence from an adoption cohort. *Science, 224,* 891–894.

Meece, J. L., Wigfield, A., & Eccles, J. S. (1990). Predictors of math anxiety and its influence on young adolescents' course enrollment intentions and performance in mathematics. *Journal of Educational Psychology, 82,* 60–70.

Meehan, P., Lamb, J. A., Saltzman, L. E., & O'Carroll, W. (1992). Attempted suicide among young adults: Progress toward a meaningful estimate of prevalence. *American Journal of Psychiatry, 149,* 41–44.

Meehl, P. (1962). Schizotaxia, schizotypy, schizophrenia. *American Psychologist, 17,* 827–838.

Meehl, P. (1989). Schizotaxia revisited. *Archives of General Psychiatry, 46,* 935–944.

Meichenbaum, D. (1977). *Cognitive–behavior modification: An integrative approach.* New York: Plenum Press.

Meichenbaum. D. (1990). Cognitive perspective on teaching self–regulation. *American Journal of Mental Retardation, 94,* 367–369.

Melton, G. B. (1987). Fear, prejudice, and neglect: Discrimination against mentally disabled persons. *American Psychologist, 42,* 1007–1026.

Meltzoff, A. (1990). Towards a developmental cognitive science: The imlications of cross–modal matching and imitation for the development of representation and memory in infancy. *Annals of the New York Academy of Sciences, 608,* 1–7.

Meltzoff, A. N., & Moore, M. K. (1977). Imitation of facial and manual gestures by human neonates. *Science, 198,* 75–78.

Meltzoff, A. N., & Moore, M. K. (1994). Imitation, memory, and the representation of persons. *Infant Behavior and Development, 17,* 83–91.

Melzack, R. (1970). Phantom limbs. *Psychology Today,* 63–68.

Melzack, R. (1973). *The puzzle of pain.* New York: Basic Books.

Melzack, R. (1980). Psychological aspects of pain. In J. Bonica (Ed.), *Pain.* New York: Raven.

Melzack, R., & Wall, P. D. (1965). Pain mechanisms: A new theory. *Science, 150,* 971–979.

Melzack, R., & Wall, P. D. (1983). *The challenge of pain.* New York: Basic Books.

Menninger, K., Mayman, M. & Pruyser, P. (1963). *The vital balance.* New York: Viking.

Merckelbach, H., Arntz, A., & deJong, P. (1991). Conditioning experiences in spider phobics. *Behavior Research and Therapy, 29,* 333–335.

Merluzzi, T., Taylor, C. B., Boltwood, M., & Gotestam, K. G. (1991). Opioid antagonist impedes exposure. *Journal of Consulting and Clinical Psychology, 59,* 425–430.

Merriam, A. P. (1971). Aspects of sexual behavior among the Bala (Basongye). In D. S. Marshall, & R. C. Suggs (Eds.) *Human sexual behavior: Variations in the ethnographic spectrum.* New York: Basic Books.

Merskey, H. (1973). The perception and measurement of pain. *Journal of Psychosomatic Research, 17,* 251–255.

Merton, R. K. (1957). The self-fulfilling prophecy. *Antioch Review, 8,* 193–210.

Merton, R. K. (1957). *Social theory and social structure.* Glencoe, Ill.: Free Press.

Mervis, C. B., & Rosch, E. (1981). Categorization of natural objects. *Annual Review of Psychology, 32,* 89–115.

Messer, S., Sass, L. H., & Woolfolk, R. L., (Eds.). (1988). *Hermeneutics and psychological theory.* New Brunswick, NJ: Rutgers University Press.

Messer, S., & Winokur, M. (1980). Some limits to the integration of psychodynamic and behavior therapy. *American Psychologist, 35,* 818–827.

Messick, S., & Jungeblut, A. (1981). Time and method in coaching for the SAT. *Psychological Bulletin, 89,* 191–216.

Metropolitan Life Insurance Company. (1983). 1983 Metropolitan height and weight tables. *Statistical Bulletin, 64,* 2–9.

Meyer, D., & Schvaneveldt, M. (1976). Facilitation in recognizing pairs of words: Evidence of a dependence between retrieval operations. *Journal of Experimental Psychology, 90,* 227–34.

Michaelis, P. R., & Wiggins, R. H. (1982). A human factors engineer's introduction to speech synthesizers. In A. Badre & B. Shneiderman (Eds.) *Directions in human/computer interaction.* Norwood, NJ: Ablex.

Michaels, C. F., & Carello, C. (1981). *Direct perception.* Englewood Cliffs, NJ: Prentice–Hall.

Michaels, J. W., Blommel, J., Brocato, R., Linkous, R., & Rowe, J. S. (1982). Social facilitation and inhibition in a natural setting. *Replication in Social Psychology, 2,* 21–24.

Michelson, L., & Marchione, K. (1991). Behavioral, cognitive, and pharmacological treatments of panic disorder with agoraphobia: Critique and synthesis. *Journal of Consulting and Clinical Psychology, 59,* 100–114.

Mickley, G. A., Ferguson, J. L., Mulvihill, M. A., & Nemeth, T. J. (1991). Early neural grafts transiently reduce the behavioral effects of radiation induced fascia dentata granule cell hypoplasia. *Brain Research, 550,* 24–34.

Middlebrooks, J. C., & Green, D. M. (1991). Sound localization by human listeners. *Annual Review of Psychology, 42,* 135–159.

Middleton, D., & Edwards, D. (1990). Introduction. In D. Middleton & D. Edwards (Eds.), *Collective remembering.* London: Sage.

Miklowitz, D., Velligan, D., Goldstein, M. J., Neuchterlein, K., Gitlin, M., Ranlett, G., & Doane, J. (1991). Communication deviance in families of schizophrenic and manic patients. *Journal of Abnormal Psychology, 100,* 163–173.

Mikulincer, M., Florian, V., & Weller, A. (1993). Attachment styles, coping strategies, and posttraumatic psychological distress: The impact of the Gulf War in Israel. *Journal of Personality and Social Psychology, 64,* 817–826.

Milgram, S. (1963). Behavioral study of obedience. *Journal of Abnormal and Social Psychology, 67,* 371–378.

Milgram, S. (1965). Some conditions of obedience and disobedience to authority. *Human Relations, 18,* 57–76.

Milgram, S. (1974). *Obedience to authority: An experimental view.* New York: Harper & Row.

Milgram, S., Bickman, L, & Berkowitz, L. (1969). Note on the drawing power of crowds of different size. *Journal of Personality and Social Psychology, 13,* 79–82.

Miller, B.C., & Sollie, D.L. (1986). Normal stresses during the transition to parenthood. In R. H. Moos (Ed.), *Coping with Life Crises: An Integrated Approach.* New York: Plenum Press.

Miller, C. B., Rothblum, E., Barbour, L., Brand, P. A., & Felicio, D. (1991). Social interactions of obese and nonobese women. *Journal of Personality, 58,* 365–380.

Miller, D. T., & Ross, M. (1975). Self-serving biases in attribution of causality: Fact or fiction? *Psychological Bulletin, 82,* 213–225.

Miller, D. T., & Turnbull, W. (1986). Expectancies and interpersonal processes. *Annual Review of Psychology, 37,* 233–256.

Miller, G. A. (1956). The magical number seven, plus or minus two: Some limits in our capacity for processing information, *Psychological Review, 63,* 81–97.

Miller, G. A., Galanter, E., & Pribram, K.H. (1960). *Plans and the structure of behavior.* New York: Holt, Rinehart & Winston.

Miller, I. J., Jr. (1995). Anatomy of the peripheral taste system. In R.L. Doty (Ed.), *Handbook of olfaction and gustation.* New York: Marcel Dekker.

Miller, J. G. (1984). Culture and the development of everyday social explanation.

Journal of Personality and Social Psychology, 46, 961–978.

Miller, J. G. (1994). Cultural diversity in the morality of caring: Individually oriented versus duty–based interpersonal moral codes. *Cross–cultural Research, 28,* 3–39.

Miller, L. C., Bettencourt, B. A., DeBro, S., & Hoffman, V. (1993). Negotiating safer sex: Interpersonal dynamics. In J. Pryor and G. Reeder (Eds.), *The social psychology of HIV infection.* Hillsdale, NJ: Erlbaum.

Miller, N. (1951). Learnable drives and rewards. In S. S. Stevens (Ed.), *Handbook of experimental psychology* (pp. 435–472). New York: John Wiley.

Miller, N., & Campbell, D. T. (1959). Recency and primacy in persuasion as a function of the timing of speeches and measurement. *Journal of Abnormal and Social Psychology, 59,* 1–9.

Miller, N. E. (1985). The value of behavioral research on animals. *American Psychologist, 40,* 423–440.

Miller, N. E. (1992). Some examples of psychophysiology and the unconscious. *Biofeedback and Self–Regulation, 17,* 3–16.

Miller, N. E. (1983). Behavioral medicine: Symbiosis between laboratory and clinic. *Annual Review of Psychology, 34,* 1–31.

Miller, S.A., Manhal, M., & Mee, L. (1991). Parental beliefs, parental accuracy, and children's cognitive performance: A search for causal relations. *Developmental Psychology, 27,* 267–276.

Miller, T. W., & Kraus, R. F. (1990). An overview of chronic pain. *Hospital and Community Psychiatry, 41,* 433–440.

Miller, W. A., Ratliff, F., & Hartline, H. K. (1961). How cells receive stimuli. *Scientific American, 222–238.*

Mills, M. (1995). *Characteristics of personals ads differ as a function of publication readership SES.* Paper presented at the annual convention of the Human Behavior and Evolution Society, June, Santa Barbara, California.

Mills, M., & Melhuish, E. (1974). Recognition of mother's voice in early infancy. *Nature, 252,* 123–124.

Milner, B., Corkin, S., & Teuber, H. L. (1968). Further analysis of the hippocampal amnesic syndrome: Fourteen year follow-up study of H.M. *Neuropsychologia, 6,* 215–234.

Milner, P. (1991). Brain–stimulation reward: A review. *Canadian Journal of Psychology, 45,* 1–36.

Mineka, S., & Sutton, S. K. (1992). Cognitive biases and the emotional disorders. *Psychological Science, 3,* 65–69.

Minsky, M. (1975). A framework for representing knowledge. In P. H. Winston (Ed.), *The psychology of computer vision.* New York: McGraw–Hill.

Minuchin, S. (1974). *Families and family therapy.* Cambridge, MA: Harvard University Press.

Mirsky, A. F., & Duncan, C. C. (1986). Etiology and expression of schizophrenia: Neurobiological and psychosocial factors.

Annual Review of Psychology, 37, 291–319.

Mischel, W. (1968). *Personality and assessment.* New York: John Wiley.

Mischel, W. (1973). Toward a cognitive social learning reconceptualization of personality. *Psychological Review, 39,* 351–364.

Mischel, W. (1979). On the interface of cognitive and personality: Beyond the person–situation debate. *American Psychologist, 34,* 740–754.

Mischel, W. (1984). Convergences and challenges in the search for consistency. *American Psychologist, 39,* 351–364.

Mischel, W. (1990). Personality dispositions revisited and revised: A view after three decades. In L. Pervin (Ed.), *Handbook of personality: Theory and research* (pp. 111–134). New York: Guilford Press.

Mischel, W., & Mischel, H. N. (1976). A cognitive social–learning approach to morality and self–regulation. In T. Lickona (Ed.), *Moral development and behavior: Theory, research, and social issues.* New York: Holt, Rinehart, & Winston.

Mistlin, A., & Perrett, D. (1990). Visual and somatosensory processing in the macaque temporal cortex: The role of "expectation." *Experimental Brain Research, 82,* 437–450.

Mistry, J., & Rogoff, B. (1985). A cultural perspective on the development of talent. In F. D Horowitz & M. O'Brien (Eds.), *The gifted and talented: Developmental perspectives* (pp. 125–144). Washington, DC: American Psychological Association.

Misumi, J., & Peterson, M. F. (1985). The performance–maintenance (PM) theory of leadership: Review of a Japanese research program. *Administrative Science Quarterly, 30,* 198–223.

Mitchell, J. E., Pyle, R., Eckert, E., Hatsukami, D., Pomeroy, C., & Zimmerman, R. (1990). A comparison study of antidepressants and structured intensive group psychotherapy in the reatment of bulimia nervosa. *Archives of General Psychiatry, 47,* 149–157.

Mitchell, S. A. (1988). *Relational concepts in psychoanalysis: An integration.* Cambridge, MA: Harvard University Press.

Mitler, M. M., & Hajdukovic, R. (1991). Relative efficacy of drugs for the treatment of sleepiness in narcolepsy. *Sleep, 14,* 218–220.

Mobilization for Animals. (1984). *Direct action program 1984.* Columbus, Ohio.

Modestin, J. (1992). Multiple personality disorder in Switzerland. *American Journal of Psychiatry, 149,* 88–92.

Modgil, S. & Modgil, C., (Eds). (1982). *Jean Piaget: Consensus and controversy.* New York: Holt, Rinehart, & Winston.

Moeller, G., & Applezweig, M. M. (1957). A motivational factor in conformity. *Journal of Abnormal Social Psychology, 55,* 114–120.

Moerk, E. L. (1986). Environmental factors in early language acquisition. In G. J.

Whitehurst (Ed.), *Annals of Child Development* (Vol. 3). Greenwich, Conn.: JAI Press.

Moerk, E. L. (1989). The LAD was a lady and the tasks were ill–defined. *Developmental Review, 9,* 21–57.

Moerk, E. L. (1992). *A first language taught and learned.* Baltimore, MD: Brookes.

Moloney, D. P., Bouchard, T., & Segal, N. (1991). A genetic and environmental analysis of the vocational interests of monozygotic and dizygotic twins reared apart. *Journal of Vocational Behavior, 39,* 76–109.

Money, J. (1987). Sin, sickness, or status? Homosexual gender identity and psychoneuroendocrinology. *American Psychologist, 42,* 384–399.

Money, J., & Ehrhardt, A. A. (1972). Gender–dimorphic behavior and fetal sex hormones. In E. B. Astwood (Ed.), *Recent Progress in Hormone Research,* Vol 28. New York: Academic Press.

Money, J., & Ehrhardt, A. A. (1972). *Man & woman. Boy & girl.* Baltimore, MD: Johns Hopkins University Press.

Money, J., Schwartz, M., & Lewis, V. G. (1984). Adult heterosexual status and fetal hormonal masculinization and demasculinization. *Psychoneuroendocrinology, 9,* 405–414.

Monroe, S. M., & Simons, A. D. (1991). Diathesis–stress theories in the context of life stress research: Implications for the depressive disorders. *Psychological Bulletin, 110,* 406–425.

Montemayor, R., & Eisen, M. (1977). A developmental sequence of self–conceptions from childhood to adolescence. *Developmental Psychology, 13,* 314–319.

Montgomery, S. (1994). Long–term treatment of depression. *British Journal of Psychiatry, 165,* 31–36.

Montgomery, S. A. (1994). Antidepressants in long–term treatment. *Annual Review of Medicine, 45,* 447–457.

Monti, P., Rohsenow, D., Rubonis, A., & Niaura, R. (1993). Cue exposure with coping skills treatment for male alcoholics: A preliminary investigation. *Journal of Consulting and Clinical Psychology, 61,* 1011–1019.

Moore, K. L. (1993). *Before we are born.* (4th. ed.). Philadelphia: Saunders.

Moos, R. H. & Billings, A. G. (1982). Conceptualizing and measuring coping resources and processes. In L. Goldberger and S. Breznitz (Eds.), *Handbook of stress.* New York: Macmillan.

Moos, R. H. & Schaefer, J. A. (1986). Life Transitions and Crises. In R. H. Moos and J. A. Schaefer (Eds.), *Coping with life crises: An integrated approach.* New York: Plenum Press.

Moray, N. (1969). *Attention: Selective processes in vision and hearing.* London: Hutchinson.

Moreland, R. L. (1985). Social categorization and the assimilation of new group members. *Journal of Personality and Social Psychology, 48,* 1173–1190.

Morelli, G., Rogoff, B., Oppenheim, D., &

Goldsmith, D. (1992). Cultural variation in infants' sleeping arrangements: Questions of independence. *Developmental Psychology, 28,* 604–613.

Morgan, H. G., & Russell, G.F.M. (1975). Value of family background and clinical features as predictors of long–term outcome in anorexia nervosa: Four–year follow–up study of 41 patients. *Psychiatric Medicine, 5,* 355–371.

Morgan, J. (1986). *From simple input to complex grammar.* Cambridge, MA: MIT Press.

Morgan, J. & Travis, L. (1989). Limits on negative information in language input. *Journal of Child Language, 16,* 531–552.

Morgan, J. L. (1990). Input, innateness, and induction in language acquisition. *Developmental Psychobiology, 23,* 661–678.

Morris, N. (1986). Working memory,1974–1984: A review of a decade of research. *Current Psychological Research & Reviews, 5,* 281–295.

Morris, R. G. & Baddeley, A. D. (1988). Primary and working memory functioning in Alzheimer–type dementia. *Journal of Clinical and Experimental Neuropsychology, 10,* 279–296.

Morris, R. G., Craik, F. I., & Gick, M. L. (1990). Age differences in working memory tasks: The role of secondary memory and the executive system. *Quarterly Journal of Experimental Psychology: Human Experimental Psychology, 42,* 67–86.

Morrison, E. E., & Moran, D. T. (1995). Anatomy and ultrastructure of the human olfactory neuroepithelium. In R. L. Doty (Ed.), *Handbook of olfaction and gustation* (pp. 75–83). New York: Marcel Dekker.

Morse, J. M. & Morse, R. M. (1988). Cultural variation in the inference of pain. *Journal of Cross–Cultural Psychology, 19,* 232–242.

Morse, J. M. & Park, C. (1988). Differences in cultural expectations of the perceived painfulness of childbirth. In K. Michaelson (Ed.), *Childbirth in America: Anthropological Perspectives.* South Hadley, MA: Bergin & Garvey.

Moscovici, S. (1985). Social influence and conformity. In G. Lindzey and E. Aronson (Eds.), *Handbook of social psychology,* Reading, MA: Addison–Wesley.

Moser, P .W. (1987). Are cats smart? Yes, at being cats. *Discover,* 77–88.

Moskowitz, J. M., Malvin, J. H., Schaeffer, G. A., & Schaps, E. (1985). Evaluation of jigsaw, a cooperative learning technique. *Contemporary Educational Psychology, 10,* 104–112.

Motley, M. (1980). Verification of Freudian slips and semantic prearticulatory processing via laboratory–induced Spoonerisms. In V. Fromkin (Ed.), *Errors in linguistic performance: Slips of the tongue, ear, pen, and hand.* New York: Academic Press.

Motley, M. T. (1985). Slips of the tongue. *Scientific American, 253,* 116–127.

Mould, D. E. (1990). A reply to Page:

Fraud, pornography, and the Meese commission. *American Psychologist, 45,* 777–778.

Mowrer, O. H. (1947). On the dual nature of learning: A reinterpretation of conditioning and problem–solving. *Harvard Educational Review, 17,* 102–148.

Mowrer, O. H. (1960). *Learning theory and behavior.* New York: John Wiley.

Moyer, K. E. (1983). The physiology of motivation: Aggression as a model. In C. James Scheirer & Anne M. Rogers (Eds.), *G. Stanley Hall Lecture Series* (Vol. 3.) Washington, DC: American Psychological Association.

Muehlenhard, C. L. (1988). Misinterpreted dating behaviors and the risk of date rape. *Journal of Social and Clinical Psychology, 6,* 20–37.

Mueller, C. W. (1983). Environmental stressors and aggressive behavior. In R. G. Green & E. I. Donnerstein (Eds.), *Aggression.* New York: Academic Press.

Mulholland, D. J., Watt, N., Philpott, A., & Sarlin, N. (1991). Academic performatnce in children of divorce: Psychological resilience and vulnerability. *Psychiatry, 54,* 268–280.

Mullen, B., & Hu, L. (1989). Perceptions of ingroup and outgroup variability: A meta–analytic integration. *Basic and Applied Social Psychology, 10,* 233–252.

Muller, W. E., Stoll, L., Schubert, T., & Gelbmann, C. (1991). Central cholinergic functioning and aging. *Acta Psychiatrica Scandinavica, 83* (supplement), 34–39.

Mumaw, R., & Pellegrino, J. (1984). Individual differences in complex spatial processing. *Journal of Educational Psychology, 76,* 920–939.

Mumford, D. B. (1993). Eating disorders in different cultures. *International Review of Psychiatry, 5,* 109–113.

Mumpower, J. L., & Cooke, S.W. (1978). The development of interpersonal attraction in cooperating interracial groups: The effects of success–failure, race and competence of groupmates, and helping a less competent groupmate. *International Journal of Group Tensions, 8,* 18–50.

Muran, J.C. (1991). A reformulation of the ABC model in cognitive psychotherapies: Implications for assessmentand treatment. *Clinical Psychology Review, 11,* 399–418.

Murdock, G.P. (1957). World ethnographic sample. *American Anthropologist, 59,* 664–687.

Murphy, G. L., & Medin, D.L. (1985). The role of theories in conceptual coherence. *Psychological Review, 92,* 289–316.

Murphy, J., & Slorach, N. (1983). The language development of preschool hearing children of deaf parents. *British Journal of Disorders of Communication, 18,* 118–126.

Murphy, J. M. (1976). Psychiatric labeling in cross–cultural perspective. *Science, 191,* 1019–1028.

Murphy, S. T., & Zajonc, R. (1993). Affect, cognition, and awareness: Affective priming with optimal and suboptimal stimulus exposures. *Journal of Personality and Social Psychology, 64,* 723–739.

Murray, H. A. (1938). *Explorations in personality.* New York: Oxford University Press.

Murray, H. A. (1943). *Thematic Apperception Test.* Cambridge, MA: Harvard University Pres.

Murray, R. M., Clifford, C. A., & Gurling, H. M. (1983). Twin and adoption studies: How good is the evidence for a genetic role? *Recent Developments in Alcoholism, 1,* 25–48.

Murrey, G. J., Cross, H. J., & Whipple, J. (1992). Hypnotically created pseudomemories: Further investigation into the "memory distortion or response bias" question. *Journal of Abnormal Psychology, 101,* 75–77.

Musselman, D. (1994). Cerebrospinal fluid study of cannabinoid users and normal control subjects. *Psychiatry Research, 52,* 103–105.

Musso, A., Blanchard, E. B., & McCoy, G. C. (1991). Evaluation of thermal biofeedback treatment of hypertension using 24–hour ambulatory blood pressure monitoring. *Behaviour Research and Therapy, 29,* 469–478.

Myers, D. G. (1993). *Social psychology.* (4th ed.). New York: McGraw–Hill.

Myerson, J., Ferraro, F. R., Hale, S., & Lima, S. (1992). General slowing in semantic priming and word recognition. *Psychology and Aging, 7,* 257–270.

Myhrer, T., Utsikt, L., Fjelland, J., & Iversen, E. (1992). Differential rearing conditions in rats: Effects on neurochemistry in neocortical areas and cognitive behaviors. *Brain Research Bulletin, 28,* 427–434.

Myhrer, T., Utsikt, L., Fjelland, J., Iversen, E., & Fonnum, F. (1992). Differential rearing conditions in rats: Effects on neurochemistry in neocortical area and cognitive behaviors. *Brain Research Bulletin, 28,* 427–434.

Na, C., Doraiswamy, P. M., Lee, K., & Krishnan, K. R. (1991). Magnetic resonance imaging in botanical psychiatry. *Progress in Neuro Psychopharmacolgy and Biological Psychiatry, 15,* 581–593.

Nadeau, R. L. (1991). *Mind, machines, and human consciousness.* Chicago: Contemporary Books.

Nadler, A., & Ben–Shushan, D. (1989). Forty years later: Long–term consequences of massive traumatization as manifested by holocaust survivors from the city and the kibbutz. *Journal of Consulting and Clinical Psychology, 57,* 287–293.

Nadon, R., Hoyt, I. P., Register, P. A., & Kihlstrom, J. F. (1991). Absorption and hypnotizability: Context effects reexamined. *Journal of Personality and Social Psychology, 60,* 144–153.

Nahemow, L., & Lawton, M. P. (1975). Similarity and propinquity in friendship formation. *Journal of Personality and Social Psychology, 32,* 205–213.

Narabayashi, H., et al. (1963). Stereotaxic amygdalotomy for behavior disorders. *Archives of Neurology, 9,* 1016.

Nash, M. R. (1988). Hypnosis as a window on regression. *Bulletin of the Menninger Clinic, 52,* 383–403.

Nathan, S. G. (1986). The epidemiology of the DSM–III psychosexual dysfunctions. *Journal of Sex & Marital Therapy, 12,* 267–81.

Nathans, J. (1987). Molecular biology of visual pigments. *Annual Rievew of Physiology, 10,* 163–194.

National Research Council. (1989). Obesity and eating disorders. In *Diet and health: Implications for reducing chronic disease risk* (pp. 563–592). Washington, DC: National Academy Press.

Natsoulas, T. (1991). Consciousness and commissurotomy: III. Toward the improvement of alternative conceptions. *Journal of Mind and Behavior, 12,* 1–32.

Negandhi, A. R. (1973). *Management and economic development: The case of Taiwan.* The Hague: Martinus Nijhoff.

Neher, A. (1991). Maslow's theory of motivation: A critique. *Journal of Humanistic Psychology, 31,* 89–112.

Neisser, U. (1967). *Cognitive psychology.* New York: Appleton–Century–Crofts.

Neisser, U. (1976). *Cognition and reality.* San Francisco: Freeman.

Neisser, U. (1978). Anticipations, images, and introspection. *Cognition, 6,* 169–174.

Neisser, U. (1991). A case of misplaced nostalgia. *American Psychologist, 46,* 34–36.

Nelson, A. (1985). Psychological equivalence: Awareness and response–ability in our nuclear age. *American Psychologist, 40,* 549–556.

Nelson, K. (1987). What's in a name? Reply to Seidenberg and Petitto. *Journal of Experimental Psychology: General, 116,* 293–296.

Nelson, K. E. (1991). Varied domains of development: A tale of LAD, MAD, SAD, DAD, and RARE and surprising events in our RELMS. In F. S. Kessel, M. H. Bornstein, and A. J. Sameroff (Eds.), *Contemporary constructions of the child: Essays in honor of William Kessen* (pp. 123–142). Hillsdale, NJ: Erlbaum.

Nemiah, J. C. (1985a). Anxiety states (anxiety neuroses). In H.I. Kaplan & B.J. Sadock (Eds.), *Comprehensive textbook of psychiatry.* (4th ed.). Baltimore, MD: Williams & Wilkins.

Nesbitt, E. B. (1973). An escalator phobia overcome in one session of flooding in vivo. *Journal of Behavior Therapy and Experimental Psychiatry, 4,* 405–406.

Neugarten, B. L. (1977). Personality and aging. In J.E. Birren & K.W. Schaie (Eds.), *Handbook of the psychology of aging.* New York: Academic.

Neugarten, B. L., Havighurst, R. J., & Tobin, S. S. (1968). Personality and patterns of aging. In B.L. Neugarten (Ed.), *Middle age and aging.* Chicago: University of Chicago Press.

Neutra, M., & Leblond, C. P. (1969). The golgli apparatus. *Scientific American,* 100–107.

Newcomb, T. M. (1956). The predictions of interpersonal attraction. *American Psychologist, II,* 575–586.

Newcomb, T. M. (1961). *The acquaintance process.* New York: Holt, Rinehart, & Winston.

Newcombe, N., & Dubas, J. S. (1992). A longitudinal study of predictors of spatial ability in adolescent females. *Child Development, 63,* 37–46.

Newell, A. (1969). Heuristic programming: Ill–structured problems. In J.Aronofsky (Ed.), *Progress in Operations Research,* Vol. 3. New York: John Wiley.

Newell, A., & Simon, H. A. (1972). *Human problem solving.* Englewood Cliffs, NJ: Prentice–Hall.

Newman, E. A., & Hartline, P. H. (1982). The infrared "vision" of snakes. *Scientific American,* 116–127.

Newman, H. G., Freeman, F. N., & Holzinger, K. J. (1937). *Twins: A study of heredity and environment.* Chicago: University of Chicago Press.

Newman, J. P., Patterson, C. M., Howland, E. W., & Nichols, S. L. (1990). Passive avoidance in psychopaths: The effects of reward. *Personality and Individual Differences, 11,* 1101–1114.

Newport, E. L., Gleitman, H., & Gleitman, L.R. (1977). Mother, I'd rather do it myself: Some effects and noneffects of maternal speech style. In C. Snow & C. A. Ferguson (Eds.), *Talking to children: Language input and acquisition.* Cambridge, England: Cambridge University Press.

Newsom, C., Flavall, J., & Rincover, A. (1983). Side effects of punishment. In S. Axelrod & J. Apsche (Eds.), *The effects of punishment on human behavior.* New York: Academic.

Newsome, W. T., Britten, K. H., & Moushon, J. A. (1989). Neuronal correlates of a perceptual decision. *Nature, 341,* 52–54.

Newton, T. L., & Contrada, R. J. (1992). Repressive coping and verbal autonomic response dissociation: the influence of social context. *Journal of Personality and Social Psychology, 62,* 159–167.

Nibuya, M., & Kanba, S. (1990). Biological aspects of anxiety. *Journal of Mental Health, 36,* 25–30.

Nicholson, J. (1984). *Men and women: How different are they?* Oxford: Oxford University Press.

Nicholson, N. L., & Blanchard, E. B. (1993). A controlled evaluation of behavioral treatment of chronic headache in the elderly. *Behavior Therapy, 24,* 395–408.

Nicol, S. E., & Gottesman, I. I. (1983).

Clues to the genetics and neurobiology of schizophrenia. *American Scientist, 71,* 398–404.

Niedenthal, P., & Cantor, N. (1986). Affective responses as guides to category–based inferences. *Motivation & Emotion, 10,* 217–232.

Niedenthal, P., Setterlund, M., & Wherry, M. B. (1992). Possible self–complexity and affective reactions to goal–relevant evaluation. *Journal of Personality and Social Psychology, 63,* 5–16.

Nigg, J. T., & Gold, H. H. (1994). Genetics of personality disorders: Perspectives from personality and psychopathology research. *Psychological Bulletin, 115,* 346–380.

Nigg, J. T., Lohr, N. E., Westen, D, Gold, L. J., & Silk, K. (1992). Malevolent object representations in borderline personality disorder and major depression. *Journal of Abnormal Psychology, 101,* 61–67.

Nilsson, O., Brundin, P., & Bjorklund, A. (1990). Amelioration of spatial memory impairment by intrahippocampal grafts of mixed septal and raphe tissue in rats with combined cholinergic and serotonergic denervation of the forebrain. *Brain Research, 515,* 193–206.

Nisbett, R. (1993). Violence and U.S. regional culture. *American Psychologist, 48,* 441–449.

Nisbett, R. E., Borgida, E., Crandall, R., & Reed, H. (1976). Popular induction: Information is not necessarily informative. In J. S. Carroll & J. W. Payne (Eds.), *Cognition and social behavior.* Hillsdale, NJ: Erlbaum.

Nisbett, R. E., & Gordon, A. (1967). Self–esteem and susceptibility to social influence. *Journal of Personality and Social Psychology, 5,* 268–276.

Nisbett, R. E., Krantz, D.H., Jepson, C., & Kunda, Z. (1983). The uses of statistical heuristics in everyday inductive reasoning. *Psychological Review, 90,* 339–363.

Nisbett, R. E., & Ross, L. (1980). *Human inference: Strategies and shortcomings of social judgment.* Englewood Cliffs, NJ: Prentice–Hall.

Nisbett, R. E., & Wilson, T. D. (1977). Telling more than we can know: verbal reports on mental processes. *Psychological Review, 84,* 231–259.

Nolen–Hoeksema, S., Girgus, J., & Seligman, M.E.P. (1992). Predictors and consequences of childhood depressive symptoms: A 5–year longitudinal study. *Journal of Abnormal Psychology, 101,* 405–422.

Noll, R. (1994). Hypnotherapy for warts in children and adolescents. *Journal of Developmental and Behavioral Pediatrics, 15,* 170–173.

Norman, W. T. (1963). Toward an adequate taxonomy of personality attributes: Replicated factor structure in peer nomination personality ratings. *Journal of Abnormal and Social Psychology, 66,* 574–583.

Novak, M. A., & Harlow, H. F. (1975).

Social recovery of monkeys isolated for the first year of life: rehabilitation and therapy. *Developmental Psychology, 11,* 453–465.

Noyes, R., Garvey, M., Cook, B., & Suelzer, M. (1991). Controlled discontinuation of benzodiazepine treatment for patients with panic disorder. *American Journal of Psychiatry, 148,* 517–523.

O'Brien, M., Huston, A. C., & Risley, T. R. (1983). Sex–typed play of toddlers in a day care center. *Journal of Applied Developmental Psychology, 4,* 1–9.

O'Leary, A. (1990). Stress, emotion, and human immune function. *Psychological Bulletin, 108,* 363–382.

O'Leary, D., Schlagger, B., & Tuttle, R. (1994). Specification of neocortical areas and thalamocortical connections. *Annual Review of Neuroscience, 17,* 419–439.

O'Malley, S. S., & Maisto, S. A. (1985). Effects of family drinking history and expectancies on responses to alcohol in men. *Journal of Studies on Alcohol, 46,* 289–297.

O'Sullivan, C. S., & Durso, F. T. (1984). Effect of schema–incongruent information on memory for stereotypical attributes. *Journal of Personality and Social Psychology, 47,* 55–70.

O'Sullivan, G., Noshirvani, H., Marks, I., & Monteira, W. (1991). Six–year follow–up after exposure and clomipramine therpay for obsessive compulsive disorder. *Journal of Clinical Psychiatry, 52,* 150–155.

Oakhill, J., & Garnham, A. (1993). On theories of belief bias in syllogistic reasoning. *Cognition, 46,* 87–92.

Oakhill, J., Johnson–Laird, P. N., & Garnham, A. (1989). Believability and syllogistic reasoning. *Cognition, 31,* 117–140.

Oatley, K., & Jenkins, J. M. (1992). Human emotion: Function and dysfunction. *Annual Review of Psychology, 43,* 55–85.

Oberle, K., Paul, P., Wry, J., & Grace, M. (1990). Pain, anxiety and analgesics: A comparative study of elderly and younger surgical patients. *Canadian Journal on Aging, 9,* 13–22.

Offer, D., & Offer, J. (1975). *From teenage to young manhood: A psychological study.* New York: Basic Books.

Offer, D., Ostrov, E., & Howard, K. I. (1981). *The adolescent: A psychological self–portrait.* New York: Basic Books.

Offer, D., Ostrov, E., Howard, K., & Atkinson, R. (1990). Normality and adolescence. *Psychiatric Clinics of North America, 13,* 377–388.

Ogata, N., Voshii, M., & Narahashi, T. (1989). Psychotropic drugs block voltage–gated ion channels in neuroblastoma cells. *Brain Research, 476,* 140–144.

Ogbu, J. (1991). Minority coping responses and school experience. *Journal of Psychohistory, 18,* 434–456.

Ohman, A., Fredrikson, M., Hugdahl, K., & Rimmo, P. (1976). The premise of equipotentiality in human classical conditioning. *Journal of Experimental Psychology General, 105,* 313–337.

Okasha, A., El Akabaw, A. S., Snyder, K. S., Wilson, A. K., Youssef, I., & El Dawla, A. S. (1994). Expressed emotion, perceived criticism, and relapse in depression: A replication. *American Journal of Psychiatry, 151,* 1001–1005.

Olds, J., & Milner, P. (1954). Positive reinforcement produced by electrical stimulation of septal areas and other regions of rat brains. *Journal of Comparative and Physiological Psychology, 47,* 419–427.

Oliner, S., & Oliner, P. (1988). *The altruistic personality: Rescuers of Jews in Nazi Europe.* New York: Free Press.

Olivier, B., Mos, J., VanderHeyden, J., & VanderPoel, G. (1992). Preclinical evidence for the anxiolytic activity of 5 ht sub 3 receptor antagonists: A review. *Stress Medicine, 8,* 117–136.

Olson, D. (1985). Circumplex model VII: Validation and FACES III. *Family Process, 25,* 337–351.

Olson, G. B. (1981). Perception of melodic contour through intrasensory matching and intersensory transfer by elementary school students. *Journal of Educational Research, 74,* 358–362.

Olson, J. (1992). Self–perception of humor: Evidence for discounting and augmentation. *Journal of Personality and Social Psychology, 62,* 369–377.

Olson, J. M. (1992). Self–perception of humor: Evidence for discounting and augmentation effects. *Journal of Personality and Social Psychology, 62,* 369–377.

Olson, J. M., & Zanna, M. (1993). Attitudes and attitude change. *Annual Review of Psychology, 44,* 117–154.

Olson, S. L. (1989). Predicting long–term developmental outcomes from maternal perceptions of infant and toddler behavior. *Infant Behavior and Development, 12,* 77–92.

Olster, D. H., & Blaustein, J. D. (1989). Development of steroid–induced lordosis in female guinea pigs: Relationship to neural estrogen and progestin receptors. *Brain Research, 484,* 168–175.

Olweus, D. (1980). Familial and temperamental determinants of aggressive behavior in adolescent boys: A causal analysis. *Developmental Psychology, 16,* 644–666.

Omark, D. R., Omark, M., & Edelman, M. (1975). Formation of dominance hierarchies in young children. In T.R. Williams (Ed.), *Psychological anthropology.* The Hague: Mouton.

Orne, M. T., Sheehan, P. W., & Evans, F. J. (1968). *Journal of Personality and Social Psychology, 9,* 189–196.

Ornstein, R. E. (1986). *The psychology of consciousness.* (2nd ed.) New York: Penguin Books.

Oro, A. & Dixon, S. (1987). Prenatal cocaine and metamphetamine exposure: Maternal and neonatal correlates. *Journal of Pediatrics, 111,* 571–578.

Ortony, A., Clore, G. L, & Collins, A. (1988). *The cognitive structure of emotions.* New York: Cambridge University Press.

Ortony, A., & Turner, T. J. (1990). What's basic about basic emotions? *Psychological Review, 97,* 315–331.

Oskamp, S. (1991). Factors influencing household recycling behavior. *Environment & Behavior, 23,* 494–519.

Ost, L. (1991). Acquisition of blood and injection phobia and anxiety response patterns in clinical patients. *Behavior Research and Therapy, 29,* 323–332.

Ostfeld, B., & Katkz, P A. (1969). The effect of threat severity in children of varying socioeconomic levels. *Developmental Psychology, 1,* 205–210.

Otto, M. W., Pollack, M., Sachs, G., & Reiter, S. (1993). Discontinuation of benzodiazepine treatment: Efficacy of cognitive–behavioral therapy for patients with panic disorder. *American Journal of Psychiatry,* 1485–1490.

Packard, J. (1986). Tone production in nonfluent aphasic Chinese speech. *Brain & Language, 29,* 212–223.

Packwood, J., & Gordon, B. (1975). Steropsis in normal domestic cat, Siamese cat, and cat raised with alternating monocular occlusion. *Journal of Neurophysiology, 38,* 1485–1499.

Page, R. C. (1989). Marathon group therapy with illicit drug users. In S. Einstein (Ed.), *Drug and alcohol use: Issues and factors.* New York: Plenum Press.

Paivio, A. (1991). Dual coding theory: Retrospect and current status. *Canadian Journal of Psychology, 45,* 255–287.

Palkes, H., Stewart, M., & Kahana, B. (1968). Porteus maze performance after training in self-directed verbal commands. *Child Development, 39,* 817–826.

Pallak, M. S., & Pittman, T. S. (1972). General motivational effects of dissonance arousal. *Journal of Personality and Social Psychology, 21,* 349–358.

Papez, J. W. (1937). A proposed mechanism of emotion. *Archives of Neurology and Psychiatry, 38,* 725–743.

Park, B., & Rothbart, M. (1982). Perception of out–group homogeneity and levels of social categorization: Memory for the subordinate attributes of in–group and out–group members. *Journal of Personality and Social Psychology, 2,* 1051–1068.

Park, S., & Holzman, P. S. (1993). Association of working memory deficit and eye tracking dysfunction in schizophrenia. *Schizophrenia Research, 11,* 55–61.

Parke, R. D., & Slaby, R. G. (1983). The development of aggression. In P. H. Mussen (Ed.), *Carmichael's Manual of Child Psychology,* Vol. 4: *Socialization, personality, and social development.* New York: John Wiley.

Parker, D. E. (1980). The vestibular apparatus. *Scientific American,* 98–111.

Parker, J., & Asher, S. (1987). Peer relations and later personal adjustment: Are low–accepted children at risk"? *Psychological Bulletin, 102,* 357–389.

Parkes, C. M. & Brown, R. J. (1971). Health after bereavement: A controlled study of young Boston widows and widowers. *Psychosomatic Medicine, 34,* 449–460.

Parks, C., & Hollon, S. (1988). Cognitive assessment. In A. Bellack & Michel Hersen (Eds.), *Behavioral assessment: A practical handbook,* (pp. 161–212) (3rd ed.). Elmsford, NY: Pergamon.

Parloff, M. B., London, P., & Wolfe, B. (1986). Individual psychotherapy and behavior change. *Annual Review of Psychology, 37,* 321–349.

Parrot, A. (1990). Institutional response: How can acquaintance rape be prevented? In A. Parrot & L. Bechhofer (Eds.), *Acquaintance rape: The hidden crime.* New York: John Wiley & Sons.

Parsons, T. (1951). *The social system.* Glencoe, IL: Free Press.

Pascual–Leone, A. (1993). Modulation of motor cortical outputs to the reading hand of braille readers. *Annals of Neurology, 34,* 33–37.

Pascual–Leone, A., Cammarota, A., Wassermann, E., & Brasil–Neto, J. (1994). Modulation of cortical motor output maps during development of implicit and explicit knowledge. *Science, 263,* 1287–1289.

Pascual–Leone, A., & Torres, F. (1993). Plasticity of the sensorimotor cortex representations of the reading finger in Braille. *Brain.*

Patchen, M. (1982). *Black–white contact in schools: Its social and academic effects.* West Lafayette, IND: Purdue University Press.

Patterson, D. G., & O'Gorman, E. C. (1989). Sexual anxiety in sexual dysfunction. *British Journal of Psychiatry, 155,* 374–378.

Patterson, G. R., & Bank, L. (1986). Bootstrapping your way in the nomological thicket. *Behavioral Assessment, 8,* 49–73.

Paulus, P. B. et al. (1988). *Prison crowding: A psychological perspective.* New York: Springer–Verlag.

Paunonen, S. V., Jackson, D. N., Trzebinski, J., & Forsterling, F. (1992). Personality structure across cultures: A multimethod evaluation. *Journal of Personality and Social Psychology, 62,* 447–456.

Pavlov, I. P. (1927). *Conditioned reflexes.* New York: Oxford University Press.

Pavone, L., Meli, C., Nigro, F., Lisi, R. et al. (1993). Late diagnosed phenylketonuria patients: Clinical presentation and results of treatment. *Developmental Brain Dysfunction, 6,* 184–187.

Pearce, J. M. (1987). A model for stimulus generalization in Pavlonian conditioning. *Psychological Review, 94,* 61–73.

Pearlson, G., Harris, G., Powers, R. E., Barta, P., Camargo, E., Chase, G., Noga,

J. T., & Tune, L. (1992). Quantitative changes in mesial temporal volume, regional cerebral blood flow, and cognition in Alzheimer's disease. *Archives of General Psychiatry, 49,* 402–408.

Pedersen, D. M., & Wheeler, J. (1983). The Muller–Lyer illusion among Navajos. *Journal of Social Pschology, 121,* 3–6.

Pedersen, N., McClearn, G., Plomin, R., & Nesselroade, J. R. (1991). The Swedish adoption/twin study of aging: An update. *Acta Geneticae Medicae et Gemellogiae: Twin Research, 40,* 7–20.

Pederson, D. R., Moran, G., Sitko, C., Campbell, K., Ghesquire, K., & Acton, H. (1990). Maternal sensitivity and the security of infant–mother attachment: A q–sort study. *Child Development, 61,* 1974–1983.

Peele, S. (1986). Implications and limitations of genetic models of alcoholism and other addictions. *Journal of Studies on Alcohol, 47,* 63–73.

Peele, S. (1990). Research issues in assessing addiction treatment efficacy: How cost effective are Alcoholics Anonymous and private treatment centers? *Drug & Alcohol Dependence, 25,* 179–182.

Penfield, W., & Rasmussen, T. (1950). *The cerebral cortex of man.* New York: Macmillan.

Pennebaker, J. (1980). Self–perception of emotion and internal sensation. In D. M. Wegner and R. R. Vallacher (Eds.), *The self in social psychology.* New York: Oxford University Press.

Pennebaker, J. (1992). Putting stress into words: Health, linguistic and therapeutic implications. *Behavior Research & Therapy, 31,* 539–548.

Pennebaker, J., Colder, M., & Sharp, L. K. (1990). Accelerating the coping process. *Journal of Personality and Social Psychology, 58,* 528–537.

Pennebaker, J., Kiecolt, G., Janice, K., & Glaser, R. (1988). Confronting traumatic experience and immunocompetence: A reply to Neale, Cox, Valdimarsdottir, and Stone. *Journal of Consulting and Clinical Psychology, 56,* 638–639.

Penner, L., & Rioux, S. (1995) *The prosocial personality and memories of parents.* Nags Head Invitation Conference on the Social Sciences, Highland Beach, June.

Perdue, C., Dovidio, J., Gurtman, M., & Tyler, R. (1990). Us and them: Social categorization and the process of intergroup bias. *Journal of Personality and Social Psychology, 59,* 475–486.

Perdue, C., & Gurtman, M. (1990). Evidence for the automaticity of ageism. *Journal of Experiment/al Social Psychology, 26,* 199–216.

Perlmutter, M. (1978). What is memory aging the aging of? *Developmental Psychology, 14,* 330–345.

Perlmutter, M. (1983). Learning and memory through adulthood. In M.W. Riley, B.B. Hess, & K. Bond (Eds.), *Aging in society: Selected reviews of recent research.* Hillsdale, NJ: Erlbaum.

Perlmutter, M., Dams, C., Berry, J., Kaplan, M., Pearson, D., & Verdonik, J. (1990). Aging and memory. *Annual Review of Gerontology and Geriatrics, 7,* 57–92.

Perlmutter, M., Kaplan, M., & Nyquist, L. (1990). Development of adaptive competence in adulthood. *Human Development, 33,* 185–197.

Perlmutter, M. & Nyquist, L. (1990). Relationship between self–reported physical and mental health and intelligence performance across adulthood. *Journal of Gerontology, 45,* 145–155.

Perls, F. S., Hefferline, R. F. & Goodman, P. (1969). *Gestalt therapy: Excitement and growth in the human personality.* New York: Julian Press.

Perris, E. E., Myers, N. A., & Clifton, R. K. (1990). Long–term memory for a single infancy experience. *Child Development, 61,* 1796–1807.

Perry, G. D., & Bussey, K. (1979). The social learning theory of sex differences: Imitation is alive and well. *Journal of Personality and Social Psychology, 37,* 1699–1712.

Perry, J. C., & Cooper, S. H. (1987). Empirical studies of psychological defense mechanisms. In R. Michels & J. O. Cavenar, Jr. (Eds.), *Psychiatry.* Philadelphia: J.B. Lippincott.

Perry, J. C., & Cooper, S. H. (1987). Empirical studies of defense mechanisms: I. Clinical Interview and life vignette ratings. *Archives of General Psychiatry, 46,* 444–460.

Perry, P. J., Miller, D. D., Arndt, S., & Cadoret, R. (1991). Clozapine and norclozapine plasma concentrations and clinical response of treatment–refractory schizophrenic patients. *American Journal of Psychiatry, 148,* 231–235.

Persons, J. (1992). Psychotherapy outcome studies do not accurately represent current models of psychotherapy: A proposed remedy. *American Psychologist, 46,* 99–106.

Peselow, E., Robins, C.J., Sanfilipo, M. P., Block, P., & Fieve, R. (1992). Sociotropy and autonomy: Relationship to antidepressant drug treatment response and endogenous–nonendogenous dichotomy. *Journal of Abnormal Psychology, 101,* 479–486.

Peskin, J. (1982). Measuring household production for the GNP. *Family Economics Review, 3,* 16–25.

Peskin, J. (1992). Ruse and representations: On children's ability to conceal information. *Developmental Psychology, 28,* 84–89.

Peterson, A. C. (1988). Adolescent development. *Annual Review of Psychology, 39,* 583–607.

Peterson, C. (1988). Explanatory style as a risk factor for illness. *Cognitive Therapy and Research, 12,* 119–132.

Peterson, C., & Seligman, M.E.P. (1984). Causal explanations as a risk factor for depression: Theory and evidence. *Psychological Review 91,* 347–374.

Peterson, C., Seligman, M., & Vaillant, G. (1988). Pessimistic explanatory style is a risk factor for physical illness: A thirty–five–year longitudinal study. *Journal of Personality & Social Psychology, 55,* 23–27.

Peterson, G., & Peters, D. (1985). The socialization values of low–income Appalachian White and rural Black mothers: A comparative study. *Journal of Comparative Family Studies, 16,* 75–91.

Peterson, J. (1925). *Early conceptions and tests of intelligence.* Yonkers–on–Hudson, NY: World Book Co.

Peterson, L. R. and Peterson, M. J. (1959). Short–term retention of individual items, *Journal of Experimental Psychology, 61,* 12–21.

Peterson, S. B. (1989). A microcomputer lab for psychology based on a hierarchical learning model. *Behavior Research Methods, Instruments, and Computers, 21,* 130–133.

Pettigrew, J. D. (1972). The neurophysiology of binocular vision. *Scientific American,* 84–95.

Pettigrew, T. (1958). Personality and socio–cultural factors in intergroup attitudes: A cross–national comparison. *Journal of Conflict Resolution, 2,* 29–42.

Petty, R. (1995).Attitude change. In A. Tesser (Ed.), *Advanced social psychology.* New York: McGraw-Hill.

Petty, R., & Cacioppo, J. (1981). *Attitudes and persuasion: Classic and contemporary approaches.* Dubuque, Iowa: W. C. Brown.

Petty, R., & Cacioppo, J. (1986). *Communication and persuasion: Central and peripheral routes to attitude change.* New York: Springer-Verlag.

Petty, R., & Cacioppo, J. T. (1986). The elaboration likelihood model of persuasion. In L. Berkowitz (Ed.), *Advances in Experimental Social Psychology, 19,* 123–205.

Petty, R., & Krosnick, J. (1994). *Attitude strength: Antecedents and consequences.* Hillsdale, NJ: Erlbaum.

Pfaffman, C. (1955). Gustatory nerve impulses in rat, cat and rabbit. *Journal of Neurophysiology, 18,* 429–440.

Phillips, C. D., & Dinitz, S. (1982). Labeling and juvenile court dispositions: Official responses to a cohort of violent juveniles. *Sociological Quarterly, 23,* 267–278.

Phillips, K. A., Gunderson, J., Hirschfeld, R. M., & Smith, L .E. (1990). A review of the depressive personality. *American Journal of Psychiatry, 147,* 830–837.

Piaget, J. (1926). *The language and thought of the child.* New York: Humanities Press, 1951.

Piaget, J. (1932). *The moral judgment of the child* (M. Gabrain, Trans.). New York: Free Press.

Piaget, J. (1951). *Play, dreams, & imitation in childhood.* New York: W. W. Norton

Piaget, J. (1954). *The construction of reality in the child* (M.Cook, Trans.). New York: Basic Books.

Piaget, J. (1970). Piaget's theory. In P. Mussen, (Ed.), *Carmichael's manual of child psychology*. New York: John Wiley.

Piaget, J. (1972). Development and learning. In C.S. Lavatelli & F. Stendler (Eds.), *Readings in child behavior and development*. (3rd ed.). New York: Harcourt Brace Jovanovich.

Piaget, J. & Inhelder, B. (1956). *The child's conception of space* (F. J. Langdon & J. L. Lunzer, Trans.). London: Routledge & T.K. Paul.

Piaget, J., & Inhelder, B. (1969). *The psychology of the child*. New York: Basic Books.

Pickar, D. (1988). Perspectives on a time–dependent model of neuroleptic action. *Schizophrenia Bulletin, 14,* 255–268.

Pickar, D., Owen, R. R., Litman, R. E., Konicki, E., Gutierrez, R., & Rapaport, M. (1992). Clinical and biologic response to clozapine in patients with schizophrenia: Crossover comparison with fluphenazine. *Archives of General Psychiatry, 49,* 345–353.

Pickens, R., Svikis, D., McGue, M., Lykken, D., Heston, L., & Clayton, P.(1991). Heterogeneity in the inheritance of alcoholism: A study of male and female twins. *Archives of General Psychiatry, 48,* 19–28.

Piers, G., & Singer, M. (1953). *Shame and guilt: A psychoanalytic and a cultural study*. Springfield, Ill.: C. Thomas.

Pihl, R., Peterson, J., & Finn, P. (1990). Inherited predisposition to alcoholism: Characteristics of sons of male alcoholics. *Journal of Abnormal Psychology, 99,* 291–301.

Piliavin, J. A., et al. (1981). *Emergency intervention*. New York: Academic Press.

Piliavin, J. A., Piliavin, J., & Rodis, J. (1975). Costs, diffusion, and the stigmatized victim. *Journal of Personality and Social Psychology, 32,* 429–438.

Pilisuk, M., Montgomery, M. B., Parks, S H., & Acredolo, C. (1993). Locus of control, life stress, and social networks: Gender differences of the health status of the elderly. *Sex Roles, 28,* 147–166.

Pillard, R. C., Poumadere, J., & Carretta, R. A. (1981). Is homosexuality familial? A review, some data, and a suggestion. *Archives of Sexual Behavior, 10,* 465–73.

Pillard, R. C., Poumadere, J., & Carretta, R. A. (1982). A family study of sexual orientation. *Archives of Sexual Behavior, 11,* 511–520.

Pillemer, D .B. (1984). Flashbulb memories of the assassination attempt on President Reagan. *Cognition, 16,* 63–80.

Pillemer, D. B. (1990). Clarifying flashbulb memory concept: Comment on McCloskey, Wible, & Cohen (1988). *Journal of Experimental Psychology: General, 119(1),* 92–96.

Pinker, S. (1994). *The language instinct: How the mind creates language*. New York: HarperCollins.

Piper, W. E., Joyce, A., McCallum, M., &

Azim, H. (1993). Concentration and correspondence of transference interpretations in short–term psychotherapy. *Journal of Consulting and Clinical Psychotherapy, 61,* 586–595.

Plomin, R. (1989). Environment and genes: Determinants of behavior. *American Psychologist, 44,* 105–111.

Plomin, R. (1990). *Nature and nurture*. Pacific Grove, CA: Brooks–Cole.

Plomin, R., & Bergeman, C. S. (1991). The nature of nurture: Genetic influence on environmental meaasures. *Behavioral and Brain Sciences, 14,* 373–427.

Plomin, R., Chipuer, H., & Loehlin, J. C. (1990). Behavioral genetics and personality. In L. Pervin (Ed.), *Handbook of personality: Theory and research* (pp. 225–243). New York: Guilford Press.

Plomin, R., & DeFries, J. (1980). Genetics and intelligence: Recent data. Intelligence, 4, 15–24.

Plomin, R., Reiss, D., Hetherington, E.M., & Howe, G.W. (1994). Nature and nurture: Genetic contributions to measures of the family environment. *Developmental Psychology, 30,* 32–43.

Plomin, R., Reiss, D., Hetherington, E. M., & Howe, G. W. (1994). Nature and nurture: Genetic contributions to measures of the family environment. *Developmental Psychology, 30,* 32–43.

Plomin, R., & Rende, R. (1991). Human behavioral genetics. *Annual Review of Psychology, 42,* 161–190.

Plomin, R., Willerman, L., & Loehlin, J. C. (1976). Resemblance in appearance and the equal environments assumption in twin studies of personality. *Behavior Genetics, 6,* 43–52.

Plous, S. (1991). An attitude survey of animal rights activists. *Psychological Science, 2,* 194–196.

Plutchik, R. (1980). *Emotions: A psycho-evolutionary synthesis*. New York: Harper & Row.

Plutchik, R. (1991). Emotions and evolution. In K.T. Strongman (Ed.), *International Review of Studies on Emotion*, Vol.1 (pp. 37–58). New York: John Wiley.

Pollock, V. E., Briere, J., Schneider, L., Knop, J., Mednick, S., & Goodwin, D. W. (1990). Childhood antecedents of antisocial behavior: Parental alcoholism and physical abusiveness. *American Journal of Psychiatry, 147,* 1290–1293.

Ponds, R., Brouwer, W., & Van Wolffelaar, P. (1988). Age differences in divided attention in a simulated driving task. *Journal of Gerontology, 43,* 151–156.

Poon, L., Clayton, P. M., Martin, P., johnson, M. A., Courtenay, B., Sweaney, A., Merriam, S., Pless, B. S., & Thielman, S. (1992). The Georgia Centenarian study. *International Journal of Aging and Human Development, 34,* 1–17.

Poortinga, Y. H. (1975). Limitations on intercultural comparison of psychological data. *Nederlands Tijdschrift van de Psychologie, 30,* 23–39.

Pope, H., Ionescu–Pioggia, M., Aizley, H., &

Varma, D. (1990). Drug use and life style among college undergraduates in 1989: A comparison with 1969 and 1978. *American Journal of Psychiatry, 147,* 998–1001.

Pope, H., McElroy, S., Keck, P., & Hudson, J. (1991). Valproate in the treatment of acute mania. *Archives of General Psychiatry, 48,* 62–68.

Pope, K., Tabachnick, B., & Keith–Spiegel, P. (1987). Ethics of practice: The beliefs and behaviors of psychologists as therapists. *American Psychologist, 42,* 993–1006.

Popper, K. (1963). *Conjectures and refutations: The growth of scientific knowledge*. New York: Basic Books.

Porcerelli, J., Hill, K., & Dauphin, V. B. (1995). Need–gratifying object relations and psychopathology. *Bulletin of the Menninger Clinic, 59,* 99–106.

Posner, R. M., Boies, S., Eichelman, W. H., & Taylor, R. L. (1969). Retention of visual and name codes of single letters. *Journal of Experimental Psychology, 79.*

Pospisil, L. (1963). *Kapauka Papuan political economy*. New Haven, Conn.: Yale University Publications in Anthropology, No. 67.

Post, R. M. (1992). Transduction of psychosocial stress into the neurobiology of recurrent affective disorder. *American Journal of Psychiatry, 149,* 999–1010.

Powers, D. E. (1993). Coaching for the SAT: A summary of the summaries and an update. *Educational Measurement Issues and Practice, 12,* 24–30.

Powers, W. T. (1973). *Behavior: The control of perception*. Chicago: Aldine.

Prakash, P. (1984). Second language acquisition and critical period hypothesis. *Psycho–Lingua, 14,* 13–17.

Pratto, F., & John, O. (1991). Automatic vigilance: The attention–grabbing power of negative social information. *Journal of Personality and Social Psychology, 61,* 380–391.

Premack, A., & Premack, D. (1983). *The mind of an ape*. New York: Norton.

Premack, A. J., & Premack, D. (1972). Teaching language to an ape. *Scientific American, 227,* 92–99.

Premack, D. (1962). Reversibility of the reinforcement relation. *Science, 136,* 235–237.

Premack, D. (1965). Reinforcement theory. In D. Levine (Ed.), *Nebraska Symposium on Motivation*. Lincoln: University of Nebraska Press.

Premack , D., & Woodruff, G. (1978). Chimpanzee problem–solving: A test for comprehension. *Science, 202,* 532–535.

Prentky, R. A. (1980). *Creativity and psychopathology*. New York: Praeger.

Preti, G., Cutler, W. B., Garcia, G. R., Huggins, M., & Lawley, J. J. (1986). Human axillary secretions influence women's menstrual cycles: The role of donor extract from females. *Hormones and Behavior, 20,* 474–482.

Previc, F. (1991). A general theory concerning the prenatal origins of cerebral lateralization in humans. *Psychological Review, 98,* 299–334.

Pribram, K. H. (1980). The biology of emotions and other feelings. In R. Plutchik and H. Kellerman (Eds.), *Emotion: theory, research, and experience,* Vol. I: Theories of emotion. New York: Academic Press.

Pribram, K. H. & Gill, M. M. (1976). *Freud's Project reassessed.* New York: Basic Books.

Price, D. L., Cork, L. C., Struble, R. G., Whitehouse, P. J., Kitt, C. A., & Walker, L. C. (1985). The functional organization of the basal forebrain cholinergic system in primates and the role of this system in Alzheimer's disease. In D.S. Olton, E. Gamzu, & S. Corkin (Eds.), *Memory dysfunctions: An integration of animal and human research from preclinical and clinical perspectives.* New York: New York Academy of Sciences.

Price, K. O., Harburg, E., & Newcomb, T. M. (1966). Psychological balance in situations of negative interpersonal attitudes. *Journal of Personality and Social Psychology, 3,* 265–270.

Price, L. H., Charney, D. S., Delgado, P., & Heninger, G. (1991). Serotonin function and depression: Neuroendocrine and mood responses to intravenous L-tryptophan in depressed patients and healthy comparison subjections. *American Journal of Psychiatry, 148,* 1518–1525.

Price-Williams, D. (1974). Kinship concepts and relational thinking among rural Hawaiian children. *Personality and Social Psychology Bulletin, 1,* 419–422.

Price-Williams, D. (1975). *Explorations in cross-cultural psychology.* San Francisco: Chandler & Sharp.

Price-Williams, D. (1981). Concrete and formal operations. In R.H. Munroe, R.L. Munroe, & B.D. Whiting (Eds.), *Handbook of cross-cultural human development.* New York: Garland Press.

Price-Williams, D., Gordon, W., & Ramirez, M. (1969). Skill and conservation: A study of pottery-making children.. *Developmental Psychology, 1,* 769.

Price-Williams, D. R. (1985). In G. Lindzey and E. Aronson (Eds.), *Handbook of social psychology.* Reading, MA: Addison-Wesley.

Prien, R. F. (1988). Somatic treatment of unipolar depressive disorder. In A. J. Frances and R. E. Hales (Eds.), *Review of Psychiatry,* Vol. 7. Washington, DC: American Psychiatric Press.

Prochaska, J. D. (1984). *The transtheoretical approach: Crossing traditional boundaries of therapy.* Homewood, Ill.: Dow Jones-Irwin.

Putnam, F. W. (1991). Dissociative disorders in children and adolescents: A developmental perspective. *Psychiatric Clinics of North America, 14,* 519–531.

Putnam, H. (1973). Reductionism and the nature of psychology. *Cognition, 2,* 131–146.

Pyle, R. L., Mitchell, J. E., Eckert, E. D.,

Halvorson, P. A., Neuman, P. A., & Goff, G. M. (1983). The incidence of bulimia in freshman college students. *International Journal of Eating Disorders, 2,* 75–85.

Quay, H. C., Routh, D. K., & Shapiro, S. K. (1987). Psychopathology of childhood: From description to validation. *Annual Review of Psychology, 38,* 491–532.

Quitkin, F., Harrison, W., Stewart, J., & McGrath, P. (1990). Response to phenelzine and imipramine in placebo nonresponders with atypical depression: A new application of the crossover design. *Archives of General Psychiatry, 48,* 319–323.

Raaijmakers, J. G., & Shiffrin, R. M. (1992). Models for recall and recognition. *Annual Review of Psychology, 43,* 205–234.

Rachman, S. J. (1978). *Fear and courage.* San Francisco: Freeman.

Raichle, M. (1983). Positron emission topography. *Annual Review of Neuroscience, 6,* 249–267.

Raichle, M. (1994). Images of the mind: Studies with modern imaging techniques. *Annual Review of Psychology, 45,* 333–356.

Rain, A., & Venables, P. H. (1984). Electrodermal nonresponding, antisocial behavior, and schizoid tendencies in adolescents. *Psychophysiology, 21,* 424–433.

Rallison, M. (1986). *Growth disorders in infants, children, and adolescents.* New York: John Wiley.

Ralston, D., Gustafson, D., Elsass, P. & Cheung, F. (1992). Eastern values: A comparison of managers in the United States, Hong Kong, and the People's Republic of China. *Journal of Applied Psychology, 77,* 664–671.

Ramachandran, V..S. (1988). Perceiving shape from shading. *Scientific American, 259,* 76–83.

Rand, C. S., & Kuldau, J. M. (1990). The epidemiology of obesity and self-defined weight prolem in the general population: Gender, race, age, and social class. *International Journal of Eating Disorders, 9,* 329–343.

Randhawa, B. (1991). Gender differences in academic achievement: A closer look at mathematics. *Alberta Journal of Educational Research, 37,* 241–257.

Rao, S. M., Huber, S. J., & Bornstein, R. A. (1992). Emotional changes with multiple sclerosis and Parkinson's disease. *Journal of Consulting and Clinical Psychology, 60,* 369–378.

Rapaport, D., Gill, M., & Schafer, R. (1945). *Manual of diagnostic testing. II. Diagnostic testing of personality and ideational content.* Chicago: Year Book Publishers.

Rapee, R. (1987). The psychological treatment of panic attacks: Theoretical conceptualization and review of evidence. *Clinical Psychology Review, 7,* 427–438.

Rapee, R. (1991). Generalized anxiety disor-

der: A review of clinical features and theoretical concepts. *Clinical Psychology Review, 11,* 419–440.

Rapee, R. M., Brown, T. A., Antony, M., & Barlow, D. (1992). Response to hyperventilation and inhalation of 5.5% carbon dioxide-enriched air across the DSM-III-R anxiety disorders. *Journal of Abnormal Psychology, 101,* 538–552.

Rapoport, J. L., Ryland, D., & Kriete, M. (1992). Drug treatment of canine acral lick. *Archives of General Psychiatry, 49,* 517–521.

Rasey, H. W., & Iversen, I. H. (1993). An experimental acquisition of maladaptive behavior by shaping. *Behavior Therapy and Experimental Psychiatry, 24,* 37–43.

Raskin, R., & Novacek, J. (1991). Narcissism and the use of fantasy. *Journal of Clinical Psychology, 47,* 490–499.

Ray, D. W., Wandersman, A., Ellison, J., & Huntington, D. E. (1982). The effects of high density in a juvenile correctional institution. *Basic and Applied Social Psychology, 2,* 95–108.

Ray, O. S., Ksir, C. (1993). *Drugs, society & human behavior.* (6th. ed.) St. Louis: Mosby-Year Book.

Read, P. B. (1982). Foreword. In D.H. Feldman (Ed.), *New directions for child development:* No. 17 (1–4), *Developmental approaches to giftedness and creativity.* San Francisco: Jossey-Bass.

Read, S. J., & Marcus-Newhall, A. (1993). Explanatory coherence in social explanations: A parallel distributed processing account. *Journal of Personality and Social Psychology, 65,* 429–447.

Reber, A. S. (1992). The cognitive unconscious: An evolutionary perspective. *Consciousness and Cognition, 1,* 93–133.

Recanzone, G. H., Schreiner, C. E., & Merzenich, M. M. (1993). Plasticity in the frequency representation in the primary auditory cortex following discontinuous training in adult owl monkeys. *Journal of Neuroscience.*

Reder, L., & Ritter, F. E. (1992). What determines initial feeling of knowing? Familiarity with question terms, not the answer. *Journal of Experimental Psychology: Learning, Memory, & Cognition, 18,* 435–451.

Reed, G. M. (1989). Stress, coping , and psychological adaptation in a sample of gay and bisexual men with AIDS. Unpublished doctoral dissertation, University of California, Los Angeles.

Reeve, R. A., & Brown, A. L. (1985). Metacognition reconsidered: Implications for intervention research. *Journal of Abnormal Child Psychology, 13,* 343–56.

Regan, D., & Fazio, R. (1977). On the consistency between attitudes and behavior: Look to the method of attitude formation. *Journal of Experimental Social Psychology, 13,* 28–45.

Regan, J. W. (1971). Guilt, perceived injustice, and altruistic behavior. *Journal of*

Personality and Social Psychology, 18, 124–32.

Reich, A. (1960). Pathologic forms of self–esteem regulation. *Psychoanalytic Study of the Child, 15,* 215–232.

Reich, J. (1986). The epidemiology of anxiety. *Journal of Nervous and Mental Disease 174,* 129–136.

Reid, W. H. (1985). The antisocial personality: A review. *Hospital and Community Psychiatry, 36,* 831–837.

Reifman, A., Larrick, R., & Fein, S. (1991). Temper and temperature on the diamond: The heat–aggression relationship in major league baseball. *Personality & Social Psychology Bulletin, 17,* 580–585.

Reiman, P. & Chi, M.T.H. (1989). Human expertise. In K. J. Gilhooly (Ed.), *Human and machine problem solving.* New York: Plenum Press.

Reinisch, J. M. (1981). Prenatal exposure to synthetic progestins increases potential for aggression in humans, *Science, 211,* 1171–1173.

Reis, H. J., & Shaver, P. (1988). Intimacy as an interpersonal process. In S. Duck (Ed.), *Handbook of personal relationships: Theory, relationships and interventions.* New York: John Wiley.

Reisenzein, R. (1983). The Schachter theory of emotion: Two decades later. *Psychological Bulletin, 94,* 239–264.

Reisman, D. (1980). Egocentrism: Is the American character changing? *Encounter, 55,* 19–28.

Reisman, J. M. (1966). *The development of clinical psychology.* Englewood Cliffs, NJ: Prentice–Hall.

Rescorla, R. A. (1988). Pavlovian conditioning: It's not what you think it is. *American Psychologist, 43,* 151–160.

Rescorla, R. A., & Holland, P. C. (1982). Behavioral studies of associative learning in animals. *Annual Review of Psychology, 33,* 265–308.

Rescorla, R. A., & Wagner, A. R. (1972). A theory of Pavlovian conditioning: Variations in the effectiveness of reinforcement and non–reinforcement. In A. H. Black & W. F. Prokasy (Eds.), *Classical conditioning: II. Current research and theory.* New York: Appleton.

Rest, J. R. (1983). Morality. In J.H. Flavell & E. M. Markman (Eds.), *Handbook of child psychology: Vol. 3. Cognitive development.* New York: John Wiley.

Reynolds, C. F. III, Kupfer, D. J., Buysee, D. J., et al. (1991). Subtyping DSM–III–R primary insomnia: A literature review by the DSM–IV work group on sleep disorders. *American Journal of Psychiatry, 148,* 432–438.

Rhodes, N., & Wood, W. (1992). Self–esteem and intelligence affect influenceability: The mediating role of message reception. *Psychological Bulletin, 111,* 156–171.

Ricco, R. B. (1989). Operational thought and the acquisition of taxonomic relations involving figurative dissimilarity.

Developmental Psychology, 25, 996–1003.

Richards, B. J. (1990). Language development and individual differences: A study of auxiliary verb learning. Cambridge: Cambridge University Press.

Richards, J. B., Sabol, K. E., & Freed, C. R. (1990). Conditioned rotation: A behavioral analysis. *Physiology and Behavior, 47,* 1083–1087.

Richards, R. & Kinney, D. K. (1990). Mood swings and creativity. *Creativity Research Journal, 3,* 202–217.

Richards, R., Kinney, D. K., Daniels, H., & Linkins, K. (1992). Everyday creativity and bipolar and unipolar affective disorder: Preliminary study of personal and family history. *European Psychiatry, 7,* 49–52.

Richards, R., Kinney, D., Lunde, I., Benet, M., & Merzel, A. (1988). Creativity in manic–depressives, cyclothymes, and their normal relatives, and control subjects. *Journal of Abnormal Psychology, 97,* 281–288.

Richardson, J.T.E., & Zucco, G. M. (1989). Cognition and olfaction: A review. *Psychological Bulletin, 105,* 352–360.

Richman, A. L., Miller, P. M., & LeVine, R. (1992). Cultural and educational variations in maternal responsiveness. *Developmental Psychology, 28,* 614–621.

Rickels, K., Downing, R., Schweizer, E., & Hassman, H. (1993). Antidepressants for the treatment of generalized anxiety disorders: A placebo–controlled comparison of imiprimine, trazodone, and diazepam. Archives *of General Psychiatry, 50,* 884–895.

Ricks, M. H. (1985). The social transmission of parental behavior: Attachment across generations. In I. Bretherton & E. Waters (Eds.), Growing points of attachment theory and research. *Monographs of the Society for Research in Child Development, 50,* (1–2, Serial No. 209), 211–227.

Ridley, R., & Baker, H. F. (1991). Can fetal neural transplants restore function in monkeys with lesion–induced behavioural deficits? *Trends in Neurosciences, 14,* 366–370.

Riesen, A. H. (1960). The effects of stimulus deprivation on the development and atrophy of the visual sensory system. *American Journal of Orthopsychiatry, 30,* 23–36.

Riesen, A. H. (1965). Effects of early deprivation of photic stimulation. In S. Osler & R. Cooke (Eds.), *The biosocial bases of mental retardation.* Baltimore, MD: John Hopkins University Press.

Riley, A. J. (1991). Sexuality and the menopause. *Sexual and Marital Therapy, 6,* 135–145.

Rimmerman, A., Finn, H., Schnee, J., & Klein, I. (1992). The rehabilitation of persons with severe mental illness in adult homes: The NYPCC study. *Psychosocial Rehabiliation Journal, 15,* 55–66.

Rinn, W. E. (1984). The neuropsychology of facial expression: A review of the neurological and psychological mechanisms for producing facial expressions. *Psychological Bulletin, 95,* 52–77.

Riordan, C. (1978). Equal–status interracial contact: A review and revision of the concept. *International Journal of Intercultural Relations, 2,* 161–185.

Riordan, R. J. & Beggs, M. S. (1988). Some critical differences between self–help and therapy groups. *Journal for Specialists in Group Work, 13,* 24–29.

Rips, L. (1990). Reasoning. *Annual Review of Psychology, 41,* 321–353.

Robben, H. S., Webley, P., Weigel, R., & Warneryd, K–E. (1990). Decision frame and opportunity as determinants of tax cheating: An international experimental study. *Journal of Economic Psychology, 11,* 341–364.

Robertson, J., & Robertson, J. (1971). Young children in brief separation: A fresh look. *Psychoanalytic study of the child, 26,* 264–315.

Robin, A. A. (1958). A controlled study of the effects of leucotomy. *Journal of Neurology, Neurosurgery and Psychiatry, 21,* 262–269.

Robins, L. H., & Kulbok, P. A. (1988). Epidemiologic studies in suicide. In A. J. Frances and R.E. Hales (Eds.), *Review of psychiatry,* Vol. 7. Washington, DC: American Psychiatric Press.

Robinson, B. W., et al. (1969). Dominance reversal resulting from aggressive responses evoked by brain telestimulation. *Physiology and Behavior, 4,* 749–752.

Robinson, F. P. (1961). *Effective study.* New York: Harper & Row.

Robinson, N. M. (1978). Mild mental retardation: Does it exist in the People's Republic of China? *Mental Retardation, 16,* 295–299.

Roche, S. M., & McConkey, K. M. (1990). Absorption: Nature, assessment, and correlates. *Journal of Personality and Social Psychology, 59,* 91–101.

Rock, I. (1984). *The logic of perception.* Cambridge, MA: MIT Press.

Rock, I., & Harris, C. S. (1967). Vision and touch. *Scientific American, 216,* 96–104.

Rodeheaver, D., & Datan, N. (1988). The challenge of double jeopardy: Toward a mental health agenda for aging women. *American Psychologist, 43,* 648–654.

Rodin, J. & Salovey, P. (1989). Health psychology. *Annual Review of Psychology, 40,* 533–579.

Rodin, J., Schank, D., & Striegel–Moore, R. (1989). Psychological features of obesity. *Medical Clinics of North America, 73,* 47–66.

Roediger, H. L. (1990). Implicit memory: Retention without remembering. *American Psychologist, 45*(9), 1043–1056.

Rogers, C. (1959). A theory of therapy, personality, and interpersonal relationships, as developed in the client–centered framework. S. Koch (Ed.), *Psychology: A study of a science,* Vol. 3. New York: McGraw–Hill.

Rogers, C. R. (1951). *Client–centered therapy: Its current practice, implications, and theory.* Boston: Houghton Mifflin.

Rogers, C. R. (1961). *On becoming a person: A therapist's view of psychotherapy.* Boston: Houghton Mifflin.

Rogers, C. R. (1980). *A way of being.* Boston: Houghton Mifflin.

Rogers, C. R. & Sanford, M. A. (1985). Client–centered psychotherapy. In H. I. Kaplan, H., & B. J. Sadock (Eds.), *Comprehensive textbook of psychiatry.* (4th ed.). Baltimore, MD: Williams & Wilkins.

Rogler, L. H., Cortes, D. E., & Malgady, R. G. (1991). Acculturation and mental health status among hispanics: Convergence and new directions for research. *American Psychologist, 46,* 585–592.

Rogoff, B., & Lave, J. (Eds.) (1984). *Everyday cognition: Its development in social context.* Cambridge, MA: Harvard University Press.

Rohner, R. (1975). Parental acceptance–rejection and personality development: A universalist approach to behavioral science. In R. W. Brislin et al. (Eds.), *Cross–cultural perspectives on learning* (pp. 251–269). New York: Sage.

Rohner, R. (1975). *They love me, they love me not.* New Haven, Conn.: HRAF Press.

Rohner, R. P. (1986). *The warmth dimension: Foundations of parental acceptance–rejection theory.* Beverly Hills, CA: Sage Publications, Inc.

Rollin, B. E. (1985). The moral status of research animals in psychology. *American Psychologist, 40,* 920–926.

Romney, K., & Romney, R. (1963). The Mixtecans of Juxtlahuaca, Mexico. In B. Whiting (Ed.), *Six cultures: Studies in child rearing* (pp. 541–691). New York: John Wiley.

Ron, M. (1989). Psychiatric manifestations of frontal lobe tumours. *British Journal of Psychiatry, 155,* 735–738.

Rosch, E. (1973). On the internal structure of perceptual and semantic categories. In T. E. Moore (Ed.), *Cognitive development and the acquisition of language.* New York: Academic Press.

Rosch, E. (1978). Principles of categorization. In E. Rosch & B. Lloyd (Eds.), *Cognition and categorization.* New York: John Wiley.

Roscoe, A. K., & Myers, R. D. (1991). Hypothermia and feeding induced simultaneously in rats by perfusion of neuropeptide Y in preoptic area. *Pharmacology, Biochemistry & Behavior, 39,* 1003–1009.

Roseman, I., Spindel, M., & Jose, P. (1990). Appraisals of emotion–eliciting events: Testing a theory of discrete emotions.

Journal of Personality and Social Psychology, 59, 899–915.

Rosen, A. B., & Rozin, P. (1993). Now you see it, now you don't: The preschool child's conception of invisible particles in the context of dissolving. *Developmental Psychology, 29,* 300–311.

Rosen, J., Reynolds, C. F. III, Yeager, A. L., Houck, P. R., & Hurwitz, L. F. (1991). Sleep disturbances in survivors of the nazi holocaust. *American Journal of Psychiatry, 148,* 62–66.

Rosen, J. C., & Gross, J. (1987). The prevalence of weight reducing and weight gaining in adolescent girls and boys. *Health Psychology, 6,* 131–147.

Rosen, K. S., & Rothbaum, F. (1993). Quality of parental caregiving and security of attachment. *Developmental Psychology, 29,* 358–367.

Rosenberg, M. (1979). *Conceiving the self.* New York: Basic Books.

Rosenblatt, A., Greenberg, J., Solomon, S., Pyszczynski, T., & Lyon, D. (1989). Evidence for terror management theory: I. The effects of mortality salience on reactions to those who violate or uphold cultural values. *Journal of Personality and Social Psychology, 57,* 681–690.

Rosenblatt, P. C. (1966). A cross–cultural study of child rearing and romantic love. *Journal of Personality and Social Psychology, 4,* 336–338.

Rosenhan, D. L. (1973). On being sane in insane places. *Science, 179,* 252–258.

Rosenhan, D. L. et al. (1981). Emotion and altruism. In J. P. Rushton and R.M. Sorrentino (Eds.), *Altruism and helping behaviors.* Hillsdale, NJ: Erlbaum.

Rosenman, R. H. (1990). Type A behavior patterns: A personal overview. *Journal of Social Behavior and Personality, 5,* 1–24.

Rosenthal, R. (1966). *Experimenter effects in behavioral research.* New York: Appleton–Century–Crofts.

Rosenthal, R. (1991). Teacher expectancy effects: A brief update 25 years after the Pygmalion experiment. *Journal of Research in Education, 1,* 3–12.

Rosenthal, R., & Jacobson, L. (1968). *Pygmalion in the classroom: Teacher expectation and pupils' intellectual development.* New York: Holt, Rinehart & Winston.

Rosenwald, G. (1988). The multiple case study method. *Journal of Personality, 56,* 239–264.

Rosenzweig, M. R. (1984). Experience, memory, and the brain. *American Psychologist, 39,* 365–376.

Rosenweig, M. R., Bennett, E. L., & Diamond, M. C. (1972). Brain changes in response to experience. *Scientific American, 226,* 22–29.

Rosenzweig, M. R., & Leiman, A. L. (1989). *Physiological psychology.* (2nd ed.). New York.: McGraw–Hill.

Rosette, H. (1980). The effects of alcohol on the fetus and offspring. In O. Kalant (Ed.), *Research advances in alcohol and*

drug problems: Vol. 5. Alcohol and drug problems in women. New York: Plenum Press.

Ross, C. A., Anderson, G., Fleisher, W., & Norton, G. R. (1991). The frequency of multiple personality disorder among psychiatric inpatients. *American Journal of Psychiatry, 148,* 1717–1720.

Ross, C. A., Miller, S. D., Reagor, P., Bjornson, L., Fraser, G., & Anderson, G. (1990). Structured interview data on 102 cases of multiple personality disorder from four centers. *American Journal of Psychiatry, 147,* 596–601.

Ross, L. (1977). The intuitive psychologist and his shortcomings: Distortions in the attribution process. *Advances in Experimental Social Psychology, 10,* 173–220.

Ross, L., Greene, D., & House, P. (1977). The false consensus phenomenon: An attributional bias in self–perception and social perception processes in the debriefing paradigm. *Journal of Experimental Social Psychology, 13,* 279–301.

Ross, M., & Fletcher, G.J.O. (1985). Attribution and social perception. In G. Lindzey and E. Aronson (Eds.), *Handbook of social psychology.* Reading, MA: Addison–Wesley.

Ross, M., & Sicoly, F. (1979). Egocentric biases in availability and attribution. *Journal of Personality and Social Psychology, 37,* 322–336.

Ross, R. J., Ball, W. A., Sullivan, K. A., et al. (1989). Sleep disturbance as the hallmark of posttraumatic stress disorder. *American Journal of Psychiatry, 146,* 697–707.

Ross, S. M., & Ross, L. E. (1971). Comparison of trace and delay classical eyelid conditioning as a function of interstimulus interval. *Journal of Experimental Psychology, 91,* 165–167.

Rossi, P. J. (1968). Adaptation and negative after effect to lateral optical displacement in newly hatched chicks. *Science, 160,* 430–432.

Roth, M. (1978). Epidemiological studies. In R. Katzman, R. D. Terry, & K. L. Bick (Eds.), *Alzheimer's disease: Senile dementia and related disorders.* New York: Raven.

Rothblum, E. (1992). The stigma of women's weight: Social and economic realities. *Feminism and Psychology, 2,* 61–73.

Rotter, J. (1971). External control and internal control. *Psychology Today,* June, 40–45.

Rotter, J. B. (1954). *Social learning and clinical psychology.* New York: Englewood Cliffs, NJ: Prentice–Hall.

Rotter, J. B. (1966). Generalized expectancies for internal versus external control of reinforcement. *Psychological Monographs* (Whole No.609).

Rotter, J. B. (1990). Internal versus external control of reinforcement: A case history of a variable. *American Psychologist, 45,* 489–493.

Rotton, J. et al. (1979). The air pollution experience and physical aggression. *Journal of Applied Social Psychology, 9,* 397–442.

Rowland, N. E. (1991). Biological factors in eating and its disorders. *Bulletin of the Psychonomic Society, 29,* 244–249.

Roy, A. (1993). Genetic and biologic risk factors for suicide in depressive disorders. *Psychiatric Quarterly, 64,* 345–358.

Roy, A., Karoum, F., & Pollack, S. (1992). Marked reduction in indexes of dopamine metabolism among patients with depression who attempt suicide. *Archives of General Psychiatry, 49,* 447–450.

Rubenstein, C. (1982). Psychologiy's fruit flies. *Psychology Today, 16,* 83–84.

Rubin, D. C., & Kozin, M. (1990). Vivid memories. *Cognition, 16,* 81–85.

Rubin, Z. (1970). Measurement of romantic love. *Journal of Personality and Social Psychology, 16,* 265–273.

Rubin, Z. (1973). *Liking and loving: An invitation to social psychology.* New York: Holt, Rinehart & Winston.

Ruisel, I. (1992). Social intelligence: Conception and methodological problems. *Studia Psychologica, 34,* 281–296.

Rumbaugh, D. M. (1992). Learning about primates' learning, language, and cognition. In G. G. Brannigan & M. R. Merrens (Eds.), *The undaunted psychologist: Adventures in research.* New York: McGraw–Hill.

Rumbaugh, D. M., & Gill, T. V. (1977). Lana's acquisition of language skills. In D. M. Rumbaugh (Ed.), *Language learning by a chimpanzee: The Lana project* (pp. 165–192). New York: Academic Press.

Rumelhart, D. (1984). Schemata and the cognitive system. In R.S. Wyer & T.K. Srull (Eds.), *Handbook of social cognition,* Vol. 1. Hillsdale, NJ: Erlbaum.

Rumelhart, D. E., McClelland, J. L., & the PDP Research Group (1986). *Parallel distributed processing: Explorations in the microstructure of cognition.* Cambridge, MA: MIT Press.

Rundus, D. (1971). Analysis of rehearsal process in free recall. *Journal of Experimental Psychology, 89,* 63–77.

Runyan, W. M. (1984). *Life histories and psychobiography: Explanations in theory and method.* New York: Oxford University Press.

Rushton, J. P. (1986). Altruism and aggression: The heritability of individual differences. *Journal of Personality and Social Psychology, 50,* 1192–1198.

Rushton, J. P. (1989). Genetic similarity, human altruism, and group selection. *Behavioral and Brain Sciences, 12,* 503–559.

Rushton, W.A.H. (1961). Rhodopsin measurement and dark adaptation in a subject deficient in cone vision. *Journal of Physiology, 156,* 193–205.

Rushton, W.A.H. (1962). Visual pigments in man. *Scientific American,* 120–132.

Russek, M. (1971). Hepatic receptors and the neurophysiological mechanisms controlling feeding behavior. In S. Ehrenpreis (Ed.), *Neurosciences Research,* Vol. 4. New York: Academic Press.

Russell, D. (1991). Wife rape. In A. Parot & L. Bechhofer (Eds.), *Acquaintance rape: The hidden crime* (pp.129–139). New York: John Wiley.

Russell, J. A. (1991). Culture and the categorization of emotions. *Psychological Bulletin, 110,* 426–450.

Russell, J. A. (1991). In defense of a prototype approach to emotion concepts. *Journal of Personality and Social Psychology, 60,* 37–47.

Russell, J. A. (1994). Is there universal recognition of emotion from facial expression? A review of the cross–cultural studies. *Psychological Bulletin, 115,* 102–141.

Russell, J. D., & Roxanas, M. (1990). Psychiatry and the frontal lobes. *Australian & New Zealand Journal of Psychiatry, 24,* 113–132.

Russell, M. J. (1976). Human olfactory communication. *Nature, 260,* 520–522.

Ruston, J. P. (1975). Generosity in children: Immediate and long–term effects of modeling, preaching, and moral judgment. *Journal of Personality and Social Psychology, 31,* 459–466.

Rutter, M., Quinton, D., & Liddle, C. (1983). Parenting in two generations: Looking backwards and looking forwards. In N. Madge (Ed.), *Families at risk* (pp. 60–98). London: Heineman.

Ryan, E. B. (1992). Beliefs about memory changes across the adult life span. *Journal of Gerontology, 47,* 41–46.

Ryder, R., & Bartle, S. (1991). Boundaries as distance regulators in personal relationships. *Family Process, 30,* 393–406.

Rymer, R. (1992). Annals of science: A silent childhood. I. *New Yorker,* April 13, 41–81.

Rymer, R. (1992). Annals of science: A silent childhood. II. *New Yorker,* April 20, 43–77.

Rymer, R. (1993). *Genie: An abused child's flight from silence.* New York: HarperCollins.

Sachs, B., Zindrick, M., & Beasley, R. (1993). Reflex sympathetic dystrophy after operative procedures on the lumbar spine. *Journal of Bone and Joint Surgery,* 75–A, 721–725.

Sacks, O. (1973). *Awakenings.* London: Duckworth.

Sacks, O. (1993). A neurologist's notebook: To see and not see. *New Yorker,* May 10, 59–73.

Sadock, B. J. (1985). Group psychotherapy, combined individual and group psychotherapy, and psychodrama. In H. I. Kaplan & B. J. Sadock (Eds.), *Comprehensive textbook of psychiatry.* (4th ed.). Baltimore, MD: Williams & Wilkins.

Saegert, S., & Winkel, G. H. (1990). Environmental psychology. *Annual Review of Psychology, 41,* 441–477.

Sagi, A. (1990). Attachment theory and research from a cross–cultural perspective. *Human Development, 33,* 10–22.

Sagi, A., van IJzendoorn, M. H., Aviezer, O., Donnell, F., & Mayseless, O. (1994). Sleeping out of the home in a kibbutz communal arrangement: It makes a difference for infant–mother attachment. *Child Development, 65,* 971–991.

Sahney, V., & Warden, G. (1991). The quest for quality and productivity in health services. *Frontiers in Health Services Management, 7.*

Salkovskis, P. M., Jones, D. R., & Clark, D. M. (1986). Respiratory control in the treatment of panic attacks: Replication and extension with concurrent measurement of behavior and PCPs. *British Journal of Psychiatry, 148,* 526–532.

Salthouse, T. (1985). Speed of behavior and its implications for cognition. In J. E. Birren & K. W. Schaie (Eds.), *Handbook of the psychology of aging* (2nd ed.). New York: Van Nostrand Reinhold.

Salthouse, T. (1992). The information-processing perspective on cognitive aging. In R. Sternberg & C. Berg (Eds.), *Intellectual development.* Cambridge: Cambridge University Press.

Salthouse, T. A. (1994). The nature of the influence of speed on adult age differences in cognition. *Developmental Psychology, 30,* 240–254.

Salzman, J. P., Salzman, C. Wolfson, A. N. & Banese, M. (1993). Association between borderline personality structure and history of childhood sexual abuse in adult volunteers. *Comprehensive Psychiatry, 34,* 254–257.

Sameroff, A., Seifer, R., Baldwin, A., & Baldwin, C. (1993). Stability of intelligence from preschool to adolescence: The influence of social and family risk factors. *Child Development, 64,* 80–97.

Sande, G. N., Goethals, G. R., & Radloff, C. E. (1988). Perceiving one's own traits and others': The multifaceted self. *Journal of Personality and Social Psychology, 54,* 13–20.

Sandler, J. & Rosenblatt, B. (1962). The concept of the representational world. *Psychoanalytic Study of the Child, 17,* 128–145.

Sano, K. (1962). Sedative neurosurgery: With special reference to postero–medical hypothalamotomy. *Neurologia Medico–Chirurgica, 4,* 112–142.

Sano, M. (1991). Basal ganglia diseases and depression. *Neuropsychiatry, Neuropsychology, & Behavioral Neurology, 4,* 41–48.

Sapir, E. (1947). *Culture, language, and personality.* Berkeley: University of California Press.

Saraswathi, T., & Dutta, R. (1988). Current trends in developmental psychology: A life span perspective. In J. Pandey (Ed.),

Psychology in India: The state-of-the-art, Vol. 1, *Personality and mental processes* (pp. 93–152). London: Sage.

Sarnat, H. B., & Netsky, M. G. (1974). *Evolution of the nervous system.* New York: Oxford University Press.

Sarter, M., & Markowitsch, H. J. (1985). Involvement of the amygdala in learning and memory: A critical review, with emphasis on anatomical relation. *Behavioral Neuroscience, 99,* 342–380.

Sartre, J. P. (1971). Being and nothingness: An essay in phenomenological ontology, H.E. Barnes (Trans.). New York: Citadel Press.

Satel, S. L., Southwick, S. M., & Gawin, F. H. (1991). Clinical features of cocaine-induced paranoia. *American Journal of Psychiatry, 148,* 495–498.

Saunders, J. B. (1989). The efficacy of treatment for drinking problems. *International Review of Psychiatry, 1,* 121–137.

Savage-Rumbaugh, E. S. (1990). Language acquisition in a nonhuman species: Implications for the innateness debate. *Developmental Psychobiology, 23,* 599–620.

Savage-Rumbaugh, E. S., Pate, J. L., Lawson, J., Smith, S. T., & Rosenbaum, S. (1983). Can a chimpanzee make a statement? *Journal of Experimental Psychology: General, 112,* 457–492.

Savage-Rumbaugh, E. S., Rumbaugh, D. M., & Boysen, S. (1978). Symbolic communiction between two chimpanzees. *Science, 201,* 641–644.

Savage-Rumbaugh, S., McDonald, K., Sevcik, R., Hopkins, W., & Rupert, E. (1986). Spontaneous symbol acquisition and communicative use by pygmy chimpanzees (pan paniscus). *Journal of Experimental Psychology: General, 115,* 211–235.

Savin-Williams, R. C., & Small, S. A. (1986). The timing of puberty and its relationship to adolescent and parent perceptions of family interactions. *Developmental Psychology, 22,* 342– 47.

Sayette, M., & Mayne, T. (1990). Survey of current clinical and research trends in clinical psychology. *American Psychologist, 45,* 1263–1266.

Scarr, S., & Carter-Saltzman, L. (1982). Genetics and intelligence. In R.J. Sternberg (Ed.), *Handbook of human intelligence* (pp. 792–896). New York: Cambridge University Press.

Scarr, S., & Eisenberg, M. (1993). Child care research: Issues, perspectives, and results. *Annual Review of Psychology, 44,* 613–644.

Scarr, S., Pakstis, A. J., Katz, S. H., & Barker, W. B. (1977). The absence of a relationship between degree of white ancestry and intellectual skills within a black population. *Human Genetics, 39,* 69–86.

Scarr, S., & Weinberg, R. A. (1976). IQ test performance of black children adopted by white families. *American Psychologist, 31,* 726–739.

Scarr, S., & Weinberg, R. A. (1983). The Minnesota adoption studies: genetic differences and malleability. *Child Development, 54,* 260–267.

Scarr, S., & Yee, D. (1980). Heritability and educational policy: Genetic and environmental effects on I.Q., aptitude, and achievement. *Educational Psychologist, 15,* 1–22

Scerbo, A., Raire, A., O'Brien, M., & Chan, C. J. (1990). Reward dominated and passive avoidance learning in adolescent psychopaths. *Journal of Abnormal Child Psychology, 18,* 451–463.

Schab, F. R. (1991). Odor memory: Taking stock. *Psychological Bulletin, 109,* 242–251.

Schachter, F. F., Shore, E., Hodapp, R., Chalfin, S., & Bundy, C. (1978). Do girls talk earlier? Mean length of uterance in toddlers. *Developmental Psychology, 14,* 388–392.

Schachter, S. & Singer, J. (1962). Cognitive, social, and physiological determinants of emotional state. *Psychological Review, 69,* 379–399.

Schacter, D., Cooper, L.A., & Valdiserri, M. (1992). Implicit and explicit memory for novel visual objects in older and younger adults. *Psychology and Aging, 7,* 299–308.

Schacter, D. L. (1992). Understanding implicit memory: A cognitive neuroscience approach. *American Psychologist, 47,* 559–569.

Schaie, K. W. (1988). Ageism in psychological research. *American Psychologist, 43,* 179–183.

Schaie, K. W. (1990). Intellectual development in adulthood. In J.E. Birren & K.W. Schaie (Eds.), *Handbook of the psychology of aging.* (3rd ed.). New York: Van Nostrand Reinhold.

Schaie, K. W., & Willis, S. L. (1986). *Adult development and aging.* (2nd ed.). Boston: Little, Brown.

Schaller, M. (1992). In-group favoritism and statistical reasoning in social inference: Implications for formation and maintenance of group stereotypes. *Journal of Personality and Social Psychology, 63,* 61–74.

Scheff, T. J. (1970). Schizophrenia as ideology. *Schizophrenia Bulletin, 1,* 15–20.

Scheier, M., & Carver, C. (1993). On the power of positive thinking: The benefits of being optimistic. *Current Directions in Psychological Science, 2,* 26–30.

Scheier, M. F., Matthews, K. A., Owens, J., Magovern, G. J., Lefebvre, R.C., Abbott, R., & Carver, C. S. (1989). Dispositional optimism and recovery from coronary artery bypass surgery: The beneficial effects on physical and psychological well-being. *Journal of Personality and Social Psychology, 57,* 1024–1040.

Scheper-Hughes, N. (1979). *Saints, scholars, and schizophrenics: Mental illness in rural Ireland.* Berkeley: University of California Press.

Scher, S., & Cooper, J. (1989). Motivational basis of dissonance: The singular role of behavioral consequences. *Journal of Personality and Social Psychology, 56,* 899–906.

Scherer, K., & Wallbott, H. (1994). Evidence for universality and cultural variation of differential emotion response patterning. *Journal of Personality & Social Psychology, 66,* 310–328.

Scheuer, M., & Pedley, T. (1990). The evaluation and treatment of seizures. *New England Journal of Medicine, 323,* 1468–1474.

Schiavi, R., Schreiner-Engel, P., Mandeli, J., Schanzer, H., & Cohen, E. (1990). Healthy aging and male sexual function. *American Journal of Psychiatry, 147,* 766–771.

Schiavi, R. C., Schreiner-Engel, P., White, D., & Mandeli, J. (1991). The relationship between pituitary-gonadal function and sexual behavior in healthy aging men. *Psychosomatic Medicine, 53,* 363–374.

Schiele, J. H. (1991). An epistemological perspective on intelligence assessment among African American children. *Journal of Black Psychology, 17,* 23–36.

Schiff, M., Duyme, M. Dumaret, A., & Tomkiewicz, S. (1982). How much could we boost scholastic achievement and IQ scores? A direct answer from a French adoption study. *Cognition, 12,* 165–96.

Schiffman, H. R. (1990). *Sensation and perception.* (3rd. ed.). New York: John Wiley.

Schiffman, H. R. (in press). *Sensation and perception.* (4th. ed.) New York: John Wiley.

Schiffman, S. S. (1974). Physio-chemical correlates of olfactory quality. *Science, 185,* 112–117.

Schiller, P. H. (1965). Monoptic and dicroptic visual masking by patterns and flashes. *Journal of Experimental Psychology, 69,* 193–199.

Schlesser, M. A., & Altshuler, K. Z. (1983). The genetics of affective disorder: Data, theory, and clinical applications. *Hospital and Community Psychiatry, 34,* 415–422.

Schmitt, R. C. (1957). Density, delinquency, and crime in Honolulu. *Sociology and Social Research, 41,* 274–276.

Schmitt, R. C. (1966). Density, health, and social disorganization. *American Institute of Planners Journal, 32,* 38–40.

Schnapf, J.,. Kraft, T., Nunn, B., & Baylor, D. (1989). Transduction in primate cones. *Neuroscience Research, Suppl 10,* 9–14.

Schneider, D. (1974). The sex-attractant receptor of moths. *Scientific American,* 28–35.

Schneider, W., & Pressley, M. (1989). *Memory development between 2 and 20.* New York: Springer-Verlag.

Schneider, W., & Shiffrin, R. M. (1977). Controlled and automatic human information processing: I. Detection, search, and attention. *Psychological Review, 84,* 1–54.

Schneier, F., Johnson, J., Hornig, C., Liebowitz, M. R., & Weissman, M. (1992). Social phobia: Comorbidity and morbidity in an epidemiological sample. *Archives of General Psychiatry, 49,* 282–288.

Schnell, L., Schneider, R., Kolbeck, R., Barde, Y., & Schwab, M. E. (1994). Neurotrophin–3 enhances sprouting of corticospinal tract during development and after adult spinal cord lesion. *Nature, 367,* 170–173.

Schradle, S. B. & Dougher, M. J. (1985). Social support as a mediator of stress: Theoretical and empirical issues. *Clinical Psychology Review, 5,* 641–661.

Schreiber, R., & de Vry, J. (1993). 5 ht sub (1A) receptor ligands in animal models of anxiety, impulsivity, and depression: Multiple mechanisms in action? *Progress in Neuro–Psychopharmocology and Biological Psychiatry, 17,* 41–54.

Schreiner, L., & Kling, A. (1953). Behavioral changes in following rhinencephalic injury in cats. *Journal of Neurophysiology, 16,* 643–658.

Schrieber, F. (1974). *Sybil.* New York: Warner Books.

Schroeder, S. R., Schroeder, C. S., & Landesman, S. (1987). Psychological services in educational settings to persons with mental retardation. *American Psychologist, 42,* 805–808.

Schuckit, M. (1984). Relationship between the course of primary alcoholism in men and family history. *Journal of Studies on Alcohol, 45,* 334–338.

Schuckit, M. (1987). Biological vulnerability to alcoholism. *Journal of Consulting and Clinical Psychology, 55,* 301–309.

Schuckit, M. A. (1994). Low level of response to alcohol as a predictor of future alcoholism. *American Journal of Psychiatry, 151,* 184–189.

Schultz, T., & Schliefer, M. (1983). Towards a refinement of attribution concepts. In J. Jaspars, F. Fincham, & M. Hewstone (Eds.), *Attribution theory and research: Conceptual, developmental, and social dimensions* (pp 37–62). New York: Academic Press.

Schuster, D. T. (1990). Fulfillment of potential, life satisfaction, and competence: Comparing four cohorts of gifted women at midlife. *Journal of Educational Psychology, 82,* 471–478.

Schwartz, G. E. (1987). Personality and health: An integrative health science approach. In V.P. Makosky (Ed.), *The G. Stanley Hall Lecture Series,* Vol. 7. Washington, DC: American Psychological Association.

Schwartz, S. H. (1977). Normative influences on altruism. In L. Berkowitz (Ed.), *Advances in experimental social psychology,* Vol. 10. New York: Academic Press.

Schwartzwald, J., Bizman, A., & Raz, M. (1983). The foot–in–the–door paradigm: Effects of second request size on donation probability and donor generosity. *Personality and Social Psychology Bulletin, 9,* 443–450.

Scialfa, C., Garvey, P. M., Tyrell, R., & Leibowitz, H. (1992). Age differences in dynamic contrast thresholds. *Journal of Gerontology, 47,* 172–175.

Scogin, F., & McElreath, L. (1994). Efficacy of psychosocial treatments for geriatric depression: A quantitative review. *Journal of Consulting and Clinical Psychology, 62,* 69–74.

Scott, E. M. (1980). Narcissism and alcoholism: Theoretical opinions and some clinical examples. *Psychotherapy Theory, Research, and Practice, 17,* 110–113.

Scott, J. P. and Fuller, J. J. (1965). *Genetics and social behavior of the dog.* Chicago: University of Chicago Press.

Scoville, W. B., & Milner, B. (1957). Loss of recent memory after bilateral hippocampal lesions. *Journal of Neurology, Neurosurgery, and Psychiatry, 20,* 11–21.

Scribner, S. (1986). Thinking in action: some characteristics of practical thought. In R. J. Sternberg & R. K. Wagner (Eds.), *Practical intelligence: Nature and origins of competence in the everyday world* (pp.13–40). New York: Cambridge University Press.

Scully, D., & Bart, P. (1973). A funny thing happened on the way to the orifice: Women in gynecology textbooks. In J. Huber (Ed.), *Changing women in a changing society.* Chicago: University of Chicago Press.

Seagall, M., Campbell, D., & Herskovits, M. (1966). *The influence of culture on visual perception.* New York: Bobbs Merrill.

Searle, J. (1974). Chomsky's revolution in linguistics. In G. Harmon, (Ed.), *On Noam Chomsky.* New York: Anchor Books.

Searle, J. (1984). *Minds, brains, and science.* Cambridge, MA: Harvard University Press.

Searle, J. (1987). Minds, brains and programs. In Rainer Born (Ed.), *Artificial intelligence: The case against.* London: Croom Helm.

Sears, D. (1988). Symbolic racism. In P. Katz & D. A. Taylor (Eds.), *Eliminating racism: Profiles in controversy.* New York: Plenum Press.

Sears, D. O. (1985). Political socialization. In F. I. Greenstein and N.W. Polsby (Eds.), *Handbook of political science,* Vol. 2. Reading, MA: Addison–Wesley.

Sears, D. O. (1986). College sophomores in the laboratory: Influences of a narrrow data base on social psychological view of human nature. *Journal of Personality and Social Psychology, 51,* 515–530.

Sederer, L. (1992). Judicial and legislative responses to cost containment. *American Journal of Psychiatry, 149,* 1157–1161.

Seelinger, G., & Schuderer, B. (1985). Release of male courtship display in *Periplaneta americana*: Evidence for female contact sex pheromone. *Animal Behaviour, 33,* 599–607.

Seeman, P., & Lee, T. (1975). Antipsychotic drugs: Direct correlation between clinical potency and presynaptic action on dopamine neurons. *Science, 188,* 1217–1219.

Segal, M. W. (1974). Alphabet and attraction: An unobtrusive measure of the effect of propinquity in a field setting. *Journal of Personality and Social Psychology, 30,* 654–657.

Segall, M. H. (1988). Cultural roots of aggressive behavior. In M. H. Bond (Ed.), *The cross–cultural challenge to social psychology.* Newbury Park, CA: Sage.

Seidenberg, M. S. & Petitto, L. A. (1987). Communication, symbolic communication, and language: Comment on Savage–Rumbaugh, McDonald, Sevcik, Hopkins, & Rupert (1986). *Journal of Experimental Psychology: General, 116,* 279–287.

Seidman, S., & Reider, R. (1994). A review of sexual behavior in the United States. *American Journal of Psychiatry, 151,* 330–341.

Sekular, R., & Blake, R. (1994). *Peception.* (3rd ed.). New York: McGraw–Hill.

Seligman, L. (1975). Skin potential as an indicator of emotion. *Journal of Counseling Psychology, 22,* 489–493.

Seligman, M.E.P. (1970). On the generality of the laws of learning. *Psychological Review, 77,* 406–418.

Seligman, M. E. P. (1971). Phobias and preparedness. *Behavior Therapy, 193,* 323–325.

Selman, R. L. (1980). *The growth of interpersonal understanding.* New York: Academic Press.

Selye, H. (1936). A syndrome produced by diverse nocuous agents. *Nature, 138,* 32.

Selye, H. (1976). *The stress of life.* New York: McGraw–Hill.

Sergent, J., & Signoret, J. L. (1992). Varieties of functional deficits in prosopagnosia. *Cerebral Cortex, 2,* 375–388.

Serpell, R. (1989). Dimensions endogenes de l'intelligence chez les A–chewa et autres peuples africans. In J. Retschitzky, M. Bossel–Lagos, & P. Dasen (Eds.), *La recherche interculturelle.* Paris: L'Harmattan.

Sethi, S., & Seligman, M. (1993). Optimism and fundamentalism. *Psychological Science, 4,* 256–259.

Sewell, K. W., Adams–Webber, J., Mitterer, J., & Cromwell, R. L. (1992). Computerized repertory grids: Review of the literature. *International Journal of Personal Construct Psychology, 5,* 1–23.

Shantz, C. U. (1983). Social cognition. In J. H. Flavell & E. M. Markman (Eds.), *Handbook of child psychology: Vol. 3. Cognitive Development.* New York: John Wiley.

Shapiro, S., & Vukovich, K. R. (1970). Early experience effects upon cortical dendrites: A proposed model for development. *Science, 167,* 292–294.

Shaver, P., Hazan, C., & Bradshaw, D. (1988). Love as attachment. In R. J. Sternberg & M.L. Barnes, *The psychology of love*. New Haven, Conn.: Yale University Press.

Shaver, P., Schwartz, J., Kirson,D. & O'Connor, G. (1987). Emotion knowledge: Further exploration of a prototype approach. *Journal of Personality and Social Psychology, 52*, 1061–1086.

Shaw, B. F., & Segal, Z. V. (1988). Introduction to cognitive theory and therapy. In A. J. Frances and R. E. Hales (Eds.), *Review of Psychiatry*, (Vol. 7.) Washington, DC: American Psychiatric Press.

Shea, M. T., Elkin, I., Imber, S., & Sotsky, S. (1992). Course of depressive symptoms over follow–up: Findings from the National Institute of Mental Health Treatment of Depression Collaborative Research Program. *Archives of General Psychiatry, 49*, 782–787.

Shedler, J., & Block, J. (1990). Adolescent drug use and psychological health: A longitudinal inquiry. *American Psychologist, 45*, 612–630.

Shedler, J., Mayman, M., & Manis, M. (1993). The illusion of mental health. *American Psychologist, 48*, 1117–1131.

Sheehy, G. (1976). *Passages*. New York: E. P. Dutton.

Sheldon, A., & Strange, W. (1982). The acquisition of /r/ and /l/ by Japanese learners of English: Evidence that speech production can precede speech perception. *Applied Psycholinguistics, 3*, 243–261.

Sher, K. J., Walitzer, K. S., Wood, P. K., & Brent, E. E. (1991). Characteristics of children of alcoholics: Putative risk factors, substance use and abuse, and psychopathology. *Journal of Abnormal Psychology, 100*, 427–448.

Sherif, M. (1935). A study of some social factors in perception. *Archives of Psychology, 87*, 27.

Sherif, M. (1947). Group influence upon the formation of norms and attitudes. In T.M. Newcombe & E.L. Hartley (Eds.), *Readings in social psychology*. New York: Holt, Rinehart, & Winston.

Sherif, M. et al. (1961). *Intergroup conflict and cooperation: The Robber's Cave experiment*. Norman: University of Oklahoma Press.

Sherif, M., & Sherif, C. W. (1979). Research on intergroup relations. In W. G. Austin and S. Worchel (Eds.), *The social psychology of intergroup relations*. Monterey, CA: Brooks/Cole.

Sherman, G. F., Galaburda, A. M., & Geschwind, N. (1982). Neuroanatomical asymmetries in non–human species. *Trends in Neurosciences, 5*, 429–431.

Sherman, S. J., Judd, C. M., & Park, B. (1989). Social cognition. *Annual Review of Psychology, 40*, 281–326.

Sherwin, B. (1993). *Menopause myths and realities*. Washington, DC: American Psychiatric Press.

Shields, J. (1962). *Monozygotic twins brought up apart and brought up together*. London: Oxford University Press.

Shiffrin, R. M., & Schneider, W. (1977). Controlled and automatic human information processing: II. Perceptual learning, automatic attending and a general theory. *Psychological Review, 84*(2), 127–190.

Shimada, M., & Otsuka, A. (1981). Functional hemispheric differences of kanji processing in Japanese. *Japanese Psychological Review, 24*, 472–489.

Shimizu, N., Oomura, Y., Novin, D., Grijalva, C., & Cooper, P. H. (1983). Functional correlations between lateral hypothalamic glucose–sensitive neurons and hepatic portal glucose–sensitive units in rats. *Brain Research, 265*, 49–54.

Shorey, H. H. (1976). *Animal communication by pheromones*. New York: Academic Press.

Showers, C., & Cantor, N. (1985). Social cognition: A look at motivated strategies. *Annual Review of Psychology, 36*, 275–305.

Shrom, S. H., Lief, H. I., & Wein, A. J. (1979). Clinical profile of experience with 130 consecutive cases of impotent men. *Urology, 13*, 511–15.

Shulman, M. E. (1988). Cost containment in clinical psychology: Critique of Biodyne and the HMOs. *Professional Psychology Research and Practice, 19*, 298–307.

Shultz, T. R., & Ravinsky, F. B. (1977). Similarity as a principle of causal inference. *Child Development, 48*, 1522–1558.

Shweder, R. (1991). *Thinking through cultures: Expeditions in cultural psychology*. Cambridge, MA: Harvard University Press.

Shweder, R. A. (1980). Scientific thought and social cognition. In W.A. Collins (Ed.), Development of cognition, affect, and social relations: Minnesota *Symposium on Child Development*, Vol. 13. Hillsdale, NJ: Erlbaum.

Shweder, R. A. & Bourne, E. J. (1982). Does the concept of the person vary cross–culturally? In A.J. Marsella and G.M. White (Eds.), *Cultural conceptions of mental health and therapy*. Boston: D. Reidel.

Siegel, R. K. (1990). *Intoxication*. New York: Pocket Books.

Siegel, S. (1984). Pavlonian conditionaing and heroin overdose: Reports by overdose victims. *Bulletin of the Psychonomic Society, 22*, 428–430.

Siegler, R. S. (1989). Mechanisms of cognitive development. *Annual Review of Psychology, 40*, 353–379.

Siegler, R. S. (1991). *Children's thinking*. (2nd ed.). Englewood Cliffs, NJ: Prentice–Hall Press.

Sifneos, P. (1973). The prevalence of alexithymic characteristics in psychosomatic patients. *Psychotherapy and Psychosomatics, 22*, 255–262.

Sifneos, P. (1987). *Short–term dynamic psychotherapy: Evaluation and technique*, (2nd ed.) New York: Plenum.

Sigall, H., Page, R., & Brown, A. C. (1971). Effort expenditure as a function of evaluation and evaluator attractiveness. *Representative Research in Social Psychology, 2*, 19–25.

Sillars, A. L., & Zietlow, P. (1993). Investigations of marital communication and lifespan development. In N. Coupland & J. Nussbaum (Eds.), *Discourse and lifespan identity: Language and language behaviors*, Vol. 4 (pp. 237–261). Newbury Park, CA: Sage Publications.

Silverstein, B., Perdue, L., Peterson, B., Vogel, L., & Fantini, D. A. (1986). Possible causes of the thin standard of bodily attractiveness for women. *International Journal of Eating Disorders, 5*, 907–916.

Silverstein, L. B. (1991). Transforming the debate about child care and maternal employment. *American Psychologist, 46*, 1025–1032.

Simmons, F. B., Epley, J. M., Lummis, R. C., Guttman, N., Frishkopf, L. S., Harmon, L. D., & Zwicker, E. (1965). Auditory nerve: Electrical stimulation in man. *Science, 148*,104–106.

Simmons, L. W. (1990). Pheromonal cues for the recognition of kin by female field crickets, Gryllus bimaculatus. *Animal Behaviour, 40*, 192–195.

Simmons, R. G. & Blythe, D. A. (1987). *Moving into adolescence*. Hawthorne, NY: Aldine.

Simon, H. A. (1978). Information–processing theory of human problem solving. In W. K. Estes (Ed.), *Handbook of learning and cognitive processes*. Hillsdale, NJ: Erlbaum.

Simon, H. A. (1990). A mechanism for social selection and successful altruism. *Science, 150*, 1665–1668.

Simon, R. (1985). Family therapy. In H. I. Kaplan & B. J. Sadock (Eds.), *Comprehensive textbook of psychiatry*. (4th ed.). Baltimore, MD: Williams & Wilkins.

Simons, H. W., Berkowitz, N. N., & Moyer, R. J. (1970). Similarity, credibility, and attitude change: A review and a theory. *Psychological Bulletin, 73*, 1–16.

Simonton, D. K. (1991). Emergence and realization of genius: The lives and works of 120 classical composers. *Journal of Personality and Social Psychology, 61*, 829–840.

Simpson, G. M., & May, P.R.A. (1985). Schizophrenia: Somatic treatment. In H. I. Kaplan, & B. J. Sadock (Eds.), *Comprehensive textbook of psychiatry*. (4th ed.). Baltimore, MD: Williams & Wilkins.

Simpson, J., Gangestad, S., & Lerma, M. (1990). Perception of physical attractiveness: Mechanisms involved in the maintenance of romantic relationships. *Journal of Personality and Social Psychology, 59*, 1192–1201.

Simpson, J., Rholes, W., & Nelligan, J. (1992). Support seeking and support giving within couples in an anxiety–provoking situation: The role of attachment styles. *Journal of Personality and Social Psychology, 62*, 434–446.

Singer, J. L. (1975). *The inner world of daydreaming.* New York: Harper & Row.

Singer, J. L. (1986). Is television bad for children? *Social Science, 71*, 178–182.

Singer, J. L. (1990). *Repression and dissociation: Implications for personality theory, psychopathology, and health.* Chicago: University of Chicago Press.

Singer, J. L., & Kolligian, J., Jr. (1987). Personality: Developments in the study of private experience. *Annual Review of Psychology, 38*, 533–574.

Singer, J. L., & Singer, D. G. (1981). Television, imagination, and agggression: A study of preschoolers. Hillsdale, NJ: Erlbaum.

Singh, M. P. and Agrawal, P. (1987). Effect of nutrition on intellectual development. *Perspectives in Psychological Researches, 10*, 25–29.

Siuta, J. (1990). Fantasy–proneness: Toward cross–cultural comparisons. *British Journal of Experimental and Clinical Hypnosis, 7*, 93–101.

Skeels, H. M. (1966). Adult states of children with contrasting early life experiences: A follow–up study. *Monographs of the Society for Research in Child Development, 31*, (serial No. 105), 70.

Skinner, B. F. (1938). *The behavior of organisms.* New York: Appleton–Century–Crofts.

Skinner, B. F. (1948). *Walden Two.* New York: Macmillan.

Skinner, B.F. (1951). How to teach animals. *Scientific American, 185*, 26–29.

Skinner, B.F. (1953). *Science and human behavior.* New York: Macmillan.

Skinner, B.F. (1957). *Verbal behavior.* New York: Appleton–Century–Crofts.

Skinner, B. F. (1977). Hernstein and the evolution of behaviorism. *American Psychologist, 32*, 1006–1012.

Skinner, B. F. (1987). Whatever happened to psychology as the science of human behavior? *American Psychologist, 42*, 780–786.

Skinner, B. F. (1990). Can psychology be a science of mind? *American Psychologist, 45*, 1206–1210.

Skodak, M., & Skeel, H. M. (1949). A final follow–up study of one hundred adopted children. *Journal of Genetic Psychology, 75*, 85–125.

Slade, L. A., & Rush, M. C. (1991). Achievement motivation and the dynamics of task difficulty choices. *Journal of Personality and Social Psychology, 60*, 165–172.

Sloboda, J. A. Hermelin, B. & O'Connor, N. (1985). An exceptional music memory. *Music Perception, 3*, 155–169.

Smetana, J., Yau, J., Restrepo, A., & Braeges, J. (1991). Adolescent–parent conflict in married and divorced families. *Developmental Psychology, 27*, 1000–1010.

Smith, C., & Lloyd, B. (1978). Maternal behavior and perceived sex of infant: Revisited. *Child Development, 49*, 1263–1265.

Smith, C. A., & Ellsworth, P. (1985). Patterns of cognitive appraisal in emotion. *Journal of Personality and Social Psychology, 48*, 813–838.

Smith, C. A., & Lazarus, R. S. (1993). Appraisal components, core relational themes, and the emotions. *Cognition and Emotion, 7*, 233–269.

Smith, D. J., Robertson, B., Monroe, P. J., Taylor, D. A., et al. (1992). Opioid receptors mediating antinociception from b–endorphin and morphine in the periaqueductal gray. *Neuropharmacology, 31*, 1137–1150.

Smith, J. (1988). The dangers of perinatal cocaine use. *American Journal of Maternal Child Nursing, 13*, 174–179.

Smith, K. (1984). Drive: In defence of a concept. *Behaviorism, 12*, 71–114.

Smith, L. (1992). On prediction and control: B. F. Skinner and the technological ideal of science. *American Psychologist, 47*, 216–223.

Smith, M. B. (1978). Perspectives on selfhood. *American Psychologist, 33*, 1053–1063.

Smith, M. B. (1988). Can there be a human science? *Symposium of the American Psychological Association*, Atlanta, G.

Smith, M. L., & Glass, G. V. (1977). Meta–analysis of psychotherapy outcome studies. *American Psychologist, 32*, 752–760.

Smith, M. L., Glass, G. V., & Miller, T. I. (1980). *The benefits of psychotherapy.* Baltimore: Johns Hopkins University Press.

Smith, P. K., & Daglish, L. (1977). Sex differences in parent and infant behavior. *Child Development, 48*, 1250–54.

Smith, R. E., & Swinyard, W. R. (1983). Attitude–behavior consistency: The impact of product trial versus advertising. *Journal of Marketing Research, 20*, 257–267.

Smith, R. J. (1990). Pessimism and depression east and west. *American Psychologist, 45*, 73–74.

Smith, S. (1988). Calculating Prodigies. In L. K. Obler & D. Fein (Eds.), *The exceptional brain: Neuropsychology of talent and special abilities* (pp.19–47). New York: Guilford Press.

Smith, V. L. & Ellsworth, P. C. (1987). The social psychology of eyewitness accuracy: Misleading questions and communicator expertise. *Journal of Applied Psychology, 72*, 294–300.

Smith–Rosenberg, C. (1975). The female world of love and ritual: Relations between women in 19th century America. *Signs*, Autumn, 1–29.

Smuts, B. (1990). Social relationships and ritualized greetings in adult male baboons (Papio cynocephalus anubis). *International Journal of Primatology, 11*, 147–172.

Snyder, C. R., & Higgins, R. (1988). Excuses: Their effective role in the negotiation of reality. *Psychological Bulletin, 104*, 23–35.

Snyder, D. K., Wills, R. M., & Grady–Fletcher, A. (1991). Long–term effectiveness of behavioral versus insight–oriented marital therapy: A 4–year follow–up study. *Journal of Consulting and Clinical Psychology, 59*, 138–141.

Snyder, M., & Ickes, W. (1985). In G. Lindzey and E. Aronson (Eds.), *Handbook of social psychology*, Reading, MA: Addison–Wesley.

Snyder, M., Tanke, E. D., & Berscheid, E. (1977). Social perception and interpersonal behavior: On the self–fulfilling nature of social stereotypes. *Journal of Personality and Social Psychology, 35*, 656–666.

Snyder, S. H. (1976). The dopamine hypothesis of schizophrenia: Focus on the dopamine receptor. *American Journal of Psychiatry, 133*, 197–202.

Sobal, J., & Stunkard, A. (1989). Socioeconomic status and obesity: A review of the literature. *Psychological Bulletin, 105*, 260–275.

Solomon, L. Z. (1982). The effects of bystander's anonymity, situational ambiguity, and victim's status on helping. *Journal of Social Psychology, 117*, 285–294.

Solomon, S., Greenberg, J., & Pyszczynski, T. (1991). A terror management theory of social behavior: The psychological functions of self–esteem and cultural worldviews. In L. Berkowitz (Ed.), *Advances in Experimental Social Psychology, 24*, 93–159.

Sommer, R., & Sommer, B. A. (1983). Mystery in Milwaukee: Early intervention, I.Q., and psychology textbooks. *American Psychologist, 38*, 982–985.

Sorenson, P. W., Hara, T. J., & Stacey, N. E. (1991). Sex pheromones selectively stimulate the medial olfactory tracts of male goldfish. *Brain Research, 558*, 343–347.

Spangler, W. D., & House, R. J. (1991). Presidential effectiveness and the leadership motive profile. *Journal of Personality and Social Psychology, 60*, 439–455.

Spanos, N. P., Burgess, C. A., Cross, P. A., & MacLeod, G. (1992). Hypnosis, response bias, and suggested negative hallucinations. *Journal of Abnormal Psychology, 101*, 192–199.

Spanos, N. P., Stenstrom, R. J., & Johnston, J. C. (1988). Hypnosis, placebo, and suggestion in the treatment of warts. *Psychosomatic Medicine, 50*, 245–260.

Spearman, C. (1904). General intelligence, objectively determined and measured. *American Journal of Psychology, 15*, 201–293.

Spearman, C. (1927). *The abilities of man:*

Their nature and measurement. New York: Macmillan.

Spector, I., & Carey, M. P. (1990). Incidence and prevalence of the sexual dysfunctions: A critical review of the empirical literature. *Archives of Sexual Behavior, 19,* 389–408.

Speicher, B. (1994). Family patterns of moral judgement during adolescence and early adulthood. *Developmental Psychology, 30,* 624–632.

Spelke, E., Hirst, W., & Neisser, U. Skills of divided attention. *Cognition, 4,* 215–230.

Spence, A. P. (1989). *Biology of human aging.* Englewood Cliffs, NJ: Prentice–Hall.

Spence, D. P. (1967). Subliminal perception and perceptual defense: Two sides of a single problem. *Behavioral Science, 12,* 183–193.

Spence, M. R. & Decasper, A. J. (1987). Prenatal experience with low–frequency maternal–voicesounds influences neonatal perception of maternal voice samples. *Infant Development and Behavior, 10,* 133–142.

Spencer, M. B., & Markstrom–Adams, C. (1990). Identity processes among racial and ethnic minority children in America. *Child Development, 61,* 290–310.

Sperling, G. (1960). The information available in brief visual presentations. *Psychological Monographs, 74,* 1–29.

Sperry, R. (1984). Consciousness, personal identity and the divided brain. *Neuropsychologia, 22,* 661–673.

Sperry, R. W. (1956). The eye and the brain. *Scientific American,* 48–52.

Spillman, L. (1994). The Mermann grid illusion: A tool for studying human perceptive field organization. *Perception, 23,* 691–708.

Spirduso, W. & MacRae, P. (1990). Motor performance and aging. In J.E. Birren & K.W. Schaie (Eds.), *Handbook of the psychology of aging.* (3rd ed.). New York: Van Nostrand Reinhold.

Spiro, M. (1965). *Context and meaning in cultural anthropology.* New York: Free Press.

Spitz, R. A. (1945). Hospitalism: An inquiry into the genesis of psychiatry conditions in early childhood. *The Psychoanalytic Study of the Child, 1,* 53–74.

Spitzer, R., Williams, J.B.W., Gibbon, M.,& First, M. (1992). The structured clinical interview for DSM–III–R (SCID) I: History, rationale, and description. *Archives of General Psychiatry, 49,* 624–629.

Spray, D. (1986). Cutaneous temperature receptors. *Annual Review of Physiology, 48,* 625–638.

Spreen, O., Tupper, D., Risser, A., Tuokko, H., & Edgell, D. (1984). *Human developmental neuropsychology.* New York: Oxford University Press.

Squire, L. R. (1982). The neuropsychology of human memory. *Annual Review of Neuroscience, 5,* 241–273.

Squire, L. R. (1986). Mechanisms of memory. *Science, 232,* 1612–1619.

Squire, L. R. (1987). *Memory and brain.* New York: Oxford University Press.

Squire, L. R. (1989). On the course of forgetting in very long–term memory. *Journal of Experimental Psychology: Learning, Memory, and Cognition, 15,* 241–245.

Squire, L. R. & Zola–Morgan, S. (1991). The medial temporal lobe memory system. *Science, 253,* 1380–1386.

Srivastava, A., Borries, C., & Sommer, Volker. (1991). Homosexual mounting in free–ranging female langurs *(Presbytis entellus–R). Archives of Sexual Behavior, 20,* 487–512.

Sroufe, L. A. (1983). Individual patterns of adaptation from infancy to preschool. In M. Perlmutter (Ed.), *Minnesota symposium on child psychology:* Vol 16. Hillsdale, NJ: Erlbaum.

Sroufe, L. A., Cooper, R. G., & DeHart, G. (1992). *Child development: Nature and course* (2nd ed.). New York.: McGraw–Hill.

Sroufe, L. A. & Fleeson, J. (1986). Attachment and the construction of relationships. In W. W. Hartup & Z. Rubin (Eds.), *Relationships and development* (pp.51–72). Hillsdale, NJ: Erlbaum.

Sroufe, L. A., & Waters, E. (1977). Attachment as an organizational construct. *Child Development, 48,* 1184–1199.

Srull, T. K., & Wyer, R. S., Jr. (1989). Person memory and judgment. *Psychological Review, 96,* 58–83.

St. George–Hyslop, P. Tanzi, R., Polinsky, R., Haines, J., Nee, L., Atkins, P., Myers, R., Feldman, R., Pollen,D., Drachman, D., Growdon, J., Bruni, A., Foncin, J., Salmon, D., Prommelt, P., Amaducci, L., Sorbi, S., Piacentini, S., Stewart, G., Hobbs, W., Conneally, M., & Gusella, J. (1987). The genetic defect causing familiar Alzheimer's disease maps on chromosome 21. *Science, 20,* 885–90.

Stasser, G., & Taylor, L. (1991). Speaking turns in face–to–face discussions. *Journal of Personality and Social Psychology, 60,* 675–684.

Stattin, H., & Magnusson, D. (1989). The role of early aggressive behavior in the frequency, seriousness, and types of later crime. *Journal of Consulting and Clinical Psychology, 57,* 710–718.

Stearns, P. (1994). *American cool: Constructing a twentieth–century emotional style.* New York: New York University Press.

Stein, B. E., & Meredith, M. A. (1990). Multisensory integration: Neural and behavioral solutions for dealing with stimuli from different sensory modalities. *Annals of the New York Academy of Sciences, 608,* 51–70.

Stein, J., Newcomb, M., & Bendler, P. (1994). Psychosocial correlates and predictors of AIDS risk behaviors, abortion, and drug use among a community sample of young adult women. *Health Psychology, 13,* 308–318.

Stein, Z., & Susser, M. (1975). Public health and mental retardation: New power and new problems. In M. Begab & S. Richardson (Eds.), *The Mentally retarded and society: A social science perspective.* Baltimore, MD: University Park Press.

Steinberg, H., & Sykes, E. A. (1985). Introduction to symposium on endorphins and behavioral processes; Review of literature on endorphins and exercise. *Pharmacology, Biochemistry, and Behavior, 23,* 857–862.

Steinberg, L. (1988). Reciprocal relation between parent–child distance and pubertal maturation. *Developmental Psychology, 24,* 122–128.

Steinberg, L., Lamborn, S. D., Darling, N., & Mounts, N. S. (1994). Over–time changes in adjustment and competence among adolescents from authoritative, authoritarian, indulgent, and neglectful families. *Child Development, 65,* 754–770.

Steinhausen, H. C., Willms, J., & Spohr, H. L. (1993). Long–term psychopathological and cognitive outcome of children with fetal alcohol syndrome. *Journal of the American Academy of Child and Adolescent Psychiatry, 32,* 990–994.

Stemmer, N. (1990). Skinner's Verbal Behavior, Chomsky's review, and mentalism. *Journal of the Experimental Analysis of Behavior, 54,* 307–315.

Sternberg, R. J. (1985). *Beyond IQ: A triarchic theory of human intelligence.* New York: Cambridge University Press.

Sternberg, R. J. (1985). The black–white differences and Spearman's g: Old wine in new bottles that still doesn't taste good. *The Behavioral and Brain Sciences, 8,* 244.

Sternberg, R. J. (1985). Human intelligence: The model is the message. *Science, 4730,* 1111–17.

Sternberg, R. J. (1985). Implicit theories of intelligence, creativity, and wisdom. *Journal of Personality and Social Psychology, 49,* 607–627.

Sternberg, R. J. (1988). Triangulating love. In R. Sternberg & M. L. Barnes (Eds.), *The psychology of love.* New Haven, Conn.: Yale University Press.

Sternberg, R. J., Conway, B. E., Ketron, J. L., & Bernstein, M. (1981). People's conceptions of intelligence. *Journal of Personality and Social Psychology, 41,* 37–55.

Sternberg, R. J., & Davidson, J. E. (1985). Cognitive development in the gifted and talented. In F. D. Horowitz & M. O'Brien (Eds.), *The gifted and talented: Developmental perspectives* (pp. 37–73). Washington, DC: American Psychological Association.

Sternberg, R. J., & Grajek, S. (1984). The nature of love. *Journal of Personality and Social Psychology, 47,* 312–329.

Sternberg, R. J., & Salter, W. (1982). Conceptions of intelligence. In R. J. Sternberg (Ed.), *Handbook of human intelligence* (pp.3–28). New York: Cambridge University Press.

Sternberg, R. J., & Wagner, R. K. (1993). The geocentric view of intelligence and job performance is wrong. Current *Directions in Psychological Science, 2,* 1–5.

Sternberg, R. J. (Ed.). (1984). *Mechanisms of cognitive development.* New York: Freeman.

Sternberg, S. (1975). Memory scanning: New findings and current controversies. *Quarterly Journal of Experimental Psychology, 27,* 1–32.

Stevens, A., & Coupe, P. (1978). Distortions in judged spacial relations. *Cognitive Psychology, 10,* 422–237.

Stevens, C. F. (1979). The neuron. *Scientific American, 241,* 54–65.

Stevens, S. S. (1961). Psychophysics of sensory function. In W. Rosenblith (Ed.), *Sensory communication* (pp.1–33). Cambridge, MA: MIT Press.

Stevens, S. S. (1975). *Psychophysics: Introduction to its perceptual, neural, and social prospects.* New York: John Wiley.

Stevens, S. S., & Newman, E. B. (1934). The localization of pure tone. *Proceedings of the National Academy of Sciences, 20,* 593–596.

Stewart, W. A. (1969). On the use of Negro dialect in the teaching of reading. In J. C. Baratz & R. W. Schuy (Eds), *Teaching black children to read* (pp. 156–219). Washington, DC: Center for Applied Linguistics.

Stipek, D., & Gralinski, J. (1991). Gender differences in children's achievement–related beliefs and emotional responses to success and failure in mathematics. *Journal of Educational Psychology, 83,* 361–371

Stoddard, D. M. (Ed.). (1980). *Olfaction in mammals.* New York: Academic Press.

Stoel–Gammon, C. (1988). Prelinguistic vocalizations of hearing–impaired and normally hearing subjects: A comparison of consonantal inventories. *Journal of Speech and Hearing Disorders, 53,* 302–315.

Stoel–Gammon, C., & Otomo, K. (1986). Babbling development of hearing–impaired and normally hearing subjects. *Journal of Speech and Hearing Disorders, 51,* 33–41.

Stogdill, R. & Coons, A. (1957). *Leader behavior: Its description and measurement.* Columbus, Ohio: Ohio State University Bureau of Business Research.

Stokes, J. P. (1985). The relation of social network and individual difference variables to loneliness. *Journal of Personality and Social Psychology, 48,* 981–990.

Stokes, P. E., Maas, J. W., Davis, J.M., Koslow, S. H., Casper, R.C., & Stoll,P. M. (1987). Biogenic amine and metabolite levels in depressed patients with high versus normal hypothalamic–pituitary–adrenocortical activity. *American Journal of Psychiatry, 144,* 868–872.

Stone, M. H. (1989). Murder. Psychiatric *Clinics of North America, 12,* 643–651.

Storms, M. D. (1973). Videotape and the attribution process: Reversing actors' and observers' points of view. *Journal of Personality and Social Psychology, 27,* 165–175.

Strang, D. J. (1972). Conformity, ability, and self–esteem. *Representative Research in Social Psychology, 3,* 97–103.

Stratton, G. M. (1897). Vision without inversion of the retinal image. *Psychological Review, 4,* 341–360.

Strauman, T. (1992). Self–guides, autobiographical memory, and anxiety and dysphoria: Toward a cognitive model of vulnerability to emotional distress. *Journal of Abnormal Psychology, 101,* 87–95.

Strauman, T. (1994). Self–representations and the nature of cognitive change in psychotherapy. *Journal of Personality Integration, 4,* 291–316.

Strauman, T., Lemieux, A., & Coe, C. (1993). Self–discrepancy and natural killer cell activity: Immunological consequences of negative self–evaluation. *Journal of Personality and Social Psychology, 64,* 1042–1052.

Straus, A. S. (1977). Northern Cheyenne ethnopsychology. *Ethnos, 5,* 326–357.

Straus, A. S. (1982). The structure of the self in Northern Cheyenne culture. In B. Lee (Ed.), *Psychosocial theories of the self.* New York: Plenum Press.

Strauss, J., Carpenter, W. T., & Bartko, J. (1974). The diagnosis and understanding of schizophrenia, III: Speculations on the processes that underlie schizophrenic symptoms and signs. *Schizophrenia Bulletin, 1,* 61–69.

Strauss, J., & Ryan, R. M. (1987). Autonomy disturbances in subtypes of anorexia nervosa. *Journal of Abnormal Psychology, 96,* 254–258.

Strayer, D. L., & Kramer, A. F. (1990). Attentional requirements of automatic and controlled processing. *Journal of Experimental Psychology Learning, Memory, and Cognition, 16*(1), 67–82.

Strayer, J. (1993). Children's concordant emotions and cognitions in response to observed emotions. *Child Development, 64,* 188–201.

Streissguth, A., Barr, H., Johnson, Martin, D., & Kirchner, G. (1985). Attention and distraction at age 7 years related to maternal drinking during pregnancy. *Alchoholism: Clinical and experimental research, 9,* 195.

Streissguth, A., Sampson, P., & Barr, H. (1989). Neurobehavioral dose–response effects of prenatal alcohol exposure in humans from infancy to adulthood. *Annals of the New York Academy of Sciences, 562,* 145–158.

Stricker, G. (1991). Ethical concerns for alcohol research. *Journal of Consulting and Clinical Psychology, 59,* 256–257.

Stricker, G. & Healey, B.J. (1990). Projective assessment of object relations: A review of the empirical literature. *Psychological Assessment, 2,* 219–230.

Strickland, L. H., Barefoot, J. C., & Hockenstein, P. (1976). Monitoring behavior in the surveillance and trust paradigm. *Representative Research in Social Psychology, 7,* 51–57.

Striegel–Moore, R. H., Silberstein, L. R., & Rodin, J. (1986). Toward an understanding of risk factors for bulimia. *American Psychologist, 41,* 246–263.

Stroebel, C. F. (1985). Biofeedback and behavioral medicine. In H. I. Kaplan & B. J. Sadock (Eds.), *Comprehensive textbook of psychiatry.* Baltimore, MD: Williams & Wilkins.

Struckman–Johnson, C. (1990). Male victims of acquaintance rape. In A. Parrot & L. Bechhofer (Eds.), *Acquaintance rape: The hidden crime.*

Strupp, H., & Binder, J. L. (1984). *Psychotherapy in a new key: A guide to time–limited dynamic psychotherapy.* New York: Basic Books.

Strupp, H. H., & Blackwood, G. L., Jr. (1985). Recent methods of psychotherapy. In H. I. Kaplan, & B. J. Sadock (Eds.), *Comprehensive textbook of psychiatry.* (4th ed.). Baltimore, MD: Williams & Wilkins.

Stumpf, H. (1993). The factor structure of the Personality Research Form: A cross–national evaluation. *Journal of Personality, 61,* 1–26.

Stunkard, A., Sorensen, T.I.A., Harris, C., Teasdale, T. W., Chakraborty, R., Schull, W., & Schulsinger, F. (1986). An adoption study of human obesity. *New England Journal of Medicine, 314,* 193–198.

Stuss, D. T., & Benson, D. F. (1984). Neuropsychological studies of the frontal lobes. *Psychological Bulletin, 95,* 3–28.

Stuss, D.T., Gw, C.A. & Hetherington, C.R. (1992). "No longer Gage": Frontal lobe dysfunction and emotional changes. *Journal of Consulting and Clinical Psychology, 60,* 349–359.

Suarez–Orozco, M., Spindler, G., & Spindler, L. (1994). *The making of psychological anthropology II.* Fort Worth, Tex.: Harcourt Brace Jovanovich.

Sullivan, H. S. (1953). *The interpersonal theory of psychiatry.* New York: W. W. Norton.

Sulloway, F. (1994). Born to rebel: Radical thinking in science and social thought. *Unpublished manuscript,* Cambridge, MA: MIT.

Super, C. M. (1981). Cross–cultural research on infancy. In H.C. Triandis & A. Heron (Ed.), *Handbook of cross–cultural psychology: Vol. 4. Developmental psychology.* Boston: Allyn & Bacon.

Super, C. M., & Harkness, S. (1980). *Anthropological perspectives on child development.* San Francisco: Jossey–Bass.

Surman, O. S., Gottlieb, S. K., Hackett, T. P., & Silverberg, E.L. (1983). Hypnosis in the treatment of warts. *Advances, 1,* 19–24.

Sutker, P., Winstead, D., Galina, Z., & Allai, A. (1991). Cognitive deficits and psycopathology among former prisoners of war and combat verterans of the Korean conflict. *American Journal of Psychiatry, 148,* 67–72.

Svartberg, M., & Stiles, T. C. (1991). Comparative effects of short–term psychodynamic psychotherapy: A meta–analysis. *Journal of Consulting and Clinical Psychology, 59,* 704–714.

Svenson, O. (1981). Are we all less risky and more skillful than our fellow drivers? *Acta Psychologia, 47,* 143–148.

Swann, W. (1984). Quest for accuracy in person perception: A matter of pragmatics. *Psychological Review, 91,* 457–477.

Swann, W. (1990). To be adored or to be known: The interplay of self–enhancement and self–verification. In R. M. Sorrentino & E.T. Higgins (Eds.), *Handbook of motivation and cognition.* Vol. 2, (pp. 408–448). New York: Guilford Press.

Swann, W., Stein–Seroussi, A., & Giesler, R. B. (1992). Why people self–verify. *Journal of Personality and Social Psychology, 62,* 392–401.

Swann, W., Wenzlaff, R., Krull, D. S., & Pelham, B. (1992). Allure of negative feedback: Self–verification strivings among depressed persons. *Journal of Abnormal Psychology, 101,* 293–306.

Swedo, S., Leonard, H., Kruesi, M., Rettew, D., Listwak, S., et al. (1992). Cerebrospinal fluid neurochemistry in children and adolescents with obsessive–compulsive disorder. *Archives of General Psychiatry, 49,* 29–36.

Swets, J. A. (1992). The science of choosing the right decision threshold in high–stakes diagnostics. *American Psychologist, 47,* 522–532.

Swift, W. J., Andrews, D., & Barklage, N. E. (1986). The relationship between affective disorder and eating disorders: A review of the literature. *American Journal of Psychiatry, 143,* 290–299.

Szapocznik, J., Rio, A., Murray, E., Cohen, R., Scopetta, M., et al. (1989). Structural family versus psychodynamic child therapy for problematic Hispanic boys. *Journal of Consulting and Clinical Psychology, 57,* 571–578.

Szasz, T. (1974). *The myth of mental illness: Foundations of a theory of personal conduct,* (Rev. ed.). New York: Harper & Row.

Szasz, T. (1989). *Law, liberty, and psychiatry: An inquiry into the social uses of mental health practices.* Syracuse, NY: Syracuse University Press.

Szeto, H., Wu, D., Decena, J., & Cheng, Y. (1991). Effects of single and repeated marijuana smoke exposure on fetal EEG. *Pharmacology, Biochemistry, and Behavior, 40,* 97–101.

Szeto, H. H., Wu, D.L., Decena, J. A., & Cheng, Y. (1991). Effects of single and repeated marijuana smoke exposure on fetal EEG. *Pharmacology, Biochemistry, and Behavior, 40,* 97–101.

Szymusiak, R., Iriye, T., & McGinty, D. (1989). Sleep–waking discharge of neurons in the posterior lateral hypothalamic area of cats. *Brain Research Bulletin, 23,* 111–120.

Tajfel, H. (1974). Social identity and intergroup behavior. *Social Science Information, 13,* 65–93.

Tajfel, H. (1981). *Human groups and social categories: Studies in social psychology.* Cambridge: Cambridge University Press.

Tajfel, H. (1982). *Social identity and intergroup relations.* Cambridge: Cambridge University Press.

Tajfel, H., & Turner, J. C. (1979). An integrative theory of intergroup conflict. In W. Austin and S. Worchel (Eds.), *The social psychology of intergroup relations.* Monterey, CA: Brooks/Cole.

Tallal, P. (1991). Hormonal influences in developmental learning disabilities. Special issue: Neuroendocrine effects on brain development and cognition. *Psychoneuroendocrinology, 16,* 203–211.

Tamminga, C., Thaker, G., Buchanon, R., Kirkpatrick, B., Alphs, L., Chase, T., & Carpenter, W. T. (1992). Limbic system abnormalities identified in schizophrenia using positron emission tomography with fluorodeoxyglucose and neocortical alterations with deficit syndrome. *Archives of General Psychiatry, 49,* 522–530.

Tamura, T., Nakatani, K., & Yau, K.–W. (1989). Light adaptation in cat retinal rods. *Science, 245,* 755–758.

Tan, C. C. (1991). Occupational health problems among nurses. *Scandinavian Journal of Work, Environment, and Health, 17,* 221–230.

Tanabe, T., Iino, M., & Tagaki, S. F. (1975). Discrimination of odors in olfactory bulb, pyriform–amygdaloid areas and orbito–frontal cortex of the monkey. *Journal of Neurophysiology, 38,* 1284–1296.

Tanaka, J. W. & Taylor, M. (1991). Object categories and expertise: Is the basic level in the eye of the beholder? *Cognitive Psychology, 23,* 457–482.

Tanner, J. M. (1978). *Fetus into man: Physical growth from conception to maturity.* Cambridge, MA: Harvard University Press.

Tassinary, L. G., & Cacioppo, J. (1992). Unobservable facial actions and emotion. *Psychological Science, 3,* 28–33.

Taylor, D. M., & Jaggi, V. (1974). Ethnocentrism and causal attribution in a South Indian context. *Journal of Cross–Cultural Psychology, 5,* 162–171

Taylor, E. H. (1990). The assessment of social intelligence. *Psychotherapy, 27,* 445–457.

Taylor, M., Cartwright, B., & Carlson, S. M. (1993). A developmental investigation of children's imaginary companions. *Developmental Psychology, 29,* 276–285.

Taylor, S. (1991). *Health psychology.* (2nd ed.). New York: McGraw–Hill.

Taylor, S. E., & Brown, J. D. (1988). Illusion and well–being: A social psychological perspective on mental *health. Psychological Bulletin, 103,* 193–210

Taylor, S., & Crocker, J. (1980). Schematic bases of social information processing. In E.T. Higgins, P.Herman, & M. Zanna (Eds.), *Social cognition: The Ontario Symposium.* Hillsdale, NJ: Erlbaum.

Taylor, S. E., & Koivumaki, J. H. (1976). The perception of self and others: Acquaintanceship, affect, and actor–observer differences. *Journal of Personality and Social Psychology, 33,* 403–408.

Taylor, S. E., & Fiske, S. T. (1975). Point of view and perceptions of causality. *Journal of Personality and Social Psychology, 32,* 439–445.

Taylor, S. E., & Fiske, S. T. (1978). Salience, attention, and attribution: Top of the head phenomena. In L. Berkowitz (Ed.), *Advances in experimental social psychology,* Vol. ll. New York: Academic Press.

Teitelbaum, P. (1961). Disturbances in feeding and drinking behavior after hypothalamic lesions. *Nebraska Symposium on Motivation, 39–68.*

Tellegen, A., Lykken, D. T., Bouchard, T. J. Jr., Wilcox, K. J., & Rich, S. (1988). Personality similarity in twins reared apart and together. *Journal of Personality and Social Psychology, 54,* 1031–1039.

Teplin, L. A. (1984). Criminalizing mental disorder: The comparative arrest rate of the mentally ill. *American Psychologist, 39,* 794–803.

Terman, L. M. (1925). *Genetic studies of genius: Vol. 1. Mental and physical traits of a thousand gifted children.* Stanford, CA: Stanford University Press.

Terman, L. M., & Oden, M. H. (1947). *Genetic studies of genius: Vol. 4. The gifted child grows up: Twenty–five years' follow–up of a superior group.* Stanford, CA: Stanford University Press.

Terman, L.M., & Oden, M.H. (1959). *Genetic studies of genius: Vol. 5. The gifted group at mid–life.* Stanford, CA: Stanford University Press.

Terrace, H. S. (1979). How Nim Chimsky changed my mind. *Psychology Today, 3 ,* 65–76.

Tesser, A. (1991). Social versus clinical approaches to self psychology: The self–evaluation maintenance model and Kohutian object relations theory. In R.C. Curtis (Ed.), *The relational self: theoretical convergences in psychoanalysis and social psychology* (pp. 257–281). New York: Guilford Press.

Tetlock, P., Armor, D., & Peterson, R. S. (1994). The slavery debate in antebellum America: Cognitive style, value conflict, and the limits of compromise. *Journal of Personality and Social Psychology, 66,* 115–126.

Tetlock, P., Peterson, R., McGuire, C., Change, S., & Feld, P. (1992). Assessing political group dynamics: A test of the groupthink model. *Journal of Personality and Social Psychology, 63,* 403–425.

Tetlock, P. E. (1986). Psychological advice on foreign policy: What do we have to contribute? *American Psychologist, 41,* 557–567

Thase, M., Simons, A. D., Cahalane, J., McGeary, J., & Harden, T. (1991). Severity of depression and response to cognitive behavior therapy. *American Journal of Psychiatry, 148,* 784–789.

Thase, M. E., Simons, A. D., McGeary, J., Cahalane, J., Hughes, C., Harden, T., & Friedman, E. (1992). Relapse after cognitive behavior therapy of depression: Potential implications for longer courses of treatment. *American Journal of Psychiatry, 149,* 1046–1052.

Thigpen, C. H., & Cleckley, H. (1954). *The three faces of Eve.* Kingsport, TN: Kingsport Press.

Thomas, D. R. (1993). A model for adaptation–level effects on stimulus generalization. *Psychological Review, 100,* 658–673.

Thomas, W., & Znaniecki, F. (1927). *The Polish peasant in Europe and America.* New York: Alfred A. Knopf.

Thompson, D. A., & Campbell, R. G. (1977). Hunger in humans induced by 2–Deoxy–D–Glucose: Clucoprivic control of taste preference and food intake. *Science, 198,* 1065–1068.

Thoren, P., Floras, J., Hoffman, P., & Seals, D. (1990). Endorphins and exercise: Physiological mechanisms and clinical implications. *Medicine & Science in Sports & Exercise, 22,* 417–428.

Thorndike, E. (1898). Animal intelligence: An experimental study of associative processes in animals. *Psychological Monographs, 2* (Whole No.8).

Thurstone, L. L. (1938). Primary mental abilities. *Psychometric Monographs,* Vol. 1. Chicago: Chicago University Press.

Thurstone, L. L., & Thurstone, T. G. (1962). *Primary mental abilities.* Chicago: Science Research Associates.

Thyer, B. A. (1980). Prolonged in vivo exposure therapy with a 70–year–old woman. *Journal of Behavior Therapy and Experimental Psychiatry, 11.*

Tienari, P. (1991). Interaction between genetic vulnerability and family environment: The Finnish adoptive family study of schizophrenia. *Acta Psychiatrica Scandinavica, 84,* 460–465.

Tinbergen, N. (1951) *The study of instinct.* Oxford: Clarendon Press.

Tizard, B. & Hodges, J. (1978). The effects of early institutional rearing on the development of eight–year old children. *The Journal of Child Psychology and Psychiatry, 19,* 99–108.

Tolliver, L. M. (1983). Social and mental health needs of the aged. *American Psychologist, 38,* 316–18.

Tolman, E. C. (1948). Cognitive maps in rats and men. *The Psychological Review, 55,* 189–208.

Tolman, E. C., & Honzik, C. H. (1930). Insight in rats. *University of California Publications in Psychology, 4,* 215–232.

Tomkins, S. S. (1962). *Affect, imagery, consciousness,* Vol. I: *The positive affects.* New York: Springer–Verlag.

Tomkins, S. S. (1970). Affect as the primary motivational system. In M. B. Arnold (Ed.), *Feelings and emotions: The Loyola Symposium.* New York: Academic.

Tomkins, S. S. (1980). Affect as amplification: Some modifications in theory. In R. Plutchik & H. Kellerman (Eds.), *Emotion: Theory, research, and experience,* Vol. I: *Theories of emotion.* New York: Academic Press.

Tomkins, S. S. (1986). Script theory. In J. Aronoff, A. I. Radin, and R. Zucker (Eds.), *The emergence of personality* (pp. 147–216). New York: Springer.

Tomlinson–Keasey, C. and Little, T. D. (1990). Predicting educational attainment, occupational achievement, intellectual skill, and personal adjustment among gifted men and women. *Journal of Educational Psychology, 82,* 442–455.

Tooby, J., & Cosmides, L. (1990). On the universality of human nature and the uniqueness of the individual: The role of genetics and adaptation. *Journal of Personality, 58,* 17–68.

Tooby, J., & Cosmides, L. (1992). The psychological foundations of culture. In J.H. Barkow, L. Cosmides, & J. Tooby (Eds.), *The adapted mind: Evolutionary psychology an the generation of culture* (pp. 19–136). New York: Oxford University Press.

Torgersen, S. (1988) Genetic factors in anxiety disorders. *Archives of General Psychiatry, 40,* 1085–1089.

Torrey. E. F. (1986). *Witchdoctors and psychiatrists: The common roots of psychotherapy and its future.* New York: Aronson.

Towler, G. (1986). From zero to 100: Coaction in a natural setting. *Perceptual and Motor Skills, 62,* 377–378.

Traiwick, M. (1990). The ideology of love in a Tamil family. In O. M. Lynch (Ed.), *Divine passions: The social construction of emotion in India.* Berkeley: University of California Press.

Trandis, H. (1990). Cross–cultural studies of individualism and collectivism. In J. Berman (Ed.), *Nebraska symposium on motivation, 1989* (pp. 42–133). Lincoln: University of Nebraska Press.

Triandis, H. (1977). Some universals of social behavior. *Personality and Social Psychology Bulletin, 4,* 1–16.

Triandis, H. (1989). The self and social behavior in differing cultural contexts. *Psychological Bulletin, 96,* 506–520.

Triandis, H. (1993). An etic–emic analysis of individualism and collectivism. *Journal of Cross–Cultural Psychology, 24,* 366–383.

Triandis, H. (1993). Collectivism and individualism as cultural syndromes. *Cross–Cultural Research: The Journal of Comparative Social Science, 27,* 155–180.

Triandis, H. (1994). *Culture and social behavior.* New York: McGraw–Hill.

Triandis, H., Bontempo, R., Villareal, M. T., & Asai, M. (1988). Individualism and collectivism: Cross–cultural perspectives on self–ingroup relationships. *Journal of Personality and Social Psychology, 54,* 323–338.

Triandis, H.,Davis, E. E. and Takezawa, S. I. (1965). Some determinants of social distance among American, German, and Japanese students. *Journal of Personality and Social Psychology, 2,* 540–551.

Triandis, H., Malpass, R. S., & Davidson, A. R. (1973). Psychology and culture. In P. Mussen and M. Rosenzweig (Eds.), *Annual Review of Psychology, 24,* 355–378.

Triandis, H. (Ed.) (1980). *Handbook of cross–cultural psychology,* 6 vols. Boston: Allyn & Bacon.

Triplett, N. (1897). The dynamogenic factors in pacemaking and competition. *American Journal of Psychology, 9,* 507–533.

Trivers, R. (1972). Parental investment and sexual selection. In B. Campbell (Ed.), *Sexual selection and the descent of man: 1871–1971* (pp. 136–179). Chicago: Aldine.

Trivers, R. L. (1971). The evolution of reciprocal altruism. *Quarterly Review of Biology, 46,* 35–57.

Trivers, R. L. (1983). The evolution of cooperation. In D. L. Bridgeman (Ed.), *The nature of prosocial behavior.* New York: Academic Press.

Tronick, E., Morelli, G., & Ivey, P. (1992). The Efe forager infant and toddler's pattern of social relationships: Multiple and simultaneous. *Developmental Psychologist, 28,* 568–577.

Tuber, S. (1992). Empirical and clinical assessment of children's object relations and object representations. *Psychoanalytic Psychology, 4,* 145-159.

Tucker, D. M., Novelly, R. A., & Walker, P. J. (1987). Hyperreligiosity in temporal lobe epilepsy: Redefining the relationship. *Journal of Nervous and Mental Disease, 175,* 181–184.

Tucker, P. & Jones, D. M. (1991). Voice as interface: An overview. *International Journal of Human–Computer Interaction, 3,* 145–170.

Tuddenham, R. D. (1962). The nature & measurement of intelligence. In L. Postman (Ed.), *Psychology in the making: Histories of selected research problems* (pp. 469–525). New York: Alfred A. Knopf.

Tulving, E. (1972). Episodic and semantic memory. In E. Tulving and W. Donaldson (Eds.), *Organization of memory* (pp. 381–403). New York: Academic Press.

Tulving, E. (1987). Multiple memory systems and consciousness. *Human Neurobiology, 6*(2), 67–80.

Tulving, E. (1991). Memory research is not a zero-sum game. *American Psychologist, 46*(1), 41–42.

Tulving, E., & Thomson, D. M. (1973). Encoding specificity and retrieval processes in episodic memory. *Psychological Review, 80,* 359–380.

Turkheimer, E. (1991). Individual and group differences in adoption studies of IQ. *Psychological Bulletin, 110*, 392–405.

Turner, E. A., & Wright, J. (1965). Effects of severity of threat and perceived availability on the attractiveness of objects. *Journal of Personality and Social Psychology, 2*, 128–132.

Turner, J. R., Sherwood, A., & Light, K. (Eds.). (1992). *Individual differences in cardiovascular response to stress.* New York: Guilford Press.

Turner, S., Beidel, D., & Jacob, R. (1994). Social phobia: A comparison of behavior therapy and atenolol. *Journal of Consulting and Clinical Psychology, 62*, 350–358.

Turner, V. (1969). *The ritual process.* Chicago: Aldine.

Tuszynski, M., U, H.S., Yoshida, K., & Gage, F. (1991). Recombinant human nerve growth factor infusions prevent cholinergic neuronal degeneration in the adult primate brain. *Annals of Neurology, 30*, 625–636.

Tversky, A., & Kahneman, D. (1973). Availability: A heuristic for judging frequency and probability. *Cognitive Psychology, 5*, 207–232.

Tversky, A., & Kahneman, D. (1974). Judgment under uncertainty: Heuristics and biases. *Science, 185*, 1124–1131.

Tversky, A., & Kahneman, D. (1981). Extensional vs. intuitive reasoning: The conjunction fallacy in probability judgment. *Psychological Review, 90*, 293–315.

Tye, M. (1991). *The imagery debate.* Cambridge, MA: MIT Press.

Tyler, L. E. (1965). *The psychology of human differences.* New York: Appleton–Century–Crofts.

Tzeng, O. J., Hung, Cohen, & Wang. (1979). Visual lateralization effect in reading Chinese characters. *Nature, 282*, 499–501.

Udry, J. R., Billy, J. O. G., Morris, N. M., Groff, T. R., & Raj, J. H. (1985). Serum androgenic hormones motivate sexual behavior in adolescent boys. *Fertility and Sterility, 43*, 90–94.

Uleman, J. S. & Bargh, J. A. (Eds.). (1989). *Unintended thought.* New York.: Guilford Press.

Ulrich, R. E. (1991). Animal rights, animal wrongs, and the question of balance. *Psychological Science, 2*, 197–201.

Ulrich, R. S. (1984). View through a window may influence recovery from surgery. *Science, 224*, 420–421.

Urban, J., Carlson, E., Egeland, B., & Sroufe, L. A. (1991). Patterns of individual adaptation across childhood. *Development and Psychopathology, 3*, 445–460.

Urist, J. (1980). Object relations. In R.W. Woody (Ed.), *Encyclopedia of Clinical Assessment*, Vol. 2 (pp. 821–833). San Francisco: Jossey Bass.

Uusi–Oukari, M., & Korpi, E. R. (1991). Specific alterations in the cerebellar GABA–sub(A) receptors of an alcohol–sensitive ANT rat line. *Alcoholism: Clinical and Experimental Research, 15*, 241–248.

Vaillant, G. (1977). *Adaptation to life.* Boston: Little, Brown.

Vaillant, G. (1990). Natural history of male psychological health: XII. A 45–year study of predictors of successful aging at age 65. *American Journal of Psychiatry, 147*, 31–37.

Vaillant, G., & Perry, J. C. (1985). Personality disorders. In H. I. Kaplan & B.J. Sadock (Eds.), *Comprehensive textbook of psychiatry.* (4th ed.) Baltimore, MD: Williams & Wilkins

Vaillant, G., & Vaillant, C. O. (1990). Determinants and consequences of creativity in a cohort of gifted women. *Psychology of Women Quarterly, 14*, 607–616..

Vaillant, G., & Vaillant, C. (1990). Natural history of male psychology health: XII. A 45–year study of predictors of successful aging at age 65. *American Journal of Psychiatry, 147*, 31–37.

Valenstein, E. S. (1986). *Great and desperate cures.* New York: Basic Books.

Valenstein, E. S. (1988). The history of lobotomy: A cautionary tale. *Michigan Quarterly, 27*, 417–437.

Valins, S. (1966). Cognitive effects of false heart–rate feedback. *Journal of Personality and Social Psychology, 4*, 400–408.

Vallerand, R. J., Pelletier, L. G., Blais, M. R., Briere, N. M., Senecal, C., & Vallieres, E. F. (1993). On the assessment of intrinsic, extrinsic, and a motivation in education: Evidence on the concurrent and construct validity of the Academic Motivation Scale. *Educational and Psychological Measurement, 53*, 159–172.

van IJzendoorn, M., & Kroonenberg, P. (1988). Cross–cultural patterns of attachment: A meta–analysis of the strange situation. *Child Development, 59*, 147–156.

van Someren, M. (1984). Learning mechanisms in AMBER. *Communication and Cognition, 17*, 67–85.

Vance, E. B., & Wagner, N. D. (1976). Written descriptions of orgasm: A study of sex differences. In R. Green (Ed.), *Archives of Sexual Behavior*, Vol. 5.

Vanden Belt, A., & Peterson, C. (1991). Parental explanatory style and its relationship to the classroom performance of disabled and nondisabled children. *Cognitive Therapy & Reserach, 15*, 331–341.

Varley, C. K. (1984). Attention deficit disorder (the hyperactivity syndrome): A review of selected issues. *Developmental and Behavioral Pediatrics, 5*, 254–258.

Vaughn, B. E., Stevenson–Hinde, J., Waters, E., & Kotsaftis, A. (1992). Attachment security and temperament in infancy and early childhood: Some conceptual clarifications. *Developmental Psychology, 28*, 463–473.

Verbrugge, L. M. (1989). The twain meet: Empirical explanations of sex differences in health and mortality. *Journal of Health and Social Behavior, 30*, 282–304.

Vernon, P. A., & Mori, M. (1992). Intelligence, reaction times, and peripheral nerve conduction velocity. Special Issue: Biology and intelligence. *Intelligence, 16*, 273–288.

Vernon, P. A., & Weese, S. E. (1993). Predicting intelligence with multiple speed of information–processing tests. *Personality and Individual Differences, 14*, 413–419.

Veroff, J., Douvan, E., & Kulka, R. A. (1981). *The Inner American: A self–portrait from 1957 to 1976.* New York: Basic Books.

Veroff, J., Kulka, R., & Douvan, E. (1981). *Mental health in America: Patterns of help–seeking from 1957–1976.* New York: Basic Books.

Viken, R. J., Rose, R. J., Kaprio, J., & Koskenvuo, M. (1994). A developmental genetic analysis of adult personality: Extroversion and neuroticism from 18 to 59 years of age. *Journal of Personality and Social Psychology, 66*, 722–730.

Vinogravdov, S., & Yalom, I. (1989). *Concise guide to group psychotherapy.* Washington, DC: American Psychiatric Press.

Vives, F., & Oltras, C. M. (1992). Plasma levels of beta–endorphin, ACTH, glucose, free fatty acids and lactata in athletes after running races of different distances. *Medical Science Research, 20*, 67–69.

Vokey, J. R., & Read, D. (1985). Subliminal messages: Between the devil and the media. *American Psychologist, 11*, 1231–1239.

Volavka, J., Cooper, T., Crobor, P., Bitter, I., Meisner, M., et al. (1992). Haloperidol blood levels and clinical effects, agpaloperidol blood levels and clinical effects. *Archives of General Psychiatry, 49*, 354–361.

Von Dras, D., & Blumenthal, H. T. (1992). Dementia of the aged: Disease or atypical accelerated aging? Biopathological and psychological perspectives. *Journal of the American Geriatrics Society, 40*, 285–294.

Von Hofstein, C. (1982). Eye–hand coordination in the newborn. *Developmental Psychology, 18*, 450–61.

Von Ijzendoorn, M. (in press). Attachment representations in mothers, fathers, adolescents, and clinical groups: A meta–analytic search for normative data. *Journal of Consulting and Clinical Psychology.*

Von Senden, M. (1960). *Space and sight.* (Public Health transcript). New York: Free Press.

Vormbrock, J. (1993). Attachment theory as applied to wartime and job–related marital separation. *Psychological Bulletin, 114*, 122–144.

Vygotsky, L. (1978). *Mind in society: The development of higher psychological processes*, M.Cole, V. John-Steiner, S. Scribner, & E. Souberman (Eds.). Cambridge: Cambridge University Press.

Wachtel, P. (1977). *Psychoanalysis and behavior therapy: toward an integration*. New York: Basic Books.

Wachtel, P. L. (1987). *Action and insight*. New York: Guilford Press.

Wagman, M. (1991). *Artificial intelligence and human cognition: A theoretical comparison of two realms of intellect*. New York: Praeger.

Wagner, A. W., & Linehan, M. M. (1994). Relationship between childhood sexual abuse and topography of parasuicide among women with borderline personality disorder. *Journal of Personality Disorders, 8*, 1–9.

Wagner, R. V. (1985). Psychology and the threat of nuclear war. *American Psychologist, 40*, 531–535.

Wagstaff, G. F. (1984). The enhancement of witness memory by "hypnosis": A review and methodological critique of the experimental literature. British *Journal of Experimental and Clinical Hypnosis, 2*, 3–12.

Wakefield, J. F. (1991). The outlook for creativity tests. *Journal of Creative Behavior, 25*, 184–193.

Walberg, H. J. (1971). Varieties of adolescent creativity and the high school environment. *Exceptional Children, 38*, 111–116.

Walberg, H. J., & Shanahan, T. (1985). Productive influence on high school student achievement. *Journal of Educational Research, 78*, 357–363.

Wald, G. (1964). *The receptors of human color vision. Science, 145*, 1007–1017.

Wald, G. (1968). Molecular basis of visual excitation. *Science, 162*, 230–239.

Waldrop, M. M. (1988). Toward a unified theory of cognition. *Science, 241*, 27–29.

Walker, J. R., El-Guebaly, N., Ross, C., & Currie, R. F. (1992). Where do you turn for help? A community survey of the use of professionals, reading materials, and group programs for three problems in living. *Journal of Community Psychology, 20*, 84–89.

Walker, L. J. (1989). A longitudinal study of moral reasoning. *Child Development, 60*, 157–166.

Wallace, A.F.C. (1956). Revitalization movements. *American Anthropologist, 58*, 264–281.

Wallace, A.F.C. (1959). Cultural determinants of response to hallucinatory experiences. *Archives of General Psychiatry, 1*, 58–69.

Wallace, B. (1993). Day persons, night persons, and variability in hypnotic susceptibility. *Journal of Personality and Social Psychology, 64*, 827–833.

Wallace, P. (1977). Individual discrimination of humans by odor. *Physiology and Behavior, 19*, 577–579.

Wallach, M. A. (1970). Creativity. In P. H. Mussen (Ed.), *Carmichael's Manual of Child Psychology*, Vol. 1. (pp. 1211–1272). (3rd ed.) New York: John Wiley.

Wallach, M. A. (1985). Creativity testing and giftedness. In F.D Horowitz & M. O'Brien (Eds.), *The gifted and talented: Developmental perspectives* (pp. 99–123). Washington, DC: American Psychological Association.

Waller, N., Kojetin, B., Bouchard, T., & Lykken, D. (1990). Genetic and environmental influences on religious interests, attitudes, and values: A study of twins reared apart and together. *Psychological Science, 1*, 138–142.

Wallerstein, J., Corbin, S., & Lewis, T. (1988). Children of divorce: A 10-year study. In E. M. Hetherington & J. Arasteh (Eds.). *Impact of divorce, single parenting, and stepparenting on children* (pp. 197–214). Hillsdale, NJ: Erlbaum.

Wallerstein, R. S. (1988). One psychoanalysis or many? *International Journal of Psycho-Analysis, 69*, 5–22.

Wallerstein, R. S. (1989). The psychotherapy research project of the Menninger Foundation: An overview. *Journal of Consulting and Clinical Psychology, 57*, 195–205.

Walsh, B. T., Hadigan, C. M., Devlin, M. J., Gladis, M., & Roose, S. (1991). Long-term outcome of antidepressant treatment for bulimia nervosa. *American Journal of Psychiatry, 148*, 1206–1212.

Walster, E., Aronson, V., Abrahams, D., & Rottman, L. (1966). The importance of physical attractiveness in dating behavior. *Journal of Personality and Social Psychology, 4*, 508–516.

Walster, E., & Festinger, L. (1962). The effectiveness of 'overheard' persuasive communications. *Journal of Abnormal and Social Psychology, 65*, 395–402.

Walster, E., & Walster, G. W. (1978). *A new look at love*. Reading, MA: Addison-Wesley Publishing Company.

Walters, J. M., & Gardner, H. (1986). The theory of multiple intelligences: Some issues and answers. In R. J. Sternberg & R. K. Walters, (Eds.), *Practical Intelligence: Nature and origins of competence in the everyday world*. New York: Cambridge University Press.

Wangesteen, O., & Carlson, A. (1931). Hunger sensation after total gastrectomy. *Proceedings of the Society of Experimental Biology, 28*, 545–547.

Ward, I. L. (1984). The prenatal stress syndrome: Current status. *Psychoneuroendocrinology, 9*, 3–11.

Warren, R. (1984). Perceptual restoration of obliterated sounds. *Psychological Bulletin, 96*, 371–383.

Warren, R. M. (1970). Perceptual restoration of missing speech sounds. *Science, 167*, 392–393.

Warren, R. M., & Warren, R. P. (1970). Auditory illusions and confusions. *Scientific American, 223*, 30–36.

Warwick, Z. S., Hall, W. G., Pappas, T. N., & Schiffman, S. S. (1993). Taste and smell sensations enhance the satiating effect of both a high-carbohydrate and a high-fat meal in humans. *Physiology and Behavior, 53*, 553–563.

Wason, P., & Johnson-Laird, P. (1972). *The psychology of reasoning: Structure and content*. Cambridge, MA: Harvard University Press.

Wason, P. C. (1960). On the failure to eliminate hypotheses in a conceptual task. *Quarterly Journal of Experimental Psychology, 12*, 129–140.

Wason, P. C. (1968). Reasoning about a rule. *Quarterly Journal of Experimental Psychology, 20*, 273–281.

Waters, E., Wippman, J., & Sroufe, J. A. (1979). Attachment, positive affect, and competence in the peer group: Two studies of construct validation. *Child Development, 50*, 821–29.

Watkin, L. R., & Mayer, D. J. (1982). Organization of endogenous opiate and nonopiate pain control systems. *Science, 216*, 1185–1193.

Watson, D., & Clark, L. A. (1992). Affects separable and inseparable: On the hierarchical arrangement of the negative affects. *Journal of Personality and Social Psychology, 62*, 489–505.

Watson, D., & Tellegen, A. (1985). Toward a consensual structure of mood. *Psychological Bulletin, 98*, 219–25.

Watson, J. (1925). *Behaviorism*. New York: W. W. Norton, 1970.

Watson, J., & Rayner, R. (1920). Conditioned emotional reactions. *Journal of Experimental Psychology, 3*, 1–14.

Weale, R. (1982). *Focus on vision*. Cambridge, MA: Harvard University Press.

Weaver, C. A. (1993). Do you need a flash to form a flashbulb memory? *Journal of Experimental Psychology General, 122*, 39–46.

Weaver, E. G. (1949). *Theory of hearing*. New York: John Wiley.

Weber, M. (1924). Bureaucracy. In H. Gerth & C. W. Mills (Eds.), *From Max Weber: Essays in sociology*. New York: Oxford University Press, 1946.

Wechsler, D. (1949). *The Wechsler Intelligence Scale for Children*. New York: Psychological Corp.

Wechsler, D. (1981). *WAIS-R Manual: Wechsler Adult Intelligence Scale—Revised*. San Antonio, Tex.: Psychological Corp.

Wegner, D. (1989). *White bears and other unwanted thoughts*. New York: Viking Press.

Wegner, D., & Erber, R. (1992). The hyperaccessibility of suppressed thoughts. *Journal of Personality and Social Psychology, 63*, 903–912.

Weinberg, R. A. (1989). Intelligence and IQ: Landmark issues and great debates. *American Psychologist, 44*, 98–104.

Weinberg, R. A., Scarr, S. & Waldman, I. D. (1992). The Minnesota Transracial

Adoption Study: A follow-up of IQ test performance at adolescence. *Intelligence, 16,* 117–135.

Weinberger, D. A. (1990). The construct validity of the repressive coping style. In J. L. Singer (Ed.), *Repression and dissociation: Implications for personality, psychopathology and health.* Chicago: University of Chicago Press.

Weinberger, D. R., Berman, K. F., Suddath, R., & Torrey, E. F. (1992). Evidence of dysfunction of a prefrontal-limbic network in schizophrenia: A magnetic resonance imaging and regional cerebral blood flow study of discordant monozygotic twins. *American Journal of Psychiatry, 149,* 890–897.

Weinberger, D. R., & Wyatt, R. J. (1983). Enlarged cerebral ventricles in schizophrenia. *Psychiatric Annals, 13,* 412–418.

Weinberger, J. (1993). Common factors in psychotherapy. In G. Stricker & J.Gold (Eds.), *Comprehensive handbook of psychotherapy integration* (pp. 43–56). New York: Plenum Press.

Weinberger, J., & Hardaway, R. (1990). Subliminal separating science from myth in subliminal psychodynamic activation. *Clinical Psychology Review, 10,* 727–756.

Weinberger, J. (in press). Heart and head: Are they one? In H. Kurtzman (Ed.), *Cognition and psychodynamics.* New York: Oxford University Press.

Weinberger, J., & Silverman, L. (1988). Testability and empirical verification of psychoanalytic dynamic propositions through subliminal psychodynamic activation. *Unpublished manuscript,* H.A. Murray Center, Harvard University.

Weiner, B. (1974). *Achievement motivation and attribution theory.* Morristown, NJ: General Learning Press.

Weiner, B. (1985). An attributional theory of achievement motivation and emotion. *Psychological Review, 92,* 548–573.

Weiner, B. (1985). 'Spontaneous' causal thinking. *Psychological Bulletin, 97,* 74–84.

Weiner, H. (1985). Schizophrenia: Etiology. In H. I. Kaplan & B. J. Sadock (Eds.), *Comprehensive textbook of psychiatry.* (4th ed.). Baltimore, MD: Williams & Wilkins.

Weiner, R. D., & Coffey, C. E. (1988). Indications for use of electroconvulsive therapy. In A.J. Frances & R. E. Hales (Eds.), *Review of Psychiatry,* Vol. 7. Washington, DC: American Psychiatric Press.

Weiner, R. D., & Krystal, A. D. (1994). The present use of electroconvulsive therapy. *Annual Review of Medicine, 45,* 273–281.

Weisberg, P., & Waldrop, P. B. (1972). Fixed-interval work habits of congress. *Journal of Applied Behavior Analysis, 5,* 93–97.

Weiskrantz, L. (1986). *Blindsight: A case history and implications.* New York: Oxford University Press.

Weiskrantz, L., Warrington, E., Sanders, M. D., & Marshall, J. (1974). Visual capacity in the hemianopic field following a restricted occipital ablation. *Brain, 97,* 709–728.

Weiss, B., Dodge, K., Bates, J., & Pettit, G. (1992). Some consequences of early harsh discipline: Child aggression and a maladaptive social information processing style. *Child Development, 63,* 1321–1335.

Weiss, G., Hechtman, L., Milroy, T., & Perlman, T. (1985). Psychiatric status of hyperactives as adults: A controlled prospective 15-year follow-up of 63 hyperactive children. *Journal of the American Academy of Child Psychiatry, 24,* 211–220.

Weiss, R. S. (1986). Continuities and transformations in social relationships from childhood to adulthood. In W.W. Hartup & Z. Rubin (Eds.), *Relationships and development,* pp. 95–110. Hillsdale, NJ: Erlbaum.

Weiss, V. (1992). Major genes of general intelligence. *Personality and Individual Differences, 13,* 1115–1134.

Weisse, C. S. (1992). Depression and immunocompetence: A review of the literature. *Psychological Bulletin, 111,* 475–489.

Weissman, M. M., & Boyd, J. H. (1985). Affective disorders: Epidemiology. In H. I. Kaplan & B. J. Sadock (Eds.), *Comprehensive textbook of psychiatry.* (4th ed.). Baltimore, MD: Williams & Wilkins.

Weizenbaum, J. (1966). ELIZA—A computer program for the study of natural language communication between man and machine. *Communiction of the Association of Computing Machinery, 9,* 36–45.

Welch, R. B. (1978). *Perceptual modification.* NewYork: Academic Press.

Welford, A. (1984). Psychomotor performance. *Annual Review of Gerontology and Geriatrics, 4,* 237–74.

Wells, G. L. & Loftus, E. F. (Eds.) (1984). *Eyewitness testimony: Psychological perspectives.* Cambridge: Cambridge University Press.

Wells, G. L. & Turtle, J.W. (1987). Eyewitness testimony: Current knowledge and emerging controversies. *Canadian Journal of Behavioural Science, 19*(4), 363–388.

Werheimer, M. (1961). Psychomotor coordination of auditory and visual space at birth. *Science, 134,* 1692.

Werker, J. F. & Lalonde, C. E. (1988). Cross-language speech perception: Initial capabilities and developmental change. *Developmental Psychology, 24,* 672–683.

Werker, J. F. & Tees, R. C. (1984). Cross-language speech perception: Evidence for perceptual reorganization during the first year of life. *Infant Behavior and Development, 7,* 49–63.

Werker, J. F., & Tees, R. C. (1992). The organization and reorganization of human speech perception. *Annual Review of Neuroscience, 15,* 377–402.

Werner, E. (1979). *Cross-cultural child development: A review from the planet earth.* Monterey, CA: Brooks/Cole.

Werner, H. (1948). *Comparative psychology of mental development.* (rev. ed.). Chicago: Follett.

Wernick, R. (1980). One-eyed jacks, like the rest of us, aren't that wild. *Smithsonian,* 63–71.

Wertenbaker, L. (1981). *The eye: Window to the world.* Washington, DC: U.S. News books.

Wertsch, J., & Kanner, B. (1992). A sociocultural approach to intellectual development. In R. Sternberg & C.A. Berg (Eds.), *Intellectual development* (pp. 328–349). New York: Cambridge University Press.

Wesley, F., & Sullivan, E. (Eds.). (1986). *Human Growth and Development.* New York: Human Services Press.

West, S. G., Gunn, S. P., & Chernicky, P. (1975). Ubiquitous Watergate: An attributional analysis. *Journal of Personality and Social Psychology, 32,* 5–65.

Westen, D. (l985). *Self and society: Narcissism, collectivism, and the development of morals.* New York: Cambridge University Press.

Westen, D. (1990). Psychoanalytic approaches to personality. In L. Pervin (Ed.), *Handbook of personality: Theory and research* (pp.21–65). New York: Guilford Press.

Westen, D. (1992). The cognitive self and the psychoanalytic self: Can we put our selves together? *Psychological Inquiry, 3,* 1–13.

Westen, D. (1994). Toward an integrative model of affect regulation: Applications to social-psychological research. *Journal of Personality, 62,* 641–647.

Westen, D., Klepser, J., Ruffins, S., Silverman, M., Lifton, N., & Boekamp, J. (1991). Object relations in childhood and adolescence: The development of working representations. *Journal of Consulting and Clinical Psychology, 59,* 400–409.

Westen, D., Lohr, N., Silk, K., Gold, L., & Kerber, K. (1990). Object relations and social cognition in borderlines, major depressives, and normals: A TAT analysis. *Psychological Assessment: A Journal of Consulting and Clinical Psychology, 2,* 355–364.

Westen, D., Ludolph, P., Misle, B., Ruffins, S., & Block, M. J. (1990). Physical and sexual abuse in adolescent girls with borderline personality disorder. *American Journal of Orthopsychiatry, 60,* 55–66.

Wet, R. B. (1989). Sensuality/sexuality of the middle years. In S. Hunter & M. Sundel (Eds.), *Midlife myths: Findings and practice implications* (pp. 31–50). Newbury Park, CA: Sage Publications.

Wever, E. G., & Bray, C. W. (1937). The perception of low tones and the resonance-volley theory. *Journal of Psychology, 3,* 101–114.

Whalen, C., & Henker, B. (1991). Therapies for hyperactive children: Comparisons, combinations, and compromises. *Journal of Consulting and Clinical Psychology, 59,* 126–137.

Wheeless, L. R., Barraclough, R., & Stewart, R. (1983). Compliance–gaining and power in persuasion. In R.N. Bostrom (Ed.), *Communication Yearbook,* Vol. 7. Beverly Hills, CA: Sage.

Whipple, B., Josimovich, J.B., and Komisaruk, B. R. (1990). Sensory thresholds during the antepartum, intrapartum and postpartum periods. *International Journal of Nursing Studies, 27,* 213–221.

Whitam, F., & Mathy, R. (1991). Childhood cross–gender behavior of homosexual females in Brazil, Peru, the Philippines, and the United States. *Archives of Sexual Behavior, 20,* 151–170.

Whitbourne, S. K., & Hulicka, I. (1990). Ageism in undergraduate psychology texts. *American Psychologist, 45,* 1127–1136.

White, C. B. (1978). Moral development in Bahamian school children: A 3–year examination of Kohlberg's stages of moral development. *Developmental Psychology, 14,* 58–65.

White, R. K. (1984). *Fearful warriors: A psychological profile of U.S.–Soviet relations.* New York: Free Press.

White, R. W. (1959). Motivation reconsidered: The concept of competence. *Psychological Review, 66,* 297–333.

Whiting, B., & Edwards, C. P. (1973). A cross–cultural analysis of the behavior of children aged 3–11. *Journal of Social Psychology, 91,* 171–88.

Whiting, B. B., & Whiting, J.W.M. (1975). *Children of six cultures: A psychocultural analysis.* Cambridge, MA: Harvard University Press.

Whiting, J. (1964). The effects of climate on certain cultural practices. In W. Goodenough (Ed.), *Explorations in cultural anthropology: Essays in honor of George Peter Murdock* (pp.511–544). New York: McGraw-Hill.

Whiting, J. W. M. & Child, I. L. (1953). *Child training and personality: A cross–cultural study.* New Haven, Conn.: Yale University Press.

Whiting, J. W. M., & Whiting, B. B. (1973). Altruistic and egoistic behavior is six cultures. In L. Nader & T.W. Marekzki (Eds.), *Cultural illness and health: Essays in human adaptation.* Washington, DC: American Anthropological Association.

Whorf, B. L. (1956). *Language, thought, and reality.* Cambridge, MA: MIT Press.

Wicker, A. W. (1969). Attitudes versus action: The relationship of verbal and overt behavioral responses to attitude objects. *Journal of Soc. Issues, 25,* 41–78.

Wicklund, R. A. and Brehm, J. W. (1976). *Perspectives on cognitive dissonance.* Hillsdale, NJ: Erlbaum.

Wiebe, D. J. (1991). Hardiness and stress moderation; A test of proposed mechanisms. *Journal of Personality and Social Psychology, 60,* 89–99.

Wiegman, Kuttschreuter, M., & Baarda, B. (1992). A longitudinal study of the effects of television viewing on aggressive and prosocial behaviours. *British Journal of Social Psychology, 31,* 147–164.

Wiesel, T. N. (1982). Postnatal development of the visual cortex and the influence of environment. *Nature, 299,* 583–591.

Wiesel, T. N., & Hubel, D. H. (1960). Receptive fields of ganglion cells in the cat's retina. *Journal of Physiology, 153,* 583–594.

Wiggins, J. G. (1990). The future of addictive behaviors: The next ten years. Special issue: Psychology of addictive behavior:1990's. *Psychology of Addictive Behaviors, 4,* 33–35.

Wiggins, J. S., & Pincus, A. L. (1992). Personality: Structure and assessment. *Annual Review of Psychology, 43,* 473–504.

Wilcox, C. & Williams, L. (1990). Taking stock of schema theory. *Social Science Journal, 27(4),* 373–393.

Wilfley, D. E., Agras, W.S., Telch, C., & Rossiter, E. (1993). Group cognitive–behavioral therapy and group interpersonal psychotherapy for the non-purging bulimic individual: A controlled comparison. *Journal of Consulting and Clinical Psychology, 61,* 296–305.

Wilkins, M. C. (1982). The effect of changed material on ability to do formal syllogistic reasoning. *Archives of Psychology, 16,* 1–83.

Wilkinson, R. & Allison, S. (1989). Age and simple reaction time: Decade differences for 5,325 subjects. *Journal of Gerontology, 44,* 29–36.

Wilkinson, S. C. (1993). WISC–R profiles of children with superior intellectual ability. *Gifted Child Quarterly, 37,* 84–91.

Williams, C., & Bybee, J. (1994). What do children feel guilty about? Developmental and gender differences. *Developmental Psychology, 30,* 617–623.

Williams, C. D. (1959). The elimination of tantrum behavior by extinction procedures. *Journal of Abnormal and Social Psychology, 59,* 269.

Williams, C. L., & Berry, J. W. (1991). Primary prevention of acculturative stress among refugees: Application of psychological theory and practice. *American Psychologist, 46,* 632–641.

Williams, D. E., & Thompson, J. K. (1993). Biology and behavior: A set–point hypothesis of psychological functioning. *Behavior Modification, 17,* 43–57.

Williams, G.–J., Power, K. G., Millar, H. R., & Freeman, C. P. (1993). Comparison of eating disorders and other dietary/weight groups on measures of perceived control, assertiveness, self–esteem, and self–directed hostility. *International Journal of Eating Disorders, 14,* 27–32.

Williams, J. B. W., Gibbon, M., First, M., Spitzer, R., Davies, M., Borus, J., Howes, M., Kane, J., Pope, H., Rounsaville, B., & Wittchen, H. (1992). The structured clinical interview for DSM–III–R (SCID) II. Multisite test–retest reliability. *Archives of General Psychiatry, 49,* 630–636.

Williams, J. E., & Best, D. L. (1982). *Measuring sex stereotypes: A thirty–nation study.* Beverly Hills, CA: Sage.

Williams, J. E., & Best, D .L. (1990). *Sex and psyche: Gender and self viewed cross–culturally.* Newbury Park, CA: Sage.

Williams, J. H. (1983). The emergence of gender differences. In W. Damon (Ed.), *Social and personality development.* New York: W. W. Norton.

Williams, L. M. (1994). Recall of childhood trauma: A prospective study of women's memories of child sexual abuse. *Journal of Consulting and Clinical Psychology, 62,* 1167–1176

Williams, R. L. (1972). *The BITCH Test (Black Intelligence Test of Cultural Homogeneity).* St. Louis: Williams & Associates.

Wills, T. (1981). Downward comparison principles in social psychology. *Psychological Bulletin, 90,* 245–271.

Wilson, E. D. (1963). Phermones. *Scientific American,* 2–11.

Wilson, E. O. (1975). *Sociobiology: A new synthesis.* Cambridge, MA: Harvard University Press.

Wilson, G., & Fairburn, C. (1993). Cognitive treatments for eating disorders. *Journal of Consulting and Clinical Psychology, 61,* 261–269.

Wilson, T., Lisle, D., Schooler, J., & Hodges, S. (1993). Introspecting about reasons can reduce post–choice satisfaction. *Personality & Social Psychology Bulletin, 19,* 331–339.

Wilson, T. D., Lisle, D. J., & Schooler, J. W. (1990). Some undesirable effects of self–reflection. *Unpublished manuscript,* University of Virginia, Department of Psychology, Charlottesville.

Wilson, T. D. & Schooler, J. W. (1991). Thinking too much: Introspection can reduce the quality of preferences and decisions. *Journal of Personality and Social Psychology, 60,* 181–192.

Wilson, W., & Miller, H. (1968). Repetition, order of presentation and timing of arguments and measures as determinants of opinion change. *Journal of Personality and Social Psychology, 9,* 184–188

Winblad, B., Hardy, J., Backman, L., & Nilsson, L–G. (1985). Memory function and brain biochemistry in normal aging and in senile dementia. In D. S. Olton, E. Gamzu, & S. Corkin (Eds.), *Memory dysfunctions: An integration of animal and human research from preclinical and clinical perspectives.* New York: New York Academy of Sciences.

Winchel, R., & Stanley, M. (1991). Self-injurious behavior: A review of the behavior and biology of self–mutilation. *American Journal of Psychiatry, 148,* 306–317.

Winograd, E., & Neissier, U. (Eds.). (1993).

Affect and accuracy in recall: Studies of "flashbulb" memories. New York: Cambridge University Press.

Winslow, R. W., Franzini, L., & Hwang, J. (1992). Perceived peer norms, casual sex, and AIDS prevention. *Journal of Applied Psychology, 22,* 1809–1827.

Winson, J. (1985). *Brain and psyche: The biology of the unconscious.* New York: Anchor.

Winter, D. (1993). Power, affiliation, and war: Three tests of a motivational model. *Journal of Personality and Social Psychology, 65,* 532–545.

Winter, D. G. (1987). Enhancement of an enemy's power motivation as a dynamic of conflict escalation. *Journal of Personality and Social Psychology, 42,* 41–46.

Winter, D. G. (1987). Power motive distortion in British and German newspapers and diplomatic dispatches at the outbreak of World War I. *Unpublished paper,* Wesleyan University.

Winterbottom, M. R. (1953). The relation of childhood training in independence to achievement motivation. *Unpublished doctoral dissertation,* University of Michigan, Ann Arbor.

Wispe, L. G., & Drambarean, N. C. (1993). Physiological need, word frequency, and visual duration threshold. *Journal of Experimental Psychology, 46,* 25–31.

Witkin, H. A., Dyk, R. B., Faterson, H. F., Goodenough, D. R., & Karp, S. A. (1962). *Psychological differentiation.* London: John Wiley.

Wixom, J., Ludolph, P., & Westen, D. (1993). Quality of depression in borderline adolescents. *Journal of the American Academy of Child & Adolescent Psychiatry, 32,* 1172–1177.

Wixted, J., & Ebbesen, E. (1991). On the form of forgetting. *Psychological Science, 2,* 409–415.

Wober, M. (1987). Perceived risk of disease from alcohol, asbestos, and AIDS: Links with television viewing? *Health Education Research, 2,* 175–184.

Woike, B., & Aronoff, J. (1992). Antecedents of complex social cognitions. *Journal of Personality and Social Psychology, 63,* 97–104.

Wolosin, R. J., Esser, J., & Fine, G. A. (1975). Effects of justification and vocalization on actors' and observers' attributions of freedom. *Journal of Personality, 43,* 612–633.

Wolpe, J. (1958). *Psychotherapy by reciprocal inhibition.* Stanford, CA: Stanford University Press.

Wolpe, J. (Ed.). (1964). *The conditioning therapies: The challenge in psychotherapy.* New York: Holt, Rinehart, & Winston.

Wong, M. M., & Csikszentmihalyi, M. (1991). Affiliation motivation and daily experience: Some issues on gender differences. *Journal of Personality and Social Psychology, 60,* 154–164.

Wong, M. M., & Csikszentmihalyi, M.

(1991). Motivation and academic achievement: The effects of personality traits and the quality of experience. *Journal of Personality, 59,* 539–574.

Wood, J. M., Bootzin, R., Rosenhan, D., Nolen–Hoeksema, S., & Jourden, F. (1992). Effects of the 1989 San Francisco earthquake on frequency and content of nightmares. *Journal of Abnormal Psychology, 101,* 219–224.

Wood, R. & Bandura, A. (1989). Social cognitive theory of organizational management. Special issue: Theory development forum. *Academy of Management Review, 14,* 361–384.

Wood, W., Wong, F., & Chachere, J. G. (1991). Effects of media violence on viewers' aggression in unconstrained social interaction. *Psychological Bulletin, 109,* 371–383.

Woodall, K., & Matthews, K. (1993). Changes in and stability of hostile characteristics: Results from a 4–year longitudinal study of children. *Journal of Personality and Social Psychology, 64,* 491–499.

Woods, J. W. (1956). Taming of the wild Norway rat by rhinencephalic lesions. *Nature, 178,* 869.

Woody, C. D. (1986). Understanding the cellular basis of memory and learning. *Annual Review of Psychology, 37,* 433–493.

Worchel, S., & Brehm, J. W. (1970). Effect of threats to attitudinal freedom as a function of agreement with the communicator. *Journal of Personality and Social Psychology, 14,* 18–22.

Worthington, E. L., Jr., Martin, G. A., Shumate, M., & Carpenter, J. (1983). The effect of brief Lamaze training and social encouragement on pain endurance in a cold pressor tank. *Journal of Applied Social Psychology, 13,* 223–233.

Wright, M. R. (1989). Body image satisfaction in adolescent girls and boys. *Journal of Youth and Adolescence, 18,* 71–84.

Wyatt, G. E., Peters, S. D., & Guthrie, D. (1988a). Kinsey revisited: I. Comparisons of the sexual socialization and sexual behavior of White women over 33 years. *Archives of Sexual Behavior, 17,* 201–239.

Wyatt, G. E., Peters, S. D., & Guthrie, D. (1988b). Kinsey revisited: II. Comparisons of the sexual socialization and sexual behavior of Black women over 33 years. *Archives of Sexual Behavior, 17,* 289–332.

Wyatt, R. J., Freed, W. J., & Hoffer, B. (1985). Functional brain grafts: A distant hope for patients with irreversible brain lesions. *Integrative Psychiatry, 3,* 27–31.

Wyer, R. S., Jr., & Srull, T. K. (1986). Human cognition in its social context. *Psychological Review, 93,* 322–359.

Wylie, R. (1979). *The self–concept, Vol. 2.* Lincoln: University of Nebraska Press.

Wynne, L. C. (1961). The study of intrafamilial alignments and splits in exploratory

family therapy. In N. Ackerman et al. (Eds.), *Exploring the base for family therapy.* New York: Family Service Association of America.

Wynne, L. C., & Singer, M. T. (1963). Thought disorder and family relations of schizophrenics. *Archives of General Psychiatry, 9,* 191–198.

Wyrwicka, W. (1976). The problem of motivation in feeding behavior. In D.Novin, W. Wyrwicka, & G. Bray, *Hunger: Basic Mechanisms and Clinical Implications.* New York: Raven.

Yakimovich, D., & Saltz, E. (1971). Helping behavior: The cry for help. *Psychonomic Science, 23,* 427–428.

Yalom, I. (1975). *The theory and practice of group psychotherapy.* New York: Basic Books.

Yankelovich, D. (1981). *New rules: Searching for self–fulfillment in a world turned upside down.* New York: Random House.

Yankura, J., & Dryden, W. (1990). *Doing RET: Albert Ellis in action.* New York: Springer.

Yarrow, M. R., Waxler, C. Z., & Scott, P. M. (1971). Child effects on adult behavior. *Developmental Psychology, 5,* 300–311.

Yassa, R., Nair, N., Iskandar, H., & Schwartz, G. (1990). Factors in the development of severe forms of tardive dyskinesia. *American Journal of Psychiatry, 147,* 1156–1163.

Yehuda, R., Lowy, M., Southwick, S. M., Shaffer, D., & Giller, E. (1991). Pymphocyte glucocoricoid receptor number in posttraumatic stress disorder. *American Journal of Psychiatry, 148,* 499–504.

Yehuda, R., Southwick, S. M., & Giller, E. (1992). Exposure to atrocities and severity of chronic posttraumatic stress disorder in Vietnam combat veterans. *American Journal of Psychiatry, 149,* 333–336.

Yeomans, F. E., Hull, J. W., & Clarkin, J. C. (1994). Risk factors for self–damaging acts in a borderline population. *Journal of Personality Disorders, 8,* 10–16.

Young, I. (1992). The child client. *Children and Society, 6,* 187–203.

Young, J. (1802). On the theory of light and colors. *Philosophical Transactions of the Royal Society of London, 92,* 12–48.

Youniss, J. & Haynie, D. (1992). Friendship in adolescence. *Developmental and Behavioral Pediatrics, 13,* 59–66.

Yu, B., Zhang, W., Jing, Q., Peng., R., Zhang, G., & Simon, H. A. (1985). STM capacity for Chinese and English language materials. *Memory and Cognition, 13,* 202–207.

Yuille, J. C. (1980). A critical examination of the psychological and practical implications of eyewitness research. *Law and Human Behavior, 4,* 335–345.

Yussen, S. R., & Levy, V. M., Jr. (1975). Developmental changes in predicting one's own span of short–term memory. *Journal of Experimental Child Psychology, 19,* 502–08.

Zahn–Waxler, C., Radke–Yarrow, M., Wagner, E., & Chapman, M. (1992). Development of concern for others. *Developmental Psychology, 28,* 126–136.

Zahn–Waxler, C., Robinson, J., & Emde, R. (1992). The development of empathy in twins. *Developmental Psychology, 28,* 1038–1047.

Zajonc, R. (1980). Feeling and thinking: Preferences need no inferences. *American Psychologist, 35,* 151–175.

Zajonc, R. B. (1960). Balance, congruity and dissonance. *Public Opinion Quarterly, 24,* 280–296.

Zajonc, R. B. (1960). The process of cognitive tuning in abnormal social communication. *Journal of Psychology, 62,* 159–167.

Zajonc, R. B. (1965). *Social facilitation. Science,* 149, 269–274.

Zajonc, R. B. (1968). The attitudinal effects of mere exposure. *Journal of Personality and Social Psychology, 9,* 1–27.

Zal, H. M. (1987). Panic disorder: Is it emotional or physical? *Psychiatric Annals, 17,* 497–505.

Zanarini, M., Gunderson, J., Marino, M., Schwartz, E., & Frankenburg, F. (1990). Psychiatric disorders in the families of borderline outpatients. In P. Links (Ed.), *Family environment and borderline personality disorder* (pp.69–84). Washington, DC: American Psychiatric Press.

Zanarini, M. C., Gunderson, J. G., Marino, M. F., Schwartz, E. D., & Frankenberg, F. R. (1989). Childhood experience of borderline patients. *Comprehensive Psychiatry, 30,* 18–25.

Zanna, M. P., & Cooper, J. (1974). Dissonance and the pill: An attribution approach to studying the arousal properties of dissonance. *Journal of Personality and Social Psychology, 9,* 703–709.

Zatzick, D. F. & Dimsdale, J. E. (1990).

Cultural variations in response to painful stimuli. *Psychosomatic Medicine, 52,* 544–557.

Zborowski, M., & Herzog, E. (1952). *Life is with people.* New York: International Universities Press.

Zeanah, C. H., & Zeanah, P. D. (1989). Intergenerational transmission of maltreatment: Insights from attachment theory and research. *Psychiatry, 52,* 177–196.

Zebrowitz–McArthur, L. (1988). Person perception in cross–cultural perspective. In M.H. Bond (Ed.), *The cross–cultural challenge to social psychology,* Vol. 11 (pp. 245–265). Newbury Park, CA: Sage Publications.

Zeki, S. (1992). The visual image in mind and brain. *Scientific American, 267,* 3–76.

Zervas, I. M., Augustine, A., & Fricchione, G. L. (1993). Patient delay in cancer: A view from the crisis model. *General Hospital Psychiatry, 15,* 9–13.

Zhang, W. T. & Peng, R. X. (1983). The lateralization of hemispheric function in the recognition of Chinese characters. *Neuropsychologia, 21,* 679–682.

Ziegler, D. K. (1985). Functional brain grafts: A distant hope for patients with "irreversible" brain lesions: *Commentary. Integrative Psychiatry, 3,* 31.

Zigler, E., & Berman, W. (1983). Discerning the future of early childhood intervention. *American Psychologist,* 894–906.

Zigler, E., & Glick, M. (1988). Is paranoid schizophrenia really camouflaged depression? *American Psychologist, 43,* 294–290.

Zigler, E., Hodapp, R. M. & Edison, M. R. (1990). From theory to practice in the care and education of mentally retarded individuals. *American Journal on Mental Retardation, 95,* 1–12.

Zillman, D., Baron, R. A., & Tamborini, R. (1981). Special costs of smoking: Effects of tobacco smoke on hostile behavior. *Journal of Applied Social Psychology, 11,* 548–561.

Zillmann, D. (1978). Attribution and misattribution of excitatory reactions. In J. H.

Harvey, W. Ickes and R. F. Kidd (Eds.), *New directions in attribution research,* Vol. 2. Hillsdale, NJ: Erlbaum.

Zimbardo, P. G. (1972). Pathology of imprisonment. *Society,* 4–8.

Zimbardo, P. G. (1975). Transforming experimental research into advocacy for social change. In M. Deutsch and H.A. Hornstein (Eds.), *Applying social psychology: Implications for research, practice, and training.* Hillsdale, NJ: Erlbaum.

Zimbardo, P. G., Andersen, S. M., & Kabat, L. G. (1981). Induced hearing deficit generates experimental paranoia. *Science, 212,* 1529–31.

Zimbardo, P. G., Weisenberg, M., & Firestone, I. (1965). Communicator effectiveness in producing public conformity and private attitude change. *Journal of Personality, 33,* 233–255.

Zinbarg, R., Barlow, D., Brown, T., & Hertz, R. (1992). Cognitive–behavioral approaches to the nature and treatment of anxiety disorders. *Annual Review of Psychology, 43,* 235–267.

Zorumski, C., & Isenberg, K. E. (1991). Insights into the structure and function of GABA–benzodiazepine receptors: Ion channels and psychiatry. *American Journal of Psychiatry, 148,* 162–173.

Zubin, J., & Spring, B. (1977). Vulnerability: A new view of schizophrenia. *Journal of Abnormal Psychology, 86,* 103–126.

Zuckerman, M. (1994). *Behavioral expression and biosocial bases of sensation seeking.* New York: Cambridge University Press.

Zuckerman, M., Koestner, R., DeBoy, T., Garcia, T., Maresca, B., & Sartoris, J. (1988). To predict some of the people some of the time: A reexamination of the moderator variable approach in personality theory. *Journal of Personality and Social Psychology, 54,* 1006–1019.

Zwislocki, J. J. (1981). Sound analysis in the ear: A history of discoveries. *American Scientist, 69,* 184–192.

PHOTO CREDITS

Page 398 (center): Novovitch/Gamma Liaison. Page 398 (bottom): Allen/Gamma Liaison. Page 400: Bruno Barbey/Magnum Photos, Inc.

CHAPTER 11 OPENER: Chris Eden/Courtesy Jacob Lawrence and Francine Seders Gallery, Seattle,W.A. Page 406: Reuters/Bettmann. Figure 11.3, 11.5 and 11.6: P. Ekman Human Interaction Lab, University of California SF. Page 422 (center): Charles Krebs/Tony Stone Images/ New York, Inc. Page 413: SUPER-STOCK. Page 422 (left): Tim Davis/Tony Stone Images/ New York, Inc. Page 422 (right): John Giordano/SABA. Page 430: Alex Webb/Magnum Photos, Inc. Page 431: Peter Menzel/Stock, Boston. Page 433: W. Karel/Sygma Photo News. Page 435: Manfred Kage/Peter Arnold, Inc. Page 437: Courtesy American Heart Association. Page 439: UPI/ Bettmann. Page 440: James D. Wilson/Gamma Liaison. Page 441: Frans Lanting/Minden Pictures, Inc.

CHAPTER 12 OPENER: American Museum of Natural History Library #2385. Page 448: Bonnie Timmons/The Image Bank. Page 449: The Bettmann Archive. Page 452: Jerry Ohlinger's Movie Material Store. Page 454: Sandra Lousada/Woodfin Camp & Associates. Page 454 (margina): ©1994 Express. Page 455: © Roy Stevens. Page 456 (top): Stephen S. Myers/Courtesy Department of Library Services,American Museum of Natural History #3837(2) 16/1507. Page 456 (bottom): Susan Meiselas/Magnum Photos, Inc. Figure12.3: © 1921 Roschach: PSYCHODIAGNOSTICS, Hans Huber- Medical Publisher, Bern. Page 464: Pablo Picasso/Superstock. Page 470: Bettmann Archive. Page 473: Courtesy Jerome Kagan, Harvard University. Page 479: Charles Schneider Photography. Page 480: Werner Forman Archive, British Museum, London/Art Resource. Page 481 (top): Henri Cartier-Bresson /Magnum Photos, Inc. Page 481 (bottom): Alan Carey/The Image Works. Page 483: Alex Webb/Magnum Photos, Inc. Page 484: "The Madonna of Humility" by Lippo di Dalmasio/The National Gallery London. Page 485: Courtesy New York Public Library Picture Collection.

CHAPTER 13 OPENER: Courtesy Romare Bearden. Page 490: Lisa Quinones/Black Star. Figure 13.1: Drawing by Claudia Schieve. Figure. 13.2 : from S. Carlson, 1980, p. 189, International Journal of Neuroscience courtesy The Gordon and Breech Publishing Group. Page 496 (top): Tony Stone Images/ New York, Inc. Page 496 (center): Neil Harding/Tony Stone Images/ New York, Inc. Page 496 (bottom): Petit Format/ Nestle/ ScienceSource/ Photo Researchers. Page 497: Dr. James W. Hanson, University of Iowa Hospital and Clinics. Page 498: Schaefer/Monkmeyer Press Photo. Page 501: Tom Raymond/Tony Stone Images/ New York, Inc. Page 502: Kenneth Garrett/Woodfin Camp & Associates. Figure 13.8: From A.N. Meltzoff & M.K. Moore, Science, 1977, 198, 75-78. Page 509: Jeffry W. Myers/Stock, Boston. Page 511: Reprinted with special permission of King Features Syndicate. Figure 13.12: Elizabeth Crews. Page 514: Pierre Perrin/ GLMR Niger/Gamma Liaison. Page 515: McLaughlin/The Image Works. Figure 13.13: R. Case 1992, Neo Piagetian Theories of Child Development/INTELLECTUAL DEVELOPMENT reprinted with permission of Cambirdge University Press. Page 519 (left): UPI/ Bettmann. Page 519 (right): Jeffrey Markowitz/Sygma. Page 526: Science Source/Photo Researchers. Page 527: Prof. R.D. Terry/Peter Arnold, Inc.

CHAPTER 14 OPENER: Lincoln Perry/Courtesy Tatistcheff & Company Inc. Page 532: J. Koontz/The Picture Cube. Figure 14.1: Nina Leen/Life Magazine, copyright Time, Inc. Page 539 (left): Albert Normandin/The Image Bank. Page 539 (right): Ira Wyman/Sygma. Page 542: Francois Charton/Black Star. Page 544: Cora du Bois" The People of Alor" /courtesy University of Minnesota Press. Page 545: Nancy Sheehan/The Picture Cube. Page 546 (left): Jeff Greenberg/The Image Works. Page 546 (right): Glassman/The Image Works. Page 546: Bettmann Archive. Page 549: Champlon-Arepi/The Image Bank. Page 556: Joan Clifford/The Picture Cube. Page 560: Mark Scott/FPG International. Page 562: Cindy Karp/Black Star. Page 567: Jose Azel/Contact Press Images, Inc. Page 570: McDonald Photography/The Picture Cube.

CHAPTER 15 OPENER: Courtesy Susan Grabel. Page 579: Rosanne Percivalle/The Image Bank. Page 577: Bettmann Archive. Page 579: Eric Roth/The Picture Cube. Page 585: Callahan/Levin Represents. Page 589: Paula Lerner/Woodfin Camp & Associates. Page 590: Michael Weisbrot/Stock, Boston. Page 590: Giannia Tobtoli/Photo Researchers. Page 592: Monte Buchsbaum, M.D., Mt. Sinai Medical Center. Figure 15.4: From: Sander L. Gilman, Seeing The Insane. Page 596: Monte Buschbaum, MD , Mt. Sinai Medical Center. Page 599 (center): UPI/ Bettmann. Figure 15.6: fr. Lieberman et al, 1992; American Journal of Psychiatry. Page 599 (left): Andy King/ Sygma. Page 599 (right): Reuters/Bettmann. Page 603: Jay Belmore/The Image Bank. Page 605: David Butow/Black Star. Page 607: Peter Marlow/Magnum Photos, Inc.

Page 613 (top): Jerry Ohlinger's Movie Material Store. Page 613 (bottom): C. Blankenhorn/The Picture Cube.

CHAPTER 16 OPENER: Courtesy Mike Green. Page 622: Arlene Colins/Monkmeyer Press Photo. Page 626: from "Bergasse 19", Signmund Freud's Home and Office, Vienna 1938, the photographs of Edmund Engleman Publishers, Inc. New York. Page 628: Stacy Pickerell/Tony Stone Images/ New York, Inc. Page 632: Dr. R. Nesse (c) Andrew Sacks. Page 633: The Far Side ©1986 FARWORKS, INC./ Dist. by UNIVERSAL PRESS SYNDICATE. Reprinted with Permission. All rights reserved. Page 638: Stan Flint/The Image Bank. Page 639: Hank Morgan/ Science Source/Photo Researchers. Page 640: David Young-Wolff/PhotoEdit. Page 646: James Wilson/Woodfin Camp & Associates. Page 647: The Museum of Modern Art/ Film Stills Archive. Page 655: Anthro-Photo File. Page 656: C. Bradley Simmons/Bruce Coleman, Inc.

CHAPTER 17 Opener: Randy Stevens/courtesy Newbury Fine Arts. Page 662: Yale Interaction Library, Yale University. Page 665: Lee Snider/The Image Works. Page 667: reprinted by permission:Tribune Media Services. Page 674 (top left): US Signal Corp. /AP Wide World Photos. Page 674 (top right): Anna Flynn/Stock, Boston. Page 674 (bottom): ITN/ F.S.P./Gamma Liaison. Page 676: Elliott Erwitt/Magnum Photos, Inc. Page 679: Hubertus Kanus/Photo Researchers. Page 694 (left): Selz, Seabolt and Associates, Inc. Page 694 (right): Paul Fusco/Magnum Photos, Inc.

CHAPTER 18 OPENER: Kathy Ruttenberg/Gallery Henoch. Page 700: Keystone Paris/Sygma. Page 703 (left): Marc and Evelyne Bernheim/Woodfin Camp & Associates. Page 703 (center): Eric RobertSygma Photo News. Page 703 (right): Bill Ellzey/Comstock, Inc. Page 706: Callahan/Levin Represents. Page 710: Kitagawa Utamaro/SUPERSTOCK- Japanese British Library. Page 713: Edward Hausner/New York Times Pictures. Page 715 (left): M. Antman/The Image Works. Page 715 (right): Werner/The Image Works. Page 719: Art Wolfe/Tony Stone Images/ New York, Inc. Page 724: David Butow/Black Star. Page 725: UPI/ Bettmann. Page 727 (center): William Vandivert. Page 727 (top left): Alan Reininger/Contact Press Images, Inc. Page727 (top right): Ken Sherman/Bruce Coleman, Inc. Page730: Prof. Philip G. Zimbardo, Dept. of Psychology, Stanford University. Page 733 (top): Henri Cartier Bresson/Magnum Photos, Inc. Page 733 (bottom): Chuck O'Rear/Woodfin Camp & Associates.

Text and Illustration Credits

CHAPTER 1 Figure 1.6: Sulloway, Frank J. (1994). *Born to rebel: radical thinking in science and social thought.* Completed manuscript. Cambridge, MA: Massachusetts Institute of Technology; Figure 1.7: Data on which pie chart is based are from: American Psychological Association, Office of Research (November 1994). [Table 1: Major fields of all doctoral psychologists and new psychology doctorate recipients: 1981-1991]. Unpublished analyses. (Original source: National Science Foundation, Division of Science Resources Studies, unpublished analyses). Copyright 1994 by the American Psychological Association. Reprinted/adapted by permission.

CHAPTER 2 Table 2.1: Smetana, J., Yau, E. C., Restrepo, A., & Braeges, J. (1991). Adolescent-parent conflict in married and divorced families. *Developmental Psychology, 27*, 1000-1010. Copyright 1991 by the American Psychological Association. Reprinted/adapted by permission of the APA and the authors.; Figure 2.4: Bower, G. H. (1981). Mood and memory. *American Psychologist, 36*, 129-148. Copyright 1981 by the American Psychological Association. Reprinted by permission of the APA and the author.; Table 2.3: Izard, C. E., Libero, C., Putnam, P. & Haynes, O. M. (1993). Stability of emotion experiences and their relationship to traits of personality. *Journal of Personality and Social Psychology, 64*, 847-860. Copyright 1993 the American Psychological Association. Reprinted/adapted by permission of the APA and the authors.

CHAPTER 2 SUPPLEMENT Table 2S.4: Zahn-Waxler, C., Radke-Yarrow, M. J., Wagner, E & Chapman, M. (1992). Development and concern for others. *Developmental Psychology, 28*, 126-136. Copyright 1992 by the American Psychological Association. Reprinted/adapted by permission of the APA and the authors.

CHAPTER 3 Figure 3.4: Björklund, A. & Gage, F. (1985). Neural grafting of neurodegenerative diseases in animal models. *Annals of the New York Academy of Sciences, 457*, 53-81. Copyright 1985 by the Annals of the New York Academy of Sciences. Reprinted/adapted by permission of the Annals of the New York Academy of Sciences and the authors.; Figure 3.9: From: FUNDAMENTALS OF HUMAN NEUROPSYCHOLOGY 3/E by Kolb & Whishaw. Copyright © 1990 by W. H. Freeman and Company. Used with permission.; Figure 3.14: Reprinted with the permission of Simon & Schuster, Inc. from THE CEREBRAL CORTEX OF MAN by Wilder Penfield & Theodore Rasmussen. Copyright 1950 Macmillan Publishing Company; copyright renewed © 1978 Theodore Rasmussen.; Figure 3.16a: Reprinted/adapted from Gazzaniga, M. S. (1967, August). The split brain in man. *Scientific American.* Copyright © 1967 by Scientific American, Inc. All rights reserved.

CHAPTER 4 Figure 4.2: Sekuler, R. & Blake, R. (1994). *Perception* (3rd ed.). New York: McGraw-Hill, Inc. Reprinted/adapted by permission of McGraw-Hill, Inc.; Figure 4.3: Griffin, D. R. (1959). *Echoes of Bats and Men.* New York: Bantam Doubleday Dell Publishing Group. Reprinted by permission.; Table 4.1: Brown, R., Galanter, E. & Hess, E. H. (1962). *New Directions in Psychology.* New York: Harcourt Brace & Co. Reprinted/adapted by permission.; Figure 4.5: Guilford, J. P. (1954). *Psychometric Methods.* New York: McGraw-Hill, Inc. Reprinted/adapted by permission of McGraw-Hill, Inc.; Figure 4.6: Stevens, S. S. (1961). The psychophysics of sensory function. In W. Rosenblith (Ed.), *Sensory Communication*, 1-34. Cambridge, MA: MIT Press. Copyright 1961 by MIT Press. Reprinted/adapted by permission.; Figure 4.12: Sekuler, R. & Blake, R. (1994). *Perception* (3rd ed.) New York: McGraw-Hill, Inc. Reprinted/adapted by permission.; Figure 4.16: Sekuler, R. & Blake, R. (1994). *Perception* (3rd ed.). New York: McGraw-Hill, Inc. Reprinted by permission.; Figure 4.24: Sekuler, R. & Blake, R. (1994). *Perception* (3rd ed.). New York: McGraw-Hill, Inc. Reprinted by permission.; Figure 4.25: Wever, E. G. (1949). *Theory of Hearing.* New York: John Wiley & Sons, Inc. Reprinted/adapted by permission.; Figure 4.32: Boring, E. G. (1930). A new ambiguous figure. *American Journal of Psychology, 42*, 444-445. Copyright 1930 by University of Illinois Press. Reprinted by permission.; Figure 4.33e, *right:* Kanizsa, G. (1976). Subjective contours. *Scientific American, 234*, 48. Copyright © 1976 by Scientific American, Inc. All rights reserved. Reprinted/adapted by permssion.; Figure 4.39: De Lucia, P. R. & Hochberg, J. (1991). Geometrical illusions in solid objects under ordinary viewing conditions. *Perception and Psychophysics, 50* (6), 547-554. Copyright 1991 by the Psychonomic Society, Inc. Reprinted/adapted by permission of the authors.; Figure 4.42: Mistlin, A. & Perrett, D. (1990). Expectations and neural firing. *Experimental Brain Research, 82*, 442. Copyright 1990 by Springer-Verlag. Reprinted/adapted by permission.

CHAPTER 5 Figure 5.2: Pavlov, I. P. (1927). *Conditioned Reflexes.* New York: Oxford University Press. Reprinted by permission of Oxford University Press.; Figure 5.4: Hovland, C. I. The generalization of conditioned responses: the sensory generalization of conditioned responses with varying frequencies of time. *The Journal of General Psychology, 17*, 125-148, 1937. Reprinted with permission of the Helen Dwight Reid Educational Foundation. Published by Heldref Publications, 1319 Eighteenth St., N.W., Washington, D.C. 20036-1802. Copyright © 1937.; Figure 5.11: Weisberg, P. & Waldrop, P. B. (1972). Fixed-interval work habits of Congress. *Journal of Applied Behavior Analysis.* Copyright 1972 Journal of Applied Behavior Analysis. Reprinted by permission.; Table 5.1: Flor, H., Haag, G. & Turk, D. (1986). Longterm efficacy of emg biofeedback for chronic rheumatic back pain. *Pain*, 198-199. Copyright 1986 by Elsevier Science. Reprinted/adapted by permission of Elsevier Science and the authors.; Figure 5.12: Gray, J. A. (1988). "Gray's Three Behavioral Systems," from *The Psychology of Fear and Stress,* 2nd ed. New York: Cambridge University Press. Reprinted/adapted with the permission of Cambridge University Press and the author.; Figure 5.14: Rotter, J. (1971, June). External control and internal control: Locus of control. *Psychology Today, 42.* Reprinted with permission from Psychology Today Magazine, Copyright © 1971 (Sussex Publishers, Inc.).; Table 5.2: Vanden Belt, A. & Peterson, C. (1991). Parental explanatory style. *Cognitive Therapy and Research, 337.* Copyright 1991 by Plenum Publishing Corporation. Reprinted/adapted by permission of Plenum Publishing Corporation and the authors.; Figure 5.15: Reprinted by permission from A. Bandura, *The Young Child; Reviews of Research,* W. Hartup & N. Smothergill, Eds.(Washington, DC: National Association for the Education of Young Children, 1967), p. 45. © 1967 by NAEYC.

CHAPTER 6 Figure 6.3: Cooper, L. A. & Shepard, R. N. (1973). The time required to prepare for a rotated stimulus. *Memory and Cognition, 1*(3), 246-250. Reprinted/adapted by permission of Psychonomic Society, Inc.; Figure 6.4: Morris, R. G., Craik, F. I., Gick, M. L. (1990). Age difference in working memory tasks: the role of secondary memory and the executive system. *Quarterly Journal of Experimental Psychology: Human Experimental Psychology, 42*(1-A). Reprinted/adapted by permission of Quarterly Journal of Experimental Psychology and the authors.; Figure 6.6: Ericsson, K. A. & Chase, W. G. (1982). Exceptional memory. *American Scientist, 70*, 607-614. Copyright 1982 by American Scientist. Reprinted/adapted by permission.; Figure 6.7: Atkinson, R. C. & Shiffrin, R. N. (1968). Human memory: a proposed system and its control processes. *The Psychology of Learning and Motivation, 2.* Copyright 1968 by Academic Press, Inc. Reprinted/adapted by permission of Academic Press and the authors.; Figure 6.8: Rundus, D. (1971). Analysis of rehearsal process in free recall. *Journal of Experimental Psychology, 89*, 63-77. Copyright 1971 by the American Psychological Association. Reprinted/adapted by permission of the APA and the author.; Table 6.1: Bowers, J. S. & Schacter, D. L. (1990). Implicit memory and test awareness. *Journal of Experimental Psychology: Learning, Memory and Cognition, 16*(3), 404-416. Copyright 1990 by the American Psychological Association. Reprinted/adapted by permission of the APA and the authors.; Figure 6.11: Reprinted/adapted with permission from Squire, L. R. & Zola-Morgan, S. (1991). The medial temporal lobe memory system. *Science, 253.* Copyright 1991 American Association for the Advancement of Science. Reprinted by permission of the AAAS and the authors.; Figure 6.15: Bartlett, F. D. (1932). *Remembering: A study in experimental and social psychology.* New York: Cambridge University Press. Reprinted with the permission of Cambridge University Press.

CHAPTER 7 Table 7.1: Rosch, E. (1978). Principles of categorization. In E. Rosch & B. Lloyd (Eds.), *Cognition and Categorization* (p. 33). Hillsdale, NJ: Lawrence Erlbaum Associates, Inc. Reprinted/adapted by permission of Lawrence Erlbaum Associates. Inc. and the author.; Table 7.2: Irwin, M. H., Shafer G. N. & Reiden, C. P. (1974). *Journal of Cross-Cultural Psychology, 5*, 407-423. Copyright © 1974 by Sage Publications, Inc. Reprinted/adapted by permission of Sage Publications, Inc.; Figure 7.3: Lehman, D. R., Lempert, R. O., & Nisbett, R. E. (1988). The effects of graduate training on reasoning: Formal discipline and thinking about everyday-life events. *American Psychologist, 43*, 431-442. Copyright 1988 by the American Psychological Association. Reprinted/adapted by permission of the APA and the authors.; Figure 7.4: Lehman, D. R. & Nisbett, R. E. (1990). A longitudinal study of the effects of undergraduate training on reasoning. *Developmental Psychology, 26*, 952-960. Copyright 1990 by the American Psychological Association. Reprinted by permission of the APA and the authors.; Figure 7.5: Wason, P. C. (1968). Reasoning about a rule. *Quarterly Journal of Experimental Psychology*, 20, 273-281. Reprinted by permission of Quarterly Journal of Experimental Psychology and the author.; Figure 7.6: Griggs, R. A. & Cox, J. R. (1982). The elusive thematic-materials effect in Wason's selection task. *British Journal of Psychology*, 73, 407-420, extract. Reprinted/adapted by permission of the British Psychological Society and the authors.; Table 7.3: Edwards, W. (1977). How to use multiattribute utility measurement for social decision making. *IEEE Transactions on Systems Management and Cybernetics*, 17, 326-340. Copyright 1977 IEEE.; Table 7.4: Edwards, W. (1977). How to use multiattribute utility measurement for social decision making. *IEEE Transactions on Systems Management and Cybernetics*, 17, 326-340. Copyright 1977 IEEE.; Figure 7.11: Rumelhart, D. (1984). Schemata and the cognitive system. In R. S. Wyer & T. K. Srull (Eds.), *Handbook of Social Cognition* (p. 84). Hillsdale, NJ: Lawrence Erlbaum Associates, Inc. Reprinted/adapted by permission of Lawrence Erlbaum Associates and the author.; Figure 7.13b: From The perception of speech in early infancy by Peter D. Eimas. (1985, January). *Scientific American*, p. 47. Copyright © 1985 by Scientific American, Inc. All rights reserved.; Table 7.7: Ambady, N. & Rosenthal, R. (1993) *Journal of Personality and Social Psychology*, 64, 34. Copyright 1993 by the American Psychological Association. Reprinted/adapted by permission of the APA and the authors.; Figure 7.14: From Teaching language to an ape by Ann James Premack & David Premack. (1972, October). *Scientific American*, p. 93. Copyright 1972 by Scientific American, Inc. All rights reserved. Reprinted by permission.

CHAPTER 8 Table 8.1: Items similar to those in the Wechsler Adult Intelligence Scale - Revised. Copyright © 1981, 1955 by The Psychological Corporation. Reproduced by permission. All rights reserved.; Figure 8.3: Williams, R. L. (1972). The BITCH test (Black Intelligence Test of Cultural Homogeneity). Reprinted/adapted by permission of the author.; Figure 8.5: Posner, M. I., Boies, S., Eichelman, W. H., & Taylor, R. L. (1969). Retention of visual and names codes of single letters. *Journal of Experimental Psychology*, 1. Copyright 1969 by the American Psychological Association. Reprinted/adapted by permission of the APA and the authors.; Figure 8.6: Mumaw, R. & Pellegrino, J. (1984). Spatial transformation problems. *Journal of Educational Psychology*, 920-939. Copyright 1984 by the American Psychological Association. Reprinted by permission of the APA and the authors.; Table 8.3: Judd, T. (1988). The varieties of musical talent. In L. K. Obler & D. Fein (Eds.), *The Exceptional Brain: Neuropsychology of Talent and Special Abilities*. New York: The Guilford Press. Reprinted/adapted by permission.; Figure 8.7: Sameroff, A., Seifer, R., Baldwin, A., & Baldwin, C. (1993). The relation between multiple risk factors and child IQ at ages 4 and 13. *Child Development*, 64, 89. Copyright © 1993 by the Society for Research in Child Development. Reprinted by permission.; Table 8.4: Henderson, N. D. (1982). Correlations in IQ for pairs of people with varying degrees of genetic relatedness and shared environment. *Annual Review of Psychology*, 33. Reprinted/adapted, with permission, from the author and the Annual Review of Psychology, Volume 33, © 1982, by Annual Reviews Inc.; Table 8.5: Loehlin, J., Horn, J., & Willerman, L. (1990). Modeling IQ change: Evidence from the Texas Adoption Project. *Child Development*, 60, 993-1004. Copyright © 1990 by the Society for Research in

Child Development. Reprinted/adapted by permission.; Table 8.6: Landesman-Dwyer, S. & Butterfield, E. C. (1983). Mental retardation: Developmental issues in cognitive and social adaptation. *Origins of Intelligence: Infancy and Early Childhood*, 485. Reprinted/adapted by permission of Plenum Publishing Corporation.; Figure 8.8: Richards, R., Kinney, D., Linde, I., & Benet, M. (1988). Creativity in manic-depressives, cyclothymes, their normal relatives, and control subjects. *Abnormal Psychology*, 97, 281-288. Copyright 1988 by the American Psychological Association. Reprinted/adapted by permission of the APA and the authors.

CHAPTER 9 Figure 9.3: CHART: "A WEEK IN THE LIFE OF KATHERINE" from BEING ADOLESCENT: CONFLICT AND GROWTH IN THE TEENAGE YEARS by MIHALY CSIK-SZENTMIHALYI and REED LARSON. Copyright © 1984 by Basic Books, Inc. Reprinted by permission of Basic Books, a division of HarperCollins Publishers, Inc. and the author.; Figure 9.6: Marcel, J. (1983). Conscious and unconscious perception: Experiments in visual masking and word recognition. *Cognitive Psychology*, 15, 197-237. Copyright 1983 by Academic Press, Inc. Reprinted/adapted by permission of Academic Press and the author.; Figure 9.8: Reprinted/adapted with permission from Squire, L. R. (1986). Priming effects in amnesia. *Science*, 232, 1612-1619. Copyright 1986 American Association for the Advancement of Science.; Figure 9.10: Kripke, D. F., Simons, R. N., Garfinkel, L., & Hammond, E. C. (1979). Short and long sleep and sleeping pills: Is increased mortality associated? *Archives of General Psychiatry*, 36, 103-116. Copyright 1979 American Medical Association. Reprinted/adapted by permission.; Figure 9.11: Kripke, D. F., Simons, R. N., Garfinkel, L., & Hammond, E. C. (1979). Short and long sleep and sleeping pills: Is increased mortality associated? *Archives of General Psychiatry*, 36, 103-116. Copyright 1979 American Medical Association. Reprinted/adapted by permission.; Figure 9.13: Cartwright, R. D. (1978). *A Primer on Sleep and Dreaming*. Reading: Addison-Wesley, Inc. Reprinted by permission of the author.; Figure 9.15: Hilgard, E. R. (1986). *Divided Consciousness*, p. 190. New York: John Wiley & Sons, Inc. Reprinted by permission of the author.; Figure 9.16: Pope, H., Ionescu-Pioggia, M., Aizley, H., & Varma, D. (1990). Drug use and lifestyle among college undergraduates in 1989: A comparison with 1969 and 1978. *American Journal of Psychiatry*, 147, 998-1001. Copyright 1990 by the American Psychiatric Association. Reprinted by permission of the publisher and the authors.

CHAPTER 10 Figure 10.2: Simmons, L. W. (1990). Pheromonal cues for the recognition of kin by female field crickets, Gryllus bimaculatus. *Animal Behaviour*, 40, 192-195. Copyright 1990 by Academic Press, Ltd. Reprinted by permission.; Figure 10.8: Reprinted with permission from Thompson, D. A. & Campbell, R. G. (1977). Hunger in humans induced by 2 deoxy-d glucose: Glucoprivic control of taste preference and food intake. *Science*, 198, 1065-1068. Copyright 1977 American Association for the Advancement of Science. Reprinted by permission of the AAAS. ; Table 10.1: Rand, C. S. & Kuldau, J. M. (1990). The epidemiology of obesity and self-defined weight problems in the general population. *International Journal of Eating Disorders*, 9, 329-343. Copyright 1990 by John Wiley & Sons, Inc. Reprinted by permission of John Wiley & Sons, Inc.; Figure 10.9: Masters,

W. H. & Johnson, V. E. (1966). *Human Sexual Response*, p. 5. Boston: Little, Brown and Company. Copyright 1966 by the Masters and Johnson Institute. Reprinted by permission.; Table 10.2: Butler, C. A. (1976). New data about female sexual response. *Journal of Sex and Marital Therapy*, 2, 40-46. Copyright 1976 by Brunner/Mazel, Inc. Reprinted with permission of Brunner/Mazel, Inc. and the author.; Figure 10.10: Bancroft, J. (1984). Hormones and human sexual behavior. *Journal of Sex and Marital Therapy*, 10, 3-21. Copyright 1984 by Brunner/Mazel, Inc. Reprinted with permission of Brunner/Mazel, Inc. and the author.; Table 10.3: Whitam, F. & Mathy, R. (1991). Childhood cross-gender behavior of homosexual females I Brazil, Peru, the Phillipines, and the U.S. *Archives of Sexual Behavior*, 20, 151-170. Copyright 1991 by Plenum Publishing Corporation. Reprinted/adapted by permission of Plenum Publishing Corporation and the author.; Figure 10.11: Reprinted with permission from Gladue, B. A., Green, R., & Hellman, R. E. (1984). Neuroendocrine response to estrogen and sexual orientation. *Science*, 225, 1496-1499. Copyright 1984 American Association for Advancement of Science. Reprinted by permission of the AAAS and the author.; Table 10.4: Nathan, S. G. (1986) The epidemology of the DSM-III psychosexual dysfunctions. *Journal of Sex and Marital Therapy*, 12, 267-281. Copyright 1986 by Brunner/Mazel, Inc. Reprinted/adapted with permission of Brunner/Mazel, Inc. and the author.; Figure 10.13: Elliott, E. S. & Dweck, C. S. (1988). Goals: An approach to motivation and achievement. *Journal of Personality and Social Psychology*, 54, 5-12. Copyright 1988 by the American Psychological Association. Reprinted/adapted by permission of the APA and the author.; Table 10.5: McClelland, D. C., Atkinson, J. W., Clark, R. A., & Lowell, E. L. (1953). *The Achievement Motive*. New York: Irvington Publishers. Reprinted/adapted by permission of Irving Publishers, Inc. ©1953 by Appleton Century Crofts.

CHAPTER 11 Figure 11.2: Pennebaker, J.. Colder, M., & Sharp, L. K. (1990). Accelerating the coping process. *Journal of Personality and Social Psychology*, 58, 528-537. Copyright 1990 by the American Psychological Association. Reprinted/adapted by permission of the APA and the authors.; Figure 11.4: Reprinted/adapted with permission from Ekman, P., Levenson, R. W., & Friesen, W. V. (1983). Automatic nervous system activity distinguishes among emotions. *Science*, 221, 1208-1210. Copyright 1983 American Association for the Advancement of Science.; Figure 11.7: Fischer, K., Shaver, P., & Carnochan, P. (1990). How emotions develop and how they organize development. *Cognition & Emotion*, 4 (2), 81-127. Reprinted by permission of Lawrence Erlbaum Associates Ltd., Hove, UK and the authors.; Figure 11.8: LeDoux, J. E. (1986) In J. E. LeDoux & W. Hirst (Eds.), *Mind and Brain*. New York: Cambridge University Press. Reprinted/adapted with the permission of Cambridge University Press and the author.; Figure 11.9: Tomarken, A., Davidson, R. J., Wheeler, R. E., & Doss, R. C. (1992). Individual differences in interior brain asymmetry and fundamental dimensions of emotion. *Journal of Personality and Social Psychology*, 62, 676-687. Copyright 1992 by the American Psychological Association. Reprinted/adapted by permission of the APA and the authors.; Figure 11.10: Shedler, J., Mayman, M., & Maris, M. (1993). The illusion of mental health. *American Psychologist*, 11, 1117-1131. Copyright 1993 by the American

Psychological Association. Reprinted/adapted by permission of the APA and the authors.; Table 11.1: Plutchik, R. (1980). A general psychoevolutionary theory of emotion. In R. Plutchik & H. Kellerman, H. (Eds). *Emotion: Theory, Research, and Experience, Vol. I: Theory of Emotion.* Orlando, FL: Academic Press. Reprinted/adapted by permission of Academic Press and the author.; Figure 11.12: Buss, D. M., Larsen, R., Westen, D., & Semmelroth, J. (1992). Sex differences in jealousy: Evolution, Physiology and Psychology. *Psychological Science, 3,* 251-255. Reprinted with the permission of Cambridge University Press and the authors.; Figure 11.13: Miller, N. E. (1992). Some examples of psychophysiology and the unconscious. *Biofeedback and Self-Regulation, 17,* 3-16. New York: Plenum Publishing Corp. Reprinted/adapted by permission of Plenum Publishing and the author.; Table 11.2: Holmes, T. H. & Rahe, R. E. (1967). The social readjustment rating scale. *Journal of Psychosomatic Research, 11,* 213-218. Reprinted by permission of the publisher. Copyright 1967 by Elsevier Science Inc.; Figure 11.14: Westen, D. (1991). Social cognition and object relations. *Psychological Bulletin, 109,* 429-455. Copyright 1991 by the American Psychological Association. Reprinted/adapted by permission of the publisher. Figure 11.15: Adams, P. R. & Adams, G. R. (1984). Mount Saint Helens's ashfall: evidence for a disaster stress reaction. *American Psychologist, 39* (3), 257. Copyright 1984 by the American Psychological Association. Reprinted/adapted by permission of the APA and the authors.; Poem excerpt, p. 433: Bukowski, Charles. (1972). Excerpt from "The shoelace." *Mockingbird Wish Me Luck,* 114. Copyright © 1972 by Charles Bukowski. Reprinted from *Mockingbird Wish Me Luck* with the permission of Black Sparrow Press.; Table 11.3: Kanner, A. D., Coyne, J. C., Schaefer, C., & Lazarus, R. S. (1991). Comparison of two modes of stress measurements: Daily hassles and uplifts versus major life events. *Journal of Behavioral Medicine, 4,* 14. Reprinted with permission of Academic Press and the authors.; Figure 11.16: Cohen, S. & Williamson, G. M. (1991). Stress and infectious disease in humans. *Psychological Bulletin, 109,* 5-24. Copyright 1991 by the American Psychological Association. Reprinted/adapted by permission of the APA and the authors.; Figure 11.17: Brown, J. B. (1991). Staying fit and staying well: Physical fitness as a moderator of life stress. *Journal of Personality and Social Psychology, 61,* 555-561. Copyright 1991 by the American Psychological Association. Reprinted/adapted by permission of the APA and the author.; Figure 11.18: Cohen, S., Yttrrell, P. A. J., & Smith, A. P. (1991). Psychological stress and susceptibility to the common cold. *New England Journal of Medicine, 325,* 606-612. Copyright 1991, Massachusetts Medical Society. Reprinted by permission of *The New England Journal of Medicine* and the authors.

CHAPTER 12   Table 12.1: Emmons, R. & King, L. A. (1988). Conflict among siblings: Immediate and long-term implications for psychological and physical well-being. *Journal of Personality & Social Psychology, 54,* 1040-1048. Copyright 1988 by the American Psychological Association. Reprinted/adapted by permission of the APA and the authors.; Quotation, p. 455: Lehrer, Tom (1959). *Oedipus Rex.* Copyright © 1959 Tom Lehrer. Copyright renewed. Used by permission.; Figure 12.6: Wood, R. & Bandura, A. (1989). Impact of conceptions of ability on self-regulatory mechanisms & complex decision making. *Journal of Personality & Social Psychology, 56,*

407-415. Copyright 1990. Copyright 1988 by the American Psychological Association. Reprinted by permission of the APA and the authors.; Figure 12.7: Eysenck, H. J. (1953). *The Structure of Human Personality.* London: Methuen & Co. Reprinted by permission.; Table 12.3: McCrae, R. R. & Costa, P. T. (1990). *Personality in Adulthood,* p. 13. New York: Guilford Press. Reprinted/adapted by permission of Guilford Press and the authors.; Table 12.4: Tellegen, A., Lykken, D. T., Bouchard, T. J., Jr., Wilcox, K. J., & Rich, S. (1988). Personality similarity in twins reared apart and together. *Journal of Personality & Social Psychology, 54,* 1031-1039. Copyright 1988 by the American Psychological Association. Reprinted/adapted by permission of the APA and the authors; Table 12.5: Plomin, R., Chiperer, H. & Loehlin, J. C. (1990). *Handbook of Personality: Theory & Research,* pp. 225-243. New York: Guilford Press. Reprinted/adapted by permission of Guilford Press and the authors.; Table 12.6: Zuckerman, M., De Roy, T., Garcia T., Maresa, B., & Sartoris, J. (1988). To predict some of the people some of the time: A reexamination of the moderator variable approach in personality theory. *Journal of Personality & Social Psychology, 54,* 1013-1014. Copyright 1988 by the American Psychological Association. Reprinted/adapted by permission of the APA and the authors.; Figure 12.8: Kagan, J. & Snidman, N. (1991). Temperamental factors in human development. *American Psychologist, 46,* 856-862. Copyright 1991 by the American Psychological Association. Reprinted/adapted by permission of the APA and the authors.; Table 12.7: McCrae, R. R. & Costa, P. T. (1990). *Personality in Adulthood,* p. 88. New York: Guilford Press. Reprinted/adapted by permission of the APA and the authors.; Table 12.8: Funder, D. & Colvin, C. R. (1991). Explorations in behavioral consistency: Properties of person, situations, & behaviors. *Journal of Personality and Social Psychology, 60,* 780-782. Copyright 1991 by the American Psychological Association. Reprinted/adapted by permission of the APA and the authors.; Table 12.9: Block, J. M., Gjerde P., & Block, J. H. (1991). Personality antecedents of depressive tendencies in 18-year-olds: A prospective study. *Journal of Personality and Social Psychology, 60,* 726-738. Copyright 1991 by the American Psychological Association. Reprinted/adapted by permission of the APA and the authors.; Quotation p. 480: O'Neill, E. (1962). *Long Day's Journey into Night.* Copyright 1992. New Haven: Yale University Press. Reprinted by permission.

CHAPTER 13   Figure 13.4: Moore, K. L. (1993) *Before We Are Born* (4th ed.), 118. Philadelphia: W. B. Saunders Company. Reprinted/adapted by permission.; Figure 13.5: Frankenburg, W. K. & Dodds, J. B. (1967). The Denver Developmental Screening Test. *Journal of Pediatrics, 91,* 181-191. Copyright 1967 by Mosby-Year Book, Inc. Reprinted/adapted by permission.; Figure 13.6: Tanner, J. M., Whitehouse, R. H., & Takaishi, M. (1966). Standards from birth to maturity for height, weight, height-velocity, and weight-velocity for British children. *Archives of Disease in Childhood, 41,* 454. Copyright 1966 by BMJ Publishing Group. Reprinted/adapted by permission.; Figure 13.7: Perdue, C. & Gurtman, M. (1990). Evidence for the automacity of ageism. *Journal of Experimental and Social Psychology, 26,* 199-216. Copyright 1990 by Academic Press, Inc. Reprinted by permission of Academic Press and the authors.; Figure 13.9: Meltzoff, A. N. & Borton, R. W. (1979). Intermodal matching by human neonates. *Nature, 282,* 403-404.

Copyright 1979 Macmillan Magazines Limited. Reprinted by permission of Nature and the authors.; Figure 13.10: Bower, T. G. R. (1971). The object in the world of the infant. *Scientific American, 225,* 30-38. Copyright 1971 by Scientific American, Inc. Reprinted/adapted by permission.; Figure 13.14: Crook, T., Youngjohn, J., Larrabee, G., & Salama, M. (1992). Aging and everyday memory. *Neuropsychology, 6,* 123-136. Copyright 1992 by the American Psychological Association. Reprinted by permission of the APA and the authors.; Figure 13.15: Horn, J. & Hofer, S. (1992) Major abilities and development in the adult period. In R. Sternberg & C. Berg (Eds.), *Intellectual Development,* 44-49. New York: Cambridge University Press. Reprinted by permission.; Figure 13.16: Cerella, J. (1990). Aging and information processing rate. In J. Birren & K. W. Schaie (Eds.), *Handbook of the Psychology of Aging* (3rd ed.). Orlando, FL: Academic Press. Reprinted/adapted by permission of Academic Press and the author.; Figure 13.17: Schaie, K. W. (1990). Intellectual development in adulthood. In J. Birren and K. W. Schaie (Eds.), *Handbook of the Psychology of Aging* (3rd ed.). Orlando, FL: Academic Press. Reprinted/adapted by permission of Academic Press and the author.; Figure 13.18: Baltes, P. (1987). Theoretical propositions of life-span developmental psychology: On the dynamics between growth and decline. *Developmental Psychology, 23,* 611-626. Copyright 1987 by the American Psychological Association. Reprinted by permission of the APA and the author.

CHAPTER 14   Figure 14.2: Kagan, J. (1983) Stress and coping in early development. In N. Garmezy & M. Rutter (Eds.), *Stress, Coping and Development in Children,* 1983. New York: McGraw-Hill, Inc. Reprinted by permission.; Figure 14.3: Anisfeld, E., Carper, V., Noyzee, M., & Cunningham, N. (1990). Does infant carrying promote attachment? An experimental study of the effects of increased physical contact on the development of attachment. *Child Development, 61,* 623. Copyright © 1990 The Society for Research in Child Development. Reprinted/adapted by permission.; Table 14.1: Dozier, M. & Kosback, R. (1992). Psychophysiology in attachment interviews: Converging evidence for deactivating strategies. *Child Development, 64,* 1473-1480. Copyright 1992 © The Society for Research in Child Development. Reprinted/adapted by permission.; Table 14.2: Rohner, R. (1975). Parental acceptance-rejection and personality development: A universalist approach to behavioral science. In R. W. Brislin (Ed.), *Cross-Cultural Perspectives on Learning,* 251-269. Copyright © 1975 by Sage Publications, Inc. Reprinted/adapted by permission of Sage Publications, Inc.; Table 14.3 : Furman, W. & Buhrmester, D. (1992). Age and sex differences in perceptions of networks in personal relationships. *Child Development, 63,* 107. Copyright 1992 © The Society for Research in Child Development. Reprinted/adapted by permission.; Figure 14.5: Harter, S. & Monsour, A. (1992). Developmental analysis of conflict caused by opposing attributes in the adolescent self-portrait. *Developmental Psychology, 28,* 251-160. Copyright 1992 The American Psychological Association. Reprinted/adapted by permission of the APA and the authors.; Table 14.4: Williams, J. E. & Best, D. L. (1982). *Measuring Sex Stereotypes: A Thirty Nation Study.* Copyright © 1982 by Sage Publications, Inc. Reprinted by permission of Sage Publications, Inc.; Table 14.5: Williams, J. E. & Best, D. L. (1990). Gender and self viewed cross-culturally. *Sex and Psyche.* Copyright ©

1990 by Sage Publications, Inc. Reprinted by permission of Sage Publications, Inc.; Table 14.6: Kohlberg, L. (1969). Stage and sequence: The cognitive-developmental approach to socialization. In D. A. Goslin (Ed.), *Handbook of Socialization and Research*, 347-480. New York: Houghton-Mifflin. Copyright 1969 by David A. Goslin. Reprinted/adapted by permission.; Figure 14.8: Darley, J. & Schultz, T. R. (1990). Moral rules: Their content and acquisition. Modified, with permission, from the *Annual Review of Psychology, 41*, 532, © 1990, by Annual Reviews, Inc.; Table 14.8: Helson, R. & Moane, G. (1987). Personality change in women from college to midlife. *Journal of Personality and Social Psychology, 53,* 181. Copyright 1987 by the American Psychological Association. Reprinted/adapted by permission of the APA and the authors.

CHAPTER 15 Table 15.1: Compton, W. M., Helzer, J., Hai-Gwo, H., Eng-Kung, Y., McEvoy, L., Tipp, J., & Spitznagel, E. (1991). New methods in cross-cultural psychiatry: Psychiatric illness in Taiwan and the U.S. *American Journal of Psychiatry, 148,* 1700-1701. Copyright 1991, the American Psychiatric Association. Reprinted by permission of the publisher and the authors.; Table 15.2: American Psychiatric Association: *Diagnostic and Statistical Manual of Mental Disorders, Fourth Edition,* Washington DC, American Psychiatric Association, 1994. Reprinted/adapted by permission.; Table 15.3: American Psychiatric Association: *Diagnostic and Statistical Manual of Mental Disorders, Fourth Edition,* Washington DC, American Psychiatric Association, 1994. Reprinted/adapted by permission.; Table 15.4: American Psychiatric Association: *Diagnostic and Statistical Manual of Mental Disorders, Fourth Edition,* Washington DC, American Psychiatric Association, 1994. Reprinted/adapted by permission.; Figure 15.3: Shedler, J. & Block, J. (1990). Adolescent drug use and emotional health: A longitudinal perspective. *American Psychologist, 45,* 612-630. Copyright 1990 by the American Psychological Association. Reprinted by permission of the APA and the authors.; Table 15.5: Gottesman, I. (1991). *Schizophrenia Genesis,* p. 96. New York: W.H. Freeman and Company. Copyright © Irving I. Gottesman. Used with permission of W.H. Freeman and Company.; Figure 15.7: Swann, W. B., Wenzlaff, R., Krull, D. S., & Pelham, B. (1992). Allure of negative feedback: Self-evaluation striving among depressed persons. *Journal of Abnormal Psychology, 101,* p. 296. Copyright 1992 by the American Psychological Association. Reprinted by permission of the authors and the APA.; Figure 15.8: Beck, A. T. (1976). *Cognitive Therapy and the Emotional Disorders,* p. 256. Madison, CT: International Universities Press, Inc. Reprinted by permission.; Figure 15.9: Barlow, D. H. (1988). Current models of panic disorder and a view from emotion theory. In A. J. Frances & R. E. Hales (Eds.), *Review of Psychiatry, 7.* Washington, DC: American Psychiatric Press. Reprinted/adapted by permission of American Psychiatric Press and the author.; Figure 15.10: Rapee, R. M., Brown, J. A., Anthony, M., & Barlow, D. H. (1992). Response to hyperventilation and inhalation of 5.5% carbon dioxide-enriched air across the DSM-III-R anxiety disorders. *Journal of Abnormal Psychology, 101,* 538-552. Copyright 1992 by the American Psychological Association. Reprinted/adapted by permission of the APA and the authors.; Table 15.7: American Psychiatric Association: *Diagnostic and Statistical Manual of Mental Disorders, Fourth Edition,* Washington DC, American Psychiatric Association, 1994. Reprinted/adapted by permission.

CHAPTER 16 Figure 16.3: Camp, B. W. & Bash, M. A. S. (1981). *Thinking Aloud: Increasing Social and Cognitive Skills—A Problem-Solving Program for Children.* (Primary Level; pp. 43-46). Champaign, IL: Research Press. Copyright 1981 by the authors. Reprinted by permission.; Excerpt, p. 636-637: Beck, A. T. (1976). *Cognitive Therapy and the Emotional Disorders,* p. 256. Madison, CT: International Universities Press, Inc. Reprinted by permission.; Figure 16.7: Abrams, R., Swartz, C. M., & Vedak, C. (1989). Unilateral ECT and the lateralization theory of ECT action: Antidepressant effects of right versus left. *American Journal of Psychiatry, 146,* 1190-1192. Copyright 1989, the American Psychiatric Association. Reprinted by permission of the publisher and the authors.; Figure 16.8: Maj, M., Veltro, R., Lobrace, S., & Magliano, L. (1992). Pattern of recurrence of illness after recovering from an episode of major depression. *American Journal of Psychiatry, 149,* 795-800. Copyright 1992, the American Psychiatric Association. Reprinted by permission of the publisher and the authors.; Figure 16.9: Smith, M. L. & Glass, G. V. (September 1977). Meta-analysis of psychotherapy outcome studies. *American Psychologist,* p. 754. Copyright 1977 by the American Psychological Association. Reprinted/adapted by permission of the APA and the authors.; Beck, A. T., Sokol, L., Clark, D. A., Berchick, R., & Wright, R. (1992). A crossover study of focused cognitive therapy for panic disorder. *American Journal of Psychiatry, 149,* 778-783. Copyright 1992, the American Psychiatric Association. Reprinted by permission of the publisher and the authors.; Figure 16.10: Howard, H. I., Kopta, S. M., Krause, M. S., & Orlinsky, D. E. (1986). The dose-effect relationship in psychotherapy. *American Psychologist, 41,* 159-164. Copyright 1986 by the American Psychological Association. Reprinted/adapted by permission of the APA and the authors.

CHAPTER 17 Figure 17.1: McGuire, W. J. (1985). *Handbook of Social Psychology.* New York: McGraw-Hill, Inc. Reprinted/adapted by permission of McGraw-Hill, Inc.; Figure 17.2: Luchins, A. S. (1957). Primacy-recency in impression formation. In C. I. Hovland (Ed.), *The Order of Presentation in Persuasion,* 34-35. New Haven: Yale University Press. Copyright 1957 by Yale University Press. Reprinted by permission.; Table 17.1: Olson, J. M. (1992). Self-perception of humor. *Journal of Personality and Social Psychology, 62,* 373. Copyright 1992 by the American Psychological Association. Reprinted/adapted by permission of the APA and the author.; Figure 17.3: Jones, E. E. (1976). How do people perceive the causes of behavior? *American Scientist, 64,* 301. Copyright 1976 by American Scientist. Reprinted by permission.; Table 17.2: John, O. & Robins, R. W. (1994). Accuracy and bias in self-perception: Individual differences in self-enhancement and the role of narcissism. *Journal of Personality and Social Psychology.* Copyright 1994 by the American Psychological Association. Reprinted/adapted by permission.; Figure 17.4: Woike, B. & Aronoff, J. (1992). Complexity of social cognition. *Journal of Personality and Social Psychology, 63,* 102. Copyright 1992 by the American Psychological Association.

Association: *Diagnostic and Statistical Manual of Mental Disorders, Fourth Edition,* Washington DC, American Psychiatric Association, 1994. Reprinted/adapted by permission.

Reprinted/adapted by permission of the APA and the authors.; Figure 17.5: Winter, D. G. (1987). Enhancement of an enemy's power: Motivation as a dynamic of conflict escalation. *Journal of Personality and Social Psychology 42(1),* 41-46. Copyright 1987 by the American Psychological Association. Reprinted/adapted by permission of the APA and the author.; Figure 17.6: Kihlstrom, J. F. & Cantor, N. (1983). Mental representations of the self. In L. Berkowitz (Ed.), *Advances in Experimental Social Psychology, 15.* Copyright 1983 by Academic Press, Inc. Reprinted/adapted by permission of Academic Press and the authors.; Table 17.3: Higgins, E. T. (1987). Self-discrepancy: A theory relating self and affect. *Psychological Review, 94(3),* 319-340. Copyright 1987 by the American Psychological Association. Reprinted/adapted by permission of the APA and the author.; Figure 17.7: Strauman, T., Lemieux, A., & Coe, C. (1993) Self-discrepancy and natural killer cell activity. *Journal of Personality and Social Psychology, 64,* 1042-1052. Copyright 1993 by the American Psychological Association. Reprinted/adapted by permission of the APA and the authors.

CHAPTER 18 Table 18.1: Sears, D. O. (1986). College sophomores in the laboratory: Influences of a narrow database on social psychological views of human nature. *Journal of Personality and Social Psychology, 51(3),* 515-530. Copyright 1986 by the American Psychological Association. Reprinted/adapted by permission of the APA and the author.; Figure 18.2: Sternberg, R. J. & Barnes, M. (1988) Triangular theory of love. In R. J. Sternberg & M. Barnes (Eds.), *The Psychology of Love.* New Haven: Yale University Press. Copyright 1988 by Yale University Press. Reprinted by permission.; Figure 18.3: Buss, D. M. & Schmitt, D. P. (1993). Sexual strategies theory: An evolutionary perspective on human mating. *Psychology Review, 100 (2),* 204-232. Copyright 1993 by the American Psychological Association. Reprinted by permission of the APA and the authors.; Figure 18.4: Simpson, J., Rholes, W. S., & Nelligan, J. (1992). Support seeking and support giving within couples in an anxiety-provoking situation. *Journal of Personality and Social Psychology, 62,* 434-446. Copyright 1992 by the American Psychological Association. Reprinted by permission of the APA and the authors.; Figure 18.5: Darley, J. M. & Latane, B. (1968, December). When will people help in a crisis? *Psychology Today,* 70-71. REPRINTED WITH PERMISSION FROM PSYCHOLOGY TODAY MAGAZINE, Copyright © 1968 (Sussex Publishers, Inc.). Figure 18.7: Anderson, C. (1989). Temperature and aggression: Ubiquitous effects of heat on occurrence of human violence. *Psychological Bulletin, 106,* 74-96. Copyright 1989 by the American Psychological Association. Reprinted by permission of the APA and the author.; Figure 18.8: Milgram, S. (1965). Some conditions of obedience and disobedience to authority. *Human Relations, 18,* 63. Reprinted by permission of Alexandra Milgram.; Figure 18.10: Asch, S. E. (1955, November). Opinions and social pressure. *Scientific American, 193,* 6. Copyright © 1955 by Scientific American, Inc. Reprinted by permission.; Figure 18.12: Zimbardo, P. G. (1975). Transforming experimental research into advocacy for social change. In Deutsch and Hornsteen (Eds.), *Applying Social Psychology.* New York: Lawrence Erlbaum Associates, Inc. Reprinted/adapted by permission of Lawrence Erlbaum Associates and the author.

Name Index

Subject Index